CORE

Java™ Foundation Classes

ISBN 0-13-080301-4

90000

9 780130 803016

PRENTICE HALL PTR
CORE SERIES

Core — Visual Basic 5, Cornell & Jezak

Core — Web Programming, Hall

Core — Java™ Foundation Classes, Topley

Core — Java™ Networking, Niemeyer

CORE
Java™ Foundation Classes

KIM TOPLEY

Prentice Hall PTR, *Upper Saddle River, NJ 07458*
http://www.phptr.com

Editorial/Production Supervision: Joe Czerwinski
Acquisitions Editor: Greg Doench
Editorial Assistant: Mary Treacy
Marketing Manager: Stephen Solomon
Manufacturing Manager: Alexis Heydt
Cover Design: Design Source
Cover Design Direction: Jerry Votta
Art Director: Gail Cocker-Bogusz

© 1998 Prentice Hall PTR
Prentice-Hall, Inc.
A Simon & Schuster Company
Upper Saddle River, NJ 07458

Prentice Hall books are widely used by corporations and government
agencies for training, marketing, and resale.

The publisher offers discounts on this book when ordered in bulk quantities.
For more information, contact

Corporate Sales Department,
Prentice Hall PTR
One Lake Street
Upper Saddle River, NJ 07458
Phone: 800-382-3419; FAX: 201-236-714
E-mail: corpsales@prenhall.com

Printed in the United States of America

10 9 8 7 6 5 4 3

ISBN 0-13-080301-4

Prentice-Hall International (UK) Limited, London
Prentice-Hall of Australia Pty. Limited, Sydney
Prentice-Hall Canada Inc., Toronto
Prentice-Hall Hispanoamericana, S.A., Mexico
Prentice-Hall of India Private Limited, New Delhi
Prentice-Hall of Japan, Inc., Tokyo
Simon & Schuster Asia Pte. Ltd., Singapore
Editora Prentice-Hall do Brasil, Ltda., Rio de Janeiro

For my parents and with thanks to the twelve men who undertook the ultimate adventure, and the nine others who got so close, for a memory that has inspired me for nearly thirty years.

Contents

PART ONE:

APPENDICES

FIGURES

Preface

The term Java Foundation Classes (JFC) refers to a collection of features that are included in, or can be used with, version 1.1 of the Java Development Kit (JDK) together with some new features introduced by JDK 1.2. The JFC is such a large topic area that to cover it in one volume and give it the treatment that it deserves, and that an experienced programmer would expect, is an impossible task. So, this book doesn't attempt to describe everything that falls under the JFC banner. Instead, I have chosen to concentrate on the parts that are of most immediate interest to programmers working in the commercial Java development environment today and left out those pieces that are not yet stable or would take up too much space in this volume.

Most of this book is, therefore, concerned with the subset of the JFC that you can use with with both JDK 1.1 and JDK 1.2. Specifically, this means the AWT as it exists in JDK 1.1, which is briefly covered as introductory or refresher material, printing, a JDK 1.1 feature that is deemed to be part of the JFC, and the Swing component set, which is the book's prime concern.

In writing about Swing, I have tried to include material that is of most interest to programmers who will want to use it to create real applications. The approach taken throughout is to explain how the Swing components and the various new Swing mechanisms (such as keyboard accelerators) work, by giving an overview of each topic and then presenting examples that show the basic principles. Then, typically, I move on to show more complex use of the component or feature and how it can be used together with other components and features to solve real application-related problems. Much of the time, you can find out some of what you want to know by reading the documentation that you get with the JDK or with the Swing package, but this documentation often falls short of explaining the more complex features and how they interact. These are the things that programmers usually need to understand before they can make full use of what is available. You'll find those explanations in this book.

I have tried to write this book as I would have liked to have seen it as an experienced programmer wanting to learn about Swing. By reading the documentation, studying the source code, disassembling the class files and trying various test cases, I have tried to do more than just scratch the surface of this large and complex topic by gathering together material and examples that are not available in Sun's documentation and presenting it in an organized, focused manner.

Who This Book Is For

This book is for experienced Java programmers who want to find out about the Java Foundation Classes and, in particular, the Swing component set. Because this book is aimed at experienced programmers, you'll find that most of the examples are not trivial, with the exception of some of those in the early chapters that illustrate basic points that can't be embedded in a more complex setting for clarity. Many of the examples that you'll find in this book are intended to be used as a starting point for writing production code that you can include in your own applications and some of the material here has been included specifically to address the most common questions that have been aired in the various news and discussion groups since the early versions of Swing were released. In particular, I have tried to address the following issues that seemed to be causing most confusion:

- Creating and customizing tree components.
- Custom renderers and editors for list boxes, trees and tables.
- How to use the powerful Swing text components, including a detailed description of how they work.
- Making proper use of the internal frames feature to create multi-document applications.
- Customizing individual components by creating your own look-and-feel classes.

If you're looking for examples on how to write slick Java applets with Swing, then this book probably won't suit you. The focus in this book is entirely on writing Java applications. However, if you're already thoroughly familiar with JDK 1.1 applets, you'll find that you can use write applets using Swing very quickly and most of this book will still apply, since Swing components can be used in applets just as easily as in applications.

What You'll Need

This book is written with the assumption that you are familiar with the Java language and the core Java classes and that you can compile and run Java applications. Although this book is mainly about the Swing components, the first few chapters cover the basic principles of the Abstract Windows Toolkit (AWT), knowledge of which is a prerequisite for understanding Swing. You'll get most from this book if you have read *Core Java 1.1, Volume I—Fundamentals* by Cay S. Horstmann and Gary Cornell, also published by Prentice Hall, and you understand inner classes, which are heavily used both in the Swing source code and in the examples shown in this book. *Core Java* includes excellent coverage of this topic.

Assuming that you have a computer running Windows 95, Windows NT version 4 or later, or a version of Solaris supported by JDK 1.1 or JDK 1.2, almost everything else that you need, including versions of JDK 1.1 and JDK 1.2 and the Swing components for all of these platforms, is included on the CD-ROM, with the exception of the Swing components for use with JDK 1.1, which you will need to download from the JavaSoft web site, as described in "About the CD-ROM" below.. You will, of course, need some kind of basic development environment. However, a basic text editor that you can invoke from the command line is sufficient.

How This Book Is Organized

The book is divided into three sections. Section 1, "From AWT to Swing," (Chapters 1 through 4) describes the relationship between the Abstract Windows Toolkit and Swing. Because Swing is a development based on the AWT, some understanding of the AWT is needed before you can fully utilize the Swing components. Although there are many good books on the AWT, this book opens by presenting the fundamentals for those who are not entirely confident that they fully understand them and as revision for those who do. These early chapters are, however, written not simply as a short course on the AWT—they are written with a Swing slant to them so that as early as Chapter 2 you will meet your first Swing components. I recommend that everybody reads Chapter 1. Then, depending on your background, you should read, or at least skim, Chapters 2 through 4.

Section 2, "Using Swing to Create Better Applications" (Chapters 5 through 8) deals with the various new mechanisms and components that Swing offers that have no real parallel in the AWT. Much of this section deals with individual Swing components or Swing concepts and, to a certain extent, the chapters in this section can be read in any order. Finally, Section 3, "Advanced Topics," (Chapters 9 through 13) covers larger topic areas such as the tree and table components and the pluggable look-and-feel.

Chapter 1 introduces the Java Foundation Classes (JFC) and puts them into perspective by comparing them to the AWT. You'll learn the scope of the JFC and get a quick overview of the main features of the Swing component set. The last part of this chapter introduces you to one of the more novel features of Swing—the so-called "pluggable look-and-feel," which allows applications to adapt their appearance to suit the platform that they are running on or to take on the same appearance across all platforms. It also explains the basis of this facility, the Model/View/Controller architecture (MVC).

Chapter 2 is the first of the AWT revision chapters. This chapter begins by introducing the Swing JFrame class as the top-level window of an application and uses it to illustrate basic AWT concepts such as components, containers, position, size, color, fonts and so on. The second half of the chapter includes material on event handling and introduces Swing's JLabel and JButton classes, which allow you to include text and an image on the same component. Here, you'll also find out about Swing improvements on the AWT, such as icons and accelerator keys, which now work outside of menus, to which they were confined in JDK 1.1.

Chapter 3 is concerned with global user-interface issues, principal among which is controlling the layout of components in the interface. With this in mind, almost the whole chapter is devoted to in-depth coverage of the AWT and Swing layout managers. Layout managers are a topic that has, in the past, been given only fleeting coverage in most Java books and represents a large proportion of the questions that are asked in the Java-related Internet newsgroups. Here, I have tried to create a consistent picture of all of the layout managers and to address the most common misunderstandings by illustrating how each layout manager lays out its container and how resizing the container affects the positioning of the components.

Swing includes a useful new feature that can help with understanding problems with component layout—Graphics Debugging. This feature allows you to see how your components are drawn, line-by-line, in slow motion. Chapter 3 looks at this feature and shows you how to use it and concludes with a look at the events generated by windows and by individual components.

Chapter 4 covers the AWT Graphics object and describes how you can use it to render text and draw graphics. The main body of this chapter is devoted to building a complete Swing application that allows you to use the mouse to draw and fill colored graphic shapes. While constructing this application, you'll put into practice much of what was covered in the previous two chapters and you'll also discover how to create custom icons and components with borders. The completed application will serve as a starting point for several improvements that will be made to it in rest of the book. Chapter 4 closes with a discussion of printing, another topic that has caused much confusion in the past.

Chapter 5 shows you how to develop applications that work well when the user prefers to use the keyboard rather than the mouse and introduces focus handling and the powerful concept of Actions. Actions are often used in Swing to abstract an action to be performed from the stimulus to perform it—such as a keystroke or a button press. The second half of the chapter looks at how Swing supports scrolling using the new `JScrollPane` and `JScrollBar` components, which are much more powerful than their AWT counterparts.

Chapter 6 introduces the Swing menu system. Swing menus are more consistent than those available with AWT. Keyboard accelerators are available on any menu or menu item and you can use icons as well as, or instead of, text. You'll also see how to integrate the `Actions` that were introduced in Chapter 5 with the menu system and with another new Swing facility, the toolbar.

Chapter 7 is the first of two chapters that contain extensive coverage of dialogs. This chapter concentrates on dialogs that you can easily create using the `JOptionPane` component. These dialogs allow you to post error, warning and information messages or present options to the user and wait for a choice to be made. Two more useful standard dialogs, the file chooser and color chooser, are also covered in this chapter.

Chapter 8 shows you how to use the Swing `JDialog` class to create your own dialogs. This chapter also introduces many of the Swing components that are useful in dialogs, such as tabbed panes, list boxes, combo boxes, progress controls and sliders.

In Chapter 9, you'll find an in-depth description of the Swing text controls, starting with the simple `JTextField` and `JTextArea` components, which are related to the AWT `TextField` and `TextArea` controls. The Swing controls are underpinned by a complex but powerful document model that is covered in detail in this chapter. The description of the document model is followed by a description of two new Swing text controls—`JTextPane`, which allows multiple fonts, colors, images and event components to be mixed in a view of a document and the flexible `JEditorPane`, which adapts itself to render documents held as plain text, HTML, Rich Text Format and a potentially infinite number of other formats.

Chapter 10 describes the Swing tree control and shows you how to build a tree, how to control which parts of it are expanded or collapsed and how to traverse the tree in various different ways. This chapter also shows you a custom control based on the tree that presents a file system in a manner familiar to users of the Windows platform and it describes in detail how to customize trees using specially-developed renderers to control how the various pieces of the tree are drawn.

Chapter 11 is concerned with the table component. This component allows you to present data in a tabular form. You'll see how to determine the order of columns and their sizes and how to change the way in which the data in the table is displayed. There is also a section on table cell editors, which shows you how to present to the user a suitable interface for changing the content of the table.

Chapter 12 discusses Swing's support for multiple-document applications. Starting with a discussion of the basic components that make multiple-document applications possible, the chapter moves on to discuss desktop panes and icons and the desktop manager. You'll also see how to create a custom desktop pane that automatically cascades or tiles the windows that it manages and how to customize the desktop manager itself.

Finally, Chapter 13 returns to the theme of the pluggable look-and-feel that was first touched on in Chapter 1. This chapter shows the underlying support for changing the look-and-feel of an application, then shows you how to create your own user interface for the Swing button component. Finally, you'll see various ways to introduce look-and-feel related customizations into your application and how to create your own look-and-feel.

This book covers all of the Swing components and most of the other important Swing features. For ease of reference, the following table lists the Swing components, along with the chapters in which they are described.

Component	Chapter	Component	Chapter
Box	3	JRadioButtonMenuItem	6
BoxLayout	3	JRootPane	2
JButton	2	JScrollBar	5
JCheckBox	8	JScrollPane	5
JCheckBoxMenuItem	6	JSeparator	8
JComboBox	8	JSlider	8
JComponent	2	JSplitPane	9
JDesktopPane	12	JTabbedPane	8
JDialog	8	JTable	11
JEditorPane	9	JTextArea	9
JFrame	2	JTextField	9
JInternalFrame	12	JTextPane	9
JLabel	2	JToggleButton	8
JLayeredPane	12	JToolBar	6
JList	8	JToolTip	8
JMenu	6	JTree	10
JMenuBar	6	JViewport	5
JMenuItem	6	JWindow	2
JOptionPane	7	OverlayLayout	3
JPanel	2	ProgressMonitor	8
JPasswordField	9	ProgressMonitorInputStream	8
JPopupMenu	6	Timer	8
JProgressBar	8	UIDefaults	13
JRadioButton	8	UIManager	13

Conventions Used in This Book

Courier font is used to indicate Java code, both in the listings and in the shorter code extracts that you'll find included in the text. The same font is also used to indicate key words and class names (such as JFrame). In some cases, we show a code extract and then explain how to modify it to change its behavior. In this case, the code that is added or modified is shown in **bold courier font**.

Icons are used to call out material that is of significance and that the reader should be alerted to:

Core Note, Alert, Tip

Note: This is information that deserves special attention, such as an interesting fact about the topic at hand, or that the reader may want to keep in mind while programming.

Alert: This is information that, while useful, may cause unexpected results or serious frustration.

Tip: This is particularly useful information that will save the reader time, highlight a valuable programming tip, or offer specific advice on increasing productivity.

About the CD-ROM

The CD-ROM that accompanies this book has the following directory structure:

```
COREJFC
    JDK1.1
            CJFC11.ZIP
    JDK1.2
            CJFC12.ZIP

WINDOWS
    JDK1.1
    JDK1.2

SOLARIS
    JDK1.1
    JDK1.2
```

The COREJFC directory contains the source code and compiled class files for the examples in this book. The WINDOWS directory contains a version of JDK1.1 for Windows 95 and Windows NT (version 4 or later) and a beta version of JDK 1.2 for Windows platforms. The SOLARIS directory has the same software for use with the Solaris operating system.

Installation Instructions

Since Swing can be used either with JDK 1.1 or JDK 1.2, you have a choice as to how to use the CD-ROM. If you want to use Swing with JDK 1.1, you need to do the following:

- Install the appropriate version of JDK 1.1 for your platform.
- Download and install the appropriate version of Swing for your platform.
- Install the JDK 1.1 examples.
- Optionally compile the example source files.

On the other hand, if you are going to use Swing with JDK 1.2, then you should

- Install the version of JDK 1.2 appropriate for your platform.
- Install the examples for JDK 1.2.
- Optionally compile the example source files.

Because Swing is an integral part of JDK 1.2, you don't need to download the Swing package if you intend to work with JDK 1.2.

The installation instructions in this section use the Windows platform when presenting typical command lines. If you are installing on the Solaris platform, you should amend the command lines as appropriate.

Installing for JDK 1.1

Install the JDK

If you already have JDK 1.1 installed, you can skip this step. However, you *must* install a new JDK if you do not have version 1.1.5 or higher, because Swing is not supported on earlier versions. To install the JDK, proceed as follows:

1. Locate the subdirectory on the CD-ROM that matches your operating system (WINDOWS\JDK1.1 or SOLARIS/JDK1.1). In this direc-

tory, you will find an installation file for the JDK in a format that is appropriate for your platform. For example, for Windows, the JDK will be in a `.exe` file.

2. Install the JDK files onto your computer by executing the installation file. We recommend that you place the JDK in a directory called `jdk`. If you have an older version of the JDK, completely remove it or move it to a new location before installing the newer version.

3. Add the `jdk\bin` directory to your `PATH` variable. For example, under Windows 95, if you install the JDK in the directory `c:\jdk`, then place the following line at the end of your `AUTOEXEC.BAT` file:

```
PATH=c:\jdk\bin;%PATH%
```

Core Note

The JDK setup program will offer a default location which is different for each JDK version, such as `jdk1.1.5`. *We recommend that you install the JDK in the directory* `jdk`, *but if you are using multiple versions, go ahead and accept the default. Be careful to modify the remaining instructions in this section to reflect your choice, however.*

Download and Install Swing

If you don't already have a copy of the Swing components for JDK 1.1, you should download them from the JavaSoft web site at `http://java.sun.com`. At the time of writing, the following URL will take you to the download page for Swing:

```
http://java.sun.com/products/jfc/index.html
```

The Swing package comes as a ZIP archive which you can install simply by unpacking its contents. Choose a suitable location and unpack the archive using any utility that can handle ZIP files. If you don't have a native utility for your platform, you can use the JDK `jar` tool to unpack the archive but, in this case, you should first reboot your computer if you have just installed the JDK.

Having installed Swing, you need to add the appropriate JAR files to your CLASSPATH. Swing contains several JAR files, all of which are found in the `swing-1.0.x` directory:

```
swing.jar
```

```
windows.jar
```

```
motif.jar

multi.jar

beaninfo.jar

swingall.jar
```

Core Note

The name of the Swing directory will depend on the current version at the time that you download it. Here, we use the generic name swing-1.0.x. *You should substitute the appropriate name for the version you download - for example, you might need to use* swing-1.0.2.

You can either choose to include the minimum set of files for your platform, or you can simply add swingall.jar to your CLASSPATH. If you just want to use the standard Metal look-and-feel, you can get away with just adding swing.jar. If you want to use either the Windows or Motif look-and-feel, add windows.jar and/or motif.jar as well. If you plan to develop Java Accessibility features (a topic outside the scope of this book), you need to add multi.jar. You won't need to use beaninfo.jar file unless you need to recreate your own version of swingall.jar—see the README.txt file in the swing-1.0.x1 directory for details.

If you are going to use Swing in conjunction with a third-party development environment, or you want to be able to use all of the look-and-feels, you should add swingall.jar to your CLASSPATH. Refer to "Set the CLASSPATH variable" below for further details.

Install the Examples

The Core JFC example source files for JDK 1.1 are held in the archive COREJFC\ JDK1.1\CJFC11.ZIP. To install them, first create a directory, say C:\CoreJFCBook, and copy the archive from the CD-ROM into this directory. If you have a utility for your platform that can handle ZIP files (such as WinZip), you can go ahead and unpack the archive, making sure that the files are all installed in the C:\CoreJFCBook directory. Refer to "Unpack the Examples" below to confirm that you have unpacked the archive correctly. If you do not have such a utility, you can unpack them using the JDK jar tool.

Set the CLASSPATH variable

Next, you need to set the CLASSPATH environment variable. This must contain:

- jdk\lib\classes.zip.
- The appropriate Swing jar files.
- The directory into which you copied the Core JFC examples.

For example, under Windows 95, add a line like this to your AUTOEXEC.BAT file:

```
SET CLASSPATH=c:\jdk\lib\classes.zip;c:\swing-1.0.x\swingall.jar;c:\CoreJFCBook
```

If you use the C-shell under Solaris, place the following in your .cshrc file (as one line):

```
setenv CLASSPATH /jdk/lib/classes.zip:$HOME/swing-1.0.x/swingall.jar:$HOME/CoreJFCBook
```

assuming that you have the JDK installed in /jdk and the examples and that the Swing archives have been installed under your home directory.

Obviously, if your CLASSPATH variable is already set, you will need to modify these instructions accordingly.

Finally, log out or reboot the computer.

Unpack the Examples

If you did not unpack the examples when you installed them, you should do so now. Make the directory in which the CJFC11.ZIP file has been installed (CoreJFCBook) your working directory, then execute the following command:

```
jar xvf CJFC11.ZIP
```

This will extract all of the examples. You should now have a directory called JFCBook in your CoreJFCBook directory, with one subdirectory per chapter. A typical layout might be as follows:

```
C:\CoreJFCBook\JFCBook\Chapter2
C:\CoreJFCBook\JFCBook\Chapter3
C:\CoreJFCBook\JFCBook\Chapter4
```

and so on. If you do not have this layout, you have done something wrong and the example programs will not work. One possible problem you might have at this stage is inability to run the jar command or an error while running it. If this is the case, either your PATH variable or your CLASSPATH variable is not correctly set. Check that you have correctly followed the instructions in this section, then reboot your computer to make sure that the settings have been incorporated into your environment.

Finally, using your favorite editor or file viewer, open any of the Java source files, for example `JFCBook\Chapter2\AddExample.java`. Near the top of this file, you should see a line like this:

```
import com.sun.java.swing.*;
```

If, instead, you see this line:

```
import java.awt.swing.*;
```

then you have installed the examples for JDK 1.2 Remove the `CJFC12.ZIP` file and all of the other files in this directory, copy the `CJFC11.ZIP` file from the CD-ROM directory `COREJFC\JDK1.1` and unpack it again.

Installing for JDK 1.2

Install the JDK

Installation JDK 1.2 is the same as for JDK 1.1, so refer to "Install the JDK" under "Installing for JDK 1.1." Note that JDK 1.2 includes the Swing components, so return here after installing JDK 1.2—do not attempt to install the JDK 1.1 Swing components with JDK 1.2.

Install the Examples

The Core JFC example source files are held in the archive `COREJFC\JDK1.2\CJFC12.ZIP`. To install them, first create a directory, say `C:\CoreJFCBook`, and copy the file from the CD-ROM into this directory. If you have a utility for your platform that can handle ZIP files (such as WinZip), you can go ahead and unpack the archive, making sure that the files are all installed in the `C:\CoreJFCBook` directory. Refer to "Unpack the Examples" below to confirm that you have unpacked the archive correctly. If you do not have such a utility, you can unpack them later using the JDK `jar` tool.

Set the CLASSPATH variable

Next, you need to add the `CLASSPATH` environment variable. This must contain:

- `jdk\lib\classes.zip`.
- The directory into which you copied the Core JFC examples.

For example, under Windows 95, add the following line to your `AUTOEXEC.BAT` file:

```
SET CLASSPATH=c:\jdk\lib\classes.zip;c:\CoreJFCBook
```

If you use the C-shell under Solaris, place the following in your `.cshrc` file:

```
setenv CLASSPATH /jdk/lib/classes.zip:$HOME/CoreJFCBook
```

assuming that you have the JDK installed in `/jdk` and the examples under your home directory.

Obviously, if your `CLASSPATH` variable is already set, you will need to modify these instructions accordingly.

Finally, log out or reboot the computer.

Unpack the Examples

If you did not unpack the examples when you installed them, you should do so now. Make the directory in which the `CJFC12.ZIP` file has been installed (`CoreJFCBook`) your working directory, then execute the following command:

```
jar xvf CJFC12.ZIP
```

This will extract all of the examples. You should now have a directory called `JFCBook` in your `CoreJFCBook` directory, with one subdirectory per chapter. A typical layout might be as follows:

```
C:\CoreJFCBook\JFCBook\Chapter1
C:\CoreJFCBook\JFCBook\Chapter2
C:\CoreJFCBook\JFCBook\Chapter3
```

and so on. If you do not have this layout, you have done something wrong and the example programs will not work. One possible problem you might have at this stage is inability to run the `jar` command or an error while running it. If this is the case, either your `PATH` variable or your `CLASSPATH` variable is not correctly set. Check that you have correctly followed the instructions in this section, then reboot your computer to make sure that the settings have been incorporated into your environment.

Finally, using your favorite editor or file viewer, open any of the Java source files, for example `JFCBook\Chapter2\AddExample.java`. Near the top of this file, you should see a line like this:

```
import java.awt.swing.*;
```

If, instead, you see this line:

```
import com.sun.java.swing.*;
```

then you have installed the examples for JDK 1.2. Remove the `CJFC11.ZIP` file and all of the other files in this directory, copy the `CJFC12.ZIP` file from the CD-ROM directory `COREJFC\JDK1.2` and unpack it again.

Building and Running the Examples

The example programs on the CD-ROM have been compiled using JDK 1.1.5 and Swing 1.0.1 and also with JDK 1.2 Beta 3. It is recommended that you just use the compiled class files that you'll find with the source files in the CoreJFCBook directories. If you need to rebuild the example files, perhaps because you want to try out some modifications of your own or to use a later version of the JDK or Swing that has incompatible changes, you should follow the procedure described in this section. The examples for each chapter are held in a directory named after that chapter and all the examples in that directory must be compiled together. You must also build the examples in ascending chapter-number order, apart from those in Chapter 13, which must be built after those in the directory Cjfc. The correct build order is, therefore, as follows:

- Chapter2 through Chapter12
- Cjfc
- Chapter13

To build the examples for Chapter 2, do the following:

```
cd C:\CoreJFCBook\JFCBook\Chapter2
javac *.java
```

This process should be repeated for each chapter, in the order just shown.

Core Alert

There are dependencies between the examples for different chapters—the examples for some of the later chapters reuse classes developed earlier. If you compile the examples out of order, you will probably find that your compilations will fail because of missing classes.

To run the examples, you must have the directory C:\CoreJFCBook on your CLASSPATH. You must then supply the full class name of the example that you want to run along with any required parameters as described in the appropriate chapter. For example, to run the first example in Chapter 2, use the following command:

```
java JFCBook.Chapter2.BasicFrame
```

In some cases, you will find explicit instructions that tell you how to run particular examples. Usually, however, you just need to use the example's class name and its chapter number as shown here.

A Note on Swing Versions

Since it was first released in developer form, the Swing API has undergone dramatic changes. Unfortunately, this process is not yet complete. At the time of writing, the current version of Swing for JDK 1.1 is Swing 1.0.1. The same version is also included in JDK 1.2 Beta 3, which you will find on the CD-ROM. The text and examples in this book relate to this particular version of Swing. Because most (over 90%) of the public API was frozen when Swing 1.0.1 was released, what you read in this book will continue to apply to later versions of Swing in almost all cases.

However, two of the Swing components, `JFileChooser` and `JColorChooser` (both of which are described in Chapter 7), did not have their API frozen in Swing 1.0.1. The API of these components is expected to change before JDK 1.2 is released and these same changes will also appear in the JDK 1.1 version of Swing. Be aware, therefore, that if incompatible changes are made to these components, some of the examples on the CD-ROM that use them may not work and their source code may no longer compile with later versions of Swing and JDK 1.2. To keep you up-to-date with the latest changes, there is a Web page at the following URL that you can use to download updated examples, should this become necessary:

```
http://www.topley.demon.co.uk/corejfc.html
```

Feedback

No book is perfect and this one is unlikely to be an exception to that rule. Even though it has been through a long period of revision and technical review, there are, of course, errors still to be found and improvements still to be made. If you find an error or if there is something that you think might make the book more useful, we want to know about them. Please send comments and corrections to the following e-mail address:

```
kt@topley.demon.co.uk
```

Further Information

Java is a fast-moving subject. To keep up with developments, reading books is not enough. The best place for up-to-date information is, of course, the JavaSoft web site at:

```
http://java.sun.com
```

You can get the most recent information on Swing and download the latest version of the software from the following page:

```
http://java.sun.com/products/jfc/index.html
```

JavaSoft also provides an online Swing magazine, called "The Swing Connection," which is periodically updated and can be found at:

```
http://java.sun.com/products/jfc/swingdoc-current
```

Finally, there are several active newsgroups devoted to discussion of the Java platform. The following two groups in particular frequently discuss Swing and JFC-related issues:

```
comp.lang.java.gui
comp.lang.java.programmer
```

Acknowledgments

I seem to have spent all of my life buying and reading books. It is probably not too great an exaggeration to say that almost everything I know I have read in a book somewhere, some time. So it was only to be expected that when Java first appeared, I turned to the bookshop to help me find out about it. After examining the (then) limited number of books available on the subject, I settled on the one that stood out as most appropriate for an experienced programmer and took down from the bookshelf the copy in best condition. That book was the first edition of *Core Java,* by Cay S. Horstmann and Gary Cornell.

A little over a year later, having decided to try to make some money from books instead of spending money on them, I submitted a very basic outline for a book to a small group of publishers. The next day, I found two e-mail items waiting for me—one from Gary Cornell, the other from Greg Doench at Prentice Hall. Of course, there was a lot more work to do before a contract was agreed, but of all the people that deserve thanks for making this book possible, these two are at the head of the queue. It still amazes me that they were willing to put such faith in someone who had not yet written a book, on the strength of a vague outline and two chapters of a different book idea that never came to fruition. Throughout the writing process, which seems to have taken such a long time, I found that I could always approach either of them with questions or problems and have them addressed quickly. They helped me with all kinds of issues, from determining the scope of the book, right down to the details of the template with which the manuscript was written. But, most of all, they trusted me to deliver and it is for this that I am most grateful to them.

As the writing phase drew to a close, Greg introduced me to Jim Markham, the book's development editor. It fell to Jim to read the entire manuscript and turn what was essentially a jumble of programmer's language into more fluent sentences and paragraphs, all under pressure of time. I can't thank Jim enough for the attention he paid to this task—the book you now hold in your hands is much more readable than the collection of chapters he started with. As well as being an excellent development editor, I have to say that I used Jim frequently as a sounding board for ideas and asked him to do other things that went well beyond the bounds of his job and was never disappointed.

On the technical review front, my thanks go to Buzzy Brown (of IBM Retail Store Solutions), Blake Ragsdell and Cameron Laird, who all read parts of the manuscript at various stages of its development, for their comments which have helped improve the presentation of the technical content as well as remove several errors of fact. Special thanks, though, are due to two people who have contributed significantly to the technical side of this book. First, Rayme Jernigan read and commented on the entire manuscript as it was being overhauled for the penultimate time. Called to the task at the last minute, Rayme did an incredible job against a deadline that at first looked aggressive and then almost impossible. Nevertheless, he made it and is still alive to tell the tale! Secondly, I am indebted to Timothy Prinzing of the JavaSoft Swing development team who, at the same time as working on the Swing 1.0 release, graciously agreed to review the chapter describing the Swing Text Components, for which he was responsible. His feedback helped me to include the Swing 1.0 changes much more quickly than would otherwise have been possible and has made this a much more useful and accurate chapter.

I would also like to thank all the other people at Prentice Hall who helped with the production of this book, especially Mary Treacy for making sure that the contract details were sorted out, Yvette Raven for putting together the book's CD-ROM, and Joe Czerwinski, who answered many questions on the document template and saw the book through the production phase against a tight schedule. Despite the efforts of all of these people, and many others, as with most books of this size, there will undoubtedly be errors that remain. For these, I claim all credit.

Writing a book of this size takes a long time. In the year or so that I have devoted to this task, there have been times when I was inclined to take a long break or even consider giving up completely. Apart from my own stubbornness (and, of course, a possible breach of contract), several groups of people have inspired me to keep going with this project, possibly without realizing it. Most significantly, I would like to mention my work colleagues, Dave Martin and Tim Lowe, who made it their business to ask about the state of the book almost every day of every week and thus made it totally unacceptable to stop work and my supervisor, Polly Yee, for being understanding when asked for a few days' leave to get through a particularly busy part of the schedule.

Finally, I would like to express my gratitude to my family for putting up with my effective absence for most of the last year and for not complaining too much about the state of the study, which has been buried under books, notes and computers for the duration of this project.

CORE
Java™ Foundation Classes

FROM AWT
TO SWING

The Abstract Window Toolkit (AWT) has been available for as long as the Java language itself. The shortcomings of the AWT have been well known for a long time and developers have spent a great deal of time and effort augmenting the AWT with components of their own that provide some of the missing user interface functionality that their customers have become accustomed to. The goal of the Swing project was to enhance the AWT by providing much of that missing functionality in a common class library that was immediately portable to any platform that can support JDK 1.1. In the first part of this book, you'll see the relationship between the AWT and Swing, and you'll discover how much more powerful the Swing components are than their AWT counterparts.

Part 1 begins with an overview of Swing, then covers the fundamentals of the AWT, using Swing components to revisit AWT concepts such as position, size, visibility and color. Chapter 3 takes an in-depth look at layout managers, including the ones provided by the AWT and the new ones added by Swing. In Chapter 4, you'll learn about the graphics capabilities provided by the AWT and how these are used with Swing components. In this chapter, you'll see how to change the way you render custom components to fit in with the Swing component model and how to use the AWT printing facilities, which are considered to be part of the Java Foundation Classes.

INTRODUCTION TO THE JAVA FOUNDATION CLASSES

Topics in This Chapter

- The History of the Java Foundation Classes
- Overview of JFC Features
- The Swing Packages
- Look-and-Feel and the Model-View-Controller Architecture

Chapter 1

The Java Foundation Classes bring new capabilities to the Java programmer, foremost among which are the components in the so-called *Swing* set. This chapter begins by looking briefly at the history of the Java programming language and of the Abstract Window Toolkit in particular. The Abstract Window Toolkit, or AWT for short, provides the classes used to build an application's user interface. In both Java Development Kit (JDK) 1.0 and JDK 1.1, Java applications running under Windows looked just like Windows programs, while those running on Solaris looked the same as native applications written with the Motif toolkit. The reason for this was simply that much of the AWT is provided by code from the native platform's windowing system—the user interface components are rendered by Windows or by Motif, not by Java code. While this has its advantages, it also has drawbacks. For one thing, it is difficult to implement a single interface and map it to two (or more) host platforms that work differently. And even when you've done that, the controls themselves behave somewhat differently between the platforms. Because this behavior is part of the native windowing system, there's nothing you can do about it.

Implementing all of the user interface classes in Java gets rid of these problems at a stroke. That's exactly what the Swing components, which are the most significant part of the Java Foundation Classes (JFC), do—they replace the native implementation with a user interface library that works the same on all Java platforms.

This chapter starts by looking at the history of the Swing project and then moves on to look at the new architecture that was developed to implement the Swing controls. The power of this architecture will be shown toward the end of the chapter, when you'll see how simple it is to change the way an application built with Swing controls looks, without changing a single line of code.

What Are the Java Foundation Classes?

The Java Foundation Classes are a group of features whose implementation began with JDK 1.1 and is continued in JDK 1.2, one of the most significant parts of which, and the main concern of this book, is the Swing component set. The Swing components are all graphical user interface controls that replace most of the platform-native components provided by the JDK 1.0 and JDK 1.1 AWT. The best way to understand what the Swing components are and how they will affect the development of Java applications is to look at how the Swing project came about and at the problems with the AWT that Swing is intended to address.

In the Beginning: The Abstract Window Toolkit

Sun Microsystems released JDK 1.0 in the first half of 1996. A significant part of this new language was a package called `java.awt`, which contains the classes for the AWT.

In its early days, Java was associated very closely with the Internet and, thanks to its incorporation in Netscape's popular Web browser, the sight of cool applets written in Java became commonplace. A Web site without a Java applet of some kind soon became hard to find. While dedicated surfers searched for the next exciting applet, programmers were busy trying to meet user expectations using the facilities of the AWT—for it is the AWT that provides the user interface that, when viewed through a Web browser, becomes a Java applet.

Most of the original Java applets were of a similar, rather simple, type: moving images, dancing text, showers of pixels and just about anything that caught the eye. The aim was usually just to liven up an otherwise static Web page and attract as many callers as possible, in the hope that at least some of them might look at and, better still, buy the product or service that the Web site's owner was offering. Creating such simple applets did not really place much of a demand on the AWT. Most of the work revolved around loading and displaying sequences of images or animating some simple text. More sophisticated applets allowed user interaction using the mouse or the keyboard but, on the whole, the level of functionality required from the AWT by these applets was very low.

Alongside the applet developers, others were trying to use Java to develop weightier applications, such as office productivity tools and database client interfaces. While the applet developer was very happy with his new-found freedom of expression and got just about all he needed from the AWT, his colleagues were typically less impressed. For serious development work, AWT 1.0 simply did not stand up to scrutiny. For one thing, it was slow.

While this is not such an issue on the Internet, it assumes great importance to a user accustomed to applications written in C or C++ that usually (but with some notable exceptions) don't require you to wait a noticeable amount of time for something to happen after pressing a button. For another, the AWT simply wasn't robust enough—the implementation, particularly of the Windows version, was buggy and required developers to spend inordinate amounts of time looking for solutions to problems that weren't in their own code and having to produce work-arounds to patch up their applications and make them usable. Worst of all, though, the AWT didn't provide much variety in its range of user interface elements.

User interfaces have come a long way since the days of DOS. These days, even Unix has a windowing interface and only programmers and (some) system administrators still toil away at the shell prompt. Over the years, beginning with the introduction of Windows 3.0 and continuing up to the present day, users have become accustomed to interacting with applications using a mouse and a collection of familiar controls such as buttons, scroll bars, text fields and so on. Each release of Windows or the Motif toolkit brought new elements to the user's attention, most of which were quickly accepted and became indispensable.

Unfortunately, AWT 1.0 was not particularly sophisticated in its supply of visual controls, so developers who wanted to make their Java spreadsheet or word processor resemble existing products had to start virtually from scratch and write their own components.

Inevitably, this was a long and tiresome process, repeated in many companies around the world. The end result, of course, was that there never were that many serious Java applications developed with AWT 1.0 that made it to the marketplace, even in Beta form. By the time the development community had come to terms with creating their own components, JavaSoft had released JDK 1.1 and, along with it, version 1.1 of the AWT.

By comparison to its predecessor, AWT 1.1 was a great improvement. The Windows version was completely rewritten and was made much faster and more robust. Better integration with the user's desktop was provided and, for the first time, a Java programmer could give an application access to a printer without needing to write platform-dependent native code. The programming model was improved, too, with a better mechanism for handling events from the user interface and, with the introduction of the JavaBeans specification and its incorporation in JDK 1.1, it became possible for developers to create components that could be taken and reused elsewhere more easily and could even be incorporated into graphical application builder tools such as Microsoft Visual Basic or Borland JBuilder. But still, there remained the issue of user interface sophistication. Notwithstanding the breadth of JDK 1.1 and the immense improvement in the quality of the AWT, only two new components (a scrolling window and a pop-up menu) were added. Developers still had to produce most of their own user interface controls.

Enter Netscape

Meanwhile developers at Netscape had begun development of a set of improved user controls that were eventually released under the banner of the Internet Foundation

Classes (IFC). Implemented on top of AWT 1.0, the IFC components were a more complete set than their predecessors and included some nice features such as dialogs to allow a user to choose colors, files and fonts visually, buttons with images, sliders, bitmaps (images that load synchronously), support for animation sequences and an improved application framework that supported the nesting of parts of an application's interface inside other parts, with drawn boundaries to emphasize the nesting and grouping of components.

As well as providing improved functionality, the IFC components were different from AWT in another way. Whereas the AWT components are implemented partly in Java and partly as a platform-dependent native library, the IFC components are written entirely in Java. As a result, the IFC is immediately portable to any platform that supports Java and takes with it its look-and-feel, unlike the AWT, which adopts the appearance of its host platform.

The Swing Set: A Joint Effort

In the early part of 1997, developers from Netscape and JavaSoft began cooperating on a project that was dubbed Swing. The aim of this project was to bring together the AWT and the best parts of Netscape's IFC to produce a fully-featured, robust set of user interface classes to be released as part of JDK 1.2. Like their IFC counterparts, these components (referred to as the Swing component set) would be written entirely in Java to ensure portability and would, at some future time, allow JavaSoft to drop most of the peer model that the AWT had used for its first two releases. The peer model allowed JavaSoft to leverage native platform user interface support to get the first release of the JDK into the hands of developers very quickly. This approach had, of course, been extremely successful but was also, in part, responsible for the bad reputation of the AWT on the Windows platform.

The Swing project would soon grow far beyond a straight merge of the IFC components into the AWT, however. JavaSoft launched a *100% Pure Java* initiative, of which the Swing component set was, of course, a very good example and the number of components to be included in this set increased. The final result of this project was, as you'll see, a comprehensive new set of controls that matches the best of the competition and puts Java applications on a par with those written using the native platform libraries. Whereas the Java developer had been forced to limit the scope of the user interface or implement custom components, now the problem is more the wealth of choice available.

Swing Plus More: The Java Foundation Classes

The Swing components are, without doubt, the most notable part of what JavaSoft named the Java Foundation Classes, but they are not the whole story. Several improvements that had gone into AWT 1.1, plus a few more enhancements planned for the JDK 1.2 time frame, were brought together and placed under the JFC banner. In total, the JFC set consists of the following pieces:

- The Swing components
- The Desktop Colors feature of JDK 1.1
- The JDK 1.1 Printing facility
- The Java2D API, which supports enhanced text, color and image support
- Accessibility, which provides support for technologies that make it easier for users with disabilities to use the Java platform
- The JDK 1.1 cut-and-paste and clipboard facility, combined with a new drag-and-drop facility introduced in JDK 1.2.

The full range of JFC features is delivered as part of JDK 1.2, but JavaSoft also provides a package, called JFC 1.1 (also known as Swing 1.0), that contains the Swing components in a form suitable for use with JDK 1.1. This package allows developers to make use of the Swing components without having to wait for the final release of JDK 1.2. This book focuses on the parts of the Java Foundation Classes that are found in both the add-on package and in JDK 1.2. In addition, it covers the JDK 1.1 printing facility and a host of other features from JDK 1.1 that are closely related to the Swing components, all of which must be properly understood in order for you to make full use of Swing. This subset of the full JFC family consists mainly of the first three items just listed.

What Is the Relationship between JFC and AWT?

With the introduction of a new set of components that use a different software architecture from those already in the AWT, it is natural to wonder what will now become of the AWT itself. As early as the last Beta version of JDK 1.1, JavaSoft were signaling that there was a major change on the way for the AWT. In this last release before final customer shipment, the AWT engineers introduced a new facility called Lightweight Components. On the surface, this simply represented the ability to produce a component or a container with a transparent background. This was done by allowing developers to directly extend the `Component` and `Container` classes and a nice example of a button with rounded edges was provided in the release documentation. However, also among the documentation was a paper entitled *AWT: The Next Generation*. This paper indicated that the future of the AWT lay in the direction of lightweight components, enabling the removal of most of the troublesome peer model. It also indicated that the peer model would be retained for a while for compatibility reasons. This paper, of course, was the first public announcement of the initiative that would eventually result in the delivery of the Swing components.

In JFC 1.1 and JDK 1.2, the old AWT components and the Swing components are both supported and the AWT components continue to use the peer model. It is not clear how long this situation will continue. Some of the Swing components are actually derived from an AWT component—for example, the `JFrame` component, which provides the top-level window for an application, is derived from the AWT `Frame` class. However, every AWT component has a corresponding Swing component, so it is already possible to implement an application that does not directly depend on the AWT, apart from the top-level window.

Core Tip

Given the obvious desire on the part of JavaSoft to move away from the peer model, developers would be well advised to upgrade existing applications as soon as possible, to remove future dependence on the old AWT components.

Because the AWT infrastructure is still in place, applications written with the old AWT continue to work in JFC 1.1 and with JDK 1.2 in the same way as those using the JDK 1.0 event model continued to work in JDK 1.1. Because of the clean separation of the two sets of components and the fact that they are all ultimately derived from the `Component` class and share the same event model, it is possible to mix AWT and Swing components in a single application. Of course, it is extremely unlikely that anybody would develop a new application that relied on both sets of components, but the ability to mix allows developers to migrate from the old set to the new incrementally, retaining a working application throughout.

This feature is of enormous importance if you have spent great efforts developing your own custom components based on the AWT classes. Most importantly, it means you can continue to use them until you create Swing-based replacements. However, because of the breadth of coverage of the Swing components, it is very likely that you will be able to use them to directly replace a large proportion of your custom controls, avoiding the need to carry out any porting at all.

Core Note

You will often see references in this book to AWT components and Swing components as if they were mutually exclusive sets. Strictly speaking, this is not true, because all of the Swing components are also AWT components. What we really mean when we say AWT components is the set of components that the AWT provided in JDK 1.1.

What Do I Need to Relearn to Use the Swing Components?

The simple answer to this question is that you should be able to make basic use of some Swing components straight away. Swing does not fundamentally change the way in which Java applications are constructed. You still create a top-level window; you still use frames, components and layout managers; and you still connect them together in almost the same way as you always have (but see the discussion of JFrame in Chapter 2, " Frames, Labels, and Buttons," for an important exception). The main problem you have to overcome to use Swing proficiently is being aware of all the possibilities available to you. Instead of the handful of AWT components, each of which was very simple and required little customization, you now have a very large and very rich set of possibilities to choose from. In addition to the wide choice, many of the components are very highly customizable, especially if you are prepared to spend time implementing some of the pluggable *helper* classes that can be attached to some of them. The aim of this book is to help you to do that.

As an example, consider the new Swing Combo box. This control allows a user to select from a list of possible values and shows the selected value in an input field. To see the list of possibilities, you click on a small arrow near the input control to reveal a drop-down list. If the programmer has made the Combo editable and the value you want is not in the list, or if you know the value without needing to refer to the list, you can type it directly into the input field. That's the basic functionality of the control.

However, if you are prepared to do a little work, you can provide your own way of rendering the contents of the drop-down box or of editing the input field. You don't have to restrict yourself any more to a traditional drop-down combo box containing a list of strings. For one thing, without doing very much, you can add images to the strings. Figure 1-1, for example, shows three combo boxes, one of which only uses images.

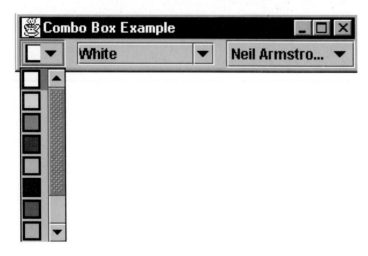

Figure 1-1 Swing combo boxes.

With slightly more effort, you can present a hierarchical view of a file system from which you could select a file to operate on. Or maybe you would prefer a drop-down scientific calculator, or, in a financial institution, a way of choosing from a selection of pricing information held on a server somewhere.

Overview of JFC Features

The JFC provides a very wide range of components and facilities. Before we start our detailed investigation, we'll spend a short time in this section looking briefly at the various parts of the Java Foundation Class API that fall within the scope of this book.

The JComponent Class

The JComponent class is the common superclass of almost all of the new Swing components. In the same way that Component provides common methods and states for all AWT components, JComponent performs several major functions for its own subclasses, several of which will be briefly described in the next few sections. JComponent is derived from the AWT Container class, which is itself a subclass of Component. Because JComponent extends Container, it is a lightweight object. It does not have a window in the native windowing system like the AWT components do and it can be transparent. The other advantage of extending Container is that a JComponent can be constructed from many different components, because it has built-in container functionality.

Core Note

It is important to understand the relationship between JComponent, Container *and* Component *and between* JComponent *and all of the other Swing classes. Appendix A contains a class hierarchy diagram that shows every component in the Swing set. It's a good idea to refer to this diagram as each new component is introduced so that you can see where it fits in the overall picture.*

JComponent enables the pluggable look-and-feel facility that will be discussed later in this chapter, by redirecting calls that would otherwise be handled by Component methods to a separate user interface object that is responsible for maintaining the component's appearance. For example, JComponent overrides the paint method and redirects it to the user interface component instead of allowing Component to process it. This issue is discussed further in "The Model/View/Controller Architecture" below and in Chapter 13, "The Pluggable Look-and-Feel." Many other Swing features are also based on support provided by the JComponent class.

Frames and Dialogs

In Swing, the top-level windows have changed. Instead of `Frame`, there is `JFrame` and, similarly, there are `JWindow` and `JDialog` classes. The difference between these Swing components and their AWT counterparts is much more than just a name change. Whereas the AWT components were straightforward containers that were special only because their native windowing system peers were top-level windows, the Swing components have a complicated internal structure that is visible to the programmer and that allows them to be much more useful when constructing user interfaces.

As an example of this, all of these containers can support a menu bar, a facility that was previously only available with a `Frame`. In addition, the main working area can be treated as if it had many independent layers. Placing components in different layers makes it possible to arrange for them to overlap, and also to ensure that some components always appear in front of others. This facility can be used to great effect to provide support for multiple document applications, which is covered in Chapter 12, "Multiple-Document Applications."

The working area of a `JFrame` can be divided in two areas using the Swing `JSplitPane` control. This component allows the user to drag a moving boundary either horizontally or vertically to adjust the space available to two components mounted on the frame. This control is useful when creating layouts like that of the Microsoft Windows Explorer, or the network news interface provided by some Web browsers, where the list of news groups and the list of items in the current news group are displayed side-by-side with a slider that allows the space available to one list to be increased at the expense of the other. `JSplitPane` is covered in Chapter 9, "Text Components," where it is used to show two different views of a single document.

Swing also provides a gamut of new support for dialogs, which were very hardly catered for at all in JDK 1.1. The old `FileDialog`, which was very limiting and fell far short of similar facilities on the native platform, has been replaced by the more powerful `JFileChooser`, which can be used on its own or as part of a larger dialog. Other extended dialog support includes `JColorChooser` for graphically selecting colors and a host of message, warning, error and information panes provided by the `JOptionPane` class.

One of the most impressive-looking Swing controls is the `JTabbedPane`, which looks and behaves like a Windows property sheet. `JTabbedPane` is especially useful in dialog boxes, where it allows the programmer to create panels of controls that control related parts of an application's configuration and present them in an uncluttered manner, separate from configuration information for other aspects of the application, while still having all of a program's configurable options available in one place.

The wide range of dialog components is discussed in Chapter 7, "Using Standard Dialogs," and Chapter 8, "Creating Custom Dialogs."

Per-Component Borders

All of the Swing components provide for the drawing of a border around their edges. Borders are managed by the following `JComponent` methods:

- `public void setBorder(Border b);`
- `public Border getBorder();`

`Border` is an interface, not a class, and the Swing set contains several standard borders that should meet most requirements.

A border can be used to group together controls that are related to each other and don't need to be closely associated with other controls on the same panel. For example, it might be appropriate to surround a group of radio buttons with a border that contains some text to describe what the buttons control, as shown in Figure 1-2. Alternatively, you can use the `setBorder` method to replace the border of a standard component, such as a text input field, with one of your own choice.

Figure 1-2   A Swing titled border grouping three radio buttons.

Borders are discussed in Chapter 4, "Graphics, Text Handling and Printing," and in Chapter 8.

Graphics Debugging

Often it can be difficult to see why complicated layouts or graphics are not being rendered properly, because the entire process happens so quickly that it is impossible to see exactly what is being done. Alternatively, you may find that sometimes your layouts are being redrawn too frequently. In both of these cases, it would be useful to have a way to either slow down the rendering process or to have a record of what was done so that it can be inspected later for redundant operations. JFC 1.1 includes a new Graphics Debugging facility that provides both of these features and JComponent provides the interface to it via the getDebugGraphicsOptions and setDebugGraphicsOptions methods. This feature is covered in detail in Chapter 3, "Managing the User Interface."

Enhanced Mouseless Operation

Swing provides an improved mechanism for allowing an application to be driven from the keyboard as well as using a mouse. JDK 1.1 introduced keyboard accelerators for menu items and a better mechanism for managing focus traversal using the Tab and Shift-Tab keys. Swing extends this by allowing actions to be triggered by particular key sequences on arbitrary components on the user interface. This new mechanism makes it almost trivial to support function keys and other types of hot keys that were very difficult to implement with JDK 1.1. JComponent provides the repository for the configuration information for this mechanism. The Swing components also provide a more flexible focus management model, including the ability to install a customized focus manager. Accelerator keys and focus management are discussed in Chapter 5, "Keyboard Handling, Actions and Scrolling."

Tooltips

A nice feature of some user interfaces is the ability to show a small help window or *tip* when the mouse pauses over a button. Typically, this window would contain text that describes what the button would do if it were pressed. Swing generalizes this mechanism by making it available in all of the new components.

Simple applications can make use of the facility by supplying some text that will display in the "tip" window, as shown in Figure 1-3, by invoking the JComponent setToolTipText method. If you want to be a bit more clever, you can take control of this mechanism by providing your own component to be used instead of the default window with text, or you can arrange for the text that is shown to be dependent upon the position of the mouse relative to the control. We cover this mechanism, and show how to exploit it to the full in Chapter 8.

Enhanced Scrolling

In JDK 1.1, some of the AWT components supplied scroll bars if the information that they needed to display did not fit in the available screen space. Programmers could also create their own scrolling components using the primitive Scrollbar or the ScrollPane container, which handles most of the details of scrolling for the simplest cases.

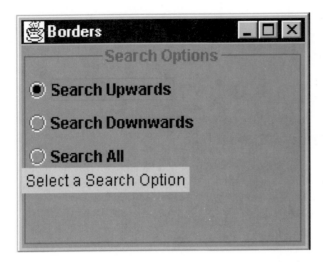

Figure 1-3   A tool tip.

By contrast, Swing components do not provide their own scroll bars—if, for example, the text in a text area could turn out to be too large to be seen on the screen at once, it is up to the programmer to provide the scrolling functionality. Fortunately, the Swing component set provides a very simple to use but extremely powerful scrolling container, JScrollPane, that fully replaces the AWT ScrollPane and can be added to any Swing component with only one line of code.

When a component is wrapped with scroll bars, it is often useful to force a particular part of the scrolled area to become visible. As an example of this, consider the case of a text control that provides a search facility. As the search progresses through the text, it is necessary to scroll the content so that matched parts of the text are in the visible region. JComponent provides a method that can be used to request that a scrolling parent object change its viewport to make some part of the calling component visible. Similarly, if the user drags an object over a scrolled list, JComponent provides the means to make the list scroll automatically, without intervention by the list itself, so that the position in which the user might want to drop the component becomes visible. Compare this to dragging files between directories in the Windows Explorer, for example. If the target directory in which the file is to be dropped is not visible, dragging the file to the top or bottom of the window that is showing the directory tree causes that window to scroll in the appropriate direction. This mechanism and the Swing scrolling controls are described in Chapter 5.

Pluggable Look-and-Feel

Without doubt one of the more interesting and novel features of the Swing architecture is the fact that the applications it produces have a platform-independent look-

and-feel to them, because the user interface is rendered not by Windows or the Motif library, but by Java code that will work the same way on every platform. As a result, you can take an application developed using Swing components on Solaris, say, and have it run with the same appearance on Windows 95. But that's only half the story.

Unlike the old AWT, the parts of the Swing classes that deal with drawing components onto the screen are not an inseparable part of each component. Instead, each control delegates its screen drawing to a separate entity that knows how to draw components of that type. For example, a button object allows a separate button-drawing class to render its image onto the screen; the button itself would be concerned only with delivering a notification to the application program that it has been pressed.

Once you have separated the rendering of components from the components themselves, it becomes possible to substitute a different rendering class that draws the button in a different way and what you can do for a button you can also do for every other interface component. From this idea comes the concept of a family of user interface classes that implement a consistent look-and-feel across all of the components. The Swing components as supplied in JFC 1.1 and JDK 1.2 come with several look-and-feel implementations, among them two that emulate the Windows and Motif look-and-feel and a third that is a cross-platform look-and-feel specifically designed for Java applications, called the *Metal* look-and-feel. All the user has to do is *plug* the appropriate look-and-feel set into the application by configuring a default for his or her platform. You'll see more on this later in this chapter and in much greater detail in Chapter 13.

Core Note

There are at least two other look-and-feel implementations available from JavaSoft but not included in the standard Swing release. One of these is a Mac look-and-feel that gives Apple Macintosh-like behavior to the application. The other is another cross-platform look-and-feel called Organic, which was originally available in the later developer prerelease versions of Swing under the name of the Java look-and-feel.

Layout Managers

Swing adds two new layout managers to those provided by the AWT. `BoxLayout` is a useful layout manager that arranges its components in either a single row or a single column. As such, it is ideal for managing groups of buttons or other components that have to remain properly aligned in one direction. It also provides the ability for the programmer to specify how its components should move and resize when the container is expanded, how much of the extra space should be used to let the components grow and how much should be left empty. The `OverlayLayout` manager can be used to arrange for components to overlap each other and to stay overlapped as their container expands. `OverlayLayout` can be used in conjunction with transparent, lightweight components to build up an interface from several layers, with each layer being composed of a different component.

Because layout managers have generally been poorly documented and a proper understanding of them can save a lot of time and effort when developing applications, this book provides an extended description of the complete set of layout managers, both the old AWT ones and the Swing ones, in Chapter 3.

Labels and Buttons

The AWT `Label` and `Button` classes were very simple and offered limited functionality. By contrast, the Swing `JLabel` and `JButton` classes are highly customizable. Labels and buttons can have both text and an image associated with them and it is possible to choose the relative positions of these items and their overall alignment in relation to the control itself. The Swing button classes are, in fact, a hierarchy that includes the Swing menu items, traditional push buttons, toggle buttons that are "sticky" (that is, they remain pressed in until pressed again), check boxes and radio buttons. All of these types of buttons share the features of `JButton`, including the ability to present an image. Among the possibilities that this opens up is the potential to represent a check box or a radio box with an image more in keeping with the application it is being used in than the default square box or the circled dot that are traditionally used. You'll see all of this functionality, and more, in Chapter 2, "Frames, Labels, and Buttons."

Menus and Toolbars

The AWT menu system was very restricted and idiosyncratic. Menus were restricted to frames, where they had to be placed directly under the caption bar and above the useful working area. Furthermore, menus and menu items were not derived from the `Component` class, which meant that they often couldn't be treated in the same way as the other components in an application. JDK 1.1 added a menu shortcut facility, but even that was disappointing because it could be used with menu items, not menus.

By contrast, the Swing menus are all derived from `JComponent` and they are all implemented entirely in Java. As a result, they behave predictably across all platforms and they don't exhibit any platform-specific peculiarities or limitations. AWT-style menu shortcuts are supported on both menus and menu items and, in addition, it is possible to attach *mnemonics* that allow a menu item to be activated with a single keystroke when it is visible and *hotkeys* that activate the menu item even when it is not visible. Figure 1-4 shows a selection of menus and menu items, with mnemonics indicated by underlines.

Swing menus also have other features that are taken for granted elsewhere. For example, you can add an image to the text on a menu item, or remove the text altogether and let the image stand alone, or you can change the font and color of the text or its background subject, of course, to constraints placed by the look-and-feel that

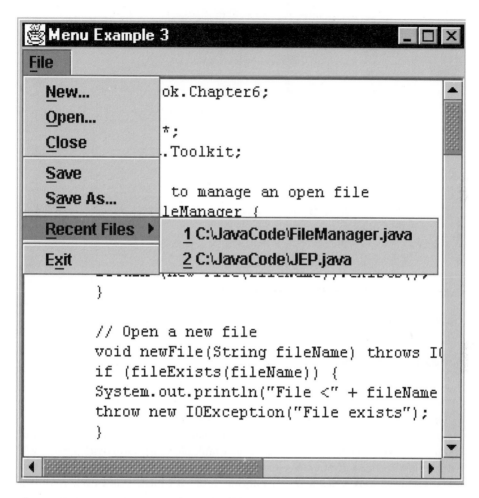

Figure 1-4 Swing menus and menu items.

the user has selected. For the benefit of the programmer, menus now post events as they are posted and removed from the screen so that they can be created and changed in a lazy manner, as they can in other windowing environments.

A relative of the menu bar is the Swing toolbar. The toolbar hosts a two-dimensional arrangement of components, usually buttons with mnemonic images, that allow very fast access to important features of the application. A typical toolbar is shown in Figure 1-5. The toolbar will usually be located under an application's menu bar but it can be placed anywhere on the application's window. Toolbars can also be configured so that they can be completely detached from the window, to float in a separate frame and can later be redocked with the frame under program or user control.

Menus and toolbars are discussed in Chapter 6, "Menus and Toolbars."

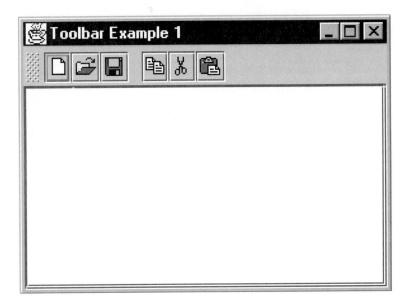

Figure 1-5   The Swing Toolbar.

Text Controls

Swing provides lightweight replacements for the AWT TextField and TextArea controls that provide all the functionality of their predecessors, including the ability to detect and track changes to their content as they are made. The Swing components are, however, built on a complex infrastructure that makes it possible to create more complex text controls that can render text in multiple fonts and colors, possibilities that the AWT does not offer. Swing includes the JTextPane control, which supports text in various styles and can intermix text with images and even AWT and Swing components, to create documents with embedded functionality, and JEditorPane, which can display documents encoded in many different input formats, including HTML. Chapter 9 contains a detailed look at the Swing text components and the underlying support that makes their powerful functionality possible.

Data Selection and Display Controls

One area in which Swing is much more complete than the AWT is its provision of controls for selecting and displaying data. Where the AWT provided the List and Choice controls, Swing has JList and JComboBox, which do everything that their predecessors do and more. Both of these Swing controls can handle large amounts of data easily, whereas on some platforms the AWT components do not cope well with large lists. The Swing controls can also be customized to represent the data they contain in various ways, including the use of images as well as or instead of text and they can also hold selections that are not limited to the strings that the AWT components require. These components are both described in Chapter 8.

Swing also has two data display controls that have no precedent in the AWT. JTree is a very flexible control for displaying data organized in a hierarchical form. As such, it can be used to display, for example, a graphical representation of a file system or anything else with a similar structure. JTable is used to display data that is organized in two-dimensional row and column form and therefore is a natural choice for representing data returned from queries made to a database. Among the facilities of JTable is the ability for the user to rearrange and resize the columns in the table. Both JTable and JTree can be customized in various different ways and they can both allow the user to edit the data being displayed.

Core Note

Both JTree *and* JComboBox *merit chapters of their own (they are described in Chapter 10, "The Tree Control," and Chapter 11, "The Table Control," respectively).*

Timers

JDK 1.1 had no support for timers. If you needed one, the best you could do was to create a separate thread that slept for the required time and then resumed to perform a delayed action or to post an event to another thread. Swing provides the Timer class that allows you to create either a one-off timer that fires once and then stops, or a repeating heartbeat timer. We look at timers and see an example of their use in Chapter 8.

Support for Applets

You can use Swing classes in applets in the same way as you can use AWT classes. In fact, there is very little that we will say about Swing in this book that doesn't apply equally to applications and applets. For this reason, you won't find any applet-specific examples in this book—there simply is no need to make the distinction between these two environments with Swing any more than there is with AWT. There are, however, a couple of points to know about Swing and applets.

First, Swing applets must be based on the JApplet class instead of Applet. JApplet is, in fact, a subclass of Applet. Secondly, JApplet has the same internal structures as the JFrame class that you'll see in Chapter 2. This means that you can have an applet with a layered display and even a menu bar if you want one. Of course, the security restrictions that apply to applets in JDK 1.1 still apply when you use Swing classes in applets, although there are changes in JDK 1.2 that make it possible to relax some of the restrictions under certain circumstances. This is not, however, a Swing issue.

The Swing Packages

The JFC 1.1 product is an add-on to JDK 1.1 that contains the Swing components in a collection of packages, the names of which all start with `com.sun.java.swing`. In JDK 1.2, the same packages exist, but the package name has been changed to `java.awt.swing`. In the code shown in this book, the Swing packages are always assumed to be at `com.sun.java.swing`, etc, which is appropriate for those using JDK 1.1. However, all of the examples are included twice on the CD-ROM, so if you intend to use JDK 1.2, you can install a suitable set of source and class files.

The reason for this duality is to allow applets and applications to be written using the Swing components before the final release of JDK 1.2, or by those who don't want to (or can't) move to JDK 1.2 immediately. The alternative was to place the new components in the `java.awt.swing` package straight away and issue this as an add-on to JDK 1.1, to be naturally superceded by JDK 1.2. However, for security reasons, packages starting with `java` should not be downloadable to browsers. Since this means it would not be possible for the owner of an applet to have the browser download both the Swing-based applet and the Swing classes (in a JAR file), the only alternative would be to require anybody who wanted to view a Swing-enabled applet to obtain and install the `java.awt.swing` packages themselves. Obviously, this is not an inviting prospect for applet writers, since a significant number of their potential customers would not be inclined to do this and therefore the applet's impact would be correspondingly reduced.

By issuing the Swing components in a package structure that is outside the core Java hierarchy, it is possible to have the browser download the Swing JAR along with the applet, or for the applet supplier to create a subset of the Swing JAR that contains only the Swing facilities that the applet requires and have that downloaded to minimize startup time.

Here are the packages that are common to JFC 1.1 and JDK 1.2, grouped by functionality.

- `com.sun.java.swing`
- `com.sun.java.swing.border`
- `com.sun.java.swing.event`
- `com.sun.java.swing.plaf`
- `com.sun.java.swing.plaf.basic`
- `com.sun.java.swing.plaf.metal`
- `com.sun.java.swing.plaf.motif`
- `com.sun.java.swing.plaf.multi`
- `com.sun.java.swing.plaf.windows`
- `com.sun.java.swing.preview`

- `com.sun.java.swing.table`
- `com.sun.java.swing.text`
- `com.sun.java.swing.text.html`
- `com.sun.java.swing.text.rtf`
- `com.sun.java.swing.tree`
- `com.sun.java.swing.undo`

Core Note

The Swing release also contains a package called `com.sun.java.acces-sibility` *that provides support for Java Accessibility in the Swing components. Although the Swing components in JFC 1.1 and JDK 1.2 do implement this support, Accessibility is not covered in this book, so does not appear in this package list.*

com.sun.java.swing and com.sun.java.swing.preview

This package contains the Swing components themselves and many of the interfaces that they use. The classes and interfaces in this package follow a naming convention that helps to identify what type of object they are. For example, the GUI components themselves have names that begin with a `J` (although `Box` is an exception to this rule, because it is not derived from `JComponent`); there is a Swing component to replace every AWT component and usually you can deduce its name by just adding the `J` prefix. A notable exception to this rule is `Choice`, which is replaced by `JList`, a Swing component that also supercedes the AWT `List` control.

Many GUI components and other classes are closely related to each other and have much of their code in a shared base class; these shared classes all have names that start with `Abstract`. Examples of this are `AbstractButton`, which is the base class for all of the Swing buttons (and even for menu items) and `AbstractAction`, which is a basic implementation of the `Action` interface that will be introduced in Chapter 5. As their names suggest, these classes are all abstract.

Many Swing components are composed of several parts; a typical component is made up of a class that represents the control itself (such as `JButton`), a class that knows how to draw the component on the screen and another class that represents the state of the component, known as the component's *model*. The Swing package contains several interfaces that define the methods that the model provides as well as actual implementations of those interfaces that are used by real components. Buttons, for instance, have a model that implements the `ButtonModel` interface. The actual implementation of this model that all of the Swing buttons use is in a class called `DefaultButtonModel`. This naming scheme, whereby a basic, but complete, implementation of an interface is placed in a class whose name is that of the interface with the added prefix `Default`, extends to the other model interfaces and their implementations in the Swing package and is also used in some of the other packages.

The Swing package also contains some classes that are used in the implementation of new mechanisms that can be used with the components themselves. For example, Swing introduces a more flexible focus management mechanism that allows much finer tuning than the mechanism provided in JDK 1.1. The basic methods that make up a Swing focus manager are contained in the abstract `FocusManager` class and there is a complete implementation of a specific focus management policy in the class `DefaultFocusManager`. Similarly, there are classes that support the new API for managing keyboard accelerators and the pluggable look-and-feel mechanism that will be described later in this chapter.

As the deadline for the first official Swing release approached, JavaSoft moved some components from the Swing package into a `preview` package, reflecting the fact that their API was not yet stable. This package is called `com.sun.java.swing.preview`. If you are going to be making use of Swing with JDK 1.1, bear in mind that the programming interface of the components in the `preview` package is very likely to change. This could cause compatibility problems if you plan to move to JDK 1.2 later.

com.sun.java.swing.table and com.sun.java.swing.tree

Swing provides two powerful components that allow you to present collections of data in the form of a tree or a table. The classes for the components themselves, `JTree` and `JTable`, reside with the other GUI components in the Swing package, but both components are sufficiently complex that their data model classes and the other helper classes that are required to make them useful are held in separate packages to avoid cluttering the Swing package and to make it easier to see what is available from `JTree` and `JTable` themselves. Like many of the Swing components, these controls are highly configurable and, by replacing or extending the *renderers* that draw parts of their screen representation, you can fundamentally change they way these controls look. The renderer interfaces are held alongside the tree and table support classes in the `com.sun.java.swing.tree` or `com.sun.java.swing.table` package as appropriate, while the default implementations are look-and-feel specific and so reside in the look-and-feel packages.

The Text Packages

The Swing text components are much more complex than those in the AWT. While you can regard the relatively simple `JTextField` and `JTextArea` controls as straightforward replacements for `TextField` and `TextArea`, in implementation terms they are very different. All of the text controls are derived from the base class

JTextComponent, which resides in the com.sun.java.swing.text package. JTextComponent itself is only a generic wrapper for the large collection of classes that keep track of the content of a text control and how it should be rendered when displayed, the classes that actually display the text and those that react to user input from the keyboard or the mouse. All of these classes reside in the com.sun.java.swing.text package.

The Swing package itself contains three other text components—JPasswordField, JTextPane and JEditorPane, which all rely on support from the classes in the text package. In addition to this, JEditorPane can be configured to render text stored in various different forms, including HTML and Rich Text Format (RTF), for which it uses classes in the com.sun.java.swing.text.html and com.sun.java.swing.text.rtf packages.

A common requirement in sophisticated text management applications, such as word processors, is to be able to undo changes made to the text. The text components are all implemented in such a way that changes made to the control's data model are recorded as transactions that can be reversed (in the right order) or re-applied after being reversed (from the right initial state), so that it is possible to expose to the user an undo/redo facility. The com.sun.java.swing.undo package contains classes that work with the information provided by the text components to make it easier to provide this support.

com.sun.java.swing.border

This package contains all of the standard borders that Swing provides, together with the Border interface that borders must implement, and an abstract base class, AbstractBorder, that forms the basis of all of the Swing borders and that can be used to create new ones.

As you'll see in Chapter 8, borders are not usually created directly. Instead, so that border instances can be shared between components whenever possible, a new border is usually created by using the BorderFactory class, which arranges to satisfy a request for a new border by returning an existing instance if it can be shared. BorderFactory resides in the Swing package.

com.sun.java.swing.event

The Swing components bring with them many new events and event listener classes. Just as the usual AWT events are all held in the java.awt.event package, the Swing events and their listeners reside in com.sun.java.swing.event. Among the new events are ChangeEvent, which reports an unspecified change of state in its source (see the discussion of progress bars and sliders for example of this event) and TreeModelEvent that is generated when the content of a tree's data model changes. While some of the events, such as ChangeEvent, extend the existing

AWTEvent that is the basis of the events in `java.awt.event`, the majority of them,   like   TreeModelEvent are not component-based and are therefore derived directly from `java.util.EventObject` instead. This reflects the fact that most of the events in this package represent things that happen inside a component or as a result of some operation performed by the component on itself, possibly as an indirect result of user interaction, rather than arising directly from actions at the user interface. Changes to the tree's data content can, for example, occur if the user is allowed to edit the tree contents, but the source of the event is the tree's data model itself reporting that it has been changed rather than the tree component, which is just the visual representation of the data.

com.sun.java.swing.plaf

As you already know, a major feature of the Swing components is their ability to be rendered in different ways depending on the look-and-feel packages that are installed on a particular system. This is made possible by placing all of the code that knows how to draw the component in a separate class from the one that the application interacts with, so that it can be changed at run time without affecting code in the application that is holding references to the component objects themselves. In order for this to work, there must be a well-defined interface between each component type and the class that implements its look-and-feel. The `com.sun.java.swing.plaf` contains all of these interfaces (`plaf` stands for Pluggable Look-And-Feel).

All of the objects in this package are actually abstract classes that both specify the actual look-and-feel interface and, in some cases, contain prototypical implementations of some of it. All of them are derived from `com.sun.java.swing.plaf.ComponentUI`, which represents the generic interface (or minimum contract) between a component and its user interface class. The amount of usable code in these classes that could form part of a real look-and-feel class implementation varies from class to class.

This package also contains classes that wrap default values stored by look-and-feel implementations that are used by the user interface classes. For example, many components have several associated colors that are used to fill part of their screen representation. The colors that a control uses will, of course, depend on the look-and-feel, so they are stored separately by each look-and-feel. Instead of storing the colors as a `java.awt.Color` object, however, the color is wrapped with an instance of `com.sun.java.swing.plaf.ColorUIResource` and there are similar classes to wrap fonts and other resources. In Chapter 13, you'll see why these wrapper classes are used.

It is important to realize that this package does not contain any actual look-and-feel implementation: it just stores the classes that define the interfaces that these implementations use.

The Look-and-Feel Packages

Several packages provide the user interface classes for the look-and-feel implementations supplied with Swing. All of these classes reside below com.sun.java.swing.plaf. The com.sun.java.swing.plaf.motif package, for example, contains classes that know how to render all of the Swing components and react to mouse, keyboard and focus changes in such a way as to make the components look and feel as if they were part of a Motif desktop application. Similarly, the com.sun.java.swing.plaf.windows package provides the Windows 95 and Windows NT 4.0 look-and-feel, while the com.sun.java.swing.plaf.metal package contains a custom look-and-feel designed specifically by JavaSoft for Java applications that need to look the same on all platforms.

The com.sun.java.swing.plaf.basic package does not provide a look-and-feel implementation that the user can elect to use. Instead, it provides a set of user interface classes, one for each Swing component, that can be used (by programmers) either directly or as the basis for a more customized one in a real look-and-feel package. For example, the user interface class for the JTree component, com.sun.java.swing.plaf.basic.BasicTreeUI, is used as the base class for the tree user interface for Windows (WindowsTreeUI in the com.sun.java.swing.plaf.windows package), Motif (MotifTreeUI in com.sun.java.swing.plaf.motif) and for the Metal look-and-feel (MetalTreeUI in com.sun.java.swing.plaf.metal). You'll see examples of the available user interfaces and how they render various components later in this chapter and throughout this book.

Core Alert

Sometimes, the only way to make a Swing component do exactly what you want it to do is to make use of an interface that is look-and-feel specific. You'll see several examples where this is the case in this book. Strictly speaking, JavaSoft has not finally frozen the interface between the Swing components and their look-and-feel implementations, so if you plan on using this interface, be prepared to evolve your software as you migrate to later releases of Swing. It is likely that these interfaces will stabilize when the final release of JDK 1.2 appears.

com.sun.java.swing.plaf.multi

By default, a component only has a single user interface associated with it at any time. However, by using the *multiplexing* look-and-feel provided by the com.sun.java.swing.plaf.multi package, it is possible for more than one user interface from any of the other look-and-feel packages, or from a custom package, to be connected to a single component at one time. This can be useful if, for example, you want a text component to be able to draw its content on the screen and also to be able to "read" that content through a sound card. This is particularly important in an application that uses the Java Accessibility features to make itself more usable by those with sight impairments, for example.

The implementation of the look-and-feel in this package is such that this requirement can be satisfied without any other look-and-feel package knowing that it is being used in connection with another one to manage a single component.

The Model-View-Controller Architecture

The major difference between the Swing components and their AWT counterparts is that the Swing controls are written entirely in Java and, as a result, do not depend on any code provided by the host windowing system to provide their visual appearance or their functionality. On its own, this change makes it possible to create controls that look the same on any platform. However, the controls have not simply been re-implemented in Java—they have, in fact, been completely redesigned using a paradigm that is well-known in object-oriented programming, called the model-view-controller architecture, or MVC for short.

To avoid getting lost in obscure and abstract discussions, let's look at what the MVC architecture means in terms of a concrete example and then show why this particular way of implementing components is so useful. At the end of the chapter, when you've seen what has been done and why it has been done, you'll find some examples of the results, and you'll be able to decide for yourself whether or not it was actually worthwhile! If, after this, you're sold on the idea of having a customized appearance to your applications, or even to somebody else's applications, in Chapter 13 you'll see in more detail how to go about implementing your own look-and-feel.

An MVC Component: a Button

To see what the MVC architecture is and how it relates to the Swing components, let's look at how you might go about designing a component that represents a button. A button is a control that has pieces that represent all three parts of the MVC architecture and it is also simple and well-understood, so it should be easy to use it to examine and assess a new component architecture.

Fundamentally, a button is an object that does little more than sit on a user interface and wait for you to click it. When it has been clicked, it changes its appearance so that it looks pushed-in, generates an event for some interested party to catch, then redraws itself to look popped-out again. It couldn't be much simpler in principle, but there is a little more to it than this straightforward description would suggest. Before going any further, read back over the first part of this paragraph. By and large, what I've told you is what the button looks like while it is being used: it starts in a popped-up state, it changes appearance so that it appears to be pushed in, and then it pops back out again. These few words actually describe what the *view* part of a Swing component is supposed to know about—how the component should look at any given time.

Core Note

Here and throughout the book you'll find descriptions of components and how they behave. Swing poses a particularly difficult problem for authors in that there is no single way for a component to look or behave—exactly what it looks like or what it does can depend crucially on the look-and-feel that is being used. In this book, unless indicated otherwise, the descriptions match the way components look and behave when the Metal look-and-feel is selected.

In this case, you can see that the button has two different representations that the view has to be able to reproduce. In fact, though, there are more than that. Buttons are not always in an active state: if you create a form with several fields that need to be filled in, with an OK button to be pressed when the form is complete, it makes little sense to offer the possibility for the user to be able to actually press it until all mandatory fields have been completed. To implement this kind of functionality, the button (along with other components) can be either enabled or disabled at any given time. Naturally, the button will only respond to a click when it is enabled. Having a software switch that records the state of the button is useful for the programmer, but of no use to the user, who can't see it, so to make it clear when the button can and can't be pressed, it is normal for the view to render it differently. Thus, there are three different ways to draw a button (only three, because a pressed-in disabled button should not be possible!). More could be added to this, but for now it should be clear that the view has to render the button differently depending on its state.

The state of the button is, of course, something that would be part of any component that represented it. In fact, the button's total state is the *model* part of the MVC architecture. So far, you've seen two items that are legitimate parts of the model—whether the button is pressed in and whether it is enabled. If you started looking more closely at the problem, you would soon see that there are a few more attributes that you would need to have; those attributes would all be held in the model.

You now know that the button holds its state in the model and that the view uses the model to decide how to draw the button. The other important feature of the button is that its state can change—when you click on it with the mouse, or give it the focus and press the space or return key, the button is activated. Obviously, something must be monitoring the mouse and the keyboard and the fact that the button has received or lost the focus, in order to notice that a state change is necessary. The part of the component that receives and responds to input is the *controller*.

Let's represent all of this with a diagram. Figure 1-6 shows a representation of the various pieces of the button in the MVC architecture and it also shows how the state of the various pieces can change. When the button is created, all three pieces come into existence and get connected together; you'll see later how this is done. The model adopts an initial state: Usually, the button isn't pressed and in this case it will start life enabled. When the button first becomes visible, the view uses the model's initial state to draw it in the appropriate way.

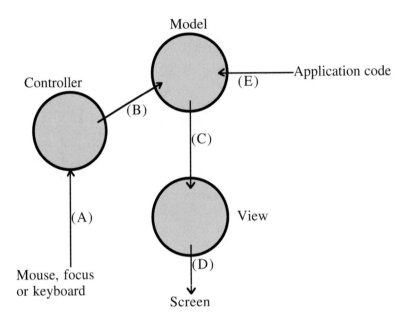

Figure 1-6 A button as an MVC component.

Now suppose that the user clicks the button with the mouse. This action is detected by the controller, which interprets it as a request to click the button. A click actually requires two steps—first, the button is pressed and then it is released. When the mouse button is pressed, the controller tells the model to change its state to reflect the fact that the button itself has been pressed. The button now needs to be redrawn so that it looks pressed in. To make this happen, the model notifies the view that its state has changed, by generating an *event* that the view has registered to receive. On receipt of this event, the view queries the model for its new state and redraws the button accordingly.

When the user releases the mouse button, the controller detects it and changes the model again so that the button's state indicates that it is not pressed. This caus-es the model to generate another event to the view, as a result of which the button will be redrawn in its *up* state. This particular state change, from *pressed* to *not pressed* also causes the model to generate another event that can be delivered to application code to indicate that the button has been clicked. This is the only piece of this interaction that is important to code outside the button: The rest has only been visible inside the button.

Now suppose the button were disabled instead of enabled. What difference would this have made? When the mouse is pressed over the button, the controller will still detect it and will attempt to change the model's state to reflect this. However, the fact that the button is disabled is held within the model. When the model is disabled it doesn't allow the button's pressed state to be changed, so no event will be generated to the view and the button's appearance won't change. As far as the user is concerned, the button press was ignored.

There is another way in which the button's state can change: Code in the application can change the enabled state of the button, or it can programmatically perform a *click* as if the mouse had been pressed and then released. Disabling the button is an action performed by the model and, of course, causes an event to the view, which will make the button be redrawn with the usual "grayed-out" appearance. Similarly, clicking the button is performed as a two-step interaction with the model in which a mouse press and a mouse release are simulated, without going through the controller. The model, of course, doesn't know which piece of software is changing its state—be it controller or application code, it still sends events to the view and, if necessary, generates the event for the button click.

The MVC Button Implementation in Swing

What has just been described is the purist approach to the MVC architecture in which there are three pieces of software that separately implement the model, the view and the controller and which get bound together when the button is created. You have also seen that application code can directly change the model to click the button or change its enabled state.

In practice, while this exact architecture is used for some components (for example the text components that you'll see in Chapter 9), many of the Swing controls are built slightly differently. In these cases, the view and the controller are merged into one entity that implements the functions of both. Also, applications usually don't have to interact directly with the model. Instead, the component itself often (but not always) exposes methods that manipulate the model, so that the almost always deals only with the component.

What do we mean by 'the component' here? Isn't the whole thing the component? In fact, the component is usually made up of several pieces; in the case of the button, these are as follows:

1. An instance of a class that implements the model. In the case of an ordinary button, this class is called `DefaultButtonModel`.

2. An instance of a class that knows how to draw the button that fulfills the role of the view. A class called `BasicButtonUI` does this job for ordinary buttons. As you'll see in Chapter 13, the button's border is provided by yet another class, which we consider to be part of the view for the purposes of this discussion.

3. An instance of a class that responds to user input, in the role of controller. For the button, this role is played by the BasicButtonListener class.

4. A wrapper class that provides the programming interface to the button and hides the other pieces. The Swing class that represents a button is JButton.

Core Note

You can see that the button actually has separate view and controller classes. Many other components do not.

In this case, when we speak of the "the component," we would be referring to the JButton instance, because this is what the application program would almost always interact with. However, all of the Swing components that have a model provide a method that allows applications to access it directly if they need to. For some controls, there is no way to change the model via the component—you have to go directly to the model.

Using MVC to Enable the Pluggable Look-and-Feel Architecture

The MVC architecture is the cornerstone of the pluggable look-and-feel feature in Swing. If you wanted to take a button and make it look different and, perhaps, make it respond to different keys or mouse events, you would need to modify the controller and the view. You wouldn't change the model, because you need the same button states—after all, this is still a button, no matter how you draw it and you wouldn't want to change the programming interface to the wrapper component either because if you did, you would make it difficult to substitute your button for an existing one. So, if you wanted to be able to substitute one button look-and-feel for another easily, you would need to design your components in such a way that the view and controller could be removed and replaced by another one without disturbing anything else. This, of course, is one reason why the view and controller are often implemented as a single unit.

Core Note

You can change the button's model for another one if you want to, provided that it implements the same interface as the default model. This is, however, an application issue and is not strictly part of the pluggable look-and-feel architecture because it does not affect the button's appearance.

Plugging in new view-controller units means having a well-defined interface between this part and the component itself and having an interface that tells the component that the look-and-feel specific part is being changed. In fact, the actual interface that is needed will depend on the type of component because, as you can imagine, a tree control is vastly more complex than a button. There is, however, a core set of methods that is required by every pluggable unit. This core set is specified in Swing by the abstract class `com.sun.java.swing.plaf.ComponentUI`. The suffix `UI` here is common to all of the classes in `com.sun.java.swing.plaf` that specify an interface between a particular component and its view-controller implementation. Other examples are `TreeUI`, `TableUI`, `LabelUI` and so on. Each of these is an abstract class that is derived from `ComponentUI`.

Core Note

In cases where the view and controller are separate, the view class, naturally enough, is the one that has the `UI` suffix.

If you wanted to change the way a Swing component looks or behaves, you would write a class that implemented all the methods in the corresponding `UI` class for that type of component and arrange for it to be plugged in at run time. For example, to create a new look-and-feel for a tree, you would have to implement a class that provided all the methods of `TreeUI`. The Swing packages, as we know, contain several look-and-feel packages. These packages all consist of a set of classes that implement (or inherit) all of the methods of all of the `UI` classes in the `com.sun.java.swing.plaf` directory.

The `ComponentUI` class has only a very small number of methods; every pluggable component module must, of course, provide all of them:

```
public abstract class ComponentUI() {
    public static ComponentUI createUI(JComponent c);
    public void installUI(JComponent c);
    public void uninstallUI(JComponent c);
    public void update(Graphics g, JComponent c);
    public void paint(Graphics g, JComponent c);
    public Dimension getPreferredSize(JComponent c);
    public Dimension getMinimumSize(JComponent c);
    public Dimension getMaximumSize(JComponent c);
    public boolean contains(JComponent c, int x, int y);
}
```

The gory details of how the actual pluggable look-and-feel mechanism works are not discussed in this chapter, because most of the time, you don't really need to know how the component is created in order to use it. These details are important only if you want to create a replacement look-and-feel, so we'll confine ourselves to a basic outline here. If you want to know more, you'll find complete coverage in Chapter 13.

The first three methods deal with creating a UI object for a control and connecting it to the component. When, for example, a button is created, the `createUI` method of the button UI class for the look-and-feel that happens to be active is called. This is a static method and its job is to return an object that can be plugged into a `JButton`. If the Metal look-and-feel is selected, the `createUI` method of `MetalButtonUI` will be called and it will return a new `MetalButtonUI`, which will be installed into the `JButton`. To tell the new `MetalButtonUI` object that this has happened and to let it know which component it is associated with, its `installUI` method is called. As you can see, this method receives a reference to the component into which the UI class is being installed as an argument.

It is possible to replace the `UI` after the component has been created. If this is happening, the old `UI` class is disconnected from the component by calling its `uninstallUI` method, then the `installUI` method of the replacement `UI` is invoked. The job of creating `UI` classes for components, based on the currently selected look-and-feel, is carried out by a class called `UIManager` that resides in the `com.sun.java.swing` package.

The remaining methods are invoked when the component is in use and they deal with things that only the look-and-feel class can know about. Clearly, drawing the component is very look-and-feel specific, so most (but not all) of this is handled by the UI class's `update` and `paint` methods. Similarly, a component's size can depend on how it is being drawn, so the `JComponent` methods that determine how big a component can be or wants to be do their job by calling the corresponding method in the UI class. Finally, the `contains` method, as its name suggests, determines whether a given point is "inside" the component; if the drawn shape of the component is irregular, deciding whether a point is inside or not cannot be done by generic code—instead, the question is passed to the UI class, which knows how the component is drawn.

Selecting the Look-and-Feel

When an application starts, its `UIManager` needs to know which of the available look-and-feel classes to use. The user can determine the selected UI by editing the file `swing.properties`. This file resides in the `lib` directory of the user's Java installation so that, for example, if the Java software has been installed in `C:\java`, this file will be called `C:\java\lib\swing.properties`.

The content of this file is a set of `property = value` lines, which will be described in Chapter 13. The only line of interest here is the following one:

```
swing.defaultlaf = com.sun.java.swing.plaf.metal.MetalLookAndFeel
```

The `swing.defaultlaf` property must be set to the name of the class that provides the look-and-feel support. This example selects the Metal look-and-feel. To select Motif, use this line:

```
swing.defaultlaf = com.sun.java.swing.plaf.motif.MotifLookAndFeel
```

and to use the Windows look-and-feel, you need this line:

```
swing.defaultlaf = com.sun.java.swing.plaf.windows.WindowsLookAndFeel
```

If `swing.properties` doesn't exist, or it doesn't contain a `swing.defaultlaf` property, the cross-platform Metal look-and-feel will be used.

Core Note

If you are using JDK 1.2, these lines will, of course, need to be changed to look like this:

```
swing.defaultlaf = java.awt.swing.plaf.metal.MetalLookAndFeel
swing.defaultlaf = java.awt.swing.plaf.motif.MotifLookAndFeel
swing.defaultlaf = java.awt.swing.plaf.windows.WindowsLookAndFeel
```

When you are running the examples in this book or developing your own programs, you'll find it useful to switch between the various look-and-feel classes to see how a program looks with the different styles installed. Chapter 13 shows you how to give an application the ability to switch its look-and-feel on command, but, if you aren't using a program that can do that, the only way around it is to stop the program, edit `swing.properties` and then start the application again. To save time, I keep all three of the above lines in my file and comment out the two that I don't want by placing a "#" at the start of the line. Here's what my file looks like when I want to run an example with the Motif look-and-feel:

```
#swing.defaultlaf = com.sun.java.swing.plaf.metal.MetalLookAndFeel
swing.defaultlaf = com.sun.java.swing.plaf.motif.MotifLookAndFeel
#swing.defaultlaf = com.sun.java.swing.plaf.windows.WindowsLookAndFeel
```

One Application, Three Disguises

To conclude this chapter, let's see how a typical Swing application's appearance changes when its look-and-feel is switched, by looking ahead to a program that will be developed in Chapter 10. This program demonstrates the Swing tree component by using it to display a view of a file system on a PC. The meaning of what you're actually seeing here is not really important—what is important is the way in which the tree's content is presented. Look carefully at Figures 1-7, 1-8, and 1-9 and notice the differences in the way that the trees are drawn. As you look at these figures,

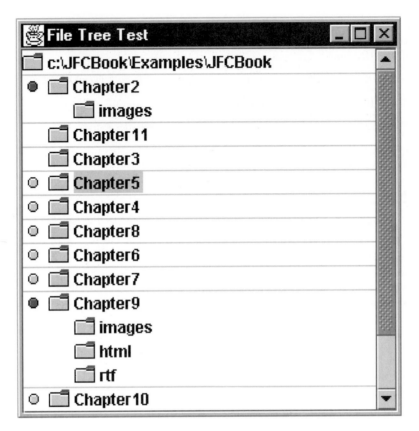

Figure 1-7   The Metal look-and-feel.

remember that the program was only written once and no code was changed between these three screen shots.

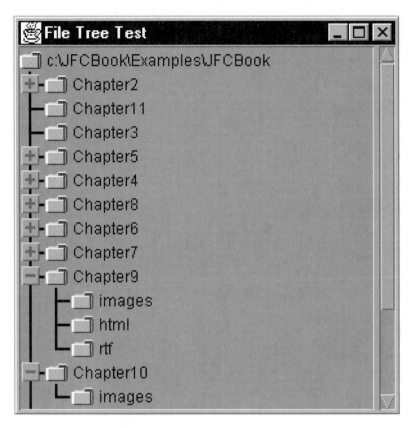

Figure 1-8   The Motif look-and-feel.

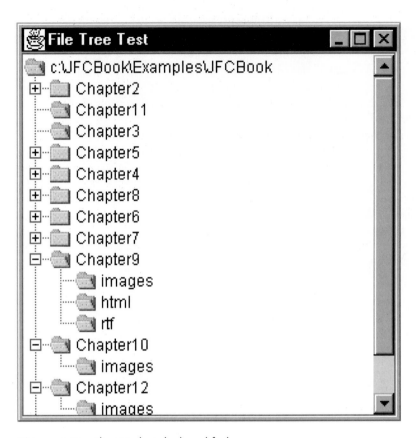

Figure 1-9   The Windows look-and-feel.

Summary

This chapter introduced the Java Foundation Classes and, in particular, the Swing component set, which is the major new feature of JFC 1.1. It presented the history of the JFC and described how the Swing components relate to their AWT predecessors.

You also saw the major features of the Swing set and were introduced to the "core" class, `JComponent`, which makes most of them possible. After a brief description of the Swing packages, you were shown the architecture of the Swing components and how this architecture makes it possible to change the appearance of a component or of a complete application without changing any application code.

In the rest of this book, you'll be introduced to all of the Swing components and to many of the new facilities that Swing provides. The next chapter, however, covers some basic ground by discussing the fundamentals of the AWT, and then introduces two of the simpler Swing controls—`JLabel` and `JButton`.

FRAMES, LABELS AND BUTTONS

Topics in This Chapter

- The JFrame Class
- Components, Containers and Layout Managers
- Events and Event Listeners
- Labels, Buttons and Images

Chapter 2

This chapter presents both an introduction to some of the Swing components and a review of the fundamentals of the Abstract Window Toolkit, covering the information that you'll be needing throughout the book. You'll first be introduced to the `JFrame` class, which is the Swing component that acts as your application's main window. You'll see how to create a `JFrame` and how to control its location, size and its colors.

Within the frame, you'll want to place other components that make up your application's user interface. Before you can begin building your interface, you need to know how you can control and customize these components. You'll look at the properties that all of the Swing components expose and see the difference between a simple component and a container. You'll also have a brief look at the job of the layout manager, which controls the locations of components within containers, in preparation for a thorough discussion of this topic in the next chapter.

The second part of this chapter takes a close look at two of the simplest but most commonly used Swing components—labels and buttons. The Swing versions of these components are more powerful than their AWT counterparts because, among other things, they can display images as well as text. In the course of discussing these components, you'll find a review of the AWT event model and you'll see how the Swing `ImageIcon` class makes it much easier than ever before to load images for use with labels and buttons.

If you are already familiar with the Abstract Window Toolkit, you will find a lot of this chapter familiar, but you'll also find some things that are completely new and much that has changed since JDK 1.1.

The Shell of an Application: The JFrame Class

When you start any Java program with a graphical user interface (GUI), you see a window where the application will display its output and into which the user will type input with the keyboard or point and click with the mouse. When you use the Swing components, this top-level window is implemented by `com.sun.java.swing.JFrame`. Like some of the other Swing components, `JFrame` is derived from an AWT control; other examples of this are `JDialog` and `JWindow`. Figure 2-1 shows how the components that are introduced in this chapter are related to each other and to the heavyweight AWT controls that you are familiar with. In this diagram, the shaded rectangles represent AWT controls and all the others are Swing components. This diagram shows clearly that `JFrame` is derived from the familiar AWT `Frame` class.

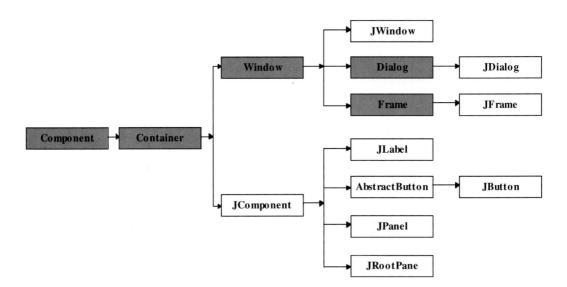

Figure 2-1   A basic AWT and Swing component hierarchy.

Creating a frame and making it visible are very simple tasks in Java. It can be done as easily as this:

```
package JFCBook.Chapter2;

import com.sun.java.swing.*;

public class BasicFrame {
```

```
      public static void main(String[] args) {
        JFrame f = new JFrame("Simple Frame");
        f.setSize(250, 200);
        f.setVisible(true);
      }
}
```

Running this trivial program under Windows 95, using the command

```
java JFCBook.Chapter2.BasicFrame
```

produces the result shown in Figure 2-2.

Figure 2-2   The Swing JFrame.

The string that is supplied to the constructor is used as the frame's caption.
Alongside it on the caption bar are the *minimize, maximize* and *close* buttons that top-
level windows usually have. If you try the minimize and maximize buttons, you will
find that they both work as you expect—the minimize button causes the frame to
iconify and the maximize button makes it grow to fill the entire screen. When the
frame is full-screen sized, the maximize button changes to another one that allows
you to restore the frame to its original size. Furthermore, if you move the mouse to
the lower right corner of the frame, the cursor changes as it normally does to show

that you can drag the mouse to resize the frame. Move the mouse over the caption bar and drag it, and you will find that the frame moves around the screen. In short, this is a fully-fledged application window, created with only three lines of code.

Sizing the Application Frame and Making It Visible

Having created the frame, the next step is to set its size:

```
f.setSize(250, 100);
```

When the frame is first created, its internal width and height are both zero and they will stay that way until you do something to change them. If you removed this line from the example code and ran it again, you would get a frame with the caption bar just large enough to contain the usual buttons and a small part of the caption text and the application icon at the far left.

Unfortunately, a frame cannot make an intelligent guess as to how large you would like it to be. Even if you create a frame with some useful content, it still won't enlarge itself so that you can actually see what it contains – it is always necessary to explicitly size a frame to make its content visible. You don't, however, have to tell it the exact size that you want, as you'll see later.

All frames start out invisible, allowing you to create and add other elements of the user interface away from the user's eyes. This trivial application does not have any more content to add to the frame, so you can just make it visible right after setting its size:

```
f.setVisible(true);
```

Once the frame is visible, the user can interact with it using the mouse. You've seen that it behaves as a normal top-level window in every respect, apart from one. If you click the close button, you would probably expect the frame to disappear and the application to terminate. In fact, the window does disappear, but the application continues running, with nothing to do.

When you press the close button, the Java libraries notify your application by generating an event that you can choose to intercept. In this example, no arrangement was made to receive the event and, as a result, the request to close the window is handled by default code in the JFrame class, which simply makes the window invisible again.

Core Note

If you're familiar with JDK 1.1, you will have noticed that this is different from the behavior of Frame, *which doesn't close unless the application processes the event caused by pressing the close button and takes explicit action to allow the close to proceed. As you'll see in Chapter 3, "Managing the User Interface," you can, if you wish, make* JFrame *adopt the JDK 1.1* Frame *behavior. If you're porting code from JDK 1.1 to use Swing classes, this is one of several important differences that you need to look out for.*

In real-world applications, you need to be careful to take proper action when the user tries to close the top-level window: at the very least, your application might need to save any data the user has entered that has not yet been written away. You'll find out more about events and how to handle them later in this chapter and you'll see exactly what happens when the user clicks the frame close button in Chapter 3. In the meanwhile, if you want to stop this simple application, you'll have to go to the command line prompt at which you started it and kill it from there (`Ctrl-C` usually works with both DOS and Unix; if this doesn't work, try the `DEL` key).

Position and Color

There are a couple of other things that we did not do to the frame before we made it visible that the Java libraries have done for us. Most obviously, how did the frame know where to appear? If you don't tell a frame where it should be, the platform-specific toolkit implementation is free to choose a default position for you. Current implementations place the frame at the top-left corner of the screen, so starting more than one application with default positioning results in them being overlaid on top of each other.

Sometimes, of course, you need to place a top-level window in a specific position on the screen. This is most commonly the case with dialogs, which allow the user to customize an application or control its behavior at certain critical points. Dialogs are usually placed on top of the application window and are often arranged to be centered over it. To allow you to influence a window's position, Java provides the `setBounds` method, which lets you specify its size and position at the same time.

> ### Core Note
>
>
>
> *There are three Swing classes that can act as top-level windows—*`JWindow`*,* `JDialog` *and* `JFrame`*. This book will always refer to* `JDialog` *and* `JFrame` *using their class names or, less formally, as* dialog *or* frame*. When describing a feature that applies equally to dialogs and frames, the more general term* window *is often used. Do not confuse this use of the word* window *with the Swing* `JWindow` *class, which we won't say much about in this book.* `JWindow` *is used almost exclusively to create popups but, as you'll see later, not all popups are created this way. In this book, the unadorned term* window *will never be used to mean* `JWindow`*.*

If you had wanted to start the application and have its frame appear 30 pixels down and 40 pixels to the right of the top left-hand corner of the screen, you would have replaced the `setSize` line that was used earlier with the following:

```
f.setBounds(40, 30, 250, 200);
```

Note, however that, strictly speaking, the requested position is only a *hint* to the windowing system about where it should place a window—nothing is guaranteed. On Unix, for example, the window manager may be operating a policy that totally disregards the application's placement request in favor of a common policy enforced across the user's desktop.

The other thing that the Java libraries did was to set the frame's colors. These colors are not arbitrary—they depend on the look-and-feel that is selected. Each look-and-feel has a set of colors that it uses for particular parts of the user interface. These colors are all grouped together in the look-and-feel's `UIDefaults` table, along with a host of other properties that vary between different look-and-feel implementations. You can read more about this table and how it is used by Swing components in Chapter 13, "The Pluggable Look-and-Feel." Both the Windows and Motif look-and-feel give the application's frame a gray background, whereas the Metal look-and-feel has the capability of supporting several colors schemes or *themes*. The Metal color scheme installed by default also has a gray frame background. You'll see more about how the frame's color is actually determined when you look at the `JFrame` class in more detail a bit later in the chapter.

Components and Their Properties

At the top of the class hierarchy for all user interface elements is the `java.awt.Component` class. `Component` is an abstract class, so you can't actually instantiate it. The only way to create one is to use one of the Swing or AWT controls that are derived from it, or to create your own subclass. In JDK 1.0, it wasn't possible to directly subclass `Component,` because its constructor had package scope. If you wanted to create a custom component, you had to extend one of the AWT controls. With JDK 1.1, this restriction was removed, but subclassing `Component` (or, as you'll see later its derived class `Container`) produces a different result from subclassing an AWT control.

All of the AWT controls have a corresponding window in the native windowing system. The connection between the Java code that implements the AWT control and the windowing system is provided by a so-called *peer* class, of which there is one for each type of AWT component and whose methods are implemented in native code. A control created by directly subclassing `Component` is referred to as a *lightweight component*, because it does not have an associated window in the native windowing system or a peer class, and therefore incurs less system overhead. Instead of having its own window, a lightweight component borrows an area of its parent's window, an important consequence of which is that, if a lightweight component chooses not to fill in its background, then the contents of its parent will show through. This means that it can be transparent, a fact that can be used to great effect in many of the Swing controls that are discussed in this book.

With only a few exceptions, the Swing components are all derived from `JComponent`, which is a subclass of `Component` and, therefore, almost all of the

Swing components are lightweight. Given that `Component` is the ultimate ancestor of all of the Swing user interface elements, any and all of its methods and fields are applicable to all of the Swing controls. If you want to know the features of a Swing control or how to make it behave in a particular way, the first place to look is in the API definition for `JComponent` and then at those of `Container` and `Component`.

Core Alert

Keep in mind at all times that `JComponent` is the ancestor of most, but not all, of the Swing components. The important exceptions to this rule are `JFrame`, `JDialog`, `JWindow` and `JApplet`, which are all derived directly from their AWT counterparts. As a result, these components are not lightweight. The most important consequence of this, however, is that you can't do with them many of the useful things that you can do with `JComponent`s, such as directly assign key accelerators (see Chapter 5, "Keyboard Handling, Actions and Scrolling," for a discussion of key accelerators). These classes are, however, all derived from `Component`, so most of what is said in this section applies equally to them.

A component, lightweight or otherwise, has several important properties, among which are the following:

- Position
- Size
- Background and foreground colors
- Font
- Visibility
- Enabled or disabled status.

Position

A component's position is specified in x and y coordinates. In Java, all coordinates are measured in pixels relative to an absolute coordinate space that has the top left-hand corner of the screen as the origin ($x = 0$, $y = 0$) and where x coordinates increase as you move from left to right and y coordinates increase as you move toward the bottom of the screen. The coordinates of a `JFrame` that sits directly on the desktop are, as you have already seen, given relative to the top left-hand corner of the screen and are therefore absolute values. However, a typical application is made up of many components that reside inside the frame. It is not convenient to specify the coordinates of these components as absolute values, because they would all have to be adjusted if the frame's position were changed.

To avoid this problem, the position of a nested component is measured relative to that of its parent. As the parent moves, its coordinates may change, but those of its children will still be correct. To calculate the absolute coordinates of any child component, you simply add its coordinates to those of its parent.

You can retrieve the coordinates of a component relative to its parent using either the getLocation or getBounds methods of Component. The first of these returns a Point object that contains only the component's x and y coordinates, while the second returns a Rectangle containing both the position and the size of the component. These methods work equally well for both a top-level frame and a component mounted on a container.

Core Note

A container *is a component that can contain other components, of which* JFrame *is an example. Containers are discussed in detail later in this chapter.*

If you want to get the position of a component relative to the screen (that is, its absolute position), you can use the getLocationOnScreen method which, like getLocation, returns a Point. For a top-level window (JFrame, JDialog or JWindow), getLocation and getLocationOnScreen return the same result. The example in Listing 2-1 shows how these methods are used. You can try this example using the command

```
java JFCBook.Chapter2.ComponentPosition
```

Listing 2-1   Measuring a component's position

```
package JFCBook.Chapter2;

import com.sun.java.swing.*;
import java.awt.*;

public class ComponentPosition {
  public static void main(String[] args) {
    JFrame f = new JFrame("Simple Frame");
    JButton b = new JButton("Press");
    Container cp = f.getContentPane();
    cp.setLayout(new FlowLayout());
    cp.add(b);
    f.setBounds(40, 50, 250, 200);
    f.setVisible(true);
    System.out.println("Frame position is " + f.getLocation());
    System.out.println("Frame screen position is " + f.getLocationOnScreen());
    System.out.println("Content pane position is " + cp.getLocation());
```

```
System.out.println("Content pane screen position is " + cp.getLocationOnScreen());
    System.out.println("Button position is " + b.getLocation());
    System.out.println("Button screen position is " + b.getLocationOnScreen());
    }
}
```

This code creates a frame and places a button on it. You use the `setLayout` method to associate a *layout manager* with a container. Layout managers apply policies to arrange components within a container and determine how big each component should be. Here, the `FlowLayout` manager is used to control the positioning of the button. As a result, as you will see in Chapter 3 where layout managers are discussed in detail, it will appear just under the caption bar and will be horizontally centered in the frame, as shown in Figure 2-3.

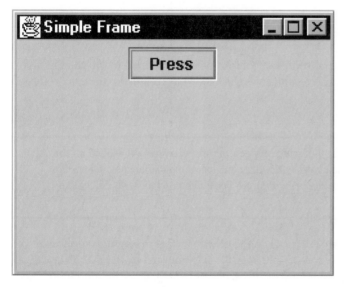

Figure 2-3 Placing a button on a JFrame.

The button is placed on the frame as follows:

```
Container cp = f.getContentPane();
cp.setLayout(new FlowLayout());
cp.add(b);
```

The `add` method belongs to the `java.awt.Container` class; it arranges for the button to become a child of a part of the frame called its *content pane*. Notice that the button was not added directly to the frame. If you're used to the JDK 1.1

Frame class, this may look a bit strange to you. Exactly what the content pane is and when to use it are covered later in this chapter. In terms of Figure 2-3, the content pane occupies the whole of the frame apart from its caption bar and the gray border around the outside—in other words, it is the lighter colored rectangular area in the middle of the frame. Here, then, we have a button sitting on top of the content pane that resides inside the JFrame. In fact, as you'll see, there is more to it than just these three components, but this simplified description will suffice to illustrate how coordinates are managed.

The output from this program is as follows:

```
Frame position is java.awt.Point[x=40,y=50]
Frame screen position is java.awt.Point[x=40,y=50]
Content pane position is java.awt.Point[x=0,y=0]
Content pane screen position is java.awt.Point[x=44,y=73]
Button position is java.awt.Point[x=86,y=5]
Button screen position is java.awt.Point[x=130,y=78]
```

Here you can clearly see the relationships described earlier. Looking first at the content pane and the button, you can see that the content pane's absolute screen coordinates are ($x = 44$, $y = 73$), while those of the button are ($x = 130$, $y = 78$). The position of the button relative to the content pane is obtained by subtracting these component pairs, giving the result ($x = 86$, $y = 5$), which is indeed the value returned by getLocation.

Core Note

The actual coordinates that you see if you run this example will depend on the resolution of your display. While the absolute values may differ, the relationships between the sets of components that are being described here will still be the same.

Now prepare for a surprise. Look at the coordinates of the frame and those of the content pane. The frame is at ($x = 40$, $y = 50$), as requested by the setBounds call in the program, and the content pane is located at ($x = 44$, $y = 73$). Subtracting these two, we should find that the coordinates of the content pane relative to the frame are ($x = 4$, $y = 23$) but the reported coordinates of the pane are ($x = 0$, $y = 0$), which is apparently impossible. In fact, though, as hinted above, the frame, content pane and button are not the only three components involved here. The frame is not actually the parent of the content pane and the content pane's coordinates shown above are not relative to the frame, but to another container that you haven't seen yet. The mystery will be fully explained when you see the complete structure of JFrame later in this chapter.

It is rare to need to specify a fixed position for a component other than a top-level window, because you usually allow a layout manager to decide where exactly components are placed within their container, given constraints such as *place it on the east side* or *divide the container into four equal rectangles and place this component in the top-left corner.* If you wanted to control a component's position and size yourself, however, you would use the `Component setBounds` method, as shown in Listing 2-1, and supply the component's *x* and *y* coordinates relative to the container and its required width and height, in pixels. This method has an overloaded variant that allows you to use a `Rectangle` object to supply the same information. Thus, the following two lines are equivalent:

```
f.setBounds(40, 50, 250, 200);
f.setBounds(new Rectangle(40, 50, 250, 200));
```

If you want to change the position of a component without changing its size, you can use the `setLocation` method, which accepts either a pair of *x* and *y* values or a `Point` structure:

```
f.setLocation(20, 30);
f.setLocation(new Point(20, 30));
```

If your component is derived from `JComponent` (which is usually the case if it isn't an old-style AWT control), you can use two new forms of `getLocation` and `getBounds` methods:

```
public Point getLocation(Point pos);
public Rectangle getBounds(Rectangle rect);
```

The reason for these methods is to save repeated allocation of new `Point` and `Rectangle` objects by allowing the caller to create one instance and reuse it for several calls. If you use the original `getLocation` method, for example, the code that implements it has to create a new `Point` object on each call. Often, you will call this method in a loop, to get the positions of a set of components. If the position of each component is only used once, a lot of wasteful memory allocation and freeing will be performed. It is more efficient to allocate a single `Point` object and pass it to the `getLocation` method each time around the loop. In other words, code that used to look like this:

```
JComponent[] comp = ..... ;  // Get a list of components (not shown)
for (int i = 0; i < count; i++) {
   Point p = comp[i].getLocation();    // Allocates new Point
   System.out.println("Position is " + p);
}
```

can now be written more efficiently like this:

```
JComponent[] comp = ..... ;  // Get a list of components (not shown)
Point p = new Point();          // Use this Point throughout
for (int i = 0; i < count; i++) {
    p = comp[i].getLocation(p);
    System.out.println("Position is " + p);
}
```

The value returned from both these methods is the object that you supply to them, which allows most of the code to remain unchanged from the original.

Core Alert

If you intend to specify absolute positions or sizes for components that you add to a container, you probably want to remove the layout manager like this:

```
setLayout(null);
```

because almost all layout managers will override size and position specifications and place components according to their own layout policy.

Size

Like its position, a component's size is measured in pixels. Unlike position, which is usually stated relative to another component, size is an absolute quantity. A component's size can be obtained using either the getSize or getBounds methods, the former returning a Dimension object containing the width and height and the latter a Rectangle object that also contains the position. Again, if your component is derived from JComponent, you can use two new forms of these methods:

```
public Dimension getSize(Dimension size);
public Rectangle getBounds(Rectangle rect);
```

You saw the new getBounds method in the previous section. As before, you would use the getSize method when you need to make repeated calls to get the sizes of several components and you can use the same Dimension object each time.

When a component is created, it may adopt a natural size, or it may start with no size at all. In general, components like buttons that are initialized with user-defined content (the label in the case of the button), are able to adopt a size suitable for their content, while components such as JPanel (a simple container that replaces the AWT Panel and Canvas classes) that has no natural initial size will start out with its width and height both zero.

The size of a component is almost always constrained by the size of the container it resides in and is usually fixed by the container's layout manager. The layout manager and the container work together to set a suitable initial size and to adjust a component's size, as necessary, should the container be resized.

Resizing a Frame

Most applications allow the user to resize the top-level window and the JFrame class supports this by providing the usual resizing decoration at the bottom right of the window. Sometimes, though, you would prefer the user not to be able to change the frame size. This is particularly often the case for dialogs, which are usually laid out with a fixed size in mind and do not react well when the size is changed. If you want to stop a frame (or dialog) being resized, you can use the `setResizable` method. The following creates a frame that doesn't have resize handles:

```
JFrame f = new JFrame("Fixed size frame");
f.setResizable(false);
```

Core Note

While frames on Unix systems have visible resize handles provided by the window manager, on Windows this is not the case. The fact that a `JFrame` *is not resizable on a Windows system is not obvious until you move the mouse over an edge or over the corner. Usually, this would cause the cursor to change to indicate the directions in which you can drag the edge to change the size. This doesn't happen if the frame is not resizable.*

This should stop you resizing the frame. However, the frame still has a maximize button that allows you to make the frame occupy the entire screen and a minimize button, which means that the frame can be iconified. While the latter is probably not a problem, the former certainly is if your application's carefully thought-out component layout won't stand being blown up to full size. If you must have your frame at its initial size only, your only recourse is to catch the event that is generated when the frame's size changes and force the frame back to its original shape. You can find out about this event in the "Component Events" section of Chapter 3.

Background and Foreground Colors

All components have two associated colors, one that dictates the color of its background, the other that of its foreground. The default colors associated with a component are initially set when it is created and depend on the component involved and on the look-and-feel implementation that the user has selected. Both the foreground and background colors can (at least in theory) be changed by the programmer.

In most cases, it is obvious what is meant by the terms foreground and background in relation to a given component. For buttons and text-based components, the foreground color is used to render the text itself, while the rest of the component takes on the background color, apart from the normal shading effects that serve to give these components their three-dimensional appearance. In most cases, the colors used to provide the shading are derived directly from the background color, so changing the background color automatically adjusts the shading to preserve the three-dimensional effect without any extra work on the part of the programmer.

Core Note

Some components, like JPanel, *which is a simple container, consist entirely of background and therefore do not use their foreground color at all. Since* JPanel *is ultimately derived from* Component, *it still has a foreground color, which the programmer can set. Although of no use to* JPanel, *this property can still be put to some use if the* JPanel *is used as the basis of a custom component that can ascribe some meaning to the foreground color.*

The Java Foundation Classes introduce the concept of a lightweight component that has a transparent background, allowing whatever is behind the component to show through. Transparent components make no use of their background color. All of the Swing components (apart from JFrame, JWindow, JDialog and JApplet, none of which are lightweight components) have an isOpaque method that returns false if they are transparent.

Core Note

Lightweight components were actually introduced by JDK 1.1, but were then deemed to be part of the Java Foundation Classes. The Swing components are the first standard components in the Java core packages to be lightweight.

You set a component's colors using the setForeground and setBackground methods, both of which take an argument of type java.awt.Color. The following code extract creates a text input field and sets both its background and foreground colors.

```
JTextField tf = new JTextField("Text");
tf.setForeground(Color.white);
tf.setBackground(Color.blue);
```

After these statements have been executed, the text field will be initialized to show white text on a blue background. You can use the same methods to change the text field's background and foreground colors at any time, as shown in Listing 2-2.

Listing 2-2   Setting and changing component colors

```
package JFCBook.Chapter2;

import com.sun.java.swing.*;
import java.awt.*;

public class ColorChange {
        public static void main(String[] args) {
```

```
JFrame f = new JFrame("Simple Frame");
JTextField tf = new JTextField("Text");
tf.setForeground(Color.white);
tf.setBackground(Color.blue);
f.getContentPane().setLayout(new BorderLayout());
f.getContentPane().add(tf, "North");
f.setBounds(40, 50, 200, 100);
f.setVisible(true);
try {
  Thread.sleep(10000);
} catch (InterruptedException e) {
  // Ignore
}
tf.setForeground(Color.red);
tf.setBackground(Color.black);
tf.repaint();
  }
}
```

You can run this example using the command

```
java JFCBook.Chapter2.ColorChange
```

The text field in this example starts out with white text on a blue background; after 10 seconds, the foreground and background are changed to red and black, respectively. Sometimes, changing a component's colors does not result in any change to its appearance. If you want the change to be immediate, you can either make the change while the component is not visible and then make it visible, or force the color change to be made by invoking the `repaint` method, which causes the component to redraw itself, as shown in Listing 2-2.

Core Alert

As you know from Chapter 1, "Introduction to the Java Foundation Classes," the appearance of a control is determined entirely by the look-and-feel that you are using. Setting a control's foreground and background colors is only a hint as to how you would like it to appear, but there is no guarantee that it will have any effect. You have just seen that text fields honor the background and foreground colors in the default look-and-feel for your platform (in fact they do this in all three of the standard Swing look-and-feel implementations) but, by contrast, the Swing button class (`JButton`) ignores the background color when the Windows or Motif look-and-feel is installed, since these look-and-feels consider the button to be transparent. The Metal look-and-feel, however, implements an opaque button which will use your supplied background color.

You'll also notice something else new in listing 2-2: to make the text field fill the frame horizontally, we used a `BorderLayout` manager and attached the text field in the `North` of the content pane. You'll see the `BorderLayout`, and the other layout managers, in Chapter 3. The result is shown in Figure 2-4.

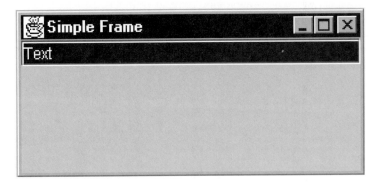

Figure 2-4   A text field on a Jframe.

Methods that deal with colors all accept an argument of type `java.awt.Color`. A `Color` object encapsulates a single, specific color, either one of a small predefined set defined by AWT or a custom color created by the application. The `Color` class defines the following fixed set of standard colors, shown in Table 2-1.

Table 2-1 Standard Colors			
Color.black	Color.blue	Color.cyan	Color.darkGray
Color.gray	Color.green	Color.lightGray	Color.magenta
Color.orange	Color.pink	Color.red	Color.white
Color.yellow			

If these colors don't meet your needs, you can define one of your own by creating a `Color` object and describing your color in terms of red, green and blue (RGB) values. The RGB system represents a color in terms of the levels of its red, green and blue components. Each of these components is specified as a value from 0 to 255 inclusive, where 0 means none of that color is used, while 255 uses as much as possible. A color that has only one nonzero component produces one of the three basic colors in the RGB model:

```
Color r = new Color(255, 0, 0);       // Red
Color g = new Color(0, 255, 0);       // Green
Color b = new Color(0, 0, 255);       // Blue
```

This form of the constructor requires the red, green and blue values as integers, in that order. Using it, you can, for example, create various shades of gray by specifying three numerically equal components, ranging from `Color(0, 0, 0)`, which is black, to `Color(255, 255, 255)`, which produces white. The standard gray (`Color.gray`) is equivalent to `Color(128, 128, 128)` and light gray is `Color(192, 192, 192)`. Some other common colors, all from the predefined set shown in Table 2-1, include:

```
Yellow        Color(255, 255, 0)
Magenta       Color(255, 0, 255);
Cyan          Color(0, 255, 255);
```

Reducing the color levels from 255 while keeping the nonzero components equal produces a darker shade of the same color. For example,

```
Color(255, 255, 255)
```

produces white, while

```
Color(192, 192, 192)
```

gives a shade of gray, and

```
Color(140, 140, 140)
```

also results in gray, but with a darker hue. Another way to produce related colors, without worrying about exactly how they are generated, is to use the `brighter` and `darker` methods of `Color`. For example:

```
Color yellow = Color.yellow;
Color darkerYellow = yellow.darker();
Color brighterYellow = yellow.brighter();
```

This technique is useful when drawing components with shadows, where the darker color would be used to render the part of the component in shadow and the brighter color the more illuminated part.

The `Color` class also has two other constructors:

```
public Color(int rgb);
```

```
public Color(float r, float g, float b);
```

The first form requires an RGB value specified as a single integer, constructed as follows:

```
RGB value = (red value << 16) | (green value << 8) | (blue value)
```

This is the form in which the color value is actually stored by the `Color` object, together with a fourth component that determines how transparent the color is to appear. This fourth component (called the *alpha value*) occupies the top 8 bits of the encoded color and is always initialized to 255, so that the color is fully opaque. The second constructor is given red, green and blue values as floating-point numbers in the range 0.0 to 1.0 inclusive. These values are simply multiplied by 255 and converted integers that are then used to create the RGB value in the usual way.

Core Note

RGB is only one way to define colors. There are various other color models that describe colors in terms of, for example, hue, saturation and brightness or their cyan, magenta and yellow components. JDK 1.2 has some particularly powerful extensions to color handling in the Java 2D package, which is beyond the scope of this volume. Understanding the RGB color space is enough to allow you to make full use of the Swing components.

If you really could freely specify the RGB values independently, then it would seem that you could construct a total of $256 \times 256 \times 256 = 16,777,216$ different colors. Of course, not every video card can cope with so many colors at the same time. Many cards in common use allocate 8 bits per pixel, allowing a maximum of 256 colors on display at any one time. The actual colors used are usually programmable, so the host operating system is responsible for choosing which 256 of the possible 16 million colors are actually available at any given time.

What usually happens is something like this. First, the operating system (or windowing system if the operating system does not take direct responsibility for managing the graphics card) reserves a number of colors for itself. Windows, for example, always reserves 20 fixed colors. Then, colors are allocated to applications based on their requests until all 256 colors have been used up. What happens when all of the available colors have been used up, so that the exact color requested is not available and cannot be added to the active set? There are two techniques available to try to resolve this situation.

First, the application could be allocated the closest available color based on the host environment's determination of *closest*. This is the only real solution if you are just drawing lines in a color that is not available. If you are filling areas of screen, however, there is a second possibility—the windowing system or the graphics driver may choose to approximate your color by *dithering*, which involves using combinations of different colors to cover the area in such a way that the eye is fooled into seeing a color that is actually not present but is a good approximation to the color that was requested. For example, a properly constructed pattern of a darkish color with interspersed dots of white can give the illusion of a lighter version of the dark color.

In practice, you have little control over the way in which your colors are actually represented on the screen. Fortunately, for many purposes, it is possible to stick with the standard color set, which Java maps to the closest colors on your platform.

Core Tip

If you are using JDK 1.2, the Java 2D package gives you much greater control over colors than is available in JDK 1.1.

Colors and the Look-and-Feel

All of the Swing components have default colors, which usually depend on the look-and-feel installed. If your application never changes the colors of the standard components, you don't really need to worry about how they are determined, because you can be sure that they will be consistent across the user interface and will fit in with the look-and-feel in use.

However, if you are using a third-party component that doesn't behave well in the presence of multiple user interface styles or you are creating a component of your own, you will need to explicitly set colors that match the rest of the application. In JDK 1.1, it was normal to use the SystemColor class to determine appropriate colors for a component. This class defines a set of colors based on the role that those colors play in the user interface. For example, you can find out, in a platform-independent way, the appropriate color to use for your component's background if it plays the role of a user interface control like a button, or the color that your main window's caption is using, by referencing static members of the SystemColor class like SystemColor.control, which is the color used for the background of dialogs and typical controls that are used in a dialog. Furthermore, on systems that allow the user to customize these colors, using these special values allows the program to fit in with the user's chosen color scheme because they don't represent fixed colors. Thus, for example, in the default Windows setup, using SystemColor.control gives a gray color, but if the user has tailored the desktop so that dialogs have a pink background, then a component whose background is set to the value SystemColor.control will appear pink instead of gray.

This arrangement doesn't work when a single platform can support more than one look-and-feel, because the colors supplied by the SystemColor class are correct only for the platform's native look-and-feel. In other words, an application that contained a component that based its colors on SystemColor would integrate well on a Windows system when the Windows look-and-feel is in use, but might look completely wrong if the application used the Metal look-and-feel.

Since the default colors clearly depend on the look-and-feel, they are now managed by the look-and-feel classes. Instead of using the JDK 1.1 SystemColor class, you should instead use the getColor method of the UIManager class, which is defined as follows:

```
public static Color getColor(Object key);
```

This method uses the `key` value to look up a color in the `UIDefaults` table of the currently active look-and-feel and returns the corresponding `Color` object. The key values for the standard look-and-feel classes are all strings; you'll see the complete set, and find out more about the `UIDefaults` table, when the Swing look-and-feel support is discussed in Chapter 13. Using this mechanism, you can set a component's background to the look-and-feel's control color using the following line of code:

```
comp.setBackground(UIManager.getColor("control"));
```

You'll see this construction used in several of the examples in this book.

Font

The `Component` class provides a font property that can be set or read using the following methods:

```
public synchronized void setFont(Font f);
```

```
public Font getFont();
```

The actual font initially assigned to a component is a default which, like the set of fonts available, depends on the host system and also on the look-and-feel. The point at which a component has a valid font varies from component to component. In general, you should not assume that the component has an associated font, unless you give it one, until you have added it to a container and made the container visible (or at least called the `pack` method of the container that will be described shortly). If you use the `getFont` method earlier than this, you are likely to be returned `null`.

If you want to change a component's font, you will need to create a `Font` object that describes the characteristics of the new font that you want. The `Font` class has only one constructor:

```
public Font(String name, int style, int size);
```

The name distinguishes one particular font from a set (or family) of similar font styles. In practice, in JDK 1.1, Java supports only a small number of font names. You can get the complete list by using the `getFontList` method of the `java.awt.Toolkit` class, as shown in Listing 2-3.

Note

For users of JDK 1.2, there is a more powerful font handling in the Java2D package.

Listing 2-3   Getting the system font list

```
package JFCBook.Chapter2;
import com.sun.java.swing.*;
import java.awt.*;

public class FontListExample {
  public static void main(String[] args) {
    String[] list = Toolkit.getDefaultToolkit().getFontList();
    for (int i = 0; i < list.length; i++) {
      System.out.println(list[i]);
    }
  }
}
```

This program produces the following results on my system:

```
Dialog
SansSerif
Serif
Monospaced
Helvetica
TimesRoman
Courier
DialogInput
ZapfDingbats
```

All of these strings can be used as valid first arguments to the Font constructor. The names are actually platform-independent, so they work anywhere. Before being used, they are mapped to the names of real fonts on the host system. This mapping is both platform and locale-dependent: that is, it may be different based on the operating system you are using and on your choice of language and country.

The mapping from name to font is determined by the file font.properties, which is installed along with the JDK software; if you installed the JDK in the directory c:\java, then you will find this file in the directory c:\java\lib. Since the chosen font depends on the mapping, which itself depends on the availability of fonts on your system, you cannot be certain what the font you finally get will look like. The font names TimesRoman, Courier, and Helvetica are retained from JDK 1.0 for compatibility reasons. New applications should use the preferred names Serif, Monospaced and SansSerif instead.

Following the font name, you specify the font style. Here, there are four possibilities—Font.PLAIN, Font.BOLD, Font.ITALIC | Font.BOLD. Font.ITALIC, which produce the obvious results, assuming once again that a suitable font is available. The last argument gives the required font size in points.

To make this somewhat abstract discussion more concrete, let's look at how it works in practice. On a Windows system, the default font mappings are shown in Table 2-2.

Table 2-2	Standard Fonts
Type	*Font*
Dialog	Arial, Wingdings or Symbol
DialogInput	Courier, Wingdings or Symbol
Serif	Times New Roman, Wingdings or Symbol
SansSerif	Arial, Wingdings or Symbol
ZapfDingbats	Wingdings
Monospaced	Courier New, Wingdings or Symbol

The list of names on the right is in order of preference; for example, if a dialog font is requested, then the platform's Arial font will be used, but if this font is not found, the next choice is Wingdings, followed by Symbol.

Now suppose you want to create a button whose label has a 14-point bold, Serif font. The code would look like this (the JButton class will be described later in this chapter):

```
JButton b1 = new JButton("Bold, 14-point, Serif");
b1.setFont(new Font("Serif", Font.BOLD, 14));
```

and the resulting button would be as shown on the left of Figure 2-5. Once you've worked out how to do this, it's easy to make changes and see what the results are. Here are a couple more examples, which can also be seen in Figure 2-5:

```
JButton b2 = new JButton("Plain, 12-point Monospaced");
b2.setFont(new Font("Monospaced", Font.PLAIN, 12));
JButton b3 = new JButton("Italic, 14-point SansSerif");
b3.setFont(new Font("SansSerif", Font.ITALIC, 14));
```

Figure 2-5   Buttons with various fonts.

What happens, then, if you use a font or a font size that isn't known on the system that you're running? What you get is a system-chosen substitute font that approximates what you asked for as closely as possible. In the case of a large font size, it may be possible to provide a font of the correct size if the given name maps to a TrueType font. Here are two buttons with rather unusual fonts requested for them:

```
JButton b1 = new JButton("Unlikely font");
b1.setFont(new Font("UnlikelyFont", Font.BOLD, 14));
JButton b2 = new JButton("Plain, 120-point DialogInput");
b2.setFont(new Font("DialogInput", Font.PLAIN, 120));
```

Of course, I don't have a font called `UnlikelyFont` on my system, but Java does manage to draw the button; in this case, it substitutes a 14-point, bold SansSerif font. As for the 120-point `DialogInput` font, this maps to Courier, which is a TrueType font on my system; as a result, what I actually got was a 120-point Courier font! Figure 2-6 shows the buttons that result from this code extract. Because of the large font, the second button is wider than the screen and thus does not render very well.

Figure 2-6   Using fonts that don't exist.

As far as using fonts in connection with standard components is concerned, you've now seen just about all you need to know. This subject will be revisited in Chapter 4, "Graphics, Text Handling, and Printing," and the topic of text in general is fully covered in Chapter 9 "Text Components."

Visibility

All components have a visibility attribute that partly controls whether or not they can be seen. A component can be seen only if its visible property is set to `true` and the container in which it resides is also visible. Components are created with their visibility attribute initialized to `true`, except for the top-level containers `JFrame`, `JWindow` and `JDialog`, which are all initially invisible. Thus, when you create a top-level window and build up a user interface by adding components (and possibly other containers) to it, the top-level window is initially invisible, which prevents any of the components being seen. When you have finished constructing the user interface and make the top-level window visible, all of the other components also appear because they were created with their visibility attribute set to `true`.

You can get and set this attribute using the following methods:

```
public boolean isVisible();

public boolean setVisible(boolean state);
```

There is also another related method:

```
public boolean isShowing();
```

that indicates whether the component is actually visible on the screen. This is true if the component itself and all of its parent containers are visible. The example in Listing 2-4 illustrates this point.

Listing 2-4   Setting and changing component visibility

```java
package JFCBook.Chapter2;

import com.sun.java.swing.*;
import java.awt.*;

public class VisibilityExample {
   public static void main(String[] args) {
      JFrame f = new JFrame("Visibility Example");
      f.getContentPane().setLayout(new FlowLayout());

      JButton b1 = new JButton("First");
      JButton b2 = new JButton("Second");
      b2.setVisible(false);
      JButton b3 = new JButton("Third");

      f.getContentPane().add(b1);
      f.getContentPane().add(b2);
      f.getContentPane().add(b3);
      System.out.println("Button 1 visible? " + b1.isVisible());
      System.out.println("Button 1 showing? " + b1.isShowing());
      f.pack();
      f.setVisible(true);
      System.out.println("Button 1 visible? " + b1.isVisible());
      System.out.println("Button 1 showing? " + b1.isShowing());

      try {
         Thread.sleep(5000);
         System.out.println("Make button 2 visible");

         b2.setVisible(true);

         Thread.sleep(5000);
```

```
    } catch (Exception e) {};

    System.out.println("Force container layout");

    f.pack();
  }
}
```

Here is the output from this program, which you can run using the command

`java JFCBook.Chapter2.VisibilityExample`

```
Button 1 visible? True
Button 1 showing? False
Button 1 visible? True
Button 1 showing? True
Make button 2 visible
Force container layout
```

In this example, button 1 is visible when created (i.e., its visibility attribute is `True`), but it is not showing because its parent is invisible. The parent is invisible because it is a top-level window. The first two lines of output show the state of button 1 before the top-level window is made visible. Immediately after the top-level window becomes visible, we look at the button's state again. Now, as you might expect, the button is both visible and showing. Note that a component is considered to be showing even if you can't see it because it is obstructed by other windows.

This example also shows another effect of the visibility attribute. Button 2 was made invisible just after it was created. When the frame appears on the screen, you see only buttons 1 and 3. You will also notice that no space has been left for button 2. Five seconds later, the program makes button 2 visible but it doesn't actually appear, because it has no screen space allocated to it. To force it to appear, you have to make the container lay itself out again by invoking the `validate` method of `Container`; containers and layouts will be discussed in the next section, when this will make more sense to you. The important point to note is that the process of deciding where components should go on the user interface ignores invisible components.

Enabled or Disabled Status

Sometimes, you need to arrange to make a component inactive so that the user can't make any use of it. For example, you may have a dialog box that allows the user to customize some aspect of the application by filling in one or more fields and then pressing a button marked OK. If the dialog box doesn't supply defaults for every field, it wouldn't make sense for the user to be able to press the OK button immediately. If you allowed this, you would just have to post an error message and make the user try again, until all of the required fields had been filled in. A simpler and clearer alternative is to make the OK button unavailable until it can be legally pressed.

One possible solution to this problem is to make the OK button invisible. However, it is considered bad style to create interfaces in which components come and go according to circumstance, because it is confusing for the user. The accepted practice in this situation is to make the button appear unusable by *graying* it out. You can achieve this by disabling it with the setEnabled method, passing it the argument false. To re-enable the component later, you simply call setEnabled(true). The example in Listing 2-5 shows how a button's appearance changes as you enable and disable it. You can run it using the command

```
java JFCBook.Chapter2.DisableExample
```

Listing 2-5   Enabling and Disabling Components

```java
package JFCBook.Chapter2;

import com.sun.java.swing.*;
import java.awt.*;

public class DisableExample {
  public static void main(String[] args) {
    JFrame f = new JFrame("Disable Example");
    JButton b = new JButton("OK");
    b.setFont(new Font("SansSerif", Font.BOLD, 18));
    f.getContentPane().add(b);
    f.setSize(200, 200);
    f.setVisible(true);

    for (;;) {
      try {
        Thread.sleep(5000);
        b.setEnabled(false);
        Thread.sleep(5000);
        b.setEnabled(true);
      } catch (Exception e) {};
    }
  }
}
```

You'll notice that the button's label becomes less distinct when it is disabled (see Figure 2-7) and if you try to press the button when it is in this state it won't react. A button can be configured to notify application code when it has been pressed (as we will see below), but when it is disabled, pressing it does not generate any notification—it is just as if the user had not tried to click the button.

Any component can be disabled, since all components inherit the setEnabled method from java.awt.Component. The precise effect of disabling a component in terms of its visual effect varies from control to control, but the result is always the same—any active feature that the component possesses is suppressed when it is disabled. For many components, there is no active feature to disable and so the component ignores the request. Typically, containers are not affected by being disabled.

Figure 2-7 A disabled button.

Containers and Layout Managers

User interfaces are created by grouping together components and placing them in a logical order inside a *container*. The container's job is to provide the screen space for its child components and to arrange for them to be drawn onto the screen when they are visible, while the actual positioning of components within the container is a matter for the container's layout manager. This section looks at the important features of containers and layout managers, in preparation for more complete coverage in Chapter 3.

Containers

A container is an extension of `Component` that has the ability to contain other components. Since a container is itself a component, a container can also be a parent to other containers, making it possible to create hierarchical arrangements of components and most applications have several containers within the top-level frame. The base class from which all containers are derived is `java.awt.Container`. Like `Component`, this class is abstract, so it cannot be used directly. Instead, you must either create your own container by subclassing it, in which case you would create a lightweight container, or you can use one of the standard ones, of which `JPanel` is an example.

Once you have a container, you usually add components to it to create part of a user interface. To make this possible, `Container` has an add method with several overloaded forms:

```
public Component add(Component comp);

public Component add(String name, Component comp);

public Component add(Component comp, int index);

public void add(Component comp, Object constraints);

public void add(Component comp, Object constraints, int index);
```

You can also remove components, using the following methods:

```
public void remove(int index);

public void remove(Component comp);

public void removeAll();
```

Why are there so many ways to add a component to a container, and how do you choose the correct one? As far as the container is concerned, there are really only two distinct variants of add: one variant supplies an index and the other does not. The container does not make use of either the optional constraints argument or the `String` argument in the second form above. That information, if it is present, is passed to a layout manager.

A container maintains a list of all the components that have been added to it, but it does not act alone in creating the user interface—it delegates the responsibility for positioning its child components and of determining their sizes to the layout manager. Exactly what layout managers do and how they influence your choice of add method is discussed shortly but, for now, note that some of them are sensitive to the order in which components are added to the container.

For example, if you use a layout manager that arranges components in a straight line, left-to-right, across the container, then you need to be aware of the fact that the layout manager places the first component in the list to the left of the container, the second to its right and so on. If you add the components in this order, you can simply used the single-argument add method as follows.

```
JFrame f = new JFrame("Add Example");
Container cp = f.getContentPane();
cp.setLayout(new FlowLayout());
cp.add(new JButton("Left"));
cp.add(new JButton("Middle"));
cp.add(new JButton("Right"));
```

You'll see what the setLayout and the getContentPane methods do shortly. This code arranges three buttons left to right, in the manner suggested by the associated text strings. Now suppose, some time later, you want to add another button between the middle and right ones. If you just did this:

```
cp.add(new JButton("Middle Right"));
```

the button would go to the end of the list and be added to the right of the button labeled Right. To deal with this, you need to know that the container associates an index with each of its children that reflects its position in its internal component list. In this case, the button marked Left has index 0, Middle has index 1 and Right has index 2. To force the new button to be placed between Middle and Right, you must make it occupy the location with index 2. To do this, you use one of the add methods that accepts an index, for example:

```
cp.add(new JButton("Middle Right"), 2);
```

This causes the Right button to move to index 3. Listing 2-6 shows this mechanism in action and Figure 2-8 shows the result of running the program using the command

```
java JFCBook.Chapter2.AddExample
```

Listing 2-6   Adding a component between existing components

```
package JFCBook.Chapter2;

import com.sun.java.swing.*;
import java.awt.*;

public class AddExample {
    public static void main(String[] args) {
        JFrame f = new JFrame("Add Example");
        Container cp = f.getContentPane();
        cp.setLayout(new FlowLayout());
        cp.add(new JButton("Left"));
        cp.add(new JButton("Middle"));
        cp.add(new JButton("Right"));
```

continued

```
        f.pack();
        f.setVisible(true);

        try {
           Thread.sleep(5000);
        } catch (Exception e) {
        }

        cp.add(new JButton("Middle Right"), 2);
        f.pack();
    }
}
```

Figure 2-8   Using indexing to insert a component in a container.

Layout Managers

`Container` is a relatively simple class. Aside from assisting with changes in layout when its own size is changed, we have already seen just about everything that a container is required to do. It is the layout manager that undertakes the complex task of creating a suitable arrangement of components within a container so that the screen representation appears as the programmer intended. There is a fairly varied selection of layout managers, all of which are discussed in detail in Chapter 3. Having chosen a suitable layout manager, you use the `setLayout` method to associate it with a container. Here's an example that creates a frame and assigns a `FlowLayout` manager with it:

```
JFrame f = new JFrame("FlowLayout");
f.getContentPane().setLayout(new FlowLayout());
```

Let's find out exactly what a layout manager's job is by trying to imitate one. In order to do the job of a layout manager, create a frame and remove its default layout manager:

```
JFrame f = new JFrame("No layout manager: 1");
f.getContentPane().setLayout(null);
```

Now suppose you want to add two buttons to this container. First, you need to create them and add them using the `add` method:

```
JButton b1 = new JButton("Left");
JButton b2 = new JButton("Right");
f.getContentPane().add(b1);
f.getContentPane().add(b2);
```

Here, you use the simplest variant of `add`, because you don't have a layout manager to look at any constraints. You are going to explicitly manage the buttons yourself, so the order in which the container holds them internally is of little interest. That's the end of the easy part. Here is where the layout manager would normally take over. To make a reasonable layout, you have first to ensure that the frame is large enough to contain both buttons, with some empty space allocated around them to avoid an over-crowded appearance. To determine the size of the buttons, you can use the `getSize` method that you saw when discussing components:

```
Dimension b1Size = b1.getSize();
Dimension b2Size = b2.getSize();
```

Now let's say that you want to place the buttons next to each other, with `GAP_SIZE` pixels between the buttons and between the end buttons and the edges of the frame, where `GAP_SIZE` is a constant that will (arbitrarily) have the value 8. Recall from the beginning of this chapter that the frame size includes not only the main area, usually referred to as the *client area*, but also the caption bar and the frame surroundings at the sides and bottom of the frame. The actual sizes of these pieces depend on the look-and-feel in use (and whether or not the container has been given a border), so you wouldn't want to hard-code it into the application. Instead, you can get this information in the form of an `Insets` object using the `Container` `getInsets` method:

```
Insets i = f.getInsets();
```

With this information and the sizes of the buttons, you can calculate and set the frame size as follows:

```
Dimension fSize = new Dimension(b1Size.width + b2Size.width +
i.left + i.right + 3 * GAP_SIZE,
        Math.max(b1Size.height, b2Size.height)
        + i.top + i.bottom + 2 * GAP_SIZE);
f.setSize(fSize);
```

Finally, you need to place the buttons on the container, for which you can use the `setLocation` method, and then make the frame visible:

```
b1.setLocation(GAP_SIZE, GAP_SIZE);
b2.setLocation(b1Size.width + 2 * GAP_SIZE, GAP_SIZE);

f.setVisible(true);
```

Notice that when you're placing the buttons you don't need to take account of the frame's insets, because you are adding the buttons to the frame's content pane, whose position already accounts for the insets. Remember that a component's position is specified relative to that of its parent, not of the frame that it resides in. You do, of course, take the insets into consideration when calculating the size of the frame itself.

Running this code with the command

```
java JFCBook.Chapter2.NoLayoutExample1
```

produces the result shown in Figure 2-9.

Figure 2-9   An attempt to lay out a container without a layout manager.

As you can see, this is not quite what was intended—the frame is, as nearly as is possible, of zero size. There are certainly no buttons in sight! What exactly went wrong here? Obviously, the frame size was wrong. Since the frame size was deduced from the sizes of the frame's insets and that of the buttons, you need to look further at how those were obtained. Let's look at the buttons. Their size was obtained by using the `getSize` method, which does indeed return the size of the button. The trouble is, the button doesn't automatically assume any convenient size when it is created: Unless you do something to make it do otherwise, the button is happy to have zero width and height. Setting the initial size of the button is one of the jobs of the layout manager. In other words, in this case it is our job.

How would you go about finding out what the size of the button should be? You can't know this in advance—it depends on the button's look-and-feel (which can be changed if you allow it) and on the size of the font used for the button's label. While all of this could be hard-coded for this particular example, you couldn't use this approach in the real world. Fortunately, there is a solution. Every `Component` has a `getPreferredSize` method that returns the size that the component thinks is most appropriate for its current configuration. Each component provides its own implementation of this method, since the details depend entirely on the component itself—a button is clearly different from a frame, for example.

Core Note

In fact, for the Swing components, the result depends not only on the component itself, but also on which look-and-feel is installed, so the `getPreferredSize` *method for Swing components is actually delegated to the look-and-feel part of the component's implementation, as you'll see in Chapter 13.*

To take this into account, it is necessary to change two lines of our example code:

```
Dimension b1Size = b1.getPreferredSize();
Dimension b2Size = b2.getPreferredSize();
```

The result this time is slightly better, as you can see from Figure 2-10. You can run this version of the program with the command

```
java JFCBook.Chapter2.NoLayoutExample2
```

Figure 2-10   A second attempt to lay out a container without a layout manager.

Now the top halves of two buttons are visible, but the bottoms are clipped by the frame. Given that our button size must now be correct, this leads us to conclude that the insets returned by the frame were wrong. If you investigate a little, perhaps by running the Java debugger, you will find that the insets returned have zero in all fields, as if the caption bar and the other frame decorations were not present. Why has this happened?

Here, we have run into a little piece of Java AWT history. The original AWT components are all *heavyweight*, which is to say that they have an associated window in the native platform windowing system. As you create components and change their attributes, the AWT classes take care of reflecting these changes in the real window. But since Java can run on more than one platform, it is necessary to map the Java requests to the native windowing system requests in different ways. To make this easier to handle, the platform-specific parts of the AWT are separated out into a toolkit that is installed along with the Java class libraries on each system. There is a toolkit for Windows, one for X-Windows, another for the Macintosh and there are various third-party ports for other platforms.

To manage the interaction between the pure Java part of the interface that resides in the `java.awt` package and the native windowing system, there is a `java.awt.peer` package, which contains a *peer* class for each component in `java.awt`. Therefore, when you create a `Frame` object, you will eventually get an instance of `java.awt.peer.FramePeer` assigned to your frame. All of the peer classes are real Java classes, but their methods are all native and typically written in C or C++.

Returning to the case of the frame, recall that, although `JFrame` is a Swing component, it is derived directly from the pre-Swing `Frame` class, which is peer-based. Therefore, even for `JFrame`, the size of its caption bar and decorations is platform-dependent, because Windows caption bars are not necessarily the same size as those used by your Window manager on Unix. To find out how big the frame's insets are, the `getInsets` method is passed from `JFrame` to `java.awt.peer.FramePeer`. Or, rather, it would be if the frame's peer had been created. In fact, AWT delays the creation of the peer object for as long as possible. Normally, this object is created for the frame just before the frame is made visible for the first time [i.e., when `setVisible(true)` is called for the first time for the frame]. In our example, when `getInsets` is called, we have not yet called `setVisible`, so the peer does not exist and the getInsets method will return an Insets object with all of its members set to zero.

Obviously, it isn't possible to wait until after setVisible has been called to get the sizes that we need—if we did that, the user would see our layout being constructed on the screen. At best, this would produce an unprofessional flashing effect. So, what normally happens when a layout manager tackles this problem?

The layout manager is an integral part of the AWT infrastructure; layout manager methods are called at appropriate points to size and place the components. In particular, when setSize(true) is first called and the frame's peer object has been created, the layout manager is called to lay out the components in the frame. Now, of course, the frame's peer exists and the getInsets method returns correct values. In fact, the layout manager won't attempt to lay out the container until this time, unless we force it to, because it won't be called.

If we want to persist with the mechanism we are using for sizing the container, we have to force the frame's peer to be created much earlier. Fortunately, this can be done by calling the frame's addNotify method, which has the effect of creating the peer. This call must be made before getting any size information, so it must be called after you add both of the buttons to the container (for a very good reason that you'll see shortly). Listing 2-7 shows the code as it would be so far.

Listing 2-7   Working with no layout manager

```
package JFCBook.Chapter2;

import com.sun.java.swing.*;
import java.awt.*;

public class NoLayoutExample3 {
  public static void main(String[] args) {
    JFrame f = new JFrame("No layout manager: 3");
    f.getContentPane().setLayout(null);

    JButton b1 = new JButton("Left");
    JButton b2 = new JButton("Right");
    f.getContentPane().add(b1);
    f.getContentPane().add(b2);
    f.addNotify();

    Dimension b1Size = b1.getPreferredSize();
    Dimension b2Size = b2.getPreferredSize();
    System.out.println("b1: " + b1Size);
    System.out.println("b2: " + b2Size);

    Insets i = f.getInsets();
    Dimension fSize = new Dimension(
```

```
                  b1Size.width + b2Size.width + i.left
                  + i.right + 3 * GAP_SIZE,
                  Math.max(b1Size.height, b2Size.height)
                  + i.top + i.bottom + 2 * GAP_SIZE);
          f.setSize(fSize);

          b1.setBounds(GAP_SIZE, GAP_SIZE, b1Size.width, b1Size.height);
          b2.setBounds(b1Size.width + 2 * GAP_SIZE, GAP_SIZE,
                  b2Size.width, b2Size.height);

          f.setVisible(true);
      }

      private static final int GAP_SIZE = 8;
  }
```

If you try this version using the command

```
java JFCBook.Chapter2.NoLayoutExample3
```

you will find that it actually produces the desired result (see Figure 2-11) but before moving on, let's look at one other little assumption that was made along the way. You'll recall that the second version of this code got the buttons' preferred sizes by calling getPreferredSize. I said earlier that a button's optimal size depends on many things, including the size of the font on the button's face and you may also recall that you were cautioned against relying on the results of getFont before a component was visible. The reason for this is simply that getFont returns null until the component's peer is created. Unless the button knows the size of its font, how can it get its preferred size? How, in fact, did the second version of the code work as well as it did?

Figure 2-11 A successful attempt to lay out a container without a layout manager.

Simply put, the answer was luck. Because the examples use JButtons, there is no need to worry about peer objects for the buttons. All of the Swing components (with the exception of top-level components like JFrame) are written entirely in Java and don't have a peer in the native windowing system. Instead, they occupy space on the window of their parent; if you go far enough up the component hierarchy, you reach a container such as JFrame that has a real window. The pure Java components do not rely on the native platform libraries to tell them which font to use: This information is stored in the look-and-feel's `UIDefaults` table. Hence, the `JButton` was able to know its preferred size straight away. Had old-style `Buttons` been used instead, however, there would still have been a problem, because these are heavy-weight objects that return a zero preferred size until their peers are created. You can verify this by modifying the code for the second example to use two `Buttons` instead of two `JButtons`.

Incidentally, the way in which the third example was created actually fixed this problem: It works for both `JButton` and `Button`. This is because invoking the `addNotify` method for a container causes the `addNotify` method for all of its child components to be called as well. As a result of this, the peer components for the `Button` objects would be created when that of the frame is made. For this to work, though, it is necessary to call `addNotify` after you have added the components to the container. For the actual example with `JButtons`, it was not critical to put the `addNotify` where it is, of course.

Finally, after a few difficulties, you have a working layout, so perhaps you don't need layout managers after all. But now suppose you want to improve the design and put a text field above the two buttons. To do this, you need to add the text field, calculate its size, factor that size into the calculation of the frame's size, change the code that places the buttons and add code to size and place the text field. In fact, you have to do this whenever you add a new component to your layout. The amount of code affected is not always proportional to the number of components added either—it is more closely related to the number of components already present so, as things get more complex, it becomes more and more costly to add something new.

If you think, despite this, that you can get things right and you know exactly what components you need and where to put them before you start coding for the first time, you then run up against the second problem, which you can see by running our example code and then resizing the frame. Of course, the buttons stay exactly where they are. This might be acceptable in this case, but in general it is not. Suppose that part of your user interface is a text area that displays a user's document. If the user resizes the frame, the odds are that he wants to see more of the document. What you should do is make the text area take up any spare space. What our example code does is to leave the spare space empty.

You could implement this by overriding the frame's `setSize` and `setBounds` methods so that you get the opportunity to resize the components when the frame changes size, but this just introduces more code that is tied to your exact layout and makes it even harder to adjust according to changing needs.

I hope by now you are convinced that working without a layout manager is not a simple thing to do and is usually undesirable. Later in this book (in Chapter 12, "Multiple-Document Applications"), you will see an example of a container that deliberately does not use a layout manager, and you'll revisit some of the problems that have been exposed here. But, except in special cases, a layout manager is by far the best way to manage a container.

Setting the Initial Size of a Container

One of the things that a layout manager can help with is establishing the initial size of the container that it is managing. As you saw in the previous section, working this out involves knowing how large each component within the container needs to be and how the components should be laid out relative to each other. To find a container's ideal size, you just call its getPreferredSize method. As you know, every component has a getPreferredSize method and the Container class overrides the default implementation provided by Component by delegating the request to its layout manager. This makes sense because, while the container could certainly discover the required sizes for each of its children, only the layout manager knows how the components will be positioned and this information is vital in working out the target size of the container.

The container passes the request to the layout manager by invoking its preferredLayoutSize method, passing itself as the only argument. To determine the container size, the layout manager usually needs to process each component within the container and usually uses the getComponentCount and getComponents methods of Container to discover how many components there are and to obtain a list of them.

```
public int getComponentCount();

public Component[] getComponents();
```

Using this list, it invokes the getPreferredSize method of each component. It may also ask for each component's minimum and maximum tolerable sizes by calling its getMinimumSize and getMaximumSize methods. Having obtained all the necessary information, the layout manager can determine the best size for the container itself.

The most common way to cause a frame to set its initial size is to call the pack method of the java.awt.Window class, from which Frame, JFrame and Dialog are all derived. This method is basically equivalent to the following line of code:

```
setSize(getPreferredSize());
```

In other words, establish the preferred size of the container and then set the container to that size. The pack method also has the side effect of creating the frame's peer and the peer objects of any other heavyweight components within the frame.

Laying Out the Container

Determining the preferred size of the container and laying out the components within the container are actually two separate facets of the layout manager's job. Often, as in the case of pack, the former immediately precedes the latter, but this is not always the case.

A layout manager lays out a container when its `layoutContainer` method is called. Like the `preferredLayoutSize` method, the layout manager is passed a reference to the container. This time, however, it has to work within the current size of the container, which it can obtain using `getSize`. In deciding how to arrange the components, the layout manager might take into account some of the following factors:

- The preferred size of each of the components
- The maximum or minimum size of each component
- Constraints supplied with each component when it was added to the container
- Global settings, such as horizontal and vertical gaps to be maintained between components, specified when the layout manager is created or using layout-manager specific methods after creation and the container's insets.

Which of these is used depends entirely on the layout manager in use. In Chapter 3, the layout policies of most of the current layout managers and the way in which they use the information supplied by individual components and by the program itself will be discussed.

A Closer Look at JFrame

In JDK 1.1, you can create a frame, select a layout manager and add a component to it using code like this:

```
Frame f = new Frame("A Frame");
f.setLayout(new FlowLayout());
f.add(new Button("Press"));
```

In the examples shown so far, however, you've seen some slightly more complex code being used to do the same thing. Unfortunately, if you try to convert your JDK 1.1 to use Swing components in the obvious way, like this:

```
JFrame f = new JFrame("A JFrame");
f.setLayout(new FlowLayout());
f.add(new JButton("Press"));
```

you'll get a `java.lang.Error` exception when you run the program. Instead of being a simple container, the Swing `JFrame` component is really a compound object, whose structure is shown in Figure 2-12.

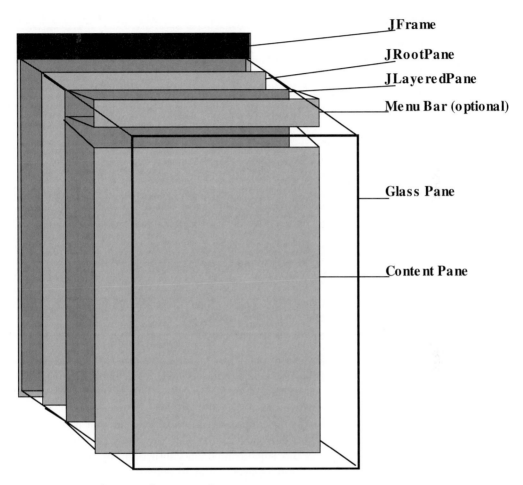

Figure 2-12 The internal structure of a JFrame.

When created, the JFrame has a single child container, which is an instance of the class JRootPane, automatically added to it. The JRootPane can manage up to four other components: a layered pane, a content pane, a menu bar and a glass pane. Figure 2-12 shows how these components are organized.

Core Tip

Ever looked at a sophisticated user interface and wondered how it has been con-structed? Sometimes resizing the frame and watching how the components move and resize can give you a clue, but there is a much simpler way. Click with the mouse somewhere in the frame and press CTRL + SHIFT + F1. This prints the component hierarchy for the frame. Here's what it looks like for a simple JFrame.

```
com.sun.java.swing.JFrame[frame0,0,0,200x200,
        layout=java.awt.BorderLayout,resizable,title=Frame]
    com.sun.java.swing.JRootPane[,4,23,192x173,layout=
                    com.sun.java.swing.JRootPane$RootLayout]
        com.sun.java.swing.JPanel[null.glassPane,0,0,192x173,hidden,
                            layout=java.awt.FlowLayout]

com.sun.java.swing.JLayeredPane[null.layeredPane,0,0,192x173]
        com.sun.java.swing.JPanel[null.contentPane,0,0,192x173,
                        layout=java.awt.BorderLayout]
```

You'll actually see two copies of this output—the first is generated when you press the F1 key and the second when you release it.

The JRootPane is managed in such a way that it always covers the entire surface of the JFrame, except for the caption bar and the frame resize bars. In other words, the JRootPane occupies all of the JFrame apart from its insets. This is the same as the usable area of the AWT Frame. Layered on top of the JRootPane is a JLayeredPane, which will be described in detail in Chapter 12. For now just note that JLayeredPane is a container that allows you to arrange components that over-lap each other in such a way that some components always appear in front of other ones, giving the appearance of distinct layers within its bounds. The JRootPane adds to the JLayeredPane a content pane, which again covers its entire area by default. The content pane is a JPanel, which serves as the working area of the frame. Optionally, you can also add a menu bar to the JRootPane. If you do this, the JRootPane arranges for the menu bar to always appear at the top of the JLayeredPane and for the content pane to occupy the rest of it. The glass pane is always present and covers the entire JLayeredPane, but is invisible by default.

The content pane plays the role of the working area of the frame: All of the user elements in the frame should be added to the content pane instead of to the frame itself. You can get a reference to the content pane using the following JFrame method:

```
public Container getContentPane();
```

The proper way to add components to a JFrame is as follows:

```
JFrame f = new JFrame("A JFrame");
Container cp = f.getContentPane();
cp.add(new JButton("Press"));
```

This code adds the button to the frame's content pane, not to the frame itself; the JFrame should only ever have a single child, namely the JRootPane that it was created with. For compatibility with the AWT Frame class, the content pane has the same layout manager as Frame itself (a BorderLayout, which is described in Chapter 3). If you need a different layout manager, you change the layout manager of the content pane, not of the JFrame:

```
JFrame f = new JFrame("A JFrame");
Container cp = f.getContentPane();
cp.setLayout(new FlowLayout());
    // NOT f.setLayout(new FlowLayout());
```

The default content pane is a simple JPanel, which is opaque. If you want to change the background color of the JFrame, you need to do something like this:

```
f.getContentPane().setBackground(Color.green);
```

This sets the background color of the content pane only. If you add a menu bar to the frame (see Chapter 6, "Menus and Toolbars"), its background color will need to be set separately if you want it to match that of the content pane.

As a general rule, whenever you would have applied an operation to the frame in JDK 1.1 that would have affected its contents (but not its size or visibility), you should now invoke it on the content pane of the JFrame instead.

Core Note

If you wish, you can make JFrame *behave a bit more like* Frame *by using the* setRootPaneCheckingEnabled *method. if you call this with argument false, you can add components to the* JFrame *itself instead of adding them to the content pane. If you are going to do this, you should probably also remove the* JRootPane *as well using the* setRootPane *method. The following code creates a* JFrame *that behaves just like a* Frame:

```
JFrame f = new JFrame("Frame-like JFrame");
f.setRootPane(null);
f.setRootPaneCheckingEnabled(false);
```

This practice is not recommended and should be used only as a short-term porting aid.

Labels

Almost every user interface uses labels and buttons. If you are familiar with the AWT in JDK 1.1, you will be aware of the `java.awt.Label` and `java.awt.Button` classes. In JDK 1.1, these are both simple controls. As far as the label is concerned, about all that you can do is set the text on the label and align it left, right or in the center. You have about the same level of control over a button, the only difference being that the button is an active component that can cause your program to perform some action in response to the user pressing it.

The corresponding Swing components are called `JLabel` and `JButton`; like all of the new controls, they are reasonably compatible with their predecessors. As well as providing the same features as `Label` and `Button`, they also have quite a lot of new functionality that you'll see later in this chapter. Labels are used to attach descriptive text to a control that can't describe itself; a typical use of a label is to place it next to a text input field to indicate what should by typed in the text area. On the other hand, you might use a button to allow the user to clear the input field or, on a form, to indicate that the user would like the form's content processed. Figure 2-13 shows a typical form designed in this way. You can run this example for yourself using the command

```
java JFCBook.Chapter2.LabelExample1
```

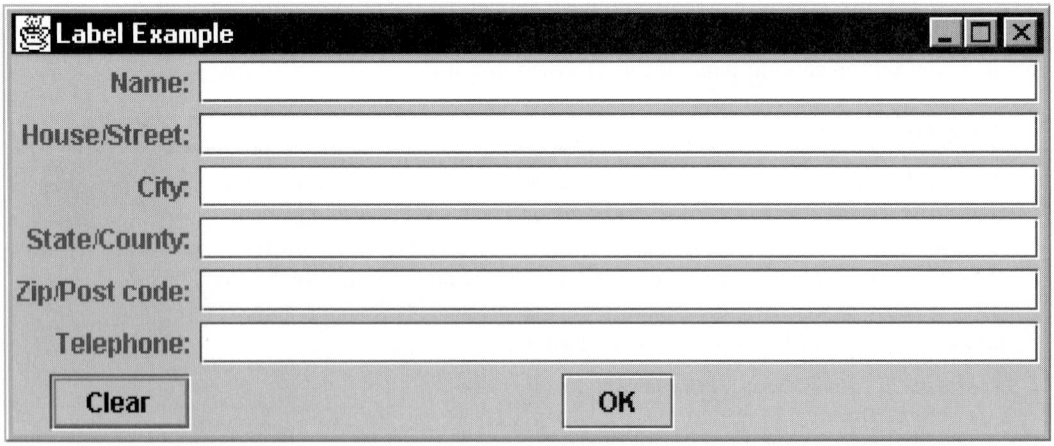

Figure 2-13   An input form created with labels.

There are several ways to create a label. For now, let's look at the three simplest forms of the constructor:

```
public JLabel();

public JLabel(String text);

public JLabel(String text, int horizontalAlignment);
```

The first constructor creates a label with no text. Obviously, for this to be useful you need to use the label's setText method before you make it visible. The second variant supplies the text, while the third supplies both the text and specifies how the text will be aligned relative to the label. JLabel allows you to control both the horizontal and vertical alignment of its text. You can specify the horizontal alignment using this constructor, or you can use the methods setHorizontalAlignment and setVerticalAlignment, both of which take a string argument. The horizontal alignment must be one of SwingConstants.LEFT, SwingConstants.RIGHT or SwingConstants.CENTER and the vertical alignment SwingConstants.TOP, SwingConstants.CENTER or SwingConstants.BOTTOM. If you don't explicitly set the alignment, the text will be aligned to the left and centered vertically. The example in Listing 2-8 constructs a small number of labels with different horizontal and vertical text alignments.

Core Note

The SwingConstants *interface defines a number of useful position and alignment constants that are used by many of the Swing components. Because these components all import these constants by implementing the* SwingConstants *interface, it is also possible to think of them as belonging to the individual component so that, for example, you can use* JLabel.CENTER *as an alternative to* SwingConstants.CENTER *if you wish.*

Listing 2-8   Aligning the text on a label

```
package JFCBook.Chapter2;

import com.sun.java.swing.*;
import java.awt.*;

public class LabelExample2 {
  public static void main(String[] args) {
    JFrame f = new JFrame("Label Example 2");
    Container cp = f.getContentPane();
    cp.setLayout(new GridLayout(0, 1));
    cp.add(new JLabel("Left-aligned           ", SwingConstants.LEFT));
    cp.add(new JLabel("Center-aligned", SwingConstants.CENTER));
    cp.add(new JLabel("Right-aligned", SwingConstants.RIGHT));

    JLabel l = new JLabel("Top-aligned");
    l.setVerticalAlignment(SwingConstants.TOP);
    cp.add(l);
    l = new JLabel("Bottom-aligned");
```

continued

```
        l.setVerticalAlignment(SwingConstants.BOTTOM);
        l.setHorizontalAlignment(SwingConstants.RIGHT);
        cp.add(l);
        f.pack();
        f.setVisible(true);
    }
}
```

When you run this program using the command

```
java JFCBook.Chapter2.LabelExample2
```

it won't be apparent that the bottom two labels have strings with top and bottom alignment, because the `pack` method is used to size the frame. As a result of this, all of the labels were made just the right height to fit the text, so the text appears to be vertically centered in each label. If you make the frame larger, however, you will see the difference between the bottom two labels, as shown in Figure 2-14.

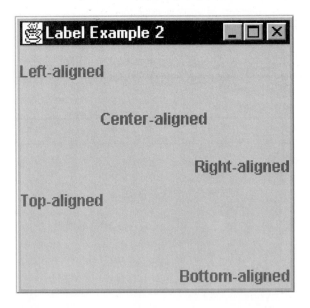

Figure 2-14 Labels with varying text alignments.

An interesting difference between `JLabel` and `Label` is that the former can be either transparent or opaque. By default, it is transparent, so it takes on the background color of the container that it resides in (as was the case in Figure 2-14) and changing its background color using `setBackground` has no visible effect. You can, however, use the `JComponent` `setOpaque` method to make the label opaque and make use of its assigned background color.

Event Handling

`JLabel` is useful for adding text to the user interface, but it is entirely passive. Both the AWT and Swing also have active components that react to the user's actions by sending events to the applications that they are a part of. Before looking at an active Swing component, the `JButton`, this section introduces you to the AWT event model and shows you what events there are and how to receive them.

Events and Listeners

Whenever something of interest happens within a component, it creates and delivers an *event*. Events are encapsulated in classes and are delivered to *event listeners*. In order to receive a component's events, you must register an event listener of the appropriate type on that component. All events are ultimately derived from `java.util.EventObject`, which is a simple class that contains only two methods in addition to its constructor. Here is its definition:

```
public class EventObject implements java.io.Serializable {
    public EventObject(Object source);
    public Object getSource();
    public String toString();
}
```

As its name suggests, the `getSource` method retrieves a reference to the object that generated the event. Note that it returns an `Object`, not a `Component`. This is because events are a general concept—they can be created and delivered by any type of object, not just AWT components. All of the events that are generated by the AWT are, however, derived from a subclass of `EventObject` called `java.awt.AWTEvent`. Apart from defining several new constants used in the low-level event handling performed within components, this class adds two things to `EventObject`—an identifier and a *consumed* status, which is used to indicate that the events should not be processed any further. The integer identifier can be obtained from an `AWTEvent` using its `getID` method. Identifiers are used to distinguish specific events types within a family of related events, each family being assigned its own subclass of `AWTEvent`. Let's look at an example to see how this works in practice.

When the mouse is over a component, anything that you do with the mouse results in the delivery of a `MouseEvent`, with the component itself as the source. There are seven reasons for the mouse to generate an event. One way to deal with this would be to create seven different classes, one for each type of mouse event. However, if this were the general approach, there would be a large number of mouse-related event classes, each containing very similar information. For example, all of the mouse events contain the coordinates of the mouse and flags indicating which mouse button is pressed. The only real difference between all of these events is a single integer describing the exact reason for the event. Instead of generating seven event classes, there is a single MouseEvent class that includes one of the following identifiers:

```
MouseEvent.MOUSE_PRESSED

MouseEvent.MOUSE_RELEASED

MouseEvent.MOUSE_CLICKED

MouseEvent.MOUSE_MOVED

MouseEvent.MOUSE_DRAGGED

MouseEvent.MOUSE_ENTERED

MouseEvent.MOUSE_EXITED
```

Given this, you might think that to process a mouse event you would need to write code that looks something like this:

```
public void receivedMouseEvent(MouseEvent evt) {
    switch (evt.getID()) {
    case MouseEvent.MOUSE_PRESSED:
      // Handle mouse button down
      break;
    case MouseEvent.MOUSE_RELEASE:
      // Handle mouse button up
      break;
    // etc, etc
    }
}
```

In fact, code like this does exist, but it should not be within your application, because the event delivery mechanism examines each event on your behalf and delivers each type of message to the appropriate method of your registered event listener.

Along with each class of event, there is an associated interface that listeners wanting to receive events of that type must implement. Each of these interfaces is derived from the interface java.util.EventListener, which does not itself declare any methods or constants. Within a listening interface, there is one method for each distinct value of the event identifier; therefore, there are seven methods associated with mouse events. Usually, one event class has one associated listener interface but, exceptionally, MouseEvent has two—MouseListener and MouseMotionListener, both in the package java.awt.event and declared as follows.

```
public interface MouseListener extends EventListener {
  public void mouseClicked(MouseEvent e);
  public void mousePressed(MouseEvent e);
  public void mouseReleased(MouseEvent e);
  public void mouseEntered(MouseEvent e);
  public void mouseExited(MouseEvent e);
}

public interface MouseMotionListener extends EventListener {
  public void mouseDragged(MouseEvent e)
  public void mouseMoved(MouseEvent e);
}
```

As you can probably guess, MOUSE_PRESSED events are delivered to the mousePressed method, MOUSE_RELEASED events to mouseReleased and so on. Each of these methods is passed a reference to the original MouseEvent, which contains information relating to that specific occurrence of the event.

Registering to Receive Events

The last piece of the event model that you need to know about is how to become a listener. Each object that can deliver events defines a method to allow you to register a listener to receive them. Since all components can generate mouse events, the registration methods for these events are defined by Component:

```
public void addMouseListener(MouseListener l);

public void addMouseMotionListener(MouseMotionListener l);
```

Each time you invoke one of these methods, the component adds your listener to its internal list of listeners for mouse or mouse motion events. From the component's point of view, delivering an event can be accomplished by traversing its list of registered listeners and calling the appropriate method on each of them. For example, if a MOUSE_PRESSED event occurs, the component calls the mousePressed method of every object registered by a call to addMouseListener. If you no longer wish to receive events from a component, you can use the corresponding remove method to remove yourself from the component's internal list.

It is no coincidence that the name of the event, the names of the identifiers, the name of the listening interface (or interfaces) and of the methods within that interface are closely linked. This is an example of a design pattern that was introduced for the benefit of JavaBeans and has been used throughout the event model. You will probably find that it makes the job of remembering which events go with which listeners very easy. You'll find definitions of all of the events and listener interfaces in the java.awt.event and com.sun.java.swing.event packages.

Event Handling Example

To conclude this short discussion of the event model, let's now look at a short program that demonstrates the delivery of mouse events—see Listing 2-9.

Listing 2-9   Receiving mouse events

```
package JFCBook.Chapter2;

import com.sun.java.swing.*;
import java.awt.*;
import java.awt.event.*;

public class EventExample1 {
  public static void main(String[] args) {
    JFrame f = new JFrame("Events 1");
    JButton b1 = new JButton("OK");
    JButton b2 = new JButton("Cancel");
    f.getContentPane().setLayout(new FlowLayout());

    f.getContentPane().add(b1);
    f.getContentPane().add(b2);

    // Add listeners
    MouseListener l = new ExampleMouseListener();
    MouseMotionListener m = new ExampleMouseListener();
    b1.addMouseListener(l);
    b2.addMouseListener(l);
    b1.addMouseMotionListener(m);
    b2.addMouseMotionListener(m);

    f.pack();
    f.setVisible(true);
  }
}

// Mouse listener class
class ExampleMouseListener implements MouseListener,
            MouseMotionListener {
  // MouseListener interface
  public void mousePressed(MouseEvent evt) {
    System.out.println("Mouse pressed: " + evt);
  }

  public void mouseReleased(MouseEvent evt) {
    System.out.println("Mouse released: " + evt);
```

```
  }

  public void mouseClicked(MouseEvent evt) {
    System.out.println("Mouse clicked: " + evt);
  }

  public void mouseEntered(MouseEvent evt) {
    System.out.println("Mouse entered: " + evt);
  }

  public void mouseExited(MouseEvent evt) {
    System.out.println("Mouse exited: " + evt);
  }

  // MouseMotionListener interface
  public void mouseMoved(MouseEvent evt) {
    System.out.println("Mouse moved: " + evt);
  }

  public void mouseDragged(MouseEvent evt) {
    System.out.println("Mouse dragged: " + evt);
  }
}
```

In this example, two buttons are created next to each other on the content pane of a frame. To catch the mouse events that happen on these buttons, both the MouseListener and MouseMotionListener interfaces are implemented in a single class (ExampleMouseListener) and the addMouseListener and addMouseMotionListener methods of Component, of which JButton is a subclass, are used to register one instance of this class to receive mouse events and another to receive mouse motion events. Notice that this means that a single listener catches events from more than one component. This is a very common programming practice.

If you start the program using the command

```
java JFCBook.Chapter.EventExample1
```

and move the mouse over one of the buttons, you will see a burst of output as the mouse's motion is reported by a stream of events. Here is a short (abbreviated) extract that is typical of what you might see:

```
Mouse entered: java.awt.event.MouseEvent[MOUSE_ENTERED,(39,22),mods=0,clickCount=0] on Button [..]
Mouse moved: java.awt.event.MouseEvent[MOUSE_MOVED,(39,22),mods=0,clickCount=0] on Button [..]
Mouse moved: java.awt.event.MouseEvent[MOUSE_MOVED,(40,21),mods=0,clickCount=0] on Button [..]
Mouse moved: java.awt.event.MouseEvent[MOUSE_MOVED,(40,20),mods=0,clickCount=0] on Button [..]
Mouse moved: java.awt.event.MouseEvent[MOUSE_MOVED,(40,19),mods=0,clickCount=0] on Button [..]
Mouse moved: java.awt.event.MouseEvent[MOUSE_MOVED,(40,18),mods=0,clickCount=0] on Button [..]
```

```
Mouse moved: java.awt.event.MouseEvent[MOUSE_MOVED,(41,18),mods=0,clickCount=0] on Button [..]
Mouse moved: java.awt.event.MouseEvent[MOUSE_MOVED,(44,18),mods=0,clickCount=0] on Button [..]
Mouse moved: java.awt.event.MouseEvent[MOUSE_MOVED,(47,16),mods=0,clickCount=0] on Button [..]
Mouse exited: java.awt.event.MouseEvent[MOUSE_EXITED,(51,16),mods=0,clickCount=0] on Button [..]
Mouse entered: java.awt.event.MouseEvent[MOUSE_ENTERED,(0,15),mods=0,clickCount=0] on Button [..]
Mouse moved: java.awt.event.MouseEvent[MOUSE_MOVED,(0,15),mods=0,clickCount=0] on Button [..]
Mouse moved: java.awt.event.MouseEvent[MOUSE_MOVED,(1,15),mods=0,clickCount=0] on Button [..]
Mouse moved: java.awt.event.MouseEvent[MOUSE_MOVED,(1,16),mods=0,clickCount=0] on Button [.]
Mouse moved: java.awt.event.MouseEvent[MOUSE_MOVED,(1,18),mods=0,clickCount=0] on Button [..]
Mouse moved: java.awt.event.MouseEvent[MOUSE_MOVED,(3,22),mods=0,clickCount=0] on Button [..]
Mouse exited: java.awt.event.MouseEvent[MOUSE_EXITED,(7,27),mods=0,clickCount=0] on Button [..]
```

If you look carefully, you'll notice that the mouse moved over one of the buttons (the left one, in fact) for a short while, then moved out and onto the right button, where it stayed for a while before leaving. As you can see, each event records the event identifier, the position of the mouse relative to the component that receives the event, the keyboard modifiers (there weren't any pressed in this example) and the number of mouse clicks represented by the event, which is nonzero only for a MOUSE_CLICKED event.

Now try something a little different. Move the mouse over the left button and press the left mouse button. With the left mouse button pressed, move the mouse outside the button. You'll see a stream of MOUSE_DRAGGED messages as the mouse moves, as you might expect. However, these MOUSE_DRAGGED messages continue to be delivered as the mouse moves outside the button, even though it is no longer over the component that they are being delivered to. You can even move the mouse outside the frame and continue to get events. If you move the mouse around to the left of the button and keep moving left, you'll get negative coordinates reported. These MOUSE_DRAGGED events will continue to be delivered until the mouse button is released.

Incidentally, this example also shows why there are separate interfaces to receive mouse events and mouse motion events. Most applications are interesting only in hearing about mouse clicks and, maybe, the times at which the mouse enters or leaves a component. If they had to receive such a large number of redundant mouse motion events, performance would be badly impacted. For this reason, it is possible to register to receive the more useful mouse events without being swamped by the motion of the mouse.

Core Note

You will notice that five methods were implemented to be able to receive mouse events (and another two to get mouse motion events). You are obliged to provide all five methods in the MouseListener *interface no matter how many of the event types you are actually interested in receiving, because the Java compiler requires this of a class that claims to implement the interface. In many cases, however, you won't actually want to handle all of the events received by a given interface and you might prefer not to have to implement dummy methods for the events that you don't want. To cater for this situation, adapter classes are provided for some event interfaces. You can find out about adapter classes in the next chapter.*

Using Buttons

Now that you know how events are handled, this section will show you how to create a button and handle the event generated when the button is pressed.

Creating a Simple Button

The JButton class replaces the AWT Button object. As with the JLabel, you can do everything with a JButton that you could do with its predecessor, but as you'll see, you can also do a lot more. The simplest way to create a button is to use one of the following two constructors:

```
public JButton();

public JButton(String label);
```

Core Tip

As a general rule, Swing components have many more constructors than their AWT counterparts, but in this book, only the most useful constructors are shown in the text. It is recommended that you look at the API documentation for each component as you meet it for information on the other constructors, as well as some of the less important methods that there isn't space to cover here.

As with JLabel, you have the choice of setting the button's text immediately, or using the setText method later. Unlike the label, though, you don't have the choice of setting the alignment in the constructor; such an option is less likely to be useful, since buttons almost always have their text centered and this is the default. You can, of course, use the setHorizontalAlignment and setVerticalAlignment methods if you really want to change the alignment. In reality, though, the real utility of these two methods is in conjunction with icons, as you'll see later.

Handling Button Presses

You've already seen examples in this chapter in which buttons have been used to demonstrate how components are placed on frames. Now that you have seen how events are handled, you can add the code needed to handle a button press.

When the user presses a JButton, several things happen. First, the act of pushing the mouse button causes a MOUSE_PRESSED event to be delivered to the JButton; in response to this, it redraws itself so that it appears to be pushed in. When the mouse button is released, a MOUSE_RELEASED and a MOUSE_CLICKED event are delivered. These events cause the JButton to render itself in its normal state and then generate an ActionEvent. Note that the JButton receives and responds to all of the mouse events itself. Even though you could register to receive these events yourself, there would be little point in doing so. Instead, you need to register to catch the ActionEvent by creating an ActionListener and using the button's addActionListener method to register it. The ActionListener interface is defined as follows:

```
public interface ActionListener extends EventListener {
    Public void actionPerformed(ActionEvent e);
}
```

This interface only has a single method, which receives the ActionEvent. As well as the getSource and getID methods inherited from its superclasses, this event type has two methods of its own:

```
public int getModifiers();
```

```
public String getActionCommand();
```

The getModifiers method returns a mask indicating which control keys were pressed at the time that the button was clicked; this mask is constructed by "OR-ing" together the appropriate values from the following list:

```
ActionEvent.ALT_MASK
```

```
ActionEvent.CTRL_MASK,
```

```
ActionEvent.META_MASK
```

```
ActionEvent.SHIFT_MASK
```

You can, for example, use this facility to assign a different meaning to a button press that happens when certain keys on the keyboard are also pressed. In most applications, though, this would not be very useful, because users are not accustomed to using keyboard keys (even modifier keys) in conjunction with buttons.

The getActionCommand method returns a string associated with the button earlier using setActionCommand. If you don't ever call setActionCommand, then getActionCommand returns the text of the label that appears on the button. This string is intended to help you decide how to action the button click. To see how, let's look at alternative ways of responding to a button press.

When your listener's actionPerformed method is entered, you need to work out why you were called. In the simplest possible case, you may have attached your ActionListener to only one button, in which case you know why you have been called and what to do. If your listener serves more than one button (as was the case in the example above), or perhaps a button and another component that generates an ActionEvent, you need some way to identify which of these components originated the event. One way is to use the getSource method; this returns a reference to the component in the form of an Object. If you saved a reference to your JButton object when you created it, you can write code like this:

```
public void actionPerformed(ActionEvent evt) {
   Object o = evt.getSource();
   if (o == (Object)myButton) {
     // It was the button
   } else {
     // It was something else
   }
}


// Instance variables
JButton myButton = new JButton("OK");
```

This is fine if you save references to all of the objects to which you attach listeners. Sometimes, it is inconvenient to save a reference, or to access the reference from the event handler. Fortunately, there is another way. If you use the setActionCommand method to associate a string with the button, you can retrieve the same string from the ActionEvent in the event handler and use it to decide what to do. Here is an example:

```
ActionListener l; // Initialize "l": not shown here

JButton b = new JButton("OK");
b.setActionCommand("OK");
b.addActionListener(l);

b = new JButton("Cancel");
b.setActionCommand("Cancel");
b.addActionListener(l);
```

Your `actionPerformed` method would then look something like this:

```
public void actionPerformed(ActionEvent evt) {
   String cmd = evt.getActionCommand();
   if (cmd.equals("Cancel")) {
     // It was the Cancel button
   } else {
     // It was the OK button
   }
}
```

Using this method, you don't need to store a reference to the button anywhere. If you need to change the button's state in the event handler, you can use the reference returned by the `getSource` method to do so. You may be thinking that you could have omitted the `setActionCommand` completely, because the `getActionCommand` would return the button's label anyway. You would be right, as long as the label continued to read `Cancel`. But suppose that you want your application to work in languages other than English. If the button's label were changed to the Japanese equivalent of `Cancel`, the event handler shown above would not work, unless you changed the `Cancel` string there as well.

Of course, you could use a single string to set both the label and perform the comparison in the event handler, but this is not always possible, because the initialization of the button and the event handler are not always contained in the same class. Also, in internationalized applications, the label text is not compiled into the program; instead, it is usually obtained from a separate text file or Java class file, which is selected based on the language in use. It would be inconvenient, and often difficult to arrange, to have the correct version of the label available at initialization time and in the event handler. It is much easier to use the `setActionCommand` method, as in our example, because this string is never seen by the user and so can be in any language you choose.

Now let's have a look at an example of a button in use. The code in Listing 2-10 creates a frame with a button and a text field on its content pane. You can run this example using the command

```
java JFCBook.Chapter2.RandomNumbers
```

When you press the button, a random number is generated and displayed in the text area (see Figure 2-15).

Figure 2-15   Using a JButton.

Listing 2-10   Reacting to button presses

```java
package JFCBook.Chapter2;

import com.sun.java.swing.*;
import java.awt.*;
import java.awt.event.*;
import java.util.Date;

public class RandomNumbers implements ActionListener {
  public RandomNumbers(Container c) {
    // Create and display the user interface
    // on the container that we are passed
    JButton b = new JButton("Press Me");

    t.setEditable(false);
    b.requestFocus();
    b.addActionListener(this);

    c.setLayout(new BorderLayout());
    c.add(b, "East");
    c.add(t, "Center");
  }

  public void actionPerformed(ActionEvent evt) {
    // Button pressed: generate a random number
    double r = Math.random();
    Date d = new Date();

    r *= d.getTime() - lastDate.getTime();
    lastDate = d;
    t.setText(new Double(r).toString());
  }

  public static void main(String[] args) {
    JFrame f = new JFrame("Random Numbers");
    RandomNumbers r = new RandomNumbers(f.getContentPane());

    f.addWindowListener(new WindowAdapter() {
      public void windowClosing(WindowEvent evt) {
        System.exit(0);
      }
    });

    f.pack();
    f.show();
  }

  private JTextField t = new JTextField(20);
  private Date lastDate = new Date();
}
```

As you can see, when the user interface is created, an `ActionListener` is registered to catch the button's events. Unlike our last example, though, this one doesn't use
a separate class to receive the event. Instead, it creates a class that encapsulates the processing behind the user interface and has that implement the `ActionListener`
interface. This makes it possible to put the code that creates the user interface and the
code that handles the events from that interface into a single class, which is the ideal
situation since it allows us to present a *black box* interface to our `RandomNumbers`
class—given a container to reside in, it is entirely self-sufficient.

Core Note

*A black box is something that provides a service according to defined interface but
doesn't require you (and perhaps doesn't allow you) to know the implementation
details of the service provider. Object-oriented programming is, by and large, all
about producing black box implementations in the form of classes with private or
protected variables and methods—the less your client knows about how you do
your job, the fewer assumptions they will make that could be invalid if the implementation is changed later.*

Having registered the `RandomNumbers` class as the `ActionListener` and
made the frame visible, you just need to wait for the user to press the button. When
he or she does so, the `actionPerformed` method will be entered. In this case, of
course, there is only one place that an `ActionEvent` can come from, so you know
when you receive it that the button has been pressed. The response to this is to calculate the time since the last time the button was pressed and use this to generate a
random number that is then displayed in the text field.

In this example, you see, for the first time, one of the Swing text components,
`JTextField`, which provides a way to read or display a single line of text. As
you'll see later in this book, the `JTextField`, like `JButton`, generates an
`ActionEvent` when the `Return` key is pressed. In our example, there is no possibility of confusing an event from the text field with one from the button, for two reasons. First, `setEditable(false)` was used to put the `JTextField` into a mode
in which it is output-only. Since the user won't be allowed to type into this field, it will
never generate an event. Making the text field write-only was, of course, the appropriate thing to do because it is only being used to display random numbers—it was
never intended to be used to accept input. Secondly, even if this line were removed
and the text field were allowed to generate an event, there would still be no problem.
Because an `ActionListener` has not been registered on the `JTextField`, no
events would be delivered to the `RandomNumbers` class. Remember that events are
only delivered if you register to receive them.

Incidentally, you may be wondering about the following piece of code from
Listing 2-10:

```
f.addWindowListener(new WindowAdapter() {
  public void windowClosing(WindowEvent evt) {
    System.exit(0);
  }
});
```

This is a compact way of arranging for an application to exit and you'll see it in many of the examples in this book. It uses an adapter class to process Window events from the application's top-level frame and intervenes only to catch the event that is generated when the user clicks on the close button. If you want to know more about how it works, look ahead to the "Working with the Application Window" section in Chapter 3.

Core Note

In JDK 1.1, a `Frame` would not close when the window close button was pressed unless the application handled the event that this button generated and allowed the window to close. By contrast, it is possible to arrange for a `JFrame` (or a `JDialog`, which will be discussed in Chapter 7, "Using Standard Dialogs"), to automatically hide or dispose itself without application intervention. See the "Working with the Application Window" section in Chapter 3 for more on this.

Mnemonics

Usually, you activate a button by "pressing" it with the mouse or, if the application is properly implemented, you might use the TAB key to move the keyboard focus to the button and then press it using the space bar. The `JButton` provides another way for you to activate it, by means of a *mnemonic*.

You define a mnemonic for a button by calling its `setMnemonic` method, passing it a single character representing the key that you want to activate the button. The button will be activated when the user presses the selected key in conjunction with the ALT modifier key, whenever the keyboard focus is on the button or in the top-level window that contains it. You can, for example, make the button in the RandomNumbers example respond to the key sequence ALT + p by adding the line of code shown in bold face type:

```
b.requestFocus();
b.addActionListener(this);
b.setMnemonic('p');

f.add(b, "East");
```

If, as in this case, the letter you choose appears in the label of the button, then it will be shown underlined to indicate to the user that a shortcut exists (see Figure 2-16). A letter that is not part of the label would, of course, be a bad choice because the user would not know that there is a possible shortcut, but the key would still work. Note also that we purposely specified a lowercase 'p' even though the button has an uppercase one. This does not stop the letter 'P' being underlined on the button and it doesn't make any difference to the mnemonic either because mnemonics are case-insensitive when you assign them, so the following lines of code are equivalent:

```
b.setMnemonic('p');
b.setMnemonic('P');
```

To activate this button, you press ALT + p without pressing the SHIFT key, even if the mnemonic assigned was an uppercase letter.

Figure 2-16   A JButton with a mnemonic added.

There is a similar facility to this offered by the JLabel component that you'll see during the discussion of text components in Chapter 9, "Text Components," and there is also a more general mechanism for keyboard shortcuts that will be discussed in Chapter 5.

Focus and Border Drawing

There are a couple of other facilities that JButton provides that are covered here for the sake of completeness. Both of these are properties that are either enabled or disabled. Like all such properties, you control them with a method that accepts a boolean value. These properties and the associated methods are summarized in Table 2-3.

In Chapter 8, "Creating Custom Dialogs," you'll see how to set a different border from a set supplied in the com.sun.java.swing.border package.

Images on Components: Icons

So far, you have seen a button with just a text label, but JButton can do better than this. Like several of the controls in the Swing set, it can host an image as well as (or instead of) the text string. JButton inherits this ability from its superclass

Table 2-3 JButton Border and Focus Methods	
Method	**Description**
`public void setFocusPainted(boolean)`	If you move the focus to a button, it highlights itself by drawing a dashed box around its label to make it clear, mainly for the benefit of keyboard users, that the focus is on the button and that pressing the space bar would activate it. You can, however, use `setFocusPainted(false)` to disable this highlighting action.
`public boolean isFocusPainted()`	Returns `true` if the button highlights the fact that it has the focus.
`public void setBorderPainted(boolean)`	By default, a button draws a border that suits the type of button it is. A `JButton` draws the familiar three-dimensional border, whereas other components derived from `AbstractButton`, such as radio boxes and checkboxes, do not need borders. Using the `setBorderPainted` method, you can stop a button that would normally draw a border from doing so.
`public void isBorderPainted()`	Returns `true` if the button will draw a border.

`AbstractButton`, from which several other types of buttons are also derived, including radio buttons and checkboxes. Bear in mind that everything in this section applies to all types of buttons, not just to `JButton`, and also to `JLabel` (even though it is not a subclass of `AbstractButton`). In fact, as you'll see in Chapter 6, menu items are also derived from the `AbstractButton` class and so they also support the facilities that are described here.

What Is an Icon?

Earlier, you saw two of `JButton`'s constructors. In fact, there are two more:

`public JButton(Icon icon);`

`public JButton(String label, Icon icon);`

Both of these constructors have an extra element that specifies the inclusion of an `Icon`. `Icon` is an interface that provides a way to implement a user-defined area within a larger control. Here is its definition:

```
public interface Icon {
   public void paintIcon(Component c, Graphics g, int x, int y);
   public int getIconWidth();
   public int getIconHeight();
}
```

The basic idea when creating an icon is to provide a class that implements this interface. This class might fill a rectangular area with a solid color, draw some complex graphics, show some text or display an image. The important thing is that the class must provide the getIconWidth and getIconHeight methods to allow the host component (in this section, this will be JButton or JLabel) to allocate the necessary space for it, and the paintIcon method. The host component will typically obtain the Icon's size while it is calculating how much screen space it needs for itself and will call the paintIcon method when its own paint method is called. As you'll see in Chapter 4, the Graphics object that is passed to the paintIcon method is used to gain access to the host component's surface and the Component argument to extract attributes, such as colors, from the component that the icon is being drawn on. There is an example implementation of an Icon in Chapter 4.

The Swing set includes an implementation of Icon called ImageIcon, an extremely useful class that can load images and render them on the surface of a button or any other JComponent that accepts an Icon. ImageIcon has many constructors, of which the following are three examples:

```
public ImageIcon(String fileName);

public ImageIcon(URL url);

public ImageIcon(Image img);
```

The first constructor requires a file name, which may be either an absolute or a relative name. Note, however, that if it is a relative name, it is interpreted relative to the current directory of the application. Since image files are usually stored near the application's class files, this constructor can only usefully be used when you have an absolute file name or you are in control of the application's current directory. This form is of no use for applets, which usually have no access to file store.

The second constructor is probably the most useful one, since it works both for applications and applets and can be used to access image files that are close to the associated class files. In the examples below, you'll see how to use this constructor. The last constructor assumes that you have already created an Image object and hence have dealt with the issues of locating the image file itself. The ImageIcon class can deal with any type of image file that the Java libraries can handle. At present, this means that it can load GIF and JPEG images.

Adding Icons to Buttons and Labels

Once you have an Icon (whether an ImageIcon or any other type), you can place it on a button or a label. The example in Listing 2-11 shows two buttons, each with both an image and a text string.

Listing 2-11   Adding images to buttons

```
package JFCBook.Chapter2;

import com.sun.java.swing.*;
import java.awt.*;
import java.awt.event.*;

public class ImageButtonsExample1 extends JPanel {
  public ImageButtonsExample1() {
    super(true);    // Double buffer
    setLayout(new GridLayout(2, 1, 4, 4));

    ok = new JButton("OK",
      new ImageIcon(getClass().getResource("images/ok.gif")));
    cancel = new JButton("Cancel",
      new ImageIcon(getClass().getResource("images/cancel.gif")));

    ok.setFont(new Font("Dialog", Font.BOLD, 14));
    cancel.setFont(new Font("Dialog", Font.BOLD, 14));

    add(ok);
    add(cancel);
  }

  public static void main(String[] args) {
    JFrame f = new JFrame("Image Buttons 1");
    f.getContentPane().add(new ImageButtonsExample1());
    f.pack();
    f.setVisible(true);
    f.addWindowListener(new WindowAdapter() {
      public void windowClosing(WindowEvent e) {
        System.exit(0);
      }
    });
  }

  JButton ok;
  JButton cancel;
}
```

Although it may not be immediately obvious, the code that creates the buttons uses the ImageIcon constructor that accepts a URL argument:

```
ok = new JButton("OK", new ImageIcon(getClass().getResource("images/ok.gif")));
```

The `getResource` method of `java.lang.Class` takes a file name and returns a URL that resolves to it. This method works by locating the image file using the class loader that loaded the class file for this example; since this class loader knows how to find the class file, it can also find other files that are located close to the class file. In this example, `getResource` takes the name of the package to which the class belongs, replaces the dots in the name by forward slashes (even on a Windows platform, because URLs use forward slash as their separator) and then adds the partial file name specified to form the second half of a URL.

Since this example resides in the class `JFCBook.Chapter2`, the second part of our URL would be `JFCBook/Chapter2/images/ok.gif`. The first part of the URL is the location at which the class loader found the class itself. Let's look at two cases. First, suppose that our class was loaded from local file storage using the entry `C:\CoreJFCBook` in the `CLASSPATH` variable. Then the actual file must reside in `C:\CoreJFCBook\JFCBook\Chapter2\images/ok.gif` and the URL returned would be something equivalent to `file:///C:/CoreJFCBook/JFCBook/Chapter2/images/ok.gif`. On the other hand, if the class file has been downloaded from a host with a `CODEBASE` of `http://www.myhost.com/java`, then the URL generated would be `http://www.myhost.com/java/JFCBook/Chapter2/images/ok.gif`.

Whatever the URL looks like, the truth of the matter is that you don't need to care. Using the `getResource` method in this way allows the class file to be independent of the user's current directory when the application is running and it avoids any assumptions about where the class was loaded from, since the same line works whether the class is in local file storage, on a Web server or in a JAR file. Figure 2-17 shows what this program looks like when it is running. The command to run this program is:

```
java JFCBook.Chapter2.ImageButtonsExample1
```

As you can see, both buttons have both an image and text on them. The text is placed to the right of the image, and the text-image combination is both vertically and horizontally centered. To see this more clearly, make the window larger in both directions and you will find that the image and text stay close together in the middle of each button.

Figure 2-17   Buttons with images.

It is possible to change the way in which these elements are arranged relative to each other and relative to the button itself, using the following four methods of `JLabel` or `AbstractButton`:

```
setHorizontalTextPosition(int pos)

setVerticalTextPosition(int pos)

setHorizontalAlignment(int align)

setVerticalAlignment(int align)
```

You have already seen the `setHorizontalAlignment` and `setVerticalAlignment` methods, which set the position of the text and icon combination relative to the button as a whole. Setting these to `SwingConstants.LEFT` and `SwingConstants.TOP` respectively would, not surprisingly, place the image and text in the top left-hand corner of the button. By default, they reside in the center.

The `setHorizontalTextPosition` and `setVerticalTextPosition` methods deal with placing the text relative to the icon. The possible arguments for the former are `SwingConstants.LEFT`, `SwingConstants.CENTER` and `SwingConstants.RIGHT` and for the latter `SwingConstants.TOP`, `SwingConstants.CENTER` and `SwingConstants.BOTTOM`. To see how this works, let's consider a few examples. If the horizontal position is given as `SwingConstants.LEFT` and the vertical position as `SwingConstants.CEN-TER`, then the text and icon are placed with their centers aligned and the text to the left of the icon. If the horizontal position is `SwingConstants.RIGHT`, the positions are reversed.

If the vertical position is `SwingConstants.TOP`, then the text is above the icon and is to the left of it if the horizontal position is `SwingConstants.LEFT`, directly above it if it is `SwingConstants.CENTER` and to the right of it if it is `SwingConstants.RIGHT`. These arrangements are vertically flipped if the vertical position is `SwingConstants.BOTTOM`. Finally, if both positions are `SwingConstants.CENTER`, then the text is placed directly over the image.

The example program shown in Listing 2-12 creates a frame with sixteen buttons on it, each with different values for text alignment and overall alignment.

Listing 2-12   Positioning images and text on a button

```java
package JFCBook.Chapter2;

import com.sun.java.swing.*;
import java.awt.*;
import java.awt.event.*;

public class ImageButtonsExample2 extends JPanel {
```

continued

```
public ImageButtonsExample2() {
  super(true);    // Double buffer

  ImageIcon okIcon =
        new ImageIcon(getClass().getResource("images/ok.gif"));
  ImageIcon cancelIcon =
        new ImageIcon(getClass().getResource("images/cancel.gif"));

  setLayout(new GridLayout(4, 5, 4, 4));
  add(makeButton("L,C/L,C", okIcon, LEFT, CENTER, LEFT, CENTER));
  add(makeButton("R,C/R,T", okIcon, RIGHT, CENTER, RIGHT, TOP));
  add(makeButton("L,T/C,B", okIcon, LEFT, TOP, CENTER, BOTTOM));
  add(makeButton("R,B/L,T", okIcon, RIGHT, BOTTOM, LEFT, TOP));
  add(makeButton("C,T/C,B", okIcon, CENTER, TOP, CENTER, BOTTOM));
  add(makeButton("C,B/L,T", okIcon, CENTER, BOTTOM, LEFT, TOP));
  add(makeButton("C,C/L,T", okIcon, CENTER, CENTER, LEFT, TOP));

  add(makeButton("L,C/L,C", cancelIcon, LEFT, CENTER, LEFT, CENTER));
  add(makeButton("R,C/R,T", cancelIcon, RIGHT, CENTER, RIGHT, TOP));
  add(makeButton("L,T/C,B", cancelIcon, LEFT, TOP, CENTER, BOTTOM));
  add(makeButton("R,B/L,T", cancelIcon, RIGHT, BOTTOM, LEFT, TOP));
  add(makeButton("C,T/C,B", cancelIcon, CENTER, TOP, CENTER, BOTTOM));
  add(makeButton("C,B/L,T", cancelIcon, CENTER, BOTTOM, LEFT, TOP));
  add(makeButton("C,C/L,T", cancelIcon, CENTER, CENTER, LEFT, TOP));
}

JButton makeButton(String label, ImageIcon icon,
        int hTextPosition,
        int vTextPosition,
        int halign,
        int valign) {
  JButton b = new JButton(label, icon);
  b.setFont(new Font("serif", Font.BOLD, 14));
  b.setHorizontalTextPosition(hTextPosition);
  b.setVerticalTextPosition(vTextPosition);
  b.setVerticalAlignment(valign);
  b.setHorizontalAlignment(halign);

  return b;
}

// Shortened names for text positions and alignments
private static final int LEFT      = SwingConstants.LEFT;
private static final int RIGHT = SwingConstants.RIGHT;
private static final int CENTER = SwingConstants.CENTER;
private static final int TOP       = SwingConstants.TOP;
private static final int BOTTOM = SwingConstants.BOTTOM;
```

```
public static void main(String[] args) {
  JFrame f = new JFrame("Image Buttons 2");
  f.getContentPane().add(new ImageButtonsExample2());
  f.pack();
  f.addWindowListener(new WindowAdapter() {
    public void windowClosing(WindowEvent e) {
      System.exit(0);
    }
  });
  f.setVisible(true);
  }
}
```

You can run this example for yourself with the command:

`java JFCBook.Chapter2.ImageButtonsExample2`

The result of running this program is shown in Figure 2-18.

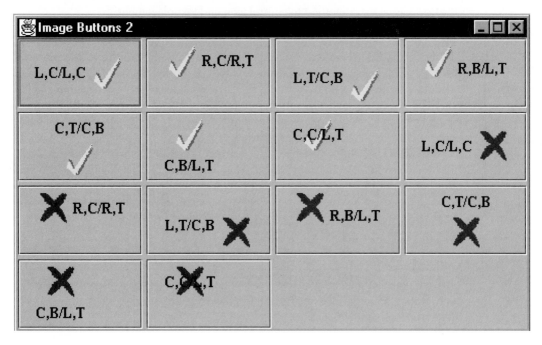

Figure 2-18   Button text and icon alignment options.

If you resize the window, you can see exactly how the specified relationships between the text and image and between the text-image combination as a whole and the button are maintained. For reference, the parameters used to set up these buttons are encoded within the text part of the label. The first two letters specify the horizontal and vertical text position, while the last two are the horizontal and vertical alignment. Thus, for example, the top left-hand button bearing the label "L, C/L, C" was created with the following settings:

Horizontal text position	SwingConstants.LEFT
Vertical text position	SwingConstants.CENTER
Horizontal alignment	SwingConstants.LEFT
Vertical alignment	SwingConstants.CENTER

As a result, the text should appear to the left of the image, but on the same horizontal level. The text/image combination will be placed against the left edge of the button, with its center line vertically aligned with the middle of the button. This is borne out by the actual appearance of this button in Figure 2-18.

Spacing and Margins

JLabel has an extra method to control icon and text placement:

```
setIconTextGap(int gap)
```

This method determines the distance between the icon and the text in pixels. If the text and icon are aligned horizontally (i.e., the horizontal alignment is SwingConstants.CENTER), this is the horizontal distance between them. On the other hand, if one is above the other and they are vertically aligned, this is the vertical separation. If the two parts are arranged diagonally, then this distance governs both the horizontal and vertical gaps between them.

You cannot control the distance between the text and the icon in the case of a button, but you can set the button's margin. The margin is the distance between the button's border and the space occupied by its text and/or icon; it is specified as an Insets object, so it does not have to be the same on all sides. You can set or retrieve the current value of the margin using the following methods of AbstractButton:

```
public void setMargin(Insets margin);

public Insets getMargin();
```

If you don't set a margin, a look-and-feel-dependent default is used. On the other hand, setting a margin does not guarantee that it will be used—this is at the discretion of the look-and-feel.

Context-sensitive Icons

The JButton and JLabel constructors just described allow you to associate a single icon with each of them. In fact, though, there can be four icons for every button and two icons for a label, although only one can be seen at any time. In addition to the normal icon, you can explicitly specify an icon to be used when the button or label is in a disabled state. You use the following methods to set or retrieve the disabled icon:

```
public void setDisabledIcon(Icon icon);

public Icon getDisabledIcon();
```

When either a button or a label is disabled, the disabled icon is substituted for the normal one and the text, if there is any, is rendered in such a way as to make it appear "grayed out." If you don't specify an icon to be used in the disabled state, then a suitable one will be generated from the normal icon.

A different disabled icon can be used for a button depending on whether it is selected or not. This has no real meaning for ordinary buttons, but it can be used with radio buttons and checkboxes, which are discussed in Chapter 8. The following two methods are used to manipulate this icon:

```
public void setDisabledSelectedIcon(Icon icon);

public Icon getDisabledSelectedIcon();
```

In the case of a button, you can also specify icons to be used when the button is pressed and when the cursor is over the button—the *rollover icon*. If either of these is not set, the button uses the normal icon instead. A useful way to use the rollover and pressed icons is to supply a color image to be used for both and another identical image with less color, or a gray-scale version of the rollover image, as the normal image. If you do this, then the button has a low-profile appearance until the mouse pointer moves over it, at which point it takes on its colored appearance and attracts the user's attention. Listing 2-13 shows how you would modify the first icon example to arrange for the button images to be gray scale when the mouse is not over the button.

Listing 2-13   Using a different image when a button is activated

```
package JFCBook.Chapter2;

import com.sun.java.swing.*;
import java.awt.*;
import java.awt.event.*;

public class ImageButtonsExample3 extends JPanel {
  public ImageButtonsExample3() {
    super(true);    // Double buffer
    setLayout(new GridLayout(2, 1, 4, 4));

    ok = new JButton("OK",
          new ImageIcon(getClass().getResource("images/ok_inactive.gif")));
```

continued

```
cancel = new JButton("Cancel",
        new ImageIcon(getClass().getResource("images/cancel_inactive.gif")));

ok.setFont(new Font("Dialog", Font.BOLD, 14));
cancel.setFont(new Font("Dialog", Font.BOLD, 14));

Icon okIcon =
        new ImageIcon(getClass().getResource("images/ok.gif"));
Icon cancelIcon =
        new ImageIcon(getClass().getResource("images/cancel.gif"));

ok.setPressedIcon(okIcon);
ok.setRolloverIcon(okIcon);
cancel.setPressedIcon(cancelIcon);
cancel.setRolloverIcon(cancelIcon);

add(ok);
add(cancel);
}

public static void main(String[] args) {
    JFrame f = new JFrame("Image Buttons 3");
    f.getContentPane().add(new ImageButtonsExample3());
    f.pack();
    f.setVisible(true);
    f.addWindowListener(new WindowAdapter() {
        public void windowClosing(WindowEvent e) {
            System.exit(0);
        }
    });
}

JButton ok;
JButton cancel;
}
```

First, two gray-scale versions of the images used in the first example were created using a graphics manipulation program and their names were substituted in the button constructors. This ensures that the buttons have gray-scale images when they are not active. Next, an icon is created from each of the original image files and the appropriate methods are used to make these the pressed and rollover icons. You'll have to run this example for yourself, because the effect can't be seen properly in a book without using color diagrams, for obvious reasons. The appropriate command is java JFCBook.Chapter2.ImageButtonsExample3

Here are the methods that are used in connection with the extra icons available with labels and buttons. Only the first two of these can be used with `JLabel`.

```
public void setDisabledIcon(Icon)

public Icon getDisabledIcon()

public void setDisabledSelectedIcon(Icon)

public Icon getDisabledSelectedIcon()

public void setRolloverIcon(Icon)

public Icon getRolloverIcon()

public void setRolloverSelectedIcon(Icon)

public Icon getRolloverSelectedIcon()

public void setPressedIcon(Icon)

public Icon getPressedIcon()
```

Summary

This chapter introduced three of the simpler Swing components. You have seen that Swing applications use a new top-level container called `JFrame` that is similar to, but subtly different from, the AWT `Frame` class. Later in this book, you'll see how to fully exploit the new features that `JFrame` provides to make up for what might seem at the moment to be a rather annoying programming interface.

You have also seen the basic properties that all AWT and Swing components share and learned that, in many cases, the exact appearance and behavior of components depends heavily on the look-and-feel that the user has chosen to use. You have seen examples of code that produces different results when run with the Metal look-and-feel than with the Motif and Windows versions, which underlines the need to test applications with all of these look-and-feels before considering them completed.

This chapter also briefly examined the topic of containers and layout managers. In the next chapter, you'll take a very detailed look at all of the Swing layout managers, which are the key to producing a good user interface. Swing retains all of the layout managers provided by AWT and also introduces a couple of new ones that will make your job much easier when creating many common layouts.

MANAGING THE USER INTERFACE

Topics in this Chapter

- Layout Managers
- Using the DebugGraphics Feature
- Window and Component Events

Chapter 3

So far, you've seen how to create a top-level window and created some simple user interfaces by placing components on the frame's content pane. As you know, the way in which components are laid out within a container and how that layout changes when the container's size is changed is controlled by the container's layout manager. In the previous chapter, you had a brief introduction to the job of the layout manager. Here, you'll have a close look at all of the Swing layout managers, many of which are inherited from the AWT. It is very important to understand how the different layout managers work, so their layout policies will be described in some detail and you'll also see how they handle unusual situations.

After completing the survey of layout managers, the discussion of event handling that began in the last chapter will be continued with a look at the various events that can be generated by operations performed on windows and by moving, resizing, showing and hiding windows and components in general.

Layout Managers

The Abstract Window Toolkit has always provided layout managers. Layout managers are a subject you either love or hate. Some people like and use the ones provided with JDK 1.1 and produce professional-looking applications with them, while others insist that the standard layout managers are difficult to understand or don't suit their needs and implement their own. Both points of view are, of course, valid. The layout managers that came with JDK 1.0 and JDK 1.1 are not perfect and there are cases in which it is necessary to write your own. Much of the problem, however, stems from the fact that some of them, particularly the more complex ones like GridBagLayout, are not properly understood. In this chapter, you'll see the strengths and weaknesses of all of the original AWT layout managers and also become acquainted with two new ones introduced by Swing.

The FlowLayout Manager

When you create a JPanel object, it has associated with it an instance of what is probably the simplest of all of the AWT layout managers, the FlowLayout manager, which has a very simple, but effective layout policy. Given a set of components, it lays them out side-by-side starting near the top of the container and working downward as each row is filled. Within each row, the components are, by default, arranged as evenly as possible around the center of that row. The horizontal and vertical gaps between components on a row and between rows can be set when the FlowLayout manager is created or using its setVgap and setHgap methods.

The most important aspect of FlowLayout's layout policy is the fact that it allows each component to occupy its *ideal* space, otherwise known as its *preferred size*; you will see later, when discussing the BorderLayout manager, why this is such a useful feature. A FlowLayout is almost never used to manage a complete application window or a dialog box. Instead, it is common to find it managing panels that represent discrete areas of the user interface, while itself being managed by a more sophisticated layout manager.

Let's now look at an example of a FlowLayout manager in action. This example shows six buttons that need to be placed next to each other with a small gap between them. In order to show how FlowLayout reacts to a change in the size of its container, it creates a JPanel and allows the FlowLayout to manage it. The code required to create and place these buttons is shown in Listing 3-1. You can run this program using the command:

```
java JFCBook.Chapter3.FlowLayoutExample
```

Listing 3-1   Using the FlowLayout Manager

```
package JFCBook.Chapter3;

import com.sun.java.swing.*;
import java.awt.*;
import java.awt.event.*;

public class FlowLayoutExample {
  public static void main(String[] args) {
    JFrame f = new JFrame("FlowLayout");
```

```
   JPanel p = new JPanel();
   Insets margin = new Insets(5, 14, 5, 14);

   p.setLayout(new FlowLayout(FlowLayout.CENTER, 4, 4));
   for (int i = 1; i <= 6; i++) {
      JButton b = new JButton("" + i);
      b.setMargin(margin);
      p.add(b);
   }

   f.getContentPane().add(p);
   f.addWindowListener(new WindowAdapter() {
      public void windowClosing(WindowEvent evt) {
         System.exit(0);
      }
   });

   f.pack();
   f.setVisible(true);
   }
}
```

The example creates a `JPanel` and associates with it a `FlowLayout` manager that aligns its components evenly around the center and with 4-pixel horizontal and vertical space. The `JPanel` object is, of course, created with a `FlowLayout` manager, which would have laid out its component centrally and with the default 5-pixel horizontal and vertical gaps; in this example, the default layout manager was replaced for the purposes of illustration. `FlowLayout` has three different constructors:

```
public FlowLayout();

public FlowLayout(int align);

public FlowLayout(int align, int hgap, int vgap);
```

Here, the third form, which allows both the alignment and the spacing between the components to be specified, is used. The *align* argument takes the value `FlowLayout.CENTER` to center the components, or either of `FlowLayout.LEFT` or `FlowLayout.RIGHT` to align them toward one of the sides.

The results of running this program are shown in Figure 3-1. As you can see, the buttons are evenly spread across the window and are centered, so that the gaps at each side of the window are of equal size. Had left- or right-alignment of the components been requested by passing `FlowLayout.LEFT` or `FlowLayout.RIGHT` as the first argument of the constructor, there would not have been any difference in the layout at this stage. The vertical gap applies between rows of components; in this case, since there is only one row of buttons, this gap is used to determine the space left between the buttons and the edges of the window.

Figure 3-1   The FlowLayout manager.

This example creates a window of exactly the size needed to hold the buttons and the requested horizontal and vertical spaces between them, by using the pack method of java.awt.Window, a superclass of JFrame. This method asks the layout manager to establish the space requirements of each of its components (and containers if it contains any) and then to size the window to exactly match these requirements. Let's look at how this mechanism works.

In our example, the JFrame's content pane contains a JPanel, so the layout manager of the JFrame asks the JPanel for its preferred size. This request is interpreted by the JPanel's layout manager, which is the FlowLayout manager installed in Listing 3-1. The FlowLayout manager, in turn, asks each of its container's components, namely the six buttons, for their preferred sizes and computes its own space requirements based on the values returned by the buttons and the inter-component gaps it has been asked to provide. This value is returned to the JFrame's layout manager, which then resizes the frame to accommodate the JPanel (and therefore its buttons) and the frame's own overhead (i.e., the caption bar and the decorations around the side and bottom of the window).

This, however, is not the end of the process. The resizing of the window marks its contents as *invalid*. The effect of this is to cause the JFrame's layout manager to allocate space to the JPanel and then to tell the JPanel's layout manager to lay out its own components. Since the window has been sized exactly as requested by the JPanel's FlowLayout manager, it will find that it has exactly enough room to lay out the buttons and provide the 4-pixel gaps above, below and around them. This results in the neat layout shown in Figure 3-1. This use of pack to create an initial window of exactly the right size for its components is common to most Java applications. You will also see this method used for exactly the same purpose in connection dialog boxes later in this book.

Core Note

This discussion has been deliberately simplified a little to make the important points clear. In fact, the JFrame *is, as you have already seen, not directly connected to the* JPanel *because of the intervening* JRootPane *and the content view. The part played by these containers in this discussion has not been mentioned because they behave in the same way as the* JFrame's *layout manager and simply pass requests to the* JPanel. *If there were, for example, a menu bar associated with the* JRootPane, *the situation would be slightly more complex, but the principles would remain the same.*

If you now stretch the window by grabbing its right-hand side and moving it to the right, leaving its height unchanged for now, you will observe the FlowLayout manager in action as it redistributes the buttons over the larger window space. When you enlarge the window, FlowLayout has to distribute the extra space somehow. The way in which each layout manager handles the distribution of extra space, or the lack of space, is one of the things that differentiates it from other layout managers. In this situation, because the layout manager was created specifying center alignment, it will allocate the extra space equally at both sides of the window, keeping the buttons tightly bunched together in the center. The more you increase the size of the window, the more obvious this effect becomes, as shown in Figure 3-2. Notice that the button's sizes are not changed in this operation and that the gaps between the buttons are also the same as they were in the original layout.

Figure 3-2 Resizing a container with a FlowLayout using center alignment.

Suppose, instead, the FlowLayout had been created using the following line of code:

```
p.setLayout(new FlowLayout(FlowLayout.LEFT, 4, 4));
```

In this case, instead of allocating the extra space equally to both sides, it would all have been placed on the right-hand side of the window, leaving the buttons on the left side of the window and 4 pixels from its inner edge. Similarly, if FlowLayout.RIGHT had been specified, the extra space would be added to the left-hand gap and the buttons would have moved, as a group, to the right-hand side of the window.

Now grab the bottom of the window and pull it downward, making the window taller but leaving the horizontal size unchanged. Since this increases the vertical size available in the window you might, based on what you have just seen, expect that the buttons would now move downward, leaving equal space between themselves and the top and bottom of the window. But, as Figure 3-3 shows, this is not the case: The buttons stay in place, as if invisible strings attached them to the top of the window. Even after resizing, the distance between the top of the buttons and the top of the window remains fixed at the initial 4 pixels.

Figure 3-3   The FlowLayout Manager increasing vertical space.

You can make life a little more difficult for `FlowLayout` by giving it too little horizontal space to lay out all of its buttons side-by-side. When this happens, as many buttons as will fit are allocated to the top row, separated by the required horizontal gaps, and the rest of the buttons are moved onto a second row. In Figure 3-4, the window has been resized in such a way as to allow four buttons to fit on the top row and, as a result, the last two have been moved to the second row.

Figure 3-4   The FlowLayout Manager with too little horizontal space.

`FlowLayout` manages the second row using the same rules as it used for the first one: The buttons are separated by the specified horizontal gap and are then aligned as specified in the constructor. You could, theoretically continue this process of making the window taller and narrower. Eventually, you would probably hit a minimum size constraint on the top-level frame imposed by your platform. On Windows, for example, the frame has to be wide enough to show the controls on the caption bar and a few letters of the caption itself and you can't make it narrower than this minimum. If you could make the frame just wider than one button, then all the buttons would be arranged vertically in six rather trivial rows, all individually centered (or left- or right-aligned, as appropriate).

You could, of course, go further than this. You might wonder what would happen if the window were too narrow to accept even a single button. One possibility is for FlowLayout to resize the buttons so that they fit within the reduced space available. However, FlowLayout always lays out components at their preferred size. Instead of making the buttons fit the window, it renders them at full size and, as a result, they are clipped at the right by the edge of the window. Similarly, if the window is too small vertically, the buttons at the bottom will be clipped. You can see an example of this in Figure 3-5.

Figure 3-5   The FlowLayout Manager with too little vertical space.

In this example, the buttons were all of approximately equal size, but what happens if not all of the components are so closely matched? In a slightly modified version of Figure 3-1, let's see what happens when the third and fourth buttons are taller and wider than the other four. You can try this example using the command:

```
java JFCBook.Chapter3.FlowLayoutExample2
```

In the initial configuration of the window, the buttons are still rendered in a straight line, but notice that they are arranged such that their centers line up horizontally. The vertical gap now represents the space between the window and the top and bottom edges of the largest components.

Figure 3-6   The FlowLayout Manager with components of unequal size.

Resizing the window so that there are now three buttons in each row results in the configuration shown in Figure 3-7. The rows are now of equal width, with the vertical distance between them determined by the constructor's vertical gap parameter. As you might expect by now, if you make the window too small by dragging the bottom upwards, the entire layout is preserved, but the buttons at the bottom are clipped by the window.

Figure 3-7   The FlowLayout Manager with components arranged in two rows.

The BorderLayout Manager

As useful as FlowLayout is, it isn't really capable of managing a complete user interface, except in the simplest cases. The main shortcoming of FlowLayout is that it is essentially one-dimensional, preferring to lay out components left-to-right and creating vertical distributions only when there is insufficient horizontal space. You have no real control over the way in which FlowLayout distributes components when this happens and no way to force it to create a two-dimensional arrangement of controls. By contrast, the BorderLayout manager is very suited to more generalized arrangements of components and is the default layout manager for the AWT Frame, Window and Dialog containers and for the content pane of the Swing JFrame, JWindow and JDialog containers.

A BorderLayout can manage from one to five components. Each component is explicitly assigned to one of the four edges of the container or to its center. Listing 3-2 shows an example that creates a fully populated container with five buttons.

Listing 3-2   Using the BorderLayout Manager

```
package JFCBook.Chapter3;

import com.sun.java.swing.*;
import java.awt.*;
import java.awt.event.*;

public class BorderLayoutExample1 {
  public static void main(String[] args) {
    JFrame f = new JFrame("Border1");
    Container cp = f.getContentPane();
    cp.add(new JButton("N"), "North");
    cp.add(new JButton("S"), "South");
    cp.add(new JButton("E"), "East");
    cp.add(new JButton("W"), "West");
    cp.add(new JButton("C"), "Center");
    f.pack();
    f.addWindowListener(new WindowAdapter() {
      public void windowClosing(WindowEvent evt) {
        System.exit(0);
      }
    });
    f.setVisible(true);
  }
}
```

You can run this example using the command:

```
java JFCBook.Chapter3.BorderLayoutExample1
```

that produces the result shown in Figure 3-8. As you would expect from their designations, the buttons are indeed placed at the compass points and in the center of the frame's content pane.

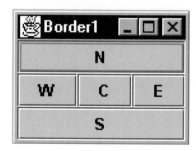

Figure 3-8   A fully-populated BorderLayout
Manager.

The code shown in Listing 3-2 uses an overloaded version of the `Container` `add` method that accepts one of the compass points or the word `Center` as a second argument. In JDK 1.0, the component and position designator were supplied in a different order and, for compatibility, this form is still allowed, so that the two lines

```
cp.add(new JButton("N"), "North");    // JDK 1.1 style
cp.add("North", new JButton("N"));    // JDK 1.0 style
```

are equivalent. In JDK 1.1, the first form of the `add` method is defined as:

```
public void add(Component c, Object constraints);
```

where the second parameter is an object passing constraints in a form acceptable to the container's layout manager. In the case of `BorderLayout`, you must supply a `String` argument from the set shown above; later, you will also see this form of the `add` method used in connection with the `GridBagLayout` manager, which requires a constraints object of a different type. To complete the story, you can also just write:

```
cp.add(new JButton("C"));
```

which places the button in the center position.

Returning to Figure 3-8, you can see that this is very different from the layout produced by `FlowLayout`. Aside from the fact that the components are not laid out in a straight line, it is clear that they are not all of the same size, despite the fact that they were all potentially of the same size when created, since their labels are almost identical. When laying out the container, `BorderLayout` asks each component for its preferred size. The components in the north and south positions are always assigned their requested preferred heights, while those in the east and west always get their preferred widths. After this has been done, the component in the center is given whatever space is left, which may sometimes be no space at all.

As is shown in Figure 3-8, this usually means that the north and south components are stretched horizontally, while the east and west ones are stretched vertically. The fate of the center component depends entirely on the size of the container; it may appear at its correct size, expanded or squashed. You can see this effect in action if you resize the container. Note particularly that, when the container is too small to give one of the components its preferred size when `BorderLayout` would normally have done so, that component begins to overlap its opposite number in the container, as you can see with the buttons in the north and south of Figure 3-9.

Figure 3-9   A fully-populated BorderLayout manager with too little vertical space.

The discussion so far has assumed that all five possible components are present. This need not, of course, be the case. Normally, the BorderLayout is used in situations where you require a large working area that should be allocated as much space as possible, with some buttons or input controls underneath or alongside it. The large working area is ideally suited to the center position, while the buttons can be placed on a panel at one of the other positions, probably in the south. This panel counts as one component and, since it uses the FlowLayout as its layout manager by default, it lays out the buttons neatly across the bottom of the container. An example of this can be produced with the code in Listing 3-3.

Listing 3-3   BorderLayout with an expandable component in the center position

```
package JFCBook.Chapter3;

import com.sun.java.swing.*;
import java.awt.*;
import java.awt.event.*;

public class BorderLayoutExample2 {
   public static void main(String[] args) {
      JFrame f = new JFrame("Border2");
      f.getContentPane().setLayout(new BorderLayout(0, 4));
      f.getContentPane().setBackground(Color.black);
      JTextArea t = new JTextArea(10, 30);
      t.setText("Some text");
      JPanel p = new JPanel(true);
      p.add(new JButton("Clear"));
      p.add(new JButton("Cut"));
      p.add(new JButton("Paste"));
      p.add(new JButton("Copy"));
      f.getContentPane().add(t, "Center");
      f.getContentPane().add(p, "South");
      f.pack();
      f.addWindowListener(new WindowAdapter() {
         public void windowClosing(WindowEvent evt) {
            System.exit(0);
         }
      });
      f.setVisible(true);
   }
}
```

This example, which you can run with the command

```
java JFCBook.Chapter3.BorderLayoutExample2
```

produces the layout shown in Figure 3-10. Note that this example creates its own `BorderLayout`, replacing the one automatically assigned to the container on creation:

```
f.getContentPane().setLayout(new BorderLayout(0, 4));
```

This form of the constructor allows you to specify the horizontal and vertical gaps between the components. In our case, for the purposes of illustration, no horizontal gap and a 4-pixel vertical gap were requested.

Figure 3-10   A BorderLayout manager with an expandable center component.

Resizing the container causes `BorderLayout` to resize both components. If you enlarge the container, any extra vertical space goes entirely to the text area, while the button panel's height remains constant, which is exactly what you would want to happen. If you make the container too small, however, you will eventually start losing buttons. There is little that you can do about this as a programmer—if the user makes the window too small to show everything, there is no sensible way out. It is, however, important to distribute spare space where the user would prefer it to be if the container is enlarged. In this case, it is clearly better to allocate spare room to the text area. This is the reason for assigning the text area to the center position. Had it been placed in the north position, leaving the center slot unoccupied, then any extra space would have been shared equally between the text area and the button panel, resulting in the button area growing at the same rate as the text area itself.

One case in which the `BorderLayout` doesn't work so well can be seen if you change the location of the button panel from the south to the east or the west. The results of this apparently trivial change are shown in Figure 3-11.

Figure 3-11   Inappropriate use of the BorderLayout manager.

Here you can see the `FlowLayout` that is managing the button panel following its normal policy of laying out the buttons horizontally whenever possible. When the application starts, every component and container gets the chance to suggest its preferred size. If the layout managers can conform to these requests, they will do so. Here, `FlowLayout` asks for enough space to lay out its buttons horizontally. Because this example sizes the frame using `pack`, which asks the frame to find its own ideal size, the `FlowLayout`'s size request is passed indirectly to the content pane. The `BorderLayout`, which is managing it, complies with this request and allocates the horizontal space required for the panel. It also satisfies the text area's request for both horizontal and vertical space and constructs the content pane in such a way as to suit both containers. Simple though this might be for `BorderLayout`, it does not produce the desired results!

If you need to produce a container that must have components stacked vertically, as would be better in this case, you should not use the `FlowLayout` manager. Instead, you should choose either the `GridLayout` or `GridBagLayout` managers that are described next or, better still in most cases, the `BoxLayout` manager described later in this chapter.

The GridLayout Manager

Our third layout manager, `GridLayout`, is, as its name suggests, used for laying out components in a gridlike configuration. A container managed by `GridLayout` is divided into a number of equally-sized cells, into each of which is placed one component. As the container is resized, the individual cells grow or shrink proportionately, as do the components that they contain.

`GridLayout` has four configurable parameters that can be used to exercise control over its behavior. The first two are the familiar horizontal and vertical gaps that you've already seen in connection with `FlowLayout` and `BorderLayout`. The gap values are applied around the edges of each cell. The other two parameters specify the number of rows and columns in the grid that `GridLayout` will create. All of these parameters can be set when the layout manager is created or modified later using the `setVgap`, `setHgap`, `setRows` and `setColumns` methods. Here is an example that creates a `GridLayout` with 2 rows and 3 columns:

```
GridLayout g = new GridLayout(2, 3);
```

If, as in this example, you don't specify the horizontal and vertical gaps, then there will be no gaps between the grid cells. The following line creates the same grid as above, but with 2-pixel gaps in both directions:

```
GridLayout g = new GridLayout(2, 3, 2, 2);
```

The `GridLayout` manager is very useful when you need to create layouts that look something like the keys on a pocket calculator. This is demonstrated in the following example, which uses a `GridLayout` to produce a simple but recognizable interface for a calculator. See Listing 3-4.

Listing 3-4   Producing a calculatorlike layout with GridLayout

```
package JFCBook.Chapter3;

import com.sun.java.swing.*;
import java.awt.*;
import java.awt.event.*;

public class GridLayoutExample1 {
  public static void main(String[] args) {
    JFrame f = new JFrame("Calculator");
    JTextField t = new JTextField();
    JPanel p = new JPanel(true);
    p.setLayout(new GridLayout(5, 4, 2, 2));
    p.add(new JButton("1"));       // Top row
    p.add(new JButton("2"));
    p.add(new JButton("3"));
    p.add(new JButton("="));

    p.add(new JButton("4"));       // 2nd row
    p.add(new JButton("5"));
    p.add(new JButton("6"));
    p.add(new JButton("+"));

    p.add(new JButton("7"));       // 3rd row
    p.add(new JButton("8"));
    p.add(new JButton("9"));
    p.add(new JButton("-"));

    p.add(new JButton("0"));       // 4th row
    p.add(new JButton("."));
    p.add(new JButton("C"));
    p.add(new JButton("*"));

    p.add(new JButton("MR"));      // Last row
    p.add(new JButton("MC"));
    p.add(new JButton("M+"));
    p.add(new JButton("/"));

    f.getContentPane().add(t, "North");
    f.getContentPane().add(p, "Center");

    f.pack();
    f.addWindowListener(new WindowAdapter() {
      public void windowClosing(WindowEvent evt) {
        System.exit(0);
      }
    });
    f.setVisible(true);
  }
}
```

You can run this example with the command:

```
java JFCBook.Chapter3.GridLayoutExample1
```

The result is shown in Figure 3-12. Note that all of the cells are of the same size, which means that the single-letter buttons have been stretched slightly to match the size of those with two-letter labels.

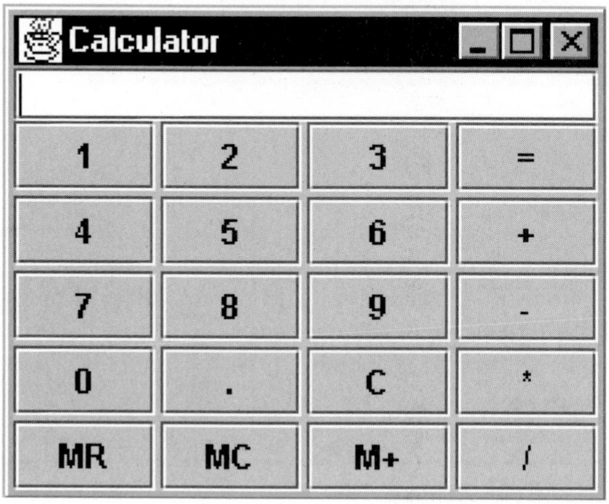

Figure 3-12   A rough-and-ready calculator using GridLayout.

As always, the interesting feature of a layout manager is how it reacts to the container being resized. In this respect, GridLayout is very different from both FlowLayout and BorderLayout. Whereas those two layout managers tried to maintain their components' preferred sizes (at least to the extent to which they originally honored the preferred size), GridLayout always divides the container space into equally-sized cells. As a result, if the container is too small in either direction, then each component will be reduced in size proportionately in that direction. Conversely, extra space is distributed evenly, causing each component to grow a little. This effect is shown in the Figure 3-13, where the calculator has been stretched horizontally, but compressed vertically, resulting in wide, thin buttons.

You don't need to specify both the row and column count when you create a GridLayout. If you supply 0 as either the row or the column count, the missing value is calculated based on the total number of components added to the container. For example, you can create the same layout manager as that in Figure 3-12 with either of the following lines of code:

```
GridLayout g1 = new GridLayout(5, 0);
GridLayout g2 = new GridLayout(0, 4);
```

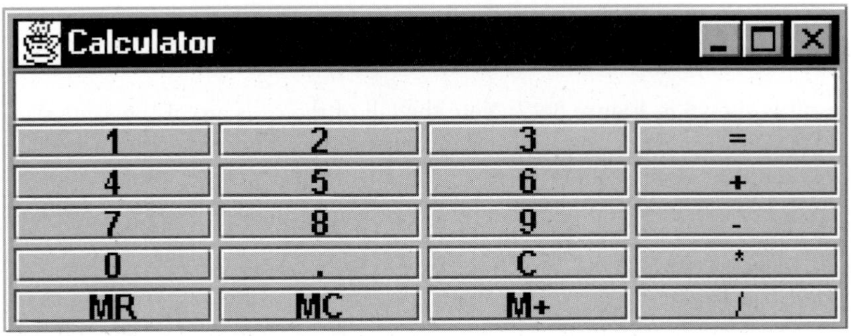

Figure 3-13   A GridLayout with too little space.

Since 20 components are added to the container, it is a simple matter to calculate the unspecified dimension in either case. You can't, of course, supply both the row and column count as zero; if you try, you will get an `IllegalArgumentException`.

Whether or not you actually supply both dimensions, you are not obliged to supply enough components to fill the entire grid. To illustrate what happens when you supply too few, Listing 3-5 creates a 3-row by 3-column grid and then adds only 8 components to it.

Listing 3-5   A GridLayout with an empty cell

```
package JFCBook.Chapter3;

import com.sun.java.swing.*;
import java.awt.*;
import java.awt.event.*;

public class GridLayoutExample2 {
  public static void main(String[] args) {
    JFrame f = new JFrame("GridLayout 2");
    f.getContentPane().setLayout(new GridLayout(3, 3));
    f.getContentPane().setBackground(Color.black);
    for (int i = 0; i < 8; i++) {
      JLabel l = new JLabel("" + i, SwingConstants.CENTER);
      l.setForeground(Color.yellow);
      f.getContentPane().add(l);
    }

    f.pack();
    f.addWindowListener(new WindowAdapter() {
      public void windowClosing(WindowEvent evt) {
        System.exit(0);
      }
```

```
    });
    f.setVisible(true);
  }
}
```

GridLayout always lays out components in the order in which they were added, filling the top row, then moving on to the second row and so on. When you don't supply enough components to occupy every cell, the last cell or cells are simply left empty. If you requested a specific number of rows, either in the constructor or via setRows, that number of rows will always be created, even if some of them are completely empty, because it is possible to add components after the container has been laid out for the first time. The code in Listing 3-5, therefore, results in a layout with the bottom right cell empty, as shown in Figure 3-14.

Figure 3-14   A GridLayout with an extra cell.

Having looked at the simple cases, let's briefly examine some slightly less obvious ones. First, what happens if you don't specify one of the dimensions and don't add a number of components that can be divided evenly by the other dimension? For example, suppose you do the following:

```
JFrame f = new JFrame("GridLayout 3");
f.getContentPane().setLayout(new GridLayout(3, 0));
f.getContentPane().setBackground(Color.black);
for (int i = 0; i < 4; i++) {
  JLabel l = new JLabel("" + i, SwingConstants.CENTER);
  l.setForeground(Color.yellow);
  f.getContentPane().add(l);
}
```

You can try this example using the command:

```
java JFCBook.Chapter3.GridLayoutExample3
```

Here there are four labels that need to be distributed over three rows. Obviously, there must be at least two columns, so GridLayout constructs a 3-row by 2-column grid into which it places the four labels starting from the top left. At the end of the second row, all four labels have been placed, so there are none left to place on the bottom row. Nonetheless, since the constructor calls for three rows, the empty bottom row remains.

What about specifying both dimensions and then supplying too many components? In this case, GridLayout retains the required number of rows and adds more columns until it has enough room to accommodate all of the components, again leaving unoccupied cells to the bottom right, as in the following code extract:

```
JFrame f = new JFrame("GridLayout 4");
f.getContentPane().setLayout(new GridLayout(3, 3));
f.getContentPane().setBackground(Color.black);
for (int i = 0; i < 10; i++) {
   JLabel l = new JLabel("" + i, SwingConstants.CENTER);
   l.setForeground(Color.yellow);
   f.getContentPane().add(l);
}
```

Here, there are nine available cells and 10 components to place in them. GridLayout resolves this by creating three rows as requested, but allocates four columns to each row, then lays out the labels from the top left, leaving the two cells at the bottom right empty, as shown in Figure 3-15.

Figure 3-15   A GridLayout with more items than requested cells

What about the problem of creating a panel of buttons arranged vertically that we examined at the end of our discussion of BorderLayout? As it happens, GridLayout is better suited to creating a layout of this form than FlowLayout, which we tried in the last section, because, provided you request one column and the correct number of rows to accommodate all of the buttons, GridLayout is guaranteed to lay the buttons out vertically and to keep them that way no matter what happens to the container's shape. In most cases, you can arrange for a panel like this to preserve its horizontal size by, for example, placing it on the east or west side of a container managed by BorderLayout provided that there is also a center component. But even in this case the panel will grow vertically if the user resizes the window in that direction. Since GridLayout always allocates extra space to its managed components, this will cause the buttons to grow vertically even though their horizontal size will remain constant. Whether or not this is acceptable depends on the application.

To create a panel in which the buttons do not grow in either direction, you need to use either the GridBagLayout manager, which we discuss next, or, probably best of all, the BoxLayout manager that we cover immediately afterwards.

Complete Flexibility with GridBagLayout

GridBagLayout is, without doubt, the most complex of all the AWT layout managers. This complexity arises because of the number of configurable options that it provides, which give you almost total control over the way in which your container is laid out. For all the apparent complexity, though, once you grasp the basic ideas, GridBagLayout becomes surprisingly easy to use. In this section you'll see all of the options available, how they change the way in which components are laid out and how they move and resize in response to changes in the container's shape.

GridBagLayout is superficially similar to GridLayout, in that it creates and manages a grid configuration within a container. However, there are two significant differences that make GridBagLayout a much more powerful tool. First, the columns and rows managed by GridBagLayout can all be of different sizes. Secondly, whereas GridLayout confines each component to one cell, GridBagLayout does not: A component can occupy a rectangular area of any size within the container, provided that it does not overlap other components.

To make this latter point clearer, consider Figure 3-16, which shows a container divided up into a 3-row by 4-column grid, occupied by three buttons and a text field. In terms of cells, the buttons labeled ONE and TWO have both been configured to occupy one row and two columns, button THREE has been configured to occupy two rows and two columns and the text field occupies one row and all four columns of the grid. These row and column constraints are stated to GridBagLayout when the container is constructed—the layout manager does not determine how many cells a component will cover. It does, however, decide how large each of these cells will be.

Figure 3-16 Explicit placement of objects with GridBagLayout.

In this case, button ONE occupies the top two cells on the left. No other component could occupy any of the area within these two cells, even if they had enough available space: No cell can be occupied by more than one component. Furthermore, you will notice that, unlike `GridLayout`, it is possible to arrange for components to be smaller in the size than the cell area to which they are allocated and, as we shall see, it is possible to determine how a component that is smaller than its assigned cell space is aligned within that space; in this case, all of the components are aligned to the center of their respective areas.

The simplest way to use `GridBagLayout` is simply to create and add components to a container that it manages. This is perfectly valid, as the example in Listing 3-6 shows.

Listing 3-6   A GridBagLayout with no explicit constraints

```
package JFCBook.Chapter3;

import com.sun.java.swing.*;
import java.awt.*;
import java.awt.event.*;

public class GridBagLayoutExample1 {
  public static void main(String[] args) {
    JFrame f = new JFrame("GridBagLayout 1");
    f.getContentPane().setLayout(new GridBagLayout());
    for (int i = 0; i < 3; i++) {
      JButton b = new JButton("" + i);
      f.getContentPane().add(b);
    }

    f.pack();
```

```
    f.addWindowListener(new WindowAdapter() {
      public void windowClosing(WindowEvent evt) {
        System.exit(0);
      }
    });
    f.setVisible(true);
  }
}
```

The result of running this program, using the command

```
java JFCBook.Chapter3.GridBagLayoutExample1
```

is a frame with three buttons side-by-side, tightly packed next to each other. If you resize the frame, the buttons remain together as a single unit and retain their original size. Making the container larger results in the extra space being evenly distributed around the buttons, leaving the center of the row of three buttons exactly in the center of the container. Similarly, if you make the frame too small, the buttons still move themselves so that they are centered in the container, resulting in clipping at the edges. See Figure 3-17.

Figure 3-17   Basic GridBagLayout: resizing the frame.

This is, of course, a rather trivial and unusual way to use `GridBagLayout`. The key to making use of the power of the `GridBagLayout` is the two-argument form of the `Container add` method that was used in conjunction with `BorderLayout` which, as you may recall, has the following signature:

```
public void add(Component c, Object constraints);
```

In the case of `BorderLayout`, the constraint object was supplied in the form of a `String`. For `GridBagLayout`, the constraints are supplied in an instance of a dedicated class called `GridBagConstraints`. All the members of `GridBagConstraints` are public, so to configure a `GridBagLayout`, you simply create a constraints object and set the member variables directly. Here are the public variables of `GridBagConstraints`:

```
public int anchor

public int fill

public int gridheight

public int gridwidth

public int gridx

public int gridy

public Insets insets

public int ipadx

public int ipady

public double weightx

public double weighty
```

It might look like there are a lot of constraints to set here, but in fact you'll find that you can set many of them once and then reuse the settings for more than one component, changing only a small number of items each time you add a component. When you add a component to a container managed by GridBagLayout, you pass both the component and the constraints to the add method. The GridBagLayout then takes its own copy of the GridBagConstraints object and associates that with the component, so you can reuse your copy without affecting the settings of components added earlier.

To demonstrate how the GridBagConstraints object is used, let's write the code that generates the component layout shown in Figure 3-16. So that you can see the effects of changing the various possible constraint settings, the code will be developed in stages.

The most obvious constraints you need to set for each component are its position and its size, which are specified by the gridx, gridy, gridwidth and gridheight members. The grid cells have *x* and *y* coordinates assigned to them, with gridx = 0 and gridy = 0, indicating the cell at the top left of the layout; *x* values increase toward the right and *y* values increase as you move downward. The gridwidth and gridheight values describe how many cells in the corresponding direction the component should occupy. A component must, as has been said earlier, have sole occupancy of the cells it covers.

Core Note

The grid cell coordinates refer to grid locations, not pixel values.

Once you have created your `GridBagConstraints` object, you add the corresponding component to the container using the `add` method, passing the constraints object as well. Here's an example that configures button ONE as shown in Figure 3-16:

```
JPanel p = new JPanel(true);
p.setLayout(new GridBagLayout());
GridBagConstraints c = new GridBagConstraints();
JButton b = new JButton("ONE");
c.gridx = 0;
c.gridy = 0;
c.gridwidth = 2;
c.gridheight = 1;
p.add(b, c);    // b = component, c = constraints
```

This is not the only way to associate constraints with a component. Before JDK 1.1, it was necessary to use the `GridBagLayout` `setConstraints` method, because the variant of the `add` method used above did not exist in the earlier release. In JDK 1.0, this code would have been written like this—do not be surprised if you see code like this carried over from applications that have not been fully ported to JDK 1.1:

```
Panel p = new Panel();
GridBagLayout l = new GridBagLayout();
p.setLayout(l);
GridBagConstraints c = new GridBagConstraints();
Button b = new Button("ONE");
c.gridx = 0;
c.gridy = 0;
c.gridwidth = 2;
c.gridheight = 1;
l.setConstraints(b, c);          // Component, constraints
p.add(b);
```

I think you'll agree that the newer method is simpler, saving a line of code for each code added, as well as being much clearer.

At this stage, the other members of the `GridBagConstraints` object will be left at their default values and look at the rest of the code to create the layout shown in Figure 3-16. This first version will be straightforward and will only use what you have seen so far; later, the code will be refined to create exactly the layout shown above and make it behave properly when the container is resized. Listing 3-7 shows the first attempt.

Listing 3-7   A GridBagLayout with simple constraints

```
package JFCBook.Chapter3;

import com.sun.java.swing.*;
import java.awt.*;
import java.awt.event.*;

public class GridBagLayoutExample2 extends JPanel {
  public GridBagLayoutExample2() {
    super(true);    // Double-buffer
    this.setLayout(new GridBagLayout());
    this.setOpaque(true);
    this.setBackground(UIManager.getColor("control"));
    GridBagConstraints c = new GridBagConstraints();
    JButton b = new JButton("ONE");
    c.gridx = 0;
    c.gridy = 0;
    c.gridwidth = 2;
    c.gridheight = 1;
    this.add(b, c);    // Button ONE added

    c.gridy++;
    b = new JButton("TWO");
    this.add(b, c);    // Button TWO added

    c.gridx = 2;
    c.gridy = 0;
    c.gridwidth = 2;
    c.gridheight = 2;
    b = new JButton("THREE");
    this.add(b, c);    // Button THREE added

    c.gridx = 0;
    c.gridy = 2;
    c.gridwidth = 4;
    c.gridheight = 1;
    this.add(new JTextField(35), c);    // Text field
  }

  public static void main(String[] args) {
    JFrame f = new JFrame("GridBagLayout 2");
    JPanel p = new GridBagLayoutExample2();
    f.getContentPane().add(p);
    f.pack();
    f.addWindowListener(new WindowAdapter() {
      public void windowClosing(WindowEvent evt) {
```

```
            System.exit(0);
        }
    });
    f.setVisible(true);
    }
}
```

That's all there is to it! First, a custom panel (based on JPanel) is created and a GridBagLayout is assigned to manage it. You will notice that we are not required to specify the size of the grid, because the layout manager can deduce the number of cells required from the constraints objects it is given as the components are added.

Since each component is added along with associated components that include its position, you don't need to add them in any particular order. Usually, the calls that add the components are ordered in such a way as to minimize changes in the GridBagConstraints object as you move from one component to the next. As noted earlier, GridBagLayout takes a private copy of the constraints passed with each add call, so it is perfectly safe to use only one GridBagConstraints object to lay out the entire container, modifying it as you go. In this example, each time a component is added, only the constraints that must be changed are actually modified—often just one of gridx, gridy, gridwidth and gridheight.

If you now run the example code, you will see that we have already done enough to obtain a layout that at least resembles the one we were trying to achieve—see Figure 3-18. The command to do this is:

```
java JFCBook.Chapter3.GridBagLayoutExample2
```

Figure 3-18   GridBagLayout: with simple constraints.

While this layout may look approximately correct, you will see a major problem if you make the window larger. When you do this, the entire layout stays frozen in the middle of the container with the extra space distributed symmetrically around it. This happens because the defaulted constraints parameters that have been associated with each component tell GridBagLayout to allocate them their preferred sizes and never to assign any more space than that. As a result, when the container is enlarged, the extra room cannot be allocated to any of the components, so it is left around the outside.

Before seeing how to allocate the extra space more sensibly, let's look at some convenient shorthand that you can use to make your layout more readable and more maintainable. You will often find when laying out containers that you will place components in order along a row, or down a single column. To do this, you would probably increment either gridx or gridy, leaving all of the other constraints unchanged. Since this is such a common operation, GridBagConstraints provides a constant value, RELATIVE, that can be assigned to either gridx or gridy. The effect of using this is to place the component affected one cell to the right of the previous cell if used in gridx or one cell below the previous one if used in gridy. So, for example, the following extract produces a row of buttons along the top of the container.

```
JPanel p = new JPanel();
GridBagConstraints c = new GridBagConstraints();
p.setLayout(new GridBagLayout());
c.gridx = GridBagConstraints.RELATIVE;
p.add(new JButton("1"), c);
p.add(new JButton("2"), c);
p.add(new JButton("3"), c);
```

Each time a button is added, GridBagLayout adds one to the x coordinate it used the previous time, resulting in a straight line of buttons. You could create a vertical set of buttons in the same way by setting gridy to GridBagConstraints.RELATIVE instead. Setting both gridx and gridy to this value is the same as setting just gridx. The results of running this code are the same as the code shown in Listing 3-6. The reason that this happens is that, if you don't supply a GridBagConstraints object in an add call, the default constraints have both gridx and gridy set to RELATIVE, which is effectively the same as the example we showed above.

A similar useful shorthand is available for the gridwidth and the gridheight members. Here, you can use the constant GridBagConstraints.REMAINDER in the gridwidth member to create a component that spans the rest of the container to the right of its starting point, no matter where that might be. Similarly, using this constant in gridheight forces the component to stretch to the bottom of the container. This facility allows you to create components that span the right number of columns or rows even if you add extra components to the layout, resulting in a change in the number of components in the direction concerned.

As an example of this, in the panel of buttons created in Listing 3-7, the text field was made to stretch under all of the buttons by hard-coding gridwidth to the value 4. This works until you insert a new control on one of the other rows, creating a container with five columns instead of four. If you instead change the gridwidth to GridBagConstraints.REMAINDER, then the text field would always span all of the bottom row.

A problem with the layout obtained from this first version of the code is that buttons ONE and TWO are placed right up against each other. Button THREE has been placed a respectable distance away, but only because of the fact that the text field forced the container to be wider than the sum of the widths of the buttons. You can arrange for some space to be left around the component by using the insets member of the GridBagConstraints object. By default, this member is null, which requests no external padding. You can change this by creating a java.awt.Insets object specifying the amount of space needed above, below, to the left and to the right of the component. The constructor of this object is defined as follows:

```
public Insets(top, left, bottom, right);
```

If you want to create a space around a component with 1 pixel above, 2 pixels to the left, 3 pixels below and 4 pixels to the right, you would do the following:

```
GridBagConstraints c = new GridBagConstraints();
// Other initializations not shown
// …
c.insets = new Insets(1, 2, 3, 4);
```

Once you have created an Insets object, you can reuse it, since all of its members are public and GridBagLayout copies this object when it copies the associated GridBagConstraints object. To obtain a suitable space around the buttons and text area in our code example, you simply add the following line after the GridBagConstraints object has been created and before it is first used:

```
c.insets = new Insets(4, 3, 4, 3);
```

This changes the initial layout to that shown in Figure 3-19; although it is difficult to see, you now have 4 pixels above and below each component and 3 pixels to both the left and the right.

Figure 3-19   GridBagLayout: with extra space around the components.

Now that you have the proper spacing around the outside of the buttons, the next issue to be addressed is the behavior when the container is resized. To stop the entire layout huddling together in the middle of the container, as they do with the constraints that are currently applied, you need to allow the cells in which the components reside to expand or contract in sympathy with the rest of the container. This is most apparent in the case of the text field, which remains stubbornly the same size no matter how the container is reshaped. The text area should always span the bottom of the container, but you would not want it to grow vertically.

The `weightx` and `weighty` members of the `GridBagConstraints` object control how the cells themselves resize when the container is reshaped. These fields are both floating-point numbers and the ratio of each individual entry's value to the total of all of the values across the container or down the container determines the proportion of the extra space that will be allocated to each cell.

Let's look at an example to see how this works, by setting the values of `weightx` for each component as follows:

Button ONE:	0.4
Button TWO	0.4
Button THREE	0.6
Text Area	1.0

Bearing in mind that button ONE is above button TWO and should remain horizontally aligned with it, it makes sense for their `weightx` values to be the same. Looking at the layout of the container as shown in the diagram above, you can see that these values make the total value of `weightx` across each row equal to 1.0. Now suppose that the container expands horizontally by 10 pixels. Then the extra space allocated to each cell is as follows:

Cell containing ONE:	$(0.4/1.0) \times 10$ = 4 pixels
Cell containing TWO:	$(0.4/1.0) \times 10$ = 4 pixels
Cell containing THREE:	$(0.6/1.0) \times 10$ = 6 pixels
Cell containing text area:	$(1.0/1.0) \times 10$ = 10 pixels

It is actually not necessary that the sum of the `weightx` values across the container (or of the `weighty` values) add up to 1.0: They can actually add up to any value at all, because it is the ratio of each column's value to the total that counts. Now that there is some flexibility in the horizontal direction, the `GridBagLayout` will allocate all of the available space in that direction to cells and not leave it unused.

If `weighty` values were left zero, the layout would expand nicely horizontally, but would continue to be squashed into the middle of the container if it were expanded vertically. In order to stop this happening, you need to set sensible values of `weighty` for each component. As noted earlier, you wouldn't want the text field to grow in the vertical direction, so you would probably choose to allocate all of the extra space to the buttons. To do this, you set the `weighty` value of the text area to `0.0` (so that it gets no extra space) and that of the buttons to any nonzero values. To distribute the vertical space equally between them, our example uses the value 0.5 (it could equally well have used 3.0 or 0.7 or any other positive value). After these changes, the code looks like that shown in Listing 3-8, where the changes just described are highlighted in bold.

Listing 3-8   GridBagLayout with per-cell expansion constraints

```
package JFCBook.Chapter3;

import com.sun.java.swing.*;
import java.awt.*;
import java.awt.event.*;

public class GridBagLayoutExample4 extends JPanel {
  public GridBagLayoutExample4() {
    super(true);     // Double-buffer
    this.setLayout(new GridBagLayout());
    this.setOpaque(true);
    this.setBackground(UIManager.getColor("control"));
    GridBagConstraints c = new GridBagConstraints();
    JButton b = new JButton("ONE");
    c.gridx = 0;
    c.gridy = 0;
    c.gridwidth = 2;
    c.gridheight = 1;
    c.weightx = 0.4;
    c.weighty = 0.5;
    c.insets = new Insets(4, 3, 4, 3);
    this.add(b, c);   // Button ONE added

    c.gridy++;
    b = new JButton("TWO");
    this.add(b, c);   // Button TWO added

    c.gridx = 2;
    c.gridy = 0;
    c.gridwidth = 2;
    c.gridheight = 2;
    c.weightx = 0.6;
    b = new JButton("THREE");
    this.add(b, c);   // Button THREE added
```

continued

```
        c.gridx = 0;
        c.gridy = 2;
        c.gridwidth = 4;
        c.gridheight = 1;
        c.weightx = 1.0;
        c.weighty = 0.0;
        this.add(new JTextField(35), c);    // Text field
    }

    public static void main(String[] args) {
        JFrame f = new JFrame("GridBagLayout 4");
        JPanel p = new GridBagLayoutExample4();
        f.getContentPane().add(p);
        f.pack();
        f.addWindowListener(new WindowAdapter() {
            public void windowClosing(WindowEvent evt) {
                System.exit(0);
            }
        });
        f.setVisible(true);
    }
}
```

This looks correct, but if you run this code and resize the window in both directions, you find that the text area does not behave as expected, as you can see from Figure 3-20, which shows the result. The command you need to run this version of the example is:

```
java JFCBook.Chapter3.GridBagLayoutExample4
```

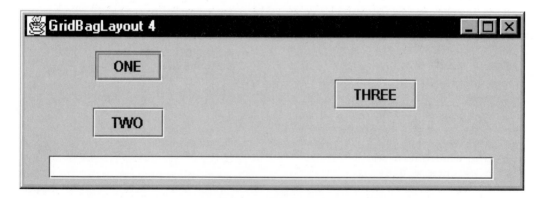

Figure 3-20   GridBagLayout: with cells that can expand or contract.

While the buttons have improved their behavior, moving away from the edges of the container in the initial configuration and also moving when the container grows, the text area, although it stays attached to the bottom of the container as required, does not expand to take up the extra horizontal space available to it. So what has gone wrong here?

The problem has arisen because the distinction between the terms *cell* and *component* has not yet been made clear. The `weightx` and `weighty` values control the extent to which the grid *cells* expand when the container grows, but, they have no direct effect on the size of the *component* within each cell. In fact, all of the cells in the container grew when the window was expanded, including the cells across which the text field lies. However, the text field didn't grow at all. This is because the growth of a component within its assigned cell or cells is controlled by the `fill` member of the `GridBagConstraints` object, which has the following possible values:

`GridBagConstraints.NONE`	Do not grow
`GridBagConstraints.HORIZONTAL`	Grow horizontally only
`GridBagConstraints.VERTICAL`	Grow vertically only
`GridBagConstraints.BOTH`	Grow in both directions

When you create a `GridBagConstraints` object, its `fill` value is set to `GridBagConstraints.NONE`, so that the associated component will not resize within its cell, even if the cell grows. To make the text area take up all of the horizontal space available to it, you need to set its `fill` value to `GridBagConstraints.HORIZONTAL`. Changing the initialization of the constraints object for the text area as follows produces the required result:

```
c.gridx = 0;
c.gridy = 2;
c.gridwidth = 4;
c.gridheight = 1;
c.weightx = 1.0;
c.weighty = 0.0;
c.fill = GridBagConstraints.HORIZONTAL;
this.add(new JTextField(35), c);       // Text field
```

Now the text area would occupy of the bottom of the container (less the 8-pixel insets) no matter how the container is resized.

There are three more members of the `GridBagConstraints` object. First, let's look at the `ipadx` and `ipady` values. When `GridBagLayout` is laying out the container, it considers the minimum size of each component as one of the constraints used to decide how to allocate space; for example, if there is a choice as to how to allocate a few pixels, it is better to allocate them to a component that would otherwise be below its designer's stated minimum size than to give them to a component that would not be. The `ipadx` and `ipady` values can be set to increase the values taken as the minimum sizes for a component when performing this calculation. For example, if a button indicates that its minimum size is 30 pixels wide and 20 pixels high and the associated constraints object has `ipadx` set to 4 and `ipadx` set to 2, then the minimum size of the button will be taken to be 38 pixels across and 24 pixels high. Furthermore, the component will not be made smaller than this.

The last constraint is the `anchor` value. This field comes into play when the component is smaller than the cell area allocated to it, in either the horizontal or vertical direction. If this is the case, then the `anchor` value determines how the component will be aligned within the available space. By default, the component is anchored to the center of its display area, so that the extra space is distributed symmetrically around it. However, you can instead choose to anchor the component to any of the eight principal compass points, by using one of the possible `anchor` values from the following set:

```
GridBagConstraints.NORTH

GridBagConstraints.SOUTH

GridBagConstraints.NORTHEAST

GridBagConstraints.SOUTHEAST

GridBagConstraints.NORTHWEST

GridBagConstraints.SOUTHWEST

GridBagConstraints.EAST

GridBagConstraints.WEST
```

The default value, as noted above, is `GridBagConstraints.CENTER`.

As an example of how this works, the following simple program (Listing 3-9) creates a 2-by-2 grid and places a button in each cell. The buttons are all anchored to the outside of their cells so that, if you resize the container, they all stay in their respective corners and move away from each other as the container expands, as shown in Figure 3-21. The command to run this example is:

```
java JFCBook.Chapter3.GridBagLayoutExample6
```

Listing 3-9   GridBagLayout using anchor constraints

```
package JFCBook.Chapter3;

import com.sun.java.swing.*;
import java.awt.*;
import java.awt.event.*;

public class GridBagLayoutExample6 extends JPanel {
    public GridBagLayoutExample6() {
```

```
      super(true);     // Double-buffer
      this.setLayout(new GridBagLayout());
      this.setOpaque(true);
      this.setBackground(UIManager.getColor("control"));
      GridBagConstraints c = new GridBagConstraints();

      c.gridx = 0;
      c.gridy = 0;
      c.gridwidth = 1;
      c.gridheight = 1;
      c.weightx = 0.5;
      c.weighty = 0.5;
      c.insets = new Insets(4, 3, 4, 3);
      c.anchor = GridBagConstraints.NORTHWEST;
      this.add(new JButton("ONE"), c);

      c.gridx++;
      c.anchor = GridBagConstraints.NORTHEAST;
      this.add(new JButton("TWO"), c);

      c.gridx = 0;
      c.gridy++;
      c.anchor = GridBagConstraints.SOUTHWEST;
      this.add(new JButton("THREE"), c);

      c.gridx++;
      c.anchor = GridBagConstraints.SOUTHEAST;
      this.add(new JButton("FOUR"), c);
   }

   public static void main(String[] args) {
      JFrame f = new JFrame("GridBagLayout 6");
      JPanel p = new GridBagLayoutExample6();
      f.getContentPane().add(p);
      f.pack();
      f.addWindowListener(new WindowAdapter() {
         public void windowClosing(WindowEvent evt) {
            System.exit(0);
         }
      });
      f.setVisible(true);
   }
}
```

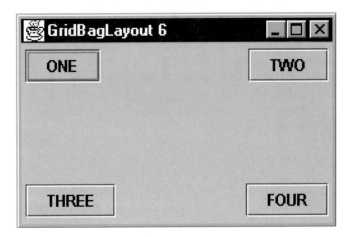

Figure 3-21 GridBagLayout: anchoring components to the side of a cell.

There is, of course, a connection between the anchor and fill values for a cell. If a cell has a fill value that allows its component to expand in any given direction, the anchor constraint for that direction is effectively nullified. Suppose, for example, you place a text field in a cell and set the cell's fill constraint to GridBagConstraints.HORIZONTAL, so that it expands horizontally. Applying an anchor constraint like GridBagConstraints.WEST would now not make sense, because the component is growing horizontally and so will automatically stay anchored to the west (and east) side of its cell. It is, however, still meaningful to apply vertical anchor constraints like GridBagConstraints.NORTH, because the component is not going to grow vertically.

To recap, Table 3-1 summarizes the fields of GridBagConstraints and how they affect how the cells and components of a container are laid out by GridBagLayout. Be very careful to distinguish between *cell* and *component* in the descriptions that follow: The term "cell" refers to the grid squares allocated to a component, whereas the term "component" refers to the space within that cell actually occupied by the component; these two are usually not the same thing, unless the fill member is set to GridBagConstraints.BOTH.

Table 3-1   Fields of the GridBagConstraints object

Field	*Description*
gridx and gridy	These members give the x and y coordinates of the top left-hand corner of a cell in which a component will reside. The top left-hand corner of the container has x and y coordinates 0; x coordinates increase to the right and y coordinates increase downward. You can use the special value GridBagConstraints.RELATIVE for

	`gridx` to indicate the next cell to the right of the previous component and as `gridy` to indicate the next cell below the previous component. This is useful when working across a row or down a column.
`gridwidth` and `gridheight`	The number of cells allocated to the component, horizontally and vertically. For example, a component that requires a space 2 cells wide by 3 cells high would have `gridwidth` set to 2 and `gridheight` set to 3. If you assign the value `GridBagConstraints.REMAINDER` to `gridwidth`, this component will be the last in its row and its cells will occupy all of the remaining space to the right-hand edge of the container. Similarly, using this value in the `gridheight` member makes the component be the last in its column, stretching to the bottom of the container.
`insets`	An `Insets` object that specifies padding to be added around the outside of the component. This value may be `null` if no external padding is required.
`ipadx` and `ipady`	The amount to be added to a component's declared minimum size to create the minimum size of the component's cell area. The actual size added is $2 \times$ `ipadx` horizontally and $2 \times$ `ipady` vertically, because the space is added to both sides of the component.
`fill`	This value is used if the component's preferred size is smaller than the space allocated to its cells and describes whether and how the component will grow to occupy this extra space. If the component is not required to grow at all, use `GridBagConstraints.NONE`, which is the default value. To make the component grow horizontally or vertically (but only in the stated direction), use `GridBagConstraints.HORIZONTAL` or `GridBagConstraints.VERTICAL`. To make the component grow in both directions, use `GridBagConstraints.BOTH`.
`anchor`	Controls how the component is placed within its cell if it doesn't occupy all of the available space. By default, this field is set to `GridBagConstraints.CENTER`, which places spare room evenly around the outside of the component. The other possible values move the component to one of the eight available compass points: `GridBagConstraints.NORTH`, `GridBagConstraints.NORTHEAST`, `GridBagConstraints.EAST`, `GridBagConstraints.SOUTHEAST`, `GridBagConstraints.SOUTH`, `GridBagConstraints.SOUTHWEST`, `GridBagConstraints.WEST` or `GridBagConstraints.NORTHWEST`.
`weightx` and `weighty`	These fields are both used to control how the component's cells expand to occupy any extra space available. If either value is 0.0, the cell does not expand in that direction. The total space for each cell in each row is determined by the ratio of the cell's `weightx` to the sum of all of the `weightx` values in that row and similarly for the columns. To make all cells resize by the same amount, use identical, nonzero `weightx` or `weighty` values for all cells in the row or column (the actual value is not important); to make cell A expand twice as fast as cell B in the horizontal direction, give cell A a `weightx` that is twice the value of the `weightx` for cell B.

Now that you've seen all aspects of `GridBagLayout`, let's look at how you might create the more complex layout shown in Figure 3-22 in a `JPanel` and then test it by placing it in the content pane of a `JFrame` so that you can see how it behaves when resized.

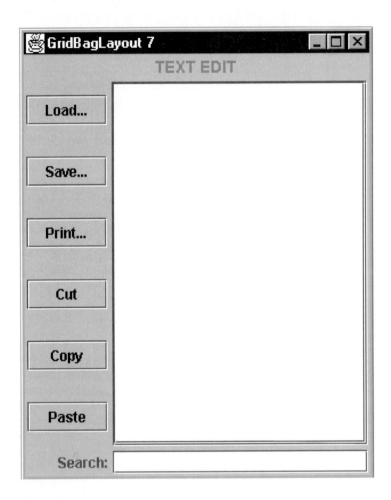

Figure 3-22   GridBagLayout: a typical form layout.

First, let's review what is required of this layout. At the top is a text heading; clearly, the correct component to use for this is a `JLabel`, which should stretch across the top of the container, but retain a fixed height when the container expands. For this component, you would want `weightx = 1.0` and `weighty = 0.0` so that the cells occupied by the label expand as much as possible horizontally but remain a constant vertical size.

The text area, shown as the large white area in Figure 3-22, is the one that should grow as much as possible in both directions when the user expands the window. Thus, you need to set both `weightx` and `weighty` to 1.0 and `fill` to `GridBagConstraints.BOTH`. Recall, however, that setting `weightx` and `weighty` to nonzero values will allow the cells occupied by the text area to expand, but the text area itself would remain stranded in the middle of its allocated area if `fill` were not changed, because its default value is `GridBagConstraints.NONE`, which stops the component resizing. The text field at the bottom of the container has the same resize requirements as the text area, except that it should not expand vertically so the same constraints can be used for both, with a change to `weighty` (from 1.0 to 0.0) for the text field. That leaves the buttons and the "Search" label.

Taking the label first, it should not resize in the horizontal direction after it has been placed, but it should occupy all of the space available initially. Accordingly, you should set `weightx = 0.0` and `weighty = 0.0` to prevent any resizing and `fill = GridBagConstraints.BOTH` to make the label fill all of the space available, to make the text appear to be close to the text input field that it refers to. You might wonder why `GridBagConstraints.HORIZONTAL` wasn't used to achieve this. That setting would also work, but `GridBagConstraints.BOTH` is preferable when the cells are constrained not to expand, because it ensures that all of the vertical space is used, resulting in proper vertical alignment of the centers of both the label and the adjacent text field, which also has the `GridBagConstraints.BOTH` setting for the same reason.

That leaves only the buttons. All of the buttons should have the same vertical and horizontal size and retain their initial sizes under all circumstances. Since the same font is going to be used on all of these buttons, their heights will be the same when they first appear but, since the text on the buttons is not all of the same width, they would not all occupy the same horizontal space. To be sure that they do the `fill` constraint should be to set `GridBagConstraints.HORIZONTAL`, which forces all of the buttons to expand horizontally to fill the column that they reside in, thus making them all of the same size. It is also necessary to ensure that this column remains of fixed size, which can be arranged by setting `weightx` to 0.0.

As for the vertical layout of the buttons, there are two choices. One possibility is to allow each cell to expand so that the buttons get equally spread over the vertical space available and get further apart as the height of the window is increased. This is the configuration shown in the diagram above. To achieve this, `weighty` should be set to 1.0 for every button. Actually, any nonzero value would do, as long as each button has the same value; if the values differ, the buttons with larger `weightx` values would get more space allocated to their cells and so would appear to be spaced further apart than those with smaller values. An alternative is to keep all of the buttons packed tightly together, separated by a constant distance and aligned toward the top of the text area. To achieve this, you would just set `weighty` to 0.0 for every button.

To make the layout pretty, suitable insets have been added around the components, resulting in the code shown in Listing 3-10.

Listing 3-10   Implementing a form-type layout with GridBagLayout

```java
package JFCBook.Chapter3;

import com.sun.java.swing.*;
import java.awt.*;
import java.awt.event.*;

public class GridBagLayoutExample7 extends JPanel {
  public GridBagLayoutExample7(boolean pack, boolean buffer) {
    super(buffer);    // Double-buffer if needed
    this.setLayout(new GridBagLayout());
    this.setOpaque(true);
    this.setBackground(UIManager.getColor("control"));
    GridBagConstraints c = new GridBagConstraints();
    double buttonWeighty = pack ? 0.0 : 1.0;
    int buttonCount = pack ? 7 : 6;

    JTextArea ta = new JTextArea(20, 30);
    JTextField tf = new JTextField(20);
    JLabel l = new JLabel("TEXT EDIT", SwingConstants.CENTER);
    l.setFont(new Font("SansSerif", Font.BOLD, 14));
    l.setForeground(Color.green);
    JLabel s = new JLabel("Search:", SwingConstants.RIGHT);

    // Heading label
    c.gridx = 0;
    c.gridy = 0;
    c.gridwidth = GridBagConstraints.REMAINDER;
    c.gridheight = 1;
    c.weightx = 1.0;
    c.weighty = 0.0;
    c.fill = GridBagConstraints.BOTH;
    c.insets = new Insets(2, 2, 2, 2);
    this.add(l, c);

    // Text area
    c.gridx = 1;
    c.gridy = 1;
    c.gridwidth = GridBagConstraints.REMAINDER;
    c.gridheight = buttonCount;
    c.fill = GridBagConstraints.BOTH;
    c.weightx = 1.0;
    c.weighty = 1.0;
    this.add(new JScrollPane(ta), c);

    // Text field
    c.gridx = 1;
    c.gridy = buttonCount + 1;
    c.gridwidth = GridBagConstraints.REMAINDER;
```

```
      c.gridheight = 1;
      c.fill = GridBagConstraints.BOTH;
      c.weightx = 1.0;
      c.weighty = 0.0;
      this.add(tf, c);

      // Search label
      c.gridx = 0;
      c.gridwidth = 1;
      c.fill = GridBagConstraints.BOTH;
      c.weightx = 0.0;
      c.weighty = 0.0;
      this.add(s, c);

      // The buttons
      c.gridx = 0;
      c.gridy = 1;
      c.fill = GridBagConstraints.HORIZONTAL;
      c.weightx = 0.0;
      c.weighty = buttonWeighty;
      this.add(new JButton("Load..."), c);

      c.gridy = GridBagConstraints.RELATIVE;
      this.add(new JButton("Save..."), c);
      this.add(new JButton("Print..."), c);
      this.add(new JButton("Cut"), c);
      this.add(new JButton("Copy"), c);
      this.add(new JButton("Paste"), c);
   }

   public static void main(String[] args) {
      JFrame f = new JFrame("GridBagLayout 7");
      boolean pack = false;
      if (args.length > 0 && args[0].equals("packed")) {
         pack = true;
      }

      JPanel p = new GridBagLayoutExample7(pack, true);

      f.add(p);
      f.pack();
      f.addWindowListener(new WindowAdapter() {
         public void windowClosing(WindowEvent evt) {
            System.exit(0);
         }
      });
      f.setVisible(true);
   }
}
```

In order to allow you to try out both ways of laying out the buttons, Listing 3-10 allows you to supply an argument that determines which layout choice you want to see. To see the layout that allows the buttons to spread out, type

```
java JFCBook.Chapter3.GridBagLayoutExample7
```

To see the buttons tightly packed at the top and to verify that they stay that way when the container is resized, use this command:

```
java JFCBook.Chapter3.GridBagLayoutExample7 packed
```

The packed button layout is shown in the Figure 3-23.

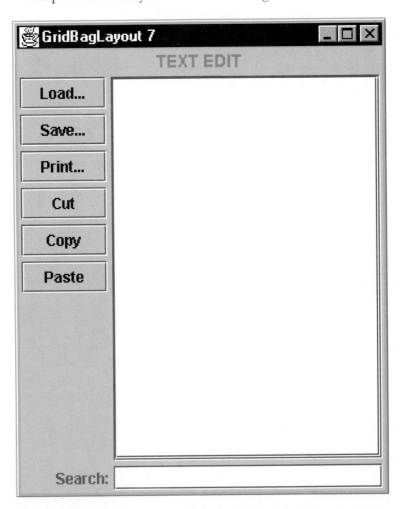

Figure 3-23   GridBagLayout: a form layout with the buttons kept together.

Box and BoxLayout

The `BoxLayout` manager is very useful if you want to lay out a single row or a single column of components within a container. You can use a `BoxLayout` with any container, or you can use the `Box` container, which comes with a `BoxLayout` as its default layout manager. To create a `Box`, you have to specify the axis along which its child components will be laid out:

```
public Box(int axis);
```

where axis is either `BoxLayout.X_AXIS` for a horizontal arrangement or `BoxLayout.Y_AXIS` for a vertical one. As you add components to the `Box`, they are arranged in order, either from left to right or from top to bottom. The interesting thing about `BoxLayout`, like all layout managers, is the way in which it sizes its child components and how it allocates extra space. For the sake of simplicity, let's assume for now that you want to lay out components in a `Box` (or any other container) which has a `BoxLayout` configured to organize them horizontally (i.e., `BorderLayout.X_AXIS`). The `BoxLayout` tries to give each component its preferred size. In a horizontal arrangement, the components are laid out from the left of the container, with the first component flush against the left side of the container, the second immediately to its right, and so on. When all of the components have been added, any spare space appears to the right. Resizing the container horizontally does not cause the components to relocate: The free space to the right increases or decreases according to the change in the container's size. Figure 3-24 shows a number of configurations created using `BoxLayout`; the one described here is labeled "1: Nothing" and there is a similar vertical arrangement labeled "5: Nothing."

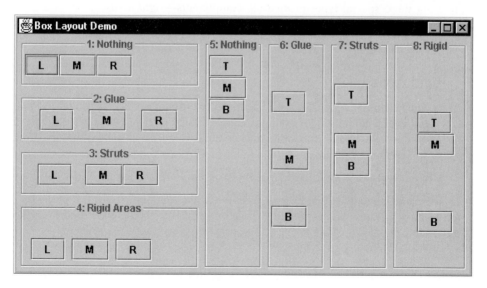

Figure 3-24   Various BoxLayout configurations.

To run this example, type

```
java JFCBook.Chapter3.BoxLayoutDemo
```

Resize the window both horizontally and vertically: You'll find that the components in these two configurations stay where they are, while the empty space to the right of and below them changes. If you make the window so small that there isn't enough space for all of the components, you'll see that their horizontal size remains the same—they do not get compressed and, as a result, they get clipped to fit within the available space.

Here is the code used to generate the horizontal version of this arrangement:

```
public JPanel createFirstBoxPane() {
    JPanel p = new JPanel();
    this.addTitledBorder(p, "1: Nothing");
    p.setLayout(new BoxLayout(p, BoxLayout.X_AXIS));
    p.add(new JButton("L"));
    p.add(new JButton("M"));
    p.add(new JButton("R"));

    return p;
}
```

As you can see, the container we're using here is not a Box, but a JPanel. To associate a BoxLayout with it, you use the setLayout method as normal, but note that the BoxLayout constructor is passed not only the required orientation, but also a reference to the container that it is managing as its first argument.

The BoxLayout allows you to change the way in which extra space is distributed by using three special types of invisible components—*rigid areas*, *struts* and *glue*. You create these components using static methods declared by the Box class and add them to the BoxLayout's container to get the desired effects.

Rigid Areas

As its name suggests, a rigid area is a fixed-size, two-dimensional component. Adding it to a horizontal container, for example, causes a horizontal gap equal to its width to be left in the layout and ensures that the container is at least as high as the rigid area itself. You create a rigid area using the following Box method:

```
public static Component createRigidArea(Dimension d);
```

The panel labeled "4: Rigid Areas" has three rigid areas, one to the left of the button labeled "L" and two between the three buttons. Here is the code used to create this area:

```
public JPanel createFourthBoxPane() {
  JPanel p = new JPanel();
  this.addTitledBorder(p, "4: Rigid Areas");
  p.setLayout(new BoxLayout(p, BoxLayout.X_AXIS));

  // The rigid areas make the pane larger top to bottom
  // and space the buttons out
  p.add(Box.createRigidArea(horzRigidAreaDim));
  p.add(new JButton("L"));
  p.add(Box.createRigidArea(horzRigidAreaDim));
  p.add(new JButton("M"));
  p.add(Box.createRigidArea(horzRigidAreaDim));
  p.add(new JButton("R"));

  return p;
}
```

As you can see, the rigid areas are added to the container exactly as if they were ordinary components. The rigid areas in this example are all of the same size, declared as follows:

```
private static Dimension horzRigidAreaDim = new Dimension(8, 40);
```

As a result, we are adding a rigid area that is 8 pixels wide and 40 pixels high. This causes the left button to be 8 pixels from the left side of the container and creates an 8-pixel gap between the three buttons. Again, any spare space appears to the right of the rightmost button. A secondary effect of adding this component is to ensure that the panel is at least 40 pixels high; it could, of course, be higher if there were a component in that layout that exceeded 40 pixels in the vertical direction. There is a similar vertical construction in panel number 8. This time, there are two rigid areas, one on either side of the button labeled "T." These two rigid areas dictate the space around this button and also influence the width of the panel.

Struts

Struts are very similar to rigid areas, except that they are one-dimensional. A horizontal strut introduces a fixed-size horizontal gap in the layout, but has no effect on the vertical size of the container because it has zero height. Similarly, a vertical strut introduces a vertical space of fixed size and does not have any effect in the horizontal direction. You create these struts using one of the following Box methods:

```
public static Component createVerticalStrut(int height);
public static Component createHorizontalStruct(int width);
```

Panel 3 has 16-pixel horizontal struts around the button labeled "L," which caus-es a gap of this size to appear on each side of it. The other two buttons are arranged next to each other because they don't have any intervening spacer component and the remaining free space appears to the right, as always. The code for this particular panel is similar to that for the previous two:

```
public JPanel createThirdBoxPane() {
  JPanel p = new JPanel();
  this.addTitledBorder(p, "3: Struts");
  p.setLayout(new BoxLayout(p, BoxLayout.X_AXIS));

  // The struts ensure that the "L" button is
  // a fixed distance from the left and the "M"
  // button the same distance from the "L" button
  p.add(Box.createHorizontalStrut(strutWidth));
  p.add(new JButton("L"));
  p.add(Box.createHorizontalStrut(strutWidth));
  p.add(new JButton("M"));
  p.add(new JButton("R"));

  return p;
}
```

The exact effect of a horizontal strut depends on the orientation of the container. Here we've seen a horizontal strut enforcing a separation between two components. You can also use a horizontal strut in a vertical container, in which case it enforces a minimum container width. Similarly, you can create vertical struts that have the cor-responding effects in the other direction.

Glue

The last spacer component that Box provides is *glue*. You create glue using one of the following methods:

```
public static Component createGlue();
public static Component createHorizontalGlue();
public static Component createVerticalGlue();
```

Glue is perhaps the wrong term for this component because it suggests something sticky. In fact, a glue component expands to take up as much space as it can. Horizontal glue occupies as much horizontal space as it can and vertical glue does the same in the direction of the Y axis. Glue created using createGlue expands in both directions.

Panels 2 and 6 show glue in use. Here is the implementation of panel 2:

```
public JPanel createSecondBoxPane() {
  JPanel p = new JPanel();
  this.addTitledBorder(p, "2: Glue");
  p.setLayout(new BoxLayout(p, BoxLayout.X_AXIS));

  // These buttons align around the center
  p.add(Box.createGlue());
  p.add(new JButton("L"));
  p.add(Box.createGlue());
  p.add(new JButton("M"));
  p.add(Box.createGlue());
  p.add(new JButton("R"));
  p.add(Box.createGlue());

  return p;
}
```

The four glue components take all of the extra space and divide it equally between themselves. As a result, this arrangement produces three evenly-spaced buttons. If there were one glue component to the left of the button labeled "L" and the rest of the glue were removed, all of the free space would be taken up by the glue on the left of the container, so the buttons would all be packed tightly together on the right. On the other hand, placing glue to the left of the left button and the right of the right button would distribute the spare space equally on each side, leaving the three buttons huddled together in the center of the container.

Watching Component Layout and Drawing with DebugGraphics

If you've ever had problems with the Abstract Window Toolkit and wondered why your applications interface wasn't being drawn properly, or tried to develop a custom component and spent hours wondering why a part of your control was missing or drawn incorrectly, the new DebugGraphics feature is sure to be able to help you. This is, quite simply, one of the best new ideas in the Java Foundation Classes and, as is usually the case with Java, it is very easy to use it when you need to: You don't have to spend a long time trying to enable it or configure it properly.

The basic idea is that, since all rendering operations in Java are performed by operations on a Graphics object (about which you learn more in the next chapter), it is possible to capture all of these operations and control the way they are performed by providing a subclass of Graphics that intercepts every operation on a component and can then report it to the user. In Swing, the DebugGraphics class performs this function. The best way to see what it does is to observe it in action.

The layout created in Listing 3-10 was fairly complicated, so let's use it to show how easy it is to turn on graphics debugging and what happens as a result. Look at the code in Listing 3-11.

Listing 3-11   Using DebugGraphics to view component drawing on the screen

```
package JFCBook.Chapter3;

import com.sun.java.swing.*;
import java.awt.*;
import java.awt.event.*;

public class DebugGraphicsExample1 {
  public static void main(String[] args) {
    JFrame f = new JFrame("DebugGraphicsExample 1");
    boolean pack = false;
    if (args.length > 0 && args[0].equals("packed")) {
      pack = true;
    }
    RepaintManager.currentManager(f.getRootPane()).
         setDoubleBufferingEnabled(false);
    JPanel p = new JFCBook.Chapter3.GridBagLayoutExample7(pack,
false);

    p.setDebugGraphicsOptions(DebugGraphics.FLASH_OPTION);

    f.getContentPane().add(p);
    f.pack();
    f.addWindowListener(new WindowAdapter() {
      public void windowClosing(WindowEvent evt) {
        System.exit(0);
      }
    });
    f.setVisible(true);
  }
}
```

The `main` method of this example is almost the same as that which was used to test the original layout. However, the following important line has been added:

```
p.setDebugGraphicsOptions(DebugGraphics.FLASH_OPTION);
```

The `setDebugGraphicsOption()` method belongs to the `JComponent` class; debugging can therefore be enabled on any class that is derived from

JComponent. Here, debugging is enabled by invoking this method against the
JPanel. The effect of calling this method on an object is to set the debugging
options specified for that object and, if that object is a container, for all of the components contained within that container. If any of these components is also a container, the options are cascaded down into that container's children as well. Thus,
turning on graphics debugging for a container switches it on for all of the components
contained within it, no matter how deeply nested.

When you run the example code in Listing 3-11, you will see the frame appear and
then the panel will start to lay itself out. However, the drawing operations will proceed much more slowly than usual and, as each line is drawn, it will flash red. With
debugging enabled, you can now watch all of the drawing operations in action at a
speed slow enough to allow you to see what is going on. The command needed to run
this example is:

```
java JFCBook.Chapter3.DebugGraphicsExample1
```

Core Alert

You may be wondering about this strange-looking line of code in the above example:

```
RepaintManager.currentManager(f.getRootPane()).
        setDoubleBufferingEnabled(false);
```

*As you'll see later, Swing components provide graphics double-buffering—that is,
they can be drawn into an off-screen buffer first and then copied directly to the
screen. This technique can reduce flashing effects caused by components redrawing themselves on the screen. It is possible to use DebugGraphics with double-buffering, but you haven't seen how to do that yet, so the above line is included
to turn off the double-buffering for everything in the frame's root pane.*

Configuring Graphics Debugging

The setDebugGraphicsOptions method takes a single integer argument
made up of a bitmask constructed by ORing together with some of the following
constants:

```
DebugGraphics.FLASH_OPTION
```

```
DebugGraphics.LOG_OPTION
```

```
DebugGraphics.BUFFERED_OPTION
```

Each time you call setDebugGraphicsOptions, the mask you supply is combined with the current settings, rather than overwriting it, so that the two calls

```
p.setDebugGraphicsOptions(DebugGraphics.FLASH_OPTION);
p.setDebugGraphicsOptions(DebugGraphics.LOG_OPTION);
```

result in both of these options being enabled. To clear all options (and hence turn debugging off), use the following line:

```
p.setDebugGraphicsOptions(DebugGraphics.NONE_OPTION);
```

If you select FLASH_OPTION, then graphics operations on the screen will cause the flashing effects that were shown in the example above. By default, each operation flashes twice, with each flash lasting for 100 milliseconds. You can change the number of flashes and the duration of each using the following static methods of the DebugGraphics class:

```
public static void setFlashTime(int flashTime);
public static void setFlashCount(int flashCount);
```

You can also use the setFlashColor method to change the flash color if red is not to your taste. The example in Listing 3-12 makes each operation display 4 flashes, each lasting 250 milliseconds, in green. This version of the program takes much longer to run, of course, since every graphics call now takes one second to perform. Try it out with the command

```
java JFCBook.Chapter3.DebugGraphicsExample2
```

Listing 3-12   Using a customized DebugGraphics setup

```
package JFCBook.Chapter3;

import com.sun.java.swing.*;
import java.awt.*;
import java.awt.event.*;

public class DebugGraphicsExample2 {
  public static void main(String[] args) {
    JFrame f = new JFrame("DebugGraphicsExample 2");
    boolean pack = false;
    if (args.length > 0 && args[0].equals("packed")) {
      pack = true;
    }
    RepaintManager.currentManager(f.getRootPane()).
          setDoubleBufferingEnabled(false);
    JPanel p = new JFCBook.Chapter3.GridBagLayoutExample7(pack,
false);
```

```
   p.setDebugGraphicsOptions(DebugGraphics.FLASH_OPTION);
   DebugGraphics.setFlashTime(250);    // 1/4 second
   DebugGraphics.setFlashCount(4);
   DebugGraphics.setFlashColor(Color.green);

   f.getContentPane().add(p);
   f.pack();
   f.addWindowListener(new WindowAdapter() {
     public void windowClosing(WindowEvent evt) {
       System.exit(0);
     }
   });
   f.setVisible(true);
  }
}
```

Since `setFlashColor`, `setFlashTime` and `setFlashCount` are all static methods, the settings they establish are effective for every component: it is not possible to customize these settings on a per-component basis. If you want to find out what settings are in effect, there are the corresponding static methods `flashColor`, `flashTime` and `flashCount` that take no arguments and return the obvious data types:

```
public static Color flashColor();
public static int flashTime();
public static int flashCount();
```

Graphics Debug Logging

While it will often be sufficient to watch components flash as they draw themselves, some problems cannot be so easily debugged. For cases like this, you can use the `LOG_OPTION` setting. When you enable this, every graphics operation causes a message to be written to a logging stream. By default, this output goes to your application's DOS or Unix command line window (in fact to your program's standard output stream). If you want to capture the output in a file, you can use the `DebugGraphics` static `setLogStream` method:

```
public static void setLogStream(PrintStream stream);
```

Listing 3-13 sets the debug options so that all of the graphics operations are written to a file whose name you supply on the program's command line.

Listing 3-13   Saving DebugGraphics output in a file

```
package JFCBook.Chapter3;

import com.sun.java.swing.*;
import java.awt.*;
import java.awt.event.*;
import java.io.*;

public class DebugGraphicsExample3 {
  public static void main(String[] args) {
    JFrame f = new JFrame("DebugGraphicsExample 3");

    if (args.length != 1) {
      System.err.println("Please supply an output file name");
      System.exit(0);
    }

    PrintStream s = null;

    try {
       s = new PrintStream(new FileOutputStream(args[0]));
    } catch (Exception e) {
      System.err.println("Failed to create output file <" + args[0] + ">: " + e);
      System.exit(0);
    }

    JPanel p = new JFCBook.Chapter3.GridBagLayoutExample7(true, false);

    p.setDebugGraphicsOptions(DebugGraphics.LOG_OPTION);
    DebugGraphics.setLogStream(s);

    f.getContentPane().add(p);
    f.pack();
    f.addWindowListener(new WindowAdapter() {
      public void windowClosing(WindowEvent evt) {
         System.exit(0);
      }
    });
    f.setVisible(true);
  }
}
```

A typical command line for running this program would be:

```
java JFCBook.Chapter3.DebugGraphicsExample3 c:\temp\debugout
```

Writing the results to a file is much quicker than directing them to your screen and not turning on the flashing option also saves a lot of time. Beware, however, that this example produces a lot of output: when I ran it, I got more than 1000 lines, an extract of which is shown below.

```
Graphics(0-1) Setting color: com.sun.java.swing.plaf.ColorUIResource[r=0,g=0,b=0]
Graphics(0-1) Setting font:
com.sun.java.swing.plaf.FontUIResource[family=Dialog,name=Dialog,
style=plain,size=12]
Graphics(1-1) Setting color: com.sun.java.swing.plaf.ColorUIResource[r=192,g=192,b=192]
Graphics(1-1) Filling rect: java.awt.Rectangle[x=0,y=0,width=69,height=23]
Graphics(1-1) Setting font:
com.sun.java.swing.plaf.FontUIResource[family=Dialog,name=Dialog,
style=plain,size=12]

Graphics(1-1) Setting color: com.sun.java.swing.plaf.ColorUIResource[r=192,g=192,b=192]
Graphics(1-1) Filling rect: java.awt.Rectangle[x=0,y=0,width=69,height=23]
Graphics(1-1) Setting color: com.sun.java.swing.plaf.ColorUIResource[r=0,g=0,b=0]
Graphics(1-1) Drawing string: "Paste" at: java.awt.Point[x=18,y=16]
Graphics(0-1) Translating by: java.awt.Point[x=0,y=0]
Graphics(0-1) Setting color: java.awt.Color[r=255,g=255,b=255]
Graphics(0-1) Drawing line: from (0, 0) to (0, 22)
Graphics(0-1) Drawing line: from (1, 0) to (66, 0)
Graphics(0-1) Setting color: java.awt.Color[r=128,g=128,b=128]
Graphics(0-1) Drawing line: from (1, 21) to (67, 21)
Graphics(0-1) Drawing line: from (67, 0) to (67, 20)
Graphics(0-1) Setting color: java.awt.Color[r=0,g=0,b=0]
Graphics(0-1) Drawing line: from (0, 22) to (68, 22)
Graphics(0-1) Drawing line: from (68, 22) to (68, 0)
Graphics(0-1) Translating by: java.awt.Point[x=0,y=0]
```

It is interesting, and a little strange, that the setLogStream method requires a PrintStream object to write to, since PrintStream has been officially deprecated since JDK 1.1. As a result, if you compile the code in Listing 3-13 you get warnings about the use of deprecated APIs. Perhaps in the future this method will be changed to take a PrintWriter argument.

Debugging Off-Screen Graphics Operations

Showing graphics operations on the screen with colored flashes is very useful, except when you perform all of your drawing in an off-screen buffer. This is actually a very common situation, especially with JFC components, which flash much less if not rendered directly to the screen. Indeed, JPanel actually has a constructor option which allows it to double-buffer all of its rendering. Setting FLASH_OPTION for such a panel would not be of any use, which is why this double-buffering was not enabled in the examples you've seen so far in this section.

To deal with this, you can set the BUFFERED_OPTION flag. When you do this, a separate frame appears in which the contents of a component's off-screen buffer are shown; the operations performed in this buffer are then shown in this frame, as Listing 3-14 demonstrates.

Core Alert

In Swing 1.0 this feature isn't working. The drawing all takes place off-screen and the layout appears on the screen, but the frame that should show what is happening as the graphics operations take place does not appear. Hopefully, this bug will be fixed before JDK 1.2 is released.

Listing 3-14   Using DebugGraphics to watch off-screen drawing

```
package JFCBook.Chapter3;

import com.sun.java.swing.*;
import java.awt.*;
import java.awt.event.*;
import java.io.*;

public class DebugGraphicsExample4 {
  public static void main(String[] args) {
    JFrame f = new JFrame("DebugGraphicsExample 4");
    JPanel p = new JFCBook.Chapter3.GridBagLayoutExample7(true, true);

    p.setDebugGraphicsOptions(DebugGraphics.FLASH_OPTION |
            DebugGraphics.BUFFERED_OPTION);

    f.getContentPane().add(p);
    f.pack();
    f.addWindowListener(new WindowAdapter() {
      public void windowClosing(WindowEvent evt) {
        System.exit(0);
      }
    });
    f.setVisible(true);
  }
}
```

OverlayLayout Manager

OverlayLayout is a Swing layout manager that allows you to place components in a container in such a way that their *alignment points* are all in the same place. It returns a preferred size for the container that would be just large enough to contain all of its children.

Each component has an alignment attribute for each axis, given as a floating-point number in the range 0.0 to 1.0. These values can be set with the setAlignmentX and setAlignmentY methods of Component and can be read using getAlignmentX and getAlignmentY. By default, these attributes are both initialized to 0.5f, which implies center alignment in each direction.

To understand how the OverlayLayout manager works, let's confine ourselves to a container that has two child components, each the same size and both with default alignment values and let's consider only the x-axis. The first thing that OverlayLayout tries to do is to place the alignment points of its children on top of each other. Since our two children both have center alignment, their horizontal midpoints will be placed over each other and, because they are the same size, they will, in fact, be placed exactly on top of each other. That takes care of the relative positioning. What about positioning within the container? Here, the story is a little more complex.

When considering how to lay out the container, OverlayLayout uses the minimum acceptable size of each component to determine how big its container needs to be, then works out where the alignment point would be based on minimum sizes. Using this information, it calculates the overall alignment position as the ratio of the x coordinate of the alignment point to the minimum required size of the container. When the container is finally sized and the components placed, this ratio is multiplied by the actual size of the container to determine the real location of the alignment point, then the components are all placed relative to that point.

By now, you're probably confused, so let's try an example to make it clearer. We'll take the case of two panels that both have minimum widths of 28 pixels and preferred widths of 56. Panel A has an X alignment of 0.25 and panel B an X alignment of 0.75. These strange sounding numbers are actually chosen to make the following arithmetic easier!

To work out what will happen, remember that the OverlayLayout wants to place the alignment point of A over the alignment point of B. Now suppose that each component were at its minimum size of 28 pixels. The alignment point of A is 0.25 of the way along its side, or 7 pixels in from its left edge, while the alignment position of B is 0.75 of the way along its side, or 21 pixels in from its own left edge. Therefore, the OverlayLayout must place the point 7 pixels from the left of A over the point 21 pixels from the left of B. In order to achieve this, the left edge of B must be to the left of the left edge of A. Suppose that the left edge of B were placed at x coordinate 0 within its container. Then, the point 7 pixels from the left of A would need to lie over the point 21 pixels from the left of B, which would be at x coordinate 21.

Therefore, A would need to start at x coordinate $(21 - 7) = 14$. Since each component is assumed to be at its minimum size of 28 pixels, it follows that B would cover the area from $x = 0$ to $x = 27$ and A would occupy the range from $x = 14$ to $x = 41$. The alignment point in this case is at $x = 21$ and the container must be at least 42 pixels wide to cover both components. With this information, the `OverlayLayout` calculates the total alignment as $21/42 = 0.5$. In other words, the alignment point will reside in the middle of the x-axis of the container.

A similar size calculation is performed based on the components' preferred width to arrive at the preferred width of the container, but the total alignment value is not recalculated. Since each component has a preferred width of 56 pixels, the alignment point of A will be 14 pixels from its left edge (remember its alignment requirement is 0.25) and that of B will be 42 pixels along. Thus, the alignment point will be 42 points from the left of the container and A will start 14 pixels to the left of it. Since A is going to be 56 pixels wide at its preferred size, it will stretch 14 pixels to the left of the alignment point and 42 points to the right of it. Since the alignment point is 42 points from the left of the container, the total required size will be $42 + 42 = 84$ pixels and this will be the preferred width of the container. Not surprisingly, this is twice the minimum size.

Now suppose that the container is finally sized at its preferred size. We know that the total alignment ratio is 0.5, so the alignment point will be placed at 0.5×84 (the actual width) $= 42$, as required. If the container grows beyond its preferred size, the alignment point will remain in the middle of the x-axis and the components will shift along accordingly, while staying at their preferred sizes. Given this size, we know that A should be placed at $x = (42 - 14) = 28$ and B should be at $x = 0$.

Core Alert

In practice, the calculations performed by `OverlayLayout` only work properly if the component's maximum size is exactly the same as its preferred size. This happens because of the way the component sizes are calculated when the container size is known. To see the problem, suppose we constrained both panels to be 128 pixels wide by making this the maximum size. In calculating the size of component A, `OverlayLayout` works out the ascent and descent values of the container and the maximum ascent and descent of the component. The ascent is the distance of the alignment point from the left of the container and the descent is its distance from the right of the container. If the container is at its preferred width of 84, then the alignment point is centered and both the ascent and descent are 42 pixels. The maximum ascent of a component is calculated as its maximum size multiplied by its requested alignment. In the case of A, this is $128 \times 0.25 = 32$. The final ascent of A is then taken to be the lesser of its own ascent and the ascent of the container, which comes out as 32. The x coordinate of A is then given by the container ascent less its own ascent—i.e., $42 - 32 = 10$. But we know that the correct x coordinate for A is actually 28, not 10! However, if the maximum size of A were the same as its preferred size (i.e., 56), then its ascent would be $56 \times 0.25 = 14$ and the x coordinate would then be $42 - 14 = 28$, which is the correct result.

Because these calculations are performed independently along each axis, these two components might be offset from each other along the x-axis, but their relative x positions will always be such that their alignment points are over each other. Listing 3-15 shows an example that is exactly like the one that has just been described, but in which the same alignment constraints are applied on both the x and y axes at the same time. Because the same constraints are applied and the components being used for illustration are both square and the same size as each other, you get the same result along each axis, as you can see from Figure 3-25.

Listing 3-15   Offset alignment with the OverlayLayout manager

```
package JFCBook.Chapter3;

import com.sun.java.swing.*;
import java.awt.*;

public class OverlayLayoutExample {
  public static void main(String[] args) {
    JFrame f = new JFrame("OverlayLayout Example");
    JPanel p = new JPanel();
    p.setLayout(new OverlayLayout(p));
    p.setBackground(Color.black);

    JPanel p1 = new JPanel();
    JPanel p2 = new JPanel();
    p1.setMinimumSize(new Dimension(28, 28));
    p2.setMinimumSize(new Dimension(28, 28));
    p1.setPreferredSize(new Dimension(56, 56));
    p2.setPreferredSize(new Dimension(56, 56));
    p1.setMaximumSize(new Dimension(56, 56));
    p2.setMaximumSize(new Dimension(56, 56));

    p1.setBackground(Color.white);
    p2.setBackground(Color.green);
    p1.setAlignmentX(0.25f);
    p2.setAlignmentX(0.75f);
    p1.setAlignmentY(0.25f);
    p2.setAlignmentY(0.75f);

    p.add(p1);
    p.add(p2);

    System.out.println("Minimum panel size is " + p.getMinimumSize());
    System.out.println("Preferred panel size is " + p.getPreferredSize());
```

continued

```
f.getContentPane().setLayout(new FlowLayout());
f.getContentPane().add(p);
f.setSize(200, 200);
f.setVisible(true);

System.out.println("Panel size: " + p.getSize());
System.out.println("p1 bounds: " + p1.getBounds());
System.out.println("p2 bounds: " + p2.getBounds());
    }
}
```

Figure 3-25   Using the OverlayLayout manager.

You can try this example for yourself with the command:

```
java JFCBook.Chapter3.OverlayLayoutExample.
```

In Figure 3-25, the lighter-colored panel is A and the darker one is B. So that you can see what is happening, the location and size of both panels are printed when the layout has been completed. Here is the result:

```
Minimum panel size is java.awt.Dimension[width=42,height=42]
Preferred panel size is java.awt.Dimension[width=84,height=84]
Panel size: java.awt.Dimension[width=84,height=84]
p1 bounds: java.awt.Rectangle[x=28,y=28,width=56,height=56]
p2 bounds: java.awt.Rectangle[x=0,y=0,width=56,height=56]
```

As you can see, the minimum and preferred sizes of the container agree with the calculations that were shown earlier, as do the actual size and locations of the components.

An interesting feature of this example is the use of the JComponent methods setMinimumSize, setPreferredSize and setMaximumSize. In JDK 1.1, the minimum, preferred and maximum sizes of a component were controlled entirely by the component and were usually calculated by the component based on what it was being asked to display. For example, a label with a long text string would need more space than one with a short string and would request greater width. In Swing, the same is true, but the calculations are now performed by a component's look-and-feel specific UI class rather than by the component itself. Often, these calculations, which are required frequently by layout managers, would be expensive. To save having to repeat the same process, the results can now be cached (computed once and then saved) on a per-JComponent basis using these new methods. Once these values have been set, the usual getMinimumSize, getPreferredSize and getMaximumSize methods don't go to the component's user interface class—instead, they retrieve the saved value. As a side effect of this, you can now apply any constraints you want on the size of a JComponent without needing to change or subclass its implementation by setting appropriate minimum, preferred and maximum sizes of your own.

CardLayout Manager

The last of the standard layout managers is the CardLayout. As its name suggests, this manager takes a set of components (normally containers) and lays them out on top of each other like cards, so that only one of them is visible at any given time. Even in JDK 1.1, CardLayout was a relatively primitive implementation of this idea, which is often seen in Windows applications in the form of a property sheet. As you'll see later, the Swing classes incorporate a much more powerful component called JTabbedPane that provides all the functionality of Windows property sheets and hence effectively replaces CardLayout for many purposes. Since CardLayout is likely to be used less and less in the future, not much space is devoted to it here.

The quickest way to explain how this layout manager works is to show an example. The code in Listing 3-16 creates a frame, on which eight labels are mounted. Since the layout manager of the frame's content pane is changed from BorderLayout to CardLayout, only one of these labels will be visible at any one time. The layout manager sizes the content pane so that it is large enough to hold all of the labels. In a real application, each card would almost certainly be a panel, on which a set of related controls would be grouped. For example, you might group together controls relating to color control on one card, font selection on another card and so on. For the purposes of this example, a simple label is sufficient to illustrate how CardLayout works.

Listing 3-16   Using the CardLayout layout manager

```java
package JFCBook.Chapter3;

import com.sun.java.swing.*;
import java.awt.*;
import java.awt.event.*;

public class CardLayoutExample {
  public static void main(String[] args) {
    JFrame f = new JFrame("CardLayout Example");
    Container cp = f.getContentPane();
    CardLayout l = new CardLayout();
    cp.setLayout(l);

    cp.add(new JLabel("First", JLabel.CENTER), "First");
    cp.add(new JLabel("Second", JLabel.CENTER), "Second");
    cp.add(new JLabel("Third", JLabel.CENTER), "Third");
    cp.add(new JLabel("Fourth", JLabel.CENTER), "Fourth");
    cp.add(new JLabel("Fifth", JLabel.CENTER), "Fifth");
    cp.add(new JLabel("Sixth", JLabel.CENTER), "Sixth");
    cp.add(new JLabel("Seventh", JLabel.CENTER), "Seventh");
    cp.add(new JLabel("Last", JLabel.CENTER), "Eighth");

    f.setSize(300, 300);
    f.addWindowListener(new WindowAdapter() {
      public void windowClosing(WindowEvent evt) {
        System.exit(0);
      }
    });
    f.setVisible(true);

    for (;;) {
      try {
        Thread.sleep(1000);
        double r = Math.random();
        if (r > 0.9) {
          l.last(cp);
        } else if (r < 0.1) {
          l.first(cp);
        } else if (r > 0.5) {
          l.next(cp);
        } else {
          l.previous(cp);
        }
      } catch (Exception e) {
        // Ignore any exception
      }
    }
  }
}
```

This example can be run using the command:

```
java JFCBook.Chapter3.CardLayoutExample
```

You will notice that each label is added with a string constraint. In this case, these constraints happen to match the text on the labels themselves (with the exception of the last one), but this need not be the case: the labels are arbitrary, but they must be unique.

Once all the cards have been added, the frame is made visible and then the program enters a loop, in which the top card is changed at random every second. The loop demonstrates the methods of CardLayout that make it possible to change the card on view. The first and last methods select the first and last cards added, respectively, no matter what was on view before. For relative selection, you can use the next and previous methods, both of which wrap when they reach the end and beginning of the set, respectively.

Not shown in Listing 3-16 is the show method. This method accepts a String argument that selects a card to be shown. This argument must match one of the constraints given when adding a component to the container managed by the CardLayout. In this example, the line

```
l.show("Eighth");
```

would select the card containing the label "Last."

Working without a Layout Manager

You have now seen all of the AWT and Swing layout managers. In almost all circumstances, you will be able to find a layout manager that is suitable for every part of your application's interface and, in a large majority of cases, the default layout manager for a container is the correct choice. However, occasionally there will be times when none of the standard layout managers suffice. In some circumstances, it is necessary to work without a layout manager at all. This is perfectly legal and it can be achieved as shown by the following example:

```
JPanel p = new JPanel();
p.setLayout(null);     // No layout manager
```

Think carefully before you decide that none of the standard layout managers is suitable for you. Working without a layout manager probably involves more work than you think, as you'll see during the discussion of the Swing JLayeredPane control in Chapter 12 "Multiple Document Applications."

Working with the Application Window

So far, you have seen how to lay out the components that make up an application's user interface, This section deals with some of the general issues relating to the management of the interface as a whole and of the top-level window in particular. First, you'll see how the application's window interacts with the desktop and discover the events that are delivered in response to changes in the top-level window's state. Then, you'll look at how an application can detect that its top-level window is being moved or resized. Finally, you'll discover how to implement an interface that doesn't require the user to use a mouse for every operation; this may not seem important if you are proficient with the mouse but, in some environments, using the mouse can actually slow the user down and a keyboard interface is preferable.

Reacting to Changes in the Window State

Much of an application's logic is concerned with laying out the user interface and then reacting to the user's interaction with its controls. In the real world, though, it is often necessary to take into account interactions with the user's desktop. For example, the user might use your application for a while, then switch to another one, only to return later, or he or she might iconify the application for a while. In many cases, you might want to modify the way your application behaves at these times.

Window Events

The AWT allows you to detect these changes by delivering window events to the top-level window. Window events are instances of the `java.awt.event.WindowEvent` class and can be processed by classes that implement the `WindowListener` interface. Table 3-2 summarizes the set of window events and the `WindowListener` interface methods that are invoked when they are received.

Table 3-2   Window Events and Listener Methods

Event	Listener Method
WINDOW_OPENED	windowOpened
WINDOW_ACTIVATED	windowActivated
WINDOW_DEACTIVATED	windowDeactivated
WINDOW_ICONIFIED	windowIconified
WINDOW_DEICONIFIED	windowDeiconified
WINDOW_CLOSING	windowClosing
WINDOW_CLOSED	windowClosed

Every `WindowEvent` has an identifier field from the set shown in Table 3-2; you can get the identifier using the `getID` method that `WindowEvent` inherits from `java.awt.AWTEvent`. You can also use the `getWindow` method to find out which window caused the event. The easiest way to describe when these events occur and how to handle them is by using an example. The code in Listing 3-17 implements a bare-bones application that just listens for events on its top-level window. As each event is received, a message is written to the application's console window.

Listing 3-17   Handling Window Events

```java
package JFCBook.Chapter3;

import com.sun.java.swing.*;
import java.awt.*;
import java.awt.event.*;

public class WindowEventsExample1 implements WindowListener {
  // WindowListener Interface
  public void windowActivated(WindowEvent e) {
    System.out.println("Window Activated");
  }

  public void windowDeactivated(WindowEvent e) {
    System.out.println("Window Deactivated");
  }

  public void windowOpened(WindowEvent e) {
    System.out.println("Window Opened");
  }

  public void windowClosing(WindowEvent e) {
    System.out.println("Window Closing");
    e.getWindow().dispose();
  }

  public void windowClosed(WindowEvent e) {
    System.out.println("Window Closed");
    System.exit(0);
  }

  public void windowIconified(WindowEvent e) {
    System.out.println("Window Iconified");
  }

  public void windowDeiconified(WindowEvent e) {
    System.out.println("Window Deiconified");
```

continued

```
    }

    public static void main(String[] args) {
        JFrame f = new JFrame("Window Events");
        JLabel l = new JLabel(" Window Test");
        f.addWindowListener(new WindowEventsExample1());

        f.getContentPane().add(l, "Center");
        f.pack();
        f.setVisible(true);
    }
}
```

The WindowEventsExample1 class exists only to implement the WindowListener interface; when this program is started with the command

```
    java JFCBook.Chapter3.WindowEventsExample1
```

it creates a small frame then registers an instance of the class as a WindowListener on itself, using the addWindowListener method:

```
    f.addWindowListener(new WindowEventsExample1());
```

This method is declared by the java.awt.Window class, which is the parent of all of the top-level windows and is thus inherited by JFrame; you cannot, however, register a window listener with some other component that is not derived from Window. When the window first appears on the screen, two lines are printed:

```
    Window Opened
    Window Activated
```

The first line is caused by the delivery of a WINDOW_OPENED event; this event is only delivered once in the lifetime of a window, at the point that it first becomes visible on the screen. A window is activated and receives a WINDOW_ACTIVATED event when it becomes the foreground application. On the Windows platform, this event is not actually triggered until the user clicks with the mouse somewhere inside the window, whereas under X-Windows, with some Window Managers it may be sufficient to simply move the mouse over the application window, while with others you may need to click to activate the window.

Core Note

The situation is not even as clear-cut as described, because, some window managers can be configured to work either way.

If you now move the mouse outside the application window, you may see the message

```
Window Deactivated
```

indicating the receipt of a WINDOW_DEACTIVATED event. If you had to click to receive the WINDOW_ACTIVATED message, you will need to click somewhere outside the window to see this message. The intent of this event is to notify the application that it is no longer in the foreground—the user has turned his or her attention elsewhere. What you do with this message depends entirely on your application. One possibility might be to reduce the priority of background threads if you have any, especially if those threads are performing tasks that might consume a lot of system resources.

If you now iconify the application, two events are delivered:

```
Window Iconified
Window Deactivated
```

The WINDOW_ICONIFIED event is delivered as the application is minimized. In many cases, you won't make much use of this event. Applications that do a lot of rendering on their main window, for example, programs that draw 3-dimensional graphics or animate images, might use this event to stop drawing on the screen, because none of the drawing will be visible. Once an application is iconified, it is no longer in the foreground, which explains the receipt of a WINDOW_DEACTIVATED event. As you might now expect, deiconifying the application produces another pair of events:

```
Window Deiconified
Window Activated
```

These events would be used to reverse the effects of the previous pair. An application that had stopped drawing while it was iconified would now allow itself to draw again, but would not need to take any explicit action to refresh the screen, because the paint method of all of the components on the window will be called as soon as the window is visible again.

Lastly, press the application's close button. This will result in the delivery of another three events:

```
Window Closing
Window Deactivated
Window Closed
```

The first message indicates the receipt of a WINDOW_CLOSING event, and the last shows that a WINDOW_CLOSED event has been sent. Between these two events, since the window is being destroyed, it is clearly becoming inactive, so a WINDOW_DEACTIVATED event is sent for the benefit of applications that properly manage state changes based on window events.

Window Closing Events

Whereas you can't do much other than react passively to the other window events, you can take some action in response to a WINDOW_CLOSING event that influences the future course of events. This event is delivered to indicate a *request* by the user to close the window (and to terminate the application if this is not a dialog window). If this is a convenient time to do this, the application can respond in one of three ways within the windowClosing method.

First, it can simply exit; secondly, it can hide the application window by calling setVisible(false) or, thirdly, it can destroy the window by invoking its dispose method. If either of the last two courses is taken, the window close is allowed to proceed and a WINDOW_CLOSED event will subsequently be delivered. It is, of course, up to the application to exit on receipt of the WINDOW_CLOSED event if this is the appropriate thing to do: Nothing in the Java libraries will terminate your application when the main window is closed.

There is, however, an extra complication to the handling of these events for both JFrame and JDialog. After the WINDOW_CLOSING event has been received by any listeners, a JFrame or a JDialog may hide or dispose itself of its own accord, whether or not the listener wanted it to. What it actually does depends on its *default close operation*, a property that can have one of the following three values:

```
WindowConstants.DO_NOTHING_ON_CLOSE

WindowConstants.HIDE_ON_CLOSE

WindowConstants.DISPOSE_ON_CLOSE
```

Both JFrame and JDialog have methods that allow this setting to be read or changed:

```
public int getDefaultCloseOperation();

public void setDefaultCloseOperation(int mode);
```

The default setting is WindowConstants.HIDE_ON_CLOSE. Here is what actually happens in the case of JFrame and JDialog. When the user presses the frame or dialog close button, a WINDOW_CLOSING event is delivered to all registered listeners, as described above. If any listener chooses to go ahead with the close by disposing the dialog, the window will close. After all listeners have seen the event, JFrame and JDialog check their default close operation. If it is set to WindowConstants.DO_NOTHING_ON_CLOSE, no further action will be taken. If it is WindowConstants.HIDE_ON_CLOSE, the frame or dialog will just be hidden; in this case, the program could make it visible again later. If the close operation is set to WindowConstants.DISPOSE_ON_CLOSE, then the window will be disposed and will no longer be usable (but the JFrame or JDialog object can still be used, although not to make the window visible again).

If you want to control exactly what happens to your frames and dialogs and you do not want them to be hidden or closed unless you explicitly request it, you should set the close operation to `WindowConstants.DO_NOTHING_ON_CLOSE`. If you accept the default setting or you explicitly request dispose on close, the frame or dialog will be hidden or disposed, but your application will not, of course, exit. This may be suitable behavior for dialogs, but it is almost certainly not what you want for your application's main window, which should normally cause the application to exit when it is closed. For the main window, therefore, the recommended setting is to do nothing. In most of the examples in this book, a listener is registered to exit when the top-level frame is closed by user request.

Core Note

This behavior is different from that of the AWT `Frame` *and* `Dialog` *classes, which don't support this feature and therefore stay visible unless closed or disposed of explicitly, as described earlier. This behavior also doesn't apply to the AWT* `Window` *or the Swing* `JWindow` *classes, which are relatively rarely used directly by the programmer. One reason why these two are different is that they don't have any window manager controls to allow the user to request that they be closed.*

Event-Handling Adapters

If you don't want to act on all of the window events, you can avoid implementing empty interface methods by using the `java.awt.event.WindowAdapter` class, which defines the empty methods for you. To use an adapter, you create a derived class based on the adapter in which you override just the methods for the events you want to provide your own handling for. For example, if you want to exit when the user closes the top-level window, you can use code that looks like that shown in Listing 3-18.

Listing 3-18   Using a WindowAdapter to terminate the application

---

```
package JFCBook.Chapter3;

import com.sun.java.swing.*;
import java.awt.*;
import java.awt.event.*;


public class WindowEventsExample2 extends JFrame {
  public WindowEventsExample2(String title) {
    super(title);
    JLabel l = new JLabel(" Window Test");

    this.getContentPane().add(l, "Center");
    pack();
```

continued

```
   }

   public static void main(String[] args) {
      WindowEventsExample2 w = new WindowEventsExample2("Window
Events 2");
      w.addWindowListener(new WindowEventsListener1());

w.setDefaultCloseOperation(WindowConstants.DO_NOTHING_ON_CLOSE);

      w.setVisible(true);
   }
}

class WindowEventsListener1 extends WindowAdapter {
   public void windowClosing(WindowEvent e) {
      System.out.println("Window Closing");
      e.getWindow().dispose();
   }

   public void windowClosed(WindowEvent e) {
      System.out.println("Window Closed");
      System.exit(0);

}
```

Here, an instance of `WindowEventsListener1` is registered to catch window
events on our window. This class extends `WindowAdapter` and overrides only the
`windowClosing` and `windowClosed` methods, so that it will only take action
when the window is being closed. In this case, the window is actually closed by disposing of it in `windowClosing` . In this example, default behavior of the frame is
explicitly overridden by using `setDefaultCloseOperation` so that it won't
close unless it is told to do so. Note that we don't need to arrange in advance for the
listener class to have a reference to the frame, because it can use the `getWindow`
method of the `WindowEvent` class to find out which window is closing.

We can, and frequently do, abbreviate the above example by using inner classes.
If you're not familiar with inner classes, you can find out about them by reading *Core
Java 1.1 Volume I: Fundamentals*, also published by Prentice Hall. When you know
about inner classes, you can simply use the code shown in Listing 3-19.

Listing 3-19   Using an inner class to handle events

```
package JFCBook.Chapter3;

import com.sun.java.swing.*;
import java.awt.*;
import java.awt.event.*;

public class WindowEventsExample3 extends JFrame {
   public WindowEventsExample3(String title) {
     super(title);
     JLabel l = new JLabel(" Window Test");

     this.getContentPane().add(l, "Center");
     pack();
   }

   public static void main(String[] args) {
     WindowEventsExample3 w = new WindowEventsExample3("Window
Events 3");
     w.addWindowListener(new WindowAdapter() {
        public void windowClosing(WindowEvent e) {
          System.out.println("Window Closing");
          e.getWindow().dispose();
        }

        public void windowClosed(WindowEvent e) {
          System.out.println("Window Closed");
          System.exit(0);
        }
     });

w.setDefaultCloseOperation(WindowConstants.DO_NOTHING_ON_CLOSE);
     w.setVisible(true);

   }
}
```

Many of the event-listening interfaces have corresponding adapter classes that you can use in this way.

Movement of Components

Window events allow you to detect most of what the user is doing to the top-level window but you can't use them to react to attempts by the user to move your window around on the screen, for example. You might think that this is an esoteric thing to want to do, but it can be important for some applications. Suppose that you want to implement your own desktop toolbar that attaches itself to one side of the screen and changes its orientation depending on where it is. You probably want to allow the user to relocate the toolbar by dragging it around the screen. When the user stops dragging the toolbar, you need to relocate it against the nearest edge of the screen and change its size and orientation to match that of the edge you are now attached to.

To allow you to conveniently implement this kind of behavior, each component can generate a `ComponentEvent` when it is moved, resized, hidden or shown. The `java.awt.event.ComponentEvent`, like all AWT events, has an identifier that describes the specific event and an interface (`ComponentListener`) to allow you to create an event listener. Table 3-3 summarizes the various events, the listener interface methods that receive them and the conditions under which each event is generated.

Table 3-3   Component Events

Event	Listener Method	Description
COMPONENT_SHOWN	componentShown	Generated when the component first becomes visible and subsequently on every use of `setVisible(true)`
COMPONENT_HIDDEN	componentHidden	Delivered after use of `setVisible(false)`
COMPONENT_MOVED	componentMoved	Generated when the component is moved by `setLocation`, `setBounds` or by the layout manager when the component's container is first laid out or resized
COMPONENT_RESIZED	componentResized	Sent when the component's size is changed using `setSize` or `setBounds` or when the layout manager initially sizes or subsequently resizes the component

These events apply to `all` components, not just to windows. Because of this, you can, if you wish, decouple logic that might be needed after some of your internal components are moved around in your window from the code that actually moves them. Many applications won't allow independent movement of parts of the user interface, but for those that do, this can be an invaluable feature. Later in this book, you'll see how to implement applications that contain internal frames, each of which might show, for example, a view of a word processing file. The internal frame can be moved around by the user without reference to the application since the code to handle the movement is part of the internal frame itself. If you need to know about the movement, perhaps to adjust the location or size of the other frames, you can do this by monitoring component events generated by the frames.

So that you can detect which component is involved in a component event, the ComponentEvent class includes the following method:

```
public Component getComponent();
```

The use of this method is demonstrated in Listing 3-20, which shows component events generated when a button is moved around inside a container under program control.

Listing 3-20   Handling Component Events

```
package JFCBook.Chapter3;

import com.sun.java.swing.*;
import java.awt.*;
import java.awt.event.*;

public class ComponentEventsExample implements ComponentListener {
  // ComponentListener interface
  public void componentMoved(ComponentEvent e) {
    Component c = e.getComponent();
    Point p = c.getLocation();
    System.out.println("Component moved to (" + p.x + ", " + p.y + ")");
  }

  public void componentResized(ComponentEvent e) {
    Component c = e.getComponent();
    Dimension d = c.getSize();
    System.out.println("Component resized: width " + d.width + ", height " + d.height);
  }

  public void componentShown(ComponentEvent e) {
    System.out.println("Component made visible");
  }

  public void componentHidden(ComponentEvent e) {
    System.out.println("Component made invisible");
  }
```

continued

```
public static void main(String[] args) {
  JFrame f = new JFrame("Component Events");
  JButton b = new JButton("Do not press...");
  b.addComponentListener(new ComponentEventsExample());

  f.getContentPane().add(b, "Center");
  f.setSize(300, 200);
  f.addWindowListener(new WindowAdapter() {
    public void windowClosing(WindowEvent evt) {
      System.exit(0);
    }
  });
  f.setVisible(true);

  try {
    Thread.sleep(5000); // Delay a bit
    b.setVisible(false);// Hide
    Thread.sleep(5000); // Delay a bit
    b.setSize(100, 100);      // Change size
    Thread.sleep(5000); // Delay a bit
    b.setLocation(20, 20);    // Move ourselves
    Thread.sleep(5000); // Delay a bit
    b.setVisible(true); // Appear again
    Thread.sleep(5000); // Delay a bit
    b.setLocation(30, 40);    // Move ourselves
    Thread.sleep(5000); // Delay a bit
    b.setSize(80, 80);  // Change size
    Thread.sleep(5000); // Delay a bit
  } catch (Exception e) {
    System.out.println(e);
  }

  System.exit(0);
  }
}
```

Running this program produces the following output:

```
Component resized: width 292, height 173
Component made invisible
Component resized: width 100, height 100
Component moved to (20, 20)
Component made visible
Component moved to (30, 40)
Component resized: width 80, height 80
```

The first line is produced when the frame's layout manager places and sizes the button within the frame. The second line is caused by our `setVisible(false)` call, at which point the button will disappear. The subsequent changes of size and position requested by `setSize` and `setLocation` are responsible for the next two lines. Notice that the correct size and location are reported. Note also that component events continue to be delivered even when the component is invisible. Finally, there are events reporting that the component is being made visible again and then being moved and resized to its final configuration.

Summary

This chapter presented all of the Swing layout managers. Making the correct choice of layout manager can considerably simplify your job, as can a proper understanding of what each layout manager is trying to achieve. Our survey of layout managers showed you how each layout manager lays out its container and how constraints can be used to influence the placement of individual components. You've looked quite closely at how layout managers respond to resizing of their containers, what their limitations are and how they behave in unusual situations.

You also saw an interesting tool for debugging component layout in the `DebugGraphics` feature of `JComponent`. This feature will also be of use if you plan to implement a new user interface for a Swing component, a topic covered in Chapter 13 or render complex graphics, which are the subject of the next chapter.

GRAPHICS, TEXT HANDLING AND PRINTING

Topics in This Chapter

- The Graphics Context, Lines, Shapes and Fills
- Properties and Property Change Events
- Borders and Icons
- Drawing and Printing Graphics and Text

Chapter 4

In the last two chapters, you have seen both text and images used in conjunction with buttons and labels. All you had to do to get your text or image drawn was to pass it to the component's constructor and the component arranged for it to appear. In this chapter, you'll see how to draw text and graphics of your own. The chapter begins by looking at the `JPanel` and `Graphics` classes. `JPanel` will be used as a drawing area and the methods of the `Graphics` class will be used to draw on it.

When you've seen how to use the primitive graphics operations, you'll build a complete application around them, concentrating on the details of the user interface and how to build components in a reusable manner. During the development of this application, you'll see how to implement a custom border, a very simple custom component and some icons that don't depend on images.

Next, you'll learn how to draw text and see how alike text and graphics handling are in Java. Armed with this knowledge, in the last part of this chapter you'll see how to use the printer to print an image of an application, a single component from that application, or a complete text file.

Working with Graphics

In this section, you're going to see how to draw text and graphics. In order to draw, you need something to draw on and something to draw with. The best thing to draw on is something that's naturally blank—like `JPanel`. In earlier chapters, you have used JPanel as a container and arranged components on top of it, but it is equally useful as an empty area that you can draw on.

If you're familiar with JDK 1.1, you might think it strange to use a container like JPanel for something as simple as drawing. After all, the AWT provided a simpler object, Canvas, derived from Component, that was used as the traditional surface for drawing on and as one of the starting points for creating custom components. Swing doesn't have a JCanvas, however. A JCanvas class would have been derived from JComponent, as JPanel is. Since JComponent is already a container, there is little to gain by retaining a separate JCanvas class so, although it made an appearance in the early releases of Swing, it soon disappeared. Now, wherever you would have used Canvas, you should probably use JPanel.

There is, however, another possible choice if you want something to draw on—JComponent. What JComponent and JPanel have in common that make them useful as a drawing area is that they both occupy screen space but don't draw anything onto themselves when they appear. There are only two real differences between them:

- JComponent is abstract, which means that you need to create a subclass to get something to draw on. JPanel is not abstract, so you can just create one whenever you need to.

- JPanel can be opaque and will fill its background with a specified color if you need it to. JComponent has no painting logic at all and so is always transparent.

As you'll see, the first difference is not at all important, because you will need to subclass JPanel if you want to draw on it. The choice between JPanel and JComponent really comes down to the second difference. If you want your drawing surface to be transparent, you might as well use JComponent. Otherwise, you can save yourself the trouble of writing the code to fill in the background by using JPanel. The examples in this chapter all use JPanel, but the same techniques work if you want to use JComponent as your starting point.

The Graphics Context

Every component, JPanel included, has an associated *graphics context,* which gives direct access to the screen space that it occupies. The graphics context is represented by the java.awt.Graphics class. Graphics is an abstract class, so you can't create an instance of it for yourself—the only way to get one is from a component. If you're going to draw on a JPanel (or a JComponent), the simplest way to get an appropriate Graphics object is to subclass it and override its paintComponent method, which is called to allow the component to update its on-screen representation. The only argument that this method receives is a Graphics object that covers its on-screen area.

The Graphics class has a large number of methods that allow you to draw on the surface of the component, all of which will be covered in the first part of this chapter. To get started, let's use the drawString method to place a short piece of text onto a JPanel. Listing 4-1 shows how this is done.

Listing 4-1   Drawing Text

```
package JFCBook.Chapter4;

import com.sun.java.swing.*;
import java.awt.*;
import java.awt.event.*;

public class DrawText extends JPanel {
   public void paintComponent(Graphics g) {
      super.paintComponent(g);
      g.setColor(getForeground());
      g.drawString("Core Java Foundation Classes", 20, 80);
   }

   public static void main(String[] args) {
      JFrame f = new JFrame("Drawing Text");
      JPanel panel = new DrawText();
      f.getContentPane().add(panel);
      f.setSize(250, 200);
      f.setVisible(true);
   }
}
```

The first line of the paintComponent method is there to make JPanel draw the background—this is the only thing that JPanel does in its own paintComponent method. If this weren't done, the panel would be transparent and the text would be drawn on the background of the frame (which, at least in the Windows look-and-feel, would have the same color by default, so you wouldn't see any difference). As you can see, apart from this, it only takes two lines of code to draw some text onto a component—one to set the drawing color and the other to draw the string itself. The drawString method is given the string to be drawn and the position at which the string is to appear on the component's surface as x and y coordinates. The coordinate system used by the Graphics class is very simple: Each pixel in the area described by the graphics context is uniquely described by its x and y coordinates. By default, the origin of this coordinate system is at the top left of the component from which the graphics context was obtained. The x coordinate increases as you move to the right and the y coordinate increases as you move down (i.e., towards the bottom of the screen). This is, of course, the same as the coordinate system used to place components on the screen and in containers. The result of running this simple program using the command

```
java JFCBook.Chapter4.DrawTest
```

is shown in Figure 4-1.

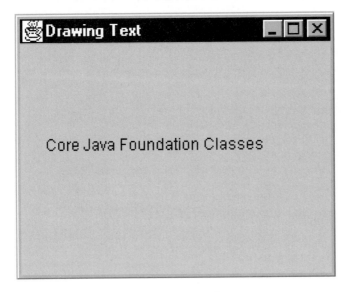

Figure 4-1   Drawing Text on a Jpanel.

You may be surprised at how little had to be done to get this string to appear on the JPanel. For example, how was the font to be used determined? It wasn't explicitly specified in the paintComponent method. When you use Graphics methods to draw text, lines and shapes, you never directly specify things like font or color—those attributes often need to be the same for many graphics operations performed one after another, so instead of passing them as arguments to each call, they are held within the graphics context itself.

Graphics Context Properties

The Graphics object stores five properties that you can regard as persistent—that is, they don't change between invocations of Graphics methods, unless those methods are explicitly intended to change them. The five properties are shown in Table 4-1.

Table 4-1	Graphics Context Properties
Property	**Description**
Font	The font to be used for text rendering.
Color	The color used for text rendering and by line, shape and fill operations.
Origin	The location within the component of the point whose coordinates are to be considered to be given by $x=0$, $y=0$. By default, the graphics context has its origin at the top left of the component, but it is possible to move the origin elsewhere. The Graphics class stores the current location of the origin.
Clip	Graphics operations (line drawing, text rendering etc.) are all carried out in conjunction with a graphics context and usually can reach anywhere on the surface of the component. Sometimes, however, it is useful to restrict or *clip* the area that can be affected by graphics operations and the Graphics object stores the current clip.
Drawing mode	The drawing mode controls how the pixels in a graphics operation interact with those already in the drawing area. By default, new pixels are painted over the old ones and completely replace them. You can, however, arrange to have new pixels combined with existing ones in such a way that they can be removed later by performing the same operation again.

You'll probably notice straight away that the first two of these properties are very similar to properties of JComponent. This is, of course, no coincidence. When the paintComponent method of a JComponent is invoked, the Graphics object is initialized as shown in Table 4-2.

Table 4-2	Graphics settings in the paintComponent method
Property	**Initial Value**
Font	The font selected into the JComponent
Color	The JComponent's foreground color
Origin	The top-left corner of the JComponent
Clip	Covers the area that needs to be redrawn, often the entire component
Drawing mode	Set to normal drawing mode

Because the component's current font and foreground color are selected when the `paintComponent` method is entered, there was no need to do anything special about selecting the font before drawing the text in Listing 4-1 (but see the discussion following regarding the foreground color). You'll see how the origin, clip and drawing mode are used later in this chapter. For now, only the font and color properties will be used.

Notice that a graphics context contains only one color, whereas components have two—background and foreground. `Graphics` only needs one color because it doesn't strictly recognize the concept of foreground and background. When you draw text, for example, the pixels that represent the characters in the font are written onto the screen in the appropriate locations and with the color selected into the graphics context. Other pixels, which you might consider to be in the background color, are not affected by this operation—their color does not change. The same is true when you use `Graphics` methods to draw lines and other shapes—only the pixels that make up the shape being drawn are affected and each operation involves only one color. Usually, of course, you will draw or render text in the foreground color of the component that you are using, but this is only a convention and is not an assumption made by the `Graphics` class.

As well as using the default settings, you can change the font or color in the graphics context using the following methods:

```
public void setColor(Color color);

public void setFont(Font font);
```

There are also corresponding methods that allow you to read the current settings:

```
public Color getColor();

public Font getFont();
```

According to Table 4-2, the panel's foreground color should have been selected into the `Graphics` object, so why was it necessary to use the `setColor` method in Listing 4-1 to explicitly set a color before drawing the string? In fact, this shouldn't have been necessary, but in order to fill the background, the `paintComponent` method of `JPanel` was called. This method changes the `Graphics` object by selecting the background color, so it was necessary to switch back to the foreground color before drawing the text

Core Note

This behavior of `JPanel` *could reasonably be considered to be a bug, because it is different from what happens in JDK 1.1. However, as you'll see later in this section, the detailed mechanics of component painting have changed with Swing and there are other assumptions that you could make in JDK 1.1 that don't hold true when you try to apply them to Swing components.*

The modified version of our first example shown in Listing 4-2 draws the same text in green using a 16-point bold and italic font. The result of running this program is shown in Figure 4-2, where you can see that the font and color have both changed, although you can't really see that the text is green!

Listing 4-2   Changing Graphics properties

```
package JFCBook.Chapter4;

import com.sun.java.swing.*;
import java.awt.*;
import java.awt.event.*;
public class DrawColoredText extends JPanel {
  public void paintComponent(Graphics g) {
    super.paintComponent(g);
    g.setFont(new Font("SansSerif", Font.ITALIC | Font.BOLD, 16));
    g.setColor(Color.green);
    g.drawString("Core Java Foundation Classes", 20, 80);
  }

  public static void main(String[] args) {
    JFrame f = new JFrame("Colored Text");
    JPanel panel = new DrawColoredText();
    f.getContentPane().add(panel);
    f.setSize(280, 200);
    f.setVisible(true);
  }
}
```

You'll learn more about changing the properties of the Graphics object in the rest of this section and you'll see other ways to get a Graphics object for a component in "Graphics Context as a View of a Component." The topic of drawing text is also covered more fully later in this chapter.

Drawing Lines and Shapes

As well as holding properties, the Graphics class provides methods for drawing lines, arcs and ovals and for filling shapes with solid colors.

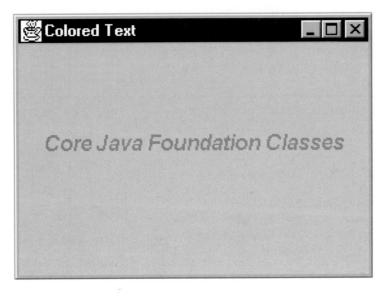

Figure 4-2   Changing the font and color in a Graphics object.

Straight Lines

The simplest possible graphics operation you could perform would be to plot a single point. Yet Java does not provide a method to do this. Instead, there is a line-drawing method that can draw a point as a special case:

```
public void drawLine(int x1, int y1, int x2, int y2);
```

This method draws a straight line, one pixel wide, between the points $(x1, y1)$ and $(x2, y2)$, in the color currently selected into the graphics context. To draw a single point, you specify a start and end point that are the same. The code in Listing 4-3 draws a set of vertical, horizontal and diagonal dashed lines in three different colors by calling drawLine in a loop. You can see a gray-scale reproduction of the results of this program in Figure 4-3. To run it for yourself, use the command:

```
java JFCBook.Chapter4.DrawLines
```

Listing 4-3   Drawing Lines

```
package JFCBook.Chapter4;

import com.sun.java.swing.*;
import java.awt.*;
import java.awt.event.*;

public class DrawLines extends JPanel {
  public void paintComponent(Graphics g) {
    super.paintComponent(g);

    for (int i = 0; i < 10; i++) {
      g.setColor(Color.black);
      g.drawLine(20 * i + 10, 40, 20 * i + 20, 40);
      g.setColor(Color.white);
      g.drawLine(40, 20 * i + 10, 40, 20 * i + 20);
      g.setColor(Color.red);
      g.drawLine(20 * i + 10, 20 * i + 10, 20 * i + 20, 20 * i
+ 20);
    }
  }

  public static void main(String[] args) {
    JFrame f = new JFrame("Line Drawing");
    JPanel panel = new DrawLines();
    f.getContentPane().add(panel);
    f.setSize(250, 250);
    f.setVisible(true);
  }
}
```

Polygons, Polylines and the Graphics Origin

As well as drawing points and individual lines, you can also draw outlines made up of
several lines that are joined together (i.e., each line starts where the previous one
ends) using the drawPolyline method. You give this method two arrays of integers, one containing the x coordinates and the other the y coordinates of each point
in the shape, and a single integer that specifies how many points there are. There is
a similar method called drawPolygon that takes the same set of arguments, but
draws a closed shape by connecting together the first and last points drawn.
Alternatively, you can encapsulate the points in a java.awt.Polygon object and
pass that to drawPolygon.

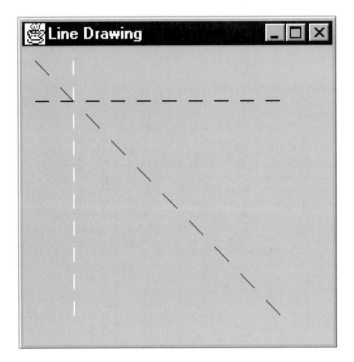

Figure 4-3   Using drawLine to draw straight lines.

```
public void drawPolyline(int[] xPoints, int[] yPoints, int nPoints);

public void drawPolygon(int[] xPoints, int[] yPoints, int nPoints);

public void drawPolygon(Polygon p);
```

You create a `Polygon` object by specifying the vertices in the same way as you would give them to `drawPolygon`:

```
public Polygon(int[] xPoints, int[] yPoints, int nPoints);
```

Listing 4-4 is an example that has a version of the `paintComponent` method that demonstrates the difference between `drawPolygon` and `drawPolyline`.

The two arrays hold the x and y coordinates of all of the points in both shapes; both methods traverse these arrays from the first entry to the last, so the vertices of these shapes will be at the points (100, 20), (50, 50), (100, 80), (150, 60) and (170, 30), relative to the origin of the graphics context.

Listing 4-4   Polygons and polylines

```
package JFCBook.Chapter4;

import com.sun.java.swing.*;
import java.awt.*;
import java.awt.event.*;

public class Polygons extends JPanel {
    public void paintComponent(Graphics g) {
        super.paintComponent(g);
        int[] xValues = { 100, 50, 100, 150, 170 };
        int[] yValues = { 20, 50, 80, 60, 30 };

        g.setColor(Color.black);
        g.drawPolyline(xValues, yValues, xValues.length);

        g.translate(0, 30);
        g.setColor(Color.white);
        g.drawPolygon(xValues, yValues, xValues.length);
    }

    public static void main(String[] args) {
        JFrame f = new JFrame("Polygons and Polylines");
        Polygons c = new Polygons();
        f.getContentPane().add(c);
        f.setSize(250, 200);
        f.addWindowListener(new WindowAdapter() {
            public void windowClosing(WindowEvent evt) {
                System.exit(0);
            }
        });
        f.setVisible(true);
    }
}
```

This example first selects black as the drawing color and draws a polyline. Next, the intention is to change the drawing color to something else (in this case white) and use the same set of points to draw a polygon. This would demonstrate that the polygon closes itself by joining the first and last points and that the polyline does not. But if this were all that were done, because the same sets of coordinates are used, the polygon would be drawn on top of the first shape, completely obscuring it. To make the polygon separate from the polyline, you could create another array of points offset from the first set by a constant amount. However, there is a more convincing way. Since the coordinates are measured relative to the origin of the graphics context, why not use the same coordinate arrays and simply relocate the origin? This can be done using the Graphics translate method:

```
public void translate(int x, int y);
```

This moves the origin to the point (x, y) relative to its current position. Any subsequent drawing is done using coordinates relative to this new origin, so, in this example, the polygon is drawn with each vertex 30 pixels directly below the corresponding one in the polyline. You can see the result in Figure 4-4, which clearly demonstrates that the drawPolygon method closes up the shape that it is drawing, while drawPolyline does not.

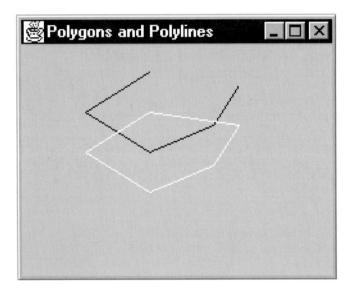

Figure 4-4   Drawing polygons and polylines.

Incidentally, you can move the origin as many times as you like and the effect is, of course, cumulative: If the following lines were added at the end of the paintComponent method just shown:

```
g.translate(0, 30);
g.setColor(Color.green);
g.drawPolygon(xValues, yValues, xValues.length);
```

then the result would be a green polygon 60 pixels below the first polyline. You can also supply negative values for x and y, and you can even move the origin right off the surface of the component by giving negative coordinates or by making one or both coordinates larger than the size of the component. When you do this, those parts of the polygon or polyline that end up being outside the bounds of the component are simply not drawn—this is called "clipping", because the edges of the component "clip off" any drawing that spills over them to the outside. You will see why it is useful to move the origin off the surface of the component in Chapter 5 "Keyboard Handling, Actions and Scrolling," when you'll see how to view drawings and images that are too large to be all on the screen at the same time.

Drawing Rectangles

There are also methods for drawing rectangles, arcs and ovals. Here are the three methods that can be used to draw rectangles:

```
public void drawRect(int x, int y, int width, int height);

public void drawRoundRect(int x, int y, int width, int height,
                          int arcWidth, int arcHeight);

public void draw3DRect(int x, int y, int width, int height,
                          boolean raised);
```

The parameters of the drawRect method are obvious, those of the drawRoundRect method less so. This method draws a rectangle in which the four corners are 90-degree arcs facing outward, so that the edges appear rounded; you use the arcWidth parameter to specify the horizontal diameter (not radius) of each arc and arcHeight to give the vertical diameter. The example in Listing 4-5 shows how this works in practice:

| Listing 4-5   Drawing rectangles |

```
package JFCBook.Chapter4;

import com.sun.java.swing.*;
import java.awt.*;
import java.awt.event.*;

public class Rectangles extends JPanel {
  public void paintComponent(Graphics g) {
    super.paintComponent(g);
    g.setColor(Color.white);
    g.drawRect(10, 10, 80, 60);

    g.translate(0, 70);
    g.setColor(Color.black);
    g.drawRoundRect(10, 10, 80, 60, 16, 8);

    g.translate(90, -70);
    g.setColor(Color.lightGray);
```

continued

```
    g.draw3DRect(10, 10, 80, 60, true);

    g.translate(0, 70);
    g.draw3DRect(10, 10, 80, 60, false);
  }

  public static void main(String[] args) {
    JFrame f = new JFrame("Rectangles");
    Rectangles c = new Rectangles();
    f.getContentPane().setBackground(UIManager.getColor("control"));
    f.getContentPane().add(c);
    f.setSize(200, 200);
    f.addWindowListener(new WindowAdapter() {
      public void windowClosing(WindowEvent evt) {
        System.exit(0);
      }
    });
    f.setVisible(true);
  }
}
```

The rounded rectangle has an arcWidth of 16 and an arcHeight of 8, so that the corners will appear to be quadrants of an ellipse that is twice as long as it is tall; each arc will extend in by 8 pixels and downward by 4 pixels, as you can see from Figure 4-5. If we made arcWidth and arcHeight equal, the corners would be circular.

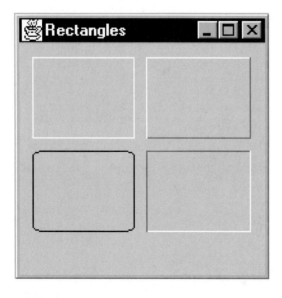

Figure 4-5 Drawing 3D rectangles and rectangles with rounded corners.

The `draw3DRect` method draws a rectangle with a shaded border that makes it look either raised up or pressed into the surface that it is drawn onto. In JDK 1.1, you might have used this method to create button outlines or a border around a group of controls, but with Swing, there is a better way to do this—see our discussion of borders in Chapter 8.

Whichever of these methods you use, the rectangle will actually be one pixel wider and higher than the width and height that you specify. In other words, if you ask for a rectangle with width 20 and height 10, it will actually cover a space 21 pixels wide and 11 pixels high, counting the pixel lines themselves. As a consequence, if you were to do this:

```
g.drawRectangle(10, 10, 20, 1);
```

your rectangle would be 2 pixels high and 21 pixels wide; if you specify a height of zero, you actually get a single-pixel line. The situation changes when you create a filled rectangle, as you will see in "Color Fills."

Arcs and Ovals

You can draw curved lines using the `drawOval` and `drawArc` methods.

```
public void drawOval(int x, int y, int width, int height);

public void drawArc(int x, int y, int width, int height,
                            int startAngle, int arcAngle);
```

The `drawOval` method draws a circle or an ellipse, wholly contained within the rectangle described by its arguments and drawn such that its center coincides with that of the rectangle. If the width and height arguments are equal, you get a circle. Similarly, `drawArc` creates an arc of a circle or an ellipse inside its bounding rectangle. The code in Listing 4-6 and the results in Figure 4-6 show how these methods work. To show how the shape is related to its bounding rectangle, we used the `drawRect` method to show the bounding rectangle in addition to that shape itself.

Listing 4-6   Drawing Arcs and Ovals

```
package JFCBook.Chapter4;

import com.sun.java.swing.*;
import java.awt.*;
import java.awt.event.*;

public class Arcs extends JPanel {
  public void paintComponent(Graphics g) {
    super.paintComponent(g);
    g.setColor(Color.white);
    g.drawRect(10, 10, 80, 40);
```

continued

```
      g.setColor(Color.black);
      g.drawOval(10, 10, 80, 40);
      g.setColor(Color.white);
      g.drawRect(10, 80, 80, 80);
      g.setColor(Color.black);
      g.drawOval(10, 80, 80, 80);

      g.translate(100, 0);
      g.setColor(Color.white);
      g.drawRect(0, 0, 80, 40);
      g.setColor(Color.black);
      g.drawArc(0, 0, 80, 40, -90, 90);
      g.setColor(Color.white);
      g.drawRect(0, 60, 80, 40);
      g.setColor(Color.black);
      g.drawArc(0, 60, 80, 40, 0, 90);
      g.setColor(Color.white);
      g.drawRect(0, 120, 80, 40);
      g.setColor(Color.black);
      g.drawArc(0, 120, 80, 40, 90, -90);

      g.translate(100, 0);
      g.setColor(Color.white);
      g.drawRect(0, 0, 40, 40);
      g.setColor(Color.black);
      g.drawArc(0, 0, 40, 40, -90, 90);
      g.setColor(Color.white);
      g.drawRect(0, 60, 40, 40);
      g.setColor(Color.black);
      g.drawArc(0, 60, 40, 40, 0, 90);
      g.setColor(Color.white);
      g.drawRect(0, 120, 40, 40);
      g.setColor(Color.black);
      g.drawArc(0, 120, 40, 40, 90, -90);
   }

   public static void main(String[] args) {
      JFrame f = new JFrame("Arcs and Ovals");
      Arcs c = new Arcs();
      f.getContentPane().setBackground(UIManager.getColor("control"));
      f.getContentPane().add(c);
      f.setSize(300, 200);
      f.addWindowListener(new WindowAdapter() {
         public void windowClosing(WindowEvent evt) {
            System.exit(0);
         }
      });
      f.setVisible(true);
   }
}
```

The results of drawing the ellipse and the circle are exactly as you would expect—the shape fills the bounding rectangle, touching all four sides. The arcs are a little less obvious. First, what you get is actually an arc taken from a complete ellipse or circle drawn within the rectangle that you specify; if you want to get an arc that fills a particular rectangle, you have to compute the size of a larger rectangle that would contain the entire circle or ellipse of which your arc is a part and specify that as the bounding rectangle.

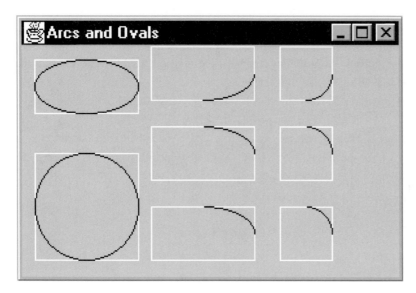

Figure 4-6   Drawing arcs and ellipses.

The `startAngle` and `arcAngle` parameters describe which part of the arc is drawn; both are specified in degrees. If you think of the bounding rectangle as the face of a clock, zero degrees is at the 3 o'clock position; positive values correspond to counter-clockwise rotation and negative values to clockwise rotation. For example, the first arc drawn is created as follows:

```
g.drawArc(0, 0, 80, 40, -90, 90);
```

The ellipse of which this arc is a part is 80 pixels wide and 40 pixels high. The arc starts 90 degrees clockwise from 3 o'clock—that is, at 6 o'clock, and turns 90 degrees counter-clockwise—that is, back to the three o'clock position. Because a 90-degree segment from an ellipse that starts on the *y*-axis and ends on the *x*-axis is being used, the whole arc is a quadrant and therefore occupies one quarter of the bounding rectangle. This arc is shown at the top of the second column in the diagram. There are, of course, two ways to draw any given arc, depending on which end of the arc you start with. The next two examples illustrate this:

```
g.drawArc(0, 60, 80, 40, 0, 90);
g.drawArc(0, 120, 80, 40, 90, -90);
```

The first line creates an arc starting at 3 o'clock, rotating 90 degrees counter-clockwise, while the second arc start 90 degrees counterclockwise from 3 o'clock and rotates back 90 degrees to produce the same result. The third column shows the same arcs taken from a circle rather than an ellipse.

Color Fills

As well as drawing outlines, you can also easily draw shapes that are filled with solid color. You can draw rectangles, polygons, ovals and arcs that are filled with the color currently selected into the graphics context using methods that are the same as the line-drawing variants apart from the name:

```
public void fill3DRect(int x, int y, int width, int height,
                       boolean raised);

public void fillArc(int x, int y, int width, int height,
                    int startAngle, int arcAngle);

public void fillOval(int x, int y, int width, int height);

public void fillPolygon(int[] xPoints, int[] yPoints,
                        int nPoints);

public void fillPolygon(Polygon p);

public void fillRect(int x, int y, int width, int height);

public void fillRoundRect(int x, int y, int width, int height,
                          int arcWidth, int arcHeight);
```

Notice that there is no `fillPolyline` method: a filled polyline would, of course, be the same as filling the polygon drawn with the same arguments, so it is sufficient to provide just `fillPolygon`. Most of these methods are simple and produce obvious results; the example in Listing 4-7 creates filled rectangles, polygons and ovals.

Listing 4-7   Drawing filled shapes

```
package JFCBook.Chapter4;

import com.sun.java.swing.*;
import java.awt.*;
import java.awt.event.*;

public class Fills extends JPanel {
  public void paintComponent(Graphics g) {
    super.paintComponent(g);
```

```
    g.setColor(Color.white);
    g.drawRect(10, 10, 80, 40);
    g.setColor(Color.gray);
    g.fillRect(10, 10, 80, 40);
    g.setColor(Color.white);
    g.drawRect(10, 80, 80, 80);
    g.setColor(Color.gray);
    g.fillOval(10, 80, 80, 80);

    g.translate(100, 0);
    g.setColor(Color.white);
    g.drawRect(0, 0, 80, 40);
    g.setColor(Color.gray);
    g.fillArc(0, 0, 80, 40, -60, 90);
    g.setColor(Color.white);
    g.drawRect(0, 60, 80, 40);
    g.setColor(Color.gray);
    g.fillArc(0, 60, 80, 40, 0, 45);
    g.setColor(Color.white);
    g.drawRect(0, 120, 80, 80);
    g.setColor(Color.gray);
    g.fillArc(0, 120, 80, 80, 135, -135);

    g.translate(100, 0);
    int[] xPoints = { 30, 0, 30, 60, 80 };
    int[] yPoints = {  0, 30, 60, 45, 15 };
    Polygon p = new Polygon(xPoints, yPoints, xPoints.length);
    g.setColor(Color.white);
    g.drawPolygon(p);
    g.setColor(Color.gray);
    g.fillPolygon(p);
  }

  public static void main(String[] args) {
    JFrame f = new JFrame("Filled Shapes");
    Fills c = new Fills();
    f.getContentPane().setBackground(UIManager.getColor("control"));
    f.getContentPane().add(c);
    f.setSize(300, 280);
    f.addWindowListener(new WindowAdapter() {
      public void windowClosing(WindowEvent evt) {
        System.exit(0);
      }
    });
    f.setVisible(true);
  }
}
```

For clarity, the corresponding bounding boxes have again been drawn in white. If you look carefully at the polygon and the rectangle in Figure 4-7, you will see that the right and lower parts of the bounding shapes are not affected by the filling operation; this means, for example, the filled rectangles are one pixel narrower and shorter than their drawn counterparts. The other shapes fill to the same boundary as they would draw. Notice that a filled oval and a filled arc are basically identical—both draw what you might think of as a segment of a pie chart, with the filled area bounded by the curved edge and the two lines joining its end to the center of the bounding rectangle.

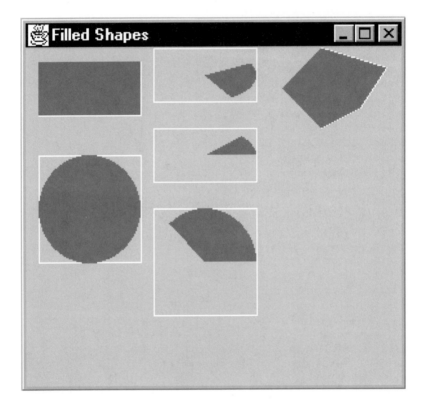

Figure 4-7   Drawing filled shapes.

You can also draw filled 3D rectangles and more complex polygons, as Listing 4-8 illustrates. You can see the results of running this example in Figure 4-8.

Listing 4-8 Drawing filled 3D shapes

```
package JFCBook.Chapter4;

import com.sun.java.swing.*;
import java.awt.*;
import java.awt.event.*;

public class Fill3D extends JPanel {
  public void paintComponent(Graphics g) {
    super.paintComponent(g);
    g.setColor(Color.white);
    g.fill3DRect(10, 10, 80, 40, false);
    g.fill3DRect(10, 100, 80, 40, true);

    g.translate(100, 0);
    g.setColor(Color.gray);
    int[] xPoints = { 120, 60, 0, 240, 180, 120, 240, 240 };
    int[] yPoints = { 0, 200, 100, 100, 200, 0, 0, 100 };
    Polygon p = new Polygon(xPoints, yPoints, xPoints.length);
    g.fillPolygon(p);
  }

  public static void main(String[] args) {
    JFrame f = new JFrame("3D Fills");
    Fill3D c = new Fill3D();
    f.getContentPane().setBackground(UIManager.getColor("control"));
    f.getContentPane().add(c);
    f.setSize(400, 280);
    f.addWindowListener(new WindowAdapter() {
      public void windowClosing(WindowEvent evt) {
        System.exit(0);
      }
    });
    f.setVisible(true);
  }
}
```

Filled 3D rectangles are rendered by filling them with the currently selected color when they are raised and with a contrasting color when they are not. The 3D effect is achieved by drawing edges on the bottom and right sides that consist of the alternate color. In our example, the current color is white, so the rectangle is white when raised. The boundary in this case is rendered in a grayish color. When the rectangle is drawn with the `raised` parameter set to `false`, these colors are exchanged.

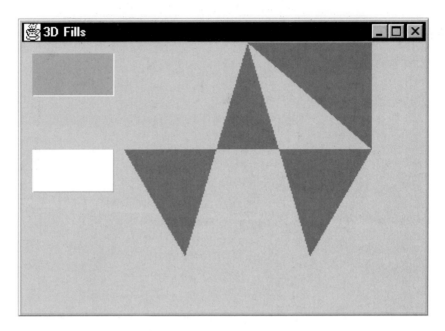

Figure 4-8 Drawing filled 3D shapes.

The polygon that is used in this example is not as trivial as the one that was filled in our earlier example, because the bounding line crosses itself, creating an enclosed area to the top right. You might wonder whether this area should be considered to be inside or outside the shape. Since it is wholly enclosed by the shape's boundaries, you might think that it is inside and hence should be filled, but in fact it is not. When deciding which areas of a shape should be filled, a simple rule is used: The area is filled if it can be reached from outside the shape by crossing an odd number of lines; this is known as the *alternating rule*.

Points of intersection are counted according to how many times the pen that draws the shape crosses the intersection point. In this example, you should be able to see that the unfilled area can always be reached by crossing exactly two lines. If you are curious about the three vertices of this area, you should convince yourself, by looking at the definitions of the points that make up the shape, that each vertex is visited exactly twice by the drawing pen:

Vertex at $x = 120, y = 0$:	start point (first visit)
	End of line from $x = 180, y = 0$ (second visit)
Vertex at $x = 240, y = 100$:	End of line from $x = 0, y = 100$ (first visit)
	End of line from $x = 240, y = 0$ (second visit)
Vertex on the line $y = 100$:	Part of line from $x = 0, y = 100$ to $x = 240, y = 100$ (first visit)
	Part of line from $x = 180, y = 200$ to $x = 120, y = 0$ (second visit)

There is one final filling method that hasn't yet been mentioned in this section:

```
public void clearRect(int x, int y, int width, int height);
```

This is a convenience method that clears the rectangle described by its parameters to the background color of the component from which the `Graphics` object was obtained. It isn't very useful unless you are implementing new components, because this is about the only case in which you don't need to explicitly specify the color used for the fill operation.

Although the methods that you have seen in this chapter allow you to draw and fill shapes with ease, they are a little restricted in that the resulting shapes are always drawn with a one-pixel wide boundary and are aligned horizontally or vertically. You cannot, for example, draw an ellipse with a 4-pixel wide dashed edge inclined at 45 degrees to the horizontal. If you need to do this, you will have need to use the JDK 1.2 Java 2D API, which is beyond the scope of this volume.

Graphics Context as a View of a Component

So far, all of our examples have only used a single graphics context at a time. It is, however, possible to obtain more than one `Graphics` object from the same component and perform operations on each of them to affect the one component. Suppose, for example, that you wanted to run a sequence of graphics operations on one component in two separate drawing colors to compare the results. You could do this by using the same `Graphics` object twice, changing the color when we move from the first to the second. This is less convenient, however, if you want to specify the graphics operations in real-time using the mouse or if the color is not the only attribute that you want to be different. In cases like this, it is more convenient to use a dedicated `Graphics` object.

Getting a Second Graphics Object Using the Create Method

You can get a second (or third, or more) graphics context in two ways. First, you can call the `JComponent` `getGraphics` method, which will give you a new `Graphics` object that covers the entire component. The `getGraphics` method is discussed in the next section. Secondly, if you want a copy of an existing graphics context, you can clone it using the `Graphics` `create` method:

```
public Graphics create();
public Graphics create(int x, int y, int width, int height);
```

The first of these methods creates an exact copy of the graphics context to which it applies; the second creates a new graphics context that corresponds to a rectangular subset of the area covered by the original context. If you create a context using the second form of `create`, you cannot use it to draw outside of its smaller area.

Once created, each `Graphics` object is independent, so changes you make to one object are not reflected in any of the others. In this sense, each graphics context is an independent view of the original component, with the capability to affect it in different ways, even when performing the same operations. Since you can change any of the attributes of each graphics context individually, the same operations invoked on two `Graphics` objects could be realized in different colors, in different positions on the same object, with different painting modes and so on.

Listing 4-9 illustrate this by drawing the same shape in two copies of the same graphics context and shows that the result depends on which graphics context is used by moving the origin of the second context and drawing the same shape as is drawn in the original `Graphics` object, but using a different color.

Listing 4-9   Using two Graphics objects with one component

```java
package JFCBook.Chapter4;

import com.sun.java.swing.*;
import java.awt.*;
import java.awt.event.*;

public class GraphicsCreate extends JPanel {
  public void paintComponent(Graphics g) {
    super.paintComponent(g);
    int[] xPoints = { 120, 60, 0, 240, 180, 120, 240, 240 };
    int[] yPoints = { 0, 200, 100, 100, 200, 0, 0, 100 };
    Polygon p = new Polygon(xPoints, yPoints, xPoints.length);
    Dimension d = getSize();
    int width = d.width;
    int height = d.height;

    Graphics secondContext = g.create(width/2, 0, width/2, height);

    g.setColor(Color.black);
    g.fillRect(0, 0, width/2, height);
    g.setColor(Color.white);
    g.fillPolygon(p);

    secondContext.setColor(Color.white);
    secondContext.fillRect(0, 0, width/2, height);
    secondContext.setColor(Color.black);
    secondContext.fillPolygon(p);

    secondContext.dispose();
  }

  public static void main(String[] args) {
```

```
    JFrame f = new JFrame("Graphics create method");
    GraphicsCreate c = new GraphicsCreate();
    f.getContentPane().setBackground(UIManager.getColor("control"));
    f.getContentPane().add(c);
    f.setSize(500, 280);
    f.addWindowListener(new WindowAdapter() {
      public void windowClosing(WindowEvent evt) {
        System.exit(0);
      }
    });
    f.setVisible(true);
  }
}
```

The `paintComponent` method is passed a graphics context that covers the whole component, so this example uses the component's `getSize` method and then creates a second copy of the graphics context that covers only the right half of the component, by using the `create` method applied to the original `Graphics` object. The original `Graphics` object is then used to fill the background with black and then draw the same polygon as was used in Listing 4-8 with a white pen.

The second context was derived from the original `Graphics` object but was clipped to the right half of the component and therefore can be used to access only that part. The origin of this context is the top left of the area of the component that it covers, not the top left of the component itself. So, when this context is filled with white and then the same polygon is drawn from the same points with a black pen, the result is a color-inverted image of the left side of the component on the right side, as shown in Figure 4-9.

The important point to note about this example is that the actual drawing code is the same in both cases. To effect the differences required, all that is necessary is to adjust the properties of the graphics context.

The last part of this example shows something you haven't seen yet in this chapter:

```
secondContext.dispose();
```

This method explicitly disposes of the `Graphics` object. Whenever you acquire a `Graphics` object yourself by using `create` or the `getGraphics` method that you'll see in the next section, you must release it in this way when you have finished with it. On some platforms, the Java `Graphics` object is linked to an underlying windowing system resource, of which there may be a limited number. If you don't dispose of `Graphics` objects that you allocate, you could degrade or cripple the system that you are running on by using up this critical resource.

This rule does not, however, apply to `Graphics` objects that are passed to you from elsewhere. Therefore, you must not dispose of the `Graphics` object that you use in the `paintComponent` method—that object is disposed of by the code in the Java libraries that allocated it in the first place.

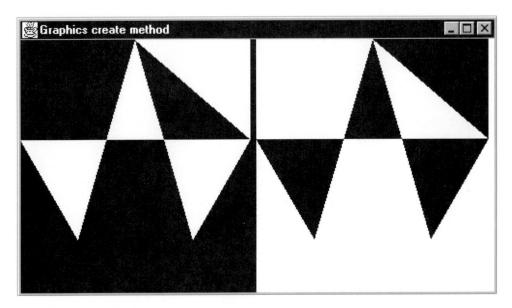

Figure 4-9   Drawing with two Graphics objects.

The getGraphics method

The create method allows you to "clone" an existing Graphics object and make changes to it that don't affect the original graphics context. This method is useful if you already have a Graphics object, but there are times when you will need to draw on a JComponent and you won't have a Graphics object on hand. So far, all of the drawing you have seen has been inside the paintComponent method, where the JComponent provides a Graphics object that lets you draw on its surface. Suppose, however, that you were implementing an application that drew shapes on a component in response to mouse movements. When the mouse moves, you get an event and you'll need to draw on the component immediately. Here, you don't have a Graphics object to work with.

You can get a graphics context for any JComponent (or, in fact, any AWT Component) using its getGraphics method:

```
public Graphics getGraphics();
```

The Graphics object returned by this method always covers the entire surface of the component unlike the one you get in paintComponent, which might be clipped if only some of the component needs to be repainted. You use it just like any other Graphics object, but there are a few important points you need to be aware of.

First, until the component has been realized, it doesn't have a graphics context at all. Until you have made the top-level window of your application visible, or at least called its pack method, you can't rely on any of your components having a valid graphics context and getGraphics may return null.

Second, any drawing you do on a component outside of its `paintComponent` method should be considered temporary. The reason for this is simple. Suppose you render a line of text onto a `JPanel` by invoking `getGraphics` to get a graphics context and then use `drawString` to draw directly onto its surface. This text will, of course, be drawn. Now suppose that the user covers your panel with another application and then uncovers it again. When the panel is uncovered, it will be cleared by the windowing system and the panel's `paintComponent` method will be called to draw the component again. Unless you have arranged for the `paintComponent` method to know about the text you drew, it won't be able to recreate it and the text will be lost.

To demonstrate this, Listing 4-10 shows another way of implementing the code you first saw in Listing 4-2.

Listing 4-10   Drawing text onto a JPanel using its graphics context

```
package JFCBook.Chapter4;

import com.sun.java.swing.*;
import java.awt.*;
import java.awt.event.*;

public class DirectText {
  public static void main(String[] args) {
    JFrame f = new JFrame("Drawing Text");
    JPanel panel = new JPanel();
    f.getContentPane().add(panel);
    f.setSize(280, 200);
    f.setVisible(true);

    try {
      Thread.sleep(5000);
    } catch (InterruptedException e) {
    }
    Graphics g = panel.getGraphics();
    g.setColor(Color.yellow);
    g.setFont(new Font("SansSerif", Font.BOLD | Font.ITALIC, 16));
    g.drawString("Core Java Foundation Classes", 20, 80);
  }
}
```

If you run this program, using the command

```
java JFCBook.Chapter4.DirectText
```

you'll first see an empty frame then, after a few seconds, the string "`Core Java Foundation Classes`" will appear. Now cover the frame up by moving another window and expose it again, or iconify and de-iconify it. The text disappears. There is, of course, no way to get this text back.

To make this program work at all, there is a 5-second delay before the string is drawn. This delay is necessary because the JPanel's paintComponent method is called shortly after the frame is made visible. As you know, this is just going to fill the panel with its background color, which will wipe out any text that has been drawn directly onto it with drawString. In fact, since the code in the main method and the code in paintComponent run in different threads, it is possible, on some platforms, that you could make this example work even without a 5-second delay if the panel's painting occurs before the string is drawn. Even if this does work sometimes, it is unlikely to work reliably because it relies on timing.

Core Alert

In fact, there are strict rules that govern access to Swing components from different threads of an application—see Appendix B, "Swing Components and Multithreading," for a detailed discussion of this topic.

You should not, however, conclude from this that drawing directly onto a component using a graphics context obtained from getGraphics is not useful. As long as you arrange for the paintComponent method to draw the same thing when the component needs to be repainted, direct drawing can improve the performance of your application. You'll see an example of this in "A Graphics Application" later in this chapter.

The Relationship between Graphics and JComponent Properties

As you saw in Table 4-2, some of the properties of a Graphics object, namely color and font, are similar to those of JComponent. In fact, since you get a Graphics object from a JComponent, there is a relationship between these properties. As you already know, the Graphics object passed to a JComponent's paintComponent method has its color set to the foreground color of the JComponent and its font is the font currently selected into the JComponent. If you're familiar with the AWT, you'll recognize this as the normal state when the paint method of an AWT Component is called. The same is true of graphics contexts created from this Graphics object using create, because create just makes an exact copy of the context that it is given.

Core Note

If you're confused by the various methods being described here, you'll find everything much clearer when you've read the section "Component Painting: Swing versus AWT" of this chapter.

You need to be careful, however, when you use `getGraphics` to obtain a Graphics object for a component. If you apply this to a heavyweight AWT Component, you would get back an object initialized with the font and foreground color of the `Component`, exactly as you would get in the `Component` paint method. However, this is not true for `JComponent`. If you call `getGraphics` on a `JComponent`, the color and font in the returned `Graphics` object are not related to those of the `JComponent`.

The code in Listing 4-11 demonstrates how different the properties of a `JComponent` are from those of the `Graphics` object returned by `getGraphics`.

Listing 4-11　Properties of a graphics context returned by getGraphics

```
package JFCBook.Chapter4;

import com.sun.java.swing.*;
import java.awt.*;

public class GetGraphics {
  public static void main(String[] args) {
    JFrame f = new JFrame("Graphics Context");
    Component cp = f.getContentPane();
    cp.setBackground(Color.black);
    cp.setForeground(Color.yellow);
    JLabel l = new JLabel("Hello");
    l.setOpaque(true);
    f.getContentPane().add(l);
    System.out.println("Label graphics: " + l.getGraphics());
    System.out.println("Label font is: " + l.getFont());
    l.setForeground(Color.yellow);
    l.setBackground(Color.green);
    f.setSize(300, 300);
    f.setVisible(true);

    System.out.println("\nFrame made visible");
    System.out.println("Label graphics: " + l.getGraphics());
    System.out.println("Label font is: " + l.getFont());

    System.out.println("\nChange label font...");
    l.setFont(new Font("SansSerif", Font.BOLD, 16));
    Graphics g = l.getGraphics();
    System.out.println("Label graphics color is " + g.getColor());
    System.out.println("Label graphics font is " + g.getFont());
    System.out.println("Label font is " + l.getFont());
```

continued

```
     System.out.println("Label foreground color is " + l.getForeground());
     System.out.println("Label background color is " + l.getBackground());

     System.out.println("\nChange graphics color to red...");
     g.setColor(Color.red);
     System.out.println("Label graphics color is " + g.getColor());
     System.out.println("Label foreground: " + l.getForeground());
     System.out.println("label background: " + l.getBackground());

     System.out.println("\nChange label background to green, foreground to blue...");
     l.setBackground(Color.green);
     l.setForeground(Color.blue);
     System.out.println("Label foreground color is " + l.getForeground());
     System.out.println("Label background color is " + l.getBackground());
     System.out.println("Label graphics color is " + g.getColor());
     Graphics g1 = l.getGraphics();
     System.out.println("Second label graphics: color is " + g1.getColor());

     g.dispose();
     g1.dispose();
   }
}
```

This program produces the following output (on a Windows platform):

```
Label graphics: null
Label font is: com.sun.java.swing.plaf.FontUIResource[family=Dialog,name=Dialog,
style=plain,size=12]

Frame made visible
Label graphics: com.sun.java.swing.SwingGraphics[font=java.awt.Font[fami-
ly=Dialog,name=Dialog,style=
plain,size=12],color=java.awt.Color[r=0,g=0,b=0]]
Label font is:
com.sun.java.swing.plaf.FontUIResource[family=Dialog,name=Dialog,style=plain,
size=12]

Change label font...
Label graphics color is java.awt.Color[r=0,g=0,b=0]
Label graphics font is java.awt.Font[family=Dialog,name=Dialog,style=plain,size=12]
Label font is java.awt.Font[family=SansSerif,name=SansSerif,style=bold,size=16]
Label foreground color is java.awt.Color[r=255,g=255,b=0]
Label background color is java.awt.Color[r=0,g=255,b=0]

Change graphics color to red...
Label graphics color is java.awt.Color[r=255,g=0,b=0]
```

```
Label foreground: java.awt.Color[r=255,g=255,b=0]
label background: java.awt.Color[r=0,g=255,b=0]

Change label background to green, foreground to blue...
Label foreground color is java.awt.Color[r=0,g=0,b=255]
Label background color is java.awt.Color[r=0,g=255,b=0]
Label graphics color is java.awt.Color[r=255,g=0,b=0]
Second label graphics: color is java.awt.Color[r=0,g=0,b=0]
```

This code creates a frame and a `JLabel` and places the `JLabel` on the frame. Before the frame is made visible, `getGraphics` is called to get a graphics context; as noted above, this returns `null`. The label's font is also obtained, for comparison with the one that will be returned from the `Graphics` object later.

Core Note

You may be surprised that the label's font turns out not to be an instance of `java.awt.Font`, but of `com.sun.java.swing.plaf.FontUIResource`. This class also represents a font—you'll see in Chapter 13 exactly why the label doesn't return a `java.awt.Font` object.

When the frame is made visible, `getGraphics` is called again and this time it returns a meaningful `Graphics` object. You can see that the font in the `Graphics` object is the same as you get by invoking `getFont` on the label. You'll soon see, however, that this is just coincidence. The next step is to change the label's font by calling `setFont` on it. The font is changed to 16-point, bold, SansSerif and a new `Graphics` object obtained using `getGraphics`. Now, the font obtained from the label and the graphics object are printed, along with the color in the font and the foreground and background colors of the label. You can see that there is no relationship at all between the fonts and colors: The `Graphics` object still has the original font and has black as the selected color, whereas the label itself has a green background and a yellow foreground.

Core Note

Actually, the state of the `Graphics` object is not as random as you might think. Because all `JComponent`s are lightweight, they don't strictly have a graphics context of their own—instead, they share the context of the heavyweight container that they are contained in. When `getGraphics` is called for a `JComponent`, it returns the `Graphics` object of its heavyweight container, with that container's font and color selected. In this case, then, the `JLabel` is getting the `Graphics` object of the `JFrame`, which is a heavyweight subclass of `Frame`. You should not, however, build applications that rely on this knowledge!

This example also illustrates the less surprising fact that changing the properties of a Graphics object doesn't affect the JComponent that it was derived from. This is true whether the Graphics object is returned by getGraphics or create, or is passed as the argument to the paintComponent method. To show this, the selected color of the Graphics object is changed to red and the label's foreground and background are fetched again. As you can see, they are unchanged by this operation. Further changes to the label's foreground and background are also not reflected in the Graphics object, or in a new Graphics object obtained after the color changes have been made.

The moral of this example is that you can't rely on the color and font when you obtain a Graphics object using getGraphics—always explicitly select the color and font that you want.

Component Painting: Swing Versus AWT

If you're familiar with how components are painted in the JDK 1.1 AWT, you will probably have been surprised that the examples in this section have been overriding a method called paintComponent instead of the more usual paint method that is used with the AWT. In fact, component drawing is slightly different for Swing components. To end this section, let's summarize how AWT components are painted and compare that with what happens in Swing.

Painting AWT Components

There are two methods that are involved in drawing AWT components:

```
public void update(Graphics g);
public void paint(Graphics g);
```

Although it can be overridden, the update method usually just fills the component with its background color and then calls paint to draw whatever should be in the foreground. The update method is called when a component's size is changed, because this operation doesn't necessarily cause the host windowing system to clear its background automatically. If, however, it can be determined that the background has already been cleared, update is skipped and paint is called directly. This will be the case if the application window is iconified and reopened, or if it is obscured and then exposed.

Both methods are passed a Graphics object initialized with the component's font and its *foreground* color selected.

Painting Swing JComponents

JComponents are, of course, just Components with some extra software layered on top. The update and paint methods of the JComponent class are called just as they are for Component, but JComponent overrides the Component implementations of these methods to provide the same functionality in a different way that is more suited to Swing components that can have associated borders and may be drawn differently when different look-and-feel classes are installed.

Figure 4-10 shows the logical flow of control through the JComponent painting mechanism.

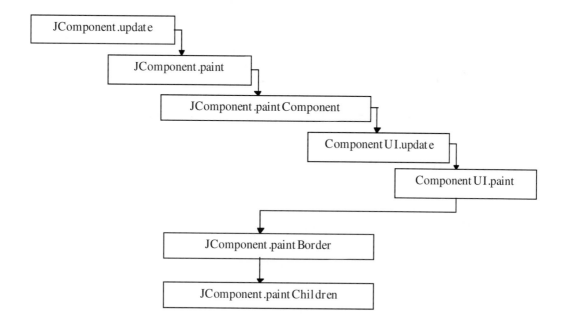

Figure 4-10   JComponent drawing logic.

First, the update method of Component is overridden so that it just calls paint directly, without clearing the background. This is necessary, of course, because Swing components can be transparent. As a result, they must fill their own backgrounds during the execution of the paint method if this is required.

The JComponent paint method is rather complex, because it implements double-buffering if required and it also tries to optimize the drawing process by only redrawing those parts of the component that need to be redrawn. Cutting through all the details, paint essentially does the following:

- If graphics debugging is enabled and the component has a UI class associated with it, it creates a copy of the Graphics object it is passed and uses it for the rest of the paint method. This object is an instance of the SwingGraphics class, which wraps a Graphics object and provides its own handling of the graphics clip.

- Selects the component's foreground color and font into the Graphics object
- Calls the paintComponent method
- Calls the paintBorder method
- Calls the paintChildren method if the component has children.

The second step is necessary because, as noted, the Graphics object passed into the paint method actually belongs to the JComponent's heavyweight container, so it will not have the JComponent's color and font selected into it. This step makes it possible for the paintComponent method to behave like the AWT Component's paint method, as all of our examples in this chapter have.

In the simple case of JPanel, the JComponent paintComponent method is overridden—all it does is fill the panel with its background color if it is opaque. If it is transparent, paintComponent does nothing. However, most JComponents need to do something other than fill their backgrounds, but what exactly they draw depends on the look-and-feel installed. As you know from Chapter 1, "Introduction to the Java Foundation Classes," almost all of the Swing components have an associated pluggable look-and-feel class associated with them that will actually draw the component. All of these classes are derived from the Swing class com.sun.java.swing.plaf.ComponentUI, which you saw in Chapter 1. The JComponent paintComponent method arranges for the UI class to paint the component by calling the ComponentUI update method. By default, this fills the component with its background color (if it is opaque), leaving the background color selected in the Graphics object, then calls the UI class's paint method to do the rest of the drawing.

Since UI classes are often going to be third-party classes that implement custom look-and-feels, paintComponent protects itself from changes that the update or paint methods might make to the Graphics object by passing a freshly-made copy of it to the update method, which will actually implement the UI class's painting logic.

After the component has been painted, paintBorder is called to add the border around the outside, if there is one and finally the paintChildren method is called to paint any lightweight children that this component might have. Remember that JComponent is derived from Container, so any JComponent can, theoretically, have child components associated with it.

Note that the same Graphics object is passed to paintComponent, paintBorder and paintChildren. This means that if you override paintComponent or implement your own border (as will be done later in this chapter), you must not make any persistent changes to the Graphics object. If you need to change the selected color, the font, the graphics origin or the clip, you must either restore them before your method returns, or, probably simpler, create a copy of the Graphics object using create and use that instead. If you fail to do this, the border or any children that there might be will probably not be drawn properly.

A Graphics Application

You've learned quite a lot about the Graphics class in this chapter. Now, you're going to put what you know into practice and develop an application that allows you to use the mouse to draw graphics objects onto a drawing area. This is the first real application that you've seen in this book, so quite a lot of time is going to be spent looking in great detail at how it works and why certain design decisions were made. As well as using much of what has been covered in the preceding sections, the opportunity will also be taken to introduce some important new features along the way. Let's first look at what the completed application looks like after it's been used for a while (see Figure 4-11).

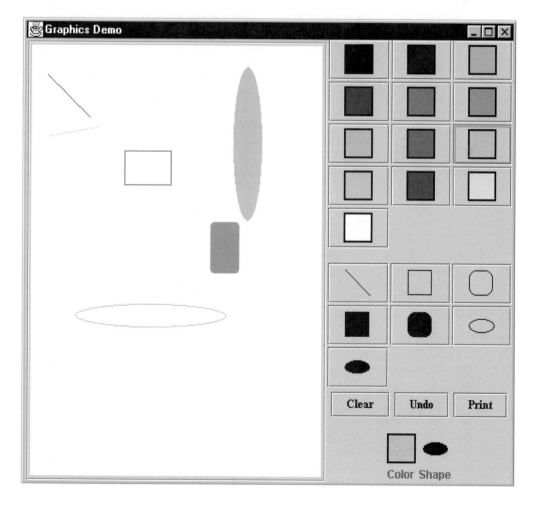

Figure 4-11   A graphics application.

As you can see, the left-hand side of the application's frame is the drawing area, or *canvas* as we'll call it here. Here, you can draw any of the shapes available on the buttons that reside on the right and you can choose from the colors shown on the buttons at the top right. If you want to run this application for yourself, just type the command:

```
java JFCBook.Chapter4.GraphicsDemo
```

When the program starts, the shapes and colors that are initially selected are shown at the bottom right; if you place the mouse over the scribbling area then press and hold down any button and drag; you'll find that the cursor changes to a hand shape and a thin black line follows it. When you're happy with your line, just release the mouse. If you want to draw a different shape, select it from the selection available in the right-hand panel by pressing on the appropriate button and a copy of the shape will appear at the bottom right where the line used to be. When you're drawing any of the shapes, you move the mouse to where you want to start and press to establish the starting point. As you move the mouse, an impression of what the shape would look like appears and becomes permanent only when you release the mouse button. You'll find that the color of the shape changes when you've let go of the mouse button. For reasons that will be discussed when looking at the implementation, the outline shape you draw when you're moving the mouse is not in the color selected from the buttons at the top right.

If you get bored with your drawing, you can start again by pressing the Clear button. If you want to remove the last shape you drew, press the Undo button. You can use the Undo button repeatedly, each time removing the most recently drawn shape, until you've cleared the entire canvas. Last, but by no means least, if you're pleased with your artwork, you can use the Print button to send it to the printer if you've got one. Notice that these buttons are only enabled when they could be useful: if the drawing area is empty, they are all disabled.

Now that you've seen what the application does, let's have a look at its component parts and what they are individually expected to do. The first thing to look at is how the user interface is constructed.

The User Interface

The application is hosted in a JFrame, laid on top of which is a JPanel that covers its entire surface. You could, perhaps, manage without this panel, but it's there for a very good reason: The JPanel class implements graphics double-buffering. This is a useful thing, because there are a lot of components displayed and that can lead to unsightly flashing effects as the screen is redrawn when you resize the window or expose it when it has been obscured. If you use a JPanel with buffering enabled, the components all draw themselves into a copy of the panel held off-screen and the result is then copied to the screen in one fast operation, which avoids the flashing.

On top of this, the drawing area is implemented as a custom component that has the lightweight JPanel as its base, while the controls all reside on a home-grown subclass of JPanel (GraphicsDemoPane) that is itself overlaid with another four JPanels: one for the color buttons, a second for the shape selection buttons, a third for the Clear, Undo and Print buttons and a fourth for the two status indicators

Why so many panels? Couldn't everything just be placed onto one, saving some memory? You could implement the control section as a single panel and manage the whole thing with a GridBagLayout layout manager, but it would be exceedingly complex to do so. Once you'd got it working, the odds are that you would want to add another control or two. After doing this a few times, you would quickly regret your decision to simplify things by removing the odd panel. As a general rule, it is probably better to aim for a larger number of simpler items than a smaller number of complex ones. The odds are that you'll need to modify the smaller pieces (by adding a new shape or a new color) more often than the larger pieces (for example adding a new set of buttons), so you start with something simpler to change by adopting this approach.

As well as this, of course, there is a natural affinity between all of the color buttons and all of the shape buttons that suggests that they should be handled as separate groups. Furthermore, if you resized the application, you would want the buttons within each group to stay closely bunched together and the space between the groups to increase if it had to—this gives a much better effect than allowing large gaps to appear between the buttons, because gaps tend to dispel the impression that there is a logical grouping of controls. Keeping related buttons on the same panel makes it much simpler to ensure that they stay close together—all you have to do is make sure that the panel doesn't get larger.

The drawing canvas is, in fact, slightly more involved than it might at first appear. Although it looks like a white JPanel, you'll notice that it has a grooved border on a gray background (or at least it's gray with the default desktop settings under Windows—your setup may be different). The Swing components support the addition of various borders as we shall see in Chapter 8, "Creating Custom Dialogs," and we could just add a standard border to a JPanel to create this effect. However, since this chapter is all about how to draw, the opportunity has been taken to show you how to implement your own border. Even though JPanel has the ability to host a border, the drawing area will be based not directly on JPanel, but on a derived class called BorderedCanvas. The reason for this will become clear later.

But that isn't all there is to say about the innocuous looking white drawing area, because it also contains all the logic to turn mouse movements into the drawing of shapes and it handles the printing as well. Of course, not all of this functionality will be required in all of the applications where you might use a canvas with a border, so in true object-oriented style, the drawing and printing logic is added not to BorderedCanvas but to a derived class called GraphicsBorderedCanvas. This class will be examined in great detail below.

If all of the drawing functionality is in the canvas, then all of the control is in the panels! In other words, while the canvas can handle its own drawing by responding directly to the mouse, it won't know what shape to draw or what color to draw it in, without input from the buttons on GraphicsDemoPane. How should this communication be implemented? At the lowest level, when a button is pressed, it needs to call an appropriate routine exported by the drawing canvas that causes it to change its drawing color or to start using a different drawing shape. All that is necessary is to define a set of such routines, implement them in the `GraphicsBorderedCanvas`, ensuring that they are public, and add code to `GraphicsDemoPane` to call them as necessary. In fact, that is exactly what is done, but this idea has been taken one step further: The methods needed have been grouped together as a Java interface. If the necessary methods had simply been added to the public interface of `GraphicsBorderedCanvas`, there would have been code like this somewhere in the implementation of `GraphicsDemoPane`:

```
GraphicsBorderedCanvas c;       // Initialized elsewhere
Color newColor;                 // New color to draw in

c.setColor(newColor);           // Change drawing color
```

As you can see, with this code the `GraphicsDemoPane` could only be used to drive a `GraphicsBorderedCanvas`, because of the explicit dependency on it in the first line of this extract. But suppose, in a few months' time, you decide to redesign the user interface of the drawing canvas while retaining the same programmatic interface. You could just throw away our existing `GraphicsBorderedCanvas` class and implement another one with the same name, or use a different name and modify the above lines of code in `GraphicsDemoPane`, but there is a better way. If the necessary control functions were encapsulated in an interface, you can have `GraphicsBorderedCanvas` implement that interface and then reference the interface instead of a specific class. In our case, the interface is called `GraphicOps`, so the extract shown above would be replaced with this:

```
GraphicOps o;                   // Initialized elsewhere
Color newColor;                 // New color to draw in

o.setColor(newColor);           // Change drawing color
```

Since `GraphicsBorderedCanvas` implements `GraphicOps`, you can legally write this:

```
o = new GraphicsBorderedCanvas(.....);
```

and, in a few months, you could write a second application in which you reuse exactly the same `GraphicsDemoPane` implementation and write this in the application's main method:

```
o = new GraphicsBorderedCanvasVersion2(.....);
```

If you wanted to be a bit more clever, you could even allow the user to run one copy of the application and choose which flavor of drawing canvas to use, based on a command line argument or a configuration file. The correct component would be loaded by creating the required implementation of GraphicOps in the application's main method. Neither the canvas nor the button panel need know that there is an element of plug-and-play going on here. Putting this another way, the button panel needs something to send commands to when its buttons are pressed. It doesn't care what exactly it is sending commands to, as long as the recipient is prepared to receive the commands. This is exactly the scenario in which you should automatically think of using an interface, because all that matters is that the target object should implement certain named methods that respond to the commands being sent.

GraphicOps is not the only interface between these two parts of the application. The canvas reacts to commands from the button panel, but the button panel also needs to have certain information about the state of the canvas, because the Clear, Undo and Print buttons should only be enabled when it is not empty. Since shapes appear on the canvas in response to mouse events delivered to the canvas, the button panel can't know when shapes appear and, even if it could, it would also have to keep track of how many there are so that it could disable the buttons when the Undo button had been pressed enough times to clear the canvas. Ideally, you don't really want to make the button panel that knowledgeable about what is happening on the canvas, so you need to arrange for the canvas to tell the button panel when something of interest has happened. This could be done by inventing another interface that would allow the canvas to call the button panel when the number of shapes on its surface changes, but there is a better solution that uses a general mechanism provided by JComponent.

Properties and Property Change Events

So far, care has been taken to develop the drawing canvas in such a way that its implementation details are not visible from outside, so that the implementation can be changed or a different component with the same interface substituted later. If you think of the drawing canvas as a self-contained component, then it is clear that the number of shapes that have been drawn should be regarded as a property of the canvas that a user of the component can obtain by using a public method provided by the canvas. But in this case, the canvas is also required to inform its users when the value of this property changes—in other words, it needs to generate an event.

JComponent provides a set of methods that allows you to create a property and allows users to register for notification when the value of the property changes. Here are their definitions:

```
public void addPropertyChangeListener(PropertyChangeListener l);

public void removePropertyChangeListener(PropertyChangeListener l);

public void addVetoableChangeListener(VetoableChangeListener l);

public void removeVetoableChangeListener(VetoableChangeListener l);
```

As you can see, when you register a listener you don't say which properties you are interested in: You are notified of changes to all of the component's properties. If you don't want to receive further notifications, you cancel your registration. The listener interfaces each have one method:

```
public interface PropertyChangeListener extends
java.util.EventListener {
   void propertyChange(PropertyChangeEvent evt);
}

public interface VetoableChangeListener extends
java.util.EventListener {
   void vetoableChange(PropertyChangeEvent evt)
        throws PropertyVetoException;
}
```

All of the information about the changed property is encapsulated in the PropertyChangeEvent object. Each event contains the name of the property concerned, and the values before and after the change. You can extract these values using the following accessor methods:

```
public String getPropertyName();

public Object getNewValue();

public Object getOldValue();
```

There are two types of property—bound and constrained. The difference between these two is that a component may change a bound property at any time and simply notify its listeners that the value has changed, whereas a constrained property may only be changed if all of the listeners agree to it. To receive notification of a bound property change, you use the addPropertyChangeListener method; the addVetoableChangeListener method is used to receive notification of changes to constrained properties. A listener may veto a change to a constrained property by throwing a PropertyVetoException.

To return to the problem at hand, what is needed is to create a property that contains the number of shapes on the canvas and to implement the canvas so that it notifies registered listeners when a new shape is drawn or when one or all of the shapes is removed. You'll see the details of how this is done when you look at the implementation of the canvas. Because the property change listeners shouldn't be able to stop us drawing or removing shapes, this property will be bound but not constrained.

Creating the User Interface

You can see how the user interface is created by examining the program's main method and the constructor of its GraphicsDemo object, which implements the application's top-level window (see Listing 4-12).

Listing 4-12   The shell of the graphics demo application

```java
package JFCBook.Chapter4;

import com.sun.java.swing.*;
import com.sun.java.swing.border.*;
import java.awt.*;
import java.awt.event.*;

public class GraphicsDemo extends JFrame {
  public GraphicsDemo(String title) {
    super(title);
    Container cp = this.getContentPane();
    JPanel p = new JPanel(true);
    cp.setBackground(UIManager.getColor("control"));
    p.setLayout(new BorderLayout());
    cp.add(p);

    // Create the canvas in which the
    // drawing will be done.
    GraphicsBorderedCanvas c = new GraphicsBorderedCanvas();

    // Create the border and associate it with the canvas.
    Border bd = new EdgedBorder(UIManager.getColor("control"));
    c.setBackground(Color.white);
    c.setBorder(bd);

    p.add(c, "Center");

    // Create the right-hand panel that
    // holds the color buttons.
    GraphicsDemoPane gp = new GraphicsDemoPane();
    p.add(gp, "East");

    // Connect panel to canvas so that
    // it can enable/disable buttons.
    c.addPropertyChangeListener(gp);

    // Connect the canvas to the panel
    // so that it can action button presses.
    gp.setDrawingArea(c);

    // Select the initial color and shape
    // from the button panel.
    gp.selectTools();
  }

  public static void main(String[] args) {
```

continued

```
        GraphicsDemo f = new GraphicsDemo("Graphics Demo");
        f.setSize(550, 500);
        f.addWindowListener(new WindowAdapter() {
          public void windowClosing(WindowEvent evt) {
            System.exit(0);
          }
        });
        f.setVisible(true);
      }
  }
```

The main method just creates the top-level window, arranges for the application to exit when the close button is pressed and makes it visible. The real initialization takes place in the constructor, which is extremely simple. First, it creates the JPanel that performs the double buffering and arranges for it to cover the frame by placing it in the center of the frame. This works because the frame's layout manager is BorderLayout, which gives all of the frame's space to the center component if there are no others. Next, the drawing canvas (including its border) and the button panel are created and placed on the buffering panel. As these two objects are created, their constructors are executed and they create their own user interface components, as you'll see when you look at their implementations.

Another BorderLayout is used to manage the main panel, placing the drawing canvas in the center and the buttons in the east, so that the canvas gets as much of the available space as possible and the button panel gets only what it needs. Furthermore, if the user expanded the window, all of the extra space would go to the canvas, so that the buttons stay in their original configuration.

Having created and placed the user interface components, the next step is to make the logical connection between the canvas and the button panel. This is achieved with only two lines of code:

```
    // Connect panel to canvas so that
    // it can enable/disable buttons
    c.addPropertyChangeListener(gp);

    // Connect the canvas to the panel
    // so that it can action button presses
    gp.setDrawingArea(c);
```

The first line registers the button panel to receive property change events from the canvas; as you'll see, the GraphicsDemoPane class that contains the buttons implements the PropertyChangeListener interface, so it can be registered using the canvas' addPropertyChangeListener method, which is inherited from JComponent. Similarly, the GraphicsBorderedCanvas implements the GraphicOps interface and can be supplied as an argument to the button panel's setDrawingArea method. With these two steps completed, the application is fully operational. The last step is to select the initial drawing shape and color, which is achieved by calling the button panel's `selectTools` method, which will be discussed later. What should strike you about this code is that it knows remarkably little about what each part of the user interface does—its only job is to create the two pieces and connect them to each other. If you had alternative implementations of these pieces in different classes, it would be very simple to modify this code to switch over and use them—one line of code would change for each piece that you want to substitute: It couldn't be much simpler.

The Drawing Canvas

The drawing canvas is where the real action in this program takes place. In principle, its job is very easy—all it has to do is monitor the mouse and draw shapes in the selected color. In fact, though, there are a few problems to solve to make this work smoothly. Let's look at what we have to do to make this component behave as the user expects.

First, you have to make the drawing canvas look right. As you can see from the screen shot of the application (Figure 4-11), the canvas consists of a white drawing area surrounded by a grooved border on a colored background. The first problem is to write the code that creates this appearance. Secondly, how do you go about actually drawing the graphics shapes on the canvas? The obvious solution is to start drawing a shape when the user presses a mouse button and to place it in its final position when the button is released. In between, to give the appearance that the shape is adjusting itself to the way that the user moves the mouse, you need to keep removing and redrawing the shape so that one point remains where the user first pressed the mouse button, while the other follows the mouse pointer itself.

This might sound easy, but what happens if the shape crosses over a shape that is already there? When you remove the shape to redraw it as the user continues to move the mouse, you have to somehow replace the pixels of the existing shape that have been erased. Not only that but, as you saw earlier in this chapter, just drawing on the canvas is not good enough. If the user iconifies the window or obscures part of it, you lose what you have done—how can it be recreated when the window is reopened or exposed again?

As you have seen before, the code to draw on a component is usually placed in its `paintComponent` method, which is called whenever it is necessary to show the component's contents. Therefore, it is necessary to remember enough about what the user has done to create the drawing to be able to reconstruct it from scratch inside the `paintComponent` method. On the other hand, if `paintComponent` were called each time the user moved the mouse, it would end up doing far too much work and, worse, the performance would be very bad—the user would probably notice that the shape being drawn was very slow to follow the mouse pointer. So, as well as being able to reconstruct the entire picture if necessary, it is a good idea to render directly onto the canvas as the mouse moves.

The problems of drawing the outline of the canvas and managing the shapes drawn inside it are actually quite separate; as noted earlier, this is recognized in the implementation by creating a subclass of JPanel called BorderedCanvas that is responsible for drawing the border and subclassing that to create GraphicsBorderedCanvas, which is responsible for all of the logic to do with drawing the shapes. These two components are discussed separately later in this chapter.

The Button Panel

The three sets of buttons and the state indicators on the button panel are managed on a set of four panels that sit within the main button panel. Each of these panels needs to stay at its preferred size, so that the buttons on each subpanel stay close to each other as the top-level frame is expanded by the user. The button panel is implemented by the GraphicsDemoPane class, which is derived from JPanel. When this panel is created, it is placed in the East position of the BorderLayout manager, which ensures that its horizontal size will not increase no matter how big the window gets.

What about the vertical size? In the East position, the panel will grow with the window. Since each sub-panel is required to stay the same size, something else is needed to take up the extra space. This can be achieved by adding a transparent JPanel between the Clear/Undo/Print buttons and the status indicators. Having done this, we make sure that all of the extra space goes to this canvas and none to the four panels by managing the GraphicsDemoPane with a GridBagLayout layout manager and constraining everything such that only the JPanel can expand to occupy extra space.

The top two sets of buttons are arranged in grids with three buttons in each row. This sort of layout is naturally managed by the GridLayout layout manager, which makes sure that the buttons are arranged uniformly so that they line up nicely and arranges for them to be all of the same size. This gives a better visual impression than the ragged arrangement that would result if each button were allowed to be just large enough to surround the text or icon that it contains. The same applies to the panel that contains the Undo, Clear and Print buttons.

The fourth panel, containing the symbols and text that indicate the current drawing shape and color, is implemented using two JLabels, with text and an icon on each. Here, you could choose to make the labels expand to fill all of the space available or have them stay together in the center of the area that they occupy. If you wanted the former effect, you would use a GridLayout manager, while a FlowLayout would produce the latter. The implementation shown here uses the FlowLayout, so these two components will always appear close together.

As well as laying out the buttons, it is necessary to provide the code that responds to the buttons when they are pressed and the icons that appear on their surfaces also need to be drawn. You've already seen that you can decorate buttons and labels with images, but the icons that are used in this example program are not image files—instead, they are custom icons that are rendered directly, rather than by using the ImageIcon class. You'll see how this is done later in this chapter.

The layout of the button panel is handled in the constructor of the GraphicsDemoPane class. The complete implementation of this class is shown in Listing 4-13.

Listing 4-13   The graphics demo's button panel

```java
package JFCBook.Chapter4;

import com.sun.java.swing.*;
import java.awt.*;
import java.awt.event.*;

public class GraphicsDemoPane extends JPanel
        implements PropertyChangeListener {
  public GraphicsDemoPane() {
    super(true);        // Double buffer

    this.setLayout(new GridBagLayout());
    GridBagConstraints c = new GridBagConstraints();
    c.gridx = 0;
    c.gridy = 0;
    c.gridwidth = 1;
    c.gridheight = 1;
    c.weightx = 0.0;
    c.weighty = 0.0;
    c.fill = GridBagConstraints.NONE;
    c.anchor = GridBagConstraints.CENTER;

    // Create and add the button panel
    JPanel colorPanel = new JPanel();
    colorPanel.setLayout(new GridLayout(0, 3, 2, 2));
    colorButtons = new JButton[buttonColors.length];
    for (int i = 0; i < buttonColors.length; i++) {
      JButton button = new JButton(new
                        ColorFillIcon(buttonColors[i]));
      colorButtons[i] = button;
      colorPanel.add(button);
      button.putClientProperty(DRAW_COLOR, buttonColors[i]);

      button.addActionListener(new ActionListener() {
        public void actionPerformed(ActionEvent evt) {
          JButton b = (JButton)evt.getSource();
```

continued

```
          Color color = (Color)b.getClientProperty(DRAW_COLOR);
          Icon g = b.getIcon();
          colorLabel.setIcon(g);
          graphicOps.setColor(color);
        }
    });
  }

  this.add(colorPanel, c);

  // Create and add the shape selection panel
  JPanel shapePanel = new JPanel();
  shapePanel.setLayout(new GridLayout(0, 3, 2, 2));
  shapeButtons = new JButton[shapeList.length];
  for (int i = 0; i < shapeList.length; i++) {
    JButton button = new JButton(new
GraphicShapeIcon(shapeList[i]));
    shapeButtons[i] = button;
    shapePanel.add(button);
    button.putClientProperty(DRAW_SHAPE, new Integer(shapeList[i]));

    button.addActionListener(new ActionListener() {
      public void actionPerformed(ActionEvent evt) {
        JButton b = (JButton)evt.getSource();
        int shape =
          ((Integer)b.getClientProperty(DRAW_SHAPE)).intValue();
        shapeLabel.setIcon(b.getIcon());
        graphicOps.setShape(shape);
      }
    });
  }

  c.gridy++;
  c.insets = new Insets(16, 0, 0, 0);
  this.add(shapePanel, c);

  // Add a dummy component that takes
  // all the spare space in the
  // right-hand panel
  c.gridy++;
  c.weighty = 1.0;
  c.insets = new Insets(0, 0, 0, 0);
  this.add(new JPanel(), c);

  // Add the "Clear" and "Undo" buttons
  c.gridy++;
```

```
c.weighty = 0.0;
JPanel buttonPanel = new JPanel();
clearButton = new JButton("Clear");
undoButton = new JButton("Undo");
printButton = new JButton("Print");
Font font = new Font("Serif", Font.BOLD, 12);
clearButton.setFont(font);
undoButton.setFont(font);
printButton.setFont(font);
buttonPanel.add(clearButton);
buttonPanel.add(undoButton);
buttonPanel.add(printButton);
this.add(buttonPanel, c);

clearButton.addActionListener(new ActionListener() {
  public void actionPerformed(ActionEvent evt) {
    graphicOps.clearCanvas();
  }
});

undoButton.addActionListener(new ActionListener() {
  public void actionPerformed(ActionEvent evt) {
    graphicOps.removeLast();
  }
});

printButton.addActionListener(new ActionListener() {
  public void actionPerformed(ActionEvent evt) {
    graphicOps.printCanvas();
  }
});

// Place labels with the currently selected
// color and shapes underneath the color panel
c.gridy++;
c.weighty = 0.0;
c.weightx = 1.0;
c.fill = GridBagConstraints.BOTH;
c.insets = new Insets(8, 0, 0, 0);
JPanel lowerPanel = new JPanel();
this.add(lowerPanel, c);
lowerPanel.setLayout(new FlowLayout(FlowLayout.CENTER, 4, 4));

colorLabel.setVerticalTextPosition(SwingConstants.BOTTOM);
colorLabel.setHorizontalTextPosition(SwingConstants.CENTER);
colorLabel.setHorizontalAlignment(SwingConstants.CENTER);
colorLabel.setVerticalAlignment(SwingConstants.BOTTOM);
```

continued

```
    lowerPanel.add(colorLabel);

    shapeLabel.setVerticalTextPosition(SwingConstants.BOTTOM);
    shapeLabel.setHorizontalTextPosition(SwingConstants.CENTER);
    shapeLabel.setHorizontalAlignment(SwingConstants.CENTER);
    shapeLabel.setVerticalAlignment(SwingConstants.BOTTOM);
    lowerPanel.add(shapeLabel);

    // Disable clear/undo/print buttons
    clearButton.setEnabled(false);
    undoButton.setEnabled(false);
    printButton.setEnabled(false);
  }

  // Associate drawing area
  public void setDrawingArea(GraphicOps graphicOps) {
    this.graphicOps = graphicOps;
  }

  // Select initial color and shape
  public void selectTools() {
    colorButtons[0].doClick();    // Draw with black
    shapeButtons[0].doClick();    // Draw a line
  }

  // PropertyChangeListener Interface
  public void propertyChange(PropertyChangeEvent evt) {
    if (evt.getPropertyName().equals(GraphicOps.SHAPE_PROPERTY)) {
      int count = ((Integer)evt.getNewValue()).intValue();
      boolean state = (count > 0);

      clearButton.setEnabled(state);
      undoButton.setEnabled(state);
      printButton.setEnabled(state);
    }
  }

  // Labels showing the current color and current shape
  protected JLabel colorLabel = new JLabel("Color");
  protected JLabel shapeLabel = new JLabel("Shape");

  // Clear, undo and print buttons
  protected JButton clearButton;
  protected JButton undoButton;
  protected JButton printButton;

  // Coloring buttons
```

```
private static Color[] buttonColors = {
        Color.black, Color.blue,
        Color.cyan, Color.darkGray,
        Color.gray, Color.green,
        Color.lightGray, Color.magenta,
        Color.orange, Color.pink,
        Color.red, Color.yellow,
        Color.white };
private JButton[] colorButtons;

// Shape buttons
private static int[] shapeList = {
        GraphicOps.DRAWN_LINE,
        GraphicOps.DRAWN_RECT,
        GraphicOps.DRAWN_ROUND_RECT,
        GraphicOps.FILLED_RECT,
        GraphicOps.FILLED_ROUND_RECT,
        GraphicOps.DRAWN_OVAL,
        GraphicOps.FILLED_OVAL };
private JButton[] shapeButtons;

// Connection to drawing area
private GraphicOps graphicOps;

// Property names
private static final String DRAW_COLOR = "Draw_color";
private static final String DRAW_SHAPE = "Draw_shape";
}
```

The complete panel is managed by a GridBagLayout. If you read through the code, you'll see that each of the four subpanels (colorPanel, shapePanel, buttonPanel, and lowerPanel) are constrained so that they don't grow vertically, by setting the weighty member of their GridBagConstraints object to 0.0. The other component in this panel, the JPanel, has a weighty value of 1.0. Because it is the only component with a nonzero weighty, it gets all of the extra vertical space when the GraphicsDemoPane grows.

Most of this code should be familiar from the ground that has been covered in previous chapters. Each of the color and shape buttons is created with an icon on its surface, for example:

```
JButton button = new JButton(new ColorFillIcon(buttonColors[i]));
```

The ColorFillIcon is a custom icon that draws a colored square with a black border; the color of the square is taken from the constructor argument. Similarly, the shape buttons use another custom icon:

```
JButton button = new JButton(new GraphicShapeIcon(shapeList[i]));
```

You'll see how these icons are implemented later. After creating each of the color selection buttons, the following line of code is executed:

```
button.putClientProperty(DRAW_COLOR, buttonColors[i]);
```

and something almost identical happens when the shape selection buttons are created:

```
button.putClientProperty(DRAW_SHAPE, new
Integer(shapeList[i]));
```

The constants DRAW_COLOR and DRAW_SHAPE are actually strings, defined as follows:

```
private static final String DRAW_COLOR = "Draw_color";
private static final String DRAW_SHAPE = "Draw_shape";
```

What is going on here? When any of these buttons is pressed, two things need to happen—the status indicator on the bottom of the button panel needs to change to show the new shape or color that will be used for drawing and the drawing canvas also needs to be told which color or shape it is to draw with. We find out about the button click when the event handler for the ActionEvent that the button generates is entered. To do what needs to be done, it is necessary to work out which button has been pressed and, from that information, get the icon that was drawn on its surface and the color associated with the button.

As you know, the ActionEvent contains a reference to the object that caused the event. Given that this allows us to find the original button, our job will be made much easier if it is possible to find both the icon and the color directly from the button itself. Getting the icon is easy, because JButton has a getIcon method that it inherits from its superclass AbstractButton. It is, however, more difficult to get the color that the icon uses to paint its surface. It isn't the color of the button itself, so calling getForeground or getBackground on the JButton is of no use. The icon, however, knows which color it uses and must store it internally. One approach would be to add a method to the ColorFillIcon class that would return the color; if this method were called getColor, there would then be code like this in the event handler:

```
JButton b = (JButton)evt.getSource();
Icon g = b.getIcon();
Color c = ((ColorFillIcon)g).getColor();
```

While this would work, it means that a ColorFillIcon (or a derived class) must be used to draw the color on the button. This prevents you from substituting a more interesting icon that doesn't implement the getColor method at later date. You have seen this issue before with the connection between the drawing canvas and the button panel. As a general rule, it is not a good idea to restrict your future options: whenever you can retain flexibility without incurring unacceptable cost, it is usually better to do so. Ideally we would want to be able use any class that implements `Icon` to provide the decoration for our button.

Fortunately, there is a better solution available that makes use of another facility provided by `JComponent`, which allows you to associate arbitrary, user-defined properties with a component by defining an arbitrary key and then using the `JComponent putClientProperty` method to store the associated value under that key. You can retrieve the value later by invoking the `getClientProperty` method with the same key. Here are the definitions of these methods:

```
public void putClientProperty(Object key, Object value);

public Object getClientProperty(Object key);
```

In this case, you need to store the color associated with the button, so all you have to do is decide on a suitable key and supply the `Color` as the `value` argument. The key can, of course, be anything you like, as long as it is an instance of a class. For clarity, the actual implementation uses the string "Draw_color" as the key. Since this string will be used both when the color value is stored and when it is retrieved, the private constant `DRAW_COLOR` is defined to avoid having to use the actual string more than once. Now, when the button is created, the associated color is stored as a `Color` object in the property table of the `JButton`:

```
button.putClientProperty(DRAW_COLOR, buttonColors[i]);
```

In the event handler, the `getClientProperty` method is given the same property name to retrieve the value. Here is the implementation of the event handler for each of the color buttons

```
public void actionPerformed(ActionEvent evt) {
   JButton b = (JButton)evt.getSource();

   Color color = (Color)b.getClientProperty(DRAW_COLOR);
   Icon g = b.getIcon();
   colorLabel.setIcon(g);
   graphicOps.setColor(color);
}
```

As noted earlier, getting the icon is much simpler. Having obtained the icon, you then simply call the `setIcon` method of the color indicator label at the bottom of the screen to change the picture that it shows. Note that this method is given exactly the same instance of the icon that is being used for the button itself. This is quite alright because, as you'll see when you look at its implementation, our icon, like all icons, doesn't know which component it is associated with—one icon can be used to render the same drawing on as many objects as you like.

The last thing that the event handler does is to invoke the `setColor` method to pass the color to the drawing canvas. This method is part of the `GraphicOps` interface that was mentioned earlier. You'll see shortly what this interface looks like.

The event handler for the shape buttons is almost identical. In this case, it is necessary to retrieve the icon and work out which shape the user wants to select. You can, of course, use the same mechanism to store and retrieve the shape as long as it is represented as an object, but how exactly should the shape be represented? Since whatever it is that represents the shape is going to be passed to the drawing canvas via the GraphicOps interface, the most obvious thing to do is to try to use whatever it is that we defined for that interface. Here is how GraphicOps is defined:

```java
public interface GraphicOps {
    public void setColor(Color color);  // Set drawing color
    public void setShape(int shape);     // Set drawing shape
    public void clearCanvas();           // Clear drawing area
    public void removeLast();            // Remove last item
    public void printCanvas();           // Print everything
    public int getShapeCount();          // Get number of shapes

    // Constants
    public static final int DRAWN_LINE        = 0;
    public static final int DRAWN_RECT        = 1;
    public static final int DRAWN_ROUND_RECT  = 2;
    public static final int FILLED_RECT       = 3;
    public static final int FILLED_ROUND_RECT = 4;
    public static final int DRAWN_OVAL        = 5;
    public static final int FILLED_OVAL       = 6;

    // Property for count of graphic shapes
    public static final String SHAPE_PROPERTY = "shape_property";
}
```

The first part of this definition declares the methods that can be used to cause the drawing canvas to take some action. You have already seen that the setColor method is used by the event handler for the color buttons. The shape buttons need to call the setShape method, which requires an integer argument from the list of constants defined by the interface to specify which shape is to be drawn. Unfortunately, the primitive type int is not an object, so it can't be passed directly to putClientProperty; instead, an instance of the wrapper class Integer is created and used instead, as the following code extract from the constructor illustrates:

```java
JButton button = new JButton(new
GraphicShapeIcon(shapeList[i]));
shapeButtons[i] = button;
shapePanel.add(button);
button.putClientProperty(DRAW_SHAPE, new
                                Integer(shapeList[i]));
```

In this case, the string "Draw_shape" is used as the key to store the shape identifier. The event handler for the shape buttons simply has to extract the stored value and unwrap it from the Integer object to obtain an int again:

```
public void actionPerformed(ActionEvent evt) {
   JButton b = (JButton)evt.getSource();
   int shape =
((Integer)b.getClientProperty(DRAW_SHAPE)).intValue();
   shapeLabel.setIcon(b.getIcon());
   graphicOps.setShape(shape);
}
```

The rest of the constructor should be very easily understood. Notice that the event handlers associated with the Clear, Undo and Print buttons just call the appropriate methods in the GraphicOps interface to get the canvas (or whatever class has been substituted for it) to perform the required action—they don't take any further part in the processing themselves. You may be surprised to see, for example, that the Clear button doesn't disable itself and the other two buttons. This would be a logical thing to do because, when it has invoked the clearCanvas method, there won't be any more shapes on the canvas. It is, of course, not necessary to do this because, as you'll see when you look at the implementation of the canvas in more detail, clearing the canvas causes a PropertyChangeEvent to be generated. Since the button panel implements this interface and is registered to be informed of these events (as you saw in the description of the GraphicsDemo class), any appropriate actions can be handled when this event is processed.

You'll notice that when the methods in the GraphicOps interface are called, they are invoked against the field graphicOps. This field contains a reference to the class that implements the GraphicOps interface—in our case, this is, of course, the GraphicsBorderedCanvas. It was initialized when the constructor of the GraphicsDemo class called our setDrawingArea method, which is implemented as follows:

```
// Associate drawing area
public void setDrawingArea(GraphicOps graphicOps) {
   this.graphicOps = graphicOps;
}

// Connection to drawing area
private GraphicOps graphicOps;
```

When the constructor is complete, the button panel and all of its subpanels are initialized with all of their buttons and labels in place and event handlers attached. Only one element is missing—the two status indicators at the bottom of the panel that show which shape is to be drawn and which color to use have been created, but they don't have an associated icon, because the constructor only associates a text label for each of them:

```
// Labels showing the current color and current shape
protected JLabel colorLabel = new JLabel("Color");
protected JLabel shapeLabel = new JLabel("Shape");
```

How are the correct icons for these labels set? The choice of initial shape and color is arbitrary; the implementation chooses black as the color and starts by drawing a straight line. As it happens, these correspond to the first color button and the first shape button. Since references to all of these buttons were stored as they were created, the icons could be obtained directly like this:

```
colorLabel.setIcon(colorButtons[0].getIcon());
shapeLabel.setIcon(shapeButtons[0].getIcon());
```

The problem with this is not that it wouldn't work, but rather that it only does part of the job. As well as setting the label icons, it is also necessary to tell the canvas which color and shape to use, by calling the `setColor` and `setShape` methods of the `GraphicOps` interface. To do this, of course, you need the color and shape associated with these buttons. You could use the values that were used to initialize the buttons in the first place, in which case you would write the following:

```
colorLabel.setIcon(colorButtons[0].getIcon());
shapeLabel.setIcon(shapeButtons[0].getIcon());
graphicOps.setColor(buttonColors[0]);
graphicOps.setShape(shapeList[0]);
```

Since this code uses the `graphicOps` field, it can't be placed in the constructor, since `graphicOps` is not set until the `setDrawingArea` method is called. There is, however, a more elegant method that doesn't rely on this code knowing how the buttons were initialized. What we are trying to do is to set the labels to show the current color and shape selected for the drawing area and inform the drawing area of our initial choice. Exactly the same work also needs to be done if the user were to press the buttons, so why not logically press the buttons ourselves? This can be done by using the `doClick` method of `AbstractButton`; when you invoke this method, it generates the `ActionEvent` that would have been fired had the user actually pressed the button. As you already know, when this event is received, the button event handlers that were discussed earlier do the job of setting the label icons and invoking the appropriate methods in the `GraphicOps` interface. This reduces our implementation to the following two lines, which are placed in the `selectTools` method:

```
public void selectTools() {
   colorButtons[0].doClick();   // Draw with black
   shapeButtons[0].doClick();   // Draw a line
}
```

As with the more direct mechanism, this method can't be called from the constructor, because the event handlers will try to call the drawing canvas's `setColor` and `setShape` methods through `graphicOps`, which isn't yet initialized. Instead, this routine is invoked from the `GraphicsDemo` class after the canvas and button panel have been connected by calling `setDrawingArea`.

The last method in this class is the one that receives the `PropertyChangeEvent` from the drawing canvas. When you register to receive these events, you get notified of all changes to any property that the component has. As you saw earlier, the `PropertyChangeEvent` has methods that allow the listener to get the name of the property whose value has changed and the new and old values. The property name forms part of the interface between the canvas and its listener, so it was declared as the constant `SHAPE_PROPERTY` in the `GraphicOps` interface. The value of this property is the number of shapes on the canvas at the completion of the operation that generated the event; since a property has to be an object, it is encoded as an `Integer`. Here is the code that processes this event:

```
// PropertyChangeListener Interface
public void propertyChange(PropertyChangeEvent evt) {
   if (evt.getPropertyName().equals(GraphicOps.SHAPE_PROPERTY)) {
      int count = ((Integer)evt.getNewValue()).intValue();
      boolean state = (count > 0);

      clearButton.setEnabled(state);
      undoButton.setEnabled(state);
      printButton.setEnabled(state);
   }
}
```

First, the `getPropertyName` method is used to extract the name of the property that generated the event. As you'll see, `GraphicsBorderedCanvas` only generates a property change event when the number of shapes on its surface changes, but its superclasses (in particular `JComponent` itself) generate events of their own, so it is important to make sure that the event that has been received is of interest, by ensuring that it is a change to `SHAPE_PROPERTY`. Having done this, the new value of the property can be extracted using `getNewValue` and converted from `Integer` to an `int`. Since all that has to be done with this value is to enable the Clear, Undo and Print buttons if there are any shapes on the canvas and disable them if there are not, it is only necessary to check whether the shape count is positive and act accordingly.

Implementing a Custom Border

In order to physically separate the drawing canvas from the button panel, it is wrapped with a border. All of the Swing components can be rendered with a border simply by choosing one from the standard set that will be shown in Chapter 8 and calling the component's `setBorder` method. This section shows you how to implement a custom border that will be used in the application's user interface.

Every border implements the `java.swing.border.Border` interface, which has only three methods:

```
public Insets getBorderInsets(Component comp);

public void paintBorder(Component comp, Graphics g, int x,
                        int y, int width, int height);

public boolean isBorderOpaque();
```

If a component's `setBorder` method has been called, the component will need to allocate space for the border around its outer edge and draw the border when it paints itself. The `getBorderInsets` method allows the border to tell its host component how much screen space it will need; it is up to the component to supply this space. When the component's `paint` method is called, it calls the border's `paintBorder` method, passing a reference to itself and the `Graphics` object that gives access to its screen area. Passing a reference to the component makes it possible to implement borders that act differently depending on the component that they are drawing on. For example, the border might make use of the component's foreground and background color. You can also implement borders that can be shared among many components; all of the standard Swing borders are implemented in this way, as you'll see in Chapter 8.

The `x, y, width` and `height` arguments describe the outside of the rectangle on the component's surface within which the border must render itself. In most cases, the border will be drawn on the outer edge of the component, so *x* and *y* will both be zero and the width and height values will be the width and height of the component itself. Finally, the `isBorderOpaque` method indicates whether the border paints the area of the component's background that it covers.

That's all there is to the `Border` interface. A real border needs a bit more than that, however. At the very least, it needs to know what color it should use to draw itself. How this is achieved depends on the border implementation: you could decide to use a fixed color, use the look-and-feel dependent color `UIManager.getColor("control")` that is the usual background for components (other than windows), use the color associated with the component on which the border is being drawn, or pass the drawing color or colors to the border object's constructor. The last of these methods is the one that will be used for the border that you'll see in this section. However, to allow this border to be shared among many components, if the color supplied to the constructor is `null`, the actual color used when filling the background will be taken from the background color of the component on which the border is being drawn.

A close-up view of the border that will be implemented in this section is shown in Figure 4-12. This border provides a small colored edge to its host component, the color of which is passed as an argument to our border object's constructor or obtained from the component, onto which it draws a rectangular groove. To create the grooved effect, two rectangles will be drawn, one pixel wide and offset from each other by one pixel horizontally and vertically. These rectangles will be drawn in contrasting colors, one light and one dark, to give the effect of a shadow on one side of the groove. You can see this clearly in the enlarged view shown in Figure 4-12.

Figure 4-12 An enlarged view of the border.

Given the color of the solid edge, suitable colors for the groove rectangles can be obtained by applying the darker and brighter methods of the Color class to it:

```
lightShadow = edgeColor.brighter();
darkShadow = edgeColor.darker();
```

While this works well enough as a default, the border will also provide a method that allows specific shadow colors to be supplied. Building in flexibility like this costs very little, enhances the usability of your class, and increases the likelihood of it being reused in the future.

Listing 4-14 shows the implementation of our border, in a class called EdgedBorder.

Listing 4-14   The graphics demo's custom border

```
package JFCBook.Chapter4;

import com.sun.java.swing.*;
import com.sun.java.swing.border.*;
import java.awt.*;

public class EdgedBorder implements Border {
  public EdgedBorder(Color edgeColor) {
    this.edgeColor = edgeColor;
  }

  // Set explicit shadow colors
```

continued

```java
  public void setShadowColors(Color lightShadow, Color
darkShadow) {
    this.lightShadow = lightShadow;
    this.darkShadow = darkShadow;
  }

  // Border interface
  public Insets getBorderInsets(Component comp) {
    return new Insets(BORDER_PAD, BORDER_PAD, BORDER_PAD, BOR-
DER_PAD);
  }

  public void paintBorder(Component comp, Graphics g, int x,
int y, int width,
                    int height) {
    Color saveColor = g.getColor();
    int totalBorder = 2 * BORDER_PAD;

  // Use the component color if a null color has been supplied
    if (edgeColor == null) {
      edgeColor = comp.getBackground();
      lightShadow = null;
      darkShadow = null;
    }

    // Determine the border colors if
    // they have not been supplied
    if (lightShadow == null) {
      lightShadow = edgeColor.brighter();
      darkShadow = edgeColor.darker();
    }

    // Draw the colored edge on which the shadow resides
    g.setColor(edgeColor);
    g.fillRect(x, y, width, BORDER_PAD);
    g.fillRect(x, y + height - BORDER_PAD, width, BORDER_PAD);
    g.fillRect(x, y + BORDER_PAD, BORDER_PAD, height - totalBorder);
    g.fillRect(x + width - BORDER_PAD, y + BORDER_PAD,
          BORDER_PAD, height - totalBorder);

    // Draw the shadow
    g.setColor(lightShadow);
    g.drawRect(x + OUTER_PAD + 1, y + OUTER_PAD + 1,
          width - 2 * OUTER_PAD - 1,
          height - 2 * OUTER_PAD - 1);
    g.setColor(darkShadow);
    g.drawRect(x + OUTER_PAD, y + OUTER_PAD,
          width - 2 * OUTER_PAD - 1,
```

```
            height - 2 * OUTER_PAD - 1);

   // Restore graphics context color
   g.setColor(saveColor);

}

public boolean isBorderOpaque() {
   return true;
}

private Color edgeColor;
private Color lightShadow;
private Color darkShadow;

// Constants
private static final int OUTER_PAD = 2;
private static final int BORDER_SIZE = 2;
private static final int INNER_PAD = 2;
private static final int BORDER_PAD =
      OUTER_PAD + BORDER_SIZE + INNER_PAD;
}
```

As you might expect, it is very simple. A constructor is provided to set the color of the solid edge, along with a method to override the default choice of groove colors with those preferred by the programmer and the three methods required by the Border interface. The border is of fixed size: It is always 6 pixels wide and has a 2-pixel wide groove in the middle of it. The private constants OUTER_PAD, BOR-DER_SIZE and INNER_PAD determine the widths of the three parts of the border and BORDER_PAD, being the sum of the three, is the border's total width. Because the border is of constant size, the implementation of the getBorderInsets method is very simple. Likewise, the isBorderOpaque method simply returns true.

To paint the border, the paintBorder method first draws the edge in the selected color by dividing the border space allocated to it into two vertical and two horizontal rectangles. Although in practice the border will usually be drawn on the outside of the host component, this simplifying assumption cannot be made in the general case, so the code that fills the rectangles uses the starting coordinates of the border's assigned area as well as the width and height to determine the size and position of each rectangle.

Core Note

To see a case in which the border would not be drawn on the outside edge of the component, look ahead to the description of the CompoundBorder *class in Chapter 8, "Creating Custom Dialogs."*

Finally, the drawRect method is used to draw two one-pixel wide rectangles in the middle of the border edge, using the colors that were selected (or were given) for the groove. Note that the Graphics object passed by the host component is used to draw the border. In order to avoid assumptions about which color is selected in this Graphics object, the initial color is saved before our color is installed and restored when drawing is complete, in case the component assumes that the selected color is the same on return as it was on entry to paintBorder.

The Bordered Canvas and the Graphics Clip

The main drawing area consists of a JPanel with a border and some added drawing logic. As noted earlier, the code that will handle mouse events and actually draw new shapes is contained in a class called GraphicsBorderedCanvas, which is derived from a direct subclass of JPanel called BorderedCanvas. As you know, JPanel itself can directly host a border of any sort, so why create an intermediate class instead of deriving GraphicsBorderedCanvas directly from JPanel?

The reason that BorderedCanvas exists is to provide one small piece of functionality that could be placed in GraphicsBorderedCanvas, but is better implemented elsewhere so that it can be re-used in conjunction with an improved GraphicsBorderedCanvas without having to copy code. To see what this piece of functionality is, you need to look forward a little to the implementation of the drawing code in GraphicsBorderedCanvas.

Suppose that the application is running and the user starts drawing a line. As long as the line stays within the canvas, all is well. But suppose the user moves the mouse outside the canvas. This will cause the line that the user is drawing to cross the border. Since the border is actually a part of the JPanel that the GraphicsBorderedCanvas is derived from, the space occupied by the border is as much a part of the component as the blank drawing area in the middle and nothing will prevent the drawing code in GraphicsBorderedCanvas drawing a line straight across it.

The Graphics Clip

Fortunately, there is a simple solution to this problem. One of the attributes of the graphics context is the *clip*, which constrains the area within which graphics operations are effective. If you get a graphics context by calling getGraphics, the clip covers the whole of the component (or image), so you can use drawing primitives to change any part of the source of the graphics context. You can, however, set a different clip using one of the following methods of the Graphics class:

```
public void clipRect(int x, int y, int width, int height);

public void setClip(int x, int y, int width, int height);

public void setClip(Shape clip);
```

A graphics context always has a current clip. If you use `clipRect`, the current clip is set to the intersection of the rectangle described by its arguments and the current clip. Suppose that you invoke `getGraphics` on a component that is 100 pixels wide and 200 pixels high. Initially, the `Graphics` object that is returned has a clip that covers all of this area. If you now do this:

```
g.clipRect(10, 10, 50, 60);
```

then the clip is reduced to the rectangle whose vertices are at (10, 10), (59, 10), (59, 69), (10, 69), which is the rectangle specified in the `clipRect` call. Calling `clipRect` again can only make the clip smaller, not larger, since the resulting clip is the intersection of the current clip with the requested one. Executing this line:

```
g.clipRect(0, 0, 60, 70);
```

leaves the clip unchanged, despite that fact that it requests the inclusion of an area to the left of and above the current clip. To make the clip larger, you must use the `setClip` method. The first form shown, like `clipRect`, supplies a rectangular area that becomes the new clip, whatever the current clip might be. The second form takes a `Shape` argument. `Shape` is an interface that provides a method that returns the bounding box of the class that implements it. Using this form, you can create a nonrectangular clip:

```
int[] xPoints = { 10, 50, 100, 70, 30};
int[] yPoints = { 60, 20, 70, 90, 80);
Polygon p = new Polygon(xPoints, yPoints, xPoints.length);
JPanel c = new JPanel();
c.setSize(200. 200);
Graphics g = c.getGraphics();
g.setClip(p); // Polygon implements Shape
```

Once you set a clip, graphics operations that fall outside the range of the clip are ignored. If a graphics operation falls partly inside and partly outside the clip, only those parts covered by the clip are actually performed—the areas outside the clip are unaffected. This can save the time required to draw the pixels outside the clip and it can also stop unwanted changes to the graphics context.

The BorderedCanvas Class

How does the graphics clip help with the problem of protecting the border of the drawing area? Quite simply, the easiest way to stop the user drawing lines and shapes into the border area is to set a graphics clip that excludes the border before the drawing code (which is in the mouse event handler of `GraphicsBorderedCanvas`, as you'll see later) turns mouse movements into shapes. If this is done, then the fact that the user moves the mouse out of the main area of the drawing canvas won't matter— the drawing code can ignore the fact that it is attempting to draw into the border, because the graphics clip will prevent the parts of the operation that cover the border being actually performed.

The problem is, though, where should the clip be applied? The most obvious solution is to put it in the mouse handling code at the point that a shape is being drawn. Naturally, this would work. The drawing code has access to the component it is drawing on, so it can get hold of the size of the border and compute the appropriate clip. However, if this were made a generic function of a class that supports a border and an enclosed, safe, drawing area, the same class could be used again for something other than the GraphicsBorderedCanvas used in this application. To make this possible, an intermediate class, BorderedCanvas, is implemented, as shown in Listing 4-15.

Listing 4-15   The bordered canvas

```
package JFCBook.Chapter4;

import com.sun.java.swing.*;
import com.sun.java.swing.border.*;
import java.awt.*;

public class BorderedCanvas extends JPanel {
   // Clip the graphics context to exclude the border
   protected void excludeBorder(Graphics g, Border border, int width, int height) {
      Rectangle r = AbstractBorder.getInteriorRectangle(this, border,
                        0, 0, width, height);
      g.clipRect(r.x, r.y, r.width, r.height);
   }

   // Override getGraphics() to clip for derived class
   public Graphics getGraphics() {
      Dimension d = getSize();

      Graphics g = super.getGraphics();

      Border border = getBorder();
      if (border != null) {
         excludeBorder(g, border, d.width, d.height);
      }

      return g;
   }
}
```

As you can see, there really is very little to this class. As you would expect, it is derived from JPanel, so it carries with it the ability to host a border. There is no drawing code, because it doesn't need to add to the behavior of JPanel, which will fill the component with its background color whenever needed as well as inheriting the code to draw the border from `JComponent`. The only useful thing this class does is to override the `Component getGraphics` method.

When new shapes are being drawn on the canvas, the mouse event handler of `GraphicsBorderedCanvas` will need a `Graphics` object that gives access to the drawing area. If this code were being called from inside the `paintComponent` method, it would already have a `Graphics` object. However, in an event handler, the only way to get a `Graphics` object for a component is to call `getGraphics`. Because `GraphicsBorderedCanvas` is derived from `BorderedCanvas`, when it calls `getGraphics`, it will actually invoke the `BorderedCanvas` version of that method, which adjusts the clip to exclude the component's border area by calling its internal `excludeBorder` method.

The `excludeBorder` method needs to get the size of the canvas and the size of the border and subtract the border dimensions from those of the canvas to determine the size of the rectangular area in the middle of the canvas on which it is safe to draw. The dimensions of the border could be obtained by calling its `getBorderInsets` method, but it isn't necessary to do this work ourselves because the `AbstractBorder` class provides a convenience method to perform this calculation for us.

`AbstractBorder` is the base class from which all of the standard Swing borders are derived. It supplies the static `getInteriorRectangle` method that accepts as arguments a component, a `Border`, the x and y positions at which the border will be rendered on the component and the width and height of the outside of the border and returns a `Rectangle` object describing the area inside the border. As you can see from Listing 4-15, the `excludeBorder` method uses the `Rectangle` returned by `getInteriorRectangle` to set the clip as required.

The Drawing Area and Its Contents

The last major part of this application is the `GraphicsBorderedCanvas`, which is derived from the `BorderedCanvas` class that has just been described. Before starting the implementation, let's look at what it needs to do:

1. It must allow a suitable border to be attached and it must render that border when it is on the screen.

2. When the user presses the left mouse button, it must start drawing the currently selected shape. As the user drags the mouse, it must draw the outline of the shape as it would appear if the mouse button were released.

3. When the mouse button is released, the shape should become a permanent part of the canvas.

4. It must be possible to change the drawing color and the current shape.

5. It must be possible to undo the last drawing operation, clear the canvas and print the content of the canvas.

Drawing the Border

Drawing the border is the simplest issue to address, because it is almost free. When the canvas is created, the GraphicsDemo class associates a border with it, as follows:

```
// Create the canvas in which the
// drawing will be done.
GraphicsBorderedCanvas c = new GraphicsBorderedCanvas();

// Create the border and associate it with the canvas
Border bd = new EdgedBorder(UIManager.getColor("control"));
c.setBackground(Color.white);
c.setBorder(bd);
```

After creating the GraphicsBorderedCanvas, a suitable border is created and the setBorder method, which is inherited from JComponent, is used to connect the border to the canvas. The border's color is passed to its constructor; since the colors to be used for the shadow are not explicitly supplied, they are defaulted to, for example, light and dark gray on Windows platforms with the default desktop settings. Finally, the canvas background is set to white. The setBackground method is inherited from Component and this color is actually used to fill the background in the paintComponent method of JPanel, which will be called from the paintComponent method of GraphicsBorderedCanvas.

Drawing in Response to the Mouse

Items 2 and 3 are related, so they will be dealt with together. The basic problems to be solved are how to use the mouse to trigger the proper drawing of shapes, how to make the shape expand or contract to follow the mouse, and how to make the shape appear permanently on the canvas when the mouse button is released. Before looking at the details of handling the mouse events, it is necessary to decide how to represent the shapes that have been drawn and the one currently being created.

The simplest thing to do would be to catch the initial mouse press and remember where the mouse is at this point; then when the user drags the mouse, draw the appropriate shape between the current mouse position and the starting point. Suppose the user is drawing a line. When the mouse is pressed, its location would be stored. When the mouse moves a short distance, a line would be drawn between the start point and the new mouse location. But what happens when the mouse moves again? According to this algorithm, another line would be drawn from the start point to the mouse cursor. But, if these three points are not in a straight line, there would now be two lines and, the more the user moves the mouse, the more lines there would be. Obviously, the last line drawn must be removed before drawing another one. How can this be done when the Graphics class doesn't have an unDrawLine method? Perhaps the line can be removed by drawing it again in the background color. This would work, except that if there are already other shapes on the screen and the line crosses any of them, they will be damaged whenever the mouse is moved and sweeping a line across a shape could completely wipe it out!

The problem can be solved by changing the `Graphics` *paint mode*. By default, when you draw lines or fill shapes, the new pixels just overwrite the old ones, so you have no memory of what was there before. If you want to remove your drawing, you need to have remembered what you overwrote, but the `Graphics` drawing methods don't do this for you. However, if you switch to *exclusive-or* drawing mode, you get a reversible drawing operation without having to remember what was underneath your shape. To set this mode, you use the `setXORMode` method, which is defined as follows:

```
public void setXORMode(Color alt);
```

When you have set this mode, you are effectively drawing with a pen of a different color, generated by combining the color that you started with and the *alternation color* that you supply as an argument to `setXORMode`. Usually, when you draw in XOR mode, you set the current color to the one you want to draw with (which will be referred to as the drawing color) and specify the background color as the alternate color. Now, when you draw on top of the background, the color used is the drawing color. This is the same as if you used the default drawing mode. However, if you draw on top of pixels that are already in the drawing color, they are changed to the alternation color—in other words, they take on the background color. If you draw on a pixel of any other color, you get a pixel of a different (unspecified) color but, if you draw on top of it again, it goes back to its original color. Let's clarify this with an example in which the drawing color is black and the background is white.

Table 4-3 shows what happens when you draw twice on the same pixels, when the current color is black, and the background and the alternate color are both white. The alternate color and the drawing color are set like this:

```
g.setXORMode(Color.white);
g.setColor(Color.black);
```

Table 4-3   Using XOR Graphics Mode

Existing Color	Drawing color	After First Drawing Operation	After Second Drawing Operation
White	Black	Black	White
Black	Black	White	Black
Red	Black	(Unpredictable)	Red
Green	Black	(Unpredictable)	Green

As you can see, when you draw on the background with a black pen, you get black. When you repeat the process, you get white again, so the background reappears. In other words, drawing the same shape twice on the background first makes it appear and then removes it. Similarly, drawing with black on black produces a white result first time, then returns to black; again, performing the same operation twice is the same as not performing it at all. If you draw on any other color, you get an undefined color after the first operation and, after the same operation, the original color returns. Therefore, by using XOR mode you can draw a shape and then remove it by just drawing it again.

If you find this hard to remember, let's look at it in a slightly different way. Let's call the alternate color *alt* and the drawing color *draw*. When you set XOR mode, you effectively create a new pen whose color is given by the expression

```
alt ^ draw
```

and you exclusive-OR this color with that of the color of the pixels that you draw over; in other words, the resulting color for any pixel that you draw over is

```
pixel ^ alt ^ draw
```

If you repeat the operation, the resulting color will be

```
pixel ^ (alt ^ draw) ^ (alt ^ draw)
```

Since the result of exclusive-ORing anything with itself is zero, the last two bracketed terms vanish, leaving us with *pixel* – that is, the original color. This explains why drawing twice returns the original state. If you draw once over a pixel that is the same as the alternate color (which is the background color in our case), the color you end up with is

```
alt ^ alt ^ draw
```

which is, of course, just *draw*; that is, drawing over the background once produces pixels of the drawing color. Drawing on pixels of the drawing color results in

```
draw ^ alt ^ draw
```

and again the two *draw* terms cancel out, leaving *alt*, which is the background color. Finally, drawing on any color *other*, gives

```
other ^ alt ^ draw
```

It isn't easy to see what this color represents because I haven't told you how the exclusive-or operation is performed. If you assume that it is done by exclusive-ORing the pixel values, you would still need to know how colors are encoded as pixels. If the default RGB model is used, you would get one result, but you would get a different result with a different color model. Because of this and because the API specification doesn't describe how the exclusive-or operation is done, it is necessary to regard the result of drawing over colors other than the alternate color and the drawing color as undefined, with the caveat that repeating the operation restores the original color.

That clears up the mechanics of drawing each shape and making the shape follow the mouse as it moves without destroying what is already there. As you have seen before, though, just drawing shapes as you go along is not enough. At any time, the user can close or obscure the window, which causes some or all of its content to be lost. When the window is reopened or made visible again, you will have to repaint all of the shapes that the user has drawn so far. In order to do this, the necessary information about each shape must be stored so that they can all be redrawn later. This is what has to be saved for each shape:

- Its color.
- Its start and end positions.
- What the shape is (line, rectangle etc.).
- Whether it is drawn or filled.

Obviously, storing this information requires a new class. There will be one instance of this class for each shape that the user draws and they will be stored in the order in which the user created them, so that shapes that obscure each other will always be drawn in the same way. It's easy to see how the color and the start and end positions should be stored, but what about the shape and fill? You could define a data member for these and use the constants defined in the GraphicOps interface to describe the shape, but there is a more natural way to do this that you've probably seen before. This method involves defining an abstract base class, that will be called DrawnShape, which contains the data members and an abstract method to do the drawing. There will then be a derived class for each real shape that will implement its own drawing method appropriately. Listing 4-16 shows how the base class is defined.

Listing 4-16   A basic class for drawing shapes

```
package JFCBook.Chapter4;

import java.awt.*;

public abstract class DrawnShape {
    public DrawnShape(Color color, int x, int y, String text) {
        this.color = color;
        this.x1 = x;
        this.y1 = y;
        this.x2 = x;
        this.y2 = y;
        this.text = text;
    }
```

continued

```
public abstract void draw(Graphics g);

public void changeEnd(int x, int y) {
   x2 = x;
   y2 = y;
}

public void makePermanent() {
   perm = true;
}

public boolean isPermanent() {
   return perm;
}

public Rectangle getBoundingBox() {
   rect.width = x2 > x1 ? x2 - x1 + 1: x1 - x2 + 1;
   rect.height = y2 > y1 ? y2 - y1 + 1: y1 - y2 + 1;
   rect.x = x1 < x2 ? x1 : x2;
   rect.y = y1 < y2 ? y1 : y2;

   return rect;
}

// Get the text for the shape
public String getText() {
   return text;
}

protected Color color;// Pen color
protected int x1;  // Start...
protected int y1;  // ... point
protected int x2;  // End...
protected int y2;  // ... point
protected boolean perm; // Permanent or not
protected String text;// Description
protected Rectangle rect = new Rectangle();
}
```

Let's look first at the fields of this class. The color field holds the color in which
this shape is drawn, while $x1, x2, y1$ and $y2$ hold the coordinates of the two points that
define the shape. If this shape is a line, these are the coordinates of its two ends. All
of the other shapes that can be drawn are defined in terms of their bounding rectangles; in these cases, $(x1, y1)$ is the point at which the left mouse button was pressed
to start the definition of the shape and $(x2, y2)$ is the point at which it was released.

The perm field records whether the shape is permanent or not. While the shape is being drawn, it is considered temporary, so this field is initially set to false. A shape becomes permanent when the user releases the left mouse button. The state of this field determines the way in which the shape is drawn, as you'll see later. The text field is not used by our simple application—it was added in anticipation of future enhancements. The idea is that you can associate a string with each shape that you can use to describe it in some interaction with the user. For example, when the user places the mouse over the Undo button on the button panel, you might want to display a message describing what will be undone if the button is pressed. The text field is where you would store this message.

Having seen the fields, the purpose of most of the methods should be obvious. The constructor initializes the object according to its arguments. Notice that you supply only the starting coordinate: The end coordinate is set to the same value, so the shape initially consists of just a single point.

The makePermanent and isPermanent methods set and query the permanent attribute. Since a shape won't become temporary once it has been made permanent, there is no need for a makeTemporary or a setPermanent(boolean state) method.

The last of the methods actually supplied by the base class is getBoundingBox, which returns a Rectangle that exactly bounds the shape. This is used in the GraphicsBorderedCanvas class to redraw only the affected region of the screen when the Undo button is pressed to remove the shape from the canvas. Finally, the changeEnd method changes the $x2$ and $y2$ values; it is called as the user moves the mouse.

The draw method is the one that will actually draw the shape, using the graphics context passed as an argument. The size, position and color of the shape are the current values held in the object. Every shape uses a different Graphics method to do its drawing, so each derived class will have its own implementation of this draw. Here is the derived class that draws a straight line.

```
package JFCBook.Chapter4;

import java.awt.*;

public class DrawnLine extends DrawnShape {
  public DrawnLine(Color color, int x, int y) {
    super(color, x, y, "draw line");
  }

  public void draw(Graphics g) {
    g.setColor(color);
    g.drawLine(x1, y1, x2, y2);
  }
}
```

As you can see, this class inherits most of its functionality from DrawnShape; its constructor is given the drawing color and the starting point and passes these to DrawnShape, along with some descriptive text. All of the derived classes have a constructor that looks like this one. The only method that differs from class to class is draw, which, in this case, selects the drawing color and draws a line between the two endpoints. The coordinates of the endpoints are, of course, held by DrawnShape and are accessible here because they are protected.

All of the other classes have a slightly more complex draw method. Here, for example, is the implementation of FilledRectangle:

```
package JFCBook.Chapter4;

import java.awt.*;

public class FilledRectangle extends DrawnShape {
    public FilledRectangle(Color color, int x, int y) {
        super(color, x, y, "draw filled rectangle");
    }

    public void draw(Graphics g) {
        int width = x2 > x1 ? x2 - x1 : x1 - x2;
        int height = y2 > y1 ? y2 - y1 : y1 - y2;

        g.setColor(color);
        if (perm) {
            g.fillRect(Math.min(x1, x2), Math.min(y1, y2), width, height);
        } else {
            g.drawRect(Math.min(x1, x2), Math.min(y1, y2), width, height);
        }
    }
}
```

The draw method has to be more complex here because all of the drawing methods of Graphics, apart from drawLine, accept a start position and a width and height, the latter two of which must be positive. If the user starts the rectangle at the point (50, 50) and drags the mouse to (100, 100) then releases the left mouse button, it is necessary to draw a rectangle starting at (50, 50) that is 50 pixels in each direction. The width and height values are, naturally, computed by subtracting the starting coordinates from the last ones. Now suppose that the user started at (50, 50) and moved the mouse to (20, 20). Now the end coordinates are less than the starting ones, so you might be tempted to call fillRect with start coordinates (50, 50), width –30 and height –30. Unfortunately, this would not work: fillRect takes a negative width or height as zero, so you would get just a single point.

To draw the rectangle you want in this case, you have to give fillRect the end coordinate and calculate the absolute values of the coordinate differences to get the width and the height. In general, the *x* value given to fillRect must be the smaller of the starting and ending *x* values and similarly for the *y* value.

You'll also notice that sometimes the filled rectangle is drawn by calling drawRect, which only draws the outline. In fact, the complete filled rectangle is only drawn when the shape is permanent, that is, when the user has released the mouse button. This implementation was chosen because drawing the outline is much faster than filling the shape, which produces a much faster response as the user moves the mouse across the screen.

Here is the complete implementation of the canvas's paintComponent method:

```
public void paintComponent(Graphics g) {
    super.paintComponent(g);                // Paint the background

    int len = drawingOps.size();
    for (int i = 0; i < len; i++) {
      DrawnShape d = (DrawnShape)drawingOps.elementAt(i);
      if (d.isPermanent()) {
        g.setPaintMode();
      } else {
        g.setXORMode(getBackground());
      }
      d.draw(g);
    }
}
```

As the user draws each shape, the appropriate subclass of DrawnShape is created to represent it and is added to the Vector drawingOps. This vector holds all of the shapes in the order in which they were drawn, so it is possible to reconstruct the content of the canvas by drawing each shape in the vector starting from the first entry. As you can see, a check is made as to whether the entry is permanent or temporary to set the appropriate drawing mode in the graphics context. Because all of the drawing objects are subclasses of DrawnShape, this code doesn't care exactly how the shape is drawn—it just invokes the object's draw method.

There's one small point that needs to be made in connection with the paintComponent method. You'll remember that the BorderedCanvas class was invented so that shapes that are drawn through the boundary area don't end up corrupting the border by drawing over it and that this problem was solved by returning a Graphics object from the getGraphics method that was clipped to exclude the border. If the user has drawn such a shape, then won't the paintComponent method redraw it? Since the Graphics object that it gets includes the border, doesn't this mean that the shape will be drawn over the border, spoiling the work done by BorderedCanvas?

The analysis of the last paragraph is correct, but it overlooks one small point. As you know, when a component is being drawn, its content is rendered by its paintComponent method and then the border is drawn on top by calling paintBorder. That, of course, is the saving grace—if paintComponent draws into the border area, it won't matter because the border will be redrawn on top of it. However, this wouldn't help at the time that the original shape was being drawn, because it would be too expensive to redraw the border from inside the mouse event handler, so the use of a clipped `Graphics` object in the event handler is the best solution.

Core Note

You could argue that there is still a problem if the border is transparent because the shape would be seen underneath it. In all probability, this is actually correct—you should be able to see through a transparent border to the shapes underneath. In this case, you should also be able to see this part of the shape as it is being drawn, but that arranging for that would be too expensive in performance terms.

Now let's see how the mouse is handled. Initially, there will be no shape being drawn and no mouse buttons pressed. When the user presses the left mouse button over the canvas, the appropriate subclass of `DrawnShape` needs to be created to record the drawing color and the shape's starting position. To catch mouse button events, `GraphicsBorderedCanvas` implements the `MouseListener` interface and, because the mouse is going to be tracked as it moves, it also implements `MouseMotionListener`. The left mouse button is handled in the `mousePressed` method.

```
public void mousePressed(MouseEvent evt) {
   if ((evt.getModifiers() & MouseEvent.BUTTON1_MASK) != 0) {
      currentShape = getNewShape(evt.getX(), evt.getY());
      setCursor(Cursor.getPredefinedCursor(Cursor.HAND_CURSOR));
      drawingOps.addElement(currentShape);
      drawShape();
   }
}
```

The first check verifies that the left mouse button is the one that is pressed; if it is, a new object to represent the shape being drawn is created and then added to the `drawingOps` vector. So that the object can be accessed quickly when handling the mouse motion events, a reference to it is also saved in the instance variable `currentShape`. The cursor is also changed so that it looks like a hand, to make it clear to the user that the mouse press has been registered. Finally, the method `drawShape` is called to put the shape, at the moment just a point, onto the screen. Here is how `drawShape` is implemented:

```
public void drawShape() {
   if (currentShape != null) {
      Graphics g = getGraphics();
      if (currentShape.isPermanent()) {
         g.setPaintMode();
      } else {
         g.setXORMode(getBackground());
```

```
      }
      currentShape.draw(g);
      g.dispose();
   }
}
```

As you can see, this method is very similar to `paintComponent`, except that only the current shape is drawn. Note also that the graphics context is obtained using `getGraphics` which, as you know, is overridden by `BorderedCanvas` to return a context that is clipped to prevent drawing over the border. Finally, after using the graphics context , it is released by invoking `dispose`.

To create an object for the new shape, the `getNewShape` method is used. This method is simply a switch statement that creates an object of the appropriate type; since these objects are all derived from `DrawnShape`, this method returns a reference to an object of that type. This is the only place where the exact nature of the object is known, because Java takes care of dispatching the `draw` call to the `draw` method of the actual object's class.

```
protected DrawnShape getNewShape(int x, int y) {
   switch (drawingShape) {
   case GraphicOps.DRAWN_LINE:
     return new DrawnLine(drawingColor, x, y);
   case GraphicOps.DRAWN_RECT:
     return new DrawnRectangle(drawingColor, x, y);
   case GraphicOps.DRAWN_ROUND_RECT:
     return new DrawnRoundedRectangle(drawingColor, x, y);
   case GraphicOps.FILLED_RECT:
     return new FilledRectangle(drawingColor, x, y);
   case GraphicOps.FILLED_ROUND_RECT:
     return new FilledRoundedRectangle(drawingColor, x, y);
   case GraphicOps.DRAWN_OVAL:
     return new DrawnOval(drawingColor, x, y);
   case GraphicOps.FILLED_OVAL:
     return new FilledOval(drawingColor, x, y);
   default:
     throw new IllegalArgumentException("Illegal shape - " +
             drawingShape);
   }
}
```

Selecting and Changing the Current Drawing Shape and Color

The type of the shape to create is obtained from the instance variable `drawingShape`. This variable is set in the `setShape` method, which is also part of the GraphicOps interface and is called from the button panel when a shape button is pressed. This method and setColor that is called by the button panel when a color button is pressed are shown below:

```
public void setColor(Color color) {
   // Set drawing color
   drawingColor = color;
}

public void setShape(int shape) {
   // Set drawing shape
   drawingShape = shape;
}
```

As the mouse moves, the mouseDragged method is called. Here, the mouse position is extracted and passed to the method changeEnd to set the new ending position of the shape. It is also necessary to remove the old drawing of the shape and paint a new one. Because exclusive-or mode is being used, the old drawing of the shape can be removed by calling drawImage again before invoking changeEnd, so that it draws the same shape and therefore reinstates what was there before. Here is the implementation:

```
public void mouseDragged(MouseEvent evt) {
   if (currentShape != null) {
      drawShape();    // Remove shape
      currentShape.changeEnd(evt.getX(), evt.getY());
      drawShape();    // Redraw it
   }
}
```

Note that mouse events will continue to be received even if the user drags the mouse outside the window. There is no problem with this—the code always draws a shape that ends where the mouse is, but the part that is not on the drawing canvas will be clipped. When the user releases the mouse (inside or outside the window), the mouseReleased method is entered and we make the shape permanent.

```
public void mouseReleased(MouseEvent evt) {
   if ((evt.getModifiers() & MouseEvent.BUTTON1_MASK) != 0) {
      if (currentShape != null) {
         drawShape();    // Remove shape
         currentShape.changeEnd(evt.getX(), evt.getY());
         currentShape.makePermanent();
         drawShape();    // Redraw it

         // Inform listeners
         int count = drawingOps.size();
         firePropertyChange(SHAPE_PROPERTY, new Integer(count - 1),
                  new Integer(count));
```

```
        currentShape = null;

    setCursor(Cursor.getPredefinedCursor(Cursor.DEFAULT_CURSOR));
        }
    }
}
```

As before, the shape is removed from the display first, then the final mouse position is recorded. This time, though, before the shape is redrawn, it is made permanent. This causes the final draw operation to be done in paint mode, so the true color of the shape will appear and, if it is a filled shape, the filled version rather than the outline will appear for the first time. The mouse cursor is also switched back to the default shape.

Since the shape has now become permanent, a property change event has to be sent to registered listeners. The number of shapes now on the canvas is obtained from the vector that stores them and the `firePropertyChange` method of `JComponent` is used to generate the event, sending the number of shapes before and after this one was created as the old and new values of the property. This method is defined as follows:

```
protected void firePropertyChange(String propertyName,
                        Object oldValue, Object newValue);
```

There is a similar method that generates an event for a change to a constrained property, which has a slightly different definition:

```
protected void fireVetoableChange(String propertyName,
                    Object oldValue, Object newValue) throws
                    PropertyVetoException
```

When this latter method is called, the `propertyChange` method of each registered listener is invoked; if any of them vetoes the change by throwing a `PropertyVetoException`, the exception is propagated back to the owner of the property (i.e. the caller of `fireVetoableChange`) so that any changes made in anticipation of the property changing can be reversed. Since the property that we are using is not constrained, `firePropertyChange` is the appropriate method to use. As you know, this event will be received by the button panel and, if the count of shapes is positive, it will cause the Undo, Clear and Print buttons to be enabled.

Undoing Drawing Operations

The `GraphicsBorderedCanvas` has some other minor duties to perform for the button panel. When the Undo button is pressed, the last shape that was drawn must be removed from the canvas. This is handled in the `removeLast` method, which is part of the `GraphicOps` interface:

```
public void removeLast() {
   // Remove last drawn item
   if (drawingOps.isEmpty() == false && currentShape == null)
{
      int count = drawingOps.size();

      DrawnShape d = (DrawnShape)drawingOps.lastElement();
      drawingOps.removeElementAt(count - 1);
      Rectangle r = d.getBoundingBox();
      repaint(r.x, r.y, r.width, r.height);

      // Inform listeners
      firePropertyChange(SHAPE_PROPERTY, new Integer(count),
                 new Integer(count - 1));
   }
}
```

The last permanent shape can easily be found from the Vector class, and it can equally be easily removed from the Vector. Notice that removeLast is ignored if a shape is currently being drawn (currentShape not null) to avoid having to write some more complicated logic; the user could cause this to happen by holding the left mouse button down, the navigating to the Undo button using the Tab key and activating it. If special action were not taken and the last shape in drawingOps were simply removed, there would be an inconsistency because the shape currently being drawn would not be there.

Having removed the shape from our stored list, it must be removed from the canvas. Since this shape was permanent, it was drawn in paint mode, not XOR mode, so it can't be removed by being redrawn. Instead, it is necessary to arrange for the entire canvas to be repainted so that the shape or shapes under the removed one will be redrawn properly. Because there may be a lot of shapes on display, this could be a time-consuming operation, so a short cut is used. Instead of just calling repaint, which would clear the canvas and redraw everything, the getBoundingBox method of DrawnShape that you saw earlier is used. This method returns a Rectangle just large enough to contain the shape; the information in this object is used to invoke a different version of repaint:

```
Rectangle r = d.getBoundingBox();
repaint(r.x, r.y, r.width, r.height);
```

The effect of this is that the paintComponent method will be called with a graphics context whose clip is set to allow drawing only within the bounding box of the removed shape. This saves time because drawing operations outside this area can be ignored and it also reduces flashing of the screen, because only the rectangular area occupied by the removed shape is cleared. Here you can see why it was important to use clipRect in the getGraphics method of BorderedCanvas—we didn't want to render this optimization useless by resetting the clip to cover the entire canvas area.

After removing the shape, a property change event is generated because there is now one fewer shape on the screen. This may cause the Undo, Clear and Print buttons to be disabled. Similar to this is the `clearCanvas` method, which handles the Clear button. Here, a property change event is sent in which the new value is zero, which will cause these buttons to be disabled. This method also removes all of the shapes from the `drawingOps` vector and calls `repaint` to have the canvas repainted. This time, since there will be no shapes to draw, the variant of `repaint` that takes no arguments is used, so that the entire canvas is cleared.

```
public void clearCanvas() {
   // Remove everything from the drawing area
   int count = drawingOps.size();
   drawingOps.removeAllElements();

   // Inform listeners
   firePropertyChange(SHAPE_PROPERTY, new Integer(count),
           new Integer(0));

   repaint();
}
```

That only leaves the Print button, which is handled by the `printCanvas` method. Since you haven't yet seen how to print from Java, the discussion of this method is deferred until later in this chapter.

Implementing Custom Icons

In Chapter 2, "Frames, Labels and Buttons," you saw how to add images to buttons and labels by using the `ImageIcon` class, which loads an image and renders it onto the component. You can, however, draw a graphic on a label or a button using any class that implements the `Icon` interface. In this section, you will see how simple it is to create a custom icon by looking at how the `ColorFillIcon` and `GraphicShapeIcon` classes that are used to decorate the buttons in our graphics application are implemented.

Any class that you want to use as an icon must implement the `java.swing.Icon` interface that you first saw in Chapter 2:

```
public interface Icon {
   public void paintIcon(Component comp, Graphics g, int x, int y);
   public void int getIconWidth();
   public int getIconHeight();
}
```

This interface is very similar to the `Border` interface that you saw earlier in this chapter. The only real difference is that the class implementing `Icon` can fill the entire area allocated to it, not just the border area. The `getIconWidth` and `getIconHeight` methods are invoked by the host component to find out how much space the icon needs to draw itself. When the component is painted, it calls the icon's `paintIcon` method, passing it a component, a graphics context and the coordinates of the top left corner of the area allocated to the icon. The icon is responsible for rendering itself in this area and must not use more space than it asked for. The area reserved for the icon will have been cleared to the component's background color, so it is possible to create a non-rectangular icon by not rendering the entire icon area. The `GraphicShapeIcon` (Listing 4-17) is an example of this.

Listing 4-17   An icon that displays a graphical shape

```java
package JFCBook.Chapter4;

import com.sun.java.swing.*;
import java.awt.*;

public class GraphicShapeIcon implements Icon {
  public GraphicShapeIcon(int shape) {
    this.shape = shape;
  }

  public GraphicShapeIcon(int shape, int fullWidth, int fullHeight) {
    this.shape = shape;
    this.fullWidth = fullWidth;
    this.fullHeight = fullHeight;
    this.width = fullWidth - 2 * PAD;
    this.height = fullHeight - 2 * PAD;
    this.arcSize = fullWidth/2;
  }

  // Icon interface
  public int getIconWidth() {
    return fullWidth;
  }

  public int getIconHeight() {
    return fullHeight;
  }

  public void paintIcon(Component comp, Graphics g, int x, int y) {
    Color c = g.getColor();
    g.translate(x + PAD, y + PAD);
    g.setColor(Color.black);

    switch(shape) {
    case GraphicOps.DRAWN_LINE:
      g.drawLine(0, 0, width - 1, height - 1);
```

```
            break;

        case GraphicOps.DRAWN_RECT:
            g.drawRect(0, 0, width - 2, height - 2);
            break;

        case GraphicOps.DRAWN_ROUND_RECT:
            g.drawRoundRect(0, 0, width - 2, height - 2, arcSize, arcSize);
            break;

        case GraphicOps.FILLED_RECT:
            g.fillRect(0, 0, width - 1, height - 1);
            break;

        case GraphicOps.FILLED_ROUND_RECT:
            g.fillRoundRect(0, 0, width - 1, height - 1, arcSize, arcSize);
            break;

        case GraphicOps.DRAWN_OVAL:
            g.drawOval(0, height/4, width, height/2);
            break;

        case GraphicOps.FILLED_OVAL:
            g.fillOval(0, height/4, width, height/2);
            break;
        }

        g.setColor(c);
        g.translate(-(x + PAD), -(y + PAD));
    }

    private int shape;

    // Constants
    public static final int FULLWIDTH = 32;
    public static final int FULLHEIGHT = 32;
    public static final int PAD = 2;
    public static final int WIDTH = FULLWIDTH - 2 * PAD;
    public static final int HEIGHT = FULLHEIGHT - 2 * PAD;
    public static final int ARC_SIZE = FULLWIDTH/2;

    // Sizes for this instance
    private int fullWidth = FULLWIDTH;
    private int fullHeight = FULLHEIGHT;
    private int width = WIDTH;
    private int height = HEIGHT;
    private int arcSize = ARC_SIZE;
}
```

A GraphicShapeIcon is created by giving its constructor an integer that specifies the shape to be drawn, from the values declared by the GraphicOps interface. A second constructor that allows the size of the icon to be changed is also provided; this facility will be used when menus are added to this application later in this book. The paintIcon method is very simple: the shape is drawn by switching based on the integer passed to the constructor. Each case draws the appropriate shape, being careful to ensure that it stays within the fixed area that it requested via its getIconWidth and getIconHeight methods. To make this simple, the origin of the graphics context is moved to the top left hand corner of this area.

It is very important to note that the color initially selected into the graphics context on entry is saved before the color used to draw the shape is installed and is restored before the method completes. Similarly, the origin is restored after the drawing has been completed, by reversing the translation performed at the start of the method. If you forget to do this, you will find that the component that your icon is being drawn onto won't render properly.

The ColorFillIcon, shown in Listing 4-18 is similar, but allows more configuration.

Listing 4-18   An icon that shows a color-filled square

```java
package JFCBook.Chapter4;

import com.sun.java.swing.*;
import java.awt.*;

public class ColorFillIcon implements Icon {
  public ColorFillIcon(Color fill,
        int width, int height, int borderSize) {
    this.fillColor  = fill;
    this.borderSize = borderSize;
    this.width = width;
    this.height= height;
    this.shadow= Color.black;
    this.fillWidth  = width - 2 * borderSize;
    this.fillHeight = height - 2 * borderSize;
  }

  public ColorFillIcon(Color fill, int size) {
    this(fill, size, size, BORDER_SIZE);
  }

  public ColorFillIcon(Color fill) {
    this(fill, DEFAULT_SIZE, DEFAULT_SIZE, BORDER_SIZE);
  }

  // Set nondefault shadow color
  public void setShadow(Color c){
```

```
    shadow = c;
  }

// Change the main color
  public void setFillColor(Color c) {
    fillColor = c;
  }

  // The Icon interface
  public int getIconWidth() {
    return width;
  }

  public int getIconHeight() {
    return height;
  }

  public void paintIcon(Component comp, Graphics g, int x, int y) {
    Color c = g.getColor();

    // Draw the border
    if (borderSize > 0) {
      g.setColor(shadow);
      for (int i = 0; i < borderSize; i++) {
        g.drawRect(x + i, y + i, width - 2 * i - 1, height - 2 * i - 1);
      }
    }

    // Fill the remainder of the icon
    g.setColor(fillColor);
    g.fillRect(x + borderSize, y + borderSize, fillWidth, fillHeight);

    g.setColor(c);

  }

  // Icon state
  protected int width;           // Color fill width
  protected int height;          // Color fill height
  protected Color fillColor;     // Color to fill with
  protected Color shadow;        // Shadow color
  protected int borderSize;      // Border size in pixels
  protected int fillHeight;      // Height of area to fill
  protected int fillWidth;       // Width of area to fill

  // Constants
  public static final int BORDER_SIZE = 2;
  public static final int DEFAULT_SIZE = 32;
}
```

The most general constructor allows you to tailor the width and height of the colored area, the width of the border area, which can be removed entirely by making it zero pixels wide, and the color to be used to fill the center of the icon. Two other constructors allow you to construct a square icon of specified size or a 32-pixel square icon, with a fill color of your choice. The border is colored black, unless the `setShadow` method is used to change the color. The rest of this class follows the same pattern as `GraphicShapeIcon`, except that calculated values are used instead of constants in the `getIconWidth`, `getIconHeight` and `paintIcon` methods. There is also a method that allows the fill color of the icon to be changed. Calling this method and then repainting the component that hosts the icon will have the effect of changing the icon's color.

In these examples, the `Component` argument passed to the `paintIcon` method hasn't been used. This argument is passed so that you can create icons that use information from the component that they are drawing on, such as the component's background color.

Rendering Text

In Java, rendering text is just like drawing graphics, with one minor difference: whereas the lines that you draw with the graphics drawing methods are all one pixel wide (unless you use the JDK 1.2 Java 2D API), text lines are much wider. While you can describe where to start a line by naming a single pixel, how do you specify the starting point of a text string that is 12-pixels high? You might think that you could draw a rectangle around the text and specify the coordinates of its top left-hand corner. This would be perfectly reasonable, but it's not how it is actually done in Java.

Fonts and Font Metrics

Let's tackle what should be a reasonably simple exercise to see what issues arise when trying to handle drawing text. The aim is to create a panel of a given size and render a string onto it in such a way that it is both horizontally and vertically centered on the canvas. Obviously, to do this it is necessary to know the height and width of the string as it will appear when drawn and this is our first problem—how is it possible to know how large it will be? If you think about it, you will realize that the size of the string depends on the font you're using to render it—obviously, a string drawn in a 24-point font will be much larger in both directions than the same string drawn in a 12-point font. Also, since most of today's fonts are proportional, you can't just take the width of one character from the font (if you could discover that somehow) and multiply it by the number of characters in the string to get the total length, because the characters in the font are not all the same width.

Fortunately, there is a simple solution to this problem. Once you have a `Font` object, you can acquire a different kind of object, called `FontMetrics`, that gives

you all the information you need about your font. There are three ways to get a
FontMetrics object. First, you can use the getFontMetrics method of the
Toolkit class, like this:

```
Font f = new Font("Serif", Font.PLAIN, 12);
FontMetrics fm = Toolkit.getDefaultToolkit().getFontMetrics();
```

On the other hand, if you have a Graphics object on hand, you can use one of
its two getFontMetrics methods:

```
// "comp" is assumed to be a Component
Graphics g = comp.getGraphics();
FontMetrics fm1 = g.getFontMetrics();

Font f = new Font("Serif", Font.PLAIN, 12);
FontMetrics fm2 = g.getFontMetrics(f);
```

When you don't give it an argument, as in the first case, getFontMetrics
returns a FontMetrics object for whichever font is currently selected into the
graphics context. On the other hand, if you hand it a font, it gives you the
FontMetrics for that font, as does the Toolkit getFontMetrics method.

Core Note

If you're wondering what would be the difference between asking for the
FontMetrics *object of a given font via* Graphics *and via* Toolkit, *the*
answer is that today there would be no difference. But there is at least a philo-
sophical difference. At the moment, it is only possible to use one toolkit implemen-
tation in a program, but suppose you could use two at the same time; let's label
them A *and* B. *Now if* A *is the default toolkit and your* Graphics *object comes*
from a component realized by toolkit B, *then the* FontMetrics *object*
obtained from Toolkit.getDefaultToolkit().getGraphics()
belongs to toolkit A, *while that from* g.getFontMetrics() *belongs to tool*
kit B *and there is no reason to suppose that these are the same, even for the*
same font name, style and point size.

How do you choose between these methods? The second one is obviously easiest
to use when you have an initialized Graphics object and you want to render text in
its selected font, as might be the case in the paintIcon method of a component
(you'll see an example of this below). You might use the third method in the same
place if you sometimes wanted to render in a different font on the same component,
or if the string is going to be drawn in more than one font. The only possible problem with using either of these methods is that you need a Graphics object to use
them, but you know that components don't have Graphics objects associated with
them until just before they appear on the screen. In some cases, you can't wait that
long to get font information because you might want to determine the size of a can-

vas based on the size of what you are trying to draw on it. In these circumstances, you would need to use the `Toolkit getFontMetrics` method.

What exactly does a `FontMetrics` object tell us? To start with, it has a `stringWidth` method that returns the width of a string when it is rendered in the font from which the `FontMetrics` object was obtained. Here's an example:

```
Font f = new Font("Serif", Font.BOLD, 24);
FontMetrics fm = Toolkit.getDefaultToolkit().getFontMetrics(f);
String s = "Hello, world";
int width = f.stringWidth(s);
```

`width` will be set to the width, in pixels, of the string "Hello, world" if it were rendered using the font represented by `f` on a component managed by the default tool kit. Note carefully that this is *not* strictly the width of that string when rendered in a 24-point, bold "Serif" font, but rather in the font that your system uses when you ask for such a thing—remember that Java maps generic names like "Serif" to actual fonts based on what it has available to it. It doesn't promise to provide a 24-point font, or even a bold font for that matter.

So much for the width, what about the height? This is equally simple, because `FontMetrics` provides a `getHeight` method that returns the height of the font:

```
int height = fm.getHeight();
```

Now that you have the width and height of the string, it seems that you know all you need to know to center the string in the canvas, assuming you also know the size of the canvas. But you're not quite there yet. Recall that strings are drawn with the `Graphics drawString` method that looks like this:

```
public void drawString(String text, int x, int y);
```

The problem, of course, is to calculate the `x` and `y` arguments so that the string is centered on the canvas. You can't do this yet, because you don't know which point of the string the coordinates describe. You can get this last piece of information from Figure 4-13.

Figure 4-13 shows the various measurements that distinguish one font from another. First, you know that different characters in a font are not necessarily all the same width; each character has its own width, known as the *advance*. When laying out characters, the `drawString` method draws a character, then adds its advance value to its `x` coordinate to get the starting `x` coordinate of the next character. The total width of the string, as returned by `stringWidth`, is the sum of the advance values for each character in the string.

Running along under the characters is the *baseline*. If you think of the screen as a lined page and you wrote on the page longhand, the lines on the page would be lined up with the baseline of the font. Any individual character extends some way above and possibly some way below the baseline; the extent to which it rises above the baseline is its *ascent* and the distance that it stretches below is the *descent*. Just as different characters have different widths, so they can have different ascent and descent

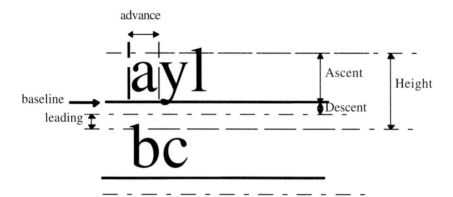

Figure 4-13   Font measurements.

values. Java doesn't actually give you access to the ascents and descents for every individual character. Instead, each font has a constant value that bounds the ascent and descent of most alphanumeric characters in the font; it is these bounding values that we refer to when we speak of a font's ascent and descent. Some characters will, of course, exceed these bounds, so there is a *maximum ascent* and a *maximum descent* associated with each font and there is also a maximum advance value that is large enough to cover every character in the font.

Core Note

In the JDK 1.2 Java 2D API, you can get access to per-character font information.

The final ingredient is the distance between lines on the page. Each font has a value called *leading* that gives the minimum advised extra space to allow between lines. The total of the font ascent, descent and leading values is the font's *height*. As shown in the diagram, we usually render successive lines so that the baseline of each line is `height` pixels below the baseline of the line above it. Since most characters are no higher than the font ascent and do not drop below the font descent, this arrangement means that there will be little vertical overlap between the characters of one line and those of the line below it, but this is not guaranteed because some of the characters may exceed these bounds and hence run into each other. Of course, if the baselines were separated by the leading space plus the maximum ascent and descent, then there would never be any overlap, but the lines would be too far apart most of the time.

`FontMetrics` stores values for all of the font attributes that we have just described and provides public methods that allow you to get access to them. It also has a few methods, like `stringWidth`, which return the widths of strings and characters. These methods are summarized in Table 4-4.

Table 4-4   FontMetrics Class Methods

Method	Description
public int getAscent	Gets the font ascent.
public int getDescent	Gets the font descent.
public int getHeight	Returns the font height (ascent + descent + leading).
public int getLeading	Returns the recommended interline gap.
public int getMaxAdvance	Gets the maximum width of all characters in the font.
public int getMaxAscent	Returns the ascent of the tallest character in the font.
public int getMaxDescent	Gets the maximum distance that any character stretches below the baseline.
public int[] getWidths	Returns the widths of the first 256 characters in the font (or fewer if the font has fewer characters).
public int bytesWidth (byte[] data, int off, int len)	Returns the length of the string made up of the bytes in the entries `off` through `off + len - 1` of the array `data`. Since all Java strings are made up of 16-bit Unicode characters and bytes are 8 bits long, each byte is logically extended on the left with 8 zero bits to create a Unicode character.
public int charsWidth (char[] data, int off, int len)	This method is the same as `bytesWidth` except that it accepts 16-bit Unicode characters and so does not need to zero-pad its input array.
public int charWidth(char c)	Returns the width of the single character given as an argument.
public int charWidth(int c)	Same as the previous method. The least significant 16 bits of the integer argument are taken as a 16-bit Unicode character.

Now let's return to the problem of the text and the canvas. The x and y coordinates supplied to `drawString` are those of the baseline at the left end of the string being rendered. In order to center the string horizontally, you need to calculate the width of the string, subtract this from the width of the canvas to get the amount of extra horizontal space and distribute this equally on the left and right sides of the string. If the canvas is cWidth pixels wide, the text is in a `String` variable called str and you have a suitable `FontMetrics` object in fm, then the string's starting x coordinate will be?

```
(cWidth - fm.stringWidth(str))/2
```

To center the string vertically, you need to decide what this actually means. It could mean placing the font baseline at the vertical midpoint of the canvas. If you choose this definition, then the y coordinate for `drawString` is simply:

```
cHeight/2
```

assuming that `cHeight` holds the height of the canvas. If you adopt this definition, however, you will find that most of the text ends up above the center of the canvas, because comparatively few characters have descenders. Instead, you get a better result if you average the ascent and the descent values and place the midpoint of those two extremes in the center of the canvas. This is slightly complex, because you have to supply the coordinates of the font's baseline.

Imagine that the text is surrounded by a bounding box that extends above and below the baseline by the amount of the font ascent and descent, respectively. The height of this box is then `(fm.getAscent() + fm.getDescent())`. You want to center this box in the canvas, so half of it will be above the center of the canvas and half will be below. Therefore, the top of this box will be at y coordinate `(cHeight/2) - (fm.getAscent() + fm.getDescent())/2`. Since you need the y coordinate of the baseline, not the top, you need to add `fm.getAscent()` to the y coordinate of the top of the bounding box, giving the result:

```
(cHeight + fm.getAscent() - fm.getDescent())/2
```

Now let's put this into practice by implementing the canvas and text as a subclass of `JPanel`. The code is shown in Listing 4-19.

Listing 4-19   Drawing centered text

```java
package JFCBook.Chapter4;

import com.sun.java.swing.*;
import java.awt.*;
import java.awt.event.*;

public class TextCanvas extends JPanel {
  public TextCanvas(String text) {
    this.text = text;
    setBackground(UIManager.getColor("control"));
  }

  public void paintComponent(Graphics g) {
    super.paintComponent(g);
    Dimension d = getSize();
    int cWidth = d.width;
    int cHeight = d.height;

    g.setColor(getForeground());
    FontMetrics fm = g.getFontMetrics();
    g.drawString(text, (cWidth - fm.stringWidth(text))/2,
      ((cHeight + fm.getAscent() - fm.getDescent())/2));
```

continued

```
    }

    // Test code
    public static void main(String[] args) {
      try {
        int fontNumber;
        Font font;
        JFrame f = new JFrame("Text Canvas Test");
        if (args.length != 2) {
          System.err.println("Usage: TextCanvas <string> <font>");
          System.exit(1);
        }

        TextCanvas c = new TextCanvas(args[0]);
        fontNumber = Integer.parseInt(args[1]);

        switch(fontNumber) {
        case 0:
          font = new Font("Serif", Font.BOLD, 12);
          break;
        case 1:
          font = new Font("Dialog", Font.PLAIN, 8);
          break;
        case 2:
          font = new Font("SansSerif", Font.BOLD, 24);
          break;
        case 3:
          font = new Font("MonoSpaced", Font.PLAIN, 16);
          break;
        default:
          throw new NumberFormatException();
        }
        c.setFont(font);

        f.getContentPane().add(c);
        f.setSize(200, 150);
        f.addWindowListener(new WindowAdapter() {
          public void windowClosing(WindowEvent evt) {
            System.exit(0);
          }
        });
        f.setVisible(true);
      } catch (NumberFormatException e) {
        System.err.println("The font must be in the range 0 through 3");
        System.exit(1);
      }
    }

  protected String text;   // The text string
}
```

Most of this listing is actually just the test code in the main method—the real code is all in the paintComponent function and you should be able to see that it implements the scheme worked out above. Note that the background color is set to the look-and-feel default color for controls. To get the background painted in this color, you just need to call super.paintComponent from the component's paintComponent method. Painting the background is the only thing that JPanel does in this method; it also leaves the background color selected in the graphics context, so the foreground color is selected before drawing the string.

This program requires two arguments—a quoted string and a font number in the range 0 to 3. You can see how these numbers correspond to actual fonts from the listing. Here is an example of how to run it:

```
java JFCBook.Chapter4.TextCanvas "Hello, world" 0
```

This produces a frame containing our control, with the words "Hello, world" rendered in a 12-point, bold, serif font in the middle of it. Try resizing the frame to demonstrate that the text remains anchored to the center of it no matter what you do to it.

What you have implemented here is a very simple custom JFC component. You might find it instructive to try to improve it in various ways. For example, the paintComponent method always gets the FontMetrics object and recalculates the position of the text, a process that takes time. If you wanted to be clever, you could calculate the text position only when it needed to change—for example, once when you first paint the component, and then subsequently only when you change the font, text or size of the component. For this, you will need to override the setFont, setSize and setBounds methods and implement a setText method to allow the user to change the text after the component has been constructed; for completeness, you should also implement a getText method.

Working with Multiple Fonts

So far, you've seen how to create a component that handles only one font. If you want to work with more than one font, you have to try much harder, because drawString can only handle a single font each time it is called. To create a label that changes fonts, you need to treat the string as a collection of smaller parts, each of which is in only a single font. Of course, this brings with it the issue of how to represent a change of font within a string. At the moment, there is no common way to do this in Java. Fortunately, the Java2D API includes a class called StyledString that solves this problem and there is also a variant of drawString that renders a StyledString just as simply as drawString ordinary strings. Unless you are going to use JDK 1.2, the only way to render multifont strings is to create your own component and a format of your own that specifies the font changes, or to use the JTextPane and JEditorPane components that we'll discuss in Chapter 9, "Text Components."

Simulating Disabled Text

As a further example of how simple it is to render text in Java and to produce useful effects with very little code, this section will show how to modify the TextCanvas class to create one that has an enabled and a disabled state, as many of the Swing components do. The difference between these two states is that when it is enabled, the label is shown in the normal foreground color, but when it is disabled it appears *grayed out*.

To produce this effect, all that is necessary is to modify the paintComponent method. The first change that needs to be made is to check whether the component is enabled or not by calling the isEnabled method of its Component superclass. If this returns true, the text is drawn exactly as it was before. However, if it returns false, something slightly different needs to be done.

Grayed-out text is produced by superimposing two copies of the text, one in a color slightly brighter than that of the background (*not* the foreground) and one slightly darker, with one copy offset one pixel to the right of and below the other. This produces the impression of a groove carved in the surface of the control in the shape of the original text. The effect works best when the background is a grayish color, as it often is on the Windows platform.

The only other change to make is to override the setEnabled method. Here, the superclass method is called to pass on the new state to it (so that isEnabled returns the right value), followed by a call to repaint so that the component's paintComponent method is called to redraw the text in its new state. This step is necessary because Component does nothing when setEnabled is called other than to store the new state setting. The modified paintComponent method, which incorporates some tidying up to avoid repeating the same calculations, and the modified setEnabled method are shown below. The important changes are highlighted in bold.

You invoke this program in the same way as the other one, for example:

```
java JFCBook.Chapter4.DisabledText "Press" 1
```

Once started, it loops until you close it, flipping itself between enabled and disabled state every 5 seconds.

```
public void paintComponent(Graphics g) {
    super.paintComponent(g);
    Dimension d = getSize();
    int cWidth = d.width;
    int cHeight = d.height;
    boolean enabled = isEnabled();
    FontMetrics fm = g.getFontMetrics();
    int xpos = (cWidth - fm.stringWidth(text))/2;
    int ypos = (cHeight + fm.getAscent() - fm.getDescent())/2;

    if (enabled == true) {
```

```
      g.setColor(getForeground());
      g.drawString(text, xpos, ypos);
   } else {
      g.setColor(getBackground().brighter());
      g.drawString(text, xpos + 1, ypos + 1);
      g.setColor(getBackground().darker());
      g.drawString(text, xpos, ypos);
   }
}

// Override setEnabled to cause repaint()
public void setEnabled(boolean b) {
   super.setEnabled(b);
   repaint();
}
```

Figure 4-14 shows a magnified view of the disabled text, which shows how it achieves the desired effect.

Figure 4-14　　Disabled text.

Note carefully how colors for the text in its disabled state are generated:

```
g.setColor(getBackground().brighter());
g.drawString(text, xpos + 1, ypos + 1);
g.setColor(getBackground().darker());
g.drawString(text, xpos, ypos);
```

The brighter and darker methods of java.awt.Color are useful for generating new colors that are closely related to an existing color, without needing to worry about what that color is. These methods work by multiplying the red, green and blue components of the color by the same constant value (greater than 1 for brighter and less than 1 for darker), so that their ratios are unchanged, to produce the effect of actually lightening or darkening it rather than changing it to a different color.

Printing Graphics and Text

Printing in Java is a multistep process: You have to get access to the printer, prepare to print a page, draw what you want to print onto the page and then have the printer print what you have drawn. After repeating this operation for as many pages as necessary, you finally release the printer. In this section, you'll see how to use the printing API by looking at three simple examples.

Printing Components and Containers

The printing API operates at several levels; although you always initiate printing in the same way, there are several things you can do when you have access to the printer. In this section, the printing support provided by the Component and Container classes will be used to produce hardcopy of a single component or a complete application. Listing 4-20 shows the code for the first example.

Listing 4-20   Printing Java Components

```
package JFCBook.Chapter4;

import com.sun.java.swing.*;
import java.awt.*;
import java.awt.event.*;
import java.util.Properties;

public class PrintingExample1 extends JFrame {
    public PrintingExample1(String title, Component comp) {
        super(title);
        scrolledObject = comp;

        JScrollPane p = new JScrollPane();
        p.setViewportView(comp);

        this.getContentPane().add(p, "Center");
        JPanel panel = new JPanel();
        button1 = new JButton("Print All...");
        button1.setMnemonic('A');
        panel.add(button1);

        button2 = new JButton("Print Image...");
        button2.setMnemonic('I');
        panel.add(button2);

        this.getContentPane().add(panel, "South");
```

```
ActionListener l = new ActionListener() {
  public void actionPerformed(ActionEvent evt) {
    Properties props = new Properties();
    button1.setEnabled(false);
    button2.setEnabled(false);

    PrintJob pj = Toolkit.getDefaultToolkit().getPrintJob(
          PrintingExample1.this,
          "Print test 1",
          props);
    if (pj != null) {
      System.out.println("Returned properties: " + props);
      JButton b = (JButton)evt.getSource();
      Component c;

      Graphics g = pj.getGraphics();
      if (b == button1) {
        c = PrintingExample1.this;
      } else {
        c = scrolledObject;
      }

      // Print in the center of the page
      Dimension od = c.getSize();         // Object size
      Dimension pd = pj.getPageDimension();    // Page size

      g.translate((pd.width - od.width)/2,
          pd.height - od.height)/2);

      if (b == button1) {
        c.printAll(g);
      } else {
        c.print(g);
      }

      g.dispose(); // Prints here
      pj.end();    // Release printer
    }

    button1.setEnabled(true);
    button2.setEnabled(true);
  }
};

button1.addActionListener(l);
button2.addActionListener(l);
```

continued

```
        }

    public static void main(String[] args) {
        ImageIcon icon = new ImageIcon(
        PrintingExample1.class.getResource("images/lem.jpg"));

        JFrame f = new PrintingExample1("Printing Test 1", new JLabel(icon));
        f.setSize(300, 200);
        f.addWindowListener(new WindowAdapter() {
            public void windowClosing(WindowEvent evt) {
                System.exit(0);
            }
        });
        f.setVisible(true);
    }

    JButton button1;     // The "Print All.." button
    JButton button2;     // The "Print Image..." button
    Component scrolledObject;     // The object in the scroll pane
}
```

The application frame contains a `JScrollPane` in which an image is displayed by mounting it on a `JLabel` which is its viewport (scrolling and `JScrollPane` are discussed in detail in Chapter 5, "Keyboard Handling, Actions and Scrolling"). Below the scrolled pane are two buttons that allow you to request a hardcopy of either the entire application or just the image. The interesting code in this application is in the `actionPerformed` method of the inner class that implements the `ActionListener` attached to the two buttons.

The first step is to get access to the printer using the `getPrintJob` method of `Toolkit`:

```
Properties props = new Properties();
button1.setEnabled(false);
button2.setEnabled(false);

PrintJob pj = Toolkit.getDefaultToolkit().getPrintJob(
        PrintingExample1.this,
        "Print test 1",
        props);
```

The `getPrintJob` method is defined as follows:

```
public PrintJob getPrintJob(Frame frame, String title, Properties props);
```

When this method is invoked, it posts a dialog that allows you to choose the printer that you want to use and to set printer-specific options. The dialog that you see and the options that you might be able to change depend on the operating system that you are using. On Windows, you see a dialog that allows you to select a printer and then shows your driver's usual printing dialog box. On Unix you see a dialog that allows you to select the printer or a file to print to and to choose the type of paper in use. In Java, to create a dialog box you must have a `Frame` that can act as its parent, so the `getPrintJob` method requires a `Frame` argument. Usually, you will pass the application's `JFrame` object here. The second argument to `getPrintJob` is a string that becomes the title of the dialog box.

Whichever platform you are using, the dialog box will have buttons that allow you to proceed with or cancel the print operation. If you decide to proceed, `getPrintJob` returns a `PrintJob` object that you can use to drive the printer; if you press the `Cancel` button, `null` is returned instead, so be careful to check for this when you implement printing support in your applications.

The final argument to `getPrintJob` is a `Properties` object that allows you to pass configuration information to the printing dialog box. The content of this object is currently platform-dependent. On Windows, it is completely ignored and is unchanged when `getPrintJob` returns. On Unix, you can specify any of the properties shown in Table 4-5.

Table 4-5 Printer Properties for Unix

Property	*Meaning*
`awt.print.numCopies`	Number of copies to print
`awt.print.paperSize`	Type of paper to use (e.g. "A4")
`awt.print.destination`	"printer" or "file"
`awt.print.orientation`	"portrait" or "landscape"
`awt.print.fileName`	Name of the file for the printed output, if `awt.print.destination` is "file."

When the dialog box is displayed, the properties you supply are reflected in the options that are initially selected. If any of these options are subsequently changed, the change is reflected in the `Properties` object when `getPrintJob` returns. The example code shown above prints the properties that are returned; if you're using Windows, you won't see anything interesting here.

Once you have a `PrintJob` object, you can use it to get a graphics context that represents a single page of printed output. The `getGraphics` method returns a `Graphics` objects that implements the `java.awt.PrintGraphics` interface:

```
Graphics g = pj.getGraphics();
```

The `PrintGraphics` interface has only a single method, which allows you to retrieve a reference to the `PrintJob` from which it was obtained:

```
public interface PrintGraphics {
   public PrintJob getPrintJob();
}
```

It is unlikely that you'll need to make much use of this method; the real value of the `PrintGraphics` interface is that it allows you to check whether a `Graphics` object that you are given is a graphics context for the printer or not by using code like this:

```
Graphics g;

if (g instanceof PrintGraphics) {
   // Code specific to printing
}
```

We'll see a case in which we can use this construction later. Using the `Graphics` object, you can use any drawing primitive to write text or draw graphics on the page, as we'll see shortly. Our example makes use of the `print` and `printAll` methods of `java.awt.Component` to print either the image or the frame and its contents:

```
public void print(Graphics g);

public void printAll(Graphics g);
```

The `print` method prints only the component on which it is invoked, whereas `printAll` prints a container and all of its child components recursively. This example chooses between the two based on which button was pressed. If the entire application is to be printed, the `printAll` method of the application frame is invoked; otherwise, it just calls `print` on the `JLabel`, in response to which the label renders itself, including the image, to the printer. When a complete page has been rendered, the `Graphics` object's `dispose` method is invoked, which causes the page to be printed. To print several pages, you repeat this process. The following code would print 20 pages of output:

```
PrintJob pj = Toolkit.getDefaultToolkit().getPrintJob(f,
"Print 20 pages", props);
if (pj != null) {
   for (int i = 0; i < 20; i++) {
      Graphics g = pg.getGraphics();

      // Render page using "g": not shown

      g.dispose();      // Print the page
   }
   pj.end();   // Release the printer
}
```

Finally, as just shown, when printing is complete, you must call the `end` method of your `PrintJob` object to release the printer. If you forget to do this, you may find that you won't be able to use the printer any more, because it is locked to the last program that called `getPrintJob`.

The `Graphics` object returned from `getGraphics` covers the entire page, so if you simply call `print` or `printAll`, the result will be printed at the top left-hand corner of the page. In our example, a more pleasing result is produced by centering the output both horizontally and vertically:

```
// Print in the center of the page
Dimension od = c.getSize();                 // Object size
Dimension pd = pj.getPageDimension();       // Page size

g.translate((pd.width - od.width)/2, (pd.height - od.height)/2);
```

The `getPageDimension` method returns the size of the printed page in pixels, so you can use its return value to change the location in which the component or container will be drawn by moving the origin of the graphics context in such a way that the center of the object being printed is in the center of the page. `PrintJob` also has a `getPageResolution` method that returns the number of pixels per inch that the printer can print:

```
public Dimension getPageDimension();

public int getPageResolution();
```

If you experiment with these methods, you'll probably find that the values that they return don't match the actual capabilities of your printer. For example, you will find that the page size returned by `getPageDimension` is not consistent with the number of pixels that your printer can print on a page. This is not an error: this method is not supposed to return the actual size of the page. Instead, it returns the size of an imaginary sheet of paper whose shape is in proportion to the actual paper size, but scaled to make it similar to the resolution of your screen. For example, if you used legal-sized paper (8.5 in $\times$ 14 in) on a 300-dpi printer, you would expect to have 2550 pixels across and 4200 pixels down the page. In fact, on my Unix system, `getPageDimension` returns an apparent size of 612 pixels horizontally and 1008 vertically. You will notice that 4200/2550 and 1008/612 are both 1.647 (approximately), so the aspect ratio of the page is preserved, but the actual size is not.

The reason for this apparently strange behavior is that it allows you to use the same `paintComponent` method to render graphics or text either to the screen or to the printer. Indeed, the default implementation of the `Component print` method just calls `paint` directly; the component's paint code will render the component to the printer without realizing it. However, if the actual dimensions of the page were reported and the `PrintGraphics` object honored them, a component whose size looks reasonable when drawn on the screen would be only about a third of its original size when drawn to the printer. To save you the trouble of modifying your `paintComponent` method to rescale its output for the printer, the `PrintGraphics` object does the rescaling for you.

In order for this to work consistently for code that bases its actions on the size of the surface it is drawing on (such as rendering text, as you'll see later), it is necessary to present an apparent page size that results in the same appearance on the printer as will appear on the screen. Most of the time, however, you can ignore the reasoning behind this and just use the page size returned by getPageDimension without worrying about how it is derived. The only case in which you need to be careful about the page size is when you want to leave a fixed-size margin around the outside of the page, as you'll see when rendering text at the end of this chapter.

Printing the Contents of the GraphicsBorderedCanvas

Now that you know how to use the printer, the GraphicsDemo application can be completed by implementing its Print button. As you've seen, once you've completed the formalities of gaining access to the printer, you have a Graphics object that will reflect any operations you perform on the printer when you dispose it. The GraphicsBorderedCanvas will reproduce all of the shapes that you have drawn on it if you call its paintComponent method, so this seems to be the obvious way to implement the Print button. The code is shown in Listing 4-21.

Listing 4-21   Printing Graphics objects

```
// Print the canvas contents
public void printCanvas() {
   if (drawingOps.isEmpty() == false) {
     // Locate the frame
     Container c = this.getTopLevelAncestor();
     if (c != null && c instanceof Frame) {
       Properties props = new Properties();
       PrintJob pj =
         Toolkit.getDefaultToolkit().getPrintJob((Frame)c,
             "Print Drawn Graphics",
             props);
       if (pj != null) {
         Graphics g = pj.getGraphics();
         Dimension pd = pj.getPageDimension();
         Dimension od = this.getSize();
         g.translate((pd.width - od.width)/2,
           (pd.height - od.height)/2);
         paintComponent(g);

         g.dispose();     // Printing happens here
         pj.end();
       }
     }
   }
}
```

The getPrintJob method requires a Frame object as its first argument. Here, we are developing code that is part of a component that can potentially be reused in many applications, so it is not desirable to rely on the application having a global variable that holds a reference to its top-level frame. Instead, it is better to use the getTopLevelAncestor method of JComponent, which returns the top-level container in which the component resides. This method works by looking at the component itself; if it is not a Window or an Applet, it looks at the component's parent, and so on, until it reaches the top of the component hierarchy. In fact, since you can't add a Window to another container, a Window is always bound to be at the top of the hierarchy. You could, of course, point getTopLevelAncestor at a component that doesn't have a parent, or does not have an ancestor that is a Window; if you do this, it just returns null.

The object returned from getTopLevelAncestor is a Window or an Applet, not a Frame, because for example, our component could also be contained within a Dialog; both Frame and Dialog are subclasses of Window. Since you must pass a Frame to getPrintJob, it follows that you can't create a print dialog that is a child of another dialog, so the GraphicsBorderedCanvas would not be able to print its contents in the (unlikely) event that it were mounted in a dialog box. Since Frame is a subclass of Window, you can cast the Window reference to a Frame reference provided that the object actually is a Frame. To be sure that this is so, you use the instanceof operator. You could also have just directly cast the returned object to Frame, provided you catch the exception that would be generated if you had been returned a Dialog or an Applet:

```
Window w = this.getTopLevelAncestor();
if (w != null) {
  try {
    Properties props = new Properties();
    PrintJob pj =
      Toolkit.getDefaultToolkit().getPrintJob((Frame)w,
          "Print Drawn Graphics",
          props);
    if (pj != null) {
      // Code omitted
    }
  } catch (ClassCastException e) {
    // Can't print from a Dialog
  }
}
```

As in the previous example, this code takes the trouble to center the output on the page by subtracting the canvas size from the apparent size of the printing area and dividing by two.

Finally, the paintComponent method is called to render the complete canvas onto the printer. But what about the border—if you recall, the GraphicsBorderedCanvas includes a border provided by its superclass

BorderedCanvas. The border won't be drawn on the printer, because it is rendered by the BorderedCanvas paintBorder method that is inherited from JComponent, not by paintComponent. Instead, a blank area where the border would have been drawn will be present, but you're unlikely to notice this because the canvas is centered in the printed page anyway.

Printing Text

Printing text is almost as simple as printing graphics because text is also rendered using a Graphics method, but, unlike graphics, the text is not completely self-describing, because the width and height of a string depend on the font being used. This section illustrates how to deal with the text by showing a program that prints the content of a text file. Unfortunately, a large proportion of the code for this example deals with parsing the text file into words, a task that a real-word processing program probably wouldn't have to deal with because it would not be likely to store the document content in an ASCII file. Since the aim of this section is to concentrate on printing, the code that handles the reading and parsing of data from the file won't be discussed here. The code is shown in Listing 4-22.

Listing 4-22   Printing Text

```java
package JFCBook.Chapter4;

import com.sun.java.swing.*;
import java.awt.*;
import java.awt.event.*;
import java.io.*;
import java.util.*;

public class PrintingExample2 {
  static void print() {
    // Print the file content
    text.setText("Printing file...");

    Properties props = new Properties();

    PrintJob pj = Toolkit.getDefaultToolkit().getPrintJob(frame,
                    "Print File",
                    props);
    if (pj == null) {
      text.setText("Printing canceled");
      return;
    }
    int screenResolution =
Toolkit.getDefaultToolkit().getScreenResolution();
    int topMargin = screenResolution;          // 1 inch
```

```
      int leftMargin = screenResolution/2;        // 0.5 inches


   Dimension pageSize = new Dimension(pj.getPageDimension());
   pageSize.width -= 2 * leftMargin;
   pageSize.height -= 2 * topMargin;

// Use try/finally to release PrintJob even if we get an exception
   try {
      String data;
      Graphics g = null;
      int line = fontAscent;              // Pixel line on page
      int column = 0;   // Pixel column on page
      int maxLine = pageSize.height - fontHeight;
      int tabGap = 8 * fm.stringWidth(" ");
      boolean isTab;         // True when we find a Tab

      BufferedReader r = new BufferedReader(new FileReader(file));
      text.setText("Printing started");

      while((data = r.readLine()) != null) {
        if (data.equals("")) {
          data = " ";
        }
        StringTokenizer st = new StringTokenizer(data, " \t", true);
        while (st.hasMoreElements() == true) {
          String token = (String)st.nextElement();
          isTab = token.equals("\t");
          int stringWidth;

          if (isTab == true) {
            int nextCol = ((column + tabGap)/tabGap) * tabGap;
            stringWidth = nextCol - column;
          } else {
            stringWidth = fm.stringWidth(token);
          }

          if (column + stringWidth > pageSize.width) {
            line += fontHeight;
            column = 0;
            if (isTab == true) {
              stringWidth = tabGap;
            }
            if (line > maxLine) {
              g.dispose();        // Flush page
              g = null;
            }
          }

          if (g == null) {
```

continued

```
          g = pj.getGraphics();        // Access to printer
          g.translate(leftMargin, topMargin); // Skip margins
          g.clipRect(0, 0, pageSize.width, pageSize.height);
          g.setFont(font);
          line = fontAscent;
          column = 0;
          if (isTab == true) {
            stringWidth = tabGap;
          }
        }

        if (isTab == false) {
          g.drawString(token, column, line);
        }
        column += stringWidth;
      }

      // End of line: go to next line
      column = pageSize.width;
    }

    if (g != null) {
      g.dispose();      // Print the last page
    }
  } catch (Exception e) {
    System.out.println("Exception while reading file data: " + e);
  } finally {
    // Always terminate the print job
    pj.end();
    text.setText("Printing completed");
  }
}

public static void main(String[] args) {
  if (args.length != 1) {
    System.out.println("Please supply one file name");
    System.exit(1);
  }

  file = new File(args[0]);
  if (file.canRead() == false) {
    System.out.println("Cannot read " + args[0]);
    System.exit(1);
  }

  font = new Font("serif", Font.PLAIN, 12);
  fm = Toolkit.getDefaultToolkit().getFontMetrics(font);
  fontHeight = fm.getHeight();
  fontAscent = fm.getAscent();
```

```
text.setEditable(false);
frame.getContentPane().add(text, "Center");
text.setText("Press \"Print\" to print file \"" + args[0] + "\"");
frame.getContentPane().add(button, "East");
button.addActionListener(new ActionListener() {
  public void actionPerformed(ActionEvent evt) {
    print();
  }
});

frame.pack();
frame.addWindowListener(new WindowAdapter() {
  public void windowClosing(WindowEvent evt) {
    System.exit(0);
  }
});
frame.setVisible(true);
}

static JFrame frame = new JFrame("Printing Example 2");
static JTextField text = new JTextField(40);
static JButton button = new JButton("Print...");
static File file;
static Font font;
static FontMetrics fm;
static int fontHeight;
static int fontAscent;
}
```

The `main` method deals with creating the simple user interface for this program, which just allows the user to start printing by pressing a button; the name of the file to be printed is supplied on the command line, for example:

```
java JFCBook.Chapter4.PrintingExample2 myfile.txt
```

For the string `myfile.txt`, substitute the absolute path name of any file you would like to have printed—for example:

```
java JFCBook.Chapter4.PrintingExample2 /etc/passwd

java JFCBook.Chapter4.PrintingExample2 c:\autoexec.bat
```

The printing work is carried out in the `print` method. Apart from the mechanics of reading the file, the issues to be dealt with in this method are:

- Leaving suitable side and top/bottom margins around the text.
- Constructing each line of output and wrapping at the end of each line.
- Detecting when the end of a page is reached.

Here, as in the previous examples, the first thing to do is to get a `PrintJob` object for the printer and return without doing anything if the user cancels the print operation. Using this object, you can get the effective size of the page in pixels. When you print, you will use a `Graphics` object that corresponds to a single page of output. By default, the graphics context will have its origin at the top left of the page and is not clipped (unlike a graphics context for a component, which is clipped to the component's boundary). In order to create margins, you need to move the origin to the top left of the area you want to print and set a clip that exposes only that area. If you implement the code that constructs each line of output correctly, you shouldn't even try to print into the margins, so setting a clip should not actually be necessary, but we do it anyway to illustrate how it would be done. If you were implementing a real word processor, you would probably want to set the clip because you might have embedded objects (such as graphics) in your document: If the graphic were too large for the page or margin size selected, it might not be possible to ensure that the graphic did not draw onto the margin by any other means.

Since the margin and page size are both constant, you can compute the appropriate origin position and the size of the clipping rectangle once and apply them at the start of every page. In this case, suppose you want to leave a 0.5 in margin on each side and a 1 in margin at the top and the bottom. Although you can get the printer resolution using the `PrintJob getPageResolution` method, this is not the correct thing to do. Remember, we said that the `Graphics` object for the printer deals in terms of screen coordinates and translates them to printer coordinates transparently. Because of this, you need to translate dimensions into pixels by using the screen resolution, not the resolution of the printer. Thus, you can calculate the margin and the clip as follows:

```
PrintJob pj = Toolkit.getDefaultToolkit().getPrintJob(frame, Print File", props);
   if (pj == null) {
     text.setText("Printing canceled");
     return;
   }
int screenResolution = Toolkit.getDefaultToolkit().getScreenResolution();
   int topMargin = screenResolution;            // 1 inch
   int leftMargin = screenResolution/2;          // 0.5 inches


   Dimension pageSize = new Dimension(pj.getPageDimension());
   pageSize.width -= 2 * leftMargin;
   pageSize.height -= 2 * topMargin;
```

The value returned from `getScreenResolution` is the number of pixels per inch, so to leave a one-inch gap, you need to move that many pixels in the required direction, which is the value to which the variable `topMargin` is set. Similarly, `leftMargin` is set to half the screen resolution, to give a 0.5 in horizontal margin. The page size is obtained using `getPageDimension` and the margins are applied by subtracting twice the top margin from the height and twice the left margin from the width.

Having acquired a `PrintJob`, it is essential to release it when printing is completed, so the printing is enclosed in a `try/catch/finally` block that invokes the end method in the `finally` clause:

```
try {
   // Printing code not shown
} catch (Exception e) {
   System.out.println("Exception while reading file data: " + e);
} finally {
   // Always terminate the print job
   pj.end();
   text.setText("Printing completed");
}
```

Since the data to be printed is from a file, we are exposed to getting an `IOException` and this construction ensures that the printer is released no matter how the printing code terminates.

Printing the file content is a matter of constructing each output line and writing it to the `Graphics` object. The number of words that can be placed onto a line depends on the font in use and the size of each word as measured in that font. In the main method, a 12-point, plain Serif font was selected and a `Font` and `FontMetrics` object for it. From the `FontMetrics` object, you can get the font ascent, which determines the distance to the font's baseline and the font height, which is the distance between the baselines of successive lines.

The main loop of this code processes a single line from the file. Having read a line, the `java.util.StringTokenizer` class is used to break it into words, separated by spaces or tabs. Since it is necessary to get both complete words and all of the spaces and tabs that separate them, the `StringTokenizer` is configured to delimit the words and the delimiters by passing `true` as the third argument. The inner loop then processes each token as it is returned by `StringTokenizer`. For each word, its size must be computed by using the `stringWidth` method of `FontMetrics`, then it is necessary to work out whether it fits on the current line. If it doesn't, it is necessary to move to the next line and, if the current list is the last one that will fit on the page, a new page must be started.

The current horizontal and vertical position are tracked using the variables `column` and `line`, respectively; the variable `maxLine` is initialized to the height of the usable area of the page (excluding the margins) less the height of the font. The fact that the end of the page has been reached can be detected by comparing `line` to `maxLine`. Similarly, the end of the current line can be detected as follows:

```
column + stringWidth > pageSize.width
```

Here, `stringWidth` is the width of the token in the current font, unless the token is a tab character. In the case of a tab, the column position has to be advanced to the next tab stop. In a real-word processing application, the positions of tab stops would be configurable; for simplicity, in this example, tab stops are defined to occur on eight-character boundaries, so the distance to the next tab stop can be computed as follows:

```
int nextCol = ((column + tabGap)/tabGap) * tabGap;
stringWidth = nextCol - column;
```

The variable tabGap is the number of pixels between tab stops; it is set to eight times the size of a space character:

```
tabGap = 8 * fm.stringWidth(" ");
```

To write some text onto the page, you need a Graphics object. At the start of processing the input file, you don't yet have a Graphics object. In fact, you don't want to get one until you find some text to print, because calling dispose on a Graphics object for a printer causes the printer to print an empty page. You need to get a new Graphics object when there is some text to print and when the bottom of a page is reached with more text still to come. To avoid getting a Graphics object when one is not strictly, a reference to the Graphics object is held in a local variable that is set to null at the start of the main loop and whenever the end of a page is reached. When it is necessary to print some text, this variable is checked and, if it is null, the current position must be at the top of a new page, so a new graphics context is acquired. If this were not done, an extra empty page would be printed if the file were empty or if its content ends exactly on a page boundary. Here is the code that acquires a graphics context:

```
if (column + stringWidth > pageSize.width) {
  line += fontHeight;
  column = 0;
  if (isTab == true) {
    stringWidth = tabGap;
  }
  if (line > maxLine) {
    g.dispose(); // Flush page
    g = null;
  }
}

if (g == null) {
  g = pj.getGraphics(); // Access to printer
  g.translate(leftMargin, topMargin); // Skip margins
  g.clipRect(0, 0, pageSize.width, pageSize.height);
  g.setFont(font);
  line = fontAscent;
  column = 0;
  if (isTab == true) {
    stringWidth = tabGap;
  }
}

if (isTab == false) {
  g.drawString(token, column, line);
}
column += stringWidth
```

This code first checks whether the current word forces a move to the next line, and moves down a line if it does. If the page is now full, `dispose` is called to print the page, and the local variable g is set to `null` to indicate that there is no valid graphics context. Next, the value of g is checked. If it is `null`, a `Graphics` object for the printer is obtained and its origin and the clip are set to exclude the margins. The `line` and `column` variables are also reset so that the current position is at the top and left of the page. Notice that, if the previous line ended because of a tab character, the new line is indented by the size of a tab stop by setting `stringWidth` to `tabGap`.

The last thing that needs to be done to initialize the `Graphics` object is to select the chosen font. This is very important, because the printer graphics context doesn't have any font selected at all. If you forget to select a font and then invoke the `drawString` method, you will get a `NullPointerException`.

Once the graphics context has been prepared, the current word is rendered with `drawString`, using the `line` and `column` variables to specify the position, and then the current position is moved past the word just printed by adding its size to `column`. Note that tab characters are not actually rendered as spaces– all that happens is that `column` is increased by the value of `stringWidth`, which was previously set to the distance to the next tab stop. Since it has already been verified that there is enough room on the line for this word (or tab), there is no need to check for line overflow here.

When the entire input file has been processed, there may be a partial page that needs to be printed. This situation can be detected by checking to see whether there is an active `Graphics` object and, if so, the last page is printed by invoking `dispose` on it.

The code shown here assumes that the printer actually prints the pages in the order in which you generate them. This is not always the case, however. You can use the `lastPageFirst` method of `PrintJob` to get the printing order; as its name suggests, it returns `true` if pages appear in reverse order. If the printer is going to reverse the order of your pages, you might want to compensate by generating them last page first.

Summary

In this chapter, you've seen how to use a component's graphics context to draw graphics and text onto its surface. You discovered that there are subtle differences between the way in which the `Graphics` object is initialized when dealing with lightweight components like those derived from `JComponent`.

This chapter also developed a complete working application, one that will be used in the next few chapters to demonstrate some more of the new Swing features. During the construction of this application, you saw how custom borders are constructed and you also saw how to create a custom component of your own, albeit a very simple one.

Finally, you saw the support that the AWT provides for printing and how to print user interface components and text, taking care to break the text at the margins and at page boundaries.

Part 2

USING SWING TO BUILD BETTER APPLICATIONS

Now that you've seen the basics of Swing and the AWT, Part 2 introduces some of the Swing mechanisms and components that help you create more professional applications. All of the things that you will see in this part could, of course, be provided in an AWT-based application, provided that you were prepared to implement the yourself. With Swing, these features are available for nothing - all you have to do is make proper use of them.

Keyboard and focus handling is a feature that is often not properly handled by AWT applications. Before Swing, it was difficult to implement shortcut keys, a feature that users of other platforms are accustomed to, because the JDK 1.1 event model made it more difficult than it had been in JDK 1.0 to catch key events that should be processed outside of the component that happens to have the focus. Swing solves this problem in an elegant manner by providing a registry of keystrokes that works independently of the component that has the focus. It also provides a more flexible focus manager to make it possible to control the tabbing order of a user interface more easily.

An application of any complexity will need a well-designed menu system. Swing provides a much more comprehensive (and more regular) menu system than the AWT. The Swing menu system comes with keyboard mnemonics that allow to activate visible menu items and hotkeys that let you access facilities from menus without having to navigate the menu hierarchy. For the more frequently-used features, you can mirror menu items with toolbar buttons. The Swing toolbar feature lets you add a toolbar to your application that can be fixed or allowed to float around the screen and subsequently re-dock with the application.

Finally, Part 2 describes at length how Swing supports dialogs. Whereas the AWT was light on common dialogs such as information, warning and error message boxes, Swing has a full complement of them, each of which is highly customizable. It also has dialogs that allow the user to choose files and colors and a whole set of components (such as lists, combo boxes and tabbed panes) that you can use to build dialogs of your own.

KEYBOARD HANDLING, ACTIONS AND SCROLLING

Topics in This Chapter

- Handling the Focus
- Keyboard Events and Shortcuts
- Using Actions to Respond to Events
- JScrollPane, JViewport and JScrollBar
- Logical Scrolling and Keyboard Scrolling

Chapter 5

This chapter looks at several Swing mechanisms that you can use to build better applications. The main theme of the first half of the chapter is the need to be able to operate the application without using a mouse. This is often a difficult area for software developers to get right because they rarely use the keyboard to navigate around an application, but to the expert user the ability to get quickly to the parts of the application that they use the most is of great importance. Getting to a piece of the application quickly usually means using accelerator keys or shifting the input focus manually with the Tab key until a particular control is reached. This chapter looks at the basic mechanisms that the Swing focus manager offers and shows how much simpler it is to create key accelerators with Swing than it was with JDK 1.1.

The use of keyboard accelerators leads naturally to the concept of Actions, which encapsulate application functionality in a way that is independent of the manner in which it is accessed. This chapter looks at using Actions as targets for accelerator keys, but later you'll see that they can be used with menus and toolbars as well.

The second half of the chapter looks at the powerful Swing scrolling components, JScrollPane and JViewport. JScrollPane is much more useful than its AWT counterpart (ScrollPane). You'll see how to arrange for a component to be scrolled and how to customize the appearance and operation of JScrollPane. Finally, the two halves of the chapter are brought together by an example that shows how you can arrange for the user to be able to scroll a view using only the keyboard.

Implementing Mouseless Operation

One of the things that often separates software developers from users is the extent to which they make use of the mouse. Software developers probably use the mouse most of the time and would be lost (or at least would slow down noticeably) without it; by contrast, many nonprogrammers find the mouse too slow to use—they quickly become familiar with the parts of an application that they want to use and learn how to use the keyboard to activate those controls that they use most frequently. Once you have learned where the most frequently-used accelerator keys are on the keyboard, the odds are that you can use them to do something much faster than you could by moving the mouse right across the screen to access the same control (or pull down a menu) and then activate it.

For example, while writing this book, I invariably used CTRL+S to save what I had done rather than moving the mouse to the File menu, clicking to make it drop down, dragging the mouse down to Save and then clicking again. Using a keyboard accelerator like this is much faster and more convenient. Unfortunately, writing an application that works well both with the mouse and the keyboard is not quite trivial. In this section, you'll see how keyboard events are handled by Java programs as well as two features that, when properly used, will allow you to produce an application that works well for keyboard users—focus handling and keyboard accelerators.

Focus Handling

Mouse users are often unaware of what the concept of focus is; a mouse user wanting to press a button will move the pointer over the button and click it. For the keyboard user, though, this simple operation breaks down into two steps. First, you have to convince the application that you want to do something with the button and, secondly, you have to carry out the operation. Getting the application to direct the next action to the button is called giving the button the focus. Think of the focus as being the place to which keyboard operations will be directed. To make it possible to drive an application using only the keyboard, you must be able to reach every active component using only the keyboard and you must be able to activate the component with the keyboard as well.

Simple Focus Management

The Swing components provide support for both focus handling and keyboard activation, but your application still has to make proper use of these facilities to make them useful. Consider the example in Listing 5-1, which creates a frame with a button and a text input field. For the purposes of illustration, whatever you type in the text area will appear on the frame's caption and, for convenience, you can use the button to clear out the text area.

Listing 5-1   Automatic Focus Handling

```java
package JFCBook.Chapter5;

import com.sun.java.swing.*;
import java.awt.*;
import java.awt.event.*;

public class FocusExample1 extends JFrame implements ActionListener {
  public FocusExample1() {
    super("Focus 1");

    b = new JButton("Clear");
    t = new JTextField(35);

    this.getContentPane().add(t, "Center");
    this.getContentPane().add(b, "West");

    b.addActionListener(this);
    t.addActionListener(this);
  }

  // ActionListener interface
  public void actionPerformed(ActionEvent e) {
    if (e.getSource() == b) {
      // The button has been pressed
      t.setText("");    // Clear the text field
    } else {
      // Return pressed in the text field
      this.setTitle(t.getText());
      t.setText("");
    }
  }

  public static void main(String[] args) {
    FocusExample1 f = new FocusExample1();
    f.pack();
    f.addWindowListener(new WindowAdapter() {
      public void windowClosing(WindowEvent evt) {
        System.exit(0);
      }
    });
    f.setVisible(true);
  }

  private JButton b;    // The button
  private JTextField t; // The text field
}
```

Run this program using the command

```
java JFCBook.Chapter5.FocusExample1
```

and try to use it *without using the mouse*. You will find that the text area is ready to receive input straight away, because the initial focus has been assigned to this component automatically. Now type something and press the return key and your text will appear on the caption bar. So far, so good. Now type some more into the text area. Suppose that you wanted to use the Clear button to discard the text you have just typed. With the mouse, you simply move the pointer over the button and click, but if you can't use the mouse, how can you get to the button?

The focus can be moved between components by using Tab to go forward and Shift-Tab to move backward. In this case, since there are only two components, you can use either key to move to the button. When you get the focus onto the button, notice that it highlights itself—this is typical visual feedback when a component has the focus. Now that you're over the button, how do you "click" it? The JButton class is keyboard-aware: if you press the space bar, it acts as if you had clicked it with the mouse. Do this now and your text will disappear. To type some more text, just tab back to the text area and notice that the button loses its highlighting.

Using the requestFocus Method

What you have just seen was *free* functionality: the correct component got the focus when the application started and both components reacted properly when they received the focus and the keyboard was used to activate them. This example used features built into Swing components, but it is possible to do better. After pressing the button to clear the text field, the button retains the focus, but there is little use for this. What does the user want to do next? It is unlikely that the next action will be to press the button again—far more likely than this is that the user wants to type some more text. So, why not pass the focus back to the text area so that the user can do this without pressing tab again? To allow you to do this, every component has a requestFocus method that can be used to pass it the focus. By adding a single line of code to the last example, the focus can be moved directly back to the text area after the button has done its job:

```
public void actionPerformed(ActionEvent e) {
  if (e.getSource() == b) {
    // The button has been pressed
    t.setText("");      // Clear the text field
    t.requestFocus();   // Give focus to the text area
  } else {
    // Return pressed in the text field
    this.setTitle(t.getText());
    t.setText("");
  }
}
```

You can try this example using the command

```
java JFCBook.Chapter5.FocusExample2
```

Selecting the Component with Initial Focus

Another use for requestFocus is to force the focus to be given to a specific component when the application starts. It was fortunate that the text area was allocated focus in this simple application; let's show a case in which the automatic choice is perhaps not the best. Suppose you were presented with a choice like that shown in Figure 5-1.

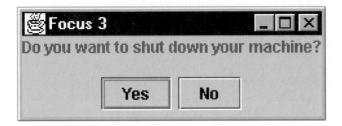

Figures 5-1   The dangers of the wrong initial focus assignment.

The question and the choices are reasonable; the problem is that the Yes button has the default keyboard focus, as you can see because it is highlighted. Now, if you press the space bar, perhaps accidentally, your machine will be closed down (not really—this *is* just an example!) and you probably won't be very amused. What we really wanted to do was to give the initial focus to the No button. Then, if the user accidentally activated it, all that would happen is that the frame would go away.

To fix this problem, perhaps the initial focus should be assigned when the user interface is created, as shown in the following code extract:

```
public FocusExample4() {
   super("Focus 4");

   l = new JLabel("Do you want to shut down your machine?",
         SwingConstants.CENTER);

   // Add some space around the label
   BorderLayout m = new BorderLayout(10, 10);
   this.getContentPane().setLayout(m);

   b1 = new JButton("Yes");
   b2 = new JButton("No");
```

```
JPanel p = new JPanel();
p.add(b1);
p.add(b2);

this.getContentPane().add(l, "Center");
this.getContentPane().add(p, "South");

b1.addActionListener(this);
b2.addActionListener(this);

b2.requestFocus();
}
```

Unfortunately, this simple solution doesn't work: the Yes button will still have the initial focus. To see this for yourself, use the command

```
java JFCBook.Chapter5.FocusExample4.
```

This happens because the focus isn't assigned until the window is about to appear on the screen, so any request made before this time is lost. The initial focus is *always* assigned to the first component added to the container, assuming that it can accept the focus. If it can't, the next component is tried and so on, until a component that can accept the focus is found. This search travels down through as many container levels as necessary to find a focusable component. This implies that it is possible to influence whether a component can accept the focus—you'll see exactly how this is done in "Component Tabbing Order" below. As a simple rule, remember that active components like JButton can accept the focus, while passive ones like JLabel usually cannot. So to get the focus to the correct place in this example, we just need to be careful about how we add children to our JPanel: the component that should receive the initial focus should be added first, as the code in Listing 5-2 shows.

Core Note

Notice the careful wording—"while passive ones like JLabel usually cannot." As you'll see in the discussion on tabbing order, even a JLabel can be made to accept the focus. You'll even see an example of this in "Handling Keyboard Input" later in this chapter.

Listing 5-2   Selecting the component that gets the initial focus

```
package JFCBook.Chapter5;

import com.sun.java.swing.*;
import java.awt.*;
import java.awt.event.*;

public class FocusExample5 extends JFrame implements ActionListener{
  public FocusExample5() {
    super("Focus 5");

    l = new JLabel("Do you want to shut down your machine?",
                                    SwingConstants.CENTER);

    // Add some space around the label
    BorderLayout m = new BorderLayout(10, 10);
    this.getContentPane().setLayout(m);

    b1 = new JButton("Yes");
    b2 = new JButton("No");

    JPanel p = new JPanel();

    // Add "No" button first to give it initial focus
    JPanel buttonPanel = new JPanel();
    buttonPanel.setLayout(new BorderLayout());
    buttonPanel.add(b2, "East");
    buttonPanel.add(b1, "West");
    p.add(buttonPanel);


    this.getContentPane().add(l, "Center");
    this.getContentPane().add(p, "South");

    b1.addActionListener(this);
    b2.addActionListener(this);
  }

  // ActionListener interface
  public void actionPerformed(ActionEvent e) {
    if (e.getSource() == b1) {
      // Yes pressed
      l.setText("Machine being shut down....");
    } else {
      // No pressed - go away
      System.exit(0);
```

(Continued)

```
    }
  }

  public static void main(String[] args) {
    FocusExample5 f = new FocusExample5();
    f.pack();
    f.addWindowListener(new WindowAdapter() {
      public void windowClosing(WindowEvent evt) {
        System.exit(0);
      }
    });
    f.setVisible(true);
  }

  private JButton b1;   // The "Yes" button
  private JButton b2;   // The "No" button
  private JLabel l;    // The label
}
```

Unfortunately, because the buttons are hosted by a `JPanel` that uses a `FlowLayout` manager, changing the order in which they are added to the panel would also reverse their order on the display, so that the No button would now appear on the left. Since the user interface order should not be dictated by an implementation detail, this problem is solved by using a `BorderLayout` instead of `FlowLayout`, because this allows us to specify where the button should go, independently of the order in which they are added to the container

Just doing this would have another undesirable effect—the buttons would be stretched horizontally to fill the entire panel, because there will only be east and west components and `BorderLayout` will allocate all of the available space to them. To avoid this problem, we create a new panel with a `BorderLayout` onto which we mount the buttons, then mount this panel onto the original one. Now the new panel will be allowed to occupy only the space that it needs because its parent is managed by `FlowLayout`, as a result of which it will be just large enough to contain the two buttons, which won't need to be stretched. You can try this example and verify that the focus is set correctly with the command

```
java JFCBook.Chapter5.FocusExample5
```

Focus Events

Movement of the focus can be monitored by registering to receive *focus* events, which are delivered when a component gains or loses the focus. These events are most often useful to component developers, who can use them to change a component's appearance to indicate whether it owns the focus.

Core Note

There is a good example of this in Chapter 13, "The Pluggable Look-and-Feel," in which you'll see how to implement a new user interface for a button that changes depending on whether the button has the focus.

To receive focus events, you need an object that implements the `FocusListener` interface and register it with the component or components that you want to monitor. The possible focus events and the corresponding listener interface methods are shown in Table 5-1.

Table 5-1:   Focus Events

Event	Method	Meaning
FOCUS_GAINED	focusGained	Delivered when a component receives the input focus
FOCUS_LOST	focusLost	Delivered when the input focus moves elsewhere

Each of these methods gets a `FocusEvent` as its only argument. This event has two interesting properties. First, since it extends `ComponentEvent`, you can use the `getComponent` method to discover the component to which the event relates. Secondly, in the case of the `FOCUS_LOST` event, you can use the `isTemporary` method to determine whether the focus has been permanently or temporarily lost. We'll use the code in Listing 5-3 to demonstrate both the use of focus events and the concept of temporary and permanent loss of focus.

Listing 5-3   Adding a help message using focus events

```
package JFCBook.Chapter5;

import com.sun.java.swing.*;
import java.awt.*;
import java.awt.event.*;

public class FocusExample6 extends JFrame implements ActionListener{
   public FocusExample6() {
     super("Focus 6");

     this.getContentPane().setBackground(UIManager.getColor("control"));

     l = new JLabel("Do you want to shut down your machine?",
                                    SwingConstants.CENTER);
     l.setFont(new Font("sansserif", Font.BOLD, 14));
```

```java
h = new JLabel(" ", SwingConstants.LEFT);
h.setFont(new Font("serif", Font.BOLD, 12));
b1 = new JButton("Yes");
b2 = new JButton("No");

this.getContentPane().setLayout(new GridBagLayout());
GridBagConstraints c = new GridBagConstraints();

c.gridx = 0;
c.gridy = 0;
c.gridwidth = GridBagConstraints.REMAINDER;
c.gridheight = 1;
c.weightx = 1.0;
c.weighty = 1.0;
c.fill = GridBagConstraints.BOTH;
c.insets = new Insets(20, 20, 20, 20);
this.getContentPane().add(l, c);     // The message text

// Add the 'Yes' and 'No' buttons
// 'No' MUST be added first so that it gets focus
c.gridx = 1;
c.gridy = 1;
c.gridwidth = 1;
c.weighty = 0.0;
c.fill = GridBagConstraints.NONE;
c.anchor = GridBagConstraints.CENTER;
c.insets = new Insets(4, 4, 4, 4);
this.getContentPane().add(b2, c);   // No button - must be
                                    // before Yes

c.gridx = 0;
this.getContentPane().add(b1, c);

c.gridx = 0;
c.gridy = 2;
c.gridwidth = GridBagConstraints.REMAINDER;
c.fill = GridBagConstraints.HORIZONTAL;
this.getContentPane().add(h, c);     // The help area

b1.addActionListener(this);
b2.addActionListener(this);

// Catch focus events
FocusListener f = new FocusListener() {
  public void focusGained(FocusEvent e) {
    JButton b = (JButton)e.getComponent();
    if (b == b1) {
```

```
            h.setText("Press this button to shut down your system");
        } else {
            h.setText("Press this button to cancel system shutdown");
        }
    }

    public void focusLost(FocusEvent e) {
        JButton b = (JButton)e.getComponent();
        String type = e.isTemporary() ? "temporarily" : "permanently";
        String blabel = (b == b1) ? "\"Yes\"" : "\"No\"";

        System.out.println("The " + blabel + " button has " + type + " lost focus.");
    }
};

b1.addFocusListener(f);
b2.addFocusListener(f);
}

// ActionListener interface
public void actionPerformed(ActionEvent e) {
    if (e.getSource() == b1) {
        // Yes pressed
        l.setText("Machine being shut down....");
    } else {
        // No pressed - go away
        System.exit(0);
    }
}

public static void main(String[] args) {
    FocusExample6 f = new FocusExample6();
    f.pack();
    f.addWindowListener(new WindowAdapter() {
        public void windowClosing(WindowEvent evt) {
            System.exit(0);
        }
    });
    f.setVisible(true);
}

private JButton b1;    // The "Yes" button
private JButton b2;    // The "No" button
private JLabel l;    // The label
private JLabel h;    // The "help" label
}
```

This example extends the one used above by adding a "help" message below the buttons, as shown in Figure 5-2. The idea is to show help for the currently focused button. When a button gets the focus, its help text is written to the JLabel that is used to implement the help area. To implement this, we create a FocusListener that reacts to FOCUS_GAINED events by extracting the reference to the component concerned from the FocusEvent and using that to choose between two different help messages. Since the No button gets the focus when the application is started, its message will appear without needing to write any special code.

Figure 5-2   Adding a help message using focus events.

If you tab between the two buttons, you will see the help message change and you will also see messages like this in the window in which you started the program:

```
The "No" button has permanently lost focus.
The "Yes" button has permanently lost focus.
The "No" button has temporarily lost focus.
The "No" button has permanently lost focus.
```

These messages are generated by the focusLost method, based on the value returned by isTemporary when applied to each FocusEvent. When you tab between the buttons, you will notice that the previous button loses the focus permanently; to give it back, you would need to tab back into that button. A temporary loss of focus occurs when you switch to a different application, causing this one to be deactivated, or when you iconify the application. The difference in the case of a temporary loss of focus is that you don't need to tab back into the button for it to get the focus again—the focus will return (with another FOCUS_GAINED event) when you reactivate or deiconify the application.

AWT Component Tabbing Order

As has been said, you can move the focus between components using the Tab or Shift-Tab keys. But how do you know which is the next component to receive the focus? Every container has a defined tabbing order that dictates the order in which the focus moves between components. When you press Tab, the focus moves to the next component in the tabbing order and with Shift-Tab it moves to the previous component. The determination of the tabbing order in JDK 1.1 was simple—it was the same as the order in which the components were added to the container so, in the example in Listing 5-2, you would expect the tabbing order to be the No button followed by the Yes button, which is what you get. If a container is added inside another container, when that container is reached in the tabbing order, its first eligible component gets the focus, and so on. Determination of the tabbing order in Swing is, however, slightly more complex.

Swing Component Tabbing Order

The default Swing tabbing order within a container is more natural than that of the AWT because it is based on the visual layout of the container, not on the order in which components were added to the container. Thus, for example, if a container has a single row of buttons, the tabbing order for that container would start with the button on the left and proceed from left to right, so that all of the buttons would be traversed in left-to-right order. If this container had two rows of buttons, the tabbing order would be across the top row, then to the leftmost button on the second row and across the second row from left-to-right. This would be true whether or not the buttons were added to the container in this order. The example in Listing 5-4 shows the difference between the default AWT and Swing tab order.

Listing 5-4   Illustrating Swing and AWT tab order

```
package JFCBook.Chapter5;

import com.sun.java.swing.*;
import java.awt.*;
import java.awt.event.*;

public class TabOrder extends JFrame {
  public TabOrder(String title) {
    super(title);

    JPanel mainPanel = new JPanel();
    mainPanel.setLayout(new GridBagLayout());
    GridBagConstraints c = new GridBagConstraints();
```

continued

```java
// Do the left column: the labels
c.gridx = 0;
c.gridy = GridBagConstraints.RELATIVE;
c.insets = new Insets(2, 2, 2, 2);

mainPanel.add(new JLabel("Name:", JLabel.RIGHT), c);
mainPanel.add(new JLabel("Street:", JLabel.RIGHT), c);
mainPanel.add(new JLabel("City:", JLabel.RIGHT), c);
mainPanel.add(new JLabel("Zip:", JLabel.RIGHT), c);
mainPanel.add(new JLabel("E-mail:", JLabel.RIGHT), c);

// Middle column: the text fields
c.gridx = 1;
c.weightx = 1.0;
c.fill = GridBagConstraints.HORIZONTAL;
for (int i = 0; i < 5; i++) {
  mainPanel.add(new JTextField(32), c);
}

// Right side: two buttons
c.gridx = 2;
c.weightx = 0.0;
mainPanel.add(new JButton("OK"), c);
mainPanel.add(new JButton("Cancel"), c);

// Add the main panel to the frame
getContentPane().add(mainPanel);
}

public static void main(String[] args) {
  String title = "Tab Order (Swing style)";
  if (args.length > 0 && args[0].equals("awt")) {
    DefaultFocusManager.disableSwingFocusManager();
    title = "Tab Order (AWT style)";
  }

  JFrame f = new TabOrder(title);
  f.pack();
  f.addWindowListener(new WindowAdapter() {
    public void windowClosing(WindowEvent evt) {
      System.exit(0);
    }
  });
  f.setVisible(true);
}
}
```

This example creates a form on which there are five input fields stacked vertically. To the left of each field is a label that indicates what is to be typed into each field and to the right of the input fields are two buttons. You can run this example using either of the following two commands:

```
java JFCBook.Chapter5.TabOrder

java JFCBook.Chapter5.TabOrder awt
```

If you use the first command, the Swing focus manager is used. The second command disables the Swing focus manager, so you can use it to see how this layout would be handled by the AWT. You'll see how to disable the Swing focus manager in "Controlling the Focus Mechanism" later in this chapter. Both commands create the same layout, as shown in Figure 5-3; only the caption bar title differs between the two commands.

Figure 5-3   A form to show Swing/AWT tab order differences.

Whichever form of the command you use, the focus is assigned initially to the text field labeled Name. This might surprise you—shouldn't the first component added to the container, which is the Name label, get the initial focus? The initial focus goes to the first *eligible* component in the container, not the first component. The label is not eligible because its isFocusTraversable method returns false. Here is how this method is defined by Component:

```
public boolean isFocusTraversable();
```

Inactive components like JLabel return false from this method, while buttons, text fields and other components that can accept the focus all return true. To determine the initial focus component, the container is scanned from the first component added to find the first component for which isFocusTraversable returns true. In this case, the first text field will therefore get the initial focus. If you are creating a custom component, you should override isFocusTraversable to indicate whether your component can accept the focus. If it can't, it won't appear in its container's tabbing order and any focus-moving operations will ignore it.

If you run the AWT version of the command and keep pressing the Tab key, you'll find that the focus moves down the list of text fields until it reaches the bottom, then passes to the OK button and the Cancel button and finally back to the Name text field again. This is probably the order that you want, because the user will most likely fill in the form from the top down and use Tab to get between the fields, then Tab over to the OK button and press it. You get this order free because the text fields were all added in the order in which you want them to be filled in, followed by the OK button and then the Cancel button and, as you know, the AWT tabbing order matches the order in which the components were added to the container.

If you now run the Swing version of this command (by omitting the "awt" argument on the command line), you'll immediately see a difference. The focus starts in the same place, but pressing Tab moves it to the OK button, followed by the Street field, the Cancel button and then the City field. This happens because the Swing tabbing order is determined by the final layout of the container, not by the way in which the components were added.

Core Note

Even though Swing's tabbing order is determined by layout, the initial focus still goes to the first component added to the container.

To determine the default tabbing order, the Swing focus manager compares each pair of components in the container, looking at their x and y components. If the y components are "close"—such as, within 10 pixels of each other, it orders the components based on the x coordinate, so that the component with the lower x coordinate comes first. If the y coordinates are not close, then the ordering is based on the y coordinate, with the lower y coordinate coming before the higher one. Put simply, components on the same row (or nearly the same row) are ordered from left to right and come before components on a lower row, but after components on a higher row.

In this example, then, the components on the top row all have the same y coordinate that is lower than that of any other component, so the tab order will traverse the top row first and, within that row it will travel from low to high x coordinates—in other words, from left to right. Often, this will be what you want and it is probably more natural than the AWT arrangement most of the time. This example, of course, has been chosen to highlight one case in which it does not produce the desired result.

Changing the Default Tabbing Order

With the AWT, to change the tabbing order, you have to change the order in which the components are added to the container. With Swing, you can change the tabbing order in two ways:

- Move components into a different container
- Explicitly set next and previous components for particular components where the order is wrong.

Using a Container to Change the Tabbing Order

The tabbing order only makes sense within a single container—you can't jump from one arbitrary component in one container to an arbitrary component in another one. But you can use containers to change the tabbing order. Here, for example, you could move the buttons onto a panel of their own. What happens then is that the panel is considered on its own as a member of the main form's tabbing order. Suppose you did this by changing the code shown in Listing 5-4 to this, where the modifications are highlighted in bold:

```
for (int i = 0; i < 5; i++) {
  mainPanel.add(new JTextField(32), c);
}

// Right side: two buttons on a separate panel
JPanel buttonPanel = new JPanel();
buttonPanel.setLayout(new GridBagLayout());
c.gridx = 2;
c.weightx = 0.0;
c.anchor = GridBagConstraints.NORTH;
c.gridheight = GridBagConstraints.REMAINDER;
mainPanel.add(buttonPanel, c);

// Put the buttons on the panel
c.gridx = 0;
c.weightx = 1.0;
c.gridheight = 1;
buttonPanel.add(new JButton("OK"), c);
buttonPanel.add(new JButton("Cancel"), c);

// Add the main panel to the frame
getContentPane().add(mainPanel);
```

The tabbing order for the form would then be:

- Name field
- Button Panel
- Street Field
- City Field
- Zip field
- E-mail field

Note that the button panel appears second in the tabbing order because of its position in the form's geometry—its *y* coordinate is the same as that of the first text field and its x coordinate is greater, so it comes after the first text field and before the second one. You can see what happens with this change in place with the command:

```
java JFCBook.Chapter5.TabOrder2
```

You'll find that the tab order has indeed changed—after the text field. The OK button gets the focus, followed by the Cancel button, then the rest of the text fields in order. This is different, but not correct. You get this tab order because the first Tab takes the focus from the Name field to the button panel (see the order above), where it starts following the tab order of that panel. Inside the panel, the tab order is the OK button followed by the Cancel button, because of their respective y coordinates. When the end of this order has been reached, the focus moves out of the panel and back up to the original form, where it goes first to the Street field and then continues through the original order shown in the list above.

There is, however, another way to regroup these components so that the correct tabbing order is obtained. The problem with the first attempt was that the button panel was on the main panel and therefore was counted in its tabbing order. The simplest way to get around this is to move it off the main panel and place it on the content pane alongside the main panel. The tabbing order within the main panel will then be the text fields in top-to-bottom order. On the button panel, the tabbing order will be the OK button followed by the Cancel button. Finally, the main panel will be traversed before the button panel because their y coordinates are equal and the main panel's x coordinate is lower. Listing 5-5 shows the implementation of this idea.

Listing 5-5   Using containers to change the tab order

```java
package JFCBook.Chapter5;

import com.sun.java.swing.*;
import java.awt.*;
import java.awt.event.*;

public class TabOrder3 extends JFrame {
  public TabOrder3(String title) {
    super(title);

    JPanel mainPanel = new JPanel();
    mainPanel.setLayout(new GridBagLayout());
    GridBagConstraints c = new GridBagConstraints();

    // Do the left column: the labels
    c.gridx = 0;
    c.gridy = GridBagConstraints.RELATIVE;
    c.insets = new Insets(2, 2, 2, 2);
```

```
      mainPanel.add(new JLabel("Name:", JLabel.RIGHT), c);
      mainPanel.add(new JLabel("Street:", JLabel.RIGHT), c);
      mainPanel.add(new JLabel("City:", JLabel.RIGHT), c);
      mainPanel.add(new JLabel("Zip:", JLabel.RIGHT), c);
      mainPanel.add(new JLabel("E-mail:", JLabel.RIGHT), c);

      // Middle column: the text fields
      c.gridx = 1;
      c.weightx = 1.0;
      c.fill = GridBagConstraints.HORIZONTAL;
      for (int i = 0; i < 5; i++) {
        mainPanel.add(new JTextField(32), c);
      }

      // Right side: two buttons on a separate panel
      JPanel buttonPanel = new JPanel();
      buttonPanel.setLayout(new GridBagLayout());
      c.gridx = 2;
      c.weightx = 0.0;
      c.anchor = GridBagConstraints.NORTH;
      c.gridheight = GridBagConstraints.REMAINDER;

      // Put the buttons on the panel
      c.gridx = 0;
      c.weightx = 1.0;
      c.gridheight = 1;
      buttonPanel.add(new JButton("OK"), c);
      buttonPanel.add(new JButton("Cancel"), c);
      c.weighty = 1.0;
      buttonPanel.add(new JPanel(), c);

      // Add the main panel and the button panel to the frame
      getContentPane().add(mainPanel, "Center");
      getContentPane().add(buttonPanel, "East");
  }

  public static void main(String[] args) {
    String title = "Tab Order";
    JFrame f = new TabOrder3(title);
    f.pack();
    f.addWindowListener(new WindowAdapter() {
      public void windowClosing(WindowEvent evt) {
        System.exit(0);
      }
    });
    f.setVisible(true);
  }
}
```

Here, the button panel is added to the content pane directly. Because the content pane is managed by a `BorderLayout`, the add line for the main panel is changed to specify the `Center` position and the button panel is added in the `East` position. In order to make the `OK` and `Cancel` buttons stay at the top of the button panel, a dummy panel is added to the button panel. The `GridBagLayout` manager will expand this panel to take up the empty space at the bottom, as you saw in a similar example in Chapter 3. If you run this version of the program using the command

```
java JFCBook.Chapter5.TabOrder3
```

you'll find that the text fields and buttons are traversed in the correct order.

Changing the Tabbing Order Explicitly

Swing offers another way to change the tabbing order of `JComponents`: the `setNextFocusableComponent` method:

```
public void setNextFocusableComponent(Component acomp);
```

You can use the `setNextFocusableComponent` method to explicitly specify which component gets the focus after the one to which the method is applied. This method belongs to `JComponent`, so although you can give it any `Component` as an argument, you can't set up tabbing *from* an AWT `Component` this way, because it doesn't have a `setNextFocusableComponent` method. This method, then, is only really useful when you are only using Swing components (which is probably the normal case).

To arrange the tabbing order required for our example, you would leave all of the text fields and components on the original panel and set them up as before. Then, you would apply `setNextFocusableComponent` to the `Name` field, pointing it to the `Street` field. Similarly, you apply this method to the `Street` field and point it to the `City` field and so on. The `E-mail` field would then be pointed to the `OK` button and the `OK` button to the `Cancel` button. You do not apply `setNextFocusableComponent` to the last component in the tabbing order, so it wouldn't be invoked against the `Cancel` button itself. Listing 5-6 shows how this works.

Listing 5-6   Using setNextFocusableComponent

```
package JFCBook.Chapter5;

import com.sun.java.swing.*;
import java.awt.*;
import java.awt.event.*;

public class TabOrder4 extends JFrame {
  public TabOrder4(String title) {
```

```
super(title);

JPanel mainPanel = new JPanel();
mainPanel.setLayout(new GridBagLayout());
GridBagConstraints c = new GridBagConstraints();

// Do the left column: the labels
c.gridx = 0;
c.gridy = GridBagConstraints.RELATIVE;
c.insets = new Insets(2, 2, 2, 2);

mainPanel.add(new JLabel("Name:", JLabel.RIGHT), c);
mainPanel.add(new JLabel("Street:", JLabel.RIGHT), c);
mainPanel.add(new JLabel("City:", JLabel.RIGHT), c);
mainPanel.add(new JLabel("Zip:", JLabel.RIGHT), c);
mainPanel.add(new JLabel("E-mail:", JLabel.RIGHT), c);

// Middle column: the text fields
c.gridx = 1;
c.weightx = 1.0;
c.fill = GridBagConstraints.HORIZONTAL;
JTextField textFields[] = new JTextField[5];
for (int i = 0; i < 5; i++) {
  textFields[i] = new JTextField(32);
  mainPanel.add(textFields[i], c);
}

// Explicitly set tab order for the text fields
for (int i = 0; i < 4; i++) {
  textFields[i].setNextFocusableComponent(textFields[i + 1]);
}

// Right side: two buttons
c.gridx = 2;
c.weightx = 0.0;
JButton okButton = new JButton("OK");
mainPanel.add(okButton, c);
JButton cancelButton = new JButton("Cancel");
mainPanel.add(cancelButton, c);

// Place the buttons in the tabbing order
textFields[4].setNextFocusableComponent(okButton);
okButton.setNextFocusableComponent(cancelButton);


// Add the main panel to the frame
getContentPane().add(mainPanel);
```

(Continued)

```
    }

    public static void main(String[] args) {
        String title = "Tab Order 4";
        JFrame f = new TabOrder4(title);
        f.pack();
        f.addWindowListener(new WindowAdapter() {
            public void windowClosing(WindowEvent evt) {
                System.exit(0);
            }
        });
        f.setVisible(true);
    }
}
```

You can try this example for yourself with the command:

```
java JFCBook.Chapter5.TabOrder4
```

Core Alert

In Swing 1.0, `setNextFocusableComponent` *(and hence the example in Listing 5-6) doesn't work properly due to bugs in the Swing focus manager. If you try this example with Swing 1.0, you'll see exceptions when you try to use the Tab key. This being the case, it is recommended that you use the other methods described in this chapter to control tab order until this bug is fixed.*

Controlling the Focus Mechanism

The focus mechanism is controlled by the Swing focus manager, implemented in the class `DefaultFocusManager`, which is derived from the basic focus manager class `FocusManager`. `FocusManager` is an abstract class, defined as follows:

```
public abstract class FocusManager {
    public FocusManager();
    public static FocusManager getCurrentManager();
    public static void setCurrentManager(FocusManager aFocusManager);
    public static void disableSwingFocusManager();
    public static boolean isFocusManagerEnabled();
    public abstract void processKeyEvent(Component focusedComponent,
                KeyEvent anEvent);
    public abstract void focusNextComponent(Component aComponent);
    public abstract void focusPreviousComponent(Component aComponent);
}
```

The FocusManager class itself provides complete implementations of the four static methods, which are all concerned with managing focus managers. The three abstract methods are placeholders for code that implements the response of a particular focus manager to key strokes and determines how the focus moves from one component to another, either forward (in the case of focusNextComponent) or backward (for focusPreviousComponent). Concrete implementations of these three methods that implement the policies that have been described in this section are provided by DefaultFocusManager.

You've already seen the focus policy operated by DefaultFocusManager, which gets control when key presses occur within a component. These keys are passed to the processKeyEvent method, which must either return having done nothing with them, or handle them as a focus-changing stimulus and consume the KeyEvent that it received. As an example, DefaultFocusManager usually consumes all KeyEvents that contain the Tab key and does nothing with the others. KeyEvents that are not consumed are processed by the component in the usual way.

In this section it is the four static methods that are of interest. The getCurrentManager and setCurrentManager methods allow you to get and change the focus manager that your application uses. The definition of these methods seems to imply that there is a single focus manager in operation at any given time, but this is not strictly true. In fact, there is one focus manager per thread group within the application: All threads in a thread group share the same focus manager.

Core Note

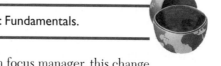

Thread groups are discussed in Core Java 1.1, Volume I: Fundamentals.

If you use setCurrentManager to install a custom focus manager, this change affects only the threads in the same thread group as the one that made the call: threads in other thread groups, if there are any, continue to use the previous focus manager. This design is probably motivated by the implementation of Web browsers, which isolate each applet in a single thread group: a change of focus manager by an applet would then only affect that applet.

In practice, it is unlikely that a Java *application* will want to have thread groups with different focus managers because, in fact, the focus manager is only useful when processing events. Events are handled by AWT event handling threads in the thread group in which the application starts. If you create a new thread group and change its focus manager, this will have no effect because AWT events will not be processed in that thread group and so the new focus manager will not be invoked there.

Initial Selection of Focus Manager

When a Swing application starts, there is actually no active focus manager. A focus manager is created only when the getCurrentManager method of FocusManager is invoked, which is usually when a key press is processed by the processKeyEvent method of JComponent. This method looks in a hash table that maps thread groups to focus managers. Since this table is initially empty, the first key event will create a focus manager for the calling thread group and enter it into the hash table. Subsequent calls to getCurrentManager from the same thread group will return this focus manager instance.

The default focus manager is not entirely hard-wired into an application—it is, in fact, a property held under the symbolic name FocusManager.FOCUS_MANAGER_CLASS_PROPERTY in the application's UIDefaults table. You'll see in Chapter 13 how to change the value of this property. By doing so, you can install your own custom focus manager that is automatically selected for all thread groups. By default, of course, the value of this property is com.sun.java.swing.DefaultFocusManager. The subject of writing custom focus managers is beyond the scope of this book. It is not, however, a difficult task. The information presented in this section, together with the source code for the FocusManager and DefaultFocusManager classes, should be enough to enable you to write one of your own.

Disabling the Focus Manager

If you want to disable the Swing focus manager and use the AWT one instead, as was done in Listing 5-4, you can use the disableSwingFocusManager method to do so. This method, like setCurrentManager, applies only to the thread group containing the thread that invoked it, so it is most useful if it is invoked as soon as the application starts. The isFocusManagerEnabled method allows you to check whether the Swing focus manager is enabled. This method returns true if the AWT manager is not enabled, which means that the Swing manager or a custom focus manager is active in the current thread group.

The Swing focus manager is actually disabled not by installing a subclass of FocusManager that implements AWT focus manager semantics, but by installing a special focus manager called DisabledFocusManager which has empty implementations for processKeyEvent, focusNextComponent and focusPreviousComponent. Of these, only the first matters in this case—because it is empty, it never consumes Tab keys, so they are passed to the AWT focus manager.

One reason to switch off the Swing focus manager is to provide compatibility with the AWT tabbing order in an application that uses Swing components but does not want the extended Swing focus manager facilities. It can also be a good idea to switch the Swing focus manager off if you are mixing Swing and AWT components, because you cannot use the setNextFocusableComponent method with AWT components to correct the default tabbing order when it doesn't suit your application.

Handling Keyboard Input

Having seen how to control the keyboard focus, this section will briefly show you how the keyboard itself is seen by Java applications. Most Java programs will probably not

deal this directly with keyboard input, since Swing provides several standard components that allow the user to type text into an application and a higher-level mechanism
that allows direct handling of keys that will be described later in this chapter. You will
probably only need to handle keyboard events for yourself if you plan to write a custom component that reacts to keyboard input or you want to create a custom look-and-
feel for one or more of the Swing components that interact with the keyboard.

Key Events

All keyboard activity is turned into one of three keyboard events, delivered as a
`java.awt.event.KeyEvent` object: KEY_PRESSED, KEY_RELEASED and
KEY_TYPED. While the purpose of these events might seem obvious from their
names, there are a few subtleties to consider as will become evident if you run the
program shown in Listing 5-7 using the command:

```
java JFCBook.Chapter5.KeyExample
```

Listing 5-7   Receiving Key Events

```
package JFCBook.Chapter5;

import com.sun.java.swing.*;
import java.awt.*;
import java.awt.event.*;

public class KeyExample implements KeyListener {
  KeyExample(JTextArea t) {
    this.t = t;
  }

  // KeyListener Interface
  public void keyPressed(KeyEvent e) {
    showKeyEvent(e);
  }

  public void keyReleased(KeyEvent e) {
    showKeyEvent(e);
  }

  public void keyTyped(KeyEvent e) {
    showKeyEvent(e);
  }

  // Describe a key event
```

(Continued)

```java
  private void showKeyEvent(KeyEvent e) {
    t.append(e + " [action? " + e.isActionKey() + "]\n");
  }
  public static void main(String[] args) {
    JFrame f = new JFrame("Key Events");
    JTextArea t = new JTextArea(20, 80);
    KeyExample k = new KeyExample(t);
    JLabel l = new JLabel("Press keys here", SwingConstants.CENTER) {
      public boolean isFocusTraversable() {
        return true;
      }
    };

    f.addWindowListener(new WindowAdapter() {
      public void windowClosing(WindowEvent evt) {
        System.exit(0);
      }
    });

    l.addKeyListener(k);
    l.addMouseListener(new MyMouseAdapter(l));

    f.getContentPane().add("South", l);
    f.getContentPane().add("Center", new JScrollPane(t));
    f.pack();
    f.show();
  }

  // Instance data
  private JTextArea t;     // The text area
}

//
// This adapter class ensures that we can pass the focus to the label
//class MyMouseAdapter extends MouseAdapter {
  MyMouseAdapter(Component c) {
    this.c = c;
  }

  public void mousePressed(MouseEvent e) {
    c.requestFocus();
  }

  private Component c;  // Component to get focus
}
```

Following a familiar pattern, this program creates a window with an empty text area and a label below it, then attaches a listener to the label. Since the idea is to capture keyboard actions on the label, the program creates an object that implements the KeyListener interface, which is defined as follows:

```
public interface KeyListener extends EventListener {
    public void keyTyped(KeyEvent e);
    public void keyPressed(KeyEvent e);
    public void keyReleased(KeyEvent e);
}
```

The important thing to realize about KeyEvents is that they are only delivered to the component that has the keyboard focus. In this example, we want keyboard input to be directed to the label, so we use the same technique that we showed earlier, namely adding the label to the container before the text area to assign the initial focus to the label without any need for the mouse to be clicked over it. In this case, that would not be enough on its own, because an ordinary JLabel claims not to be able to accept the keyboard focus, so the initial focus would still be given to the text area. To get around this problem, a subclass of JLabel with an overridden isFocusTraversable method is used instead. Because this method will always return true and the label is the first component in the frame, it will be assigned the initial focus. For good measure, a MouseAdapter that gives the focus to the label when it is clicked on has been added, so that you can continue typing in the label if you accidentally give the focus to the text area by clicking on it.

When you run the program, move the mouse anywhere over the application window . There is no need to click the mouse. You will find that you can press keys and view the events they generate in the text area. Start by pressing the A key on the keyboard (without the SHIFT key) and releasing it. This produces the following output in the text area (some of the program's output has been deleted for clarity):

```
java.awt.event.KeyEvent[KEY_PRESSED,keyCode=65,keyChar='a'] on [.] [action? false]
java.awt.event.KeyEvent[KEY_TYPED,keyCode=0,keyChar='a'] on [.] [action? false]
java.awt.event.KeyEvent[KEY_RELEASED,keyCode=65,keyChar='a'] on[.] [action? false]
```

Pressing and releasing this key generated three events. The KEY_PRESSED and KEY_RELEASED events are generated at the times at which their names suggest and the KEY_TYPED message is produced somewhere in between. Both of these messages have two attributes, called keyCode and keyChar. The keyCode attribute is a number (known as a virtual key code) assigned to the key on the keyboard which has been pressed or released, while keyChar represents the Unicode character produced by that key. The KEY_PRESSED event shows that pressing the 'A' key generates a keyChar of 'a' and a keyCode of 65;. You will also notice that the KEY_RELEASED event contains the same values.

The set of values that can be returned as the keyCode attribute can be found in the Java API documentation for the KeyEvent class. Each value has a symbolic representation that should be used in code: You should *not* rely on the actual numeric values. Typical examples of values that you might find in keyCode are:

KeyEvent.VK_A	The "A" key.
KeyEvent.VK_0	The key "0" on the main keyboard.
KeyEvent.VK_NUMPAD0	The key "0" on the keyboard number pad
KeyEvent.VK_F1	Function key F1.
KeyEvent.VK_DELETE	The DELETE key
KeyEvent.VK_PRINTSCREEN	The PRINT SCREEN key
KeyEvent.VK_SHIFT	The SHIFT key
KeyEvent.VK_ENTER	The ENTER key

Now look at the KEY_TYPED event. This contains the same keyChar value as the KEY_PRESSED event, but the keyCode is set to 0. This is one of the differences between these two events: the KEY_TYPED event never carries the keyCode associated with the actual key pressed.

Next, press the shift key and the "A" key together, so that you type an uppercase "A", then release both keys. This time, you will see the following:

```
java.awt.event.KeyEvent[KEY_PRESSED,keyCode=16,keyChar='',Modifiers=Shift] on [.]
                                                              [action? false]
java.awt.event.KeyEvent[KEY_PRESSED,keyCode=65,keyChar='A',modifiers=Shift] on [.]
                                                              [action? false]
java.awt.event.KeyEvent[KEY_TYPED,keyCode=0,keyChar='A',modifiers=Shift] on [.]
                                                              [action? false]
java.awt.event.KeyEvent[KEY_RELEASED,keyCode=65,keyChar='A',modifiers=Shift] on [.]
                                                              [action? false]
java.awt.event.KeyEvent[KEY_RELEASED,keyCode=16,keyChar=''] on [.] [action? false]
```

Core Note

If you see an uppercase A in the text area, you have inadvertently shifted the keyboard focus into the text area. Return it to the label by clicking the mouse over it and try again. Note that, in this special case, pressing Tab *to navigate back to the label doesn't work because the* JTextArea *component swallows the* Tab *character before the keyboard navigation mechanism sees it. You can, however, use* Tab *with the* CTRL *key pressed to return the focus to the label.*

The exact order of the KEY_RELEASED events depends on the order in which you release the Shift and "A" so may differ from that shown above. Notice that there are KEY_PRESSED and KEY_RELEASED events for both the Shift and A keys, and a single KEY_TYPED event for the single effective keystroke. Comparing the KEY_TYPED event with the previous one, you will notice that keyChar now has the value "A" rather than "a", but the keyCode in the KEY_PRESSED and KEY_RELEASED events is still 65. This is because the key code represents the key itself and is independent of any modifiers, such as Shift, applied by other keys.

The KEY_TYPED event also indicates that the Shift key was pressed. The state of the Shift, Ctrl, Alt and Meta keys (or as many as are defined on your particular keyboard) is encoded in the modifiers attribute of the KeyEvent object as an OR of the values SHIFT_MASK, CTRL_MASK, ALT_MASK, and META_MASK defined by the class InputEvent, which is the superclass of KeyEvent (and, incidentally, of MouseEvent as well). This mask is also supplied with the KEY_PRESSED and KEY_RELEASED events (assuming, in the case of KEY_RELEASE, that the Shift key is released after the "A" key, which was not the case in the example above).

If you now press and hold down the "A" key (without Shift) for slightly longer than before so that the key starts to repeat, and then release it, you see a different set of events:

```
java.awt.event.KeyEvent[KEY_PRESSED,keyCode=65,keyChar='a'] on [.] [action? false]
java.awt.event.KeyEvent[KEY_TYPED,keyCode=0,keyChar='a'] on [.] [action? false]
java.awt.event.KeyEvent[KEY_PRESSED,keyCode=65,keyChar='a'] on [.] [action? false]
java.awt.event.KeyEvent[KEY_TYPED,keyCode=0,keyChar='a'] on [.] [action? false]
java.awt.event.KeyEvent[KEY_PRESSED,keyCode=65,keyChar='a'] on [.] [action? false]
java.awt.event.KeyEvent[KEY_TYPED,keyCode=0,keyChar='a'] on [.] [action? false]
java.awt.event.KeyEvent[KEY_PRESSED,keyCode=65,keyChar='a'] on [.] [action? false]
java.awt.event.KeyEvent[KEY_TYPED,keyCode=0,keyChar='a'] on [.] [action? false]
java.awt.event.KeyEvent[KEY_RELEASED,keyCode=65,keyChar='a'] on [.] [action? false]
```

Here there are four pairs of KEY_PRESSED and KEY_TYPED events, followed by the single KEY_RELEASED, as you might expect. This underlines, however, that it is incorrect to assume that a KEY_PRESSED will be followed by a KEY_RELEASED event before the next KEY_PRESSED. The set of keys that repeat and the rate at which they repeat is platform-dependent and cannot be controlled by the Java application.

Not all keys on the keyboard have a valid Unicode encoding. To see how Java deals with this, press and release the F1 key. You should see the following output:

```
java.awt.event.KeyEvent[KEY_PRESSED,keyCode=112,F1] on [.] [action? true]
java.awt.event.KeyEvent[KEY_RELEASED,keyCode=112,F1] on [.] [action? true]
```

Since function keys do not have a Unicode encoding, no KEY_TYPED event is generated for them. Note also that the value of the keyChar attribute is not shown; in fact, this field would have the value KeyEvent.CHAR_UNDEFINED. Another difference you will see here is that this key has the attribute action set to true. Several keys on the keyboard, including the function keys, the cursor movement keys, PAGE UP, PAGE DOWN, PRINT SCREEN and so on, which request an action on the part of the application rather than supply information to be stored, are tagged as action keys in this way.

The KeyEvent class supplies methods for extracting the various attributes in a form usable by an application. The keyCode and keyChar attributes can be extracted using the getKeyCode and getKeyChar methods, while the modifiers can be obtained using the getModifiers method inherited from InputEvent. Alternatively, the state of individual modifier keys can be obtained using the isAltDown, isControlDown, isMetaDown and isShiftDown, methods, while isActionKey returns the action attribute; these last five methods all return a boolean.

Whether you decide to monitor just KEY_TYPED events or act upon KEY_PRESSED and KEY_RELEASED events depends on the functionality your component or application needs to provide. If you only act upon KEY_TYPED events, you will not be able to detect action keys and other keys that do not generate Unicode characters. In this case, you would examine the keyChar attribute and possibly the modifiers to handle a keystroke. Note that keyChar is a Unicode character, so your code would look something like this:

```
public void keyTyped(KeyEvent e) {
   char key = e.getKeyChar();
   boolean controlPressed = e.isControlDown();

   if (key == 'x' && controlPressed  == true) {
      // CTRL + X pressed
      // Perform 'cut' operation
   } else if (key == 'c' && controlPressed == true) {
      // CTRL + 'C' pressed
      // Perform 'copy' operation
   } else if (key == 'v' && controlPressed == true) {
      // CTRL + 'V' pressed
      // Perform 'paste' operation
   }
}
```

If you need greater keyboard control, you will need to process KEY_PRESSED and KEY_RELEASED events. In this case, you could choose to inspect the keyChar attribute for Unicode characters and if this has the value KeyEvent.CHAR_UNDE-FINED you would look at the value of keyCode. The following code extract shows how you might handle a KEY_PRESSED event.

```
public void keyPressed(KeyEvent e) {
   char key = e.getKeyChar();
   int keyCode = e.getKeyCode();
   int modifiers = e.getModifiers();

   if (key != KeyEvent.CHAR_UNDEFINED) {
      // Process Unicode character
   } else if (keyCode == KeyEvent.VK_F1) {
      // F1 is pressed
   } else if (keyCode == KeyEvent.VK_PRINTSCREEN) {
      if (modifiers & InputEvent.ALT_MASK) {
         // Alt + PrintScreen
         // Could also have used isAltDown()
      } else {
         // Just PrintScreen
      }
   }
}
```

Keyboard Shortcuts

Directly handling keyboard events was the only way to respond to user key presses in JDK 1.1, but because of the way events are handled, it is very difficult to provide some of the features expected of a professional application without doing a lot of work. The most obvious example of this is providing support for accelerator keys that work wherever the keyboard focus is. Suppose, for example, you want to write an application that can provide help when the user presses the F1 key. To be useful, this feature has to work no matter where the user is typing and irrespective of the keyboard focus.

KeyStrokes

The problem with this in JDK 1.1 is that the KEY_PRESSED event will only go to the component that has the focus—which could be any component in the application window. In order to implement a help system based on the F1 key, you would have to register keyboard listeners on each and every component, then specifically check for either F1 or forward key events that a component doesn't want to process itself to another part of the application that looks for appropriate key presses, such as F1. This is highly undesirable, because it complicates the application and doesn't work very well (and perhaps not at all) if you use third-party components in your application, because you may not be able to gain access to the internals of these components in order to register key listeners.

JComponent provides a mechanism that makes it very easy to intercept the key events that you are interested in and dispatch them to an event handler, no matter where the keyboard focus is when the appropriate keys are pressed. This mechanism is activated using the following JComponent method:

```
public void registerKeyboardAction(ActionListener action,
                    KeyStroke stroke, int condition);
```

The arguments passed to this method are:

- Action. The action to be performed when the given key combination is pressed and the specified condition is satisfied.
- Stroke. Specifies the key to be pressed or released and the state of the modifier keys.
- Condition. Indicates where the focus can be for this action to be triggered.

The key combination is specified using a KeyStroke object. The KeyStroke class provides five static methods that all create a KeyStroke object:

```
public static KeyStroke getKeyStroke(int keyCode, int modifiers, boolean onKeyRelease);
public static KeyStroke getKeyStroke(char keyChar);
public static KeyStroke getKeyStroke(int keyCode, int modifiers);
public static KeyStroke getKeyStroke(String representation);
public static KeyStroke getKeyStrokeForEvent(KeyEvent anEvent);
```

The first form of the getKeyStroke method allows you to specify all three of a key stroke's attributes—a key, the modifier state and a boolean specifying whether the key stroke is deemed to have occurred when the key is pressed (when false) or when it is released (true). For example, to create a KeyStroke that describes pressing the F1 key with no modifier keys pressed, use the following:

```
KeyStroke ks = KeyStroke.getKeyStroke(KeyEvent.VK_F1, 0, false);
```

The modifiers are specified as a combination of the values Input Event.SHIFT_MASK, InputEvent.ALT_MASK, InputEvent.META_MASK, and InputEvent.CTRL_MASK. For example, the following creates a KeyStroke that can be used to trigger an action when the PRINT SCREEN key is pressed, but only if the ALT key is also pressed:

```
KeyStroke ks = KeyStroke.getKeyStroke(KeyEvent.VK_PRINTSCREEN,
                                      InputEvent.ALT_MASK, false);
```

The second form of this method allows you to conveniently create a KeyStroke from a Unicode character:

```
KeyStroke ks = KeyStroke.getKeyStroke(' ');
```

The KeyStroke returned from this invocation would cause an event if the space bar is pressed with no keyboard modifiers; you cannot use this form to handle a key that does not have a valid Unicode encoding. To do that, you use, the third form, which accepts a key code and modifiers and creates a KeyStroke that activates when the key that generates that key code is pressed. Thus, the following two lines are equivalent:

```
KeyStroke ks = KeyStroke.getKeyStroke(KeyEvent.VK_PRINTSCREEN,
                                      InputEvent.ALT_MASK, false);
KeyStroke ks = KeyStroke.getKeyStroke(KeyEvent.VK_PRINTSCREEN,
                                      InputEvent.ALT_MASK);
```

The fourth variant of getKeyStroke, which accepts a string description of a key sequence, is not currently implemented and always returns null. Finally, you can use getKeyStrokeForEvent to create a KeyStroke that corresponds to the key sequence that generated the specified event. The key code and modifiers are extracted from the KeyEvent and the condition is set so that that KeyStroke specifies pressing the key if the event is KEY_PRESSED and releasing it if it is KEY_RELEASED. If the event is KEY_TYPED, the key is taken from the keyChar field of the event, the modifier field is set to 0, and the key must be pressed to cause an event to occur.

```
    // (4) 'F1' only when text area focused
    ActionListener 14 = new ActionListener() {
      public void actionPerformed(ActionEvent evt) {
        System.out.println("F1 pressed in the text area");
      }
    };
    tf.registerKeyboardAction(14,
          KeyStroke.getKeyStroke(KeyEvent.VK_F1, 0, false),
          JComponent.WHEN_FOCUSED);
  }
}
```

This example program creates a JFrame with two colored panes one above the other. On the upper pane there is a button labeled 'A' and a text field and on the bottom pane are three buttons labeled "B," "C" and "D," as shown in Figure 5-4.

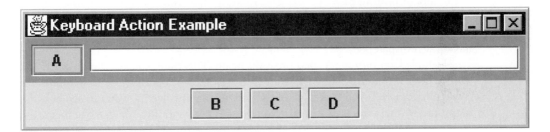

Figure 5-4 Using accelerator keys.

You can run this example using the command:

```
java JFCBook.Chapter5.KeyboardActionExample
```

After the user interface has been created, keyboard actions are registered for four different cases; each action has a corresponding inner class that implements the ActionListener interface, providing an actionPerformed method that prints a message that allows us to see when the action has been triggered and exactly which action was selected. Later in this section, you'll see a more useful way of processing actions generated from the keyboard, which also generalizes to menu, button and toolbar operations. Here are the keyboard actions that are registered and when they should be triggered; the numbers correspond to those in Listing 5-8.

1. The F1 key is pressed within the focused window.
2. The "A" key is pressed or the "D" key is released when the focus is in the lower pane.

3. The F1 key is pressed when the focus is in the lower pane.

4. The F1 key is pressed when the text field has the focus.

You may find the registerKeyboardAction lines slightly confusing: It can be a little difficult to see the exact conditions under which the action will be triggered. If you read these lines in a particular way, however, everything will become clear. Let's take the following example:

```
lowerPane.registerKeyboardAction(13,
        KeyStroke.getKeyStroke(KeyEvent.VK_F1, 0, false),
        JComponent.WHEN_ANCESTOR_OF_FOCUSED_COMPONENT);
```

This action is triggered when the F1 key is pressed if lowerPane is the ancestor of the focused component. To see this, first read the keystroke description (the second argument to registerKeyboardAction), then the JComponent against which the action is registered, and finally the condition applied (the last argument). The lowerPane is the ancestor of the focused component when the focus is directed to any of buttons "B," "C" or "D." To verify that the action occurs when one if these buttons has the focus, click any of them with the mouse and press the F1 key. This produces the message 'F1 somewhere in lower pane," showing that the correct action was dispatched.

Next, click on button "A" and press F1 again. This time, you see the message "F1 somewhere in main window," as shown in Figure 5-5, because the first action has been performed. If you look at all of the actions that involve F1, you can see how the appropriate operation is selected. If you press F1 when button "A" has the focus, the key event that this generates will actually be processed by the JComponent part of the JButton "A." There is no keyboard action registered against button "A" for F1, so the button's parent is inspected next. In this case, the parent is upperPane. Since there are no actions registered on the upper pane, the next place to look is this pane's parent, which is the frame's content pane. Again, this has no registered action. The search continues upward until the JFrame's JRootPane is reached, which has keyboard action (1) associated with it. This explains why you see the message "F1 somewhere in main window."

Figure 5-5   F1 key detected on button "A."

Now click in the text area and again click on F1. This time, you see the message "F1 pressed in the text area." It is easy to see that this is correct, because the fourth action is supposed to be performed when you press F1 when the text field has the focus.

Lastly, click on any button in the lower pane. Now press the "A" key and hold it down. When you release it, you will see the message "A released or D pressed on lower pane button," indicating that one of the actions labeled (2) has been activated. You get the same message if you press the "D" key, but this time you don't have to wait until you release the key. Again, you can see that this is the correct result by imitating the logic used by the JComponent class when searching for an appropriate action. Suppose that you clicked on button "B" and then pressed the "D" key. The KEY_PRESSED event will go to button "D," which doesn't have a handler for it (there are no actions registered against button "D"). Next, the parent of button "D"— namely lowerPane—is inspected. This has the following actions associated with it:

```
lowerPane.registerKeyboardAction(12,
        KeyStroke.getKeyStroke(KeyEvent.VK_A, 0, true),
        JComponent.WHEN_ANCESTOR_OF_FOCUSED_COMPONENT);
    lowerPane.registerKeyboardAction(12,
        KeyStroke.getKeyStroke(KeyEvent.VK_D, 0, false),
        JComponent.WHEN_ANCESTOR_OF_FOCUSED_COMPONENT);
```

Of these, only the second has the correct keystroke –the "D" key has just been pressed. Finally, the condition is checked: This action is selected if lowerPane is the parent of the focused component. Since the focused component is button "B," the condition is met so the action is performed.

The search order for actions is as follows:

1. Check the focused JComponent for any action matching the keystroke.

2. Scan upward through the ancestors of the focused JComponent for actions that match the keystroke and also have either the condition WHEN_ANCESTOR_OF_FOCUSED_COMPONENT or the condition WHEN_IN_FOCUSED_WINDOW.

3. Check all JComponents in the same window as the focused component for actions that match the keystroke and have condition WHEN_IN_FOCUSED_WINDOW.

Note that only one action is ever performed for each registered keystroke. Thus, despite the fact that there is, for example, an action registered for F1 that covers the whole window, it won't be triggered if F1 is pressed when the focus is in the text area or in one of the buttons on the lower pane, because those actions will be located first.

Removing and Managing KeyStrokes

JComponent also has a few other methods that deal with keyboard actions. You can remove a registered keyboard action using the method:

```
public void unregisterKeyboardAction(KeyStroke);
```

The argument passed to this method is the reference to the KeyStroke originally obtained from registerKeyboardAction. Notice that when you register a keyboard action, you specify a KeyStroke and a condition, but when you unregister you specify only the KeyStroke. This is because the actions are held in a Hashtable associated with the JComponent in which the KeyStroke reference is the key. If you want to register two actions for the same KeyStroke, you must create two KeyStroke objects. This is the correct way to do it (assuming l1 and l2 are two different implementations of ActionListener):

```
KeyStroke k1 = KeyStroke.getKeyStroke('A');
KeyStroke k2 = KeyStroke.getKeyStroke('A'),
registerKeyboardAction(l1, k1, WHEN_FOCUSED);
registerKeyboardAction(l2, k2, WHEN_IN_FOCUSED_WINDOW);
```

This will create two entries in the Hashtable, because k1 and k2, which are the keys to the Hashtable, are different objects, so when you do this:

```
unregisterKeyboardAction(k1);
```

you remove only the WHEN_FOCUSED action. On the other hand, do not be tempted to try this shortcut:

```
KeyStroke k1 = KeyStroke.getKeyStroke('A');
registerKeyboardAction(l1, k1, WHEN_FOCUSED);
registerKeyboardAction(l2, k1, WHEN_IN_FOCUSED_WINDOW);
```

This won't work: Because the same KeyStroke object has been used in both cases, the same key will be used twice to access the Hashtable, so the second action will overwrite the first and the listener l1 will never be called. You can remove all registered keyboard actions from a JComponent using the resetKeyboardActions method, which doesn't require any arguments.

If you want to know what actions are registered against a component, you can use the method getRegisteredKeyStrokes:

```
public KeyStroke[] getRegisteredKeyStrokes();
```

When you have a KeyStroke object, you can retrieve the associated action and the condition for that action using the following methods:

```
public ActionListener getActionForKeyStroke(KeyStroke)
public int getConditionForKeyStroke(KeyStroke)
```

Note that these are JComponent methods, not KeyStroke methods, because the action and condition are stored in the JComponent, not in the KeyStroke.

Keystrokes and Actions

The KeyStroke class and the supporting functionality in JComponent is one of the improvements in Swing that make it easier to write keyboard-aware applications. The Swing architects wanted to make it easy for developers to make application functions that would naturally be placed on menus (and, as you'll see later, on toolbars) available via keyboard accelerators. As you'll see, the design they came up with was a very clever one.

Providing the KeyStroke class goes some way toward satisfying this aim, since it is very easy to link any action to a keystroke: Only one line of code is needed to arrange for an appropriate event handler to be invoked. The other problem that needed to be solved was how to represent the actions themselves.

Actions

If you've written applications for JDK 1.1, you've probably connected application logic to buttons and menu items by writing an ActionListener and placing the code that performs the required function in the actionPerformed method, or in another method invoked from there. Sometimes, the fact that an event has occurred tells you all that you need to know. For example, if the user selects a menu item that says Exit, you can assume that he/she wants to terminate the application. You might, in this case, verify that this is really intended, but you won't need any more information. In most cases, though, the action will involve changing the state of something and the problem is to know how to locate that something from within the event handler.

To see why this can be a problem, remember that an action triggered from a button (or a menu item, as you'll find out later in this chapter), causes the actionPerformed method of the registered listener to be invoked, with an ActionEvent as its only argument. From the event, you can determine the component that caused the event and the string that you may have associated with that component using setActionCommand. The action command is often used to tell you which of several possible application functions is required (e.g., open a file, save a file, etc.). Where can other types of information be stored? Since the event contains a reference to the source component, you could consider storing any information you need there. If it is a JComponent, you could, for example, use the putClientProperty method to save arbitrary information that can be retrieved in the event handler using getClientProperty. You've already seen this technique in the graphics drawing program back in Chapter 4, "Graphics, Text Handling, and Printing."

```
JButton button = new JButton(new
ColorFillIcon(buttonColors[i]));
colorButtons[i] = button;
colorPanel.add(button);
button.putClientProperty(DRAW_COLOR, buttonColors[i]);
button.addActionListener(new ActionListener() {
  public void actionPerformed(ActionEvent evt) {
    JButton b = (JButton)evt.getSource();

    Color color = (Color)b.getClientProperty(DRAW_COLOR);
    Icon g = b.getIcon();
    colorLabel.setIcon(g);
    graphicOps.setColor(color);
  }
});
```

Here, each button corresponds to a color; when the button is pressed, you need to know which color has been selected. While this could have been encoded in a string in some way and stored in the button using `setActionCommand`, it would be tedious to parse the string back into a color in the event handler. Instead, a reference to the information is stored in the `JComponent` that caused the event, where it could easily be retrieved. It is easy to see that information that is needed in an event handler cannot always be conveniently represented as a string, so some solution of this kind will be needed in most cases.

While the solution adopted here was perfectly workable for this application, things aren't always so simple. Storing the information along with the source of the event works well when there is only one source. Sometimes, however, there will be more than one source of the same event. In this chapter, you have already seen how to make it possible for users to activate application functionality from the keyboard. What is the source of the event in this case? The whole point of the `KeyStroke` mechanism described in this chapter is that it should work no matter where the keyboard focus is—you might, therefore, get the `F1` key pressed when the mouse is pointing anywhere at all in the application window. What actually happens is that the event appears to come from the component against which the keyboard action was registered (i.e., the `JComponent` on which `registerKeyboardAction` was performed). It might be that you could store the information that you need inside that component. But suppose you also have the `Help` function on a menu. Now, the event can happen in two ways, with two different sources. If you want to continue storing the information with the source components, you now have to save it twice. But that isn't the end of the story.

What if you want a `Help` button on your application's toolbar? You might (stretching a point) even want a separate `Help` button on the application window itself, making a total of four sources for the same event. Obviously, it will be very inconvenient to have to write the same code four times and a nightmare to maintain it should you need to change anything later. Clearly, there has to be a better way to store information that relates to processing an application event for use by the event handler. The solution to this provided by Swing is the `Action` interface and an implementation of it called `AbstractAction`. Here is how the `Action` interface is defined:

```
public interface Action extends ActionListener {
    public Object getValue(String key);
    public void putValue(String key, Object value);
    public void setEnabled(boolean b);
    public boolean isEnabled();
    public void addPropertyChangeListener(PropertyChangeListener listener);
    public void removePropertyChangeListener(PropertyChangeListener listener);
}
```

Not all of the methods associated with `Action` will be described in this section, since many of them are aimed specifically at menus and toolbars. The main point to note here is that `Action` extends `ActionListener`. This has two consequences. First, any class that implements `Action` must also implement `ActionListener`, so it must provide an `actionPerformed` method in addition to those shown above. Secondly, you can use an `Action` anywhere that you can use an `ActionListener`. In other words, you can use an `Action` as the target of a registered keyboard action or to process a button press. As you'll see shortly, you can also use an `Action` to handle menu and toolbar events.

The AbstractAction Class

How does `Action` help with the problem of storing information needed by event handlers? Actually, on its own it doesn't, but the `AbstractAction` class does. `AbstractAction` is an implementation of `Action` in which all of the methods, apart from the `actionPerformed` method, are provided but do nothing. You can think of `AbstractAction` as a prototypical `Action`: It is used in the same way as event adapters like `MouseAdapter` are, by providing a way for you to write only that part of an interface that you want to use, while defaulting the rest. Unlike event adapters, however, it is an abstract class: To use it, you must subclass it and implement `actionPerformed`. This is perfectly reasonable—what use would an `Action` be without a method to process the action when it occurs?

Here is how the `AbstractAction` class is defined:

```
public abstract class AbstractAction implements Action,
                              Cloneable, Serializable {
    public AbstractAction();
    public AbstractAction(String name);
    public AbstractAction(String name, Icon icon);
    public abstract void actionPerformed(ActionEvent evt);
    public synchronized void setEnabled(boolean enabled);
    public boolean isEnabled();
    public Object getValue(String key);
    public synchronized void putValue(String key, Object value);
    public synchronized void
```

```
        addPropertyChangeListener(PropertyChangeListener 1);
public synchronized void
        removePropertyChangeListener(PropertyChangeListener 1);
}
```

To pass information to an event handler, you can create an instance of a subclass of `AbstractAction` that stores that information when it is created. In the event handler, you can easily retrieve whatever you stored because the "`this`" pointer in the `actionPerformed` method points to your original `AbstractAction` object. Furthermore, you can solve the problem of performing the same action in response to an event from more than one source by simply registering one `Action` (i.e. one instance of your subclass of `AbstractAction`) to process the event no matter where it comes from.

You have two ways to store information in a subclass of `AbstractAction`. The most obvious way is to define the storage yourself within your subclass and pass the information to be stored to the constructor. This information can then be used in the `actionPerformed` method. The `FontChangeAction` that you'll see in the next section is an example of this approach.

`AbstractAction` also provides a limited form of internal storage that allows you to store arbitrary objects under named keys using the `putValue` and `getValue` methods. While you can store anything you like using these methods, they are most commonly used to store one or both of a text string and an `Icon` that are associated with the `Action`. As you'll see in the next chapter, you can add `Actions` to Swing menus and toolbars and when you do this, the menu looks for the text string to use as the label of a menu item and the toolbar needs the `Icon` to mount on a button. These values are held under well-known keys. Here is the complete set of keys defined by the `Action` interface:

```
DEFAULT

NAME

SHORT_DESCRIPTION

LONG_DESCRIPTION

SMALL_ICON
```

The `SMALL_ICON` value is used to store an `Icon` that can be used by toolbars and menus. The `Object` stored under this key must, of course, be of type `Icon`. The `NAME` value is the string used to set the text of a menu item created using the `Action`. The other keys are available for use but have no preassigned meanings.

You can store the text label or the `Icon` when you create an `AbstractAction` using the last two constructors that you saw earlier. If you specify the name parameter, it is stored under the `NAME` key and similarly if you supply an `Icon`, it becomes the `SMALL_ICON` value.

At the end of this chapter, the graphics application from Chapter 4 will be rewritten to show exactly how to use `Actions` and how to share `Actions` between multiple sources. For now, let's clarify what has just been said with a simpler example.

Using Actions with Keyboard Accelerators

The following code creates a simple user interface with a text label and three buttons that can be used to change the font of the text on the label. The setMnemonic method could be used to attach keyboard accelerators to these buttons, but for the purposes of this example, KeyStroke objects that map F2 to the Bold key, F3 to the Italic key and F4 to the Plain key are used instead, as shown in Figure 5-6.

Figure 5-6   Using keyboard shortcuts and actions together.

To see how to use an Action, let's look at what the event handler that will handle the button press or the keystroke will need to do. When the user causes the event to occur the font associated with the label must be changed. To do this, the event handler will need a reference to the label and to the font to be associated with it. To store this information, you would create a class derived from AbstractAction and pass the label and font to its constructor, which stores them within the object. Here is the implementation of this class:

```
class FontChangeAction extends AbstractAction {
  public FontChangeAction(Font f, Component c) {
    this.font = f;
    this.comp = c;
  }

  public void actionPerformed(ActionEvent evt) {
    comp.setFont(font);
  }

  protected Font font;          // Font to select
  protected Component comp;     // Component whose font is to change
}
```

One of these action objects will be created, with appropriate associated font, for each of the function keys and the `registerKeyboardAction` method will be used to map a keystroke to its corresponding action, as shown in the code for the application itself (Listing 5-9). The command

```
java JFCBook.Chapter5.ActionExample
```

can be used to run this example.

Listing 5-9   Using an Action to implement a keyboard accelerator

```java
package JFCBook.Chapter5;

import com.sun.java.swing.*;
import java.awt.*;
import java.awt.event.*;

public class ActionExample extends JPanel {
  public ActionExample() {
    this.setLayout(new BorderLayout());

    JLabel l = new JLabel("Bold = F2; Italic = F3; Plain = F4",
            SwingConstants.CENTER);
    this.add(l, "Center");
    JPanel buttonPanel = new JPanel();
    this.add(buttonPanel, "South");

    Font boldFont = new Font("Dialog", Font.BOLD, 14);
    Font italicFont = new Font("Dialog", Font.ITALIC, 14);
    Font plainFont = new Font("Dialog", Font.PLAIN, 14);
    l.setFont(plainFont);

    JButton boldButton = new JButton("Bold");
    boldButton.setFont(boldFont);

    JButton italicButton = new JButton("Italic");
    italicButton.setFont(italicFont);

    JButton plainButton = new JButton("Plain");
    plainButton.setFont(plainFont);

    buttonPanel.add(boldButton);
    buttonPanel.add(italicButton);
    buttonPanel.add(plainButton);

    FontChangeAction boldAction = new FontChangeAction(boldFont, l);
```

```
      FontChangeAction italicAction = new FontChangeAction(italicFont, 1);
      FontChangeAction plainAction = new FontChangeAction(plainFont, 1);

      // Associate actions with buttons
      boldButton.addActionListener(boldAction);
      italicButton.addActionListener(italicAction);
      plainButton.addActionListener(plainAction);

      // Attach actions to keystrokes over the whole panel
      this.registerKeyboardAction(boldAction,
            KeyStroke.getKeyStroke(KeyEvent.VK_F2, 0, false),
            JComponent.WHEN_IN_FOCUSED_WINDOW);
      this.registerKeyboardAction(italicAction,
            KeyStroke.getKeyStroke(KeyEvent.VK_F3, 0, false),
            JComponent.WHEN_IN_FOCUSED_WINDOW);
      this.registerKeyboardAction(plainAction,
            KeyStroke.getKeyStroke(KeyEvent.VK_F4, 0, false),
            JComponent.WHEN_IN_FOCUSED_WINDOW);
   }

   public static void main(String[] args) {
      JFrame f = new JFrame("Action Example");
      ActionExample e = new ActionExample();
      f.setContentPane(e);
      f.addWindowListener(new WindowAdapter() {
         public void windowClosing(WindowEvent evt) {
            System.exit(0);
         }
      });
      f.setSize(300, 150);
      f.setVisible(true);
   }
}
```

As you can see, the `boldAction` object is created with a reference to the text label and the bold font and then registered to receive the event generated by the F2 key using the following line of code:

```
this.registerKeyboardAction(boldAction,
      KeyStroke.getKeyStroke(KeyEvent.VK_F2, 0, false),
JComponent.WHEN_IN_FOCUSED_WINDOW);
```

When the F2 key is pressed, the `actionPerformed` method of the `boldAction` object is entered. The ActionEvent passed to this method will indicate which component had the focus when the F2 key was pressed but, as we know, this is not really of any interest here. Instead of using that information, this method just performs the font change in one simple line of code, using the information that was stored when the action was created:

```
public void actionPerformed(ActionEvent evt) {
   comp.setFont(font);
}
```

I think you'll agree that this couldn't be much simpler: There is no need to worry about which component actually generated the event and you don't need to search for information stored with that component (or elsewhere) when the user interface was created. As a bonus, the same object can be used to act as the ActionListener for the buttons themselves, so the same code is executed whether a button or a function key is used to change the font.

More use will be made of the Action interface and the AbstractAction class later in this chapter and the next, where you will see how to use them in conjunction with menus and toolbars.

Scrolling Components

Most sophisticated user interfaces use scrollable areas in some way. Sometimes you'll want to display large graphics or images and for this you'll need a means of creating a canvas that allows you to scroll its contents. Fortunately, the Swing set includes a component called JScrollPane that fulfills most of the requirements you're likely to come across for scrolling and, if this isn't sufficient, you can create your own scrolling component by interacting directly with the JScrollBar component that JScrollPane uses. This section looks at both of these possibilities.

The JScrollPane and JViewport Classes

JScrollPane is a composite component that, in its simplest form, allows you to attach scrollbars to any component and manages the scrolling itself without any further intervention from your application code. This gives you a very simple way to allow a user with a small screen to view an image or graphic that would otherwise be too large to display. You can see how JScrollPane works by looking at a simple example (see Listing 5-10).

Listing 5-10 Scrolling an image

```
package JFCBook.Chapter5;

import com.sun.java.swing.*;
import java.awt.*;
import java.awt.event.*;

public class ScrollExample1 extends JFrame {
  public ScrollExample1() {
    super("Scroll Example 1");
    JScrollPane p = new JScrollPane(
                JScrollPane.VERTICAL_SCROLLBAR_AS_NEEDED,
                JScrollPane.HORIZONTAL_SCROLLBAR_AS_NEEDED);
    this.getContentPane().add(p);
    ImageIcon icon = new ImageIcon(getClass().getResource("images/bridge.jpg"));
    JLabel l = new JLabel(icon);
    p.setViewportView(l);
  }

  public static void main(String[] args) {
    JFrame f = new ScrollExample1();
    f.setSize(250, 200);
    f.setVisible(true);
    f.addWindowListener(new WindowAdapter() {
      public void windowClosing(WindowEvent e) {
        System.exit(0);
      }
    });
  }
}
```

This example creates a frame on which it places a JScrollPane. In the display area or *viewport* of this component we want to display an image. You know that images can by displayed easily using the ImageIcon class in conjunction with a JLabel, so this technique is used here to place a JLabel in the viewport of the JScrollPane. This is all that needs to be done to make the scrolling work.

You can run this example using the command:

```
java JFCBook.Chapter5.ScrollExample1.
```

When you do this, you'll see the image in the window with scrollbars to the right of and below it, as shown in Figure 5-7. If you click in these scrollbars you'll find that the image moves as expected. More than this, if you resize the window until it becomes larger then the image, one or both of the scrollbars become unnecessary and disappears.

Figure 5-7   Using JScrollPane to scroll a large image.

JScrollPane has four constructors:

```
public JScrollPane();

public JScrollPane(int vsbpolicy, int hsbpolicy);

public JScrollPane(Component comp);

public JScrollPane(Component comp, int vsbpolicy, int hsbpolicy);
```

The second of these constructors allows you to specify which of the scrollbars you want and when they should be displayed; the first argument refers to the vertical scrollbar and the second to the horizontal one. The following values are possible:

```
HORIZONTAL_SCROLLBAR_ALWAYS

VERTICAL_SCROLLBAR_ALWAYS

HORIZONTAL_SCROLLBAR_AS_NEEDED

VERTICAL_SCROLLBAR_AS_NEEDED

HORIZONTAL_SCROLLBAR_NEVER

VERTICAL_SCROLLBAR_NEVER
```

These constants are part of the ScrollPaneConstants interface, which is implemented by JScrollPane, so you would normally write them as JScrollPane.HORIZONTAL_SCROLLBAR_ALWAYS, etc. If you use the first constructor, then you get scrollbars only when they are needed. No matter how you create the JScrollPane, you can change the scrollbar policy at any time using the setHorizontalScrollBarPolicy and setVerticalScrollBarPolicy methods, which accept the constants shown above as their argument.

Creating a JScrollPane is the first step; the other thing you have to do is give it something to scroll. One way to do this is to use the setViewportView method, which takes a Component as its argument. Using this method, you can theoretically scroll almost anything you can display on the screen, including another JScrollPane! Once you've given it something to display, the JScrollPane takes care of everything, including whether or not to display scrollbars, how large the slider in the scrollbar should be, and which part of the scrolled object should be visible at any given time. The other way to do it is to use the third or fourth constructor, which take the Component to be scrolled as the first argument, so you don't need to call setViewportView yourself.

While you can use JScrollPane in this simple way, you can do more with it if you take a closer look at how it is constructed, as shown in Figure 5-8.

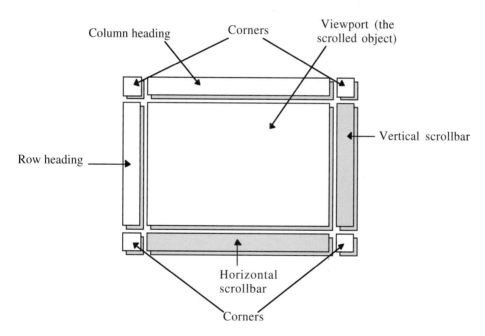

Figure 5-8   Component parts of JScrollPane.

The JScrollPane can have up to nine separate components, most of which are entirely optional. The most obvious of these, of course, are the scrollbars which, when present, are placed at the bottom and the right of the display area. Usually, these are just JScrollBar components but, as we'll see later, you can supply your own scrollbars if you need to. The other piece that is always present is the scrolling area, which is referred to as the viewport. The scrolled component is not laid directly on top of the `JScrollPane` itself; instead, the `setViewportView` method creates an instance of the `JViewport` class that will actually occupy the scrolled area, and passes the object to be scrolled to it. In fact, it is not the `JScrollPane` itself that manages the scrolling, but the `JViewport`—more about this in a moment.

Corners

So far, you have seen enough pieces to create the scrolling control you saw in Listing 5-10. In addition to these parts, you can supply components for the *corners* and for the *row and column headings*.

When you have scrollbars, each of them extends only to the bottom or to the right of the viewport so that, if you have two of them, there will be a gap in the bottom right corner where the two scrollbars meet. This area will normally be blank and will be the same color as the background of the `JScrollPane` itself (which is not necessarily the same color as the component in the viewport). You can enhance the appearance of the scroll pane by supplying a component to fill this area using the `setCorner` method:

```
public void setCorner(String key, Component corner);
```

The component you supply can be anything you like; usually, it will be a graphic of the appropriate size, or, as you'll see in a moment, you can create a custom component that adjusts itself according to the space it is given. The `key` argument specifies which of the four corners the component should occupy and must be one of the following:

JScrollPane.LOWER_RIGHT_CORNER

JScrollPane.LOWER_LEFT_CORNER

JScrollPane.UPPER_RIGHT_CORNER

JScrollPane.UPPER_LEFT_CORNER

Each corner is displayed only if it is requested and it is necessary to do so. If a corner is necessary but you don't supply one using `setCorner`, then the background of the `JScrollPane` will appear in the area that it would occupy. The lower right-hand corner, for example, is necessary only if there are two scrollbars; if there were only a vertical scrollbar, it would extend to the bottom of the scroll pane, making a corner unnecessary. Similarly, the upper right corner is needed only if the vertical scrollbar and the column heading component are present.

Row and Column Headings

The row and column headings are added using the following two methods:

```
public void setColumnHeaderView(Component heading);
public void setRowHeadingView(Component heading);
```

Again, you can use any component as a row or column heading; usually, you would use an image of the appropriate size or supply a custom component that draws an appropriate graphic as you'll see in the next example.

The column heading is placed across the top of the display area and it scrolls horizontally in step with the display area itself, but it never scrolls vertically. This allows you to keep some descriptive text or graphic in line with something in the scrolled area itself. For example, if your scrolled object is a spreadsheet, you can supply the column headings as the column header component and they will remain on view as you scroll the spreadsheet up and down, but move left to right as you scroll it sideways so that the headings remain over their assigned columns. Similarly, the row heading is attached to the left side of the scroll pane and scrolls vertically but not horizontally.

Core Note

This technique is used to good effect in Chapter 11, "The Table Control," to provide headings for a JTable.

The layout of the scroll pane itself is managed by an invisible layout manager called ScrollPaneLayout. Its job is to place the parts of the pane that have been requested and to ensure that they are sized appropriately as the scroll pane itself is initially sized or subsequently resized.

When the user moves the slider in a scrollbar, an event is generated that is handled by the JScrollPane's UI component. In response to this event, it decides how far and in which direction the component in the viewport should be moved and affects the move by calling the viewport's setViewPosition method, which acts like the translate method of the Graphics class that was used to move graphics around on a canvas in Chapter 4. In fact, the setViewPosition method works by translating the origin of the graphics context of the component being scrolled and then having that component repaint itself. Thus, for example, if the user moves the slider in the vertical scrollbar downward, the scrolled component should move upwards, so the JViewport translates the graphics origin by a negative amount in the y direction, so that more of the component falls above the top of the scrolled area. You'll see more clearly how this works when you see how to implement a scrolling component of your own at the end of this section.

Customizing the JScrollPane Component

Given that the JViewport's job is to affect the scrolling of the component that it contains, you won't be surprised to know that the row and column headings are, in fact, wrapped with a JViewport component as well. When you use the setViewportView, setRowHeaderView, or setColumnHeaderView methods, you supply a Component and the JScrollPane creates the corresponding JViewport object (if it doesn't already have one), adds your component to it, and then adds it to its own layout in the appropriate location. You can, if you wish, create your own JViewport objects and assign them to the scroll pane yourself by using the following JScrollPane methods:

```
public void setViewport(JViewport view);

public void setRowHeader(JViewport view);

public void setColumnHeader(JViewport view);
```

If you use these methods, it is your responsibility to suitably initialize the JViewport by adding to it the component to be scrolled. The next example shows how this is done and also demonstrates most of the ways in which you can customize JScrollPane. The idea is to create a scrolling canvas with two custom corners at the top right and bottom left, and row and column headings that are engraved with markings approximately every half-inch, so that they look like rulers attached to the top and side of the image that will be placed in the scrolling area. The rulers and the corners are all simple custom components that demonstrate how to attach your own controls to a scrolled pane. Figure 5-9 shows what this example program looks like when you run it using the command:

```
java JFCBook.Chapter5.ScrollExample2
```

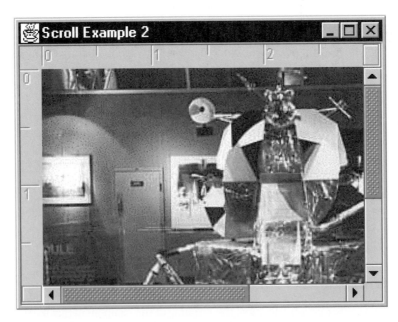

Figure 5-9   Using row and column headers with JScrollPane.

Let's first look at Listing 5-11 and see how the application window and the JScrollPane are created.

| Listing 5-11 | Adding custom row and column headers to JScrollPane |

```java
package JFCBook.Chapter5;

import com.sun.java.swing.*;
import java.awt.*;
import java.awt.event.*;

public class ScrollExample2 extends JFrame {
  public ScrollExample2() {
    super("Scroll Example 2");
    JScrollPane p = new JScrollPane(JScrollPane.VERTICAL_SCROLLBAR_AS_NEEDED,
        JScrollPane.HORIZONTAL_SCROLLBAR_AS_NEEDED);
    this.getContentPane().add(p);

    ImageIcon icon = new ImageIcon(getClass().getResource("images/lem.jpg"));
    JLabel l = new JLabel(icon);
    l.setHorizontalAlignment(SwingConstants.LEFT);
    l.setVerticalAlignment(SwingConstants.TOP);
    p.setViewportView(l);

    RulerPane hrc = new RulerPane(RulerPane.HORIZONTAL_RULE,
              l.getPreferredSize().width, 0);
    JViewport hr = new JViewport();
    hr.add(hrc);
    hr.setSize(hrc.getPreferredSize());

    RulerPane vrc = new RulerPane(RulerPane.VERTICAL_RULE,
              0, l.getPreferredSize().height);
    JViewport vr = new JViewport();
    vr.add(vrc);
    vr.setSize(vrc.getPreferredSize());

    p.setColumnHeader(hr);
    p.setRowHeader(vr);

    p.setCorner(JScrollPane.UPPER_RIGHT_CORNER, new RuledCorner());
    p.setCorner(JScrollPane.LOWER_LEFT_CORNER, new RuledCorner());
  }

  public static void main(String[] args) {
    JFrame f = new ScrollExample2();
    f.setSize(250, 200);
    f.setVisible(true);
    f.addWindowListener(new WindowAdapter() {
      public void windowClosing(WindowEvent e) {
        System.exit(0);
      }
    });
  }
}
```

This code starts very much like the previous example in Listing 5-10; it creates a JScrollPane with the scrollbars visible only as needed and mounts it on a JFrame. The main method creates the frame itself and sets its initial size. Also, as before, the image is loaded by using a JLabel and an ImageIcon and setViewportView is used to assign it as the main viewport. Since this method is used instead of setViewport, the JScrollPane creates its own JViewport and mounts the JLabel on top of it, then places the JViewport in the viewport position. You'll notice that the alignment properties of the JLabel are set so that the ImageIcon stays at its top left; if this hadn't been done, the image would detach itself from the top or left side of the scrolled area if the JScrollPane were resized to the extent that it had spare space in the viewport and would appear to move away from the ruler.

The next step is to create the components that will become the horizontal and vertical rulers and their corresponding viewports and attach them to the pane:

```
RulerPane hrc = new RulerPane(l.getPreferredSize().width, 0);
JViewport hr = new JViewport();
hr.add(hrc);

RulerPane vrc = new RulerPane(0,
l.getPreferredSize().height);
JViewport vr = new JViewport();
vr.add(vrc);

p.setColumnHeader(hr);
p.setRowHeader(vr);
```

As you'll see, the rulers are derived from JPanel. Since all we want to do is draw on them, it makes sense to use a simple component as the base for these objects. To show how the setColumnHeader and setRowHeader methods are used, we create our own viewports, add the rulers to them and then attach them as the row and column headings.

Adding Corners

This example creates two custom components to act as the top right and bottom left corners and adds to the scroll pane:

```
p.setCorner(JScrollPane.UPPER_RIGHT_CORNER, new
        RuledCorner());
p.setCorner(JScrollPane.LOWER_LEFT_CORNER, new RuledCorner());
```

Each of these corners will appear as long as the scrollbar to which it is adjacent is visible; since the scrollbars are only shown when they are needed, the bottom-left corner, for example, will disappear when the scroll pane is wide enough to show the entire image. When this happens, the vertical ruler (i.e., the row heading view) will extend to the bottom of the scroll pane.

The corner itself is just a panel on which an etched border is drawn, as shown in Listing 5-12. Since `JPanel` can host a border, all this class does is add an etched border to itself, choosing colors that contrast with the color of its own background. You've already seen this technique used in Chapter 4 and you can find a complete description of Swing borders in Chapter 8, "Building Custom Dialogs." Note that the border color is adjusted to fit in with any change to the background color by overriding the `setBackground` method.

Listing 5-12   Creating a custom corner for JScrollPane

```
class RuledCorner extends JPanel {
  RuledCorner() {
    setBackground(UIManager.getColor("control"));
    addBorder();
  }

  public void setBackground(Color color) {
    super.setBackground(color);
    addBorder();
  }

  protected void addBorder() {
    Color background = getBackground();
    setBorder(BorderFactory.createEtchedBorder(background.brighter(),
                      background.darker()));
  }
}
```

Adding Horizontal and Vertical Rulers

The last piece of this example is the `RulerPane` class, which provides an etched ruler along the top and the left side of the scroll pane. The constructor allows you to specify the orientation and its initial size. You'll notice that when the rulers were created, the width of the horizontal ruler and the height of the vertical one were specified so that they matched the corresponding dimension of the image. Since the size of the frame (and therefore indirectly of the rulers) is fixed in the `main` method, these sizes are not actually used in this particular example, but they could be of use if this class were reused elsewhere. The other dimension of the rulers is not set; instead, it will default based on the size of the ruler's markings, which itself depends on the size of the font used to draw the numbers that appear every inch along it.

The ruler markings are drawn in a way that you should be now very familiar with: by using two contrasting colors, you get the effect of an etched ruler face. This effect is applied to both the markings and the numbers. The marks are of two lengths:

Every inch, there is a long mark accompanied by the number of inches along the ruler, and there is a shorter mark to indicate half-inches. The ruler is calibrated by using the getScreenResolution   method of java.awt.Toolkit, which returns the number of pixels per inch of the screen. This value may only be approximate, however, so the ruler you see on the screen may not be very accurate.

Listing 5-13 shows the code for the RulerPane class.

Listing 5-13   Creating a custom ruler for JScrollPane

```
class RulerPane extends JPanel {
  RulerPane(int orientation, int width, int height) {
    this.width = width;
    this.height = height;
    this.orientation = orientation;

    setFont(new Font("Dialog", Font.PLAIN, 12));
    resolution = getToolkit().getScreenResolution();
    computeSizes();

    setBackground(UIManager.getColor("control"));
    setSize(width, height);
  }

  public void setBackground(Color color) {
    super.setBackground(color);
    lightShadow = null;    // Recalculate shadow colors
  }

  public void setFont(Font f) {
    super.setFont(f);
    fm = null;       // Recalculate sizes
  }

  public Dimension getPreferredSize() {
    computeSizes();
    return new Dimension(width, height);
  }

  public void paintComponent(Graphics g) {
    Dimension d = getSize();
    Rectangle r = g.getClipBounds();
    int markPosition = 0;

    if (lightShadow == null) {
      Color color = getBackground();
```

```
   lightShadow = color.brighter();
   darkShadow = color.darker();
}

if (fm == null) {
  computeSizes();
}

int ascent = fm.getAscent();

g.setColor(getBackground());
g.fillRect(r.x, r.y, r.width, r.height);

if (orientation == VERTICAL_RULE) {
  int marks = d.height/resolution + 1;
  int startPosition = r.y;
  int endPosition = r.y + r.height;

  for (int i = 0; i < marks && markPosition <= endPosition; i++) {
    String s = (new Integer(i)).toString();

    if (markPosition >= startPosition) {
      g.setColor(lightShadow);
      g.drawLine(0, markPosition + 1, longMark + 1,
           markPosition + 1);
      g.drawString(s, LEFT_GAP + 1,
           markPosition + ascent + 1);
      g.setColor(darkShadow);
      g.drawLine(0, markPosition, longMark, markPosition);
      g.drawString(s, LEFT_GAP, markPosition + ascent);
    }
    markPosition += resolution/2;

    if (markPosition >= startPosition) {
      g.setColor(lightShadow);
      g.drawLine(0, markPosition + 1, shortMark + 1,
           markPosition + 1);
      g.setColor(darkShadow);
      g.drawLine(0, markPosition, shortMark, markPosition);
    }
    markPosition += resolution/2;
  }
} else {
  int marks = d.width/resolution + 1;
  int startPosition = r.x;
  int endPosition = r.x + r.width;
```

(Continued)

```
      for (int i = 0; i < marks && markPosition <= endPosition; i++) {
        String s = (new Integer(i)).toString();

        if (markPosition >= startPosition) {
          g.setColor(lightShadow);
          g.drawLine(markPosition + 1, 0, markPosition + 1,
              longMark + 1);
          g.drawString(s, markPosition + LEFT_GAP + 1, ascent + 1);
          g.setColor(darkShadow);
          g.drawLine(markPosition, 0, markPosition, longMark);
          g.drawString(s, markPosition + LEFT_GAP, ascent);
        }
        markPosition += resolution/2;

        if (markPosition >= startPosition) {
          g.setColor(lightShadow);
          g.drawLine(markPosition + 1, 0, markPosition + 1,
              shortMark + 1);
          g.setColor(darkShadow);
          g.drawLine(markPosition, 0, markPosition, shortMark);
        }
        markPosition += resolution/2;
      }
    }
  }

  void computeSizes() {
    fm = getToolkit().getFontMetrics(getFont());

    int fontHeight = fm.getHeight();
    longMark = fontHeight;
    shortMark = longMark/2;
    if (orientation == HORIZONTAL_RULE) {
      height = longMark + BOTTOM_GAP;
    } else {
      width = longMark + RIGHT_GAP;
    }
  }

  int width;      // Width in pixels
  int height;   // Height in pixels
  int orientation;    // Horizontal or vertical
  int resolution;   // Pixels per inch
  Color lightShadow;    // Light shadow color
  Color darkShadow;   // Dark shadow color
  FontMetrics fm;   // Font sizes
  int longMark;   // Size of inch mark
```

```
   int shortMark;      // Size of other marks

   public static final int HORIZONTAL_RULE = 1;
   public static final int VERTICAL_RULE = 2;

   static final int BOTTOM_GAP = 4;
   static final int RIGHT_GAP = 4;
   static final int LEFT_GAP = 2;
}
```

Most of this code should be fairly obvious. The `computeSizes` method determines how long the inch and half-inch marks should be, based on the size of the font in use. The ruler is padded by a few extra pixels so that the inch marks don't cut right across it. The sizes calculated here, along with the number of pixels per inch, are used to determine the length of each mark and the spacing between them that are used in the `paintComponent` method.

Before drawing the ruler markings, the background is cleared. This is necessary because the ruler is scrolled horizontally or vertically by the `JViewport` as the image itself moves. You'll note that at the start of the `paintComponent` method the `getClipBounds` method is called. This method will tell us which part of the ruler is actually visible within the column or row heading viewport. To achieve the scrolling effect, the ruler is made to move relative to the viewport by translating the graphics origin in the direction of motion of the ruler, but the clipping rectangle is set so that only the part of the ruler visible inside the viewport is drawn.

At any given time, then, only a part of the ruler is on the screen. Drawing the rest of the ruler won't do any harm because the drawing operations will fall outside the clipping rectangle, but they are a waste of time, so the loop in which the ruler is drawn does nothing if it would draw in the area before the start of the clipping rectangle and terminates when it reaches the end of the clipped area.

Logical Scrolling and Forcing Visibility of an Area

The scrolling you've seen so far has been pixel-based—each time the scrollbar is clicked, the scrolled area moves either by 1 pixel or by the size of its visible area (so-called block scrolling). If you make the scroll pane larger, the block scroll will move a larger amount, but each click will still move the content the same distance. Sometimes, this is not convenient. Listing 5-14 demonstrates this. It creates a panel on which nine images are drawn (using `JLabel`s as before), arranged in a 3-by-3 grid. These pictures are not all of the same size and the example code deliberately uses a `GridBagLayout` and allows each row and column to occupy the natural size for the pictures that they contain, so that the rows and columns are all of different sizes.

Listing 5-14   Pixel scrolling of multiple images in a grid

```java
package JFCBook.Chapter5;

import com.sun.java.swing.*;
import java.awt.*;
import java.awt.event.*;

public class ScrollExample3 extends JFrame {
  public ScrollExample3() {
    super("Scroll Example 3");
    JScrollPane p = new
JScrollPane(JScrollPane.VERTICAL_SCROLLBAR_AS_NEEDED,
          JScrollPane.HORIZONTAL_SCROLLBAR_AS_NEEDED);
    this.getContentPane().add(p);
    labels = new JLabel[imageNames.length];

    for (int i = 0; i < imageNames.length; i++) {
      labels[i] =
          new JLabel(new ImageIcon(getClass().getResource(imageNames[i])));
      labels[i].setHorizontalAlignment(SwingConstants.LEFT);
      labels[i].setVerticalAlignment(SwingConstants.TOP);
    }

    JPanel pictures = new JPanel();
    pictures.setBackground(UIManager.getColor("control"));
    pictures.setLayout(new GridBagLayout());
    GridBagConstraints c = new GridBagConstraints();
    c.gridwidth = 1;
    c.gridheight = 1;
    c.gridx = 0;
    c.gridy = 0;
    c.insets = new Insets(4, 4, 4, 4);
    c.fill = GridBagConstraints.BOTH;

    for (int i = 0; i < labels.length; i++) {
      pictures.add(labels[i], c);
      c.gridx++;
      if ((c.gridx % 3) == 0) {
        c.gridx = 0;
        c.gridy++;
      }
    }

    p.setViewportView(pictures);
    p.getViewport().setBackingStoreEnabled(true);

  }
```

```
public static void main(String[] args) {
  JFrame f = new ScrollExample3();
  f.setSize(250, 200);
  f.setVisible(true);
  f.addWindowListener(new WindowAdapter() {
    public void windowClosing(WindowEvent e) {
      System.exit(0);
    }
  });
}

private static final String[] imageNames = {
    "images/p1.jpg", "images/p2.jpg", "images/p3.jpg",
    "images/p4.jpg", "images/p5.jpg", "images/p6.jpg",
    "images/p7.jpg", "images/p8.jpg", "images/p9.jpg" };
private JLabel[] labels;
}
```

If you run this program using the command:

```
java JFCBook.Chapter5.ScrollExample3
```

when the pictures appear you will find it awkward to view any one picture (see Figure 5-10). It takes too long to bring a picture conveniently into view if you scroll by one pixel, while block scrolling by clicking near the ends of the scrollbars is too coarse, and you inevitably have to adjust the scroll position one pixel at a time. This remains true even if you enlarge the scroll pane to fill the entire screen, because even if you get one picture properly positioned, it is just as difficult to align the next one.

In order to speed up scrolling, the JViewport backing store facility has been enabled with this line of code:

```
p.getViewport().setBackingStoreEnabled(true);
```

When you enable backing store, the component in the viewport is rendered into an off-screen buffer and then the visible part drawn to the screen. This allows much of the cost of drawing the component to be paid once; the scrolling action then only involves copying part of the saved image of the component onto the viewport. While this noticeably speeds up the scrolling, it doesn't make it easier to look at any given picture.

Fortunately, there are a couple of things that can be done to improve this situation. The first thing to do is to stop performing pixel scrolling and use logical scrolling instead. This will make it easier to find any particular picture using the scrollbars. The second improvement is to make use of the JComponent scrollRectToVisible method that makes the viewport scroll to bring a particular component into view. To show how these two features work, the example above will be amended to incorporate both of them.

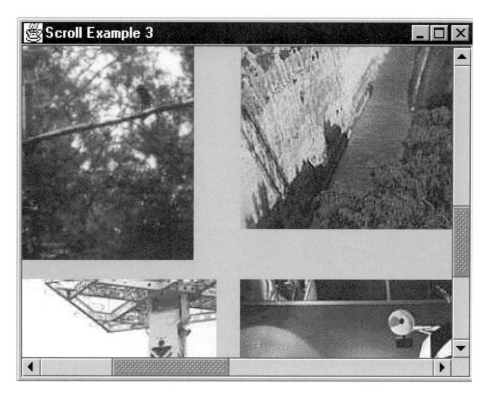

Figure 5-10   A scrolling grid of images.

Logical Scrolling

The idea behind logical scrolling is to move the display area by an amount that depends not on the size of the viewport, but on what is displayed within it. In our case, since we have a grid of pictures, it makes sense to change the block scrolling behavior so that scrolling down moves the next picture below up to the top left of the view port and so on. With this arrangement, a single click in any direction moves the viewport by one picture and aligns it exactly within the window so that its top left-hand corner is visible, no matter what the relative sizes of the pictures are.

There are actually two ways to implement logical scrolling. One of them involves directly controlling the scroll bars and the other involves implementing an interface that will be used by the JScrollPane to find out how the scrolled area should move. Since these are such different techniques, both of them will be shown here.

Logical Scrolling By Extending JScrollBar

The first method of implementing logical scrolling involves taking direct control of the scrolling mechanism, which requires an understanding of how it works. This is the more involved of the two techniques. Under normal circumstances, the alternative mechanism (using the `Scrollable` interface) is preferable. This method, however, has the merit of illustrating how the `JScrollPane` and scrollbars work.

Each scrollbar is an instance of the `JScrollBar` class. When you create a `JScrollPane`, depending on the scrollbar policy, it will create zero, one or two scrollbars by invoking its own `createHorizontalScrollBar` and `createVerticalScrollBar` methods, the default implementations of which return a `JScrollBar`. The `JScrollBar` has a simple scrolling model that is based around the concepts of view size and extent size.

The view size is simply the size of the object being scrolled; since a scrollbar only manages one direction of motion, the vertical scrollbar considers only the height of the object in the viewport, while the horizontal one considers the width. By contrast, the extent size is the height or width of the viewport itself and measures how much of the scrolled object you can see at any one time. If the extent size is smaller than the view size, a scrollbar will be shown if it has been requested; if the extent is larger than the view size, the scrollbar will be removed unless you configure the scroll pane such that it always shows the scrollbar. The ratio of the view size to the extent size determines the size of the slider in the scrollbar on most platforms, so that you can see how much of the actual object is on view.

The other values that control the scrollbar are its maximum and minimum values. As the scrollbar moves, the top or left extremity of the slider indicates the current value of the scrollbar. By default, the minimum value is zero, and the maximum value is the size of the object being scrolled, in pixels. However, since the height or width of the slider represents one extent, the top or left part of the scrollbar cannot indicate a value greater than (maximum – extent). For example, if you have a 200-pixel high object displayed in a 60-pixel high viewport, the minimum value will be 0 and the maximum will be 199, but the slider will represent 60-pixels of view, so its upper end will represent the value 200 – 60 = 140 when it is right at the bottom of the scrollbar.

The extent size, view size, maximum and minimum values are set automatically when the `JScrollPane` is sized. If you take direct control over the scrollbars you can, of course, manage them yourself by using the `JScrollBar` `setValues` method that allows you to set the maximum, minimum and current values and the extent size explicitly. You can also cause the slider to move to a new position by using the `setValue` method and get the current value using `getValue`. You'll see more about this later in this chapter.

When you click to move the scrollbar's slider, it moves by either a small amount, known as the unit increment, or a larger amount, the block increment. By default, the unit increment is 1 pixel and the block increment is the extent size, so that clicking on the arrow at either end shifts the view by one pixel in that direction, while clicking in the scrollbar near the arrow moves the view a complete viewport's distance. To decide how far to move, the scrollbar calls the following methods:

```
public int getUnitIncrement(int direction);

public int getBlockIncrement(int direction);
```

The direction argument takes the value +1 if the scrollbar is moving to the right or downward and −1 if it is moving to the left or upwards. Note that this is the direction of movement of the slider in the scrollbar, *not* of the content of the viewport, which moves in the opposite direction. The value returned from these methods is always positive or zero and represents the distance to move in that direction; if you mistakenly return a negative value, you'll find that the scrollbar doesn't behave as you might have expected it to! To implement logical scrolling, you have to make the block increment depend on the current position of the object in the viewport, which requires you to override the `getBlockIncrement` method. In order to do this, you create a subclass of `JScrollBar` and have the `JScrollPane` create instances of this subclass instead of `JScrollBar`. Since the scrollbars are created by calling methods of `JScrollPane`, it follows that it is also necessary to subclass `JScrollPane` to be able to attach custom scrollbars. The new scrolled pane subclass will be called `PictureScrollPane` and the scrollbar class `PictureScrollBar`.

Now let's consider what will happen when you click on a scrollbar. First, the `getBlockIncrement` method will be called and will return the distance by which the slider will move; the scroll pane then computes the new scrollbar value based on what was returned to it and adjusts the scrollbar accordingly. This also results in the viewport itself being scrolled, but there is no need to do anything extra to make that happen. In order to decide how far to move the slider, it is necessary to know where each picture begins within the viewport and where the scrollbar currently is.

For example, considering only the vertical scrollbar, suppose there are three rows of pictures starting at pixel offsets 0, 100, and 180 from the top of the scrolled object. When the `JScrollPane` first appears, the top picture will be at the top left of the viewport. If you now click to move the slider downward by a block, you want to place the second row of pictures at the top of the viewport, which requires a downward scroll of 100 pixels. This result is arrived at by subtracting the scrollbar's current value from the offset of the next row of pictures. Things can be slightly trickier, though, because the user could now click on the down arrow a few times, making the viewport scroll by individual pixel amounts, or the slider could be dragged down the scrollbar and dropped at a new position. In all of these cases, however, it is still possible to determine how far the slider should move next by subtracting the scrollbar's current value from the pixel offset of the next row of pictures. The only problem is to figure out where the next row of pictures starts.

If you know the pixel offsets of the pictures, you can compare the current slider value to these offsets to determine which is the next row; which way the list of offsets is traversed depends, of course, on whether the slider is moving upwards or downward. For example, in the example being considered here, suppose that the slider has been moved to position 20 and then the user clicks to move down a block. Since the next picture is at pixel offset 100, the right thing to do is to move down 80 pixels.

Now suppose the slider is dragged down to position 140. When this is done, neither `getUnitIncrement` not `getBlockIncrement` is called—instead, the scrollbar's value changes directly to that which corresponds to its new position, in this case 140, and the top of the viewport ends up cutting the second row of pictures into two. If you were now to click to move down a block, by scanning the list of picture offsets, that the next row of pictures would be found at pixel offset 180, so the next action would be to move down by 40 pixels. From here, it isn't possible to go down any further. If the user clicked to move up a block, our `getBlockIncrement` method would be called with its direction argument set to –1 and would look for the largest picture offset that is smaller than the current slider value, in this case 100. Because the current value is 180, it would return a block increment of 80 (and *not* –80).

We've summarized the basic idea, now let's see the implementation. First, let's look at the application's initialization code, which is shown in Listing 5-15.

Listing 5-15   Logical scrolling and forced scrolling: application initialization

---

```
package JFCBook.Chapter5;

import com.sun.java.swing.*;
import java.awt.*;
import java.awt.event.*;

public class ScrollExample4 extends JFrame {
  public ScrollExample4() {
    super("Scroll Example 4");
    picturePane = new PictureScrollPane(
        JScrollPane.VERTICAL_SCROLLBAR_AS_NEEDED,
        JScrollPane.HORIZONTAL_SCROLLBAR_AS_NEEDED,
        imageNames, PICTURES_PER_ROW);
    this.getContentPane().add(picturePane, "Center");

    // Add buttons to bring numbered picture into view
    JPanel panel = new JPanel();
    panel.setBackground(UIManager.getColor("control"));
    JPanel buttonPanel = new JPanel();
    buttonPanel.setLayout(new GridLayout(0, PICTURES_PER_ROW, 4, 4));
    panel.add(buttonPanel);

    Font f = new Font("Serif", Font.BOLD, 14);
    for (int i = 0; i < imageNames.length; i++) {
```

(Continued)

```
        JButton b = new JButton("" + i);
        b.setFont(f);
        buttonPanel.add(b);
        b.addActionListener(new ActionListener() {
          public void actionPerformed(ActionEvent evt) {
            JButton button = (JButton)evt.getSource();
            int index = button.getActionCommand().charAt(0) - '0';
            picturePane.makeVisible(index);// Make picture visible
          }
        });
    }
    this.getContentPane().add(panel, "East");
  }

  public static void main(String[] args) {
    JFrame f = new ScrollExample4();
    Dimension d = Toolkit.getDefaultToolkit().getScreenSize();
    f.setSize(3*d.width/4, 3*d.height/4);
    f.setVisible(true);
    f.addWindowListener(new WindowAdapter() {
      public void windowClosing(WindowEvent e) {
        System.exit(0);
      }
    });
  }

  private static final String[] imageNames = {
      "images/p1.jpg",  "images/p2.jpg",      "images/p3.jpg",
      "images/p4.jpg",  "images/p5.jpg",      "images/p6.jpg",
      "images/p7.jpg",  "images/p8.jpg",      "images/p9.jpg" };


  private static final int PICTURES_PER_ROW = 3;      // Pictures on each row

  private PictureScrollPane picturePane;              // The picture panel
}
```

Here, as before, a scroll pane is created and mounted on the top-level window. But there are some differences this time. Most obviously, a PictureScrollPane is created instead of a JScrollPane. This example also adds a panel of buttons, one for each picture; these buttons will be used when you see how to move directly to a particular picture without using the scrollbars later in this section. The other difference is that the list of image names is now passed to the PictureScrollPane so that it can construct the panel of pictures, instead of doing it ourselves and simply adding the completed panel as the viewport.

The reason for this change is that the scrollbars need to know exactly where each row and column of pictures has been placed. Since the scrollbars are created by the PictureScrollPane class, it seems natural for it to know where the pictures have been placed and the simplest and most object-oriented way to achieve this is to have it be completely responsible for constructing and managing the picture panel. The only information it needs to do this is the list of pictures and the number of pictures that should appear on each row. In this case, there are nine pictures (a fact that the scroll pane can deduce from the length of the array of picture names), so we choose to allow three pictures per row, as in the previous example. Figure 5-11 shows what the application looks like when it is running.

Figure 5-11   A scrolling grid with buttons to bring grid cells into view.

Before looking at the implementation of the PictureScrollPane class, let's look a bit more closely at what happens when the scrollbar is clicked near one of its ends. As noted earlier, to decide how far to move, you need the current value of the scrollbar and the offsets of each row of pictures. This calculation is performed in the getBlockIncrement method of the PictureScrollBar class. Getting the current value of the scrollbar is simply a matter of invoking the PictureScrollBar getValue method, but what about the picture offsets? Even though the scrollbar is attached to the JScrollPane, this association is not directly known to the scrollbar—it has never been told what component it is controlling, so it doesn't know how to get information about the pictures. But remember that each scrollbar is created by the PictureScrollPane when its overridden createHorizontalScrollBar or createVerticalScrollBar method is called. This seems to give us the opportunity to tell the scrollbars where to get the information they need. This is certainly a feasible solution: the PictureScrollBar constructor could be defined so that it takes a reference to the PictureScrollPane as an argument and a method would be added to PictureScrollPane that would return the picture offsets as an array to the scrollbars; this function would be called from within the scrollbar's getBlockIncrement method.

There is, however, a neater solution that allows the whole PictureScrollPane to be packaged as a single logical entity. Instead of creating a new public PictureScrollBar class and then inventing a way to give it access to information stored in the PictureScrollPane, the scrollbar can be implemented as an inner class of PictureScrollPane, so that it automatically has access to its members without spoiling the encapsulation of the information held by the scroll pane class and without adding any unnecessary publicly-visible functionality. Listing 5-16 shows the implementation of PictureScrollPane, together with its in-built scrollbars.

Listing 5-16   A custom scroll pane that can handle logical scrolling

```
class PictureScrollPane extends JScrollPane {
  public PictureScrollPane(int vsbPolicy, int hsbPolicy,
        String[] imageNames, int picturesPerRow) {
    super(vsbPolicy, hsbPolicy);

    this.picturesPerRow = picturesPerRow;

    // Create labels for all of the pictures
    labels = new JLabel[imageNames.length];

    for (int i = 0; i < imageNames.length; i++) {
      labels[i] = new JLabel(new
ImageIcon(getClass().getResource(imageNames[i])));
      labels[i].setHorizontalAlignment(SwingConstants.LEFT);
      labels[i].setVerticalAlignment(SwingConstants.TOP);
    }

    JPanel pictures = new JPanel();
```

```
pictures.setBackground(UIManager.getColor("control"));
pictures.setLayout(new GridBagLayout());

GridBagConstraints c = new GridBagConstraints();
c.gridwidth = 1;
c.gridheight = 1;
c.gridx = 0;
c.gridy = 0;
c.insets = new Insets(4, 4, 4, 4);
c.fill = GridBagConstraints.BOTH;

for (int i = 0; i < labels.length; i++) {
  pictures.add(labels[i], c);
  c.gridx++;
  if ((c.gridx % picturesPerRow) == 0) {
    c.gridx = 0;
    c.gridy++;
    rows++;
  }
}

// Correct row count if we haven't
// filled the last row
if (c.gridx != 0) {
  rows++;
}

setViewportView(pictures);
getViewport().setBackingStoreEnabled(true);
}

public JScrollBar createVerticalScrollBar() {
  return new PictureScrollBar(JScrollBar.VERTICAL);
}

public JScrollBar createHorizontalScrollBar() {
  return new PictureScrollBar(JScrollBar.HORIZONTAL);
}

public void makeVisible(int index) {
  try {
    JComponent c = labels[index];
    Dimension d = c.getSize();
    labels[index].scrollRectToVisible(new Rectangle(0, 0, d.width,
                d.height));
  } catch (Exception e) {
    System.out.println("Illegal index: " + index);
```

(Continued)

```java
    }
}

// Inner class to implement custom scrollbar functionality
class PictureScrollBar extends JScrollBar {
  public PictureScrollBar(int orientation) {
    super(orientation);
  }

  public int getBlockIncrement(int direction) {
    int value = getValue();
    int targetValue;
    int index;

    if (positions == null) {
      // Cache the image positions
      getImagePositions();
    }

    for (index = 0; index < positions.length; index++) {
      if (value <= positions[index]) {
        break;
      }
    }

    if (direction > 0) {
      if (index < positions.length - 1) {
        index++;
      } else if (index == positions.length) {
        // Already as far right as we can go
        return 0;
      }
    } else {
      if (index > 0) {
        index--;
      }
    }

    targetValue = positions[index];  // Where we need to scroll to

    // Always return positive value
    return (targetValue - value) * direction;
  }

  public int getUnitIncrement(int direction) {
    return 1;
  }
```

```
    // Helper to cache the positions of the images
    private void getImagePositions() {
       if (getOrientation() == JScrollBar.HORIZONTAL) {
          positions = new int[picturesPerRow];
          for (int i = 0; i < picturesPerRow; i++) {
             if (labels[i] != null) {
                positions[i] = labels[i].getLocation().x;
             }
          }
       } else {
          positions = new int[rows];
          for (int i = 0; i < rows; i++) {
             if (labels[i * picturesPerRow] != null) {
                positions[i] =    labels[i *
picturesPerRow].getLocation().y;
             }
          }
       }
    }

    private int[] positions;
 }

 private JLabel[] labels;          // Pictures, one per JLabel
 private int picturesPerRow;       // Pictures in each row
 private int rows;                 // Number of rows
}
```

The constructor contains the code to create the picture panel that was shown in the previous example. There then follow the overridden createVerticalScrollBar and createHorizontalScrollBar methods that allow custom scrollbars to be attached to the scrolled pane; these two methods return instances of our PictureScrollPane class, initialized with the correct orientation. The makeVisible method helps to provide the functionality offered by the button panel on the main frame, as you'll see later.

The rest of this class is the implementation of the PictureScrollBar class, which is derived from JScrollBar and overrides the getUnitIncrement and getBlockIncrement methods to provide the logical scrolling. The getUnitIncrement method is trivial—it just returns 1, causing the viewport to move by 1 pixel in the appropriate direction. All of the real work of this class is in getBlockIncrement. You've already seen a description of how this method works in principle. Since this class could manage either a vertical or a horizontal scrollbar, there are two slightly different pieces of code, in the getImagePositions method, that achieve the same thing in a slightly different way. In the case of a horizontal scrollbar, the x coordinates of the picture columns are found by invoking getLocation on the three pictures on the top row; since the pictures are arranged in columns, this returns the x coordinates of all the pictures. Similarly, the vertical scrollbar finds the y locations of the pictures in the left-hand column.

Since the pictures won't move once they have been placed on the panel, the getBlockIncrement method only invokes getImagePositions the first time it is called, saving the resulting array of offsets in the positions array for future use. Using this array and the current value of the scrollbar, obtained using getValue, the index of the picture that occupies the top-left corner of the viewport can be located. As described earlier, it is then a simple matter to locate the picture that should next be made visible and, with that information and the values in the positions array, the distance by which the scrollbar should be moved can be calculated with a simple subtraction.

Forcing Visibility of Part of a Scrolled Area

The last piece of the PictureScrollPane class is the makeVisible method. When the user presses one of the nine buttons at the top right of the main frame, the actionPerformed method that you saw in the ScrollExample4 class above is invoked. The number on the face of the button is converted to an image index by simple subtraction and the makeVisible method is called. Pressing the button is supposed to make the corresponding picture come into view in the viewport and, as you can see, not much work is needed to achieve this.

The makeVisible method uses the index it is given to find the label on which the picture is mounted by using the label array, then uses getSize to construct a rectangle that exactly covers the picture. With the reference to the JLabel and a rectangle that covers the entire picture, you just need to use the scrollRectToVisible method of JLabel (which it inherits from JComponent) to make the label visible in the viewport. When this method is invoked, JComponent looks at its parent to see if it is a JViewport; if it isn't, it continues with that component's parent, until it finds a viewport or reaches the top-level frame. If it finds a JViewport, it calls its setViewPosition method to adjust the position of the view within the viewport so that the supplied rectangle is visible.

Implementing Logical Scrolling with the Scrollable Interface

What you have just seen works and demonstrates how to create custom scrollbars for use with a JScrollPane. In this section, you'll see what is often a simpler way to achieve the same result. The problem with the last approach is that the scrollbars had to have knowledge of the content of the picture pane. This is not really a very natural thing to do—it would be much better if the picture pane had some way to tell the scroll pane how much it should scroll by. This requirement is satisfied by the Scrollable interface. If the object that you place in the viewport of a JScrollPane implements Scrollable, then the scroll pane will delegate certain actions to it. Here is how this interface is defined:

```
public interface Scrollable {
  public Dimension getPreferredScrollableViewportSize();
  public boolean getScrollableTracksViewportHeight();
  public boolean getScrollableTracksViewportWidth();
  public int getScrollableUnitIncrement(Rectangle visibleRect, int orientation,
                        int direction);
  public int getScrollableBlockIncrement(Rectangle visibleRect, int orientation,
                        int direction);
}
```

Our revised implementation no longer needs to extend `JScrollPane`, because there is no need to create custom scrollbars. Instead, it will use a standard `JScrollPane` and the object to be placed in the viewport, called `PictureGallery`, will be a subclass of `JPanel` that implements the `Scrollable` interface. All of the information about the pictures will be embedded in `PictureGallery`; the only extra method that it exposes over and above the methods of `Scrollable`, will be `makeVisible`, which will be used as it was in Listing 5-15.

Let's first look at how the application that uses this new mechanism is implemented. The code is shown in Listing 5-17.

Listing 5-17   A revised application using logical scrolling

```
package JFCBook.Chapter5;

import com.sun.java.swing.*;
import java.awt.*;
import java.awt.event.*;
import JFCBook.Chapter5.PictureGallery;

public class ScrollExample4a extends JFrame {
  public ScrollExample4a() {
    super("Scroll Example 4A");

    // Create the gallery of pictures and add it to the scroll pane
    final PictureGallery pg = new PictureGallery(imageNames,
PICTURES_PER_ROW);

    picturePane = new JScrollPane(pg,
JScrollPane.VERTICAL_SCROLLBAR_AS_NEEDED,
                    JScrollPane.HORIZONTAL_SCROLLBAR_AS_NEEDED);
    picturePane.getViewport().setBackingStoreEnabled(true);

    this.getContentPane().add(picturePane, "Center");

    // Add buttons to bring numbered picture into view
```

(Continued)

```java
    JPanel panel = new JPanel();
    panel.setBackground(UIManager.getColor("control"));
    JPanel buttonPanel = new JPanel();
    buttonPanel.setLayout(new GridLayout(0, PICTURES_PER_ROW, 4, 4));
    panel.add(buttonPanel);

    Font f = new Font("Serif", Font.BOLD, 14);
    for (int i = 0; i < imageNames.length; i++) {
      JButton b = new JButton("" + i);
      b.setFont(f);
      buttonPanel.add(b);
      b.addActionListener(new ActionListener() {
        public void actionPerformed(ActionEvent evt) {
          JButton button = (JButton)evt.getSource();
          int index = button.getActionCommand().charAt(0) - '0';
          pg.makeVisible(index);         // Make picture visible

        }
      });
    }
    this.getContentPane().add(panel, "East");
  }

  public static void main(String[] args) {
    JFrame f = new ScrollExample4a();
    Dimension d = Toolkit.getDefaultToolkit().getScreenSize();
    f.setSize(3*d.width/4, 3*d.height/4);
    f.setVisible(true);
    f.addWindowListener(new WindowAdapter() {
      public void windowClosing(WindowEvent e) {
        System.exit(0);
      }
    });
  }

  private static final String[] imageNames = {
          "images/p1.jpg",       "images/p2.jpg",      "images/p3.jpg",
          "images/p4.jpg",       "images/p5.jpg",      "images/p6.jpg",
          "images/p7.jpg",       "images/p8.jpg",      "images/p9.jpg" };


  private static final int PICTURES_PER_ROW = 3;    // Pictures on each row

  private JScrollPane picturePane;                   // The picture panel
}
```

You'll notice that this is simpler than the original version in Listing 5-15. Instead of creating a custom JScrollPane, an instance of PictureGallery is created, with the list of images and number of pictures per row as arguments to the constructor, and it is simply installed in the JScrollPane like any other component. The JScrollPane checks whether the object in the viewport implements Scrollable when it needs to—it is not necessary to tell it. The other change you'll notice here is that the buttons' Action handlers direct the makeVisible call to the PictureGallery, because it is no longer implemented by the scroll pane. In other words, all of the operations performed by the application and the JScrollPane are now directed at one object that implements the real functionality of the application.

The PictureGallery implementation is actually very similar to that of PictureScrollPane. The code is shown in Listing 5-18.

Listing 5-18   A panel of pictures implementing the Scrollable interface

```
package JFCBook.Chapter5;

import com.sun.java.swing.*;
import java.awt.*;
import java.awt.event.*;

public class PictureGallery extends JPanel implements Scrollable {
   public PictureGallery(String[] imageNames, int picturesPerRow) {
      this.picturesPerRow = picturesPerRow;

      // Create labels for all of the pictures
      labels = new JLabel[imageNames.length];

      for (int i = 0; i < imageNames.length; i++) {
         labels[i] = new JLabel(new
ImageIcon(getClass().getResource(imageNames[i])));
         labels[i].setHorizontalAlignment(SwingConstants.LEFT);
         labels[i].setVerticalAlignment(SwingConstants.TOP);
      }

      setBackground(UIManager.getColor("control"));
      setLayout(new GridBagLayout());

      GridBagConstraints c = new GridBagConstraints();
      c.gridwidth = 1;
      c.gridheight = 1;
      c.gridx = 0;
      c.gridy = 0;
```

(Continued)

```java
    c.insets = new Insets(4, 4, 4, 4);
    c.fill = GridBagConstraints.BOTH;

    for (int i = 0; i < labels.length; i++) {
      add(labels[i], c);
      c.gridx++;
      if ((c.gridx % picturesPerRow) == 0) {
        c.gridx = 0;
        c.gridy++;
        rows++;
      }
    }

    // Correct row count if we haven't
    // filled the last row
    if (c.gridx != 0) {
      rows++;
    }
  }

  public void makeVisible(int index) {
    try {
      JComponent c = labels[index];
      Dimension d = c.getSize();
      labels[index].scrollRectToVisible(new Rectangle(0, 0, d.width, d.height));
    } catch (Exception e) {
      System.out.println("Illegal index: " + index);
    }
  }

  // Implementation of the Scrollable interface
  public Dimension getPreferredScrollableViewportSize() {
    return getPreferredSize();
  }

  public boolean getScrollableTracksViewportWidth() {
    return false;
  }

  public boolean getScrollableTracksViewportHeight() {
    return false;
  }

  public int getScrollableUnitIncrement(Rectangle visibleRect,
                int orientation, int direction) {
    return 1;
  }
```

```
public int getScrollableBlockIncrement(Rectangle visibleRect,
                int orientation, int direction) {
  int value;
  int targetValue;
  int index;
  int offsetType;

  if (positions == null) {
    // Cache the image positions
    getImagePositions();
  }

  offsetType = orientation == SwingConstants.VERTICAL ? Y_OFFSETS : X_OFFSETS;
  value = orientation == SwingConstants.VERTICAL ? visibleRect.y : visibleRect.x;

  for (index = 0; index < positions.length; index++) {
    if (value <= positions[offsetType][index]) {
      break;
    }
  }

  if (direction > 0) {
    if (index < positions[offsetType].length - 1) {
      index++;
    } else if (index == positions[offsetType].length) {
      // Already as far right as we can go
      return 0;
    }
  } else {
    if (index > 0) {
      index—;
    }
  }

  targetValue = positions[offsetType][index]; // Where we need to scroll to

  // Always return positive value
  return (targetValue - value) * direction;
}

// Helper to cache the positions of the images
private void getImagePositions() {
  positions = new int[OFFSET_TYPES][];
  positions[X_OFFSETS] = new int[picturesPerRow];
  positions[Y_OFFSETS] = new int[rows];

  for (int i = 0; i < picturesPerRow; i++) {
    if (labels[i] != null) {
```

(Continued)

```
        positions[X_OFFSETS][i] = labels[i].getLocation().x;
      }
    }

    for (int i = 0; i < rows; i++) {
      if (labels[i * picturesPerRow] != null) {
        positions[Y_OFFSETS][i] = labels[i *
picturesPerRow].getLocation().y;
      }
    }
  }

  private int[][] positions;              // x and y picture offsets
  private JLabel[] labels;                // Pictures, one per JLabel
  private int picturesPerRow;             // Pictures in each row
  private int rows;                       // Number of rows
  private static final int X_OFFSETS = 0;
  private static final int Y_OFFSETS = 1;
  private static final int OFFSET_TYPES = Y_OFFSETS + 1;
}
```

The constructor is almost identical to that of PictureScrollPane, except that it has fewer arguments and does not need to initialize its superclass. You'll notice also that this class now implements the makeVisible method that was in PictureScrollPane, but the code is, in fact, identical.

The rest of this class implements the Scrollable interface. The methods of most interest are the last two: the others are not of any real use here and just return standard values—you'll find a description of them at the end of this section. The getScrollableUnitIncrement and getScrollableBlockIncrement methods are the ones that JScrollPane uses to work out how far to move when a unit or block scroll is required. Each of them gets three parameters:

visibleRect	the portion of the viewport that is currently visible

orientation	indicates which scrollbar is involved:
	    SwingConstants.HORIZONTAL or
	    SwingConstants.VERTICAL

direction	1 or –1, as before

An important difference between these methods and the getUnitIncrement and getBlockIncrement methods is context: in the previous example, these methods were invoked against a particular scrollbar. Here, the new methods have a parameter that indicates which scrollbar is being moved. This makes a small difference to us, because the information used to decide how far to move, namely the offsets of the picture rows and columns, was held separately in each scrollbar—the vertical scrollbar knew about vertical offsets and the horizontal one about horizontal offsets. Now, this is no longer feasible: The `PictureGallery` object has to know about both sets of offsets and `getScrollableBlockIncrement` has to use the correct set when deciding how far to move. Note that the `getScrollableUnitIncrement` method is trivial, as it was in the previous implementation.

Instead of creating a single one-dimensional array of picture offsets in each scrollbar, `PictureGallery` builds a two-dimensional array, with one row for horizontal offset and one for vertical offsets. The code that builds this array is fundamentally the same as it was earlier, except that it now stores both the *x* and *y* offsets of each picture.

When the `getScrollableBlockIncrement` method is called, it uses the `orientation` argument to determine which row of the positions array to use. Once this is done, the algorithm used to find the offset of the next picture to scroll to is identical to that shown in Listing 5-16. Notice, however, that the current value of the scrollbar is now obtained differently. In the earlier example, the scrollbar value was obtained by calling its `getValue` method. Here, the scrollbar object is not directly available, but the same information is available in the `visibleRect` parameter, which describes the part of the scrollable that is actually visible in the viewport at the point of the call. This means that the horizontal scrollbar's value is given by the `x` value of `visibleRect` and the vertical scrollbar's value by its `y` member variable.

More About The Scrollable Interface

This example didn't use the other three methods in the `Scrollable` interface, but they are worth knowing about because there are some common problems that you can use them to help with.

The `getPreferredScrollableViewportSize` allows you to specify how big you would like the scroll pane's viewport to be. Usually, the viewport should be either as large as the application's frame will allow it to be, or it should take the preferred size of the object that it is scrolling. Often, these are the same thing. In the example above, the preferred size of the `PictureGallery` was returned by this method. In fact, this won't really be used here, because the size of the application frame was explicitly set and the size of the `JScrollPane` is absolutely determined by that in this case. However, had the `pack` method been used to size the frame, the size allocated to the `JScrollPane` would depend on its preferred size, which is determined by the result of the `getPreferredScrollableViewportSize` method if its viewport implements `Scrollable`. You'll see an example of this method in use in Chapter 11, "The Table Control," because `JTable` has a setPreferredScrollableViewportSize method that allows you to specify the size of the viewport in which your table should be displayed if it needs to be scrolled.

The other two methods, getScrollableTracksViewportWidth and getScrollableTracksViewportHeight control what happens when the JScrollPane is resized. If these methods return false, the size of the scrolled object is unaffected by the size of the scroll pane itself. But suppose you return true from getScrollableTracksViewportWidth. If this happens, then the scrolled object's width is always set to match the width of the scroll pane's viewport—so there will never be a horizontal scrollbar. When the scroll pane is expanded, the viewport will grow horizontally by the same amount. You can use this to ensure that text is never cropped on the right, for example, but for this to be useful, you must have a text control that does word wrapping, such as the JTextArea control that you'll see in Chapter 9. The same behavior can be obtained in the vertical direction using the getScrollableTracksViewportHeight.

Listing 5-19 shows a simple example in which the get ScrollableTracksViewportWidth method is used. This example defines a class called TextFlow that extends the JTextArea control. Its constructor has three arguments—the string to be displayed, a boolean that indicates whether it should perform line wrapping and a boolean that specifies what it is to return to getScrollableTracksViewportWidth. Because JTextArea implements the Scrollable interface, it is only necessary to override the get ScrollableTracksViewportWidth method itself—all of the other methods in the interface are already implemented.

To see the difference between returning true and false, the example creates two TextFlow objects and mounts them side-by-side in a frame. The left-hand object will line wrap and will return true from getScrollableTracksViewportWidth, while the right-hand one returns false and does not line wrap.

Core Note

You'll find out more about the JTextArea *control in Chapter 9, "Text Components."*

Listing 5-19   Tracking viewport width

```
package JFCBook.Chapter5;

import com.sun.java.swing.*;
import java.awt.*;
import java.awt.event.*;

public class TextFlow extends JTextArea implements Scrollable {
  public TextFlow(boolean tracksViewport, boolean lineWrap, String text) {
    super();
    super.setLineWrap(lineWrap);
    setText(text);
    this.tracksViewport = tracksViewport;
  }

  // Scrollable implementation
  public boolean getScrollableTracksViewportWidth() {
    return tracksViewport;
  }

  public static void main(String[] args) {
    JFrame f = new JFrame("Text Flow");
    Dimension d = Toolkit.getDefaultToolkit().getScreenSize();
    f.setSize(7 * d.width/8, 3 * d.height/4);
    f.getContentPane().setLayout(new GridLayout(0, 2));
    f.getContentPane().add(new JScrollPane(new TextFlow(true, true, text)));
    f.getContentPane().add(new JScrollPane(new TextFlow(false, false, text)));
    f.setVisible(true);
    f.addWindowListener(new WindowAdapter() {
      public void windowClosing(WindowEvent e) {
        System.exit(0);
      }
    });
  }

  protected boolean tracksViewport;
  protected static String text = "\"Houston, Tranquility Base here.\nThe
Eagle has Landed\"\n" +
      "\n\n\"Roger, Tranquility, we copy you on the ground.\n" +
      "You got a bunch of guys about to turn blue.\n" +
      "We're breathing again. Thanks a lot\"\n";
}
```

When the example starts, the window is wide enough to accommodate all of the text, so there are no scrollbars. If you narrow the window enough so that some of the text lines are too wide to fit, the difference between the two text panes becomes apparent, as shown in Figure 5-12.

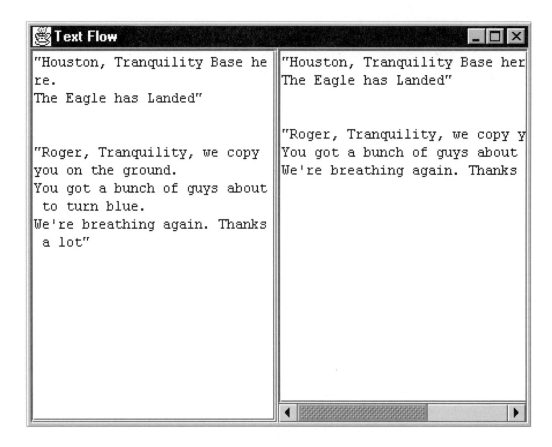

Figure 5-12   Text areas with and without word wrap in a scroll pane.

The left-hand text area's width always tracks that of the scroll pane. As a result, it is being made narrower and narrower. Since some of the lines are now too long to fit, it word-wraps onto the next line, but nothing is lost. By contrast, the right-hand text area's width does not get adjusted as the scroll pane gets smaller—instead, it stays constant. When the scroll pane's viewport becomes too small to show all of the text pane, a horizontal scrollbar is added to allow the rest of the text to be accessed.

Implementing Scrolling with JScrollBar

JScrollPane gives you a very simple and quick way to add scrolling to an application; if you are prepared to do a bit more work, you can, as you have seen, produce a more sophisticated user interface. But there are times when it isn't convenient to use JScrollPane. For example, you may have noticed that the examples so far create the object to be scrolled and then pass it to JScrollPane to manage. This is fine if what you want to scroll can be created in one step like this, but this might not always be possible. Consider what would happen if you wanted to produce a scrolling view onto the results of a database query that had produced thousands of rows of data. Having all that data in memory would be costly enough; adding to that by producing a graphical representation of that data, possibly very much larger than the original, could easily make the application impractical or, at best, impossible to use because of its resource requirements.

In this situation, you can improve matters if you process only enough data to fill the scrolling area and possibly a bit more to allow the user to scroll around a bit before you have to create more information to display. This doesn't fit very well with the JScrollPane model, however. To make this work, you need to directly manage the scrolling area, which means adding your own scrollbars to the component that you use to display the data.

The example in this section illustrates how scrollbars work by showing an application that has a canvas on which there is a gray-scale pattern that starts black at the top and gradually lightens until, after 1024 pixel lines, it has turned completely white. A pattern of 1024 lines is not that huge, so JScrollPane could actually be used to manage it, but we'll forsake the simpler implementation and use this program to demonstrate how scrollbars work and how scrolling speed can be maximized by copying the scrolled data rather than regenerating it every time the scrollbar moves.

First let's look at how the application's frame is constructed (Listing 5-20) and what the finished product looks like (Figure 5-13).

Listing 5-20   Handling scrolling directly with JScrollBar: application initialization

```
package JFCBook.Chapter5;

import com.sun.java.swing.*;
import java.awt.*;
import java.awt.event.*;

public class ScrollExample5 extends JFrame {
  public ScrollExample5(String title) {
    super(title);
    JScrollBar vsb = new JScrollBar(JScrollBar.VERTICAL);
```

(Continued)

```
    ScrollingCanvas c = new ScrollingCanvas(vsb);
    this.getContentPane().add(c, "Center");
    this.getContentPane().add(vsb, "East");
    ((JPanel)getContentPane()).setDoubleBuffered(false);
    getRootPane().setDoubleBuffered(false);
  }

  public static void main(String[] args) {
    JFrame f = new ScrollExample5("Scroll Example 5");
    Dimension d = Toolkit.getDefaultToolkit().getScreenSize();
    f.setSize(3 * d.width/4, 3 * d.height/4);
    f.addWindowListener(new WindowAdapter() {
      public void windowClosing(WindowEvent evt) {
        System.exit(0);
      }
    });
    f.setVisible(true);
  }
}
```

Figure 5-13   A large pattern to be scrolled with a scrollbar.

The main frame consists of a vertical `JScrollBar` and a subclass of `JPanel` that will actually handle the scrolling. Despite its name, `JScrollBar` doesn't actually do any scrolling. Instead, it provides an interface that allows the user to specify how far and in which direction the content of the canvas should be scrolled; in our case, it is the job of the `ScrollingCanvas` to manage the scrolling in response to the movement of the scrollbar. The scrollbar has five attributes that determine is appearance at any given time. These attributes are listed in Table 5-2.

Table 5-2 JScrollBar Attributes

Attribute	Description
Orientation	`JScrollBar.HORIZONTAL` or `JScrollBar.VERTICAL`
Value	The value represented by the slider's current position
Minimum	The lowest value that the slider can take
Maximum	The value represented by the bottom or right-most end of the slider when it is at its lowest or right-most point
Extent	The size of the visible part of the object being scrolled

When the `ScrollingCanvas` is created, the maximum and minimum values will be set. Since these depend on what is being scrolled, they are not set in the application's `main` method; instead, these values are set by the canvas, which knows how large an object it is going to represent. The extent is more difficult to set, because it depends on how tall the canvas will be. Naturally, the canvas doesn't know its height until it has been placed on the frame and the application window sized. Subsequently, the user could resize the application window, which would result in the canvas growing or shrinking; if this happened, it would be necessary to change the scrollbar's extent accordingly. To make this possible, the `ScrollingCanvas` class overrides the `Component` methods `setSize` and `setBounds`. When either of these methods is called, the extent will be set by calling the scrollbar's `setVisibleAmount` method.

As you saw in the previous example, the scrollbar's slider moves either to an absolute position if the user drags it, or changes position by the unit or block increment amounts. To implement logical scrolling, the `getUnitIncrement` and `getBlockIncrement` methods were overridden so that these values could be context-dependent. If pixel scrolling is sufficient, as it is in this case, you can either let the scrollbar use default values for these increments, or set them explicitly using `setUnitIncrement` and `setBlockIncrement`. In this example, the unit increment will be defaulted (to 1 pixel). When it comes to block scrolling, the default is to have the scrollbar move the scrolled object by the size of the visible area. Often, though, this will be confusing for the user: It is better to have some overlap so that the user can pick up looking at the information where they were before they scrolled it. For example, if you have a window that holds 32 lines of text, instead of scrolling up 32 lines on any click, you might choose to scroll by only 30 lines, so that the bottom two lines appear at the top of the screen to give reading continuity. This idea will be implemented here by setting the block increment to be 8 pixels less than the visible area. Since the height of the visible area can change, it is necessary to adjust the block increment whenever the height of the canvas changes.

To ensure that the size of the visible region and the block increment are adjusted together, both operations are encapsulated in a single method called change ScrollBar. Here is its implementation, together with an illustration of how it is called from the setBounds method; there is a similar call in the setSize methods.

```
public void setBounds(int x, int y, int width, int height) {
    super.setBounds(x, y, width, height);
    canvasHeight = height;
    canvasWidth = width;
    changeScrollBar();
}

// Keep visible size and block increment in step
public void changeScrollBar() {
    scrollBar.setVisibleAmount(canvasHeight);
    scrollBar.setBlockIncrement(canvasHeight - OVERLAP);
}
```

Once the scrollbar and the canvas have been created and initialized, the next problem to solve is how the canvas will find out that the scrollbar's slider has been moved. When its value changes, the scrollbar generates an AdjustmentEvent. In order to be notified of these changes, the canvas registers itself with the scrollbar as an AdjustmentListener by calling the JScrollBar addAdjustmentListener method. The AdjustmentListener interface contains only one method:

```
public void adjustmentValueChanged(AdjustmentEvent evt)
```

All of the information that describes the adjustment is contained in the AdjustmentEvent. Like the other AWT events, this one is derived from java.awt.AWTEvent, so it contains an identifier and the source of the event. The identifier is always set to the value ADJUSTMENT_VALUE_CHANGED and the event source, in this case, will always be the vertical scrollbar. As well as these generic attributes, it also has a type and a value. The value is the current value of the scrollbar; it doesn't matter whether the value was changed by dragging or by clicking on or near the movement arrows of the scrollbar. This value can be obtained from the event using its getValue method. Note that the incremental amount by which the scrollbar's value has changed is not contained in the event. If you want to know why the value changed, you can extract the event type with the getAdjustmentType method, which returns one of the following values, all defined by the `java.awt.event.AdjustmentEvent` class as shown in Table 5-3.

Table 5-3   Adjustment Event Types

Attribute	Description
UNIT_INCREMENT	Slider moved down by a click on the scrollbar arrow
UNIT_DECREMENT	Slider moved up by a click on the scrollbar arrow
BLOCK_INCREMENT	Slider moved down by a click inside the scrollbar
BLOCK_DECREMENT	Slider moved up by a click inside the scrollbar
TRACK	Slider dragged to a new position

In this example, it isn't necessary to know how the scrollbar's value changed, so only its new value will be used.

The last, and most important, part of the `ScrollingCanvas` is its `paintComponent` method. Before seeing how this works, let's remind ourselves of what needs to be drawn on the canvas. If you could see the entire scrolled object in one go on the screen, you would see 1024 pixels lines, each of which is painted in a single shade of gray. The color starts out being black at the top and gradually lightens until it is white at the bottom. The gradually changing color is produced by starting with a `Color` object created as follows:

```
new Color(0, 0, 0)
```

and incrementing each of the red, green and blue values by the same amount as we move down the canvas. Since there are 1024 pixel lines and only 256 possible values for each color component, the color value should be changed on every 4th pixel line.

In reality, only a part of the canvas will be on display at any given time. If the pixel lines of the pattern were numbered 0 through 1023 with 0 at the top, then the value of the scrollbar will indicate which line should be drawn at the top of the canvas and the canvas's height determines the number of lines to draw. The color of the pixel line *offset* pixels from the top of the pattern is `Color(offset/4, offset/4, offset/4)`, so the part of the pattern visible on the screen could be drawn as follows:

```
public void paintComponent(Graphics g) {
  int value = scrollBar.getValue();

  for (int i = 0; i < canvasHeight; i++, value++) {
    g.setColor(new Color(value/4, value/4, value/4));
    g.drawLine(0, i, canvasWidth - 1, i);
  }
}
```

While this works, it is very slow. Since the color changes only every fourth pixel line, the paintComponent method could be improved by drawing a filled rectangle instead of four pixel lines, remembering to treat the first one differently if it doesn't start on a 4-pixel boundary. While this would speed it up a bit, there is a simpler way to make an improvement to the scrolling speed. Once a section of the pattern has been drawn, when the scrollbar moves, what you really want to do is literally scroll the existing pattern upward or downward, preserving the part that remains within the viewport. The newly exposed part would then be filled in using code very much like that shown above. For example, if the viewport is 200 pixels high and the scrollbar is moved down by 20 pixels, the bottom 180 pixel lines, which won't need to change, should be copied up to the top of the canvas and new content should be drawn only on the bottom 20 pixel lines. The copyArea method of Graphics allows us to do just that:

```
public void copyArea(int x, int y, int width, int height, int dx, int dy)
```

This method copies the content of the rectangle described by the first four parameters to a new location, offset from the original by dx pixels horizontally and dy pixels vertically, where positive values correspond to movement to the right and downward respectively and overlapping moves are handled properly. Using this function, you can calculate how much of the content of the canvas can be preserved and move it quickly to its new location, then draw only the new part as a continuous pattern at the top or bottom of the canvas.

To allow the calculation of the offsets to be performed, the current value of the scrollbar and its previous value are recorded in the fields topLine and lastLine respectively; the difference between these two gives the amount of movement. Provided this distance is not greater than the height of the canvas, we can copy (canvasHeight - movement distance) pixel lines can be copied using copyArea. The implementation is shown in Listing 5-21.

Listing 5-21   Direct scrollbar handling

```
class ScrollingCanvas extends JPanel implements AdjustmentListener {
    ScrollingCanvas(JScrollBar sb) {
        scrollBar = sb;
        sb.setMaximum(MAX_VALUE);
        sb.setMinimum(0);
        sb.addAdjustmentListener(this);
    }

    // Draw the content of the canvas
    public void paintComponent(Graphics g) {
        int drawFromValue = 0;        // Value to draw from
        int drawFromScan = 0;         // y-position in canvas to draw from
        int drawHeight = canvasHeight; // Amount to draw
```

```
    // If there is any overlap with what is on screen, copy that amount
    int delta = lastTopLine - topLine; // Negative if scrolling down

    if (delta < 0) {
      // Scrolling downward
      int overlap = canvasHeight + delta;     // Size of common area
      if (overlap > 0) {
        g.copyArea(0, -delta, canvasWidth, overlap, 0, delta);
        drawFromValue = topLine + overlap;
        drawFromScan = overlap;
        drawHeight = -delta;
      }
    } else if (delta != 0) {
      // Scrolling downward
      int overlap = canvasHeight - delta;     // Size of common area
      if (overlap > 0) {
        g.copyArea(0, 0, canvasWidth, overlap, 0, delta);
        drawFromValue = topLine;
        drawFromScan = 0;
        drawHeight = delta;
      }
    }

    if (drawHeight + drawFromValue > MAX_VALUE) {
      drawHeight = MAX_VALUE - drawFromValue;
    }

    // Draw the part that was not visible before
    if (drawHeight > 0) {
      // Round down to block-size boundary
      int offset = drawFromValue % BLOCK_SIZE;
      if (offset != 0) {
        drawFromValue -= offset;
        drawFromScan -= offset;
        drawHeight += offset;
      }

      Color color;
      int total = (drawHeight + BLOCK_SIZE - 1)/BLOCK_SIZE;
      int value = drawFromValue/BLOCK_SIZE;
      for (int i = 0; i < total; i++) {
        color = new Color(value, value, value);
        g.setColor(color);
        value++;
        g.fillRect(0, drawFromScan, canvasWidth, BLOCK_SIZE);
        drawFromValue += BLOCK_SIZE;
        drawFromScan += BLOCK_SIZE;
      }
    }
  }
}
```

(Continued)

```java
   // Adjustment Listener interface
   public void adjustmentValueChanged(AdjustmentEvent evt) {
      if (evt.getID() == AdjustmentEvent.ADJUSTMENT_VALUE_CHANGED) {
         // Scrollbar moved: repaint the canvas
         lastTopLine = topLine;            // Save current top line
         topLine = evt.getValue();         // Set new top line
         repaint();
      }
   }

   // Override size-setting methods to set
   // correct scrollbar visible size and
   // block increment values.
   public void setSize(int width, int height) {
      super.setSize(width, height);
      canvasHeight = height;
      canvasWidth = width;
      changeScrollBar();
   }

   public void setSize(Dimension d) {
      super.setSize(d);
      canvasHeight = d.height;
      canvasWidth = d.width;
      changeScrollBar();
   }

   public void setBounds(int x, int y, int width, int height) {
      super.setBounds(x, y, width, height);
      canvasHeight = height;
      canvasWidth = width;
      changeScrollBar();
   }

   // Keep visible size and block increment in step
   public void changeScrollBar() {
      scrollBar.setVisibleAmount(canvasHeight);
      scrollBar.setBlockIncrement(canvasHeight - OVERLAP);
   }

   private int topLine;                 // Top line on the canvas
   private int lastTopLine;             // Previous value of the top line
   private int canvasHeight;            // Height of the canvas
   private int canvasWidth;             // Width of canvas
   private JScrollBar scrollBar;        // Associated scrollbar
   private final int MAX_VALUE = 1023;  // Maximum value
   private final int OVERLAP = 8;       // Overlap for block scrolls
   private final int BLOCK_SIZE = 4;    // Size of each rectangle
}
```

In the `paintComponent` method, the `drawFromScan`, `drawFromValue` and `drawHeight` variables describe the area that can't be copied. The first of these is the pixel line, relative to the top of the canvas, of the first line that can't be copied; `drawFromValue` is the offset down the original pattern of the corresponding line and `drawHeight` is the number of lines that need to be drawn. To see how these values are used, let's look at an example. When the frame first appears, nothing can be copied because the canvas is blank; it is simple to recognize this situation, because the current and previous values of the scrollbar are equal, so as much of the pattern as will fit on the canvas is drawn. Now suppose that the canvas is 200 pixels high and it is scrolled up by 20 pixels. Since the difference between the old and new values is 20 pixels, (200 – 20) = 180 pixels worth can be copied from pixel line 20 of the canvas up to pixel line 0; this will, of course, represent pixel lines 20 through 199 of the original pattern. It would then be necessary to draw the bottom 20 lines (i.e., lines 200 through 219 of the pattern) using the usual graphics primitives. In this case, `drawFromScan` would be set to 180, `drawFromValue` to 200 and `drawHeight` to 20. If the pattern were now scrolled down by 10 pixels, 190 rows of pixels from the top of the canvas would be copied to the bottom and the top 10 lines would be drawn from scratch. Here, `drawFromScan` would be set to 0, `drawFromValue` set to 10 and `drawHeight` also set to 10.

Scrolling with the Keyboard

At the beginning of this chapter, you saw how important it is to allow users to operate an application using only the keyboard. When the user interface includes scrollbars, it is essential that it is possible for the user to operate them without resorting to the mouse. If you've used a word processor, you're probably used to being able to move up and down a document using the PAGE UP and PAGE DOWN keys as well as dragging or clicking the scrollbars. Fortunately, Swing makes it easy to imitate this behavior in your own applications.

To show how to implement keyboard-controlled scrolling, let's modify the example used to show logical scrolling in Listing 5-15.

Recall that this example consisted of an extended `JScrollPane`, called `PictureScrollPane`, that arranges images in a grid and allows the user to scroll to picture boundaries as well as a single pixel at a time. To make this example complete, the application that uses this component is going to be extended so that the following key sequences can be used to drive the scrollbars:

- PAGE UP.—Scroll up by one picture
- PAGE DOWN.—Scroll down by one picture
- SHIFT + PAGE UP.—Scroll left by one picture
- SHIFT + PAGE DOWN.—Scroll right by one picture

- UP arrow key.—Scroll up one pixel
- DOWN arrow key.—Scroll down by one pixel
- LEFT arrow key.—Scroll left by one pixel
- RIGHT arrow key.—Scroll right by one pixel

What you need to do is to arrange to capture the key events just listed and perform the corresponding operation on either the horizontal or vertical scrollbar. To catch the key event, the key management facilities that were shown at the beginning of this chapter can be used to arrange for the appropriate combination of keys to be detected and processed as an Action. The Action will then perform the required operations on the scrollbar.

Let's suppose for a moment that the proper key sequences have been registered. What should be done when the action is triggered? If the PAGE UP or PAGE DOWN key has been used, the correct scrollbar should be moved in the correct direction by the correct block increment, while if one of the arrow keys is pressed, the scrollbar should be moved by one pixel in the right direction. To correctly process the action, then, the following information needs to be available:

- Which scrollbar is involved (horizontal or vertical)
- Whether to move by a pixel or by the size of a picture (i.e., a unit- or block-sized move)
- Which direction the scrollbar should move in—i.e., whether the scrollbar value should increase or decrease.

Recall from the last chapter that the keyboard action is handled by an ActionListener. In this case, since it is necessary to store several pieces of information to describe what is to be done, we choose to create a subclass of AbstractAction that will describe which scrollbar to operate on and what to do with it, and register this as the ActionListener for the key event. Listing 5-22 shows the definition of this class.

Listing 5-22   A scrolling Action

```
// Class to handle scrolling actions
class ScrollBarAction extends AbstractAction {
  ScrollBarAction(JScrollPane pane, int orientation, int type, int direction) {
    this.pane = pane;
    this.orientation = orientation;
    this.type = type;
    this.direction = direction;
  }

  public void actionPerformed(ActionEvent evt) {
    JScrollBar bar;
```

```
   if (orientation == JScrollBar.HORIZONTAL) {
     bar = pane.getHorizontalScrollBar();
   } else {
     bar = pane.getVerticalScrollBar();
   }

   if (bar != null && bar.isVisible() == true) {
     int delta;

     delta = type == UNIT ? bar.getUnitIncrement(direction) :
                 bar.getBlockIncrement(direction);

     if (direction == DECREASE) {
       delta = -delta;
     }

     bar.setValue(delta + bar.getValue());
   }
 }

 // Constants
 public static final int UNIT = 0;          // Unit change
 public static final int BLOCK = 1;         // Block change

 public static final int INCREASE = 1;
 public static final int DECREASE = -1;

 private JScrollPane pane;        // Target scroll pane
 private int orientation;         // Orientation of scrollbar
 private int type;                // UNIT or BLOCK change
 private int direction;           // INCREASE or DECREASE
}
```

When one of these objects is created, it is given a reference to the JScrollPane object that has the scrollbars, the scrollbar that needs to be manipulated (as JScrollBar.HORIZONTAL or JScrollBar.VERTICAL), the scroll type (BLOCK or UNIT) and the direction of change (INCREASE or DECREASE). This information is stored within the object and used when the event occurs.

Why store the JScrollPane and the scrollbar orientation instead of directly storing a reference to the JScrollBar? This is done to make this class more generally useful: As you know, you are not obliged to use both scrollbars when you create a JScrollPane and, even if you allow both to be present, one or both may not be visible if the JScrollPane is created in such a way that it shows only those scrollbars which are needed at any given time.

An alternative approach might be to get the JScrollBar reference and store it with the ScrollBarAction object, but this would mean making an assumption about the implementation of JScrollPane: Suppose that the scrollbar reference returned by getHorizontalScrollBar or getVerticalScrollBar is null when the scrollbar is not in use? If the scrollbar is initially in this state, you won't ever be able to get a reference to it. To avoid making this assumption, a reference to the JScrollPane is stored and used to get the scrollbar reference when it is needed.

When the correct key sequence occurs, the actionPerformed method of the ScrollBarAction object is invoked. Using the information stored when the object was constructed, it is a simple matter to decide which scrollbar is affected and what type of scrolling is required. First, a reference to the scrollbar is obtained and then a check is made that it is not null and, if so, that the scrollbar is visible. To decide how far to move, the getUnitIncrement or getBlockIncrement method of the scrollbar is called. These return the appropriate increments as positive numbers. As you already know, this works even if logical scrolling is being used. Once you have the distance by which to move, you can set the new scrollbar value using its setValue method. Incidentally, setValue ensures that the scrollbar is always in a legal position, so there is no need to write code to verify this—you can just add or subtract the distance by which the scrollbar is to move to the current value and be sure that the scrollbar won't get out of range.

Now let's look at the application code that registers the keyboard actions. The code for the earlier example (ScrollExample4) is used and modified slightly, renaming it to ScrollExample6 as shown in Listing 5-23; the changes that have been are highlighted.

Listing 5-23   Using the keyboard to scroll

```
package JFCBook.Chapter5;

import com.sun.java.swing.*;
import java.awt.*;
import java.awt.event.*;

public class ScrollExample6 extends JFrame {
  public ScrollExample6() {
    super("Scroll Example 6");
    picturePane = new
PictureScrollPane(JScrollPane.VERTICAL_SCROLLBAR_AS_NEEDED,
        JScrollPane.HORIZONTAL_SCROLLBAR_AS_NEEDED,
        imageNames, PICTURES_PER_ROW);
    this.getContentPane().add(picturePane, "Center");

    // Add buttons to bring numbered picture into view
    JPanel panel = new JPanel();
    panel.setBackground(UIManager.getColor("control"));
    JPanel buttonPanel = new JPanel();
    buttonPanel.setLayout(new GridLayout(0, PICTURES_PER_ROW, 4, 4));
    panel.add(buttonPanel);

    Font f = new Font("Serif", Font.BOLD, 14);
```

```
for (int i = 0; i < imageNames.length; i++) {
  JButton b = new JButton("" + i);
  b.setMnemonic('0' + i);    // Accelerator for button
  b.setFont(f);
  buttonPanel.add(b);
  b.addActionListener(new ActionListener() {
    public void actionPerformed(ActionEvent evt) {
      JButton button = (JButton)evt.getSource();
      int index = button.getActionCommand().charAt(0) - '0';
      picturePane.makeVisible(index);// Make picture visible
    }
  });
}
this.getContentPane().add(panel, "East");

// Register keyboard actions
// Down key
picturePane.registerKeyboardAction(new ScrollBarAction(picturePane,
        JScrollBar.VERTICAL,
        ScrollBarAction.UNIT,
        ScrollBarAction.INCREASE),
      KeyStroke.getKeyStroke(KeyEvent.VK_DOWN,
          0, false),
      JComponent.WHEN_IN_FOCUSED_WINDOW);
// Up key
picturePane.registerKeyboardAction(new ScrollBarAction(picturePane,
        JScrollBar.VERTICAL,
        ScrollBarAction.UNIT,
        ScrollBarAction.DECREASE),
      KeyStroke.getKeyStroke(KeyEvent.VK_UP,
          0, false),
      JComponent.WHEN_IN_FOCUSED_WINDOW);
// Left key
picturePane.registerKeyboardAction(new ScrollBarAction(picturePane,
        JScrollBar.HORIZONTAL,
        ScrollBarAction.UNIT,
        ScrollBarAction.DECREASE),
      KeyStroke.getKeyStroke(KeyEvent.VK_LEFT,
          0, false),
      JComponent.WHEN_IN_FOCUSED_WINDOW);
// Right key
picturePane.registerKeyboardAction(new ScrollBarAction(picturePane,
        JScrollBar.HORIZONTAL,
        ScrollBarAction.UNIT,
        ScrollBarAction.INCREASE),
      KeyStroke.getKeyStroke(KeyEvent.VK_RIGHT,
          0, false),
      JComponent.WHEN_IN_FOCUSED_WINDOW);
// Page up key
picturePane.registerKeyboardAction(new ScrollBarAction(picturePane,
        JScrollBar.VERTICAL,
        ScrollBarAction.BLOCK,
        ScrollBarAction.DECREASE),
```

(Continued)

```
                    KeyStroke.getKeyStroke(KeyEvent.VK_PAGE_UP,
                            0, false),
                    JComponent.WHEN_IN_FOCUSED_WINDOW);
    // Page down key
    picturePane.registerKeyboardAction(new ScrollBarAction(picturePane,
                    JScrollBar.VERTICAL,
                    ScrollBarAction.BLOCK,
                    ScrollBarAction.INCREASE),
                    KeyStroke.getKeyStroke(KeyEvent.VK_PAGE_DOWN,
                            0, false),
                    JComponent.WHEN_IN_FOCUSED_WINDOW);
    // Page up key + SHIFT
    picturePane.registerKeyboardAction(new ScrollBarAction(picturePane,
                    JScrollBar.HORIZONTAL,
                    ScrollBarAction.BLOCK,
                    ScrollBarAction.DECREASE),
                    KeyStroke.getKeyStroke(KeyEvent.VK_PAGE_UP,
                            InputEvent.SHIFT_MASK, false),
                    JComponent.WHEN_IN_FOCUSED_WINDOW);
    // Page down key + SHIFT
    picturePane.registerKeyboardAction(new ScrollBarAction(picturePane,
                    JScrollBar.HORIZONTAL,
                    ScrollBarAction.BLOCK,
                    ScrollBarAction.INCREASE),
                    KeyStroke.getKeyStroke(KeyEvent.VK_PAGE_DOWN,
                            InputEvent.SHIFT_MASK, false),
                    JComponent.WHEN_IN_FOCUSED_WINDOW);
  }

  public static void main(String[] args) {
    JFrame f = new ScrollExample6();
    Dimension d = Toolkit.getDefaultToolkit().getScreenSize();
    f.setSize(3*d.width/4, 3*d.height/4);
    f.setVisible(true);
    f.addWindowListener(new WindowAdapter() {
      public void windowClosing(WindowEvent e) {
        System.exit(0);
      }
    });
  }

  private static final String[] imageNames = {
      "images/p1.jpg",  "images/p2.jpg",     "images/p3.jpg",
      "images/p4.jpg",  "images/p5.jpg",     "images/p6.jpg",
      "images/p7.jpg",  "images/p8.jpg",     "images/p9.jpg" };


  private static final int PICTURES_PER_ROW = 3;     // Pictures on each row

  private PictureScrollPane picturePane;              // The picture panel
```

The first change was to add keyboard accelerators to the panel of buttons that allow us to directly scroll to a particular picture. With this modification, ALT+0 can now be used to view the top left picture, ALT+1 to view the one to its right and so on.

Eight keyboard actions were also added using the JComponent register KeyboardAction method. Each registration is accompanied by a description of the key sequence required and a ScrollBarAction object that will handle the event; this should all be familiar from the examples at the beginning of this chapter. Since keyboard scrolling should work whenever the application is in the foreground, the keyboard events should be registered so that they are activated from anywhere within the JFrame. Unfortunately, JFrame is not a JComponent, so registerKeyboardAction can't be used on it. However, it can be applied it to any JComponent in the JFrame provided that the action is configured to apply whenever the application window has the focus. Since the application window is the JFrame, this is equivalent to registering the action against the JFrame. In this case, the key events were registered against the PictureScrollPane. You can verify that this works by running this example using the command:

```
java JFCBook.Chapter5.ScrollExample6
```

and using the arrow and page keys to scroll without using the mouse.

Summary

This chapter showed how important it is to pay proper attention to proper tabbing order and when to help the user by moving the focus automatically as the application's state changes. It also explored the various ways of handling the keyboard, from catching individual key events at the lowest level, to the powerful keystroke mechanism that allows you to handle accelerator keys without having to attach key listeners to every component on the screen that might acquire the focus. This facility dovetails nicely with the topic of Actions, which were used here only to provide ActionListeners for accelerator keys. In the next chapter, you'll see how the Action mechanism is used in conjunction with the menu bar and with toolbars and how you can conveniently connect various parts of the user interface to application logic using an Action.

In the second part of the chapter, you saw how to scroll images and components using the built-in scrolling support and how to customize both the appearance and the operation of the JScrollPane component. Finally, we looked at the more primitive JScrollBar, which can be used independently of JScrollPane, and how to use Actions to drive scrollbars from the keyboard.

MENUS AND TOOLBARS

Topics in This Chapter

- The Menu Bar and The Menu System
- Using Actions and Menus together
- Customizing Menus and Using Popup Menus
- Using Toolbars
- Implementing Floating and Docking Toolbars

Chapter 6

This chapter looks at how to give the user fast access to application functionality by showing you how to add menus and toolbars. The Swing menu system is much more powerful and more configurable than the AWT menus. You can, for example, add shortcuts on the menu bar and you can change the appearance of both the menu bar and the menus themselves. You'll see how to use various types of menu item and how to populate menus as needed.

In a deep menu hierarchy, it can sometimes be time-consuming to find the menu item that you want. To make it easier to control an application, Swing provides the toolbar, on which you can mount buttons and other components. This chapter shows you how to create toolbars and how to arrange for them to float over the application window and dock again on request.

The Menu Bar and the Menu System

The Swing menu system is, in many ways, similar to the one that you have probably used when developing AWT applications. Swing retains the concepts of the menu bar, menus and menu items and it also has popup menus, which were first introduced with JDK 1.1. But while the basic building blocks are the same, you'll see in this section that the implementation is much more generalized than it was in AWT 1.1 and, therefore, there is much more that you can do with Swing menus.

Adding a Menu Bar to an Application

Almost all applications have a menu bar and most have an extensive set of menus that provide a way (usually not the only way) to access the application's functionality. Creating menus in other programming languages can be a tricky process, but in Java it is easy. The first step is to create a menu bar and attach it to the application window. Creating the menu only takes one line of code:

```
JMenuBar mb = new JMenuBar();
```

A menu bar is actually just another JComponent, so you could place it anywhere on the application window, but normally you attach it to a JFrame using the setJMenuBar method:

```
JFrame f = new JFrame("Menu Example");
f.setJMenuBar(mb);
```

As you already know, JFrame is a compound container that houses several components, one of which is the content pane on which an application's user interface is mounted. If you use the setJMenuBar to attach the menu bar, the JFrame arranges for it to adapt its preferred height and to appear at the top of the frame, just underneath the caption bar and immediately above the content pane.

A menu bar can house one or more menus and each menu can hold any number of menu items or other menus. You add a new menu by creating an instance of JMenu and placing it on the menu bar:

```
JMenu fileMenu = new JMenu("File");
mb.add(fileMenu);
```

Menus appear on the menu bar from left to right, in the order in which they are added. On their own, menus are not useful. To make them usable, you add menu items that correspond to actions that the application can perform:

```
JMenuItem newItem = new JMenuItem("New...");
JMenuItem openItem = new JMenuItem("Open...");
JMenuItem closeItem = new JMenuItem("Close");
fileMenu.add(newItem);
fileMenu.add(openItem);
fileMenu.add(closeItem);
```

When you create a menu or a menu item, the string supplied to the constructor is used to represent the object. For example, the string File supplied when we created the JMenu object appears on the menu bar in place of the menu itself.

If you move the mouse over this word and click it, the menu will drop down, revealing the menu items that it contains. Figure 6-1 shows an example of an application with two menus, as it would appear just after the user had clicked on the word File. You can try this example for yourself using the command:

```
java JFCBook.Chapter6.MenuExample1
```

Figure 6-1   An application with a menu bar.

The file menu in this example was created using statements very similar to those just shown; each menu item added results in another entry on the menu. You will notice that there are separators between some of the menu items. Separators are commonly used to group together menu items that implement related functions, such as opening and closing files. You can add a separator to a menu using the addSeparator method:

```
fileMenu.addSeparator();
```

The Recent Files menu item is different from all of the others in that it has a small arrow pointing to the right. This is an example of a *cascading* drop-down menu. If you moved the mouse pointer down over it and let it hover there for a short while, a new menu would drop down to the right, where the arrow is pointing.

Core Note

The gesture needed to drop down a cascading menu is actually look-and-feel dependent. With the Windows look-and-feel, hovering the mouse over the menu item is sufficient, but Motif requires you to press a mouse button to make the sub-menu appear and to hold the button down as you move the mouse onto the sub-menu to stop it from disappearing.

This submenu will be used to hold the names of files that have recently been used in this application. When this test program starts up, the submenu contains only one item, labeled Empty, which represents an empty file list (see Figure 6-1). You create a sub-menu by adding a JMenu object to the menu instead of a JMenuItem. This is possible because JMenu is actually derived from JMenuItem, so it is valid to supply a JMenu as an argument to a method whose signature is:

```
public JMenuItem add(JMenuItem);
```

Here is the code used to create the submenu:

```
JMenu fileListMenu = new JMenu("Recent Files");
fileMenu.add(fileListMenu);
JMenuItem emptyListItem = new JMenuItem("Empty");
emptyListItem.setEnabled(false);
fileListMenu.add(emptyListItem);
```

The second line of this extract adds the new JMenu to its parent JMenu to create a cascaded menu; the label associated with the submenu (Recent Files) is used to represent it on the parent File menu. The dummy file entry is added in the same way as any other menu item, but to make it clear that this is not a real file name (so that it doesn't appear that a file called Empty has recently been opened), the label is grayed out by disabling the menu item. You'll see later what the effect of disabling a menu item is, other than the obvious visual feedback that we get.

Handling Events from Menus

When the user clicks on an item on the menu bar, the corresponding menu drops down; a selection occurs when the user clicks on an individual menu item. At this point, two things happen—an event is generated to notify the application of the user's choice and the menu disappears. The source of the event is the JMenuItem that the user selected. Since JMenuItem is actually derived from AbstractButton, which is the parent class of JButton, it uses the same notification mechanism as all of the Swing buttons—it generates an ActionEvent.

To receive notification of a menu selection, you register an ActionListener on each JMenuItem and then handle the event as you would an event from a button. In particular, you can find out which item the user has selected by getting a reference to the menu item from the `ActionEvent` using the `getSource` method and then invoking `getActionCommand`, as was done with buttons in Chapter 2, "Frames, Labels, and Buttons." Alternatively, you can avoid string comparisons by attaching a single listener to each menu item. You'll see both of these techniques in the following example.

A Simple File Editor

The example application in this section is a very simple file editor. Most of the work is done by the standard `JTextArea` component; our interest will be not in how the text is manipulated, but in how to manage the opening and closing of files using menus. The menu bar of this application contains only a `File` menu, which is the same as the one you saw in the previous example. The difference here is that this menu will be functional. Listing 6-1 shows the implementation of the class `MenuExample2`, which contains the user interface for this application.

Listing 6-1   A menu for a simple file editor

```
package JFCBook.Chapter6;

import com.sun.java.swing.*;
import java.awt.*;
import java.awt.event.*;
import java.io.*;
import java.util.*;

public class MenuExample2 extends JFrame {
  public MenuExample2(String title) {
    super(title);

    JMenuBar mb = new JMenuBar();
    this.setJMenuBar(mb);

    JMenu fileMenu = new JMenu("File");
    mb.add(fileMenu);

    newItem = new JMenuItem("New...");
    openItem = new JMenuItem("Open...");
    closeItem = new JMenuItem("Close");
    fileMenu.add(newItem);
    fileMenu.add(openItem);
    fileMenu.add(closeItem);

    fileMenu.addSeparator();
```

continued

```java
saveItem = new JMenuItem("Save");
saveAsItem = new JMenuItem("Save As...");
fileMenu.add(saveItem);
fileMenu.add(saveAsItem);

fileMenu.addSeparator();

fileListMenu = new JMenu("Recent Files");
fileMenu.add(fileListMenu);
emptyListItem = new JMenuItem("Empty");
emptyListItem.setEnabled(false);
fileListMenu.add(emptyListItem);

fileMenu.addSeparator();

JMenuItem exitItem = new JMenuItem("Exit");
fileMenu.add(exitItem);
exitItem.addActionListener(new ActionListener() {
  public void actionPerformed(ActionEvent evt) {
    closeWindow();
  }
});

this.getContentPane().add(new JScrollPane(textArea = new JTextArea(20,40)));
fileManager = new FileManager();

// Processing for "New..." menu item
newItem.addActionListener(new ActionListener() {
  public void actionPerformed(ActionEvent evt) {
    String name = getFileName("New File", FileDialog.SAVE);
    if (name != null) {
      if (fileManager.isFileOpen()) {
        // Close any open file
        try {
          fileManager.closeFile(textArea.getText());
        } catch (Throwable e) {
          // Ignore any exception
        }
      }
      try {
        fileManager.newFile(name);
        textArea.setText("");
        addRecentFile(name);
      } catch (IOException e) {
        // Do nothing - message already printed
      }
    }
```

```
      }
    });

    // Processing for "Open..." menu item
    openItem.addActionListener(new ActionListener() {
      public void actionPerformed(ActionEvent evt) {
        String name = getFileName("Open File", FileDialog.LOAD);
        if (name != null) {
          try {
            String text = fileManager.openFile(name);
            textArea.setText(text);
            addRecentFile(name);
          } catch (IOException e) {
            // Do nothing - message already printed
          }
        }
      }
    });

    // Processing for "Close..." menu item
    closeItem.addActionListener(new ActionListener() {
      public void actionPerformed(ActionEvent evt) {
        try {
          fileManager.closeFile(textArea.getText());
          textArea.setText("");
        } catch (IOException e) {
          // Do nothing - message already printed
        }
      }
    });

    // Processing for "Save..." menu item
    saveItem.addActionListener(new ActionListener() {
      public void actionPerformed(ActionEvent evt) {
        try {
          fileManager.saveFile(textArea.getText());
        } catch (IOException e) {
          // Do nothing - message already printed
        }
      }
    });

    // Processing for "Save As..." menu item
    saveAsItem.addActionListener(new ActionListener() {
      public void actionPerformed(ActionEvent evt) {
        if (fileManager.isFileOpen()) {
          String name = getFileName("Save As File", FileDialog.SAVE);
```

continued

```
          if (name != null) {
            try {
              fileManager.saveAsFile(name,
                  textArea.getText());
            } catch (IOException e) {
              // Do nothing - message already printed
            }
          }
        }
      }
    });

    // Create the handler for the recent file list
    menuListener = new ActionListener() {
      public void actionPerformed(ActionEvent evt) {
        JMenuItem mi = (JMenuItem)(evt.getSource());
        String fileName = mi.getActionCommand();
        try {
          String text = fileManager.openFile(fileName);
          textArea.setText(text);
          addRecentFile(fileName);
        } catch (IOException e) {
          // Do nothing - message already printed
        }
      }
    };
}

// Add a name to the recent file list
public void addRecentFile(String fileName) {
  int offset;

  // Check whether this file is already in the file list
  if ((offset = recentFiles.indexOf(fileName)) == -1) {
    // Not present - add it at the beginning
    recentFiles.insertElementAt(fileName, 0);
    if (recentFiles.size() > RECENT_FILES) {
      // List was full - remove the last (oldest) item
      recentFiles.removeElementAt(RECENT_FILES);
    }
  } else {
    // Already present: move this item to the front of the list
    recentFiles.removeElementAt(offset);
    recentFiles.insertElementAt(fileName, 0);
  }

      // Rebuild the file menu
```

```
    buildRecentFileMenu();
}


// Build the recent file menu
public void buildRecentFileMenu() {
  int size = recentFiles.size();

  fileListMenu.removeAll();

  for (int i = 0; i < size; i++) {
    String fileName = (String)(recentFiles.elementAt(i));
    JMenuItem mi = new JMenuItem(fileName);
    fileListMenu.add(mi);
    mi.addActionListener(menuListener);
  }
}

// Get a file name
public String getFileName(String title, int mode) {
  FileDialog fd = new FileDialog(this, title, mode);
  fd.setFile("*.*");
  fd.setDirectory(directory);

  fd.setVisible(true);

  String dir = fd.getDirectory();
  String file = fd.getFile();
  if (dir == null || file == null) {
    return null;
  }
  directory = dir;

  String separator = System.getProperty("file.separator");
  if (dir.endsWith(separator)) {
    return dir + file;
  } else {
    return dir + System.getProperty("file.separator") + file;
  }
}

// Take any action needed to close the application
public void closeWindow() {
  try {
    fileManager.closeFile(textArea.getText());
  } catch (IOException e) {
    System.out.println("Failed to write data on close.");
```

continued

```
      }
      System.exit(0);
   }

   public static void main(String[] args) {
      JFrame f = new MenuExample2("Menu Example 2");
      f.pack();
      f.setVisible(true);
      f.addWindowListener(new WindowAdapter() {
         public void windowClosing(WindowEvent evt) {
            MenuExample2 frame = (MenuExample2)(evt.getSource());
            frame.closeWindow();
         }
      });
   }

   JMenuItem newItem;
   JMenuItem openItem;
   JMenuItem closeItem;
   JMenuItem saveItem;
   JMenuItem saveAsItem;
   JMenuItem emptyListItem;
   JMenu fileListMenu;
   JTextArea textArea;
   FileManager fileManager;
   String directory = "";           // Current directory

   ActionListener menuListener;

   // Recently-used file list
   static final int RECENT_FILES = 4;
   Vector recentFiles = new Vector(RECENT_FILES);
}
```

The constructor builds the user interface by adding a JTextArea and a menu bar to a JFrame. After adding all of the menu items to the file menu, ActionListeners that handle the New, Open, Close, Save, Save As and Exit operations are added. The implementation of the actionPerformed methods of these listeners is not going to be explored in any great detail, because they don't tell us much about the menu system. The important point to note about these methods is that, since there is a separate one for each menu item, each of them can do its own job without needing to work out which menu item caused it to be invoked. You'll also notice that this code does not directly deal with the details of reading and writing files; this job is delegated to a small helper class (FileManager) that isn't shown here. You can find the code for this class on the CD-ROM that accompanies this book. In general, it is good practice to separate user interface code from application logic like this as much as possible.

Core Note

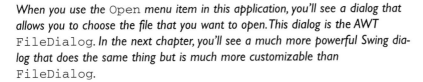

When you use the `Open` *menu item in this application, you'll see a dialog that allows you to choose the file that you want to open. This dialog is the AWT* `FileDialog`. *In the next chapter, you'll see a much more powerful Swing dialog that does the same thing but is much more customizable than* `FileDialog`.

Maintaining the Recent Files Menu

The most interesting part of this application from the point of view of this chapter is the way in which the `Recent Files` menu is maintained. When the application starts, this menu will be empty. An empty drop-down menu appears as a box that's almost too small to see, so to make it clear that the recent file list is empty, a menu with a single item on it that says "Empty" is created and, since this isn't a real file name, it is disabled so that the user can't activate it. The code that does this was shown at the start of this section and is placed here again for reference:

```
emptyListItem.setEnabled(false);
```

As files are opened, each file name should be added to this submenu. For convenience, the menu items should be arranged so that the most recently used file is at the top. When the menu is full, the oldest entry will be dropped. In this example, an arbitrary limit of four items (defined as `RECENT_FILES`) is placed on this menu. The logic that maintains the menu is contained in the `addRecentFile` and `buildRecentFileMenu` methods. The file names are kept in a vector called `recentFiles`, which starts empty. Each time a file is opened, the `addRecentFile` method inserts its name at the front of the vector. When the vector is full, the oldest entry, which is always the one at the end—that is, the entry with index `RECENT_FILES`—should be discarded. This simple algorithm, as stated, doesn't work if a file that is already on the list is reopened, because there would then be two entries for the same file. To cater for this, we first check whether the file is already in the list and, if it is, the entry is removed and then added again to the front. All of these operations can be performed very easily using the `Vector` class.

The `buildRecentFileMenu` creates the `Recent Files` menu itself from the vector of file names. The menu items should reflect the order of elements in the vector, with the first entry in the vector appearing at the top of the menu. When the vector is reordered, it is necessary to change the order of the items on the `Recent Files` menu. It is possible to change the order of items in a menu without completely reconstructing it and, for the sake of completeness, you'll see how to do this later in "Adding and Removing Menu Items." This example takes a simpler approach and empties and repopulates the menu whenever a change is made. Although this will take slightly longer than the method you'll see later, it makes it easier when accelerator keys whose values depend on the position of the associated menu item in the Recent Files menu are added later. Since the menu will be manipulated comparatively rarely, the slightly higher run-time cost is more than offset by the saving in implementation complexity.

When the content of the file list changes, all of the menu items in the Recent Files menu are removed using the JMenu removeAll method, then a new JMenuItem is added for each entry in the vector. Note that this simple algorithm solves the problem of what to do with the dummy Empty entry that should only exist until a file is opened, because it will be removed the first time the removeAll method is called and will not be recreated because it is not in the list of open files.

Receiving Menu Events

To use the Recent Files menu, the user pops it up, selects the file to open, and clicks on it with the mouse. This will generate an ActionEvent. To handle the event, an ActionListener is attached to each of the menu items as it is created. Since all of these menu items will be processed in exactly the same way, in this case it makes more sense to attach the same listener to all of them. When the menu item is selected, the listener's actionPerformed method extracts the file name as follows:

```
menuListener = new ActionListener() {
  public void actionPerformed(ActionEvent evt) {
    JMenuItem mi = (JMenuItem)(evt.getSource());
    String fileName = mi.getActionCommand();
    try {
      String text = fileManager.openFile(fileName);
      textArea.setText(text);
      addRecentFile(fileName);
    } catch (IOException e) {
      // Do nothing - message already printed
    }
  }
};
```

The source of the event is the menu item itself. Since JMenuItem extends AbstractButton, the AbstractButton getActionCommand method can be used to obtain the command associated with the button. Since an action command was not explicitly set, this method retrieves the button's label, which is the file name on the menu item. This is, of course, one example in which it is acceptable to use the menu item text rather than an action command, because there are no internationalization concerns over the value of the text in the menu item—it will always be a file name.

Adding and Removing Menu Items

You've seen some of the methods that can be used to maintain menus. Let's now look at the complete set. When you create a new menu it is, of course, empty. To add some menu items, you would normally use the add method that has four different forms:

```
public JMenuItem add(JMenuItem menuItem);

public JMenuItem add(Action a);

public void add(String s);

public Component add(Component c);
```

As you saw in Listing 6-1, you can also add a separator at the end of a menu using the addSeparator method:

```
public void addSeparator();
```

When you use the add method, the new menu item is always placed at the end of the menu.

The first form of add is the one that you have already seen in use in this chapter. When you use this form, you have to create your own JMenuItem. Often, this is the most convenient way to add a menu item, because you'll probably want to add an ActionListener, for which you will need access to the JMenuItem object, as you saw in the buildRecentFileMenu method in Listing 6-1. The second form is a variant on the first in which you pass an Action instead of a JMenuItem. This form is described further in "Using Actions with Menus" below.

The third variant is given only the string to be used as the menu item's label and creates a JMenuItem itself. This JMenuItem is, however, not returned to you, so you cannot easily add an action listener or customize the menu item in any way. This form is obviously inferior to the first two ways of creating a menu item and it is not recommended.

The last version of the add method allows you to add a Component of any sort to the menu. However, adding a Component in this way does not create a JMenuItem. The Component is physically a part of the menu, but is not managed by the menu system in any way. You can use this method to place custom separators or other objects on the menu, provided that you manage them yourself. This is, in effect, a way for the JMenu to allow other objects to occupy its screen space and could be regarded as an open-ended mechanism for extending the menu system.

As well as adding entries at the end of a menu, you can also insert an entry at any given position using the insert method:

```
public JMenuItem insert(JMenuItem menuItem, int pos);

public JMenuItem insert(Action a, int pos);

public void insert(String s, int pos);
```

These methods work in the same way as add, except that the new menu item occupies the position given by the pos argument. The position is counted from the top of the menu and is numbered from 0. Every item on the menu is counted, including separators and Components, if there are any. Consider, for example, the following code extract:

```
JMenu menu = new JMenu("File");
menu.add(new JMenuItem("New..."));
menu.add(new JMenuItem("Open..."));
menu.addSeparator();
menu.add(new JMenuItem("Exit"));
```

When this menu is constructed, the menu items occupy positions 0, 1 and 3 and the separator is in position 2. The following statement:

```
menu.insert(new JMenuItem("Close"). 2);
```

would add a Close menu item in position 2, which is immediately below the Open item, displacing the separator to position 3 and the Exit item to position 4. You can insert a separator at a given position using the following method:

```
public void insertSeparator(int pos);
```

Note that there is no form of the insert method that allows the insertion of a Component.

Menu items can be deleted using the remove method which, like add and insert, has several forms:

```
public void remove(JMenuItem menuItem);
```

```
public void remove(Action a);
```

```
public void remove(int pos);
```

If you want to remove everything from a menu (including any Components added with the add method), you can use the removeAll method, which you saw in Listing 6-1:

```
public void removeAll()
```

To show how these methods can be used to manipulate a menu, let's see how to implement the Recent Files menu without using the removeAll method that was shown in Listing 6-1. The idea behind this revised implementation is to place a newly-opened file at the top of the menu. If it was already in the menu, the existing item must be moved from its existing location to the top. If it was not in the menu, a new menu item is created and inserted at the top of the menu. If this makes the menu grow beyond the maximum size of RECENT_FILES, the last item is removed. Here is how the addRecentFile method would look when implemented in this way:

```
// Add a name to the recent file list
public void addRecentFile(String fileName) {
   int offset;

   // Remove the empty item if it is present
   if (emptyListItem != null && fileListMenu.getItem(0) == emptyListItem) {
     fileListMenu.remove(0);
     emptyListItem = null;
```

```
  }

  // Check whether this file is already in the file list
  if ((offset = recentFiles.indexOf(fileName)) == -1) {
    // Not present - add it at the beginning
    recentFiles.insertElementAt(fileName, 0);

    // Add a menu item as well
    JMenuItem mi = new JMenuItem(fileName);
    mi.addActionListener(menuListener);
    fileListMenu.insert(mi, 0);
    if (recentFiles.size() > RECENT_FILES) {
      // List was full - remove the last (oldest) item
      recentFiles.removeElementAt(RECENT_FILES);

      // Also remove the last menu item
      fileListMenu.remove(RECENT_FILES);
    }
  } else {
    // Already present: move this item to the front of the
list
    recentFiles.removeElementAt(offset);
    recentFiles.insertElementAt(fileName, 0);
    // Move the menu item
    JMenuItem mi = fileListMenu.getItem(offset);
    fileListMenu.remove(offset);
    fileListMenu.insert(mi, 0);
  }
}
```

Notice that the first part of this code takes care of getting rid of the dummy Empty entry that should only be present until the first file is opened. Without this code, the Empty entry would get pushed down the menu until it disappeared off the bottom when the menu had been filled up. The operations on the menu exactly parallel the changes made to the vector of open files and use the same indexing to locate a menu item from the corresponding file name. If the new file is in the vector, its position within the vector is obtained and that position is used as the index to remove the corresponding menu item, then place it at the front of the menu, by inserting it at position 0. This code implicitly assumes that the menu only contains menu items: If separators or other components were added, it would no longer work because the positions of the file menu items would be incorrect.

This code uses the JMenu getItem method to get the JMenuItem at a given position in the menu. Again, the position used here counts everything in the menu, not just menu items.

Menu Mnemonics

The implementation so far falls far short of being complete. There are a number of improvements that will be made in the next few sections that give the application a more professional appearance. The first change is to add mnemonics to the menus and menu items. Windows and Motif applications usually supply mnemonics (often called shortcuts) for all of their menu items, which appear as an underlined letter on the menu or the menu bar. For example, the file menu on the menu bar usually appears with its first letter underlined. To activate the file menu, you either click with the mouse on the word File, or you press F together with the ALT key; either of these actions makes the file menu drop down. Similarly, it is normal to add mnemonics to the items that appear on the application's menus.

You can add a shortcut to a menu item using a form of the constructor that accepts a mnemonic argument:

```
public JMenuItem(String title, int mnemonic)
```

Using this method, you can create an Open menu item with a suitable mnemonic like this:

```
openItem = new JMenuItem("Open...", 'O');
```

A mnemonic works only if the corresponding menu item is visible on the screen.

Core Note

The AWT menus use an extra class called MenuShortcut *to implement mnemonics. This class is not used with Swing menus.*

While this mechanism works for menu items, it can't be used for menus because JMenu doesn't have a constructor that accepts a mnemonic, despite the fact that it is derived from JMenuItem that does. Instead, you have to use the setMnemonic method. Since this method is actually implemented by AbstractButton, which is also a superclass of JMenuItem, you can also use it as an alternative to passing the shortcut to a menu item's constructor. To arrange for the file menu to drop down in response to the key sequence ALT+F requires the following two lines of code:

```
JMenu fileMenu = new JMenu("File");
fileMenu.setMnemonic('F');
```

Core Note

The menu mnemonics are the same mnemonics that you saw in connection with buttons in Chapter 2, "Frames, Labels and Buttons," which should not surprise you because both JMenu *and* JMenuItem *are derived from* AbstractButton. *As before, these mnemonics are case-insensitive when you associate them with a menu or menu item. At the keyboard, you do not press the* SHIFT *key in conjunction with* ALT *to activate the mnemonic.*

Our example also has a submenu on the file menu; a mnemonic can be added to this in the same way:

```
fileListMenu = new JMenu("Recent Files");
fileListMenu.setMnemonic('R');
```

Mnemonics on menus and menu items work only when they are visible, so to activate the Recent Files list, you first need to pop down the file menu using ALT+F, then activate the recent file list using ALT+R.

The letter used as the mnemonic for a menu or menu item is usually the first letter of its label. If this is not unique, however, you need to choose another letter. Choosing the first letter of the label makes it easy for the user to remember the appropriate key sequence. This doesn't work very well for menus in which the menu items are not fixed, like the Recent File list. Figure 6-2 shows a typical screenshot of this file list.

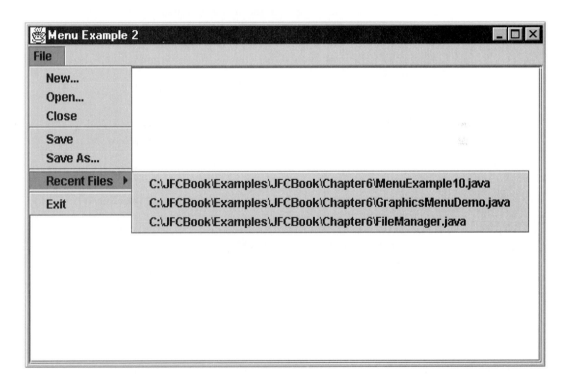

Figure 6-2   A menu with a recently-used file list.

Here, the first letter is always "C," which couldn't be used anyway because it is ambiguous.

Whatever choice was made here, it would not be especially useful, because the user needs to know the key sequence in advance, but the content of the recent file list is not fixed—it depends on how the application has been used. In cases like this, what the user might want to do with a mnemonic would be to open the second, third or fourth most recently used file, without having to remember the file name and guess the shortcut. The best way to cater for this is to label the files with their position in the list, starting with 1, and arrange for the position to be the shortcut key. With this arrangement, the user can open the files on the recent file list using ALT+1, ALT+2, ALT+3 and so on.

The implementation of this idea is relatively simple, but it contains a small twist. If a mnemonic were added to each menu item on the recent file menu, it would work, but it wouldn't appear on the menu item unless there happened to be a 1 (or 2 etc.) in the file name. To make it appear there, the ordinal needs to be included in the label of the menu item so that it gets underlined when the shortcut is attached to it. Since the action command associated with a menu item is used to determine which file to open and since the action command has the same value as the label by default, code is now needed to arrange that the action command is explicitly set to the file name, because the default action command is the menu item text, which is no longer simply the file name. Here is a modified implementation of the buildRecentFileMenu method that enables these mnemonics, with the changed lines highlighted:

```
// Build the recent file menu
public void buildRecentFileMenu() {
  int size = recentFiles.size();

  fileListMenu.removeAll();

  for (int i = 1; i <= size; i++) {
    String fileName = (String)(recentFiles.elementAt(i - 1));
    JMenuItem mi = new JMenuItem();
    mi.setActionCommand(fileName);
    mi.setText(i + " " + fileName);
    mi.setMnemonic('0' + i);
    fileListMenu.add(mi);
    mi.addActionListener(menuListener);
  }
}
```

You can run a version of the application with this modification in place using the command:

```
java JFCBook.Chapter6.MenuExample3
```

If you open several files in succession and then try the key sequence ALT +F, ALT + R, ALT+2, you will now find that the second most recently used file is opened.

Core Alert

Swing 1.0.1 has a nasty bug that passes through the keys that correspond to the menu shortcut to whichever component in the frame has the focus after the menu processed them. If you have a later version of Swing you can see whether or not it has this bug by running the example you have just seen. If it has, then you'll see the accelerator keys appear in the text area after they have activated the corresponding menu or menu item.

Checkbox and Radio Button Menu Items

The menu items that have been used so far all cause a fixed action to be performed when they are activated. There are two other types of menu items that allow you to specify changes in an application's state. As the names *checkbox* and *radio button* suggest, these menu items allow you to place a checkbox or a set of radio buttons on a menu. Typically, you use these to control parameters that are either on or off, or parameters that have a fixed set of values.

The use of a checkbox menu item can easily be illustrated by enhancing our editor application. Up to now, it has been assumed that every file is opened with the intention of changing it and writing it back but sometimes you might want just to read the file and protect yourself against accidentally writing it back. In other words, you want to specify whether you want the file to be open for writing or not. This type of `true` or `false` state is ideally suited to a checkbox menu item.

Creating a checkbox menu item is just as simple as creating an ordinary one:

```
JCheckBoxMenuItem writeItem = new JCheckboxMenuItem("Enable writing", true);
fileMenu.add(writeItem);
```

These statements create a checkbox menu item with its state initialized to `true` and add it to the `File` menu. When you drop down this menu it appears as shown in Figure 6-3.

When you click on this menu item, it inverts its state and generates an `ActionEvent`. You can obtain the state of the menu item using the `getState` method and, if you wish, you can use the `setState` method to change the state yourself:

```
public boolean getState();

public void setState(boolean newState);
```

In this example, the state of the checkbox menu item will be checked when a new file is opened. If writing has been disabled, the state of the `JTextArea` is changed so that its content cannot be edited and the `FileManager` object is notified that the user doesn't want to write to the file, so that when the file is closed, the `write`

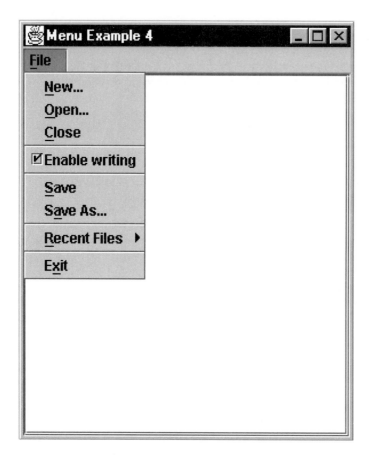

Figure 6-3   A checkbox menu item.

operation that would usually be performed will be skipped. If, however, the New menu item is used to open a file, it is appropriate to assume that the user wants to write to the file, so the setting of this checkbox is ignored. Because the state of the menu item is inspected only when it is needed, there is no need to know, in this case, when the user changes it, so an `ActionListener` isn't registered against it. Here is the code that is affected by this change.

```
// Processing for "New..." menu item
newItem.addActionListener(new ActionListener() {
   public void actionPerformed(ActionEvent evt) {
      String name = getFileName("New File", FileDialog.SAVE);
      if (name != null) {
         if (fileManager.isFileOpen()) {
            // Close any open file
            try {
               fileManager.closeFile(textArea.getText());
```

```
        } catch (Throwable e) {
           // Ignore any exception
        }
      }
      try {
         fileManager.newFile(name);
         textArea.setText("");
         textArea.setEditable(true);// Always writable
         writeItem.setState(true);     // Check writable box
         fileManager.setWritable(true);// Allow writes to file
         addRecentFile(name);
      } catch (IOException e) {
         // Do nothing - message already printed
      }
    }
  }
});

// Processing for "Open..." menu item
openItem.addActionListener(new ActionListener() {
  public void actionPerformed(ActionEvent evt) {
     String name = getFileName("Open File", FileDialog.LOAD);
     if (name != null) {
        try {
           String text = fileManager.openFile(name);
           textArea.setText(text);
           // Enable for writing if allowed to
           textArea.setEditable(writeItem.getState());
           fileManager.setWritable(writeItem.getState());
           addRecentFile(name);
        } catch (IOException e) {
           // Do nothing - message already printed
        }
     }
  }
});
```

RadioButtonMenuItems are just like ordinary JRadioButtons, which will be examined in Chapter 8, except that they reside on a menu. To ensure that only one of the radio buttons is selected at any time, you place then in a ButtonGroup. You'll see an example of this type of menu item under "Enhancing Menus" later.

Changing Menu State

In all of the versions of the editor application so far, the items on the File menu have been available at all times. However, this can be confusing for the user. For example, when you start the application, the menu looks like the one shown in Figure 6-4.

Figure 6-4   Initial state of the editor menu.

This menu implies that you can save or close a file, but this doesn't make sense because there is no file to close or write to. In a properly-implemented application, only those actions that make sense at any given time are available on the application's menu. You can control whether a menu item is available for use by enabling or disabling it using the setEnabled method. When you disable a menu item, it appears grayed out and doesn't respond when you move the mouse over it or click on it.

There are other cases in which menu items should be disabled. Clearly, the Close item should be available only when there is an open file. It should only be possible to save a file if all of the following are true:

- A file is open
- The user has not disabled using the checkbox menu item
- The file is actually writeable (i.e., the user has permission to write to it).

To find out whether or not a file can be written to, our FileManager class has a canWrite method that returns true or false when used just after the file has been opened. After a file has been opened, a check is made to find out whether or not it can be written to. If not, the Save and Save As menu items are disabled. Since the state of the Enable write menu item is only looked at when a file is opened, it is disabled after opening a file, so as not to give the impression that a change in its state would be honored while there is an open file. It is reenabled when the file is closed. The Close menu item is enabled only when there a file open.

The initial menu item state is set in the constructor by disabling the Close, Save As and Save items:

```
// Set initial state of menu items
closeItem.setEnabled(false);
saveItem.setEnabled(false);
saveAsItem.setEnabled(false);
```

In response to the New menu item, having created a new file, the Close, Save and Save As menu items are enabled, because a newly-created file should be writable, and the checkbox that allows the user to make the file read-only is disabled:

```
fileManager.newFile(name);
textArea.setText("");
textArea.setEditable(true);          // Always writable
writeItem.setState(true);            // Check writable box
fileManager.setWritable(true);       // Allow writes to file
closeItem.setEnabled(true);          // Allow file close
writeItem.setEnabled(false);         // Disable checkbox

boolean canWrite = fileManager.canWrite();

saveItem.setEnabled(canWrite);
saveAsItem.setEnabled(canWrite);
addRecentFile(name);
```

The actionPerformed method that handles file Open is similar, but in this case the Save and Save As menu items are enabled only if the file can be written (i.e. the user has write access to it) and the Enable write menu item is also checked. The text area is also made editable or not on the same condition:

```
// Enable for writing if allowed to
boolean canWrite = fileManager.canWrite() &&
    writeItem.getState();

textArea.setEditable(canWrite);
fileManager.setWritable(writeItem.getState());
closeItem.setEnabled(true);          // Allow file close
writeItem.setEnabled(false);         // Disable checkbox

saveItem.setEnabled(canWrite);
saveAsItem.setEnabled(canWrite);
addRecentFile(name);
```

The same code is also added to the actionPerformed method that handles selection of a file from the recent file list. Finally, the menu item state is reset when the file is closed:

```
// Reset state of menu items
closeItem.setEnabled(false);
saveItem.setEnabled(false);
saveAsItem.setEnabled(false);
writeItem.setEnabled(true);
```

You can see this code in action by starting the application with the command:

```
java JFCBook.Chapter6.MenuExample5
```

and pulling down the File menu, which now looks like Figure 6-5.

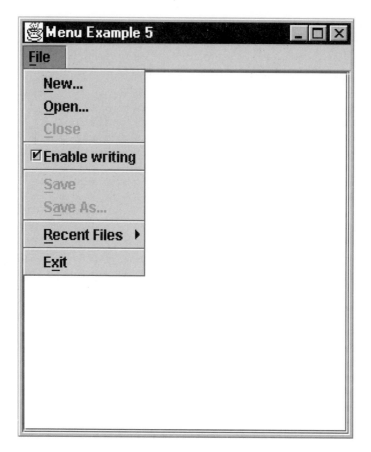

Figure 6-5 The editor menu with only the available items enabled.

Here, the Close, Save and Save As menu items are disabled. If you open a file to which you have write access, these items become enabled and the Enable writing item is disabled as in Figure 6-6.

Closing the file reverts the menu to its original state. If you clear the Enable writing flag or open a file to which you only have read access, the Save and Save As items remain disabled, as shown in Figure 6-7, and you'll find that you can't modify the text in the text area either.

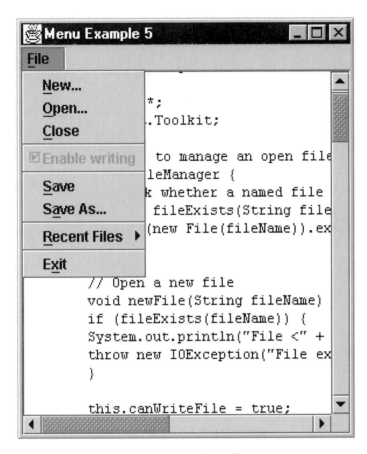

Figure 6-6   The editor menu when a file is open.

Core Note

To arrange to have read-only access to a file that you own, use the following commands under Unix:

```
chmod u-w filename
chmod u+r filename
```

If you are using Windows, use the Windows Explorer to find the file, right-click on it, select Properties, check "Read-only" and the click OK.

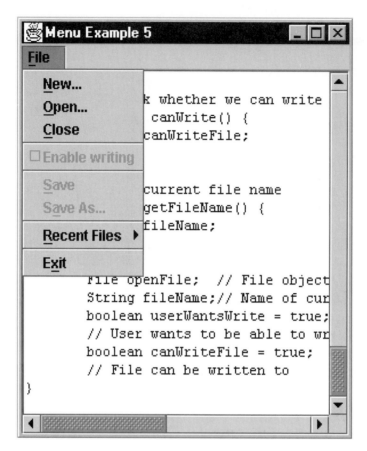

Figure 6-7   The `editor` menu with a read-only file open.

Disabling a menu item not only grays out the menu and stops it responding to the mouse; it also disables any shortcut associated with that menu item. Therefore, when there is no file open, `ALT+C`, `ALT+S` and `ALT+A` won't work.

Another Way to Change the Menu State

In the last section, the state of menu items was changed as soon as a change in the application state occurred, so that the menus would appear correct if they were used. In complex applications, though, most of this work would be wasted because the number of application state changes that might affect the state of a menu usually far exceeds the number of times that the menu is actually dropped down. As well as wasting time, the method we used before also has the effect of spreading menu-handling code all over the application.

Instead of taking this approach, you can instead change the state of menu items only when the menu is dropped down. This allows you to keep the menu-handling code together and also avoids unnecessary menu updates. The menu system provides a MenuEvent that is posted whenever a menu is selected, deselected, or canceled. To catch a MenuEvent, you must register a MenuListener with the JMenu object for the menu. Here is the definition of the MenuListener interface:

```
public interface MenuListener extends EventListener {
    public void menuCanceled(MenuEvent e);
    public void menuDeselected(MenuEvent e);
    public void menuSelected(MenuEvent e);
}
```

Core Note

The menuCanceled *method does not, at present, appear to be used.*

A menu is selected when it is posted and deselected when it disappears. The only state associated with the MenuEvent is a reference to the source JMenu object, which can be obtained using the getSource method. Here is how you might implement a MenuListener for the File menu:

```
// Processing for the "File" menu
fileMenu.addMenuListener(new MenuListener() {
    public void menuSelected(MenuEvent evt) {
        boolean fileOpen = fileManager.isFileOpen();

        // Allow close only if we have an open file
        closeItem.setEnabled(fileOpen);

        // Similarly, allow "Enable write" only if no open file
        writeItem.setEnabled(fileOpen == false);

        // If we have an open file, enable Save and Save As
        // if the user has selected Enable Write AND the
        // file can be written to.
        boolean canSave = (fileOpen && writeItem.getState() &&
                fileManager.canWrite());

        saveItem.setEnabled(canSave);
        saveAsItem.setEnabled(canSave);
    }
    public void menuDeselected(MenuEvent evt) {
        // Not used
    }
    public void menuCanceled(MenuEvent evt) {
        // Not used
    }
});
```

You can try this code using the command:

```
java JFCBook.Chapter6.MenuExample6
```

When a menu is posted, a MenuEvent will be posted from the JMenu. When this event is passed to the listener's menuSelected method, the state of all of its menu items is adjusted based on the application's internal state. Therefore, the menu items' state will be correct when the menu is displayed, but may be out-of-date when it is not. This doesn't matter, of course, because the user can't see that the menu items are in the wrong state.

As well as implementing the MenuListener, all of the code that enables and disables menu items that were introduced in the previous section can be removed. Using a MenuListener is obviously cleaner—the code is all in one place and it is much more easily understandable. We recommend using this technique whenever possible.

Using Actions with Menus

So far in this chapter, menu items have been created directly and ActionListeners have been added to them to handle the event generated when the menu item is selected. In the last chapter, you saw how useful the concept of an Action was when handling events from the keyboard, since Actions make it possible to combine an ActionListener with some state information needed when the action is to be performed. A useful feature of the JMenu class is that it allows you to add an Action directly to a menu:

```
public JMenuItem add(Action action);
```

In order for this to work properly, you have to create an Action with an appropriate text string, which is then used as the label of the menu item. For example, you can use the AbstractAction class to create a suitable Action. Here's how you might add an Action to process the Save operation:

```
JMenu menu = new JMenu("File");
  .

  .
JMenuItem mi = menu.add(new AbstractAction("Save…") {
  public void actionPerformed(ActionEvent evt) {
    // Process save operation (not shown)
  }
});
```

When this code is run, a Save item will appear on the File menu. When this item is selected, the actionPerformed method shown will be executed. Since the add method returns a JMenuItem, you can treat this menu item in the same way as any other that you might create. In particular, you can add shortcut keys if required. You'll see in more detail how to make use of Actions on menu bars in the next section and also in "Using Actions with Menu Bars and Toolbars."

Menu Accelerators

You've seen how to add mnemonics to menus and menu items that allow you to activate them from the keyboard when they are visible. Swing also provides menu accelerators that work the same way as mnemonics, except that the menu item does not need to be visible for the associated action to be carried out. To attach an accelerator to a menu item, you use the JMenuItem setAccelerator method:

```
public void setAccelerator(Keystroke keyStroke);
```

The keyStroke argument specifies the key sequence that causes the action associated with the menu item to be performed. When this key sequence is detected, an ActionEvent is delivered to all ActionListeners registered on the associated menu item.

Core Note

You can't attach an accelerator to a JMenu. It wouldn't make any sense to do so anyway, because there is no functionality associated with a JMenu (other than to post its associated menu items). If you try to attach one, you will get an exception.

To show how menu accelerators work, let's add them to our editor application. On the File menu, there are three candidates for accelerators—the New item, the Open item and the Exit item. The Recent Files item also has a mnemonic, but it can't have an accelerator because it is a JMenu, not a JMenuItem. These accelerators are so common in Windows applications that they are almost always assigned the following key sequences:

New	CTRL + N
Open	CTRL + O
Exit	CTRL + X

However, as will be explained shortly, it is not possible to use CTRL+X in the case of the example application being used in this section, so instead the key sequence CTRL+E will be used.

Attaching accelerators is very simple—here are the lines that would be added to our file editor application to add these three accelerators:

```
newItem.setAccelerator(KeyStroke.getKeyStroke(KeyEvent.VK_N,
                 InputEvent.CTRL_MASK, false));
openItem.setAccelerator(KeyStroke.getKeyStroke(KeyEvent.VK_O,
                 InputEvent.CTRL_MASK, false));
exitItem.setAccelerator(KeyStroke.getKeyStroke(KeyEvent.VK_E,
                 InputEvent.CTRL_MASK, false));
```

If you run this version of the example using the command:

```
java JFCBook.Chapter6.MenuExample6A
```

and then drop down the `File` menu, you'll see that the accelerator keys are displayed on their associated menu items, as shown in Figure 6-8.

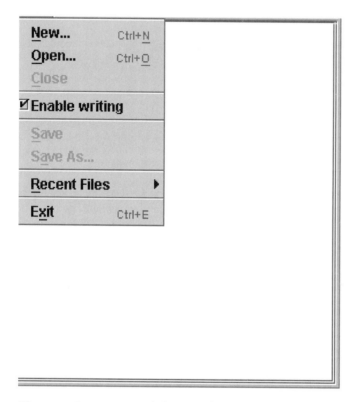

Figure 6-8   A menu with three accelerator keys.

If you now dismiss the `File` menu and then press CTRL+N or CTRL+O, you'll see the `FileDialog` associated with the `New` and `Open` menu items appear. Similarly, CTRL+E will cause the application to exit. An accelerator key that causes the application to exit can be a very dangerous facility. In a full-scale application, you would probably want to display a dialog asking the user to confirm this particular action. Dialogs are the subject of the next two chapters.

Finally, why was it not possible to use CTRL+X as an accelerator for the Exit menu item? Accelerators are just `KeyStrokes` that are automatically registered to catch keys in the window with which the menu is associated. If CTRL+X were used, a `KeyStroke` would be registered to catch this key sequence if it happened anywhere in the main window by using the `JComponent.WHEN_IN_FOCUSED_WINDOW` setting (refer back to Chapter 5, "Keyboard Handling, Actions and Scrolling," for a description of `KeyStrokes`). As you'll recall from Chapter 5, this action will not be triggered if the focus is in another component that has registered to catch the same key sequence with the flag `JComponent.WHEN_FOCUSED`. In the case of this example, the focus will always be in the text area, which registers CTRL+X as an accelerator that performs the delete action. Thus, it would never be passed to the menu handling code.

Enhancing Menus

You've now seen most of the ways in which you can use menus in an application. This section will show you various ways in which you can change the appearance of a menu without changing its functionality.

Changing Color and Font of Menu Items

As you know, menus and menu items are basically buttons with slightly different user interfaces and modified behavior. They do, therefore, inherit some of the features of a button. In particular, you can change the color and font of any menu or menu item just by treating it as a standard component. Therefore, if you'd like to create a menu item that uses a 14-point bold italic dialog font and has white text on a green background, you can do it as shown in Listing 6-2.

Listing 6-2   A customized menu item

```
public class MenuExample7 extends JFrame {
  public MenuExample7(String title) {
    super(title);

    JMenuBar mb = new JMenuBar();
    this.setJMenuBar(mb);

    JMenu fileMenu = new JMenu("File");
    fileMenu.setMnemonic('F');
    mb.add(fileMenu);

    JMenuItem newItem = new JMenuItem("New...", 'N');
    JMenuItem openItem = new JMenuItem("Open...", 'O');
    JMenuItem closeItem = new JMenuItem("Close", 'C');
    fileMenu.add(newItem);
    fileMenu.add(openItem);
    fileMenu.add(closeItem);

    // Set custom font and colors
    newItem.setFont(new Font("Dialog", Font.BOLD | Font.ITALIC, 14));
    newItem.setForeground(Color.white);
    newItem.setBackground(Color.green);
```

continued

```
    this.getContentPane().add(new JScrollPane(new JTextArea(20, 40)));
  }

  public static void main(String[] args) {
    JFrame f = new MenuExample7("Menu Example 7");
    f.pack();
    f.setVisible(true);
    f.addWindowListener(new WindowAdapter() {
      public void windowClosing(WindowEvent evt) {
        System.exit(0);
      }
    });
  }
}
```

Figure 6-9 shows what the File menu now looks like (not, of course, in color!)

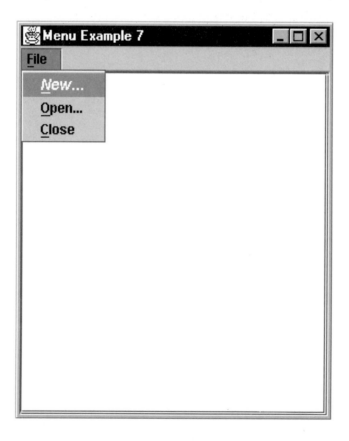

Figure 6-9   A customized menu item.

Although you can't see that the background is green, you can see that it has changed and that the menu item's label is in bold italic.

Menus and Menu Items with Icons

Another, more useful, technique is to add icons to a menu. Using the `ImageIcon` class (or any other class that implements the `Icon` interface), you can associate an icon with any menu or menu item. You can even create a menu or menu item without a text label if you think that the icon is descriptive enough.

You can place an icon on a menu item using one of the following constructors:

```
public JMenuItem(Icon icon);

public JMenuItem(String text, Icon icon);
```

The `JMenu` class doesn't have a constructor that accepts an icon, so to place an icon on a menu, you need to use the `setIcon` method inherited from `AbstractButton`. This method also works for `JMenuItem`. Here, for example, is how you might modify the previous example to include icons on the menu bar and in the `File` menu itself:

```
JMenuItem newItem = new JMenuItem("New...", 'N');
JMenuItem openItem = new JMenuItem("Open...", 'O');
JMenuItem closeItem = new JMenuItem("Close", 'C');
fileMenu.add(newItem);
fileMenu.add(openItem);
fileMenu.add(closeItem);

fileMenu.setIcon(new ImageIcon(getClass().getResource("images/folder.gif")));
newItem.setIcon(new ImageIcon(getClass().getResource("images/new.gif")));
openItem.setIcon(new ImageIcon(getClass().getResource("images/open.gif")));
```

Figure 6-10 how it looks when the `File` menu has been pulled down. You can try this for yourself with the command:

```
java JFCBook.Chapter6.MenuExample8
```

As you can see, by default the text label appears to the left of the icon. Since menu items are really just like buttons, you can change the relative positions and alignment of the text and the icon using the `setHorizontalAlignment`, `set VerticalAlignment`, `setHorizontalTextPosition` and `setVertical TextPosition` methods that you saw in Chapter 2. Here, for example, the icon for the `File` entry on the menu bar is moved to the left of the text, which is the conventional position for the Windows environment.

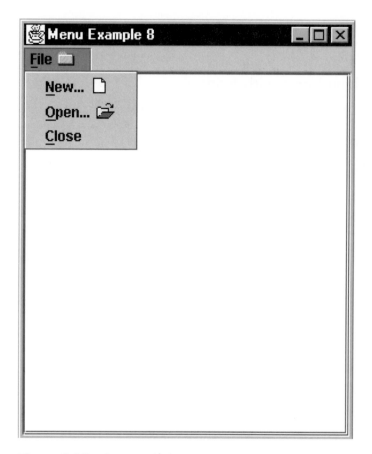

Figure 6-10   A menu with icons.

```
fileMenu.setIcon(new ImageIcon(getClass().getResource("images/folder.gif")));
fileMenu.setHorizontalTextPosition(SwingConstants.RIGHT);

newItem.setIcon(new ImageIcon(getClass().getResource("images/new.gif")));
newItem.setVerticalTextPosition(SwingConstants.BOTTOM);
newItem.setHorizontalTextPosition(SwingConstants.CENTER);

openItem.setIcon(new ImageIcon(getClass().getResource("images/open.gif")));
openItem.setVerticalTextPosition(SwingConstants.BOTTOM);
openItem.setHorizontalTextPosition(SwingConstants.CENTER);
```

The text on the menu items can also be made to appear directly underneath the corresponding images, as you can see in Figure 6-11. This is not, of course, to everybody's taste! To make the boundaries between the menu items clearer in this example, separators have been added.

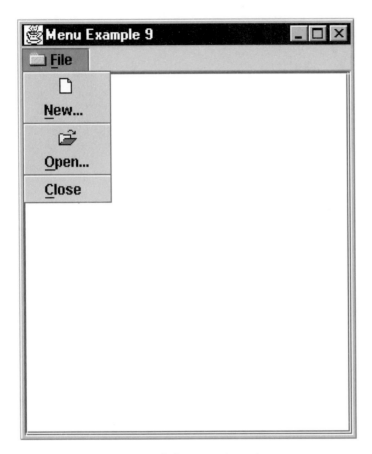

Figure 6-11   A menu with the icons above the text.

If you add an `Action` that has both text and an icon associated with it to a menu, the icon will automatically be drawn on the menu item associated with the `Action`, with the text to the right of the icon. You can also add an `Action` with an icon and no associated text to get an icon-only menu item.

Icons with Checkbox and Radio Button Menu Items

Icons can be used with all types of menu items, including `JCheckboxMenuItem` and `JRadioButtonMenuItem`. With both of these types, as with `JMenuItem`, you can either associate the icon when you create the menu item, or later using the `setIcon` method. Listing 6-3 provides an example that shows the use of a group of `JRadioButtonMenuItems` with icons.

Listing 6-3   Radio Button Menu items with icons

```java
package JFCBook.Chapter6;

import com.sun.java.swing.*;
import java.awt.*;
import java.awt.event.*;
import java.util.*;
import JFCBook.Chapter4.ColorFillIcon;

public class RadioButtonMenuExample extends JFrame {
  public RadioButtonMenuExample(String title) {
    super(title);

    colorList.put("White", Color.white);
    colorList.put("Black", Color.black);
    colorList.put("Yellow", Color.yellow);
    colorList.put("Green", Color.green);
    colorList.put("Red", Color.red);
    colorList.put("Orange", Color.orange);
    colorList.put("Grey", Color.gray);
    colorList.put("Pink", Color.pink);

    JMenuBar menuBar = new JMenuBar();
    JMenu menu = new JMenu("Colors");
    menuBar.add(menu);
    ButtonGroup group = new ButtonGroup();

    JRadioButtonMenuItem rb = null;
    Color color = Color.black;

    Action action = new AbstractAction() {
      public void actionPerformed(ActionEvent evt) {
        JRadioButtonMenuItem mi = (JRadioButtonMenuItem)evt.getSource();
        String newColor = mi.getActionCommand();
        mainPanel.setBackground((Color)colorList.get(newColor));
      }
    };

    Enumeration keys = colorList.keys();
    while (keys.hasMoreElements()) {
      String label = (String)keys.nextElement();
      color = (Color)colorList.get(label);
      Icon icon = new ColorFillIcon(color, 16, 16, 1);
      rb = new JRadioButtonMenuItem(label, icon);
```

```
         rb.setSelected(false);
         rb.addActionListener(action);
         menu.add(rb);
         group.add(rb);
      }

      rb.setSelected(true);
      mainPanel = this.getContentPane();
      mainPanel.setBackground(color);
      this.setJMenuBar(menuBar);
   }

   public static void main(String[] args) {
      JFrame f = new RadioButtonMenuExample("Radio Button Menu
Example");
      f.setSize(300, 300);
      f.addWindowListener(new WindowAdapter() {
        public void windowClosing(WindowEvent evt) {
           System.exit(0);
        }
      });
      f.setVisible(true);
   }

   Hashtable colorList = new Hashtable();
   Container mainPanel;
}
```

Figure 6-12 shows what this example looks like when you run it and pull down the Colors menu item. The command required to run this example is:

```
java JFCBook.Chapter6.RadioButtonMenuExample
```

The program creates a JFrame with a single menu and populates it with JRadioButtonMenuItems. Each of these menu items is labeled with a color and has an associated icon, created using the ColorFillIcon class that was implemented in Chapter 4, "Graphics, Text Handling, and Printing," filled with the color associated with the menu item. As each menu item is created, it is added to a ButtonGroup. As you'll see in Chapter 8, "Creating Custom Dialogs," the ButtonGroup manages a set of buttons and ensures that only one of them is selected at any time. An Action, implemented using the AbstractAction class, is also associated with each of the menu items, illustrating the JRadioButtonMenuItem addActionListener method, which it inherits from AbstractButton. After creating the menu, the last entry is selected and the background color of the frame's content pane is set to the corresponding color.

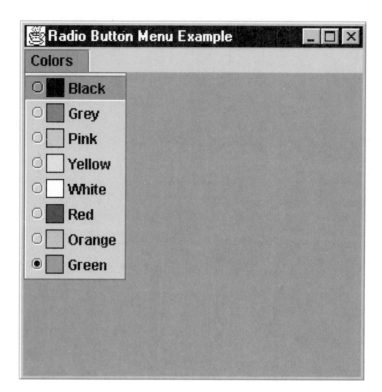

Figure 6-12   Radio Button menu items with icons.

When you click on an item on the Color menu, the previously selected item is deselected and an ActionEvent is sent to the newly selected menu item, causing the actionPerformed method of the associated Action to be entered. The ActionEvent delivered by a JRadioButtonMenuItem, like any other, contains a reference to the event source, which in this case is the menu item. This reference is used to get the text from the menu item and hence the color associated with it, which is used to change the content pane's background color.

Changing the Menu Bar Border

A final cosmetic technique that you can apply to menus is to change the border of the menu bar. By default, the menu bar has a look-and-feel specific border that separates it from the frame it is mounted on. You can use the setBorderPainted method to completely remove the border:

```
JMenuBar mb = new JMenuBar();
mb.setBorderPainted(false);                    // No border
```

Alternatively, you can use `setBorder` to replace the default border with one of your own choice. For example, you can opt for a lowered Bevel border as follows:

```
JMenuBar mb = new JMenuBar();
this.setJMenuBar(mb);
mb.setBorder(BorderFactory.createBevelBorder(BevelBorder.LOWERED));
```

which produces the result shown in Figure 6-13.

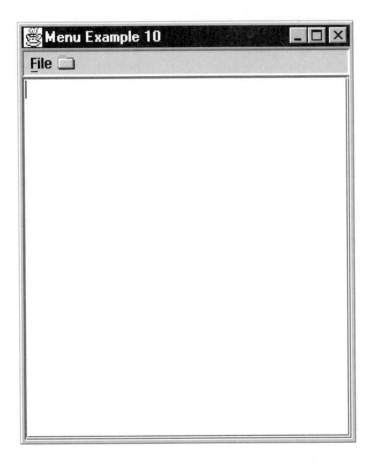

Figure 6-13   A menu bar with a customized border.

Core Note

The JMenu *API contains provisions for tear-off menus, which are detachable from the menu bar and remain floating above the desktop, like the floating toolbars that are described at the end of this chapter. At the time of writing, this feature has not yet been implemented.*

Context-Sensitive Menus

Sometimes it is useful to be able to create a menu that comes into existence for long enough for the user to make a selection from it, then disappears. Since such a menu is not intended to exist for very long and its availability might depend on the application's state, it would not be appropriate for it to be permanently attached to the menu bar. To create a transient menu like this, you use the `JPopupMenu` class.

Creating a JPopupMenu

In most respects, a `JPopupMenu` is the same as a `JMenu`: You add menu items, and even submenus, to it in the same way and you receive the same menu events and action events as you would from a menu attached to the menu bar. The only time that you need to take special action for a popup menu is when you create it and when you destroy it.

The user causes a popup menu to appear using a mouse operation that is platform-dependent. On the Windows platform, for example, pressing and then releasing the right mouse button almost always produces a popup with menu items that depend on the context in which the menu appears. To avoid the need to code a platform-dependent gesture into applications, the `MouseEvent` class provides the `isPopupTrigger` method that returns `true` when the event describes an action that the user might expect to produce a popup. When this method returns `true`, the application will typically generate an appropriate popup menu and place it at the current mouse location.

To illustrate how to manage a popup menu, let's look at a simple example. The program in Listing 6-4 creates an empty frame and monitors mouse events. When the popup trigger is received, it posts a popup menu where the mouse is located. Since this example is only intended to demonstrate the mechanics of managing popups, it doesn't contain any useful application code: The menu items are only connected to a trivial event handler that allows you to see that the menu is actually doing something.

Listing 6-4   Creating a popup menu

```
package JFCBook.Chapter6;

import com.sun.java.swing.*;
import java.awt.*;
import java.awt.event.*;

public class PopupExample extends JPanel
        implements MouseListener, ActionListener {
  public PopupExample() {
    this.addMouseListener(this);
```

```
}

// MouseListener interface
public void mousePressed(MouseEvent evt) {
  if (evt.isPopupTrigger()) {
    createPopup(evt.getPoint());
  }
}

public void mouseReleased(MouseEvent evt) {
  if (evt.isPopupTrigger()) {
    createPopup(evt.getPoint());
  }
}

public void mouseClicked(MouseEvent evt) {
  if (evt.isPopupTrigger()) {
    createPopup(evt.getPoint());
  }
}

public void mouseEntered(MouseEvent evt) {
}

public void mouseExited(MouseEvent evt) {
}

// Create and post the popup
protected void createPopup(Point point) {
  JMenuItem mi;

  popup = new JPopupMenu();

  mi = popup.add(new JMenuItem("Copy"));
  mi.addActionListener(this);
  mi = popup.add(new JMenuItem("Cut"));
  mi.addActionListener(this);
  mi = popup.add(new JMenuItem("Paste"));
  mi.addActionListener(this);

  JMenu submenu = new JMenu("Colors");
  for (int i = 0 ; i < colors.length; i++) {
    mi = new JMenuItem(colors[i]);
    sub-menu.add(mi);
    mi.addActionListener(this);
  }
  popup.add(submenu);
```

continued

```
      popup.show(this, point.x, point.y);
   }

   public void actionPerformed(ActionEvent evt) {
      JMenuItem mi = (JMenuItem)evt.getSource();
      System.out.println("Menu item <" + mi.getActionCommand() + "> activated");
   }

   public static void main(String[] args) {
      JFrame f = new JFrame("Popup Example");
      f.setContentPane(new PopupExample());
      f.setSize(300, 300);
      f.addWindowListener(new WindowAdapter() {
         public void windowClosing(WindowEvent evt) {
            System.exit(0);
         }
      });
      f.setVisible(true);
   }

   private JPopupMenu popup;
   private String[] colors = {
      "Black", "White", "Green", "Orange", "Pink", "Red", "Blue", "Cyan", "Gray"
   };
}
```

When you run this example, nothing happens until you make the appropriate gesture with the mouse. On the Windows platform, for example, you need to press and then release the right mouse button. Since you don't actually know when writing the application which mouse event should pop up the menu, isPopupTrigger is called whenever the user presses and releases the mouse. When this method returns true, the popup menu is created and posted. If you run this example using the command:

```
java JFCBook.Chapter6.PopupExample
```

and then popup the menu, you get a result that looks like Figure 6-14.

To post the menu, the JPopupMenu show method is used. This method is defined as follows:

```
public void show(Component invoker, int x, int y);
```

The menu is placed at co-ordinates (x, y) relative to the component given as the first argument; usually, this component will be the application's top-level frame or possibly the component whose mouse event handler posts the menu.

If you move the mouse over any menu item and click on it, you'll find that the usual ActionEvent is fired (as shown by the message in the window from which you started the program) and, in addition to this, the popup menu disappears. If you move the mouse over the Colors item and post the Colors submenu, you'll

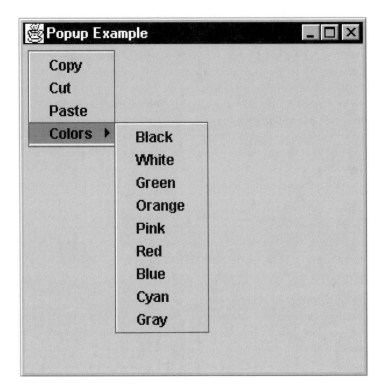

Figure 6-14   Popup menus.

notice that both of the menus disappear when you make a selection. This functionality is built into the JPopupMenu.

Managing a Popup Menu

If you look carefully at the code for this example, a couple of questions should occur to you. First, what happens if the user brings up a popup menu by, say, clicking the right mouse button, then immediately does the same elsewhere in the frame? Looking at the code in the mouse event handlers, you would expect a second popup to appear alongside the first one—after all, the code doesn't do anything to make the first popup disappear and it doesn't check whether there is a popup before creating another one. The second question you might ask is how should the user dismiss a popup if he/she doesn't want to make a selection from the menu?

The answer to the first question is that there is no need to check whether there is a popup active before creating another one, because the JPopupMenu does this for you. When you make a popup menu visible, it checks whether there is already one visible and, if there is, the original one is canceled and disappears. This makes the handling of popup menus very simple—you don't need to retain any state information at all.

The user can dismiss a popup menu without making a selection by clicking the mouse anywhere inside the application frame but outside of the popup. Because this is all done automatically, you don't need to be concerned about if or when the popup disappears: Once you make it visible, you can forget about it and just handle selections in the event handlers connected to the menu items. If you want to discard the menu yourself at any time (perhaps because you want it to be visible for only a fixed amount of time), you can do so by making it invisible using `setVisible(false)`. A popup menu also disappears if its parent frame is made invisible under program control [using `setVisible(false)` on the frame] or the frame is minimized and doesn't reappear if the frame is made visible again. Note that a popup that becomes invisible by virtue of being automatically canceled by any means described here, or because `setVisible(false)` is invoked, can be made visible again later—the popup is not destroyed as long you maintain a reference to it.

Choosing the Location for a Popup Menu

Usually, popup menus are placed wherever the mouse happens to be pointing because most popups are brought into being by a mouse event. Being careful over the choice of your popup's location can, however, make a slight difference to your application's performance. The reason for this is that, if you create your popup in such a way that it is entirely contained by your application's frame (or by the dialog if you are using a `JDialog`—see the next two chapters), the `JPopupMenu` is created inside a lightweight container (actually a `JPanel`), whereas if any part of it would lie outside the frame, a heavyweight `Window` is used instead. It is, therefore, usually preferable to try to arrange for your popup menu to lie inside the application frame, unless it is critical that it appear next to the mouse pointer under all circumstances.

To show how simple it is to arrange for your popups to be lightweight, let's amend the example in Listing 6-4 so that the popup always appears inside the frame, if at all possible. Looking first at the `createPopup` method of Listing 6-4, you'll see that the popup is currently placed at the current mouse position. The modified version will use the mouse location and the size of the popup, together with the size of the frame, to deduce a nearby location that bounds the popup inside the frame. So that you can use this logic elsewhere, it will all be encapsulated in a single method called `getSuitableLocation`. Here is how the end of the `createPopup` method will look after this modification, with changes in bold:

```
popup.add(subMenu);

// Try to make the popup lightweight
point = getSuitableLocation(point, popup.getPreferredSize(),
this);

popup.show(this, point.x, point.y);
System.out.println("Popup is: " + popup.getParent());
```

The last line has been added only so that you can see that the popup is actually hosted in a `JPanel` when it has been successfully relocated.

The `getSuitableLocation` method is given the initial location for the popup, relative to the panel (**NOT** the frame), the size of the popup and a reference to the panel. The implementation of this method is quite straightforward, but it does introduce a couple of new methods that you haven't seen before.

```
// Get a suitable location for a JPopupMenu to make it lightweight
protected Point getSuitableLocation(Point point, Dimension d, Component c) {
  // First locate the parent JFrame or JDialog
  Component topLevel = c;
  while (topLevel != null && !(topLevel instanceof JFrame) &&
                !(topLevel instanceof JDialog)) {
    topLevel = topLevel.getParent();
  }

  if (topLevel != null) {
    int newX;     // New proposed x co-ordinate
    int newY;     // New proposed y co-ordinate

    // We have a top-level parent
    Rectangle parentBounds = topLevel.getBounds();
                // Parent bounds, screen-relative

    // Get proposed location, relative to the screen
    SwingUtilities.convertPointToScreen(point, c);

    if (point.x + d.width > parentBounds.x + parentBounds.width) {
      // Popup overhangs to the right
      newX = parentBounds.x + parentBounds.width - d.width;
    } else {
      newX = point.x;
    }

    if (point.y + d.height > parentBounds.y + parentBounds.height) {
      // Popup ends below frame
      newY = parentBounds.y + parentBounds.height - d.height;
    } else {
      newY = point.y;
    }

    // Change location only if necessary AND if
    // we can make the popup fit inside the frame
    if (newX >= 0 && newY >= 0) {
      point.x = newX;
      point.y = newY;
    }
```

```
    // Convert back to relative coordinates
    SwingUtilities.convertPointFromScreen(point, c);
  }

  return point;
}
```

The basic idea is simple: If the popup overhangs the frame to the right, move it left so that it is within the frame by changing the x coordinate to be that of the right of the frame minus the width of the popup. The same applies to the y coordinate, except that the frame height and popup height are used. The first problem is to find the enclosing frame or dialog. That problem is solved by following up the parent chain of the panel (or whatever component is passed in) until a frame or dialog is found. If neither is found, the original co-ordinates are returned unchanged.

When the frame has been found, its bounds are obtained. Since these are in terms of screen coordinates, it is now necessary to convert the proposed location of the popup into screen-relative coordinates. To do this, the method convertPointToScreen from the utility class SwingUtilities is used. This method requires a point and the component relative to which the point's co-ordinates are measured. Having converted the coordinates so that they are compatible with those of the frame, the necessary adjustments are made based on the widths and heights of the popup and the frame and the new location is converted back to the original coordinate space using the convertScreenToPoint method and then returned to the caller.

Note that it is possible that the popup can't be placed in such a way that it will always be bounded by the frame: It could be wider or taller than the frame. In this case, the original location is used unchanged.

To see that this algorithm works, you can try a modified version of the example in Listing 6-4 with the command:

```
java JFCBook.Chapter6.PopupExample2
```

First, try creating a popup near the middle of the frame and notice that it appears where you click and that the message written to the window from which you started the program says that the popup is a PanelPopup, which is the lightweight version. Now try creating a popup near the bottom right corner. You'll find that the popup appears above and to the left of where you click and that it is fully bounded by the frame. As before, it will be a PanelPopup.

Now resize the frame so that its height is very small and click inside it to create a new popup. In this case, the popup cannot be bounded by the frame, so it will appear where you click and it will be a WindowPopup, which is the heavyweight version.

Placing a Popup Menu on the Desktop

Instead of using the show method to create a popup at a position specified relative to some component within your application, you can also post a menu at an absolute location relative to the desktop using the JPopupMenu setLocation method. If you use this method, you must also invoke the JPopupMenu setInvoker method to associate the popup menu with your application's frame, by passing a reference to any component within the frame. A popup created and placed in this way won't be visible until you call setVisible(true).

Listing 6-5 shows how a popup menu can be placed on the desktop. This example is similar to the one you saw in Listing 6-4, except that the popup menu now contains just the list of colors that was originally on a submenu and activates the popup followed by selecting one of the colors that will actually change the background color of the application.

You'll notice that the createPopup method builds the menu by adding Actions to the JPopupMenu instead of building individual JMenuItems. This approach is very convenient here, because it makes it possible to store the color name (which appears on the menu), the color value, and a reference to the component whose background color is going to be changed in the ColorChangeAction, which is, as you would expect, derived from AbstractAction. This method of attaching Actions to menus should by now be familiar to you. Storing all this information together makes the implementation of the actionPerformed method trivial.

Listing 6-5   Placing a Popup Menu on the Desktop

```
package JFCBook.Chapter6;

import com.sun.java.swing.*;
import java.awt.*;
import java.awt.event.*;
import java.util.Hashtable;

public class PopupExample3 extends JPanel
        implements MouseListener {
  public PopupExample3() {
    this.addMouseListener(this);
  }

  // MouseListener interface
  public void mousePressed(MouseEvent evt) {
    if (evt.isPopupTrigger()) {
      createPopup(evt.getPoint());
    }
  }
}
```

continued

```java
public void mouseReleased(MouseEvent evt) {
  if (evt.isPopupTrigger()) {
    createPopup(evt.getPoint());
  }
}

public void mouseClicked(MouseEvent evt) {
  if (evt.isPopupTrigger()) {
    createPopup(evt.getPoint());
  }
}

public void mouseEntered(MouseEvent evt) {
}

public void mouseExited(MouseEvent evt) {
}

// Create and post the popup
protected void createPopup(Point point) {
  JMenuItem mi;

  popup = new JPopupMenu();
  for (int i = 0 ; i < colors.length; i++) {
    popup.add(new ColorChangeAction(colors[i],
           colorValues[i], this));
  }

  Dimension d = popup.getPreferredSize();
  Dimension screenSize = Toolkit.getDefaultToolkit().getScreenSize();

  popup.setLocation((screenSize.width - d.width)/2, (screenSize.height - d.height)/2);
  popup.setInvoker(this);

  popup.setVisible(true);

}

// An Action that sets the background of a given
// component to a given color.
public class ColorChangeAction extends AbstractAction {
  public ColorChangeAction(String name, Color color, Component comp) {
    super(name);
    this.color = color;
    this.comp = comp;
  }
```

```
   public void actionPerformed(ActionEvent evt) {
      comp.setBackground(color);
      comp.repaint();
   }

   protected Color color;
   protected Component comp;
}

public static void main(String[] args) {
   JFrame f = new JFrame("Popup Example");
   f.setContentPane(new PopupExample3());
   f.setSize(300, 300);
   f.addWindowListener(new WindowAdapter() {
      public void windowClosing(WindowEvent evt) {
         System.exit(0);
      }
   });
   f.setVisible(true);
}

private JPopupMenu popup;
private String[] colors = {
   "Black", "White", "Green", "Orange", "Pink", "Red", "Blue", "Cyan", "Gray"
};
private Color[] colorValues = {
   Color.black, Color.white, Color.green, Color.orange, Color.pink, Color.red, Color.blue,
      Color.cyan, Color.gray
};
}
```

The createPopup method builds the JPopupMenu and calls setInvoker passing it a reference to the main panel, which is used by JPopupMenu to find the application frame. The location of the popup is, in this example, calculated by getting its preferred size and the size of the screen and arranging for it to be centered in the screen. The setLocation method is used to specify the correct absolute location for the popup and then setVisible is used to make it appear. If you run this example using the command:

```
java JFCBook.Chapter6.PopupExample3
```

and click and release the mouse inside the frame (or do whatever your platform considers to be the popup trigger), you'll find that the popup appears in the middle of the screen and that selecting a color changes the background color of the panel accordingly. If you pop up the menu and then click again inside the frame, you'll find that the popup vanishes.

Popup Menu Events

Like windows, popup menus generate events. However, since popups are sometimes panels and sometimes windows, they don't generate `WindowEvents`. Instead, they have a dedicated event called `com.sun.java.swing.event.PopupMenuEvent` and a listener interface `com.sun.java.swing.event.PopupMenuListener`, which is defined as follows:

```
public interface PopupMenuListener extends EventListener {
   public void popupMenuWillBecomeVisible(PopupMenuEvent e);
   public void popupMenuWillBecomeInvisible(PopupMenuEvent e);
   public void popupMenuCanceled(PopupMenuEvent e);
}
```

The `PopupMenuEvent`, as you might expect, is derived from `EventObject`. The only useful information it contains is the source of the event, which is the `JPopupMenu`. The reference to the event source can, as usual, be obtained using the `getSource` method of `EventObject`. You can register to receive these events using the `JPopupMenu addPopupMenuListener` method and remove the listener using `removePopupMenuListener`.

The `popupMenuWillBecomeVisible` method is called just before the popup menu appears on the screen. A typical use for this method is to construct the content of the `JPopupMenu` as late as possible, in the same way that you saw earlier how menus are often manipulated just before they become visible. This method is actually invoked before the size of the popup has been determined and, therefore, you can do anything you need to at this point. Taking this strategy to its extreme, you could create an empty `JPopupMenu`, register a listener on it, then make it visible using show or `setVisible` and populate in the `popupMenuWillBecomeVisible` method. Such a technique might be useful for a popup whose content is very dependent on the state of the application—you could create a single `JPopupMenu` when the application starts and populate it as needed. As was said earlier, you can reuse a `JPopupMenu` as many times as you wish by using `setVisible` to make it appear and disappear.

Similarly, `popupMenuWillBecomeInvisible` is called just before the popup menu vanishes. This method is analogous to the `windowClosing` method of `WindowListener`, except that you cannot stop the popup menu closing. Finally, the `popupMenuCanceled` method is invoked when the popup is aborted because another popup was created, the user clicked outside the popup or the application frame was iconified.

Toolbars

A menu system is a very powerful way to present the commands available to a user of an application, but it can take time to navigate a hierarchy of menus to find the command you want. With good menu design, it is possible to minimize this problem by placing the functions that most users will need most frequently on a top-level menu so that only two mouse clicks are needed to reach them and, of course, these functions will have associated keyboard accelerators. Many users (myself included) don't have very good memories for function keys and prefer to use the mouse no matter how fast a keyboard accelerator might be: After all, if they can't remember which key to press, it's going to be faster for them to go to the menu than to consult the manual or the online help. For these users, a toolbar is a good solution. Instead of burying commands in a hierarchy of menus, you create buttons for the most common ones and place them on a toolbar underneath the menu bar where they can be reached quickly.

The Swing set contains a new component that makes it very simple to create toolbars. The `JToolBar` class is a container that you can add to your application's top level window (or any other window) and fill with buttons. The toolbar takes care of arranging the buttons left to right (or top to bottom if you want a vertical toolbar) and even creates the buttons for you if you add an `Action` instead of a button. As well as attaching itself to an application window, a toolbar can also be made to float independently of the application in its own frame so that the user can place it in any convenient location on the screen and it can be reattached to the application window later if required.

Creating and Populating a Toolbar

Creating a toolbar is extremely simple—only one line of code is necessary:

```
JToolBar toolBar = new JToolBar();
```

This produces an unpopulated horizontal toolbar with a grooved border. Adding buttons to the toolbar is equally simple: You just treat it as a container and use the `add` method to line the buttons up from left to right or, if your toolbar is a vertical one, from top to bottom. The example in Listing 6-6 shows a toolbar that might be useful in a file editor application.

Listing 6-6   A typical toolbar

```
package JFCBook.Chapter6;

import com.sun.java.swing.*;
import java.awt.*;
import java.awt.event.*;

public class ToolBarExample1 extends JFrame {
  public ToolBarExample1(String title) {
    super(title);

    // Create the toolbar
    JToolBar toolBar = new JToolBar();

    // Create the buttons to populate it
    JButton newButton = new JButton(
          new ImageIcon(getClass().getResource("images/new.gif")));
    JButton openButton = new JButton(
          new ImageIcon(getClass().getResource("images/open.gif")));
    JButton saveButton = new JButton(
          new ImageIcon(getClass().getResource("images/save.gif")));
    JButton copyButton = new JButton(
          new ImageIcon(getClass().getResource("images/copy.gif")));
    JButton cutButton = new JButton(
          new ImageIcon(getClass().getResource("images/cut.gif")));
    JButton pasteButton = new JButton(
          new ImageIcon(getClass().getResource("images/paste.gif")));

    // Add the buttons to the toolbar
    toolBar.add(newButton);
    toolBar.add(openButton);
    toolBar.add(saveButton);
    toolBar.addSeparator();
    toolBar.add(copyButton);
    toolBar.add(cutButton);
    toolBar.add(pasteButton);

    // Add a text area where we would show the file
    JTextArea textArea = new JTextArea(10, 40);

    Container cp = this.getContentPane();
    cp.add(toolBar, "North");           // Put the toolbar at the top
    cp.add(new JScrollPane(textArea), "Center");    // Text area gets the rest
  }

  public static void main(String[] args) {
```

```
    JFrame f = new ToolBarExample1("Toolbar Example 1");
    f.addWindowListener(new WindowAdapter() {
      public void windowClosing(WindowEvent evt) {
        System.exit(0);
      }
    });
    f.pack();
    f.setVisible(true);
  }
}
```

This example creates a horizontal toolbar with six buttons grouped into two logical areas. As you can see, you can use the addSeparator method to group related buttons on the toolbar; unlike the menu addSeparator method, this just adds some padding between the buttons rather than drawing a line. Figure 6-15 shows what this example looks like when you run it using the command:

```
java JFCBook.Chapter6.ToolBarExample1
```

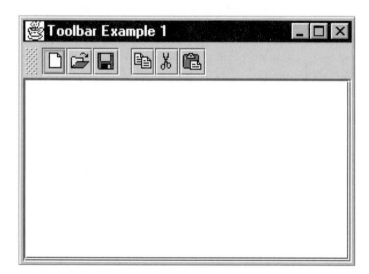

Figure 6-15   A frame with a toolbar.

The toolbar was populated with six buttons that were created in the usual way. Since this example is only intended to demonstrate how to create a toolbar, there isn't any processing associated with these buttons. If you wanted to make this application do something useful, you would create ActionListeners and connect them to the buttons; the creation of the buttons and their connection to application logic is, of course, nothing to do with the toolbar. You can, however, make the toolbar do some of this work for you if you use Actions, as you'll see later.

Whereas the menu bar has a special method to attach it to a JFrame (setJMenuBar), the toolbar does not. You just treat JToolBar as an ordinary component and place it wherever you want to. Conventionally, the toolbar goes underneath the menu bar (if there is one), but you could place it at the bottom or along the side of the frame if that suits your application layout better. Some applications might even have more than one toolbar—there is an example of this later in this chapter.

Once you've created a toolbar, you have some control over its appearance. You can determine its orientation using the setOrientation method:

```
JToolBar hToolBar = new JToolBar();
hToolBar.setOrientation(JToolBar.HORIZONTAL);
JToolBar.vToolBar = new JToolBar();
vToolBar.setOrientation(JToolBar.VERTICAL);
```

You can also remove the toolbar's border or select a different one from the default, as you'll see in the next example.

Buttons are the most common objects to be found on the toolbars. JToolBar is, however, just a container, so you can actually add any component you want to it. Listing 6-7 adds a label and a list box to a toolbar. List boxes and combo boxes, which will be described in detail in Chapter 8, "Creating Custom Dialogs," are commonly found on the toolbars of real applications. Listing 6-7 also shows a toolbar without a border and another with a Bevel border, as shown in Figure 6-16.

Listing 6-7   A frame with customized toolbars

```
package JFCBook.Chapter6;

import com.sun.java.swing.*;
import com.sun.java.swing.border.*;
import java.awt.*;
import java.awt.event.*;

public class ToolBarExample2 extends JFrame {
  public ToolBarExample2(String title) {
    super(title);

    // Create a toolbar with large insets
    JToolBar toolBar1 = new JToolBar();
    toolBar1.setMargin(new Insets(8,8,8,8));
    addActions(toolBar1);

    // Create a toolbar with default insets, no border
```

```
    JToolBar toolBar2 = new JToolBar();
    toolBar2.setBorderPainted(false);
    addActions(toolBar2);

    // Create a toolbar with a nondefault border and a Combo Box
    JToolBar toolBar3 = new JToolBar();
    toolBar3.setBorder(new BevelBorder(BevelBorder.RAISED));
    addActions(toolBar3);
    toolBar3.add(new JLabel(" Font:", SwingConstants.RIGHT));

    JList lb = new JList(new String[] {
            "Dialog", "Dialog Input", "Courier",
            "Helvetica", "WingDings" });
    toolBar3.add(lb);

    Container cp = this.getContentPane();
    cp.setBackground(UIManager.getColor("control"));
    cp.add(toolBar1, "North");
    cp.add(toolBar2, "Center");
    cp.add(toolBar3, "South");
}

public void addActions(JToolBar toolBar) {
    toolBar.add(newAction);
    toolBar.add(openAction);
    toolBar.add(saveAction);
    toolBar.add(copyAction);
    toolBar.add(cutAction);
    toolBar.add(pasteAction);
}

public static void main(String[] args) {
    JFrame f = new ToolBarExample2("Toolbar Example 2");
    f.addWindowListener(new WindowAdapter() {
        public void windowClosing(WindowEvent evt) {
            System.exit(0);
        }
    });
    f.setSize(500, 300);
    f.setVisible(true);
}

static Class thisClass = ToolBarExample2.class;
static Action newAction = new NullAction("New",
            new ImageIcon(thisClass.getResource("images/new.gif")));
static Action openAction = new NullAction("Open",
            new ImageIcon(thisClass.getResource("images/open.gif")));
```

continued

```
static Action saveAction = new NullAction("Save",
        new ImageIcon(thisClass.getResource("images/save.gif")));
static Action copyAction = new NullAction("Copy",
        new ImageIcon(thisClass.getResource("images/copy.gif")));
static Action cutAction = new NullAction("Cut",
        new ImageIcon(thisClass.getResource("images/cut.gif")));
static Action pasteAction = new NullAction("Paste",
        new ImageIcon(thisClass.getResource("images/paste.gif")));
}
```

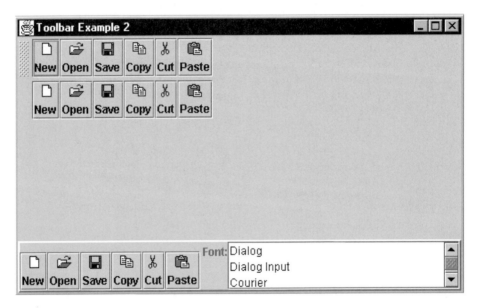

Figure 6-16   Customized toolbars.

The addActions method shown in Listing 6-7 adds the six buttons that appear on the toolbars, but there isn't a JButton in sight. Instead of creating the buttons directly, this example creates objects derived from AbstractAction and puts those on the toolbar. When you add an Action of any sort to a toolbar, the toolbar invokes its getValue method with the key Action.SMALL_ICON to get the associated icon and also looks for text stored under the key Action.NAME, then creates a JButton for itself, passing the text and icon to it. You are not required to supply both of these attributes. If both text and an icon are supplied, the text will appear below the icon and the combination will be centered in the button. Whenever you create an Action and add it to a toolbar, you should supply an appropriate icon. The use of Actions with toolbars and menus is better than the alternative of creating your own buttons, as the example in the next section will show.

Core Note

The developer versions of Swing only placed the icon associated with an Action
*on the toolbar button that it created. The text, if any, was added starting with
Swing 1.0. This might be considered a backward step, because there is (at least at
present) no way to request that the text be ignored so that you can get a button
with an icon and no text. If you are using* Actions *to attach the same code to a
menu and a toolbar, you need the text to be present for the benefit of the menu
item, so it is not really acceptable to not supply a text label. Furthermore, creating
separate* Actions *for the menu and toolbar defeats the aim of* Actions. *In
Swing 1.0, there is no sensible way around this problem [other than to subclass*
JToolBar *and reimplement the* add(Action a) *method] while using*
Actions.

Incidentally, the NullAction class that is used in this example is not a Swing
class, but a trivial subclass of DefaultAction that just writes a message when its
actionPerformed method is called. This example doesn't do anything useful
when these buttons are pressed, but it is necessary to provide a concrete Action to
the toolbar and DefaultAction can't be used directly because it is abstract. Here
is the implementation of NullAction:

```
// An action that does nothing other
// than log the fact that it was invoked
public class NullAction extends AbstractAction {
  NullAction(String name, Icon icon) {
    super(name, icon);
  }

  public void actionPerformed(ActionEvent evt) {
    System.out.println("Action performed");
  }
}
```

Using Actions with Menu Bars and Toolbars

One of the benefits of Actions is that you can create a single Action and use it to
give the user access to an application feature in several different ways. This section
illustrates the use of Actions to create menu bars and toolbars that use the same
code by adding a menu bar and a toolbar to the GraphicsDemo application that you
saw in Chapter 4. After the changes in this section have been made, the application
will look like Figure 6-17.

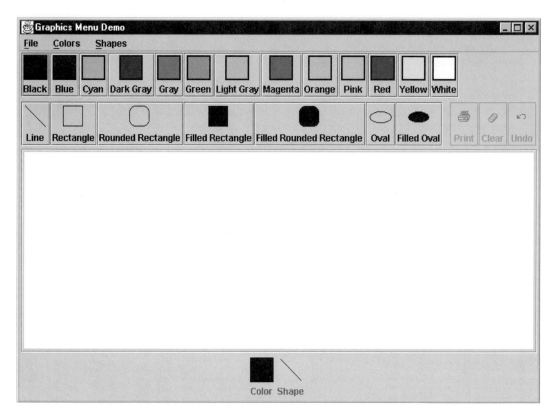

Figure 6-17   The Graphics Demo application with a toolbar.

Restructuring the Graphics Application User Interface

As you can see from Figure 6-17, all of the color and shape buttons that were on a separate panel alongside the drawing area have been placed on a pair of toolbars just below the new menu bar, along with the `Print`, `Clear` and `Undo` buttons. Also, the labels that used to be at the bottom of the right-hand part of the interface have now moved underneath the `GraphicsBorderedCanvas`, because they take up less space there.

> **Core Note**
>
> *In Figure 6-17, you can see the effect of the Swing 1.0 change that adds the label as well as the icon to a toolbar button created using an `Action`. The same `Actions` are used to create the menu items as well, so the text labels must be present in the `Action` and hence will also appear on the toolbar buttons.*

In Chapter 4, three classes were involved in providing the user interface: GraphicsBorderedCanvas provided the drawing area, GraphicsDemoPane housed the buttons and labels, and GraphicsDemo enclosed the other two, placing the drawing area to the left of the buttons and labels. In the revised application, all of the buttons on GraphicsDemoPane are removed and a pair of toolbars are added at the top. This arrangement could be implemented by using the existing GraphicsBorderedCanvas, a reduced version of GraphicsDemoPane and a new pane to hold the toolbars. While this would certainly make the job of laying out the user interface simple, it turns out to be inconvenient in other ways.

The GraphicsDemoPane as implemented in Chapter 4 contained the logic for handling the color and shape buttons and their effects on the buttons and labels at the bottom of the interface. When the buttons are migrated to the toolbars, it is easier to keep the code that is executed from the toolbar within the same class as that which implements the lower part of the display. For this reason, the GraphicsBorderedCanvas class is left unchanged and two new classes are created: GraphicsMenuDemoPane to replace GraphicsDemoPane and GraphicsMenuDemo to replace GraphicsDemo.

In terms of layout, GraphicsMenuDemoPane will now cover the entire JFrame, apart from the menu bar, and GraphicsBorderedCanvas will be placed on top of it, between the toolbars that occupy the upper part of the pane and the labels at the bottom. In this way, most of the application logic is kept together and, as you'll see, this maximizes code reuse between the toolbar and the menu bar.

Listing 6-8 shows the implementation of the GraphicsMenuDemo class, which replaces GraphicsDemo from Chapter 4.

Listing 6-8 The Graphics Demo with a toolbar

```
package JFCBook.Chapter6;

import com.sun.java.swing.*;
import com.sun.java.swing.border.*;
import java.awt.*;
import java.awt.event.*;
import JFCBook.Chapter4.GraphicsBorderedCanvas;
import JFCBook.Chapter4.EdgedBorder;

public class GraphicsMenuDemo extends JFrame {
   public GraphicsMenuDemo(String title) {
      super(title);
      this.getContentPane().setBackground(UIManager.getColor("control"));

      // Create the canvas in which the
      // drawing will be done.
      GraphicsBorderedCanvas c = new GraphicsBorderedCanvas();
```

continued

```java
// Create the border and associate it with the canvas
Border bd = new EdgedBorder(UIManager.getColor("control"));
c.setBackground(Color.white);
c.setBorder(bd);

// Create the pane that holds the user interface
// including the toolbars
GraphicsMenuDemoPane gp = new GraphicsMenuDemoPane(c);
gp.setBackground(UIManager.getColor("control"));

// Connect panel to canvas so that
// it can enable/disable buttons
c.addPropertyChangeListener(gp);

// Connect the canvas to the panel
// so that it can action button presses
gp.setDrawingArea(c);

// Select the initial color and shape
// from the button panel.
gp.selectTools();

// Create the menu bar
JMenuBar mb = new JMenuBar();
this.setJMenuBar(mb);

// Build the File menu
JMenu fileMenu = new JMenu("File");
mb.add(fileMenu);
fileMenu.setMnemonic('F');
gp.buildFileMenu(fileMenu);
fileMenu.addSeparator();
JMenuItem mi = new JMenuItem("Exit", 'x');
mi.addActionListener(new ActionListener() {
  public void actionPerformed(ActionEvent evt) {
    System.exit(0);
  }
});
fileMenu.add(mi);

// Add GraphicsMenuDemoPane menus to the menu bar
gp.addToMenuBar(mb);

this.getContentPane().add(gp);
}
```

```
   public static void main(String[] args) {
      GraphicsMenuDemo f = new GraphicsMenuDemo("Graphics Menu Demo");
      Dimension d = f.getPreferredSize();
      f.setSize(d.width, 500);
      f.addWindowListener(new WindowAdapter() {
         public void windowClosing(WindowEvent evt) {
            System.exit(0);
         }
      });
      f.setVisible(true);
   }
}
```

Much of this code is unchanged from Chapter 4. The two major differences are the way in which GraphicsBorderedCanvas and GraphicsMenuDemoPane are handled and the fact that the new version has a menu bar to manage. In the original implementation, there was an extra pane on which the drawing area was placed in the center and the GraphicsDemoPane to the east. Now, it is only necessary to create a GraphicsMenuDemoPane and add it to the frame's content pane. The GraphicsBorderedCanvas is passed to the GraphicsMenuDemoPane's constructor and is controlled by that object.

The menu bar poses an interesting problem that is typical of complex applications. While it is usually practical to divide a user interface into different functional areas and arrange to manage each area with a single class (and possibly other related classes) with little or no direct interaction between the various areas, this approach often does not work for menus, because there is only one menu bar that many parts of the application might want to use. In this case, the menu bar will have a File menu with an Exit command that should be controlled from the GraphicsMenuDemo class. In addition to this, the list of drawing shapes and colors should appear as separate menus and the Print, Undo and Clear functions should also be available on the File menu.

This type of arrangement is typical of real applications: Some parts of the application will want to create menus that they manage entirely themselves, while other parts need to add menu items to existing menus, usually the File menu. The solution adopted here is to create the menu bar in the GraphicsMenuDemo class and add to it a File menu that contains the Exit command. To allow the GraphicsMenuDemoPane to add its own items to the File menu, a buildFileMenu method is implemented in GraphicsMenuDemoPane; this method is then called with the File menu JMenu object as its argument. Similarly, to allow extra menus to be added, the GraphicsMenuDemoPane implements a method called addToMenuBar that will be called with the JMenuBar object as its argument. If there were other parts of the application that needed to add new menus or new menu items, you would add methods with these names to their classes and call them when the application is initialized.

You can easily extend this design pattern to other applications with a more complex menu structure. In the longer term, the JavaBeans API will eventually include a formal mechanism for menu merging, which will allow a component that is being imported into an application to add its own menus and menu items to the applications menu in a standard way. Until this feature is available, it is necessary to use an ad hoc solution like the one implemented here.

Now let's look at the GraphicsMenuDemoPane, which provides almost the entire user interface. In terms of components, it is derived from JPanel and is assigned a BorderLayout manager. On top of this, there are three other JPanels in the North, Center and South positions. The Center position is occupied by the GraphicsBorderedCanvas that is passed to the GraphicsMenuDemoPane constructor. Placing this in the center ensures that it uses any space not used by the other two panes, so that they both retain their original sizes should the user make the application window larger. In the North position there is a JPanel that will hold two JToolBars, one above the other; this pane will also have a BorderLayout manager to maintain the relative positions of the two toolbars. Finally, the South position is occupied by yet another JPanel on which will be the labels that show the current color and drawing shape to the right. Listing 6-9 shows the implementation of GraphicsMenuDemoPane, the first part of which shows how the user interface is created. Refer to Figure 6-17 to see where each component is being placed. Don't worry about the lines that use the setFloatable method—they just make sure you can't accidentally detach the toolbars by clicking on them. You'll see exactly how this works later in this chapter.

Listing 6-9   Creating the toolbar and labels for the Graphics Demo

```
package JFCBook.Chapter6;

import com.sun.java.swing.*;
import java.awt.*;
import java.awt.event.*;
import java.beans.*;
import JFCBook.Chapter4.GraphicShapeIcon;
import JFCBook.Chapter4.ColorFillIcon;
import JFCBook.Chapter4.GraphicOps;

public class GraphicsMenuDemoPane extends JPanel
        implements PropertyChangeListener {
  public GraphicsMenuDemoPane(Component c) {
    super(true);        // Double buffer
    this.setLayout(new BorderLayout());

    // Create and add the toolbar pane
    JPanel toolBarPane = new JPanel();
```

```
this.add(toolBarPane, "North");
toolBarPane.setLayout(new BorderLayout());
colorToolBar = new JToolBar();
colorToolBar.setFloatable(false);

shapeToolBar = new JToolBar();
shapeToolBar.setFloatable(false);

toolBarPane.add(colorToolBar, "North");
toolBarPane.add(shapeToolBar, "South");

// Add the pane that will contain the graphics
this.add(c, "Center");

// Add the pane with the current shape/color
JPanel labelPane = new JPanel();
this.add(labelPane, "South");

colorLabel.setVerticalTextPosition(SwingConstants.BOTTOM);
colorLabel.setHorizontalTextPosition(SwingConstants.CENTER);
colorLabel.setHorizontalAlignment(SwingConstants.CENTER);
colorLabel.setVerticalAlignment(SwingConstants.BOTTOM);
labelPane.add(colorLabel);

shapeLabel.setVerticalTextPosition(SwingConstants.BOTTOM);
shapeLabel.setHorizontalTextPosition(SwingConstants.CENTER);
shapeLabel.setHorizontalAlignment(SwingConstants.CENTER);
shapeLabel.setVerticalAlignment(SwingConstants.BOTTOM);
labelPane.add(shapeLabel);

// Create Action objects for the clear, undo and print buttons
clearAction = new AbstractAction("Clear",
           new ImageIcon(getClass().getResource("images/clear.gif"))){
  public void actionPerformed(ActionEvent evt) {
    graphicOps.clearCanvas();
  }
};

undoAction = new AbstractAction("Undo",
         new ImageIcon(getClass().getResource("images/undo.gif"))) {
  public void actionPerformed(ActionEvent evt) {
    graphicOps.removeLast();
  }
};

printAction = new AbstractAction("Print",
         new ImageIcon(getClass().getResource("images/print.gif"))){
```

continued

```
   public void actionPerformed(ActionEvent evt) {
     graphicOps.printCanvas();
   }
};

clearAction.setEnabled(false);
undoAction.setEnabled(false);
printAction.setEnabled(false);

// Create actions for color changes
colorActions = new ColorAction[colorList.length];
for (int i = 0; i < colorList.length; i++) {
  colorActions[i] = new ColorAction(colorList[i], colorNames[i],
          new ColorFillIcon(colorList[i]));
}

// Create actions for shape changes
shapeActions = new ShapeAction[shapeList.length];
for (int i = 0; i < shapeList.length; i++) {
  shapeActions[i] = new ShapeAction(shapeList[i], shapeNames[i],
          new GraphicShapeIcon(shapeList[i]));
}

JButton b;

// Add actions to the toolbars
for (int i = 0; i < colorActions.length; i++) {
  b = colorToolBar.add(colorActions[i]);
  b.setToolTipText((String)colorActions[i].getValue(Action.NAME));
}

// Add shapes to the shape toolbar
for (int i = 0; i < shapeActions.length; i++) {
  b = shapeToolBar.add(shapeActions[i]);
  b.setToolTipText((String)shapeActions[i].getValue(Action.NAME));
}

// Add a separator and then the print/clear/undo actions
shapeToolBar.addSeparator();
b = shapeToolBar.add(printAction);
b.setToolTipText("Print...");
b = shapeToolBar.add(clearAction);
b.setToolTipText("Clear");
b = shapeToolBar.add(undoAction);
b.setToolTipText("Undo");

}
```

```
// Associate drawing area
public void setDrawingArea(GraphicOps graphicOps) {
  this.graphicOps = graphicOps;
}

// Select initial color and shape
public void selectTools() {
  colorLabel.setIcon((Icon)colorActions[0].getValue(Action.SMALL_ICON));
  graphicOps.setColor(colorActions[0].getColor());
  shapeLabel.setIcon((Icon)shapeActions[0].getValue(Action.SMALL_ICON));
  graphicOps.setShape(shapeActions[0].getShape());
}

// PropertyChangeListener Interface
public void propertyChange(PropertyChangeEvent evt) {
  if (evt.getPropertyName().equals(GraphicOps.SHAPE_PROPERTY)) {
    int count = ((Integer)evt.getNewValue()).intValue();
    boolean state = (count > 0);

    clearAction.setEnabled(state);
    undoAction.setEnabled(state);
    printAction.setEnabled(state);
  }
}

// Add to the application's file menu
public void buildFileMenu(JMenu fileMenu) {
  JMenuItem mi;

  mi = fileMenu.add(clearAction);
  mi.setMnemonic('l');
  mi = fileMenu.add(undoAction);
  mi.setMnemonic('U');
  mi = fileMenu.add(printAction);
  mi.setMnemonic('P');
  fileMenu.addSeparator();

  JCheckBoxMenuItem cmi;
  cmi = new JCheckBoxMenuItem("Show color toolbar", true);
  cmi.addActionListener(new ToolBarViewAction(cmi, colorToolBar));
  fileMenu.add(cmi);

  cmi = new JCheckBoxMenuItem("Show shape toolbar", true);
  cmi.addActionListener(new ToolBarViewAction(cmi, shapeToolBar));
  fileMenu.add(cmi);
}
```

continued

```
// Add new menus to application's menu bar
public void addToMenuBar(JMenuBar mb) {
  JMenu mn;

  // Add the colors menu
  mn = new JMenu("Colors");
  mn.setMnemonic('C');
  for (int i = 0; i < colorActions.length; i++) {
    mn.add(colorActions[i]);
  }
  mb.add(mn);

  // Add the shapes menu
  mn = new JMenu("Shapes");
  mn.setMnemonic('S');
  for (int i = 0; i < shapeActions.length; i++) {
    mn.add(shapeActions[i]);
  }
  mb.add(mn);
}

// Labels showing the current color and current shape
protected JLabel colorLabel = new JLabel("Color");
protected JLabel shapeLabel = new JLabel("Shape");

// Toolbars for shapes and colors
protected JToolBar colorToolBar;          // Color tools
protected JToolBar shapeToolBar;          // Shape tools

// Coloring buttons
private static Color[] colorList = {
        Color.black, Color.blue,
        Color.cyan, Color.darkGray,
        Color.gray, Color.green,
        Color.lightGray, Color.magenta,
        Color.orange, Color.pink,
        Color.red, Color.yellow,
        Color.white };
private String colorNames[] = {
      "Black",    "Blue",      "Cyan",          "Dark Gray",
      "Gray",     "Green",     "Light Gray",    "Magenta",
      "Orange",   "Pink",      "Red",           "Yellow",
      "White" };
private ColorAction[] colorActions;

// Shape buttons
```

```
   private static int[] shapeList = {
           GraphicOps.DRAWN_LINE,
           GraphicOps.DRAWN_RECT,
           GraphicOps.DRAWN_ROUND_RECT,
           GraphicOps.FILLED_RECT,
           GraphicOps.FILLED_ROUND_RECT,
           GraphicOps.DRAWN_OVAL,
           GraphicOps.FILLED_OVAL };
   private static String[] shapeNames = {
           "Line",
           "Rectangle",
           "Rounded Rectangle",
           "Filled Rectangle",
           "Filled Rounded Rectangle",
           "Oval",
           "Filled Oval" };
   private ShapeAction[] shapeActions;

   // Actions for the print/undo/clear buttons
   private Action clearAction;
   private Action undoAction;
   private Action printAction;

   // Connection to drawing area
   private GraphicOps graphicOps;

   //
   // Inner classes ColorAction, ShapeAction, ToolBarViewAction
   // - shown below
   //
         .
         .
         .
}
```

Creating the Menus and the Toolbar Using Actions

Having gotten the broad outline of the user interface in place, it's now time to add the code that connects the menus and the toolbar to the code that actually performs the work of the application. In Chapter 4, everything was controlled by JButtons, so all of the application logic was contained in or accessed from ActionListeners attached to these buttons. In its revised form, most of the functions of the application can be accessed in two ways—either from the toolbar or from a menu. It is, of course, possible to continue to create simple ActionListeners and attach the same listener wherever it needs to be accessed (i.e., to a menu item and a

toolbar button), but the implementation shown here encapsulates the logic from the
ActionListener in a class that implements the Action interface and reuses that
class wherever the action formerly provided by the ActionListener is needed.
To see why this is better, let's look at how the Clear, Undo and Print buttons are
implemented.

In the constructor of GraphicsMenuDemoPane, after creating the user interface as shown in Listing 6-9, Actions are created for these three buttons:

```
// Create Action objects for the clear, undo and print buttons
clearAction = new AbstractAction("Clear",
    new ImageIcon(getClass().getResource("images/clear.gif"))) {
  public void actionPerformed(ActionEvent evt) {
    graphicOps.clearCanvas();
  }
};

undoAction = new AbstractAction("Undo",
    new ImageIcon(getClass().getResource("images/undo.gif"))) {
  public void actionPerformed(ActionEvent evt) {
    graphicOps.removeLast();
  }
};
printAction = new AbstractAction("Print",
    new ImageIcon(getClass().getResource("images/print.gif"))) {
  public void actionPerformed(ActionEvent evt) {
    graphicOps.printCanvas();
  }
};

clearAction.setEnabled(false);
undoAction.setEnabled(false);
printAction.setEnabled(false);
```

If you compare this to the implementation in Chapter 4, you'll find that the
actionPerformed methods here are unchanged. So what is the benefit of creating
an Action object? In the case of these three buttons, there are two main benefits.

The first is encapsulation. Instead of requiring you to create separate menu items
and buttons to which you would connect the ActionListener and which would
then be added to the menu and the toolbar, the Swing API allows Actions to be
added directly to menus and toolbars. Furthermore, as you have seen, the
AbstractAction class allows you to associate a text name and an icon with the
action by passing them to the constructor. When you add an Action of any type to
a menu, the text string is extracted from the Action and used as the label of the
menu item and, similarly, when you assign an Action to a toolbar, the icon is used
on the button that appears on the button. This means that you can almost completely
specify an Action at the time of its creation and then just quote a reference to it later

in whatever context you want to use it. To show how this works in practice, here is part of the implementation of the buildFileMenu method of GraphicsMenuDemoPane, in which we add the Clear, Undo and Print actions to the File menu:

```
// Add to the application's file menu
public void buildFileMenu(JMenu fileMenu) {
   JMenuItem mi;

   mi = fileMenu.add(clearAction);
   mi.setMnemonic('l');
   mi = fileMenu.add(undoAction);
   mi.setMnemonic('U');
   mi = fileMenu.add(printAction);
   mi.setMnemonic('P');
   fileMenu.addSeparator();

   // Further code shown later
}
```

As you can see, the menu entries are created by simply adding the AbstractAction for each function directly to the File menu. The code that creates the menu entries (and, elsewhere, the toolbar buttons) does not need to know how to connect them to application logic—the connection is already made through the Action. The definition of this variant of the JMenu add function used here is as follows:

```
public JMenuItem add(Action);
```

The return value is a reference to the JMenuItem that has been created for us. In our case, this reference is used only to add a keyboard accelerator for the action using the setMnemonic method that you saw earlier in this book in connection with JButtons. This is done by using the JMenuItem setMnemonic method, for example:

```
mi.setMnemonic('l');
```

It would be nice if the JMenuItem add(Action) method allowed you to specify a shortcut along with the Action, or, better, if AbstractAction stored an accelerator key that would be automatically assigned to the menu by the add method. With the current implementation of Swing menus, you are forced to do this yourself.

The second benefit of using an Action becomes evident when you remember how the Clear, Undo and Print buttons are used. When the application starts, these three toolbar buttons are all disabled. They only become enabled when a shape is drawn on the GraphicsBorderedCanvas and they can later become disabled again after, for example, the Clear button is pressed. In this version of the application, it is also necessary to enable and disable the corresponding menu items to keep them in step with the state of their corresponding buttons. If Actions hadn't been used, this would have meant retaining references to the three JMenuItems and the three JButtons on the toolbar and changing their states at the same time. Instead of this, however, it is now possible to just keep references to the AbstractAction objects and use the setEnabled method of the Action interface to enable and disable the action itself. When you do this, the change in state of the Action is propagated to both the corresponding menu item and the toolbar button. As well as reducing the amount of state that needs to be saved, this facility also allows most of the application to deal in terms of application-related objects (i.e., an AbstractAction object that describes an action to be performed by the application) and allows the application to enable and disable access to a feature by changing the state of the application object, rather than by directly manipulating a part of the user interface.

Now let's look at how the color and shape buttons on the toolbar and the corresponding menu items are implemented. After the discussion above, you probably won't be surprised to find that Actions are used to encapsulate the logic for these buttons as well. As you already know, when an Action is added to a menu, the text associated with it is used as the label of the menu item. Similarly, when an Action is added to a toolbar, the toolbar uses the Action interface's getValue method to get an icon to display on the toolbar button. You've already seen an icon that can be used for both the shape and color buttons—the ColorFillIcon and GraphicShapeIcon classes that were developed in chapter 4 to decorate the JButtons that we used in the earlier implementation. Here, instead of creating a button and assigning it the appropriate icon, the icon is assigned to an Action and the Action is then placed on the toolbar.

Unlike the Print, Clear and Undo buttons, which are self-describing because they have dedicated actionPerformed methods that don't need any information over and above the fact that they have been entered, it is necessary retain some state for each color and shape button. In Chapter 4, you saw that the actionPerformed method for each of these buttons needed to know the color or shape that the button was associated with so that it could change the state of the GraphicsBorderedCanvas and it also needed access to the button's icon to change the icon displayed on the labels that show the current drawing color or shape. This information was obtained by having the actionPerformed handler extract the source of the button press from the ActionEvent. It could then obtain the icon by casting the event source to a JButton and using the JButton getIcon method. The shape number or color was also stored with the button, by making use of the JComponent getClientProperty and putClientProperty methods. Here is the original implementation of the actionPerformed method for a color selection button:

```
public void actionPerformed(ActionEvent evt) {
    JButton b = (JButton)evt.getSource();

    Color color = (Color)b.getClientProperty(DRAW_COLOR);
    Icon g = b.getIcon();
    colorLabel.setIcon(g);
    graphicOps.setColor(color);
}
```

In our revised implementation, a new color can be selected from either a menu item or a button on the toolbar. Since menu items and toolbar buttons are both instances of the `AbstractButton` class, and since `AbstractButton` is derived from `JComponent`, one possibility is to attempt to preserve the technique used in the earlier implementation by rewriting the code like this:

```
public void actionPerformed(ActionEvent evt) {
   AbstractButton b = (AbstractButton)evt.getSource();

   Color color = (Color)b.getClientProperty(DRAW_COLOR);
   Icon g = b.getIcon();
   colorLabel.setIcon(g);
   graphicOps.setColor(color);
}
```

To make this work, it would be necessary to associate the color or shape number and the icon with both the menu item and the toolbar button when they are created. However, we have chosen not to add an icon to our menu items, so the `getIcon` method will not provide the desired result if a new color or a new shape is selected from the menu. To continue to use this method, there would be no choice but to add icons to the menu. There is, however, a much better solution: instead of associating the information that is needed when the action is triggered with the source of the action, it should instead be associated with the action itself. This is, of course, the solution that was used in the first example in this chapter that used the `AbstractAction` class.

In order to add an action to a menu or a toolbar, you have to create a class that implements the `Action` interface by providing the `actionPerformed` method, the text label and the icon. For the simple case of the `Print`, `Clear` and `Undo` actions, it was sufficient to use a subclass of the Swing `AbstractAction` class (which implements `Action` and therefore provides a way to store the label and the icon), to which only an `actionPerformed` method was added. To save the additional information needed for the color and shape buttons, as you saw earlier in this chapter, you need to do slightly more than this and implement subclasses of `AbstractAction` that also have a field to hold a color or a shape number. It isn't necessary to take any special action for the icon, because `AbstractAction` itself can store the icon. Here are the two classes that are used to implement the `Action`s for the color and shape menu items and toolbar buttons; these are actually implemented as inner classes of `GraphicsMenuDemoPane`, so they can directly access the `graphicOps` member:

```
// Action to handle color change
class ColorAction extends AbstractAction {
   ColorAction(Color color, String name, Icon icon) {
      super(name, icon);
      this.color = color;
   }
```

```
    public void actionPerformed(ActionEvent evt) {

colorLabel.setIcon((Icon)this.getValue(Action.SMALL_ICON));
      graphicOps.setColor(color);
    }

    public Color getColor() {
      return color;
    }

    private Color color;                    // The associated color
  }

  // Action to handle shape change
  class ShapeAction extends AbstractAction {
    ShapeAction(int shape, String name, Icon icon) {
      super(name, icon);
      this.shape = shape;
    }

    public void actionPerformed(ActionEvent evt) {

shapeLabel.setIcon((Icon)this.getValue(Action.SMALL_ICON));
      graphicOps.setShape(shape);
    }

    public int getShape() {
      return shape;
    }

    private int shape;                // The associated shape
  }
```

As you can see the `actionPerformed` methods of both these classes perform the same function as the versions shown above, but are more compact and deal only with local data. Furthermore, the same code is used whether the action is performed as a result of selection from the toolbar or the menu. The `ColorAction` class hasa constructor that accepts a `Color`, the text label and an `Icon`. The last two of these arguments are passed directly to the `AbstractAction` constructor: Only the color is stored by `ColorAction` itself. `ShapeAction`, likewise, saves the shape number and passes the text label and the icon to its superclass. Creating the actions for each of the color and shape buttons and adding them to the two toolbars is now very simple:

```
// Create actions for color changes
colorActions = new ColorAction[colorList.length];
for (int i = 0; i < colorList.length; i++) {
  colorActions[i] = new ColorAction(colorList[i], colorNames[i],
        new ColorFillIcon(colorList[i]));
}

// Create actions for shape changes
shapeActions = new ShapeAction[shapeList.length];
for (int i = 0; i < shapeList.length; i++) {
  shapeActions[i] = new ShapeAction(shapeList[i], shapeNames[i],
        new GraphicShapeIcon(shapeList[i]));
}

JButton b;

// Add actions to the toolbars
for (int i = 0; i < colorActions.length; i++) {
  b = colorToolBar.add(colorActions[i]);
  b.setToolTipText((String)colorActions[i].getValue(Action.NAME));
}

// Add shapes to the shape toolbar
for (int i = 0; i < shapeActions.length; i++) {
  b = shapeToolBar.add(shapeActions[i]);
  b.setToolTipText((String)shapeActions[i].getValue(Action.NAME));
}
```

Having created the actions, the `add` method is used to arrange for an appropriate button to appear on the toolbar and, as a bonus, a tool tip is added by extracting the text from the action and invoking `setToolTipText` on the newly-created toolbar button. Once they have been created, the exact same `Action` objects can also be used to create the Shapes and Colors menus that appear on the menu bar:

```
// Add new menus to application's menu bar
public void addToMenuBar(JMenuBar mb) {
  JMenu mn;

  // Add the colors menu
  mn = new JMenu("Colors");
  mn.setMnemonic('C');
  for (int i = 0; i < colorActions.length; i++) {
    mn.add(colorActions[i]);
  }
  mb.add(mn);

  // Add the shapes menu
  mn = new JMenu("Shapes");
  mn.setMnemonic('S');
```

```
    for (int i = 0; i < shapeActions.length; i++) {
      mn.add(shapeActions[i]);
    }
    mb.add(mn);
}
```

Again, after creating the new menus, they are populated with menu items by simply adding the `Actions`. This automatically creates the menu item with the correct label and connects it to the correct `Action`, so that the `actionPerformed` method will be invoked when the menu item is selected.

Enabling and Disabling Functionality Using Actions

Using `Actions` instead of directly manipulating buttons has another effect on the code. In Chapter 4, it was necessary to register to receive notification of changes to the `SHAPE_PROPERTY` of the `GraphicsBorderedCanvas` in order to keep track of the number of shapes on the canvas and therefore enable the `Print`, `Clear` and `Undo` buttons as necessary. Now that `Actions` are being used, the `propertyChange` method changes to enable or disable the `Actions` associated with the functions that these buttons and menu items provide, rather than the menu items and toolbar buttons themselves:

```
// PropertyChangeListener Interface
public void propertyChange(PropertyChangeEvent evt) {
   if (evt.getPropertyName().equals(GraphicOps.SHAPE_PROPER-
TY)) {
      int count = ((Integer)evt.getNewValue()).intValue();
      boolean state = (count > 0);

      clearAction.setEnabled(state);
      undoAction.setEnabled(state);
      printAction.setEnabled(state);
   }
}
```

Changing the enabled state of the action causes the menu item and the toolbar button to which it is connected to make the same state change. The `propertyChange` method doesn't know which user interface elements are being affected by its actions of course—it can simply assume that disabling the action stops the corresponding facility from being activated from the user interface and enabling it to make the facility available again.

Making Toolbars Selectable

Finally, a piece of gloss was added to this version of the application. The interface now uses two toolbars, which take up quite a bit of screen space. Some users might want to free as much of the screen as possible for use by the application proper, in this case to maximize the area occupied by the drawing canvas. In part, the situation has already been improved by comparison to the original implementation because the buttons that occupied the right-hand side of the interface have been removed, allowing more of the horizontal screen area to be used. If screen space is at a premium, things could be improved further if it were possible to remove the toolbars too. This wouldn't make the application useless—all the functions of the toolbars can still be accessed from the menus, which take up far less space. In a real-world application, quite a bit of the commonly used functionality will also be available via keyboard accelerators.

To allow the user to decide whether the toolbars are to be shown, two checkbox menu items have been added to the `File` menu at the end of the `buildFileMenu` method (this code wasn't shown when this method was described earlier in this section):

```
public void buildFileMenu(JMenu fileMenu) {
    .
    .
    .

    JCheckBoxMenuItem cmi;
    cmi = new JCheckBoxMenuItem("Show color toolbar", true);
    cmi.addActionListener(new ToolBarViewAction(cmi, colorToolBar));
    fileMenu.add(cmi);

    cmi = new JCheckboxMenuItem("Show shape toolbar", true);
    cmi.addActionListener(new ToolBarViewAction(cmi, shapeToolBar));
    fileMenu.add(cmi);
}
```

Again, an `Action` is used to process changes in state of the checkbox menu item. When the state of the checkbox is changed it is necessary to know which toolbar is affected. To ensure that this information is available, a subclass of `AbstractAction` is created to store a reference to the toolbar and to handle the state change. This class is an inner class of `GraphicsMenuDemoPane`, implemented as follows.

```
// Action to handle showing and hiding of toolbars
class ToolBarViewAction extends AbstractAction {
    ToolBarViewAction(JCheckBoxMenuItem cmi, JToolBar tb) {
        this.cmi = cmi;
        this.tb = tb;
    }

    public void actionPerformed(ActionEvent evt) {
        tb.setVisible(cmi.getState());
        GraphicsMenuDemoPane.this.validate();
    }

    protected JCheckboxMenuItem cmi;
    protected JToolBar tb;
}
```

References to both the checkbox menu item and the toolbar are stored in the `ToolBarViewAction` object. When the checkbox changes state, the `actionPerformed` method of the `ToolBarViewAction` is called. All that is necessary is to get the state of the checkbox (using the reference stored in the object) and change the toolbar's visibility to match that state, so that when the checkbox is ticked the toolbar is visible and vice versa. Changing the state of the toolbar isn't quite enough, though. To have the space occupied by the toolbar reused by the canvas, it is necessary to make the top-level pane's layout manager lay it out again. To make this happen, the following line of code is needed:

```
GraphicsMenuDemoPane.this.validate();
```

Since this code is executed in an instance of an inner class of `GraphicsMenuDemoPane`, the expression `GraphicsMenuDemoPane.this` resolves to a reference to the `GraphicsMenuDemoPane` itself. Invoking the `validate` method on a container causes the layout manager to redo its layout, provided that it is already marked as invalid. Changing the visibility of a component in the container, as will have happened in this case, is enough to make the container be invalid.

Floating and Docking Toolbars

The toolbars that have been shown so far have been attached to the application window, but you can also arrange for a toolbar to float. A floatable toolbar may start life attached to the application frame and then be detached, or it may be created in a floating state.

Creating a Floating Toolbar

There are several methods that you need to use if you want to create floating toolbars:

```
public void setFloatable(boolean b);

public void setFloating(boolean b, Point p);

public void setFloatingLocation(int x, int y);
```

A toolbar must be *floatable* in order for it to become detached from the application frame. You use the `setFloatable` method to make the toolbar floatable. In fact, by default, all toolbars are floatable so, if you don't want your application's toolbar to float, you need to use `setFloatable(false)`. Assuming that a toolbar is floatable, it won't actually detach itself until `setFloating` is called. This method serves the dual purpose of detaching the toolbar from the frame when its first argument is `true` and re-attaching or *docking* it later when it is called with its first argument set to `false`. The `setFloatingLocation` method is used to control where the toolbar is placed when it is detached. You'll see how this method is used at the end of this chapter.

Floating and docking toolbars are actually supported not by JToolBar itself, but by the basic toolbar UI class. The setFloatable method belongs to JToolBar, but the other two, along with some others that you'll see shortly, are provided by the BasicToolBarUI class, not by JToolBar. Fortunately, however, the various look-and-feel implementations either use the basic toolbar UI class directly or extend it, so their toolbars are all built around BasicToolBarUI. Therefore, all three standard look-and-feels support floating and docking toolbars. You'll notice that all the examples in this section check that the UI is an instance of BasicToolBarUI before attempting to use either of the last two methods, to avoid an exception should a new look-and-feel with a separate UI be introduced.

Although you can detach and reattach floatable toolbars under program control, it is usually the user that controls whether the toolbar is floating or docked. When it is docked, as you have seen, the toolbar normally resides near the top of the application frame. When it is floating, however, it is housed in a separate top-level frame that the user can drag around the screen with the mouse. The example in Listing 6-10 shows how to create a toolbar that the user can detach from the frame.

Listing 6-10   Creating a floating toolbar

```
package JFCBook.Chapter6;

import com.sun.java.swing.*;
import com.sun.java.swing.plaf.basic.BasicToolBarUI;
import com.sun.java.swing.border.*;
import java.awt.*;
import java.awt.event.*;

public class ToolBarExample4 extends JFrame {
  public ToolBarExample4(String title) {
    super(title);

    JToolBar toolBar = new JToolBar();
    toolBar.setMargin(new Insets(8, 12, 8, 12));
    addActions(toolBar);

    // Set various floating control attributes:
    if (toolBar.getUI() instanceof BasicToolBarUI) {
      BasicToolBarUI ui = (BasicToolBarUI)(toolBar.getUI());
      ui.setDockingColor(Color.orange);
      ui.setFloatingColor(Color.green);
      toolBar.setFloatable(true);
    }

    JTextArea textArea = new JTextArea(10, 40);
```

continued

```
    Container cp = this.getContentPane();
    cp.setBackground(UIManager.getColor("control"));
    cp.add(toolBar, "North");                    // Put the toolbar at the top
    cp.add(new JScrollPane(textArea), "Center");// Text area gets the rest
  }

  public void addActions(JToolBar toolBar) {
    toolBar.add(newAction);
    toolBar.add(openAction);
    toolBar.add(saveAction);
    toolBar.add(copyAction);
    toolBar.add(cutAction);
    toolBar.add(pasteAction);
  }

  public static void main(String[] args) {
    JFrame f = new ToolBarExample4("Toolbar Example 4");
    f.addWindowListener(new WindowAdapter() {
      public void windowClosing(WindowEvent evt) {
        System.exit(0);
      }
    });
    f.pack();
    f.setVisible(true);
  }

  static Class thisClass = ToolBarExample4.class;
  static Action newAction = new NullAction("New",
          new ImageIcon(thisClass.getResource("images/new.gif")));
  static Action openAction = new NullAction("Open",
          new ImageIcon(thisClass.getResource("images/open.gif")));
  static Action saveAction = new NullAction("Save",
          new ImageIcon(thisClass.getResource("images/save.gif")));
  static Action copyAction = new NullAction("Copy",
          new ImageIcon(thisClass.getResource("images/copy.gif")));
  static Action cutAction = new NullAction("Cut",
          new ImageIcon(thisClass.getResource("images/cut.gif")));
  static Action pasteAction = new NullAction("Paste",
          new ImageIcon(thisClass.getResource("images/paste.gif")));
}
```

You can run this example using the command:

```
java JFCBook.Chapter6.ToolBarExample4
```

If you look at Listing 6-10, you'll see that the toolbar was made floating by calling `setFloatable(true)`. This was strictly unnecessary, because this is the default. Before this method was called, though, a check was made that the toolbar's UI class is an instance of `BasicToolBarUI`. The UI class reference is obtained from the component using the `getUI` method, which you'll find out more about in Chapter 13, "The Pluggable Look and Feel." If this example program is ever run with a look-and-feel whose toolbar is implemented with a different UI class, it won't be able to control some aspects of floating and docking that might be provided by that look-and-feel. The explicit check that is made here is made not so that `setFloatable` can be used (because `setFloatable` is a `JToolBar` method and so is always available). It is necessary because the UI class reference must be cast to a `BasicToolBarUI` reference before it can be used in conjunction with the `setDockingColor` and `setFloatingColor` methods, which belong to the UI class. These methods will be discussed shortly. Casting without an explicit check would risk a `ClassCastException` sometime in the future.

Detaching the Toolbar

To make the toolbar float, place the mouse over the ridged area to the left of the buttons, press a mouse button and drag the toolbar.. When you do this, you'll find that a color-filled rectangle appears over the toolbar and then follows the mouse around. In this case, the rectangle will be either green or orange—the exact color will depend on where it is on the screen. If you move the colored rectangle away from the edges of the frame or right outside the main window and release the mouse, the toolbar re-appears in a frame of its own and you can move it elsewhere by dragging on its caption bar, as shown in Figure 6-18.

Figure 6-18   A floating toolbar.

Core Note

This works for the Metal look-and-feel. For the Windows and Motif look-and-feel, you need to place the mouse in the blank area to the right of the buttons and drag.

Docking the Toolbar

Once the toolbar has been detached, you can move it anywhere on the screen by dragging it with its caption bar and continue to use it buttons. If you want to dock it back onto the frame, you need to drag it back to the place on the frame where you want it to reattach itself and then release the mouse button, dropping it into its new location. However, you can't make the toolbar dock if you drag it by its caption bar. To make the toolbar eligible for docking, you have to hold down the mouse over the toolbar itself, somewhere between or outside the buttons, but not in the caption bar. With the Metal look-and-feel, you can drag the mouse by the ridged area to the left of the buttons as before. With other look-and-feels, you'll probably find that the frame is tightly wrapped around the buttons and that there isn't any convenient location to drag with the mouse. If you can't find a place in the toolbar where you can place the mouse and drag, resize the toolbar frame first to create some more space around the buttons. When you manage to find the correct location, a colored copy of the toolbar appears and follows the mouse as you drag it around the screen. When you release the mouse, the toolbar moves to its new location.

If you move the colored frame over the application window into a position in which it could reattach itself to the window (or *dock* with the window), it changes color to indicate that it would dock if released. You can use the `set FloatingColor` and `setDockingColor` methods to set the colors that will be used when the outline is being dragged. In the example in Listing 6-10, the frame will be orange if it would dock when the mouse is released and green if it would not. If, in this example, the toolbar does not turn green or orange as you drag it, it won't dock because you don't have the mouse in the correct position—almost certainly, the mouse is over the caption bar.

Docking and Docking Constraints

To determine whether the toolbar can dock with the frame, it invokes the toolbar UI's `canDock` method as it moves:

```
public boolean canDock(Component c, Point p)
```

If this method returns `true`, then the toolbar reattaches itself by passing its current location as the second argument to the following method:

```
private String getDockingConstraint(Component c, Point p);
```

The first argument is the container that was the parent of the toolbar when it was first added to the application. In most cases, this will be the content pane of the application's `JFrame` and the position is relative to this container.

This method returns a string that can be used as a position constraint by a `BorderLayout`, which makes the assumption that the container is managed by a `BorderLayout`. If the toolbar is close enough to the top of the container, this method will return the string `North` and the toolbar will dock in the North position, while if it is close to the bottom it docks to the South. If neither of these apply, then it docks either to the East or the West depending on whether it is near enough to either of these sides. If the toolbar docks to the North or South, it will be oriented horizontally and it will be vertical if it docks against the left or right edges. The meaning of 'close enough' is determined by a parameter called the *docking sensitivity*. If the mouse position at the time that you release the mouse is nearer than the docking sensitivity pixels from one of the sides, in the order listed above, then the toolbar will dock against that side. At the present time, there is no way to control the value of the docking sensitivity—it is always the height of the toolbar if it is horizontal or its width if it is vertical.

Creating a Floating ToolBar That Will Not Dock

While most toolbars will probably be attached to the application frame at least some of the time, it is sometimes useful to be able to create a toolbar that starts life floating. It is a simple matter to create such a toolbar, as you can see from Listing 6-11. The toolbar in this example also has another characteristic that may sometimes be useful—it will never dock with the application window.

Listing 6-11   Creating a toolbar that is initially floating and will never dock

```
package JFCBook.Chapter6;

import com.sun.java.swing.*;
import com.sun.java.swing.plaf.basic.BasicToolBarUI;
import com.sun.java.swing.border.*;
import java.awt.*;
import java.awt.event.*;

public class ToolBarExample5 extends JFrame {
  public ToolBarExample5(String title) {
    super(title);

    ToolBar toolBar = new JToolBar();
    JTextArea textArea = new JTextArea(10, 40);
    Container cp = this.getContentPane();
    cp.setBackground(UIManager.getColor("control"));
    cp.add(toolBar, "North");                   // Put the toolbar at the top
    cp.add(new JScrollPane(textArea), "Center"); // Text area gets the rest
    toolBar.setMargin(new Insets(8, 12, 8, 12));
    toolBar.setUI(new NonDockingToolBarUI());
    addActions(toolBar);

    // Set various floating control attributes:
    BasicToolBarUI ui = (BasicToolBarUI)(toolBar.getUI());
```

continued

```
      ui.setDockingColor(Color.orange);
      ui.setFloatingColor(Color.green);
      toolBar.setFloatable(true);
      ui.setFloatingLocation(200, 300);
      ui.setFloating(true, null);
   }

   public void addActions(JToolBar toolBar) {
      toolBar.add(newAction);
      toolBar.add(openAction);
      toolBar.add(saveAction);
      toolBar.add(copyAction);
      toolBar.add(cutAction);
      toolBar.add(pasteAction);
   }

   public static void main(String[] args) {
      JFrame f = new ToolBarExample5("Toolbar Example 5");
      f.addWindowListener(new WindowAdapter() {
        public void windowClosing(WindowEvent evt) {
          System.exit(0);
        }
      });
      f.pack();
      f.setVisible(true);
   }

   // Inner class that implements our private toolbar UI
   public class NonDockingToolBarUI extends BasicToolBarUI {
      public boolean canDock(Component c, Point p) {
        return false;
      }
   }

   static Class thisClass = ToolBarExample5.class;
   static Action newAction = new NullAction("New",
             new ImageIcon(thisClass.getResource("images/new.gif")));
   static Action openAction = new NullAction("Open",
             new ImageIcon(thisClass.getResource("images/open.gif")));
   static Action saveAction = new NullAction("Save",
             new ImageIcon(thisClass.getResource("images/save.gif")));
   static Action copyAction = new NullAction("Copy",
             new ImageIcon(thisClass.getResource("images/copy.gif")));
   static Action cutAction = new NullAction("Cut",
             new ImageIcon(thisClass.getResource("images/cut.gif")));
   static Action pasteAction = new NullAction("Paste",
             new ImageIcon(thisClass.getResource("images/paste.gif")));
}
```

If you run this example using the command:

```
java JFCBook.Chapter6.ToolBarExample5
```

you'll find that the toolbar appears in its own frame below the application main window. As usual, you can drag it around with its caption bar and place it anywhere you want. You can also drag it from within the toolbar and a green rectangle will follow the mouse around the screen. However, the rectangle will never turn orange and the toolbar will never dock with the application. Let's see how this is achieved.

Making the toolbar refuse to dock is very simple. This example creates its own toolbar UI class derived from `BasicToolBarUI` and attaches it to the `JToolBar`. The reason for inventing this class is to override the `canDock` method so that it always returns `false`, which will ensure that the toolbar will never dock with its frame.

Making the toolbar start life floating is also simple, but there are a few points you need to be careful about. In principle, to make the toolbar float, you just call `setFloating` with the first argument set to `true`. The second argument, which will be discussed shortly, can be `null` in this case because it is ignored when the first argument is `true`. This causes the toolbar to float at the location set by the `setFloatingLocation` method, which is also invoked in Listing 6-11. The coordinates given to `setFloatingLocation` are relative to the screen, not to the application frame. Therefore, in this case, the toolbar will always appear 200 pixels to the right and 300 pixels down from the top left-hand corner of the screen.

The most important thing to remember when you create a floating toolbar like this is that you must have used the `add` method to add the toolbar to the application frame before letting it float—that's why the code that controls the floating attributes in Listing 6-11 is at the end of the constructor—the `setFloating` method must be called after this line(in this example):

```
cp.add(toolBar, "North");       // Put the toolbar at the top
```

Finally, what about the second argument of the `setFloating` method? The full definition of this method is:

```
public void setFloating(boolean floating, Point position);
```

As well as being used to detach a toolbar, this method is also used to reattach a floating toolbar to the frame by invoking it with the `floating` argument set to `false`. In this case, the second parameter specifies the position *relative to the application frame* at which the toolbar would like to dock. This location is not, necessarily, however, where the toolbar will be placed. In fact, this position is passed to the `getDockingConstraint` method that you saw earlier, which uses it as a hint to decide which side of the container the toolbar should dock with. The constraint returned by this method will determine the toolbar's actual docked location.

Unfortunately, there is a small problem with this implementation. While it is true that this toolbar won't dock while it is being dragged around, you can nevertheless make it dock by clicking the close button on its floating frame. When this happens, the toolbar is docked without calling `canDock` to check whether or not it should. If you really don't want the toolbar to dock under any circumstances, you need to take control of what happens when the floating frame is closed.

There are two things you could do in this situation. First, you could let the toolbar disappear (and not dock). If you do this, you will need some other mechanism within the application to make it visible again—perhaps a menu item or a set of checkboxes that control which optional elements of the user interface are accessible. The second possibility is to ignore the user's request to close the frame. Here, you'll see how to do the second of these two. Once you know how to do that, implementing the first doesn't require any new techniques.

When the user clicks on the close button, the floating frame closes without any intervention from the application or from the toolbar UI class because, as you saw in Chapter 2, by default frames hide themselves automatically when the close button is pressed. Obviously, this behavior needs to be changed. To do this, it is necessary to change the default close behavior of the frame, but the frame is held as a private member of the toolbar UI class, so it is not possible to get a reference to it, even from a derived toolbar UI class. Fortunately, `BasicToolBarUI` follows a common Swing design pattern—it calls a protected method to create the frame. Because of this, the `NonDockingToolBarUI` class from the Listing 6-11 can be changed to override this method (called `createFloatingFrame`) and change the frame's close behavior to DO_NOTHING_ON_CLOSE.

This change arranges for the toolbar to remain visible on the screen, but it doesn't prevent it from docking. The docking behavior is cause by a listener for `WindowEvents` that the toolbar UI class registers on the floating frame. When this listener's `windowClosing` method is entered, it calls `setFloating(false, null)` to dock the toolbar. Again, the problem is to stop this listener's `windowClosing` method being called. The listener is created by another protected method called `createFrameListener`, so the same solution is possible here—override this method and return a listener that ignores all `WindowEvents`. You can see the implementation of both of these methods in the revised `NonDockingToolBarUI` class shown in Listing 6-12 and you can run this example to verify that the floating toolbar cannot be closed or docked using the command:

```
java JFCBook.Chapter6.ToolBarExample6
```

Listing 6-12   Creating a toolbar that is initially floating and will never dock

---

```
public class NonDockingToolBarUI extends BasicToolBarUI {
  public boolean canDock(Component c, Point p) {
    return false;
  }

  // Don't allow autoclose
  protected JFrame createFloatingFrame(JToolBar toolbar) {
```

```
    JFrame f = super.createFloatingFrame(toolbar);
    f.setDefaultCloseOperation(JFrame.DO_NOTHING_ON_CLOSE);
    return f;
  }

  // Don't dock on frame close
  protected WindowListener createFrameListener() {
    return new WindowAdapter() {
    };
  }
}
```

Summary

This chapter started by looking at the Swing menu system and concluded by looking at the toolbar, a kind of single-level graphical menu that is often placed below the menu bar to allow fast access to frequently-used features of an application. In between, it described the various types of menu items that can be used to populate menus and showed how you can arrange to handle the user's menu selections.

You also saw that you can use Actions, which were first introduced in Chapter 5, "Keyboard Handling, Actions and Scrolling" as menu items and with toolbars. You saw how the text and icon from the Action are used to create menu items and toolbar buttons and how changing the state of the Action results in the same state change on the menu or the toolbar.

Finally, the graphical demo application from Chapter 4 was reworked to show menus and toolbars in action, and you saw how to create docking and floating toolbars and how to control the conditions under which a floating toolbar will reattach itself to the application frame.

Menus and toolbars are useful for allowing the user exercise simple control over an application, but occasionally you need to allow the user to supply a lot of information at once. To make this possible, you can use free-standing windows called dialogs, which are the subject of the next two chapters.

USING STANDARD DIALOGS

Chapter 7

In this chapter, you'll see how to use dialog boxes to allow your application to interact with the user. Whereas JDK 1.1 provided only the most basic support for dialogs, JFC 1.1 contains a very wide selection of controls that can be used directly or tailored with only a few lines of code to satisfy the needs of many applications, including message and information dialogs and controls that allow the user to select files and colors.

The chapter starts by introducing the powerful JOptionPane component, which can be used to create free-standing dialog boxes or, as you'll see in the next chapter, as part of a more complex dialog layout. JOptionPane allows you to create simple dialogs that ask the user for input or inform the user of some condition that needs attention. In their most basic forms, these controls can be created with only a single line of code.

This chapter also takes a long look at JFileChooser and JDirectoryPane which offer the ability to select files from a file system. You'll find out how to select the directory in which the dialog will start and how to tailor the control so that it applies filters to the content of the directory before displaying its content to the user.

Finally, you'll see the simple, but very pretty, JColorChooser, which allows color selection to be made graphically.

Basic Dialogs

A dialog is a free-standing window associated with an application that appears only when it is needed. There are several reasons for using dialogs. Most commonly, you would show a dialog when the user wants to change the application's behavior in some way; this type of dialog would contain a list of things that the user can configure along with input fields, checkboxes and other controls that allow the required settings to be specified. Other types of dialog just show a message to which the user must respond, or present the user with a simple set of alternatives, one of which must be chosen before the application will continue. The Java Foundation Classes provide a rich set of dialogs that allow basic interaction with the user without the need to write a great deal of code. At the other end of the scale, it is also possible to build extremely complex dialog boxes of the type that you see in full-scale applications like Microsoft Word. This section looks at the basic dialogs and shows how you can customize them to meet your needs—the more complex dialogs are left for Chapter 8, "Creating Custom Dialogs."

The Message Dialog

If you just want to create a very simple dialog, you'll probably be able to find what you want among the sets provided by the Swing JOptionPane class. If you can't directly use what you find there, the odds are that you can use some of the techniques that you'll see in this chapter to create what you want from one of these basic dialogs. The simplest dialog that JOptionPane offers is a message dialog. In its most basic form, this displays an on-line message and a button labeled OK. Once it has been created, the dialog stays on view until the user presses the button. While the dialog is displayed, the user can't interact with the application in any other way.

Creating a Basic Message Dialog

Listing 7-1 shows how easily a simple message dialog can be created.

Listing 7-1   A JOptionPane message dialog

```
package JFCBook.Chapter7;

import com.sun.java.swing.*;
import java.awt.*;
import java.awt.event.*;

public class MessageDialogExample1 extends JFrame {
  public MessageDialogExample1(String title) {
    super(title);
    this.getContentPane().setBackground(Color.gray);
  }

  public void changeColor(Color targetColor, String colorName) {
```

```
      JOptionPane.showMessageDialog(this, "Press OK to change the
background color to "
                        + colorName);
      this.getContentPane().setBackground(targetColor);
      this.getContentPane().repaint();
   }

   public static void main(String[] args) {
      MessageDialogExample1 f = new
MessageDialogExample1("Message Dialog Example 1");
      f.setSize(200, 200);
      f.setLocation(100, 100);
      f.addWindowListener(new WindowAdapter() {
        public void windowClosing(WindowEvent evt) {
           System.exit(0);
        }
      });
      f.setVisible(true);

      f.changeColor(Color.black, "black");
      f.changeColor(Color.white, "white");
   }
}
```

This small program creates a frame with a gray background and then pops up a dialog informing you that the background is about to change to black. The Metal look-and-feel version of this dialog is shown in Figure 7-1. Notice that the dialog appears as an independent frame and that it is located above the application's main window; the positioning is determined entirely by JOptionPane and is not under your control.

The message itself is in the right-hand side of the window and underneath it is the OK button. When you press this button, the dialog disappears and the frame's background color changes as advertised. A second dialog box then appears and the process repeats itself.

Core Note

The exact appearance of any of these dialog boxes is ultimately determined by the look-and-feel itself. For simplicity, the descriptions that you'll see in this chapter assume that the Metal look-and-feel is in use.

The code that creates this dialog box is extremely simple:

```
JOptionPane.showMessageDialog(this,
   "Press OK to change the background color to " + colorName);
```

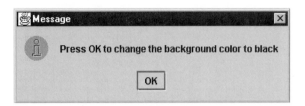

Figure 7-1   A JOptionPane message dialog.

This static method provides the simplest way to create a message dialog: you specify only the message to display and the frame to which the dialog belongs, which is usually the application's main window. This is the window relative to which the dialog's position is determined. Once the dialog has been displayed, the user can't do anything other than dismiss it and, furthermore, the application window (or windows if it has more than one) won't respond to the mouse or the keyboard. This type of dialog is called a *modal* dialog. As you'll see later, it is also possible to create *nonmodal* dialogs that allow you to continue to interact with the application while they are visible.

If you look at the `changeColor` method of Listing 7-1, you'll see that, according to the way the code is written, the pane's color is changed immediately after the dialog has been posted.

In fact, though, the color change doesn't happen until you press the OK button. What actually happens is that the `showMessageDialog` method creates and displays the dialog and retains control until you dismiss it. This is slightly unusual in Java: Normally, you create a window and continue execution; user actions on that window are usually handled elsewhere in an event handler. Of course, being able to wait until the user has responded to the dialog makes programming a lot simpler.

Core Note

In fact, there is quite a bit going on behind the scenes here, because the `showMessageDialog` *method can't simply block until the dialog is dismissed. Since everything in Java is actually event-driven, simply blocking would be fatal if the dialog were created in the AWT event-handling thread, because this thread would be unable to handle any more events. Since the only way to unblock the thread is to press the OK button, the application would be deadlocked forever, because the button press can only be processed by the blocked thread. The majority of dialog boxes used in real applications are created as a result of user actions, typically from menus. Because these user actions are handled as events, dialogs are most often created in the AWT event thread and are therefore open to this potential deadlock. To solve this problem, the Swing dialog classes create a new thread to handle events while the application itself (i.e., the usual AWT event thread) remains blocked. This relieves you of the need to worry about where you create your dialogs, and avoids a major problem with dialogs that existed in earlier versions of the JDK.*

The declaration of this simple form of the showMessageDialog method is as follows:

```
public static void showMessageDialog(Component comp, Object message);
```

In Listing 7-1, the application frame was used as the first argument, but, as you can see, all that you're bound to supply is a reference to a Component, not strictly a JFrame. If you wish, you can supply any component within the application window; the code that creates the dialog looks at the parents and grandparents of this component until it finds the top-level window, then places the dialog relative to that window. Therefore, the same result could have been obtained by saying

```
JOptionPane.showMessageDialog(this.getContentPane( ),
            "Press OK to change the background color to "
            + colorName);
```

However, to save the time it would take to traverse the component hierarchy and locate the top-level window, it is recommended that, whenever possible, you pass a reference to the top-level window when creating a dialog.

You can also supply null as the first argument to this method. If you do this, the dialog is posted in a frame that is not connected to the application window at all. The positioning of this frame is determined by JOptionPane and is unlikely to bear any predictable relationship to the position of your application. This feature, which also applies to all the other dialog creation methods in this chapter, is useful if you have to create a dialog in code that does not have a handle on the application's window, or if your application doesn't have a window at all, but does its work silently in the background until something goes wrong.

Our example used a String to display a message, but the type of the second argument is actually declared as Object, which means that you can pass an instance of any Java class as the message. This might seem rather strange at first; you'll see what happens if you pass something other than a String in the next chapter.

Customizing the Message Dialog

This basic method doesn't allow much control over what the user sees. You can create a greater variety of dialogs without much extra work using a second form of showMessageDialog:

```
public static void showMessageDialog(Component comp,
    Object message, String title, int messageType);
```

Using this method, you can supply your own title for the dialog and specify one of several message types. The message type must be chosen from the following set of values:

```
JOptionPane.PLAIN_MESSAGE

JOptionPane.INFORMATION_MESSAGE

JOptionPane.WARNING_MESSAGE

JOptionPane.QUESTION_MESSAGE

JOptionPane.ERROR_MESSAGE
```

This parameter is used to select one of several icons that is placed next to the message text. If you specify JOptionPane.PLAIN_MESSAGE, you don't get an icon; this is equivalent to the first form of showMessageDialog, except that you can supply the dialog's title. Strictly speaking, the particular icon that is associated with each of these values depends on the look-and-feel associated with the application. If you use the Metal look-and-feel, you get the familiar-looking icons shown in the Figure 7-2.

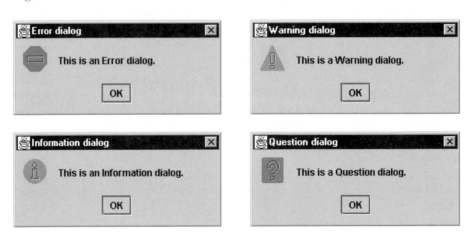

Figure 7-2   Variations on the JOptionPane message dialog.

If you don't like any of the standard icons, you can use the third variant of showMessageDialog to supply your own; this form has a single extra Icon parameter:

```
public static void showMessageDialog(Component comp,
    Object message, String title, int messageType, Icon icon);
```

Listing 7-2 shows an example that posts a message box indicating that a file save operation has been completed. As always, the ImageIcon class is used to quickly create an Icon from an image stored in a file. You can, of course, create an icon in many other ways, including using graphics operations to draw a suitable picture.

Listing 7-2   A message dialog with a custom icon

```
package JFCBook.Chapter7;

import com.sun.java.swing.*;
import java.awt.*;
import java.awt.event.*;

public class MessageDialogExample3 {
  public static void main(String[] args) {
    JFrame f = new JFrame("Message Dialog Example 3");
    JOptionPane.showMessageDialog(f, "File Save Completed",
            "File has been saved successfully",
            JOptionPane.INFORMATION_MESSAGE,
            new
ImageIcon(MessageDialogExample3.class.getResource("images/save.gif")));
    System.exit(0);
  }
}
```

Figure 7-3   Using a custom icon with JOptionPane.

Notice that a value for the message type is still supplied, even though a custom icon is being used (Figure 7-3). We said that the purpose of this parameter is to select a suitable icon, so why is it necessary to supply a value when the icon that it implies is being replaced with our own? The reason is that, while the standard look-and-feel implementations use the message type only to select the icon (and therefore won't make any use of it in this case), it is perfectly possible to create a different look-and-feel for this dialog box that makes other changes to its appearance which depend on the message type. For example, you might vary the background color to reflect the urgency of the message, using, perhaps, red for an error and white for a simple information message. You'll see many similar examples of apparently redundant information when we look at the other types of dialog box. Incidentally, since convenience methods are being used to create dialogs, you never get a reference to the dialog itself and so you don't have the opportunity to change the background color or other attributes of the dialog box yourself. This is the price you pay for simplicity. If you want more control over the appearance of the dialog, you need to use the more complex interfaces that are described in the next chapter.

The Confirm Dialog

The message dialog is useful if you want to inform the user of some event, but there's no way to get any feedback from it. If you want the user to be able to allow or cancel what your application is about to do, you can use a Confirm dialog. In its simplest form, this displays a message and three buttons labeled Yes, No and Cancel. You might use a dialog like this if your application has an open file whose content has been modified but not saved when the user tries to close the application. To avoid unintended loss of data, you could post a confirm dialog asking whether the user wants to save the data. In response to the answer Yes, the data would be saved and the application would then terminate, No would cause the application to exit without saving the data, while Cancel would withdraw the request to close the application. The simplest way to create such a dialog is to use the following JOptionPane method:

```
public static int showConfirmDialog(Component comp, Object message);
```

As with showMessageDialog, this produces a modal dialog. Unlike showMessageDialog, however, this method provides a return value that reflects the user's response to the dialog. The possible return values, and their meanings, are as follows:

JOptionPane.CLOSED_OPTION.	The user dismissed the dialog without pressing any of the buttons.
JOptionPane.CANCEL_OPTION.	The Cancel button was pressed.
JOptionPane.NO_OPTION.	The No button was pressed.
JOptionPane.YES_OPTION.	The Yes button was pressed.

Listing 7-3 shows how you could use a dialog box to implement the policy described in the previous paragraph and Figure 7-4 shows how this dialog is rendered by the Metal look-and-feel.

Listing 7-3   The JOptionPane confirm dialog

```
package JFCBook.Chapter7;

import com.sun.java.swing.*;

public class ConfirmDialogExample1 {
  public static void main(String[] args) {
    JFrame f = new JFrame("Confirm Dialog Example 1");
    int response = JOptionPane.showConfirmDialog(f,
        "Do you want to save the changes you have made to
        this file?");

    switch (response) {
    case JOptionPane.YES_OPTION:
      System.out.println("Yes - save data and exit");
      break;
    case JOptionPane.NO_OPTION:
      System.out.println("No - exit without saving data");
      break;
    case JOptionPane.CANCEL_OPTION:
      System.out.println("Cancel - do not exit");
      break;
    case JOptionPane.CLOSED_OPTION:
      System.out.println("Close - treat as cancel: do not exit");
      break;
    }
    // Just an example: exit anyway!
    System.exit(0);
  }
}
```

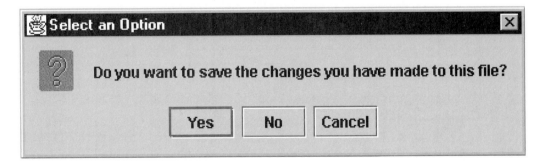

Figure 7-4   The JOptionPane confirm dialog.

In this case, if the user closes the dialog without responding to the question, the program behaves as if he/she had pressed `Cancel`. This is usually the safest course of action because it would (if this were a real application) avoid accidental loss of data.

If you want to get slightly more sophisticated, there are three more variants of `showConfirmDialog` that allow you greater control over the appearance of the dialog box. The simplest of these allows you to specify the dialog's title and restrict the set of buttons on display:

```
public static int showConfirmDialog(Component comp,
        Object message, String title, int optionType);
```

The `title` parameter replaces the default string ("Select an Option") supplied by the two-argument form of this method; `optionType` determines which buttons are displayed and takes one of the following values:

```
JOptionPane.OK_CANCEL_OPTION
```

```
JOptionPane.YES_NO_OPTION
```

```
JOptionPane.YES_NO_CANCEL_OPTION
```

```
JOptionPane.DEFAULT_OPTION
```

It should be obvious what the result of using the first three of these constants will be. Using `JOptionPane.DEFAULT_OPTION` produces a dialog with a single button labeled OK. The OK button is always equivalent to "Yes." If you create a dialog with `JOptionPane.OK_CANCEL_OPTION`, the possible return values from `showConfirmDialog` are CLOSED_OPTION, CANCEL_OPTION and OK_OPTION. The actual value of `OK_OPTION` is the same as `YES_OPTION`, so you can use them interchangeably in your code. It makes more sense to check against `OK_OPTION` when you create a dialog with `OK_CANCEL_OPTION` or `DEFAULT_OPTION`; in fact, using `DEFAULT_OPTION` is not recommended, because you can obtain the same result with greater clarity using `showMessageDialog`.

You can incorporate an icon using by supplying an extra message type parameter, from the list that was shown with the description of `showMessageDialog`:

```
public int showConfirmDialog(Component comp,
        Object message, String title, int optionType,
        int messageType);
```

and, not surprisingly, you can also supply your own icon:

```
public int showConfirmDialog(Component comp, Object message,
        String title, int optionType, int messageType,Icon icon);
```

As before, the look-and-feel decides how the message type parameter is used when you supply your own icon. Incidentally, if you use this form, it is perfectly legal to supply a `null Icon` parameter: the default look-and-feel provides the icon implied by the message type. Thus, the following two lines produce the same result:

```
JOptionPane.showConfirmDialog(f, "Exit now?", "Exit dialog",
        JOptionPane.OK_CANCEL_OPTION, JOptionPane.QUESTION_MESSAGE);
JOptionPane.showConfirmDialog(f, "Exit now?", "Exit dialog",
        JOptionPane.OK_CANCEL_OPTION, JOptionPane.QUESTION_MESSAGE, null);
```

The Option Dialog

The Option dialog box is basically the same as the Confirm dialog, except that it allows you complete control over the buttons that appear on it. If you use the Confirm dialog box, the possible button arrangements are:

- OK
- OK and CANCEL
- YES and NO
- YES, NO and CANCEL

In many cases, none of these choices are appropriate. For example, suppose your application needs to make a connection over a network to a host that cannot be reached at present. In this situation, you might want to offer the user the choice between retrying the connection or aborting the entire operation, so you would like to have two buttons that say `Abort` and `Retry`. You can do this with an Option dialog. There is only one method that creates a modal Option dialog:

```
public static int showOptionDialog(Component comp, Object
        message, String title, int optionType, int messageType,
        Icon icon, Object options[], Object initialValue);
```

Much of this rather long list of arguments should be familiar from what you have already seen. Only the last two arguments are new. The `options` array determines what appears at the bottom of the dialog box. Usually, you would supply a list of strings, each of which causes a button to be created with one of the strings as its label. The button whose label matches `initialValue` is given the initial keyboard focus. Listing 7-4 shows you how to create the dialog box for the network application mentioned above:

Listing 7-4   The JOptionPane option dialog

```
package JFCBook.Chapter7;

import com.sun.java.swing.*;

public class OptionDialogExample1 {
  public static void main(String[] args) {
    JFrame f = new JFrame("Option Dialog Example 1");
    int option = JOptionPane.showOptionDialog(f,
      "Attempt to connect to remote host has failed.
          Do you want to retry?",
      "Connection Failed", JOptionPane.DEFAULT_OPTION,
      JOptionPane.ERROR_MESSAGE, null,
      new String [] { retryString, abortString }, retryString);

    switch (option) {
    case JOptionPane.CLOSED_OPTION:
      System.out.println("Close - treat as retry");
      break;
    case 0:
      System.out.println("Retry");
      break;
    case 1:
      System.out.println("Abort");
      break;
    }

    System.exit(0);
  }

  protected static final String retryString = "Retry";
  protected static final String abortString = "Abort";
}
```

The first three arguments of showOptionDialog are self-explanatory. The fourth argument specifies which of the standard buttons are required. Since this example is using showOptionDialog in order to be able to directly control these buttons, none of the standard buttons are actually needed. Provided that something is supplied in the options argument, it doesn't matter what the value of the optionType argument is, since it won't be used. The special value JOptionPane.DEFAULT_OPTION is normally used in cases like this.

The message type and icon parameters are used here as they are elsewhere; this example creates an error dialog with the default icon. Finally, an array of strings that become the button labels is passed as the `options` argument and the `Retry` button is selected as the default, by giving its label as the last argument. Figure 7-5 shows the resulting dialog.

Figure 7-5   The JOptionPane option dialog.

What about the return value from this method? If the user closes the dialog without clicking on one of the buttons, the return value is `JOptionPane.CLOSED_OPTION`; otherwise, it returns the index number of the button that has been pressed, counting the left-most button as 0, the next as 1 and so on. In this example, the `Retry` button causes a return value of 0 and `Retry` generates 1. There is no possible confusion between a button being pressed and the dialog box being closed because `JOptionPane.CLOSED_OPTION` has the value –1.

You aren't restricted to any particular number of buttons in an Option dialog: You can have as many as you like, provided that there is room on the screen for them. Also, you can supply an empty `options` array. If you do this, then `optionType` determines which buttons are displayed, as is the case with the Confirm dialog. In fact, a Confirm dialog is actually implemented as an Option dialog with a null `options` parameter.

The Input Dialog

The last of the basic dialogs that Swing provides is the Input dialog, which allows you to prompt the user for arbitrary input, usually in the form of a string. There are four different ways to create these dialogs:

```
public static String showInputDialog(Object message);

public static String showInputDialog(Component comp, Object message);

public static String showInputDialog(Component comp, Object message,
        String title, int messageType);

public static Object showInputDialog(Component comp, Object message,
        String title, int messageType, Icon icon,
        Object[ ] selectionValues, Object initialSelectionValue);
```

The first three forms generate a dialog box with a text field into which the user can type a string. The first form, is equivalent to the second variant, in which the `comp` argument is supplied as `null`. As before, this creates a dialog with no associated top-level frame. The `message` parameter can be used to prompt the user as to the type of information required and, as usual, you can either accept a default title (in this case `Input`) and a question mark icon or, using the third form of the method, supply your own. Here are examples of both of these cases:

```
String fileName = JOptionPane.showInputDialog(f,
    "Please supply the name of the file to open:");

fileName = JOptionPane.showInputDialog(f,
    "File Open failed - Please supply an alternative name:",
    "File Open Failed",
    JOptionPane.ERROR_MESSAGE);
```

Figure 7-6 shows one of the input dialogs that would be created by the code extract above.

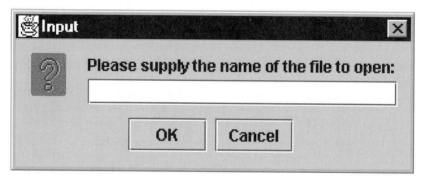

Figure 7-6   The JOptionPane input dialog.

All Input dialog boxes come with OK and Cancel buttons: `showInputDialog` doesn't provide any arguments that allow you to specify the labels or the number of buttons.

If the user presses the OK button or hits RETURN in the text field, the return value is whatever has been typed into the input field. If the user didn't actually type anything, you get an empty string—not a `null` string. A `null` string is returned only if the user closes the dialog or presses Cancel.

The fourth form of this dialog box allows you to supply a set of possible responses and to select the initial value. This produces a dialog with a combo box or a list box, depending on the number of possible responses, instead of a text field:

```
String colorName = (String)JOptionPane.showInputDialog(f,
        "Which color would you like to use for the background?:",
        "Background Color Selection",
        JOptionPane.QUESTION_MESSAGE,
        null,
        choices,
        choices[0]);

public static final String[] choices = {
        "Red", "Orange", "Yellow", "Green", "Blue",
        "White", "Black", "Grey", "Pink" };
```

Figure 7-7 shows what this code extract produces with the Metal look-and-feel. The Metal look-and-feel supplies a combo box when there are less than 20 selections and a list box if there are 20 or more, so in this case the color choices are placed in a combo box. You can run this example with the command:

```
java JFCBook.Chapter7.InputDialogExample2
```

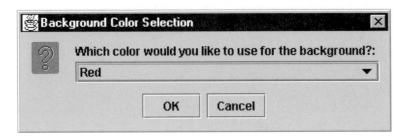

Figure 7-7 The JOptionPane input dialog with a combo box.

All of the strings in the `choices` array appear in the combo or list box and the one supplied as the last argument is selected as the one that is returned if the user presses the OK button. The display field of the choice box is read-only, so the user cannot type an arbitrary value into it. However, it is possible to type characters into this field and these are used to search the list of options; for example, typing the letter o locates `Orange` and makes it the current selection. Note, however, that only one letter is used, so that typing g followed by r locates `Red`, not `Green`.

Notice that this form of `showInputDialog` accepts a list of `Objects` and returns an `Object`, which must be cast to the appropriate actual type to make it useful. In the overwhelming majority of cases, you will use a string here, but it is possible to supply a list of objects of any kind; each entry in the list is turned into a string by calling its `toString` method and the result is added to the combo box. However, when the user makes a selection, the value returned by `showInputDialog` is not the string that the user saw but the `Object` that generated that string. This can be demonstrated by creating a list of `Font` objects instead of `Strings`:

```
Font selectedFont = (Font)JOptionPane.showInputDialog(f,
        "Please select a font:",
        "Background Color Selection",
        JOptionPane.PLAIN_MESSAGE,
        null,
        choices,
        choices[0]);
```

```
public static final Font[] choices = {
        new Font("DialogInput", Font.PLAIN, 12),
        new Font("DialogInput", Font.PLAIN, 14),
        new Font("Dialog", Font.PLAIN, 12),
        new Font("Dialog", Font.BOLD, 12),
        new Font("Serif", Font.ITALIC, 12),
        new Font("Serif", Font.BOLD | Font.ITALIC, 12)
};
```

The dialog box that appears when you execute the command:

```
java JFCBook.Chapter7.InputDialogExample3
```

Figure 7-8 contains string versions of the `Font` objects. Unfortunately, the result of applying `toString` to a `Font` does not produce a very useful result (except perhaps to the programmer), but it does clearly show that the combo box contains a representation of the objects that it was passed.

Figure 7-8   The JOptionPane input dialog with an object rather than a string.

Choosing a font description and pressing `OK` causes `showInputDialog` to return and the result is printed. The output is, not surprisingly, the same as the entry that was selected from the dialog. It is clear, however, that what was returned was a `Font` object, not a `String`, because anything other than a `Font` would cause the assignment to the variable `selectedFont` to throw a `ClassCastException`.

Core Tip

One moral of this story is that, if you intend to create classes that might be used as part of a user selection in an Input dialog, you should provide a user-friendly `toString` *method.*

This short survey of the `JOptionPane` class has by no means exhausted all of its possibilities. As powerful as it is for creating common dialogs with ease, it is even more useful as part of a custom dialog, as you'll see in Chapter 8.

The File Selection Dialog

The simple dialog boxes that you have seen so far are very useful for simple interactions that require a yes/no response or a single line of input from the user. Most programs have more complex requirements than this, and almost every application needs to manipulate files. Swing provides two components that provide a flexible user interface to allow the user to select files, including the ability to filter according to file type and other criteria so that only files that are relevant to the user's task are presented as possible choices. This section takes a close look at both of these components.

Core Alert

The `JFileChooser` *component described in this section is in the* `com.sun.java.swing.preview` *package, which means that its API is not frozen and may change. While the description of* `JFileChooser` *that follows is correct at the time of writing, it is possible that some of the API will have changed by the time you need to use it. It is recommended that you refer to the* `JFileChooser` *documentation for the latest information.*

JFileChooser and JDirectoryPane

In Chapter 6, "Menus and Toolbars," you saw how to use the menu system to allow the user to open a file. The file selection dialog that was used in Chapter 6 was, in fact, the AWT `FileDialog`, which has been available since JDK 1.0. The `FileDialog` class is simply a Java wrapper around the file selection dialog box offered by whatever platform the application is running on, so it will be familiar to users of the platform. But, for various reasons, it hasn't been possible for programmers to take full advantage of the facilities of the file dialogs offered by either Windows or Motif. Swing replaces the old `FileDialog` class with the platform-independent JFileChooser, which is implemented completely in Java and provides features that are very similar to the powerful Windows File Open dialog. As you'll see, the JFileChooser derives much of its functionality from a reusable component called JDirectoryPane, which is capable of displaying the contents of a file system directory. JDirectoryPane is, however, a free-standing component that you can take advantage of to create custom dialogs to allow the user to navigate the file system without necessarily having to open a file. Custom dialogs are described in the next chapter.

The most basic Swing file selection dialog can be created with just two lines of code:

```
JFileChooser chooser = new JFileChooser();
int result = chooser.showDialog(parentFrame);
```

The first line creates a JFileChooser object that will show all of the files and subdirectories in the user's home directory.

Core Note

On platforms that support it, the home directory that the JFileChooser starts in is the user's home directory. Where this concept doesn't exist (for example on Windows 95), the content of the Java installation directory is displayed instead.

A JFileChooser is not itself a complete dialog—in fact, it is just a JComponent that needs to be hosted inside a dialog box or, perhaps, an application window. You can easily use a JFileChooser to create a complete dialog box by using its showDialog method, which produces a modal dialog that returns when the user has made a selection or dismissed the dialog. Figure 7-9 shows what a basic JFileChooser dialog looks like in the Metal look-and-feel. You can run this example for yourself using the command:

```
java JFCBook.Chapter7.FileChooserExample1
```

When you create a dialog using JFileChooser, the JDirectoryPane part of it draws the pictorial representation of the directory, while the JFileChooser itself adds the controls that show the current directory and file name and enables you to navigate the file system and make a selection or close the dialog. Once you have a JFileChooser, you can use the methods of its associated JDirectoryPane object, which allow you to control what will be displayed in the directory view, and of the JFileChooser, which can be used to customize the appearance of the other controls on the dialog. To use the JDirectoryPane methods, you need to get a reference to it using the getDirectoryPane method. Here is a typical code sequence that shows how this is done:

```
JFileChooser chooser = new JFileChooser();
JDirectoryPane pane = chooser.getDirectoryPane();
```

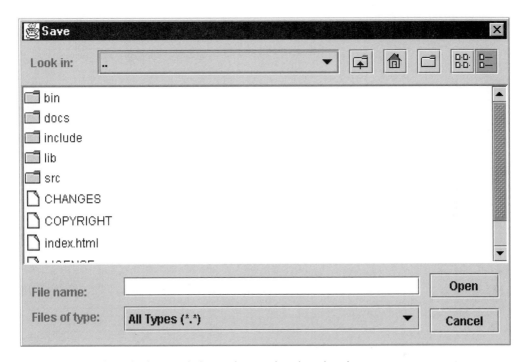

Figure 7-9   The JFileChooser dialog in the Metal Look-and-Feel.

At the top of the dialog shown in Figure 7-9 is a box that shows the name of the directory whose contents are shown in the JDirectoryPane. To the right of these are several buttons that will be familiar to Windows users. The first button allows you to move up one level in the directory structure, if there is anywhere to go. The second button moves you to the user's home directory (or what passes for it on your platform) and the third button allows you to create a new directory in the directory view. If you press this button, you should recognize the dialog box that it produces as the Input dialog that you saw earlier in this chapter (see Figure 7-10). The last two buttons control the way in which the files are displayed, showing either a plain listing or a listing with more detailed information (file size, etc.).

Core Note

In Swing 1.0.1, the last two buttons are not yet implemented.

At the bottom of the dialog, the text field contains the name of the currently selected item relative to the directory; if you haven't yet selected anything, this field will be empty. Beneath this is a combo box that lists all of the file *filters* that you can apply to the JDirectoryPane. By default, this box contains a single entry that

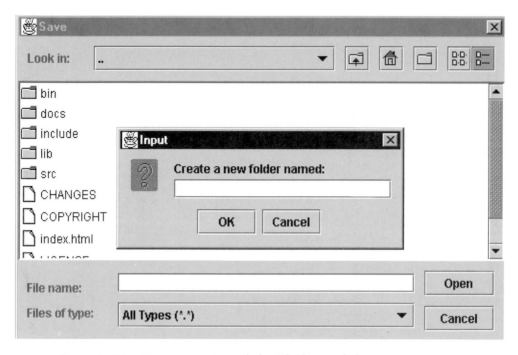

Figure 7-10   Directory creation with the JFileChooser dialog.

results in everything in the directory being shown. You'll see later how to add filters to this list. Finally, to the right of the combo box are two buttons, labeled Open and Cancel, that allow you to accept the selected file or dismiss the dialog without selecting anything.

The descriptions of JFileChooser and JDirectoryPane in this chapter and the next relate to their appearance when either the Metal or the Windows look-and-feel is selected. The Motif appearance is slightly different, but essentially the same facilities are available. The button that is described here as the Open button is labeled OK by the Motif JFileChooser. Figure 7-11 shows the same JFileChooser as Figure 7-9, but with the Motif look-and-feel selected.

If you select a file from the directory pane and press Open, showDialog returns 0; on the other hand, if you press Cancel or close the dialog window, –1 is returned. You can also select a file by typing its name into the text field below the directory pane and pressing RETURN. Unlike the basic dialogs you have seen so far, you don't get the selected file as the return value from the showDialog method. To find out which file the user selected, you use the JFileChooser getSelectedFile method:

```
TypedFile selectedFile = chooser.getSelectedFile();
```

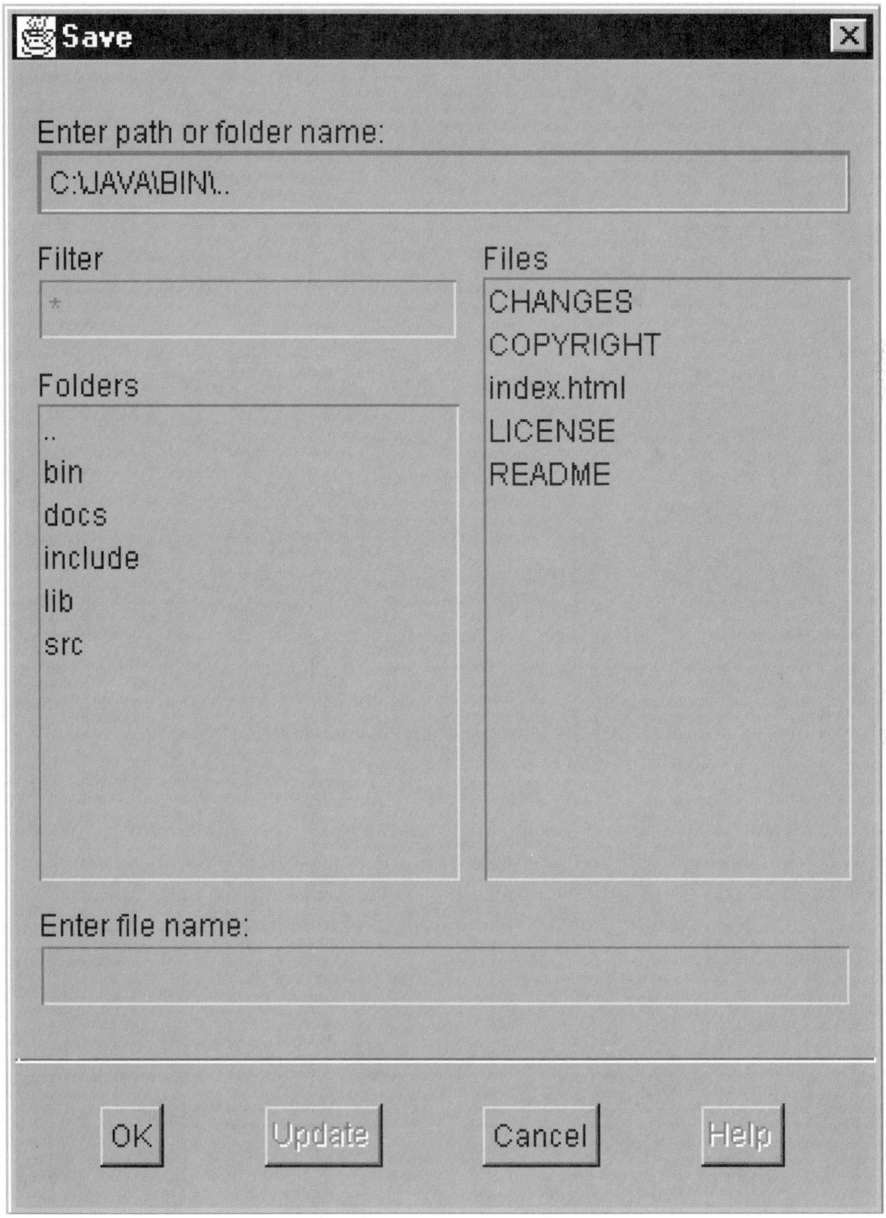

Figure 7-11   The JFileChooser dialog in the Motif Look-and-Feel.

If no file was selected, this method returns `null`, which you might think means that you don't strictly need to check the return value from `showDialog`. Why not just do this?

```
int result = chooser.showDialog(parentFrame);
TypedFile selectedFile = chooser.getSelectedFile();
if (selectedFile != null) {
  // File was selected
} else {
  // No file was selected
}
```

Unfortunately, this doesn't work. If the user highlights a file and then presses `Cancel`, `showDialog` correctly returns –1, but `getSelectedFile` will still return a `TypedFile` object for the highlighted file, as you can verify by trying it out for yourself with the `FileChooserExample1`. To avoid this problem, always check both the return value of `showDialog` and check that `getSelectedFile` returns a nonnull value.

You have probably noticed that `getSelectedFile` doesn't return the file name in the form of a `String`—it returns a `TypedFile` instead. The `TypedFile` class is derived from `File`, which makes it a lot more useful than a simple file name. You can, for example, use the `TypedFile` object to determine whether the selected file can be opened for reading or writing. If you need to know the name of the selected file, you can use the `File` method `getPath` to get the complete path or `getName` to get the last component of the file's name. You'll learn a lot more about the `TypedFile` class later in this chapter.

The `JDirectoryPane` allows you to select a range of files from the directory view. To do this, select the file at one end of the range. Then, while holding down the SHIFT key, click on the file at the other end of the range. The two files that you clicked and all the ones in between will be selected. Listing 7-5 shows an example program that demonstrates how to handle multiple file selection, which you can run with the command:

```
java JFCBook.Chapter7.FileChooserExample2
```

Listing 7-5   The JFileChooser dialog with multiple selection

```
package JFCBook.Chapter7;

import com.sun.java.swing.*;
import com.sun.java.swing.preview.*;
import java.util.Vector;

public class FileChooserExample2 {
  public static void main(String[] args) {
```

```
JFrame parentFrame = new JFrame("File Chooser Example 2");
JFileChooser chooser = new JFileChooser();
JDirectoryPane pane = chooser.getDirectoryPane();
int result = chooser.showDialog(parentFrame);

if (result == 0) {
  Vector selectedFiles = pane.getSelectedFiles();
  int length = selectedFiles.size();
  System.out.println(length + " file(s) selected");
  if (length > 0) {
    for (int i = 0; i < length; i++) {
      System.out.println("\t" +
((TypedFile)selectedFiles.elementAt(i)).getPath());
      }

    System.out.println("getSelectedFile returns " +
        pane.getSelectedFile());
  }
 }
}
}
```

When you press Open, showDialog will return 0 and getSelectedFile returns a File object for the second file that you clicked. If you want to be able to process all of the selected files, you need to use the getSelectedFiles method, which returns a Vector, each element of which is a TypedFile representing one selected file. There isn't a method that allows you to determine in advance how many files have been selected, so a program that wants to allow multiple selection must always call getSelectedFiles, even if the resulting Vector will only return one item. If there are no files selected, getSelectedFiles does not return null. Instead, it returns a Vector with no elements.

Of course, you are not obliged to support the selection of multiple files—you could just call getSelectedFile and use the file at the top of the selection. If you are going to do this, you should also ensure that the JDirectoryPane doesn't allow the user to select more than one file at a time. To do this, you need to change the mode of its associated ListSelectionModel, which can be arranged by adding the following code before you invoke showDialog:

```
// Allow single selection only
ListSelectionModel listModel = pane.getListSelectionModel();
listModel.setSelectionMode(ListSelectionModel.SINGLE_SELECTION);
```

You can try this out by running a modified version of the previous example with the command:

```
java JFCBook.Chapter7.FileChooserExample2a
```

You'll find that holding down the SHIFT key while clicking on files now has no effect—only the last file you click on is selected. You'll find out more about `ListSelectionModel`, which is the selection model used by the `JList` control, in the next chapter.

> **Core Note**
>
> *At the time of writing, it was possible to select multiple individual files in the* `JDirectoryPane` *by holding down the CTRL key as you click. However, only the last selected file was returned by* `getSelectedFiles`. *This is, of course, very misleading for the user. You can fix it by setting the list selection mode to* SINGLE_SELECTION, *or to* SINGLE_INTERVAL_SELECTION, *which allows the SHIFT key to work as described above.*

Changing the JFileChooser's Appearance

There is a limited set of ways in which you can change the default settings of the `JFileChooser`. If, as would almost always be the case, you want it to start by displaying files from some location other than the home directory, you need to use one of the following two constructors:

```
public JFileChooser(String path);
public JFileChooser(File directory);
```

These constructors cause the `JDirectoryPane` to show the content of the directory whose name is `path` or that is represented by the given `File` object. Note that these really must be directories—if you supply file arguments, you just get an empty directory view. As well as selecting the directory, you can also change the text displayed on various parts of the dialog box using the following `JFileChooser` methods:

```
public void setOkayTitle(String title);
public void setCancelTitle(String title);
public void setLocationTitle(String title);
public void setTypesTitle(String title);
public void setPrompt(String prompt);
```

The `setOkayTitle` and `setCancelTitle` methods change the text on the Open and Cancel buttons respectively, to values more suitable for the task that the user is performing. For example, if the dialog box is prompting for a file in which to save data, you might want to use:

```
chooser.setOkayTitle("Save to File");
```

On the other hand, if your application is an image previewer, the Open button might be better changed as follows:

```
chooser.setOkayTitle("Preview Image");
```

The other three methods change the strings on three of the labels on the `JFileChooser`. The *Location Title* is the string that appears to the left of the box that contains the name of the `JDirectoryPane`'s current directory at the top left of the dialog box. By default, this string reads `Look in`; in an image viewer dialog box, you might want to change this to `Find images in`. Similarly, you can change the *Prompt*, which appears to the left of the file-name box below the directory view and initially reads `File Name` and the *Types Title* that appears to the left of the combo box at the bottom of the dialog and is set to `Files of Type` by default.

Controling which Files Are Displayed in the Directory View

When you create a `JFileChooser`, it shows all objects of all types in the directory whose contents are displayed in the directory view and the combo box that holds the list of file-name filters contains just one entry, labeled:

```
All Types (*.*)
```

Sometimes, you'll want to show only a subset of the files in a directory. This subset might be based on file type, or it might depend on the content of the file, usually denoted by its file-name suffix. A front-end to a Java development environment, for example, might want to show only Java source and class files, so would filter out files whose names don't end in `.java` or `.class`. You can use methods provided by both `JFileChooser` and `JDirectoryPane`, in conjunction with the `FileType` interface, to use filters that include or exclude files based on arbitrary criteria.

Using Standard Filters

The simplest way to create a filter is to use one of the following predefined constants defined by the `FileType` interface:

```
FileType.SharedComputer

FileType.SharedFloppyDrive

FileType.SharedFolder

FileType.SharedGenericFile.

FileType.SharedHardDrive

FileType.SharedHidden
```

The meaning of most of these constants is obvious from their names. To add one of these filters to a `JFileChooser`, use the `addChoosableFileType` method:

```
public void addChoosableFileType(FileType fileType);
```

Each time you call this method, you add one filter to the JFileChooser's Files of Type combo box. Here's an example that adds two filters, one that shows only floppy drives, the other showing hard drives:

```
chooser.addChoosableFileType(FileType.SharedFloppyDrive);
chooser.addChoosableFileType(FileType.SharedHardDrive);
```

Alternatively, you can add a set of filters in one call using setChooseable FileTypes, as shown in Listing 7-6.

Listing 7-6   The JFileChooser dialog with standard filters

```
package JFCBook.Chapter7;

import com.sun.java.swing.*;
import com.sun.java.swing.preview.*;

public class FileChooserExample3 {
  public static void main(String[] args) {
    JFrame parentFrame = new JFrame("File Chooser Example 3");
    JFileChooser chooser = new JFileChooser();
    JDirectoryPane pane = chooser.getDirectoryPane();

    FileType[] fileTypes = new FileType[] {
        FileType.SharedFolder,
        FileType.SharedHardDrive
    };
    pane.setKnownFileTypes(fileTypes);
    chooser.setChoosableFileTypes(fileTypes);
    int result = chooser.showDialog(parentFrame);
  }
}
```

This example creates two filters, one that selects folders, the other selecting hard disk drives. You'll notice that another method called setKnownFileTypes is also called with the same list of file types; you'll see what this method is used for later. When you run this program (it's called JFCBook.Chapter7.FileChooserExample3), the JFileChooser's combo box will be set up as shown in the Figure 7-12.

Notice first of all that the All Types (*.*) entry is still there.

The setChooseableFileTypes method replaces any filters that were previously associated with the dialog apart from this one, which is always present. Notice also that there is an entry in the combo box for both of the filters that were added. If you select each entry in the combo box in turn, you'll see how the directory view's

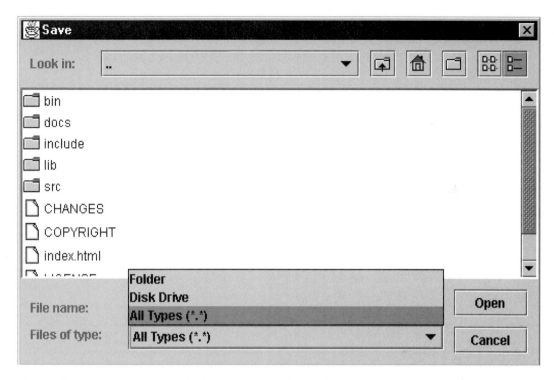

Figure 7-12   Additional types in the JFileChooser file type box.

content changes according to the filter. If you're wondering how to find a directory that contains some hard disk drives, this is easily done if you're using the Windows platform: just start in any directory and keep hitting the button to go up the directory hierarchy. Eventually you'll reach the root directory of the drive on which your starting directory resides. If you go up one more time, you'll see all of the drives installed on your machine.

Suffix Filters

Probably the most common way in which you'll want to filter the JFileChooser display is based on file-name suffix. Two additional variants of addChoosableFileType allow you to do this:

```
public void addChoosableFileType(String presentationName,
                    String extension, Icon icon);
public void addChoosableFileType(String presentationName,
                    String[] extension, Icon icon);
```

The *presentation name* is the name that appears in the Files Of Type box and *extension* consists of one or more file suffixes that are recognized by this filter. The first form is a convenience method that is simpler to use if you only want to filter one type of file. The *icon* is used to indicate files of this type in the directory listing. Listing 7-7 shows an example that allows you to select Java source or class files.

| Listing 7-7   Using suffix filters with JFileChooser |

```
package JFCBook.Chapter7;

import com.sun.java.swing.*;
import com.sun.java.swing.preview.*;

public class FileChooserExample4 {
  public static void main(String[] args) {
    JFrame parentFrame = new JFrame("File Chooser Example 4");
    JFileChooser chooser;

    if (args.length == 1) {
      chooser = new JFileChooser(args[0]);
    } else {
      chooser = new JFileChooser();
    }
    JDirectoryPane pane = chooser.getDirectoryPane();

    FileType[] fileTypes = new FileType[] {
                FileType.SharedFolder,
                FileType.SharedHardDrive
    };
    pane.setKnownFileTypes(fileTypes);
    chooser.setChoosableFileTypes(fileTypes);

    chooser.addChoosableFileType("Java Source Files", ".java", icon);
    chooser.addChoosableFileType("Java Class Files", ".class", icon);

    int result = chooser.showDialog(parentFrame);
  }

  protected static final ImageIcon icon =
        new ImageIcon
        (FileChooserExample4.class.getResource("images/j.gif"));
}
```

To run this example, use the command:

```
java JFCBook.Chapter7.FileChooserExample4 dirname
```

where *dirname* is the name of a directory containing some Java source and class files, such as `C:\java\src\java\awt` (assuming you have the Java source installed here). When the directory first appears (be patient—it may take a few seconds), you'll find all the files in the directory listed. You'll also notice that the Java files now have a green J instead of the usual file icon. Now open the `Files of Type` box and you'll see two new entries for `Java Source Files` and `Java Class Files`. Selecting either of these items changes the display so that only files of that type (and folders) are displayed. You can also supply an array of strings to `addChoosableFileType`, in which case files whose suffix matches any of those supplied will be displayed. This allows you to create a filter for Java Files that shows both source and class files, but no other files.

Core Note

At the time of writing, the suffix that you supply to `addChoosableFileType` *must include the period character. This may not, however, be intended. It is possible that the requirement to supply this character will be removed at some stage.*

How Filters Work

By using the standard filters, you can control the content of the `JFileChooser`'s directory view based on the type of each object in the directory or on its file-name suffix. If you want to filter based on other criteria, such as file size, modification time, readability and so on, then you have to create a custom filter. Custom filters are simple to write and can be as powerful as you need them to be. A custom filter is simply an implementation of the FileType interface, which is defined as follows:

```
public interface FileType {
   public abstract String getPresentationName()
   public abstract boolean testFile(File file);
   public abstract Icon getIcon();
   public abstract boolean isContainer();
}
```

To see how to write a filter, let's look at how the `JDirectoryPane` works. Like most of the Swing components, `JDirectoryPane` has an associated model: in this case, the model is provided by the `DirectoryModel` class. When you create a `JDirectoryPane` object, or when you change either its current directory or the active filter, the `DirectoryModel`'s `getTypedFilesForDirectory` method is used to scan the directory and create a `Vector` of `TypedFile` objects for the files and other objects in the directory that match the `DirectoryModel`'s currently selected filter. This filter is used to populate the `JList` control embedded in the `JDirectoryPane` that provides the view that you see.

Creating the list of files to be displayed requires a two-step process for each item in the directory. First, the item's type must be identified. Then, if the item matches the currently selected filter, it is added to the set of objects to be returned. The process of identifying an item produces a `TypedFile` object that encapsulates the item itself, a representation of its type (as a `FileType` object) and an icon that can be used to represent the item visually. As was noted earlier, `TypedFile` is a subclass of `File`; its full definition is as follows:

```
public class TypedFile extends File {
   public TypedFile(String path, FileType type);
   public TypedFile(String path, String name, FileType type);
   public FileType getType();
   public void setType(FileType type);
   public Icon getIcon();
   public String toString();
}
```

The `DirectoryModel`'s `getTypedFilesForDirectory` method is passed a `File` object that represents the directory and it uses the `list` method of this class to get a list of the names of all of the objects in this directory. It then processes each name in this list as follows.

First, a `TypedFile` object is created. As we've said, this object encapsulates both the file and its type. Since the type is not known yet, it is initially set to a value that would cause an exception to be thrown if the `getType` method were called. In order to determine the correct type, the `TypedFile` object is then passed to up to three sets of objects that implement the `FileType` interface, in the following order:

1. A set of `FileTypes` that always takes precedence, known as override types. These types recognize floppy disks and hard disks.

2. The set of registered known types. Initially, there is nothing in this list. You can add items to this list by calling the `DirectoryModel`'s `addKnownFileType` or `setKnownFileTypes` method, but, since you don't normally interact directly with the `DirectoryModel`, the usual way to add a type is to call the `addKnownFileType` or `setKnownFileTypes` methods of `JDirectoryPane`.

3. A set of *cleanup* types that recognize folders and treat anything else as a plain file.

To find out whether a `FileType` object recognizes the type of a file, `DirectoryModel` passes its `TypedFile` object to the `FileType`'s `testFile` method. Because `TypedFile` is a subclass of `File`, this method can access the underlying file or its name and can perform any checks it needs to in order to determine if the file is of a type that it recognizes. Often, this will just mean examining the name of the file. If this method returns `true`, then the file's type has been recognized and the `TypedFile` object's type is set by calling its `setType` method, passing it the `FileType` that recognized it.

If an object is not a disk and its type is not recognized by any of the types registered using `addKnownFileType` or `setKnownFileTypes`, the cleanup types will ensure that it will be classed as a folder if it is a directory, or as a plain file otherwise. Therefore, at the end of this process, the `TypedFile` will have a valid type associated with it.

Having identified the file type, the next step is to determine whether the file matches the filtering criteria set by the `JDirectoryPane`. There are two filters that can be set to control which items from a directory are returned from the `getTypedFilesForDirectory` method; these filters are set using the following `DirectoryModel` methods:

```
public void setShownType(FileType t);
public void setHiddenRule(FileType rule);
```

If the file is a container (that is, its `isContainer` method, as implemented by its `TypedFile` object, returns `true`), then it will always be included. If it is not, then its type is compared to the file type set using `setShownType`. The job of the filter set by this method is to select only those files that should be returned in the directory content collection; this is the filter that is set when you make a selection from the combo box on the `JFileChooser`. Thus, for example, if you choose the `Hard Drives` entry from our earlier example, this filter would be `FileType.SharedHardDrive`. Any items that do not have this file type will not be included in the returned collection, but, at this stage, folders will still be included, no matter what the filter is. If no filter has been set because `setShownType` has never been called (as is the case when you create a default `DirectoryModel`, usually by creating a default `JFileChooser`), then this filter will let everything through.

It is very important to note that this step does *not* involve executing the filter's `testFile` method against the file again. Because the file has already been typed, to determine whether its type matches the `Shown Type` filter, it is only necessary to compare its `FileType` against the one set by `setShownType`. If they are the same filter, the file should be shown. If they are different filters, the file will not be shown.

If the file is still a candidate after the `ShownType` filter has been applied, its file type is compared to that set with `setHiddenRule`. If the filter matches, then the file will be excluded. This filter can be used to omit files (and folders) whose name begins with a period ("."), for example, by using the `SharedHidden` file type:

```
setHiddenRule(FileType.SharedHidden); // Hide names starting with '.'
```

Both `DirectoryModel` and `JDirectoryPane` have `setHiddenRule` methods, but only `DirectoryModel` has `setShownType`. If you want to set the shown-type filter, you need to get a handle on the underlying `DirectoryModel` and operate on it directly:

```
chooser.getDirectoryPane().getModel().setShownType(FileType.SharedFolder);
```

Any objects that pass through both filters are included in the collection
returned from `getTypedFilesForDirectory` and will appear in the
`JDirectoryPane`'s directory view.

Creating a Custom Filter

To see how all of this works in practice, let's write a filter that recognizes uncompiled
Java source files. Determining whether something is a Java source file is simple: We
just check whether the last five characters of its file name are ".java." This much is
already provided by the standard suffix filter that you have already seen. To determine whether the file has been compiled, our filter will look for a corresponding class
file in the same directory. Since the idea is to detect uncompiled Java files, this filter
will allow through files whose names end in `.java` for which there is no corresponding `.class` file. Implementing the `testFile` method, then, will be very
straightforward. As well as this, you have to provide `getIcon`,
`getPresentationName` and `isContainer` methods. A small, green letter J will
be used as the icon for the filter. As was the case in Listing 7-7, the icon will be loaded
using the `ImageIcon` class. The presentation name is a short description of what
class of objects the filter selects; this name is used in the filter combo box on the
`JFileChooser`. Finally, `isContainer` returns `true` if this file type can contain
other objects; a `FileType` that detects folders would be implemented to return
`true`, whereas one for a plain file, like this one, would return `false`. The implementation of this filter is shown in Listing 7-8.

Core Note

You are not obliged to supply an icon. If the `getIcon` *method returns* `null`,
the `JDirectoryPane`'s *look-and-feel implementation supplies a default
icon—the one used for generic files.*

Listing 7-8   A custom filter for the JFileChooser dialog

```
package JFCBook.Chapter7;

import com.sun.java.swing.*;
import java.io.*;

public class UncompiledJavaFileType implements FileType {
  protected UncompiledJavaFileType() {
```

```
    }

    public Icon getIcon() {
        return icon;
    }

    public String getPresentationName() {
        return "Uncompiled Java Source Files";
    }

    public boolean isContainer() {
        return false;
    }

    public boolean testFile(File target) {
        if (target.isFile() && target.getName().endsWith(".java")) {
            String pathName = target.getPath();
            int nameSize = pathName.length();
            String classFileName =
                    pathName.substring(0, nameSize - 4) + "class";
            File classFile = new File(classFileName);
            return classFile.exists() == false || classFile.isFile() == false;
        }
        return false;
    }

    // Our icon: a small 'J'
    protected static final ImageIcon icon =
        new ImageIcon
        (UncompiledJavaFileType.class.getResource("images/j.gif"));

    // A concrete instance to use as a constant
    public static final UncompiledJavaFileType
        UncompiledJavaFile = new UncompiledJavaFileType();
}
```

Notice that a single instance of this filter is created and a reference to it saved it in the public static variable `UncompiledJavaFile`. Since every copy of this filter would be identical (the constructor has no parameters and there is no state to be changed at any time), it doesn't make sense to create more than one instance, so the constructor is protected to stop code outside the package from creating separate instances. The same pattern is used by all of the standard filters that you've already seen in this chapter.

To test this filter, add it to the list of filters associated with a JFileChooser:

```
FileType[ ] fileTypes = new FileType[ ] {
        UncompiledJavaFileType.UncompiledJavaFile,
        new FileType.ExtensionBased("Java Source Files",
          ".java", sourceIcon),
        new FileType.ExtensionBased("Java Class Files",
          ".class", classIcon),
        FileType.SharedHardDrive
};
pane.setKnownFileTypes(fileTypes);
chooser.setChooseableFileTypes(fileTypes);
```

You can see how the filter works by using the following command:

```
java JFCBook.Chapter7.FileChooserExample5 dirname
```

where *dirname* is the path name of a directory that contains some Java source and class files. Make sure that at least one of the Java source files does not have a corresponding class file. When the program starts, it creates a JFileChooser for that directory. The filter combo box initially has the All Types (*.*) filter selected, so you'll be able to see everything in your chosen directory. If you open up the combo box by clicking on the down arrow, you should find that it has an entry labeled Uncompiled Java Source Files. If you select this filter, the directory view should change so that only the uncompiled source files in this directory are shown—see Figure 7-13. If you see only folders, then either there are no Java source files in the directory, or they have all been compiled.

Notice also that there were two new filters shown in the previous example. The filter FileType.ExtensionBased is the filter that selects files based on their suffix. It is used automatically when you invoke the suffixed-based form of addChoosableFileType. In this example, all of the filters are being supplied together in a single call of setChoosableFileTypes, so it is necessary to create instances of these filters. The icons used here are, as you will have seen by running the example, a small green J for source files and an orange C for class files.

It is also important to be aware of the fact that the order of filters is very important. You must place more specific types earlier in the list than less specific ones. In this case, an uncompiled Java source file is more specific than a Java source file, so its filter comes earlier in the list of choosable types. If the order had been reversed, every Java source file would have been considered just a Java source file and the filter for uncompiled source files would not be entered, because the file type would already have been identified.

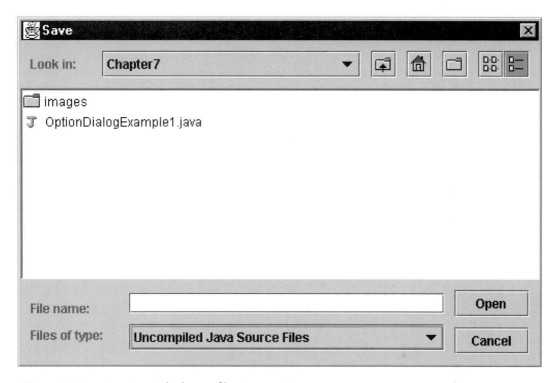

Figure 7-13   A custom JFileChooser filter in operation.

Known File Types and Choosable File Types

At this point, it is important to make a very clear distinction between setting the *known* file types and the *choosable* file types. Even though you pass one or more `FileType` objects in each case, and on many occasions you'll supply the same set, they are used in different ways.

The known file types, set using the `JDirectoryPane` method `setKnownFileTypes`, are used to determine the type of each file and to select which icon will be used to display it. The file types in this set do *not* decide whether a particular file will be included in the directory view—this is determined entirely by the file types passed to `setShownType` and `setHiddenRule`. The filter passed to `setShownType` determines whether a file will be displayed, but does not determine its icon.

The set of file types that can be used as filters is determined using the JFileChooser setChooseableFileTypes and addChoosableFileType methods, which populate the combo box from which the shown filter is selected. Let's look at some examples that illustrate the importance of understanding the difference between these two sets of file types and of understanding how the various filters operate.

Run the example JFCBook.Chapter7.FileChooserExample3 again; this example showed what happens if you add a Folder filter to the list of choosable file types. If you navigate to a directory that contains both files and other directories with the All Files filter in place and then activate the Folder filter, the files will disappear, as you might expect. Now suppose you want to show just the files and hide the folders. You might be tempted to create an extra filter for generic files and add it, like this:

```
FileType[ ] fileTypes = new FileType[ ] {
        FileType.SharedFolder,
        FileType.SharedHardDrive,
        FileType.SharedGenericFile
};
pane.setKnownFileTypes(fileTypes);
chooser.setChooseableFileTypes(fileTypes);
```

If you run this modified example (it's called JFCBook.Chapter7.FileChooserExample3a) and select the File filter, the result probably won't be what you expect—the directories are still there. This happens because, as was indicated in the description of the filtering process, the file type from the combo box is used as the file filter, but it is not applied to containers, so it isn't possible to exclude directories by choosing an item from the combo box. In fact, there is no way for the user to have directories hidden by using the controls provided by JFileChooser. If you want to hide directories, you have to set the hidden file rule:

```
chooser. setHiddenRule(FileType.SharedFolder);
```

Now, the directories will be included in the set returned by the first filtering operation, but will be excluded by the hidden file rule.

Core Alert

To emphasize again a point made earlier about the order of FileType objects, it is essential that more specific types appear before less specific ones in the list of known file types. This is why the FileType. SharedGenericFile entry was added to the end of the list shown above, not at the beginning. This FileType will identify any kind of file system object as a file, so if it were placed at the top of the list, everything would appear to be a plain file, even folders!

To see why you must distinguish the file types passed to `setKnownFileTypes` and those given to `setChooseableFileTypes`, let's see what happens when you forget to invoke the first of these two methods. Run the example program `JFCBook.Examples.FileChooserExample6`, giving it the name of a directory containing some Java source files on its command line. This example is actually a modified version of the program used to test the uncompiled Java source file filter, but which doesn't declare any known file types. Here's the modified piece of code:

```
FileType[] fileTypes = new FileType[] {
    UncompiledJavaFileType.UncompiledJavaFile,
    new FileType.ExtensionBased("Java Source Files",
            ".java", sourceIcon),
    new FileType.ExtensionBased("Java Class Files",
            ".class", classIcon),
    FileType.SharedHardDrive
};

// The line 'pane.setKnownFileTypes(fileTypes)' has been removed
chooser.setChoosableFileTypes(fileTypes);
int result = chooser.showDialog(parentFrame);
```

You should see a problem straight away: Even though the Java source file filter is in place, all of the files in the directory, including Java source files, have the icon normally used for ordinary files. Now select the `Java Source Files` filter from the combo box. This time, only the Java source files are shown and they have the correct icon. How does this happen?

To understand this, remember that the icon associated with a file is determined only by the filter in the *known* file list that recognizes it. In this example, we didn't add our filter to this list. As a result, when the `DirectoryModel` was creating the list of files to return to `JDirectoryPane`, it couldn't pass any of them to our Java source file filter. Instead, the Java source files end up being passed to the "cleanup" file types and are recognized as ordinary files. This explains why you see the ordinary file icon when the dialog box first appears. The Java source filter (along with the other filters) has only been declared using `setChooseableFileTypes` and therefore has only been used, so far, to populate the `JFileChooser` combo box.

When you select the `Java Source Files` filter from the combo box, the `JFileChooser` calls the `DirectoryModel`'s `setShownType` method, passing it the `FileType.ExtensionBased` object that selects files with suffix `.java`. As a side effect, the `setShownType` method enters this object in the known file types list before performing the filtering process again. Now, the files in the directory are all scanned again and passed to the list of known file types to be categorized. This time, because the Java source file type appears in the known file list, its file type is recognized, so the correct icon is extracted.

Taking Control of the Dialog

The examples you have seen so far have just created a JFileChooser, initialized it to show an entire directory or the file types selected according to certain rules, and used it to create a modal dialog. Once the dialog has been displayed, because showDialog blocks, you can, apparently, do nothing until the user selects a file and control is returned to you. This is not quite true, however. Even though the application is blocked in showDialog, there are several ways in which it can still influence events inside the dialog.

Suppose your application has posted a file selection dialog so that the user can select a file into which some data will be written. When the user has chosen a file, the application will extract the file name, open the file for writing and write the data. Suppose, however, that the user doesn't have permission to write to the file that he/she has chosen. What will happen is that the application will fail when opening the file and, presumably, post a message dialog alerting the user to the problem, then show the file selection dialog again so that another file can be chosen. It would be neater to detect the problem during the process of selecting the file, so that showDialog only returns when a writable file has been chosen.

To make this possible, it is necessary to get control when the user has made a selection and pressed the OK button before showDialog returns. At this point, it is possible to check whether the file is writable and post an error message if it is not. Then, you would need to be able to stop showDialog returning control to the user if the selected file cannot be used. Fortunately, all of this can be achieved by overriding the JFileChooser's performOkay method, which is called when the user presses the Open button. This method receives no arguments and doesn't provide a return value:

```
public void performOkay();
```

Core Note

There is also a performCancel *method that can be overridden to intercept the* Cancel *button.*

In order to override the performOkay method, you have to subclass JFileChooser. The sample code in Listing 7-9, creates a class called MyFileChooser that allows the selection of a file, but posts an error message if the item selected is either not a file, or cannot be written to.

```
Listing 7-9    Handling JFileChooser dialog button actions
```

```
package JFCBook.Chapter7;

import com.sun.java.swing.*;
import com.sun.java.swing.preview.*;
import java.io.File;

public class FileChooserExample7 {
   public static void main(String[] args) {
      JFrame parentFrame = new JFrame("File Chooser Example 7");
      File directory = null;
      JFileChooser chooser = new MyFileChooser(parentFrame);

      if (args.length > 0) {
         directory = new File(args[0]);
      }

      chooser.getDirectoryPane().setCurrentDirectory(directory);

      int result = chooser.showDialog(parentFrame);

      System.exit(0);
   }
}

// This example class catches attempts to open unwritable files
class MyFileChooser extends JFileChooser {
   MyFileChooser(JFrame f) {
      this.frame = f;
   }

   public void performOkay() {
      TypedFile selectedFile = getSelectedFile();
      if (selectedFile != null && (selectedFile.canWrite() == false ||
          selectedFile.isFile() == false)) {
         // Post an error message and return
         JOptionPane.showMessageDialog(frame,
            "You do not have permission to write to that file",
            "File not Writable",
            JOptionPane.ERROR_MESSAGE);

         // Return - causes the dialog to stay posted
         return;
      }

   // No file selected, or file can be written - let OK action continue
      super.performOkay();
   }

   // A frame to post dialogs relative to
   JFrame frame;

}
```

To try this example, use the command:

```
java JFCBook.Chapter7.FileChooserExample7 dirname
```

where *dirname* is the name of a directory with some files in it, one of which you do not have write-access to, or of a directory containing a subdirectory. If you don't supply a directory name, the `JFileChooser` displays the user's home directory or the Java installation directory as usual. The `main` method creates an instance of `MyFileChooser`, then uses the `JFileChooser` `setCurrentDirectory` method to choose the initial directory; if you pass `null` as the argument, the chooser starts in the home directory.

The interesting code in this example is in the overridden `performOkay` method, in which the `File` object for the currently selected file is obtained. If it turns out that it isn't a file, or it cannot be written to for any reason, a message dialog is posted. When the user dismisses this dialog, `showMessageDialog` completes and `performOkay` simply returns to whatever called it. On the other hand, if the selected file is acceptable, the `performOkay` method of `JFileChooser` is called. This method sets up the return value and causes the original `showDialog` call to return. Suppressing this call causes the dialog to remain posted, allowing the user to make another selection.

As an alternative, you could choose to allow the user to cancel the entire file selection process if the chosen file turned out to be unacceptable. To do this, you need to replace the message dialog with a Confirm dialog containing an `OK` button and a `Cancel` button. Pressing the `Cancel` button should then dismiss both the error message and the file selection dialog. The problem is, how can you cause the file dialog to act as if it had been canceled from within the `performOkay` handler if the user presses the `Cancel` button of the Confirm dialog? Fortunately, this is easy to do—all you need to do is call the `JFileChooser`'s `performCancel` method and it behaves as if its own `Cancel` button had been pressed, dismissing the dialog and returning –1 to `showDialog`. Listing 7-10 shows another `JFileChooser` subclass that implements this policy. You can try this example using the command:

```
java JFCBook.Chapter7.FileChooserExample8
```

Listing 7-10   Allowing the user to cancel a JFileChooser selection in case of an error

```java
// This example class catches attempts to open unwritable files
// and allows the interaction to be cancelled if required.
class DismissFileChooser extends JFileChooser {
  DismissFileChooser(JFrame f) {
    this.frame = f;
  }

  public void performOkay() {
```

```
  TypedFile selectedFile = getSelectedFile();
  if (selectedFile != null && (selectedFile.canWrite() == false ||
      selectedFile.isFile() == false)) {
    // Post an option dialog
    int response = JOptionPane.showConfirmDialog(frame,
        "You do not have permission to write to that file",
        "File not Writable", JOptionPane.OK_CANCEL_OPTION,
        JOptionPane.ERROR_MESSAGE);

    if (response == JOptionPane.CLOSED_OPTION ||
          response == JOptionPane.CANCEL_OPTION) {
      // Carry out the cancel action - drops the dialog
      performCancel();
      return;
    } else {
      // Return - causes the dialog to stay posted
      return;
    }
  }

  // No file selected, or file can be written - let OK action continue
  super.performOkay();
}

// A frame to post dialogs relative to
JFrame frame;
}
```

Listening to JFileChooser Events

Another way to respond to user actions in a `JFileChooser` or its associated
`JDirectoryPane` is to register to receive the `ActionEvents` that are generated.
These events are sent to `ActionListeners` when any of the following happens:

- The Open button is pressed
- The Cancel button is pressed
- A file or directory is selected by a single mouse click
- A double-click occurs on a file or directory

The source of all these events is the `JDirectoryPane`; to receive them, you
must register an `ActionListener` with the `JDirectoryPane` itself. To determine which action caused the event, you have to look at the event's action command.
By default, the values of the action command string for each event are as follows:

Table 7-1   JDirectoryPane Action Events

Event	Default Action Command
Open button	OKAY
Cancel button	CANCEL
Mouse click	null
Double-click on a file	doubleClick
Double-click on a directory	doubleClickContainer

If you intend to use these action events, it is best not to hard-code the strings in the above table. Instead, you can get the correct values, or set replacement strings of your own, using the following methods:

Table 7-2   JDirectoryPane Action Event Methods

Get Method	*Set methods*
public String getOkayCommand()	public void setOkayCommand(String command)
public String getCancelCommand()	public void setCancelCommand(String command)
public String getActionCommand()	public void setActionCommand(String command)
public String getDoubleClickCommand()	public void setDoubleClickCommand(String command)
public String getDoubleClickContainerCommand()	public void setDoubleClickContainerCommand (String command)

The events for the `Open` and `Cancel` actions are generated from the default implementations of the `performOkay` and `performCancel` methods that you saw in the previous section. If you override these methods, the events won't be posted unless you invoke the superclass method. In some cases, such as `performOkay`, it is not appropriate to do this if you don't want the operation to proceed, as was the case in our earlier example where the `Open` action was suppressed if the file selected was not writable.

Double-Click Selection

You can use the events generated by `JDirectoryPane` to implement a common shortcut that is missing in the current implementation. Most users are accustomed to being able to select a file from a file chooser by simply double-clicking on it. A double click, as you know, generates an `ActionEvent` but doesn't select the file. The example shown in Listing 7-11 implements this feature as an extension of `JFileChooser`.

Listing 7-11   Using a double click to select a file

```java
package JFCBook.Chapter7;

import com.sun.java.swing.*;
import com.sun.java.swing.preview.*;
import java.awt.event.*;
import java.io.File;

public class FileChooserExample9 {
  public static void main(String[] args) {
    JFrame parentFrame = new JFrame("File Chooser Example 9");
    File directory = null;
    JFileChooser chooser = new DoubleClickFileChooser();

    if (args.length > 0) {
      directory = new File(args[0]);
    }

    chooser.getDirectoryPane().setCurrentDirectory(directory);

    int result = chooser.showDialog(parentFrame);
    System.out.println("Selected file is "  +
          chooser.getSelectedFile().getPath());
    System.out.println("File chooser " +
          (result == 0 ? " selected a file" : " was cancelled"));

    System.exit(0);
  }
}

class DoubleClickFileChooser extends JFileChooser
          implements ActionListener {
  DoubleClickFileChooser() {
    getDirectoryPane().addActionListener(this);
    getDirectoryPane().setActionCommand("mouseClick");
  }

  public void actionPerformed(ActionEvent evt) {
    if (evt.getActionCommand().equals(getDirectoryPane().getDoubleClickCommand())) {
      // This is a double click: call performOkay
      // to dismiss the dialog.
      performOkay();
    }
  }
}
```

The DoubleClickFileChooser is a trivial extension of JFileChooser that just registers to receive events from its own JDirectoryPane. When the user double-clicks on a file, an ActionEvent with the command returned by the getDoubleClickCommand method will be received. When this happens, all that is necessary is to call the performOkay method, which does everything that pressing the Open button would do.

The only catch in this example is that it is necessary to use the setActionCommand method to set a non-null action command for single mouse clicks. If this were not done, the first of the two clicks on the file to be selected would generate an ActionEvent in which the action command would be null (refer to Table 7-1 to see why this is so). Establishing a non-null action command for this case avoids the need to check for null in the event handler.

Choosing Colors

Many applications will need to allow their users to customize the way they appear and, in many cases, color plays an important part of the user interface. The graphics application developed in Chapter 4 and improved in Chapter 6 is an example of this. To keep things simple, this application offered only a limited set of colors for the user to draw with. Ideally, it would have used a dialog box that offered a free choice of colors, not just the handful of standard colors declared by java.awt.Color. Swing provides a simple, yet powerful, dialog that makes it easy for the user to pick colors and for the programmer to give the user that choice.

The JColorChooser class makes it possible to display a color dialog and get the user's selection with just a single line of code:

```
Color selectedColor = JFileChooser.showDialog(parentFrame,
                         "Choose a color", Color.red);
```

The showDialog method displays a modal dialog with the title "Choose a color," with red as the initially selected color. Figure 7-14 is a gray-scale reproduction that gives you some idea what this control looks like, but it really must be seen to be appreciated—it's certainly one of the most attractive components I've ever come across. You can see this dialog for yourself using the command:

```
java JFCBook.Chapter7.ColorChooserExample
```

Core Alert

Like JFileChooser, *the* JColorChooser *component is in the* com.sun.java.swing.preview *package, which means that its API is not frozen and may change. While the description of* JColorChooser *that follows is correct at the time of writing, it is possible that some of the API will have changed by the time you need to use it. It is recommended that you refer to the* JColorChooser *documentation for the latest information.*

Figure 7-14   The JColorChooser dialog box.

The rectangle at the bottom right shows the currently selected color. There are two ways to change this color. One way is to type directly into the three text boxes that give the hue, saturation and brightness (HSB) values. As you type, the selected color changes accordingly. It's easier, though, to use the color swatch. You change the hue by clicking the mouse in the circular area and dragging the small circle that appears. The color in the square in the middle changes to reflect the hue represented by the mouse position. In the bottom right-hand corner, the saturation and brightness are both zero. As you move across to the left, the saturation increases linearly to its maximum of 100 percent. Similarly, the brightness increases as you move up. You can vary the saturation and brightness by dragging a small cross-hair over the square. When you're happy with the color you've chosen, press "OK" and `showDialog` returns a `Color` object that represents it. If you press "Cancel," `showDialog` returns `null`, while the "Reset" button returns the display to the initial color supplied as the third argument to `showDialog`.

You'll see from Figure 7-14 that this chooser is built with a `JTabbedPane` (a control that you'll see in the next chapter) that allows you to choose whether to use HSB or RGB values. If you click on the RGB tab, you get three sliders to adjust the red, green and blue values individually, as shown in Figure 7-15.

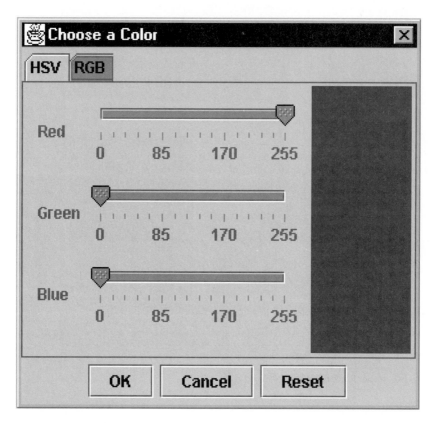

Figure 7-15   The JColorChooser dialog box showing RGB values.

Summary

This chapter introduced the Swing standard dialogs. These dialogs can be created very quickly, while still allowing the possibility of customization to meet particular needs. JOptionPane offers a comprehensive set of dialogs for direct interaction with the user, ranging from simple error messages to more complex interactions involving user input. JOptionPane also allows the programmer to create dialogs of open-ended complexity by allowing arbitrary components to be included.

The JFileChooser dialog exploits the capabilities of the JDirectoryPane control to display a set of files and allows the user to move around the file system to find a particular file and then select it. With only a modest amount of work, it is possible to add filtering to the dialog so that only files of particular types are displayed and to customize the way each entry in the dialog is presented. Finally, you saw the `JColorChooser` dialog, which presents an attractive way for the user to select colors.

In the next chapter, you'll see how to create your own dialogs, incorporating some of the controls that were introduced in this chapter together with a collection of new ones, many of which have no counterparts in the AWT component set.

CREATING CUSTOM DIALOGS

Topics in This Chapter

- Custom Dialog Boxes with JDialog
- Using JFileChooser
- Tabbed Panes and Borders
- Swing Controls Often Used in Dialogs

Chapter 8

The last chapter reviewed the built-in dialog classes that come with the Swing package. When these dialogs aren't sufficient for your needs, you need to create your own. This chapter looks at the `JDialog` class, which is the basis of all custom dialogs, and uses it to construct examples of the two basic types of dialog: *modal* and *nonmodal*.

Whereas dialog support in AWT is very basic, Swing contains a very powerful set of information, error and warning dialogs wrapped up in the `JOptionPane` class, which were introduced in the previous chapter. The facilities provided by `JOptionPane` can also be used as part of a larger dialog, as you'll see here. This chapter also looks at many of the new Swing components that are useful in dialogs, including the most powerful dialog component of all, the `JTabbedPane`, and also demonstrates how to use and customize the list box and combo box controls that present lists of choices to the user.

Creating Custom Dialog Boxes

The dialogs that you have seen so far have all been created with a static convenience method that hides what goes on behind the scenes. In a large number of cases, you won't need to look any further than this, because the standard dialog boxes are sufficiently general that they can be used unchanged much of the time. If you want to construct your own dialogs, however, you have to build a custom dialog by using the `JDialog` class.

The JDialog Class

JDialog is a Swing component derived from the AWT Dialog class, which is itself
an instance of Window. Like JFrame, it is not a JComponent and, also like
JFrame, it has a JRootPane with a content view, glass pane and an optional menu
bar.

Core Note

The AWT Dialog *class didn't allow you to have a menu bar. In Swing, there is
very little difference between* JFrame *and* JDialog, *but the differences that
exist are important ones, as you'll see.*

The JDialog class has four constructors:

```
public JDialog(Frame f);
public JDialog(Frame f, boolean modal);
public JDialog(Frame f, String title);
public JDialog(Frame f, String title, boolean modal);
```

Each of these constructors produces a dialog box which, when shown, looks just
like a JFrame, except that it doesn't have the controls on the caption bar necessary
to allow the user to iconify or maximize it. As you'll see, dialogs are usually designed
with a fixed set of controls and are intended to be used only at their natural size. Each
constructor requires a Frame argument. This argument is not, however, used to create a parent-child relationship between the JDialog and the Frame. The
JDialog is an independent window, in the sense that it is not confined to the
boundaries of the Frame as a child component would be; indeed, dialogs are normally placed near to, but not entirely covering, their related Frame. However, a relationship is created between the JDialog and the Frame, which has two effects:

- The JDialog is always in front of its Frame. If you try to move the
  Frame over the JDialog, it appears to move behind it instead.

- If you iconify the Frame, the JDialog is iconified with it; deiconifying the Frame also deiconifies the JDialog.

The existence of these relationships is the main reason why you can't use a Frame
or a JFrame instead of a JDialog: You can't reproduce this behavior with a
JFrame or a Frame.

A JDialog also has a title, which appears on the caption bar; if you use one of
the forms of the constructor that doesn't supply a title, it will be blank unless you
use the setTitle method (inherited from Dialog) to explicitly set it. Two of the
constructors have a boolean parameter that allows you to specify whether the
dialog is modal or nonmodal; if you don't use one of these two constructors, the dialog is nonmodal.

Core Alert

There is a JDialog *method called* setModal *that is supposed to change the modality of a dialog. However, at least in JDK 1.1, this method does not actually work.*

When a modal dialog is displayed, it effectively takes over control of the application, in the sense that the user can't interact with the application's main window or any other windows it might have created. A modal dialog is typically used where you need to have the user respond immediately. If it wouldn't make sense to carry on without the user acknowledging the dialog and, possibly, providing some information, then you should use a modal dialog. By contrast, a nonmodal dialog doesn't stop the user accessing the rest of the application and is typically used to implement toolboxes that remain displayed until the user dismisses them.

Core Note

Some platforms have the concept of system-modal and application-modal dialogs. Java modal dialogs are application-modal. A system-modal dialog not only prevents interaction with the other windows of the application that posted it – it stops the user using any window of any application window other than the dialog itself. Java doesn't support system-modal dialog boxes.

Once you have created a dialog box, you display it using the show method. This method makes the dialog visible and brings it to the front of the window stacking order (it does this even if the dialog is already visible). If the dialog is not modal, the show method then returns. However, in the case of a modal dialog, show blocks until the user dismisses the dialog. You've already seen this behavior in all of the standard dialogs that were shown in the last chapter: they have all stayed posted until the user pressed OK or Cancel (or the equivalent). When the dialog disappears, the method that was used to post it (for example the JColorChooser showDialog method) typically returns a value that represents the choice that the user made from the dialog, or describes whether the dialog was canceled.

Core Note

If you are familiar with JDK 1.0, you may remember that windows, frames, dialogs and indeed all components used the show *and* hide *methods to render themselves visible or invisible. In JDK 1.1, these methods were deprecated for most components in favor of* setVisible, *meaning that the* show *method should no longer be used. The exception to this rule was* Dialog, *which retained a* show *method. The* Dialog show *method has the special behavior for modality that we described above. In fact, for modeless dialogs you can get away with using* setVisible *provided you don't need to force the dialog to the top of the stacking order if it is already on display.*

This mechanism is, of course, very convenient for the programmer because it allows the code that drives a modal dialog to be very simple:

```
// Get a new color from the user
Color selectedColor = JColorChooser.showDialog(f,
                    "Choose a new drawing color", Color.black);

// "selectedColor" is now the color that the user chose.
```

Things are not so simple when you use JDialog directly, however. Here is the definition of its show method:

```
public void show();
```

As you can see, it doesn't accept any arguments and, worse, it doesn't have a return value, so how do you get an answer back from a dialog box that you manage yourself? In fact, since show blocks until the dialog is dismissed, how can you get control to manage the dialog box and dismiss it at all? After all, just placing an OK button on a JDialog won't achieve anything—that button won't make the dialog go away unless you do something to arrange for that to happen.

So how is a dialog dismissed? There are two ways to get rid of a dialog:

1.   Call setVisible(false);
2.   Call dispose();

Both of these cause the dialog to disappear from the screen and, if it was a modal dialog, the show method will return. The difference between them is, however, an important one. If you call dispose, you can't use the dialog again, although the JDialog object continues to exist. If you use setVisible(false), the dialog drops out of view, but you can reuse it by calling show again. Some applications create a new dialog each time they need to use it. These applications would then use dispose to dismiss the dialog. In many cases, however, creating a dialog is an expensive operation. To minimize the overhead of managing frequently-used dialogs, smart applications create them either when they start, or when the dialog is needed for the first time, and then just hide them using setVisible(false). The next time the dialog is required, it can be popped up immediately by calling show.

Core Alert

If you adopt the lazy technique described here, remember to dispose *all of your dialog boxes before your application terminates. On some platforms, dialogs take up resources that aren't released unless you invoke* dispose, *not even if the program ends.*

A Simple Modal Dialog

You now know that either `dispose` or `setVisible(false)` can be used to get rid of a dialog, but how do you get to call either of these methods and how can a value be returned to the caller of `show`? To see exactly how this works, let's look at how to implement a modal dialog box that displays a message and allows the user to respond either `OK` or `Cancel`. This is, of course, a little like the confirm dialog that you saw in the previous chapter. When you've seen the basic principles involved in creating a custom modal dialog, the next step will be to create a better one by using some features of `JOptionPane` that you haven't seen yet.

Our simple dialog is derived from `JDialog`. This dialog allows the programmer to specify the frame that the dialog is associated with, the caption bar title and the message that the dialog displays. The message is displayed in bold font above the `OK` and `Cancel` buttons. Once the dialog is on display, it remains there until one of these buttons is pressed, or the window is closed using the `close` button on its caption bar, at which point the `show` method returns. The programmer can then use the dialog's `getValue` method to retrieve the result, which will be one of `OK_OPTION`, `CANCEL_OPTION` or `CLOSED_OPTION`, as defined by the `JOptionPane` class. You'll find the implementation of this dialog in Listing 8-1, while Figure 8-1 shows what it looks like. You can try this example for yourself with the command:

```
JFCBook.Chapter8.SimpleConfirmDialog
```

Listing 8-1   Creating a basic confirmation dialog with JDialog

```
package JFCBook.Chapter8;

import com.sun.java.swing.*;
import java.awt.*;
import java.awt.event.*;

public class SimpleConfirmDialog extends JDialog {
    public SimpleConfirmDialog(Frame f, String title, String message) {
        super(f, title, true);
        JPanel panel = new JPanel();
        JButton okButton = new JButton("OK");
        cancelButton = new JButton("Cancel");
        panel.add(okButton);
        panel.add(cancelButton);
        this.getContentPane().add(panel, "South");

        JLabel label = new JLabel(message, SwingConstants.CENTER);
        label.setFont(new Font("Dialog", Font.BOLD, 14));
        this.getContentPane().add(label, "Center");
```

continued

```java
    this.pack();

    // Arrange to catch window closing events
    // and also set initial focus
    this.addWindowListener(new WindowAdapter() {
      public void windowClosing(WindowEvent evt) {
        returnValue = JOptionPane.CLOSED_OPTION;
        SimpleConfirmDialog.this.setVisible(false);
      }
      public void windowOpened(WindowEvent evt) {
        cancelButton.requestFocus();
      }
    });

    // Catch the OK button
    okButton.addActionListener(new ActionListener() {
      public void actionPerformed(ActionEvent evt) {
        returnValue = JOptionPane.OK_OPTION;
        SimpleConfirmDialog.this.setVisible(false);
      }
    });

    // Catch the Cancel button
    cancelButton.addActionListener(new ActionListener() {
      public void actionPerformed(ActionEvent evt) {
        returnValue = JOptionPane.CANCEL_OPTION;
        SimpleConfirmDialog.this.setVisible(false);
      }
    });
  }

  // Get the return value
  public int getValue() {
    return returnValue;
  }

  public static void main(String[] args) {
    JFrame f = new JFrame("Test SimpleConfirmDialog");
    f.setSize(300, 100);
    f.addWindowListener(new WindowAdapter() {
      public void windowClosing(WindowEvent evt) {
        System.exit(0);
      }
    });
    f.setVisible(true);

    SimpleConfirmDialog d = new SimpleConfirmDialog(f, "Delete files",
              "This will erase all of your files. Proceed?");
```

```
    d.show();

    System.out.println("Dialog value is " + d.getValue());
  }

  protected int returnValue = JOptionPane.CLOSED_OPTION;
  protected JButton cancelButton;
}
```

The main method demonstrates how this dialog is used: Create an instance and then pop it up using its show method. The show method is inherited from Jdialog and, since the dialog is modal, it will block the calling thread until the dialog is dismissed. Before it does this, however, it arranges for another thread that will handle AWT events to be started. As noted in the last chapter, most dialogs are started from the AWT event thread and, if they simply were blocked, no further events would be processed, resulting in the application appearing to lock up. The creation of a new AWT event thread avoids this possibility.

Figure 8-1   A basic confirmation dialog.

Once the dialog has been displayed, nothing more will happen until the user presses a button or dismisses the dialog, either of which will cause an event to be generated. To catch these events, the dialog box's constructor registered listeners for the ActionEvents that will be delivered from the buttons and the WindowEvent that will occur if the user dismisses the dialog box. Whichever of these happens, the event handler does the same things:

1. It stores a return value in the dialog's returnValue member; each of the event handlers stores a different value, which indicates how the dialog was dismissed.

2. It drops the dialog by calling setVisible(false). This causes the thread blocked in show to resume and the code that originally posted the dialog box will receive control again.

The key to creating your own modal dialog boxes, then, is to use event handlers to manage the user's interaction with the dialog and to allow it to be dismissed when appropriate. If you need to return any values to the code that invoke the dialog, you must save them in the event handlers and provide a way for the invoking thread to retrieve them. Usually, the return value or values are members of the dialog class and member functions, like the `getValue` method in this example, are provided to allow the results to be accessed.

Creating Custom Dialogs with JOptionPane

The last chapter demonstrated how useful `JOptionPane` can be when you want to post messages or obtain input from the user. Up to now, its static convenience methods have been used to create modal dialogs that return the result of the interaction with the user directly to the calling thread. `JOptionPane` also allows you to create you own dialogs. You can use one of its many constructors to create one of several possible panes that can be incorporated into more sophisticated dialogs; here is the complete set of `JOptionPane`'s constructors:

```
JOptionPane()

JOptionPane(Object message)

JOptionPane(Object message, int messageType)

JOptionPane(Object message, int messageType, int optionType)

JOptionPane(Object message, int messageType, int optionType,
          Icon icon)

JOptionPane(Object message, int messageType, int optionType,
          Icon icon, Object[] options)

JOptionPane(Object message, int messageType, int optionType,
          Icon icon, Object[] options, Object initialValue)
```

You should recognize these constructors from the discussion of `JOptionPane` in the last chapter. Using them, you can create a custom dialog equivalent to any of the message, confirm and option dialogs that were shown earlier. The only dialog type that you won't be able to find in this list is the form of the input dialog that provides a combo box or a list box of possible values. The last constructor above looks similar, but in fact the `options` array is used to add a set of buttons to the dialog and the `initialValue` indicates the one that is initially selected. To create a dialog pane with a combo box, you use any of the constructors above and then add the combo box using the `setSelectionValues` and `setInitialSelectionValue` methods.

Creating a Dialog and Returning a Value

When you've created an option pane, you can either use the JOptionPane createDialog method to create a dialog box that contains only the pane, or you can use it as part of your own dialog, providing your own JDialog box and probably other components as well. The choice you make determines the way in which you get results from the dialog, so both variations will be shown in this chapter.

The JOptionPane createDialog method is defined as follows:

```
public JDialog createDialog(Component c, String title);
```

The component you supply as the first argument determines the frame that controls the dialog; if it isn't itself a frame, createDialog searches upwards through the parents and grandparents of this component until it finds one. The title argument becomes the dialog's caption.

When you use the convenience methods like showOptionDialog shown in the last chapter, the dialog is displayed immediately. The createDialog method, however, doesn't do this: you need to invoke show to present the dialog to the user. Before doing that, you might want to use setSelectionValues and setInitialSelectionValue to add an input component such as a combo box or a list box. The code below creates the same dialog box as the showInputDialog convenience method, as shown in the example in Chapter 7:

```
JFrame f = new JFrame("Option Pane Example 1");
JOptionPane pane = new JOptionPane(
   "Which color would you like to use for the background?:",
   JOptionPane.QUESTION_MESSAGE,
   JOptionPane.OK_CANCEL_OPTION,
   null);

pane.setSelectionValues(choices);
pane.setInitialSelectionValue(choices[0]);

JDialog d = pane.createDialog(f, "Background Color Selection");
```

If you look back to the description of the most general form of the showInputDialog method and the example of it that was shown in the last chapter, you'll find that it returned the user's color choice as an object of the type that was supplied to populate the list or combo box, which was a String. This code, however, uses a JDialog, so it will be popped up using the show method, which doesn't return a value. So how is it possible to get the results of the dialog?

A dialog of this sort can return two things: the *return* value and the *input* value. The return value indicates which button was pressed to dismiss the dialog, whereas the input value is the item that was selected from the combo box. Dialogs that don't have a combo box or a list box don't have a meaningful input value. You can retrieve these values using the following methods:

```
public Object getValue();
```

```
public Object getInputValue();
```

Both of these methods return an `Object`, but in a real application, you can't do very much with an `Object`: you need to know its actual type. The object returned by `getInputValue` is always of the same type as the ones that you supplied with `setSelectionValues` because, in fact, it *is* one of those values, but the type of the value returned by `getValue` is not so simple to predict.

If, as in the example above, you allow `JOptionPane` to supply the buttons at the bottom of the dialog, then `getValue` will return an `Integer`, whose value corresponds to the button that was pressed to close the dialog—that is, `JOptionPane.OK_OPTION`, `JOptionPane.CANCEL_OPTION`, and so on. However, if you supply an `options` parameter, what you get is the object that corresponds to the button that was pressed. In the example shown above, in which the `JOptionPane` supplied the buttons based on the `optionType` argument, this is how the return value and the input value would be handled:

```
Integer returnValue = (Integer)d.getValue();
String inputValue = (String)d.getInputValue();
```

Now suppose that you create a `JOptionPane` in which you specify the strings for the buttons explicitly using the `options` argument with the same options as were used in Listing 7-4, as in the following case:

```
JFrame f = new JFrame("Option Pane Example 2");
JOptionPane pane = new JOptionPane(
  "Connection to remote host has failed: retry or abort?",
  JOptionPane.QUESTION_MESSAGE,
  JOptionPane.DEFAULT_OPTION,
  null,
  options, options[0]);

JDialog d = pane.createDialog(f, "Connection Failure");

d.show();

String returnValue = (String)pane.getValue();

System.out.println("Return value is <" + returnValue + ">");
```

This gives us the same dialog box as the code in Listing 7-4 in the last chapter, with buttons labeled `Retry` and `Abort`. Because the buttons have been specified by supplying `String` labels, the return value from `getValue` is itself a `String`. This is actually a particular example of a more general rule as far as option panes are concerned. If you look back to the `JOptionPane` constructors at the start of this section and to the definitions of the convenience routines that were shown at the beginning of the last chapter, you'll see that the options argument, and the initial option, are both defined not as String, but as Object. What happens if you supply something other than a String? Here are the rules:

- If you supply a String, a JButton is created and the string becomes its label.
- If you supply a Component, that Component is mounted on the dialog pane in place of the button.
- If you supply any other Object, it is converted to a String using its toString method and the result becomes the label of a JButton.

When you dismiss the dialog by pressing one of the buttons (or your Component), the value returned by getValue, will, by default, be the same object that created the button or Component. That is, a String returns a String, a Component returns a Component and anything else returns itself, having been represented on a button as a String. But this is not quite the end of the story, because this is what happens *by default*: If you supply a Component, you can arrange for something different to happen and, in fact, you must do something to make anything happen at all.

When you supply something other than a Component, the JOptionPane creates a button with the appropriate label and arranges to catch the ActionEvent that is generated when that button is pressed. When this ActionEvent is caught, the JOptionPane's event handler has to store a return value and arrange for the dialog box to be dismissed, in much the same way as was shown in Listing 8-1. The event handler actually saves the return value using the JOptionPane setValue method, which is defined as follows:

```
public void setValue(Object value);
```

As you might expect, this method takes an Object; the event handler actually supplies the original object from the options list that created the button. Invoking this method on a dialog creating using createDialog causes the dialog to be disposed, not just hidden.

Core Alert

The fact that pressing one of the buttons causes the dialog to be dismissed means that you can't reuse it: A dialog created using createDialog *is a one-shot object, just like the dialogs created using* showOptionDialog *and the other convenience methods.*

Core Note

The mechanism by which the dialog is dismissed is an interesting one. In Listing 8-1, our event handlers set the appropriate return value and then closed the dialog by directly calling `setVisible(false)`. `JOptionPane` *doesn't do it this way. Instead,* `setValue` *stores the new value and then fires a* `PropertyChangeEvent` *on the property name* `value`. *When creating the* `JDialog` *object, the* `createDialog` *method registered a* `PropertyChangeListener` *for this event. When this listener's* `propertyChange` *method is entered, one of the things it does is to hide and dispose the dialog. This apparently circuitous mechanism is essential, because, as you'll see later, you can create* `JOptionPane` *objects and use them in your own dialogs that weren't created by* `createDialog`. *It wouldn't be correct for the* `setValue` *method to directly hide or dispose the dialog, because you may want to perform error checking or carry out further interaction with the user when one of the dialog's buttons is pressed. As a result of this, when you create a custom dialog using a* `JOptionPane`, *you must handle the* `PropertyChangeEvent` *and take appropriate action. An example of this appears later in this chapter.*

The situation is different if you supply a `Component` among your options list. When you do this, the `JOptionPane` does nothing other than add it to the pane. It doesn't arrange for anything to be done when the component is activated to close the dialog—after all, it doesn't know what the component does. It certainly can't register an `ActionListener`, because `Component` doesn't have an `addActionListener` method! It is your responsibility to arrange for the object to invoke `setValue` on the `JOptionPane` to which it has been added when it was activated. Since your object is calling `setValue`, it can pass anything it likes as the value to store and, when the dialog's show method returns, the object returned by `getValue` will be whatever was stored by `setValue`. Obviously, the code that extracts the dialog's return value has to know what type to expect.

Core Note

Since the `options` *list is just an array of* `Objects`, *there is no requirement for them to be all of the same type. If you wish, you can supply a mixture of* `Strings`, `Components`, `Integers` *or anything else. The flip side of this, of course, is that the code that calls* `getValue` *has to be able to cast the returned value to the appropriate type and the correct cast will depend on which option was actually selected.*

Using the JOptionPane Message Parameter

You will also have noticed that, even though the examples that have been shown so far always supply the message part of these dialogs as a `String`, the message argument is actually defined as an `Object`. Like the `options`, if you supply a `Component`, it will just be mounted on the dialog where the message string would have gone—above the buttons and to the right of the icon, if there is one. You can also supply an `Icon`, which will be mounted on a `JLabel` and used. Anything other than a `String`, an `Icon` or a `Component` is converted to a `String` using its `toString` method and the resulting String used as the text on a `JLabel`.

The ability to supply a `Component` allows you to place customized labels incorporating text and an icon, for example, in addition to the standard icon provided by the `JOptionPane` itself. In fact, the message parameter is more powerful than that. In Java, an array is an `Object`, so you can supply an array where an `Object` is required, provided that the code that interprets the `Object` is prepared to accept an array. `JOptionPane` will allow you to supply an array of `Object`s as the message parameter. Each entry in this array can itself be a `String`, an `Icon`, a `Component` or another `Object`. When an array is supplied, the objects in the array are stacked above each other on the `JOptionPane`, with the first entry at the top. You'll see an example of this in the next section.

Core Note

This applies equally to the convenience methods that were shown in the last chapter.

Creating a `JOptionPane` and then using `createDialog` to display it offers you a few more options over how you handle the return value from the dialog but, as you have seen, it is also more complicated than it is when using the static convenience methods, where the type of the return value is more easily remembered. On balance, it's probably only worth creating your own `JOptionPane` if you're going to use it as part of a more complex dialog box.

Using ToolTips to Create an Image Map Dialog

This section will show you how to implement a dialog that allows the user to make a selection by using an image, in effect creating the Java equivalent of an HTML image map. The image map will be a `Component`, which will be used to demonstrate how to use a custom component and a `JOptionPane` together to build a complete dialog. In the course of creating this dialog, you'll also find out more about how to make effective use of tooltips. First, let's look at what the finished product looks like (Figure 8-2).

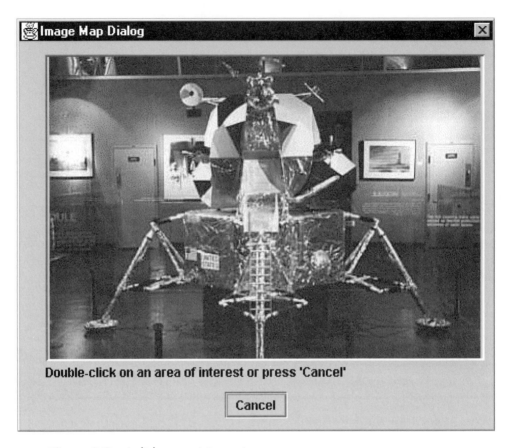

Figure 8-2   A dialog containing an image map.

Figure 8-2 shows a modal dialog derived from JDialog made up of two independent parts. The top half is our image map object, implemented in a class called ImageMap, and the bottom is created using JOptionPane. Before looking at how this dialog is implemented, let's describe how it is supposed to work.

The Image Map Dialog

From the user's point of view, this particular dialog offers the ability to select part of the picture and receive some information about it. This example implements only the dialog itself: it won't supply any actual information, but it does return a string that indicates what the user wanted information about. When the dialog is posted, the user moves the mouse over the image to an area of interest. As the mouse moves, nothing special happens, but if it remains stationary for a short period over a region of the picture for which there is information available, a tooltip appears, giving a brief description of the area under the mouse. You can try this out for yourself using the command:

```
java JFCBook.Chapter8.ImageMapDialogExample
```

The picture used here shows a mock-up of an Apollo Lunar Module in the Visitor Center of the John F. Kennedy Space Center in Florida. If you move the mouse just about anywhere over the Lunar Module and let it rest for a second or so, you'll see a tooltip appear. Move it over the upper part of the vehicle, for example, and you'll probably see the text "Ascent Stage" appear. Move it over one of the triangular windows and the text changes to "LM Pilot Position" or "Commander's Position." Double-click the mouse over an area with a tooltip and the dialog disappears but the content of the tooltip that describes the area clicked on is printed. Finally, if you didn't find the picture very inspiring and just pressed the `Cancel` button, the dialog will be dismissed and "null" will be printed, indicating that nothing was selected.

The implementation of the image map itself will be shown later in this section. First, however, let's concentrate on the dialog itself. In order to see how the dialog works, you need to know what information the dialog requires to create the image map and what feedback the image map provides to the dialog.

The image map class is supplied with the location of an image to load and an array of objects that specify the parts of the picture that are to respond to the mouse and the text that should be displayed when the mouse hovers over any particular area. Each such area is described by an instance of a class called `MapSection` that you'll see later on. To create the image map, the constructor for the dialog class, which is called `ImageMapDialog`, is passed a Uniform Resource Locator (URL) for the image and an array of `MapSection` objects. In addition, it is also given a reference to its controlling frame, the string to use in its title and a boolean flag telling it whether to be modal or not.

The constructor's main job is to lay out the contents of the dialog and to register to receive events from its active parts. Here, the dialog consists of an `ImageMap`, a message and a single button. You already know that you can create the message and the button together as a `JOptionPane`. In fact, the `JOptionPane` can also host the `ImageMap`. As noted earlier, the message parameter supplied to the `JOptionPane` constructor can be an array. In this case, you can arrange for the `ImageMap` to appear above the message by passing as the `JOptionPane`'s message parameter an array consisting of a reference to the `ImageMap` as the first element of the array and the `String` message as the second. The entire dialog, then, is just a `JOptionPane` added to the content pane of a `JDialog`.

To create the `Cancel` button, the form of the `JOptionPane` that allows a list of buttons to be given as options is used:

```
JOptionPane(Object message, int messageType, int optionType,
            Icon icon, Object[] options);
```

In this case, since one button is required, the following, simpler constructor could have been used:

```
JOptionPane(Object message, int messageType, int optionType)
```

Had this been done, JOptionPane.CANCEL_OPTION would have been used as the optionType argument. Visually, this would have achieved the same result as with the more complex constructor. The more complex constructor is used here for no reason other than to demonstrate yet another variant of the versatile JOptionPane component.

The complete ImageMapDialog class constructor implementation is shown, along with that of the rest of the class, in Listing 8-2.

Listing 8-2   A dialog that hosts an image map

```java
package JFCBook.Chapter8;

import com.sun.java.swing.*;
import java.awt.*;
import java.awt.event.*;
import java.beans.*;
import java.net.URL;

public class ImageMapDialog extends JDialog
     implements ActionListener, PropertyChangeListener {
  public ImageMapDialog(Frame f, String title, boolean modal,
        URL imageURL, MapSection[] map) {
    super(f, title, modal);
    ImageMap imageMap = new ImageMap(new ImageIcon(imageURL),
map);
    imageMap.addActionListener(this);

    Object[] message = new Object[] { imageMap,
        "Double-click on an area of interest or press 'Cancel'" };
    optionPane = new JOptionPane(message,
            JOptionPane.PLAIN_MESSAGE,
            JOptionPane.DEFAULT_OPTION,
            null,
            options,
            options[0]);

    optionPane.addPropertyChangeListener(this);

    this.getContentPane().add(optionPane, "Center");
    this.pack();
    this.setResizable(false);
  }

  // This method gets the result of the dialog
```

```
public String getValue() {
  String selectedValue = null;
  String returnValue;

  returnValue = (String)optionPane.getValue();
  if (returnValue.equals(okString)) {
    selectedValue = (String)optionPane.getInputValue();
  }

  return selectedValue;
}

// ActionListener for ImageMap
public void actionPerformed(ActionEvent evt) {
  optionPane.setInputValue(evt.getActionCommand());
  optionPane.setValue(okString);
}

// PropertyChangeListener for JOptionPane
public void propertyChange(PropertyChangeEvent evt) {
  if (evt.getPropertyName().equals(JOptionPane.VALUE_PROPERTY)) {
    this.setVisible(false);
  }
}

protected JOptionPane optionPane;
private static String[] options = { "Cancel" };
private static String okString = "OK";
}
```

You'll notice that this class implements both the `ActionListener` and `PropertyChangeListener` interfaces and that the constructor registers the dialog to receive action events from the `ImageMap` and property change events from the `JOptionPane`. The job of the dialog is to connect together these two different pieces and arrange for them to work together and it does this by handling events from both of them. The `ImageMap` generates an `ActionEvent` when the user double-clicks on an area for which it has associated text; the `ActionEvent` that is delivered has the text that appears in the tooltip as its action command. A double click indicates that the user has made a selection and that the dialog should now be dismissed. Similarly, the dialog should be dropped if the user presses the `Cancel` button.

As you saw in the previous section, the `JOptionPane` handles the `Cancel` button itself: When it is pressed, the event is caught and causes the `JOptionPane`'s `setValue` method to be invoked. When you supply your own options using `Strings`, as is the case here, the value set with `setValue` is a `String` and, in this case, it will be `Cancel`, the label of the button. As well as storing this value, setValue also generates a `PropertyChangeEvent`, which is why the `ImageMapDialog` was registered to receive these events. When this event occurs, the event handler (see `propertyChange` in Listing 8-2) drops the dialog by calling `setVisible`(false).

If the user double-clicked on a part of the image with associated text, the `ActionEvent` from `ImageMap` will be processed in the `actionPerformed` method of `ImageMapDialog`, because it was registered as an `ActionListener`. Again, this method needs to cause the dialog to be dismissed, but it also needs to arrange for the text returned from the image map to be available to the code that invoked the dialog.

As you know, a modal dialog is invoked using the `show` method, which blocks until the dialog has completed but doesn't return a value. Instead, the dialog usually supplies a method (or methods) to allow the results of the dialog to be retrieved. In the case of `ImageMapDialog`, a `getValue` method is provided, which will return the text provided by the image map, or `null` if the `Cancel` button was pressed.

Core Note

Do not confuse the `getValue` *method provided by* `ImageMapDialog` *with the* `getValue` *method of* `JOptionPane`. *In this example, the* `JOptionPane` *is encapsulated inside the* `ImageMapDialog` *and is not accessible to users of the latter. The job of* `ImageMapDialog` *is to extract the information stored inside the* `JOptionPane` *when its own* `getValue` *method is called.*

How will `getValue` get this information? Remember that `getValue` will be called some time after the dialog has been dismissed and the only information it can work with is whatever was stored by whichever event handler dismissed the dialog. One possibility is to create a `String` member of `ImageMapDialog` in which the `String` from the `ActionEvent` is saved when the image is double-clicked. If the `Cancel` button were pressed, this member would be set to `null`. That is a perfectly acceptable solution—no matter how the dialog was dismissed, the text will be held in this `ImageMapDialog` member. This example, however, uses a slightly different method, which illustrates the use that can be made of mechanisms provided by `JOptionPane`.

You've already seen that the `Cancel` button causes the `JOptionPane` setValue method to be called, with `Cancel` as its argument. When the dialog completes, you can determine that this happened by calling the `JOptionPane` getValue method. As you know, this returns an `Object`, but if this object is cast to a `String`, you can tell that the `Cancel` button was pressed by looking at the value. In order to be able to distinguish the `Cancel` button in this way, you have to arrange for the action taken when the user double-clicks the image to store a different value. As you can see by looking at the `actionPerformed` method, in this case setValue is called with the argument OK. This has two important effects. First, because the value being passed when both the Cancel button is pressed and the image is double-clicked is of type String, it is always safe when calling the JOptionPane getValue method to cast the returned object to String. Had an Integer been used instead when the image was double-clicked, it would have made the ImageMapDialog's getValue method harder to implement. The second effect of calling the JOptionPane setValue method when the image is double-clicked, and the more important one from the point of view of this example, is that, just like the one performed internally by JOptionPane when the Cancel button was pressed, it causes a PropertyChangeEvent to be generated. This event is received by the same propertyChange method, which again dismisses the dialog by making it invisible.

Core Note

The propertyChange *method checks that the event it has received is actually for a change in the "value" property of the* JOptionPane *before dismissing the dialog. This is very important, because* JComponents *have many properties that can generate property change events and it is not safe to assume that the only event you will receive is the one you are interested in.*

So, when the dialog is dismissed using the Cancel button, the JOptionPane getValue method returns Cancel and when the image was double-clicked it returns OK. The user of ImageMapDialog needs to see a return value of null in the first case and the String associated with the area of the image map that was clicked in the second. The fact that the JOptionPane getValue method returns different values in these two cases allows the ImageMapDialog getValue method to distinguish them and return null in the first case, but how will it get the text from the image map? It can only get this if it was stored somewhere within the dialog before it was dismissed.

Where should this text be stored? Again, it could be stored in a private member within ImageMapDialog, but this would require another method to be implemented to retrieve its value when getValue returns OK. Another possibility is to backtrack on the design just described and save the text itself instead of the constant string OK when the image is double-clicked. This would allow the text to be retrieved using the JOptionPane getValue method. This is a much better solution—the ImageMapDialog getValue method would then look something like this:

```
String returnValue = (String)optionPane.getValue();
return returnValue.equals("Cancel") ? null : returnValue;
```

Again, however, this example forsakes this simple solution in favor of a slightly more complex one that is more general. Instead of either of these possibilities, the text from the image map is saved in the JOptionPane using its setInputValue method and is later extricated by getValue using getInputValue. This solution makes it easier to change the dialog to include, for example, a combo box that contains all the pieces of text that the image map could generate. If the user made a choice from the combo box, the JOptionPane would save that choice using setInputValue, exactly as has been done in this case, and the ImageMapDialog getValue method could continue to use getInputValue to retrieve the text whether it came from the image or the combo box.

Implementing the Image Map

That's all there is to the ImageMapDialog class. Now let's look at the image map itself. Here, the problem is to create a component that can render a graphic and respond to the mouse by generating a tooltip whose content depends on where the mouse is. Fortunately, all of this functionality is provided by Swing: All that is necessary is to exploit it in the right way.

First, let's address the issue of rendering the image. This is very straightforward – you've already seen (Chapter 2) that the JLabel class allows you to draw an image onto its surface if you supply it in the form of an ImageIcon. To give a pleasing effect, a border around the outside of the image, use one of the borders that you'll see later in this section. Since any JComponent can render a border, it is very easy to arrange for the JLabel to wrap one around the image.

Having arranged for the image to be drawn on the label, the next problem is to show tooltips at appropriate times. Again, JComponent provides the means for doing this. To see how to make this work, let's look at how the tooltip mechanism itself works. Recall from Chapter 1 and Chapter 6 that you can associate a fixed tooltip with a JComponent by using its setToolTipText method, for example:

```
JLabel label = new JLabel(icon);
label.setToolTipText("This is an Apollo Lunar Module");
```

All of the tooltips in the application are managed by the ToolTipManager. When you set a tooltip for a JComponent, the setToolTipText method declares the JComponent to the ToolTipManager, which registers itself to receive mouse events from it. When the mouse enters any of the JComponents it is managing, it invokes its getToolTipText method, which is defined as follows:

```
public String getToolTipText(MouseEvent evt);
```

Since this method gets a MouseEvent, if you override it, you can return a string that depends on the position of the mouse. Once the mouse has entered a component, the ToolTipManager registers to receive MouseMotionEvents. As the mouse tracks over the JComponent, the ToolTipManager continues to call the getToolTipText method.

When the mouse has been inside the component for a short time (by default this is 500 ms, but it can be changed using the ToolTipManager setInitialDelay method), the tooltip is displayed in a window that floats over the component, near the mouse pointer. This tip stays posted until the mouse leaves the component or until it remains stationary for a relatively long period (4 seconds by default). As long as the mouse continues to move inside the boundary of the component, the getToolTipText method is called every time the mouse moves. If it returns the same text as is currently displayed, the tooltip window is left unchanged: It doesn't track the mouse pointer. If the text changes, the old window is hidden and a new one is posted at the mouse's new location. Finally, if getToolTipText returns null, the tooltip is dismissed completely.

You can control many aspects of the global behavior of tooltips using the ToolTipManager object. There is only one of these objects and you can get a reference to it using the static method ToolTipManager.sharedInstance. The most important methods of this class are shown in Table 8-1.

Table 8-1   ToolTipManager methods

Method	Effect
public void setEnabled(boolean cond);	Determines whether tooltips are displayed. If you set this to false, no tooltips will appear.
public void setInitialDelay(int delay);	The delay in milliseconds before which a tooltip will appear after the mouse enters a component. By default, ToolTipManager waits _ second before showing a tooltip. It won't display one at all if the mouse leaves the component before this initial time elapses.
public void setDismissDelay(int delay);	The time for which the tooltip remains visible. Once the tooltip is displayed, it will remain on view for this interval and then disappear. However, this interval is extended if the mouse moves. This delay is 4 seconds by default.
public void setReshowDelay(int delay);	The time within which a tooltip will be reshown at once if the mouse re-enters a component that was showing a tooltip when it left. Initially, this is set to 500 milliseconds, so that if the mouse reenters less than _ second after leaving, the usual _ second initial delay won't apply.

To set the amount of time for which a tooltip remains visible to 3 seconds instead of 4, for example, use the following:

```
ToolTipManager.sharedInstance().setDismissDelay(3000);
```

When you call setToolTipText, the string you supply is stored as a property of the JComponent; the default implementation of getToolTipText simply reads and returns this property, so you get a constant tool tip that doesn't follow the mouse. To create an image map, you need to override the getToolTipText method and check the mouse position against the set of areas defined by the image map as having associated text. If the mouse is inside one of these areas, the associated text is returned from getToolTipText. If it is not, null is returned and the tooltip window vanishes.

Listing 8-3 shows the implementation of the ImageMap class, which is derived from JLabel. Because JLabel is a JComponent, it is capable of showing tooltips. JLabel is subclassed rather than being used directly so that its getToolTipText method can be overridden. The constructor creates the image map's user interface by creating an ImageIcon with the supplied image and surrounding it with a border to improve the component's overall appearance. It also saves the array of MapSection objects for later use and remembers the size of the border, which it obtains from the border's getBorderInsets method. Finally, it calls setToolTipText to set an empty tooltip string. This step is necessary so that the ToolTipManager registers to receive the mouse events that will eventually cause it to begin calling the ImageMap's getToolTipText method.

Listing 8-3   An image map class

```
package JFCBook.Chapter8;

import com.sun.java.swing.*;
import com.sun.java.swing.border.*;
import java.awt.*;
import java.awt.event.*;

public class ImageMap extends JLabel implements MouseListener {
  public ImageMap(Icon image, MapSection[] map) {
    super(image);

    this.map = map;

    Border border = BorderFactory.createLoweredBevelBorder();
    this.setBorder(border);
    this.setToolTipText("");

    Insets insets = border.getBorderInsets(this);
    xoffset = insets.left;
    yoffset = insets.top;;
  }

  public String getToolTipText(MouseEvent evt) {
```

```
      Point pt = new Point(evt.getX() - xoffset, evt.getY() - yoffset);
      for (int i = 0; i < map.length; i++) {
        if (map[i].area.contains(pt)) {
          return map[i].text;
        }
      }
      return null;
    }

    public void addActionListener(ActionListener l) {
      this.l = l;
      this.addMouseListener(this);
    }

    public void removeActionListener(ActionListener l) {
      if (this.l == l) {
        this.l = null;
        this.removeMouseListener(this);
      }
    }

    // Mouse Listener interface
    public void mouseClicked(MouseEvent evt) {
      if (evt.getClickCount() == 2) {
        String text = getToolTipText(evt);
        if (text != null) {
          l.actionPerformed(new ActionEvent(this,
              ActionEvent.ACTION_PERFORMED, text));
        }
      }
    }

    public void mouseEntered(MouseEvent evt) {
    }

    public void mouseExited(MouseEvent evt) {
    }

    public void mousePressed(MouseEvent evt) {
    }

    public void mouseReleased(MouseEvent evt) {
    }

    protected MapSection[] map;
    protected int xoffset;
    protected int yoffset;
    protected ActionListener l;
}
```

As the mouse tracks over the ImageMap, its getToolTipText method is called. This method extracts the mouse position from the accompanying MouseEvent and adjusts it to account for the size of the border. This is essential, because the mouse position is reported relative to the top-left corner of the label, which is outside the border, but the map data contains coordinates measured relative to the image itself, which is inside the border. The mouse position, offset by the border insets, is used to search the array of MapSection objects passed to the constructor. MapSection is a trivial class, defined like this:

```
public class MapSection {
  public MapSection(Polygon area, String text) {
    this.area = area;
    this.text = text;
  }

  public String text;
  public Polygon area;
}
```

To find out whether or not the mouse is inside an area described by a MapSection object, you just need to use the Polygon's contains method, passing it the mouse position as the argument. If the mouse is inside one of these areas, the corresponding text is used as the return value of getToolTipText; if it isn't, null is returned and no tooltip will be displayed. In the case of the Apollo Lunar Module picture, many of the areas overlap each other. For example, both windows have their own tooltips, as does the entire ascent stage. To make sure that the correct tooltip is returned, you need to organize the MapSection objects so that the smaller areas are found before the larger ones. In this case the MapSection objects for the windows appear before the enclosing one for the ascent stage.

The other thing the ImageMap must do is respond to double clicks with the mouse. The ImageMap class allows a single object to register as an ActionListener; this could be generalized to allow more than one listener, but one listener suffices for this example. If an ActionListener is registered, the ImageMap starts listening to its own mouse events. When the user clicks the mouse, the ImageIcon's mouseClicked method will be invoked. If the MouseEvent represents a double click, the mouse position is extracted and passed to getToolTipText to locate the tooltip for the mouse's location. If there is one, an ActionEvent is created and posted to the ActionListener. This event will show the ImageMap as its source and has the tooltip text as its action command.

Custom Dialogs with JFileChooser

In the last chapter some time was spent looking at the JFileChooser class and using its showDialog method to explore its features. In this section, you'll see how you can use JFileChooser in a custom dialog by creating a useful dialog that allows you to preview text files. A JFileChooser will be used to give a view of the file system; the user will be able to select a file by clicking on it and, if it is a file (not a directory) and it turns out to be readable, a preview of the first 20 lines of the file will appear in a small window alongside the directory listing. Finally, by double-clicking the file or pressing the Open button, the user can choose the file as the result of the dialog. The finished dialog box is shown in the Figure 8-3.

Core Alert

The JFileChooser *component described in this section is in the* com.sun.java.swing.preview *package, which means that its API is not frozen and may change. While the description of* JFileChooser *that follows is correct at the time of writing, it is possible that some of the API will have changed by the time you need to use it. It is recommended that you refer to the* JFileChooser *documentation for the latest information.*

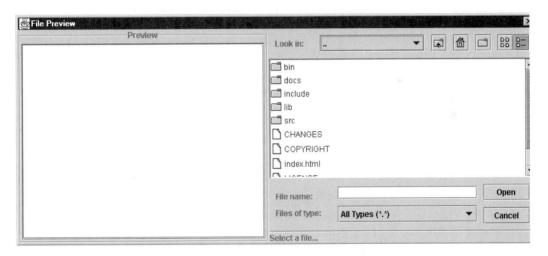

Figure 8-3   A file preview dialog.

Laying out the Dialog

In this dialog, the left-hand side is a JTextArea component, which provides an easy way to display the contents of the file. Since we don't want the user to be able to change the file contents, the text area is made noneditable. Surrounding the text area is another Swing border. This one is a *titled border*, which allows you to choose the border style (here an *etched border* is being used) and overlays onto it a text string. As you'll see later in this chapter, you can control both the font and location of the border title. Borders are very useful in breaking up the content of dialog boxes into discrete areas. You can achieve a similar effect with the JSeparator component, which simply draws a horizontal or vertical line; JSeparator is actually the object added to menus by the JMenu addSeparator method. Finally, the majority of the right side of the dialog is occupied by the JFileChooser. The code that is used to create this dialog is shown in Listing 8-4.

Listing 8-4   A file content previewer

```
package JFCBook.Chapter8;

import com.sun.java.swing.*;
import com.sun.java.swing.border.*;
import com.sun.java.swing.preview.*;
import java.awt.*;
import java.awt.event.*;
import java.io.*;

public class FilePreviewDialog extends JDialog
          implements ActionListener {
  public FilePreviewDialog(Frame f, String title) {
    this(f, title, null);
  }

  public FilePreviewDialog(Frame f, String title, String dir) {
    super(f, title, true);       // Modal dialog
    chooser = new JFileChooser(dir);
    pane = chooser.getDirectoryPane();
    pane.addActionListener(this);

    chooser.setOkayCommand(OPEN);
    pane.setActionCommand(ACTION);
    pane.setDoubleClickCommand(DOUBLE);
    pane.setDoubleClickContainerCommand(CONTAINER);

    textArea = new JTextArea(LINES, COLUMNS);
    textArea.setEditable(false);
    textArea.setFont(new Font("Dialog", Font.BOLD, 10));

    JPanel controlPanel = new JPanel();
    controlPanel.setLayout(new BorderLayout());
    controlPanel.add(chooser, "Center");
    JPanel commentPanel = new JPanel();
    commentPanel.setLayout(new BorderLayout());
    commentArea = new JLabel("Select a file...", SwingConstants.LEFT);
    commentPanel.add(new JSeparator(), "North");
    commentPanel.add(commentArea, "South");
    controlPanel.add(commentPanel, "South");

    JPanel textPanel = new JPanel();
    textPanel.setLayout(new BorderLayout());
```

```java
    textPanel.add(new JScrollPane(textArea), "Center");
    textPanel.setBorder(BorderFactory.createTitledBorder(BorderFactory.createEtchedBorder(),
                   "Preview", TitledBorder.CENTER,
                   TitledBorder.TOP));
    this.getContentPane().add(controlPanel, "Center");
    this.getContentPane().add(textPanel, "West");
    this.pack();

    this.addWindowListener(new WindowAdapter() {
      public void windowClosing(WindowEvent evt) {
        // Dismiss the dialog
        FilePreviewDialog.this.setVisible(false);
      }
    });
  }

  // Get the name of the selected file, or null if none selected
  public String getFileName() {
    return fileName;
  }

  // Handle events from the JFileChooser
  public void actionPerformed(ActionEvent evt) {
    File selectedFile = chooser.getSelectedFile();
    if (selectedFile == null) {
      return;
    }

    String command = evt.getActionCommand();
    if (command.equals(ACTION)) {
      // Single click on something
      if (selectedFile.isFile() && selectedFile.canRead()) {
        // It's a file: show the preview
        previewFile(selectedFile);
        commentArea.setText("Double-click to select this file.");
      } else {
        // Clear text area if not a readable file
        textArea.setText("");
        if (selectedFile.isFile() == false) {
          commentArea.setText("Not a file.");
        } else {
          commentArea.setText("File is not readable.");
        }
      }
    } else if (command.equals(DOUBLE) || command.equals(OPEN)) {
      // Double click on a file
      if (selectedFile.isFile() && selectedFile.canRead()) {
        // Double-clicked a file: choose it and dismiss
        fileName = selectedFile.getPath();
        setVisible(false);
      }
    } else if (command.equals(CONTAINER)) {
```

continued

```java
        // Double click on a container
        textArea.setText("");
        commentArea.setText("Select a file...");
      }
    }

    protected void previewFile(File f) {
      textArea.setText("");
      try {
        BufferedReader br = new BufferedReader(new FileReader(f));
        for (int i = 0; i < LINES; i++) {
          String s = br.readLine();
          if (s == null) {
            break;
          }
          textArea.append(s);
          textArea.append("\n");
        }
        br.close();
      } catch (Throwable t) {
        textArea.setText("");
        commentArea.setText("Failed to read file contents.");
      }
    }

    public static void main(String[] args) {
      String dir = null;
      if (args.length > 0) {
        dir = args[0];
      }

      JFrame f = new JFrame();
      FilePreviewDialog d = new FilePreviewDialog(f, "File Preview", dir);
      d.show();
      d.dispose();
      System.out.println("Selected file is " + d.getFileName());
      System.exit(0);
    }

    protected JFileChooser chooser;
    protected JDirectoryPane pane;
    protected JTextArea textArea;
    protected JLabel commentArea;
    protected String fileName = null;
    protected static final int LINES = 20;
    protected static final int COLUMNS = 40;
    protected static final String OPEN = "OPEN";
    protected static final String ACTION = "ACTION";
    protected static final String DOUBLE = "DOUBLE";
    protected static final String CONTAINER = "CONTAINER";
}
```

Most of the constructor should be self-explanatory. Several panels are used to create the required layout effect. All of the panels are assigned a `BorderLayout` instead of their natural `FlowLayout`, so that the components within the panels and the panels mounted on other panels can be precisely placed and the distribution of space to each component can be controlled as required. The component in the center position grows as necessary to fit in with everything else in the same container. For example, the `JFileChooser` will be expanded horizontally to span the space available to it and, because a `BorderLayout` is used to manage the dialog's content pane, the `JFileChooser`'s height is effectively controlled by the height of the `JTextArea`, which resides on another panel to its left. Similarly, the width of the `JLabel` beneath the `JFileChooser` is always the same as that of the `JFileChooser` and grows as the dialog expands horizontally. This label is used to display informational messages.

Core Alert

You'll notice that there is a `JSeparator` *in the North position of the panel on which the* `JLabel` *resides. Placing it in this position means that it gets the height that it asks for and is stretched horizontally to the full width of the container. As you can see, the result is a horizontal line. However* `JSeparator` *can also be used to create a vertical separator. Here's its only constructor:*

```
public JSeparator();
```

How does it know whether you want a horizontal or a vertical line? When you create it, it doesn't know how it should be oriented, and neither does it care. It only matters when the time comes to render itself, in its `paint` *method, at which time its height and width are fixed. All that it then does is draw a grooved rectangle that fits around the inside of the space that it's been allocated. If this space is wider than it is tall, you get the effect of a horizontal line. However, you need to be careful when using* `JSeparator`, *because it assumes that the space it is allocated is narrow in one direction or the other. When asked its preferred size, it requests a width of 0 and height 2, but its final allocation depends on the layout manager. If, for example, you placed a* `JSeparator` *in an area that could expand both horizontally and vertically as its container changed size, then your separator would grow into a rectangle with a grooved border instead of a line. For this reason, it is usual to use* `JSeparator` *with a* `BorderLayout`, *in any position other than the Center.*

Handling Events from the JFileChooser

Once the dialog has been created, nothing happens until the user clicks on something in the `JFileChooser`. To see what should then happen, let's walk through how you might expect this dialog to be used. The dialog would be created by an application that makes some use of text files, perhaps an editor of some sort. When it's created, it is given the name of the directory that it should initially display the contents of. This directory name is, of course, passed directly to the JFileChooser.

When the dialog is displayed, the intention is that the user should be able to click once on a plain file to have its content displayed in the JTextArea. Double-clicking on a file would have the same effect as pressing the JFileChooser OK button – the file becomes selected as the result of the dialog, which is then dismissed. Clicking once on a directory has no effect (other than highlighting it), while clicking twice makes the JFileChooser descend into it, updating its display accordingly. If the user clicks on a file that cannot be read, or on some object that is not a file, a message will appear at the bottom right of the dialog explaining why the file preview does not appear. If a file is successfully previewed, however, a message instructing the user to double-click to select it is displayed.

The controlling application displays this dialog using the blocking show method. When the dialog is dismissed, the application must have a way to extract the name of the file that the user chose. In this case, a method called getFileName is supplied that returns the selected file's full path name, or null if the dialog was canceled using the Cancel button or by closing its window.

In order to provide the functionality just described, it is necessary to detect the user's actions in the JFileChooser. Here is what we need to be able to do:

- When the user highlights something with a single mouse click, its name needs to be extracted and checked to see whether it is a readable file. If it is not a file, or it cannot be read, the text area should be cleared. Either way, an appropriate message should be written to the message area at the bottom right of the dialog.

- If the user double-clicks on a directory, the JFileChooser will automatically update its view and descend into that directory, but it still is necessary for us to get control in order to clear the file preview area and display a different message.

- Finally, if the user double-clicks a file that is readable, the file's name needs to be stored where it can later be retrieved by the getFileName method and the dialog should be dismissed. The same thing needs to happen if the Open button is pressed.

Table 7-1 in the last chapter listed the action events that JDirectoryPane generates. If you look back to that table, you'll see that these events correspond to the items just listed. Therefore, in order to be able to provide this functionality, the dialog is registered as an ActionListener of the JDirectoryPane.

The action command that is delivered with each ActionEvent allows you to determine exactly what caused the event. To make the code easier to read, instead of using the default action commands associated with the JDirectoryPane, one of which is a null string (see Table 7-1), replacement action commands are set using the `setActionCommand`, `setDoubleClickCommand` and `setDoubleClickContainer` methods. When an `ActionEvent` is received from the `JDirectoryPane`, the action that is taken is based on which of these preset strings is in the `actionCommand` field. Listing 8-5 shows the dialog's `actionPerformed` method.

Listing 8-5 Handling buttons in the file preview dialog

```
// Handle events from the JFileChooser
public void actionPerformed(ActionEvent evt) {
  File selectedFile = chooser.getSelectedFile();
  if (selectedFile == null) {
    return;
  }

  String command = evt.getActionCommand();
  if (command.equals(ACTION)) {
    // Single click on something
    if (selectedFile.isFile() && selectedFile.canRead()) {
      // It's a file: show the preview
      previewFile(selectedFile);
      commentArea.setText("Double-click to select this file.");
    } else {
      // Clear text area if not a readable file
      textArea.setText("");
      if (selectedFile.isFile() == false) {
        commentArea.setText("Not a file.");
      } else {
        commentArea.setText("File is not readable.");
      }
    }
  } else if (command.equals(DOUBLE) || command.equals(OPEN)) {
    // Double click on a file
    if (selectedFile.isFile() && selectedFile.canRead()) {
      // Double-clicked a file: choose it and dismiss
      fileName = selectedFile.getPath();
      setVisible(false);
    }
  } else if (command.equals(CONTAINER)) {
    // Double click on a container
    textArea.setText("");
    commentArea.setText("Select a file...");
  }
}
```

First, the `getSelectedFile` method is used to get a `TypedFile` object for the file or directory that the user has clicked or double-clicked. Since `TypedFile` is a subclass of `java.io.File`, its `isFile` and `canRead` methods can be used to find out what we want to know about the selected object. The first thing to do is to work out what type of event has occurred, by looking at the event's `actionCommand` field. If the user has just clicked on an object, this field will be set to the value passed to the `setActionCommand` method. Here, the code checks whether the user has selected a readable file and, if so, the file's content is read into the preview area and a suitable message written to the `JLabel`. The code used to show the file content in the preview area is very simple—you can find it in the `previewFile` method in Listing 8-4. If the object is not a file or it is not readable, the file preview area is cleared and a message explaining why the file could not be previewed is displayed.

Core Note

You'll see in the next chapter that the Swing text components have methods that allow you to initialize them from the content of a file. This example, however, uses the brute force method!

Double-clicking a file is a request to select it as the result of the dialog. In this case, the action command will be set to the value supplied to `setDoubleClickCommand`. Another way to reach this state is to press the Open button, which can also be detected by looked at the action command. Again, we check that this is a readable file and, if it is, the name of the selected file is saved in the dialog's `fileName` field, then the dialog is dismissed. This causes the `show` method to return control to the application, which can use the `getFileName` method to extract the selected file's name.

The last case to deal with is a double-click on a container—that is, on a directory. Here, the `JFileChooser` will update its display and the event-handling code only has to clear the preview area and write a new message to the label.

Using Nonmodal Dialogs

All the dialogs that you have seen so far have been modal. These are what the user usually thinks of as a dialog: They pop up from a menu, toolbar or other button, stay around until a choice has been made, then go away. From the programming point of view, modal dialogs are usually very simple to handle because the application loses control until the `show` method returns, at which point the result of the dialog is immediately available. There is no need to arrange for event handlers and synchronization between the dialog and the application: This is all left to the implementor of the dialog and you've seen how this is handled in the last two examples. By contrast, nonmodal dialogs usually stay open until the user explicitly dismisses them.

The other major difference between modal and nonmodal dialogs is, of course, that non-modal dialogs don't lock out the rest of the application (or the system) while they're on display. For this reason, the most common use of a nonmodal dialog is as a toolbox. If you've ever used a graphics or photo editor program, you'll be very familiar with the nonmodal dialogs that float over the main window with drawing and coloring tools that you can choose from at any time and then use in the application.

Having seen how to build modal dialogs, you don't need to learn anything new to create a nonmodal one. To make a dialog nonmodal, you simply pass `false` as the third argument to the `JDialog` constructor. With a nonmodal dialog, the `show` method doesn't block, so the application continues to execute in parallel with the dialog. This raises the issue of how to get results from the dialog to the application. You can still have a `get` method that the dialog exports to allow any changed values to be extracted, but how would the application know that it was worth using it?

The usual solution to issues like this is to use an event to notify the dialog's users that something has changed in its state. The Swing classes make extensive use of the concept of bound properties that was introduced in JDK 1.1 for JavaBeans. You've already seen many examples of this, among them the graphics drawing application in Chapter 4, "Graphics, Text Handling, and Printing." Essentially, the idea is that a component declares a set of properties, whose names are part of the component's public interface. Interested parties can register to receive `PropertyChangeEvents` whenever any of these properties changes. The `PropertyChangeEvent` will contain the name of the affected property and its old and new values, both defined as `Object`. To make use of these events you do, of course, need to know the actual type of each property. In terms of nonmodal dialogs, it makes sense to adopt one of two approaches:

- If the dialog only allows the user to change a small number of values and these values might often be changed independently of each other, define each of them as a bound property and fire a `PropertyChangeEvent` as each of them changes.

- If the dialog has many configurable values, either group them together and define a property for each group, or define a single property that covers everything that the dialog can change. An event would be generated for each group, or for the whole dialog, when any value in the group or in the whole dialog changed. Since each event would report the change of one value among many, or possibly of several values, and the event only allows one changed value to be included, the old and new values in the event would normally be passed as `null`, which requires the listener to get the new values by querying the dialog box using some kind of `get` method.

Since this property-based mechanism is used extensively in the Swing components themselves, support for it has been included in the `JComponent` class in the form of the following methods:

- `addPropertyChangeListener`. Registers a listener to receive property change events from the component

- `removePropertyChangeListener`. Reverses the registration performed by the previous method

- `firePropertyChange`. Generates a `PropertyChangeEvent` and posts it to all registered listeners. There are several overloaded forms that allow you to use primitives and objects of different types as the old and new values of the property. The most general form of this method is `firePropertyChange(String, Object, Object)`.

Before we show an example of a nonmodal dialog that uses property events to communicate changes, we need to explain one small problem. The methods listed above are defined in the `JComponent` class, so they are available to any object derived from `JComponent`. Unfortunately, `JDialog` is derived not from `JComponent`, but from `Dialog`, so `JDialog` does not inherit any of these methods. If you want to use this mechanism, then, it appears that you need to implement it yourself. In the example we'll look at below, we show you how to do this. Using properties in this way is worth the small amount of extra work you have to do, because it makes your dialog consistent with other components and it is, of course, essential if you want your dialog to be JavaBeans compatible.

A Color Toolbox as a Nonmodal Dialog

Now let's look at an example. Our nonmodal dialog is going to be a toolbox that contains twelve buttons, each with an associated color. The user selects a color by pressing the appropriate button and the dialog's bound property COLOR_PROPERTY changes to the newly selected color. You could use such a toolbox with the graphics program from Chapter 4, for example, instead of the toolbar that was added to it in Chapter 6, "Menus and Toolbars." A simple program that just draws random lines continuously on a frame will be used to demonstrate this dialog and the property change mechanism that it uses. The lines will be drawn in the current drawing color and the frame will register to receive property change events from the dialog. If the property being changed is COLOR_PROPERTY, the new color will be extracted from the event and the frame will start drawing in that color. Figure 8-4 shows how the program looks when it is running.

Before looking at the dialog itself, let's see how the test program uses it (Listing 8-6).

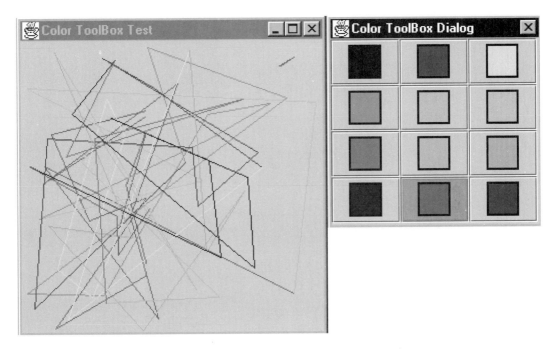

Figure 8-4 A color toolbox.

Listing 8-6 A program that uses a dialog containing color selection buttons

```
package JFCBook.Chapter8;

import com.sun.java.swing.*;
import java.awt.*;
import java.awt.event.*;
import java.beans.*;

public class ColorToolBoxTest extends JFrame implements
          PropertyChangeListener {
  public ColorToolBoxTest(String title) {
    super(title);
  }

  // This method draws random lines
```

continued

```java
public void draw(JPanel p) {
  int lastX = 0;
  int lastY = 0;
  Graphics g = p.getGraphics();

  try {
    for (;;) {
      Thread.sleep(250);
      Dimension d = p.getSize();

      int nextX = (int)(Math.random() * d.width);
      int nextY = (int)(Math.random() * d.height);
      g.setColor(drawingColor);
      g.drawLine(lastX, lastY, nextX, nextY);
      lastX = nextX;
      lastY = nextY;
    }
  } catch (Throwable t) {
  }
}

// PropertyChangeListener interface
public void propertyChange(PropertyChangeEvent evt) {
  if (evt.getPropertyName().equals(ColorToolBoxDialog.COLOR_PROPERTY)) {
    drawingColor = (Color)evt.getNewValue();
  }
}

public static void main(String[] args) {
  ColorToolBoxTest f = new ColorToolBoxTest("Color ToolBox Test");
  JPanel p = new JPanel();
  f.getContentPane().add(p);

  final ColorToolBoxDialog toolBox = new ColorToolBoxDialog(f,
                "Color ToolBox Dialog");
  toolBox.addPropertyChangeListener(f);

  f.setSize(300, 300);
  f.addWindowListener(new WindowAdapter() {
    public void windowClosing(WindowEvent evt) {
      toolBox.dispose();
      System.exit(0);
    }
  });
```

```
    f.setVisible(true);

    // Display the dialog box to the right of the frame
    Point pt = f.getLocationOnScreen();
    toolBox.setLocation(pt.x + f.getSize().width, pt.y);
    toolBox.show(); // Not modal, so returns...

    // Start drawing
    f.draw(p);

    System.exit(0);
}

// The current drawing color
protected static Color drawingColor = Color.black;
}
```

The line drawing is done by an infinite loop in the `draw` method; as you can see, before each `drawLine` call, it selects the current drawing color into the `Graphics` context. The dialog itself is created in the `main` method and the frame object is registered to receive `PropertyChangeEvents` from it, then the dialog is placed to the right of the frame by getting the frame's location relative to the screen and adding its width. When a dialog is created, it is associated with a frame but, as has already been said, this is not a parent-child relationship: The dialog is a top-level window, so its coordinates are specified relative to the screen itself, not to the frame. Like modal dialogs, non-modal dialogs disappear when their associated frame is iconized and are restored when the frame is opened again.

The frame's `propertyChange` method is very simple: It looks at the property name and, if the changed property is `COLOR_PROPERTY`, it gets the new color from the event and uses it to change its own current drawing color. The `propertyChange` event will almost certainly be received in a different thread from the one in which the drawing is being performed, so there is a possibility that the event thread will update the drawing color as the main thread is reading it. Because only one value is involved here, this is not a problem: Either the drawing thread gets the old color on this pass or it gets the new one. Either way, it will get the new color on the next cycle of its loop. This is a special case, however. If the processing of a property change event would involve updating more than one item of state that could be used by other code in the application at the same time, it would be necessary to synchronize access so that the event handler could consistently update the object's state without conflicting with the rest of the application. Now let's look at the dialog box itself, the code for which is shown in Listing 8-7.

Listing 8-7   A dialog containing color selection buttons

```java
package JFCBook.Chapter8;

import com.sun.java.swing.*;
import java.awt.*;
import java.awt.event.*;
import java.beans.*;

public class ColorToolBoxDialog extends JDialog {
  public ColorToolBoxDialog(Frame f, String title) {
    super(f, title, false);            // Not a modal dialog
    colorPanel = new HelperPanel();
    this.getContentPane().add(colorPanel);

    colorPanel.setLayout(new GridLayout(ROWS, COLUMNS));
    this.addWindowListener(new WindowAdapter() {
      public void windowClosing(WindowEvent evt) {
        ColorToolBoxDialog.this.setVisible(false);
      }
    });

    // Add buttons to the toolbox
    JToggleButton b = null;
    for (int i = 0; i < actions.length; i++) {
      b = this.add(actions[i]);
    }

    // Select the last button
    b.doClick();

    this.pack();
  }

  // Gets the current color
  public Color getSelectedColor() {
    return currentColor;
  }

  // Delegate property listener methods to the JPanel
  public void addPropertyChangeListener(PropertyChangeListener l) {
    colorPanel.addPropertyChangeListener(l);
  }

  public void
removePropertyChangeListener(PropertyChangeListener l) {
    colorPanel.removePropertyChangeListener(l);
```

```
    }

    // Add an action to the toolbox and return a toggle button
    protected JToggleButton add(Action a) {
      Icon icon = (Icon)a.getValue(Action.SMALL_ICON);
      if (icon != null) {
        JToggleButton b = new JToggleButton(icon);
        // Use the text as a tooltip
        if (a.getValue(Action.NAME) != null) {
          b.setToolTipText((String)a.getValue(Action.NAME));
        }
        b.addActionListener(a);

        // Add to the color panel
        colorPanel.add(b);

        // Add this button to the button group
        grp.add(b);

        return b;
      }
      return null;
    }

    // Color change - fire a property change event
    protected void colorChanged(Color c) {
      oldColor = currentColor;
      currentColor = c;

      colorPanel.firePropertyChangeEvent(COLOR_PROPERTY, oldColor,
currentColor);
    }

    // Helper class that changes the drawing color
    protected class ColorChangeAction extends AbstractAction {
      protected ColorChangeAction(Color c, String text) {
        super(text, new JFCBook.Chapter4.ColorFillIcon(c));
        this.color = c;
      }

      public void actionPerformed(ActionEvent evt) {
        ColorToolBoxDialog.this.colorChanged(color);
      }

      private Color color;
    }
```

continued

```
// Our exposed property name
public static final String COLOR_PROPERTY = "COLOR_PROPERTY";

// Button group to manage the toolbox buttons
protected ButtonGroup grp = new ButtonGroup();

// The color actions
protected final ColorChangeAction[] actions = new ColorChangeAction[] {
  new ColorChangeAction(Color.black, "Black"),
          new ColorChangeAction(Color.red, "Red"),
  new ColorChangeAction(Color.yellow, "Yellow"),
          new ColorChangeAction(Color.green, "Green"),
  new ColorChangeAction(Color.orange, "Orange"),
          new ColorChangeAction(Color.pink, "Pink"),
  new ColorChangeAction(Color.gray, "Gray"),
          new ColorChangeAction(Color.lightGray, "Light Gray"),
  new ColorChangeAction(Color.cyan, "Cyan"),
          new ColorChangeAction(Color.blue, "Blue"),
  new ColorChangeAction(Color.magenta, "Magenta"),
          new ColorChangeAction(Color.darkGray, "Dark Gray")
  };

  protected Color oldColor = Color.black;
  protected Color currentColor = Color.black;
  protected HelperPanel colorPanel;

  protected static final int ROWS = 4;
  protected static final int COLUMNS = 3;
}

// Helper class to generate PropertyChangeEvents
class HelperPanel extends JPanel {
  // Expose the firePropertyChange method
  public void firePropertyChangeEvent(String name, Object oldValue, Object newValue) {
    firePropertyChange(name, oldValue, newValue);
  }
}
```

The first line of the constructor is an important one:

```
super(f, title, false);                 // Not a modal dialog
```

In this example, the third argument passed to JDialog's constructor is false, which results in the dialog being nonmodal. The main consequence of this from the application's point of view is that the show method will return as soon as the dialog has been displayed. In the case of our example, this allows it to get on with drawing its lines. On top of the `JDialog`, the constructor overlays an object called `HelperPanel`, which is a helper class derived from `JPanel`. Under ordinary circumstances, you would just use a `JPanel` and populate it directly with colored buttons, but here it is necessary to compensate for the fact that the JDK 1.1 version of Swing does not have property support available from `JDialog`. To solve this problem, the property support of `JPanel`, which is a `JComponent`, is used. Here is what happens.

When the dialog's users add or remove a property change listener, this operation is delegated to the `JPanel`; in effect, the dialog's users are registering as listeners on the `JPanel`, not the dialog.

When the dialog needs to fire a property change event, it should just invoke the `firePropertyChange` method of the panel, which will then broadcast the event to all of its registered listeners. Unfortunately, `firePropertyChange` is protected, so it can only use it from within the Swing package or from a subclass of `JPanel`, so this method is made available from within the dialog by subclassing `JPanel` and implementing a public version called `firePropertyChangeEvent` that directly calls the protected `firePropertyChange` method.

Each of the colors that appears in the dialog box is represented by an `Action`. Earlier in this book, we looked closely at `Action`s and pointed out how useful they are as a way of encapsulating functionality in such a way that it can be consistently accessed from menu bars, toolbars and buttons without needing to replicate code. This example implements an `add` method for the dialog box that allows you to pass it an `Action` and have a button appear on the dialog. When pressed, the button will invoke the `actionPerformed` method of the `Action`. You'll recall from Chapter 6 that `Action` is an interface, so you need to implement a concrete class to make use of this mechanism. Here, as before, this class is derived from `AbstractAction` by adding the mandatory `actionPerformed` method and the `color` member, which stores the color associated with the button. The constructor of this class is passed the color that it represents as both a `Color` object and a text string. From the `Color` object it generates an icon using the `ColorFillIcon` class from Chapter 4 and passes this and the text string to the `AbstractAction` constructor.

Each `Action` is added to the dialog using the `add` method. This method needs to create a button that represents the action required, add it to the dialog itself (actually to the panel), then connect the `actionPerformed` method of the `Action` to the button so that it will be invoked when the button is pressed. The text string stored in the `Action` is used to add a tooltip, while the icon will appear on the button's face.

If you add an `Action` to a `JToolBar`, you get back a `JButton`, created in much the same way as the buttons that are placed on this dialog. In our case, however, what is added and returned is not a `JButton` but a `JToggleButton`. `JToggleButton` is the same as `JButton` in all respects except that it is sticky: When you press it, it generates an `ActionEvent` and stays pressed in. Similarly, if you press it again, it generates another `ActionEvent` and pops out. This is a more natural representation for buttons in a toolbox, because the selected color can be seen by looking for the button that's depressed. To make sure that only one button is pressed at any time, they are all added to a `ButtonGroup`. This class monitors the events generated by all of the buttons it contains. If one of them generates an event that indicates it has been pressed, the `ButtonGroup` will deselect whichever button is currently pressed. You can tell whether a `JToggleButton` is pressed in or not by calling its `isSelected` method that returns true if the button is selected (i.e., pressed in). You can also use the `setSelected` method to cause the button to appear to be pressed (with argument `true`) or to make it pop up (with argument `false`). `JToggleButton` is the base upon which the Swing radio and checkbox buttons are built, as you'll see later in this chapter.

The rest of the dialog is straightforward. The `actionPerformed` method of the `Action` subclass calls the dialog's `colorChanged` method, passing it associated color as argument. This method uses the new color and the previously selected color to fire a property change event.

Tabbed Panes and Borders

Swing introduces two features that are of great use in developing complex dialogs—the *tabbed pane* control and a set of *stock borders*. Since there are so many different border styles and many variations possible on each of these styles, the tabbed pane is an appropriate way to put them all on view, so this section describes these features together.

The Tabbed Pane

The tabbed pane will be very familiar to you if you have used the Windows platform where it is known as the *tabbed dialog box* or a *property sheet*. A tabbed pane is a container that allows you to overlay several dialog sheets, on top of each other, so that only one sheet is visible at any time. In order that you can see which sheets are available and select the one you want, each of them has a label or tab at the top of it. In a fully-populated dialog box, these tabs look like cards in a card file index. Figure 8-5 shows a typical tabbed pane that shows some of the Swing borders.

For all its apparent complexity, the `JTabbedPane` is actually a very simple component. In order to create a tabbed pane, you need to do the following:

1. Create an empty tabbed pane.
2. Create a container for each sheet of the pane and populate it with the controls that you need.
3. Add each container to the pane.
4. Select the tab that should be initially displayed.
5. Mount the `JTabbedPane` in a `JDialog`.

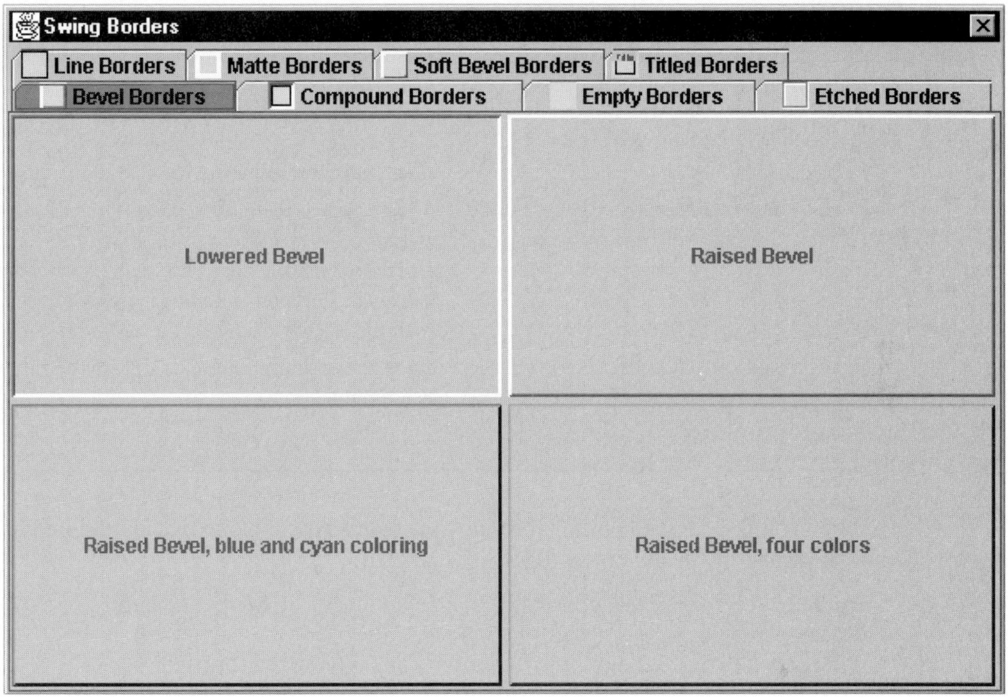

Figure 8-5   The JTabbedPane control.

Creating and Initializing a Tabbed Pane

Creating the tabbed pane is simple—it has only two constructors:

```
JTabbedPane();

JTabbedPane(int tabPlacement);
```

Each tab can be created in any way you like; usually, you'll create a JPanel and mount some controls on it. You'll see some of the more common dialog controls in the next section. When you've created each panel, you add it to the pane using one of the addTab methods shown in Table 8-2.

When you use addTab, the sheets are arranged in the same order as the addTab calls, working across the pane from left to right, then moving to the left of the second row and so on. The number of rows depends on the size of the pane and the number of tabs that you add to it. This description assumes the default tab placement, which arranges them along the top of the pane. You'll see later how to change the tab placement policy. Since JTabbedPane is not very good at working out its preferred size, it is best to explicitly size it by giving the JDialog a specific size rather than using pack.

Table 8-2 Adding sheets to a JTabbedPane

Method	Description
`public void addTab(String title, Component comp)`	Adds comp to the tabbed pane as a new sheet, with the text string `title` on its tab
`public void addTab(String title, Icon icon, Component comp)`	Adds comp to the tabbed pane. The tab will have the text string `title` and the icon on its tab. Either `title` or `icon` can be `null`. For a tab with just an icon, for example, supply `null` for the text argument
`public void addTab(String title, Icon icon, Component comp, String tip)`	Same as the above, but adds `tip` to the tab as a tooltip.

When you've added all of the tabs that you want, select the one that should be initially displayed using one of the following methods:

```
public void setSelectedIndex(int index);

public void setSelectedComponent(Component comp);
```

The index value is the number of the tab to select, where the first tab added to the pane is number 0. In the second method, you specify the component that was used to create the tab that you want selected. There are a number of other methods that you can use to insert tabs out of order or remove tabs. These, along with some other useful methods, are listed in Table 8-3.

Table 8-3 Methods used to manipulate JTabbedPane

Method	Description
`public void insertTab (String title, Icon icon, Component comp, String tip, int index)`	Adds component comp to the pane at the supplied index. If this position is already occupied, the existing tab's number and those of all following tabs are increased by 1. Either `title` or `icon` may be `null`.
`public void removeTabAt (int index)`	Removes the tab at position `index`. Any tabs that follow this tab are renumbered.
`public int getSelectedIndex()`	Gets the index of the tab at the front of the pane. This is usually used when handling the event generated when the tab on view is changed (see Listing 8-8).
`public Component getSelectedComponent()`	Gets the component for the selected tab.

`public int getTabCount()`	Gets the number of tabs in the pane.
`public int getTabRunCount()`	Returns the number of tab runs necessary to display the tabs with the current placement policy.
`public String getTitleAt(int index)`	Gets the title of the indicated tab, or `null` if there is no string title.
`public Icon getIconAt(int index)`	Gets the icon for a tab, or `null` if it doesn't have an icon.
`Public Icon getDisabledIconAt` `(int index)`	Gets the disabled icon for a tab.
`public Component getComponentAt` `(int index)`	Retrieves the component for `index`.
`Public boolean isEnabledAt` `(int index)`	Returns whether the indicated tab is enabled.
`public void setEnabledAt` `(int index, boolean enabled)`	Enables or disables a given tab. A disabled tab cannot be selected and may have a different icon (see `setDisabledIconAt`)
`public void setTitleAt` `(int index, String title)`	Sets or changes the title for tab number `index`. You can supply `null` to remove the title for the tab.
`public void setIconAt` `(int index, Icon icon)`	Sets or changes a tab's icon. Supply `null` to remove the icon.
`public void setDisabledIconAt` `(int index, Icon icon)`	Sets or changes the icon to be used when a tab is disabled. If you don't set a disabled icon for a tab, a grayed-out version of the enabled icon is used instead
`public void setComponentAt` `(int index, Component comp)`	Replaces the entire content of a tab with the supplied `Component`.
`public void setTabPlacement` `(int placement)`	Sets the tab placement to one of `JTabbedPane.TOP`, `JTabbedPane.BOTTOM`, `JTabbedPane.LEFT`, `JTabbedPane.RIGHT`
`public int getTabPlacement()`	Returns the current tab placement.
`public void setForegroundAt` `(int index, Color foreground)`	Sets the foreground color of the given tab.
`public Color getForegroundAt` `(int index)`	Returns the foreground color of a tab.
`public void setBackgroundAt` `(int index, Color background)`	Sets the background color of the given tab.
`public Color getBackgroundAt` `(int index);`	Gets the background color of a tab.
`public Rectangle getBoundsAt` `(int index)`	Gets the bounds of a tab.

Once the dialog is displayed, the user can change the active sheet by clicking on the appropriate tab. In the Windows and Motif look-and-feels, the JTabbedPane reorganizes the tabs so that the selected tabs row moves to the front. This does not, however, happen in the Metal look-and-feel.

Each time the selected tab changes, JTabbedPane generates a ChangeEvent. You can catch this event by registering a ChangeListener on the JTabbedPane. This is useful if you have dependencies between some of the sheets in the dialog, because it enables you to delay updating a sheet until it is actually on view. In the extreme case, you can avoid populating any of the sheets (apart from the first) until they are made visible. If you take this approach, there will be a delay as each sheet is created, so it may not be feasible for complex layouts.

You've now seen just about all there is to know about JTabbedPane. To see how it works in practice, look at Listing 8-8, which shows an extract from the BorderTab program that shows all of the Swing borders.

Listing 8-8   Using JTabbedPane

```
public class BorderTab extends JDialog {
  public BorderTab(Frame f, String title, int placement) {
    super(f, title, true);

    // Create a tabbed pane and add it to the dialog
    pane = new JTabbedPane(placement);
    this.getContentPane().add(pane);

    // Add the border tabs
    addBevelBorders();
    addCompoundBorders();
    addEmptyBorders();
    addEtchedBorders();
    addLineBorders();
    addMatteBorders();
    addSoftBevelBorders();
    addTitledBorders();

    pane.setSelectedIndex(0);

    this.setSize(600, 400);
  }

  // Code omitted

  public static void main(String[] args) {
    JFrame f = new JFrame("Tabbed Pane with Borders");
    final JLabel label = new JLabel("", JLabel.CENTER);
    f.getContentPane().add(label);
    f.setSize(200, 200);
```

```
// Get tab placement from command line argument
  int tabPlacement = JTabbedPane.TOP;

  if (args.length > 0) {
    String arg = args[0];
    if (arg.equals("bottom")) {
      tabPlacement = JTabbedPane.BOTTOM;
    } else if (arg.equals("left")) {
      tabPlacement = JTabbedPane.LEFT;
    } else if (arg.equals("right")) {
      tabPlacement = JTabbedPane.RIGHT;
    }
  }

  final BorderTab d = new BorderTab(f, "Swing Borders", tabPlacement);
  d.getTabbedPane().addChangeListener(new ChangeListener() {
    public void stateChanged(ChangeEvent evt) {
      JTabbedPane src = (JTabbedPane)evt.getSource();
      String title = src.getTitleAt(src.getSelectedIndex());
      label.setText(title);
    }
  });

  WindowListener l = new WindowAdapter() {
    public void windowClosing(WindowEvent evt) {
      d.dispose();
      System.exit(0);
    }
  };

  f.addWindowListener(l);
  d.addWindowListener(l);

  f.show();

  try {
    Thread.sleep(2000);
  } catch (Throwable t) {
  }

  d.setLocation(50, 50);
  d.show();

  System.exit(0);
}

// Code omitted
protected JTabbedPane pane;

}
```

This example creates a dialog box containing a JTabbedPane, each sheet of which shows a selection of borders of one particular style. On the tab for each sheet, a text description of the border style and a small icon that has an example of that border style applied to it will be displayed. The dialog constructor creates the empty JTabbedPane and adds it to the content pane of the dialog box, then calls a series of methods, each of which adds one sheet of borders. You'll see some of these methods as the corresponding border styles are described below. After adding all of the sheets, the first one (which displays bevel borders) is selected and then the dialog is explicitly sized.

To illustrate the events that are generated as the active sheet is changed, the main method creates a JFrame and mounts a JLabel onto it, then registers a ChangeListener against the tabbed pane. Note that this listener must be registered against the JTabbedPane itself, not against the dialog box. The event is processed by the stateChanged method, which gets a reference to the JTabbedPane from the source field of the event. Using this reference, the title of the selected sheet is obtained using the getSelectedIndex and getTitleAt methods and then used to set the text of the label on the application frame. As a result, if you start this application using the command:

```
java JFCBook.Chapter8.BorderTab
```

and select various sheets, you will see the text in the application's main window change as the tabs are switched.

This example also allows you to specify on the command line where you would like the tabs to be placed. Use one of the following strings to explicitly control the tab placement:

- top
- left
- bottom
- right

If you don't specify a placement, the tabs appear along the top. If you examine the code in Listing 8-8, you'll see that the command line argument is used to select a placement value (one of JTabbedPane.TOP, JTabbedPane.BOTTOM, JTabbedPane.LEFT and JTabbedPane.RIGHT) which is passed to the JTabbedPane constructor. You can also control the placement of tabs (and change it dynamically) using the setTabPlacement method. Figure 8-5 shows the tabbed pane with the tabs along the top, while Figure 8-6 shows tabs on the right, obtained using the following command line:

```
java JFCBook.Chapter8.BorderTab right
```

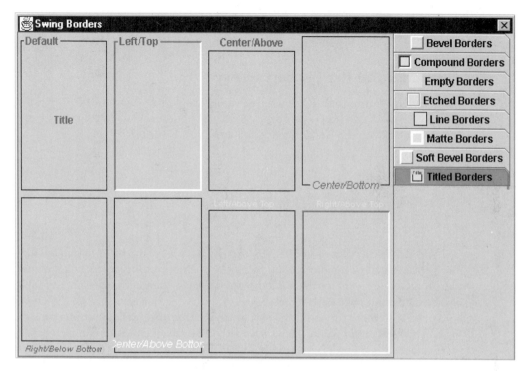

Figure 8-6   The JTabbedPane control with tabs on the right.

Swing Borders

Every Swing component derived from JComponent can be given any of a selection of standard borders, or a border that you implement yourself. The Swing borders are all classes that implement the Border interface that was examined in some detail in Chapter 4 while implementing a border for a graphics canvas. Essentially, a border takes over a certain amount of space around the edge of a JComponent. When a component has a border, it is responsible for ensuring that it does not render its usual content over the border. In AWT 1.1, you could not specify insets for a component, but some component (such as Frame) had fixed insets that could not be overridden by the programmer. By using the Swing EmptyBorder, however, you can achieve the effect of a blank region at the edge of a component, which is the same as setting component insets. This allows you to arrange for there to appear to be space around a component without relying on the layout manager for the component's container to provide it for you.

This section looks at each of the Swing border types and shows several variations on each one. The best way to see these borders for yourself is to run the BorderTab application that was used in the previous section. You'll be looking at how some of the dialog sheets in that application were implemented as we survey the various border types.

Borders and the BorderFactory

Each Swing border is implemented as a separate class in the package `com.sun.java.swing.border`. All of the border classes implement the `Border` interface, which is defined as follows:

```
public interface Border {
    public abstract void paintBorder(Component c, Graphics g,
    int x, int y, int width, int height);
    public abstract Insets getBorderInsets(Component c);
    public abstract boolean isBorderOpaque();
}
```

The `getBorderInsets` method is used by the host component to find out how much space to allow for the border. Since this method returns an `Insets` object, there is no requirement for the border to use the same amount of space on every side of the component and, as you'll see, some of the Swing borders allow you to create borders that are not symmetrical. The `isBorderOpaque` method returns `true` if the border itself either paints the background of the area it covers or completely covers that area. Some borders are transparent, `EmptyBorder` being the most obvious example. Finally, the `paintBorder` method is responsible for actually rendering the border. If you look back to Chapter 4, you'll find an implementation of a typical `paintBorder` method.

Two of the `Border` methods have a `Component` as their first argument. This allows the border to take some of its state from the component that it is rendering on. For example, borders that draw effects that rely on shadows only work properly if they can use colors that are closely related to the surface that they are drawn on. One way to approach this problem would be to create a separate border object for each component that needs a border and to configure every border with the colors that it is supposed to use by passing constructor arguments. However, this would be inefficient use of memory. By passing the host component as an argument, it is often possible to arrange for only one copy of a border type to be shared by every component that uses that border, because there is no state that needs to be separately saved for each use of that border.

Because this is true, the Swing package includes a class called `BorderFactory` that has factory methods that can create common borders and maximize border sharing. While you can always create a border using the `new` operator, it is much more efficient to use `BorderFactory` whenever it can create a suitable border for you. Even with `BorderFactory`, not all borders are shared, because it is possible to specify individual colors for some borders if you don't want to accept the defaults. For example, you can use shared Bevel borders if you want the default color scheme, which uses colors derived from those of the host component, or you can create a

Bevel border with your own chosen highlight and shadow colors. However, BorderFactory has factory methods for each case, which makes it possible to share the default bevel borders and, at least in theory, to share customized borders, created by different components, which have the same colors (even though it is not currently implemented that way).

Core Tip

To save memory, before creating a border instance using new, *check whether the* BorderFactory *can create it for you.*

Empty Border

The empty border is the most trivial border: It just leaves empty space at the edge of the component. You can use it to create insets that need not be the same on each edge of the component. There are two BorderFactory methods that create empty borders:

```
public static Border createEmptyBorder();

public static Border createEmptyBorder(int top, int left,
   int bottom, int right);
```

The first method is of questionable value, because it creates a border with zero insets—in other words, the border occupies no space at all. However, only one instance of this border is ever created. By contrast, the second method gives an empty border with arbitrary margins. A new border is created each time you call this method.

The EmptyBorder class itself has two constructors that are equivalent to the second factory method:

```
public EmptyBorder(Insets insets);

public EmptyBorder(int top, int left, int bottom, int right);
```

Line Border

This border draws a simple rectangle of given color and thickness around the edge of its host component. There are two BorderFactory methods that create line borders:

```
public static Border createLineBorder(Color color);

public static Border createLineBorder(Color color,
   int thickness);
```

The line is drawn right up against the edge of the component; if you need to leave a gap between the edge of the component and the line, you can combine a line border and an empty border using the `CompoundBorder` class, which is described later.

The `LineBorder` class itself has two constructors that do the same job as the `BorderFactory` methods:

```
public LineBorder(Color color);

public LineBorder(Color color, int thickness);
```

It also has two static methods that return shared instances of the most commonly used line borders:

```
public static Border createBlackLineBorder();

public static Border createGrayLineBorder();
```

These methods should be used if you need a 1-pixel wide black- or gray-lined border.

Etched Border

An etched border draws a 2-pixel wide groove around the edge of its host component. To give a three-dimensional effect, the groove is drawn in two colors. By default, the highlight color is slightly lighter than its host component's background and the shadow color slightly darker. The `BorderFactory` has methods to create a lowered etched border with the default colors (which is shared among all components) or a specific border with colors of your choice:

```
public static Border createEtchedBorder();

public static Border createEtchedBorder(Color highlight,
   Color shadow);
```

The `EtchedBorder` class has four constructors:

```
public EtchedBorder();

public EtchedBorder(Color highlight, Color shadow);

public EtchedBorder(int etchType);

public EtchedBorder(int etchType, Color highlight,
   Color shadow);
```

The first two produce the same borders as the factory methods. If you use the second constructor or the second factory method, then to get the proper etched effect, you need to choose the highlight and shadow colors carefully. To achieve the grooved effect of the default etched border, the shadow color must be darker than the high-light color; if you reverse these colors, making the shadow appear lighter, then the bor-der will appear raised up from the component instead of being etched into it. Another way to get a raised etched border is to use one of the last two constructors. These both have an `etchType` argument that can be either `EtchedBorder.LOWERED` or `EtchedBorder.RAISED`. To get the correct effect with the last constructor, the shadow color must be darker than the highlight color, whichever type of etched bor-der you choose. Figure 8-7 shows a selection of etched borders.

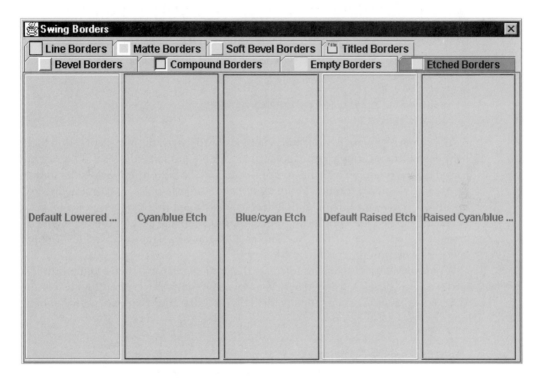

Figure 8-7   Swing etched borders.

Bevel Border and Soft Bevel Border

The bevel and soft bevel borders are similar to the etched border, except that the col-ors are used to create the impression that the region inside the border is raised above or depressed into the component's surface. The border itself is always two pixels wide. There are five factory methods for the Bevel border:

```
public static Border createBevelBorder(int type);
public static Border createBevelBorder(int type,
              Color highlight, Color shadow);
public static Border createBevelBorder(int type,
              Color highlightOuter, Color highlightInner,
              Color shadowOuter, Color shadowInner);
public static Border createRaisedBevelBorder();
public static Border createLoweredBevelBorder();
```

The `createRaisedBevelBorder` and `createLoweredBevelBorder` methods create borders with default colors derived from the background of the host component. These methods arrange for only one instance of each type to be created. The first factory method shown above takes an argument that specifies the border type; it is just a longer equivalent of one of the last two methods:

```
createBevelBorder(BevelBorder.RAISED)  is equivalent to
createRaisedBevelBorder()
```

```
createBevelBorder(BevelBorder.LOWERED)  is equivalent to
createLoweredBevelBorder()
```

You can use the other two factory methods to specify your own shadow and highlight colors. If you supply two colors, then the top and left sides of the border are each drawn as two-pixel wide lines of one color and the bottom and right sides as two-pixel wide lines of the other. On the other hand, you can give a more gradually sloping effect to the bevel if you supply four colors. If you do this, then, for a lowered bevel, the top and left corners are rendered using one line each of the highlight colors and the bottom and right one line each of the two shadow colors; for a raised bevel, the color ordering is reversed.

A plain bevel uses rectangles to create the border. You can obtain rounded corners using a soft bevel border. These borders can only be created by using the `SoftBevelBorder` constructors directly, because there are no corresponding `BorderFactory` methods:

```
public SoftBevelBorder(int type)
public SoftBevelBorder(int type, Color highlight, Color shadow);
public SoftBevelBorder(int type, Color highlightOuter, Color
       highlightInner, Color shadowOuter, Color shadowInner);
```

You can see the soft bevel borders from the `BorderTab` application in Figure 8-8.

Compound Border

As its name suggests, this border is made up of two other borders. The `CompoundBorder` accepts two instances of any of the borders (of which one or both may also be `CompoundBorders`) and arranges one of the borders inside the other one. This is especially useful if you want a border with a margin on either side

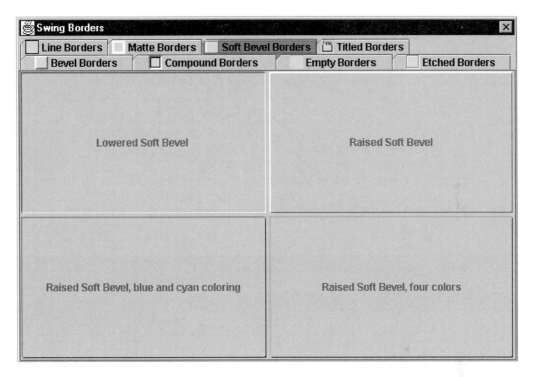

Figure 8-8   Swing soft bevel borders.

of it, since all of the borders draw themselves onto the component without leaving a gap on their outer edge. There are two factory methods:

```
public static CompoundBorder createCompoundBorder();
public static CompoundBorder createCompoundBorder(Border
outsideBorder, Border insideBorder);
```

Of these, the first is of little use, since the resulting border is completely empty. Here is an extract from the implementation of the `BorderTab` application that shows how the "Compound Border" tab was created.

```
protected void addCompoundBorders() {
    JPanel panel = new JPanel();
    panel.setLayout(new GridLayout(1, 0, HGAP, VGAP));
    panel.add(createBorderedLabel("Lowered Bevel/Lined",
        BorderFactory.createCompoundBorder(
            BorderFactory.createLoweredBevelBorder(),
            BorderFactory.createLineBorder(Color.black))));
    panel.add(createBorderedLabel("Empty/Lined",
        BorderFactory.createCompoundBorder(
            BorderFactory.createEmptyBorder(8, 8, 8, 8),
```

```
            BorderFactory.createLineBorder(Color.black)))));
      panel.add(createBorderedLabel("Etched/Raised Bevel",
         BorderFactory.createCompoundBorder(
            BorderFactory.createEtchedBorder(),
            BorderFactory.createRaisedBevelBorder()))));
```

```
   }
```

The `createBorderedLabel` method used here is a helper that creates a label and adds the give border and text to it. The code for that method is so simple that it is not shown here.

The second example is probably the most useful—a lined border with a margin on the outside; in this case, there will be a uniform 8-pixel margin all around the outside of the lined border. The borders on this tab are shown in Figure 8-9.

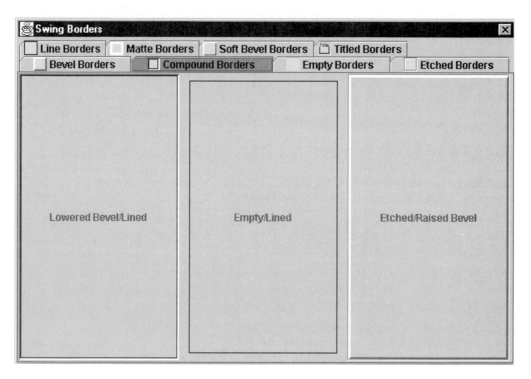

Figure 8-9 Compound borders.

Titled Border

The titled border is related to the compound border in that it (usually) takes another border as one of its arguments, then places some text near or on top of it. The text and its precise location are configurable. Here are the factory methods that you can use to create a `TitledBorder`:

```
public static TitledBorder createTitledBorder(String title);
public static TitledBorder createTitledBorder(Border border);
public static TitledBorder createTitledBorder(Border border,
    String title);
public static TitledBorder createTitledBorder(Border border,
    String title, int justification, int position);
public static TitledBorder createTitledBorder(Border border,
    String title, int justification, int position, Font font);
public static TitledBorder createTitledBorder(Border border,
    String title, int justification, int position, Font font,
    Color color);
```

The first creates an etched border and overlays the given title in the default position (see below), while the second creates a border from the given border but with no text string. This is not entirely useless, because `TitledBorder` has methods that allow you to add a title, among other things:

```
public void setBorder(Border border);
public void setTitle(String title);
public void setTitlePosition(int position);
public void setTitleJustification(int justification);
public void setTitleFont(Font font);
public void setTitleColor(Color color);
```

The remaining factory methods create borders that have the above customizable values preset.

The `position` and `justification` attributes govern where the text is placed in relation to the border. The possible values for `position` are as follows:

- TitledBorder.ABOVE_BOTTOM
- TitledBorder.ABOVE_TOP
- TitledBorder.BELOW_BOTTOM
- TitledBorder.BELOW_TOP
- TitledBorder.BOTTOM
- TitledBorder.TOP

And the possible justification values are:

- TitledBorder.CENTER
- TitledBorder.LEFT
- TitledBorder.RIGHT

You can see how these attributes, together with the font and color, affect the result from Figure 8-6, which shows the Titled Border tab of `BorderTab`.

Matte Border

This border can be used in two ways. Either it will paint a border of a solid color, which makes it the same as an empty border except that the color used does not have to be the same as the background color of the component, or it can be used to tile the border with an icon. Here are the constructors that correspond to these two cases:

```
public MatteBorder(int top, int left, int bottom, int right,
        Color color);

public MatteBorder(int top, int left, int bottom, int right,
        Icon icon);
```

The first four arguments to both constructors specify the area that the border will occupy. Figure 8-10 shows an example of each of these forms of the Matte border.

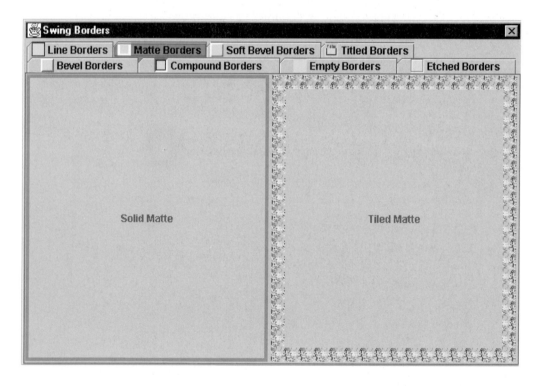

Figure 8-10   Matte borders.

There is also another, simpler constructor that requires you to specify just an icon:

```
public MatteBorder(Icon icon);
```

This form uses the width and height of the icon to determine the border insets, saving you the trouble of retrieving the width and height yourself.

Swing Components Often Used in Dialogs

This section looks at some of the Swing components that are most commonly found in dialog boxes. This is by no means a complete survey of all the controls you would ever use in a dialog, because almost any control can be used in a dialog and, similarly, the controls that are introduced here are equally useful in the application's main window. The first controls that you'll see are checkboxes and radio boxes, which allow the user to make choices—a common reason for creating a dialog box—followed by two controls that allow you to present lists of data to the user (a list box and a combo box) and a progress bar and two related controls that use a progress bar to display progress through a time-consuming operation and a slider control that can be used to change the value of a parameter with a bounded range.

Checkboxes and Radio Buttons

Checkboxes are used to allow the user to make choices that are binary in nature, whereas radio buttons allow one of several mutually exclusive alternatives to be chosen. In appearance, these controls are very similar. By default, a checkbox consists of an etched box that has a tick in it when the option it represents is selected, with some associated text that describes the option. A radio button is identical, except that the box is replaced by a small etched circle that has a colored dot in the middle when the corresponding option is enabled. Figure 8-11 shows a selection of checkboxes and radio buttons.

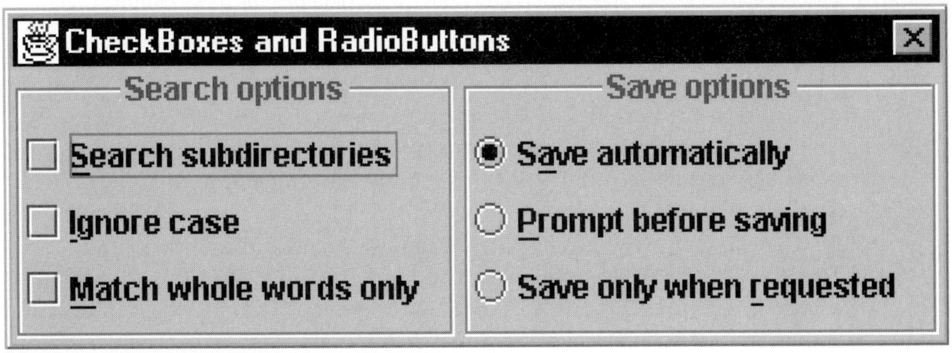

Figure 8-11   Checkboxes and radio buttons.

As you can see, a pair of titled borders has been used to separate the checkboxes and radio buttons into two logical groups. Using borders in this way is a very effective way to show the relationships between controls in a dialog.

To create a radio button, you use the `JRadioButton` class, while a checkbox can be created using `JCheckBox`. Each of these classes has several constructors that produce slightly different representations. Here, for example, are the constructors for `JRadioButton`:

```
public JRadioButton()

public JRadioButton(Icon icon)

public JRadioButton(Icon icon, boolean state)

public JRadioButton(String text)

public JRadioButton(String text, boolean state)

public JRadioButton(String text, Icon icon)

public JRadioButton(String text, Icon icon, boolean state)
```

The constructors for `JCheckBox` are identical.

If you don't specify an icon, the default icon (i.e., the square for `JCheckBox` and the circle for `JRadioButton`) is used, but if you explicitly specify an icon, the familiar square or circle will not appear. Constructors that do not supply text create a control with just an icon.

Core Note

As is often the case with Swing controls, the defaults actually depend on the selected look-and-feel. This section describes the appearance of these controls with the Metal look-and-feel.

Both `JRadioButton` and `JCheckBox` are derived from `JToggleButton`, a control that you saw earlier in this chapter, because both of them have two possible states: selected or unselected. Some of the constructors allow you to specify the initial state of the button as a boolean. If you supply the value `true`, the checkbox or radio button starts in the selected state. If you use a constructor that doesn't specify an initial state, it defaults to unselected.

Ultimately, `JToggleButton`, `JRadioButton` and `JCheckBox` are all derived from `AbstractButton`, which is the parent of the familiar `JButton` class. This means that all these buttons can be configured as flexibly as `JButton` itself and everything you know about `JButton` works for these buttons too. Thus you can, for example, change the relative positions and the alignment of the icon and the text, or add a key accelerator. You can also, of course, add a tooltip, as you can with any `JComponent`.

Radio Button and Checkbox Selection

In implementation terms, there is almost no difference between radio buttons and checkboxes, since, apart from the code that renders the user interface, they derive all of their functionality from their superclasses. In fact, radio buttons and checkboxes behave differently only if you force them to. The user expects, when confronted with a set of related radio buttons, that one and only one of them will be selected at any time. Initially, the application will select one of them to represent its default behavior and, subsequently the use can change this by clicking a different radio button. When this happens, the radio button that was initially selected should become deselected. By contrast, there is no such expectation of checkboxes: They don't represent mutually exclusive choices, so any combination of them can be selected at any given time. This difference in behavior is not enforced by the `JCheckBox` and `JRadioButton` classes—in fact, they know nothing about it.

To make a set of radio buttons behave as the user expects, you create a `ButtonGroup` and place them all in it by using its `add` method. The only job of the `ButtonGroup` is to receive events from all of the buttons that it is managing; when it receives an event indicating that one of these buttons has been selected, it just deselects the button that was selected before, if there was one. `ButtonGroup` isn't particular about the type of buttons that it manages: You can give it any combination of objects as long as they are all derived from `AbstractButton`. This means that you can make checkboxes behave like radio buttons if you wish, but it's not recommended!

Checkboxes and radio buttons are only of any use if the application does something when the user clicks on them to change their state. We've seen that you can set the initial state using the constructor; you can also change the state using the `setSelected` method and get the current state using `getSelected`:

```
public void setSelected(boolean state);

public boolean getSelected();
```

Getting Events from Checkboxes and Radio Buttons

There are two ways to be notified when the state of either a radio button or a checkbox changes. The most direct way is to exploit the fact that they are both derived from `AbstractButton`; as you know, buttons generate an `ActionEvent` when they are pressed and this remains true for both checkboxes and radio buttons. The event is, however, generated only for the button that the user actually clicks on. In the case of a checkbox, this means that you get an `ActionEvent` whenever the user selects it or deselects it. Since the `ActionEvent` doesn't tell you what state the checkbox is in, you need to use the `getSelected` method to obtain that information.

For radio buttons, the situation is slightly more complicated because selecting one button implicitly deselects another one, but an `ActionEvent` is generated only for the radio button that the user clicked: you won't get notification that the previously selected button has been deselected. In many cases, this doesn't matter because the application is probably managing the buttons as a group and can deduce the state of all of the buttons if it knows which one is selected. You do, however, have another option.

As well as generating `ActionEvents`, `JToggleButton` and its subclasses generate `ItemEvents` on every state change. An `ItemEvent` is an AWT event, derived from `java.awt.AWTEvent` and defined in the `java.awt.event` package. Like all AWT events, it has an identifier field that you can obtain using the `getID` method; only one ID value, `ITEM_STATE_CHANGE` is actually defined. In addition, it has the following methods:

```
public Object getItem();

public ItemSelectable getItemSelectable();

public int getStateChange();
```

The `getItem` method returns the object whose state actually changed. This will be the checkbox or the radio button. By contrast, `getItemSelectable` returns the `ItemSelectable` container that contains the changed item. For all toggle buttons, this method also returns the toggle button. Later in this chapter, you'll see the `JComboBox`, which is an example of an `ItemSelectable`. For a `JComboBox`, the `getItemSelectable` method returns a reference to the combo box itself and the `getItem` method returns the item that was selected from it.

For radio buttons and checkboxes, the most interesting method is `getStateChange`, which returns one of `ItemEvent.SELECTED` and `ItemEvent.DESELECTED`. If you need to monitor every state change of a set of radio buttons, you register to receive `ItemEvents` from all of them by adding an `ItemListener` using the `addItemListener` method. The `ItemListener` interface contains only one method, which corresponds to the single type of `ItemEvent` that it can receive:

```
public interface ItemListener {
  public void itemStateChanged(ItemEvent event);
}
```

Now, if you have a set of radio buttons with one selected and you click on another, the button that was initially selected receives an `ItemEvent` in which the state change is `DESELECTED` and the button that has been clicked receives an `ItemEvent` with state change `SELECTED` followed by an `ActionEvent`. The code in Listing 8-9 implements the dialog box shown in Figure 8-11.

Listing 8-9   A dialog with radio buttons

```
package JFCBook.Chapter8;

import com.sun.java.swing.*;
import com.sun.java.swing.border.*;
import java.awt.*;
import java.awt.event.*;

public class CheckRadioButtonPanel extends JPanel {
   public CheckRadioButtonPanel() {
      this.setLayout(new BorderLayout());

      JPanel checkPanel = new JPanel();
      Border b = BorderFactory.createEtchedBorder();
      checkPanel.setBorder(BorderFactory.createTitledBorder(b, "Search
options",
                     TitledBorder.TOP,
                     TitledBorder.CENTER));

      JCheckBox subDirs = new JCheckBox("Search subdirectories");
      subDirs.setMnemonic('S');
      JCheckBox ignoreCase = new JCheckBox("Ignore case");
      ignoreCase.setMnemonic('I');
      JCheckBox matchWords = new JCheckBox("Match whole words only");
      matchWords.setMnemonic('M');
      checkPanel.setLayout(new BoxLayout(checkPanel, BoxLayout.Y_AXIS));
      checkPanel.add(subDirs);
      checkPanel.add(ignoreCase);
      checkPanel.add(matchWords);
      this.add(checkPanel, "West");

      JPanel radioPanel = new JPanel();
      radioPanel.setBorder(BorderFactory.createTitledBorder(b, "Save options",
                     TitledBorder.TOP,
                     TitledBorder.CENTER));
      ButtonGroup grp = new ButtonGroup();
      JRadioButton autoSave = new JRadioButton("Save automatically");
      autoSave.setMnemonic('A');
      JRadioButton promptSave = new JRadioButton("Prompt before saving");
      promptSave.setMnemonic('P');
      JRadioButton requestSave = new JRadioButton("Save only when requested");
      requestSave.setMnemonic('R');
      radioPanel.setLayout(new BoxLayout(radioPanel, BoxLayout.Y_AXIS));
      radioPanel.add(autoSave);
      radioPanel.add(promptSave);
      radioPanel.add(requestSave);
```

continued

```java
    // Add the radio buttons to the button group
    grp.add(autoSave);
    grp.add(promptSave);
    grp.add(requestSave);

    autoSave.setSelected(true);

    ActionListener l = new ActionListener() {
      public void actionPerformed(ActionEvent evt) {
        System.out.println("Button event: " + evt);
      }
    };

    ItemListener il = new ItemListener() {
      public void itemStateChanged(ItemEvent evt) {
        System.out.println("Item event: " + evt);
      }
    };

    subDirs.addActionListener(l);
    subDirs.addItemListener(il);

    ignoreCase.addActionListener(l);
    ignoreCase.addItemListener(il);

    matchWords.addActionListener(l);
    matchWords.addItemListener(il);

    autoSave.addActionListener(l);
    autoSave.addItemListener(il);

    promptSave.addActionListener(l);
    promptSave.addItemListener(il);

    requestSave.addActionListener(l);
    requestSave.addItemListener(il);

    this.add(radioPanel, "Center");
  }

  public static void main(String[] args) {
    JFrame f = new JFrame("CheckBox/RadioButton example");

    JDialog d = new JDialog(f, "CheckBoxes and RadioButtons", true);
    CheckRadioButtonPanel p = new CheckRadioButtonPanel();
    d.getContentPane().add(p);
```

```
   d.pack();

   d.addWindowListener(new WindowAdapter() {
      public void windowClosing(WindowEvent evt) {
         System.exit(0);
      }
   });
   d.show();
   }
}
```

This example attaches both `ItemListeners` and `ActionListeners` to all of the checkboxes and radio buttons and, when the events are received, prints their contents. You can use this simple example to see how checkboxes and radio buttons generate events. Here's an extract from the program's output:

```
Item event: java.awt.event.ItemEvent[ITEM_STATE_CHANGED,item=com.sun.java.swing.
JRadioButton[,6,21,123x19,layout=com.sun.java.swing.OverlayLayout],stateChange=
DESELECTED] on com.sun.java.swing.JRadioButton[,6,21,123x19,layout=com.sun.java.s
wing.OverlayLayout]
Item event: java.awt.event.ItemEvent[ITEM_STATE_CHANGED,item=com.sun.java.swing.
JRadioButton[,6,40,138x19,layout=com.sun.java.swing.OverlayLayout],stateChange=
SELECTED] on com.sun.java.swing.JRadioButton[,6,40,138x19,layout=com.sun.java.swi
ng.OverlayLayout]
Button event: java.awt.event.ActionEvent[ACTION_PERFORMED,cmd=Prompt before saving]
on com.sun.java.swing.JRadioButton[,6,40,138x19,layout=com.sun.java.swing.OverlayLayout]
Item event: java.awt.event.ItemEvent[ITEM_STATE_CHANGED,item=com.sun.java.swing.
JCheckBox[,6,40,86x19,layout=com.sun.java.swing.OverlayLayout],stateChange=SELECTED]
 on com.sun.java.swing.JCheckBox[,6,40,86x19,layout=com.sun.java.swing.OverlayLayout]
Button event: java.awt.event.ActionEvent[ACTION_PERFORMED,cmd=Ignore case] on co
m.sun.java.swing.JCheckBox[,6,40,86x19,layout=com.sun.java.swing.OverlayLayout]
```

Initially, the 'Save automatically' radio button is selected. The first action was to click on "Prompt before saving." In response to this, a `DESELECTED` event for the top radio button was generated, followed by a `SELECTED` event and the usual `ActionEvent` for the button that was clicked on. Contrast this with the last two events, which were generated by clicking the "Ignore case" checkbox. This generates a `SELECTED` event and an `ActionEvent` for the checkbox, but there is no `DESELECT` event, because selecting a checkbox doesn't cause any other item to be deselected.

The Default Button

Sometimes you want to create a group of controls and let the user change their state, without processing any of the state changes until the user is happy with his or her selection, at which point he or she would press an OK button to have the new state processed. This is, of course, very easy to do and you have already seen all of the techniques that you need to use to do it. Swing, however, has a small refinement that can make the keyboard user's life a bit easier. Consider the dialog shown in Figure 8-12. This dialog contains a set of checkboxes that allow the user to make several independent choices. The user will move the focus around these checkboxes to change the selection, then move the focus to the button and activate it by pressing SPACE. Swing makes this last step unnecessary by making it possible to activate the OK button *without giving it the focus*. The application enables this feature by making this button the *default button* for the dialog.

Figure 8-12   A dialog with a default button.

Each JRootPane can have a default button, assigned using its setDefaultButton method:

```
public void setDefaultButton(JButton defaultButton);
```

Since each JFrame, JDialog and JApplet object has a JRootPane, this means that there can be a default button on each frame, dialog or applet. Here is how you might make a button the default button:

```
JFrame f  = new JFrame("Frame with default button");
JButton b = new JButton("OK");
f.getContentPane().add(b);
f.getRootPane().setDefaultButton(b);
```

Once the default button has been assigned, it can be activated any time the focus is within the frame, dialog or applet for which it is the default by pressing the RETURN key, whether or not the button itself has the focus. You can try this for yourself by running the example shown in Figure 8-12 by using the command:

```
java JFCBook.Chapter8.DefaultButton
```

The code for this example is not reproduced here because most of it is not related to the topic of default buttons—you can, however, find it on the CD-ROM that accompanies this book.

To demonstrate the default button, use the keyboard to move the focus around between the checkboxes and change their state. Then, leaving the focus on a checkbox, press RETURN. The dialog will disappear and a message appears in the window from which you started the example indicating that the OK button was pressed.

> **Core Alert**
>
> *The default button will not be activated if the focus is in a component that has special focus handling. Specifically, this means that it won't work if a Swing text component has the focus.*

The JList Control

The JList control is one of several Swing components that allow you to present the user with a collection of data and allow one or more of the items to be selected. This chapter looks at JList and JComboBox and later in this book you'll see the more powerful JTable and JTree components, which allow data to be presented and selected in very sophisticated ways.

JList is the simplest of all the data-handling controls. Its only purpose is to take a list of data items and present them in a vertical arrangement to the user. The basic JList doesn't even support scrolling, so you need to arrange for it to be allocated enough space in its container to display all of its contents, or add the scrolling capability yourself. Figure 8-13 shows two JList components displaying the same data; the frame has deliberately been made too small, so that the list on the left cannot display all of its content. Those items that you can't see are now completely inaccessible. The JList on the right, however, has been added to a JScrollPane, which provides a vertical scrollbar to allow access to the bottom part of the list.

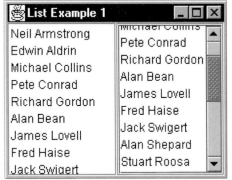

Figure 8-13   The JList control.

The code that created these two list boxes is shown below in Listing 8-10 and you can run it using the command:

```
java JFCBook.Chapter8.ListExample1
```

Listing 8-10   Creating and populating JList controls

```java
package JFCBook.Chapter8;

import com.sun.java.swing.*;
import com.sun.java.swing.border.*;
import java.awt.*;
import java.awt.event.*;
import java.util.Vector;

public class ListExample1 extends JPanel {
  public ListExample1() {
    this.setLayout(new GridLayout(1, 2));

    JPanel list1Panel = new JPanel();
    list1Panel.setBackground(UIManager.getColor("control"));
    list1Panel.setLayout(new BorderLayout());
    list1Panel.setBorder(BorderFactory.createEtchedBorder());
    JList list1 = new JList(list1Data);
    list1Panel.add(list1);

    for (int i = 0; i < list1Data.length; i++) {
      list2Data.addElement(list1Data[i]);
    }

    JPanel list2Panel = new JPanel();
    list2Panel.setBackground(UIManager.getColor("control"));
    list2Panel.setLayout(new BorderLayout());
    list2Panel.setBorder(BorderFactory.createEtchedBorder());
    JList list2 = new JList(list2Data);
    JScrollPane listScroll = new JScrollPane(list2);
    list2Panel.add(listScroll);

    this.add(list1Panel);
    this.add(list2Panel);
  }

  public static void main(String[] args) {
    JFrame f = new JFrame("List Example 1");
    f.getContentPane().add(new ListExample1());
    Dimension d = f.getPreferredSize();
    f.setSize(d.width, d.height/2);
    f.addWindowListener(new WindowAdapter() {
      public void windowClosing(WindowEvent evt) {
        System.exit(0);
      }
    });
```

```
    f.setVisible(true);
  }

  protected String[] list1Data = {
        "Neil Armstrong", "Edwin Aldrin", "Michael Collins",
        "Pete Conrad", "Richard Gordon", "Alan Bean",
        "James Lovell", "Fred Haise", "Jack Swigert",
        "Alan Shepard", "Stuart Roosa", "Edgar Mitchell",
        "Dave Scott", "Jim Irwin", "Al Worden",
        "John Young", "Charlie Duke", "Ken Mattingly",
        "Eugene Cernan", "Ron Evans", "Harrison Schmitt
  };
  protected Vector list2Data = new Vector();
}
```

It is very unlikely that you would consider creating a JList without giving it the ability to scroll, unless you are enforcing a layout policy that ensures that the control will always be large enough to show its content. Fortunately, adding scrollbars is a simple task:

```
JList list = new JList();
JScrollPane scrolledList = new JScrollPane(list);
```

You can specify the *preferred* number of rows of your list that should be made visible using the setVisibleRowCount method:

```
list.setVisibleRowCount(4);
```

Note that this method belongs to the JList control, not the JScrollPane. It only has any effect, however, if your list is mounted in a scrolling container and it will be ignored if the JScrollPane is allocated more space than it needs to show the requested number of rows.

Creating a JList Control

JList has four constructors:

```
public JList();

public JList(ListModel model);

public JList(Object[] values);

public JList(Vector data);
```

When you create a JList, you need to initialize it with some data. Contrary to what you might expect, the JList doesn't have any methods that allow you to add, remove or re-order individual items of data after the control has been created: Your only choices, as far as JList is concerned, are to associate the data with it via the constructor, or to replace its data with a completely new set of values. This is because the JList doesn't manage any data itself. In terms of the Swing Model-View-Controller architecture, JList and its UI classes implement the view part, by providing a means to display the data, but the data itself is the model part of the architecture and is managed by a separate class.

The first constructor creates a list with no data at all; to make use of this object, you will need to supply it with some data before it is displayed. There are three methods that can be used to do this:

```
public void setModel(ListModel model);

public void setListData(Object[] values);

public void setListData(Vector data);
```

These methods correspond very closely to the three remaining constructors, which supply data in various different ways; they all replace whatever data the control currently has with the new set.

JList can manage data only if presented to it in the form of a ListModel. ListModel is an interface that provides methods to allow access to a collection of data and the ability to be notified of changes to that data. Here is how it is defined:

```
public interface ListModel {
   public abstract int getSize();
   public abstract Object getElementAt(int index);
   public abstract void addListDataListener(ListDataListener l);
   public abstract void removeListDataListener(ListDataListener l);
}
```

As you can see, the getSize and getElementAt methods allow a client to find out how much data there is and makes it possible to extract each item, one at a time. It is called a list model because the data is accessed using an integer index, starting at 0 and ending at getSize() – 1. There is no provision within this interface for creating the collection in the first place, or for changing its content. The fact that the interface does not support this capability is one reason why JList cannot support it either.

The Swing package contains two implementations of this interface. AbstractListModel is a base class that is intended to be extended by adding the data handling capabilities. It provides the addListDataListener and removeListDataListener methods and manages the set of registered listeners on behalf of any class that extends it. It also provides a fireContentsChanged method that broadcasts a ListDataEvent to all registered listeners when the data content is changed and two methods (fireIntervalAdded and fireIntervalRemoved) that report changes in the items in the model that are selected, again by delivering a ListDataEvent.

There is also a subclass of AbstractListModel called DefaultListModel that is a complete implementation. It uses a Vector to store its data and clients must use Vector methods (addElement etc) to manipulate its contents. You can use a DefaultListModel to create a JList using its second constructor:

```
DefaultListModel m = new DefaultListModel();
m.addElement("Neil Armstrong");
m.addElement("Buzz Aldrin");
m.addElement("Michael Collins")
JList l = new JList(m);
```

Usually, however, you will find it more convenient to supply the data either as an array or in a Vector, as shown in Listing 8-10. Neither the array nor the Vector class implements the ListModel interface, however, so the JList constructors that accept these data types use an anonymous class to wrap them and create the appearance of a ListModel object. Here is an example of this:

```
public JList(final Vector data) {
   this(new AbstractListModel() {
     public int getSize() {
       data.getSize();
     }
     public Object getElementAt(int index) {
       return data.getElementAt(index);
     }
   });
}
```

The data model that is created from the Vector supplied as an argument is an anonymous class based on AbstractListModel. As you saw earlier, AbstractListModel implements the handling of listeners, so it is only necessary to supply the getSize and getElementAt methods. These are delegated directly to the underlying Vector. Notice that the reference to the Vector that was given to the constructor was used to access its data. This reference will actually be used long after the constructor has completed; to make this possible, it is necessary to declare the data argument final, which allows its value to be copied and stored locally with the anonymous class implementation for use later. All of this is done by the compiler.

Modifying the Content of a JList

How do you go about changing the items in a JList? Since the JList doesn't supply an API for this, you have to add or remove items from the data model itself. If you created your JList by passing an array of Objects or a Vector, you need to add, remove or change items in the Vector or you can change the contents of the array and then use the setListData method to associate the changed data with the JList. If you created the JList by populating an instance of

`DefaultListModel`, you can just make changes to it directly, because it will fire events to notify the `JList` that its content is being changed. In either case, the `JList` will update its displayed content when new data is given to it.

Selecting Items in a JList Control

Once you've supplied a `JList` with its data, it is ready to be displayed. If you wish, you can arrange for one or more of its items to be selected when it first appears, or at any other time, using the following methods:

```
public void setSelectedIndex(int index);

public void setSelectedValue(Object value, boolean scroll);

public void setSelectedIndices(int[] indices);

public void setSelectionInterval(int index1, int index2);

public void addSelectionInterval(int index1, int index2);
```

Most of these methods reference the appropriate items by index. The first two methods select a single item referenced either by index (counted from 0) or as an actual value, which must be present in the list. If you use the second method and the `JList` is hosted in a `JScrollPane`, you can ensure that the selected item is visible by passing `true` as the second argument. You can use the last three methods to select a set of items, which need not be adjacent, or to select a range of items. The `set` methods replace the current selection with the range of indices that they specify, whereas `addSelectionInterval` leaves the currently selected set selected. There are restrictions on the use of these methods, however, as you'll see below.

In the same way as `JList` doesn't manage the data that it displays, it also doesn't directly deal with remembering which items are selected at any given time. It delegates this responsibility to a class implementing the `ListSelectionModel` interface. This interface provides the means to create selections as ranges of indices. For example, the `ListSelectionModel` starts with no items selected. Under program control, the `JList` might select entry 3 (in response to `setSelectedIndex(3)`, for example, or because the user clicked on this entry), by invoking the `ListSelectionModel`'s `setSelectionInterval` method, specifying an interval from index 3 to index 3. The `ListSelectionModel` must remember that this item is selected, because the `JList` does not retain this information itself.

The `ListSelectionModel` can handle multiple selection ranges, so that it is possible to select indices 2 through 5 and 9 through 12, for example. Whether or not it allows this depends on the *list selection mode*, which is set using the `setSelectionMode` method of either `ListSelectionModel` or of `JList` itself. This method takes a single argument from the set shown in Table 8-4.

Table 8-4   List box selection modes

Setting	*Description*
ListSelectionModel. SINGLE_SELECTION	Only one item may be selected. Selecting another item causes the first to be deselected.
ListSelectionModel. SINGLE_INTERVAL_SELECTION	Allows a single range of adjacent items to be selected.
ListSelectionModel. MULTIPLE_INTERVAL_SELECTION	Allows any number of ranges of adjacent items to be selected at the same time.

If the model is in single-selection mode, calls to `setSelectedIndex` or `setSelectedValue` work as you would expect, selecting the indicated item and deselecting any other value currently selected. In this mode, however, you can't select a range of values, so the `setSelectedIndices`, `setSelectionInterval` and `addSelectionInterval` methods behave differently. The first two methods select only the last index that they are given. For example,

```
setSelectedIndices(new int[] { 1, 2, 4, 6});
```

would select index 6 only, while

```
setSelectionInterval(2, 7);
```

selects only index 7. The `addSelectionInterval` method is treated in the same way as `setSelectionInterval`.

When the model is in single-interval selection mode, a single range of values can be selected. In this mode, `setSelectedIndex` and `setSelectedValue` again work as normal and result in only the nominated value being selected. The `setSelectedIndices` method works the same way as it does in single-selection mode—only the last index is selected, even if the set supplied is a contiguous range of items; that is to say, the following call:

```
setSelectedIndices(new int[] {1, 2, 3, 4});
```

selects only item 4, while the similar call

```
setSelectionInterval(1, 4);
```

selects items 1 to 4 inclusive. As with single-selection mode, `addSelectionInterval` behaves in the same way as `setSelectionInterval`.

In multiple-selection mode, all of the methods behave as you might expect. The `setSelectedIndex` and `setSelectedValue` methods again clear all selected values and then select the single named item. The `setSelectedIndices` method selects each of the items it is given, deselecting anything already selected and `setSelectionInterval` creates a single selection consisting of the range of values it is supplied. Finally, `addSelectionInterval` adds a new range of one or more values to whatever is currently selected.

There are two other methods that allow you to manipulate the selection:

```
public void clearSelection();
public void removeSelectionInterval(int index1, int index2);
```

The first of these methods clears the entire selection, leaving nothing selected. The second removes the range of items from `index1` to `index2` inclusive from the selection. It is permissible for this range to include items that are not actually selected. Items that were initially selected but do not fall within the supplied range remain selected when this method completes.

When you create a `JList`, the `ListSelectionModel` you get by default is in multiple interval selection mode.

Core Note

The `ListSelectionModel` *never sees the data that a* `JList` *is holding. The* `JList` *just tells it which indices are to be considered selected at any given time. The Swing package includes an implementation of* `ListSelectionModel` *called* `DefaultListSelectionModel`, *which is used by* `JList`. *If you wish, you can supply your own implementation of* `ListSelectionModel` *instead of the default one using the* `JList` `setSelectionModel` *method.*

User Selections

The methods just described allow you to manipulate the selection from within an application. Often, these methods are actually called from the `JList` UI class in response to user interaction with the `JList` using the mouse.

Core Tip

You can change the colors used to render selected items using the following two methods:

```
public void setSelectionBackground(Color backColor);

public void setSelectionForeground(Color foreColor);
```

Using the mouse, a single item can be selected by clicking it, which will deselect anything currently selected.

To select a contiguous range of items, click on the item at one end of the range, then hold down the SHIFT key while clicking on the other. These two items and everything in between will be selected. The first item clicked on is referred to as the *anchor* of the selection, while the second is the *lead* item. Range selection doesn't work if the list is in single selection mode—here, the anchor and lead are always the last item clicked on.

To select items that are not adjacent to each other, use the CTRL key as you click. This causes the item clicked on to be added to the current selection without deselecting anything already selected. It can only be used, however, when the list is in multiple interval selection mode.

List Selection Events

When the user makes a selection using the mouse, the JList UI class tells the ListSelectionModel to update its set of selected objects. The ListSelectionModel changes its internal state and generates a ListSelectionEvent. To receive notification of selection changes, you need to register a ListSelectionListener using the addListSelectionListener method provided by JList. The ListSelectionListener interface has only one method:

```
public interface ListSelectionListener extends EventListener {
    public abstract void valueChanged(ListSelectionEvent evt);
}
```

The ListSelectionEvent contains the source of the event (which will be the JList), two indices that indicate a range of values between which a change has occurred and a boolean flag indicating whether the selection is still changing. You can obtain these four values using the following ListSelectionEvent methods:

public Object getSource().	Gets the source of the event.
public int getFirstIndex.	The lower index of the range within which a change has occurred.
public int getLastIndex().	The upper index of the range within which the change occurred.
public boolean getValueIsAdjusting().	Returns true if the selection is still changing.

Core Alert

You can also add a ListSelectionListener *directly to the* ListSelectionModel *using its* addListSelectionListener *method. If you do this, the source of the event you receive will be the* ListSelectionModel *itself, not the* JList

When you select a single item, both getFirstIndex and getLastIndex will return the same index. If a range of values is selected, the entire range will lie between the values returned by these methods. However, it is important to bear in mind that if an item is already selected and you select another one, you get three events, one for the deselection of the first item, one showing that the selection is moving from the first item to the second and the third showing only the second item selected.

Unless you particularly need to handle all of the events, the most convenient way to handle selections is to handle only the last event of a set. This can be identified because getValueIsAdjusting returns false only for the final event. Therefore, most event handlers connected to JList controls will probably start by checking the value returned by getValueIsAdjusting. Let's look at an example that allows you to see the events generated as you make selections. Listing 8-11 shows an extract from a modified version of our earlier example. Run this program using the command:

```
java JFCBook.Chapter8.ListExample2
```

and follow the instructions that follow to see how the events are generated.

Listing 8-11   Receiving selection events from a JList

```
public ListExample2() {
  this.setLayout(new BorderLayout());

  this.setBorder(BorderFactory.createEtchedBorder());
  JList list = new JList(listData);
  JScrollPane listScroll = new JScrollPane(list);
  list.setVisibleRowCount(8);
  this.add(listScroll);
  // Register to receive selection events
  list.addListSelectionListener(new ListSelectionListener()

    public void valueChanged(ListSelectionEvent evt) {
      JList src = (JList)evt.getSource();
      System.out.println("Change in selection between indices " +
          evt.getFirstIndex() + " and " +
          evt.getLastIndex() +
          "; value is adjusting: " +
          evt.getValueIsAdjusting());

      if (evt.getValueIsAdjusting() == false) {
        int[] selectedIndices = src.getSelectedIndices();
        System.out.print("Selected indices are: ");
        for (int i = 0; i < selectedIndices.length; i++) {
          System.out.print(selectedIndices[i] + " ");
```

```
      }

      Object[] selectedValues = src.getSelectedValues();
      System.out.println("\n\nSelected values are:");
      for (int i = 0; i < selectedValues.length; i++) {
         System.out.println("\t" + selectedValues[i]);
      }
    }
  }
});
}
```

In this example, a `ListSelectionListener` that prints the content of each `ListSelectionEvent` that it receives is registered. First, try selecting the entry for "Neil Armstrong:"

```
Change in selection between indices -1 and -1;
       value is adjusting: true
Change in selection between indices 0 and 0;
       value is adjusting: true
Change in selection between indices 0 and 0;
       value is adjusting: false
Selected indices are: 0

Selected values are:
       Neil Armstrong
```

First, notice that three events were received, in which only the last has the "value adjusting" flag set to `false`; the first two were generated as the selection moved from index –1 (which corresponds to there being no selection) to index 0. Our event handler ignores events that have the value-adjusting flag set to `true`, because they represent transient states that are usually not of interest. When you get an event of interest, you have several ways to get hold of the item that has been selected and you can also obtain other information about the current selection:

```
public int getSelectedIndex();

public int[] getSelectedIndices();

public Object getSelectedValue();

public Object[] getSelectedValues();

public int getAnchorSelectedIndex();

public int getLeadSelectionIndex();

public int getMinSelectionIndex();

public int getMaxSelectionIndex();
```

The first two methods return index information that you can also obtain from the event. These methods are more useful when used outside an event handler if you just want to see which items are currently selected, perhaps because the user clicked an OK button on the same panel. The next two methods are the ones you are likely to use most frequently. The first returns only one value, whereas the second returns all of the selected values. If your application can only handle one selected item, you should use `getSelectedValue` instead of `getSelectedValues`. Our event handler uses the latter, so that you can see exactly what is considered to be selected.

The last four methods return general information about the current selection. The terms anchor and lead were introduced earlier, while the minimum and maximum selected items are exactly as their names imply—the lowest numbered and highest number index of all the selected items. If the list is in multiple interval selection mode, there may be unselected items between these two indices.

Now scroll down to the bottom of the list and click on "Harrison Schmitt." The events that are generated this time are:

```
Change in selection between indices 0 and 0;
        value is adjusting: true
Change in selection between indices 0 and 20;
        value is adjusting: true
Change in selection between indices 20 and 20;
        value is adjusting: false
Selected indices are: 20


Selected values are:
        Harrison Schmitt
```

This is almost identical to the first case, except that now the selection starts at index 0 and moves to index 20. Notice that the second event indicates a selection change between index 0 and 20, which covers the entire list. It is important to realize that the indices in the events cover the entire area over which there has been a change: This does not imply that every item in between has changed selection state.

Next, leaving the last entry selected, hold down the SHIFT key and click on "Ken Mattingly." This results in the following output:

```
Change in selection between indices 20 and 20;
        value is adjusting: true
Change in selection between indices 17 and 20;
        value is adjusting: true
```

Here, the second event reports the range of selected values, but it still says that the selection is being adjusted. This is a feature of multiple-selections. Because you may want to add to the selection, clicking with the SHIFT button does not generate an event in which the adjusting flag is set to false. If your application allows multiple selections, you should supply an OK button (or something equivalent) so that the user can indicate that all of the required items have been selected. The same thing happens with the CTRL key. To see this, leave the current selection as it is and then click on "Al Worden" while holding down CTRL. This generates a single event:

```
Change in selection between indices 14 and 20;
        value is adjusting: true
```

In some contexts, just selecting an item by clicking on it is enough to generate an action. For example, you might display an explanatory message somewhere in a status bar when the user clicked on "Neil Armstrong" explaining that he was the first man to walk on the moon. If this grabs the user's interest, he or she might want to know more. Usually, choosing an item from a list involves selecting it and then pressing a button somewhere to confirm the selection. Most platforms allow the user to double-click on an entry as a quicker way to achieve this. If you do this with JList, you just get another ListSelectionEvent for the second click. This is because JList doesn't have any way to report a double click to you. If you want to implement double-click semantics, you need to register an event handler for mouse-clicked events and process the event yourself. Here's an example that shows how you might add this to the code above:

```
// Register for mouse events
list.addMouseListener(new MouseAdapter() {
   public void mouseClicked(MouseEvent evt) {
      if (evt.getClickCount() == 2) {
         JList l = (JList)evt.getSource();
         int index = l.locationToIndex(evt.getPoint());
         if (index > 0) {
            Object value = l.getModel().getElementAt(index);
            System.out.println("Chosen value is " + value);
         }
      }
   }
});
```

This code registers to receive mouse events from the JList. As they arrive, the first check is for a double click, then the mouse location is obtained using the getPoint method of MouseEvent. JList provides the locationToIndex method to translate a point to the index of the item at that location; this translation is not trivial because the list might be mounted in a JScrollPane. Assuming the mouse is over an item, the returned index is used to get the correct item from the JList's data model. You can try this out for yourself using the following command:

```
java JFCBook.Chapter8.ListExample3
```

Double-clicking on one of the entries in the list shows the same debugging output as before, but also indicates that the clicked entry has been chosen:

```
Change in selection between indices -1 and -1;
        value is adjusting: true
Change in selection between indices 3 and 3;
        value is adjusting: true
Change in selection between indices 3 and 3;
        value is adjusting: false
Selected indices are: 3

Selected values are:
        Pete Conrad
Change in selection between indices 3 and 3;
        value is adjusting: true
Change in selection between indices 3 and 3;
        value is adjusting: false
Selected indices are: 3

Selected values are:
        Pete Conrad
Chosen value is Pete Conrad
```

Core Note

Why is it necessary to check that the value returned by locationToIndex *was positive? Surely a mouse event is only received if you click over the* JList, *in which case you must have a valid index? Yes to the first part of that statement and no to the second: Suppose the* JList *is in a frame that is larger than the space needed for the list. Then the items will stop part way down the list leaving the bottom of it empty. If you click in this area, you are within the* JList *but not over a valid selection and in this case* locationToIndex *returns* −1.

Customizing the JList Control

To end this discussion of JList, let's look at how you can influence the way in which it renders its contents.

Controlling Cell Width

When displaying the list of items, the width of the control is determined by the space required to render its widest item. To work this out, the list has to measure the rendered size of every item of data that it will draw. If there is a lot of data in the control, this can significantly impact performance. To avoid this, you can set a fixed width using the setFixedCellWidth method; you can also make all cells be of the same height using the setFixedCellHeight method. These methods are defined as follows:

```
public void setFixedCellWidth(int width);
public void setFixedCellHeight(int height);
```

where both `width` and `height` are specified in pixels. Often, though, it is not convenient (or possible) to specify the cell sizes in pixels, because the width or height of a cell large enough to hold, say, an 8-character string depends entirely on the font in use. A better method is to let the `JList` compute the appropriate dimensions by passing typical content to the `setPrototypeCellValue` method, defined as follows:

```
public void setPrototypeCellValue(Object typicalValue);
```

If you are populating the control with 8-letter words, you can use the following to have the `JList` compute suitable cell width and height values:

```
list.setPrototypeCellValue("MMMMMMMM");
```

Using the List Cell Renderer

The `JList` controls in the examples shown so far have been populated with strings, but the constructors allow you to supply data models that can hold any type of `Object` and the methods that retrieve values from the control return an `Object` or an array of `Objects`. If a `JList` can hold any type of object, how does it represent them? There are two cases that are treated specially by default. If any item in the `JList` is an `Icon`, it is rendered directly onto its cell. This means that it is trivial to create a list whose items are all graphics instead of text. If an item is anything other than an `Icon`, its `toString` method is called and the result is drawn into the item's cell. In other words, `JList` can render icons and strings by default.

If this isn't sufficient, you can take over the rendering process yourself by replacing the `JList`'s default rendering behavior. To do this, you have to provide an implementation of the `ListCellRenderer` interface and by passing it to the `setCellRenderer` method. The `ListCellRenderer` interface has only one method:

```
public Component getListCellRendererComponent(JList list,
        Object value, int index, boolean isSelected,
        boolean hasFocus);
```

This method is invoked for each item in the list that needs to be currently on display. The arguments passed to this method include the value from the list, its index and booleans indicating whether the value is currently selected and whether it has the keyboard focus. The implementation of this method must return a `Component` that can be used to render the passed value on the screen. The `JList` will render the value by calling the returned `Component`'s `paint` method, making it draw into a `Graphics` object that covers part of the `JList`'s surface. In theory, an implementation of this method could return any sort of custom `Component` that exhibited the right behavior when its `paint` method was called. It is possible, for example, to create an object, derived from `Component` that just stores the value and the selected and focus flags and uses them only when it is asked to paint itself. Usually, though, the simplest thing to do is to create an object derived from JPanel or JLabel that you can use to draw on or that can draw itself.

The example that will be used here is another variation on the graphics drawing program from Chapter 4. In subsequent chapters, the color selection buttons that were originally on the application's main window have been removed and mounted first on a toolbar and then in a floating, non-modal dialog box. For the purposes of this example, they are going to be placed in a scrolling list. Each color will be represented by the usual colored square icon that has been used before, together with its name that will appear to the right of it. Our task will be to make the list control display both the icon and the text.

Had it been required to show just the icon, you could have simply created an array of them and directly populated the JList with them, because it can draw a list of icons without a special renderer. The code to do this would look something like this:

```
ColorFillIcon[] icons = new ColorFillIcon[] {
  new ColorFillIcon(Color.white), ColorFillIcon(Color.red),
       ColorFillIcon(Color.black)
};
JList list = new JList(icons);
```

This code would populate each entry in the list with a ColorFillIcon and the icons would appear in the list box on the screen. If the user made a selection, the getSelectedValue method would return a ColorFillIcon object.

Because the requirement here is to render both text and an icon, the list needs to store an object that holds both pieces of information. When the user selects an entry, it will be necessary to get at both the icon and the corresponding color. You'll remember from Chapter 4 that the icon is used to change the appearance of a label at the bottom of the application window and the color, preferably as a Color object, is used to actually change the drawing color. Thus, it is necessary to have in the list an object that can store the icon, the color name and the corresponding Color object.

Suppose we create a class derived from AbstractAction. As you've seen in connection with menus and toolbars, this class can store and retrieve both the text and icon and, as a bonus, you can also define an actionPerformed method that contains the code to be executed when the user selects a color. By subclassing AbstractAction, you can also add a member to hold the Color object. To implement this solution, a class called ColorChangeAction, which is derived from AbstractAction, is created. The list box is then populated with a collection of these objects, one for each color choice. The implementation of this class is shown in Listing 8-12.

Listing 8-13   An action to handle a JList selection

```
// Helper class that implements a color change action
class ColorChangeAction extends AbstractAction {
  ColorChangeAction(Color color, String name) {
    super(name, new ColorFillIcon(color));
    this.color = color;
  }

  // Action to take when this color is selected
  public void actionPerformed(ActionEvent evt) {
    System.out.println("Color chosen: " + color);
  }

  Color color;    // Associated color
}
```

The `Color` object and the color's name are passed to the constructor, which creates the `ColorFillIcon` and stores both it and the color name in the `AbstractAction` by passing the name and the icon to the `AbstractAction` constructor. The only remaining duties are to store the color itself and to implement an `actionPerformed` method. In this example, the `actionPerformed` method will just print a method to demonstrate that the code works properly: This list box is not actually going to be linked into the graphic drawing application here.

To populate the list box, an array of `ColorChangeAction` objects is created and passed to the `JList` constructor. Then, the list box is mounted in a frame and displayed. At this point, if nothing more were done, the `JList` would use its default renderer, which would represent these objects by calling the `toString` method of each of them. This would produce a rather unusable result—here's a sample of what you might see:

```
JFCBook.Chapter8.ColorChangeAction@1cc9e9
JFCBook.Chapter8.ColorChangeAction@1cc9ff
JFCBook.Chapter8.ColorChangeAction@1cca04
JFCBook.Chapter8.ColorChangeAction@1cca09
```

To produce the required display, it is necessary to implement a custom `ListCellRenderer` and substitute it for the default one by calling the `setCellRenderer` method. When the `JList` paints itself, it calls the `getListCellRendererComponent` method of the renderer for each item in the list that is going to be visible. This method returns a `Component` that can paint a proper representation of the list item. Since this example uses a text item and an icon, a `JLabel` can be used to do the actual rendering. The code shown in Listing 8-13

creates a subclass of `JLabel` that implements the `ListCellRenderer` interface
and registers that as the renderer.

Listing 8-13   A custom list cell renderer

```
package JFCBook.Chapter8;

import com.sun.java.swing.*;
import com.sun.java.swing.border.*;
import com.sun.java.swing.event.*;
import JFCBook.Chapter4.ColorFillIcon;
import java.awt.*;
import java.awt.event.*;
import java.util.Vector;

public class ListExample4 extends JPanel {
   public ListExample4() {
     this.setLayout(new BorderLayout());
     this.setBorder(BorderFactory.createEtchedBorder());
     JList list = new JList(actions);
     JScrollPane listScroll = new JScrollPane(list);
     list.setVisibleRowCount(6);
     list.setCellRenderer(new ColorActionRenderer());
     this.add(listScroll);

     // Register to receive selection events
     list.addListSelectionListener(new ListSelectionListener() {
       public void valueChanged(ListSelectionEvent evt) {
         JList src = (JList)evt.getSource();
         if (evt.getValueIsAdjusting() == false) {
           ColorChangeAction action =
                 (ColorChangeAction)src.getSelectedValue();
           System.out.println("Selected " +
                 (String)action.getValue(Action.NAME));
         }
       }
     });

     // Register for mouse events
     list.addMouseListener(new MouseAdapter() {
       public void mouseClicked(MouseEvent evt) {
         if (evt.getClickCount() == 2) {
           JList l = (JList)evt.getSource();
           int index = l.locationToIndex(evt.getPoint());
           if (index >= 0) {
             Object value = l.getModel().getElementAt(index);
```

```
            ColorChangeAction action = (ColorChangeAction)value;
            System.out.println("Chosen " +
                (String)action.getValueAction.NAME));
            action.actionPerformed(new ActionEvent(1,
                ActionEvent.ACTION_PERFORMED, null));
        }
      }
    }
  });
}

protected class ColorActionRenderer extends JLabel implements ListCellRenderer {
  public Component getListCellRendererComponent(JList list,
                Object value,
                int index,
                boolean isSelected,
                boolean hasFocus) {
    ColorChangeAction action = (ColorChangeAction)value;
    this.setOpaque(true);
    this.setIcon((Icon)action.getValue(Action.SMALL_ICON));
    this.setText((String)action.getValue(Action.NAME));
    if (isSelected) {
      this.setBackground(Color.blue);
      this.setForeground(Color.white);
      this.setFont(selectedFont);
    } else {
      this.setBackground(Color.yellow);
      this.setForeground(Color.black);
      this.setFont(normalFont);
    }

    return this;
  }

  protected final Font selectedFont = new Font("Serif", Font.BOLD, 14);
  protected final Font normalFont = new Font("Serif", Font.PLAIN, 12);
}

public static void main(String[] args) {
  JFrame f = new JFrame("List Example 4");
  f.getContentPane().add(new ListExample4());
  f.pack();
  f.addWindowListener(new WindowAdapter() {
    public void windowClosing(WindowEvent evt) {
      System.exit(0);
    }
  });
```

```
        f.setVisible(true);
    }

    // Data for the list
    ColorChangeAction[] actions = new ColorChangeAction[] {
            new ColorChangeAction(Color.white, "White"),
            new ColorChangeAction(Color.orange, "Orange"),
            new ColorChangeAction(Color.yellow, "Yellow"),
            new ColorChangeAction(Color.green, "Green"),
            new ColorChangeAction(Color.blue, "Blue"),
            new ColorChangeAction(Color.magenta, "Magenta"),
            new ColorChangeAction(Color.red, "Red"),
            new ColorChangeAction(Color.pink, "Pink"),
            new ColorChangeAction(Color.gray, "Gray"),
            new ColorChangeAction(Color.black, "Black") };
}
```

When our class's getListCellRendererComponent method is called, it will receive an object from the list box. This object is a ColorChangeAction, so the text and icon can be extracted using the AbstractAction getValue method and then used to configure the JLabel superclass. This, in itself, is enough to produce a reasonable effect, but one more thing needs to be done. When the user clicks on an entry in a list box, the background is highlighted. This highlighting is the responsibility of the cell renderer—in other words, it is our job. The JList passes an argument that indicates whether the cell that is being rendered is selected or not. This argument is used to give the JLabel either a blue background when it is selected or a yellow one if it is not. In addition, a slightly larger font is used for the selected item. Having configured the JLabel, we return a reference to it to the JList.

Core Note

This example uses specific colors to show the highlighted items. If you want to be more orthodox, you can use the JList reference passed to the getListCellRendererComponent method to obtain the usual foreground and background colors using getForeground and getBackground or the colors to be used for selection using getSelectionForeground and getSelectionBackground.

The JList uses this component to render the item's representation onto the screen by creating a Graphics object that corresponds to a part of the screen and calls the Component's paint method, passing the Graphics object as its argument. It doesn't create a container and add a Component for each item to it. This is why you only need one Component to render the contents of the entire list. If this were not so, we would have to derive our ListCellRenderer from some other class and have it create and return a new JLabel for each item to be displayed. Figure 8-14 shows what the list box looks like with this renderer.

Figure 8-14 The JList control with a custom renderer.

To allow the user to make a selection by double-clicking on it, the mouse-handling code from the previous example has been carried forward. This code extracts the selected value from the data model; since the list box was populated with ColorChangeAction objects, this value is the ColorChangeAction object for the selected object. The mouse click method generates an ActionEvent and passes it to the actionPerformed method of the ColorChangeAction. This method runs with the ColorChangeAction as its this pointer, so it has access to the color name, the icon and the Color object itself, which is what would be needed to use this list box in the graphics drawing application from Chapter 4.

The JComboBox Control

There are many similarities between JList and its close relative JComboBox. Since these controls are so similar, this section concentrates mainly on the features unique to JComboBox.

The major visible difference between these two controls is that a list box usually shows several possible choices at once, whereas a combo box will normally show only one. When you create a combo box, you get what looks like a text field with a downward-point arrow to the right of it. If you click on the arrow, a popup containing all of the possible choices appears beneath the input field. Another important difference is that a combo box may (but need not) allow the user to type into the text field a value that isn't among the list of selectable values that the combo box has been initialized with. Unlike JList, however, you can only select a single value from a JComboBox.

The Combo Box and its Data Model

Like JList, the JComboBox class gets its data from a data model, which you can supply using one of its two constructors:

```
public JComboBox(ComboBoxModel model);
public JComboBox();
```

JComboBox needs data in the form of a ComboBoxModel, which is derived from the ListModel used by the list box with the addition of the following two methods:

```
public void setSelectedItem(Object item);
public Object getSelectedItem();
```

These additional methods are needed because an editable combo box allows the user to make a choice from the data already in the model or to type a different value into the combo box. The value that the user types need not be one of the items in the combo box, so the ComboBoxModel has to be able to hold this value separately.

If you choose the first constructor, you have to supply your own data model, populated with the data that you want to appear in the combo box. The problem with this approach is that there aren't any public ComboBoxModel classes in the Swing package, so to use this constructor you would have to implement your own model (probably deriving it from DefaultListModel, with an extension to support the selected item). If you use the second constructor, the combo box uses a data model that it implements for itself. You can get a reference to this model using the getModel method and you can change the model using setModel.

Since ComboBoxModel is derived from ListModel, it has the same problem of not having any methods that allow you to add, change or remove any data. Instead, you have to use methods provided by the model to perform these tasks. If you write your own model, you can, of course, provide and use suitable methods to allow you to manage the data content without involving the combo box. Usually, though, you'll want to use the default data model that you get from the second constructor. Since the default model is not implemented by a public class, how can you put any data into it?

To solve this problem, JComboBox provides several convenience methods that allow you to manipulate data in the model. Note that these work **ONLY** if you are using the default model, because they have to use special knowledge of this model to do their jobs. If you add your own model and then try to manipulate it using these methods, you will get an exception. Here are the data manipulation methods for the default data model:

`public void addItem` `(Object anItem)`	Adds an item at the end of the list.
`public void insertItemAt` `(Object anItem, int index)`	Inserts an item at the given index.
`public void removeAllItems()`	Empties the data model.
`public void removeItem` `(Object anItem)`	Removes the given item.
`public void removeItemAt` `(int index)`	Removes the item at the given index.

As with `JList`, these methods all deal with `Object`s, not just text strings, so you can store arbitrary content in a combo box. The same rules apply as far as retrieving and displaying data are concerned: You get back one of the objects that you stored when you ask for the selected item, and the objects in the combo box are either displayed directly in the case of icons or strings, or have the results of applying the `toString` method displayed otherwise. Also like `JList`, you can create a custom cell renderer by implementing the `ListCellRenderer` interface and using the `setRenderer` method to register it with the combo box (note that this is not the same method name as that used by `JList`). In fact, any custom renderer that works with `JList` will work just as well with `JComboBox` and vice versa.

Combo Box Selection

When you have data in the combo box, you can display it and allow the user to make a selection. When the combo box first appears, the first item that you added to it is considered to be selected and appears in the combo box.

To make a choice from the combo box, the user clicks on the down arrow to make the list of possible choices appear. The area in which the choices are displayed is referred to as a "popup," despite the fact that it usually drops down below the combo box. As the mouse moves up and down the list of choices, they are highlighted, unlike the list box, which only highlights choices when the mouse is clicked. If there are too many items in the combo box to fit in the visible area of popup, a scrollbar will be added so that it can be scrolled to bring all of the choices into view. By default, the popup can display eight items, but you can change this by calling the `setMaximumRowCount` method.

When the user clicks an entry, an `ItemEvent` is generated. You can register an `ItemListener` to receive these events, in the same way as was done to receive checkbox and radio button events earlier in this chapter. Each time the user makes a selection, you get a `SELECTED` event for the new selection; you will also get a `DE-SELECTED` event for the item that was previously selected. This is even true the first time that the user makes a selection, because the first item in the list is selected automatically when the combo box is initialized. The following methods allow you to manage the selection of items in the combo box:

`public void getSelectedIndex()`	Returns the index of the selected item, counted from 0.
`public Object getSelectedItem()`	Returns the selected object.
`public Object[] getSelectedObjects()`	Returns all selected items.
`public void setSelectedIndex (int index)`	Selects the item at index.
`public void setSelectedItem (Object anItem)`	Selects the given object, which need not be in the combo box's list.

Even though there is a `getSelectedObjects` method that returns an array of objects, you can only select one item at a time from the combo box. Trying to use the SHIFT or CTRL keys to select a range of objects won't work—only the last item you click on will be considered to be selected. The array returned by `getSelectedObjects` will, therefore, have at most one entry in it. The last item to be highlighted will appear in the combo box's input area, and this item is also the one that will be returned to `getSelectedItem`, or its index to `getSelectedIndex` and that will appear in the `ItemEvent` generated when the mouse button is released.

The example in Listing 8-14 demonstrates some of the features of the combo box. It creates three combo boxes and populates two with strings and the third with colored icons.

You can see what this application looks like in Figure 8-15 and you can run it for yourself using the command:

```
java JFCBook.Chapter8.ComboBoxExample
```

Listing 8-14   The JComboBox control

```
package JFCBook.Chapter8;

import com.sun.java.swing.*;
import com.sun.java.swing.event.*;
import java.awt.*;
import java.awt.event.*;
import JFCBook.Chapter4.ColorFillIcon;

public class ComboBoxExample extends JPanel {
  public ComboBoxExample() {
```

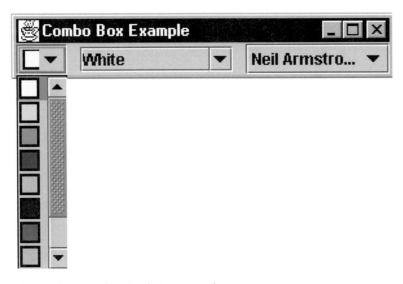

Figure 8-15   The JComboBox control.

```
this.setLayout(new BorderLayout(8, 8));

leftCombo = new JComboBox();
this.add(leftCombo, "West");
for (int i = 0; i < leftComboData.length; i++) {
  leftCombo.addItem(leftComboData[i]);
}

middleCombo = new JComboBox();
this.add(middleCombo, "Center");
for (int i = 0; i < middleComboData.length; i++) {
  middleCombo.addItem(middleComboData[i]);
}

rightCombo = new JComboBox();
this.add(rightCombo, "East");
for (int i = 0; i < rightComboData.length; i++) {
  rightCombo.addItem(rightComboData[i]);
}

middleCombo.setEditable(true);      // Make it editable

// Add item listeners
leftCombo.addItemListener(new ItemListener() {
  public void itemStateChanged(ItemEvent evt) {
    System.out.println("Left combo event: " + evt);
  }
```

continued

```java
      });

      middleCombo.addItemListener(new ItemListener() {
        public void itemStateChanged(ItemEvent evt) {
          System.out.println("Middle combo event: " + evt);
        }
      });

      rightCombo.addItemListener(new ItemListener() {
        public void itemStateChanged(ItemEvent evt) {
          System.out.println("Right combo event: " + evt);
        }
      });

      // Add action listeners
      leftCombo.addActionListener(new ActionListener() {
        public void actionPerformed(ActionEvent evt) {
          System.out.println("Left combo action event: " + evt);
        }
      });

      middleCombo.addActionListener(new ActionListener() {
        public void actionPerformed(ActionEvent evt) {
          System.out.println("Middle combo action event: " + evt);
        }
      });

      rightCombo.addActionListener(new ActionListener() {
        public void actionPerformed(ActionEvent evt) {
          System.out.println("Right combo action event: " + evt);
        }
      });
  }

  public static void main(String[] args) {
    JFrame f = new JFrame("Combo Box Example");
    ComboBoxExample c = new ComboBoxExample();
    f.getContentPane().add(c);

    f.addWindowListener(new WindowAdapter() {
      public void windowClosing(WindowEvent evt) {
        System.exit(0);
      }
    });

    f.pack();
```

```
      f.setVisible(true);


      // Start with the popup shown
      // on the left combo box
      leftCombo.showPopup();

   }

   static JComboBox leftCombo;
   static JComboBox middleCombo;
   static JComboBox rightCombo;

   public static String[] rightComboData = {
        "Neil Armstrong", "Buzz Aldrin", "Michael Collins",
        "Pete Conrad", "Richard Gordon", "Alan Bean",
        "James Lovell", "Fred Haise", "Jack Swigert",
        "Alan Shepard", "Stuart Roosa", "Edgar Mitchell"
   };

   public static String[] middleComboData = {
        "White", "Yellow", "Green", "Red", "Pink",
        "Blue", "Magenta", "Orange", "Gray", "Black"
   };

   public static Icon[] leftComboData = new Icon[] {
        new ColorFillIcon(Color.white, 16), new ColorFillIcon(Color.yellow, 16),
        new ColorFillIcon(Color.green, 16), new ColorFillIcon(Color.red, 16),
        new ColorFillIcon(Color.pink, 16), new ColorFillIcon(Color.blue, 16),
        new ColorFillIcon(Color.magenta, 16), new ColorFillIcon(Color.orange, 16),
        new ColorFillIcon(Color.gray, 16), new ColorFillIcon(Color.black, 16)
   };
}
```

All three combo boxes are populated using the addItem method; the default combo box data model is used for both combo boxes, so this method can be used to add data to the box. As you can see, the strings and the icons are added in exactly the same way. The middle combo box, which contains text strings, is made editable and, as a result, when you run this program, if you type something into the middle combo box and press return, you'll see an event containing the string that you typed appear in the window from which you started the program. If you move to the left-hand combo box and select an icon, you'll find that that icon will appear in the input box and another selection event is generated. You won't be able to type anything into the right-hand combo box because it isn't editable, which is the default state. You can change this using the setEditable method.

As well as using the mouse to make selections, you can also navigate the selection list with up and down arrow keys on the keyboard. There is, however, a difference: When you use the keyboard, you get a DESELECT event followed by a SELECT event each time you move the selection. In practice, this is not an important difference, because most applications won't consider the user to have made a choice until a selection has been made and confirmed, probably by pressing a button elsewhere on the dialog.

As this example shows, you can also add an ActionListener to a combo box. An ActionEvent is generated just after the SELECT ItemEvent, but it tells you less about what has happened than the ItemEvent does. You need to explicitly query the JComboBox to find out what has been selected. You can use the JComboBox setActionCommand method to change the action command delivered with the ActionEvent; by default, this is set to the constant string 'comboBoxChanged'.

Selecting an Entry By Prefix

A third way to navigate the choice list is to press a key corresponding to the first letter of one of its entries, which causes that entry to be selected. This method only works if the combo box is not editable and if the items in the selection list have meaningful string representations. In this example, only the right-hand combo box will respond to key selection. If there is more than one entry with the same first letter, pressing the same key repeatedly causes them all to be selected in turn. Case is ignored when matching the key you press to the entries in the combo box. It is possible to search objects that are not strings in this way, provided that the object has a toString method that returns a reasonable value. For example, if we changed our ColorFillIcon class to return the color name from its toString method, it would be possible to find a green icon by pressing "g," because the search algorithm compares the key pressed to the first character of the string returned by toString.

Note that it isn't possible to search for strings based on more than one letter, because pressing the key "A" followed by "B" results in a search for an entry that starts with "A" or "a" and then for an entry beginning with "B" or "b," not for an entry that begins "AB" (in either upper, lower or mixed case).

A Combo Box with Multiple Key Selection

If you want to improve on this feature, you can install a custom key manager by implementing the JComboBox.KeySelectionManager interface, which has only one method:

```
public abstract int selectionForKey(char key, ComboBoxModel model);
```

Keys pressed in the combo box's popup are passed to this method, together with the data from the control. This method is required to search the data in the model and return the index of the item that matches the selected key, according to its own definition of what matching means. If no entry matches, –1 should be returned. The default key selection manager does exactly that—looks for an exact match of the single given character against an entry in the model—which is why it cannot cope with searching for a string more than one character long. To implement a more powerful search, you need to remember some state between invocations of this method. Listing 8-15 shows a sample implementation of a key selection manager that implements such a search. You can try this example out by typing the command:

```
java JFCBook.Chapter8.ComboBoxSearchExample
```

Listing 8-15   Implementation of a JComboBox list-searching class

---

```
package JFCBook.Chapter8;

import com.sun.java.swing.*;
import java.awt.event.ActionEvent;
import java.awt.event.ActionListener;
import java.awt.event.KeyEvent;
import java.awt.Toolkit;

public class MultiKeySelection implements
JComboBox.KeySelectionManager,
             ActionListener {
  public MultiKeySelection() {
    searchTimer = new Timer(SEARCH_DELAY, this);
    searchTimer.setRepeats(false);   // Only one event is required
  }

  public int selectionForKey(char key, ComboBoxModel model) {
    int selectedIndex = 0;
    int modelSize = model.getSize();

    // Ignore this if our search string is at maximum size
    if (searchStringSize == MAX_SEARCH_STRING) {
      return -1;
    }

    if (key == KeyEvent.CHAR_UNDEFINED) {
      searchStringSize = 0;
      searchString = "";
      Toolkit.getDefaultToolkit().beep();
       return -1;
    }
```

continued

```
   // Stop the search delay timer
   searchTimer.stop();

   // Convert the key to lower case and store it.
   char realKey = ("" + key).toLowerCase().charAt(0);
   searchString += realKey;
   searchStringSize++;

   // Get the start point of the search
   Object selectedItem = model.getSelectedItem();
   if (selectedItem != null) {
     String searchString = selectedItem.toString();
     for (int i = 0; i < modelSize; i++) {
       if (searchString.equals(model.getElementAt(i).toString())) {
         selectedIndex = i;
         break;
       }
     }
   }

   boolean found = false;

   // Search forward from "selectedIndex", wrapping the search at the bottom
   for (int i = 0; i < modelSize; i++) {
     String entry = ((String)model.getElementAt(selectedIndex)).toLowerCase();

     if (entry.length() >= searchStringSize) {
       // Entry is no smaller than search string
       if (entry.startsWith(searchString)) {
         found = true;
         break;
       }
     }

     // Try next entry
     if (++selectedIndex == modelSize) {
       selectedIndex = 0;                 // Wrap to the top
     }
   }

   // Restart the delay timer
   searchTimer.start();
   return found == true ? selectedIndex : -1;
}

// Timer handler
```

```
public void actionPerformed(ActionEvent evt) {
  // Timer has expired: empty the search string
  searchStringSize = 0;
  searchString = "";
}

// Size of the longest search string
public static final int MAX_SEARCH_STRING = 16;

// The current search string
protected String searchString = "";

// Size of the search string
protected int searchStringSize;

// The timer that cancels a search after a pause
protected Timer searchTimer;

// The delay until we cancel a search. If no key is pressed
// for this length of time, we clear the search string.
protected static final int SEARCH_DELAY = 5000;    // 5 seconds
}
```

When you start this example, you get a frame with a single combo box in it that contains the names of many of the Apollo astronauts. The list of names will drop down without the combo box being clicked; to get the list to drop down, the JComboBox showPopup method was used. An instance of the MultiKeySelection class has been attached to this combo box, replacing the default key selection manager. Now, any key strokes that are directed at the combo box will be passed to this object's selectionForKey method.

The basic idea of this method is simple. A string containing all of the search characters that have been typed is created. Each time a new character is received, it is added to the string and then the data in the model is scanned for an item that starts with that string, ignoring case. If a match is found, the index of the matching entry is returned, which will cause it to be selected. If there is no match, –1 is returned, which leaves the current selection unchanged. The details are a little more complicated, but not too hard.

First, as key strokes are received, they are converted to lowercase and appended to the string held in the searchString field. An upper limit of 16 characters on this field keeps the search times reasonable. Any characters in excess of this limit are simply dumped. In order to perform the search, the following methods of ComboBoxModel are used:

```
public int getSize()                    Returns the number of items in the model

public Object                           Returns the indicated entry
    getElementAt(int index)
```

Where should the search start? The most logical place to start is with the currently selected item, but it isn't easy to directly find out where that is—since this code doesn't have a reference to the `JComboBox`, it can't get call `getSelectedIndex` to get the starting index. Instead, it only has access to the `ComboBoxModel`, so it call its `getSelectedItem` method, which returns the `Object` that is the current selection. If this is not `null`, it is converted to a string (remember it could be any type of object), then used as the key to search the model for the corresponding entry. If it is found, its index is the starting point. If it is not found, or its value was `null`, the search starts at the first entry.

Once the starting point is known, the search is easy: Every item is retrieved, sequentially, from the model and checked to see if it starts with the search string. Note that, again, the items in the model are `Objects`, so the code first invokes `toString` and then converts the result to lowercase before performing the comparison. Finally, if a match is found, its index is returned. If no match is found when all the entries in the model have been checked, –1 is returned.

This much code is enough to implement a search that matches on multiple keys. To see that this works, try searching for "Alan Bean" and "Alan Shepard." You'll discover that you can find them, and any other entry, by continuing to type characters until you have supplied a string that is not ambiguous. When there is more than one match, the first one found is selected (which depends on what was selected before, of course).

However, at some stage it is necessary to clean out the search string, or it would soon reach 16 characters and would be useless. It can't be cleared out when a match is found, because that would be the same as the default key selection manager. Instead, two mechanisms are used. First, if you hit any key on your keyboard that doesn't generate an ASCII character (such as a function key), you will hear a beep and the search string will be cleared. You can try this easily by type typing "Ala" then hitting F1 followed by "B." You'll immediately find Buzz Aldrin. The second method involves using a timer. Each time a key is added to the search string, a 5-second timer is started. If this timer ever expires (i.e., there hasn't been a keystroke for 5 seconds), it is assumed that the user has given up on the search and the search string is discarded.

Timers

The ability to use a timer is a new feature provided by the Swing package. In JDK 1.1, if you wanted to use a timer, you had to implement it for yourself, usually by starting a separate thread that suspended itself (using the `Thread.sleep` method) for the required length of time and then generated an event. The Swing `Timer` class allows you to create and manage as many timers as you need without worrying about the implementation details.

Creating, Starting and Stopping a Timer

To use a Swing timer, you need a timer object and an `ActionListener` that will be notified when the timer expires. The `Timer` class has only one constructor:

```
public Timer(int delay, ActionListener l);
```

The delay is specified in milliseconds. Creating the timer does not, however, make it active. Often, as is the case in Listing 8-15, you create a timer in the constructor of some other object and you don't want the timer to begin until some later point. When you need the timer to run, you use its `start` method:

```
public void start();
```

Once the timer is running, it continues until one of three things happens:

- The time interval expires
- The timer is stopped
- The timer is restarted

When the timer expires, it creates an `ActionEvent` and delivers it to any registered listeners. In Listing 8-15, the `MultiKeySelection` class acts as its own `ActionListener`, so that timer expiry is handled by its `actionPerformed` method. The listener was registered when the timer was created, but you don't have to do it this way—it is permissible to create a timer with the `ActionListener` argument passed as `null` and then add a listener later with the `addActionListener` method. You can also deregister a listener using `removeActionListener`. If the timer expires when there are no listeners registered, the event is discarded.

If the event you've been waiting for happens before the time interval is up, you can stop the timer using its `stop` method:

```
public void stop();
```

A stopped timer doesn't generate any more events, but it isn't completely useless: you can start it again using the `start` method and it will start timing from that point. Alternatively, if you want to cancel the timer and start it again immediately, you can use the `restart` method:

```
public void restart();
```

In fact, you can stop a timer and start it again just by invoking `start`, which works even when the timer is running, by resetting the interval until the timer expires. The difference between using `start` and `restart` is that `restart` cancels any pending timer expiry events that haven't yet been delivered, whereas `start` does not.

Repeating Timers and the Initial Timer Delay

By default, timers don't stop once they've delivered their expiry event—they continue to deliver timer expiry events until you explicitly stop them with the `stop` method. Actually, it is possible to arrange for the first event delivered by the timer to have a different delay from all of the other ones by using the `setInitialDelay` method:

```
public void setInitialDelay(int initialDelay);
```

Suppose you create and start a timer like this:

```
Timer tm = new Timer(500, l);          // Half second
tm.start();
```

where `l` is assumed to be an `ActionListener` declared earlier. Assuming it never gets stopped, this timer will deliver an `ActionEvent` every 500 milliseconds. If instead you do this:

```
Timer tm = new Timer(500, l);          // Half second
tm.setInitialDelay(1000);              // One second
tm.start();
```

then the first event is delivered after one second and all of the others occur at half-second intervals. If you explicitly start or restart a timer while it is running, the initial delay is used to determine when the next event is delivered so that, in the above example, restarting the timer with `restart` or `start` will cause the next event to occur after one second, with repeat events every 500 milliseconds after that.

If you don't want this repeating behavior, you can disable it using the `setRepeats` method:

```
Timer tm = new Timer(500, l);
tm.setRepeats(false);
```

This timer will deliver one event after 500 milliseconds and then stop. You can, if required, restart this timer as usual to arrange for another single event some time later. The timer in the combo box example in Listing 8-15 is of this single-shot type, because we only need it to time a single event—once that event occurs, the user's search is implicitly terminated and we don't need the timer any more.

You can change the delay or initial delay associated with a timer when it is stopped or even when it is running. The repeating delay time can be changed using the `setDelay` method:

```
public void setDelay(int delay);
```

Changing the delay when the timer is running takes effect immediately—the timer is stopped and restarted to expire after the new delay. Note that the new delay is used even if the timer has never expired and has a different initial delay. On the other hand, changing the initial delay while the timer is running has no effect at all until the next time that the timer is started using `start` or `restart`.

Merging Timer Events

Timer events are created internally and are delivered into the system event queue. When a timer event reaches the head of the queue, it is removed and your `actionPerformed` method is called. Since a timer repeats by default, if your timer delay is short and the system is busy, it is possible that several events for the same timer could be generated before any events are processed. You can avoid this situation by allowing timer events to be coalesced, so that only one event is generated at a time. If the timer expires while an earlier event is still in the queue, a new event will not be generated, but the timer will start on its next cycle. You control whether coalescing is done using the `setCoalesce` method:

```
public void setCoalesce(boolean coalesce);
```

By default, timer events will coalesce, which is appropriate if you don't need to see every event. It is recommended that you allow coalescing to occur if possible because it can stop the event queue from being filled up with timer events that will prevent your application responding to the user, since AWT events use the same queue.

Conveying Extra Information with a Timer Event

The timer that was used in Listing 8-15 didn't need to convey any information to its `actionPerformed` method—all this method needed to have was a reference to the `MultiKeySelection` object, which it got from the `this` value. If you need to deliver state information to the event handler, the only way to do it is to subclass `Timer` and store the information you need in your object. Suppose, for example, you need to store a message to be written when the timer expires. To do this, you would create a subclass that can store the message:

```
public class MessageTimer extends Timer {
   public MessageTimer(int delay, ActionListener l, String msg) {
      super(delay, l);
      this.msg = msg;
   }

   public String getMessage() {
      return msg;
   }
   protected String msg;
}
```

Now, instead of creating a `Timer`, you create a `MessageTimer`. Because a `MessageTimer` is derived from `Timer`, you can use all of the methods of `Timer` with it, including `start`:

```
Timer tm = new MessageTimer(500, l, "Timer expired...");
tm.start();
```

When the timer expires, you can retrieve the message from the `MessageTimer` object. Here's a sample event handler that just prints the message:

```
ActionListener l = new ActionListener() {
    public void actionPerformed(ActionEvent evt) {
        MessageTimer tm = (MessageTimer)evt.getSource();
        System.out.println(tm.getMessage());
    }
};
```

This code uses the fact that the source of the `ActionEvent` delivered from a timer is the `Timer` object itself which, in this case, is actually a `MessageTimer`. Using this reference, you can retrieve the message using the `getMessage` method that we implemented in the `MessageTimer` class. Note that you can't make any use of the fact that `ActionEvent` has a `getActionCommand` method, because there is no way to set the action command when creating the timer. In fact, if you call `getActionCommand` in the event handler, you get back `null`.

Core Tip

The `Timer` *class has a simple debugging facility built into it—if you call the static* `setLogTimers` *method with argument* `true`, *you'll get trace messages printed to your command window whenever a timer event is generated. You can turn this off by calling the same method with argument* `false`. *Here's an example of what you might see:* `Timer ringing: MessageTimer@1cc73c`

The Progress Bar

The Swing `JProgressBar` is a very simple, yet effective control. Its task is to give a visual representation of how far a task has progressed in proportion to how long it will take to complete. A progress bar is basically a rectangle that may or may not have a border and may be drawn either horizontally or vertically. Initially, the rectangle will usually be empty. As the application progresses through its operation, it updates the progress bar, which causes it to fill with color from left to right, or from bottom to top.

Creating and Managing a Progress Bar

Management of the progress bar is entirely the program's responsibility. After creating it, the program must configure a maximum and a minimum value and, when it starts the operation that the progress bar is tracking, it should use the `JProgressBar` `setValue` method to set the current value to the configured minimum. As the operation proceeds, `setValue` should be called with progressively larger values, working towards the maximum value at the end of the operation.

For example, suppose the application has a task that involves 50 steps, perhaps 50 iterations of a program loop. To indicate to the user how far it has progressed, it would create a JProgressBar with a minimum value of 0 and a maximum of 50. At the start of the operation, it would call setValue(0) to initialize the progress bar and then, at the end of each step, it would call it again with a value one larger than the one used in the previous step. This will cause the progress bar to fill with color at a uniform rate, assuming that each step takes an equal amount of time. Apart from calling setValue, the application doesn't need to do anything else—the JProgressBar repaints itself when necessary.

To illustrate the steps required, Listing 8-16 is a (somewhat contrived) example that creates a progress bar and increments its value every second. As you can see if you run this example yourself using the command:

```
java JFCBook.Chapter8.ProgressBarExample1
```

the setForeground method can be used to change the color used to fill the progress bar—in this case it is green. Figure 8-16 shows the progress bar after about 30 iterations of the program loop.

Listing 8-16   A Progress Bar

```
package JFCBook.Chapter8;

import com.sun.java.swing.*;
import java.awt.*;
import java.awt.event.*;

public class ProgressBarExample1 {
  public static void main(String[] args) {
    JFrame f = new JFrame("Progress Bar Example 1");
    JProgressBar b = new JProgressBar();
    b.setOrientation(JProgressBar.HORIZONTAL);
    b.setMinimum(0);
    b.setMaximum(100);
    b.setValue(0);
    b.setForeground(Color.green);
    b.setBorderPainted(true);
    f.getContentPane().add(b);
    f.pack();
    f.setVisible(true);
    f.addWindowListener(new WindowAdapter() {
      public void windowClosing(WindowEvent evt) {
        System.exit(0);
      }
    });
```

continued

```
    try {
      for (int i = 0; i <= 100; i++) {
        Thread.sleep(1000);
        b.setValue(i);
      }
    } catch (Throwable t) {
    }
  }
}
```

Figure 8-16 Progress bar.

Some of the more important methods of JProgressBar are listed in Table 8-5.

Table 8-5 JProgressBar Methods

Method	*Description*
public int getMaximum()	Returns the maximum value. By default, this is set to 100.
public int getMinimum()	Gets the minimum value, 0 by default.
public int getOrientation()	Gets the progress bar's orientation, one of JProgressBar.HORIZONTAL and JProgressBar.VERTICAL. Horizontal by default.
public int getValue()	Returns the current value. Initially returns 0.
public boolean isBorderPainted()	This is true by default, which indicates that a border will be drawn. The default border is a lowered bevel border. Since JProgressBar is a JComponent, you can change the border if you wish by using setBorder.
public boolean isOpaque()	Indicates whether or not the background will be painted. This is true by default.
public void setBorderPainted(boolean)	Enables or disables painting of a border.
public void setMaximum(int)	Sets the maximum value.

`public void setMinimum(int)`	Sets the minimum value.
`public void setOpaque(boolean)`	Determines whether or not the background will be painted or not. If set to `false`, the background of the container in which the progress bar is mounted will be visible under the progress markers.
`public void setOrientation(int)`	Makes the progress bar horizontal or vertical.
`public void setValue(int)`	Changes the current value of the progress bar. Causes the progress bar to repaint itself.

Progress Bar Events

You are not obliged to supply increasing values to `setValue`; if the values go down as well as up, the progress bar will similarly go down and up (or left and right) as appropriate. It is also possible to arrange for a progress bar to start at its maximum value and work down to its minimum. This might be appropriate if the progress bar represents free space on a disk which, in my experience, is a monotonically decreasing quantity.

It is also possible to monitor the state of a progress bar by registering a `ChangeListener` using the `addChangeListener` method. Whenever `setValue` is called, a `ChangeEvent` is posted to all registered listeners. This event reports only its source; to get the current value of the progress bar, you need to use its `getValue` method. Figure 8-17 shows a collection of progress bars configured in different ways and a text field that monitors the value of one of the bars. This text field is updated using `ChangeEvents` generated from the horizontal progress bar at the top of the diagram. Here is the code that arranges for these events to be generated and handles them when they occur:

```
northBar.addChangeListener(new ChangeListener() {
  public void stateChanged(ChangeEvent evt) {
    JProgressBar bar = (JProgressBar)evt.getSource();
    tf.setText("Value is " + bar.getValue());
  }
});
```

You can find rest of the code for this example on the CD-ROM and you can run it with the command:

```
java JFCBook.Chapter8.ProgressBarExample2
```

The progress bar at the top has a default configuration, apart from its green foreground that dictates the color of the filler. This bar's value starts at 0 and is incremented every second. The bar on the left has a raised bevel border and is also opaque; as a result, the yellow border is visible under the progress marker. Finally, the bar on the right is opaque but has no border at all. Its value starts at 100 and decreases; when it reaches zero, it is reset to 100 and the cycle begins again.

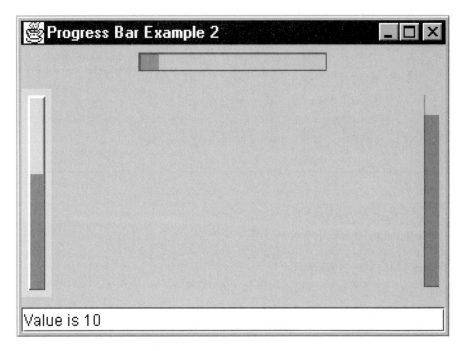

Figure 8-17   Customized progress bars.

ProgressMonitor and ProgressMonitorInputStream

Swing includes a couple of useful classes based on `JProgressBar` that create and manage their own dialog boxes. Let's look first at `ProgressMonitorInputStream`. This class looks like an ordinary input stream that can be included in a pipeline with all of the other input streams in the `java.io` package. When it's sitting in an input stream, it snoops on the data that's being read and, if it thinks that the process of reading all of the data is going to take a long time, it pops up a dialog with a message that you can configure and a progress bar that shows how far through the file the reading has progressed. Listing 8-17 shows a program that reads a file whose name you give it and counts the number of words (defined as sequences of characters separated by white space) it finds. If this process takes more than a couple of seconds, a progress monitor appears, as you can see from Figure 8-18. You can try this example for yourself using the command:

```
java JFCBook.Chapter8.WordCounter
```

You need to give it a large file so that the operation takes long enough for the progress dialog to appear. If you've got the JDK documentation installed in the directory `c:\java`, you can find a very large text file at `c:\java\docs\api\ AllNames.html`. This file is more than one megabyte long and it can take several minutes to count the number of words in it on a slow PC.

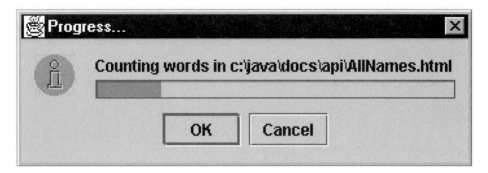

Figure 8-18   ProgressMonitorInputStream monitoring a long process.

Listing 8-17   Using ProgressMonitorInputStream

```
package JFCBook.Chapter8;

import com.sun.java.swing.*;
import java.awt.*;
import java.awt.event.*;
import java.io.*;
import java.util.*;

public class WordCounter extends JPanel implements ActionListener {
  public WordCounter() {
    this.setLayout(new GridBagLayout());
    GridBagConstraints c = new GridBagConstraints();
    Insets i = new Insets(3, 3, 3, 3);

    c.gridx = 0;
    c.gridy = 0;
    c.gridwidth = 1;
    c.gridheight = 1;
    c.insets = i;
    c.anchor = GridBagConstraints.EAST;
    c.fill = GridBagConstraints.NONE;
    c.weightx = 0.0;
    c.weighty = 0.0;
    JLabel l = new JLabel("File Name: ", JLabel.RIGHT);
    this.add(l, c);

    c.gridy = 1;
    l = new JLabel("Words Found: ", JLabel.RIGHT);
    this.add(l, c);
```

continued

```
      c.gridx = 1;
      c.gridy = 0;
      c.fill = GridBagConstraints.HORIZONTAL;
      c.weightx = 1.0;
      fileName = new JTextField(40);
      this.add(fileName, c);

      c.gridy = 1;
      wordsFound = new JLabel("          ", JLabel.LEFT);
      this.add(wordsFound, c);

      fileName.addActionListener(this);
   }

   public void actionPerformed(ActionEvent evt) {
     Thread t = new Thread() {
       public void run() {
         String name = fileName.getText().trim();
         int words = 0;
         String str;
         DataInputStream is = null;
         try {
           fileName.setEnabled(false);
           wordsFound.setText("");

           is = new DataInputStream(
             new BufferedInputStream(
               new ProgressMonitorInputStream(
                 WordCounter.this,
                 "Counting words in " + name,
                 new FileInputStream(name))));

           while ((str = is.readLine()) != null) {
             words += new StringTokenizer(str).countTokens();
             wordsFound.setText("" + words);
           }
         } catch (FileNotFoundException e) {
           JOptionPane.showMessageDialog(WordCounter.this,
                 "Cannot find " + name,
                 "File Error",
                 JOptionPane.ERROR_MESSAGE);
           wordsFound.setText("");
         } catch (IOException e) {
           JOptionPane.showMessageDialog(WordCounter.this,
                 "I/O Exception while reading " + name,
                 "File Read Error",
                 JOptionPane.ERROR_MESSAGE);
```

```
                 wordsFound.setText("");
             } finally {
                 fileName.setEnabled(true);
                 try {
                     if (is != null) {
                         is.close();// Always close!
                     }
                 } catch (IOException ioe) {
                     // Nothing to do
                 }
             }
         }
     };
     t.start();
   }

   public static void main(String[] args) {
     JFrame f = new JFrame("Word Counter");
     f.getContentPane().add(new WordCounter());
     f.addWindowListener(new WindowAdapter() {
       public void windowClosing(WindowEvent evt) {
         System.exit(0);
       }
     });
     f.pack();
     f.setVisible(true);
   }

   protected JTextField fileName;
   protected JLabel wordsFound;
}
```

Using a ProgressMonitorInputStream

Most of the implementation is uninteresting. The important line of code from the point of view of this section is this:

```
is = new DataInputStream(
   new BufferedInputStream(
       new ProgressMonitorInputStream(
         WordCounter.this,
         "Counting words in " + name,
         new FileInputStream(name))));
```

This seemingly contorted line constructs a normal stack of input streams to read from a file, but in the middle of it there is a `ProgressMonitorInputStream`. The constructor for this class is defined as follows:

```
public ProgressMonitorInputStream(Component parent,
        Object message,
        InputStream in);
```

The first argument is, as usual, a component in the frame that will be the parent of the dialog that gets popped up. In our example, the word counter is implemented as a `JPanel` that contains the components necessary to allow the user to supply the file name and to see the number of words counted as the operation proceeds and this panel as the first argument of the constructor. The second argument is the message that is displayed in the dialog box above the progress bar. This argument can be anything that can be supplied as a message to `JOptionPane`, including a string (as here), an `Icon`, a `Component`, or an array of these types of objects.

The last argument is the input stream to monitor; to the next stream in the chain, the `ProgressMonitorInputStream` is transparent—it just passes the data straight through, while keeping the dialog updated as it does so. When the input stream is closed, the dialog box disappears.

The dialog box that pops up has two buttons on it, as you can see in Figure 8-18. If you press the `Cancel` button, the next read that's issued against the input stream will fail with an `IOException`. This should cause the reader to stop whatever it's doing and, in our example, it causes an error dialog to be posted. Pressing the `OK` button or closing the dialog using the close button on its window has no effect on the program—it causes the dialog box to disappear on the assumption that you don't want to see progress for this operation any more.

Notice a very important point about this example. When the user pressed return in the text field, the `actionPerformed` method was entered. This method just created a new thread and then returned. All of the work of reading the file and counting words is carried out in this new thread. Why is this necessary? The `actionPerformed` method is executed in the AWT event thread. As you know, if this thread gets blocked, the user interface stops working, because this thread handles all repaint requests and all of the other events that keep the interface up to date. Obviously, reading a long file is going to tie this thread up for a long time, so this activity is delegated to another thread instead. If you don't do this, the `ProgressMonitorInputStream` dialog box will appear but won't be able to paint itself and the count of words on the main window won't update.

The ProgressMonitor Class

We said that the dialog box appears "after a while." What exactly did we mean by that and how does it work? The `ProgressMonitorInputStream` is actually based around a simpler class called `ProgressMonitor`, which supplies the dialog box and the code that decides whether it should be displayed or not. Here is its constructor:

```
public ProgressMonitor(Component parent,
        Object message,
        String note,
        int min,
        int max);
```

The first two arguments are these same ones as those passed to the constructor of `ProgressMonitorInputStream`. The `min` and `max` arguments set the bounds for a set of values that describe the operation in progress. In the case of the example in Listing 8-17, `min` would be zero and `max` would be the size of the file that is being read. These two values are used to construct the `JProgressBar`. The third argument is the one of interest in the example that will be shown below. The string that's supplied, if it is not `null`, is placed between the message and the progress bar. As the operation progresses, you use the following two methods to update the dialog:

```
public void setProgress(int value);

public void setNote(String note);
```

The `setProgress` method updates the progress bar with a new value, which must be between the maximum and minimum values passed to the constructor. If this value is greater than or equal to the maximum, the operation is assumed to be completed and the dialog disappears. Similarly, calling `setNote` changes the note displayed on the dialog, which allows you to report more useful status information in addition to showing total progress through the operation. If you want to use `setNote`, you must invoke the constructor with a `note` argument that is not `null`, or the dialog won't contain a note line at all.

In order to use `ProgressMonitor`, you first create one, setting its minimum and maximum values. As the operation progresses, you update it with progress using the `setProgress` method and possibly using `setNote` as well. That's all the application needs to do. When first created, the progress monitor doesn't have a dialog. It waits for a short time and monitors the progress that is reported to it. At the end of this period, it attempts to work out how long the entire operation will take and, if this predicted time is longer than another configurable value, it creates and pops up a dialog box showing the message, the note (if there is one) and the progress bar.

You can control how long `ProgressMonitor` waits before deciding how long the operation will take using `setMillisToDecideToPopup` and the time that the operation must last for using the `setMillisToPopup`:

```
public void setMillisToDecideToPopup(int delay);

public void setMillisToPopup(int delay);
```

Both methods require a time interval in milliseconds. Consider this example:

```
ProgressMonitor p = new ProgressMonitor( … params not shown …);
p.setMillisToDecideToPopup(250);
p.setMillisToPopup(1000);
```

With these values, the progress monitor will wait for 250 milliseconds before predicting the expected length of the operation. At that time if it expects the operation to take longer than 1000 milliseconds, it will create and show the dialog box. By default, the initial wait time is 500 milliseconds and the operation must be expected to last 2 seconds before a dialog will be shown.

Core Note

The progress monitor makes its prediction on the first invocation of setProgress *after the initial time limit has passed. If you don't call* setProgress *for a long time, the dialog box will not appear until you do call it.*

Once a dialog is shown, it will remain on view until the user dismisses it using the OK or Cancel buttons, or until setProgress is called with a value that exceeds the maximum value given to the constructor. If you abort the operation for any reason, you must call the progress monitor's close method to allow it to dismiss the dialog.

It is possible to demonstrate ProgressMonitor by making a change to the actionPerformed method of the previous example. Instead of having ProgressMonitorInputStream create and manage the ProgressMonitor, the new version will create its own and have it display not only the current progress but also how long it thinks the operation will take to complete. To do this, the setNote method will be used to write a text string with the current time remaining onto the dialog box. Listing 8-18 shows the new actionPerformed method.

Core Note

If you press the Cancel *button on the dialog shown by* ProgressMonitorInputStream, *the I/O operation is terminated with an exception because the ProgressMonitorInputStream is handling the I/O. If you use a* ProgressMonitor, *dismissing it has no effect on the I/O, because it isn't directly involved in it.*

Listing 8-18   Displaying extra information with a ProgressMonitor

```
public void actionPerformed(ActionEvent evt) {
  Thread t = new Thread() {
    public void run() {
        String name = fileName.getText().trim();
        int words = 0;
        int bytesRead = 0;
        String str;
        DataInputStream is = null;
        ProgressMonitor p = null;
        long startTime;
        long currentTime;
        long lastCheckTime;

        try {
          fileName.setEnabled(false);
          wordsFound.setText("");
            is = new DataInputStream(
                  new BufferedInputStream(
                       new FileInputStream(name)));

          float size = (float)new File(name).length();// Total size of file
          p = new ProgressMonitor(WordCounterTime.this,
                  "Counting words in " + name,
                  TIME_STRING,
                  0, (int)size);

          startTime = System.currentTimeMillis();
          lastCheckTime = startTime;
          while ((str = is.readLine()) != null) {
            bytesRead += str.length();
            words += new StringTokenizer(str).countTokens();
            wordsFound.setText("" + words);

            currentTime = System.currentTimeMillis();
            if (currentTime - lastCheckTime > CHECK_INTERVAL) {
              lastCheckTime = currentTime;
              float bytes = (float)bytesRead;
              float sizeLeft = size - bytes;
              int guessTime = (int)((((currentTime - startTime)/bytes) *
                        sizeLeft)/1000);
              p.setNote(TIME_STRING + guessTime + " seconds");
            }
```

continued

```
              p.setProgress(bytesRead);
            }
        } catch (FileNotFoundException e) {
          JOptionPane.showMessageDialog(WordCounterTime.this,
                    "Cannot find " + name,
                    "File Error",
                    JOptionPane.ERROR_MESSAGE);
          wordsFound.setText("");
        } catch (IOException e) {
          JOptionPane.showMessageDialog(WordCounterTime.this,
                    "I/O Exception while reading " + name,
                    "File Read Error",
                    JOptionPane.ERROR_MESSAGE);
          wordsFound.setText("");
        } finally {
          fileName.setEnabled(true);
          try {
            if (is != null) {
              is.close();// Always close!
            }
          } catch (IOException ioe) {
            // Nothing to do
          }

          if (p != null) {
            p.close();    // Close the ProgressMonitor
          }
        }
      }
    };
    t.start();
}

protected static final String TIME_STRING = "Time remaining: ";
protected static final long CHECK_INTERVAL = 500;
```

You can try this example for yourself using the command:

```
java JFCBook.Chapter8.WordCounterTime
```

To get the dialog to appear, you have to give it a file that is large enough to make the operation take longer than two seconds—the file AllNames.html used with the previous example will also work here. Figure 8-19 shows the dialog that appears while this program is running.

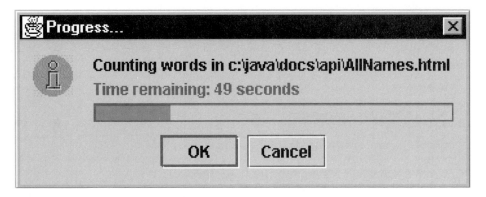

Figure 8-19   Using ProgressMonitor.

In the `actionPerformed` method, the size of the file is used as the maximum value for the `ProgressMonitor` constructor. Since this example is going to use the note field, it is necessary to pass a nonnull note argument, in this case the string "Time Remaining:" which is the first part of the message that we will later display there. Once the progress monitor is created, it isn't necessary to display it—our only duty is to call `setProgress` and `setNote` to let it do its job. As the program reads through the file, it keeps track of how many bytes have been read and how long it has been reading for.

Every 500 milliseconds, an attempt is made to work out how long the entire operation will take by calculating the average speed at which data has been read so far and multiplying this value by the number of bytes left to read. This is, of course, a very rough-and-ready mechanism, but it suffices as an estimate. Having calculated the time left, `setNote` is used to show the result on the dialog. The `setProgress` method is also called after every line of input to cause the progress bar to be updated and, initially, to give the progress monitor the opportunity to decide whether it needs to create the dialog box.

Finally, when the operation completes, or aborts for some reason, the progress monitor is closed.

The Slider Control

The slider is a simple control that allows the user to adjust the value of a setting that takes one of a continuous range of values, where the ends of the range are fixed. To create a slider, you need to specify its orientation, the maximum and minimum values that the slider can take and its initial value:

```
public JSlider(int orientation, int minimum, int maximum, int value);
```

The orientation must be either `JSlider.HORIZONTAL` or `JSlider.VERTICAL`. There is also a constructor that requires no arguments. This constructor creates a horizontal slider with a minimum of 0, maximum 100 and initial value 50. You can, however, change these defaults later using the setMaximum, setMinimum and setValue methods and you can even change the slider's orientation with setOrientation:

```
public void setMinimum(int min);

public void setMaximum(int max);

public void setValue(int value);

public void setOrientation(int orientation);
```

If you create a slider and make it visible, you get just a bare groove and a the thumbnail that moves along it. If the slider is horizontal, the left side of the groove represents the minimum value; for a vertical slider, the minimum value is at the bottom. Figure 8-20 shows two horizontal sliders.

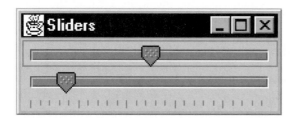

Figure 8-20   Two JSlider controls.

The slider at the top of the figure was created with the line:

```
JSlider slider = new JSlider(JSlider.HORIZONTAL, 0, 100, 50);
```

As you can see, there is no visible marking that shows the range or the current value of the slider; about all you can tell from the figure is that you are approximately in the middle of the allowed range. The slider underneath is slightly more useful because it has tick marks added. There are three methods that control the display of these marks:

```
public void setPaintTicks(boolean paint);

public void setMajorTickSpacing(int pixels);

public void setMinorTickSpacing(int pixels);
```

The first method controls whether the ticks will be shown at all; if you call it with argument false, you won't get any ticks. Enabling ticks is not, however, enough to make them appear because, by default, there aren't any to show until you call one or both of the other two methods, which determine the distance, in slider units, between successive major ticks and minor ticks. In the lower half of Figure 8-20, the tick marks were added by the following lines of code:

```
slider.setPaintTicks(true);
slider.setMajorTickSpacing(20);
slider.setMinorTickSpacing(4);
```

With these settings, you get the large tick marks at intervals of 20 and the small ones every 4 units, which means that there will be 5 short ticks to every major one and a total of 5 major ticks in all, since the total range covered is 100. Obviously, where a minor tick coincides with a major tick, you get a major tick. There is no necessary relationship between the distances between the two types of tick. You could, for example, arrange for them to be completely out of step with each other, as in this case:

```
slider.setMajorTickSpacing(20);
slider.setMinorTickSpacing(3);
```

Here, the minor ticks occur every 3 units, but the major ones are still 20 units apart. As a result, you get either 6 or 7 minor ticks, equally spaced, between the major ticks, but the result is not very useful (Figure 8-21).

Figure 8-21 JSlider with incompatible major/
minor tick values.

Changing the Slider Value and Handling Slider Events

The value associated with a slider is changed by dragging the thumbnail with the mouse, or by clicking on the grooved area, which causes the thumb to move a short distance toward the mouse. The exact distance by which the thumbnail is moved by a mouse click depends on the look-and-feel. With the Windows look-and-feel, the thumbnail moves by one tenth of the maximum value with each mouse click.

As the slider moves, it generates `ChangeEvents` that you can receive by registering a `ChangeListener` with the slider. As you saw in connection with `JProgressBar`, this event tells you nothing other than the fact that its source has changed state in some way—to get the value of the slider, you have to use its `getValue` method.

The slider generates a continuous stream of events as it is dragged by the user, but sometimes you only need to know the value when the slider has come to rest. So that you can tell when this is the case, the slider provides the `getValueIsAdjusting` method, which returns `true` while the slider is in motion. Here is a sample event handler that shows only the value when the slider comes to rest:

```
slider.addChangeListener(new ChangeListener() {
   public void stateChanged(ChangeEvent evt) {
      JSlider source = (JSlider)evt.getSource();
      if (source.getValueIsAdjusting() == false) {
         System.out.println("Slider stopped at value " +
                  source.getValue());
      }
   }
});
```

There are a couple of other things that you can do to control the movement of the thumbnail. First, if you want to ensure that it always stops opposite a tick, you can use the following method:

```
public void setSnapToTicks(boolean cond);
```

Invoking this with value `true` causes the slider to adjust the thumbnail's position after the user stops dragging it so that it always aligns with a tick; what this means in terms of the value of the slider is, of course, unclear unless you have carefully sized your control to guarantee that ticks are on, say, a boundary that causes increments of 5 in the value of the slider.

The other thing you can do is temporarily limit the range of the slider by using the `setExtent` method:

```
public void setExtent(int extent);
```

This method restricts the slider to return a value no more than `extent` less than the maximum so that, for example, if your slider has a maximum value of 99 and an extent of 20, the highest value that will be reported will be 79. If you continue to drag the slider beyond this point, no further events are generated.

As well as restricting the movement of the slider, you can also change its direction of movement using the `setInverted` method:

```
public void setInverted(boolean inverted);
```

If you call this method with argument `true`, the minimum value for a horizontal slider will be on the right and values increase as the thumbnail is dragged to the left. Similarly, in the case of a vertical slider the minimum moves to the top and the value increases as the thumbnail moves down. You can experiment with the effects of the `setSnapToTicks`, `setExtent` and `setInverted` methods by running an example in which the first and last are enabled and the extent is set to 20 on a slider with maximum and minimum values 0 and 99, respectively, using the command:

```
java JFCBook.Chapter8.Sliders3
```

The result of running this example is shown in Figure 8-22.

Figure 8-22   An inverted, filled slider.

The slider shown in Figure 8-22 is slightly different from the ones you saw in the earlier figures. If you look at Figures 8-20 and 8-21, you'll see that the track on which the slider runs is all the same color, whereas in Figure 8-22, only the part that the slider has moved over is of the darker track color—the rest is filled with the same color as the rest of the control. This effect works for the Metal look-and-feel only and is controlled by the client property `JSlider.isFilled`. To get a fill effect like this, the following line of code is required:

```
slider.putClientProperty(JSlider.isFilled, Boolean.TRUE);
```

The track shown in the earlier figures is what you get by default, or if you explicitly specify that it should not be filled as follows:

```
slider.putClientProperty(JSlider.isFilled, Boolean.FALSE);
```

Labels

As well as painting ticks, a slider can also draw labels to represent its possible values. The simplest way to get labels is to use the `setPaintLabels` method:

```
public void setPaintLabels(boolean paint);
```

Calling this method with argument `true` generates a standard set of labels, provided that you have already called `setMajorTickSpacing` with a positive value. A label is generated and placed at the location where each major tick would be drawn. You don't need to turn on painting of ticks to allow labels to be drawn, but you may find the result more readable if you do. Figure 8-23 shows a slider with the standard labels applied to it and major tick spacing set to 20. You can run this example with the command:

```
java JFCBook.Chapter8.Sliders4
```

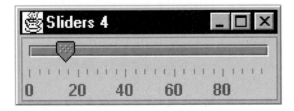

Figure 8-23   A JSlider with default labels.

The labels are actually stored in a `Hashtable`, each entry of which maps a slider value encoded as an `Integer` to the required label, held as a `Component`. When the slider is drawn, the labels in the `Hashtable` are added to it using the slider value to determine position. The standard label set is generated by a method called `createStandardLabels`, which has two variants:

```
public Hashtable createStandardLabels(int increment);
public Hashtable createStandardLabels(int start, int increment);
```

When you call `setPaintLabels`, unless you have already created a label table, it calls the first form of `createStandardLabels` with the major tick spacing as the increment and an implied start value of 10. In the examples in this section, the major tick spacing is 20 and the maximum value is 99, so this would generate labels at values 0, 20, 40, 60 and 80, which is borne out by Figure 8-23. You can change the standard table by calling either version of `createStandardLabels` yourself. The `Hashtable` that is returned should be given as the argument to the `setLabelTable` method:

```
public void setLabelTable(Dictionary labels);
```

For example, you can create labels at intervals of 10 units using this line:

```
slider.setLabelTable(slider.createStandardLabels(10));
```

or you can create labels that count in 15-unit increments starting at 5 with this line of code:

```
slider.setLabelTable(slider.createStandardLabels(5, 15));
```

The standard labels are all `JLabel` objects with the slider value rendered on them. You are not required to use the standard labels, however. You can create your own label table by constructing the appropriate `Hashtable` and using `setLabelTable` to associate with the slider. If you don't need to replace all of the labels, you can use `getLabelTable` to retrieve the current labels and change or add only your new labels:

```
public Dictionary getLabelTable();
```

One way to use `setLabelTable` is to create labels that use icons instead of or as well as text.

Summary

In this chapter, you have seen how to create your own dialog boxes using the Swing `JDialog` class. You've seen the difference between a modal and a non-modal dialog box and how to write the code to handle both types.

You also saw how you can use and customize further the `JOptionPane` and `JFileChooser` classes introduced in the last chapter and how to use them as part of more complex dialogs along with many of the controls that are most frequently used in dialog boxes, including checkboxes, radio buttons, lists, combo boxes, progress monitors and sliders. One of the more powerful ways to create a dialog box is with the `JTabbedPane` control, which allows you to have several "pages" of dialog sheets overlaid on top of each other in such a way that only one is visible at any given time. This control was used to demonstrate the collection of borders that you can apply to any Swing control.

There are two more important Swing controls that might be used in dialogs that you haven't yet seen—`JTree` and `JTable`. Both of them are sufficiently complex that they merit their own chapters in this book. Before that, however, the next chapter takes a close look at what you might up to now have considered to be simple components—text controls.

Part 3

ADVANCED TOPICS

You have now seen all of the new mechanisms that Swing provides to help create more professional-looking applications than was possible with the Abstract Windows Toolkit. You have also seen how to build sophisticated dialogs and how to make keyboard operation faster by providing suitable keyboard accelerators and by carefully controlling the keyboard focus as the user interacts with your application.

In Part 3, you'll build on the groundwork laid in the first eight chapters of this book by looking at some of the more complex and powerful of the Swing components. First, you'll see the Swing text components which, at first glance, look just like lightweight versions of their AWT counterparts. In fact, as you'll soon discover, the lightweight exterior hides a much more sophisticated framework that can be used to build more general components such as `JTextPane` and `JEditorPane`, which support documents containing multiple fonts and colors and even let you view and modify content that is not encoded as plain text. Using the material presented here, you will be able to build on this framework to build your own custom editors and file viewers.

Next, you'll find out about the `JTree` and `JTable` controls. These controls provide two different ways to display bulk data. While being extremely simple to use for mundane tasks, they are also very easy to customize for more demanding tasks. Chapters 10 and 11 are devoted to these controls; they show you not only how to handle the simple cases, but also how to develop your own renderers and editors that enable you to make radical changes to the way these controls appear and how they react to user input.

Multiple-document applications are very popular on the desktop. Swing provides a useful framework for building these applications with the `JDesktopPane` and `JInternalFrame` components. In Chapter 12, you'll see how these components work and how to extend their capabilities to provide tiling, cascading and more.

Finally, Chapter 13 opens the hood on the Swing pluggable look-and-feel mechanism to help you get the best from the ability of every Swing component to take on a new appearance without the need to change application code. Here, you'll see how the pluggable look-and-feel mechanism works, how to change the appearance of individual components, and what is involved in creating your own look-and-feel.

647

TEXT
COMPONENTS

Topics in This Chapter

Chapter 9

The Swing package includes replacements for the AWT `TextField` and `TextArea` components, which provide all of the functionality of the originals with a (nearly) compatible interface. These controls are, however, built on a very rich infrastructure that allows you to do much more with them than was possible with their predecessors. This chapter looks first at the features that `JTextField` and `JTextArea` provide for applications that want a simple input field or a simple way of displaying plain text, then moves on to examine the underlying document infrastructure and the more complex `JTextPane` and `JEditorPane` controls.

Simple Text Controls

Although the text components are built on a complex infrastructure that you'll see later, it is possible to use some of them in a very straightforward manner without having to understand what goes on under the hood. The first half of this chapter looks at the three text components to which this applies, `JTextField`, `JTextArea` and `JPasswordField`.

JTextField and JTextArea

The Swing set includes a large amount of support for text processing, much of which is new. This section looks at the JTextField and JTextArea components, which are replacements for the AWT TextField and TextArea controls.

JTextField

JTextField is a single-line text component that is commonly used to obtain a small amount of input or display a one-line message. You can create a JTextField using one of the following constructors:

```
public JTextField();

public JTextField(Document doc, String text, int cols);

public JTextField(int cols);

public JTextField(String text);

public JTextField(String text, int cols);
```

The first form creates an empty text field with no specified size; if you don't specify the size of text field, it decides for itself how wide it will be and the result you see on the screen will depend on the layout manager in use—see Chapter 3, "Managing the User Interface," for a description of the various layout managers and how they behave.

The second constructor allows you to associate a Document with the text field; a default implementation of the Document interface that is sufficient for most purposes is supplied if you use the other constructors. Just as each Swing component has a separable look-and-feel component that deals with drawing it onto the screen, the text components have the ability to incorporate different methods of holding and manipulating the text itself. In terms of the Model-View-Controller architecture introduced in Chapter 1, "Introduction to the Java Foundation Classes," the Document represents the model. Usually, unless you have special requirements, you won't need to deal with the Document associated with a text component. There is, however, one common case in which you'll need to work with the Document, which you'll see shortly. There is an in-depth description of the Document model later in the second half of this chapter.

The last three constructors are the ones you will use most often. These allow you to create a text field of a specified (or defaulted) size and with given initial content (or blank). There are a couple of important things to keep in mind if you specify the size of a text field. Suppose we do this:

```
JTextField t = new JTextField("Hello, world", 5);
```

This line creates a five-character wide text field with the text "Hello, world" in it. Since the text is more than five characters wide, you might expect that it would not fit in the text field's visible area. The text field can, however, store more characters than it can display, so you don't lose any information by doing this: You won't just get the word "Hello" in the text field, which you can prove by trying the example shown in Listing 9-1, the results of which are shown in Figure 9-1.

Listing 9-1   A simple text field

```
package JFCBook.Chapter9;

import com.sun.java.swing.*;
import java.awt.*;
import java.awt.event.*;

public class TextExample1 {
  public static void main(String[] args) {
    JFrame f = new JFrame("Text Example 1");
    JTextField tf = new JTextField("Hello, world", 5);
    tf.setScrollOffset(0);

    f.getContentPane().setLayout(new FlowLayout());
    f.getContentPane().setBackground(UIManager.getColor("control"));

    f.getContentPane().add(tf);

    f.pack();
    f.addWindowListener(new WindowAdapter() {
      public void windowClosing(WindowEvent evt) {
        System.exit(0);
      }
    });
    f.setVisible(true);
  }
}
```

Figure 9-1   A text field with too much text.

Text Size versus JTextField Size

When, as in this case, the text is too wide to fit in the display area, you can bring the rest of the text into view by scrolling left or right using the mouse or the keyboard. If you do this, you'll see that the whole string is actually in the text field. You can also use the HOME and END keys to move to the left or right ends of the text, respectively.

You will also have noticed that you could actually see more than the first five characters of the text string, despite the fact that a five-character field was created. This is because the font that is used in the text field is not constant width, so any given five-character string might or might not exactly fill the display area. In that case, what exactly do you get when you ask for five characters? What you get is a field wide enough to display five lower case "m" characters in the text field's default font. Since 'm' is a wide character, most of the strings that are displayed in this particular text field will show more than their leading five characters. You can find out how many pixels represent a column for any given text field using the `getColumnWidth` method:

```
public int getColumnWidth();
```

If you change the text field's font, the value returned by this method will change to reflect the width of the letter "m" in the new font. You can also change the number of columns in the text field, or get the current number of columns, with the following two methods:

```
public void setColumns(int columns);
```

```
public int getColumns();
```

Using `setColumns` to change the number of columns won't have any visible effect on the control unless you force the container that it resides in to lay itself out again by calling `validate` on it. Even then, this will have no effect unless the container is allowing the text control to adopt its natural size, as would be the case if it were managed by a `FlowLayout` manager.

Scrolling and Alignment

When the text is too wide to be displayed in the text field's visible area, you can control which part of it is displayed using the following methods:

```
public void setScrollOffset(int offset);
```

```
public int getScrollOffset();
```

The `setScrollOffset` method determines which part of the string appears against the left-hand boundary of the control. The offset is measured in pixels, not characters, so you will need to obtain the `FontMetrics` object for the text field's font if you want to do character-based positioning. If you set the scroll offset to zero, the text starts at the left of the visible area. Setting larger offsets causes some (or all) of the text to be logically drawn to the left of the visible area, giving the appearance of the text scrolling out of the text field to the left. Setting a negative scroll offset is the same as setting a scroll offset of zero. Note that the scroll offset is ignored if the size of the text field is larger than the text that it needs to display.

Another way to control the placement of text within the text field is to use the alignment property that is set using the `setHorizontalAlignment` method:

```
public void setHorizontalAlignment(int align);
```

The `align` argument takes one of the values `JTextField.LEFT` (the default), `JTextField.CENTER` or `JTextField.RIGHT`. Once the alignment has been set, the text stays aligned that way even if more is added to the field so that, for example, if the text is right-aligned and the user adds more to the end of it, the left side of the text moves to the left to make room. Similarly, center-aligned text remains centered as the user types new text.

Getting and Setting the Text Field Contents

Once you have a text field, you can subsequently change or retrieve the text it contains using the `setText` and `getText` methods:

```
public void setText(String text);
```

```
public String getText();
```

The text doesn't change unless the user types into the field. Sometimes, you'll fetch whatever is in the text field in response to a user action elsewhere—for example, the user might fill in a complete form consisting of several text fields and then press a button to have the form processed. On other occasions, you'll want to process the text when the user presses the RETURN key and generates an event; you'll see how this is done a little later.

JTextArea

Similar to `JTextField` but more powerful is the `JTextArea` control. This control is derived from the same parent as `JTextField` (namely `JTextComponent`), but `JTextArea` can have more than one row of text in it and is usually used in conjunction with a `JScrollPane` to make it possible to show large amounts of text in a small area. Like `JTextField`, `JTextArea` has several constructors:

```
public JTextArea();
```

```
public JTextArea(Document doc);
```

```
public JTextArea(Document doc, String text, int rows, int cols);
```

```
public JTextArea(int rows, int cols);
```

```
public JTextArea(String text);
```

```
public JTextArea(String text, int rows, int cols);
```

Apart from the Document, a JTextArea has three properties that you can set using these constructors—the initial text and the number of rows and columns in the text area. If you explicitly set either the row or column value, then the JTextArea will use the value you supply. If you don't set these values, then the column count will be calculated to match the longest line of the initial text string and the row count will equal the number of lines of text you supply (where lines of text are separated by the newline character '\n'). Setting the row and/or column values to zero in one of the constructors that allows you to specify them instructs the JTextArea to use defaults calculated in this way for whichever values are zero.

Note that the JTextArea component, unlike its AWT counterpart TextArea, does not provide scrollbars of its own; usually, you add scrollbars to a JTextArea by wrapping it in a JScrollPane, like this:

```
JTextArea textArea = new JTextArea(20, 30);
JScrollPane p = new JScrollPane(textArea);
```

Figure 9-2 shows a text area to which scrollbars have been added. If the scrollbars hadn't been added, the text that extends beyond the right of the visible area would have been inaccessible, because JTextArea doesn't perform word wrapping by default.

You can make JTextArea perform word wrapping using the setLineWrap method:

```
public void setLineWrap(boolean wrap);
```

```
public boolean getLineWrap();
```

You can see the difference that this makes by comparing Figure 9-2, which does not have word wrapping enabled, with Figure 9-3, which does.

After you've created a JTextArea, you can change the number of rows and/or columns it contains using the following methods:

```
public void setRows(int rows);
```

```
public void setColumns(int cols);
```

As with JTextField, changing these values has no effect on the component's appearance until you invoke validate on its container.

Unlike JTextField, JTextArea will expand tabs that appear in its input string. Logically, tab stops appear at constant intervals across the control. By default, there is a tab stop every 8 columns. When a tab is encountered in the string being displayed, the display position is advanced to the next tab stop. You can change the distance between tab stops using the setTabSize method:

```
public void setTabSize(int columns);
```

Figure 9-2 A text area with added scrollbars.

The tab size in the example shown in Figure 9-2 has been set to 4 columns. If you run this program using the command:

```
java JFCBook.Chapter9.TextAreaExample1
```

and then press the TAB key, you'll see the cursor jump forward by 4 columns each time you do so. If you type 2 characters and then press TAB, it jumps forward by a smaller amount that depends on the width of the characters that you typed. In pixel terms, the distance between tab stops is the number of columns you specify multiplied by the maximum advance of the font in use.

Figure 9-3   A text area with line wrapping enabled.

Non-Editable Text

Sometimes you'll use a JTextField or a JTextArea as a way of displaying information that you don't want the user to be able to edit. You might, for example, want to show the content of a text file but not allow the user to update it, or you might be presenting information that is, by its nature, read-only, such as a directory listing of a Web site on a server that you don't own. Of course, if your program doesn't have the code necessary actually write to the text file itself or to modify the content of the Web site, just allowing the user to edit the displayed representation is not actually harmful, but it is misleading. You could disable the text field using setEnabled(false), but that would cause the text to be grayed out. Instead, you can stop the user changing the text using the setEditable method, as in the following example:

```
JTextField t = new JTextField("This text cannot be edited");
t.setEditable(false);
```

You can change this attribute to suit your needs. Consider another example. You may have a dialog that consists of several fields, one of which is a search key for a database. When you open the dialog, there won't be any information in it, so you disable all of the fields apart from the one that represents the key. When the user supplies the key, you retrieve the required information from the database and populate the text fields in the dialog. Now, since the information you have relates to the search key given, you probably want to stop the user editing that field, so you call `setEditable(false)` for it and then enable the other fields to make them readable. You might, of course, be prepared to allow some of the other information to be modified and, if so, you would call `setEditable(true)` for those fields (or do nothing, because this is the default).

Text Fields and the Input Focus

Text fields are typically used in dialogs; we have already seen an example of a form that consisted of a text field for each line of a person's address and an associated label to show what information is required in each text field (see, for example, Listing 5-4 and Figure 5-3 in Chapter 5, "Keyboard Handling, Actions and Scrolling"). Now suppose that as well as using this form to create new information you want to allow it to be used for changing information: Perhaps this form is an interface to a customer database and you want to change that customer's telephone number. In the current implementation, to reach the telephone number field, you either have to move and click with the mouse or you need to move the focus through all of the text fields until you reach the last one. If you are not a mouse user, you might find it annoying to keep having to use the TAB key so often to reach the field you want to change, so the Swing text components allow you to associate an accelerator key with every component, in the same way as you can with buttons.

To associate an accelerator with a text field, you need to choose a single character that will be used to access the field and pass that to the `JTextComponent` `setFocusAccelerator` method; as was the case with buttons, you press the chosen key along with the ALT key to make the focus move. The following code extract creates a text input field and arranges for the focus to be passed to it when the user presses ALT+a:

```
JTextField t = new JTextField(35);
t.setFocusAccelerator('a');
```

While this will work, how will the user know that this accelerator is available? Unlike the button, text fields do not come with attached labels, so there won't be an underlined "a" character to alert the user to the possibility of a shortcut. But most text fields do have labels attached to them by the programmer, and there is a way to force a single letter to be underlined for this very purpose. Using the `JLabel` method `setDisplayedMnemonic`, you can give the impression that the label has an accelerator associated with it. In fact, it is the text field that has the accelerator, but the label visually represents that accelerator, which explains the name of the method itself. Here are the definitions of the `JLabel` methods that display mnemonics:

```
public void setDisplayedMnemonic(char c);

public void setDisplayedMnemonic(int k);

public int getDisplayedMnemonic();
```

The first two methods allow you to associate a mnemonic given either as a character constant (e.g., "A") or as a keycode (e.g., `VK_A`). The third method returns the mnemonic as a keycode. If no mnemonic has been set, it returns zero.

You can easily apply this idea to a form-type layout by including a couple of lines of code for each input field, as shown in Listing 9-2.

Listing 9-2   Accelerator keys for text fields

```
package JFCBook.Chapter9;

import com.sun.java.swing.*;
import java.awt.*;
import java.awt.event.*;

public class TextAcceleratorExample {
  public static void main(String[] args) {
    JLabel l;
    JTextField t;
    JButton b;
    JFrame f = new JFrame("Text Accelerator Example");
    Container cp = f.getContentPane();
    cp.setLayout(new GridBagLayout());
    cp.setBackground(UIManager.getColor("control"));
    GridBagConstraints c = new GridBagConstraints();

    c.gridx = 0;
    c.gridy = GridBagConstraints.RELATIVE;
    c.gridwidth = 1;
    c.gridheight = 1;
    c.insets = new Insets(2, 2, 2, 2);
    c.anchor = GridBagConstraints.EAST;

    cp.add(l = new JLabel("Name:", SwingConstants.RIGHT), c);
    l.setDisplayedMnemonic('n');
    cp.add(l = new JLabel("House/Street:", SwingConstants.RIGHT), c);
```

```
    l.setDisplayedMnemonic('h');
    cp.add(l = new JLabel("City:", SwingConstants.RIGHT), c);
    l.setDisplayedMnemonic('c');
    cp.add(l = new JLabel("State/County:", SwingConstants.RIGHT), c);
    l.setDisplayedMnemonic('s');
    cp.add(l = new JLabel("Zip/Post code:", SwingConstants.RIGHT), c);
    l.setDisplayedMnemonic('z');
    cp.add(l = new JLabel("Telephone:", SwingConstants.RIGHT), c);
    l.setDisplayedMnemonic('t');
    cp.add(b = new JButton("Clear"), c);
    b.setMnemonic('l');

    c.gridx = 1;
    c.gridy = 0;
    c.weightx = 1.0;
    c.fill = GridBagConstraints.HORIZONTAL;
    c.anchor = GridBagConstraints.CENTER;

    cp.add(t = new JTextField(35), c);
    t.setFocusAccelerator('n');
    c.gridx = 1;
    c.gridy = GridBagConstraints.RELATIVE;
    cp.add(t = new JTextField(35), c);
    t.setFocusAccelerator('h');
    cp.add(t = new JTextField(35), c);
    t.setFocusAccelerator('c');
    cp.add(t = new JTextField(35), c);
    t.setFocusAccelerator('s');
    cp.add(t = new JTextField(35), c);
    t.setFocusAccelerator('z');
    cp.add(t = new JTextField(35), c);
    t.setFocusAccelerator('t');
    c.weightx = 0.0;
    c.fill = GridBagConstraints.NONE;
    cp.add(b = new JButton("OK"), c);
    b.setMnemonic('o');

    f.pack();
    f.addWindowListener(new WindowAdapter() {
      public void windowClosing(WindowEvent evt) {
        System.exit(0);
      }
    });
    f.setVisible(true);
  }
}
```

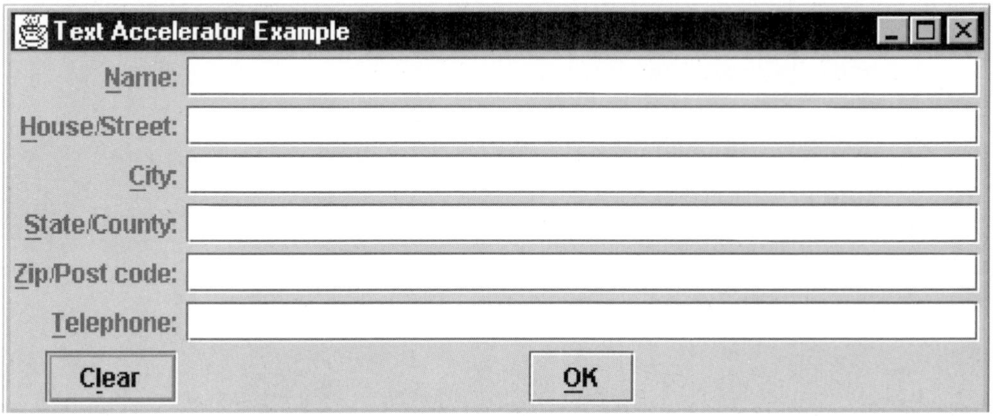

Figure 9-4   Input fields with keyboard accelerators.

Figure 9-4 shows what the finished form looks like.

Notice in this example that accelerator keys have also been assigned to the OK and Clear buttons using the setMnemonic method that you saw earlier. If you run this example, you will find that there is a visible shortcut associated with every field on the form and you should find it possible to navigate anywhere on the form without having to press more than one key (not counting the ALT key, of course).

Core Note

This example only demonstrates the setDisplayedMnemonic *and* setFocusAccelerator *methods—the* OK *and* Clear *keys do not actually work.*

There is, in fact, another way to arrange for the focus to pass to another component associated with a JLabel. You'll see that in the next section.

Password-like Field Input

Sometimes you want to allow the user to type into an input field but you don't want what has been typed to be readable by anybody else. A typical example of this would be when prompting the user for a password. There is a specialized form of the JTextField component that provides this facility. Using the JPasswordField control, you can present the same interface as a JTextField, but instead of the user's keystrokes being echoed, you can arrange for any character of your choice to appear on the screen. JPasswordField is a subclass of JTextField with the following extra methods:

```
public boolean echoCharIsSet();

public char getEchoChar();

public void setEchoChar(char c);
```

If you're familiar with the AWT `TextField` component, you'll recognize these methods. The Swing `JTextField` component doesn't have this functionality built into it, because it isn't the only way to implement a password field. Factoring this implementation into a separate class makes it possible to provide different implementations of this feature as separate subclasses of `JTextField`. If you're converting code that uses this feature of `TextField`, though, you'll need to remember to convert `TextFields` used as password fields to `JPasswordField`, but since `JPasswordField` is a subclass of `JTextField`, which is itself almost compatible with `TextField`, this should be the only change you need to make to such code. Listing 9-3 shows this mechanism in use. You can run this program with the command:

```
java JFCBook.Chapter9.PasswordExample1
```

Listing 9-3   The JPasswordField control

```
package JFCBook.Chapter9;

import com.sun.java.swing.*;
import java.awt.*;
import java.awt.event.*;

public class PasswordExample1 extends JPanel {
  public PasswordExample1() {
    JLabel l;
    JButton b;

    setLayout(new GridBagLayout());
    GridBagConstraints c = new GridBagConstraints();

    c.gridx = 0;
    c.gridy = GridBagConstraints.RELATIVE;
    c.gridwidth = 1;
    c.gridheight = 1;
    c.insets = new Insets(2, 2, 2, 2);
    c.anchor = GridBagConstraints.EAST;

    add(l = new JLabel("User name:", SwingConstants.RIGHT), c);
    l.setDisplayedMnemonic('n');
    l.setLabelFor(userName);
```

continued

```
add(l = new JLabel("Password:", SwingConstants.RIGHT), c);
l.setDisplayedMnemonic('p');
l.setLabelFor(passwordField);

c.gridx = 1;
c.gridy = 0;
c.weightx = 1.0;
c.fill = GridBagConstraints.HORIZONTAL;
c.anchor = GridBagConstraints.CENTER;
add(userName, c);

c.gridx = 1;
c.gridy = GridBagConstraints.RELATIVE;
add(passwordField, c);
passwordField.setEchoChar('-');

// Add the buttons on their own panel
c.gridx = 0;
c.weighty = 0.0;
c.weightx = 1.0;
c.gridwidth = GridBagConstraints.REMAINDER;
c.fill = GridBagConstraints.HORIZONTAL;
c.anchor = GridBagConstraints.CENTER;
JPanel p = new JPanel();
add(p, c);
p.add(b = new JButton("OK"), c);
b.setMnemonic('o');
b.addActionListener(new ActionListener() {
  public void actionPerformed(ActionEvent evt) {
    okPressed();
  }
});

p.add(b = new JButton("Clear"), c);
b.setMnemonic('c');
b.addActionListener(new ActionListener() {
  public void actionPerformed(ActionEvent evt) {
    userName.setText("");
    passwordField.setText("");
    userName.requestFocus();
  }
});
}

public void okPressed() {
  // Add code here to handle the "OK" button.
  // We just print the contents of the text fields
```

```
    System.out.println("User name: <" + userName.getText()
            + ">; password: <" +
            passwordField.getText() + ">");
  }

  public static void main(String[] args) {
    JFrame f = new JFrame("Password Example");
    f.getContentPane().setBackground(UIManager.getColor("control"));

    f.getContentPane().add(new PasswordExample1());
    f.pack();
    f.addWindowListener(new WindowAdapter() {
      public void windowClosing(WindowEvent evt) {
        System.exit(0);
      }
    });
    f.setVisible(true);
  }

  JTextField userName = new JTextField(35);
  JPasswordField passwordField = new JPasswordField(35);
}
```

Here, an ordinary JTextField is used to get the user name, and a JPasswordField for the password. The setEchoChar method is used to make the password field echo a hyphen for each character that the user types. If you don't set an echo character, the field echoes an asterisk instead. Figure 9-5 shows what the form looks like when a few characters have been typed into the password field.

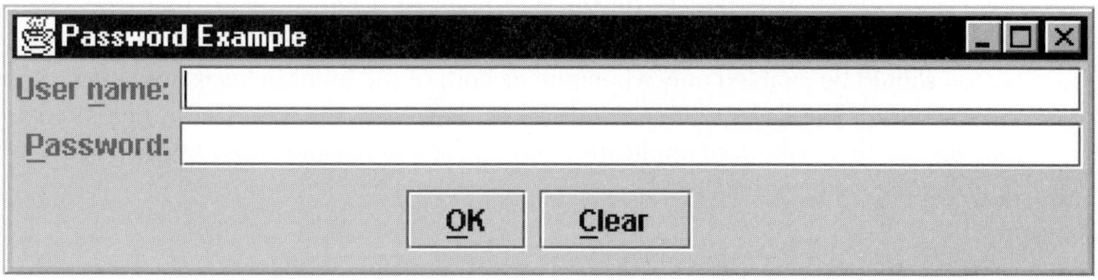

Figure 9-5 An input field for passwords.

This example also shows another way to get the focus into a text component and, at the same time, give a visual cue that this is possible. As with the previous example, the visual cue is obtained by setting a mnemonic on each label using setDisplayedMnemonic. Unlike the last example, however, you won't find setFocusAccelerator called on either of the text components, yet you can use ALT+N and ALT+P to get the focus to these fields. How does this work?

JLabel has a property called JLabel.labelFor which you can set using the following method:

```
public void setLabelFor(Component c);
```

If you set this property and you also set a mnemonic then, when the mnemonic is activated, the label will pass the focus to the component given to it by setLabelFor. In this case, this method is invoked for both labels, passing a reference to the text field with which they are associated. Since the label will direct the focus, there is no need to invoke setFocusAccelerator on the text components.

Core Tip

This facility works for any component—not just text components.

Getting Events from Text Components

If you tried using the example shown in Listing 9-3, you probably found it very unfriendly—the text fields don't react when you press RETURN and the OK button really should be enabled only when the user has typed both user name and password. It is possible to make both of these changes when you know how to get events from text fields, which is the subject of this section.

It is possible to make this code a little more user-friendly by doing something useful when the user presses RETURN in one of the text fields. For example, if this happens in the User name field, you might want to transfer the keyboard focus to the Password component and, if RETURN is pressed when the password has been typed, perhaps you should pass the focus to the User Name field if it is blank and otherwise behave as if the OK button had been pressed. Another thing you might want to do is to enable the buttons only when it is meaningful to do so: The Clear button should be enabled only when one or both of the input fields is non-empty and the OK button should not be enabled unless there is some text in both fields. Little touches like this make your application more professional and easier to use. All of this can be done using events.

Text Field Action Events

When you press RETURN in a JTextField or a JPasswordField, it generates an ActionEvent with itself as the source. As with JButton, you can handle this by holding a pointer to the text component and comparing it with the source of the event, by creating a single listener for each text component or by associating a command string with each text field by using the setActionCommand method of

JTextField, which works in the same way as it does for JButton. Here is some code that could be added to that in Listing 9-3 to process the RETURN key in the User name field:

```
userName.addActionListener(new ActionListener() {
  public void actionPerformed(ActionEvent evt) {
    // Pass focus to the password field
    passwordField.requestFocus();
  }
});
```

As you can see, using an inner class makes it almost trivial to write event handlers. In this case, the new statement creates an anonymous class and, since ActionListener is an interface, this creates an anonymous class that implements the ActionListener interface. This requires the class to implement all of the methods of this interface, of which there is only name—namely actionPerformed. The actionPerformed method is entered only when the RETURN key is pressed in the User name text field and just passes the keyboard focus to the password field.

Having seen this code, you won't be surprised at how the ActionListener for the password field is implemented:

```
passwordField.addActionListener(new ActionListener() {
  public void actionPerformed(ActionEvent evt) {
    if (userName.getText().equals("")) {
      userName.requestFocus();
    } else if (passwordField.getText().equals("") == false) {
      okPressed();
    }
  }
});
```

The only difference here is that the contents of the password field is retrieved invoking getText to decide what to do next.

Monitoring Changes in Text Component Content

Handling the RETURN key, then, is almost the same as handling button presses. The other desirable improvement is to have each button enabled only when it is appropriate to do so. Let's consider the OK button first. This should be enabled only when both the user name and password fields are nonempty. Suppose that the user types a user name and then moves the focus to the password field. As soon as one character has been typed in the password field, the user could press OK and expect the program to process the user name and password. This means that the OK button should now be enabled. But, how does the program know that a character has been typed? So far, you have only seen how to get an event when the user presses RETURN in the password field, by which time it is too late to enable the OK button!

Fortunately, the text components generate a DocumentEvent when their content is changed in any way. This event is delivered to a DocumentListener that you can register with any text component. The methods of this interface are as follows:

```
public interface DocumentListener {
   public void changedUpdate(DocumentEvent evt);
   public void insertUpdate(DocumentEvent evt);
   public void removeUpdate(DocumentEvent evt);
}
```

As you saw earlier, the Swing text components are always associated with a Document. This is not necessarily an actual document on disk, but a logical document made up of one or more *elements*. Each element can have content and attributes. For our purposes, it is necessary to track text insertion and removal, which are reported by calling the insertUpdate and removeUpdate methods.

In order to make changes to the button states, it is necessary to store persistent references to them so that they can be accessed in the DocumentListeners. The last state of each button is also stored. Initially, since there will be no text in either field, the buttons will both be disabled. Here are the declarations we add to the class shown in Listing 9-3 to define these new fields:

```
JTextField userName = new JTextField(35);
JPasswordField passwordField = new JPasswordField(35);
JButton okButton;
JButton clearButton;

// Button states
boolean okState = false;// Disabled
boolean clearState = false;    // Disabled
```

The next thing to do is define a DocumentListener that implements the insertUpdate and removeUpdate methods and a dummy changedUpdate method. The changedUpdate method reports changes to document attributes, for which we have no use in this example. This listener is registered on both text fields:

```
DocumentListener d = new DocumentListener() {
   public void changedUpdate(DocumentEvent evt) {
     // Nothing to do
   }

   public void insertUpdate(DocumentEvent evt) {
     checkButtons();
   }

   public void removeUpdate(DocumentEvent evt) {
     checkButtons();
   }
};
```

```
userName.getDocument().addDocumentListener(d);
passwordField.getDocument().addDocumentListener(d);

// Both buttons are disabled at first
okButton.setEnabled(false);
clearButton.setEnabled(false);
```

Notice that, to register the listeners, the text component's getDocument method was used to get a reference to its underlying Document object. This is the only part of the component that is actually aware that a change has been made to the text. Remember that the text can be changed by calling the setText method as well as because of keyboard input, so it is not possible for the user interface part of the text component to keep track of all changes to the document. This is about the only time you will need to use the Document object directly if you are going to use text components for simple user interface tasks.

Now, whenever any characters are added to or deleted from either of the text fields, the checkButtons method will be entered. This method checks the state of each text field using getText and determines what the proper state of each button should be:

OK button: Enabled if both fields are nonempty.

Clear button: Enabled if either field is empty.

To avoid redrawing the screen after each key press, the state of each button is changed only if it needs to be. To make this possible, the new state is compared with the state last time it was changed and setEnabled is called only if these states differ. Here is the implementation of the checkButtons method:

```
public void checkButtons() {
   // Check whether the buttons should be enabled or not
   boolean newOkState;
   boolean newClearState;
   boolean nameClear = userName.getText().equals("");
   boolean passwordClear = passwordField.getText().equals("");

   newOkState = nameClear == false && passwordClear == false;
   newClearState = nameClear == false || passwordClear == false;
   if (newOkState != okState) {
     okButton.setEnabled(newOkState);
     okState = newOkState;
   }
   if (newClearState != clearState) {
     clearButton.setEnabled(newClearState);
     clearState = newClearState;
   }
}
```

You can try out the modified version of the password program by using the command:

```
java JFCBook.Chapter9.PasswordExample2
```

Now you'll find that both of the buttons are initially disabled. As soon as you type anything into either text field, the `Clear` button is enabled, but if you delete everything it disables itself again. If you type something into the `User` name field and press RETURN, you'll see that the focus passes to the `Password` field. Type anything in here and the `OK` button will be enabled. If you clear out either the password field or the user name field, the `OK` button will be disabled again. Finally, after typing both the user name and password, you'll find that you can have them processed either by pressing RETURN in the `Password` field or by pressing the `OK` button.

Text Selection

Both `JTextArea` and `JTextField` allow you to highlight text for selection using the mouse in the normal way: Press the left button and drag over the text that you want to select. When this has been done, the program can get access to the selected text by using the `getSelectedText` method, which returns whatever text has been selected as a `String`. It is also possible to get the offsets of the start and end of the selection from the start of the text using the `getSelectionStart` and `getSelectionEnd` methods, which return the offsets as integer values. The simple example in Listing 9-4 shows how text selection works.

Listing 9-4   Selecting text from a text control

```
package JFCBook.Chapter9;

import com.sun.java.swing.*;
import java.awt.*;
import java.awt.event.*;

public class SelectedTextExample1 extends JTextArea {
  public SelectedTextExample1() {
    super(10, 40);
    setText("\"Houston, Tranquility Base here.\nThe Eagle has Landed\"\n" +
      "\n\n\"Roger, Tranquility, we copy you on the ground.\n" +
      "You got a bunch of guys about to turn blue.\n" +
      "We're breathing again. Thanks a lot\"\n");
  }

  public static void main(String[] args) {
    JFrame f = new JFrame("Selected Text 1");
    Container cp = f.getContentPane();
    cp.setBackground(UIManager.getColor("control"));
```

```
    cp.add(new JScrollPane(e = new SelectedTextExample1()), "Center");
    JPanel p = new JPanel();
    JButton b = new JButton("Read Text");
    b.setMnemonic('R');
    p.add(b);
    cp.add(p, "South");
    f.pack();
    f.addWindowListener(new WindowAdapter() {
      public void windowClosing(WindowEvent evt) {
        System.exit(0);
      }
    });
    b.addActionListener(new ActionListener() {
      public void actionPerformed(ActionEvent evt) {
        System.out.println("Selected text is:\n\t<"
          + e.getSelectedText() + ">");
        System.out.println("Selection starts at offset: " +
              e.getSelectionStart());
        System.out.println("Selection ends at offset: " +
              e.getSelectionEnd());
      }
    });
    f.setVisible(true);
  }

  static SelectedTextExample1 e;
}
```

To run this program, use the command:

```
java JFCBook.Chapter9.SelectedTextExample1
```

When the program starts, a `JTextArea`, wrapped in a `JScrollPane`, will appear with some reasonably well-known text inside it. Underneath the text is a button labeled `Read Text`. If you highlight some of the text and then press the button (or use ALT+R), the program will display the text you highlighted together with its start and end offsets. Note that these offsets are counted from 0 and that, if you press the button when you don't have any highlighted text, you get two equal offsets back. The value of the offset in this case depends on where you last clicked over the text. When you click on the text, an insertion cursor appears; if you then press the button, the start and end offsets indicate the position of this cursor. Note that, when there is some text selected, the end offset is that of the first *nonselected* character after the selection. Therefore, if you select the first 3 characters, the start offset will be zero and the end offset 3. If you type when you have text highlighted, your typing replaces that text and the resulting text is not marked as selected.

Programmatically Selecting Text

You can also select text and operate on it from within your application. A selected region is created by using the following methods:

```
public synchronized void setSelectionStart(int startOffset);

public synchronized void setSelectionEnd(int endOffset);
```

Core Alert

Be careful when using the `setSelectionEnd` *method: Its argument is the offset of the first character after the selection, not of the last character you want selected.*

You can treat a selection created in this way exactly as a selection created by the user. You can also select all of the text using the `selectAll` method.

Apart from just reading the text selection, you can write to it using the method `replaceSelection`:

```
public void replaceSelection(String content);
```

The text supplied as the `content` argument replaces whatever is currently selected. If you call this method and supply an empty replacement string, then the selected text is deleted. Note, however, that after you replace a selection, the resulting text is *not* selected.

To see some of these features in operation, use the following command:

```
java JFCBook.Chapter9.SelectedTextExample2
```

This example is similar to that in Listing 9-4, but with the following code added to the `main` method, after the frame has been made visible:

```
b.setEnabled(false);
try {
  System.out.println("Selecting all text....");
  e.selectAll();
  Thread.sleep(5000);
  System.out.println("Selecting offsets 10 to 25");
  e.setSelectionStart(10);
  e.setSelectionEnd(26);
  String text = e.getSelectedText();
  System.out.println("Selected text is <" + text + ">");
  Thread.sleep(5000);
  System.out.println("Replacing selection");
  e.replaceSelection("TRANQUILITY BASE");
  Thread.sleep(5000);
  System.out.println("Deleting selection");
```

```
      e.setSelectionStart(10);
      e.setSelectionEnd(26);
      e.replaceSelection("");
      Thread.sleep(5000);
      System.out.println("Restore original text");
      e.setSelectionStart(10);
      e.setSelectionEnd(10);
      e.replaceSelection(text);
   } catch (InterruptedException e) {
   }
```

```
   b.setEnabled(true);
```

Here, the whole text area is first selected to demonstrate the `selectAll` method. After 5 seconds, the selection is reduced to two words on the first line. Note that the selected text is highlighted just as it would be if you had selected it yourself. Next, the selected text is replaced, using `replaceSelection`, with the same text in uppercase. Notice that the new text is not selected. Therefore, to perform the next operation, namely deleting the selection, it is necessary to reset the start and end values of the range. The last step is to put the text back again. To do this, an empty selected range is created at the original start offset and then `replaceSelection` is used to put back the original words. The important thing to note about this process is that each operation first requires you to create a selection. In the case of an insertion, you create an empty selection at the insertion point.

Everything that has been covered in this section is provided by `JTextComponent` and so applies equally to both `JTextField` and `JTextArea`, and to all of the other text components in the Swing set. `JTextArea` also has three extra convenience methods that you can use to quickly replace, insert or append text:

```
   public void replaceRange(String text, int start, int end);

   public void append(String text);

   public void insert(String text, int offset);
```

The `append` method adds the supplied text at the end of the text in the `JTextArea`, while `insert` places it before the given offset. The `replaceRange` method replaces the text between the given start and end offsets with that supplied. As usual, the end offset is the offset of the character *after* the last one affected by the operation. These methods save you having to separately create the selections that would be required by `replaceSelection`.

The System Clipboard

Sometimes you need to highlight some text with a view to cutting or copying it into another application. Most windowing platforms support this by providing a clipboard onto which data from one application can be copied before being pasted into another. JTextComponent provides convenience methods that allow you to copy text between a text component and the system clipboard, thus allowing you to move text between Java applications or even to exchange text with native applications not running in a Java virtual machine.

The three methods in question are defined as follows:

```
public void copy();

public void cut();

public void paste();
```

The first two of these take the selected text and place it on the system clipboard; in the case of cut, the selected text is also removed from the text component. When there is text on the clipboard, the third method, paste, may be used to incorporate it into the same, or another, text component. The paste method replaces any current selection in the text component with the content of the clipboard. If there is no text selected, the clipboard content is placed before the insertion point (i.e., where the insertion caret appears on the screen).

To demonstrate how simple it is to use these methods Listing 9-5 shows a modified version of the text example in Listing 9-4 in which the Read Text button is replaced with Copy, Cut and Paste buttons.

Listing 9-5   Copy, cut and paste via the system clipboard

```
package JFCBook.Chapter9;

import com.sun.java.swing.*;
import java.awt.*;
import java.awt.event.*;

public class SelectedTextExample3 extends JTextArea {
   public SelectedTextExample3() {
      super(10, 40);
      setText("\"Houston, Tranquility Base here.\nThe Eagle has Landed\"\n" +
         "\n\n\"Roger, Tranquility, we copy you on the ground.\n" +
         "You got a bunch of guys about to turn blue.\n" +
         "We're breathing again. Thanks a lot\"\n");
   }

   public static void main(String[] args) {
      JFrame f = new JFrame("Selected Text 3");
      Container cp = f.getContentPane();
      cp.setBackground(UIManager.getColor("control"));
```

```
   cp.add(new JScrollPane(e = new SelectedTextExample3()), "Center");
   JPanel p = new JPanel();

   JButton b = new JButton("Copy");
   b.setMnemonic('o');
   b.addActionListener(new ActionListener() {
     public void actionPerformed(ActionEvent evt) {
       e.copy();
     }
   });
   p.add(b);

   b = new JButton("Cut");
   b.setMnemonic('u');
   b.addActionListener(new ActionListener() {
     public void actionPerformed(ActionEvent evt) {
       e.cut();
     }
   });
   p.add(b);

   b = new JButton("Paste");
   b.setMnemonic('p');
   b.addActionListener(new ActionListener() {
     public void actionPerformed(ActionEvent evt) {
       e.paste();
     }
   });
   p.add(b);

   cp.add(p, "South");
   f.pack();
   f.addWindowListener(new WindowAdapter() {
     public void windowClosing(WindowEvent evt) {
       System.exit(0);
     }
   });

   f.setVisible(true);
 }

 static SelectedTextExample3 e;
}
```

To run this example, use the command:

```
java JFCBook.Chapter9.SelectedTextExample3
```

You can now try cutting, copying and pasting text within the window. For example, highlight the words Tranquility Base on the first line and press the Copy button. Nothing appears to happen, but the text has been copied to the system clipboard. To prove this, click with the mouse anywhere else in the text area and then press Paste and you'll find that the text is inserted there. Now highlight the newly inserted text and press Cut to cause the text to be removed again. If you have another application running, activate it and paste the text into it.

Core Note

The action required to do this is platform-dependent. On some systems, you click the middle mouse button while on others, such as Windows, you press Ctrl+v.

Conversely, you can move text from an external application to the JTextArea or JTextField. First, highlight and copy text from any other application you have running. On Windows, you need to first highlight the text and then press Ctrl+c to do this, while Unix systems simply require you to highlight the text. Now click inside the text component and press the Paste button and the text will appear where you clicked with the mouse.

Text Components: Under the Hood

While discussing the text field and text area components, there have been strong hints that there is something complex lurking behind them. This section opens the hood and shows exactly how these simple controls are implemented and also looks at their more powerful cousins, JTextPane and JEditorPane.

When you use a text field, you see a rectangular area of the screen into which you can type some text. If you make a mistake while typing, you can erase and correct the mistakes. You can press RETURN to have the application process what you have typed and you can cut and paste text to and from the text field. You might think that the source code for JTextField must be very large to provide all of this, but you would be wrong: In fact, it's only about 450 lines. Actually, most of the functionality you can access through JTextField and, for that matter through JTextArea as well, is not provided by either of these controls. Instead, a variety of software components work together to give the view of a single unit that provides all of these features. The text controls are, in fact, a very good example of the Swing Model-View-Controller architecture.

Text Component Architecture

Figure 9-6 shows some of the pieces that go together to make the Swing text components. The complete picture is actually more complex than this—it wasn't possible to put everything into one diagram and still make it readable.

At the top of the diagram are the familiar JPasswordField, JTextField and JTextArea controls, together with the more complex JTextPane and JEditorPane. These are the components that actually end up on the screen and are often referred to as *editors*. At the other end of the diagram is a class called AbstractDocument, which is part of the MVC model for the text components. In between are the various MVC view components and JTextComponent which, among other things, plays part of the role of the MVC controller by responding to key events. There is also another piece of the controller, the *Caret*, that handles mouse and focus events. The caret is not shown in Figure 9-6 for the sake of clarity. Before taking a closer look at each of these areas, let's examine briefly the role that each of these pieces plays.

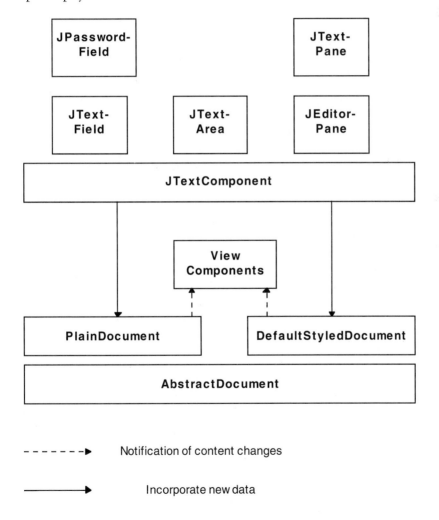

Figure 9-6   Text component architecture.

Let's suppose you have typed some characters into a JTextField. These characters will actually be stored in the *model*, which is realized, in the case of both JTextField and JTextArea, by the PlainDocument class. PlainDocument organizes the data into lines, separated by line breaks that are generated when you press RETURN; in the simple case of JTextField., there is only one line in the model and the RETURN key is not stored: Instead, it generates an event.

The keystrokes themselves don't get directly into the model via the text components themselves. Instead keyboard events are trapped by JTextComponent. As keys are pressed, JTextComponent looks at each of them and decides whether they represent a special action, such as a backspace, HOME or the RETURN key. If the key is not special (you'll see later how a key gets to be considered special) and it has a valid character code, it is passed, by default, to the model for storage.

All special keys have associated *actions* that are registered with JTextComponent; the particular set of special keys depends on the text component itself or, more accurately, on its plugged-in look-and-feel implementation. When one of these keys is found, the corresponding action is performed. One of the jobs of JTextComponent is to map the special keys to the registered actions, but the set of available actions depends entirely on the component involved.

Keyboard actions are usually implemented by what is loosely referred to as the "editor." In fact, the editor functionality is provided by another class derived from EditorKit. Simple text components, like JTextField and JTextArea, use a basic subclass of EditorKit called DefaultEditorKit, which provides code to handle common actions like moving the cursor, inserting and deleting text and so on. JTextComponent maps look-and-feel dependent key sequences to these editor-dependent actions. As you'll see later, the JTextPane control uses a more complex editor call StyledEditorKit and JEditorPane can use one of several editor kits that can be plugged in dynamically. Over and above the actions supplied by its editor kit, a text component can add some of its own. These are, of course, useful only if the corresponding look-and-feel class adds a key mapping to activate the action. As an example of this, JTextField defines an action that sends an ActionEvent containing the action command registered with it using setActionCommand, or its text content if this method has not been called. The default UI class for JTextField, BasicTextFieldIUI, adds a key mapping that activates this action when the RETURN key is pressed. This is, in fact, how a JTextField generates an ActionEvent when you press RETURN. If you need to, you can use the same interfaces as the text components themselves use to add new actions or new key mappings.

Core Note

*Be very careful to distinguish keys from actions. Actions are things that editors can do—they are services that the editor advertises using a well-known name (such as "*page-up*"), while the special keys are the way in which the user can activate those actions. In a reasonable look-and-feel implementation, the text component UI class would register with* JTextComponent *a mapping of the* PAGE UP *key to the editor's "*page-up*" action.*

As just noted, keys that are not mapped to editor actions are given to the text component to be added to the data model, which is how data gets into the text components. In fact, it is possible to override this and do something completely different with keystrokes that do not correspond to editor actions, because they are actually passed to the editor's installed action that deals with unmapped keystrokes. By replacing this action, you can receive all of these characters and handle them differently if you wish.

Mouse and focus events are monitored by the *caret*. Where text components are concerned, the mouse has two uses. First, you can click with the mouse to move the text insertion point. This position is usually marked with a thin cursor that is drawn by, and often referred to as, the caret. Clicking the mouse moves the caret to the mouse's current location. Secondly, with the mouse button pressed, you can drag the mouse to highlight text. The caret is responsible for tracking mouse movement as text is selected and arranging for the text to be highlighted. The caret itself is represented by an object that implements the `Caret` interface. By default, the caret is an instance of the `DefaultCaret` class. Highlighting of selected text is controlled by `DefaultCaret` using an instance of the `DefaultHighlighter` class, which implements the `Highlighter` interface. The caret monitors focus events to make the cursor appear when its text component has the focus and to switch it off when it does not.

The text components `JTextField`, `JTextArea`, `JPasswordField`, `JTextPane` *and* `JEditorPane` *are in the* `com.sun.java.swing` *package. All of the other classes that are discussed in this section, including* `JTextComponent`, *reside in* `com.sun.java.swing.text`. *The only exceptions to this are some of the classes used by* `JEditorPane` *which are in the* `com.sun.java.swing.text.html` *and* `com.sun.java.swing.text.rtf` *packages.*

What about displaying the content of the model on the screen? This job falls to *view* classes that depend on the text component that is in use and on the selected editor kit. The view uses information stored in the model to place the appropriate text on the screen. As you'll see, `JTextPane` and `JEditorPane` allow you to display more than just text. For documents that contain images and other nontext items, it is necessary to create a view that can render objects of these types. The view is also responsible for keeping the screen up to date as the content of the model changes, as when the user types into the control, for example.

The Document

The lowest level of a text component is the Document that underlies it. Earlier in this chapter, you saw that it is possible to associate a Document with a JTextField using one of its constructors:

```
public JTextField(Document doc, String text, int columns);
```

If you don't supply a Document of your own, a suitable default (in this case PlainDocument, a class that will be described later) is used instead. Document is actually an interface, not a class. Its function is to provide a very basic way to access and manage the data in the control. Here are the methods that make up the Document interface.

```
public String getText(int offset, int length) throws
         BadLocationException

public void getText(int offset, int length, Segment txt)
         throws BadLocationException

public int getLength()

public void insertString(int offset, String str,
         AttributeSet a) throws BadLocationException

public void remove(int offset, int len) throws
         BadLocationException

public void render(Runnable r);

public Position getStartPosition()

public Position getEndPosition()

public Position createPosition(int offset) throws
         BadLocationException

public Object getProperty(Object key)

public void putProperty(Object key, Object value)

public Element[] getRootElements()

public Element getDefaultRootElement()

public void addDocumentListener(DocumentListener l)

public void removeDocumentListener(DocumentListener l)

public void addUndoableEditListener(UndoableEditListener l)

public void removeUndoableEditListener(UndoableEditListener l)
```

These methods are described in the following sections.

Data Manipulation Methods

The first three methods allow you to get information out of the model. The model represents the document as a contiguous sequence of characters, addressable by an integral offset, where the first character has offset 0. The getText method can return a piece of the document as a String or in a Segment object, which holds the document data in the form of an array of characters. This is often more useful than a String if you want to process the individual characters efficiently. Here is its definition:

```
public class Segment {
   public Segment()
   public Segment(char[] array, int offset, int count)
   public String toString()

   public char[] array;
   public int offset;
   public int count;
}
```

Whenever you use a method like getText that supplies an initial offset and a length, the entire range must be within the bounds of the document's data. If it isn't, a BadLocationException is thrown. Only insertString is an exception to this rule, because it is allowed to add text that increases the size of the document, provided that the initial offset is no greater than the document size. For example, if the document is 80 bytes long, an insertString of any length may be done starting at any offset up to and including (but not beyond) 80. This is the only way to increase the size of the document.

As well as data, the insertString method allows you to provide *attributes* that qualify the data. Although the Document interface provides the means to specify attributes, it doesn't apply any meaning to them, nor does it specify what they actually look like, other then requiring them to be described by a class that implements the AttributeSet interface that you'll see later. A document's attributes are not considered to be part of its data and they are stored separately from it in the document model.

The getLength method returns the current size of the document, in characters.

Core Note

Here and elsewhere in this chapter the unit of storage inside a document will be referred to as a character, by which is meant a Java char type (a 16-bit Unicode character). This is just convenient shorthand, however. While the Document interface is framed in terms of char and String, no constraint is placed on how the data is actually stored within the document, much less on how it is held within the original source of the data. The storage mechanism itself will be examined later in this chapter.

Data can be removed from the document using the `remove` method, which specifies a range of characters to delete. The entire range must actually exist in the document at the time that this method is invoked, or a `BadLocationException` is thrown. Removing data from the middle of the document does not leave a hole: Anything that lies beyond the removed range is (at least logically) moved up to fill the space. For example, if a document is initially 80 bytes long and a removal of 6 bytes from offset 40 is performed, the data at offsets 46 through 79 move up to occupy offsets 40 through 73, thus reducing the total size of the model by 6 bytes.

Concurrency

Since Java provides support for multithreaded applications, the `Document` interface (informally) requires that its implementations provide a storage mechanism that can be made safe in the presence of multiple threads that want to concurrently read and write the data content. To make this possible, implementations might be expected to implement internal locking such that any operation that modifies the data is atomic with respect to read operations on the data and with respect to other write operations. In simple terms, the model would be expected to allow multiple threads to read the document at the same time, but to allow only one writer at any given time and only at a time when there are no readers.

In fact, though, this is not the way it is actually implemented. The model ensures that write operations do not collide by automatically taking a write lock before any write operation starts and releasing it when it ends. In this context, writing means changing data content, removing data from the model or adding it at the end. For efficiency, however, read operations are not locked out by this write lock—in other words, while a write is in progress, another thread can read the data. This can, of course, lead to incorrect behavior. To avoid this problem, code that must read data in an environment that could involve writers in a separate thread can use the `render` method. This method is given a `Runnable` as its only argument. Before executing the `run` method of this `Runnable`, the document is locked so that no writers can modify its content. If a writer is currently active, the thread that called `render` waits until the writer releases its write lock. Once the `run` method of the Runnable has been entered, it can assume that the document will not be modified. The lock is released when the `run` method ends. It is possible for more than one thread to use the `render` method at any time, because simultaneous read access is not harmful.

Unless you are going to be implementing your own low-level access to the `Document` model, you won't need to be concerned with the details of the `render` method, because it is used by the UI classes of all of the text components.

Positioning

The `getStartPosition` and `getEndPosition` methods return `Positions` that represent the start and end of the document, respectively. `Position` is an interface that has a single method:

```
public interface Position {
   public int getOffset();
}
```

When an object that implements the `Position` interface is created, it represents a given location within the document, specified by its offset *at that time*. If data is added to or removed from anywhere in the document before the location represented by the `Position`, the offset of that location relative the start of the document would change, rendering the offset previously obtained useless as a means of fixing a particular point in a document. A `Position`, however, remains bound to the *location* that it originally represented no matter what happens to the document. The offset that the `Position` returns from its `getOffset` method will always be the current offset of the original place in the document The `Positions` returned by `getStartPosition` and `getEndPosition` always indicate the start and end of the document, respectively.

Using the `createPosition` method, you can obtain a `Position` that tracks any arbitrary point in the document. As an example, suppose you have a document that consists of several paragraphs and you obtain a `Position` object that represents the start of the second paragraph. If you call `getOffset` at this point, you'll get the current offset of that paragraph. If, subsequently, some text is added to or removed from the first paragraph, the offset you obtained earlier will no longer represent the start of the second paragraph. However, if you invoke `getOffset` on your `Position` object, you'll get the new offset of the start of that paragraph.

Core Note

The coordinate system used in the model actually refers not to the characters, but to the positions between characters. Thus, descriptions like the "offset of a paragraph" are to be read something like "the offset of the point before the first character in the paragraph." The shorthand version is less of a mouthful than the whole truth. Bear this in mind when reading the rest of this chapter.

What happens if the data corresponding to a `Position` is removed? If this happens, the offset is changed so that the `Position` points just before the data that was removed. For example, if you create a `Position` that tracks original offset 40 and then remove the characters at offset 30 through 45, your `Position` will now track offset 30.

Document Properties

The `getProperty` and `putProperty` methods allow you to associate arbitrary values with a document. There are no rules regarding what you can use these values for. You might, for example, hold such information as the author's name. Internally, properties are used by the text components to store such things as the number of space characters represented by the tab character. Bear in mind when using these properties that, like the document data itself, they are not persistent unless you provide some means for them to be permanently stored somewhere.

The `Document` interface specifies two property names that can be used by all implementations:

```
public static final String TitleProperty;

public static final String StreamDescriptionProperty;
```

The first of these is intended to allow a document title to be stored under a common key. It is used by the HTML implementation used by `JEditorPane` to store the document title extracted from the HTML `TITLE` tag. You can retrieve the document title, if it exists, from a text component as follows:

```
JTextComponent t;    // Any text component (JTextField etc.)
String title = t.getDocument().getProperty(Document.TitleProperty);
```

If no title has been set, `null` will be returned.

The `StreamDescriptionProperty` is more abstract. In fact, no concrete meaning is assigned to it. The HTML support uses it to store the URL of the document that it belongs to, but the scope of this meaning is, of course, limited to the `com.sun.java.swing.text.html` package.

Document Elements

The `getRootElements` and `getDefaultRootElement` methods provide access to the mechanism that allows a document to contain more than just character data. Even simple documents have some form of basic structure in the form of lines and paragraphs. The simple storage mechanism used by the `Document` interface and its implementations in the Swing text package only presents a sequence of characters. The paragraph structure and other features such as mixed fonts and color are held separately in a hierarchy of *elements*. The `getDefaultRootElement` provides access to the element at the base of the tree structure, from which the entire document structure is linked. All of the document types in the Swing package have a single root element, but it is possible to create separate hierarchies that simultaneously place a different structure on the same document content. To do this, it is necessary to have separate root elements. The `getRootElements` method returns an array containing all of the root elements associated with a document. There is no guarantee, however, that a particular document type (i.e., a given implementation of `Document`) will allow the existence of more than one root element. The document types underlying the Swing text components allow only a single root element, which they create as each document is built, and the `getRootElements` method returns an array of one entry, containing the same element returned by `getDefaultRootElement`. There is a more detailed description of the `Element` interface later in this chapter.

Core Note

Even though the standard Swing Document *model implementations provide only a single root element, nothing stops you creating your own implementation that supports more than one.*

Event Listeners

The last four methods allow the registration and removal of listeners for document and undoable edit events. All changes to the document content or its structure result in the generation of document events, a fact that has already been exploited in this chapter to control buttons based on the content of a text field and to react to changes in the text field as they happen. You'll find out more about document events later on. Undoable edit events are used to indicate changes to the document that could be reversed at a later date. The event contains all the information needed to reverse the change that was made.

Content

The discussion of the Document interface skirted around the issue of where and how the data in the document is actually stored. To the user of the Document interface, the details of the storage mechanism are not actually important. In fact, the minimum requirements of an object that can provide this mechanism are described by an interface that is declared inside the AbstractDocument class. AbstractDocument is the prototypical implementation of the Document interface—it provides enough functionality to develop real document types, without itself being tied to any particular type or style of document. Since AbstractDocument is a real class, (albeit still an abstract one), it needs to deal with real data and hence must have a way to associate itself with actual document content. To create an AbstractDocument, you must supply its constructor with an object that implements the AbstractDocument.Content interface. This object contains, or will contain, the real data that the text control will manipulate.

The AbstractDocument.Content interface (which we'll refer to simply as the Content interface for brevity) is a very simple one:

```
public interface Content {
    public Position createPosition(int offset) throws BadLocationException;
    public int length();
    public UndoableEdit insertString(int where, String str) throws
            BadLocationException;
    public UndoableEdit remove(int where, int nitems) throws
            BadLocationException;
    public String getString(int where, int len) throws BadLocationException;
    public void getChars(int where, int len, Segment txt) throws
            BadLocationException;
}
```

You'll notice that some of these methods have exact parallels in the Document interface and, in fact, some of them are called more or less directly by AbstractDocument.

The StringContent Class

There is a concrete implementation of the Content interface called StringContent that is actually used by all of the text components as their underlying storage mechanism. This class uses the most basic possible mechanism for managing character data—a simple character array. By default, if you create a StringContent object using its default constructor, it allocates ten characters worth of space and initializes the size of the document it is storing to one—a single newline character. As you add data using the insertString method, the underlying storage space will be expanded if necessary.

The characters in the document are always held in a single contiguous array, even if data is removed using the remove method. Removing data from the middle of the document causes the data at the end to move up over the hole, so that the content length is reduced by the amount of data removed. This operation is performed using a data copy and the spare space at the end of the character array is left allocated for future expansion. Other implementations of the Content method, which might be more efficient, are possible, but the Swing package only provides StringContent.

Core Note

Another content class called GapContent *that manages changes more efficiently will be included as of Swing 1.0.2.*

Using a character array makes the implementation of most of the Content methods almost trivial. The only method that is not straightforward is createPosition. This method must provide the functionality offered by the method of the same name in the Document interface—namely, it must return an object that can track the location of a point in the document even when the document content changes.

When the createPosition method is invoked, it creates an object of type StickyPosition. StickyPosition is an inner class declared by StringContent; the important things about it are that it holds an offset and that it implements the Position interface by supplying a getOffset method that simply reads the stored offset. Every StickyPosition object that is created for a particular instance of StringContent is held in a Vector associated with the StringContent. If there are no changes to the document content, the offsets in these objects will remain correct. If data is added or removed, however, all of the objects in the Vector are scanned and their offset is updated to take account of the operation that has just been performed.

For example, suppose some data is inserted somewhere. To keep existing Positions valid, any StickyPosition object whose offset is the same as or greater than the starting offset of the insertion must have its offset field increased by the amount of data inserted. Similarly, if data is removed, any Position whose offset is not less than that of the start of the removal will be affected. If the Position marks a point beyond the area removed, then its offset is simply reduced by the amount of data removed. On the other hand, if the Position relates to a point inside the deleted area, its offset is changed to that of the starting point of the removal.

The insertString and remove methods, unlike their Document counterparts, return an object of type UndoableEdit. The intention here is to provide an object that encapsulates the change that was made in such a way that it can be rolled back without the software that needs the rollback to be done having to understand how it is actually performed.

Once you've created a StringContent object and passed it to AbstractDocument, you shouldn't access it directly yourself, because all changes to it must be notified to text components that are viewing the content. This job belongs to AbstractDocument, which provides, through the Document interface, the only way to access the document content. The StringContent is, however, usually created for you by the Document model implementation itself.

Elements, Attributes, and Styles

So far, you've only seen how the actual document data is stored. Using the StringContent class and an appropriate implementation of the Document interface (such as the PlainDocument class that you'll see later), you have the basis for a simple component like JTextField in which the text has one font and one color. To create more interesting documents, you need to be able to store information about document structure, fonts, colors and other attributes.

Elements

Within a document, structure is provided by Elements. An Element has three functions. First, it allows a set of attributes to be associated with a portion of a document. Because of this, it is possible to create documents with multiple fonts and colors. Second, it allows structures such as paragraphs to be established, by providing the means to mark the boundaries of paragraphs or other, arbitrary structures that your particular type of document might want. Finally, because Elements can be arranged in a hierarchical fashion, it is possible to nest Elements inside other Elements to allow, for example, font changes within a paragraph, while preserving the ability to treat the paragraph itself as a logical whole, represented by its own Element, when this is necessary.

Like Document and Content, Element is an interface. Here is its definition:

```
public interface Element {
   public AttributeSet getAttributes();
   public Document getDocument();
   public String getName();
   public int getStartOffset();
   public int getEndOffset();
   public Element getParentElement();
   public int getElementCount();
   public Element getElement(int index);
   public int getElementIndex(int offset);
   public boolean isLeaf();
}
```

The getAttributes and getDocument methods are trivial: the former returns the set of attributes associated with the Element and the latter returns a reference to the document of which it is a part. Every element has exactly one set of attributes associated with it, which may be empty. The AttributeSet interface and attributes in general are discussed later in this section. Note that the getAttributes method never returns null, even though you can create an element without specifying any attributes; in this case, getAttributes returns a reference to an empty set of attributes.

getName returns an element's name. In theory, you can give an element any name you choose when you create it. The name is actually stored as one of the attributes associated with the element. All of the Swing classes use the name attribute to indicate the type of the element, of which there are three commonly-used types—content, paragraph and section. These element types and the way in which they are used are discussed below.

Core Note

These three are not the only element types used in the Swing text controls and, in fact, new document model implementations are free to add their own types. The document type used for JTextPane, for example, adds element types for icons and components, while the HTML support has types for inline images and horizontal rules.

An element represents a contiguous chunk of a document. When an element is created, it has an associated range of document offsets that you can obtain using the getStartOffset and getEndOffset methods, both of which return integers. You might think that offsets are unreliable things to have when the document is able to change its size as a result of new content being added or because of content removal. This issue applies as much to elements as it does to the data itself. To deal with keeping track of data offsets within documents, the Position interface, which makes it possible to "tag" part of a document's content so that its actual offset can be obtained whenever necessary, is used. In the case of elements, the element itself keeps track of its own position in the document, so that the `getStartOffset` and `getEndOffset` methods always return current values.

Core Note

The responsibility for maintaining the start and end offsets of elements belongs to the Document *implementation, which creates new elements or merges adjacent elements as necessary to reflect the changing content of a document.*

The last five methods deal with traversing element hierarchies. The `Element` interface does not include methods that allow hierarchies to be created or destroyed; these matters are dealt with by the `AbstractDocument` class and its subclasses which work together to maintain the structure of a document. `AbstractDocument` defines an abstract inner class called `AbstractElement` that implements the `Element` interface and provides the framework for real elements in real documents. From this class, two real element classes are derived—`BranchElement` and `LeafElement`. As their names suggest, a `LeafElement` is the lowest level in the structure hierarchy: It may not have any child elements. `BranchElement` represents all of the other items in the hierarchy. It can have both parents and children. The differences between these two element types are clearly shown by their constructors:

```
public LeafElement(Element parent, AttributeSet a, int offs0, int offs1)

public BranchElement(Element parent, AttributeSet a)
```

Notice that both element types have associated attributes in the form of an `AttributeSet`; you'll see shortly what it means for a nonleaf element to have associated attributes. The most fundamental distinction between these two classes is that only leaf elements can directly describe content—notice that a branch element does not have an associated range of offsets that mark out the part of the document that it covers. The range of a branch element is implicitly the range covered by all of its children, be they leaf elements or other branch elements.

Every leaf element in a document has a parent within the document. In a flat document (such as `JTextField`), there is only one level of structure—the root element is the only branch element and the document content is completely described by a set of leaf elements of which the root element is the parent. The other text components have a more complex document structure.

The `getParentElement` method returns the branch element that is the direct parent of the element (branch or leaf) to which it is applied. Applying this method to the root element results in `null` being returned. `getElementCount` returns the number of elements to which the given element is parent. This method returns zero if applied to a leaf element.

The `getElement` and `getElementIndex` methods allow you to locate elements given one of two pieces of information. `getElement` returns an element given its index within its parent branch. Branch elements hold their children in ascending offset order, numbering the first entry 0. This method is useful if you want to step through all of the elements of a branch, which is typically what a rendering component (the *view*) does to display a paragraph on the screen. The `getElementIndex` method returns the index of an element given an offset into the document. This is typically used, in conjunction with the previous method, to find the element that holds the attributes for a particular location in the document. Note, however, that what this method returns is the index of one of its direct children that is `nearest` to the specified offset, even if that child does not contain the offset itself. Thus, for example, if a branch element covers offset 80 to 100 in a document and it has three children covering offsets 80–90, 91–95 and 96–100, it would return index 0 in response to any offset less than or equal to 90 and index 2 to any offset 96 and higher, even though these elements don't necessarily cover the actual offset given. It is expected that you would first use the `getStartOffset` and `getEndOffset` methods to determine whether the offset you need is within the bounds of the element before using `getElementIndex`.

Finally, the `isLeaf` method returns `true` for a leaf element and `false` for a branch, even if the branch has no children. This method is used to check whether an element *could* contain children, not whether it actually has any.

Attributes and Attribute Sets

An *attribute* is simply a property that has both a name, expressed as an `Object`, and a value, which can also be an `Object` of any kind. Attributes are always grouped together into *attribute sets* and then associated with elements to control the rendering of a document by a view. There are two interfaces that deal with attributes—`AttributeSet` and `MutableAttributeSet`. The first of these represents a read-only view of a collection of attributes and is implemented by the inner class `SmallAttributeSet` of the `StyleContext` class that you'll see later. This class is used to quickly compare whether two attribute sets are equal—two `SmallAttributeSets` are equal if and only if they are the same set. There is also another class that handles attributes. The `SimpleAttributeSet` class implements `MutableAttributeSet`, which is an extension of `AttributeSet` that allows the attributes to be changed.

Theoretically, since attributes are simply named objects, you can invent attributes of your own and store them within a document. This is, of course, only useful if you intend to write a customized viewer that can make use of these extended attributes. The viewers built into the Swing package recognize a set of attributes, whose names should be considered to be reserved. A partial list of attributes and the type and meaning of the associated values is shown in Table 9-1. These attributes are all declared as instances of four static inner classes of the `StyleConstants` class that will be described below—`ParagraphConstants`, `CharacterConstants`,

`ColorConstants` and `FontConstants` and then assigned to static variables of the `StyleConstants` class, which is how they are normally used. To reference one of these attributes, you would prefix the name in Table 9-1 by `StyleConstants`— for example:

```
StyleConstants.Alignment
```

Table 9-1 Attributes Recognized by Swing Components

Name	Data Type	Associated Value
Alignment	Integer	This attribute specifies the alignment of the paragraph with which it is associated. There are four possible values: ALIGN_CENTER: Each line in the paragraph is horizontally centered, with extra space distributed equally to the left and right ALIGN_JUSTIFIED: Each line starts at the left margin and ends at the right margin. If the line is not long enough, after word wrapping, to fill the entire line, extra spaces are distributed between words to make the last word end at the right margin. ALIGN_LEFT: Each line starts at the left margin. No attempt is made to align the end of the line. ALIGN_RIGHT: Each line ends at the right margin. This usually produces a ragged effect on the left-hand side of the document.
Bold	Boolean	If `true`, indicates that the text associated with this element should be rendered in a bold font.
ComponentAttribute	Component	Stores a `Component` to be rendered at the location corresponding to this element.
FirstLineIndent	Float	Gives the amount, in points, by which the first line of a paragraph is indented in addition to the `LeftIndent` attribute. If this attribute is positive, the first line of a paragraph has extra lead-in space. If it is negative, the first line juts out to the left of the rest of the paragraph.
FontFamily	String	Gives the name of the font family to use when rendering this element. A typical example might be `'SansSerif'`.
FontSize	Integer	The size of the font for this element, in points.

continued

Table 9-1	Attributes Recognized by Swing Components (continued)	
Foreground	Color	The color to be used for rendering foreground items (typically text) in this element.
IconAttribute	Icon	Supplies an icon to be rendered at the location occupied by this element.
Italic	Boolean	Specifies that the text should be rendered in italics, if `true`.
LeftIndent	Float	The indentation to be used for the left side of a paragraph, in points.
LineSpacing	Float	The number of points to be left between one line and the line below it. This value is added to the usual distance between the font baselines when rendering text.
RightIndent	Float	The number of points to be left between the right-hand side of a paragraph and the right side of the view.
SpaceAbove	Float	The number of points to be left above the paragraph described by this element.
SpaceBelow	Float	The number of points to be left below the paragraph described by this element. If `SpaceBelow` is specified for a paragraph and `SpaceAbove` is specified for the paragraph below it, the distance between these two paragraphs will be the sum of the two values.
Underline	Boolean	If `true`, causes the text associated with the element to be underlined when rendered.

Attribute Set Hierarchies

As you know, an element can have a single set of attributes associated with it. Typically, an attribute set might describe the font and colors used to render some text. Now suppose that you wanted to create an attribute set that is like one you already have, but differs in a minor way. For example, you might have an attribute set that defines the way in which an entire document is rendered and want to be able to change the font to bold for a few characters, then return to the usual typeface. One way to do this is to create the modified attribute set by duplicating the original set and adding the attribute `"StyleConstants.Bold = true"`. This is, of course, inefficient in terms of memory consumption. To avoid this, it is possible to arrange attributes in a hierarchy, in the sense that any attribute set can be given a *resolving parent*. When looking for an attribute in an attribute set, if the attribute set itself does not declare a value for that attribute, its resolving parent is queried for a value and so on, until either the attribute is found or an attribute set without a resolving parent is reached.

Using this mechanism, you can create an attribute set just like the normal one but with a bold font, by building one with just the bold attribute (defined as `true`) and setting its resolving parent to the style used elsewhere in the document. This approach is, of course, resilient to changes in the base attribute set: If somebody decides that all documents should be rendered in a 14-point font instead of a 12-point font, your modified attributes will continue to work and the bold text will now be in 14-point font as well.

Be careful to distinguish this logical arrangement of attribute sets, which is independent of document contents, from the hierarchy of character and paragraph attributes that you can create in a document. This topic will be discussed further later on in connection with styled documents.

The AttributeSet and MutableAttributeSet Interfaces

Now that you've seen how attribute sets are intended to be used, let's look at the `AttributeSet` and `MutableAttributeSet` interfaces. Note that there is no concept of an individual attribute object: Attributes only exist within attribute sets.

The AttributeSet Interface

The `AttributeSet` interface describes a set of attributes that must be considered read-only because it does not define any methods to change the content of the attribute set. Here is its definition.

```
public interface AttributeSet {
  public Object getAttribute(Object attrName);
  public int getAttributeCount();
  public boolean isEqual(AttributeSet attr);
  public AttributeSet getResolveParent();
  public AttributeSet copyAttributes();
  public boolean containsAttribute(Object name, Object value);
  public boolean containsAttributes(AttributeSet attributes);
  public Enumeration getAttributeNames();
  public boolean isDefined(Object attrName);
}
```

When using these methods, an important point to bear in mind is whether or not the operation includes the attribute set's resolving parent if it has one. The descriptions that follow indicate which operations take account of the content of resolving parent attribute sets.

The `getAttribute` method is used to get the value of a named attribute. It is first looked for in the attribute set itself; if it is found there, its value is returned.

Otherwise, if there is a resolving parent, the request is passed to it for resolution. Obviously, this process repeats itself if until either an ancestor of the original attribute set contains the attribute, or an attribute set with no resolving parent is found. This method effectively flattens the hierarchy of attribute sets, allowing values in child attribute sets to take precedence over values in their ancestors.

The methods `isEmpty` and `getAttributeCount` indicate whether the attribute set is empty and return the number of attributes in the set, respectively. The results do not take account of any attributes that may be found through a resolving parent.

`isEqual` compares the attribute set on which it operates with the content of another one. They are considered to be equal if they have the same number of attributes and every attribute in one set is present in the other and each individual attribute in one set has the same value as its counterpart in the other set.

`getResolveParent` returns the resolving parent of the attribute set, or `null` if it doesn't have one.

`copyAttributes` makes a duplicate copy of the attributes set on which it operates by cloning it. The returned object has a separate copy of all of the attributes that were in the original set, so that changing them would not affect the values seen through the original attribute set. It also clones the reference to the resolving parent, if there is one, so the new attribute set shares the same resolving parent. It does not, however, clone the resolving parent, so values in that parent are actually shared between the two attribute sets (and any modification would be visible in both).

The `containsAttribute` and `containsAttributes` method look for either one attribute given by name or for a set of attributes, in another attribute set. For each attribute, a check is made that it is present in the attribute set against which the method has been invoked and, if it is, whether it has the same value as that passed as an argument or in the second attribute set. If no attributes are missing and all of the values match, then `true` is returned. Note that the resolving parent of the attribute set against which the method has been invoked is consulted to locate values, if necessary, but the resolving parent of the attribute set passed as argument to `containsAttributes` is not consulted when creating the list of attributes to compare.

`getAttributeNames` gets an `Enumeration` of the names of all of the attributes in the set. It does not include attributes in the resolving parent.

Finally, `isDefined` checks whether the name attribute exists in the attribute set. It does not consult the resolving parent, so the attribute is considered not defined if it is not in the attribute set itself, even if the resolving parent can locate a definition for it.

The MutableAttributeSet Interface

If you want to be able to modify a set of attributes, you need a `MutableAttributeSet`. The `MutableAttributeSet` interface is implemented by the Swing class `SimpleAttributeSet`. Here is the definition of `MutableAttributeSet`:

```
public interface MutableAttributeSet extends AttributeSet {
    public void addAttribute(Object name, Object value);
    public void addAttributes(AttributeSet attrs);
    public void removeAttribute(Object name);
    public void removeAttributes(Enumeration names);
    public void removeAttributes(AttributeSet attrs);
    public void setResolveParent(MutableAttributeSet parent);
}
```

`addAttribute` adds the given attribute with the supplied value to the current attribute set. `addAttributes` adds all of the attributes from the supplied attribute set to the current attribute set. The set of attributes added does not include those in the resolving parent of the source set.

`removeAttribute` deletes the named attribute from the attribute set, if it is present. Only the attribute set itself is affected—the contents of the set's resolving parent, if any, are not changed. This has the following results:

- If the attribute was not defined in either the attribute set or its resolving parent, there is no change and the attribute will remain undefined.

- If the attribute was defined in the attribute set but not in its resolving parent, it will be removed and the attribute will now be undefined.

- If the attribute was defined in the resolving parent but not in the attribute set itself, no change will be made. As a result, calling `getAttribute` will continue to return the attribute from the resolving parent.

- If the attribute was defined in both the attribute set and its resolving parent, the value in the attribute set will be removed but the resolving parent will be unaffected. Therefore, a call to `getAttribute` will now return the value stored in the resolving parent, which may be different from the original.

Likewise, the two forms of `removeAttributes` delete attributes given in the form of an `Enumeration` or another attribute set. If an attribute set is given, attributes present in the resolving parent that are not present in the attribute set itself are not copied. Also note that the same cautions regarding the result of the operation apply to each individual attribute affected by this operation as apply when `removeAttribute` is used.

You set the resolving parent using the `setResolveParent` method. Note that the resolving parent of an attribute set is stored within the attribute set as an attribute called `AttributeSet.ResolveAttribute`. The value of this attribute is a reference to the resolving parent itself. If you remove this attribute the connection between the attribute set and its parent will be lost. Also, as was noted during the discussion of the `AttributeSet` interface, cloning an attribute set using `copyAttributes` causes the resolving parent to be inherited, because the attribute that defines it is copied to the new attribute set.

Core Note

In future versions of Swing, it is possible that the resolving parent of an attribute set may not be stored this way, so it is best not to rely on this implementation detail. Instead, use the `getResolveParent` *method to get the resolving parent of an attribute set.*

Styles

So far, you've seen the various attributes that are defined by the Swing text package, but you haven't yet learned how to create an attribute set. Neither the `AttributeSet` nor the `MutableAttributeSet` interfaces include methods that allow you to do this. In fact, there are two ways to obtain an attribute set.

SimpleAttributeSet

The most obvious way to create a `MutableAttributeSet` is to use the `SimpleAttributeSet` class, which is an implementation of `MutableAttributeSet` that stores attributes in a `Hashtable`, using the attribute name as the key. This class has three constructors:

```
public SimpleAttributeSet();

public SimpleAttributeSet(AttributeSet source);

private SimpleAttributeSet(Hashtable table);
```

The first constructor creates an empty set to which you can add attributes using the `addAttribute` or `addAttributes` methods, while the second initializes itself from an existing attribute set. The third form directly copies a `Hashtable` mapping attributes names to values into the `Hashtable` that the `SimpleAttributeSet` uses to hold its attributes. This last constructor is, however, private so you cannot make any use of it.

Styles and StyleContexts

The other way to create a `MutableAttributeSet` is to use the `StyleContext` class. This class is intended to allow a set of *styles* to be created and stored together, so that they can be used as the basis of a *styled document*. Storing styles in a `StyleContext` also allows the same pool of styles to be shared between documents. But what is a style?

A style is actually little more than an attribute set. Formally, `Style` is yet another interface, defined as follows:

```
public interface Style extends MutableAttributeSet {
   public void addChangeListener(ChangeListener l);
   public void removeChangeListener(ChangeListener l);
   public String getName();
}
```

A style gives you the ability to register a listener for changes to its attributes and to have a name by which you can refer to it. It does not, however, provide a method to set the name. For that, you have to use `StyleContext`. Unless you intend to implement your own `Style` class, `StyleContext` is the only way to create a style and it is also the only way to get an attribute set that has a name associated with it. If you create a style in a `StyleContext` and associate a name with it, you can use that name to refer to the style without having to save a private reference to the original object. Styles are usually given names that are meaningful to the user, such as "Heading 1," which might store the attributes for top-level headings in your document. Another advantage of naming styles is that it is easier to extend a style by asking for the base style by name and then creating a new one with the required differences and linking it to the original style via the resolving parent mechanism.

Core Note

Remember that a `Style` *is just a* `MutableAttributeSet`, *so anything you can do with an attribute set you can do with a style as well.*

Here is the definition of the `StyleContext` class:

```
public class StyleContext implements Serializable,
         AbstractDocument.AttributeContext {
   public StyleContext();
   public static final StyleContext getDefaultStyleContext()
   public void addChangeListener(ChangeListener l);
   public void removeChangeListener(ChangeListener l);
   public Style addStyle(String name, Style parent);
   public void removeStyle(String name);
   public Enumeration getStyleNames();
   public Style getStyle(String name);
   public Font getFont(AttributeSet attr);
   public Font getFont(String family, int style, int size);
   public FontMetrics getFontMetrics(Font font);
   public synchronized AttributeSet addAttribute(AttributeSet old,
            Object name, Object value);
```

```
public synchronized AttributeSet addAttributes(AttributeSet old,
        AttributeSet attrs);
public synchronized AttributeSet removeAttribute(AttributeSet old,
        Object name);
public synchronized AttributeSet removeAttributes(AttributeSet old,
        Enumeration names);
public synchronized AttributeSet removeAttributes(AttributeSet old,
        AttributeSet attrs);
public AttributeSet getEmptySet();
public synchronized void reclaim(AttributeSet attrs);
public static void writeAttributeSet(ObjectOutputStream out,
        AttributeSet attrs);
public static void readAttributeSet(ObjectInputStream in,
        MutableAttributeSet attrs);
public static void registerStaticAttributeKey(Object key);
}
```

You'll notice that these methods fall naturally into several different groups. The first nine (up to and including get Style) deal with the management of styles and the style context itself. The next three provide fast font handling by providing a layer of caching within the StyleContext and the rest deal with handling AttributeSets. In fact, the first seven of this last group of methods (from addAttribute to reclaim) define an interface called AbstractDocument.AttributeContext that you'll see later in connection with the DefaultStyledDocument class. This last set of methods is not of particular interest unless you are adding to the text component framework, so they won't be discussed any further here.

The constructor creates a StyleContext with a single style called default. This style initially has no associated attributes and no resolving parent. To create a new style, you first call the addStyle method, giving the name that you want to associate with the style and the style's resolving parent, if it needs one. The name must be unique within the StyleContext object—if you reuse an existing name, the original style will be lost. Having created the style, you can use the methods of MutableAttributeSet to set its attributes. For example, the following code extract creates a StyleContext and adds to it a style called Basic Style, which uses a 12-point SansSerif font:

```
StyleContext sc = new StyleContext();
Style basicStyle = sc.addStyle("Basic Style", null);
basicStyle.addAttribute(StyleConstants.FontFamily, "SansSerif");
basicStyle.addAttribute(StyleConstants.FontSize, new Integer(12));
```

Now suppose that you wanted to create a style for chapter headings that will be used in the same document as Basic Style. The chapter heading style will use the same font family as Basic Style, but will be bold, underlined, be followed by 12 points of vertical space and use a 16-point font. You could define this style from scratch by setting all of its attributes explicitly, but it is preferable to inherit the font family from the document's basic font by setting the resolving parent attribute to point to `Basic Style`:

```
Style chapterHeading = sc.addStyle("Chapter Heading", basicStyle);
chapterHeading.addAttribute(StyleConstants.FontSize, new Integer(16));
chapterHeading.addAttribute(StyleConstants.Bold, new Boolean(true));
chapterHeading.addAttribute(StyleConstants.SpaceBelow, new Float(12.0));
```

The `addStyle` method in this extract makes `Basic Style` the resolving parent of `Chapter Heading`. As a result, if you ask for the `FontFamily` attribute of the chapter heading style, it will return "SansSerif" even though an explicit font family isn't defined for `Chapter Heading`, because the `getAttribute` method looks for missing attributes in the resolving parent. On the other hand, the `FontSize` attribute of this style is 16, which overrides the original 12 points of the basic style.

Once you've defined a style and given it a name, you can use the `getStyle` method to get a reference to the style given the name. Similarly, `getStyleNames` returns an `Enumeration` of all of the styles in the context.

A style can be removed from the style context using `removeStyle`, which needs the name of the style as its only argument. Removing a style does not delete it: It can still be used through its original reference. For example, if the document's basic style were removed like this:

```
sc.removeStyle("Basic Style");
```

it would still be possible to use this style via the variable `basicStyle` that was initialized earlier. Furthermore, style resolution from the chapter heading style continues to work, because of the way in which style names and the resolving parent identity are stored.

When you create a style within a style context and give it a name, an attribute is added to the style context's `default` style; the name of this attribute is the name of the style itself and its value is the created style. For example, when `Basic Style` was created, the following attribute and value were placed in the style context's `default` style:

```
("Basic Style", basicStyle)
```

When `removeStyle` is called, this attribute is removed from the default attribute set of the context, but nothing else changes. As we discovered earlier, the resolving parent is an attribute of the child's attribute set, whose value is a reference to the parent. As a result, any existing references to the style itself remain valid and the `AttributeSet.ResolveAttribute` attribute in the child style is unaffected, because it stores a reference to the parent style, not its name.

AbstractDocument and PlainDocument

All of the text components in the Swing packages are based around the AbstractDocument class, which provides a basic implementation of the Document interface. You can't, however, directly create an instance of AbstractDocument because it is an abstract class and its constructors are protected. Instead, you would usually create a PlainDocument or a DefaultStyledDocument, or perhaps develop a document implementation of your own, derived from AbstractDocument.

The public methods of this class are simply implementations of those required to comply with the Document interface. The document content can be held in any object that implements the AbstractDocument.Content interface, which must be passed to the constructors:

```
protected AbstractDocument(AbstractDocument.Content content);
```

```
protected AbstractDocument(Content data, AttributeContext context)
```

Both PlainDocument and DefaultStyledDocument use the StringContent class that you've already seen to manage the data content.

The Structure of a Plain Document

JTextField and JTextArea use PlainDocument to implement their document model. Both of these components display only text and can support a single font and a single foreground color. Such a basic component doesn't require much more than the simple implementation provided by AbstractDocument; in fact, PlainDocument only has four declared methods:

```
public Element getDefaultRootElement();
```

```
public AbstractDocument.AbstractElement createDefaultRootElement();
```

```
protected void insertUpdate(DefaultDocumentEvent chng, AttributeSet attr);
```

```
protected void removeUpdate(DefaultDocumentEvent chng);
```

The getDefaultRootElement method simply returns the root element originally created by createDefaultRootElement, which is called from the constructor of AbstractDocument. Each document type is allowed to have its own root element; the only requirement is that it should implement the Element interface. As you saw earlier, AbstractDocument provides two element types, BranchElement and LeafElement, for use by its subclasses. PlainDocument creates a BranchElement to act as the root of its internal structure, while DefaultStyledDocument uses a rather trivial subclass of BranchElement called SectionElement. However, not all branch elements are used in the same way, as you'll see later when we look at styled documents. To provide a way to distinguish between them, they are given different names. Since the ability to get an element's name is provided by the Element interface, leaf elements can also be given a name. Three common element names are defined by AbstractDocument:

```
AbstractDocument.ContentElementName: "content"

AbstractDocument.ParagraphElementName: "paragraph"

AbstractDocument.SectionElementName: "section"
```

A Class That Formats Element Structures

In a plain document, all of the branch elements are paragraphs, so the root element is a paragraph. In fact, the structure of a plain document is probably much simpler than you might think. The term *paragraph*, in the context of a word processor, usually means a sequence of characters (in sentences) terminated by a newline character. This is not, however, what a paragraph is in the context of a plain document. Let's look at the internal structures created when we use both a JTextField and a JTextArea. To look at these, it is necessary to write a fairly simple program to get the Document from a text control, then extract the elements in that document and format them. Since this functionality will be needed again when looking at JTextPane, the formatting code is implemented in a class of its own and an interface is wrapped around it to allow you to manipulate a text field and a text area to see how the internal structure is affected. Listing 9-6 shows the class that will be used to display a document's content and its elements.

Listing 9-6   A class that formats document structures

```
package JFCBook.Chapter9;

import com.sun.java.swing.*;
import com.sun.java.swing.text.*;
import java.io.*;
import java.util.*;

public class ModelDisplay {
  public static String showModel(Document doc) {
    StringWriter sw = new StringWriter();
    BufferedWriter w = new BufferedWriter(sw);
    try {
      w.write("Document contains " + doc.getLength() + " characters\n");

      // Get the root element and display it.
      // We also display any elements that this
```
continued

```
    // element contains
    Element root = doc.getDefaultRootElement();
    showElement(root, w, 0);

    w.flush();
    return sw.toString();
  } catch (IOException e) {
    return "I/O Exception";
  } catch (BadLocationException e) {
    return "Bad location exception";
  }
}

protected static void showElement(Element e, Writer w, int indent)
            throws IOException, BadLocationException {
  // Show the element name first
  String name = e.getName();
  int startOffset = e.getStartOffset();
  int endOffset = e.getEndOffset();

  doIndent(w, indent);
  w.write("[ " + name + " ], start offset: " + startOffset +
            ", end: " + endOffset + "\n");

  // Display the attributes, if there are any...
  AttributeSet a = e.getAttributes();
  int attrs = a.getAttributeCount();
  if (attrs == 0) {
    doIndent(w, indent + 2);
    w.write("{ No attributes }\n");
  } else {
    Enumeration enum = a.getAttributeNames();
    while (enum.hasMoreElements()) {
      Object o = enum.nextElement();
      String ename = o.toString();
      doIndent(w, indent + 2);
      w.write("{ " + ename + " = ");
      String value = a.getAttribute(o).toString();
      w.write(value + " }\n");
    }
  }

  // If it is content, show some of the data
  if (name.equals(AbstractDocument.ContentElementName)) {
    // Display no more than CONTENT_COLUMNS characters
    int length = endOffset - startOffset;
    if (length > CONTENT_COLUMNS) {
```

```
      length = CONTENT_COLUMNS;
    }

    if (length > 0) {
      Segment s = new Segment();
      e.getDocument().getText(startOffset, length, s);
      doIndent(w, indent + 8);
      for (int i = 0; i < length; i++) {
        char c = s.array[i + s.offset];
        if (c == '\n') {
          w.write(" \\n ");
        } else if (c == '\r') {
          w.write(" \\r ");
        } else {
          w.write(s.array[i + s.offset]);
        }
      }
    }
  }
  w.write("\n");

  // Now traverse the children of this element
  int children = e.getElementCount();
  for (int i = 0; i < children; i++) {
    showElement(e.getElement(i), w, indent + 4);
  }
}

// Indent by the given amount
protected static void doIndent(Writer w, int n)
          throws IOException {
  for (int i = 0; i < n; i++) {
    w.write(" ");
  }
}

public static final int CONTENT_COLUMNS = 40;
}
```

This class only has a single public method, showModel, which takes a Document as its argument and returns a String containing an analysis of the document's content and structure. In the program that will be used to look at the internals of text components, this string will be displayed in a text area. The implementation of this class uses java.io.StringWriter, which is an output writer that places everything you write into it in a String. When you've finished writing, you just flush the output and then use the `toString` method to get back everything that you wrote to it. This is a more general and more useful solution than writing the results to the program's output stream.

The core of the `ModelDisplay` class is the static `showElement` method, which takes as arguments an element, the `Writer` to which it will send its output and the number of spaces by which each line of output should be indented. This method first prints information about the element it has been given, then invokes itself recursively for each child element, increasing the indent by 4 spaces so that the hierarchy can be clearly seen. Since every element is descended from the document's root element, to see every element `getDefaultRootElement` is used to get a starting point and then `showElement` is called with an initial indentation of zero.

For each element, the element name and its start and end offsets are printed, then the `getAttributes` method is used to see whether it has any associated attributes. If it does, each attribute is printed by using `getAttributeNames` to get an enumeration of the attribute names, then getting each attribute's associated value from the `getAttribute` method. Because an attribute can be an object of any kind, we use its `toString` method to produce a readable representation and the attributes are also indented slightly from the element description.

Having printed the attributes, the element name is examined. If it's a content element (i.e. its name as returned by `getName` is `AbstractDocument.ContentElementName`), then the next thing to do is to display some of the data so that you can see which part of the document the element represents. From the element itself, the start and end offsets have already been obtained and these are used to get the actual data using the `getText` method of `Document`. The `showElement` method wasn't given the `Document` as an argument, but a reference to it can be obtained using `Element`'s `getDocument` method. Because there could potentially be a lot of data associated with a content element, it isn't reasonable to display it all. Instead, no more that 40 characters will be printed. It is also not desirable to actually print any newline characters that are in the date—instead, a readable representation is printed so that it is obvious that a newline was present, without ruining the formatting. Both of these requirements make it more efficient to extract the document content as an array of characters rather than a `String`, so the variant of `getText` that returns a `Segment` object is used. The `Segment` class was described at the beginning of this section. It has three public members that describe the returned data:

```
public char[] array;

public int offset;

public int count;
```

The caller of `getText` doesn't supply the array into which the data is copied and the returned array should be considered read-only. The `count` field indicates how many elements of the array are valid and `offset` is the index of the character in the array that resides at the offset specified in the `getText` call. As you already know,

`AbstractDocument` uses the `StringContent` class to holds its data and it delegates the `getText` call directly to the `StringContent getChars` method. Because `StringContent` holds the complete document in a character array, it implements the `getChars` method by simply setting the `array` member of the `Segment` object to the base of its internal array and the `offset` and `count` to the same values that it is supplied as arguments, assuming that they are valid.

Having formatted both the type, data content and attributes of an element, the last task is to handle any child elements. The number of child elements that each element has can be obtained by using the `getElementCount` method. If this returns a positive value, `getElement` is called for each child element and `showElement` is recursively invoked with a larger indentation.

The Internal Structure of Simple Text Components

Having seen the implementation, let's look at how it works in practice. Figure 9-7 shows a simple application that uses the `ModelDisplay` class. On the left, there is a text field and a text area. If you type something into these components and then press one of the buttons at the bottom right, the content of the selected text component's model will be shown in the text area above the buttons.

To run this program for yourself, use the command:

```
java JFCBook.Chapter9.PlainTextModel
```

First, lets look at the text field. Into this control, the following text was typed:

```
That's one small step for man...
```

and then the `Dump Text Field` button was pressed. This produced the following result:

```
Document contains 32 characters
[ paragraph ], start offset: 0, end: 33
  { No attributes }

    [ content ], start offset: 0, end: 33
      { No attributes }
          That's one small step for man...\n
```

As you can see, the `getLength` method returns the correct size for the document, i.e., 32 characters.

Structurally, the first element (which is the root element) is a `paragraph`, covering offsets 0 to 32. The end offset is, as this example shows, the first offset after the end of the document. This paragraph has no associated attributes, but it does have a child element, which is a `content` element. This element covers the same range of offsets as the root element and, similarly, it has no attributes. The data associated with this element is the text typed into the control. Notice that the text ends with a newline character, even though one was not typed into the text field and it doesn't get counted in the size of the document.

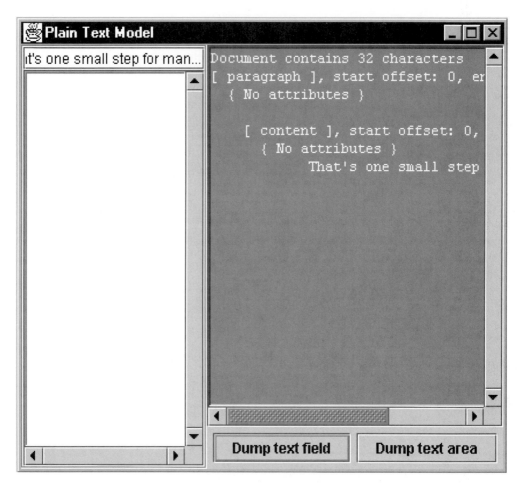

Figure 9-7   The structure of a plain document.

This is all there ever is in a JTextField. By definition, there is only one line in a text field and there is no way to assign any attributes to it. The font and the foreground color are held not in the document model, but in the JTextComponent (actually in the Component). When the text field is drawn onto the screen, the font and the foreground color are obtained using the getFont and getForeground methods, as usual.

Now let's look at the text area. This time, as you can see from Figure 9-8, there is a bit more text, in two paragraphs. Here is exactly what was typed, with the correct line and paragraph breaks:

```
Houston, Tranquility Base here.
The Eagle has landed.

Roger, Tranquility, we copy you on the
ground.
You got a bunch of guys about to turn
blue. We're breathing again.
Thanks a lot.
```

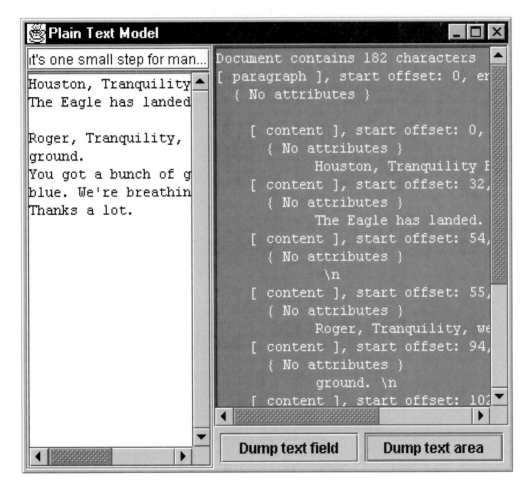

Figure 9-8   The internal structure of a text area.

Pressing the "Dump Text Area" button results in this output:

```
Document contains 182 characters
[ paragraph ], start offset: 0, end: 183
  { No attributes }

      [ content ], start offset: 0, end: 32
        { No attributes }
              Houston, Tranquility Base here. \n
      [ content ], start offset: 32, end: 54
        { No attributes }
              The Eagle has landed. \n
      [ content ], start offset: 54, end: 55
        { No attributes }
                 \n
      [ content ], start offset: 55, end: 94
        { No attributes }
              Roger, Tranquility, we copy you on the \n
      [ content ], start offset: 94, end: 102
        { No attributes }
              ground. \n
      [ content ], start offset: 102, end: 140
        { No attributes }
              You got a bunch of guys about to turn \n

      [ content ], start offset: 140, end: 169
        { No attributes }
              blue. We're breathing again. \n
      [ content ], start offset: 169, end: 183
        { No attributes }
              Thanks a lot. \n
```

Even though the text that was typed contains two paragraphs, the JTextArea's model only contains one paragraph element. This element contains all of the document's content, just as it did in the case of the JTextField. Here you can see that the paragraph element as used by JTextField and JTextArea doesn't really bear any relationship to an actual paragraph in a real document: Both of these controls use a single paragraph element as the root element and place all of the data in content elements. In terms of the logical structure, the root element is the only BranchElement and it has one LeafElement for each item of content. Notice also that, again, there are no attributes associated with any of these elements.

Turning to the content elements, you can see that each of them corresponds to one line of text and is terminated with a newline character. The last element has a newline even though one wasn't typed at the end of the text, but as with the JTextField it is not part of the document because it isn't included in the total count of characters. In a JTextArea, elements always span a complete line. As text is entered, it is split at newline boundaries and an element is added for each line.

Since there is no way to apply any formatting to the content, there is no reason to create an element shorter than one line. The paragraph break between the second and third lines of the text appears as two consecutive newline characters, one of which is in an element of its own at offset 54.

Now suppose that you were to go back and change the text a little. If the text were broken after "about to turn blue" so that the sentence "We're breathing again" appeared as a line on its own and the model contents were dumped again, you would see that the extra newline has caused a new element to be generated:

```
[ content ], start offset: 102, end: 140
    { No attributes }
            You got a bunch of guys about to turn \n
  [ content ], start offset: 140, end: 147
    { No attributes }
            blue.  \n
  [ content ], start offset: 147, end: 170
    { No attributes }
            We're breathing again. \n
```

The original element that covered all of this text has been deleted and two new ones added. There is only one element covering any part of a document even though elements are arranged hierarchically, because content elements are always leaves, so cannot be nested one inside the other. This remains true even for the more complex JTextPane and JEditorPane controls.

Document Edits and Events

Returning to the methods of PlainDocument, there are two that haven't yet been mentioned—insertUpdate and removeUpdate. These methods are invoked when some content is inserted into the document or removed from it. In more complex document types (such as DefaultStyledDocument), insertUpdate can be called as a result of an attribute change, even if no new content is added. Each of these methods is given a DefaultDocumentEvent as its first argument. Earlier in this chapter, you saw how a user of a text component could be notified when its content is changed by registering a DocumentListener, which receives DocumentEvents. Unlike other events, DocumentEvent is not a class, but an interface, defined as follows:

```
public interface DocumentEvent {
   public int getOffset();
   public int getLength();
   public Document getDocument();
   public EventType getType();
   public ElementChange getChange(Element elem);
}
```

DefaultDocumentEvent is a class that implements the DocumentEvent interface. When we looked at monitoring and reacting to document changes earlier in this chapter, the events that we received were actually DefaultDocumentEvents.

As you know, the only way to change a Document is to call either the insertString or remove methods of AbstractDocument. These methods invoke the insertString or remove methods of StringContent to change the data, but they also create a DefaultDocumentEvent, which is initialized with the offset and length of the area affected by the change. This object is then passed to either the Document's insertUpdate or its removeUpdate method. AbstractDocument doesn't implement either of these—they are provided by PlainDocument and DefaultStyledDocument. Different processing is needed for these two document types, because the structure of a style document is more complex than that of a plain document.

The job of both insertUpdate and removeUpdate is twofold. First, each of them needs to modify the element structure of the document to reflect the data being inserted or removed. In the case of plain documents, inserting text means possibly adding new elements if the new text has newlines in it, or extending the range of an element if more data is being added within a line. In the case of data removal, it may be possible to remove elements and possibly merge adjacent elements into one. The second task that these methods need to perform is to update the DefaultDocumentEvent with change records that can be used by other components to update their view of the model without having to process all of the document data from scratch. These records can also be used to allow the change to be reversed or to be reapplied later if it is subsequently removed.

JTextComponent, Keymaps and the Caret

So far, you've seen how text components store their data and how it is possible to associate attributes with parts of the document. Later in this chapter, you'll see text components that make more extensive use of the underlying infrastructure. Meanwhile, having seen the text components' model implementation, let's now examine the controller. In the MVC architecture, the controller handles user input and directs it to either the model or the view, as appropriate. For the text components, the controller is implemented partly by JTextComponent and partly by the DefaultCaret class.

The keyboard handling functions of the MVC controller are handled by JTextComponent. Its job is to map special keys to the appropriate actions. For example, in a JTextField, pressing the RETURN key doesn't generate a newline in the model. Instead, it causes an ActionEvent to be created. This is not, however, true for JTextArea. To handle special key processing, which is component-specific, JTextComponent supports the notion of a *keymap*, which determines which keys are special and what should be done with them.

Mouse- and focus-handling are controlled by an object that implements the `Caret` interface. By default, all text components use the `DefaultCaret` class to provide this functionality, but it is possible to install a custom `Caret` implementation using the `JTextComponent setCaret` method. As well as responding to events, the `Caret` implementation is responsible for drawing the cursor (also called the caret, with a lowercase "c") and for highlighting selected text.

Focus Management

`DefaultCaret` implements the `FocusListener` interface so that it can receive events when the associated text component gains and loses the focus. Text components display a caret at the point at which text would be inserted, either from the keyboard or by using the `replaceSelection` method. The caret is a separate unit that appears to be a part of a text component and, by default, it is rendered as a thin line to the left of the insertion point. The caret should be visible only when the component has the keyboard focus. To implement this, `DefaultCaret` implementation switches the caret on when it receives a focus-gained event and switches it off when the focus has been lost.

`JTextComponent` also has some focus-handling logic in it. A static inner class of `JTextComponent` called `MutableCaretEvent` registers to receive focus events from its associated component and records the text component that currently has the focus in the static `JTextComponent` member `focusedComponent`. As you'll see later, this information is used by the actions that are associated with the component's editor to allow them to be written without prior knowledge of the component on which they will operate.

Mouse Handling and the Caret

When the user clicks a mouse button in a text component that is both enabled and editable, the `Caret` for that text component grabs the keyboard focus using the `Component requestFocus` method. As was noted in the previous section, receipt of the focus will cause the caret to be turned on to show the current insertion point. The caret both marks the current insertion point and allows the user to create a selection. It is provided by a class called `DefaultCaret`, which implements the `Caret` interface:

```
public interface com.sun.java.swing.text.Caret extends java.lang.Object {
    public abstract void install(JTextComponent comp);
    public abstract void deinstall(JTextComponent comp);
    public abstract void paint(Graphics g);
    public abstract void addChangeListener(ChangeListener l);
    public abstract void removeChangeListener(ChangeListener l);
    public abstract boolean isVisible();
    public abstract void setVisible(boolean cond);
```

```
     public abstract boolean isSelectionVisible();
     public abstract void setSelectionVisible(boolean cond);
     public abstract void setMagicCaretPosition(Point pt);
     public abstract Point getMagicCaretPosition();
     public abstract void setBlinkRate(int rate);
     public abstract int getDot();
     public abstract int getMark();
     public abstract void setDot(int pos);
     public abstract void moveDot(int pos);
}
```

The way in which many of these methods are used should be obvious from their names. The `setBlinkRate` method controls the interval over which the caret flashes; its argument is specified in milliseconds. `DefaultCaret` implements this by setting a timer (using the `Timer` class that was described in Chapter 8, "Creating Custom Dialogs") that causes an `ActionEvent` to be fired when it is time to change the caret's appearance. If the flash interval is specified as zero, the caret does not blink and the visibility of the caret, which is maintained as a simple boolean, can be directly controlled using the `setVisible` method. If the caret is set to blink, its visibility is toggled when the timer that controls the caret blink fires, and the `paint` method will then be invoked to draw the caret, if it is visible.

The most interesting methods in the `Caret` interface are the last four, which handle the *mark* and the *dot*. The dot marks the current position of the caret, while the mark is the position at which the mouse was last pressed. When the user presses a mouse button, `DefaultCaret` invokes its own `setDot` method, which moves the dot and the mark to the location in the document represented by the current position of the mouse. The `setDot` method requires a document offset as its argument, but a mouse event has the mouse coordinates. Translation from mouse coordinates to a document offset is performed by using the `viewToModel` method of `JTextComponent`, which returns an offset given a `Point`.

If the user drags the mouse across the text component, each event from the mouse as it is moved causes the `Caret moveDot` method to be invoked. Like `setDot`, this method requires a document offset. The dot is moved to the offset in the document corresponding to the mouse position, leaving the mark behind. The part of the document between the mark and the dot is considered to be selected. Operations such as cut, copy and paste, as you have already seen, operate on selected text and, if you create a selection and then type some new text, it overwrites the selection. You'll see later that the selection is also used to indicate the portion of a document that is affected when new attributes are assigned. To highlight the selection, `setDot` uses the text component's associated `Highlighter`. The `setSelectionVisible` method switches the display of selected text on and off. This method could be used to show the selected text only when the component has the focus, but this is not actually implemented at Swing 1.0.1.

Core Tip

The color of the caret can be set or retrieved using the following `JTextComponent` *methods:*

```
public Color getCaretColor();

public void setCaretColor(Color color);
```

The Highlighter

`Highlighter` is another interface in the Swing text package, which allows one or more regions of a document to be highlighted at any given time and to provide the appropriate appearance when these regions are visible on the screen. Each highlight can have a different background color. There is an implementation of the `Highlighter` interface called `DefaultHighlighter` that is used by all of the standard text components. The text controller manages the highlighting of the selection, but it is possible to separately highlight other regions of text under program control by making direct use of the highlighter. For example, consider the example code shown in Listing 9-7, which creates a text field with a small amount of (by now familiar) text in it. If you run this example using the command:

```
java JFCBook.Chapter9.MouseHighlightExample
```

and then move the mouse over the text, you'll find that a green highlight appears over the character that is directly under the mouse and follows it as it moves.

Listing 9-7 Using the highlighter

```
package JFCBook.Chapter9;

import com.sun.java.swing.*;
import com.sun.java.swing.text.*;
import java.awt.*;
import java.awt.event.*;

public class MouseHighlightExample {
  public static void main(String[] args) {
    JFrame f = new JFrame("Mouse Highlight Example");
    JTextArea textArea = new JTextArea(10, 30);
    JScrollPane pane = new JScrollPane(textArea);
    f.getContentPane().add(pane);
    f.pack();
    f.addWindowListener(new WindowAdapter() {
      public void windowClosing(WindowEvent evt) {
        System.exit(0);
```

continued

```
      }
   });

   textArea.setText("Houston, Tranquility Base here.\nThe Eagle has landed.\n\n" +
            "Roger Tranquility, we copy you on the ground.\n" +
            "You got a bunch of guys about to turn blue.\n" +
            "We're breathing again. Thanks a lot\n");

   f.setVisible(true);

   // Register a mouse highlighter on the text area
   textArea.addMouseMotionListener(new MouseHighlighter(textArea));
}

// A simple highlighter that follows the mouse
protected static class MouseHighlighter extends MouseMotionAdapter {
   protected MouseHighlighter(JTextArea textArea) {
      p = new DefaultHighlighter.DefaultHighlightPainter(Color.green);
      h = textArea.getHighlighter();
      this.textArea = textArea;
   }

   // Mouse motion methods
   public void mouseMoved(MouseEvent evt) {
      int offset = textArea.viewToModel(evt.getPoint());
      if (lastHighlight != null) {
         h.removeHighlight(lastHighlight);
      }

      try {
         lastHighlight = h.addHighlight(offset, offset + 1, p);
      } catch (BadLocationException e) {
         lastHighlight = null;
      }
   }

   DefaultHighlighter.DefaultHighlightPainter p;
   Highlighter h;
   JTextArea textArea;
   Object lastHighlight;
}
}
```

The code is pretty straightforward. A custom highlighter is an implementation of the `Highlighter.HighlightPainter` interface. The `DefaultHighlighter` class provides an inner class called `DefaultHighlighter.DefaultHighlightPainter` that implements this interface and paints a highlight in the form of a rectangle filled with a solid color that is given to its constructor. In this example, the highlighter used is green, so that it can be distinguished from the one used to show selections.

To implement a highlighter that follows the mouse, you need to register a mouse listener on the text component, then use the JTextComponent viewToModel method to get the offset in the document that corresponds to the location of the mouse. In Listing 9-7, the mouse listener is implemented as an inner class that creates its own highlight painter and saves a reference to the JTextArea that it will be associated with, then registers itself as a listener on that component. When the mouse is over the component, mouse events are received. The mouse location, extracted from the mouse motion event using getPoint, is translated to a position within the document and then used to set the highlight position by using the Document addHighlight method, which supplies the start and end offset of the area covered by the highlight and the painter to be used. Each time the highlight is moved, care is taken to remove the last instance of it.

If the mouse moves outside the bounds of the text in the document, which it does, for example, as it leaves the text area window, the viewToModel method returns a location that is not valid and the addHighlight method throws a BadLocationException. When this happens, the last highlight location, stored for the purpose of clearing the previous highlight, is clear because it is guaranteed at this point that there is no highlight on the screen.

Keyboard Handling and Keymaps

JTextComponent receives all key events for a text component. There are two things that can happen when a keystroke is received—either it is treated as a special action, or it is considered to be part of the document content. Keystrokes that are not recognized by the keymap are assumed to be characters for insertion into the document, by passing them to the replaceSelection method. If there is an active selection, it is first removed and then the new character is inserted into the document. If there is no selection, the character is inserted at the location of the caret. As you'll see, though, this behavior can be overridden if necessary.

Core Note

Actually, characters that are typed into a JTextComponent *do not get processed as described here straight away. Instead, they are first offered to the focus manager, then to any* KeyListeners *registered on the component. If the key event is not consumed by this time, it is then passed to the* JTextComponent *logic that is described in this section. If* JTextComponent *does not consume the key event, it would then be checked to see if it represented a keyboard accelerator, as described in Chapter 5, "Keyboard Handling, Actions and Scrolling."*

Editor Actions and the Default Keymap

To determine whether a key represents an action, it is looked up in the text component's keymap, which is managed by `JTextComponent`. A keymap maps `KeyStrokes` to `Actions`. For any given text component, there is a set of actions that its editor can perform and a set of keys that map to those actions. However, these two are not tightly coupled to each other at compile time; instead, they are connected when the text component is created.

The set of operations that an editor can perform is fixed and determined by the editor itself. The Swing text package provides an interface called `EditorKit` that allows an editor implementation to specify the set of actions that it provides. There is also an editor implementation called `DefaultEditorKit` that provides a large selection of actions that are applicable to all of the text components and that is used as the basis of every control created by subclassing `JTextComponent`. The set of actions that an editor provides can be determined by calling its `getActions` method, which returns an array of objects that implement the `Action` interface. In the case of `DefaultEditorKit`, these objects are all instances of `TextAction`, which provides some methods that make it possible to write editor actions in such a way that they are independent of the component on which they operate, as you'll see below.

By contrast, the mapping of keystrokes to actions depends on the look-and-feel in use, so it is not built into the editors. Instead, each text component's look-and-feel implementation provides a set of bindings that map keystrokes (specified as `KeyStroke` objects) to the action names declared by the editor. `JTextComponent` takes the bindings for a particular component and the actions from its editor and maps the keystrokes from one to the actions in the other, using the action name to connect them, thus creating a keymap.

In practice, the set of actions available in a given text component comes from more than one source. `JTextComponent` gets the list of actions that it has available to it by calling its editor's `getActions` method.

Core Note

Remember that the editor is the text component itself—`JTextArea,` `JTextPane,` *etc.*

The editor will typically have a set of actions of its own and will add to those a set supplied by its superclass. For example, `JTextField` has an action called `noti-fy-field-accept` that, in the default look-and-feel, should be invoked when the user presses the RETURN key. `JTextField` creates a `TextAction` whose name is `notify-field-accept` and then calls the `getActions` method of `JTextComponent` to get its list of supported actions, which returns the action list supplied by `DefaultEditorKit`. These two sets of actions are merged into one by the `TextAction` method `augmentList` and returned as the complete set of actions for the editor. Since the actions for an editor are contained in classes such as

`DefaultEditorKit`, `JTextField` and `JTextComponent`, they are platform-independent and so do not depend on the look-and-feel installed.

The key mappings that connect keystrokes to the actions are, as we have said, dependent on the look-and-feel in use, but some of them are likely to be the same in most implementations. The most common key mappings are actually supplied by `JTextComponent` itself. As noted in the previous paragraph, `JTextComponent` gets a list of all of the actions that its associated editor can support by calling its editor's `getActions` method. It then creates a keymap that connects a default set of keys to these actions. The key mappings that this establishes constitute the *default keymap* for the component. The exact content of this map depends on the editor in use; its maximum content is shown in Table 9-2. The maximum keymap will be active if the editor supplies all of the actions in the `Action` column.

Table 9-2   The Default Keymap

Key	*Action*
BACKSPACE	delete-previous
DELETE	delete-next
HOME	caret-begin
END	caret-end
RIGHT	caret-forward
LEFT	caret-backward
UP	caret-up
DOWN	caret-down

Editor Keymaps

Keymaps, like styles, are hierarchical. The default keymap is at the top of the hierarchy and provides fallback mappings that can be overridden. After the default keymap has been created, the text component's look-and-feel class will usually add mappings of its own. Here's a typical sequence of code that might be found in a look-and-feel class.

```
Keymap parent = JTextComponent.getKeymap(JTextComponent.DEFAULT_KEYMAP);
Keymap myKeymap = JTextComponent.addKeymap("New Keymap", parent);
JTextComponent.loadKeymap(myKeymap, bindings, editor.getActions());
setKeymap(myKeymap);
```

First, the default key mapping created earlier by `JTextComponent` is obtained and then a new keymap (`myKeymap` in this example), initially empty, is added with the default keymap as its parent. The `addKeymap` method is analogous to the `addStyle` method that you saw earlier in this chapter—it creates a new keymap with the keymap passed in its second argument as its parent, and associates the new keymap with the name given by the first argument. This new keymap is empty. Its content is created by the `loadKeymap` method of `JTextComponent`, which requires three arguments—the keymap to be loaded, a list of key bindings and a set of actions. The set of actions is, again, usually obtained from the editor by calling its `getActions` method. This method will, of course, return the same set of actions that were obtained by `JTextComponent` when it established the default keymap but there are usually many more actions available than those listed in Table 9-2. These extra actions are not yet accessible because, in creating the default keymap, `JTextComponent` only mapped a limited set of keys to the editor's actions. Usually, the look-and-feel class will supply a much larger range of keys (in the `bindings` argument) than `JTextComponent`, so the new keymap will be larger then the default one. The set of keys and the actions to which they should be mapped are passed by the look-and-feel class as the second argument of `loadKeymap`.

The content of the keymap is created by matching action names from the list of bindings to the names associated with the actions in the action list. As you know, an `Action` can have several text strings associated with it but, by convention, the name of the `Action` is stored under a key given by the constant value `Action.NAME`. Each action name in the list of bindings passed to `loadKeymap` is compared to the names of the `Actions` in the action list. If a match is found, an entry is made in the keymap that connects the `KeyStroke` in the binding to the `Action`. It follows that no keymap entry will be made for an action that an editor offers unless there is a key binding entry in the `bindings` argument for it and, conversely, a key-to-action binding will be ignored if the editor in use does not support the action.

`JTextComponent` provides a convenient static inner class that is used to specify bindings to the `loadKeymap` method. Here is its definition:

```
public static class KeyBinding {
  public KeyBinding(KeyStroke key, String actionName);
  public KeyStroke key;
  public String actionName;
}
```

A text component creates a set of bindings by compiling in (or maybe generating at run time) an array of `KeyBinding` objects. Editors that provide actions usually export the action names as public variables that can be used when creating the bindings. Here's a typical declaration that binds keystrokes to actions provided by `DefaultEditorKit`:

```
static final KeyBinding[] bindings = {
  new KeyBinding(KeyStroke.getKeyStroke(KeyEvent.VK_G, KeyEvent.CTRL_MASK),
          DefaultEditorKit.beepAction),
  new KeyBinding(KeyStroke.getKeyStroke(KeyEvent.VK_R, KeyEvent.ALT_MASK),
          DefaultEditorKit.readOnlyAction),
  new KeyBinding(KeyStroke.getKeyStroke(KeyEvent.VK_W, KeyEvent.ALT_MASK),
          DefaultEditorKit.writableAction)
};
```

If these bindings were used with the `loadKeymap` call in the code extract shown above, then, in addition to the default mappings, the key sequence CTRL+G would cause a beep, ALT+R would switch the editor into read-only mode and ALT+W would switch it back to read-write mode, assuming that the editor supports these operations—which is to say that these actions appear in the set returned by the editor's `getActions` method.. These key mappings would be effective with any editor using `DefaultEditorKit`, which includes all of the standard text components. For reference, the complete set of actions provided by `DefaultEditorKit` is shown in Table 9-3.

| Table 9-3   Actions implemented by DefaultEditorKit |

Name	*Action*
`caret-backward`	Moves the caret backward one character
`beep`	Causes a 'beep'
`caret-begin`	Moves the caret to the start of the document
`caret-begin-line`	Moves the caret to the start of the current line
`caret-begin-paragraph`	Moves the caret to the start of the current paragraph
`caret-begin-word`	Moves the caret to the start of the current word
`caret-down`	Moves the caret down a line
`caret-end`	Moves the caret to the end of the document
`caret-end-line`	Moves the caret to the end of the current line
`caret-end-paragraph`	Moves the caret to the end of the current paragraph
`caret-end-word`	Moves the caret to the end of the current word
`caret-forward`	Moves the caret forward one character
`caret-next-word`	Moves the caret to the start of the next word
`caret-previous-word`	Moves the caret to the start of the previous word
`caret-up`	Moves the caret up by one line
`copy-to-clipboard`	Copies the currently selected text onto the system clipboard
`cut-to-clipboard`	Deletes the text that is currently selected and places it on the system clipboard
`default-typed`	Inserts the last key typed in the document model
`delete-next`	Deletes the character that immediately follows the caret.
`delete-previous`	Deletes the character immediately before the caret
`insert-break`	Inserts a newline into the document
`insert-content`	Places the keystroke that caused this action into the document
`insert-tab`	Inserts a tab in the document

continued

Table 9-3   Actions implemented by DefaultEditorKit (continued)

Name	Action
page-down	Moves the caret down one page
page-up	Moves the caret up one page
paste-from-clipboard	Pastes the content of the system clipboard into the document immediately before the current caret position, deleting anything currently selected
select-all	Selects the entire document
select-line	Makes the current line into the selection
select-paragraph	Makes the current paragraph into the selection
select-word	Makes the current word into the selection
selection-backward	Moves the caret backwards one position, extending the current selection
selection-begin	Extends the selection to the start of the document
selection-begin-line	Extends the selection to the start of the current line
selection-begin-paragraph	Extends the selection to the start of the current paragraph
selection-begin-word	Extends the selection to the start of the current work
selection-down	Moves the caret down one line and moves the selection with it
selection-end	Extends the selection to the end of the document
selection-end-line	Extends the selection to the end of the current line
selection-end-paragraph	Extends the selection to the end of the current paragraph
selection-end-word	Extends the selection to the end of the current word
selection-forward	Moves the caret forward one position, extending the current selection
selection-next-word	Extends the selection to the start of the next word
selection-previous-word	Extends the selection to the start of the previous word
selection-up	Moves the caret up one line and moves the selection with it
set-read-only	Makes the editor read-only
set-writable	Switches the editor into read-write mode

The last step is to connect the keymap to the text component using `setKeymap`, which is actually implemented by `JTextComponent`. This method causes the new keymap to replace the default keymap as the component's active map.

The final keymap for a text component is, therefore, the result of combining the keymap created by its look-and-feel class with the default keymap created by the `JTextComponent`. It is possible for a look-and-feel class to override entries in the default keymap, but this doesn't usually happen.

When a key event is received from the keyboard, JTextComponent converts it to a KeyStroke object using the KeyStroke getKeyStrokeForEvent method that you saw in Chapter 5 and then uses this to search the component's keymap using the getAction method of the Keymap interface. Keymap is an interface for which JTextComponent provides an implementation in the form of an inner class called DefaultKeymap. DefaultKeymap is actually the class that handles all keymap-related operations for JTextComponent. The default key mapping is held in a DefaultKeymap and the object that is returned to the look-and-feel class when it calls addKeymap is also a newly created DefaultKeymap.

DefaultKeymap holds the mapping between keystrokes and actions in a Hashtable, so the process of looking for an action corresponding to a given keystroke just involves presenting the KeyStroke object to the Hashtable. If this finds a match, the corresponding Action is returned. If it doesn't and the DefaultKeymap has a parent, the search is delegated to the parent. As a result, keystrokes that are defined in the default keymap and are not overridden by the look-and-feel class can be found and returned as if they were in the text component's own keymap.

Handling Unmapped Keys

If a keystroke has no corresponding entry in the keymap, JTextComponent uses the keymap's *default action* instead. When the default keymap for a text component is created, this action is initialized to the DefaultKeyTypedAction supplied by DefaultEditorKit, which inserts the key just received into the document as content.

You can set the default action for a Keymap using its setDefaultAction method and retrieve it using getDefaultAction:

```
public void setDefaultAction(Action a);
public Action getDefaultAction();
```

As you know, most keymaps are a hierarchy of at least two levels—the mapping established by a particular text component, which take precedence over the default mappings set up by JTextComponent itself. The keymap reference stored by the JTextComponent and returned by getKeymap refers to the component's own keymap, which has the JTextComponent keymap as its parent. When JTextComponent calls getDefaultAction on the component's keymap, it will normally be returned the DefaultKeyTypedAction installed by JTextComponent in the initial keymap, because the action associated with a keymap by default (and therefore the action associated with the keymap installed by the text component itself) is null and getDefaultAction searches up the keymap hierarchy until is finds a non-null default action. You can, however, use setDefaultAction to install your own action on the component's keymap and override the default action of placing unmapped keys into the document as content. One possible use of this mechanism would be to convert alphabetic characters to uppercase or to ignore characters that your component doesn't consider legal, such as alphabetic characters in a numeric input field.

A Keymap Example

Now let's look at the keymaps that are associated with real text components. The code in Listing 9-8 allows us to demonstrate how simple it is to modify the keymap of an existing component and also allows us to look at the keymap that comes with each of the text components in the Swing package.

Listing 9-8   Manipulating keymaps

```
package JFCBook.Chapter9;

import com.sun.java.swing.*;
import com.sun.java.swing.text.*;
import java.awt.*;
import java.awt.event.*;

public class SetKeymap extends JTextArea {
  public SetKeymap(int rows, int cols) {
    super(rows, cols);

    // Set the new keymap
    Keymap parent = JTextComponent.getKeymap(JTextComponent.DEFAULT_KEYMAP);
    Keymap myKeymap = JTextComponent.addKeymap("New Keymap", parent);
    JTextComponent.loadKeymap(myKeymap, bindings, this.getActions());
    setKeymap(myKeymap);
  }

  public static void main(String[] args) {
    JTextComponent t;

    JFrame f = new JFrame("Modified keymap");
    f.getContentPane().add(new JScrollPane(t = new SetKeymap(15, 40)));
    f.pack();
    f.addWindowListener(new WindowAdapter() {
      public void windowClosing(WindowEvent evt) {
        System.exit(0);
      }
    });
    f.setVisible(true);

    // If an argument was given, try to create an object and get its keymap
    if (args.length == 1) {
      try {
        Class cl = Class.forName(args[0]);
        Object o = cl.newInstance();
        if (o instanceof JTextComponent) {
          t = (JTextComponent)o;
        } else {
```

```
          System.out.println("Class " + args[0] + " is not a JTextComponent");
          t = null;
        }
      } catch (Throwable e) {
        System.out.println("Failed to create an instance of " + args[0]);
        t = null;
      }
    }

    if (t != null) {
      // Get the keymap and print it, including its parent
      Keymap map = t.getKeymap();
      printKeymap(map, 0);
    }
  }

  // Static method to print a keymap, with recursion
  protected static void printKeymap(Keymap m, int indent) {
    KeyStroke[] k = m.getBoundKeyStrokes();

    for (int i = 0; i < k.length; i++) {
      for (int j = 0 ; j < indent ; j++) {
        System.out.print(" ");
      }
      System.out.print("Keystroke <" +
          KeyEvent.getKeyModifiersText(k[i].getModifiers())
          + " " + k[i].getKeyCode() + "> ");
      Action a = m.getAction(k[i]);
      System.out.println((String)a.getValue(Action.NAME));
    }

    // If this keymap has a parent, print that as well
    m = m.getResolveParent();
    if (m != null) {
      printKeymap(m, indent + 2);
    }
  }

  // New key bindings
  static final JTextComponent.KeyBinding[] bindings = {
    new JTextComponent.KeyBinding(KeyStroke.getKeyStroke(KeyEvent.VK_G,
                KeyEvent.CTRL_MASK),
              DefaultEditorKit.beepAction),
    new JTextComponent.KeyBinding(KeyStroke.getKeyStroke(KeyEvent.VK_R,
                KeyEvent.ALT_MASK), DefaultEditorKit.readOnlyAction),
    new JTextComponent.KeyBinding(KeyStroke.getKeyStroke(KeyEvent.VK_W,
                KeyEvent.ALT_MASK), DefaultEditorKit.writableAction)
  };
}
```

The code in the SetKeymap constructor is almost identical to an extract that was shown earlier and, in conjunction with the static data shown at the end of the listing, replaces any key mappings that JTextArea added over and above the default mappings and replaces them with mappings for the CTRL+G, ALT+R and ALT+W key sequences. Strictly speaking, though, when adding keys to a component's keymap from outside its UI class, you should use the component's getKeymap method to get the current keymap rather than manipulating the default keymap, because other mappings may have been added since the default keymap was created. The code above would lose those mappings if it were not in a class derived directly from JTextArea. You'll see an example of the alternative method in Listing 9-14. When you run this example using the command:

```
java JFCBook.Chapter9.SetKeymap
```

you'll see a frame with a text area. Start typing in the text area, then press CTRL+G and you'll hear a short beep. Press ALT+R and try to type some more—you'll find that you can't, because the control is now read-only. The only way to reverse this is to type ALT+W which makes it writable again. You can use code like this to add entries to the keymap of any text component and, because keymaps are hierarchical, you can redefine existing behavior by adding a keymap entry that matches a keystroke defined by the control itself to do something else.

This program also does something else. In the window from which you launched this program, you'll see the complete keymap for the text area including our modification to it. Here is what you should see:

```
Keystroke <Alt 82> set-read-only
Keystroke <Alt 87> set-writable
Keystroke <Ctrl 71> beep
   Keystroke < 40> caret-down
   Keystroke < 39> caret-forward
   Keystroke < 38> caret-up
   Keystroke < 37> caret-backward
   Keystroke < 36> caret-begin
   Keystroke < 35> caret-end
   Keystroke < 127> delete-next
   Keystroke < 8> delete-previous
```

The first three entries are the ones that were added in Listing 9-8; the remainder belong to the text area itself. The number in the angled brackets is the keycode for the key that triggers the action. The keymap stores KeyStroke objects, which can be created using either keycodes or Unicode characters. If you create the KeyStroke with a keycode, the character field is not initialized and stays zero. Similarly, creating a KeyStroke with a Unicode character leaves the keycode field zero. Most of the keymap is created using keycodes, which is why you see numeric codes (and not Unicode characters) in the list above.

The code that prints the keymap takes an instance of a text component and calls `getKeymap` to obtain its keymap; this method is declared by `JTextComponent`, so it works for `JTextArea` and all the other text controls. From a `Keymap`, it is possible to get all of the registered keystrokes using the `getBoundKeystrokes` method, which returns an array of `KeyStroke` objects. To find the `Action` to which a keystroke is bound, the `Keymap getAction` method is used, passing it a `KeyStroke`.

By default, this program shows the keymap for our modified `JTextArea`, but you can supply on the command line the name of any class derived from `JTextComponent` and see its keymap. For example, if you use the following command line:

```
java JFCBook.Chapter9.SetKeymap com.sun.java.swing.JTextArea
```

you'll get the real keymap for `JTextArea`:

Keystroke < 34> page-down	Keystroke < 33> page-up
Keystroke <Shift 39> selection-forward	Keystroke <Shift 37> selection-backward
Keystroke <Ctrl 39> caret-end	Keystroke <Ctrl 88> cut-to-clipboard
Keystroke <Ctrl 37> caret-begin	Keystroke < 10> insert-break
Keystroke < 9> insert-tab	Keystroke <Ctrl 86> paste-from-clipboard
Keystroke <Ctrl 67> copy-to-clipboard	Keystroke < 40> caret-down
Keystroke < 39> caret-forward	Keystroke < 38> caret-up
Keystroke < 37> caret-backward	Keystroke < 36> caret-begin
Keystroke < 35> caret-end	Keystroke < 127> delete-next
Keystroke < 8> delete-previous	

Here, the character actually defined to map to "insert-break" is the newline. In this context, "break" means a line break. In terms of the document model, this becomes a place where one `Element` ends and another begins.

The keymap for the `JTextField` component is very similar to that of `JTextArea`:

Keystroke <Shift 39> selection-forward	Keystroke <Shift 37> selection-backward
Keystroke <Ctrl 39> caret-end	Keystroke <Ctrl 88> cut-to-clipboard
Keystroke <Ctrl 37> caret-begin	Keystroke < 10> notify-field-accept
Keystroke <Ctrl 86> paste-from-clipboard	Keystroke <Ctrl 67> copy-to-clipboard
Keystroke < 40> caret-down	Keystroke < 39> caret-forward
Keystroke < 38> caret-up	Keystroke < 37> caret-backward
Keystroke < 36> caret-begin	Keystroke < 35> caret-end
Keystroke < 127> delete-next	Keystroke < 8> delete-previous

Here, the `insert-break` action has gone and the key that was mapped to it in the `JTextArea` is now mapped to the `notify-field-accept` action. This key is actually `RETURN` and the `notify-field-accept` action maps to a `TextAction` that generates the `ActionEvent` that `JTextField` provides when the user has finished entering text. The way in which this behavior is triggered, then, is not wired into `JTextField`; in fact, its look-and-feel class installs it.

Views

The last piece of the MVC architecture for text components is the view. The view is, of course, the piece that renders the control's content onto the screen and it is the part with which you seem to interact the most. In fact, though, the view is almost entirely passive and is driven entirely by the model and the controller.

Just as the model has many constituent parts, so does the view. There isn't actually one class that you can point to and identify as being 'the view'; instead, there are several classes that are used to render different types of content. All that these classes have in common is that they are derived from the abstract class `View`. `View` has the following subclasses, which can draw particular types of content:

- `BoxView`: Renders the elements for which it is responsible in a vertical or horizontal line. It is used to arrange paragraphs in a line from the top to the bottom of a document that can provide multiple paragraphs, such as `JTextPane`.

- `CompositeView`: `CompositeView` is an abstract class that provides the ability to host other views, rather like an AWT `Container`. It is the base class for `BoxView`.

- `ComponentView`: Draws a `Component` inline with the document. Components in documents are supported by `JTextPane` and `JEditorPane`.

- `FieldView`: A view suitable for rendering a single-line text editor such as `JTextField`. This view has little work to do because it is representing a very simple text component. Its only substantial job is to align the text properly within the area assigned to it. If that area is too tall or too short, the text is vertically centered within the area available (i.e., the characters themselves do not grow to fit the height of the component). The horizontal alignment is controlled by the alignment attribute of the `JTextField`.

- `IconView`: Renders an `Icon`. This is another feature of `JTextPane`.

- `LabelView`: `LabelView`'s job is to draw a run of text from within a paragraph. The text run has a single set of attributes. This view is used only by styled documents: `JTextArea` uses the simpler `PlainView`.

- `ParagraphView:` Represents a paragraph as a vertical arrangement of lines. The content of the paragraph may have varied fonts and colors and need not be restricted to text. `ParagraphView` may need other views (such as `LabelView`, `IconView` etc.) to draw its constituent parts.

- `PasswordView:` Represents a control like `JPasswordField` by drawing each character in the model using the echo character. Distinguishes selected and unselected text using the appropriate colors.

- `PlainView:` A simple view used to render all of a document type such as `JTextArea` in which a single font and a single color are in use. This view assumes that all lines are of equal height, determined by the font in use by the component in which it is hosted.

- `WrappedPlainView:` The same as `PlainView`, but does word wrapping.

So far, this chapter has only looked at the relatively simple `JTextField` and `JTextArea` controls, which don't need complicated view support. `JTextField` uses `FieldView`, while `JTextArea` uses `PlainView` when word wrapping is turned off and `WrappedPlainView` when it is on. These views render every element of the model identically. Remember that these components consist of a single paragraph element with one or more (at least in the case of `JTextArea`) content elements and no associated attributes. The `PlainView` simply maps each element to a single line of the screen. It doesn't perform word wrapping, but just places line breaks where they were typed by the user, relying on the program to provide scrollbars if the text is too wide to fit in the display space.

You saw earlier that when you type text into a text control, it is processed by the `JTextComponent`, which delivers any keystrokes that are not mapped to actions to the default action of the component's keymap, which actually passes them to the `replaceSelection` method of `JTextComponent` for inclusion in the document model. None of this will yet have been reflected on the screen, because the text controller does not have direct access to the display and has no idea how particular keystrokes should affect what is being shown to the user. Changing the document contents, however, causes a `DocumentEvent` to be generated by the `Document` implementation, as you've already seen.

`DocumentEvents` contain information about the changes that have been made to the model. The various view components are notified when these events are generated and each view is passed only the events that relate to a part of the model that it is responsible for rendering the view of. A view always maps a single element to the screen. Therefore, because document events are always framed in terms of a set of changed elements, it is a relatively simple matter to discover which views are affected by any given document event. As a result, it is often possible to effect a change to the display very efficiently, since only the views responsible for areas of the screen that are affected by the user's actions receive the DocumentEvents and redraw their contents.

Getting Multiple Views of a Document

You've seen that the content of a text component is held in the document model and that the model notifies the view components when any changes are made to it, in response to which the text control updates its appearance. Each text component has an associated Document, but a single Document can be shared between different text components. Arranging to share one set of content between two components is simple:

```
JTextArea firstTextArea = new JTextArea(10, 20);
JTextArea secondTextArea = new JTextArea(10, 20);
secondTextArea.setDocument(firstTextArea.getDocument());
```

Here, the document that is part of the first text area is connected directly to the second, replacing the model created for it during execution of its constructor. The document isn't aware that it is connected to more than one component—in fact, it doesn't have a direct reference to its text component. Various pieces of the text component, including the views, are connected (directly or indirectly) as DocumentListeners to the document. In the example above, changes in the document will cause the model to send the same DocumentEvent to the views of both components, so they will both perform the same screen updates and, as a result, their contents will remain the same.

This feature is useful if you want to implement an application that allows multiple views of the same file. If, for example, your application allows the user to look at or edit a large file, it can be very inconvenient if the user has to page up and down the file to look at pieces of it that are logically related but not located close together. In many cases, the only way to work effectively is to see more than one piece of a file at the same time. Creating two text areas that share the same model solves this problem—just place the two text areas next to each other and give each of them scrollbars and you can have two independently controllable, but related, views of the same file. Furthermore, if you're editing the file, the text areas automatically stay in step if they share the same Document, which would not be the case if the file were opened separately in each text area.

Core Note

Assuming that this application operates by opening the file and reading it into memory, the text areas remain consistent with each other because they are being updated from the same in-memory copy of the file's contents. Changes to the file itself would then not affect either view, whether or not they share the same model, because the text area is no longer looking at the content of the file. A more sophisticated application might read only a part of the file into memory at any given time, based on the region of the file currently being operated on. This would, however, make it more difficult to view two different pieces of the same file and would require a more sophisticated model than that provided by StringContent, *to allow data to be loaded from the file only when it is needed.*

The JSplitPane Control

The Swing set provides a useful container, JSplitPane, that manages two controls either side by side or one above the other, with a divider between them. If you place the two text areas in a JSplitPane, you can drag the divider to change the space allocated to each of them as necessary. The code shown in Listing 9-9 places two empty text areas that share the same document one above the other on a frame. When the program starts, the text areas are both empty. If you start typing into one of them, the same text will appear simultaneously in the other one. Similarly, you can delete or cut text from one control and the same operation will be performed on its partner. Figure 9-9 shows what this arrangement looks like.

Listing 9-9   Two views of a JTextArea

```
package JFCBook.Chapter9;

import com.sun.java.swing.*;
import com.sun.java.swing.text.*;
import java.awt.*;
import java.awt.event.*;
import java.io.*;
import java.net.*;
```

continued

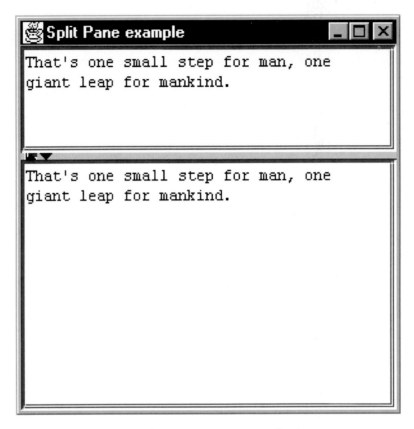

Figure 9-9   Using a JSplitPane to get two views of a document.

```
public class SplitPaneExample extends JSplitPane {
  public SplitPaneExample() {
    super(JSplitPane.VERTICAL_SPLIT, true);
    this.setOneTouchExpandable(true);

    JTextArea topPane = new JTextArea(5, 40);
    JTextArea bottomPane = new JTextArea(5, 40);
    bottomPane.setDocument(topPane.getDocument());
    this.setTopComponent(new JScrollPane(topPane));
    this.setBottomComponent(new JScrollPane(bottomPane));

  }

  public static void main(String[] args) {
    JFrame f = new JFrame("Split Pane example");

    SplitPaneExample p = new SplitPaneExample();
    f.getContentPane().add(p);
```

```
    f.setSize(300, 300);
    f.setVisible(true);
    f.addWindowListener(new WindowAdapter() {
      public void windowClosing(WindowEvent evt) {
        System.exit(0);
      }
    });
  }
}
```

Dragging the divider allows you to change the space allocated to each of the text components. In this example, as you drag the divider, the two components are continuously adjusted. It is also possible to configure the `JSplitPane` so that the divider moves separately when it is dragged, leaving the text components unchanged until you stop dragging. The choice between these two options can be made either when the pane is created, or later using the `setContinousLayout` method.

Creating a JSplitPane

Here is the full set of `JSplitPane` constructors:

- `public JSplitPane()`. Creates a pane with two buttons arranged to the left and right of a divider that is not continuously adjusting. This constructor is not useful in real applications, because you need to remove the two buttons before adding your own components.

- `public JSplitPane(int orientation)`. Creates a pane with the divider horizontal or vertical depending on the *orientation* argument, which must be one of `JSplitPane.VERTICAL_SPLIT` or `JSplitPane.HORIZONTAL_SPLIT`. The divider does not continuously adjust and there are no components added.

- `public JSplitPane(int orientation, boolean cont)`. Creates a pane with the specified orientation. The second argument determines whether the divider is continuously adjusting (if `true`) or not.

- `public JSplitPane(int orientation, boolean cont, Component first, Component second)`. Creates a pane with the specified orientation and continuous or noncontinuous layout with the supplied components installed on either side of the divider.

- `public JSplitPane(int orientation, Component first, Component second)`. Creates a pane with the specified orientation and with the supplied components installed on either side of the divider. The divider does not lay out continuously.

When the pane has a horizontal layout, the components given to the last two constructors are placed to the left and right side of the divider in that order. In the case of a vertical layout, the first component is placed above the divider and the second below it. Keep in mind that the orientation specifies the axis along which the two components are laid out, so that the orientation VERTICAL_SPLIT places the components above and below a horizontal divider.

Adding and Removing the Components

The components need not be placed when the pane is created. There are four methods that can be used to add the two children that this container can manage:

```
public void setBottomComponent(Component);

public void setLeftComponent(Component);

public void setRightComponent(Component);

public void setTopComponent(Component);
```

These methods both place the component in the appropriate location and add them to the container: You use them instead of directly adding components to the container using the add method. If the layout is horizontal, you should use the setLeftComponent and setRightComponent methods, but you can also achieve the same effect, if you wish, with setTopComponent and setBottomComponent, respectively. Although this may seem an obscure thing to do, it can save a few lines of code if the actual orientation is not known until run time. It is also possible to change the orientation at any time by using the setOrientation method, which takes immediate effect.

You can replace either or both of the child components by invoking the appropriate setXXXComponent again. Thus, for example, you could remove the top component before replacing it:

```
// Case 1: use remove method
JButton one = new JButton("One");
JSplitPane p = new JSplitPane(JSplitPane.VERTICAL_SPLIT);
p.setTopComponent(one);
p.setBottomComponent(new JButton("Two"));

// Remove and replace the top component
p.remove(one);
p.setTopComponent(new JButton("Three"));
```

or, you could just replace it directly:

```
// Case 2: no remove
JSplitPane p = new JSplitPane(JSplitPane.VERTICAL_SPLIT);
p.setTopComponent(new JButton("One"));
p.setBottomComponent(new JButton("Two"));

// Replace top component directly
p.setTopComponent(new JButton("Three"));
```

Another way to remove a component is to pass `null` to one of the `set` methods—for example `setTopComponent(null)` removes the top component. If you intend to replace both components, be careful not to remove them using the `Container removeAll` method because the divider is also a child of the `JSplitPane` and would be removed by `removeAll`, rendering the pane useless.

Controlling the Divider

There are a number of ways to control or find out about the location of the divider. The following three methods set or return the divider's current location:

```
public int getDividerLocation();

public void setDividerLocation(int pos);

public void setDividerLocation(double location);
```

The position used by the first two of these methods depends on the orientation of the `JSplitPane`. In the case of a horizontal pane with a vertical divider, the position is the x-coordinate of the left side of the divider while, for a vertical pane it is the y-component of its upper side. Attempting to set a negative position moves the divider to the far left or to the top of the pane, while using a position that is larger than the size of the pane's interior moves the divider to the far right or the bottom.

The last method uses a multiplier that must be between 0.0 and 1.0. The supplied value is multiplied by the current width or height of the split pane (less the size of the divider) to obtain an absolute position value that is then used as if the first `setDividerLocation` method had been called. This form is useful for placing the divider _ of the way across the pane, for example, using code like this:

```
pane.setDividerLocation((double)0.25);
```

You can use the two methods `getMinimumDividerLocation` and `getMaximumDividerLocation` to find the leftmost and rightmost allowed positions of a horizontal divider or the highest and lowest for a vertical divider. These bounds apply only when the divider is being dragged by the user—they are ignored by `setDividerLocation`. The `JSplitPane` tries to choose the bounds in such a way that the divider can't be used to resize either of the components so that they are smaller than their minimum sizes or larger than their maximum sizes as returned by the JComponent getMinimumSize and getMaximumSize methods. Of course, it may not be possible to ensure this if the container is too small to allocate the minimum sizes of each component, or too large to respect the maximum sizes but it is never possible to shrink a component below its minimum size by dragging the divider. There is no way to control these bounds other than by arranging for the child components to return appropriate maximum and minimum sizes, because there are no JSplitPane methods to set the minimum or maximum locations. The resetToPreferredSize method can be used at any time to reposition the divider so that both children are at their preferred sizes, if this is possible.

The getDividerSize and setDividerSize methods get and set the size of the divider. If the divider is horizontal, these methods apply to its vertical size; the divider always reaches from one side of the container to the other, so its dimension in this direction cannot be changed. If the divider is not configured to perform continuous layout, the 'ghost' divider that follows the mouse as you drag it to a new location also takes up the size set by setDividerSize.

Each time the divider moves, it stores its previous position. You can retrieve this value using the getLastDividerLocation method or set a different value with setLastDividerLocation:

```
public int getLastDividerLocation();

public void setLastDividerLocation(int pos);
```

The last divider location is important if you make the divider *one-touch expandable* using the setOneTouchExpandable method. When you do this, two small black arrows appear on the divider, pointing in its two possible directions of motion, as you can see in Figure 9-9. To see how these arrows are used, start the example shown in Listing 9-9 and move the divider to a position near the middle of the pane, then click on the arrow pointing up. This causes the divider to move right to the top, expanding the lower component to its full size in one touch (hence the name). Now press the down arrow. Instead of moving all the way to the bottom, the divider now jumps back to its last location in the middle of the pane. Clicking on the down arrow will now move the divider right to the bottom, expanding the top component completely.

The down arrow, then, moves the divider from the top, through the intermediate "last" location and then to the bottom and the up arrow reverses the order of traversal. If you interrupt the sequence and drag the divider to a new location then press one of the arrows again, the divider's position at the end of the drag becomes its new intermediate position. You can, of course, use setLastDividerLocation to change this position programmatically.

Monitoring Divider Location

There is no direct way to receive an event when the divider is moved, because the JSplitPane doesn't provide a method to get a reference to the divider itself. If this were possible, you could register a ComponentListener to be notified of

COMPONENT_MOVED events for the divider. Instead, you can detect movement of the divider by registering a ComponentListener on either of the child components; when the divider moves, both components will resize and a COMPONENT_RESIZED event will be delivered to your listener. This is not, however, a perfect solution because resizing a JSplitPane will also result in a COMPONENT_RESIZED event, even if the divider hasn't moved. This happens, for example, if you have a pane with a vertical split and you stretch it horizontally while leaving the vertical size unchanged. If you want to take action only when the divider has actually moved, use getDividerLocation on each COMPONENT_RESIZED event and store the result. You can then determine whether the divider has moved by comparing the value returned with the value that you saved while processing the previous event. Listing 9-10 shows the code necessary to track divider movement.

Listing 9-10   Monitoring movement of the JSplitPane divider

```
package JFCBook.Chapter9;

import com.sun.java.swing.*;
import java.awt.*;
import java.awt.event.*;

public class SplitPaneEventsExample {
  public static void main(String[] args) {
    JFrame f = new JFrame("Split Pane Events Example");
    JPanel leftPanel = new JPanel();
    JPanel rightPanel = new JPanel();
    final JSplitPane split = new JSplitPane(JSplitPane.HORIZONTAL_SPLIT,
                 false, leftPanel, rightPanel);
    split.setOneTouchExpandable(true);

    f.getContentPane().add(split);
    f.setSize(300, 200);
    f.addWindowListener(new WindowAdapter() {
      public void windowClosing(WindowEvent evt) {
        System.exit(0);
      }
    });

    ComponentListener l = new ComponentAdapter() {
      public void componentResized(ComponentEvent evt) {
        int location = split.getDividerLocation();
        if (location != lastLocation) {
          System.out.println("Slider moved from " + lastLocation +
              " to " + location);
          lastLocation = location;
```

continued

```
        }
    }

    protected int lastLocation = -1; // Last slider location
    };

    leftPanel.addComponentListener(l);

    f.setVisible(true);
    }
}
```

This example creates a frame onto which is mounted a `JSplitPane` with two panels to the left and right of the vertical divider. It creates an inner class that extends `ComponentAdapter` and registers that class as a `ComponentListener` on the left panel. This example takes advantage of the fact that you can use an inner class to store information by adding a field to store the previous location of the slider, which is initially set to the impossible value –1. You'll also notice that the local variable `slider` is made final so that its value can be referenced from inside the inner class.

When the frame appears on the screen, the initial position of the slider is set and the left panel is sized. This causes a `COMPONENT_RESIZED` event and the new divider location is reported. You can see this if you run this example using the command:

```
java JFCBook.Chapter9.SplitPaneEventsExample
```

If you drag the divider around, you'll see a message appear each time you let go of it in a new location. In this example, the divider does not perform continuous layout, so the event only happens when you stop dragging. In the case of a continuous layout divider, the events would be delivered in a constant stream as the divider is moved. The divider is one-touch expandable so that you can experiment with using the arrows to move the divider in each direction and see the exact x-coordinates of the positions it takes up.

Documents with Nontext Elements: JTextPane and JEditorPane

As you have seen, the Swing text components have a complex infrastructure underlying what appears to be a very simple exterior. Strictly speaking, there is far too much complexity to justify creating only the simple text field, text area and password field that you have seen so far. In fact, most of the inner workings that have been presented so far only come into play in the `JTextPane` and `JEditorPane` controls that have no counterpart in the AWT.

JTextPane is a powerful component that allows you to display text with various fonts, colors and styles and to intermix these elements with images and other components. Working with JTextPane is more complex than using JTextArea because of the need to specify attributes for each piece of the text. In this section, you'll see how to do this and how attributes can be connected to individual characters, paragraphs and to the entire document. Having seen how tedious it is to write the code that assigns these attributes, the next section introduces the JEditorPane, which displays text from HTML and RTF documents that specify attributes alongside the text in the source file.

StyledDocument and DefaultStyledDocument

JTextPane uses a document model based on an extension of AbstractDocument called StyledDocument and an implementation of this interface called DefaultStyledDocument. The methods that StyledDocument adds to those of AbstractDocument are as follows:

```
public Style addStyle(String name, Style parent);

public Style getStyle(String name);

public void removeStyle (String name);

public Color getBackground(AttributeSet attr);

public Font getFont(AttributeSet attrs);

public Color getForeground(AttributeSet attr);

public Element getCharacterElement (int pos);

public Element getParagraphElement(int pos);

public Style getLogicalStyle(int pos);

public void setLogicalStyle(int pos, Style style);

public void setCharacterAttributes(int offset, int length,
            AttributeSet attrs, boolean replace);

public void setParagraphAttributes(int offset, int length,
            AttributeSet attrs, boolean replace);
```

These methods fall into four separate groups. The first group consists of the first three methods, which manage the Styles that are used with the document. A styled document keeps its styles in a StyleContext, which was discussed earlier in this chapter. Of the three constructors of DefaultStyledDocument, two allow you to specify your own StyleContext:

```
public DefaultStyledDocument()

public DefaultStyledDocument(AbstractDocument.Content content,
            StyleContext styles);

public DefaultStyledDocument(StyleContext styles);
```

If you use the first constructor, a StyleContext with a single style called StyleContext.DEFAULT_STYLE is used. Every StyleContext has this default style when it is created, so it will also be present when you use the other two constructor and supply your own collection of styles.

The addStyle, getStyle and removeStyle methods are simply redirected directly to the document's StyleContext so you don't need to keep a separate reference to it once the document has been created.

The next three methods extract certain information from a set of attributes; they are used when rendering views of the document. The getForeground and getBackground methods return the foreground and background colors implied by the attributes in the attribute set passed as an argument, while getFont creates a Font based on the font family, font style and font size attributes (refer back to Table 9-1 for the standard attributes that can be found in an AttributeSet).

DefaultStyledDocument Attribute Structure

As you'll see when looking at the element structure of the JTextPane control, DefaultStyledDocument creates elements that manage individual characters and paragraphs. These elements are mapped differently to the leaf and branch element types than they are by PlainDocument. The getCharacterElement and getParagraphElement methods get the Element that contains a specific character at a given offset, or the entire paragraph that contains an offset.

The last four methods of the StyledDocument interface shown earlier introduce the three levels at which attributes can be held within a styled document. When a styled document is first created, it has a single empty paragraph. A paragraph may have both *paragraph attributes* and a *logical style*, while characters within a paragraph can have individual *character attributes*; character attributes can also be applied to ranges (or "runs") of characters within the paragraph. Character attributes, paragraph attributes and the logical style are arranged in order such that, to find out the value of a given attribute for a character, this attribute is first searched for in the character attributes for that character, if it has any, then in the paragraph attributes for the paragraph that it resides in, if there are any and, finally, in the paragraph's logical style.

Logical Styles and the Default Style

Logical styles are the lowest level of attribute assignment in a document. Every paragraph has a logical style that is initially the DEFAULT_STYLE from the document's StyleContext. You can set attributes that apply to the whole document simply by modifying the default style. For example, to make all of the document's text appear in a 16-point font, you would set the font size attribute of the default style to 16:

```
Style defaultStyle = doc.getStyle(StyleContext.DEFAULT_STYLE);
defaultStyle.addAttribute(StyleConstants.FontSize, new Integer(16));
```

This style is automatically applied to every paragraph in the document as it is created, so these two lines will cause all of the text to be rendered in a 16-point font. If you change the font size in the default style after the document has been created, all of the text in the document will take on the new size immediately, apart from text that has specific attributes that override the default.

While every paragraph has the same logical style when it is created, you can change the logical style for individual paragraphs using the setLogicalStyle method. When you do this, any attributes that applied to the paragraph from the default logical style are lost, unless the style you apply has the default style as its resolving parent or as a higher-level ancestor. This happens because the logical style is the last level of style in which attributes are looked for; if the paragraph has its own specific logical style, the document's logical style won't be searched for any attributes that aren't found in the paragraph. To clarify what this means, suppose that the document has a default style that specifies that all text should be rendered in italics. There are two ways that you could assign a separate logical style to an individual paragraph in this document. Suppose you want to be able to create individual paragraphs in which all of the text is green, but retain the usual formatting for the other paragraphs. One way to do this would be to create a style that has the foreground attribute set to green:

```
Style s = doc.addStyle("GreenText", null);
s.addAttribute(StyleConstants.Foreground, Color.green);
```

The style called GreenText can now be applied to any paragraph or range of characters to obtain green text. If you assign this as the logical style for the first paragraph, which currently has italic text:

```
doc.setLogicalStyle(0, s);
```

then all of the text in that paragraph will change to green, but it will also revert to plain font because the style in use only has the foreground attribute set and setting a new logical style for a paragraph replaces any earlier logical style assigned to it. Note that setLogicalStyle requires a Style and an offset. The offset is used to identify a paragraph and the style becomes the logical style for that paragraph. The offset can correspond to any character in that paragraph. Choosing zero as the offset ensures that the logical style for the first paragraph in the document is set. If you don't want to lose the italics in any paragraphs that will use green text, you could, instead, create a style that inherits whatever is in the default style for the document by changing the code as follows:

```
Style s = doc.addStyle("GreenText",
            doc.getStyle(StyleContext.DEFAULT_STYLE));
s.addAttribute(StyleConstants.Foreground, Color.green);
doc.setLogicalStyle(0, s);
```

Now, when the view renders the first paragraph and looks for the italics attribute, it will find it because it will be searched for first in the paragraph style itself and then in its resolving parent, the document default style, where it will be found. As a result, the first paragraph will be rendered with green, italic text and all of the other paragraphs will be in black italics.

Paragraph Attributes

The next level in the style hierarchy is paragraph formatting, which, like logical styles, applies to an entire paragraph. Attributes in a paragraph style take precedence over those in the paragraph's logical style or in the document's default logical style if the paragraph doesn't have a specific logical style applied to it. Paragraph styles are applied with the setParagraphAttributes method:

```
public void setParagraphAttributes(int offset, int length,
            AttributeSet attrs, boolean replace);
```

The offset and length arguments identify one or more paragraphs to which the attributes specified by attrs should be applied as paragraph attributes. Often, you'll supply an offset with a length of 1 to identify the paragraph containing a given character, but it is possible to apply the same attributes to more than one paragraph by supplying a length that covers all of the paragraphs that should be affected. A typical way in which this would happen in a word processor implementation would be to allow the user to create a selection by dragging with the mouse, then getting the start and end locations of the selection using the getDot and getMark methods of the document's Caret and using the difference between these two as the length and the offset corresponding to the mark as the starting point.

The replace argument controls what happens to any existing paragraph attributes that might be assigned to the paragraph. If this argument is true, then the new attributes completely replace those that exist. Otherwise, they are just added to the current paragraph attributes, replacing those that have the same name but leaving others unchanged. Adding paragraph attributes does not change any attributes in the paragraph's logical style, but it does mask them. What this means is the following:

- If you add paragraph attributes with replace = false, then any attributes in the paragraph's logical style that are not named in the new attribute set continue to apply to the paragraph.

- If you add paragraph attributes with `replace = true`, then all attributes applied from the paragraph's existing paragraph style are lost, but the attributes in the paragraph's style that are not overridden by the new paragraph attributes will remain.

Suppose that you want to change all of the text in a paragraph into a bold font, but you don't want to change the logical style that the paragraph is based on. Since this change is specific to this paragraph, you would apply a paragraph style to realize it. Here is what you might try:

```
Style s = doc.addStyle(null, null);
s.addAttribute(StyleConstants.Bold, new Boolean(true));
doc.setParagraphAttributes(0, 1, s, false);
```

Because this style is not going to be used again, there is no point in giving it a name and it does not have a resolving parent because it doesn't need to inherit any other attributes from another style. Now suppose that the paragraph's logical style specified italic text in black and there are also paragraph attributes applied to this paragraph that make the text red. When these new paragraph attributes have been set, you will have red text that is in italics, but is also bold because the `setParagraphAttributes` method specified `replace = false`. Had `replace = true` been specified, we would have lost the existing paragraph attributes (i.e. the red color) but retained the logical style, giving black, italic, bold text. Since what is wanted is bold, nonitalicized text with the text color left unchanged (whatever it is), it is necessary to turn off the italics. The correct code sequence is as follows:

```
Style s = doc.addStyle(null, null);
s.addAttribute(StyleConstants.Bold, new Boolean(true));
s.addAttribute(StyleConstants.Italic, new Boolean(false));
doc.setParagraphAttributes(0, 1, s, false);
```

This works because the new paragraph formatting explicitly turns off italics and overrides the italic setting in the paragraph's logical style.

Character Formatting

The last level of formatting, and the one that takes highest precedence in the formatting hierarchy, is character formatting which is applied with the `setCharacterAttributes` method:

```
public void setCharacterAttributes(int offset, int length,
              AttributeSet attrs, boolean replace);
```

Although this method has the same arguments as `setParagraphAttributes`, it only affects the exact range of characters specified by the offset and the length. Attributes set using this method override existing paragraph attributes and the paragraph's logical style. Continuing the example used above, our paragraph is currently rendered in bold, red text. Suppose that you wanted to change the second and third characters of that paragraph to blue. Since this operation affects the attributes of individual characters, character formatting is used instead of paragraph formatting and a style that has a blue foreground is created:

```
s = doc.addStyle(null, null);
s.addAttribute(StyleConstants.Foreground, Color.blue);
```

This style is going to be applied from offset 1 for two characters, but should `replace` be set to `true` or `false`? In the case of `setCharacterAttributes`, `replace` affects only character attributes applied to the same characters, not paragraph attributes. This is different from paragraph formatting, where setting `replace` to `true` loses attributes from the paragraph's logical style. Since there is currently no character formatting on these characters, it doesn't matter which value of `replace` is chosen: the text will be blue and bold, because the paragraph style specifies bold. Therefore, either of the following alternatives is acceptable:

```
doc.setCharacterAttributes(1, 2, s, true);
doc.setCharacterAttributes(1, 2, s, false);
```

Now suppose you decided to change the font of these same two characters so that the point size is 16 instead of the default. This time, you want to supplement the existing attributes, not replace them, so you would use a `replace` value of `false`.

The JTextPane Control

The `JTextPane` is a text control whose model is `DefaultStyledDocument`, so you can apply to it the logical styles, paragraph and character formatting that you saw in the last section. Many of the methods of `JTextPane` are similar to those of the model but, in several cases, there is the possibility of confusion because `JTextPane` and `DefaultStyledDocument` use the same method name but different arguments. The list below shows the methods of `JTextPane`, grouped by function:

```
public StyledDocument getStyledDocument()

public void setStyledDocument(StyledDocument doc)

public void setDocument(Document doc)

public Style addStyle(String name, Style parent)

public Style getStyle(String name)

public void removeStyle(String name)

public Style getLogicalStyle()
```

```
public StyledDocument getStyledDocument()

public void setLogicalStyle(Style style)

public AttributeSet getCharacterAttributes()

public void setCharacterAttributes(AttributeSet attr, boolean replace)

public AttributeSet getParagraphAttributes()

public void setParagraphAttributes(AttributeSet attr, boolean replace)

public AttributeSet getInputAttributes ()

public void replaceSelection(String content)

public void insertComponent(Component c)

public void insertIcon(Icon icon)

public boolean getScrollableTracksViewportWidth()

public String getUIClassID()
```

The first three methods are concerned with the underlying document. You must use a `StyledDocument` with `JTextPane`; even though there is a `setDocument` method as well as a `setStyledDocument`. If you supply anything other than a `StyledDocument`, an `IllegalArgumentException` will be thrown. You can also specify, or default, the document when you create the control. Here are the constructors:

```
public JTextPane();

public JTextPane(StyledDocument doc);
```

The first form uses a `StyledDocument` with a `StyleContext` that contains only an empty, default style. You can manage the styles in the document using the next three methods, `addStyle`, `getStyle` and `removeStyle`, which just directly call the same methods of the underlying document.

The next group of methods deals with applying attributes to the document. You've already seen `setLogicalStyle`, `setParagraphAttributes` and `setCharacterAttributes` in connection with `StyledDocument` and these versions operate in the same way, but there is an important difference. The methods of the model specify an offset, a length, an attribute set and a replace flag. The `JTextPane` methods, however only require the last two arguments—the offset and length are not specified. This is because `JTextPane` uses a different way of specifying the part of the document to which attribute changes should apply. The setLogicalStyle method is the simplest of the three—the new logical style is applied to the paragraph at the current position of the caret. In the case of the other two methods, what happens depends on whether there is any text selected.

If there is a current selection, the new attributes are applied to that selection. In the case of character attributes, this means that they replace or supplement exactly the characters that are part of the selection, while the paragraph attributes and the logical style are applied to all of the paragraphs that are part of the selection. This is really just the same as DefaultStyledDocument, because JTextPane gets the extent of the selection using the JTextComponent getSelectionStart and getSelectionEnd methods (which use the Caret getDot and getMark methods) and uses the difference between the two as the length and the selection start position as the start offset. If there isn't a selection, setParagraphAttributes applies to the paragraph that contains the caret, which is the same as setLogicalStyle.

Character attributes are, however, applied not to the document, but to a set of *input* attributes maintained by JTextPane. When the caret is moved, the input attribute set is initialized to contain the character attributes at the caret's current location. When there is no selection, the attributes supplied with setCharacterAttributes are applied instead to the input attributes; if replace is true, they completely replace the input attribute set, otherwise they just supplement the input set, in the same way as they would have affected existing character attributes in the document. These attributes remain in force until they are changed by another setCharacterAttributes call or the caret is moved. You can use the getInputAttributes method to get the current set of input attributes at any time.

The input attributes are used when you insert content into the JTextPane using its replaceSelection method, which looks like this:

```
public void replaceSelection(String text);
```

As with the attribute handling methods, the position at which this text will be inserted is implicit. If there is a current selection, the text in the selection is first removed, leaving the caret where the selection started, then the new text is inserted at the caret position. If there was no selection, the text is simply inserted at the location of the caret. In either case, the input attributes are applied to the text as character attributes.

When you replace or insert text, the paragraph attributes at the insertion point are not affected and will apply to whatever you insert. The way in which character formatting works is a little more complex, because the input attribute set picks up attributes as the caret is moved. When you move the caret to the required insertion or replacement point, the input attributes are replaced by the character attributes under the caret. If you now create a selection and replace it, or simply insert text without first creating a selection, your new text will have the character and paragraph attributes (or logical style) in force at the insertion point. This is, of course, the most logical result, because you would expect your inserted text to take on the appearance of the text that surrounds it. If, after moving the caret, you invoke `setCharacterAttributes`, the attributes you supply will supplement (or replace) the input attributes from the document and these modified input attributes will be applied by `replaceSelection`.

Suppose you create a selection that straddles an area with more than one set of character formatting. For example, if you start the selection by setting the caret to a position at which the character attributes specify red text, then make a selection by moving the caret to an area in which the character attributes give bold, black text. What are the input attributes applicable to a replacement of this selection? Should the attributes specify red text (as at the start of the selection) or bold black text (as at the end)? Replacing a selection consists of logically deleting the selected text and then inserting the new text. Deleting the text leaves the caret at the start of the selection, so the input attributes are those that were in effect at that point—that is, they specify red text.

Core Tip

If you want to insert text and be sure that you don't have any character formatting inherited from the text under the caret, you can supply replacement character formatting using the empty attribute set `SimpleAttributeSet.EMPTY`:

```
// Assumes "tp" references a JTextPane
tp.setCharacterAttributes(SimpleAttributeSet.EMPTY, true);
        // NB: true to REPLACE attributes
tp.replaceSelection("No character attributes applied");
```

The second argument to the `setCharacterAttributes` *method must be* `true` *for this to work.*

Text is not the only thing you can insert into a `JTextPane`—you can also place icons inline with the text and, to create arbitrary effects and documents that respond to user input, you can also include any `Component`. To make this possible, `JTextPane` provides the following methods:

```
public void insertComponent(Component c)
```

```
public void insertIcon(Icon icon)
```

The icon or component is inserted at the current caret position, or replaces the current selection if there is one. When you insert an icon or a component into a text flow, the bottom of the icon or component occupies the baseline of the text. Components and icons are actually inserted as attributes and their position is taken in the document by a single space character with the component or icon attached to it as a character attribute. If you want to center an icon or a component, you need to place it in a paragraph of its own and apply your own attributes. There is an example of this later in this chapter.

Core Alert

Both the `insertComponent` *and* `insertIcon` *methods clear the input attribute set when placing the icon or component, so you can't add additional formatting using the input attributes. Furthermore, any attributes in the input attribute set will, of course, be lost.*

The `getScrollableTracksViewportWidth` method overrides the `JComponent` method of this name and always returns `true`. This method is used when the `JTextPane` is controlled by a `JScrollPane` and requests that the `JViewport` should always change its width to match that of the `JScrollPane`. Since `JTextPane` implements word wrap, this is an appropriate thing to do. Like `JTextArea`, no scrollbars are provided when you create a `JTextPane`, so you would normally wrap a `JTextPane` in a `JScrollPane`.

The `getUIClassID` method is used to install the component's pluggable look-and-feel implementation. You'll see what this method does in Chapter 13, "Pluggable Look-and-Feel."

JTextPane Examples

You've seen how to create the formatting for a `JTextPane`, now it is time to look at a couple of examples. The first example creates a document that contains some text arranged in several paragraphs with several fonts and different colors and also includes an image with the text. The second example takes this a step further by replacing the image with a component that can be used to navigate around the document. These two examples have a lot of code in common. You'll see much of the code as you examine the first example, then you'll see how to change the first example to create the second version.

Using JTextPane to Display Colored Text and an Image

Let's start by looking at what the first example looks like when it is finished. You can see a screen shot in Figure 9-10.

You can run this example for yourself using the command:

```
java JFCBook.Chapter9.TextPaneExample1
```

This application is a `JTextPane` wrapped by a `JScrollPane` to provide the scrolling capability. All of the text and the attributes are held as data within the program. As you'll see, this makes the process of using `JTextPane` rather tedious. Luckily, however, you don't always have to use `JTextPane` directly—in many cases, you can use JEditorPane, which is covered later in this chapter, instead. JEditorPane accepts HTML or RTF as input, so you can embed the text and the formatting information in the same file.

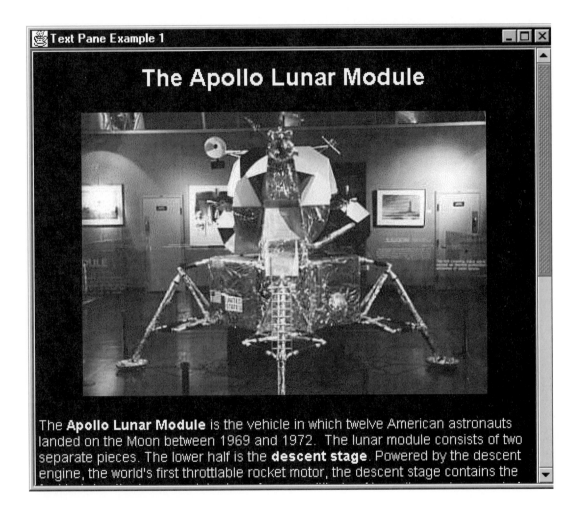

Figure 9-10   Styled Text with JTextPane.

The Application's Main Method

Let's first look at application's main method and the constructor of its class (Listing 9-11).

Listing 9-11   JTextPane Example (Part 1)

```
package JFCBook.Chapter9;

import com.sun.java.swing.*;
import com.sun.java.swing.text.*;
import java.awt.*;
import java.awt.event.*;
import java.util.*;

public class TextPaneExample1 extends JTextPane {
  public TextPaneExample1(ParagraphSpec[] paragraphs) {
    this.setBackground(Color.black);
    createStyles();      // Create the text styles
    addText(paragraphs);  // Add all of the text
  }

  // CODE OMITTED

  public static void main(String[] args) {
    JFrame f = new JFrame("Text Pane Example 1");
    f.setBackground(Color.black);
    TextPaneExample1 tp = new TextPaneExample1(paragraphs);
    JScrollPane sp = new JScrollPane(tp);
    f.getContentPane().add(sp);
    f.setSize(500, 400);
    f.addWindowListener(new WindowAdapter() {
      public void windowClosing(WindowEvent evt) {
        System.exit(0);
      }
    });
    f.setVisible(true);
  }

  // CODE OMITTED
}
```

The main method creates an instance of TextPaneExample1, which is an extension of JTextPane, and wraps it in a JScrollPane, which is then mounted in a frame. The constructor of the TextPaneExample1 class initializes the content of the text pane by giving it a black background, then defining the styles that will be required by calling the method createStyles and adding the text and formatting using the addText method. These two methods make up the majority of this example and you'll see both of them shortly. First, let's consider how the text should be represented so that it can be used to create the document that the text pane will display.

Storing the Document Text and Its Attributes

Apart from the image, the document consists of several paragraphs, each with one or more lines of text. The basic style to be used in most of the paragraphs will be the same, but some of the text within individual lines will have special formatting. The page heading and the image need to be handled specially and there is also a direct quotation at the end of the document, which should be rendered in a different style from the rest of the document.

There are many ways in which the text and the information needed to apply the attributes could be stored to obtain the desired result. The method chosen here is to arrange the text into paragraphs represented by the inner class `ParagraphSpec`. This class encapsulates a set of attributes that will set the overall style of the paragraph together with an array of `ContentSpec` classes. The `ContentSpec` class represents part of a line of text, together with its associated attributes, which will be applied to the text as character attributes. As well as the text and its attributes, a "tag" can also be associated with the text. The tag will be used in the second example.

The `ParagraphSpec` and `ContentSpec` inner classes are very simple, since they just hold data:

```
protected static class ContentSpec {
   protected ContentSpec(String tag, String style, String text) {
      this.tag = tag;
      this.style = style;
      this.text = text;
   }
   public String tag;
   public String style;
   public String text;
}


protected static class ParagraphSpec {
   protected ParagraphSpec(String style, ContentSpec[] con-
tents) {
      this.style = style;
      this.contents = contents;
   }
   public String style;
   public ContentSpec[] contents;
}
```

As you can see from the constructors, to create a paragraph, you need to supply paragraph attributes and an array of contents while to create contents, you need a tag, some character attributes and some text. As you'll see, not all of these elements are required all of the time, so certain of them can be defaulted by specifying `null`.

The idea of the tags is to allow a text string to be associated with the position within the document of the text that was defined with the tag. To make this possible, another inner class is defined to hold the tag as a text string along with the start and end positions of the text that was in the same `ContentSpec` as the tag declaration:

```
protected static class TagEntry {
    protected TagEntry(Position startPos, Position endPos) {
        this.startPos = startPos;
        this.endPos = endPos;
    }
    public Position startPos;
    public Position endPos;
}
```

Notice that the start and end values are held as `Position` objects, not as offsets. In this example, the document that is displayed won't be editable, but you might, in a more general case, want to allow this. To make it possible for the text to change and still retain a meaningful reference to places within it, it is necessary to store `Position` objects rather than offsets because, as you have seen, these change transparently as the position that they refer to moves within the document. In the discussion of the second example, you'll see that we extract a document offset from each `Position` when we need to.

Specifying the Document Styles

You have now seen all of the data structures that are needed for this example. Let's now look at how to create the document's styles. Several different styles are needed for various parts of the text. All of the styles are created and meaningful names assigned to them, in the `createStyles` method that is shown in Listing 9-12.

Listing 9-12   JTextPane example—creating styles

```
protected void createStyles() {
  StyledDocument doc = getStyledDocument();
  // Create the top-level style, with the required font
  basicStyle = doc.addStyle(Basic, null);
  StyleConstants.setFontFamily(basicStyle, "SansSerif");
  StyleConstants.setFontSize(basicStyle, 14);
  StyleConstants.setForeground(basicStyle, Color.white);
  StyleConstants.setFirstLineIndent(basicStyle, 50.0f);
  StyleConstants.setSpaceAbove(basicStyle, 6);
  StyleConstants.setSpaceBelow(basicStyle, 0);

  // Heading: centered, bold, larger font
  Style s = doc.addStyle(Heading, basicStyle);
  StyleConstants.setBold(s, true);
  StyleConstants.setFontSize(s, 24);
  StyleConstants.setAlignment(s, StyleConstants.ALIGN_CENTER);
```

```
      StyleConstants.setSpaceAbove(s, 8);
      StyleConstants.setSpaceBelow(s, 12);
      // BoldText
      s = doc.addStyle(BoldText, basicStyle);
      StyleConstants.setBold(s, true);

      // Cite - a paragraph style for quotations
      s = doc.addStyle(Cite, basicStyle);
      StyleConstants.setItalic(s, true);
      StyleConstants.setFontSize(s, 14);
      StyleConstants.setAlignment(s, StyleConstants.ALIGN_CENTER);
      StyleConstants.setSpaceAbove(s, 10);
      StyleConstants.setSpaceBelow(s, 10);
      StyleConstants.setForeground(s, Color.yellow);

      // RedText
      s = doc.addStyle(RedText, basicStyle);
      StyleConstants.setForeground(s, Color.red);

      // ImageIcon: an image of the Lunar Module
      s = doc.addStyle(ImageIcon, basicStyle);
      StyleConstants.setIcon(s, new
            ImageIcon(getClass().getResource("images/lem.jpg")));
}

// CODE OMITTED
// Style names
protected static final String Basic = "Basic";
protected static final String Heading = "Heading";
protected static final String BoldText = "BoldText";
protected static final String Cite = "Cite";
protected static final String RedText = "RedText";
protected static final String ImageIcon = "ImageIcon";

// The basic paragraph style
protected Style basicStyle;
```

This method creates the styles shown in Table 9-4.

Table 9-4	Styles Used in the First JTextPane Example

Style Name	Attributes
Basic	14-point, plain, SansSerif font; White text; 6 points above the paragraph; 0 points below; 50 points extra indent on the first line of the paragraph
Heading	Same as Basic, except 24-point, bold, SansSerif font; centered; 8 points above the paragraph; 12 points below the paragraph
BoldText	Same as Basic, except bold font
RedText	Same as Basic, except red text
ImageIcon	Same as Basic, except displays an image
Cite	Same as Basic, except 14-point, italic SansSerif font; centered; 10 points above and below the paragraph; yellow text

Some of these styles are used as paragraph attributes (Basic, Heading and Cite), and others for character formatting (BoldText, RedText). It is important to realize that some attributes, such as alignment, space above and below and extra indentation, are only honored when a style is used to format a paragraph. This is why it is possible for all of the styles to be based on the Basic style, even though the character styles can't make use of the space above and below and the 50-point indentation on the first line that the Basic style passes to Cite and Heading. In fact, though, in this case, neither Cite nor Heading actually uses many of the attributes that they inherit from the Basic style. It is, however, usually a good idea to derive styles from a common base so that shared attributes need be specified only once.

If you examine Listing 9-12 in conjunction with Table 9-4, you should be able to see how the styles are constructed. Notice that this example uses a different method of specifying attributes than the code extracts that have been shown so far in this chapter. Instead of creating a Style and using its addAttribute method to associate a value with an attribute name, the code here makes use of a set of convenience routines provided by the StyleConstants class. The advantage of these methods, which are all static, is that they are type-safe—you have to supply an object of the type that the attribute requires, whereas the addAttribute method accepts an Object as the value, which results in a ClassCastException at runtime if you supply the wrong type of object. An error when using StyleConstants is trapped at compile time instead. The complete set of convenience routines provided by StyleConstants is shown in Table 9-5.

To display the image that appears at the top of the document, the ImageIcon style will be used. It is displayed by associating an Icon with an attribute; in the case of this example, an instance of the class ImageIcon that loads and displays an image from a file will be used. The icon is placed in the text by inserting a space and giving it the ImageIcon attribute.

Table 9-5	Attribute Setting Methods Supplied by StyleConstants

Method	*Purpose*
`public static void setAlignment` `(MutableAttributeSet, int)`	Sets paragraph alignment
`public static void setBold` `(MutableAttributeSet, boolean)`	Sets the bold attribute
`public static void setComponent` `(MutableAttributeSet, Component)`	Sets the component attribute
`public static void setFirstLineIndent` `(MutableAttributeSet, float)`	Sets the paragraph first-line indent
`public static void setFontFamily` `(MutableAttributeSet, String)`	Sets the font family attribute
`public static void setFontSize` `(MutableAttributeSet, int)`	Sets the font size attribute
`public static void setForeground` `(MutableAttributeSet, Color)`	Sets the foreground color
`public static void setIcon` `(MutableAttributeSet, Icon)`	Sets the icon attribute
`public static void setItalic` `(MutableAttributeSet, boolean)`	Sets the italic attribute
`public static void setLeftIndent` `(MutableAttributeSet, float)`	Sets the paragraph left indent
`public static void setLineSpacing` `(MutableAttributeSet, float)`	Sets paragraph line spacing
`public static void setRightIndent` `(MutableAttributeSet, float)`	Sets the paragraph right indent
`public static void setSpaceAbove` `(MutableAttributeSet, float)`	Sets the space above a paragraph
`public static void setSpaceBelow` `(MutableAttributeSet, float)`	Sets the space below a paragraph
`public static void setUnderline` `(MutableAttributeSet, boolean)`	Sets the underline attribute

Building the Document

The last method to look at is `addText`, which inserts the text and its associated attributes in the document. The data structures that have been chosen make this method relatively simple to implement. You can see the code in Listing 9-13.

Listing 9-13   JTextPane example—inserting the text

```
protected void addText(ParagraphSpec[] paragraphs) {
  StyledDocument doc = getStyledDocument();

  int count = paragraphs.length;

  // Insert each paragraph
  for (int i = 0; i < count; i++) {
    ParagraphSpec p = paragraphs[i];

    int contentCount = p.contents.length;
    for (int j = 0; j < contentCount; j++) {
      // Insert each piece of content for this paragraph,
      // with its own tag (optional) and character attributes
      // (also optional)
      ContentSpec cs = p.contents[j];
      AttributeSet s = cs.style == null ?
              SimpleAttributeSet.EMPTY :
              doc.getStyle(cs.style);
      setCharacterAttributes(s, true); // Apply formatting

      int startPoint = doc.getLength();
      replaceSelection(cs.text); // Insert text
      int endPoint = doc.getLength();

      if (cs.tag != null) {
        // Insert a tag
        try {
          tagList.put(cs.tag, new
              TagEntry(doc.createPosition(startPoint),
              doc.createPosition(endPoint - 1)));
        } catch (BadLocationException e) {
          System.out.println("Unexpected bad location exception!");
          System.exit(0);
        }
      }
    }

    // At the end of the paragraph, apply the style
    // and add a newline to terminate it
    doc.setLogicalStyle(doc.getLength() - 1,
          p.style != null ? doc.getStyle(p.style) : basicStyle);

    replaceSelection("\n");
  }

  setEditable(false);    // No editing
  setCaretColor(Color.black);    // Hide the caret
}
```

This method cycles through the `paragraphs` array, which contains one entry for each paragraph in the document. To make it easier to understand the code, here is the start of the declaration of `paragraphs`:

```
protected static ParagraphSpec[] paragraphs = new ParagraphSpec[] {
    new ParagraphSpec(Heading, new ContentSpec[] {
        new ContentSpec(null, null, "The Apollo Lunar Module")
    }),
    new ParagraphSpec(Heading, new ContentSpec[] {
        new ContentSpec(null, ImageIcon, " ")
    }),
    new ParagraphSpec(Basic, new ContentSpec[] {
        new ContentSpec(null, null, "The "),
        new ContentSpec(null, BoldText, "Apollo Lunar Module"),
        new ContentSpec(null, null,
            " is the vehicle in which twelve American astronauts" +
            " landed on the Moon between 1969 and 1972. " +
            " The lunar module consists of two separate pieces." +
            " The lower half is the "),
        new ContentSpec("Descent Stage", BoldText, "descent stage"),
        new ContentSpec(null, null, ". Powered by the descent engine, the world's" +
            " first throttlable rocket motor, the descent stage contains" +
            " the fuel to bring the lunar module down from an altitude" +
            " of ten miles and a speed of 3,800 miles per hour to a" +
            " safe landing on the lunar surface.")
    }),
    // CODE OMITTED
}
```

The outer loop of `addText` processes one `ParagraphSpec` object from the `paragraphs` array, while the inner loop processes all of the `ContentSpec` objects in that paragraph. Recall that a paragraph is delimited by a newline character, so after placing all of the text for the paragraph, the outer loop adds a newline and applies the paragraph formatting:

```
doc.setLogicalStyle(doc.getLength() - 1,
    p.style != null ? doc.getStyle(p.style) : basicStyle);

replaceSelection("\n");
```

Recall that the logical style must be applied to the paragraph that it relates to. Here, an offset within that paragraph is obtained by using the length of the document. This is possible because the document content is being added sequentially, so an offset obtained in this way is always in the paragraph currently being formatted. In the data, the name of the style is stored rather than a reference to the `Style` object. This makes it possible to optimize the way in which the styles are held, perhaps by using a static `Hashtable` so that each style is created only once, no matter how many times instances of this data are created. In this example, no such optimization is actually attempted—the style is obtained by using the `getStyle` method of

`StyledDocument`. Another useful facility is the ability to specify the paragraph style as `null`, in which case the default formatting of the `Basic` style is applied. Having applied the formatting, the paragraph is terminated with a newline character, created using `replaceSelection`. This will always amount to an insertion, because there is no text selected at this stage.

Now let's look at the inner loop. Each `ContentSpec` specifies a tag, optional character formatting, specified as a style name, and some text. The code in the inner loop extracts these three values and converts the style name to a string. Again, if the style name is given as `null`, an empty set of attributes is applied; as a result, text that has a `null` character format string will have only the paragraph formatting applied to it. Having applied the character attributes (with `setCharacterAttributes`), the text is inserted using the `replaceSelection` method. The document length before and after this is done, so that the start and end offsets of the text just inserted are known. If the text has an associated tag, a `TagEntry` with the tag name and `Position` objects for the start and end offsets is created and placed in a `Hashtable` with the tag string as the key. Text that does not need to be tagged specifies the tag name as a `null` string.

Notice the second entry in the `paragraphs` array:

```
new ParagraphSpec(Heading, new ContentSpec[] {
      new ContentSpec(null, ImageIcon, " ")
  }),
```

This entry does not have a tag and the text is just a space. The attributes, however, come from the `ImageIcon` style, which has an associated `Icon`. This is the entry that causes the picture of the Lunar Module to appear underneath the document heading—the picture itself is a part of the `ImageIcon` attribute. This mechanism makes it very easy to place a picture in a document.

Creating an Active Document with JTextPane

For our second example, the image used in the first example will be replaced with the `ImageMap` that was developed to demonstrate dialogs in Chapter 8. When the `ImageMap` was created, it was implemented as a separate class so that it could easily be reused elsewhere. Since `ImageMap` is a `Component`, you can easily include it in a document by defining a style that has the `Component` attribute. Replacing the image with the image map requires the following style to be defined in place of `ImageIcon` in the `createStyles` method:

```
// Component - an image of the Lunar Module
s = doc.addStyle(ImageMap, basicStyle);
StyleConstants.setComponent(s, mapComponent);
```

and the `ImageMap` can be included simply by changing one line of the paragraphs array:

```
protected static ParagraphSpec[] paragraphs = new ParagraphSpec[] {
    new ParagraphSpec(Heading, new ContentSpec[] {
        new ContentSpec(null, null, "The Apollo Lunar Module")
    }),
    new ParagraphSpec(Heading, new ContentSpec[] {
        new ContentSpec(null, ImageMap, " ") // The image map
    }),
```

The only other thing to do is create the ImageMap object and store a reference to it in the instance variable mapComponent, where the style definition code shown above expects it to be. This is handled in the constructor before creating the styles, as you'll see below.

Replacing the image by the image map is the first change to make. The second part of the change is to make the image map active. You may recall that Chapter 8 created an image map that would display descriptions of certain parts of the Apollo Lunar Module as the mouse passed over them and, in response to a double click would fire an ActionEvent with the description as its action command. This example will catch those events and match the description to the tags that have been stored in a hash list. In the data that was used to create the JTextPane, each tag has been placed near some text that describes the corresponding piece of the lunar module; here's an example:

```
new ParagraphSpec(Basic, new ContentSpec[] {
    new ContentSpec(null, null, "Attached to the front "),
    new ContentSpec("Landing Leg", BoldText, "landing leg"),
    new ContentSpec(null, null,    " of the Apollo 11 lunar module "),
    new ContentSpec(null, RedText, "Eagle"),
    new ContentSpec(null, null, " is a plaque that reads:")
}),
```

Here, the tag Landing Leg is associated with the text "landing leg," which is rendered in bold in the document. On encountering this data, the addText method creates an entry in the hash list with key Landing Leg; the information stored with this key in the TagEntry structure is a pair of Position objects that track the start and end position of the text "landing leg." Given the text Landing Leg in the action command of an ActionEvent, it is, therefore, possible to find the position of the related text in the document. To make this useful, the text is highlighted and the JTextPane is scrolled so that the text is visible. This makes the picture of the lunar module behave like a real image map, with active hyperlinks. It is easy to see how to extend this idea to add more powerful behavior.

Now let's see how the constructor is changed to add the image map:

```
public TextPaneExample2(ParagraphSpec[] paragraphs) {
  this.setBackground(Color.black);

  // Create the image map
  mapComponent = new ImageMap(
      new ImageIcon(getClass().getResource("images/lem.jpg")),
      mapSections);
  createStyles();    // Create the text styles
  addText(paragraphs);// Add all of the text

  // Change the highlight color
  setSelectionColor(Color.green.darker());

  // Process double-clicks from the image map
  mapComponent.addActionListener(new ActionListener() {
    public void actionPerformed(ActionEvent evt) {
      jumpToTag(evt.getActionCommand());
    }
  });
}
```

The name of the class has been changed to `TextPaneExample2`, so to run this example, use the command:

```
java JFCBook.Chapter9.TextPaneExample2
```

Core Alert

In Swing 1.0.1, there was a problem that resulted in a `NullPointerException` *when adding a* `Component` *to a document. If you get a* `NullPointerException` *when running this example, you can work around it by using a temporary patch that was installed from the CD-ROM when the example programs were installed. To activate this fix, you need to add the appropriate path to the beginning of your* `CLASSPATH` *variable. If, for example, you installed the examples in the directory* `C:\CoreJFCBook`, *you should do this:*

`set CLASSPATH=c:\CoreJFCBook\JFCBook\Chapter9\bugfixes;%CLASSPATH%`

Note that this is just a temporary workaround to allow you to try this example—it is not an official JavaSoft fix and should not be used in a production environment.

The image map is created using the `ImageMap` constructor in the same way as was done in Chapter 8. The second argument to this constructor is an array of `MapSection` objects that defines the areas of the image that are active. This array is too large to show in this book, but you can find it in the source code on the CD-ROM. The `JTextComponent` method `setSelectionColor` is used to change the color used to highlight the text selection from its default gray to a dark green so that it shows up well against the black background of the control and contrasts with the white text. Finally, an `ActionListener` is attached to the `ImageMap`. When this listener gets an `ActionEvent`, the name of the area that has been double-clicked is extracted and the `jumpToTag` method, which is shown below, is invoked with this name as its argument:

```
protected void jumpToTag(String tag) {
   TagEntry ent = (TagEntry)tagList.get(tag);
   if (ent != null) {
      // Use the selection to highlight the target text
      select(ent.startPos.getOffset(), ent.endPos.getOffset() + 1);
      try {

scrollRectToVisible(modelToView(ent.startPos.getOffset())));
      } catch (BadLocationException e) {
         // Ignore.
      }
   }
}
```

This method uses the tag that it receives to get the corresponding `TagEntry` from the hash list created by `addText`, then gets the start and end positions of the associated text and converts them to document offsets using the `getOffset` method of the `Position` interface. To highlight the text, it is made the current selection using the `select` method of `JTextComponent`; this method is an alternative to the `setSelectionStart` and `setSelectionEnd` pair that were used at the start of this chapter. The last thing to do is to force the `JScrollPane` to scroll the highlighted area into view. As you saw in Chapter 5, you can force any area of a `JComponent` to be scrolled into view by using the `scrollRectToVisible` method. This method requires a `Rectangle` describing the area to be made visible. What you actually have is the offset of the start of the selected text. This can be converted to screen coordinates by calling the `modelToView` method that was mentioned earlier. This method returns a `Rectangle`, which can be passed directly to `scrollRectToVisible`.

Inside the JTextPane

The last two examples have shown how to construct documents with images and text formatting and mount them in a `JTextPane` and how the character and paragraph formatting are used to determine the attributes of each part of the document. Some of the details of this can be confusing, unless you understand the way in which the attributes are held in the underlying element structure of the document behind the `JTextPane`. To make this possible, the second example above has been extended so that it prints the complete element structure after executing the `addText` method, by using the `ModelDisplay` class that was developed earlier in this chapter. To run this example, use the command:

```
java JFCBook.Chapter9.TextPaneExample3
```

An abbreviated snapshot of the output from this example is shown below. You can see, first of all, that the top-level element in a `StyledDocument` is not a paragraph (as it was for a `PlainDocument`), but a *section*. The document has only one section and it can have associated attributes that affect all of the document. In our example, there are no attributes at the section level. Each real paragraph in the document is represented by a paragraph element. This is again different from `PlainDocument`, which represents these as content elements. A paragraph may contain several content elements.

Each paragraph element has an associated style because, in this example, every paragraph is assigned its own individual logical style. In some documents, the default logical style associated with the document when it is created would supply the attributes for most of the paragraphs. Only paragraphs that needed special formatting like the quotation near the end of this example, would have their own paragraph formatting.

```
[ section ], start offset: 0, end: 1684
   { No attributes }

     [ paragraph ], start offset: 0, end: 24
        { resolver = NamedStyle:Heading }

          [ content ], start offset: 0, end: 24
             { No attributes }
                   The Apollo Lunar Module \n
     [ paragraph ], start offset: 24, end: 26
        { resolver = NamedStyle:Heading }

          [ component ], start offset: 24, end: 26
             { resolver = NamedStyle:Basic }
             { $ename = component }
             { name = ImageMap }
             { component =
JFCBook.Chapter8.ImageMap[,0,0,0x0,invalid] }

     [ paragraph ], start offset: 26, end: 479
        { resolver = NamedStyle:Basic }

          [ content ], start offset: 26, end: 30
             { No attributes }
                   The
          [ content ], start offset: 30, end: 49
             { resolver = NamedStyle:Basic }
             { name = BoldText }
             { bold = true }
                   Apollo Lunar Module
          [ content ], start offset: 49, end: 216
```

```
{ No attributes }
        is the vehicle in which twelve American
[ content ], start offset: 216, end: 229
  { resolver = NamedStyle:Basic }
  { name = BoldText }
  { bold = true }
        descent stage
[ content ], start offset: 229, end: 479
  { No attributes }
        . Powered by the descent engine, the wor
```

Within a paragraph, the individual content elements may have special attributes, or they may just inherit those of their parent paragraph. Let's look at some examples. The first paragraph corresponds to the heading, which is in large, bold font and is centered on the display. Looking at the element structure, you can see that the paragraph occupies offsets 0 to 23 inclusive and has the logical style `Heading`, which is consistent with the data used to create it, which we saw earlier in this chapter. The content itself reads "The Apollo Lunar Module" and has no character attributes.

Compare this to the third paragraph, which contains five separate content elements. The paragraph itself covers offsets 26 to 478 and uses the `Basic` style for its paragraph formatting. This means that its text will be in a 14-point SansSerif, plain font and it will be rendered in white. Some of the text in this paragraph has no special character attributes, so will just use the paragraph formatting; this applies to the first, third and fifth content elements. However, the second and fourth elements have their own character formatting, both provided by the `BoldText` style. The output shows that the `BoldText` style has a value for the attribute called `bold` (which is the string defined by the constant value `StyleConstants.Bold`) and that this attribute is `true`. All other attributes should first be looked for in the `Basic` style (because this is listed as the resolving parent of the `BoldText` style). If you examine the rest of the output, you'll find plenty of similar examples that show how the attributes that we apply with `setCharacterAttributes` and `setLogicalStyle` are mapped onto the underlying element structure.

Editor Kits and The JEditorPane Control

Powerful though `JTextPane` is, it can be very time-consuming to create the effects that you want. Ultimately, for all but the simplest cases, you probably don't want to hard-code document content and formatting into your application. It would be much better to be able to place the text and the associated attributes in a file that is read at run time and to build a parser that would use the file contents to build a `JTextPane` with all of its associated formatting. This would make it possible to reuse the same class to display many different documents and reduce development time by cutting down on the number of compilations required to achieve the desired effect.

Fortunately, it isn't necessary to invent a format for holding text and markup in the same file, because there are several of them already in existence. Two commonly-used ones are HTML (Hypertext Markup Language) and RTF (Rich Text Format). You don't even need to write the parsers for these file formats because there is another component in the Swing set that knows how to read, display and even write files in HTML, RTF and, potentially, any other document format you like. Before looking in detail at the powerful `JEditorPane` component, let's take another, brief, look at editor kits, which `JEditorPane` relies on to do its job.

Editor Kits

The Swing text components are, as you have seen in this chapter, very complex pieces of software, yet the controls themselves (`JTextField`, `JTextArea`, `JPasswordField`, `JTextPane` and `JEditorPane`) are not large at all. This is, of course, because most of their functionality resides in other classes—the component itself is just the facade behind which a framework is built from pieces that work together to give the desired effect. You've already seen the `Document`, the `JTextComponent` and the `View`, but there is another piece that each text component uses—the editor kit.

The editor kit actually has more than one role to play. Its primary job is to provide the editing actions that the text control will allow the user to perform, but it also has a method that allows its text component to create a document of a type that the editor kit can work with and it is responsible for loading a document from a file or other external source where it can be stored persistently and for saving a (possibly modified) version of the document.

Editor Actions

This aspect of the editor kit's job has already been touched on in this chapter. It is the editor kit that provides the code that actually inserts new content in a document, deletes characters, moves the cursor around within the document, allows the user to copy, cut and paste text and so on. The actions that the simplest of the editor kits, `DefaultEditorKit`, provides were listed in Table 9-3. It is important to realize, however, that the editor kit implementation for most of these actions is very simple—the editor kit often just acts as a switching center, directing an action to the correct piece of code in the text component itself or in the model.

For example, take the case of inserting a new character in a `Document`. You'll recall from our earlier discussion that `JTextComponent` handles each keystroke it receives by looking through its keymap. If it doesn't find a specific action bound to the keystroke that it has, then it passes the key to the installed editor kit's `default-typed` action.

In the case of `DefaultEditorKit`, this action is implemented in the `actionPerformed` method of the inner class `DefaultTypedAction`. As you saw earlier, all editor kit actions are implementations of the `Action` interface, which allows them to be connected to keystrokes and also to menus and toolbars. Usually, these action classes, like `DefaultTypedAction`, are actually derived from the class `TextAction`, which is defined as follows:

```
public abstract class TextAction extends AbstractAction {
    public TextAction(String name);
    public static final Action[ ] augmentList(Action[ ] list1,
            Action[ ] list2);
    protected final JTextComponent getTextComponent(ActionEvent e);
    protected JTextComponent getFocusedComponent();
}
```

The `name` argument passed to the constructor is also the name of the action that will be implemented by a subclass of `TextAction`. `DefaultTypedAction`, for example, passes the string default-typed to this constructor.

The `augmentList` method takes two lists of `Action`s and combines them into a single list. If the original lists contain `Action`s with the same name, the `Action` from the second list will be used. This method is used by text components that want to combine `Action`s of their own with those provided by their editor kit. A typical example of this is `JTextField`, which, as you know, provides an action called notify-field-accept that generates an `ActionEvent` when the RETURN key is pressed. This action is over and above the set provided by `DefaultEditorKit`, so to make it appear in the list of supported actions for the component, which can be obtained by calling `getActions` on any text component, it must be added to the set supplied by the editor kit. The `augmentList` method is used to do this.

The `getTextComponent` method returns the text component associated with the current action. This is always the source of the `ActionEvent` if it is a text component, of the component returned by `getFocusedComponent` if it is not. The `getFocusedComponent` method returns a reference to whichever text component currently has the focus, or `null` if the focus is not in a text component. As you'll see in the next example, these last two methods allow the editor's actions to be written without being tied to any particular text component.

Adding Actions to a Text Component

As a simple illustration of how easy it is to add functionality to a text component over and above that provided by its editor kit, the next example adds to the `JTextArea` the ability to select all of its content in a single keystroke. This is often a useful facility, particularly if you want to copy an entire document or delete all of it in one go. To add an action to a text component, you need to subclass it in order to override its `getActions` method.

Core Note

`DefaultEditorKit` *actually provides an action to select all of the text in its associated document, so this example could be implemented by mapping a key sequence to that action. Instead, for the purposes of illustration, the selection action will also be implemented here.*

Listing 9-14 shows the implementation of an extended JTextArea, called SelectAllTextArea, that has the new functionality built into it.

Listing 9-14   Adding an action to a text component

```java
package JFCBook.Chapter9;

import com.sun.java.swing.*;
import com.sun.java.swing.text.*;
import java.awt.event.*;

public class SelectAllTextArea extends JTextArea {
  public SelectAllTextArea() {
    super();
    mapSelectAll();
  }

  public SelectAllTextArea(Document doc) {
    super(doc);
    mapSelectAll();
  }

  public SelectAllTextArea(Document doc, String text, int rows, int cols) {
    super(doc, text, rows, cols);
    mapSelectAll();
  }

  public SelectAllTextArea(int rows, int cols) {
    super(rows, cols);
    mapSelectAll();
  }

  public SelectAllTextArea(String text) {
    super(text);
    mapSelectAll();
  }

  public SelectAllTextArea(String text, int rows, int cols) {
    super(text, rows, cols);
    mapSelectAll();
  }

  // The overridden addActions methods provides our select-all action
  public Action[] getActions() {
    return TextAction.augmentList(super.getActions(), localActions);
  }
```

```java
// Implementation of the select-all action
public static final String selectAllAction = "select-all";

static class SelectAllAction extends TextAction {
  SelectAllAction() {
    super(selectAllAction);
  }

  // Method called to perform the action
  public void actionPerformed(ActionEvent e) {
    JTextComponent target = getTextComponent(e);
    if (target instanceof SelectAllTextArea) {
      Document doc = target.getDocument();
      target.setSelectionStart(0);
      target.setSelectionEnd(doc.getLength());
    }
  }
}

// Add a key mapping for the select-all action
protected void mapSelectAll() {
  Keymap parent = getKeymap(); // Get current keymap
  Keymap myKeymap = JTextComponent.addKeymap("SelectAllTextArea Keymap", parent);
  JTextComponent.loadKeymap(myKeymap, bindings, this.getActions());
  setKeymap(myKeymap);
}

// Local actions implemented by this control
protected static final Action[] localActions = new Action[] {
  new SelectAllAction()
};

// New key binding: ALT-A -> select all
protected static final JTextComponent.KeyBinding[] bindings = {
  new JTextComponent.KeyBinding(KeyStroke.getKeyStroke(KeyEvent.VK_A,
            KeyEvent.CTRL_MASK), selectAllAction)
};

public static void main(String[] args) {
  JFrame f = new JFrame("SelectAllTextArea");
  SelectAllTextArea ta = new SelectAllTextArea(15, 40);
  ta.setText("\"Houston, Tranquility Base here.\nThe Eagle has Landed\"\n"

    "\n\n\"Roger, Tranquility, we copy you on the ground.\n" +
    "You got a bunch of guys about to turn blue.\n" +
    "We're breathing again. Thanks a lot\"\n");
```

continued

```
    f.getContentPane().add(ta);
    f.addWindowListener(new WindowAdapter() {
      public void windowClosing(WindowEvent evt) {
        System.exit(0);
      }
    });
    f.pack();
    f.setVisible(true);
  }
}
```

The constructors all mirror and invoke those of `JTextArea`. As well as initializing the text area, they also invoke our local `mapSelectAll` method, which will be described below.

In order to add the required functionality, only two steps are required. First, the new action must be defined and implemented and then added to the component's list of actions. Secondly, a key binding must be added to make the action available to the user.

The action itself is, of course, derived from `TextAction`. In this case, it is implemented in the static inner class `SelectAllAction`, which has to define only a name for the action and the `actionPerformed` method that gets invoked when the user triggers it. The name that is chosen for the action is arbitrary, but it must be unique within the component and, of course, it should describe what the action does. In this case, the name `select-all` is used.

The action itself is implemented in the `actionPerformed` method. In principle, what actually needs to be done is very simple: When the action is triggered, all of the text in the text component needs to be selected—that's all there is to it. You already know that a selection is created using the `setSelectionStart` and `setSelectionEnd` methods of `JTextComponent` and, in this case, the start and end positions are easy to find because they are the start and end of the document itself. But, there is a problem. Using these methods requires that you have a reference to the text component. The `actionPerformed` method comes with an event source in its `ActionEvent`, but this need not be the text component, because the action may have been triggered from a menu, not from a keystroke. Fortunately, `JTextComponent` keeps track of which text component last had the focus and you can get a reference to that component using the `getTextComponent` method of `TextAction` As you can see from the implementation, a check is made that the target is a `SelectAllTextArea` before the action is performed, in case an attempt is made to invoke the action against a component that it would not apply to. This can easily happen if the action is invoked from a menu, of course.

In order for the new action to be useful, it must be mapped to a keystroke or added to a menu. In either case, this means arranging for it to appear in the list of actions returned by the `getActions` method. To make this possible, the

`JTextArea getActions` method is overridden to return a list of actions created by augmenting the original list from `JTextArea` with the `select-all` action using `augmentList`.

Adding a key mapping is also simple—in fact, you have already seen the code required to do this in Listing 9-8. In this case, however, no assumption is made about which keymap is currently installed in the `JTextArea` as was done in Listing 9-8 where the default keymap was assumed to be in place. To avoid this assumption, the `getKeymap` method of `JTextComponent` is used to extract the current keymap and then a new key binding is added. In this case, the key sequence CTRL+A is used to activate the `select-all` action. The `mapSelectAll` method that adds the mapping is called from all of our component's constructors so that the key mapping always takes place. If you were implementing a text component from scratch, you would actually add the key mapping in the text component's UI class. This example adds the mapping here to avoid having to subclass the Windows, Motif, Metal and so on. UI classes for `JTextArea` to achieve the same effect. As noted earlier, this solution is acceptable if the key sequence can be the same across all look-and-feel implementations, or if you only intend to allow your application to use a single look-and-feel.

Text Components, Documents and Editor Kits

`DefaultEditorKit` is only one of the editor kits in the Swing packages. Swing-1.0 includes four editor kits that are used by the different text components. In most cases, the editor kit associated with a text component is fixed because of implementation dependencies and cannot be changed at run time. This is not true, however, for `JEditorPane` and `JTextPane` as you'll see in the next section. The other aspect of a text component that is usually fixed is the type of document that it uses. The document type is actually connected to the editor kit, not the component itself, so each editor kit implements a `createDefaultDocument` method that returns an empty `Document` of the type that it can work with. Thus, with the exception of `JTextPane` and `JEditorPane`, every text component has a fixed editor kit and a fixed document type associated with it, as shown in Table 9-6.

Table 9-6   Components, Editor Kits and Document Types

Component	Editor Kit	Document Type
`JTextField`	`DefaultEditorKit`	`PlainDocument`
`JPasswordField`	`DefaultEditorKit`	`PlainDocument`
`JTextArea`	`DefaultEditorKit`	`PlainDocument`
`JTextPane`	Any editor kit derived from `StyledEditorKit`	Any document type derived from `DefaultStyledDocument`
`JEditorPane`	Varies	Depends on the editor kit

StyledEditorKit is a subclass of DefaultEditorKit that provides extra actions to deal with handling document attributes such as font size, family and style. The actions that it provides, over and above those of DefaultEditorKit, are listed in Table 9-7.

Table 9-7   Actions Implemented by StyledEditorKit

Name	Action
font-family-Helvetica	Select Helvetica font
font-family-Courier	Select Courier font
font-family-TimesRoman	Select Times Roman font
font-size-8	Set font size to 8 points
font-size-10	Set font size to 10 points
font-size-12	Set font size to 12 points
font-size-14	Set font size to 14 points
font-size-16	Set font size to 16 points
font-size-18	Set font size to 18 points
font-size-24	Set font size to 24 points
font-size-36	Set font size to 36 points
font-size-48	Set font size to 48 points
font-bold	Toggle bold attribute on and off
font-italic	Toggle the italic attribute on and off
font-underline	Toggles the underline attribute on and off
left-justify	Left-justify paragraph(s)
center-justify	Center paragraph(s)
right-justify	Right-justify paragraph(s)

There are two more editor kits, HTMLEditorKit and RTFEditorKit, that are used in conjunction with JEditorPane. These editor kits both create documents using DefaultStyledDocument.

Loading and Saving Text Component Content

JTextComponent provides methods that allow you to read the content of a file into a text component, edit it and then save the modified version. Here are their definitions:

```
public void read(Reader in, Object desc) throws IOException;
public void write(Writer w) throws IOException;
```

It is your responsibility to open and close the actual files—JTextComponent just takes care of moving the data between the file and the text control. The read method installs a new Document of the correct type for the current editor kit into which the content is read. These two code extracts show how you might read the content of a file into a text area and then write it out again:

```
JTextArea textArea = new JTextArea(10, 40);
try {
  Reader r = new BufferedReader(new FileReader(fileName));
  textArea.read(r, fileName);
  r.close();
} catch (Throwable t) {
  // Handle IOException or FileNotFoundException
}

// This code would normally be in an event handler
try {
  Writer w = new BufferedWriter(new FileWriter("c:\\temp\\XX"));
  textArea.write(w);
  w.flush();
  w.close();
} catch (Throwable t) {
  // Handle IOException or FileNotFoundException
}
```

The desc argument of the read method can be used to supply a description of the file being read for the benefit of advanced text components that can make use of this information. As an example of its use, JEditorPane, when configured to use HTML, expects to find the URL of the page that has been read in the document property set by this object. Usually, of course, you would let JEditorPane read the file for itself and allow it to set the URL to the one it was supplied when obtaining the page. There is more on this in the discussion of JEditorPane shortly.

Loading and Saving Using the Editor Kit

The methods that you have just seen are actually just simple wrappers that delegate the job of loading and saving the Document to the current editor kit. The EditorKit class defines the following four methods for this purpose:

```
public abstract void read(Reader in, Document doc, int pos)
                    throws IOException, BadLocationException
public abstract void write(Writer out,Document doc,int pos,int len)
                    throws IOException, BadLocationException
public abstract void read(InputStream in, Document doc, int pos)
                    throws IOException, BadLocationException
public abstract void write(OutputStream out, Document doc, int pos, int len)
                    throws IOException, BadLocationException
```

As you can see, these methods allow you to specify which `Document` to read into or write from and to specify a starting position within the document. It is important to note that the first two of these methods deal with Unicode character readers and writers, while the second two use the JDK 1.0-style 8-bit byte-based input and output streams. Usually, you will want to use the first two methods, because the text components work in terms of Unicode and the Java `Reader` and `Writer` classes correctly convert between external encodings and Unicode, taking into account locale-specific file encodings by using encoders and decoders that can be specifically applied to a given `Reader` or `Writer`, or the system default one. By contrast, the second pair of methods just translates bytes from the file into Unicode by expanding the 8-bit input stream to 16-bit Java characters by zero padding the upper 8 bits. While this may be acceptable for a document stored in ASCII format, it is often not correct when there are more than 128 characters in the character set being used.

Core Note

You can read all about Readers, Writers *and converters in* Core Java 1.1 Volume II: Advanced Fundamentals, *published by Prentice Hall.*

If you use the `JTextComponent` methods, then you are bound to supply a `Reader` or a `Writer`, so you will be (indirectly) using the first two methods above. In almost all cases, this is the right thing to do. There is, however, an exception to this rule for Rich Text Format (RTF) files, for which the second two methods must be used. The reason for this is that RTF is actually an 8-bit format that should not be passed through a decoder to turn it into Unicode—the default action of placing 8-bit bytes into 16-bit Java characters is the only appropriate thing to do for RTF files. Indeed, passing an RTF document through a byte-to-Unicode filter that does anything other than this could damage the data represented by the file, especially if it contains binary data such as an embedded image. If you're going to load or save RTF files directly using the editor kit interfaces, you must use the methods that deal with `InputStreams` and `OutputStreams`. Furthermore, since the `JTextComponent` methods don't use these forms, you can only load and save RTF files using the methods provided by the `RTFEditorKit` used by `JEditorPane`; if you try to use the `JTextComponent` methods, you'll just get an `IOException`.

Using JEditorPane

`JEditorPane` is a clever component that uses the full power of the `Document` architecture to make it possible for you to view and even edit data that need not be held in plain text format. In the Swing 1.0 release, `JEditorPane` can handle plain text files, HTML files and files encoded as RTF. To use `JEditorPane`, you need to create an instance of it and then give it some input data in the form of a file or any other resource that can be referenced using a URL. `JEditorPane` determines the type of data it has been given and configures itself appropriately by selecting the correct editor kit and installing a `Document` of the right type.

Creating a JEditorPane

`JEditorPane` has three constructors:

```
public JEditorPane();

public JEditorPane(String url) throws IOException;

public JEditorPane(URL url) throws IOException;
```

The first constructor creates a `JEditorPane` without anything to display. When you create a `JEditorPane` in this way, it installs a `DefaultEditorKit` and a `PlainDocument`, which enables it to handle simple text. The other two constructors initialize the control with the content of a specific document whose location is supplied using either a `URL` object or the string representation of a `URL`. Using these constructors is equivalent to using the default constructor followed by the corresponding form of the `setPage` method that is described below.

Opening a Document in a JEditorPane Using setPage

There are two different ways to arrange for `JEditorPane` to display a particular document. The simplest way is to give it the document's URL and let it do the rest. You'll see how to do that in this section. In the next section, you'll see how the process of initializing a `JEditorPane` actually works. When you know that, you can take more control of the way in which it loads content.

To get `JEditorPane` to display something, you need to use one of the constructors that specifies an initial document to load or one of the following methods:

```
public void setPage(String url);

public void setPage(URL url);
```

Here are two examples that result in the `JEditorPane` loading an HTML page from the Web, assuming that your computer is connected to the Internet. The first example specifies the URL in the well-known string format that you would supply to your browser:

```
JEditorPane p = new JEditorPane("http://www.prenhall.com");
```

Alternatively, you can pass an instance of the `java.net.URL` class to the constructor:

```
URL url = new URL("http://www.prenhall.com");
JEditorPane p = new JEditorPane(url);
```

These constructors are equivalent to the following uses of `setPage`:

```
JEditorPane p = new JEditorPane();

// Load new page by URL string
p.setPage("http://www.prenhall.com");

// Load new page by URL
p.setPage(new URL("http://www.prenhall.com"));
```

The second form of setPage is the more powerful of the two because you can give it a URL constructed by any means. This allows you, for example, to load HTML files (or RTF files) that are held with your Java class files in the same way as you load other resources. Listing 9-15 shows an example of this approach. This example creates a JEditorPane and gives it the URL of an HTML page that you supply as a command line argument. You can see the result of this in Figure 9-11.

Listing 9-15   Using JEditorPane to display a page of HTML

```
package JFCBook.Chapter9;

import com.sun.java.swing.*;
import com.sun.java.swing.text.*;
import java.awt.*;
import java.awt.event.*;
import java.io.*;
import java.net.URL;


public class EditorPaneExample1 extends JEditorPane {
   public static void main(String[] args) {
      try {
         if (args.length != 1) {
            System.out.println("Please supply the URL of an HTML page");
            System.exit(1);
         }

         String url = args[0];
         JFrame f = new JFrame("Editor Pane Example 1");
         JEditorPane ep = new JEditorPane();
         ep.setEditable(false);
         JScrollPane sp = new JScrollPane(ep);
         f.getContentPane().add(sp);

         System.out.println("Before loading page:");
         showInfo(ep);
```

```
        // Have the editor pane load it
        ep.setPage(url);

        System.out.println("\nAfter loading page:");
        showInfo(ep);

        f.setSize(500, 400);
        f.addWindowListener(new WindowAdapter() {
          public void windowClosing(WindowEvent evt) {
            System.exit(0);
          }
        });
        f.setVisible(true);
      } catch (IOException e) {
        System.out.println("Failed to read HTML page");
        System.exit(0);
      }
    }

  public static void showInfo(JEditorPane ep) {
      System.out.println("Document type:    " + ep.getContentType());
      System.out.println("Editor kit:    " + ep.getEditorKit().getClass().getName());
      System.out.println("Document type:    " + ep.getDocument().getClass().getName());
      System.out.println("============================");
    }
}
```

You can run thus program yourself using the command:

```
java JFCBook.Chapter9.EditorPaneExample1 url
```

where `url` is the URL of the HTML page you want to display. For example, if you installed the Swing package at `C:\swing-1.0`, you can view the top-level package list using the following command:

```
java JFCBook.Chapter9.EditorPaneExample1 file:///C:/swing-
1.0/doc/api/packages.html
```

The `JEditorPane` takes care of reading the HTML file and mapping its contents into text and attributes. Note however, that HTML is changing very rapidly and `JEditorPane` will not be able to properly represent the content of all HTML pages.

In the short term, it is probably best to use this control only to display HTML pages that you have complete control of and embed it as part of a larger application using a fixed set of pages, rather than trying to present it as part of a fully-functional Web browser written in Java.

After the `JEditorPane` is created, the program shows you how it is configured by default:

Figure 9-11   Viewing HTML with JEditorPane.

```
Before loading page:
Document type:  text/plain
Editor kit:     com.sun.java.swing.text.DefaultEditorKit
Document type:  com.sun.java.swing.text.PlainDocument
=============================
```

As noted earlier, a default JEditorPane is initialized to handle plain text documents. The document type is a MIME specification for the type of document that the editor can handle. You'll see more about this later. After the setPage operation, however, you can see that the editor has been reconfigured to handle HTML:

```
After loading page:
Document type:  text/html
Editor kit:     com.sun.java.swing.text.html.HTMLEditorKit
Document type:  com.sun.java.swing.text.html.HTMLDocument
=============================
```

If you load a page with hypertext links and click on one of them, you might expect `JEditorPane` to follow the link and load the new page, but it does not: to follow links, you have to catch `HyperlinkEvents` and load the new page yourself, as you'll see later in this chapter.

Configuring JEditorPane for Different Document Types

When you use `setPage` to load a document into a `JEditorPane`, several things happen:

- The `JEditorPane` establishes the type of the document it is about to load.
- Based on the document type, it creates and installs an instance of the appropriate editor kit.
- The `JTextComponent read` method is called to create the correct document type and load the document content.

When you understand how the complete process works, you can change parts of it to load the control in different ways and from different sources. This section explains how each of the steps listed above is performed and then shows you how to load a document from an input stream that is already open instead of using a URL.

Establishing the Document Content Type

Establishing the content type for the document to be loaded is simple when the document source is a URL—it is only necessary to open the document being loaded (via a Web server if the document is being accessed over the Internet) and then calling the `URLConnection getContentType` method. This method returns the MIME type of the object as a `String`. If the object is not being fetched from a Web server because, for example, it is in the local file system or in a JAR file, there will still be a `URLConnection` and the software that supports that `URLConnection` will assign a MIME type to the file based on some criteria. Usually, the MIME type is based on an examination of the object name's suffix or by looking at the first few bytes of its content. However the type is determined, `JEditorPane` uses it to decide how to configure itself. Typical values that will be returned for the MIME type are:

`text/plain`	Plain text, no internal structure
`text/html`	An HTML page
`text/rtf`	A document encoded in RTF format

Creating the Editor Kit

When the content type is known, the `JEditorPane` calls its own `setContentType` method:

```
public void setContentType(String mimeType);
```

The job of this method is simply to create and install the correct editor kit. You can see from the MIME type which editor kit might be a good choice for each content type, but it is not sufficient to hard code a few MIME type to content editor class mappings into the JEditorPane. Instead, there is a cache and a registry that hold these mappings.

The *registry* maps content type name to the name of the class file for the corresponding editor kit. It is initialized with four entries for the types listed above:

text/plain	com.sun.java.swing.text.DefaultEditorKit
text/html	com.sun.java.swing.text.html.HTMLEditorKit
text/rtf	com.sun.java.swing.text.rtf.RTFEditorKit
application/rtf	com.sun.java.swing.text.rtf.RTFEditorKit

Entries in the registry are created using the following method:

```
public void registerEditorKitForContentType
                (String type, String class);
```

You can use this method to install new mappings if you create editor kits of your own.

The *cache* maps object types to instances of editor kits. This cache is managed using the following methods:

```
public void setEditorKitForContentType(String type, EditorKit kit);

public EditorKit getEditorKitForContentType(String type);
```

The JEditorPane only makes direct use of the cache, not the registry. Given a MIME type, it calls getEditorKitForContentType to get a new EditorKit that it can use. This method first looks to see if it has a suitable EditorKit in the cache. If it does, it returns it. If the cache does not have an entry for it, which is always the case when a JEditorPane is first created, the MIME type is passed to the registry. If the type is recognized there, an instance of the class that it maps to is created and then installed, along with the type name, in the cache. Subsequent calls of getEditorKitForContentType with the same MIME type will now find the editor kit in the cache. If the MIME type is not recognized, an instance of DefaultEditorKit is returned. Ultimately, this means that the document will be formatted as plain text, which may or may not be useful.

Creating the Document and Loading the Document Content

Once the content type is known and the editor kit has been obtained, the hard part is over because the editor kit can handle the rest. Only two more steps need to be performed—creating the document and loading the content.

As you already know, every editor kit can create an appropriate Document object for the type of content that it can handle. All that is necessary is to call the editor kit's createDefaultDocument method and install the resulting Document in the JEditorPane using setDocument. The editor kit also knows how to load the document from an input stream or a reader, as was shown earlier in this section. Once the Document has been created, the editor kit read method is called to load the content. In fact, both of these steps are encapsulated in the JTextComponent read method, which is called directly by setPage after the editor kit has been installed by setContentType.

The example in Listing 9-15 is extremely simple, yet it creates an application that can view ordinary text files, HTML files and RTF files. If you want to see how RTF files are handled, you just need to start the program and give it the name of an RTF file—here's an example:

```
java JFCBook.Chapter9.EditorPaneExample1
file:///c:/CoreJFCBook/JFCBook/Chapter9/rtf/LM.rtf
```

When you execute this command, the JEditorPane will open the named file, determine that its content type is text/rtf and configure itself for reading RTF, as you can see from the output it produces. This file contains approximately the same data as the page that was constructed in Listing 9-11.

Core Alert

If you run this example with Swing 1.0.1, you will see a lot of messages in the window from which you run it and the image will not appear. In Swing 1.0, the RTF support is not quite perfect.

Loading a Document from an Input Stream

You've seen how simple it is to open documents in a JEditorPane when you have a URL. Sometimes, however, you won't have a URL. What happens if you just have an input stream to the source of the data? By using what you have already seen, you can easily arrange to have the JEditorPane configure itself and load whatever is on the stream for display.

As you know, to load a document you have to establish the content type, create and install an editor kit, create the correct document type and then finally read the data. Most of this is simple—the only problem is in establishing the content type. If you just have an input stream from the data source, it is almost impossible to establish the data type for certain. Often, you can guess the type by reading a few bytes from the stream and looking at them. There is, in fact, a method of URLConnection that does just that:

```
public static String guessContentTypeFromStream(InputStream is);
```

Because this method is static, you don't need to create a URLConnection object in order to use it. Unfortunately, it only guesses correctly at a small number of content types that are often returned from Web servers. It does not identify RTF documents, for example. When it can't identify the type, it returns null instead of a default guess, which at least allows you to try some guessing of your own! Of course, one approach is to supply the correct content type along with the input stream. If this isn't possible, you just have to hope that guessContentTypeFromStream properly identifies your data.

In the next example, shown in Listing 9-16, you'll see how to load a document from an input stream. To identify the type, guessContentTypeFromStream is indeed used and, if this fails, an additional check for RTF is made by looking at the first few bytes of the file. The code that does this is actually very much like that in guessContentTypeFromStream itself.

Listing 9-16   Using JEditorPane to read an input stream

```java
package JFCBook.Chapter9;

import com.sun.java.swing.*;
import com.sun.java.swing.text.*;
import java.awt.event.*;
import java.io.*;
import java.net.URLConnection;

public class StreamEditorPane extends JEditorPane {
  public void setInputStream(InputStream is) throws IOException,
               BadLocationException {
    String type = guessContentType(is);
    if (type == null) {
      // Unknown type - use plain text
      type = "text/plain";
    }
    System.out.println("File content type is " + type);

    // Set the new content type
    setContentType(type);

    // Now create the appropriate document and install it
    Document doc = getEditorKit().createDefaultDocument();
    setDocument(doc);

    // Finally, read the date from the stream
    getEditorKit().read(is, doc, 0);
  }
```

```java
// Guess the content type
protected String guessContentType(InputStream is) throws IOException {
    String type = URLConnection.guessContentTypeFromStream(is);
    if (type == null) {
        is.mark(5);
        int c1 = is.read();
        int c2 = is.read();
        int c3 = is.read();
        int c4 = is.read();
        int c5 = is.read();
        is.reset();

        if (c1 == '{' && c2 == '\\' && c3 == 'r' && c4 == 't'
            && c5 == 'f') {
            type = "text/rtf";
        }

        // Add more heuristics here
    }

    return type;
}

public static void main(String[] args) {
    if (args.length != 1) {
        System.out.println("Please supply the name of a file to read");
        System.exit(1);
    }

    try {
        InputStream is = new BufferedInputStream(new
                    FileInputStream(args[0]));

        JFrame f = new JFrame("StreamEditorPane Example");
        StreamEditorPane ep = new StreamEditorPane();

        f.getContentPane().add(ep);
        f.setSize(400, 400);
        f.addWindowListener(new WindowAdapter() {
            public void windowClosing(WindowEvent evt) {
                System.exit(0);
            }
        });
        f.setVisible(true);

        // Load the data from the stream
        ep.setInputStream(is);
```

continued

```
  } catch (FileNotFoundException e) {
    System.out.println("Failed to open file " + args[0]);
    System.exit(1);
  } catch (IOException e) {
    System.out.println("Error while reading file " + args[0]);
    System.exit(1);
  } catch (Throwable t) {
    System.out.println("Unexpected exception: " + t);
    System.exit(1);
  }
}
}
}
```

This example creates a control called `StreamEditorPane` that is derived from `JEditorPane` and that can read an input stream for data. The `main` method shows this control in use. Having created a `StreamEditorPane` and placed it on a `JFrame`, the `setInputStream` method is called to identify the type of the input stream and to load the data for display. The first thing this method does is invoke `guessContentType`. As you can see, this simple method first tries to identify the input stream type by using `URLConnection`. If this fails, it reads the first five bytes of the input stream and checks whether they contain the signature that identifies an RTF file. Notice that this is done by using the `InputStream mark` and `reset` methods, which allow you to effectively peek at the content of a stream, while leaving the data in place to be read again later. If this method cannot guess the type of the stream, it returns `null` and the data will be treated as type `text/plain`. On the other hand, if it is RTF, the type `text/rtf` will be returned.

Having identified the type, the rest is easy. The correct editor kit is created and installed by passing the content type to the `setContentType` method, which you've seen before. This method does not, however, create an appropriate document—to do that, the `createDefaultDocument` method of the newly-installed editor kit is called and the `Document` returned is installed in the `JEditorPane` using `setDocument`. Lastly, the data is read from the stream using the editor kit's `read` method, which is given the `InputStream` to use, the `Document` and the position within that document to start loading from.

You can run this example and load an RTF document using the following command:

```
java JFCBook.Chapter9.StreamEditorPane
         C:\CoreJFCBook\JFCBook\Chapter9\rtf\LM.rtf
```

You'll notice that the correct content type is identified and that the document is loaded into the editor pane.

Core Alert

As before, if you run this example with Swing 1.0.1, you will see a lot of messages in the window from which you run it and the image does not appear.

Using JEditorPane to Edit and Save Document Content

The instances of JEditorPane that you have seen so far have been made read-only using setEditable(false). However, it is possible to make a JEditorPane editable simply by calling its setEditable method with argument true, or by doing nothing because the default is for JEditorPane to be editable. When you do this, you can use it to change the content of the document and then write the changed content back. This even works for HTML and RTF, because the packages that support these formats have the ability to generate new HTML or RTF to reflect changes made by the editor.

> **Core Note**
>
> Note, however, that if you make JEditorPane editable, it disables the feature that you'll see in the next section that allows hypertext links to be followed.

The next example is a simple modification of an earlier one that allows you to edit the file and then save it. You supply the file name on the command line, edit it and then use the Save button to write back the modified content to file whose name is the one that was read with the suffix '.new' added. In the real world, of course, you would encapsulate this functionality in an application that used dialogs to allow you to choose the file to open and a different file to write the changes to, if necessary.

Listing 9-17   Using JEditorPane to edit documents

```
package JFCBook.Chapter9;

import com.sun.java.swing.*;
import com.sun.java.swing.text.*;
import java.awt.*;
import java.awt.event.*;
import java.io.*;
import java.net.URL;


public class EditorPaneExample2 extends JEditorPane {
   public static void main(String[] args) {
      try {
         JFrame f = new JFrame("Editor Pane Example 2");
         final JEditorPane ep = new JEditorPane();
         JScrollPane sp = new JScrollPane(ep);
         f.getContentPane().add(sp, "Center");

         JPanel p = new JPanel();
```

```
JButton bw = new JButton("Save (Writer)");
p.add(bw);
JButton bs = new JButton("Save (Stream)");
p.add(bs);
f.getContentPane().add(p, "South");

System.out.println("Before loading page:");
showInfo(ep);

if (args.length != 1) {
  System.out.println("Please supply a file name");
  System.exit(1);
}

fileName = args[0];

bw.addActionListener(new ActionListener() {
  public void actionPerformed(ActionEvent evt) {
    try {
      Writer w = new FileWriter(fileName + ".new");
      ep.write(w);
      w.close();
      System.out.println("Content saved to " + fileName + ".new");
    } catch (Throwable t) {
      System.out.println("Error while saving: " + t);
    }
  }
});

bs.addActionListener(new ActionListener() {
  public void actionPerformed(ActionEvent evt) {
    try {
      OutputStream o = new FileOutputStream(fileName + ".new");
      ep.getEditorKit().write(o, ep.getDocument(), 0,
              ep.getDocument().getLength());
      o.close();
      System.out.println("Content saved to " + fileName + ".new");
    } catch (Throwable t) {
      System.out.println("Error while saving: " + t);
    }
  }
});

// Have the editor pane load the document
ep.setPage("file:///" + fileName);

// Make the content editable
```

```
      ep.setEditable(true);

      System.out.println("\nAfter loading page:");
      showInfo(ep);

      f.setSize(500, 400);
      f.addWindowListener(new WindowAdapter() {
        public void windowClosing(WindowEvent evt) {
          System.exit(0);
        }
      });
      f.setVisible(true);
    } catch (IOException e) {
      System.out.println("Failed to read HTML page");
      System.exit(0);
    }
  }

  public static void showInfo(JEditorPane ep) {
    System.out.println("Document type:   " + ep.getContentType());
    System.out.println("Editor kit:    " +
            ep.getEditorKit().getClass().getName());
    System.out.println("Document type: " +
            ep.getDocument().getClass().getName());
    System.out.println("============================");
  }

  public static String fileName;
}
```

To run this example, use the command:

```
java JFCBook.Chapter9.EditorPaneExample2 filename
```

where *filename* is the *full* path name of the file you want to read, for example:

```
java JFCBook.Chapter9.EditorPaneExample2
            C:\CoreJFCBook\JFCBook\Chapter9\rtf\LM.rtf
```

The setPage method is used to load the file into the editor pane and the document is made writable using the setEditable method. There are two Save buttons in this program's user interface: One saves the content using a Writer, the other using an OutputStream. You can see how this is implemented by looking at the actionPerformed methods connected to the two buttons. The Writer case is easy, because the JTextComponent write method does all the work—all that is necessary is to create the file to be written to. The OutputStream case is a little harder. Because there isn't a JTextComponent method that writes to OutputStreams, you have to go directly to the editor kit's write method.

Why are there two Save buttons in this program? You can see the reason if you try to save an RTF file using the Writer button. Because RTF is an 8-bit format, it won't allow you to save via a Writer—if you try, you'll get an error message. To save RTF documents, you have to use an OutputStream and, as noted earlier, you can't use the JTextComponent write method to do this.

JEditorPane Events

JEditorPane can generate an event when an attempt is made to change the displayed page due to the installed editor kit detecting the activation of a hyperlink in the current document. Theoretically, any editor kit could define a meaning for this event and provide a means to jump between documents but in Swing-1.0, only the HTML editor kit makes use of it.

If an HTML page with a hypertext link in it is displayed in a JEditorPane, the HTML editor kit generates a HyperlinkEvent when the hypertext link is activated. As well as the usual source, this event contains a type field and the URL of the target of the link. You can extract these values using the following HyperlinkEvent methods:

```
public EventType getEventType();
```

```
public URL getURL();
```

There are, theoretically, three types of event that can be generated:

```
HyperlinkEvent.EventType.ENTERED
```

```
HyperlinkEvent.EventType.ACTIVATED
```

```
HyperlinkEvent.EventType.EXITED
```

In fact, though, only EventType.ACTIVATED is actually generated, at the point that the user clicks on the hypertext link.

Clicking on the link does not, however, change the active page and neither does JEditorPane register to receive this event to perform the switch. If you want to follow hypertext links, you have to register a HyperlinkListener and change to the new page yourself. The HyperlinkListener interface has only one method:

```
public interface HyperlinkListener {
    public void hyperlinkUpdate(HyperlinkEvent evt);
}
```

You register to receive these events using the following JEditorPane methods:

```
public void addHyperlinkListener(HyperlinkListener l);
```

```
public void removeHyperlinkListener(HyperlinkListener l);
```

Core Alert

Hyperlinks are followed only if the `JEditorPane` *is not editable. Therefore, you must create your editor pane like this:*

```
JEditorPane pane = new JEditorPane();
pane.setEditable(false);
```

If you leave out the second line, clicking on hyperlinks will have no effect.

The following code extract demonstrates how you might register to receive `HyperlinkEvents` and use the `ACTIVATED` event to change the active page. The variables ep and f in this code refer to the `JEditorPane` and its enclosing `JFrame`, respectively.

```
// Add a Hyperlink listener
ep.addHyperlinkListener(new HyperlinkListener() {
  public void hyperlinkUpdate(HyperlinkEvent evt) {
    System.out.println("Hyperlink event, source: " +
                  evt.getSource());
    System.out.println("URL: " + evt.getURL());
    System.out.println("=====================");

    URL thisPage = ep.getPage();
    Cursor oldCursor = f.getCursor();
    try {
      f.setCursor(Cursor.getPredefinedCursor(Cursor.WAIT_CURSOR));

      // Switch to the new page
      ep.setPage(evt.getURL());
    } catch (IOException e) {
      System.out.println("Page switch failed - revert to old page");
      try {
        ep.setPage(thisPage);
      } catch (IOException ioexc) {
        System.out.println("Failed to revert to old page");
      }
    } finally {
      f.setCursor(oldCursor);
    }
  }
});
```

The code is quite straightforward. When the event is received, the type is checked. If it is an ACTIVATED event, the cursor is changed to the WAIT_CURSOR (because the page switch could take a short time), the target URL is extracted and setPage is used to move to the new page. An attempt at error recovery is provided by saving the original page URL and attempting to restore it if the new page cannot be loaded for some reason.

You can try this code out for yourself with the following command:

```
java JFCBook.Chapter9.EditorPaneExample3 URL
```

where *URL* is the full URL of an HTML page with a hypertext link in it. If you have the Swing package installed in c:\swing-1.0, then you could use the following command line:

```
java JFCBook.Chapter9.EditorPaneExample3
            file:///C:/swing-1.0/doc/api/packages.html
```

to bring up the documentation index page and then follow the links from there. Each time you activate a link, the program prints a representation of the event that it gets and then switches to the new page. Here is some sample output showing one HyperlinkEvent:

```
Hyperlink event, source: com.sun.java.swing.JEditorPane[,0,0,489x370]
Hyperlink event type: ACTIVATED
URL: file:/c:/swing-1.0/doc/api/Package-com.sun.java.swing.html
======================
```

Note that the target of a hypertext link need not be an HTML document. Because setPage can change the style of the JEditorPane to suit the content type it is given, the target document could be HTML, RTF or plain text. Furthermore, since the document switch happens under your control, you could intervene to prevent the loading of specific documents based on their content type or some or all of the URL.

Summary

This chapter introduced the full range of Swing text controls, from the simple text input field to the powerful JTextPane and JEditorPane.

The chapter started by looking at JTextField and JTextArea as replacements for their AWT counterparts then showed a variant of JTextField called JPasswordField that doesn't echo the characters typed into it. This control replaces the passwordlike functionality of the AWT TextField that is not supported by its direct replacement JTextField.

The main theme of the second half of the chapter was an examination of the internals of the Swing text components, to reveal the underlying structures that enable the more powerful components to support multiple fonts and colors at the same time and to embed images and components in documents. While this material was very detailed, it is essential to have at least seen it in order to make best use of the `JTextPane` control. You saw an impressive use of `JTextPane` that included an image map that had the ability to move the reader to another part of the document, much like HTML hyperlinks and, finally, looked at `JEditorPane`, which is capable of rendering real HTML and Rich Text Format and has the capability to be extended to support other document encodings via suitable editor kits.

THE TREE
CONTROL

Topics in This Chapter

- Creating and Working with Trees
- A File System Tree Control
- Customizing the Tree Control
- Tree Editing
- Trees and Custom Objects

10

This chapter takes an in-depth look at `JTree`, one of the two Swing components that manage data. `JTree` is intended to represent information that has a hierarchical structure, of which the prototypical example is a file system. You'll see how simple it is to create a basic `JTree` and look at the ways in which the user can interact with the control to expose and hide data and to have the application operate on the objects that the tree's content represents.

A large part of this chapter is devoted to developing a control that allows you to display the contents of a file system in the form of a tree. While building this control, you'll learn how to use many of the tree's powerful features and, when it's finished, you'll have a component that you can extend or used directly in your own applications.

Finally, `JTree` allows you to take over the job of rendering individual display elements. The second half of this chapter looks at how this can be achieved and how to allow the user to directly edit the tree's data.

The Tree Control

The `JTree` component is the first of two controls that you'll meet in this book that are intended to present views of large amounts of data. The difference between `JTree` and the other control, `JTable`, is that the former is well-suited to handling data that is hierarchical in nature, while the latter is used with information that can be organized into rows and columns. The most familiar example of a tree control is probably the one in the left pane of Windows Explorer, which shows a directory view of a file system. Later in this section, you'll see how to implement a Java version of this control, which is pictured in Figure 10-1.

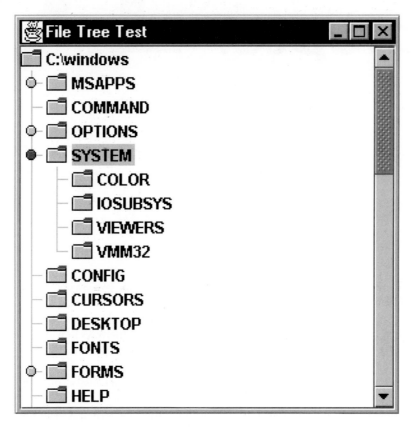

Figure 10-1   A tree showing a file system.

Tree Nodes

All trees start with a root node, which is customarily shown at the top left of the control. By default, when you create a JTree, the root is visible, together with the objects in the level immediately below it. Figure 10-1 shows a view of part of the C: drive of my laptop. In this case, the C:\WINDOWS directory is the root and the directories that reside within it are shown below and to the right of it. The Metal, Motif and Windows look-and-feel classes all represent each node in the tree using both an icon and a text string. In the case of a file system, the natural way to use the text string is to display the name of the directory that corresponds to the node, while the icon shows either an open or closed folder, depending on whether the contents of the directory are visible or not.

Core Note

The descriptions that are given in this section, unless otherwise qualified, relate to the appearance of the control when the Metal look-and-feel is installed. Installing a different look-and-feel can have a radical effect on the way the tree looks and there can even be variations within a single look-and-feel, as you'll see.

It is simple and routine to change the text string that describes the node. Changing the icon is a topic that will be left until the end of the chapter, so most of the examples will have the usual folder representation, whether or not they represent a file system.

Tree nodes may or may not have other nodes, known as *child* nodes, linked beneath them. Each node that has child nodes can be considered to be the root of a sub-tree. For example, in Figure 10-1, the node C:\WINDOWS\SYSTEM has four child nodes beneath it and can be thought of as the root of the subtree composed of itself and those nodes.

Nodes that are at the same level of the tree are displayed in a vertical line so that, in the case of a file system tree, all of the directories directly below the root are shown one above the other. As you move further to the right on the screen, you are moving further down the file system hierarchy, until you reach a node that doesn't have any nodes attached below it. Such nodes are often called *leaf* nodes, because they reside at the very end of a sequence of *branches* that join nodes to each other. In the case of JTree, however, a node that doesn't have any nodes below it need not be a leaf node, as you'll see. As far as the tree is concerned, whether or not a given node is a leaf matters only so far as it affects the icon used to represent it—leaf nodes are typically represented by a black dot or a folded sheet of paper instead of the folder used to represent the other nodes.

Nodes at the same level are typically connected to each other by a vertical dashed line as shown in Figure 10-1; each node at that level connects to the vertical line with a small horizontal dashed line. If the node does not have any nodes below it, the horizontal and vertical lines just meet at a point, as is the case with the node C:\WINDOWS\CONFIG in Figure 10-1. At the intersection point for a node that does have other nodes below it in the hierarchy is a small circle, whose color depends on whether these nodes are visible. Assuming these nodes are not visible, clicking on this circle makes the tree expand to the right to show the next level of nodes, and downward to make room for the nodes that have just become visible to be stacked vertically. In Figure 10-1, the node C:\WINDOWS\SYSTEM has been expanded in this way to show its child nodes. Notice that the node C:\WINDOWS\CONFIG has moved downward to make room for the children of C:\WINDOWS\SYSTEM, and that the circle to the left of the expanded node is not the same color as the others. Clicking on this circle will cause the child nodes to disappear and the nodes at C:\WINDOWS\CONFIG and below to move upward to occupy the free space. There is never more than one node on any given row.

Tree Appearance

To emphasize how dependent the appearance of a tree and its nodes are on the selected look-and-feel, let's look at some of the possible variations. Figure 10-1 shows a tree with the Metal look-and-feel selected. The same tree in the Windows look-and-feel is shown in Figure 10-2, while the Motif version can be seen in Figure 10-3.

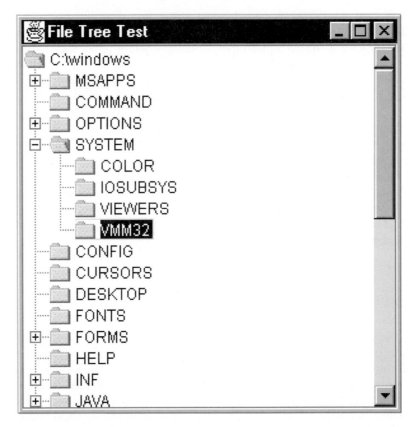

Figure 10-2   A tree as drawn by the Windows look-and-feel.

It's pretty evident that there are differences between these figures and Figure 10-1. As you can see, Windows and Motif use boxes to indicate nodes that have children. When the children are invisible, the expansion box has a plus sign to indicate that there is more of the tree to be viewed; when you open such a node to show its children, the plus sign changes to a minus sign, as you can see in the case of the C:\WINDOWS\SYSTEM node. The icons are also subtly different and the line styles vary between look-and-feel implementations.

It is even possible to have different representations of the same tree within a single look-and-feel. The tree has a client property called lineStyle that is used to control the lines drawn between nodes. This property is currently supported only by the Metal look-and-feel, but there is nothing about the mechanism used to implement it that binds it to a single look-and-feel, so you may find it implemented more widely in the future. The lineStyle property has three possible values, listed in Table 10-1.

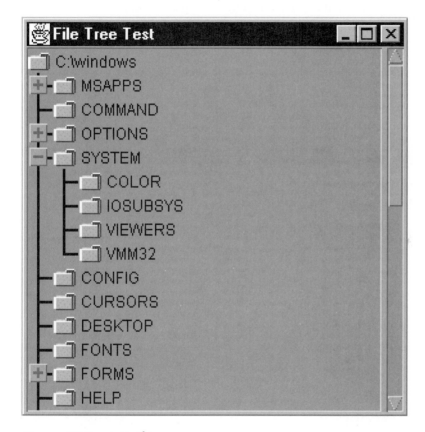

Figure 10-3   A Motif tree.

Table 10-1	LineStyle Settings

Setting	Effect
None	No lines are drawn anywhere on the tree.
Angled	Vertical lines between nodes at the same level, horizontal line to child node.
Horizontal	A single horizontal line between nodes immediately attached to the root node. This is the default setting.

Figure 10-1 shows a tree with the Angled setting, which is the most natural way to represent a file system and is most like the appearance of Windows and Motif trees. This configuration can be obtained using code like this:

```
JTree tree = new JTree();
tree.putClientProperty("JTree.lineStyle", "Angled");
```

Similar code is required to obtain the other two possible effects. The same tree rendered with lineStyle set to None is shown in Figure 10-4 and with lineStyle set to Horizontal in Figure 10-5. Because Horizontal is the default, all of your trees will look like the one in Figure 10-5 if you don't explicitly select a lineStyle (or choose a look-and-feel other than Metal). Since lineStyle is ignored by look-and-feel implementations that don't provide it, it is always safe to set a specific value no matter which look-and-feel is selected.

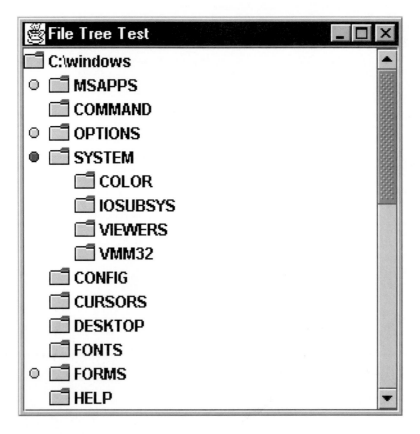

Figure 10-4   A Metal tree with line style 'None'.

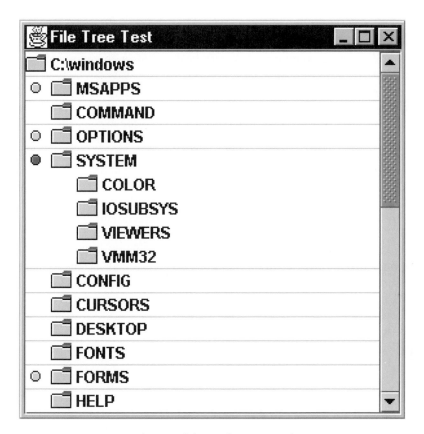

Figure 10-5   A Metal tree with line style 'Horizontal'.

Tree Node Selection

The mouse can be used to select an item from the tree by clicking on the icon or the text. Clicking twice on either of these is the same as clicking on the expansion circle—the node either expands or collapses depending on its current state. The ability to make a selection is the main reason for using a tree control. As you'll see, you can attach listeners that receive notification when a selection is made and you can also arrange to be notified when part of the tree is expanded or collapsed.

Elements of the Tree

Now let's turn to how a tree is represented in terms of data structures. The only elements of any substance in a tree are the nodes themselves—the way in which these nodes relate to each other is represented by references from one node to another.

The JTree control doesn't directly manage the nodes themselves, or remember how they are organized. Instead, it delegates this to its data model.

As with the other Swing components, JTree deals mainly with generic objects that are represented in Java by an interface. For example, any class can be used as a data model for the tree, so long as it implements the TreeModel interface and any class can participate in the model as a node in the tree so long as it implements the interface TreeNode. This design pattern has been shown before in connection with JComboBox and JList, which have data models specified as interfaces and concrete implementations of those interfaces that are used by default. The JTree (and, to some extent JTable), is a little different from JComboBox and JList in that it is not really good enough to just implement the TreeNode and TreeModel interfaces. The default implementations of these interfaces in the Swing tree package provide facilities far beyond those specified by TreeNode and TreeModel. Furthermore, in many cases, these extra facilities can be accessed directly or through the JTree object, so that there will be a loss of functionality if classes that only implement the minimal interface are used instead of the default ones. In practice, all tree nodes are likely to be instances of the class DefaultMutableTreeNode, while the model will probably be derived from DefaultTreeModel.

JTree is unlike JComboBox and JList in another way. When you create either of the latter two, you populate the model and then wait for a selection. The item that is retrieved from the control as the user's selection is of the same type as the data held within the model itself. For example, a list box populated with Strings would return a selected item of type String. With JTree, things are not so simple. The model deals in terms of nodes, but the user interface to the tree uses a class called TreePath and the immediate result of a selection is one or more TreePaths. As you'll see later, there is a way to map from a TreePath to the corresponding TreeNode, which means that it is possible, from an event listener, to get back to the original node in the data model. This node is not, however, of any direct use to the selection event handler unless some information has been stored with the node that is of meaning to the user of the tree. Suppose, for example, that you construct a tree that shows the content of a file system in a file open dialog and the user double-clicks on an item to have it returned to the tree user as the selected file. There are two ways that the interface to the user of this tree could be built—either the name of the selected file would be returned, or alternatively you could choose to return an object that represents the file that was stored with the file's node when the tree was created. The second of these alternatives is obviously more powerful. To make such an implementation possible, the tree nodes allow you to store a reference to an arbitrary object, the *user object*, with each node. How you use this is up to you—you might just choose to make it the file's name, or it might be a java.io.File object for the file.

Creating a Tree

JTree has no less than seven constructors, most of which allow you to initialize the data model with a small quantity of data taken from the more common data collection classes in the JDK:

```
public JTree();

public JTree(Hashtable);

public JTree(Vector);

public JTree(Object[]);

public JTree(TreeModel);

public JTree(TreeNode);

public JTree(TreeNode, boolean);
```

The first constructor gives you a tree with a small data model already installed; this can be useful when you write your first program that uses a tree, but after that you'll probably never use it again. The next three constructors initialize the tree from a Hashtable, a Vector, and an array of arbitrary objects. Since all of these are flat data structures, the resulting tree is also flat, consisting of a root node and the data from the object passed to the constructor attached to it, with one node per entry in the table, vector or array. Figure 10-6 shows a tree created from a Hashtable containing five entries.

Figure 10-6   A tree created from a Hashtable.

The code that was used to create this tree is shown in Listing 10-1.

Listing 10-1   Creating a Tree with a Hashtable

```
package JFCBook.Chapter10;

import com.sun.java.swing.*;
import com.sun.java.swing.tree.*;
import java.util.*;

public class HashHandleTree {
  public static void main(String[] args) {
    JFrame f = new JFrame("Tree Created From a Hashtable");
    Hashtable h = new Hashtable();
    h.put("One", "Number one");
    h.put("Two", "Number two");
    h.put("Three", "Number three");
    h.put("Four", "Number four");
    h.put("Five", "Number five");
    JTree t = new JTree(h);
    t.putClientProperty("JTree.lineStyle", "Angled");

    t.setShowsRootHandles(false);
    f.getContentPane().add(t);
    f.pack();
    f.setVisible(true);
  }
}
```

As you can see from Figure 10-6, the tree displays all of the items from the hashtable. Each item has been turned into a leaf node and added directly beneath the root node of the tree. However, since a root node was not explicitly supplied, the tree doesn't display one. A consequence of this is that you can't collapse this tree. You can force the root node to be displayed by using the JTree setRootVisible method:

```
t.setRootVisible(true);
```

This would show the root node as an open folder labeled root, with an expansion icon to the left of it. If you don't want to show the expansion icon, you can disable it using setShowsRootHandles:

```
t.setShowsRootHandles(false);
```

Figure 10-7 shows two trees, both with the root node visible. The left-hand tree was created with setShowsRootHandles(true) and the right one with setShowsRootHandles(false).

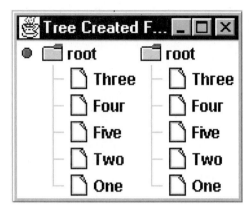

Figure 10-7   A tree with the root visible.

You can expand or collapse the tree by double-clicking on the root folder or its label. In cases like this where the root node was created automatically, the arbitrary label `root` is assigned to it. You can, if you wish, change this label or remove it entirely. You'll see how to do this later.

You'll notice that the items in the tree are not ordered in a particularly sensible way. This happens because hashtables don't maintain the order of the items that you place into them. The tree is constructed by getting an enumeration of the items in the hashtable, which doesn't guarantee any particular ordering. If you care about the order in which the data is displayed, you should use a `Vector` or an array.

Most trees will be created using one of the last three constructors, which require a complete tree model or at least the root node to have already been constructed. If you choose to supply a model, you can use the Swing `DefaultTreeModel` class, or create your own as long as it implements the `TreeModel` interface. For most purposes, `DefaultTreeModel` is more than adequate and, as mentioned earlier, it offers useful facilities over and above the basic interface, many of which will be used in this chapter.

TreeNode Interface

Whether or not you explicitly supply the model, you will need to create the root node and attach to it all the data for the tree. All nodes are based on the `TreeNode` interface, which has seven methods:

```
public Enumeration children()

public boolean getAllowsChildren()

public TreeNode getChildAt(int index)

public int getChildCount()
```

```
public int getIndex(TreeNode child)

public TreeNode getParent()

public boolean isLeaf()
```

With the exception of `isLeaf`, all of these methods are concerned with the relationship between a node and its parent and children. Every node (apart from the root node) has exactly one parent and may have any number of children. If the node is a leaf node, it doesn't have children. It is also possible to have a type of node that shouldn't be considered to be a leaf when the tree draws its on-screen representation, but still doesn't allow child nodes to be connected to it. Nodes with this property return `false` to the `getAllowsChildren`, as should any node that can only be a leaf (such as a node representing a file in a file system). Child nodes are ordered within their parent, because the ordering might be important to the data that is being represented. Because of this property, it is possible to get the `TreeNode` object for a child at a given index within the parent's collection (using `getChildAt`) or the index for a particular child node (from `getIndex`). The `getParent` method returns a node's parent node. In the case of the root node, this returns `null`. Finally, `getChildCount` returns the number of children directly connected to a node. This value does not include grandchildren and more distant descendants.

As you can see, `TreeNode` is a read-only interface. To make changes to a node or its position in the tree, you need an instance of `MutableTreeNode`, an interface that extends `TreeNode`. Usually, the nodes that you actually create will be instances of `DefaultMutableTreeNode`, which is the Swing class implementing `MutableTreeNode` so that it is usually possible to get a writable reference to any node even if you're only given a `TreeNode` reference by casting this reference to a `MutableTreeNode`. If you don't have prior knowledge of the type of node you are dealing with (perhaps because you're writing code to drive a third-party tree-based component), you should check that your `TreeNode` is an instance of `Mutable-TreeNode` before doing this.

MutableTreeNode

The `MutableTreeNode` interface adds the following methods to `TreeNode`:

```
public void insert(MutableTreeNode child, int index)

public void remove(int index)

public void remove(MutableTreeNode node)

public void removeFromParent()

public void setParent(MutableTreeNode parent)

public void setUserObject(Object userObject)
```

By contrast to `TreeNode`, these methods are entirely concerned with creating and changing the parent-child relationships between nodes. The `insert` method adds the given node as a child of the node against which it is invoked, specifying the index that should be used for the child. `DefaultMutableTreeNode` provides a more convenient way of adding children that doesn't require you to keep track of indices, as you'll see shortly. The `remove` methods disconnect a node from its parent given either the node reference or an index. Whichever variant of `remove` you use, you must invoke this method against the parent of the node that you want to remove. To remove a child node without a reference to its parent, invoke `removeFromParent` against the node itself.

The `setParent` method sets the reference from a child to its parent. You are very unlikely to want to use this method, however, because it doesn't make the parent itself aware of the child. This method is really intended for use in the implementation of the other `MutableTreeNode` methods, such as `insert`.

The last method in this interface is `setUserObject`, which associates an arbitrary object with the node. This is, in fact, the only way to make a node useful. The other methods of `MutableTreeNode` deal with the construction of the tree: This method allows you to say what the objects in the tree represent. In the examples shown above, the strings `One`, `Two`, `Three` and so on were the useful content of the tree (although 'useful' might not be the right word in the case of this trivial example). They are stored in the tree as the user objects of the nodes that represent them. If you use the `DefaultMutableTreeNode` class to create your nodes, you supply the user object to the constructor, and you can also use the `setUserObject` method to change the associated object later.

Now let's look at the `DefaultMutableTreeNode` class which, as has been said, implements a superset of the `MutableTreeNode` interface. Unless you're implementing a very lightweight tree and have special requirements, it's not worth considering implementing your own `MutableTreeNode` class. All of the examples in this chapter will directly use or derive from `DefaultMutableTreeNode`.

Core Note

While this section is concerned with tree nodes as part of the `JTree` *component, it is worth bearing in mind that the tree model can be used on its own without reference to the tree control. You could, for example, use* `DefaultTree-Model` *to implement a tree to hold information used internally by your application. If you intend to do this and memory is a concern, you might consider implementing a lightweight implementation of* `MutableTreeNode` *that suits your specific requirements.*

`DefaultMutableTreeNode` has too many methods to list them all here—refer to the API specification if you want to see what they all are. Many of them will be covered here and in the following sections.

DefaultMutableTreeNode

The first thing we're going to do with this class is to show you how to use it to build a simple tree from scratch. `DefaultMutableTreeNode` has three constructors:

```
public DefaultMutableTreeNode()

public DefaultMutableTreeNode(Object userObject)

public DefaultMutableTreeNode(Object userObject, boolean
            allowsChildren)
```

The first constructor creates a node with no associated user object; you can associate one with the node later using the `setUserObject` method. The other two connect the node to the user object that you supply. The second constructor creates a node to which you can attach children, while the third can be used to specify that child nodes cannot be attached by supplying the third argument as `false`.

Using `DefaultMutableTreeNode`, you can create nodes for the root and for all of the data you want to represent in the tree, but how do you link them together? You could use the `insert` method that we saw above, but it is simpler to use the `add` method:

```
public void add(MutableTreeNode child);
```

This method adds the given node as a child of the node against which it is invoked and at the end of the parent's list of children. By using this method, you avoid having to keep track of how many children the parent has. This method, together with the constructors, gives us all you need to create a workable tree.

To begin to create a tree, you need a root node:

```
DefaultMutableTreeNode rootNode = new DefaultMutableTreeNode();
```

Below the root node, two more nodes are going to be added, one to hold details of the Apollo lunar flights, the other with information on the manned Skylab missions. These two nodes will be given meaningful text labels:

```
DefaultMutableTreeNode apolloNode = new DefaultMutableTreeNode("Apollo");
DefaultMutableTreeNode skylabNode = new DefaultMutableTreeNode("Skylab");
```

The nodes are then added directly beneath the root node:

```
rootNode.add(apolloNode);
rootNode.add(skylabNode);
```

Under each of these nodes, a further node will be added for each mission and beneath each of these a leaf node for each crew member. There's an implementation of this in the example programs that you can run using the command:

```
java JFCBook.Chapter10.TreeExample1
```

The result of running this example is shown in Figure 10-8.

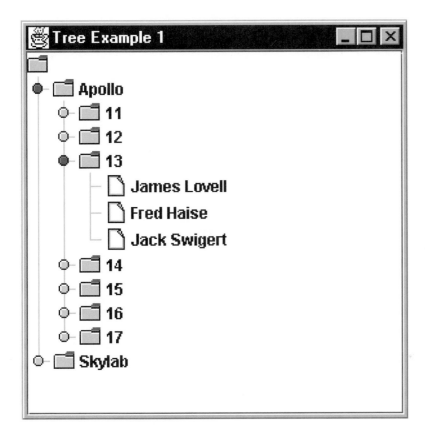

Figure 10-8   A tree built using DefaultMutableTreeNodes.

This program shows a root folder with no associated label and nodes labeled Apollo and Skylab. Clicking on the expansion icons of either of these opens it to show the numbered missions, and clicking on any of these shows the crew for that flight. Let's look at an extract from the source of this example:

```java
import com.sun.java.swing.*;
import com.sun.java.swing.tree.*;

public class TreeExample1 extends JTree {
  public TreeExample1() {
    DefaultMutableTreeNode rootNode = new DefaultMutableTreeNode();
    DefaultMutableTreeNode apolloNode =
             new DefaultMutableTreeNode("Apollo");
    rootNode.add(apolloNode);

    DefaultMutableTreeNode skylabNode =
      new DefaultMutableTreeNode("Skylab");
```

```
      rootNode.add(skylabNode);

      // CODE OMITTED

      this.setModel(new DefaultTreeModel(rootNode));
   }

   public static void main(String[] args) {
      JFrame f = new JFrame("Tree Example 1");

      TreeExample1 t = new TreeExample1();
      t.putClientProperty("JTree.lineStyle", "Angled");
      t.expandRow(0);

      f.getContentPane().add(new JScrollPane(t));
      f.setSize(300, 300);
      f.setVisible(true);
   }
}
```

This class is defined as an extension of JTree, which allows the creation of its data to be encapsulated within it. The root node and all of the child nodes are created and a tree structure is built from the nodes as described earlier. The JTree needs a data model in order to display anything, so the last step of the constructor is to install a model that contains the structure that has just been created:

```
this.setModel(new DefaultTreeModel(rootNode));
```

This creates a new DefaultTreeModel and initializes it with our root node, then uses the JTree setModel method to associate the data model with the tree. Since our class is derived from JTree, its default constructor will have been invoked at the start of our constructor. As noted earlier, this creates a tree with a model containing dummy data. When setModel is called at the end of the constructor, this data is overwritten with the real data.

Another way to create a JTree is to directly pass it the root node. If you use this method, it creates a DefaultTreeModel of its own and wraps it around the node that you pass to its constructor. Here's a short example of that:

```
DefaultMutableTreeNode rootNode = new DefaultMutableTreeNode();
DefaultMutableTreeNode apolloNode = new DefaultMutableTreeNode("Apollo");
DefaultMutableTreeNode skylabNode = new DefaultMutableTreeNode("Skylab");
rootNode.add(apolloNode);
rootnode.add(skylabNode);
JTree t = new JTree(rootNode);
```

If you look at the main method in the code extract shown above, you'll notice the following line after the tree was created:

```
t.expandRow(0);
```

This line ensures that row 0 of the tree is expanded to display the children that the node on that row contains.

Apart from when you create it, the `JTree` control doesn't deal with nodes directly. Instead, you can address items in the tree and obtain information about them using either their `TreePath` or their row number. Let's look at the row number first. The row number refers to the number of the row on the screen at which the node in question appears. There is only one node ever on any row, so specifying the row identifies a node without any ambiguity. Furthermore, provided it's actually displayed, row 0 is always occupied by the root node. The problem with using row numbers is that the row numbers for all of the others can change. When you start `TreeExample1`, the root node is on row 0, the "Apollo" node on row 1, and the "Skylab" node occupies row 2. However, if you click on the expansion icon for "Apollo," the "Skylab" node moves downward and, in this case, becomes row number 5, because the "Apollo" nodes open to show three child nodes, which will occupy rows 2, 3 and 4. Because keeping track of row numbers is not very convenient, it is more usual to deal in terms of `TreePaths` when using `JTree`.

The TreePath Class

If `DefaultMutableTreeNode` is the physical representation of a node, then `TreePath` is its logical representation. Instead of pointing you directly at the node, it tells you the node's "address" within the tree. So long as the node itself and its parents are not moved within the tree, its `TreePath` will remain constant and can always be used to address it. `TreePath` has two constructors:

```
public TreePath(Object singlePath)
public TreePath(Object[] paths)
```

A `TreePath` stores an array of objects that somehow describe the path; the second constructor sets up this array from its argument, while the first is a convenience method that creates an array of length 1 and initializes it with the single object passed as the argument. `TreePath` has the following methods:

```
public boolean equals(Object)
public Object getLastPathComponent();
public Object getPathComponent(int index);
public int getPathCount();
public Object[] getPath();
public boolean isDescendant(TreePath treePath)
public String toString()
```

None of these methods are concerned with what the objects that the `TreePath` stores actually are—they just treat them as anonymous objects. The `equals` method returns `true` if the object passed as its argument is another `TreePath` with an object array of the same length as its own and for which the result of comparing each object in its own array with the corresponding object in the other array (using the equals method the objects being compared) returns true.

The getPath method just returns the array of objects installed by the constructor, while getLastPathComponent returns the last object in the array. In the case of a TreePath representing a set of directories from a file system tree ending in a file, this method would return the object that corresponds to the file itself. Similarly, getPathCount returns the number of objects in the path and getPathComponent returns a single component of that path given its index, where 0 is the component at the root.

The isDescendant method determines whether the TreePath passed as its argument represents a descendant of the TreePath against which it is invoked. This will be true if the TreePath passed as the argument has at least as many objects in its array as the TreePath against which this method is invoked, and each of the objects in the invoked TreePath's array is equal to the corresponding object in the array of the proposed descendant. Finally, the toString method prints a readable representation of the TreePath by invoking the toString methods of each object in its array and concatenating them, separated by commas.

The TreePath doesn't care what the objects that it manipulates are, but *you* need to know what they are in order to make much use of a TreePath. The objects that TreePath actually stores are the TreeNodes for each node of the tree between the root and the object that the TreePath relates to. In most cases (and in all of the examples in this chapter), this object will actually be a MutableTreeNode. This means that, in an event handler that receives a TreePath in its event, you can access the information from the data model that the event relates to, including the user object associated with the node. You'll see when looking at the file system tree component that is developed later in this chapter why this is a useful feature.

Let's look at what a TreePath is made up of by using an example. TreeExample2 is a development of the last example in which the tree is built and then, every 30 seconds, the TreePath object for whatever is on row 4 of the tree's display is obtained and its content is printed. Here is the interesting part of this program:

```
for (;;) {
  Thread.sleep(30000);

  // Get TreePath for row 4
  TreePath p = t.getPathForRow(4);
  if (p == null) {
    System.out.println("Nothing on row 4!");
    continue;
  }

  // Print the official description of "p"
  System.out.println("===================\n" + p);
```

```
  // Now look inside
  Object[] o = p.getPath();
  for (int i = 0; i < o.length; i++) {
    System.out.println("Class: " + o[i].getClass() +
        "; value: " + o[i]);
    if (o[i] instanceof DefaultMutableTreeNode) {
      Object uo = ((DefaultMutableTreeNode)o[i]).getUserObject();
      if (uo != null) {
        System.out.println("\tUser object class: " +
            uo.getClass() +     "; value: " + uo);
      }
    }
  }
}
```

The `TreePath` for whatever is on row 4 is obtained by using the `getPathForRow` method of `JTree`. If the row is empty, as it will be when you start the program, this method returns `null`, so a message is printed and nothing further happens for another 30 seconds. Otherwise, the `TreePath toString` method is used to see its own description of itself, then `getPath` is called to get its array of objects. For each object returned in this array, its Java class and its value are printed. If any object that is obtained from the array is a `DefaultMutableTreeNode`, its `getUserObject` method is called to get the user object associated with the node and, if there is one, its class and its value are also printed. You can run this example yourself by typing:

```
javac JFCBook.Chapter10.TreeExample2
```

Following are the results of three iterations around the loop with three different directories expanded to place different objects on row 4 of the display.

```
====================
AbstractTreePath: VN 1890214 {null, Skylab, 3}
Class: class com.sun.java.swing.tree.DefaultMutableTreeNode; value: null
Class: class com.sun.java.swing.tree.DefaultMutableTreeNode; value:
        Skylab
          User object class: class java.lang.String; value: Skylab
Class: class com.sun.java.swing.tree.DefaultMutableTreeNode; value: 3
          User object class: class java.lang.String; value: 3
====================
AbstractTreePath: VN 1891634 {null, Apollo, 13}
Class: class com.sun.java.swing.tree.DefaultMutableTreeNode; value: null
Class: class com.sun.java.swing.tree.DefaultMutableTreeNode; value: Apollo
          User object class: class java.lang.String; value: Apollo
Class: class com.sun.java.swing.tree.DefaultMutableTreeNode; value: 13
          User object class: class java.lang.String; value: 13
```

```
====================
AbstractTreePath: VN 1892234 {null, Apollo, 12, Pete Conrad}
Class: class com.sun.java.swing.tree.DefaultMutableTreeNode; value: null
Class: class com.sun.java.swing.tree.DefaultMutableTreeNode; value: Apollo
       User object class: class java.lang.String; value: Apollo
Class: class com.sun.java.swing.tree.DefaultMutableTreeNode; value: 12
       User object class: class java.lang.String; value: 12
Class: class com.sun.java.swing.tree.DefaultMutableTreeNode; value: Pete Conrad
       User object class: class java.lang.String; value: Pete Conrad
```

The toString method of TreePath prints the path to the node that was on row 4. In fact, you can see that the object is actually an instance of AbstractTreePath, a subclass of TreePath implemented by the tree control's basic look-and-feel class. Next, the objects that correspond to the various parts of the path are shown. As you can see, there is one object for each node in the path, starting at the root and ending with the node that corresponds to the TreePath. As noted above, these objects are actually the nodes that were stored in the DefaultTreeModel, so they are all instances of DefaultMutableTreeNode and invoking toString on them prints the string that was supplied to the constructor that created them. Finally, each of these nodes, apart from the root node, has an associated user object that, as you can see, is the same string. This is not, however, a surprise, because the DefaultMutableTreeNode constructor that was used described its argument as the user object associated with the node. In fact, the toString method of DefaultMutableTreeNode just invokes the toString method of the user object if there is one and returns an empty string if there isn't. This explains why the DefaultMutableTreeNode returns the string passed to its constructor.

Incidentally, we now have the information needed to modify one of our earlier example programs so that the string root doesn't appear next to the root node on the display, as it did in Figure 10-7. In that example, the root nodes were not explicitly created by the program: Because each JTree was built by passing a Hashtable to its constructor, the root nodes were built for us. The string displayed for the root node is the result of invoking toString against that node. You now know that, because this node is a DefaultMutableTreeNode, its toString method will delegate to that of its user object if there is one and return an empty string otherwise. When the root nodes in Figure 10-7 were created, the string root was assigned as the user object, so to make it disappear, you just have to use the setUserObject method to set the user object to null.

Here is how you would create a tree that shows a root folder without the root label:

```
JTree t = new JTree(h);
t.setShowsRootHandles(false);
t.setRootVisible(true);

// Remove the 'root' label
Object rootNode = t.getModel().getRoot();
((DefaultMutableTreeNode)rootNode).setUserObject(null);
```

This code gets the root node from the model by using the `TreeModel getRoot` method; it gets the model itself from the `JTree` using the `getModel` method. `getRoot` actually returns an `Object`, but you know that the root node is a `DefaultMutableTreeNode`, so all you have to do is cast it and use `setUserObject` to remove the `root` string. You can use the same technique to assign an arbitrary label to the root node.

What is a Leaf?

The Metal look-and-feel displays nodes that it considers to be leaves using what looks like a sheet of paper instead of a folder icon. How does it determine that the node is a leaf? There are two methods in the `TreeNode` interface that determine whether a node is a leaf:

```
public void getAllowsChildren()
public void isLeaf()
```

If you think of the tree of Apollo and Skylab missions and their astronauts, the astronauts are represented as leaf objects. This is correct, because it is not our intention to add further nodes below those representing the astronauts. In cases like this, it is acceptable to determine that a node is a leaf simply because it doesn't actually have any children. Contrast this, however, with a file system. If a file system were represented by a tree control (an example of which you'll see later), you would expect files to be leaf objects, but you would always expect a directory to be represented as a folder, whether or not it contain any files or subdirectories. In this case, it is not sufficient to rely on the number of children that the node has.

As relying on the count of children is acceptable to determine whether a node is a leaf, the `isLeaf` method returns the appropriate answer, because the default implementation in `DefaultMutableTreeNode` returns `true` if the node that it is applied to does not have children and `false` if it does. This explains why the astronauts all appeared as leaf nodes even though nothing special was done when creating their nodes.

For nodes like directories, a more appropriate check is whether the node is *allowed* to have child nodes attached to it. If it isn't, then it must be a leaf and vice versa. The `getAllowsChildren` method is used to allow the node to return this information. `DefaultMutableTreeNode` supplies a default implementation that returns the value of the node's `allowsChildren` variable, which is initially `true`, indicating that the node is not a leaf.

The next problem, given that there are two ways to find out whether a node is a leaf, is how the tree knows which method is the appropriate one to use. This problem is handled by `DefaultTreeModel`, which maintains a boolean instance variable called `asksAllowsChildren`, which is initialized to `false` by default. `DefaultTreeModel` has two constructors:

```
public DefaultTreeModel(TreeNode rootNode);
```

```
public DefaultTreeModel(TreeNode rootNode, boolean
            asksAllowsChildren)
```

If the second constructor is used, you can supply `true` as the second argument to indicate that all nodes in the model should have their `getAllowsChildren` method called to determine whether they should be considered a leaf. If `asksAllowsChildren` is `false`, the node's `isLeaf` method is always used. To achieve the correct effect, you need to use the correct tree model constructor and set this variable appropriately.

The value of this variable is only used in the `DefaultTreeModel isLeaf` routine:

```
public boolean isLeaf(Object node);
```

This method checks the `asksAllowsChildren` variable and returns the value of either `isLeaf` or `getAllowsChildren`, having invoked it on the `TreeNode` given as the argument. This method, then, returns the correct value whichever way the tree nodes are using to indicate whether they are leaf nodes.

Core Alert

Despite appearances, the argument supplied to this method must be a `TreeNode`, *or you'll get a* `ClassCastException`.

If you are using the `getAllowsChildren` method to determine whether a node is a leaf, you need to set the node's `allowsChildren` value properly when you create it. Alternatively, you can use the `setAllowsChildren` method to change it after construction.

Expanding and Collapsing a Tree

Even if you never change the content of a tree after creating it, trees are not static objects. Once it has been displayed, the user can change a tree's appearance by expanding and collapsing nonleaf nodes to show or hide different levels of the tree. This section shows you what possibilities there are for expanding and traversing a tree and looks at the events that these actions generate.

Tree Expansion and Traversal

When a tree is first created, unless you take special action, one level of nodes is visible. By default, you'll just see the root node but, if you hide the root node using `setRootVisible(false)`, the first level of nodes below the root is shown instead. Nodes that have children are rendered with an expansion icon, which you can use to make their child nodes visible. When you click on the icon, the next level of nodes is drawn and the icon changes its appearance to indicate that a second click will reverse the process and collapse the node. Another way to expand or collapse a subtree is to double-click on the icon or the text instead of clicking the expansion box.

It is also possible to navigate the tree using the keyboard. To see how this works, run the `TreeExample1` program that was shown earlier:

```
java JFCBook.Chapter10.TreeExample1
```

When this starts, you'll see the root node and two child nodes labeled `Apollo` and `Skylab`. Provided you don't click the mouse, none of these items will be highlighted. Now press the right-arrow key on your keyboard and a small box will appear around the root node, indicating that it has been selected. Pressing the down arrow now moves the selection to the `Apollo` node and repeating it carries the selection down to `Skylab`. Similarly, the up arrow key moves the selection back up.

Now use the up and down arrow keys to highlight `Apollo` and then press the right arrow. This causes the `Apollo` node to expand and display its child nodes. With these nodes exposed, the down key now moves you not to `Skylab`, but to `11`, the first child node of `Apollo`. In fact, the up and down keys just move the selection up and down by one row on the screen. If you leave the selection on `11` and press the right arrow key, this node opens to expose the names of the crew of Apollo 11. With these nodes visible, press the left arrow key. This collapses the subtree rooted at `11`, but leaves `11` selected. So it appears that the left and right arrows just expand and collapse a node's subtree. However, if you press the right arrow with the selection on `11` to expand its child nodes, then press it again, the selection moves to the first child. In other words, the left and right arrow keys open and close a subtree if they can, but if the subtree is already open or closed, these keys behave like the up and down arrows, respectively.

You can also use the HOME, END, PAGE DOWN and PAGE UP keys to navigate a tree. The HOME key moves the selection back to the root, or whichever node is at the top of the tree if the root node is hidden, while END moves it to the last row of the tree. PAGE DOWN and PAGE UP scroll the tree down or up by a page. To see this, expand the tree completely and, if necessary, resize the window until the vertical scrollbar appears so that you have more in the viewport than can be displayed on one page, then press PAGE DOWN.

Expanding and Collapsing Nodes under Program Control

`JTree` provides a set of methods that you can use to expand or collapse parts of the tree and to find out whether a given node is expanded or not. These methods are listed in Table 10-2.

Table 10-2 Expanding and Collapsing Nodes in a Tree	
Method	*Description*
public void expandRow (int row)	Expands the node currently on the given row of the screen
public void collapseRow (int row)	Collapses the node on the given row
public void expandPath (TreePath path)	Expands the node with the given TreePath
public void collapsePath (TreePath path)	Collapses the node with the given TreePath
public boolean isExpanded (int row)	Determines whether the node on the given row is expanded
public boolean isCollapsed (int row)	Determines whether the node on the given row is collapsed
public boolean isExpanded (TreePath path)	Determines whether the node with the given TreePath is expanded
public boolean isCollapsed (TreePath path)	Determines whether the node with the given TreePath is collapsed

The isExpanded and isCollapsed methods just return a boolean that indicates whether the node is currently expanded or collapsed. You can address the node either using its screen row (which is rarely likely to be a useful option), or its TreePath, which is more useful because it is independent of how much of the tree is expanded at any given time. Notice, however, that there is no method that can be used with a TreeNode, because these are JTree methods and JTree doesn't deal with TreeNodes, except in its constructor. However, if you have a TreeNode, you can get the corresponding TreePath using the following code:

```
// This only works if "node" is a DefaultMutableTreeNode.
DefaultMutableTreeNode node = ……. // Initialize to point to a
                                   // node in the tree

TreeNode[] pathToRoot = node.getPath();
TreePath path = new TreePath(pathToRoot);
```

Given a node, the DefaultMutableTreeNode getPath method returns the ordered set of nodes that lead to it from the root of the tree. For example, in the case of TreeExample1, the ordered set of nodes that would be returned by getPath for the node corresponding to Neil Armstrong would be:

```
root
Apollo
11
Neil Armstrong
```

Using a set of nodes, you can create a `TreePath` by using the constructor that takes an array of objects—as you saw earlier, the objects that make up a `TreePath` are actually just the `TreeNodes` in the path that it represents. This is a general method for mapping from a node to a `TreePath`, but it only works with a `DefaultMutableTreeNode` because neither the `TreeNode` nor the `MutableTreeNode` interface requires the implementation of the `getPath` method that was used to get the array of nodes.

The `collapseRow` and `collapsePath` methods perform the obvious functions. Again, you must know either a row number or a `TreePath` to use these methods. Nothing happens if the node is already collapsed.

To expand a node, you use either `expandRow` or `expandPath`. If the node has any children and it is not already expanded, its immediate children are displayed. If you want to expand more of the tree, you will need to apply the expand methods to subsequent levels. If the node that is the target of these methods is not itself visible when asked to expand, the parts of the tree that lead to it will first be expanded to make it visible. For example, if the example tree were completely closed and you asked for the node `11` to be expanded, the root node would be expanded to show `Apollo` and `Skylab`, then `Apollo` would be expanded to show all of the mission numbers, including `11`, and finally `11` would expand to show `Neil Armstrong`, `Buzz Aldrin` and `Michael Collins`. In this case, expanding a node and then collapsing it does not leave the tree in the same state as it started, because the nodes above `11` would not be collapsed.

Tree Expansion Events

Every time a node in the tree is expanded or collapsed, a `TreeExpansionEvent` is generated. You can receive these events by registering a `TreeExpansionListener` on the `JTree` itself. The `TreeExpansionListener` interface has only two methods:

```
public void treeExpanded(TreeExpansionEvent event)
public void treeCollapsed(TreeExpansionEvent event)
```

The `TreeExpansionEvent` contains a source field that corresponds to the `JTree` itself and a `TreePath` that represents the node was expanded or collapsed. You can obtain the source of the events using the usual `getSource` method and the path using `getPath`:

```
public TreePath getPath();
```

Sometimes, expanding a path can generate more than one event, because it may be necessary to expand other nodes to make the target node visible. To see the events that are generated when this happens, we created a modified version of `TreeExample1` that registers a `TreeExpansionListener` and prints the events that it receives. Here is the snippet of code that was added to implement the listener:

```
t.addTreeExpansionListener(new TreeExpansionListener() {
  public void treeExpanded(TreeExpansionEvent evt) {
    System.out.println("Expansion event, path " + evt.getPath());
  }

  public void treeCollapsed(TreeExpansionEvent evt) {
    System.out.println("Collapse event, path " + evt.getPath());
  }
});
```

You can run the modified version of the program using the command:

```
javac JFCBook.Chapter10.TreeExample3
```

The code was also changed so that the tree starts with only the root visible by adding the line:

```
t.collapseRow(0);
```

If you expand and collapse nodes in the tree, you'll see the events that are generated displayed in the window from which you started the program. Notice that there is one event generated each time you expand or collapse a node. This remains true even if you open the whole tree and then collapse it by double-clicking on the root node. The event that you get contains a `TreePath` for the root: You don't get events for all of the other nodes that disappeared. This is actually reasonable, because if you expand root again, you'll find that the tree returns to its fully expanded state—in other words, the other nodes didn't actually collapse. As well as adding a listener, code was also added to expand the node corresponding to `Neil  Armstrong`, which runs after a 15-second delay. Here is the extra code for this:

```
try {
  Thread.sleep(15000);
  DefaultMutableTreeNode rootNode =
        (DefaultMutableTreeNode)t.getModel().getRoot();
  DefaultMutableTreeNode apolloNode =
        (DefaultMutableTreeNode)rootNode.getFirstChild();
  DefaultMutableTreeNode apollo11Node =
        (DefaultMutableTreeNode)apolloNode.getFirstChild();
  DefaultMutableTreeNode target =
        (DefaultMutableTreeNode)apollo11Node.getFirstChild();

  // Convert the node to a TreePath
```

```
    TreeNode[] pathToRoot = target.getPath();
    TreePath path = new TreePath(pathToRoot);

    // Expand the node
    t.expandPath(path);
} catch (InterruptedException e) {
}
```

The first problem is to find the node that needs to be opened. This is achieved by getting the root node from the tree's model and then using the `getFirstChild` method of `DefaultMutableTreeNode` to walk down through the various levels until the target is reached. `DefaultMutableTreeNode` has several methods that allow you to access related nodes—look at its API documentation to find out what they are.

Having found the target node, it must be converted to a `TreePath`, for which the technique shown earlier is used, then the node can finally be expanded. If you start the program and do nothing for 15 seconds, you'll find that the tree opens to show the crew of Apollo 11, and three events are generated, one for each level above the target that is expanded automatically:

```
Expansion event, path AbstractTreePath: VN 1888450 {null}
Expansion event, path AbstractTreePath: VN 1888453 {null, Apollo}
Expansion event, path AbstractTreePath: VN 1890108 {null, Apollo, 11}
```

Notice that no event is generated for the actual node that was explicitly expanded (`Neil Armstrong`). Since this is a leaf node, it can't actually expand. A request to expand a leaf node is equivalent to asking for it to be made visible.

Selecting Items in a Tree

If you want a tree to be useful for user feedback, you need to be allow the user to select items and to take action when those selections are made. The tree, like `JList`, has a separate selection model that offers several different selection modes. This section looks at how to control and respond to a selection within a tree.

Selection and the TreeSelectionModel

`JTree` delegates management of the selection to a selection model. By default, an instance of the class `DefaultTreeSelectionModel` is associated with the tree when it is created, but you can, if you wish, define your own selection model, as long as it implements the `TreeSelectionModel` interface. You can switch in your custom selection model using the `setSelectionModel` method. In this section, it is assumed that the default selection model is in use.

The selection model can be configured to operate in one of three different modes:

SINGLE_TREE_SELECTION. Only one node from the tree can be selected at any given time.

CONTIGUOUS_TREE_SELECTION. Any number of nodes can be selected, as long as they occupy adjacent rows.

DISCONTIGUOUS_TREE_SELECTION. Any number of nodes can be selected, with no restriction on location relative to other nodes.

The default mode is DISCONTIGUOUS_TREE_SELECTION.

Changes in the selection can be made either under program control or by the user. No matter how the selection is changed, the selection model ensures that any changes fit in with the current selection mode. Changing the selection also generates an event, as you'll see later.

The user can create or change the selection by using the mouse. Clicking on a node will make the selection contain just that single node. Clicking on another node removes the first node from the selection and selects only the item just clicked on. Selection of a single item in this way is always possible, unless there is no selection model, in which case no selection is allowed. You can create this situation with the following lines of code:

```
JTree t = new JTree()
t.setSelectionModel(null);      // No selection allowed
```

Holding down the CTRL key while clicking on a node adds that node to the selection, leaving the existing content of the selection intact. If the node clicked on is already in the selection, it is removed. However, there are some restrictions on this, depending on the selection mode:

- If the selection mode is SINGLE_TREE_SELECTION, the CTRL key is ignored—that is, if there is already a node in the selection it is de-selected and the new node replaces it.

- If the selection mode is CONTIGUOUS_TREE_SELECTION, the new node must be adjacent to the row or rows that make up the current selection. If this is not the case, the selection is cleared and the new node becomes the only member of the selection.

- If the selection mode is CONTIGUOUS_TREE_SELECTION and the first or last row in the selection is clicked with CTRL pressed, that node is removed from the selection leaving the rest of the nodes selected.

- If the selection mode is CONTIGUOUS_TREE_SELECTION and the node clicked is one of the selected nodes but is not at the top or bottom of the selected range, the selection is cleared. The node clicked is not added to the selection.

Holding down the SHIFT key while clicking creates a contiguous selection between two selected nodes. This is not allowed if the selection model is in SIN-GLE_TREE_SELECTION mode; instead, the clicked node becomes the selected node.

When a selection is made, the path most recently selected is often the one of most interest to the application. This path is called the *lead* path and its TreePath or row number can be specifically requested by the program using the getLeadSelectionPath or getLeadSelectionRow methods (see Table 10-3).

Core Note

There is one case in which the lead row is not the last row selected—see the discussion of tree selection events below for details.

There is a collection of methods, listed in Table 10-3, that can be used to query or change the selection. All of these methods are provided by the DefaultTreeSelectionModel, but they can also be accessed, for convenience, via JTree.

Table 10-3   Methods Used to Manage the Selection

Method	*Description*
public TreePath getLeadSelectionPath()	Returns the path for the lead selection
public int getLeadSelectionRow()	Returns the row number for the lead selection
public int getMaxSelectionRow()	Returns the highest selected row number
public int getMinSelectionRow()	Returns the lowest selected row number
public int getSelectionCount()	Gets the number of selected items
public TreePath getSelectionPath()	Returns the TreePath object for the first item in the selection
public TreePath[] getSelectionPaths()	Returns the TreePath objects for all of the selected items
public int[] getSelectionRows()	Returns the row numbers of all of the items in the selection
public boolean isPathSelected (TreePath path)	Returns true if the given path is selected, false if not.

continued

Table 10-3 Methods used to Manage the Selection (continued)	
Method	*Description*
public boolean isRowSelected(int row)	Returns true if the given row is selected, false if not.
public boolean isSelectionEmpty()	Returns true if there are no selected items
public void clearSelection()	Removes all items from the selection
public void removeSelectionInterval (int row0, int row1)	Removes the rows in the given range from the selection
public void removeSelectionPath (TreePath path)	Removes one path from the selection
public void removeSelectionPaths (TreePath[] paths)	Removes the listed paths from the selection
public void removeSelectionRow (int row)	Removes the given row from the selection
public void removeSelectionRows (int[] rows)	Removes the listed rows from the selection
public void addSelectionInterval (int row0, int row1)	Adds the rows in the given range to the current selection
public void addtSelectionPath (TreePath path)	Adds the given path to the selection
public void addSelectionPaths (TreePath[] path)	Adds the given set of paths to the selection
public void addSelectionRow(int row)	Adds the object on the given row to the selection
public void addSelectionRows(int[] row)	Adds the objects in the given rows to the selection
public void setSelectionInterval (int row0, int row1)	Makes the selection equal to all rows in the given range
public void setSelectionPath (TreePath path)	Makes the selection be the given path
public void setSelectionPaths (TreePath[] path)	Sets the selection to the given set of paths
public void setSelectionRow(int row)	Sets the selection to the object on the given row
public void setSelectionRows(int[] row)	Sets the selection to the objects in the given rows

The selection can span many rows of a tree; an extreme case would be opening the whole tree, clicking on the root node, then scrolling to the bottom of the tree and holding down SHIFT while clicking on the last node which, unless the tree is in SINGLE_TREE_SELECTION mode, would select every node in the tree. Keep in mind, however, that only nodes that are visible can be selected using the mouse: Selecting a node that has child nodes does not select any of the child nodes (and vice versa). Also, if you select a node or nodes in a subtree and then collapse that subtree so that those nodes are no longer visible, they become deselected and the selection passes to the root of the closed subtree, whether or not it was selected when the node was collapsed.

Tree Selection Events

A change in the selection is reported using a `TreeSelectionEvent`. To receive these events, you must register a `TreeSelectionListener` using the `addTreeSelectionListener` method of your tree's `TreeSelectionModel`, or the convenience method of the same name provided by `JTree`. The `TreeSelectionListener` interface has only one method:

```
public void valueChanged(TreeSelectionEvent evt)
```

You need to inspect the accompanying event to determine what changes were made to the selection.

`TreeSelectionEvents` tell you exactly which paths are involved in the last change of selection and whether they were added or removed from the selection. You can also get the leading path and the old leading path from the event. The important methods supplied by `TreeSelectionEvent` are shown in Table 10-4.

Table 10-4   Methods Used with Tree Selection Events

Method	*Description*
`public TreePath[] getPaths`	Returns the paths for all of the nodes that were either selected or deselected in the last selection change.
`public boolean isAddedPath` `(TreePath path)`	Assuming that `path` represents a node affected by this event, this method returns `true` if the node was added to the selection and `false` if it was removed from the selection.
`public TreePath getPath()`	Returns the first `TreePath` in the set that would be returned by `getPaths`. This is a convenience method for the case where you know there is only one path of interest.

continued

Table 10-4 Methods Used with Tree Selection Events (continued)	
Method	*Description*
`public boolean isAddedPath()`	Returns `true` if the path returned by `getPath` was added to the selection and `false` if it was removed.
`public TreePath` `    getOldLeadSelection()`	Returns that path for the node that was the leading path before this event.
`public TreePath` `    getNewLeadSelection()`	Gets the path for the node that is now the lead path.

The simplest way to understand how `TreeSelectionEvents` work is to see an example. The program `JFCBook.Chapter10.TreeSelectionEvents` uses the tree that has been used throughout this chapter, together with some code to receive and print the contents of selection event:

```
t.addTreeSelectionListener(new TreeSelectionListener() {
  public void valueChanged(TreeSelectionEvent evt) {
    System.out.println("=======\nFirst path: " + evt.getPath()
          + "; added? " + evt.isAddedPath());
    System.out.println("Lead path: " + evt.getNewLeadSelectionPath());
    System.out.println("Old Lead path: " + evt.getOldLeadSelectionPath());

    TreePath[] paths = evt.getPaths();
    for (int i = 0 ; i < paths.length; i++) {
      System.out.println("Path: < " + paths[i] + "; added? " +
        evt.isAddedPath(paths[i]));
    }
  }
});
```

The listener is added using the `addTreeSelectionListener` method of `JTree`. Another way to do this is to register with the selection model itself:

```
TreeSelectionModel m = t.getSelectionModel();
```

```
m.addTreeSelectionModel(new TreeSelectionListener() {
```

In the event handler, the various paths are extracted and displayed, along with the flag indicating whether they were added or removed from the selection. To see some typical events, run the program and open the tree by expanding the `Apollo` node, the `11` node and the `12` node; you should now have 16 rows on the screen.

First, select `Neil Armstrong`. Not surprisingly, this generates an event in which all the entries refer to this node:

```
First path: AbstractTreePath: VN 1891099 {null, Apollo, 11,
          Neil Armstrong}; added? true
```

```
Lead path: AbstractTreePath: VN 1891099 {null, Apollo, 11,
           Neil Armstrong}
Old Lead path: null
Path: < AbstractTreePath: VN 1891099 {null, Apollo, 11,
           Neil Armstrong}; added? True
```

Next, click `Buzz Aldrin`, causing this entry to be selected and the previous one deselected. This time, the event contains entries for both paths:

```
First path: AbstractTreePath: VN 1891117 {null, Apollo, 11,
           Buzz Aldrin}; added? True
Lead path: AbstractTreePath: VN 1891117 {null, Apollo, 11,
           Buzz Aldrin}
Old Lead path: AbstractTreePath: VN 1891099 {null, Apollo, 11,
           Neil Armstrong}
Path: < AbstractTreePath: VN 1891117 {null, Apollo, 11,
           Buzz Aldrin}; added? True
Path: < AbstractTreePath: VN 1891099 {null, Apollo, 11,
           Neil Armstrong}; added? false
```

Here, the first path and the lead path are the one that has just been added, the old lead path is the lead path from the previous event, and the complete set of paths affected contains both the selected and the deselected path, together with booleans that indicate which of the two has just been selected. As long as you can be sure that only one item is being selected at a time (for example, if you use single-selection mode), each event will be self-contained and will tell you all you need to know about the state of the selection, as this one does. Things aren't always so simple, however. Now that you've got one path selected, hold down the CTRL key and click on `Pete Conrad`. This gives a selection of two individual items, but the event that it generates is not so obviously informative:

```
First path: AbstractTreePath: VN 1891880 {null, Apollo, 12,
           Pete Conrad}; added? True
Lead path: AbstractTreePath: VN 1891880 {null, Apollo, 12,
           Pete Conrad}
Old Lead path: AbstractTreePath: VN 1891117 {null, Apollo, 11,
           Buzz Aldrin}
Path: < AbstractTreePath: VN 1891880 {null, Apollo, 12,
           Pete Conrad}; added? True
```

You can see that `Pete Conrad` has just been added to the selection and that `Buzz Aldrin` must also be in the selection because that entry used to be the leading path, but note that the complete set of paths reported doesn't include `Buzz Aldrin`. This is because a `TreeSelectionEvent` only reports *changes* to the selection—anything that doesn't change is not mentioned. To emphasize this further, hold down CTRL and click `Alan Bean`. This gives three selected items and the following event:

```
First path: AbstractTreePath: VN 1891898 {null, Apollo, 12,
           Alan Bean}; added? True
Lead path: AbstractTreePath: VN 1891898 {null, Apollo, 12,
           Alan Bean}
```

```
Old Lead path: AbstractTreePath: VN 1891880 {null, Apollo, 12,
          Pete Conrad}
Path: < AbstractTreePath: VN 1891898 {null, Apollo, 12,
          Alan Bean}; added? true
```

Now, there's no mention of `Buzz Aldrin` at all and the set of paths still contains only the one entry. This is, of course, because only one path changed state.

Using the mouse with no modifiers or with the `CTRL` key pressed always generates events with only either one or two entries in the paths list. You can get events with more entries if you use the `SHIFT` key to select a range of items. To see an example, hold down the `SHIFT` key and click on `Apollo`. The `SHIFT` key selects all items between itself and the top of the existing selection if it is above the selection, or the bottom of the selection if it is below it. In this case, the selection will contain the items `Apollo`, `11`, `Neil Armstrong` and `Buzz Aldrin`, the last of which was the top member of the selection before the selection changed. Here is the event that is created for this selection:

```
First path: AbstractTreePath: VN 1888449 {null, Apollo};
          added? true
Lead path: AbstractTreePath: VN 1888449 {null, Apollo}
Old Lead path: AbstractTreePath: VN 1891898 {null, Apollo, 12,
          Alan Bean}
Path: < AbstractTreePath: VN 1888449 {null, Apollo};
          added? true
Path: < AbstractTreePath: VN 1890400 {null, Apollo, 11};
          added? true
Path: < AbstractTreePath: VN 1891099 {null, Apollo, 11,
          Neil Armstrong}; added? true
Path: < AbstractTreePath: VN 1891880 {null, Apollo, 12,
          Pete Conrad}; added? false
Path: < AbstractTreePath: VN 1891898 {null, Apollo, 12,
          Alan Bean}; added? false
```

As expected, the node that was clicked on, `Apollo`, is the lead path and is listed as having been added, along with the node for `Neil Armstrong`. The list of paths also includes the two that were deselected and reports the fact that they were deselected. So far, the lead path has always been the last path that was selected and this is usually the case, but there is an exception. Hold down the `SHIFT` key again and click on `Alan Bean`, to create another block selection. You might expect that `Alan Bean` would now be the lead path, but the event says otherwise:

```
First path: AbstractTreePath: VN 1891125 {null, Apollo, 11,
          Michael Collins}; added? true
Lead path: AbstractTreePath: VN 1891117 {null, Apollo, 11,
          Buzz Aldrin}
Old Lead path: AbstractTreePath: VN 1888449 {null, Apollo}
Path: < AbstractTreePath: VN 1891125 {null, Apollo, 11,
          Michael Collins}; added? true
Path: < AbstractTreePath: VN 1890418 {null, Apollo, 12};
          added? true
```

```
Path: < AbstractTreePath: VN 1891880 {null, Apollo, 12,
           Pete Conrad}; added? true
Path: < AbstractTreePath: VN 1891898 {null, Apollo, 12,
           Alan Bean}; added? true
Path: < AbstractTreePath: VN 1888449 {null, Apollo};
           added? false
Path: < AbstractTreePath: VN 1890400 {null, Apollo, 11};
           added? false
Path: < AbstractTreePath: VN 1891099 {null, Apollo, 11,
           Neil Armstrong}; added? false
```

The lead path is, in fact, `Buzz Aldrin`, the path at the top of the block selection. For block selections, this appears to be the rule because, as you saw in the previous example, if you click above the selection with `SHIFT` held down, the path that was clicked on, which will be at the top of the new block, is the lead path.

Finally, note that a `TreeSelectionEvent` is delivered only if the selection changes. To see this, click on `Richard Gordon`. This clears the old block selection and selects just one entry. Now click on `Richard Gordon` again. This time, you don't get an event—there is nothing to report because nothing has changed. To see why this is important, double-click on `Apollo`. This delivers just one event. Double-click again and you get no event at all. Many programs allow the user to pick an object from a list by double-clicking: This isn't going to be possible if you rely on `TreeSelectionEvents` to tell you that this has happened.

To make it possible to choose an item in this way, you have to register a listener for mouse events, detect a double click and convert the mouse location to a tree path for yourself. Fortunately, `JTree` has a convenience method that converts coordinates to a path in the tree, from which, as we know, you can get the node itself if you need it. Here's an example of the code that you would use to implement this:

```
// Here, 't' is a JTree. It must be declared as final
// so that we can use it in the event handler -
//        final JTree t;
t.addMouseListener(new MouseAdapter() {
  public void mouseClicked(MouseEvent evt) {
    if (evt.getClickCount() == 2) {
      // A double click - get the path
      TreePath path = t.getPathForLocation(evt.getX(), evt.getY());

      // Add here the code to use the path.
    }
  }
});
```

If you don't need (or want) to keep track of exactly which paths have been affected by an event, you can just treat the event as notification that something has changed and query the tree model for the selected paths, as long as the model is derived from `DefaultTreeModel`. The methods that you can use, which are also implemented by `JTree` for convenience, were shown earlier in Table 10-4.

Traversing a Tree

Sometimes it is necessary to be able to traverse some or all of a tree, or to be able to search a subtree. The TreeNode interface allows you to find the parent of a given node and to get an enumeration of all of a node's children, which is all you need to implement your own searching mechanism. If all you can be sure of is that your tree is populated with TreeNodes (which is always a safe assumption), then you will have to be satisfied with the rather primitive getParent and children methods. On the other hand, if your tree is composed of DefaultMutableTreeNodes, you can make use of the following more powerful methods to traverse the tree or a subtree in various different orders:

```
public Enumeration pathFromAncestorEnumeration(TreeNode ancestor)

public Enumeration preorderEnumeration()

public Enumeration postorderEnumeration()

public Enumeration breadthFirstEnumeration()

public Enumeration depthFirstEnumeration()
```

The pathFromAncestorEnumeration method is a little different from the other four, so we deal with it separately. This method involves two nodes—the one against which it is invoked (the target node) and the one passed as an argument, which *must* be an ancestor of the first node. If it is not, an IllegalArgumentException is thrown. Assuming that the ancestor is valid, this method walks the tree between it and the target node, adding to the enumeration each node that it encounters on the way. The first entry in the enumeration is the ancestor given as an argument and the last item is the target node itself. The other items in the enumeration are returned in the order in which they were encountered in the tree—in other words, each node is the parent of the one that follows it in the enumeration.

Of the other four enumerations, depthFirstEnumeration is the same as postOrderEnumeration. To see how the others order the nodes in the subtree that they cover, Listing 10-2 shows a short program that creates a small tree and applies preorderEnumeration, postorderEnumeration and breadthFirstEnumeration to its root node. You can run this program for yourself by typing:

```
java JFCBook.Chapter10.TreeEnumerations
```

Listing 10-2   Various tree traversal enumerations

```java
package JFCBook.Chapter10;

import com.sun.java.swing.*;
import com.sun.java.swing.tree.*;
import java.util.*;

public class TreeEnumerations {
  public static void main(String[] args) {
    JFrame f = new JFrame("Tree Enumerations");
```

```
   DefaultMutableTreeNode rootNode = new DefaultMutableTreeNode("Root");

   for (int i = 0; i < 2; i++) {
     DefaultMutableTreeNode a = new DefaultMutableTreeNode("" + i);
     for (int j = 0; j < 2; j++) {
       DefaultMutableTreeNode b = new DefaultMutableTreeNode("" + i +
"_" + j);
       for (int k = 0; k < 2; k++) {
         b.add(new DefaultMutableTreeNode("" + i + "_" + j + "_" + k));
       }

       a.add(b);
     }
     rootNode.add(a);
   }

   JTree t = new JTree(rootNode);
   f.getContentPane().add(new JScrollPane(t));
   f.setSize(300, 300);
   f.setVisible(true);

   // Now show various enumerations
   printEnum("Preorder", rootNode.preorderEnumeration());
   printEnum("Postorder", rootNode.postorderEnumeration());
   printEnum("Breadth First", rootNode.breadthFirstEnumeration());
  }

  public static void printEnum(String title, Enumeration e) {
    System.out.println("===============\n" + title);
    while (e.hasMoreElements()) {
      System.out.print(e.nextElement() + " ");
    }
    System.out.println("\n");
  }
}
```

The tree that this program generates is shown in Figure 10-9; the output follows. Here is what a preorder enumeration produces:

```
===============
Preorder
Root 0 0_0 0_0_0 0_0_1 0_1 0_1_0 0_1_1 1 1_0 1_0_0 1_0_1 1_1 1_1_0 1_1_1
```

As you can see, the *preorder enumeration* starts at the root and walks down the tree as far as it can go, adding the nodes that it traverses (0, 0_0, 0_0_0) to the enumeration. Having reached the bottom of the tree, it then walks across the children of the last node it traversed and adds them (0_0_1). Next, it moves back up to 0_0 and across to its sibling 0_1, which it adds to the enumeration and then descends and traverses its children (0_1_0, 0_1_1). This completes the traversal of the 0 subtree. Next, the subtree rooted at 1 is scanned in the same order.

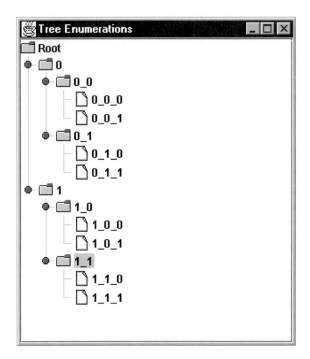

Figure 10-9   A tree to demonstrate tree traversal enumerations.

The *postorder enumeration* is very similar, except that it adds the parent nodes that it traverses as it crosses them on the way up, not on the way down. In other words, whereas the preorder traverse announced a subtree and then added its contents, postorder enumeration adds the contents and then adds the root of the subree. If you think in terms of a file system, this is like processing all of the files in a directory and then applying the operation to the directory itself, which is the required order for removing a directory and its contents (since the directory must be empty to be removed).

```
================
Postorder
0_0_0 0_0_1 0_0 0_1_0 0_1_1 0_1 0 1_0_0 1_0_1 1_0 1_1_0 1_1_1 1_1 1 Root
```

Breadth-first enumeration is much simpler to visualize—it just walks across all the nodes at each level and adds them to the enumeration, then goes down a level and lists all of the nodes at that level, and so on. In terms of the tree's display, if you open all of the subtrees so that every node in the tree is visible, you'll see that this enumeration walks vertically down the screen and, when it reaches the bottom, goes back up and across to the right one level, then back down the screen again, and so on. The effect is that you see everything at depth 0, then everything at depth 1, followed by depth 2 and so on.

```
================
Breadth First
Root 0 1 0_0 0_1 1_0 1_1 0_0_0 0_0_1 0_1_0 0_1_1 1_0_0 1_0_1 1_1_0 1_1_1
```

Changing Tree Content

Many trees will be static once you've created them, but many will not. If you need to change the content of the tree's data model, there are two ways you can do it—at the model level and at the node level. You need to handle these two possibilities slightly differently, so they are described separately in this section.

Making Changes via DefaultTreeModel

The generic `TreeModel` interface doesn't offer any way to change the content of the model—it assumes that any changes will be made at the node level. The problem with just changing the nodes is that the screen display of the tree won't be updated. It isn't sufficient just to make changes to the data—the tree's user interface class must also be told about these changes.

If you want to handle changes at the node level, you'll see what you need to do in the next section. If you don't want to go to that much trouble, however, there are two convenience methods in the `DefaultTreeModel` that do everything for you:

```
public void insertNodeInto(MutableTreeNode child,
            MutableTreeNode parent, int index)
public void removeNodeFromParent(MutableTreeNode parent)
```

These methods make the changes that their names imply by manipulating the node data directly, then they arrange for the tree's on-screen representation to be updated by invoking the `nodesWereInserted` and `nodesWereRemoved` methods of `DefaultTreeModel` that will be covered shortly. If you are making a small number of changes to the model, `insertNodeInto` and `removeNodeFromParent` are the simplest way, to do it. However, because these methods generate one event for each node you add or remove, if you are adding and changing more than a few nodes, it can be more efficient to side-step them and manipulate the nodes directly because, by doing so, you can generate fewer events.

Making Changes at the Node Level

`DefaultMutableTreeNode` has six methods that allow you to make changes to the data model:

```
public void add(MutableTreeNode child)

public void insert(MutableTreeNode child, int index)

public void remove(int index)

public void remove(MutableTreeNode child)

public void removeAllChildren()

public void removeFromParent()
```

With the exception of the last, all these are invoked against the parent to be affected by the change; `removeFromParent` is invoked on the child node to be removed from its parent. The effect of these methods is obvious from their names. All that they do, however, is to update the tree's data model and keep it in a consistent state. They do not inform the tree itself that it may need to redisplay its contents. After making any changes to the node structure, you need to invoke one of the following `DefaultTreeModel` methods to ensure that the tree's appearance matches its internal data:

```
public void reload()

public void reload(TreeNode node)

public void nodesWereInserted(TreeNode, int[] childIndices)

public void nodesWereRemoved(TreeNode, int[] childIndices,
          Object[] removedChildren)

public void nodeStructureChanged(TreeNode node)
```

The first of these methods is the most radical solution: It tells the `JTree` to discard everything that it has cached about the structure of the tree and to rebuild its view from scratch. This could be a very slow process and is not recommended. The second form of the `reload` method gives a node as a limiting point. When this method is used, the tree assumes that there may have been radical changes but that they were confined to the subtree rooted at the node given as the argument. In response, the tree rebuilds its view from that point in the hierarchy downward. This method is ideal if you make major changes under a node, such as populating it from scratch or removing all of its children. You might, for example, use this after calling `removeAllChildren` and pass the node whose children were removed as its argument:

```
// Delete everything below "node" and tell the tree about it
node.removeAllChildren();
model.reload(node); // "model" is the DefaultTreeModel
```

The method `nodeStructureChanged` is identical to `reload`.

The other two methods are used for finer control over the mechanism. You can use these to minimize the impact of any changes by informing the tree exactly which nodes were added or removed. Both of these methods require you to accumulate a list, in ascending numerical order, of the indices of all of the nodes that were added or removed and, in the latter case, a list of all of the removed nodes themselves. This is obviously more complex than just using `nodeStructureChanged`, but it can be more efficient.

These methods have the limitation that they can only inform the tree about changes in one parent node at a time. If you make changes to more than one node, for example, to several levels in the hierarchy, you need to invoke these methods once for each parent node affected, which can increase the complexity of the task.

Changing the Attributes of a Node

There is a third type of change to the tree model that hasn't been covered so far—changes to one of the nodes themselves. Suppose that you make a change to a node that doesn't affect its relationship to its neighbors but should result in its appearance changing. This might happen if you change the value of the node's user object, as might be the case if your tree represents a file system and you allow the user to rename a file or directory. When this happens, you can use one of the following `DefaultTreeModel` methods:

```
public void nodeChanged(TreeNode changedNode);

public void nodesChanged(TreeNode parentNode, int[] childIndices)
```

Notice the important difference between these two methods: When you change one node, you pass a reference to that node, but if you change several then you must pass a reference to their common parent and a set of indices that identify the affected children. If you make changes that affect nodes in several parts of the tree, then you must invoke `nodesChanged` once for each node that has had children changed.

Tree Model Events

All of the methods in the previous sections operate by generating `TreeModelEvents` that can be caught by registering a `TreeModelListener` on the tree's `DefaultTreeModel` object. Usually, events are not highly specific about exactly what has changed—the listener is expected to query the source of the event to find out what happened and this is normally acceptable for simple controls like lists, combo boxes, text fields and buttons where only one thing can have happened. But in the case of a tree, many modifications of different types can be made. If a single event that said "something has changed" were posted, it would be necessary to scan the whole tree to try and detect what happened. This would, of course, be time-consuming and might require the listener to remember a large amount of state in order to be able to perform a comparison at all.

Because of this, the `TreeModelListener` must implement four methods, each of which receives a `TreeModelEvent`:

```
public void treeNodesChanged(TreeModelEvent)

public void treeStructureChanged(TreeModelEvent)

public void treeNodesInserted(TreeModelEvent)

public void treeNodesRemoved(TreeModelEvent)
```

These listener methods are entered as a result of calling the following `DefaultTreeModel` methods:

treeNodesChanged: nodeChanged or nodesChanged was called

treeStructureChanged: reload (either variant) or nodeStructureChanged
                         was called

treeNodesInserted: nodesWereInserted was called

treeNodesRemoved: nodesWereRemoved was called

Splitting at this level is not sufficient, however, because it doesn't tell the listener what was added, removed or changed. This information is contained in the `TreeModelEvent`, which has four methods to extract it:

```
public Object getSource()

public TreePath getPath()

public Object[] getChildren()

public int[] getChildIndices()
```

Which of these methods returns meaningful values and what they mean depends on the type of event. All of the events return a valid value to `getSource`, which is a reference to the affected tree model (i.e., the `DefaultTreeModel` instance for the affected `JTree`).

In the case of an event delivered to `treeStructureChanged`, only `getPath` returns any useful information. This method gives the `TreePath` for the node and below which the change occurred. This `TreePath` corresponds to the node that was originally passed to `reload` or `nodeStructureChanged`. The `getChildren` and `getChildIndices` methods both return `null`.

For `treeNodesChanged`, `getPath` returns a `TreePath` object for the node that is the parent of the node or nodes that were affected. The `getChildIndices` and `getChildren` methods return arrays that contain one entry for each affected child of that node. The indices in the array returned by `getChildIndices` are in ascending numerical order and the array returned by `getChildren` is sorted so that corresponding entries in these two arrays match—that is, the index in entry *n* of the index array corresponds to the child in entry *n* of the child array.

Similarly, `getPath` returns the `TreePath` of the parent of the affected nodes in both `treeNodesRemoved` and `treeNodesInserted` and the `getChildIndices` and `getChildren` methods retrieve sorted and matching arrays of the affected children. Note, however, that in the case of `treeNodesRemoved`, these children have already been removed from the parent node and the indices indicate where they used to reside in the parent's list of children.

Most applications won't need to handle these events because the `JTree` look-and-feel class registers itself as a listener of the tree's model and updates the tree's appearance based on the events that it receives. You can, however, register a listener of your own if you want the tree control to cause your application to react in some special way to changes in its structure. You'll see examples of this in the rest of this chapter.

A File System Tree Control

The most obvious thing to use a tree control for is to show the content of your machine's file system, in the same way as the Windows Explorer does in the left of its two display panes. Since the file system and `JTree` are both inherently hierarchical, you might expect it to be a simple matter to create a tree control that maps a file system but, as you'll see in this section, there are a few interesting issues to tackle along the way. As the description of the implementation of this component progresses, you'll see some of the real-world problems that come up when creating new components, including the need to sometimes work around bugs in the classes that the new control is based on.

Before looking at how to implement a file system control, let's look at what the finished product looks like. Figure 10-1 shows the control mounted in a frame and running on a Windows platform. If you want to try this out for yourself, use a command like the following:

```
java JFCBook.Chapter10.FileTreeTest C:
```

You can replace the string 'C:' with the name of any directory on your system—this is the directory that becomes the root of the file tree.

Core Alert

With some versions of the JDK on the Windows platform, you'll get an exception if you use the string "C:\" instead of "C:". This happens because the File *class can't cope with being asked for a list of the files in the directory 'C:\', whereas it is happy with 'C:'. As you'll see shortly, this is not the only shortcoming in this area.*

If you run this example, you should see the directory whose name was supplied on the command line at the top of the display, followed by all of its subdirectories. Like Windows Explorer, this control only shows directories, not files. Windows Explorer shows files in its right-hand pane, which is almost identical to the Swing `JDirectoryPane`. Indeed, once you have this control, you can use it, together with the `JDirectoryPane` and the `JSplitPane` component that you saw in the last chapter to create an application that looks very much like Windows Explorer itself except, of course, that it also runs on many versions of UNIX (and other platforms).

If you move the mouse over any directory with an expansion icon to the left of it and click on the icon or double-click on the directory icon or name, it opens to reveal its subdirectories. If those subdirectories have other subdirectories, they will also have expansion icons next to them. A directory that doesn't have any subdirectories (i.e., a directory that is empty or contains only files) cannot be expanded. Again, to see the contents, you would need to connect this control to a `JDirectoryPane` and have it display the directory's contents.

Core Note

The Swing `JTree` component doesn't behave very well with respect to displaying the icon for a node that has no children. If you're using a look-and-feel with this problem, you'll find that all of the subdirectories seem to have contents but, when you click on one that actually only has files in it, the icon sign disappears. All of the standard look-and-feels currently behave this way.

Implementation Plan for the File System Control

In order to create a tree that shows a file system, a representation of the file system's directory structure must be loaded into a `DefaultTreeModel`. On the face of it, this is a relatively simple proposition: All you need is a recursive method that is given a directory, reads its contents and, each time it comes across a subdirectory, adds a node to the tree model, then invokes itself to process the content of that subdirectory. Using the methods of the `java.io.File` class, it is easy to get a list of the objects in a directory and to determine which of these objects are themselves directories. The problem with this simplistic approach is that it would scan the entire file system when the control is created. This has two obvious drawbacks—it may take a long time and it will probably take up a large amount of memory to hold all of the nodes. Most of this time and memory is probably wasted, because the odds are that the user will find what he/she is looking for fairly quickly and not look at most of what has been generated.

The ideal approach would be to start by doing only as much work as necessary to show the user the content of the directory that the control starts in. Then, whenever a directory is clicked and opened, the nodes for that directory should be created and displayed, and so on. If this can be achieved, it should be possible to create the control with only the relatively short delay required to read the top-level directory, at the cost of a small delay each time a new directory is opened. This approach is, however, too simplistic.

To see why this won't work, suppose you have a small file system with a directory structure that looks like this:

```
C:\java
C:\java\bin
C:\java\demo
     C:\java\demo\Animator
     C:\java\demo\ArcTest
     C:\java\demo\awt-1.1
     C:\java\demo\BarChart
C:\java\docs
     C:\java\docs\api
     C:\java\docs\guide
     C:\java\docs\images
     C:\java\docs\relnotes
     C:\java\docs\tooldocs
C:\java\include
     C:\java\include\win32
C:\java\lib
C:\java\src
     C:\java\src\java
          C:\java\src\java\applet
          C:\java\src\java\awt
          C:\java\src\java\bean
          C:\java\src\java\io
     C:\java\src\sun
     C:\java\src\sunw
```

To create a tree that allows the user to navigate the directory C:\java following the algorithm outlined earlier, the first step would be to build a node for C:\java itself and then child nodes would be added for the subdirectories C:\java\bin, C:\java\demo, C:\java\docs, C:\java\include, C:\java\lib and C:\java\src. If the process stopped here, the tree would indeed show the top-level directory and all of these subdirectories. However, you can see that the demo, docs, include and src directories themselves have subdirectories, so you would expect the tree to show them with an expansion icon. But, this icon is only shown if the node that it relates to has child nodes attached to it. So far, no tree nodes have been added nodes for these subdirectories, because the idea is to minimize the work that is needed to get the control created. To get the right effect, this approach will have to be modified in some way.

The only way to make the expansion icons appear is to add a child node to each directory that has subdirectories. To do this, it is necessary to scan not only the directory that the control starts in, but also the directories that are found in that directory. With this modification, nodes would be added for the subdirectories Animator, ArcTest, awt-1.1, BarChart, api, guide and so on. It isn't necessary to go any lower at this stage, because directories further down can't influence the appearance of the control when the user is only looking at the contents of the C:\java directory.

Now suppose the user clicked on the icon for C:\java\src. This would open up and reveal the nodes representing the java, sun and sunw subdirectories, but now there is the same problem again: The C:\java\src\java subdirectory and (although this hasn't been shown in detail in the file system map shown above) all the other directories have subdirectories of their own, but the expansion icons for their nodes don't appear because those directories haven't been scanned to build their child nodes. Fortunately, as you know, it is possible to get a TreeExpansionEvent when the user opens a node. This event can be used to find out which directory the user wants to look at and then all of its subdirectories can be populated, as was done with the initial directory. In fact, as you'll see, the same code can be used to handle both cases.

The approach just outlined will work, but there is a small improvement that can be made to minimize the impact of having to scan for subdirectories. The only reason to look for directories that are not going to be visible straight away is to make the expansion icon appear for a directory that will be visible. All you have to do to make the expansion icon appear is to place *one* child under the node for a directory that has subdirectories. In other words, when scanning for hidden subdirectories, it is possible to stop as soon as we have found one. This can save a lot of time if the file system has big directories, because it avoids the overhead of reading through lots of files to find subdirectories that may not exist, and also minimizes the effect of looking in directories that the user doesn't end up opening anyway. The flip side of this is, of course, that if the user does open a directory that has had a single entry placed in it, it is necessary to get rid of it before fully populating the directory, or the first entry wold appear in the directory twice.

File System Tree Control Implementation

Having seen the basic idea, let's now examine the implementation, the code for which appears in Listing 10-3.

Listing 10-3   A custom control to display a file system in a tree

---

```
package JFCBook.Chapter10;

import com.sun.java.swing.*;
import com.sun.java.swing.tree.*;
import com.sun.java.swing.event.*;
import java.io.*;
import java.util.*;

public class FileTree extends JTree {
    public FileTree(String path) throws FileNotFoundException, SecurityException
    {
```

```
  super((TreeModel)null);        // Create the JTree itself

  // Use horizontal and vertical lines
  putClientProperty("JTree.lineStyle", "Angled");

  // Create the first node
  FileTreeNode rootNode = new FileTreeNode(null, path);

  // Populate the root node with its subdirectories
  boolean addedNodes = rootNode.populateDirectories(true);
  setModel(new DefaultTreeModel(rootNode));

  // Listen for Tree Selection Events
  addTreeExpansionListener(new TreeExpansionHandler());
}

// Returns the full path name for a path, or null if not a known path
public String getPathName(TreePath path) {
  Object o = path.getLastPathComponent();
  if (o instanceof FileTreeNode) {
    return ((FileTreeNode)o).fullName;
  }
  return null;
}

// Inner class that represents a node in this file system tree
protected static class FileTreeNode extends DefaultMutableTreeNode {
  public FileTreeNode(String parent, String name) throws SecurityException,
                  FileNotFoundException {
    this.name = name;

    // See if this node exists and whether it is a directory
    fullName = parent == null ? name : parent + File.separator + name;

    File f = new File(fullName);
    if (f.exists() == false) {
      throw new FileNotFoundException("File " + fullName + " does not exist");
    }

    isDir = f.isDirectory();

    // Hack for Windows that doesn't consider a drive to be a directory!
    if (isDir == false && f.isFile() == false) {
      isDir = true;
    }
  }
```

continued

```
// Override isLeaf to check whether this is a directory
public boolean isLeaf() {
  return !isDir;
}

// Override getAllowsChildren to check whether this is a directory
public boolean getAllowsChildren() {
  return isDir;
}

// For display purposes, we return our own name
public String toString() {
  return name;
}

// If we are a directory, scan our contents and populate
// with children. In addition, populate those children
// if the "descend" flag is true. We only descend once,
// to avoid recursing the whole subtree.
// Returns true if some nodes were added
boolean populateDirectories(boolean descend) {
  boolean addedNodes = false;

  // Do this only once
  if (populated == false) {
    File f;
    try {
      f = new File(fullName);
    } catch (SecurityException e) {
      populated = true;
      return false;
    }

    if (interim == true) {
      // We have had a quick look here before:
      // remove the dummy node that we added last time
      removeAllChildren();
      interim = false;
    }

    String[] names = f.list();           // Get list of contents

    // Process the directories
    for (int i = 0; i < names.length; i++) {
      String name = names[i];
      File d = new File(fullName, name);
      try {
```

```
          if (d.isDirectory()) {
            FileTreeNode node = new FileTreeNode(fullName, name);
            this.add(node);
            if (descend) {
              node.populateDirectories(false);
            }
            addedNodes = true;
            if (descend == false) {
              // Only add one node if not descending
              break;
            }
          }
        } catch (Throwable t) {
          // Ignore phantoms or access problems
        }
      }

      // If we were scanning to get all subdirectories,
      // or if we found no subdirectories, there is no
      // reason to look at this directory again, so
      // set populated to true. Otherwise, we set interim
      // so that we look again in the future if we need to
      if (descend == true || addedNodes == false) {
        populated = true;
      } else {
        // Just set interim state
        interim = true;
      }
    }
    return addedNodes;
  }

  protected String name;              // Name of this component
  protected String fullName;          // Full path name
  protected boolean populated;        // true if we have been populated
  protected boolean interim;          // true if we are in interim state
  protected boolean isDir;            // true if this is a directory
}

// Inner class that handles Tree Expansion Events
protected class TreeExpansionHandler implements TreeExpansionListener {
  public void treeExpanded(TreeExpansionEvent evt) {
    TreePath path = evt.getPath();            // The expanded path
    JTree tree = (JTree)evt.getSource();      // The tree

    // Get the last component of the path and
    // arrange to have it fully populated.
```

continued

```
      FileTreeNode node = (FileTreeNode)path.getLastPathComponent();
      if (node.populateDirectories(true)) {
        ((DefaultTreeModel)tree.getModel()).nodeStructureChanged(node);
      }
    }

    public void treeCollapsed(TreeExpansionEvent evt) {
      // Nothing to do
    }
  }
}
```

Naturally enough, the control, called `FileTree`, is derived from `JTree`. It is a self-contained component that is given a directory name as its starting point—that's all you need to do to get a hierarchical display of the objects below that directory. The component can be placed in a `JScrollPane` and used just like any other tree.

Designing the Data Model

The constructor first invokes the `JTree` constructor, creating a tree with no data model, then starts building the contents of the control by creating a `DefaultTreeModel` that initially contains just a node for that starting directory. The first question that arises is whether to use a `DefaultMutableTreeNode` to represent the directories, or create a node class of our own. Once a node has been added to the tree, it must show the name of the directory that it represents. The text displayed by the default look-and-feel is the result of invoking `toString` on the node, so the directory's name must be stored somewhere in the node so that it can be returned when `toString` is called. One way to achieve the desired result is to have the user object associated with the node *be* the string name of the directory. In fact, though, it must be only the last component of the directory name, because displaying the full path alongside each node would produce a very unattractive and over-crowded result.

Suppose that this strategy of storing strings as the user object for each node in the tree is adopted and that the string associated with each node only represents part of the full path name. When a directory in the file system is opened to look for sub-directories, it is necessary to have the directory's complete path name, but the node representing the directory only stores its own part of the name. However, as you know, the `TreeExpansionEvent` actually contains the node's `TreePath`. Using this, it is possible to build the full path name of the node by getting the `TreeNodes` representing each hop of the path and retrieving their user objects, which, on this design, would be strings, then combining them to form the complete path name. While this would be possible, it would be a slow process. It is much more efficient to store the full path name as well as the component name.

Since only one item of private information can be stored in a DefaultMutableTreeNode, it is necessary to create a private node class to store two. Because this class is tied to the design of the tree, it is implemented as an inner class of the tree, called FileTreeNode and is derived, naturally, from DefaultMutableTreeNode. This class will store both the full path name and the node's name relative to its parent, both of which will be passed as arguments to the constructor. To achieve the correct display, the toString method will return the latter of these two values. This is, actually, quite a natural way to construct a node because the code than scans a directory to create nodes for subdirectories and will know the full path name of the directory that it is scanning. It will discover the component name by reading the directory and so will have both items available when it creates a new node.

Building the Initial Data Model

Construction of the data model begins with the node for the initial directory, to which nodes must be added for each of its immediate subdirectories. This task is delegated to a method of FileTreeNode called populateDirectories, which you'll see in a moment. When this method returns, a DefaultTreeModel initialized with the root node is created and the JTree setModel method is used to attach it to the tree. The model as created by this method is sufficient for the initial display of the tree and will remain sufficient until the user (or the application) expands one of the nodes. To handle this (likely) eventuality, the last thing the FileTree constructor has to do is register a listener for TreeExpansionEvents. The code that will handle these events is encapsulated in a separate inner class called TreeExpansionHandler to avoid cluttering FileTree with methods that aren't part of its public interface, so the constructor creates an instance of this class and registers it to receive the events. At this point, the control is fully initialized and ready to be displayed.

Apart from its constructor, FileTree only has one method of its own. The getPathName method accepts a TreePath as its argument and returns the path name of the file that it represents in the tree. You'll see why this is necessary when you see an example of this control in use. Once the tree has been created, it is managed entirely by the JTree class. All that remains for us to do is implement the inner classes FileTreeNode and TreeExpansionHandler.

Implementing the FileTreeNode Class

The FileTreeNode class is derived from DefaultMutableTreeNode so that it can be added to a tree. Earlier design considerations dictate that its constructor must have two string arguments that give the path name of the directory that it resides in and name of the object that it represents relative to that directory. From these, the full name of the object is constructed and saved in the instance variable fullName, while the relative path name is stored in the variable name. The case of the root node (the one that represents the initial directory) is a special one, because it only has a full path name. To cater for this, the name of the parent directory is allowed to be `null`, in which case the component name is stored as both the object's relative name and in the `fullName` field.

All that remains for the constructor to do is to determine whether the node's associated object in the file system is a directory or not. To do this, the object's full path name is used to create a `java.io.File` object and then its `isDirectory` method is called. The result of this call is stored in an instance variable called `isDir`, which is a `boolean`. Unfortunately, this method returns `false` if the object is not a directory *or* if it doesn't exist. Most of the time, objects will be constructed using names that have been discovered by reading the file system, which (subject to possible race conditions) should exist, but the node at the top of the tree will be built based on information supplied by the user, so it might not exist. To be safe, the existence of the object is verified by using the `exists` method and a `FileNotFoundException` is thrown if necessary. On some systems (e.g., UNIX and Windows NT), it may turn out that the user of the control doesn't have access to the directory in which the object resides, or to the object itself. On these systems, the constructor will throw a `SecurityException`. If either of these exceptions occurs while the tree is being built, they are just caught and ignored, with the result that the tree will be properly constructed but won't contain those objects that it couldn't get access to. The exception to this is the root node, which is built in the `FileTree` constructor: Any problem creating this is passed as an exception to the code creating the tree.

Core Note

A nice enhancement to this control might be to catch a `SecurityException` *and represent the object that could not be accessed in some meaningful way to the user—perhaps with an icon representing a* NO ENTRY *sign. You shouldn't find it too difficult, as an exercise, to add this functionality.*

Usually, ensuring that the object exists and then using `isDirectory` will correctly determine the object's type, but there is an exception to this rule. Rightly or wrongly, on Windows, the `File isDirectory` method considers that the root directory of a drive, that is, `C:`, `D:`, and the likes is *not* a directory. If nothing were done about this, these drives would be seen as files, so creating a `FileTree` to show the content of an entire drive would show just one entry for the drive itself! Luckily, the `isFile` method claims that a drive is not a file either, so the implementation incorporates a gross hack that makes an object with this behavior appear as a directory:

```
isDir = f.isDirectory();

// Hack for Windows which doesn't consider a drive to be a directory!
if (isDir == false && f.isFile() == false) {
  isDir = true;
}
```

There are other ways to work around this problem. For example, one possibility is to look to see whether the path name is two characters long and consists of a single letter followed by a colon. It's probably just a matter of taste which is better: The code above looks slightly more elegant than the alternative that plays around with strings.

Core Note

This is not the only problem in this area. It may be defensible to say that C: *is neither a directory nor a file, but what about* C:\? *This is, without doubt, a directory and the* isDirectory *method agrees. The trouble is that, as noted earlier, when you try to list the contents of this directory, you get back a* null *pointer! To work around this bug (and this definitely is a bug), you could try adding code to strip trailing slashes from the path name, so that* C:\ *becomes* C:, *but this would give you the original problem!*

Once it has been determined whether the object is a directory, the FileTreeNode constructor is complete and has created a viable node to insert into the tree.

FileTreeNode Icon and Text Representation

Before looking in detail at how to handle the population of subdirectories, there is a small point that needs to be dealt with. JTree has a small selection of icons that it can display for any given node—a sheet of paper representing a leaf, a closed folder, and an open folder (in the Metal look-and-feel). The choice between a sheet of paper and a folder depends on whether the node is a leaf. As you know, there are two different ways to determine whether a node considers itself to be a leaf, only one of which is usually appropriate for a particular node class: Either its isLeaf method or its getAllowsChildren method should be called. In the case of a file system, directories are never leaves, even if they are empty, so it would be normal to implement the getAllowsChildren method and have it return false if the node represents a directory and true otherwise. For flexibility, the FileTreeNode class also implements the isLeaf method, which is its inverse. Since both of these return correct answers for any node, there is no need to tell the DefaultTreeModel which method to use, so the default setting is used when we the data model is created (which means that isLeaf will be called).

The text that is rendered alongside the icon is obtained by invoking the toString method of the object that represents the node—that is, the toString method of FileTreeNode—so this method is overridden to return the name of the component.

Populating Directory Nodes

The last important piece of the FileTreeNode class is the populateDirectories method, which contains the code to create nodes to represent subdirectories. As noted earlier, sometimes it is necessary to create nodes for all of a directory's subdirectories and sometimes only one node is needed, so that the directory's icon shows that it can be expanded. In fact, these actions will always need to be carried out in pairs, one immediately after the other. To see why this is, consider the file system example that is shown above and imagine what needs to happen when the root node for the `C:\java` directory is created. The first thing to do is to get a list of the directories in the directory `C:\java`. Since all of these are going to be shown straight away, it is necessary to create nodes for each of them immediately and attach them to the root node. If any of these directories has subdirectories, a single node must be attached to them, to show that the directory is expandable. So, for each directory that is created in `populateDirectories`, there will need a second scan that creates no more than one node under it. Since both of these operations involve scanning a directory and creating a node (or nodes) to attach to the directory's node, the same code should be used for each case.

For this reason, the `populateDirectories` method takes a boolean argument called `descend`. When it is called to populate a directory that's going to be displayed, this parameter is set to `true` and the entire directory will be scanned and populated. When it is called to scan a newly-discovered subdirectory, on the other hand, `descend` will be set to `false`. If `descend` is `false`, the loop that processes each directory will terminate when it finds a subdirectory. Also, if `descend` is `false`, discovering a subdirectory doesn't cause `populateDirectories` to descend into it—which is the reason for the name. If this were not done, `populateDirectories` would always recursively descend down to the end of one path on the file system, instead of scanning only two levels.

Let's see how this works in practice. Refer to the implementation of `populateDirectories` in Listing 10-3 as you read this. When this method is first called, `descend` is set to `true`. Ignore, for a moment, the `populated` and `interim` instance variables, which are both initially `false`—you'll see how these are used in a moment. The first thing to do is create a `File` object for the node and get a list of its contents using the `list` method.

Core Note

Notice that this code is very carefully arranged so that, if it gets a `SecurityException`, *it returns having done no damage to the tree structure. This means that the tree will be incomplete, but will reflect those parts of the file system that the user has access to.*

In the case of the example file system, this will return the following list of subdirectories:

```
bin, demo, docs, include, lib, src
```

It will also return the names of any files in the `java` directory; on my machine, there are several of these, but I've left them out of this list for clarity. A

`FileTreeNode` for each of these directories must be added to the node that represents the directory being scanned. This job is carried out by the `for` loop, which makes one pass for each name in the list. Each time round the loop, it creates a `File` object for one of the above names (and the files that I haven't shown) and checks whether it represents a directory. If it doesn't, it is ignored and the next pass of the loop is started. In the case of a directory, it creates a `FileTreeNode` for it, giving the full path name of the parent (which is the name of the current node) and the component name from the list (i.e., `bin` or `demo`, etc.), then adds it underneath the node in the data mode being scanned. Next comes the interesting part. If `descend` is true, which it is for all of the directories in the last list, `populateDirectories` is called again, but this time there are two important differences:

- The `descend` argument changes to `false`.
- The node on which it operates is the new node (i.e., that for `bin`, `demo` etc.), not the top-level node.

This second call does the same things again for the subdirectory that it is dropping into, but it stops sooner—as soon as any subdirectory is found. This call is made for each of the directories in the original list (i.e., `bin`, `demo`, `docs`, `include`, `lib` and `src`). In the case of `bin`, there are no subdirectories, so it will complete the `for` loop without finding anything and just return (what happens to the `populated` and `interim` fields will be discussed below). However, the second pass of the loop calls `populateDirectories` for the `demo` node, which does have subdirectories. In this case, the `list` method returns the following set of names (and possibly some files that will be ignored because they have no bearing on how the data model is constructed):

    Animator, ArcTest, awt-1.1, BarChart

Now the `for` loop is entered and the code starts handling the subdirectory `Animator`. This turns out to be a directory, so a `FileTreeNode` is built for it and attached under the node for `C:\java\demo`. However, this time, `descend` is `false`, so `populateDirectories` is not called again to descend into this new directory. Instead, the `for` loop ends, having added exactly one child to `C:\java\demo`. Control now returns to the `for` loop of the first invocation of `populateDirectories`, where the rest of the original list of names is processed in the same way but, because here `descend` is set to `true`, the loop runs to completion.

When this loop has been completed, the state of the `C:\java` node needs to be changed to reflect that fact that all of its subdirectories have been located and nodes have been built for them. To indicate this, the `populated` field is set to `true`. When `populateDirectories` is called for a node with `populated` set to `true`, it knows that there is nothing more to do and just returns at once. As you'll see, this can happen during tree expansion. On the other hand, the nodes for the subdirectories demo, docs, include and src have all been processed by populateDirectories and have had *one* node each added. These directories are not completely processed and it will be necessary to scan them again later if the user expands them in the tree, so it would be incorrect to set populated to true. But it is also necessary to remember that a child has been attached to these nodes so that it can be discarded later before building a fully populated subtree. To distinguish this case, the instance variable interim is set to true, because this node is in an interim state. Note, however, that there is a special case here. If a scan of a subdirectory finds that it has no subdirectories at all, it is marked as populated, because there is nothing to be gained from scanning it again later.

At the end of this process, the following node structure will be as follows:

```
C:\java (populated)
    C:\java\bin (populated)
    C:\java\demo (interim)
        C:\java\demo\Animator
    C:\java\docs (interim)
        C:\java\docs\api
    C:\java\include (interim)
        C:\java\include\win32
    C:\java\lib (populated)
    C:\java\src (interim)
        C:\java\src\java
```

Note that the top-level directory is marked as populated, as are the subdirectories that don't themselves have any further directories (bin and lib). The others are marked as interim, because only one node has been created underneath them and more would need to be added before the user could be allowed to expand, say, C:\java\docs. Notice also that C:\java\include is marked as interim despite the fact that it only has one subdirectory and a node has been created for it. This is because populateDirectories stops after finding one directory, so it wasn't able to see that there weren't any more directories to find. The point of this optimization is the assumption that it is better to stop after finding one directory, on the grounds that if there is one subdirectory there is probably another and, if there isn't, there may still be a large number of files to traverse before getting to the end. Sometimes this guess will be right, other times it won't. In this case, a little more work than is strictly necessary will be done if the user opens this directory, because the node for win32 will be discarded and then put back again.

Handling Expansion of Directories

In terms of the tree as seen by the user, the node structure is now correct and the tree will display the demo, docs, include and src directories with an expansion icon and the others without one. Nothing will change until the user clicks on one of these icons. Suppose the user clicks on the node for C:\java\demo. Unless something is done, in response to this click the JTree will expand the node and show just the entry for C:\java\demo\Animator. This is, of course, wrong because there are three missing subdirectories. Here is where the TreeExpansionListener comes into play. When the user clicks on the node, the treeExpanded method of the TreeExpansionHandler inner class will be entered. The TreeExpansionEvent that it receives tells it the source of the event (i.e., the FileTree instance) and the TreePath for the node that was expanded—for instance a TreePath for C:\java\demo. To give the tree the correct appearance three new nodes must be added under the node for C:\java\demo, for which it is necessary to find the FileTreeNode for that path.

As you saw earlier in this chapter, given a TreePath, you can find the TreeNode for that path by extracting the path object for the last component in the TreePath. To get the FileTreeNode for C:\java\demo, then, the getLastComponent method is invoked on the TreePath from the event. This returns an Object that is actually the FileTreeNode for the path. Armed with this, the node for C:\java\demo can be populated by invoking populateDirectories against it, passing the argument true to have it process two levels of directory, so that the new directories that get added will get the right expansion icons.

This time, populateDirectories will start at C:\java\demo, which is marked as interim, so it starts by discarding all of its children, which cause the existing node for C:\java\demo\Animator to be removed. Then, it adds nodes for all four subdirectories of C:\java\demo and marks it as populated. Along the way, it will have looked to see if there were directories in any of these four subdirectories and marked the new nodes for the Animator, ArcTest, awt-1.1 and BarChart directories as interim if they were or populated if there were not.

Finally, adding new nodes below an existing node is not sufficient to make the tree show them. To have the tree update its view, the model's nodeStructureChanged method must be called, passing it the node for C:\java\demo, since this is the parent node beneath which all of the changes were made. The event handler has a reference to this node, but how is it possible to get hold of a reference to the model? There are two ways to do this. First, the TreeExpansionHandler is a nonstatic inner class of FileTree, which is a JTree, so the model reference can be obtained using the following expression:

```
FileTree.this.getModel()
```

This works because FileTree.this refers, by definition to the containing FileTree. A simpler way, though, is to use the fact that a reference to the JTree is provided as the source of the TreeExpansionEvent, so you can instead just do this:

```
JTree tree = (JTree)evt.getSource();
((DefaultTreeModel)tree.getModel()).nodeStructureChanged(node);
```

This is the approach taken in the implementation.

Using the File System Tree Control

The file system tree control is intended to be a black box. To use it, you decide on the starting point in the file system, then create an appropriate `FileTree`. Usually, you will want to know when the user has selected a file in the tree. Since `FileTree` is derived from `JTree`, it supports the same events, so you can receive notification of user actions by registering a listener for the `TreeSelectionEvent`, which, as you know, is generated when any change is made to the selection. What you really want to know when you get one of these events is the file name that corresponds to the node that has been selected, but the event itself only has `TreePath` objects associated with it. As you've already seen, you can get the complete set of objects that make up a `TreePath` by calling its `getPath` method. Once you've got these objects, you can invoke `toString` on each of them, then join them with the system file name separator character to get the full path name of the file. However, this would be a very slow process, so the method `getPathName` was added to `FileTree`. This method takes a `TreePath` from an event and returns the full path name that it represents, or `null` if it isn't a path in the tree. The implementation of this method, which is repeated fromListing 10-3, is very simple:

```
// Returns the full pathname for a path, or null if not a known path
public String getPathName(TreePath path) {
  Object o = path.getLastPathComponent();
  if (o instanceof FileTreeNode) {
    return ((FileTreeNode)o).fullName;
  }
  return null;
}
```

First, the user object from the last component of the `TreePath` is obtained using `getLastPathComponent`. If this `TreePath` was really obtained from an event generated by `FileTree`, the user object will be the `FileTreeNode` for the selected file. Before casting it, however, the code ensures that this is the case to protect against the application passing erroneous paths to `getPathName`. Finally, if the path really does correspond to a `FileTreeNode`, the full path name of the selected file is obtained from the `fullName` field, where it was stored when the node was constructed, and returned to the caller. If this is not a `FileTreeNode`, `null` is returned.

The test program that was used to demonstrate the `FileTree` control earlier in this chapter contains some typical code that shows how to handle file selections in the tree. You can try this code out by running the test program again using a command like this:

```
java JFCBook.Chapter10.FileTreeTest c:
```

and clicking on file names in the tree. Here is what the relevant piece of code looks like:

```
final FileTree ft = new FileTree(args[0]);

ft.addTreeSelectionListener(new TreeSelectionListener() {
  public void valueChanged(TreeSelectionEvent evt) {
    TreePath path = evt.getPath();
    String name = ft.getPathName(path);
    System.out.println("File " + name + " has been "
      + (evt.isAddedPath() ? "selected" : "deselected"));
  }
});
```

Having created the `FileTree` with its root at the location specified on the command line, a `TreeSelectionListener` is added to it. When the event occurs, the `getPath` method is used to extract the first path affected by the event. In this simple example, only one path will be handled—in the general case, you might need, if you allow it, to handle more than one simultaneous selection. The `getPathName` method of `FileTree` is invoked on the path to get the full path name of the selected file. This is all you need to know about `FileTree` to make use of it for selecting files. Here is some typical output from this program:

```
File C:\BACKUP has been selected
File C:\DRIVERS has been selected
File C:\HDU_MGR has been selected
```

Custom Tree Rendering and Editing

While the general appearance of the tree control is probably sufficient for many applications, it is possible to customize several aspects of the way in which it is rendered using various techniques that will be covered in this section. Some of these techniques work no matter which look-and-feel is installed, while others need to be tailored to work differently with different look-and-feel implementations.

As well as changing a tree's appearance, it is also possible to allow the user to edit the data represented by individual tree nodes. This topic is also covered in this section.

Changing the Appearance of a Tree's Contents

There are two ways in which you can change the appearance of the nodes of a particular tree. The most flexible option is to create your own renderer that implements the `TreeCellRenderer` interface. If you do this, you have complete control over how each node is displayed. If you just want to change the appearance of the tree slightly, the simplest thing to do is just to customize the basic look-and-feel implementation. The techniques that will be shown here can be used if you want to change the appearance of one particular tree in your application. If you want to make a change that applies to all trees, you may be able to use the simpler technique that will be described in "Changing Properties for All Trees."

Customizing the Basic Tree Cell Renderer

The default tree cell renderer is provided by the class `BasicTreeCellRenderer`, which resides in the Swing `com.sun.java.swing.plaf.basic` package. You can get a reference to the renderer using the `JTree getCellRenderer` method and you should verify that this returns a `BasicTreeCellRenderer`, then cast it and use the methods shown in Table 10-5 to change its behavior as required. The method works for all of the current look-and-feel implementations, because their tree cell renderers are all derived from `BasicTreeCellRenderer`.

Table 10-5   Basic tree cell renderer customization methods

Method	Description
public void setBackgroundNonSelectionColor(Color)	Sets the background color used when the node is not selected.
public void setBackgroundSelectionColor(Color)	Sets the color in which to draw the background of a selected node.
public void setBorderSelectionColor(Color)	Sets the color in which to draw the border of a selected node. There is no method to set the color of the border of a nonselected node because nonselected nodes do not have borders.
public void setTextNonSelectionColor(Color)	Determines the color of the text when the node is not selected.
public void setTextSelectionColor(Color)	Determines the color of the text when the node is selected.
public void setClosedIcon(Icon)	Sets the icon displayed when the node's children are not shown.
public void setOpenIcon(Icon)	Sets the icon displayed when the node's children are shown.
public void setLeafIcon(Icon)	Changes the icon displayed when the node is a leaf.

For the purposes of illustration, the next example changes the background of the tree to black and uses green text for nonselected items and white text for those that are selected. The background color for selected items will also be changed to gray. The starting point for this tree is `TreeExample1`, which was created earlier. This tree shows the crews of the Skylab space station and the Apollo lunar landing missions. The code that we added to the `main` method of the program, which we renamed `ModifyRenderer`, in Listing 10-4.

Listing 10-4   Customizing the basic tree cell renderer

```
// Get the tree's cell renderer. If it is a basic cell renderer,
// customize it.
TreeCellRenderer cr = t.getCellRenderer();
if (cr instanceof BasicTreeCellRenderer) {
  BasicTreeCellRenderer btcr = (BasicTreeCellRenderer)cr;

  // Set the various colors
  btcr.setBackgroundNonSelectionColor(Color.black);
  btcr.setBackgroundSelectionColor(Color.gray);
  btcr.setTextSelectionColor(Color.white);
  btcr.setTextNonSelectionColor(Color.green);

  // Finally, set the tree's background color
  t.setBackground(Color.black);
}
```

You can run this example for yourself with the command:

```
java JFCBook.Chapter10.ModifyRenderer
```

The result will look something like Figure 10-10.

If you look at the code, you'll see that it gets the tree's renderer and checks that it is the renderer from the basic package, or one derived from it. If it is, then the text and background colors are changed. Once these changes are made, all of the nodes in the tree will be drawn with the new settings. This is a simple way to make basic changes to the tree's appearance. To make more radical changes, you need to customize the renderer that draws each node's representation.

Core Alert

The simple approach taken in this example works well for the Metal and Motif look-and-feels, but it isn't so simple for Windows, because the icons it uses have opaque, white backgrounds. When placed against a black backdrop, these leave a white square around the icon. To solve this problem, you would need to substitute icons with transparent backgrounds using the `setClosedIcon` *and* `setOpenIcon` *methods. Furthermore, the icon used for a leaf is a black dot, which won't be visible against a black background. This would require you to supply a new leaf icon and install it using the* `setLeafIcon` *method. This code would have to be executed only if the Windows look-and-feel is selected, of course.*

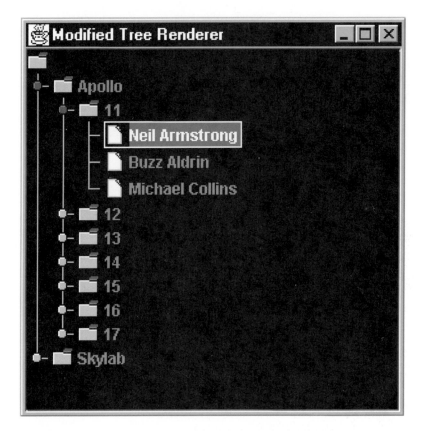

Listing 10-10   Customizing the icons and colors of tree nodes.

Implementing a New Renderer

Like the combo box and list controls, each cell of a tree is drawn by a *renderer*, which implements the `TreeCellRenderer` interface. This interface only has one method:

```
public abstract Component getTreeCellRendererComponent(JTree tree,
    Object value,
    boolean selected,
    boolean expanded,
    boolean leaf,
    int row,
    boolean hasFocus)
```

In most cases, the most important argument passed by this method is the `value`, which is the object to be formatted. The renderer is responsible for configuring a `Component` that represents this value in the tree. In terms of the default look-and-feel, this component will take the place of the folder or leaf icon and the descriptive text that appears to the right of it. The remaining arguments may be used to affect the way in which the component is rendered. For example, if the node is expanded, the default look-and-feel shows an open folder; if it is a leaf, it displays a sheet of paper. Selected rows usually have a background of a different color, while a row with the focus might be drawn with a colored line around the border.

You've just seen that you can use public methods supplied by `BasicTreeCellRenderer` to customize it to some extent. Another way to change the way a node is rendered is to subclass the basic renderer. The basic renderer is actually a subclass of `JLabel` that also implements the `TreeCellRenderer` interface. Ultimately, the `BasicTreeCellRenderer` just places the text and icon it is given on the label and, aside from some work that takes place in the `paint` method to paint the background of the cell, most of the rendering code is inherited from `JLabel`. If you subclass `BasicTreeCellRenderer`, you can do such things as changing the relative positions of the text and the icon, or changing the font in which the text is displayed by setting the label's font attribute appropriately. You can use this, for example, to switch to italics or bold when an item is selected.

The following example places the text above the icon. It also uses an italic font for selected items and a bold italic font if the item is both selected and has the focus. This example is actually an extension of Listing 10-4, which works by creating and installing a subclass of the basic renderer. The code that is changed is highlighted in bold in Listing 10-5.

Listing 10-5	Installing a customized version of the basic tree cell renderer

```
TreeCellRenderer cr = t.getCellRenderer();
if (cr instanceof BasicTreeCellRenderer) {
   CustomBasicRenderer btcr = new CustomBasicRenderer();
   t.setCellRenderer(btcr);

   // Set the various colors
   btcr.setBackgroundNonSelectionColor(Color.black);
   btcr.setBackgroundSelectionColor(Color.gray);
   btcr.setTextSelectionColor(Color.white);
   btcr.setTextNonSelectionColor(Color.green);

   // Change the row height
   t.setRowHeight(0);

   // Finally, set the tree's background color
   t.setBackground(Color.black);
}
```

As before, it is a good idea to verify that the tree has a renderer from one of the standard look-and-feels before installing a new one. This time, instead of customizing the existing renderer, a new one is created and installed using the `JTree` `setCellRenderer` method, then the customizations from the previous example are applied to it. Since the new renderer is derived from the basic renderer, these customizations will continue to be possible. Whether they work, of course, depends on whether the new renderer takes any notice of the values being changed.

The only other change is to set the cell row height. The `JTree` `setRowHeight` method changes the height of the rows managed by the cell renderer from its default. If you supply a positive value, the rows will all be of that height, whereas a zero or negative value causes the tree look-and-feel class to query the renderer for the height of each row as it draws it, which allows variable height rows. This is necessary in this case because this renderer places the text above the icon, so it will need more vertical space than it would get with the default setting.

The custom renderer itself is actually very simple—its only job is to change the way that the `JLabel` displays its content by manipulating its properties. In this example, it is implemented as an inner class, but you could make it equally well a freestanding object that can be reused. The code is shown in Listing 10-6.

Listing 10-6   A customized tree cell renderer

```
// This class is a custom renderer based on BasicTreeCellRenderer
protected static class CustomBasicRenderer extends BasicTreeCellRenderer {
  public Component getTreeCellRendererComponent(JTree tree,
               Object value,
               boolean selected,
               boolean expanded,
               boolean leaf,
               int row,
               boolean hasFocus) {
// Allow the original renderer to set up the label
    Component c = super.getTreeCellRendererComponent(tree, value, selected,
               expanded, leaf, row,
               hasFocus);

    // Now change the icon and text position
    if (c instanceof JLabel) {
      JLabel l = (JLabel)c;
      l.setHorizontalAlignment(JLabel.CENTER);
      l.setVerticalAlignment(JLabel.CENTER);
      l.setVerticalTextPosition(JLabel.TOP);
      l.setHorizontalTextPosition(JLabel.CENTER);

      // Set the font
```

```
      int type = Font.PLAIN;
      if (selected == true) {
        type = Font.ITALIC;
        if (hasFocus == true) {
          type = Font.ITALIC | Font.BOLD;
        }
      }
      l.setFont(new Font("SansSerif", type, 12));
    }

    return c;
  }
}
```

Since the intention is just to change the way in which the label created by the default renderer is configured, the first step is to invoke the default renderer and let it create the label as it would normally appear. This arranges for the appropriate text and icon to be attached to the label . The returned component is checked to be sure that it is a `JLabel` (in case somebody reimplements it one day!). If it is, the usual `JLabel` methods that you first saw back in Chapter 2, "Frames, Labels, and Buttons," are used to place the text above the icon and aligned centrally, and to align the text and icon combination so that they are in the middle of the area allocated to the cell.

Lastly, the font needs to be set. The new font is a 12-point SansSerif font to which bold and/or italic attributes depending on whether the cell is selected and whether it has the input focus. With the label correctly configured, it is just returned to the caller of this method, the tree's basic look-and-feel class.

To try this version of the example for yourself, use the command:

```
java JFCBook.Chapter10.SubClassRenderer
```

You'll see immediately that the relative positions of the text and the icon have changed. If you select an item, you'll find that the text becomes bold and italicized. Select a different item, and the previously selected item reverts to a plain font. For a more interesting effect, try selecting more than one item by using the CTRL key when selecting. You'll see the text of that all of the selected items is in italics and the most recently-selected item, which has the focus, is also in bold. Figure 10-11 shows a typical snapshot of this example.

One problem with creating a new renderer by subclassing `Basic-TreeCellRenderer` is that it may only work properly if the Metal or Windows look and-feel is installed. Because of the fact that this example uses the original renderer functionality by invoking the `getTreeCellRendererComponent` method of its superclass, there might be a problem if it were replacing the Motif look-and-feel, which has its own cell renderer that is derived from `BasicTreeCellRenderer,` because we wouldn't be using its specific `getTreeCellRendererComponent` method. Whether or not this matters depends entirely on what your customization is. You could, of course, implement a subclass for each of the look-and-feels and install the correct one at run time. There is, however, another technique that avoids having to generate more classes that you'll see in "Rendering and Editing Custom Objects" below.

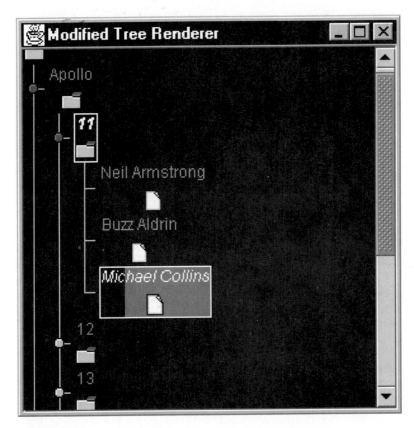

Figure 10-11   Changing text and icon positions using a custom tree renderer.

If you can't achieve the effects you need by subclassing the basic renderer, you can provide your own by implementing the `TreeCellRenderer` interface yourself. The technique for doing this is identical to the one used when creating renderers for the `JList` and `JComboBox` control, so it isn't repeated here.

Changing the Basic Look-and-Feel Specific Parts of a Tree

If your tree uses a look-and-feel that is derived from `BasicTreeUI`, you can customize more of its appearance. You can find out at run time whether a tree is using this class by getting its UI class (using getUI) and checking whether it is an instance of BasicTreeUI. If it is, you can make use of the methods shown in Table 10-6 to change the way in which the framework of the tree is drawn (but not the individual tree elements, which are controlled by the renderer, as you've already seen):

Table 10-6	Basic Tree Look-and-Feel Customization Methods

Method	*Description*
public void setLeftChildIndent(int)	Sets the horizontal distance between the left side of a node and the expansion icon for its children.
public void setRightChildIndent(int)	Sets the horizontal distance between the center of a node's expansion icon and the left side of its rendered cell.
public void setCollapsedIcon(Icon)	Sets the icon used to render the expansion icon when the node's children are not shown.
public void setExpandedIcon(Icon)	Changes the icon used as the expansion icon when the node's children are on view.

Figure 10-12 shows the various configurable parts and how they affect the way in which the tree is rendered.

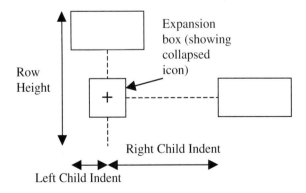

Figure 10-12   Basic Tree UI Customizable Items.

These settings are applied everywhere in the tree—you can't have different settings for different rows. The icons that you supply are used to replace the expansion icon that appears to the left of a node that has children; normally, this icon is a colored circle or small square with a plus sign (+) in it when the node is collapsed and a minus sign (–) when it is expanded. The default icons are all fairly small. If you substitute larger ones, you will need to change the right or left indent values to space the remaining elements out horizontally. If your icon is taller than the standard ones, you'll need to increase the tree's row size, which you can do with the setRowHeight method of JTree.

The next example adds some customization to TreeExample1, which was used in the previous section. New expansion icons have been substituted and, since the new icons are larger then the standard ones, it was necessary to change the right child indentation and the row height. You can run this example for yourself using the command:

```
java JFCBook.Chapter10.CustomTree
```

The result will look like that shown in Figure 10-13.

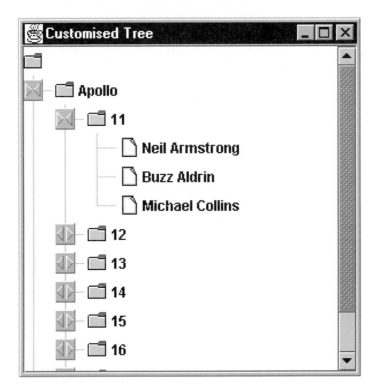

Figure 10-13   A tree with customized expansion icons.

Here's the code that was added to the main method of TreeExample1, immediately after creating the tree, to make these changes. In this code, t holds a reference to the JTree object:

```
// Get the tree's UI class. If it is a BasicTreeUI,
// customize the icons
ComponentUI ui = t.getUI();
if (ui instanceof BasicTreeUI) {
  t.setRowHeight(24);
  ((BasicTreeUI)ui).setRightChildIndent(21);
  URL expandedURL = CustomTree.class.getResource("images/closebutton.gif");
  URL collapsedURL = CustomTree.class.getResource("images/openbutton.gif");
  ((BasicTreeUI)ui).setExpandedIcon(new ImageIcon(expandedURL));
  ((BasicTreeUI)ui).setCollapsedIcon(new ImageIcon(collapsedURL));
}
```

Since these customizations only work for a look-and-feel that bases its tree UI on BasicTreeUI, the first step is to use getUI to get the UI class, which is always an instance of ComponentUI. If it turns out that it is actually a BasicTreeUI, then the row height (which is a property of JTree, not of the UI class) is changed, the new icons are loaded using the familiar ImageIcon class and then they are used to customize the expansion icons.

Changing Properties for All Trees

If all that you want to do is change the color of certain parts of a tree or the icons that it uses to represent open and closed folders and leaf nodes, and you want this change to apply to every tree in your application, you don't need to implement your own renderer or modify an existing one—instead, you can modify the UIDefaults table for the current look-and-feel, which maps property names to the values appropriate for the current look-and-feel. If you change those defaults, you can make your settings apply to everything that uses them. The tree has 10 properties that you can set. These properties, together with the types of the associated objects, are listed in Table 10-7.

Table 10-7   UIDefaults Properties for JTree

Property Name	Object Type
Tree.background	Color
Tree.backgroundNonSelectionColor	Color
Tree.backgroundSelectionColor	Color
Tree.borderSelectionColor	Color
Tree.closedIcon	Icon
Tree.hash	Color
Tree.leafIcon	Icon
Tree.openIcon	Icon
Tree.textNonSelectionColor	Color
Tree.textSelectionColor	Color

If you want to change an entry in this table, there are two possible approaches depending on the effect you want to achieve. If you want the changes to stay in place if the user dynamically switches the look-and-feel (if you allow this—see Chapter 13), you should store `Color` or `Icon` objects in the `UIDefaults` table. When a look-and-feel switch occurs, these values will not then be changed.

On the other hand, if the attributes you are setting only work with the current look-and-feel, you need to allow them to be reset to the new look-and-feel's defaults when a look-and-feel switch occurs. To achieve this, you need to wrap the attribute you are changing with an instance of `IconUIResource` in the case of an icon or `ColorUIResource` for a color. For example, to change the color of the text for a selected node to yellow only while the current look-and-feel is selected, you would proceed as follows:

```
UIDefaults defaults = UIManager.getDefaults();
defaults.put("Tree.textSelectionColor",
            new ColorUIResource(Color.yellow));
```

or to change the color of the lines that connect the nodes to white, you might do this:

```
UIDefaults defaults = UIManager.getDefaults();
defaults.put("Tree.hash", new ColorUIResource(Color.white));
```

On the other hand, the following lines makes these changes permanent:

```
UIDefaults defaults = UIManager.getDefaults();
defaults.put("Tree.textSelectionColor", Color.yellow);
defaults.put("Tree.hash", Color.white);
```

You can find out more about the `UIDefaults` table in Chapter 13. In general, it is a good idea to check whether you can carry out customization by modifying this table before using a more complex approach.

Editing a Tree's Nodes

By default, trees are read-only to the user but, if you wish, you can allow the user to change the text associated with any node in the tree with just one line of code:

```
t.setEditable(true);
```

If a tree is editable, you can edit the nodes by just selecting the node that you want to change and then clicking it again. The second click causes the node's editor to appear with the current value associated with the node displayed. By default, the editor is a text field and it shows the text that is displayed to the right of the node in the default look-and-feel. To edit the node, just change the text and press return. The editor will disappear and the new value will be installed.

Core Note

The mouse sequence needed to start the editing process depends on the editor in use. As we'll see, it is possible to configure the editor supplied with the Swing package so that it starts editing after only one click of the mouse. Furthermore, individual editors can still delay editing beyond that point. For example, the text editor requires two mouse clicks separated by a pause, followed by another pause before it becomes active.

To show how editing works, let's look at yet another version of the hard-working `TreeExample1` program, this time called `EditableTree`. The change to make it editable is just one line of code but, so that you can see what happened, a `TreeModelListener` is attached to the tree. When the editor accepts a change, it applies it to the tree model, which causes a `TreeModelEvent`. The code that was added to display the content of this event is shown below:

```
t.setEditable(true);

t.getModel().addTreeModelListener(new TreeModelListener() {
  public void treeNodesChanged(TreeModelEvent evt) {
    System.out.println("Tree Nodes Changed Event");
    Object[] children = evt.getChildren();
    int[] childIndices = evt.getChildIndices();
    for (int i = 0; i < children.length; i++) {
      System.out.println("Index " + childIndices[i] +
        ", changed value: " + children[0]);
    }
  }
  public void treeStructureChanged(TreeModelEvent evt) {
    System.out.println("Tree Structure Changed Event");
  }
  public void treeNodesInserted(TreeModelEvent evt) {
    System.out.println("Tree Nodes Inserted Event");
  }
  public void treeNodesRemoved(TreeModelEvent evt) {
    System.out.println("Tree Nodes Removed Event");
  }
});
```

The event that the listener gets will indicate that one node has changed, so of the listener methods shown above, only `treeNodesChanged` will ever be called, but you are obliged to provide the others to implement the listener interface. The event handler extracts the list of changed indices from the event and the array of changed objects. Code is included to print a set of these but, in fact, there will only ever be one. The object in the array returned by getChildren is the DefaultMutableTreeNode for the node that was edited, so printing it will cause its toString method to be called that, as you know, will print the text associated with the node. If you run this program using the command?

```
java JFCBook.Chapter10.EditableTree
```

and change the text "Apollo" to "Shuttle", you'll see the following event generated:

```
Tree Nodes Changed Event
Index 0, changed value: Shuttle
```

To edit the tree cell, click the mouse over the text of value you want to change, then pause briefly and click again. If your clicks are too close together, you'll end up expanding the node instead. If you accidentally start editing a cell and don't want to continue, click anywhere else in the control and the edit will be aborted.

Custom Cell Editors

If you allow your tree to be edited, it is up to you to carry out whatever action is implied by the change and to check that the new value is legal. One way to make it easier to get legal input values is to supply a custom editor that only offers the legal values, such as a JComboBox. The tree uses the TreeCellEditor interface to allow a customized editor to be installed.

```
public interface TreeCellEditor extends CellEditor {
    public Component getTreeCellEditorComponent(JTree tree, Object value,
        boolean isSelected, boolean expanded, boolean leaf, int row);
}
```

The TreeCellEditor interface extends CellEditor, which contains methods that are also used to create editable tables, as you'll see later in the next chapter. The getTreeCellEditorComponent returns a component that can edit a value in the tree; the initial value is passed as the second argument, along with three arguments that specify whether the node being edited is selected or expanded and whether it is a leaf. The last argument gives the screen row of the node. There is only one TreeCellEditor for each tree. As the user edits different nodes, this method is called with different values and may, if necessary, return a differently configured component. Typically, the appearance of the returned component depends on the three boolean arguments, because it occupies the same space in the tree as a cell renderer and therefore will need to draw an appropriate icon (e.g., an open or closed folder).

The methods shared with editors used with JTable (see Chapter 11, "The Table Control") are as follows:

```
public interface CellEditor {
    public Object getCellEditorValue();
    public boolean isCellEditable(EventObject);
    public boolean shouldSelectCell(EventObject);
    public boolean stopCellEditing();
    public void cancelCellEditing();
    public void addCellEditorListener(CellEditorListener);
    public void removeCellEditorListener(CellEditorListener);
}
```

These methods all deal with the mechanics of setting up an editor and starting and stopping the editing process. You don't need to implement all seven of these methods to change the text-based node editor, because most of the work is done for you in the `DefaultCellEditor` class that provides a complete implementation of an editor that can appear as either a text field, a checkbox or a combo box. Here are its three constructors:

```
public DefaultCellEditor(JTextField text);
public DefaultCellEditor(JCheckBox box);
public DefaultCellEditor(JComboBox combo);
```

To add a combo-box editor to a tree requires only a few lines of code. The `ComboTree` example, that you can run with the command:

```
java JFCBook.Chapter10.ComboTree
```

was created by adding the following to the `EditableTree` program:

```
t.setEditable(true);

final String[] values = { "Mercury", "Gemini", "Apollo",
            "Skylab", "Shuttle" };

JComboBox combo = new JComboBox();
for (int i = 0 ; i < values.length; i++) {
  combo.addItem(values[i]);
}

DefaultCellEditor editor = new DefaultCellEditor(combo);
t.setCellEditor(editor);

t.getModel().addTreeModelListener(new TreeModelListener() {
```

Because the `DefaultCellEditor` class does all of the work, all you need to do is populate the combo box that will appear in the tree and then create the `DefaultCellEditor` that will manage it. The default text editor is replaced by calling the `JTree` method `setCellEditor`. If you run this example and click once on the Apollo node, the combo box appears, as shown in Figure 10-14. Click on the arrow and the list of possible values drops down. When you select one, the drop-down closes and the editor disappears. As with the text editor, selecting a new value causes a TreeModelEvent that contains the new value.

The result will be something like that shown in Figure 10-14.

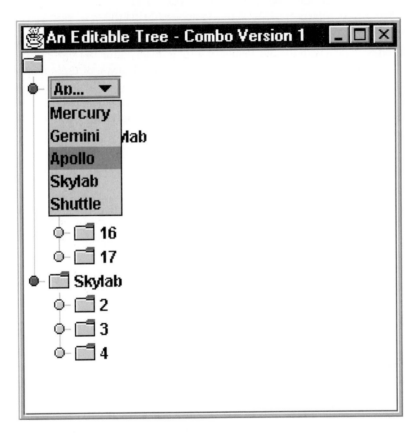

Figure 10-14   A tree with a Combo Box cell editor.

This simple example does, however, have a major flaw. As noted earlier, there is one editor that is shared amongst all of the nodes in the tree. This being the case, run the previous example again and open the tree to expose the crew of, say, Apollo 11. As you do this, be careful to click only on the expansion icons and not on the nodes themselves or on the text, to avoid initiating the editor. Now click once on the name of any crew member. In response, you'll get the same combo box offering a choice of spacecraft. This is clearly not appropriate.

To avoid this behavior, you need to create a subclass of `DefaultCellEditor` that implements the `isCellEditable` method from the `CellEditor` interface. When the user clicks with the mouse on a cell, the tree invokes this method to decide whether or not an editor should be installed on the node. If it returns `false`, no editor will appear and the node will seem to the user to be uneditable. A small change makes the previous example much more usable:

```
DefaultCellEditor editor = new DefaultCellEditor(combo) {
   public boolean isCellEditable(EventObject evt) {
      if (super.isCellEditable(evt) && evt instanceof MouseEvent) {
         TreePath path = t.getPathForLocation(((MouseEvent)evt).getX(),
                     ((MouseEvent)evt).getY());
         Object o = path.getLastPathComponent();
         String val = o.toString();
         for (int i = 0; i < values.length; i++) {
            if (val.equals(values[i])) {
               return true;
            }
         }
      }
      return false;
   }
};

editor.setClickCountToStart(2);
```

This example can be run with the command:

```
java JFCBook.Chapter10.ComboTree2.
```

This code creates a subclass of `DefaultCellEditor` in which the `isCellEditable` method is overridden.

This method receives an `EventObject` that contains the event that causes the tree to consider editing the node. If you're using the mouse, this will be a `MouseEvent`. Theoretically, it would be possible to create a look-and-feel class for the tree that allowed editing to be initiated from the keyboard, in which case the event delivered to `isCellEditable` would be a `KeyEvent`. The standard look-and-feel classes, however, do not yet support this.

The first thing the new `isCellEditable` method does is to invoke its counterpart in `DefaultCellEditor`; you'll see why this is done later. If this returns `false` or the event isn't from the mouse, `isCellEditable` returns `false` and the node will not be edited. The real problem is to decide which nodes can be allowed to be edited and which cannot.

Since the combo box in this example contains spacecraft names, one way to decide whether the node is suitable for editing is to see whether its current value is one of the possibilities in the combo box. This is not, of course, foolproof as a general algorithm, but it will work for this tree. To apply this check, it is necessary to find the node being edited and get its current value. Fortunately, the mouse event contains the coordinates of the node, so the `JTree` method `getPathForLocation` method, which returns a `TreePath` object for the node at a given position, can be used.

Core Tip

`JTree` *has a wealth of useful methods, not all of which are covered in this chapter for reasons of space. It is worthwhile reading the* `JTree` *API specification to see all of the facilities that it offers.*

Given the `TreePath`, the last component, which we know is the `TreeNode` object for the node that we are considering editing, can be extracted. Given this, the user object can be extracted using `getUserObject`. In the example, use is made of the fact that invoking `toString` on the `TreeNode` returns the user object as a string and, having obtained the value, it is simple to check whether it is in the list used to populate the combo box. If it is found, `true` is returned to allow editing to proceed.

This simple check was sufficient for our tree, because the spacecraft names only appear in one place in the tree and that the user cannot edit other nodes and introduce spacecraft names to mislead us. A more robust solution is, of course, required in a more general setting. One possible way to solve the general problem is to store information about the editability of a node in its user object or in a subclass of `DefaultMutableTreeNode` that would be used to populate the tree. A solution along these lines is simple to implement because, as you have seen, it is easy to locate the `TreeNode` and the user object from the `isCellEditable` method.

One other problem that was solved with this example was the need to not click on the node's icon or text in order to avoid starting the editor. In the code extract above, you'll see that the following line was added:

```
editor.setClickCountToStart(2);
```

This tells the `DefaultCellEditor` that it shouldn't edit the node unless it sees a mouse event with the click count 2 or greater. As a result, a single click on the node is now acceptable, and doesn't invoke the editor. In fact, this check is made by the `isCellEditable` method of `DefaultCellEditor` itself, which is the reason that its `isCellEditable` method was invoked at the start of our own.

Rendering and Editing Custom Objects

The replacement editor developed in the previous section had an implicit assumption that doesn't hold for some trees. The assumption was that the user objects associated with the tree's nodes were all strings, which was (conveniently) true in that particular example. There is no reason for this always to be true and in many cases it is useful to be able to associate an arbitrary object with a node. When the user object is not a string, the default renderer will display it properly provided that it provides a suitable toString method because, as you already know, the renderer applies this method to the node, which will in turn apply it to the user object.

While it is easy to arrange for rendering of custom user objects to work, proper editing is not so simple. Let's return to the combo box editor to see what the issue is. When the tree was built for this case, all the user objects were strings and the combo box was populated with all of the possible string values that would be meaningful for the nodes that could be edited. When the user selects a new value, the editor applies the value to the tree. Because the editor was derived from the DefaultCellEditor class, there was no need to supply the code that carried out this step. What actually happens is that the editor's stopCellEditing method is called when the edit is finished and this method informs any registered CellEditorListeners that editing is complete. The tree's UI class registers as a listener and, when it receives this event, it gets the new value from the editor by calling its getCellEditorValue method, which, in the case of our example, will return the value selected from the combo box, courtesy of code provided by DefaultCellEditor.

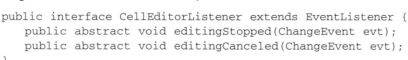

Core Note

CellEditorListener *is not a very useful interface unless you are implementing a tree UI or an editor. It consists of two methods:*

```
public interface CellEditorListener extends EventListener {
    public abstract void editingStopped(ChangeEvent evt);
    public abstract void editingCanceled(ChangeEvent evt);
}
```

The editingStopped *method is called when editing completes normally, while* editingCanceled *is invoked when editing is aborted because, for example, the user selected a different node on the tree or collapsed the branch that contained the node being edited. This interface doesn't have an event of its own—it just supplies a* ChangeEvent, *an event that has no state, but just indicates that something about the event source may have changed.*

The problem that our earlier editor would fall foul of if it had to handle custom user objects is that DefaultCellEditor applies the edited value by invoking the DefaultTreeModel valueForPathChanged method, which is defined as follows:

```
public void valueForPathChanged(TreePath path, Object value);
```

The default implementation of this method locates the DefaultMutableTreeNode for the affected path and makes the change by invoking setUserObject(value). The combo box returned a String value, so the type of the value argument to this method will be String, which means that the user object will be replaced by its own String representation. Unless the user object was originally a String (which, fortunately, it was in our example), this is a fatal mistake.

To get around this problem, you can do one of two things:

- Populate the combo box with the user objects instead of strings. This works because the combo box displays the result of invoking toString on each of its displayed items, and the selected item will be an instance of the user object type. Therefore, valueForPathChanged will be passed an object of the correct type.
- Continue to populate the combo box with strings, but override the valueForPathChanged method to substitute an appropriate object for the String when the edit is complete.

The first method is much the simpler of the two so, for the purposes of illustration, let's look at how to implement the second method.

Implementing Editing of Trees with Custom User Objects

Let's start by deciding what the user object that will be associated with a node might be. Obviously, this depends on how you are going to use the tree, but one common way to create a tree is to save a custom icon and a text string in the user object. This allows you to have a different icon for each object in the tree instead of using the default icon provided by the look-and-feel, or using a single substitute that is the same for all nodes (or at least for all leaf nodes), as you saw when looking at how to create a custom renderer earlier in this chapter. Here's the plan for this example.

Instead of populating the tree with nodes that use Strings as the user object, this example will invent an interface that allows an object to return an icon to be rendered to represent it, then create suitable objects that implement this interface and associate them with nodes in the tree. To correctly display these nodes, a custom renderer will be needed. This renderer will get the text and the icon from the user object instead of using built-in icons or substitute icons that don't depend on the object being displayed. To edit these nodes, an editor that offers a combo box interface will be used and, finally, it will be necessary to supply our own tree model in which the valueForPathChanged method is overridden.

Let's start by defining the interface:

```
// An interface that describes objects with icons
interface NodeWithIcon {
  public Icon getIcon();
}
```

All that is required of the user objects in the tree is the ability to get an icon from them. It isn't necessary to include a method in the interface to get a text description, because the `toString` method can be used for this.

Core Note

For simplicity, the implementation of this example is kept in a single source file. Because there can only be one public class or interface per source file, the above interface is declared with package scope. If you were developing a real application using the technique that we are explaining here, you would extract this interface into its own source file and make it public.

Next, let's define the user objects that will be used to populate the tree. This example is going to use a custom data model so that a new `valueForPathChanged` method can be implemented. This method will need to know how to map from a `String` to the appropriate user object that corresponds to that `String`. In other words, the data model must be aware of the meaning of the objects that it contains, so the definition of the data objects is tied to the data model by defining them in terms of an inner class of the data model itself. In fact, the data model is going to be defined in such a way that its users need only know that the items that it contains implement the `NodeWithIcon` interface, which allows us to use other data models in place of the one that will be shown here.

Listing 10-7 shows the implementation of the tree data model and the items that will be used as the user objects in the tree.

Listing 10-7   A customized tree model class

```
// This class represents the data model for this tree
class CustomTreeModel extends DefaultTreeModel {
   public CustomTreeModel(TreeNode node) {
     super(node);
     objects.put("CSM",
           new HardwareObject("CSM", "images/csmicon.gif"));
     objects.put("LM",
           new HardwareObject("LM", "images/lemicon.gif"));
   }

   public void valueForPathChanged(TreePath path, Object newValue) {
     DefaultMutableTreeNode node =
(DefaultMutableTreeNode)path.getLastPathComponent();
     String value = (String)newValue;

     // Use the string to locate a suitable HardwareObject.
     // If there isn't one, just use the string as the user object
```
continued

```
    HardwareObject object = getObjectForName(value);
    if (object != null) {
      node.setUserObject(object);
    } else {
      node.setUserObject(value);
    }
    nodeChanged(node);
    }

  // Get the HardwareObject for a given name, or null if unknown
  public HardwareObject getObjectForName(String name) {
    return (HardwareObject)objects.get(name);
  }

  // Create the set of objects that can populate the leaf nodes
  protected static class HardwareObject implements NodeWithIcon {
    protected HardwareObject(String text, String imageName) {
      this.text = text;
      this.icon = new ImageIcon(getClass().getResource(imageName));
    }

    // Return text for display
    public String toString() {
      return text;
    }

    // Return the icon
    public Icon getIcon() {
      return icon;
    }

    protected String text;
    protected Icon icon;
  }

  // Get the possible hardware types in a combo box
  public JComboBox getNamesAsCombo() {
    JComboBox combo = new JComboBox();
    Enumeration e = objects.keys();
    while (e.hasMoreElements()) {
      combo.addItem(e.nextElement());
    }
    return combo;
  }

  protected static Hashtable objects = new Hashtable();
  }
```

Let's look first at the user object class, which is called `HardwareObject`. This particular example will display two items of space hardware and allow the user to place either one of them into a particular location in the tree by offering a combo box with their names when the user clicks to start editing. To the left of the name, there will be a small picture that shows what the item actually looks like. To keep this example simple, only leaf items will be customized, so there is no need to supply extra icons for expanded and collapsed nodes. The same principles would, of course, be applied if you wanted to produce a completely general solution.

To create each `HardwareNode` object, the name of the hardware and the location of its icon must be supplied. The implementation of the `HardwareNode` class is very simple. The constructor stores the hardware name and uses the `ImageIcon` class to load the corresponding icon. The `toString` method returns the object's name and the `getIcon` method returns the icon. This method is needed because `HardwareNode` is required to implement the `NodeWithIcon` interface.

Because we don't want anything outside the data model to know how to create these user objects, two of them are built in the data model's constructor and placed in a hash table, keyed by their names. To complete the encapsulation, a method (`getObjectForName`) is provided to get a copy of the object given its name. You'll see why this method is needed later. These objects are both read-only, so it is only necessary to create one of each. Storing one copy of each in the hashtable is, therefore, acceptable, no matter how many times it might appear in the tree (and in this example it appears either once or not at all).

Thinking ahead a bit to the implementation of the cell editor, a combo box will need to be populated with the names of the possible hardware choices. Again, it isn't desirable to have the editor know how many possible choices there are or what relationship the string name that it will store might have to the objects themselves, so we implement a method within the data model (`getNamesAsCombo`) that returns a suitably populated `JComboBox` that the editor can use. This combo box is created by obtaining an enumeration of the items in the data model's internal hash table and adding one combo item per entry in the enumeration.

The valueForPathChanged Method

The only other method of the data model that still needs to be described is the one that this section opened with—`valueForPathChanged`. This method is called with a `TreePath` for the node that has been edited and the new value, which is known to be a `String`. What it needs to do is find the correct user object corresponding to the `String` and install it in the node. Finding the user object is easy— the data model has a hashtable that maps from the name to the object itself, so all that is necessary is to invoke the `getObjectForName` method to locate the object. This method only returns an appropriate answer if the string returned by the combo box was the name of one of the objects that are in the hashtable. Given the way that this example has been written, this will always be true, but if you take the code here and use it in another application which allows the combo box to be editable (probably a mistake!), the user may type a meaningless value and you won't find a corresponding object in the hashtable. To defend against this possibility, if this happens, the exact value that the user typed is stored as the user object. Whether or not this is of any use depends on the application: It does at least stop the program getting a `NullPointerException`.

Having got the object, the next step is to find the node to install it in. You already know how to do this—you just apply `getLastPathComponent` to the `TreePath` to find the node and then call `setUserObject` to install the user object. Finally, the `nodeChanged` method is called to have the data model send events to registered `TreeModelListeners`.

A Renderer for Custom Nodes

That takes care of the data model. However, this example also needs a custom cell renderer and a custom editor. The editor is almost identical to the example you saw earlier. As before, it is derived from `DefaultCellEditor` and its constructor is passed the combo box that is obtained from the data model's `getNamesAsCombo` method. All that is left to do is implement the `isCellEditable` method to determine which cells are editable. In this tree, all of the nonleaf nodes will be standard `DefaultMutableTreeNodes`. These nodes are not going to be editable—only leaf nodes can be edited. Therefore, this method just returns the result of invoking `isLeaf` on the node in question. The implementation of the cell editor, along with the rest of this example, is shown in Listing 10-8.

Listing 10-8   Rendering and editing nodes with custom icons

```
package JFCBook.Chapter10;

import com.sun.java.swing.*;
import com.sun.java.swing.tree.*;
import com.sun.java.swing.event.*;
import java.util.*;
import java.awt.Component;
import java.awt.event.*;

public class CustomIcons {
  public static void main(String[] args) {
    JFrame f = new JFrame("Custom Icons");
```

```
// Create the model with just the root node
DefaultMutableTreeNode rootNode =
            new DefaultMutableTreeNode("Apollo");
final CustomTreeModel m = new CustomTreeModel(rootNode);
final JTree t = new JTree(m);
t.putClientProperty("JTree.lineStyle", "Angled");
t.setEditable(true);
t.setRowHeight(0);      // Row height is not fixed

// Create the combo of names for the editor
JComboBox combo = m.getNamesAsCombo();

// Define a replacement editor
DefaultCellEditor editor = new DefaultCellEditor(combo) {
  public boolean isCellEditable(EventObject evt) {
    if (super.isCellEditable(evt) && evt instanceof MouseEvent) {
      TreePath path = t.getPathForLocation(((MouseEvent)evt).getX(),
            ((MouseEvent)evt).getY());
      DefaultMutableTreeNode node =
        (DefaultMutableTreeNode)path.getLastPathComponent();

      // We can edit a leaf
      return node.isLeaf();
    }
    return false;
  }
};
editor.setClickCountToStart(2);
t.setCellEditor(editor);

// Define a replacement renderer
final TreeCellRenderer oldRenderer = t.getCellRenderer();
TreeCellRenderer r = new TreeCellRenderer() {
  public  Component getTreeCellRendererComponent(JTree tree,
              Object value,
              boolean selected,
              boolean expanded,
              boolean leaf,
              int row,
              boolean hasFocus) {
    // Allow the original renderer to set up the label
    Component c = oldRenderer.getTreeCellRendererComponent(tree, value, selected,
                expanded, leaf, row,
                hasFocus);
```

continued

```
        // Now change the icon if possible necessary
        if (leaf && c instanceof JLabel) {
          JLabel l = (JLabel)c;
          Object o = ((DefaultMutableTreeNode)value).getUserObject();
          if (o instanceof NodeWithIcon) {
            // It has an icon, so use that
            l.setIcon(((NodeWithIcon)o).getIcon());
          }
        }

        return c;
      }
    };
    t.setCellRenderer(r);

    // Populate the model with a small amount of data
    DefaultMutableTreeNode hardwareNode = new DefaultMutableTreeNode("Hardware");
    rootNode.add(hardwareNode);
    String itemName = (String)combo.getItemAt(0);
    DefaultMutableTreeNode itemNode = new DefaultMutableTreeNode(
                m.getObjectForName(itemName));
    hardwareNode.add(itemNode);

    t.expandRow(0);
    t.expandRow(1);

    f.getContentPane().add(new JScrollPane(t));
    f.setSize(300, 300);
    f.setVisible(true);
  }
}
```

The Cell Renderer

Now let's turn to the cell renderer. This needs to be customized because it needs to display a specific icon for each node that has one and, conversely, it should display the standard icon if it comes across a node that does not have a special icon—that is, a node whose user object is not an instance of a class that implements the NodeWithIcon interface. In the previous example, you saw how to change the icon by subclassing BasicCellRenderer. The technique used was to let it set up the rendered component, which is known to be a JLabel, and then substitute a different icon for the standard one. Since a specific icon can be obtained from each node that implements NodeWithIcon, the same approach could be used here and, if the node doesn't implement this interface (e.g., if it is not one of our leaf nodes), the standard icon would be left in place.

The problem with this approach is that it limits us to look-and-feel classes whose cell renderers are derived from BasicTreeCellRenderer and that don't add any functionality to it that can't be lost. This time, it would be nice to be a bit more general and produce a renderer that will work in tandem with any installed renderer that creates a JLabel as its rendered component. Since this restriction effectively prevents us from implementing our renderer by subclassing an existing one, the choices are either to implement a completely new renderer, or to find some way of exploiting the existing one.

Implementing a new renderer is very unattractive—you would need to create one for every look-and-feel you might come across, so that the nonleaf nodes are rendered correctly. You might even find that a particular look-and-feel chooses to place the icon above the text, or make some other change to the way the component is displayed. A better solution is to use the renderer that's installed in the tree when it is created, by first installing our own renderer in its place and then calling the original renderer's getTreeCellRendererComponent method at the start of our own. This allows the original renderer to create the component in its usual format, then it gives us control. If the component it created is a JLabel and our node has an icon of its own, the only thing left to do is get the node's icon and install it in the JLabel. There is no need to be concerned about how the label is organized, because this is a simple trade of one icon for another. You'll find the implementation details in Listing 10-8

All of the pieces are now in place. The rest of the code just creates an instance of the tree with suitable data and displays it. Figure 10-15 shows what it looks like with one hardware item selected. If you run this example by typing the command:

```
java JFCBook.Chapter10.CustomIcons
```

you can try out editing the leaf node by double-clicking on it. You'll get a combo box with two selections in it. Notice how the text and the image both change when you change the selection. Notice also that the nonleaf nodes are not editable.

Figure 10-15   A tree node with a custom icon.

Summary

This chapter introduced the Swing tree control, one of two powerful data display components that you have at your disposal. After seeing the basic components of a tree, you learned how trees are created and how the user can manipulate them by expanding and collapsing nodes and making selections. You also saw how these actions are reflected in the tree itself and how they can be intercepted by applications and by custom components derived from the JTree class.

One of the more popular uses for a tree control is to display the content of a file system. A large portion of this chapter was devoted to creating a subclass of JTree that can show a file system in hierarchic form. The implementation of this control reveals much of the inner workings of the tree's data structures.

Finally, you saw several ways in which the tree's appearance can be customized to suit the needs of particular applications and discovered how to allow the user to edit the contents of a tree, while still making sure that only meaningful changes can be made.

THE TABLE CONTROL

Topics in This Chapter

- Tables and Table Headers
- The Table Data Model and the Column Model
- Table Selection
- Renderers and Editors
- Column- and Class-Based Rendering and Editing

Chapter 11

Next to `JTree`, `JTable` is probably the most complex control in the Swing component set. This chapter starts by showing how to create a table with only a few lines of code then, in order to allow you to exploit fully the more powerful features of tables, you'll see in detail the parts that make it up—the data model and the way in which table columns are specified and managed. You'll also learn how to control and react to the selection of cells, rows and columns within the table.

The second part of the chapter introduces table cell renderers and editors, which allow you to customize the table's appearance and shows some examples that demonstrate several useful techniques you can use as the basis for your own applications.

An Overview of the Table Control

By comparison to the `JTree` control that we saw in the last chapter, `JTable` is relatively simple, but provides enough flexibility to enable it to be used in a very simple way to quickly display information in a rough-and-ready manner, while also being capable of being configured and customized to allow the user, if necessary, to edit or interactively change the way in the data is ordered on the screen. As with the tree, tables are actually built from several parts, all of which will be examined closely in this chapter. If you just want to display a two-dimensional array of numbers, for example, you don't need to know very much about the table to be able to do so but, on the other hand, learning the details of each piece of the table allows you to create more useful tables and to present the same data in different ways depending on the needs of the user.

A Simple Table

Let's start by looking at an example of a table that was created with only a few lines of code. Because the aim is to keep this example as simple as possible, you'll see that the table has some imperfections. In fact, it is possible to create simple tables that don't have the problems that you'll see in this example, provided that the data is consistent with the defaults that the table controller uses. In this example, several of the table's columns have been made deliberately difficult for the table to handle. This, of course, gives us the opportunity to show you what can go wrong and how you can fix it. You can see the table for yourself by running the program that displays it using the command:

```
java JFCBook.Chapter11.TableExample
```

The table that this program creates is shown in Figure 11-1.

Flight	Comm...	LM Pilot	CM Pilot	Launch	Duration	Landin...	Surfac...	Moonw...	Moonw...	Sampl...
Apollo 7	Walter ...	Walter ...	Donn ...	java.uti...	936540	-	0	0	0	0.0
Apollo 8	Frank ...	Willia...	James...	java.uti...	529260	-	0	0	0	0.0
Apollo 9	James...	Russel...	David ...	java.uti...	867660	-	0	0	0	0.0
Apollo ...	Thoma...	Eugen...	John Y...	java.uti...	691380	-	0	0	0	0.0
Apollo ...	Neil Ar...	Edwin ...	Michae...	java.uti...	703080	Sea of ...	77760	9060	1	47.7
Apollo ...	Charle...	Alan B...	Richar...	java.uti...	880560	Ocean ...	113460	27900	2	75.7
Apollo ...	James...	Fred H...	Jack S...	java.uti...	514440	-	0	0	0	0.0
Apollo ...	Alan S...	Edgar ...	Stuart ...	java.uti...	777720	Fra Ma...	120600	33660	2	94.4
Apollo ...	David ...	James...	Alfred ...	java.uti...	1062720	Hadley...	240840	66780	3	169.0
Apollo ...	John Y...	Charle...	Thoma...	java.uti...	957060	Descar...	255720	72840	3	208.3
Apollo ...	Eugen...	Harris...	Ronald...	java.uti...	1086660	Taurus...	269940	79320	3	243.1

Figure 11-1   A simple table.

The data in this table is a list of the manned Apollo space flights from 1968 to 1972 and includes the flight dates, the crews, the spacecraft names and other information, some of which will be used later in this chapter.

The first thing to observe is that the table is divided into two parts—the *header* and the *body*. The header occupies the top row of the table and contains a heading for each of the columns. To make it stand out from the body, it is colored differently and each column header has a border. Figure 11-1 shows what the table looks like with the Metal look-and-feel, but the other look-and-feels have a similar distinction between the header and the body. It wasn't necessary to do anything special to create the header—it was built automatically when the table was created. However, it is possible to create your own table headers that contain custom components or have different colored background or text, as you'll see during the discussion of the table header and of table renderers that, like those used with the tree, control exactly how the various pieces of a table are represented.

The body of the table is drawn in the form of a grid, with horizontal and vertical lines bounding every cell in the table. The color of the grid lines is customizable and it is also possible to suppress the grid lines. If you don't like solid grid lines, you can provide your own alternative provided that you are prepared to override the basic look-and-feel of the table by extending the table's UI class using techniques similar to those used when customizing the tree component in the previous chapter. If you want to take this step, you should consult the API documentation for the class `BasicTableUI`.

Analyzing the Columns

The next thing to notice about this table is that some of the data is hard to read. Take, for example, the second column that should contain the name of the commander of the flight whose name is in the first column. As you can see, the column header for this column is incomplete—instead of reading `Commander`, it says `Comm...`, because the column itself is not wide enough to contain the text assigned to it. This is also true for many of the entries in that column.

Core Note

The size of the window that this program uses depends on the resolution of your display, so you may see more or less of each column depending on your monitor and the settings of your video driver.

There are several other columns that share this same problem. If you expand the window, you'll find that all of the columns get proportionately wider, which may allow you to see more of the information that you might be looking for, but this is, of course, not ideal. If you want to see exactly what is in the second column, you'll have to move the mouse until it is over the gap *in the header* between the second and third columns. When the mouse is correctly positioned, the cursor will change to a two-headed arrow (or whatever the resize cursor is on your platform). At this point, you can drag to the right with the left mouse button pressed to increase the size of the second column. As you do this, the columns in the table body adjust themselves to reflect the change made in the header and when you release the mouse button the table takes up its new configuration. When you've arranged for all of the second column to be visible, you'll see something like Figure 11-2.

...	Commander	LM Pilot	CM Pilot	Launch	Durati...	Landi...	Surfac...	Moon...	Moon...	Samp...
...	Walter Schirra	Walter ...	Donn ...	java.uti...	936540	-	0	0	0	0.0
...	Frank Borman	Willia...	James...	java.uti...	529260	-	0	0	0	0.0
...	James McDivitt	Russe...	David ...	java.uti...	867660	-	0	0	0	0.0
...	Thomas Stafford	Eugen...	John Y...	java.uti...	691380	-	0	0	0	0.0
...	Neil Armstrong	Edwin ...	Micha...	java.uti...	703080	Sea of...	77760	9060	1	47.7
...	Charles Conrad Jr	Alan B...	Richar...	java.uti...	880560	Ocean...	113460	27900	2	75.7
...	James Lovell Jr	Fred H...	Jack S...	java.uti...	514440	-	0	0	0	0.0
...	Alan Shephard Jr	Edgar ...	Stuart ...	java.uti...	777720	Fra M...	120600	33660	2	94.4
...	David Scott	James...	Alfred ...	java.uti...	10627...	Hadle...	240840	66780	3	169.0
...	John Young	Charle...	Thom...	java.uti...	957060	Desca...	255720	72840	3	208.3
...	Eugene Cernan	Harris...	Ronal...	java.uti...	10866...	Tauru...	269940	79320	3	243.1

Figure 11-2   The table after resizing the second column.

While the second column has grown, the others have had to be adjusted to create the extra space that it needed and now you'll find it harder to read what is in the other columns—as an example, the flight name in the first column has been narrowed to the point that you can no longer see it at all. In fact, if you want to read all of the information in this table, it will take you some time to adjust each column in turn so that you can see all of it and, each time you do so, you lose information elsewhere. This is, of course, partly due to the fact that this table was created using the default settings for JTable and its constituent parts but, in general, it can be tricky to arrange for all of the information to be visible at the same time. This issue will crop up again several times in the next few sections.

Next, look at the column headed Launch. This should contain the launch date of the flight, but instead it contains the start of a string representation of the GregorianCalendar object that contains the date. Within the table, each cell has a renderer that is responsible for displaying the data in that cell. The table initially contains default renderers that can display icons, booleans and numbers and a catch-all renderer for other objects that just calls the object's toString method and displays the result, which is what has happened here. To make this field display properly, you have to provide a custom renderer. You can see a similar problem in several other columns such as Duration, which currently shows the flight duration in seconds. Later in this chapter, you'll see how to display this as days, hours, minutes and seconds. The default renderers are, of course, perfectly adequate if your table consists of strings and numbers that are meaningful in their raw form (such as sales figures, etc.)—notice, for example, that the last column contains the number of pounds of moon rock collected, which displays properly as a floating-point number.

Rearranging Columns

One of the nice features of the table control is that you are not necessarily bound to use the column ordering that you are initially presented with. Unless the programmer prevents it, the user can rearrange table columns by dragging the column headers. As an example, with the example program running, move the mouse over the header of the LM Pilot column and press and hold down the left mouse button, then drag the mouse to the right, keeping the button pressed. As you move the mouse, the column header becomes detached and follows the mouse, followed by the rest of the LM Pilot column, as shown in Figure 11-3. When the header is about half-way over the CM Pilot header to its right, you'll notice that the two columns change places, so that the CM Pilot column moves into the vacant position next to the Commander column. If you now release the mouse button, the LM Pilot column will drop into its new location. If you continue dragging, you'll find that each column that you pass over will jump to the left when you have obscured half of it, leaving its former position vacant for you to drop your column into.

Flight	Comm...	LM Pilot	M Pilot	Launch	Duration	Landin...	Surfac...	Moonw...	Moonw...	Sampl...
Apollo 7	Walter ...	Walter ...	nn ...	java.uti...	936540	-	0	0	0	0.0
Apollo 8	Frank ...	Willia...	mes...	java.uti...	529260	-	0	0	0	0.0
Apollo 9	James...	Russel...	vid ...	java.uti...	867660	-	0	0	0	0.0
Apollo ...	Thoma...	Eugen...	nn Y...	java.uti...	691380	-	0	0	0	0.0
Apollo ...	Neil Ar...	Edwin ...	chae...	java.uti...	703080	Sea of ...	77760	9060	1	47.7
Apollo ...	Charle...	Alan B...	char...	java.uti...	880560	Ocean ...	113460	27900	2	75.7
Apollo ...	James...	Fred H...	ck S...	java.uti...	514440	-	0	0	0	0.0
Apollo ...	Alan S...	Edgar ...	uart ...	java.uti...	777720	Fra Ma...	120600	33660	2	94.4
Apollo ...	David ...	James...	red ...	java.uti...	1062720	Hadley...	240840	66780	3	169.0
Apollo ...	John Y...	Charle...	oma...	java.uti...	957060	Descar...	255720	72840	3	208.3
Apollo ...	Eugen...	Harris...	nald...	java.uti...	1086660	Taurus...	269940	79320	3	243.1

Figure 11-3 Dragging a table column to a new location.

Selecting Columns and Rows

As you clicked on the header of the LM Pilot column, you will have noticed that the entire column changed color. Clicking on the header of a column results in that column being selected. Like many other Swing controls, the table allows some or all of its content to be selected by the user; changes in the selection are notified to application code by events and it is possible to retrieve whatever is currently selected. Clicking on an individual cell selects the row that the cell is in and deselects anything else. If you use the CTRL key in conjunction with the mouse, you can create selections that consist of more than one row or more than one column. For example, click on the header of the first column, then hold down CTRL and click on the header of the Commander column. This results in both of these columns being selected. As long as you hold down the CTRL key, you can continue to add new columns to the selection by clicking on their headers. If you click on a column that is already selected, it becomes deselected. Releasing the CTRL key leaves the selection undisturbed, but clicking anywhere else clears it and starts a new selection.

It is possible to enable row, column or individual cell selection. By default, row selection is enabled, but the table in this example also has column selection turned on. If you click in one of the cells of the table with these settings, you'll find that the column and row that the cell is in become selected. If you click somewhere else, the selection changes to the row and column that intersect at the new cell. To deselect a row or a column, hold down CTRL to click anywhere in that row or column. If you click the cell at the intersection point with CTRL pressed, both the row and the column become deselected. With the default table settings, clicking in a cell would just select the row containing that cell.

With the default settings, it is not possible to select an individual cell, but it is possible to arrange for this behavior and, in fact, most of what has been said about selection in this overview is true only when the default settings are used, as you'll see in the section on table selection later in this chapter.

Cell Editing

You can see another potentially useful feature of JTable if you double-click any of the cells in the first column. First, the row that contains the cell will be selected, then a cursor will appear in that cell. In fact, the cell has been replaced by a text field initialized with its current value and you'll find that you can edit the cell's contents and, when you press RETURN, the cell takes on the new value. In the case of this table, this is not an especially meaningful thing to do because the table presents historical information that a user wouldn't normally want to change and editing has been allowed in the first column only, simply for illustrative purposes. If you try double-clicking the cells in any of the other columns, you'll find that you can't edit them.

Scrolling

To complete this brief introductory look at the table control, use the mouse to reduce the height of the window so that it can no longer display all of the rows of data that it contains. When you do this, a vertical scrollbar appears that allows you to scroll the table content so that you can view every row. You'll notice that the column headers stay in view at all times, because they reside in the column header part of a

`JScrollPane`. However, no matter how much you narrow the window, you won't get a usable horizontal scrollbar, even though the `JScrollPane` that the table is wrapped in has such a scrollbar available. You'll see why the table behaves like this, and how to get around it, later in this chapter.

Table Structure

Like `JTree`, the table is actually made up of several pieces, each of which will be examined closely in this chapter. Most obviously, there is `JTable` itself, which is derived from `JComponent`. `JTable` really only provides a way to present a view, in this case a tabular view, of some data; that view does not include the table header, which is managed by the related `JTableHeader` class, as shown in Figure 11-4.

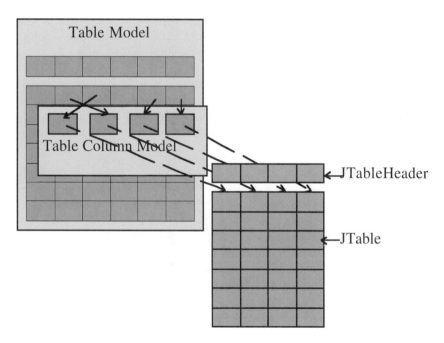

Figure 11-4   The internal structure of a table.

The table content, that is, the data itself, is held separately in the table's *data model*. Any class can be used to supply data to a table, provided that it implements the `com.sun.java.swing.table.TableModel` interface, which you'll see in the next section along with the two classes in the Swing set that implements this interface. The data model is also responsible for maintaining information about the number of columns the table has and the default headers to be used for each column.

Core Note

All of the classes and interfaces that make up the table are in the com.sun.java.swing.table *package, with the exception of* JTable *itself that resides in* com.sun.java.swing *and two events and their corresponding listener interfaces in the* com.sun.java.swing.event *package.*

Neither JTable nor JTableHeader get all of the information they need directly from the data model. Between the table and its data model is the *table column model*, which is also shown in Figure 11-4. The idea of the table column model is to map the columns in the data model to a visual representation. The mapping may involve reordering the table columns, leaving some columns out or even including duplicate columns. In Figure 11-4, for example, the data model has six columns, but the JTable itself shows only four of them. As you can see, the TableColumnModel selects which of the columns from the model will be displayed and in which order. In this case, the TableColumnModel selects columns 1, 2, 4 and 5 from the model and displays them in the order 2, 1, 4, 5.

Each column in the TableColumnModel is an object of type TableColumn. It is actually the TableColumnModel that makes it possible for the user to reorder the columns shown by the JTable; when a column is dragged to a new location, the order of TableColumn objects is changed accordingly, but the order of columns in the data model is not affected—in fact, the model is unaware of the fact that any re-ordering is taking place.

Core Note

The table model is actually not aware of which of its columns are being displayed at any given time, much less the order in which they are being viewed. This makes it much easier to provide more than one view of the same data at the same time—if one view re-orders its columns, this has no effect on the other view, which will use a different TableColumnModel. *Use will be made of this fact toward the end of this chapter, when you'll see how to fix a set of columns from a table so that they don't scroll horizontally along with the rest of it.*

The other aspect of the table that will be examined in this chapter, which isn't shown in Figure 11-4, is its selection model. The selection model remembers which rows, columns or cells are selected and the overall selection policy that the table will allow. JTable uses the same selection model, ListSelectionModel, as the JList component that you saw in Chapter 8, "Creating Custom Dialogs," so you already know a lot about how it works. Later in this chapter, you'll see how you can configure the table's selection policy and act on selection changes.

The Table Model

In order to create a table, you have to supply the data that it will display and connect the table to that data. JTable can extract data from any object that implements the TableModel interface. The first part of this section shows the TableModel interface and describes what the methods in this interface are supposed to do. You'll see them illustrated with concrete examples when specific implementations of the TableModel interface are discussed in the following paragraphs.

The TableModel Interface

The TableModel interface is defined as follows:

```
public interface TableModel {
    public int getRowCount();
    public int getColumnCount();
    public String getColumnName(int columnIndex);
    public Class getColumnClass(int columnIndex);
    public boolean isCellEditable(int rowIndex, int columnIndex);
    public Object getValueAt(int rowIndex, int columnIndex);
    public void setValueAt(Object aValue, int rowIndex, int columnIndex);
    public void addTableModelListener(TableModelListener l);
    public void removeTableModelListener(TableModelListener l);
}
```

The data that this model represents is assumed to be in tabular or grid form; each item of data occupies one cell in the grid, whose location can be specified by the index of the row and column at whose intersection the cell resides. The getRowCount and getColumnCount methods return the total number of rows and columns in the table. The table is assumed to be fully-populated at all times, so that if there are 3 rows and 4 columns, there will be 12 valid cells in the table.

The value of any data item in the table can be obtained using the getValueAt method, which is given the row and column index of the cell that contains the data. These indices are both numbered from 0, where row 0 is (logically) at the top of the grid and column 0 is (logically) at the left, as shown in Figure 11-5. The value returned from this method is an Object, so the data model can contain information of any kind. Nothing in the table component cares what the actual type of the data in the model is, apart from the renderers that display it and the editors that optionally allow the user to change it. You'll see later how these are configured.

The TableModel interface also provides the ability to modify the content of individual cells. There are two methods that are used to implement this. The isCellEditable method returns a boolean that indicates whether the content of a specific cell can be changed given its row and column index. If this method returns false, no change to the data will be allowed. If it returns true, the caller can use the setValueAt method to change the cell's value. This method is given the cell's row and column indices and the new value to be stored in the cell, as an Object. It is the responsibility of the class implementing the TableModel interface to ensure that the value being stored is acceptable—for example, if a cell should contain a positive integer, it is the table model's responsibility to ensure that the value supplied is actually a positive integer.

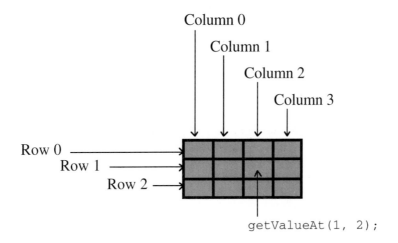

Column 0
Column 1
Column 2
Column 3

Row 0
Row 1
Row 2

getValueAt(1, 2);

Figure 11-5 The table data model.

Core Note

The TableModel interface does not specify how an unacceptable value supplied to setValueAt should be rejected. In particular, there is no expectation that this method will throw an exception. In fact, the code that makes the change to the cell content in the JTable class does not catch any exceptions, so throwing one would be fatal. The only way to reject an unacceptable value is, therefore, to ignore it, the result of which will be that the user will be able to supply an illegal value and press RETURN, but will then see the cell restored to its previous state.

No change to a cell's content is possible unless the isCellEditable method returns true and the setValueAt method is implemented to actually store the new value. It is, therefore, possible to create a read-only data model by implementing isCellEditable so that it always returns false. On the other hand, if this method can return true under any circumstances, you must implement a complementary setValueAt method, or the user will be allowed to edit the cell on the screen but will then be unable to save the new value, just as if an illegal value had been supplied.

As well as storing the table data, the model is also responsible for supplying a name for each column of the table, which can be obtained by invoking the `getColumnName` method with the column index as the only argument. In many cases, the column name that this method returns, which is always a `String`, will be directly usable in the header of the table that displays the model data, but this need not be so. For example, if you populate a table data model using a database query, the column name may be the name of a field within a database record. Since database field names are not always meaningful to the end user of the database, it is possible to substitute a more useful column name in the `TableColumn` object that maps the column from the data model, as you'll see later.

The `getColumnClass` method returns a `Class` object that describes the type of object stored in a given column. The table makes the default assumption that every row will have an object of the same type in any given colum—for instance, in the example table shown at the start of this chapter, the first column always contains a `String`. This assumption is used when selecting the appropriate renderer or editor for a cell. However, as you'll see, it is not necessary for the class returned to be more specific than `java.lang.Object`, which allows every row to have a different type of object in the column. In most tables, though, the assumption will be valid that all the objects in any given column are of the same type.

The last two methods in this interface allow the registration and removal of listeners that can be notified of changes to the table data model, including adding and removing rows or columns or changing the content of individual cells. The table supports this through the `TableModelEvent` and the `TableModelListener` interface, both of which will be discussed later. Despite the fact that it allows listeners to register to receive notification of these events, the `TableModel` interface does not provide methods that allow the number of rows or columns in the data model to be initially defined or to be changed. These facilities are not in the interface because they are not needed to implement `JTable`. Most implementations of this interface will, of course, supply methods to accomplish these tasks and you'll see examples in the discussion of the `DefaultTableModel`. Given that the table data can be modified while the table is being displayed, it is necessary for the `TableModel` to define the methods by which these changes can be notified so that `JTable` and its user interface implementation can receive these events and update the user's view of the data as it changes.

The AbstractTableModel and DefaultTableModel Classes

There are two implementations of the `TableModel` interface in the Swing table package—`AbstractTableModel` and `DefaultTableModel`, the first of which is abstract. You have seen examples of this pattern before, where a core implementation is provided in an abstract class and extended to create a basic version that is actually used within the Swing packages. In this case, though, the situation is different—even though `AbstractTableModel` is not a complete implementation and the

`DefaultTableModel` is, you are more likely to use the former to create table models, because it is easier to work with and is probably more convenient if you get your data from an external source rather than hard-coding it into your application. This section, looks at how to use the `AbstractTableModel` then, in the next section, you'll see how it differs from `DefaultTableModel`.

Using AbstractTableModel to Create a Table

The `AbstractTableModel` class provides default implementations of all of the methods of the `TableModel` interface, with the exception of the following three:

```
public int getRowCount();

public int getColumnCount();

public Object getValueAt(int rowIndex, int columnIndex);
```

These methods are the ones that deal directly with the data in the table which is, naturally enough, one of the things that cannot be built into an abstract base class. When you use `AbstractTableModel`, you supply the table data in some convenient form along with (at least) the three methods above, which allow the table itself to get access to the data and to determine how much data there is.

Creating a Basic Table

Using the `AbstractTableModel` class, you can quickly create a basic table that shows the current state of orders at a pizza shop, as shown in Listing 11-1.

Listing 11-1   Creating a table with AbstractTableModel

```
package JFCBook.Chapter11;

import com.sun.java.swing.*;
import com.sun.java.swing.table.*;
import java.awt.*;
import java.awt.event.*;

public class TableModelExample1 extends JFrame {
  public TableModelExample1(String title) {
    super(title);

    AbstractTableModel model = new AbstractTableModel() {
      // The table data
      Object[][] data = {
        { "Hot & Spicy", "False" },
```

```
      { "Cheese", "False" },
      { "Ham", "False" },
      { "New Yorker", "False" },
      { "Vegetarian", "False" }
    };

    public int getRowCount() {
      return data.length;
    }

    public int getColumnCount() {
      return data[0].length;
    }

    public Object getValueAt(int row, int col) {
      return data[row][col];
    }
  };

  JTable tbl = new JTable(model);

this.getContentPane().add(JTable.createScrollPaneForTable(tbl));
  }

  public static void main(String[] args) {
    JFrame f = new TableModelExample1("AbstractDataModel Example 1");
    f.pack();
    f.setVisible(true);
    f.setDefaultCloseOperation(JFrame.DO_NOTHING_ON_CLOSE);
    f.addWindowListener(new WindowAdapter() {
      public void windowClosing(WindowEvent evt) {
        System.exit(0);
      }
    });
  }
}
```

The data model is created as an anonymous class that is described from
AbstractTableModel. The table data is stored within the anonymous class as a
two-dimensional array of strings. This class also contains implementations for the
three methods that AbstractTableModel does not provide. It is important to
notice that, because you have to provide the method that accesses the data, it is
entirely up to you how you represent that data—a two-dimensional array is a convenient and natural way to represent the content of a table, but you can use any mechanism that works well in the context of the application, including reading data from a

file or a database. AbstractTableModel does not provide data storage—only default implementations of methods that manage the table model.

Using a two-dimensional array makes it very easy to map the data into the form required by the TableModel interface—each row of the table corresponds to a row in the array, so the row index can be mapped directly to the first index of the array and the column index to the second. If, as in this case, the data is being hard-coded into the application, this method also allows a very compact way to declare and lay out the data. For applications that show read-only data that rarely changes, this may actually be all that is ever needed. Later in this chapter, you'll see how to adapt this technique to allow the user to change the data on the fly.

An array also simplifies the task of returning the row and column counts—the number of rows can be obtained as the length of the array itself, since a two-dimensional array is actually an array of arrays, in which each entry is a reference to a single row. The number of columns is simply the length of any entry in the array. In this example, the number of columns is obtained from the number of entries in the first row of the array.

The rest of the example code is concerned with creating the table itself and the frame that it resides in, most of which should be familiar. As you'll see later, you can create a table directly from a table model by invoking a constructor that takes the model as its only argument:

```
public JTable(TableModel model);
```

Having created the table, you can then use a convenience method to wrap it with scroll bars and then place it on the frame. Figure 11-6 shows what the table looks like when this example program is run using the command:

```
java JFCBook.Chapter11.TableModelExample1
```

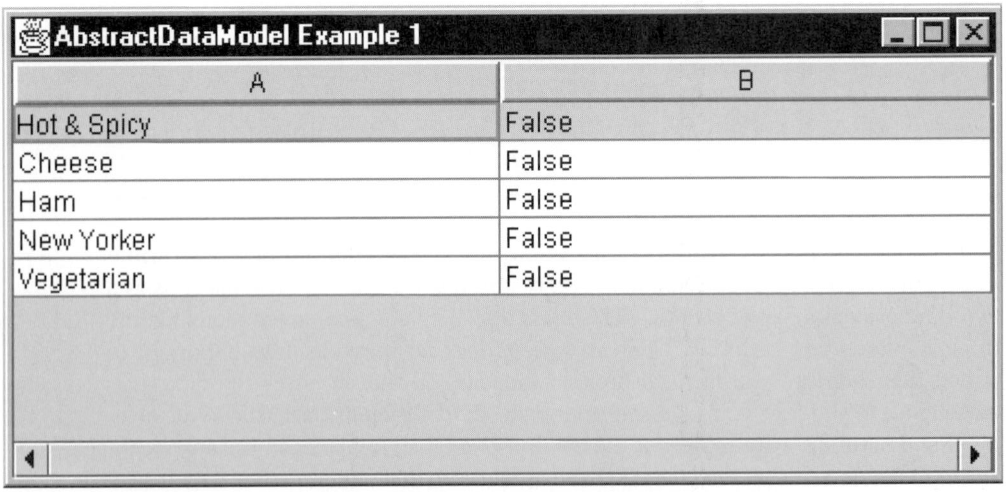

Figure 11-6   A table created with AbstractTableModel.

Refining the Table

Using remarkably little code, then, it is possible to create a basic table that shows all of the data that is hard-coded into the program. You'll also find that rows (but not columns) can be selected, that the headers can be resized and that you can swap around the two columns, as we showed with the first example in this chapter.

Nevertheless, this table has some pretty obvious shortcomings. First, the column headers are not exactly very descriptive. The table gets the column headers using the model's `getColumnName` method. The default implementation of this method provided by `AbstractTableModel` cannot, of course, provide meaningful names—instead, it just uses the letters of the alphabet to label the columns and, if there are more than 26 columns it starts again using two letters and so on. To provide usable column headers, you need to override `getColumnName`.

The second problem with this table is that the second column, which shows whether there are outstanding orders for the pizza in the first column, just contains a static string that always reads `False`. To make the table more useful, it would be better to have a checkbox here instead. In order to do this, you need to force the table to use a cell renderer that displays checkboxes instead of simple strings. The choice of renderer is, in this case, determined by the class of the object that appears in each cell, which the table determines by calling the `getColumnClass` method for each column in the table. The default implementation of this method provided by `AbstractTableModel` simply returns `Object.class`, which causes the string representation of the cell's content, obtained by calling its `toString` method, to be displayed. To make the table choose a renderer that displays a checkbox, you need to override `getColumnClass` to return `Boolean.class` for the second column.

Listing 11-2 shows a revised table model implementation that incorporates the changes just described. If you run this version of the program using the command:

```
java JFCBook.Chapter11.TableModelExample2
```

the result will look like Figure 11-7.

**Listing11-2   Making the table data model more descriptive of the
data content**

```
AbstractTableModel model = new AbstractTableModel() {
  // The table data
  Object[][] data = {
      { "Hot & Spicy", Boolean.FALSE },
      { "Cheese", Boolean.FALSE },
      { "Ham", Boolean.FALSE },
      { "New Yorker", Boolean.FALSE },
      { "Vegetarian", Boolean.FALSE }
  };

  String[] columnNames = {
    "Pizza", "Ordered?"
  };

  public int getRowCount() {
    return data.length;
  }

  public int getColumnCount() {
    return data[0].length;
  }

  public Object getValueAt(int row, int col) {
    return data[row][col];
  }

  public String getColumnName(int columnIndex) {
    return columnNames[columnIndex];
  }

  public Class getColumnClass(int columnIndex) {
    return data[0][columnIndex].getClass();
  }
};
```

The first change was made in the data array itself. Now, instead of supplying the
order status as a `String`, it is held as a `Boolean`, which is, of course, the correct
data type to use but, equally important, it makes our implementation of the
`getColumnClass` method simple—in order to get the class for a particular column, it just returns the class of whatever object is in that column in the first row of
the table. This approach is simple and clear and it works for both columns in this

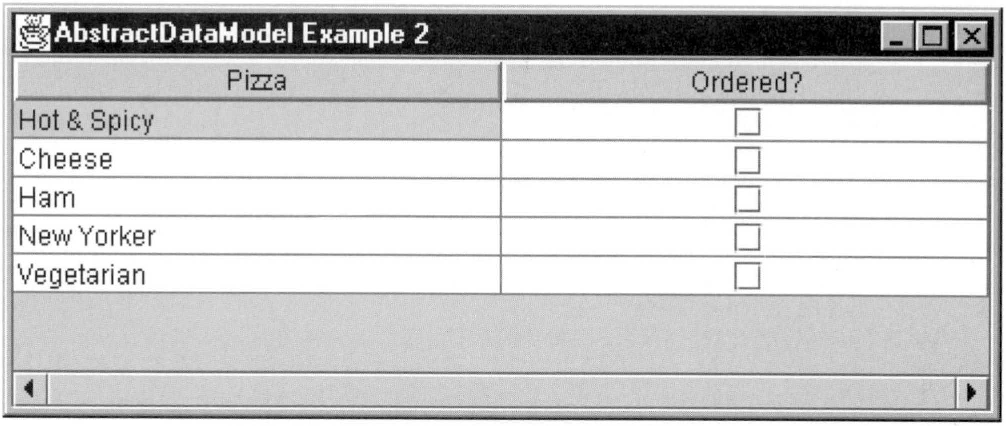

Figure 11-7   An improved version of the orders table.

particular table. However, there are cases in which it would not work. Suppose, for example, that you had a column filled with geometric shapes, all derived from an abstract base class called (for the sake of illustration) `AbstractShape`. The actual entries in the table rows will, however, be instances of concrete subclasses of `AbstractShape` (circles, lines, squares etc.). If the method shown above was used for a table like that, it would claim that all of the entries in this column are of whatever type is in the first row—perhaps a circle or a square, and so on. What it should return is the `AbstractShape.class`. For cases like this, you need to hard-code the correct result or use another array to map the columns to their data types.

The other change was the addition of an array of strings that provides the names of the table columns and a corresponding implementation of the `getColumnName` method that uses it. By keeping the array of names in the same order as the columns in the table, the name for a given column can be obtained by simply using the column index argument as the array index.

Note that this always works, even if the user reorders the table columns, because the order of columns in the table's data model is fixed—it is only the order of columns in the `TableColumn` model that changes, as was shown in Figure 11-4.

Making a Column Editable

These modifications bring us closer to a usable table but we are still not quite there—even though a checkbox is displayed in the second column, you'll find that you can't change its state, because none of the cells in the table is editable. As noted earlier in this chapter, to make a cell editable you need to arrange for the `isCellEditable` method to return `true` and you must also implement the `setValueAt` method to store a modified value in the model. Neither of these is particularly difficult in this case and the implementation is shown in Listing 11-3. To run this version of the example, type:

```
java JFCBook.Chapter11.TableModelExample3
```

The result will look something like Figure 11-8, where orders have been placed for the Hot and Spicy (my favorite) and New Yorker pizzas, simply by clicking the appropriate checkboxes.

Listing 11-3   An editable version of the orders table

```
public boolean isCellEditable(int rowIndex, int columnIndex) {
    return columnIndex == 1;
}

public void setValueAt(Object value, int rowIndex, int columnIndex) {
    if (value instanceof Boolean && columnIndex == 1) {
        data[rowIndex][columnIndex] = value;
        fireTableCellUpdated(rowIndex, columnIndex);
    }
}
```

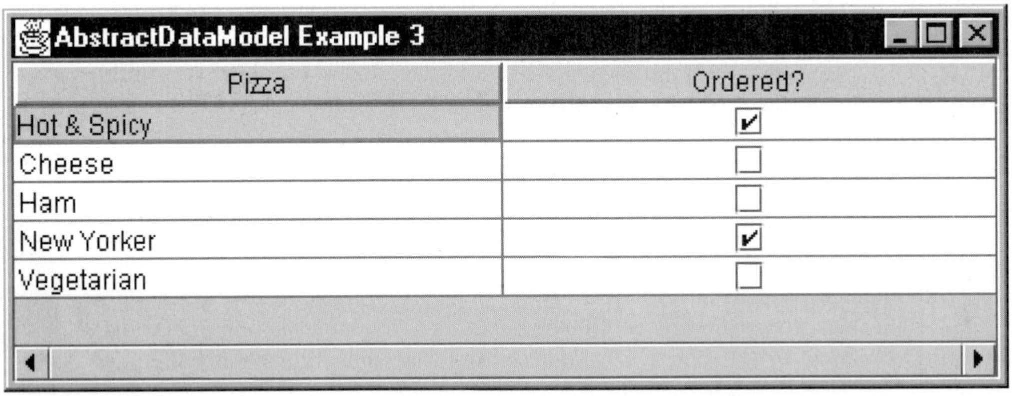

Pizza	Ordered?
Hot & Spicy	☑
Cheese	☐
Ham	☐
New Yorker	☑
Vegetarian	☐

AbstractDataModel Example 3

Figure 11-8   An editable orders table.

Since the user should only be able to edit the orders column, the isCellEditable method returns true only when it is asked about cells in column one. Even though isCellEditable allows you to specify editability at the cell level, you will almost always return only a single value for any given column, as shown here.

To make it possible to save a modified value in the table model, the setValueAt method is implemented. Before the value that the user supplied is stored, this method checks both that it is being asked to update column 1 and that the value it is given is actually a Boolean. If both of these conditions are met, the table data is updated and then the AbstractTableModel fireTableCellUpdated method is called. As you saw in the earlier description at the TableModel interface, it is possible to register for notification of various changes to the table model, one of which is changing the content of a table cell. AbstractTableModel provides several methods that generate the appropriate TableModelEvents and distribute them to registered listeners, of which fireTableCellUpdated is one. You'll see the others in the section on table-related events later in this chapter. Events like this are used to keep the table's view synchronized with its data model in the same way as TreeModelEvents are used by the tree control. In this case, the event is not strictly needed because the table is being updated via its own user interface, but had some other application code invoked setValueAt, the table view would not be changed unless an event is generated.

Sharing the Data Model between Two Views

How this event is used can be demonstrated by showing something that will be used later in this chapter, but in a modified form—constructing two tables that use the same table model. This example builds two identical tables that share the same model and places them one above the other in a frame, as shown in Figure 11-9.

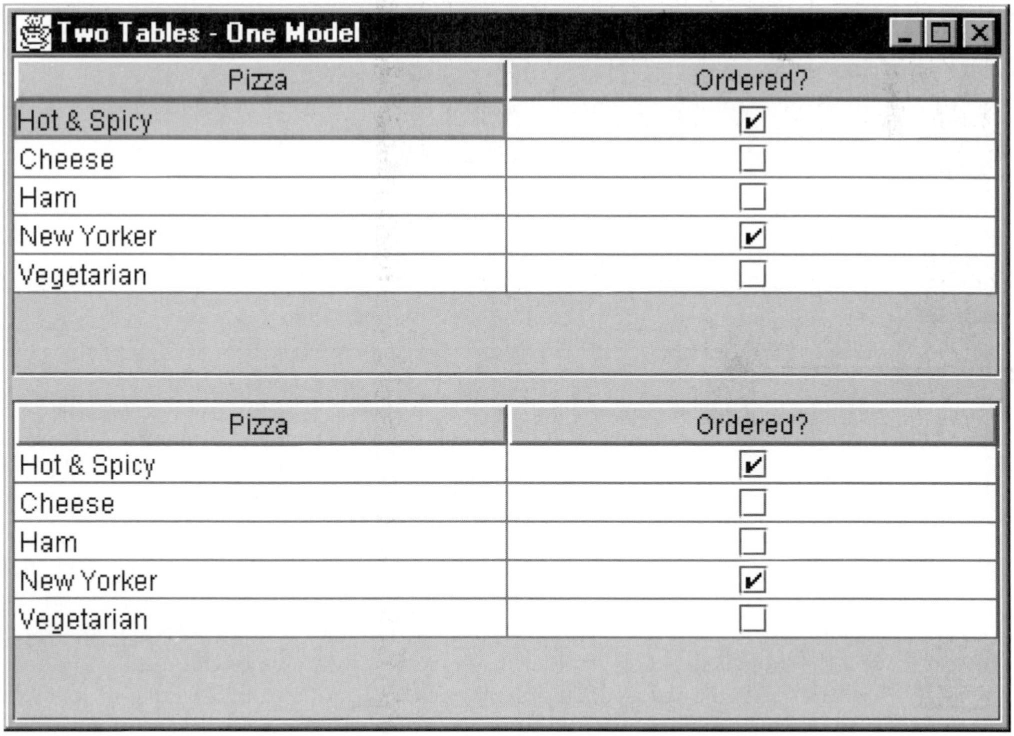

Figure 11-9 Two views of one table model.

The basic mechanics of doing this are simple enough—the model is built once and passed as an argument to two JTable constructors. To make it slightly more difficult, this example makes the top table editable and the bottom one read-only. Most of the code required to do this is the same as for the other examples that you have seen in this section. Listing 11-4 shows only the code that has been changed—it replaces the construction of a single table in Listing 11-1.

Listing 11-4   Constructing two views of a single table model

```
// Create first table
  Dimension viewportSize = new Dimension(450, 120);
  JTable tbl = new JTable(model);
  tbl.setPreferredScrollableViewportSize(viewportSize);
  JScrollPane topPane = JTable.createScrollPaneForTable(tbl);

  // Create a read-only version of the same table
  tbl = new JTable(model) {
    public boolean isCellEditable(int rowIndex, int columnIndex) {
      return false;
    }
  };
  tbl.setPreferredScrollableViewportSize(viewportSize);
  JScrollPane bottomPane = JTable.createScrollPaneForTable(tbl);

  Container pane = this.getContentPane();
  pane.setLayout(new BoxLayout(pane, BoxLayout.Y_AXIS));
  pane.add(topPane);
  pane.add(Box.createVerticalStrut(10));
  pane.add(bottomPane);
}
```

The first table is created in the same way as before, passing the table model to the constructor and then wrapping it in a scroll pane. As you'll have noticed when running the earlier examples in this chapter, left to its own devices the table would leave a lot of blank space in the scrolled area, so this is minimized by giving it a smaller preferred viewport size so that two views of the same table can be placed on the screen. The second table is created as an anonymous subclass of JTable in which the isCellEditable method is overridden so that it always returns false. So far, you have seen only the isCellEditable method of TableModel; however, when the table is deciding whether the user should be able to edit a cell, it calls its *own* isCellEditable method that, by default, directly invokes that of its table model. In this case, because the entire *table* needs to be read-only, even though the *model* allows the second column to be edited, the JTable isCellEditable method is overridden to indicate that every cell is read-only, instead of deferring to the table model. This allows the second table to be read-only while still permitting editing in the first table.

Now, if you run this program with the command:

```
java JFCBook.Chapter11.DoubleTable
```

you'll see two identical tables, one above the other. If you try to edit the cells in the right-hand column of the lower table, you'll find that you can't. However, setting and clearing checkboxes in the top table results in the same operation being performed in the bottom one (see Figure 11-9). This happens because the `fireTableCellUpdated` call in our `setValueAt` method creates a `TableModelEvent` that is caught by the user interface code of the bottom table, causing that table to be redrawn.

The DefaultTableModel Class

`AbstractTableModel` allows you to create table models in which you provide the data storage and the methods by which the data is accessed, but it doesn't deal with adding and removing rows or columns from the data or completely redefining the table content—if you need to do any of these things, you have to supply the code yourself (as will be shown in the discussion of table selection later in this chapter). If you require this functionality and you don't want to provide it for yourself, you may find it easier to use the `DefaultTableModel` class. `DefaultTableModel` is a subclass of `AbstractTableModel`, so it inherits all of the behavior you have seen so far, but it also implements the three methods that are left abstract by `AbstractTableModel`, as well as a set of additional methods that are not part of the `TableModel` interface, listed in Table 11-1.

Table 11-1	Methods Defined by DefaultTableModel in Addition to Those in TableModel

Method	*Purpose*
`public void addColumn(Object columnIdentifier);`	Adds a column at the end of the model with `null` data
`public void addColumn(Object columnIdentifier, Object[] columnData);`	Adds a column with the supplied data
`public void addColumn(Object columnIdentifier, Vector columnData);`	Adds a column with the supplied data
`public void addRow(Object[] rowData);`	Adds a row at the bottom of the table

(Continued)

Table 11-1 Methods Defined by DefaultTableModel in Addition to
Those in TableModel (continued)

Method	Purpose
`public void addRow(Vector rowData);`	Adds a row at the bottom of the table
`public Vector getDataVector();`	Extracts the table data (see Figure 11-10)
`public void insertRow(int rowIndex, Object[] rowData);`	Inserts a row with given data
`public void insertRow(int rowIndex, Vector rowData);`	Inserts a row with given data
`public void moveRow(int startIndex, int endIndex, int toIndex);`	Moves a row to a new location
`public void newDataAvailable (TableModelEvent evt);`	Tells the model that its internal data has been changed
`public void newRowsAdded (TableModelEvent evt);`	Tells the model that new rows have been added to its internal data
`public void removeRow(int rowIndex);`	Removes a row
`public void rowsRemoved (TableModelEvent evt);`	Tells the model that rows have been removed from its internal data
`public void setColumnIdentifiers (Object[] columnIdentifiers);`	Changes the model's column identifiers
`public void setColumnIdentifiers (Vector columnIdentifiers);`	Changes the model's column identifiers
`public void setDataVector(Object[][] dataValues, Object[] columnIdentifiers);`	Replaces the model's data with new data and new column identifiers
`public void setDataVector(Vector dataValues, Vector columnIdentifiers);`	Replaces the model's data with new data and new column identifiers
`public void setNumRows(int rowcount);`	Changes the number of rows in the table, truncating it with loss of data if necessary or inserting an empty row at the end.

DefaultTableModel is able to support the direct manipulation of rows and columns because it actually contains all of the data that will be used by the table, stored in the form of a Vector, in which each entry is itself a Vector that represents one row of the table and contains one element for each table column, as shown in

Figure 11-10. The order of elements in the data Vector is the same as the order of rows in the table and the elements within each row Vector are in column order. Each row Vector must, of course, be of the same length and supply a value for each column.

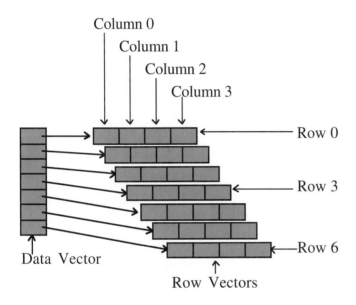

Figure 11-10 How DefaultTableModel holds the table data.

Creating a DefaultTableModel

You can construct a DefaultTableModel in a number of different ways, using any of the following constructors:

```
public DefaultTableModel();

public DefaultTableModel(int numRows, int numColumns);

public DefaultTableModel(Vector columnIds, int numRows);

public DefaultTableModel(Object[] columnIds, int numRows);

public DefaultTableModel(Vector data, Vector columnIds);

public DefaultTableModel(Object[][] data, Object columnIds);
```

You'll see later that JTable has several constructors that allow you to create a table model at the same time as the table itself. These all resolve to a use of one of the constructors shown above, but not all of the DefaultTableModel constructors are available through JTable.

Core Note

The "column identifiers" referred to when discussing constructors and the other methods of DefaultTableModel *are the names attached to the columns and usually interpreted as column headings. In terms of our earlier example,* Pizza *and* Ordered? *are the column identifiers for the Pizza table. Do not mistake this use of the term "identifier" for the identifier that can be attached to a* TableColumn *object. Although the two can have the same value, they need not.*

When studying these constructors, remember that the important features of the table model are the number of rows and columns it has, the content of each cell in the table and the values used for the table model's column headers. As you can see, not all of the constructors set all of these attributes in the table model that they create.

The first constructor creates an empty table model—one that has no rows and no columns. Before you can use a model created in this way, you will need to use the methods shown in Table 11-1, such as setDataVector, to populate it. The second one creates a table with the given number of rows and columns in which each cell has a null value. If you render a table created in this way without populating it, each cell will be empty and the column headers will be the defaults supplied by AbstractTableModel ("A", "B" and so on).

The third and fourth constructors supply the column headers in the form of an array or a vector, and the number of rows of data that the model will ultimately contain. The number of columns in the table is determined from the size of the header array or vector and the table is created with the given number of rows, with all cells initialized to null. Only the last two constructors create a viable table model in one step, providing the column headers and the data together. The first of these two supplies the data in the form of a Vector, which must be created in the same way as the table would create its own data Vector, and the column headings in a separate Vector. The second variant uses arrays instead of vectors and is very close to the method that was used earlier in this chapter to store table data in conjunction with AbstractTableModel. Whichever of these two constructors you use, the number of entries in the array or Vector of column names must be the same as the number of columns in the data array or Vector. You can, however, supply the column identifier argument as null, in which case the default column names supplied by AbstractTableModel will be used. This is not, however, likely to be very useful!

Manipulating a DefaultTableModel

Once you've created your table model, you can use the methods in Table 11-1 to operate on the table data. The addColumn methods place a new column of data at the end of the existing model. If you provide only the column identifier, the new column is created with null in all rows, while if you supply the data as well, the table rows in the new column are filled from the Vector or array supplied. If there is less data than rows in the table, the extra rows are filled with null; if there is more data than rows, the extra data is ignored. Because the order of data in the displayed table does not depend on the order in the model, it is not necessary to place new columns in any particular place in the model. Placing extra columns at the end is, therefore, perfectly acceptable. To have the new column displayed you do, of course, have to amend the `TableColumnModel`.

Core Note

You don't have to do even this if the table is creating its own `TableColumnModel` from its data, as you'll see in "The Table Control."

Similarly, you can add a new row at the bottom of the table with either of the `addRow` methods, or in an arbitrary position with `insertRow`. Unlike columns, rows are displayed in the same order as they appear in the model, so you need to place new rows where you want them to be shown in the table. If you want to remove a row of data, use `removeRow` and supply the index of the row to be deleted.

Finally, you can move existing rows with the `moveRow` method that, despite its name, can move more than one row at a time. You specify the range of rows to move with the `startIndex` and `endIndex`, arguments that must both be within the row bounds of the table and the first must not be greater than the second. To move just one row, supply its index as both `startIndex` and `endIndex`. The target location is given as `toIndex`. If `toIndex` is within the set of rows to be moved, nothing will happen—for example:

```
moveRow(1, 3, 2);
```

is legal, but it has no effect.

The result of the move depends on whether the rows are being moved towards the top or the bottom of the table. If the move is towards the top, then the row originally at `startIndex` will move to row `toIndex`, the one at `startIndex + 1` to `toIndex + 1` and so on. The row at `toIndex` and all of the others between that row and the location originally occupied by the first row affected, all move down the table by `endIndex - startIndex + 1` rows. For example, suppose the model has the following initial row order:

Row A
Row B
Row C
Row D
Row E
Row F

and the call `moveRow(3, 4, 1)` is executed. This moves rows 3 and 4 ("Row D" and "Row E") to row index 1 and row index 2, resulting in the following final arrangement:

Row A
Row D
Row E
Row B
Row C
Row F

If the move is towards the bottom of the table, the result is slightly different in that the first row moves to the location *after* the row that initially occupied row toIndex. This happens because the move is performed by removing each row in turn and moving it to its target location. As a result, when the first row to be moved has been removed, the row formerly at toIndex has moved up to occupy row toIndex - 1. Using the original row arrangement above, if the move:

```
moveRow(2, 3, 4);
```

were executed, it would be moving rows 2 and 3 ("Row C" and "Row D"). This is done by first removing "Row C," leaving this arrangement:

Row A
Row B
Row D
Row E
Row F

The removed row is then placed in row 4, which is not the original row 4:

Row A
Row B
Row D
Row E
Row C
Row F

This process is repeated for the second row to be moved—after it has been removed, the table looks like this:

Row A
Row B
Row E
Row C
Row F

Finally, "Row D" is also placed in row 4, giving the final configuration:

Row A
Row B
Row E
Row C
Row D
Row F

As you can see, "Row C" and "Row D" are after "Row E", which used to occupy row 4, the original target of the move. It is also apparent that the first moved row does not occupy row 4 in the completed table arrangement, whereas when you move rows up the table, the first moved row does occupy the target row number in the moveRow call.

All of the methods that add, insert, move or remove rows generate appropriate events so that the table's displayed view is kept up to date. This is another chore that you have to perform for yourselves with AbstractTableModel and that you don't have to worry about with DefaultTableModel.

The setColumnIdentifiers methods let you change all of the column headings at once. There is no way to change just a single column heading, but this is not likely to be necessary. If you want to change the heading displayed in a table by JTable, it is simpler (and probably more logical) to use the facilities provided by TableColumn, which don't affect the table model at all. There is one important point to notice with regard to these methods: If you supply more or less headers than the table has columns, *the size of the model is changed to reflect the number of headers you supply*. In other words, supplying few headers than there are columns results in columns at the end of the table being inaccessible, while supplying extra headers effectively creates new columns populated with null entries.

The setNumRows method allows you to change the number of rows in the table. Supplying a row count smaller than the number of rows in the table discards rows at the bottom of the table, while increasing the row count makes the table grow by adding rows at the bottom populated with null values.

To completely repopulate a table, you can use the setDataVector method. As noted earlier in this section, if you use the form of this method that supplies the data in the form of a Vector, you must construct that Vector as shown in Figure 11-10. This method, like all of the other methods of DefaultTableModel, arranges for the displayed view of the table to be brought up to date automatically.

Finally, you can use the getDataVector method to get a reference to the data that the model itself is using and manipulate it directly if you wish, rather than using the convenience methods of DefaultTableModel. This might make sense if you are going to make a large number of isolated changes or change a large number of rows or columns at a time. If you do these things using, for example, setValueAt (which DefaultTableModel implements), you will generate an event for each cell that you change and each of these events may cause the JTable to redraw itself. If you update the data vector directly, you can avoid all of these events. However, when you have finished changing the model, you must call one of the methods `newDataAvailable`, `newRowsAdded` or `rowsRemoved` to allow `DefaultTableModel` to synchronize its internal data structures and to generate events to the `JTable` to have the table view updated. Generating a single event and repainting the table once is usually much more efficient than updating once per change. Each of these methods requires you to supply a `TableModelEvent` that describes the actual changes made.

Core Note

The table doesn't actually redraw itself in the event handler when it receives an event. Instead, it uses the `repaint` *method to schedule the work sometime later. Depending on your platform and how your code is written, you may be able to complete multiple updates before the table has a chance to redraw itself for the first time. On other platforms, however, you may find that the table manages to redraw itself more frequently and, as a result, your application will run more slowly if you generate one event per change.*

Two Views of One Table Using DefaultTableModel

As an illustration of the use of the `DefaultTableModel`, let's use it to reimplement the example shown in Figure 11-9 where two views of the same table were kept in step by generating a `TableModelEvent` from within the `setValueAt` method. When using `DefaultTableModel`, there is no need for you to supply this code yourself, but you can't quite get away with using `DefaultTableModel` without any modifications. The revised implementation is shown in Listing 11-5.

Listing 11-5   Using the DefaultTableModel

```
package JFCBook.Chapter11;

import com.sun.java.swing.*;
import com.sun.java.swing.table.*;
import java.awt.*;
import java.awt.event.*;

public class DoubleTableDefault extends JFrame {
  public DoubleTableDefault(String title) {
    super(title);

    DefaultTableModel model = new DefaultTableModel(data, columnNames) {
      public boolean isCellEditable(int rowIndex, int columnIndex) {
        return columnIndex == 1;
      }
      public Class getColumnClass(int columnIndex) {
```

```
          return DoubleTableDefault.this.data[0][columnIndex].getClass();
        }
    };

    // Create first table
    Dimension viewportSize = new Dimension(450, 120);
    JTable tbl = new JTable(model);
    tbl.setPreferredScrollableViewportSize(viewportSize);
    JScrollPane topPane = JTable.createScrollPaneForTable(tbl);

    // Create a read-only version of the same table
    tbl = new JTable(model) {
      public boolean isCellEditable(int rowIndex, int columnIndex) {
        return false;
      }
    };
    tbl.setPreferredScrollableViewportSize(viewportSize);
    JScrollPane bottomPane = JTable.createScrollPaneForTable(tbl);

    Container pane = this.getContentPane();
    pane.setLayout(new BoxLayout(pane, BoxLayout.Y_AXIS));
    pane.add(topPane);
    pane.add(Box.createVerticalStrut(10));
    pane.add(bottomPane);
  }

  public static void main(String[] args) {
    JFrame f = new DoubleTableDefault("Two Tables - One Model (Default Table Model)");
    f.pack();
    f.setVisible(true);
    f.setDefaultCloseOperation(JFrame.DO_NOTHING_ON_CLOSE);
    f.addWindowListener(new WindowAdapter() {
      public void windowClosing(WindowEvent evt) {
        System.exit(0);
      }
    });
  }

  // The table data
  Object[][] data = {
    { "Hot & Spicy", Boolean.FALSE },
    { "Cheese", Boolean.FALSE },
    { "Ham", Boolean.FALSE },
    { "New Yorker", Boolean.FALSE },
    { "Vegetarian", Boolean.FALSE }
  };

  String[] columnNames = {
    "Pizza", "Ordered?"
  };
}
```

The data model is created by using the constructor that takes an array of data and an array of column names. The data itself is unchanged from Listing 11-1, except that its declaration has been moved to the class itself. In the previous examples, the data and the column names were declared inside an anonymous subclass of AbstractTableModel, because that is the natural way to use AbstractTableModel. When you use DefaultTableModel, however, you are more likely to be encapsulating data obtained from an outside source rather than using data hard-coded into the application and this example more closely reflects that.

Notice that you still have to override two methods of DefaultTableModel, so it is not possible to get away without creating a subclass. You need to implement your own isCellEditable method, because DefaultTableModel just returns true whatever arguments it is given. You also needed to supply the same implementation of getColumnClass as was used with AbstractTableModel, because DefaultTableModel simply returns Object.class for all columns. Apart from these two methods, you don't need to do anything special to use DefaultTableModel: Because it contains all of the data, it knows how many rows and columns there are and it can return the column names. Apart from the substitution of DefaultTableModel for AbstractTableModel, the rest of the code is unchanged from the earlier implementation of this example. If you run this example using the command:

```
java JFCBook.Chapter11.DoubleTableDefault
```

you'll find that it is equivalent to the previous implementation.

Table Model Events

Changes to the table model cause a TableModelEvent to be generated. JTable includes code to handle these events, so you are not obliged to handle them yourself. If you want to receive them to implement some kind of custom behavior, you need to register a TableModelListener using the addTableModelListener method of TableModel. This interface has only one method:

```
public void tableChanged(TableModelEvent evt);
```

All of the information about the change that has been made is in the TableModelEvent that the listener receives as the argument to this method. This event, like all events, has a source that is always the TableModel in which the change has occurred and four attributes that describe exactly what happened. These attributes can be obtained using the following methods:

```
public int getType();
public int getColumn();
public int getFirstRow();
public int getLastRow();
```

The event type will be one of TableModelEvent.UPDATE, TableModelEvent.INSERT, and TableModelEvent.DELETE. UPDATE implies that some of the data in the table was changed in some way. The affected area can be deduced from the values returned by the other three methods that specify a column and a range of rows. Usually, a whole column or a set of complete rows will be updated. To indicate that all columns in a row were affected, getColumn returns the special value ALL_COLUMNS. Moving a row or a set of rows within the table generates an UPDATE event in which the range of rows covers the extreme ends of the move and that has the column value ALL_COLUMNS.

If the table's structure has been fundamentally changed, then getFirstRow will return the value HEADER_ROW; when this happens, the listener should discard any assumptions it has about the state of the table and build new data structures from scratch. This event is generated, for example, when a new column is added to a model managed by DefaultTableModel.

Row insertion and removal are reported with INSERT and DELETE events in which the affected rows are returned by the getFirstRow and getLastRow methods. In the case of an insertion, these give the new row indices while for a deletion, the row numbers correspond to rows that no longer exist.

Table Columns and the Table Column Model

Now that you've seen how the table holds its data, it's time to turn to the data structures that it uses to determine how that data is displayed. The JTable class itself is only a small part of the whole control—much of what you see and what you can do with the table's representation is controlled by the TableColumn and the TableColumnModel, both of which are covered in this section.

The TableColumn Class

TableColumn is a class that holds information about how a single column from the table model will be displayed. When the table needs to render or edit any of the cells in a column, it looks in that column's TableColumn object to find out how to do it. The methods defined for this class are as follows:

```
public void setModelIndex(int modelIndex);

public int getModelIndex();

public void setWidth(int width);

public int getWidth();

public void setMinWidth(int minWidth);

public int getMinWidth();
```

```
public void setMaxWidth(int maxWidth);

public int getMaxWidth();

public void setResizable(boolean resizable);

public boolean getResizable();

public void sizeWidthToFit();

public void disableResizedPosting();

public void enableResizedPosting();

public void setIdentifier(Object identifier);

public Object getIdentifier();

public void setHeaderValue(Object value);

public Object getHeaderValue();

public void setHeaderRenderer(TableCellRenderer renderer);

public TableCellRenderer getHeaderRenderer();

public void setCellRenderer(TableCellRenderer renderer);

public TableCellRenderer getCellRenderer();

public void setCellEditor(TableCellEditor editor);

public TableCellEditor getCellEditor();

public void addPropertyChangeListener(PropertyChangeListener l);

public void removePropertyChangeListener(PropertyChangeListener l);
```

The most fundamental piece of information that a `TableColumn` object holds is the index of the column within the model that it relates to. This index can be set with the `setModelIndex` method and read with `getModelIndex`, or it can be initialized when the object is created. `TableColumn` has four constructors:

```
public TableColumn();

public TableColumn(int modelIndex);

public TableColumn(int modelIndex, int width);
```

```
public TableColumn(int modelIndex, int width,
            TableCellRenderer renderer, TableCellEditor editor);
```

The default constructor creates a `TableColumn` object that corresponds to column zero of the table model, has width of 75 pixels, and no associated renderer or editor. The other constructors let you specify the table column, the initial width, the renderer and the editor to be used for this column.

Column Width

The actual width of a column when it is displayed depends on several factors, but is constrained by the column's minimum and maximum allowed widths. If you don't use the `setMinWidth` and `setMaxWidth` methods to explicitly change them, the minimum width is 15 pixels and there is no effective maximum width (it is set to the largest allowed integer value). When a table is displayed, it tries to make each column the size returned by its `getWidth` method. If the table is not configured to automatically resize to fit the space available, this is exactly what will happen. On the other hand, if the table is constrained to fit its content within the screen space allocated to it, it adjusts the size of each column (or possibly just the last column—see "The Table Control" below) so that the total column width matches the width of its available space. In making this adjustment, however, it never exceeds the configured maximum width or makes the column narrower than its minimum width and, as a result, the table may not actually fit in the space available, or may not fill that space if all of the columns are too narrow even at their widest possible settings.

Even after you have set the width of a column, the user may be able to resize it using the mouse, as was demonstrated earlier in this chapter. You can disable this by invoking the `setResizable` method with argument `false`—by default, user resizing of all columns is allowed. Doing this does not prevent the column being resized by calling `setWidth` or as part of the table's automatic resizing mechanism if it is enabled.

An important feature to note is that the actual size of the column has nothing whatever to do with its content, unless you explicitly set the column's width with this in mind. In adjusting the size of a column, the table is only concerned with meeting its overall width constraint and, as a result, some columns may become too small for their content to be completely visible, while others are enlarged to the point that there is extra space. It is the programmer's job to ensure that the maximum, minimum and requested width of a column are set so that its contents are not lost. In general, this is not a simple task unless you know in advance the exact data that will be displayed in the table and the font in which it will be rendered. The task is made even more difficult by the possibility that a custom renderer may be used, invalidating any assumptions about the space required to show the column's data.

One way to deal with this is to compute the column's minimum size by passing each entry in each row through the renderer that will be used to display it and getting the width of each rendered cell, then setting the minimum width of the column to that value. If you absolutely must have the entire content of a column visible and you want to allow substitution of arbitrary renderers, this is probably your only option, but it is expensive in performance terms, especially if the table contains a lot of data. A possible compromise that may work in some cases is to set the column's width using the `sizeWidthToFit` method, which sets the width to the size needed to render the header of the column with the data that the header currently contains. If you can guarantee that the header text is always no narrower than the content of any cell in the column, you can use this method to calculate the width and then set the minimum width to the same value. If there is a possibility that the renderer might be changed, you will need to repeat this calculation when the change is made. The cell and header renderers are both bound properties of the column, so you can register a listener to be notified when they change, as you'll see later. If, on the other hand, you have control over the renderer and the font that will be used, you can minimize the cost of displaying the table by determining the appropriate widths in advance and then setting the columns' minimum widths appropriately.

Column Indices and Identifiers

Internally, the table always uses integer indices to locate the `TableColumn` object for a given column and almost all of the API calls are constructed in the same way, because this is the quickest way to access the data for a column. You can, however, associate an identifier with each `TableColumn` and subsequently, using `TableColumnModel` or `JTable` methods, search for a column given its identifier. This is, of course, much more expensive than the direct indexing method. Under some circumstances, you may have no choice but to do this, especially if you allow the user to reorder the columns in the table's view.

If you don't explicitly set an identifier for a column using `setIdentifier`, it uses its associated header value as a default identifier. The header value may itself be set using the `setHeaderValue` method, usually to the column name as returned by the table model's `getColumnName` method. If you don't set the header value, it defaults to `null`. It is important to realize that nothing attaches any particular meaning to the column identifier, whether it is defaulted or specifically set: In searching for a column by name, the object given as the search key is simply compared with the column's identifier using the search key's `equals` method. In particular, it is possible for more than one column to have the same identifier, in which case the first column matching the given search key is returned. In general, for performance reasons, we do not recommend addressing table columns by name unless you have no alternative but to do so.

Column and Cell Renderers

Each column can have two associated renderers—one for the header and one for all of the cells in that column. By default, the header renderer uses a subclass of `JLabel` with a raised bevel border and draws the string representation of the column's header value (as returned by getHeaderValue) centered on the label. As noted in the previous paragraph, the header value is usually initialized to the name of the column in the table model. The column header should, of course, always be something of meaning to the user; if your table model uses obscure names (such as database field names), you should use a more descriptive name instead.

Core Note

As you'll see later, you can arrange for JTable *to create the* TableColumn *objects that it needs to display the data in a table model directly from the model data. When it does this, it sets the header value in each* TableColumn *to the column name from the data model.*

The default for cells is no specific renderer at all. This results in a renderer suitable for the type of data held in the column (as returned by the model's getColumnClass method) being used for each cell in the column. Similarly, there is no default editor for a column—instead, a class-based editor is used unless you configure one via the constructor or using setCellEditor. More will be said about this in the section titled "Customized Table Rendering and Editing."

Column Properties

TableColumn has a number of bound properties that you can be notified of changes to by registering a property change listener. The complete set of properties is listed in Table 11-2.

Table 11-2   TableColumn Bound Properties

Property	Description
COLUMN_WIDTH_PROPERTY	The width of the column
CELL_RENDERER_PROPERTY	The cell renderer for the column
HEADER_RENDERER_PROPERTY	The column's header renderer
HEADER_VALUE_PROPERTY	The value used in the column's header

Under normal circumstances, you probably will not need to monitor changes to these properties. However, as was mentioned earlier, you might need to monitor changes to the header and cell renderers to allow you to recalculate the minimum width for the column if you are forced to perform exact calculations.

Selecting and Ordering Columns with the TableColumnModel

`TableColumn` holds information about only one column in a table's view. The columns that the table actually displays and the order in which it displays them are determined by its `TableColumnModel`, which is an ordered collection of `TableColumn` objects. Unlike `TableColumn`, `TableColumnModel` is an interface, not a class. The Swing table package provides an implementation of this interface, called `DefaultTableColumnModel`, which `JTable` uses unless you provide a column model of your own.

The Table Column Model

Table 11-3 lists the methods required by the `TableColumnModel` interface.

Table 11-3   The TableColumnModel Interface

Method	Purpose
`public void addColumn (TableColumn column);`	Adds a column to the end of the table
`public void removeColumn (TableColumn column);`	Removes a column from the table
`public void moveColumn (int columnIndex, int newIndex);`	Changes the location of a column
`public int getColumnCount();`	Returns the number of columns in this view of the table
`public Enumeration getColumns();`	Returns the columns in left-to-right order
`public int getColumnIndex (Object identifier);`	Gets the index for the column with the given identifier
`public TableColumn getColumn (int index);`	Returns the column at the given index
`public int getColumnIndexAtX (int xPosition);`	Gets the column for a given screen location
`public int getColumnMargin();`	Gets the margin between columns
`public void setColumnMargin (int margin);`	Sets the margin between columns
`public int getTotalColumnWidth();`	Calculates the total width of the columns including margins
`public void setColumnSelectionAllowed (boolean flag);`	Controls whether columns can be selected

`public boolean` `    getColumnSelectionAllowed();`	Returns whether columns can be selected
`public int[] getSelectedColumns();`	Returns the indices of all selected columns
`public int getSelectedColumnCount();`	Returns the number of selected columns
`public void setSelectionModel` `    (ListSelectionModel model);`	Installs a new selection model
`public ListSelectionModel` `    getSelectionModel();`	Gets the current selection model
`public void addColumnModelListener` `    (TableColumnModelListener l);`	Adds a listener for changes to the column model
`public void removeColumnModelListener` `    (TableColumnModelListener l);`	Removes a column model listener

Since `TableColumnModel` is an interface, it doesn't provide a method that allows you to create a table column model—this facility is provided instead by the constructor of `DefaultTableColumnModel`, which creates a column model with no columns in it. To get a column into the column model, you have to create the appropriate `TableColumn` object and then use the `addColumn` method to add it to the model. This process must be repeated for each column from the table model that you want a `JTable` to actually display (you'll see an example of this at the end of this section). The `addColumn` method adds the new column at the end of its internal list, which is important because the order of columns in the `TableColumnModel` is the order in which they will be displayed by the table itself. When you first create a table, therefore, you build its table column model by adding columns in the required display order.

Core Note

If you are creating a simple table that displays all of the columns in table model in the order in which they appear in that model, you can simplify your task by setting the JTable autoCreateColumnsFromModel *flag. When this flag is* true, *which it is by default,* JTable *builds a suitable* TableColumnModel *when it is first given a* TableModel *and whenever the* TableModel *changes. Note, however, that leaving this flag* true *after the table column model has been built can have some unwanted side effects as will shortly become apparent.*

Reordering Table Columns

When the table is displayed, the user can reorder the columns by dragging them around with the mouse. The reordering of columns is achieved by changing their order in the `TableColumnModel` using the `moveColumn` method. You can, of course, achieve the same effect programmatically by calling this method directly. This might be necessary if you want to add a new column to the table somewhere other than at the end: To do this, you must call `addColumn`, which always places it at the end of the column list, then use `moveColumn` to relocate it to the desired position. You can also remove a column from the column model using `removeColumn`. When you use `DefaultTableColumnModel`, adding, moving or removing a column causes an event to be generated that `JTable` uses to update the table display.

It is important to realize that the table model and the table column model are almost completely independent of each other. In particular, moving columns within or removing them from the table column model has no effect at all on the table model itself. Similarly, adding a column to the table model does not affect the table column model and won't cause the table to display the new column. However, moving columns in the table model will have an effect on the table display, because the connection between the columns in the column model and those in the table model is the index of the column in the table model: If you change the column at a particular index in the model, you will also change what that column represents in the `JTable`. Removing columns from the table model has the same effect. For this reason, as a general rule, you should avoid reordering or deleting columns from the table model.

Core Note

If you enable the `JTable autoCreateColumnsFromModel` *feature, however, changing the table model will discard and rebuild the table column model, so that the displayed version of the table will be completely rebuilt and will reflect any changes made. Any earlier manual reordering and resizing of columns by the user will also be lost. If you don't want changes to the table model to affect your table display, make sure that this flag is set to* `false` *after the table column model has been built (i.e., after the* `setModel` *method has been called or when the* `JTable` *constructor finishes if you pass the table model that way).*

Accessing Table Columns

The `TableColumnModel` interface provides several methods that allow access to the individual columns. The `getColumns` method returns an `Enumeration` that allows you to visit all of the columns in the model exactly once. Usually, you are not supposed to make any assumptions about the order of elements in an `Enumeration`, but in this case it is safe to assume that the columns are returned by the `nextElement` method in the order in which they are intended to be displayed.

The `getColumn` method returns the `TableColumn` object with the given column index, where the index reflects the display order position of the column so that the left most column as shown by `JTable` has column index 0 and is returned by `getColumn(0)`, the next to the right has column index 1 and so on. This is the most efficient way to get the `TableColumn` object for a given column, but the index that you need to use to find a particular column will change if the columns are reordered. If you need to find a particular column and you don't want to track column order changes using `TableColumnModelEvents` (which are discussed later), you can assign each column a fixed identifier using the `TableColumn setIdentifier` method that was described in the previous section, or use the table model's name for the column, and locate it using the `getColumnIndex` method that returns the column index of the first `TableColumn` with an identifier matching the one passed as an argument. You can pass the returned index to `getColumn` to get the actual `TableColumn` object.

Mouse Events

If you are processing mouse events on a table, you will need to determine which cell the mouse was over when the event occurred. To determine this, you'll need the cell's row and column number. `JTable` provides a method that returns the row number and a convenience method to access the `TableColumnModel` `getColumnIndexAtX` method, which returns the column as a column index given the mouse's X-coordinate relative to the table. Note, however, that not every position within a table corresponds to a column in the table column model. In particular, there is usually some margin space between the columns of the table; if `getColumnIndexAtX` is given a coordinate that corresponds to a margin, it returns –1. The size of the margin between columns can be set by calling the `setColumnMargin` method and passing the desired margin width in pixels. Since this affects the total width of the table, calling this method (and changing the margin) causes the `DefaultTableColumnModel` implementation to generate an event to cause `JTable` to redraw the table.

For convenience, you can use the `getTotalColumnWidth` method to calculate the horizontal space needed to display all of the columns in the table model. This value is computed by adding together the current widths of all of the columns (as returned by the `TableColumn getWidth` method) and adding the additional space required for the intercolumn margins (as returned by `getColumnMargin`). Assuming that the columns are sized appropriately for their contents, you can think of the value returned by `getTotalColumnWidth` as the "preferred" width of the entire table in its current configuration.

The last set of methods in Table 11-3 deal with column selections and events generated by the table column model, topics that are dealt with after discussion of `JTable` itself.

Using DefaultTableColumnModel

`DefaultTableColumnModel` implements all of the methods of the `TableColumnModel` interface and also provides the following convenience methods for use by subclasses:

```
protected void fireColumnAdded(TableColumnModelEvent evt);

protected void fireColumnRemoved(TableColumnModelEvent evt);

protected void fireColumnMoved(TableColumnModelEvent evt);

protected void fireColumnSelectionChanged(ListSelectionEvent evt);

protected void fireColumnMarginChanged();
```

As you can see, these are all convenience methods that you might use in a subclass to create events when the table column model or the set of selected columns changes. Unless you are intending to create your own customized column model based on `DefaultTableColumnModel`, you won't need to use any of these methods, so they are not discussed any further in this book.

To illustrate how `DefaultTableColumnModel` works, let's look at a simple example that uses the Apollo space flight data model that you first saw at the beginning of this chapter, but displays only a subset of its data. Let's start by displaying only the flight names, then add the names of the crew one by one and rearrange the columns under program control to put them in the correct order. This isn't a very spectacular or a very useful example, but it does show how the `TableColumnModel` works and emphasizes the fact that it is independent of the underlying table model. The code is shown in Listing 11-6. To run this example, use the command:

```
java JFCBook.Chapter11.TableColumnModelExample
```

Listing 11-6   The TableColumnModel

```
package JFCBook.Chapter11;

import com.sun.java.swing.*;
import com.sun.java.swing.table.*;
import JFCBook.Chapter11.TableExampleData;
import java.awt.*;
import java.awt.event.*;

public class TableColumnModelExample extends JFrame {
  public TableColumnModelExample(String title) {
    super(title);

    dataModel = new TableExampleData();

    JTable tbl = new JTable();
    tbl.setAutoCreateColumnsFromModel(false);
    tbl.setAutoResizeMode(JTable.AUTO_RESIZE_OFF);
```

```
      tbl.setModel(dataModel);

      columnModel = new DefaultTableColumnModel();
      TableColumn col = new TableColumn(0);       // Map column 0
      col.setHeaderValue(dataModel.getColumnName(0));
      columnModel.addColumn(col);
      tbl.setColumnModel(columnModel);

      this.getContentPane().add(JTable.createScrollPaneForTable(tbl));
   }

   public static void main(String[] args) {
      TableColumnModelExample f = new TableColumnModelExample
              ("Table Column Model Example");
      f.pack();
      f.setVisible(true);
      f.setDefaultCloseOperation(JFrame.DO_NOTHING_ON_CLOSE);
      f.addWindowListener(new WindowAdapter() {
        public void windowClosing(WindowEvent evt) {
          System.exit(0);
        }
      });

      // Column 0 is already displayed. Now add columns 3, 2 and 1
      // in that order and move them into place. Delay 10 seconds
      // each time.
      try {
        Thread.sleep(10000);
        TableColumn col = new TableColumn(3);
        col.setHeaderValue(f.dataModel.getColumnName(3));
        f.columnModel.addColumn(col);
        Thread.sleep(10000);
        col = new TableColumn(2);
        col.setHeaderValue(f.dataModel.getColumnName(2));
        f.columnModel.addColumn(col);
        f.columnModel.moveColumn(2, 1);
        Thread.sleep(10000);
        col = new TableColumn(1);
        col.setHeaderValue(f.dataModel.getColumnName(1));
        f.columnModel.addColumn(col);
        f.columnModel.moveColumn(3, 1);
      } catch (InterruptedException e) {
      }
   }

   protected DefaultTableColumnModel columnModel;
   protected TableModel dataModel;
}
```

This example starts by creating an instance of the data model, then builds a `JTable` based around it, but this time the table model is not passed to the `JTable` constructor. Passing it to the constructor would be a waste of time, because it would automatically generate a column model mapping all of the columns in the data model. In this case, only a small subset of the columns are going to be displayed, so a custom table column model is required. Instead, the default constructor is used to create a table with an empty model and then automatic creation of the table model is switched off to avoid the same problem when the `setModel` method is called. Automatic table resizing is also switched off so that the columns remain at their natural size. Finally, the `setModel` method is called to connect the table to its table model.

The next step is to build a custom table column model by instantiating a `DefaultTableColumnModel` object. When it is created, this model has no columns, so the first column, which maps to column 0 of the table model, is created by adding a single `TableColumn` to it. The constructor is given the index of the target column in the model. As noted above, when you create a `TableColumn` object, the associated header value is `null`, so to make the correct heading appear in the table, the column header is obtained from the model and the `TableColumn` `setHeaderValue` method is used to configure the column information. Finally, the column is added to the table column model using `addColumn`.

At this point, the table appears with only one column containing the flight name and number. Ten seconds later, a second column is created, which maps column 3 of the table model using the same technique as we used for the first one. When `addColumn` is used, the new column is placed at the end of the column list, so it displays to the right of the flight name which is, in this case, where it should be. After another ten seconds, a third column is built for the LM Pilot name. This one should appear in between the two columns already on display, but it can't be placed there directly: First `addColumn` puts it at the end of the list (in index position 2) and then `moveColumn` is used to relocate it to position 1. Finally, ten seconds later, yet another column is added and moved to the immediate right of the flight name using the same mechanism.

Table Column Model Events

Adding each column and moving it will cause two `TableColumnModelEvents` to be generated for these two changes to the table column model. However, because the table handles these events by scheduling an event to redraw itself in a separate thread, the odds are very good that you will just see each new column appear in its target location because, by the time the repaint operation begins, the new column has been both added and moved within the table.

To receive a `TableColumnModelEvent`, you need to register a `TableColumnModelListener`. Whereas in the case of the table model the listener interface was simple and the event itself was more complex, here the reverse is true—the event is simple and the listener interface has five methods to be implemented:

```
public void columnAdded(TableColumnModelEvent evt);

public void columnRemoved(TableColumnModelEvent evt);

public void columnMoved(TableColumnModelEvent evt);

public void columnMarginChanged(ChangeEvent evt);

public void columnSelectionChanged(ListSelectionEvent evt);
```

The first three methods are self-describing; the event that each method receives contains a source object (always the `TableColumnModel`), a "from" column index and a "to" column index, both of which are integers and can be obtained using the `getFromIndex` and `getToIndex` methods, respectively. When a column is added, its assigned column number is supplied as the "to" index, while column removal has the removed column's index in the "from" field. When a column is moved, the source and destination of the move are given by "from" and "to" indices, respectively and are the values supplied to the `moveColumn` method.

The last two methods are slightly different from the first three in that they don't use a `TableColumnModelEvent`. The `columnMarginChanged` method is invoked when the `setColumnMargin` method is used to change the gap between columns. The `ChangeEvent` that is supplied as the only argument carries no useful information other than the source of the event, which is the affected `TableColumnModel`. To get the new column margin, it is necessary to use the `getColumnMargin` method of the event source. Usually, this event will cause the receiver to completely redraw the table.

Finally, any change in the column selection is reported by the `columnSelectionChanged` method that is given a `ListSelectionEvent` from which the changes can be deduced. Table selection is discussed later in this chapter.

The Table Control

After a long preamble, it's finally time to look at the Swing table control itself. A lot of ground has had to be covered before a proper description of `JTable` could be presented, because much of the functionality you see when you use a table is not actually provided by the control itself. As you've already seen, the data is organized into rows and columns by a separate data model, the columns that you actually see and the order in which you see them is determined by the table's column model and even the table header itself isn't strictly part of the table control. In fact, by this point you already know as much as you need to know in order to create simple tables. In this section, you'll see what the JTable component itself adds to its component parts, then look at the table header and at how the table manages row, column and cell selection.

Creating a Table

JTable has seven constructors:

```
public JTable();

public JTable(TableModel dataModel);

public JTable(TableModel dataModel, TableColumnModel columnModel);

public JTable(TableModel dataModel, TableColumnModel
            columnModel, ListSelectionModel selModel);

public JTable(int numRows, int numColumns);

public JTable(Vector data, Vector columnNames);

public JTable(Object[][] data, Object[] columnNames);
```

The first constructor uses defaults for each part of the table—you can see the table attributes that can be customized and their default values in Table 11-4. Some of these attributes can be set at construction time, while others can only be changed using specific accessor methods. In the case of the default constructor, the table will have a DefaultTableModel with no rows and no columns, so it isn't very useful until you give it some real data using the setModel method, as was shown in Listing 11-6. The next three constructors allow you to specify one, two or all of a data model, a table column model and a selection model for the table. All of these constructors take the table size from the model.

The fifth constructor installs the default column and selection models and creates a table using a DefaultTableModel, of the size specified by its arguments in which every cell is null. The table headers for this table will be the defaults provided by DefaultTableModel—"A," "B" and so on. Again, this is not a very useful table until you populate it with some real data and assign proper column headers.

The last two constructors let you build a fully-configured table with all of its data, using DefaultTableModel, DefaultTableColumnModel and the default list selection model. If you use the Vector variant, you need to construct the data Vector as shown in Figure 11-10.

Table 11-4 shows all of the attributes of the JTable component, the method that you can use to change its value, and the default installed when the table is created. In some cases, as you have seen, the defaults can be directly overridden by choosing an appropriate constructor.

Table 11-4   JTable Attributes and Their Defaults

Attribute	Data Type	Method	Default Value
dataModel	TableModel	SetModel	DefaultTableModel with no rows and no columns.
columnModel	TableColumnModel	SetColumnModel	DefaultTableColumnModel derived from the data model.
selectionModel	ListSelectionModel	SetSelectionModel	DefaultListSelectionModel initialized with ListSelectionModel. MULTIPLE_INTERVAL_ SELECTION: Controls row selection only.
tableHeader	JTableHeader	SetTableHeader	A table header derived from the DefaultTableColumnModel that matches the table's data model.
rowHeight	Int	SetRowHeight	The height of each row—16 pixels.
rowMargin	Int	SetIntercellSpacing	Space between rows—1 pixel.
gridColor	Color	SetGridColor	The color of the grid lines— gray.
showGrid	Color	SetShowGrid	true—draws grid lines in the margins between table rows and columns.
autoResizeMode	Int	SetAutoResizeMode	Determines whether and how the table is resized to fit available space—initially set to AUTO_RESIZE_ALL_COLUMNS.
autoCreateColumns FromModel	Boolean	SetAutoCreate ColumnsFromModel	Controls whether the table builds its own table column model—initially true.
preferredViewportSize	Dimension	setPreferred Scrollable ViewportSize	The size of the viewport that the table prefers if it is wrapped by a JScrollPane—defaults to 450 pixels wide and 400 pixels high.
rowSelectionAllowed	Boolean	setRowSelection Allowed	true—allows selection of rows
cellSelectionEnabled	Boolean	setCellSelection Enabled	false—selection of individual cells is not allowed.

You'll see how these attributes are used and how you can change their values in the rest of this section and in the sections that follow. Note that there are other attributes that the table provides and convenience methods for them that actually belong to other objects, an example of which is the table selection mode, which properly belongs to the table selection model.

Table Size

One of the more perplexing features of `JTable` is how to control its size. You can take two different approaches to this—either you can make the table adopt its natural size and stay at that size, or you can allow it to adapt its size to the amount of space that is allocated to it. You make the choice by setting the `autoResizeMode` attribute, which has three possible values:

```
AUTO_RESIZE_OFF
```

```
AUTO_RESIZE_LAST_COLUMN
```

```
AUTO_RESIZE_ALL_COLUMNS
```

Note that auto-resizing works only for the *width* of the table. Every row in a table has the same height, which can be set using the `setRowHeight` method and a fixed row margin controlled by `setIntercellSpacing`. Therefore, the table's height is fixed for a given number of rows. Row heights are never changed to suit the space available.

If you select `AUTO_RESIZE_OFF`, the table doesn't take into account the amount of space that is allocated to it. Instead, each column will have the width specified in its `TableColumn` object and the total width of the table will be the sum of the individual column widths and of the column margins between them. By default, the column margin is one pixel to allow for a grid to be drawn around the cells. If the total width calculated in this way is greater than the available space, the table will be clipped on the right. Usually, however, you avoid this clipping by wrapping the table with a `JScrollPane`, which will supply a horizontal scrollbar to allow the rest of the table to be viewed. The simplest way to equip a table with scrollbars is to use the static `createScrollPaneForTable` method, of which you have seen several examples already:

```
public static JScrollPane createScrollPaneForTable(JTable table);
```

This method is preferred over direct construction of a scroll pane because the table actually consists of a body and a header. Wrapping the table directly in a scroll pane like this:

```
JTable table = new JTable(......);
JScrollPane pane = new JScrollPane(table);
```

will work, but it will only mount the table body in the scroll pane's viewport. The `createScrollPaneForTable` method does this for you and also puts the table header in the scroll pane's column header so that it lines up correctly over the table body and scrolls horizontally with it, but not vertically (refer back to chapter 5 for more information on `JScrollPane`). Later in this chapter, you'll see how to make further use of `JScrollPane` to enhance the usability of tables.

When a table is wrapped in a `JScrollPane`, it is asked for its "preferred viewport size." This is the size that the `JScrollPane` will try to allocate to the table in its scrolling area. There is no obvious way to determine the ideal size for the table's viewport. Should it be as large as the table itself? Possibly this is sometimes the best choice but if the table is very wide, creating a large viewport might distort other parts of the user interface. By default, the table asks for a viewport that is 450 pixels wide and 400 pixels high. You can, of course, adjust this using the `setPreferredScrollableViewportSize` method, as was done in Listing 11-4 in order to fit two tables stacked one above the other on one frame. If the table is short, you might find it useful to reduce the required height of the viewport like this, otherwise you will find that you have wasted space under the last row of the table, an effect that you can see by running any of the early example programs in this chapter.

Disabling automatic table resizing does not stop the user from resizing any of the tables in the column. Increasing or decreasing the size of an individual column in this mode will change the total width of the table by the same amount.

If you want the table to adapt its size to fit within the space allocated to it by a layout manager, you need to use either `AUTO_RESIZE_LAST_COLUMN` or `AUTO_RESIZE_ALL_COLUMNS`. When either of these modes is selected, the table attempts to adjust the width of its columns so that its total width is as close as possible to, and does not exceed, the space it has allocated to it on the screen. As you'll see, though, this is not always possible. Whichever mode is selected, the table first calculates the total width based on each column's width as returned by its `TableColumn` object and the column margins. If this does not match the available width, then the extra space must be allocated to one or more of the columns or, if the required width is too large, some of the columns will need to be narrowed.

Let's first consider the `AUTO_RESIZE_LAST_COLUMN` case. The basic idea of this mode is to give all of the columns their ideal size, apart from the right most one, which will be made larger or smaller by however much is necessary to make the table fit the available space. The name is, however, a misnomer, because this simple policy doesn't always work. Suppose, for example, that your table has 10 columns that each want to be 75 pixels wide (which is the default) and the intercolumn margin is 1 pixel (also the default). This table needs 760 pixels of horizontal space to be properly represented. Suppose first that constraints placed by the user interface mean that the table can only be 500 pixels wide. This being the case, you would need to reduce the size of the last column by 260 pixels, which obviously can't be done.

What actually happens here is that the table works out the maximum amount by which it can shrink the last column; that depends on that column's minimum size. Assuming that the `TableColumn` object was created with the defaults, it can't be made narrower than 15 pixels, so it is given this width, which saves 60 pixels. This saving is subtracted from the total saving required, leaving 200 pixels to save. This problem is now carried to the next column to the left—the last column but one. Again, this column wants to be 75 pixels wide and can be no less then 15 pixels across, so another 60 pixels are saved here and a shortfall of 140 pixels is carried forward. This process repeats until the shortfall has been recovered. When the table is finally laid out, its first 5 columns will be the desired 75 pixels wide, the sixth will have a width of 55 pixels and the last four will be 15 pixels across. Counting the 10, 1-pixel margins, this does indeed add up to 500 pixels. As you can see, though, `AUTO_RESIZE_LAST_COLUMN` doesn't quite mean what it says.

There are times, though, when this mechanism still fails. What would happen if there were only 100 pixels available to show the entire table? It is assumed that each column has its default minimum size of 15 pixels, so counting in the margin again, at least 160 pixels are needed to show the table. Since no column will ever be made narrower than its minimum width, every column will be 15 pixels wide and the table will occupy 160 pixels. To be able to see the whole table, you need to have wrapped it in a scroll pane. Actually, this is the only way in which you will ever see the horizontal scrollbar if you don't use `AUTO_RESIZE_OFF`—because the table tries its best to make the table fit the available space, you don't usually see a scrollbar.

There are similar problems when the available space is too large for the table. In this case, the extra space is allocated to the last column first which, in the default case, is all that needs to happen because columns have no maximum size. However, if you set a maximum size on the last column, the table won't be able to make it grow beyond that size, so it carries any extra space to the next column to the left and so on. If all of the columns have a maximum size limit, it is possible that not all of the extra space can be distributed to them, in which case there will be a gap on the right of the table.

A possible disadvantage of `AUTO_RESIZE_LAST_COLUMN` is that it affects one or more of the right most columns while leaving other columns alone, which may not be an issue if there is too much space for the table or if the table space is too small and you don't have appropriate minimum column sizes set. In some circumstances, you can get a better result by using `AUTO_RESIZE_ALL_COLUMNS`, which distributes any extra space or any shortfall over all of the columns. The algorithm here is slightly more complex, but basically it starts in the same way—calculate the total width requirement and from that work out how much extra space needs to be shared or how much needs to be clawed back. Let's start with the same situation as that above—10 columns with minimum size 15 pixels, desired size 75 pixels and a margin of 1 pixel, with a frame size of 500 pixels, resulting in a shortfall of 260 pixels. The first step is to calculate the percentage of the total space required by each column, including its margin. Since all of the columns are the same, each of them accounts for 10 percent of the required space. In principle, what happens now is that 10 percent of the shortfall is removed from each column, resulting in each of them being narrowed by 26 pixels to occupy 49 pixels each. Since this is well above the minimum width of any of the columns, this is the final outcome.

Things become more involved if one or more of the columns has a minimum width that is more than 49 pixels. In this case, the columns that can lose their entire allocation of 26 pixels will lose it, while the others will be set at their minimum sizes. Let's suppose in our example that columns 0 and 1 have a minimum size of 59 pixels each. This means that columns 2 through 9 can be reduced by 26 pixels each and columns 0 and 1 by 16 pixels, a total reduction of 240 pixels. As a result, it is necessary to lose another 20 pixels somewhere, without involving columns 0 and 1.

What happens now is that 10 percent of the remainder is deducted from the remaining columns—in other words, columns 2 through 9 are each reduced by 2 further pixels to 47 pixels each, while columns 0 and 1 are fixed at 59. However, 2 pixels have been removed from only 8 columns, not from 10—an actual saving of just 16 pixels, leaving another 4 pixels to lose from 8 columns. Since this can't be distributed evenly, what actually happens is that 1 pixel is removed from columns 2 through 5 and the remainder are left unchanged. The final configuration, then, is as follows:

Columns 0 and 1:	59 pixels + 1 margin
Columns 2–5:	46 pixels + 1 margin
Columns 6–9:	47 pixels + 1 margin

While this case worked out in the end, there are cases that can't be resolved—if all of the columns reach their minimum sizes, then the table will still be too large for its allocated area and a scrollbar is needed, or if the table is too small and the columns all reach maximum width, there will be a gap to the right.

Table Appearance

Aside from its size and the width of its columns, there are some other features of the table that affect its appearance, three of which are briefly described in this section.

Colors

Color is often an issue that is tightly-coupled to a component's look-and-feel class. In many cases, you can change the foreground and background attributes of a Swing control's underlying JComponent without making any difference to what appears on the screen because the code that draws the control prefers to use its own default colors. In the case of the table, this is not so. You can set both the foreground and the background colors of the table and its header and they will be rendered in those colors. For example, we can change the appearance of the table we created in Listing 11-6 by adding the following lines after the table is created:

```
tbl.setBackground(Color.black);
tbl.setForeground(Color.green);
tbl.getTableHeader().setBackground(Color.blue);
tbl.getTableHeader().setForeground(Color.orange);
```

You can try this modified version of the example using the command:

```
java JFCBook.Chapter11.TableColumnModelExample2
```

and you'll get a result that looks like a more colorful version of Figure 11-11. Even though the result is shown here as a gray-scale figure, you can easily see that the color scheme has changed. Notice in particular that the blue (or at least very dark gray!) background of the table header runs right across the top of the table, even though there are no table columns on the right of the frame. The first column is colored differently because it is currently selected.

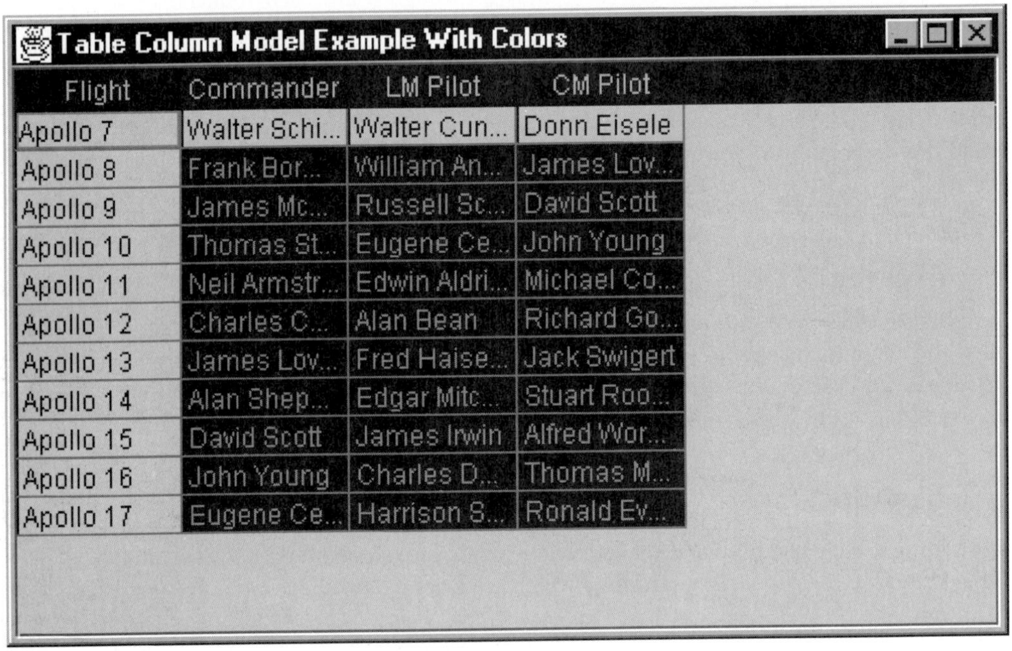

Figure 11-11   A table with customized colors.

Changing colors works as long as you use the default cell and header renderers in the Swing packages. If you install a different renderer, you may find that it doesn't honor the table's foreground or background color. Sometimes you need to use different colors for different columns or even for different cells within a column and it is the renderer's job to implement this as you'll see when looking at how table rendering is done later in this chapter.

Grid Lines and Intercell Spacing

All of the tables that have been shown so far have had horizontal and vertical grid lines around the individual cells. These lines are drawn by the table's look-and-feel class and you can completely change their appearance by implementing your own look-and-feel. Without going to this much trouble, however, you can turn grid lines on and off or change the grid color using the following JTable methods:

```
public void setShowGrid(boolean show);

public void setShowHorizontalLines(boolean show);

public void setShowVerticalLines(boolean show)

public void setGridColor(Color color);
```

Not surprisingly, the `setShowHorizontalLines` and `setShowVerticalLines` methods give you individual control over the appearance of horizontal and vertical lines, while the `setShowGrid` method can be used to either enable or disable both sets of lines in one call. Figure 11-12 shows the table from the previous section as it appears without horizontal grid lines and with red vertical lines. To see the red grid lines, use the command:

```
java JFCBook.Chapter11.TableColumnModelExample3
```

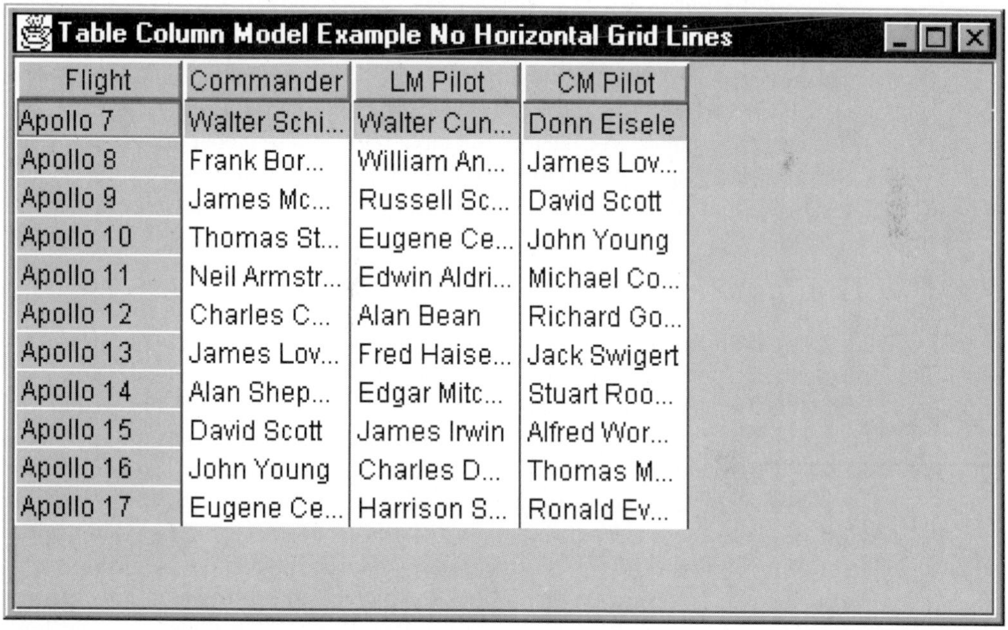
Table Column Model Example No Horizontal Grid Lines
Flight
Commander
LM Pilot
CM Pilot
Apollo 7
Walter Schi...
Walter Cun...
Donn Eisele
Apollo 8
Frank Bor...
William An...
James Lov...
Apollo 9
James Mc...
Russell Sc...
David Scott
Apollo 10
Thomas St...
Eugene Ce...
John Young
Apollo 11
Neil Armstr...
Edwin Aldri...
Michael Co...
Apollo 12
Charles C...
Alan Bean
Richard Go...
Apollo 13
James Lov...
Fred Haise...
Jack Swigert
Apollo 14
Alan Shep...
Edgar Mitc...
Stuart Roo...
Apollo 15
David Scott
James Irwin
Alfred Wor...
Apollo 16
John Young
Charles D...
Thomas M...
Apollo 17
Eugene Ce...
Harrison S...
Ronald Ev...

Figure 11-12 A table with no horizontal grid lines.

You can see from this example that the selected column always has grid lines even if they are switched off for the rest of the table and the color of these lines is not related to that set using `setGridColor`, You can't change the thickness of the grid lines—they are always one pixel across.

The grid runs down the middle of the intercell spacing that consists of the table's row and column margins. You can change the size of this spacing using the setIntercellSpacing method, which requires a Dimension object as its argument, in which the width gives the column margin and the height the row margin. The column margin actually belongs to the TableColumnModel—invoking setIntercellSpacing causes the table to change the value stored by the TableColumnModel that will, incidentally, cause an event that will make JTable redraw the whole table.

ToolTips

Since JTable is just a JComponent, it can, in principle, have tool tips. In fact, both JTable and its header provide support for tool tips supplied by the cell and header renderers that means that you could, at least in theory, provide a different tool tip for each cell in the table. Even the default renderers can give you either a column-based tool tip or a tool tip based on the class of the object in the column, which may be shared by several columns in any given table. Further discussion of this topic is postponed until the section on renderers.

Even if you don't want to get involved with configuring or writing your own renderer, you can still use the setToolTipText method that JTable inherits from JComponent to set a single tip that will be shown whenever the mouse pointer is anywhere over the table body. JTableHeader supports the same facility and can have its own tip, separate from that of the table body. These global tips are displayed if no more specific tips are available from the renderer of whichever cell the mouse pointer is over and whenever the mouse stops over the margins between cells.

The Table Header

While JTable handles displaying the data in the table, the header is managed by a separate JTableHeader object. When you first create a table, it builds its own JTableHeader based on the table column model that you give it, or the one that it builds for itself if the autoCreateColumnsFromModel flag is true, so in most cases you won't need to concern yourself with actually creating a header for your table. As you've already seen, the table header is usually mounted in the column header part of a JScrollPane so that the column headers remain visible as the table body is scrolled vertically. To make this work, the table and table header components need to be aware of each other, so that column movement and resizing, which are controlled by JTableHeader rather than by the table, result in both parts being updated consistently. The JTable setTableHeader method is used to associate a header with a table. When you call this method, it also invokes the JTableHeader setTable method so that the header and the table have consistent references to each other. It is, of course, perfectly possible to create a table that doesn't have a header—to do this, call setTable(null) before placing the table in its JScrollPane.

Creating a Table Header

It is unlikely that you will create your own table header, but should you wish to do so, you have a choice of two constructors:

```
public JTableHeader();
public JTableHeader(TableColumnModel model);
```

The first constructor creates a header using a `DefaultTableColumnModel` with no columns, which is not especially useful. The second one constructs a header based on the table column model that you supply. The column headers are taken from the header values of the individual `TableColumn` objects in the model, as returned by calling `getHeaderValue` for each column. As noted in the discussion of `TableColumn`, the header value is NOT initialized by default—it is your job to set appropriate header names, as shown in Listing 11-6, which created custom `TableColumn` objects.

If you look back to Listing 11-6, you'll see that it used the `JTableHeader` created automatically by the table. However, when new columns were added to the table column model, nothing was done to update the table header. Whether you create your own table header or use the one supplied by the table, you don't need to worry about keeping it current as you add or remove columns from the column model because it registers itself as a `TableColumnModelListener` and adjusts the displayed column headers according to the changes in the model.

JTableHeader Methods

The public methods of `JTableHeader` are shown here:

```
public void setTable(JTable table);

public JTable getTable();

public void setColumnModel(TableColumnModel model);

public TableColumnModel getColumnModel();

public void setResizingAllowed(boolean flag);

public boolean getResizingAllowed();

public void setReorderingAllowed(boolean flag);

public boolean getReorderingAllowed();

public int getDraggedColumn();
```

```
public int getDraggedDistance();

public int getResizingColumn();

public void setUpdateTableInRealTime(boolean flag);

public boolean getUpdateTableInRealTime();

public int columnAtPoint(Point point);

public String getToolTipText(MouseEvent evt);
```

The first four of these get and set the associated table and column model. Usually, these are set once and for all when the table header is created, but you can, if you wish, install a new column model at any time. In fact, it is not necessary to directly call setColumnModel once the table header is connected to the table, because JTable invokes it when you change the column model using its own setColumnModel method.

As well as rendering the table header, JTableHeader is also responsible for allowing the user to resize or re-order columns. The code that implements these features is in the header's UI class. Before allowing the user to change the columns, this code uses the getReorderingAllowed or getResizingAllowed methods to see whether the operation is permitted. By default, both resizing and column reordering are allowed. These settings only control what the user can do via the UI class—they don't prevent automatic column resizing by JTable should the table's container change size, or changes made by the application to the column order or column size via the TableColumnModel and TableColumn interfaces.

No formal mechanism is provided to allow the application to detect when a column is being moved or resized—notification is only provided when the operation is complete by a TableColumnModelEvent in the case of a column movement or a PropertyChangeEvent for the TableColumn COLUMN_WIDTH_PROPERTY for a column resize. If you want to know when these changes are taking place, the only way to do this is to register a MouseMotionListener on the JTableHeader. As the column itself or its edge is moved, your mouseDragged method will be called. During this period, you can use the getDraggedColumn method to find out whether a column drag is in progress and, if so, which column is being moved. This method returns the index of the column involved, as it was before the move started, or –1 if there is no column drag in progress. The getDraggedDistance method tells you how far (in pixels) the column has moved. If the mouse is being dragged and there is no column drag in progress, the other possibility is that a column is being resized. If this is the case, then the getResizingColumn method will return the index of the column being resized, or –1 if there isn't one.

If you're resizing or moving columns in a large table, you may be able to speed the operation up considerably by using the setUpdateTableInRealTime method.

Calling this method with argument `false` causes the table header to resize or move only the column header itself—by default, the table body is also updated as the header is modified. When real-time updates are disabled, the table body will be changed to reflect header change only when the user releases the mouse at the end of the operation.

The `columnAtPoint` method returns the index of the column at a given location, whose coordinates must be given relative to the table header itself, or –1 if location does not correspond to any column header (i.e. it is outside the header or is in the margin between the headers). This method would typically be used in a mouse-event handler to perform a custom column-based operation.

Finally, the `getToolTipText` method returns a tool tip for a particular mouse position. This method can be called directly by application code, but it is, as you saw in chapter 8, usually called by the `ToolTipManager` when necessary. `JTableHeader` provides an implementation of this method that allows you to have a separate tool tip for each column in the header. You'll see how this is done in the discussion of renderers at the end of this chapter.

Table Selection

`JTable` uses the same selection model as the `JList` component does. Since the `ListSelectionModel` has already been covered in some detail in chapter 8, including how to detect selection changes, this section just outlines the features of the table that make selection different than it would be in a list or a tree. The most important difference between `JTable` and `JList` as far as selection is concerned is that a table is two-dimensional, which gives you the possibility of selecting either rows or columns. In fact, `JTable` also allows you to select individual cells.

Because you can, at least theoretically, select rows and columns independently of each other, a table actually has two selection models—one for row selections and another for column selections. The column selection model is, as you have already seen, owned and controlled by the `TableColumnModel` installed in the table, while the row selection model belongs to the table itself. Even though these models are separate, they are not quite independent of each other, because `JTable` has access to both of them and coordinates row and column selections according to certain rules.

There are five attributes that distinguish a particular table's selection policy:

- *Row selection enabled.* This attribute belongs to the `JTable` and can be controlled using its `setRowSelectionAllowed` method. If this attribute is false, you cannot select rows from the user interface.

- *Column selection enabled.* This is an attribute of the `TableColumnModel`. `JTable` that provides the `setColumnSelectionAllowed` method to allow you to change it without having to directly access the column model.

- *Cell selection enabled*. This attribute belongs to JTable. If it is true, you can't select individual rows and columns—clicking in a cell selects only that cell. Use the setCellSelectionEnabled method to control this attribute.
- *Row selection mode*. This attribute is part of the row selection model and can take any of the values ListSelectionModel.-MULTIPLE_INTERVAL_SELECTION, ListSelectionModel.SINGLE_ INTERVAL_SELECTION and ListSelectionModel.SINGLE_SELECTION.
- *Column selection mode*. This is the column selection model's version of the row selection mode.

Theoretically, the row and column selection modes could be independently set. However, if you use the JTable setSelectionMode method, it applies the same mode to both models. If you want different row and column modes, you will need to set their modes directly as follows:

```
JTable tbl = new JTable(…);
// Set up table (not shown)
tbl.getSelectionModel().setSelectionMode(….);
            // set the row selection mode
tbl.getColumnModel().getSelectionModel().setSelectionMode(…);
            // set column selection mode
```

The following list shows all of the JTable methods that are connected with selection management. Many of these are similar to the methods that you've already seen in connection with JList and JTree, so they are not going to be discussed in detail. There are, however, a few subtle points that need to be mentioned:

```
public void setCellSelectionEnabled(boolean flag);

public boolean getCellSelectionEnabled();

public void setRowSelectionAllowed(boolean flag);

public boolean getRowSelectionAllowed();

public void setColumnSelectionAllowed(boolean flag);

public boolean getColumnSelectionAllowed();

public void setSelectionMode(int mode);

public int getSelectionMode();

public void clearSelection();
```

```
public void selectAll();

public void setSelectionBackground(Color color);

public void setSelectionForeground(Color color);

public Color getSelectionBackground();

public Color getSelectionForeground();

public void addColumnSelectionInterval(int index0, int index1);

public void addRowSelectionInterval(int index0, int index1);

public void removeColumnSelectionInterval(int index0, int index1);

public void removeRowSelectionInterval(int index0, int index1);

public void setColumnSelectionInterval(int index0, int index1);

public void setRowSelectionInterval(int index0, int index1);

public int getSelectedColumn();

public int[] getSelectedColumns();

public int getSelectedColumnCount();

public int getSelectedRow();

public int[] getSelectedRows();

public int getSelectedRowCount();

public boolean isRowSelected(int row);

public boolean isColumnSelected(int col);

public boolean isCellSelected(int row, int col);
```

The first interesting point concerns cell selection. When cell selection is enabled, clicking in any cell highlights only that cell. However, if you interrogate the selection models, you would find that the row and column that pass through that cell are actually both selected in the model, but do not appear so on the screen. This means that you need to interpret the results of the methods that retrieve the selected rows and columns differently depending on whether cell selection is enabled. In fact, the table does not record the selection status of individual cells—it infers that a cell is selected based on the state of its row and column. A cell is selected if *one* of the following is true:

- Cell selection is enabled AND its row and column are both selected.
- Cell selection is disabled AND one of its row and column are selected.

You can find out whether a cell is selected using isCellSelected, giving the cell's row and column indices as arguments. From the rules above, you can see that a cell can be considered selected even if cell selection is not enabled, because the cell selection attribute really controls the ability to select a single cell, rather than the whole row or column that the cell occupies.

The second point to make about selection is that JTable, like JList, does not provide any support for mouse double clicks, which are often used to select an object (in this case a cell, row or column) and perform some action on it. If you need this functionality, you need to implement it yourself by providing a MouseListener and registering it on the JTable. When you get a double click, you can either find the selected row and/or column using the methods in the list you have just seen, or you can determine the cell in which the mouse was clicked using the following JTable methods:

```
public int columnAtPoint(Point pt);
public int rowAtPoint(Point pt);
```

To use these methods, pass the mouse location (obtained from the MouseEvent using its getPoint method) to both of them to get the column and row of the cell. If the mouse was clicked in the margin between columns or rows, one or both of these methods will return −1.

To demonstrate some of what we have seen in this section, let's look at a simple program, based on the table that was used in Figure 11-1, that just shows how cell selection works and also traps mouse double clicks and prints the row and column of the cell under the mouse using the method outlined above. Listing 11-7 shows the code that implements the detection of mouse clicks, then locates the corresponding cell and prints its position and contents. In this extract, the variable table is a reference to a JTable created earlier.

Listing11-7   Handling mouse selection in a table

```
table.addMouseListener(new MouseAdapter() {
  public void mouseClicked(MouseEvent evt) {
    if (evt.getClickCount() == 2) {
      Point pt = evt.getPoint();
      int rowIndex = table.rowAtPoint(pt);
      int columnIndex = table.columnAtPoint(pt);
```

```
      if (rowIndex == -1 || columnIndex == -1) {
        System.out.println("Clicked outside table");
      } else {
        System.out.println("Clicked in row " + rowIndex + ", column "
          + columnIndex + ". Data is <" +
          table.getModel().getValueAt(rowIndex, columnIndex) + ">");
      }
    }
  }
});
```

You can try this example for yourself using the command:

```
java JFCBook.Chapter11.CellSelectionExample
```

If you run this example and click in any cell (but not in the left-most column), you'll find that only that cell highlights itself, instead of the whole row as was the case with the original version of this program (TableExample) at the start of this chapter. If you click in another cell, the first cell is deselected as the new one is highlighted. Now double-click in any cell and you'll find that the cell's coordinates and its content are printed in the window from which you started the program. If you double-click in the space below the table not occupied by any data, you'll see the message "Clicked outside table", indicating that the mouse was inside the bounds of the JTable component (which covers the entire frame), but outside the area occupied by valid data.

Core Alert

The last thing to try with this example is selecting two cells. First, click on any cell in the table to highlight it. Then, move the mouse to another cell in a different row and column and hold down the CTRL button while clicking. Now you'll find four cells selected, instead of two! This is, of course, a result of the fact that the table selects a cell by selecting the row and column that it resides in. Selecting two cells in different rows and columns gives two selected rows and two selected columns, which always intersect in four places. There is no way to detect which cells the user actually clicked in (unless you are prepared to monitor mouse events).

Customized Table Rendering and Editing

Like the tree component , JTable uses renderers to draw the content of its cells and editors to allow the user to provide input to the table, where this is allowed by the underlying table model. In many cases, the default renderers and editors that the table provides will be sufficient for your needs, but it is possible to improve the presentation of the table or make it easier for the user to interact with it if you provide a customized renderer or an editor designed specifically for the type of data in your particular table. This section shows you how to do both of these things.

How Table Renderers and Editors Work

Every cell in a table, including the column headers, is drawn by a renderer of some sort. When a part of the table needs to be painted or repainted, the table's UI class works out which renderer to use for each cell that it needs to draw and calls its `getTableCellRendererComponent` method to get a `Component` that can render the visual appearance of the cell. Then it arranges for it to paint itself into the area that the cell occupies. A renderer must implement the `TableCellRenderer` interface, which simply requires it to have a `getTableCellRendererComponent` method. Similarly, when the user triggers an editing session for a particular cell, the table finds the correct editor to use and places it in the table so that it takes over the space belonging to the cell to be edited. Table editors implement the `TableCellEditor` interface, which contains, among others, a similar method called `getTableCellEditorComponent` that returns an editor component for the table to use. You have already seen the details of renderers and editors used with `JTree` and you won't be surprised to learn that the table works in very much the same way, so some of the basic details will be omitted in this section to avoid repetition.

Determining the Renderer or Editor to be Used

The renderer or editor for a cell depends on whether the cell is in the header or the table body and how the table has been configured.

Let's first look at renderers. If the cell is in the header, the header renderer in the column's `TableColumn` is always used. When a `TableColumn` object is created, a default renderer that draws text on a `JLabel` with a beveled border is installed; if you want to change the appearance of your table headers, you can provide your own header renderer on a per-column basis if necessary.

Outside the header, the table looks first at the `TableColumn` object for the column that the cell is in. If this has been configured with a renderer, then it will use that. If there is no column renderer, which is the default case, then the table model's `getColumnClass` method is used to find out the type of object in the column and a renderer capable of displaying content of that type is used, if there is one. If no such renderer exists, a renderer for the type of the object's superclass is searched for. This process repeats until a suitable renderer is found. As a last resort, a default renderer for the `Object` class will be used. This renderer is created automatically by the table, along with renderers for objects of type (or derived from) `Number` and `Boolean`. These renderers are known as class-based renderers (as opposed to column-based renderers); you can add class-based renderers of your own or replace existing ones (including the table's defaults) using the following `JTable` method:

```
public void setDefaultRenderer(Class columnClass,
TableCellRenderer renderer);
```

You'll see this method used later when creating custom renderers that display dates and times properly.

The same process is used to find the correct editor for a cell, except that there is no such thing as a column header editor. As with renderers, there is no editor assigned to any column by default, but there are class-based editors for `Object`, `Number` and `Boolean` that are used if a column does not have a specific editor assigned to it. Because these editors exist, if you make a column that contains a `Boolean` value editable, you get a checkbox that you can toggle to change the state of the corresponding item in the table model. For tables containing any other kind of object, you'll see a `JTextField` in which the string version of the object (obtained by calling `toString`) will be displayed for editing. This may, of course, not be what you want to happen, in which case you need to supply your own custom editor, either to each column that needs it using the `TableColumn` `setCellEditor` method or as a class-based editor using the `JTable` method `setDefaultEditor`, which is similar to `setDefaultRenderer`.

Controlling Whether or Not a Cell Can Be Edited

As you've already seen, the table model ultimately determines whether or not the data in the table can be edited. By supplying a suitable `isCellEditable` method in your subclass of `AbstractTableModel` or `DefaultTableModel`, you can control whether any individual cell can be edited using the row and column indices passed to it. If the model disallows cell editing, it cannot be overridden. However, the reverse is not true—an editable model can be presented in such a way that the resulting table is partially or completely read-only. This is possible because the `isCellEditable` method of `JTable` is called before an editing session is started for any cell in the table. By default, this just delegates the decision to the table model, but you could implement a different policy, as was shown in Listing 11-4, which created a read-only version of a writable table using this mechanism. Intermediate policies are, of course, possible. You could, for example, make specific columns editable or even make individual cells read-only.

One thing that you can't really do is shortcut this mechanism by not providing an editor for a column that you want to be regarded as read-only if the table model allows it to be edited. You can, of course, attempt to arrange for there not to be an editor for a column by creating a `TableColumn` object in which the column editor is `null` and this is, in fact, the default. However, this does you no good because the table will use a class-based editor instead. You could attempt to defeat this strategy by removing all of the class-based editors and leave the table without an editor to use, in which case the column will not be editable, but this will make *any* column without its own editor read-only, which may not be what you want.

Configuring Renderers

Any renderer that you want to use has to implement the `TableCellRenderer` interface. The Swing package provides a class called `DefaultTableCellRenderer` that implements this interface and provides the same facilities as a `JLabel`. `DefaultTableCellRenderers` are actually used as the default class-based renderers installed by the table for `Object` and `Number`. There is also a private renderer that is installed to render `Boolean` values; the first two of these behaves like a `JLabel` and the last like a `JCheckBox`. If these standard renderers don't do what you want, you can create a custom renderer instead. This section describes both approaches.

Standard Renderers

To demonstrate how to use a standard renderer, the next example creates a simple table using `DefaultTableModel`, in which the first column should always be displayed as black text on a yellow background, regardless of the background color of the table itself. The table will use the same data as the pizza example that you have already seen in this chapter.

Up to this point, the renderer used for each column has been determined by the class of object within that column. If you look back to Listing 11-5, you'll see that the `getColumnClass` method of the `DefaultTableModel` used for this table returns the type of the object on the first row of each column as the overall type for that column. As a result, the first column's type is `String` and the second column has type `Boolean`. As you know, the table doesn't have a specific renderer for `String`, but it has one for `Object`, which would be used to render the first column. The second column would be drawn by the installed renderer for `Booleans`. In this example, to achieve special effects for one column only, a column-specific renderer will be installed. When a column has its own renderer, that renderer is used instead of the class-based one indicated by `getColumnClass`.

The implementation of this example is shown in Listing 11-8. You can run this program using the command:

```
java JFCBook.Chapter11.ColumnRendererExample
```

When you do so, you get the familiar two-column table showing pizzas and whether they have been ordered.

Listing 11-8   Using a column renderer

```
package JFCBook.Chapter11;

import com.sun.java.swing.*;
import com.sun.java.swing.table.*;
import java.awt.*;
```

```java
import java.awt.event.*;

public class ColumnRendererExample extends JFrame {
  public ColumnRendererExample(String title) {
    super(title);

    DefaultTableModel model = new DefaultTableModel(data, columnNames); {
      public Class getColumnClass(int columnIndex) {
        return data[0][columnIndex].getClass();
      }
    };

    // Create the table
    Dimension viewportSize = new Dimension(450, 120);
    JTable tbl = new JTable(model) {
      public boolean isCellEditable(int row, int column) {
        return false;
      }
    };
    tbl.setColumnSelectionAllowed(true);

    // Create the column renderer for the first column
    DefaultTableCellRenderer renderer = new DefaultTableCellRenderer();

    // Configure the renderer as we want it to be
    renderer.setBackground(Color.yellow);
    renderer.setForeground(Color.black);
    renderer.setToolTipText("Pizza Name");

    // Attach the renderer to the first column
    tbl.getColumnModel().getColumn(0).setCellRenderer(renderer);

    tbl.setPreferredScrollableViewportSize(viewportSize);
    JScrollPane pane = JTable.createScrollPaneForTable(tbl);

    this.getContentPane().add(pane);
  }

  public static void main(String[] args) {
    JFrame f = new ColumnRendererExample("Using a Column Renderer");
    f.pack();
    f.setVisible(true);
    f.setDefaultCloseOperation(JFrame.DO_NOTHING_ON_CLOSE);
    f.addWindowListener(new WindowAdapter() {
      public void windowClosing(WindowEvent evt) {
        System.exit(0);
      }
```

(Continued)

```
    });
}

// The table data
Object[][] data = {
    { "Hot & Spicy", Boolean.TRUE },
    { "Cheese", Boolean.FALSE },
    { "Ham", Boolean.TRUE },
    { "New Yorker", Boolean.FALSE },
    { "Vegetarian", Boolean.TRUE }
};

String[] columnNames = {
    "Pizza", "Ordered?"
};
}
```

In this example, the user isn't going to be allowed to change the data in the table, so the JTable isCellEditable method is overridden to return false and therefore make the entire tree read-only. This is slightly better in performance terms than leaving the decision to the table model because it saves the cost of invoking another method (the table model's isCellEditable is called from the default JTable isCellEditable method).

The major change in this example that is of interest here is the fact that it creates a column renderer for the first column. Since this column contains String values, they can be rendered using a simple DefaultTableCellRenderer, which is a subclass of JLabel and is therefore well-suited to representing String values.

As well as implementing the TableCellRenderer interface, DefaultTableCellRenderer also provides the following methods:

```
public void setBackground(Color background);

public void setForeground(Color foreground);

public void setValue(Object value);
```

Using these methods, you can supply the colors to be applied to the component when it is drawn onto the table. These colors are applied to the component when the getTableCellRendererComponent method is called to render each individual cell. You can see the results of running this example in Figure 11-13.

When this example starts, the left-hand column will appear selected and will take on the usual selection colors. If you click on the header of the right-hand column, however, you will see that the renderer for the left column is using black text on a yellow background, as required.

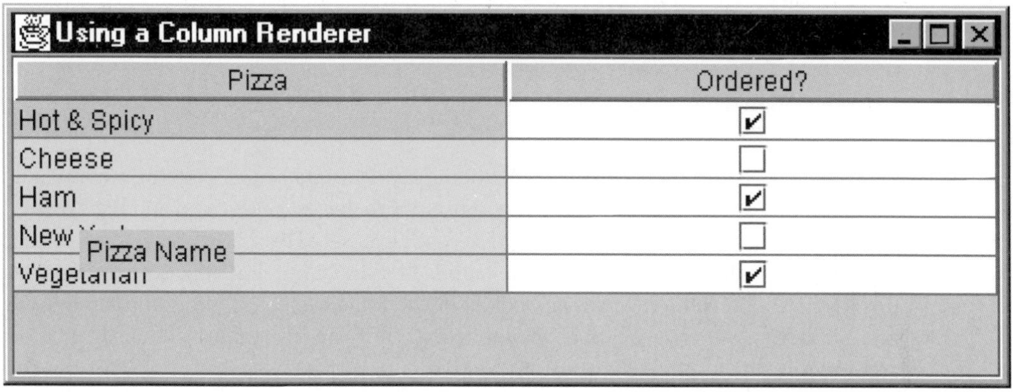

Figure 11-13 A table with a column renderer.

The colors used for selected rows and columns are attributes of the table, not of the renderer and are set using the `JTable` `setSelectionForeground` and `setSelectionBackground` methods. When you use `DefaultTableCellRenderer`, you don't need to be concerned with these extra colors, because they will be used automatically in place of any specific colors you choose with the `DefaultTableCellRenderer` `setForeground` and `setBackground` methods if the renderer is used to draw a cell in a selected column.

Because `DefaultTableCellRenderer` is really just a `JLabel`, you can do anything with it that you can do with a label. For example, you can change the text alignment, provide an icon, or even associate a tool tip with it, which will apply to every cell drawn with that renderer. The example above provides the tip "Pizza Name," which will appear if you let the mouse rest over any of the cells in the left-hand column of the table. There is an example of this in Figure 11-13.

Custom Renderers

Now that you know how renderers work, it is finally possible to improve the table that was produced in the example in Figure 11-1. If you remember, there was a problem with the way in which some of the cell content was represented—specifically, there were two types of columns that did not seem to have useful information, namely the one that contained dates and those containing elapsed times. In this section, you'll see how to develop a pair of custom renderers that can be used to convert from a `GregorianCalendar` value to a readable date and from a time interval in seconds to days, hours, minutes and seconds, so that the data can be presented as it was intended to be seen.

The key to implementing a custom renderer is the `getTableCellRendererComponent` method. This works in the same way as the `getTreeCellRendererComponent` method that you saw in the last chapter, except that it has slightly different arguments:

```
public Component getTableCellRendererComponent(JTable table,
      Object value,
      boolean isSelected,
      boolean isFocused,
      int row, int column);
```

The first two arguments are the table being used and the value from the current cell. The standard renderer uses the `table` argument to get its foreground and background colors from the table if specific colors have not been set. The `isSelected` argument is true if the cell being rendered is selected. `DefaultTableCellRenderer` uses this to choose between the ordinary colors or the table's selected foreground and background colors, which again are obtained directly from the table. The `isFocused` argument is provided to allow custom renderers to provide visual feedback for the cell in the table that is considered to have the focus—the one that was last clicked. `DefaultTableCellRenderer` uses this argument to enclose the focused cell with a border. Finally, the `row` and `column` arguments are also not used by the default renderer. They could be used to create a custom renderer that used specific attributes for cells determined on a per-row, per-column or even per-cell basis. Such a renderer would have to be created with a reference to the object or objects that hold the attributes and would use the row and/or column arguments to access the attributes as each cell is rendered.

Three of the columns in the original table contain elapsed times that are measured in seconds and were displayed that way in Figure 11-1. To convert a value held in seconds to something more readable, you need a custom renderer that knows how to do the conversion. The quickest way to build this simple renderer is to extend `DefaultTableCellRenderer`—the only thing you will have to do to create a suitable renderer is to provide the code that creates the text that will be displayed in each cell by overriding the `getTableCellRendererComponent` method. It will still be possible to change the cell's colors and associate a tool tip with it if necessary, because those capabilities are inherited from `DefaultTableCellRenderer`. Listing 11-9 shows the implementation.

Listing 11-9   A renderer for time intervals

```
package JFCBook.Chapter11;

import com.sun.java.swing.*;
import com.sun.java.swing.table.*;
import java.awt.*;

public class IntervalRenderer extends DefaultTableCellRenderer {
  public Component getTableCellRendererComponent(JTable table,
          Object value,
          boolean isSelected,
```

```
                boolean isFocused,
                int row, int column) {
    Component component = super.getTableCellRendererComponent(table,
                        value, isSelected,
                        isFocused, row, column);
    if (value != null && value instanceof Integer) {
        int interval = ((Integer)value).intValue();
        int days = interval/SECS_PER_DAY;
        interval -= days * SECS_PER_DAY;
        int hours = interval/SECS_PER_HOUR;
        interval -= hours * SECS_PER_HOUR;
        int minutes = interval/SECS_PER_MIN;
        int seconds = interval - minutes * SECS_PER_MIN;

        ((JLabel)component).setText(days + "d " + hours + "h " + minutes +
                        "m " + seconds + "s");
    } else {
        ((JLabel)component).setText(value == null ? "" : value.toString());
    }

    return component;
}

protected static final int SECS_PER_MIN = 60;
protected static final int MINS_PER_HOUR = 60;
protected static final int HOURS_PER_DAY = 24;
protected static final int SECS_PER_HOUR = SECS_PER_MIN * MINS_PER_HOUR;
protected static final int SECS_PER_DAY = SECS_PER_HOUR * HOURS_PER_DAY;
}
```

The getTableCellRendererComponent is very straightforward. First, the superclass version of this method is invoked to get the actual component that will do the rendering. This will, of course, be a JLabel. In fact, the component returned will be the DefaultTableCellRenderer itself—the local variable component will actually be set to "this." Invoking the superclass getTableCellRendererComponent allows DefaultTableCellRenderer to set the correct foreground and background colors depending on whether the cell being drawn is selected (as indicated by the isSelected argument).

The value to be converted and displayed in the cell is supplied as one of the arguments to getTableCellRendererComponent, in the form of an Integer from the table model. If, indeed, an Integer is passed, it is converted from seconds to days, hours, minutes and seconds and a suitable string showing the results is constructed. If an object of any other form is provided as the cell's value, the code just uses its toString method to get a representation of it. Either way, the resulting string is then used as the label's text field and the label is returned, to be drawn into the table.

Core Note

You'll notice that there is a check to determine whether the value supplied to the renderer is null *and an empty string is rendered if it is. There are two common cases that lead to a* null *value being supplied. Most obviously, if the table model is created using one of the constructors that doesn't fully populate it, some of the cells will contain* null *and, because of this check, they will be rendered as empty. The other case occurs when the mouse is over the table long enough for the* ToolTipManager *to ask for a tool tip. This request is passed to the renderer for the cell that the mouse is over by calling its* getTableCell RendererComponent *method. Since the reason for calling this method is only to get the* Component *that would be used for rendering and not to actually redraw the table cell, a* null *value is passed and the returned* Component, *if it is a* JComponent, *is asked for the tool tip via its* getToolTipText *method. If you are going to be writing a custom renderer, be sure to handle* null *values properly.*

The second renderer that is required takes a GregorianCalendar from the table model and converts it to a date in the appropriate form for the location in which the application is run. The same principles are used here and much of the code is the same as for the IntervalRenderer—only the details of the getTableCellRendererComponent method differ, as shown in Listing 11-10.

Listing 11-10   A renderer for dates

```
package JFCBook.Chapter11;

import com.sun.java.swing.*;
import com.sun.java.swing.table.*;
import java.awt.*;
import java.util.*;
import java.text.*;

public class DateRenderer extends DefaultTableCellRenderer {
  public Component getTableCellRendererComponent(JTable table,
                Object value,
                boolean isSelected, boolean isFocused,
                int row, int column) {
    Component component =
                super.getTableCellRendererComponent(table, value,
                isSelected, isFocused, row, column);
    if (value != null && value instanceof GregorianCalendar) {
      GregorianCalendar cal = (GregorianCalendar)value;
      ((JLabel)component).setText(dateFormatter.format(cal.getTime()));
```

```
  } else {
    ((JLabel)component).setText(value == null ? "" : value.toString());
  }

  return component;
}

protected DateFormat dateFormatter = DateFormat.getDateInstance();
}
```

Again, the first step is to call the `DefaultTableCellRenderer` `getTableCellRendererComponent` method to get the label to be rendered onto. This time, the renderer expects to get a `GregorianCalendar` object from the table model and converts it to a date (not including the time). Because the `DateFormat` class from the `java.text` package is used, the date will be represented in a form suitable for the locale of the user running the program. If the way in which the date is converted is unfamiliar to you, read the chapter on Internationalization from *Core Java 1.1 Volume II: Advanced Features*, published by Prentice Hall.

Having created the necessary renderers, it is a simple matter to install them in the table and see the results, as you can see in Listing 11-11, which shows the important changes to the original `TableExample` program that we used at the beginning of this chapter. You can find the complete source code for this program on the CD-ROM and you can run the revised program for yourself with the command:

```
java JFCBook.Chapter11.ExtendedTableExample
```

Listing 11-11   Using custom renderers

```
public ExtendedTableExample(String title) {
  super(title);
  JTable table = new JTable(new TableExampleData());
  table.setAutoResizeMode(JTable.AUTO_RESIZE_OFF);
  table.getTableHeader().setUpdateTableInRealTime(false);
  this.getContentPane().add(JTable.createScrollPaneForTable(table));

  // Fix up special renderers
  // First, a class-based renderer for GregorianCalendar
  DateRenderer dateRenderer = new DateRenderer();
  dateRenderer.setHorizontalAlignment(JLabel.CENTER);
  table.setDefaultRenderer(java.util.GregorianCalendar.class,
              dateRenderer);
```

```
// A column-based renderer for time intervals,
// used in various columns
IntervalRenderer interval = new IntervalRenderer();
interval.setHorizontalAlignment(JLabel.CENTER);
// Fix up special renderers

// Attach the interval renderer to the correct columns
TableColumnModel tcm = table.getColumnModel();
tcm.getColumn(5).setCellRenderer(interval);
tcm.getColumn(7).setCellRenderer(interval);
tcm.getColumn(8).setCellRenderer(interval);

// Set appropriate column widths
for (int i = 0; i < widths.length; i++) {
  TableColumn col = tcm.getColumn(i);
  col.setMinWidth(widths[i]);
  col.setWidth(widths[i]);
}
}
```

The listing actually shows the constructor for the program's main class where the table is created; the data is in a separate class that isn't shown here—you can find it on the CD-ROM. The two renderers are actually installed in different ways. The DateRenderer is obviously generic—it can be used for any column that contains a GregorianCalendar value, so it is installed as a class-based renderer using the JTable setDefaultRenderer method. Notice that the first parameter supplied to this method is a class object for the class that this renderer can deal with, while the second argument is an instance of the renderer. Having installed it in this way, you can be sure that it will be used for every column that contains a GregorianCalendar, unless specifically overridden on a per-column basis.

On the other hand, you don't necessarily want to treat all Integer values as if they were time intervals, so the IntervalRenderer is installed separately on each column that needs it by getting the table's column model, which was created automatically, and attaching it to columns 5, 7 and 8 using the setCellRenderer method.

Note that as each renderer was created, its setHorizontalAlignment method was called to arrange for the text that they end up drawing to be centered in the cell. This method is inherited from JLabel, from which these renderers are descended, via DefaultTableCellRenderer.

A few other important changes were also made to this program to improve the way the table looks and behaves. First, automatic resizing was turned off so that the table wouldn't be crammed into whatever space is available; since it is a wide table, you're unlikely to be able to see all of it without having to use a horizontal scroll bar unless you have a very high-resolution screen. Real-time table updates as the columns are dragged or resized were also turned off, so that the performance of these operations is improved. Lastly, at the end of the constructor the widths of each column are explicitly set, so that all of the data in that column is visible and the minimum width is also set to the same value. There is nothing magic about the way these values were determined—they were discovered by trial and error. As explained earlier, there is no simple way to calculate the correct value for column widths without incurring a performance penalty at least once by running every value in the table through its cell renderer. For a table like this with fixed data, it isn't worth the effort. You can see the table as it now looks (or at least part of it) in Figure 11-14.

Flight	Commander	LM Pilot	CM Pilot	Launch	Duration	
Apollo 7	Walter Schirra	Walter Cunningham	Donn Eisele	11-Oct-68	10d 20h 9m 0s	-
Apollo 8	Frank Borman	William Anders	James Lovell Jr	21-Dec-68	6d 3h 1m 0s	-
Apollo 9	James McDivitt	Russell Schweickart	David Scott	03-Mar-69	10d 1h 1m 0s	-
Apollo 10	Thomas Stafford	Eugene Cernan	John Young	18-May-69	8d 0h 3m 0s	-
Apollo 11	Neil Armstrong	Edwin Aldrin Jr	Michael Collins	16-Jul-69	8d 3h 18m 0s	Se
Apollo 12	Charles Conrad Jr	Alan Bean	Richard Gordon Jr	19-Nov-69	10d 4h 36m 0s	O
Apollo 13	James Lovell Jr	Fred Haise Jr	Jack Swigert	11-Apr-70	5d 22h 54m 0s	-
Apollo 14	Alan Shephard Jr	Edgar Mitchell	Stuart Roosa	31-Jan-71	9d 0h 2m 0s	Fr
Apollo 15	David Scott	James Irwin	Alfred Worden	26-Jul-71	12d 7h 12m 0s	Ha
Apollo 16	John Young	Charles Duke Jr	Thomas Mattingly	16-Apr-72	11d 1h 51m 0s	De
Apollo 17	Eugene Cernan	Harrison Schmidt	Ronald Evans	11-Dec-72	12d 13h 51m 0s	Ta

Figure 11-14   Custom date and time renderers.

Implementing Fixed Table Columns

Adding customized renderers to our original example and setting the right column widths has greatly improved it, but there is still one minor inconvenience that can be fairly easily resolved using a technique that you'll probably find useful if you're going to make use of JTable to show tables with anything but a small number of columns. The problem is that when you scroll the table horizontally to see the columns at the right-hand end, you lose sight of which flight's data you are looking at, because this information is held in the left most column, which quickly scrolls out of view. What would be useful would be to "lock" that column in place so that you can always see what data you are looking at in any particular row.

The key to solving this problem is in the scroll pane. If you look back to Chapter 5, "Keyboard Handling, Actions and Scrolling," you'll see that we described there how you can provide column and row headers for anything in a scroll pane. The table itself uses the column header to hold column headers. In this case, as many columns from the table as need to be locked should be placed in the scroll pane's row header. When this has been done, they remain fixed when you scroll the table horizontally, but still follow vertical scrolling movement.

The problem is that you can't just break the table into two pieces and display some of it as a row header. Instead, what you need to do is to create two different views *of the same table model*, as two tables, and place the columns that should be locked as a separate table in the scroll pane's row header. It is even possible to provide these separate columns with column headers, because the second table will create a JTableHeader, which can be placed above the row header part of the scroll pane, in the top left-hand corner component. This is a very neat solution that is remarkably simple to implement and also very effective.

To illustrate how it's done, let's lock the flight name and the landing site and allow the other columns to scroll horizontally. These columns are numbered 0 and 6 in the data model, so it is necessary to create two tables, whose column models contain table columns 0 and 6, and 1 through 5 plus 7 through 10 respectively. This could be done by manually creating two separate TableColumnModel objects and connecting each to its own JTable, but this example uses a shortcut that also allows us to show some of the methods of a TableColumnModel in action.

What we're going to do is to create the original table exactly as we did before. When the table model is connected to the JTable, it will build a TableColumnModel containing all of the columns in model order. This model is almost perfect for the main table. All we need to do then is to create an empty DefaultTableColumnModel and remove the two columns that are going to be locked in place from the main table's column model and add them to the table column of the second table. Doing this avoids having to create the TableColumn objects for all 11 columns ourselves. Listing 11-12 shows the constructor for the main class of the example program, which is derived from the code in Listing 11-11.

Listing 11-12   A table with fixed columns

```
public class FixedColumnsExample extends JFrame {
  public FixedColumnsExample(String title) {
    super(title);

    TableExampleData model = new TableExampleData();
    JTable table = new JTable(model);
    table.setAutoResizeMode(JTable.AUTO_RESIZE_OFF);
    table.getTableHeader().setUpdateTableInRealTime(false);
    JScrollPane pane = JTable.createScrollPaneForTable(table);
    this.getContentPane().add(pane);

    // Build a second table containing two columns from the original
    // and remove those columns from the main table. Use the same
    // model for both tables.
    JTable table2 = new JTable(model);
    table2.setAutoResizeMode(JTable.AUTO_RESIZE_OFF);
    table2.getTableHeader().setUpdateTableInRealTime(false);
```

```
    TableColumnModel tcm = table.getColumnModel();
    TableColumnModel tcm2 = new DefaultTableColumnModel();

    TableColumn col = tcm.getColumn(0);
    tcm.removeColumn(col);
    tcm2.addColumn(col);

    col = tcm.getColumn(5);
    tcm.removeColumn(col);
    tcm2.addColumn(col);

    // Set the widths of the columns for the
    // second table before we get its preferred size
    for (int i = 0; i < widths2.length; i++) {
      col = tcm2.getColumn(i);
      col.setMinWidth(widths[i]);
      col.setWidth(widths[i]);
    }
    table2.setColumnModel(tcm2); // Install new column model
    table2.setPreferredScrollableViewportSize(table2.getPreferredSize());

    // Put the second table in the row header
    pane.setRowHeaderView(table2);

    // Put the header of the second table in the top left corner
    pane.setCorner(JScrollPane.UPPER_LEFT_CORNER, table2.getTableHeader());

    // Fix up special renderers
    // First, a class-based renderer for GregorianCalendar
    DateRenderer dateRenderer = new DateRenderer();
    dateRenderer.setHorizontalAlignment(JLabel.CENTER);
    table.setDefaultRenderer(java.util.GregorianCalendar.class, dateRenderer);

    // A column-based renderer for time intervals, used in various columns
    IntervalRenderer interval = new IntervalRenderer();
    interval.setHorizontalAlignment(JLabel.CENTER);

    // Attach the interval renderer to the correct columns
    tcm.getColumn(4).setCellRenderer(interval);
    tcm.getColumn(5).setCellRenderer(interval);
    tcm.getColumn(6).setCellRenderer(interval);

    // Set appropriate column widths
    for (int i = 0; i < widths.length; i++) {
      col = tcm.getColumn(i);
      col.setMinWidth(widths[i]);
      col.setWidth(widths[i]);
    }
  }
}
}
```

The first step is to create the same table as in the previous example and wrap it in a scroll pane. Then, a second table is created, sharing exactly the same table model, so that both tables derive their content from the same data. Next, the `JTable` `getColumnModel` method is used to get the column model of the first table and then an empty replacement column model is created for the second table. Using the `TableColumnModel` `getColumn`, `removeColumn` and `addColumn` methods, the two columns that are to be locked are removed from the first table's column model and added into that of the second table, in the order that they should be displayed. Notice that, after column 0 has been removed, the second column that needs to be removed has become column 5, even though it started as column 6.

Removing the columns from the original table causes it to recreate its table header automatically, so nothing extra needs to be done to keep the header up to date. The same is true of the second table—when its new column model is installed using `setColumnModel`, it too builds an appropriate table header.

All that needs to be done now is to set the correct column widths and renderers as was done in Listing 11-11 and then put all the components where they need to be in the scroll pane. The first table and its header are already in the main scrolling area and the column header, respectively, so all that remains is to put the second table in the scroll pane's row header and its table header (which is obtained from `getTableHeader`) in the top left-hand corner component.

Note, however, that there is a subtlety about this. When the second table is placed in the row header, the row header viewport asks the table how big a viewport it would like. As you saw earlier in this section, a table always asks for a view port 450 pixels wide and 400 pixels high by default so, if nothing were done about this, the result would be a row header with a table on its left-hand side, a large gap to the right and then the second table. To avoid this, the second table's preferred size is obtained and set as the preferred viewport size. This makes the row header just large enough to contain the table. It is important to set the correct column widths before this is done, of course.

To run this example for yourself, use the command:

```
java JFCBook.Chapter11.FixedColumnsExample
```

You'll find that the table starts off looking as it did in the last example, except that the horizontal scrollbar doesn't cover all of it, as you can see in Figure 11-15. If you scroll horizontally, the left two columns stay in place, as we wanted them to. Notice also that the table headers are all correctly placed and the rows all line up neatly. If you make the window vertically smaller so that a vertical scrollbar appears, you can verify that scrolling the main table up and down works as expected—the locked columns scroll so that complete rows stay intact.

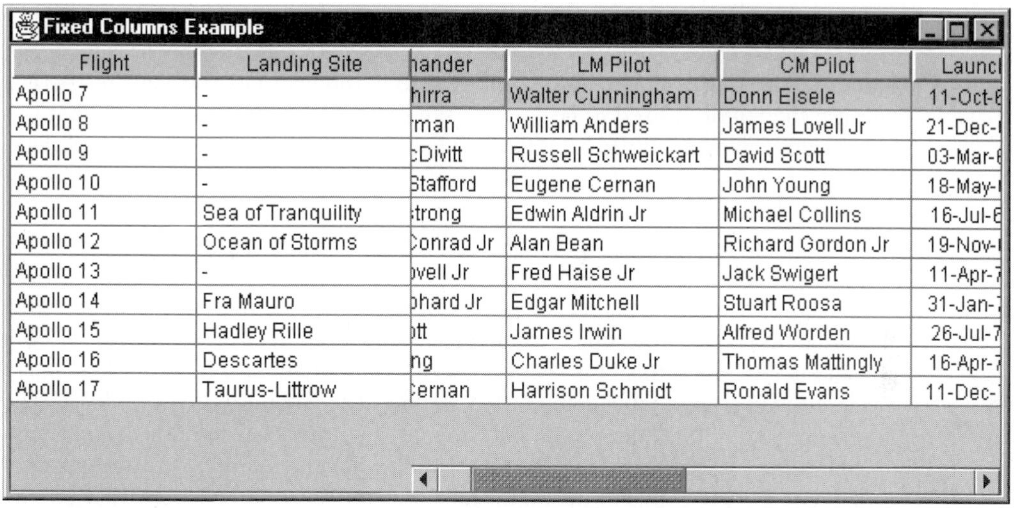

Figure 11-15   A table with two locked columns.

Using Editors

Editors are very similar to renderers. Editors implement the TableCellEditor interface for which there is the default implementation DefaultCellEditor that supports the use of a JTextField, JCheckBox or a JComboBox as an editor component. One of the methods in the TableCellEditor interface is getTableCellEditorComponent, which is almost identical to the corresponding renderer method, in that it provides a component that can be used in a table cell. The difference in this case is that this component actually becomes part of the table while editing is in progress.

When you create a table, it installs standard class-based editors so that you can edit cells whose data is of type Boolean using a JCheckBox, those of type Number with a JTextField, and those of all other types not derived from these two also with a JTextField, in which the string representation of the object appears. This latter editor is associated with the Object class. You can, of course, add class-based editors of your own using the JTable setDefaultEditor method and you can install column-based editors with the TableColumn setCellEditor method.

Because using editors is very similar to using renderers and since, as you've already seen, you can make tables editable without having to manipulate editors at all, there aren't any simple editor examples in this chapter. Instead, you're going to see a complete example that builds both a custom renderer and a custom editor.

The standard table editors all place the editing component in the cell occupied by the data being edited. Because the table dictates where the component will be rendered, editors have little control over this. But this can also be very restricting, because the editor is sized to occupy the same amount of space as the cell that it is temporarily replacing. If you want to provide the user with a more complex interface, you need to take control of the editing mechanism yourself and create a component that resides outside the table.

In this section, we'll create a simple application that displays a table that shows the names of some (fictional) people and their (imaginary) favorite colors. Because you will by now have become very adept at writing renderers, the color is going to be shown not as text but as a small icon in the second column of the table, next to each person's name. To do this, it is necessary to implement another renderer that shows a colored icon from a table column that contains the color as a `Color` object. The interesting part of this example is what happens when you click in the second column to change the person's favorite color. One option would be to use a `JComboBox` populated with a set of colors as the editor for this column—when editing is started, the combo box would appear in the cell and the user would choose one of the preset colors as the new favorite color. But that would be too easy. Instead, this example is going to pop up a dialog box with a `JColorChooser` in it and allow the user to select any color as his or her favorite directly from the chooser.

To implement this example, three pieces are needed:

- The custom renderer for icons that we'll call `IconRenderer`
- The custom editor for colors, called `ColorEditor`
- A table data model and the application itself

These three pieces will be discussed separately, starting with the application itself, the code for which is shown in Listing 11-13.

Listing 11-13   A table with a custom color editor

```
package JFCBook.Chapter11;

import com.sun.java.swing.*;
import com.sun.java.swing.table.*;
import java.awt.*;
import java.awt.event.*;
import JFCBook.Chapter11.IconRenderer;
import JFCBook.Chapter11.ColorEditor;

public class CustomEditorExample extends JFrame {
  public CustomEditorExample(String title) {
    super(title);
```

```
AbstractTableModel model = new AbstractTableModel() {
  // The table data
  Object[][] data = {
    { "John Doe", Color.green },
    { "Jane Doe", Color.yellow },
    { "John Smith", Color.blue },
    { "Fred Bloggs", Color.red }

  };

  String[] columnNames = {
    "Name", "Color"
  };

  public int getRowCount() {
    return data.length;
  }

  public int getColumnCount() {
    return data[0].length;
  }

  public Object getValueAt(int row, int col) {
    return data[row][col];
  }

  public String getColumnName(int columnIndex) {
    return columnNames[columnIndex];
  }

  public Class getColumnClass(int columnIndex) {
    return data[0][columnIndex].getClass();
  }

  public boolean isCellEditable(int rowIndex, int columnIndex) {
    return true;
  }

  public void setValueAt(Object value, int rowIndex, int columnIndex)
{
    if ((value instanceof Color && columnIndex == 1) ||
        (value instanceof String && columnIndex == 0)) {
      data[rowIndex][columnIndex] = value;
      fireTableCellUpdated(rowIndex, columnIndex);
    }
  }
```

(Continued)

```
  };

  // Create the table
  Dimension viewportSize = new Dimension(450, 120);
  JTable tbl = new JTable(model);

  // Create the class renderer for colors
  IconRenderer renderer = new IconRenderer();
  renderer.setHorizontalAlignment(JLabel.CENTER);
  renderer.setToolTipText("This is the person's favorite color");
  tbl.setDefaultRenderer(Color.class, renderer);

  // Create the class editor for colors
  ColorEditor editor = new ColorEditor(new JTextField());
  tbl.setDefaultEditor(Color.class, editor);

  tbl.setPreferredScrollableViewportSize(viewportSize);
  JScrollPane pane = JTable.createScrollPaneForTable(tbl);

  this.getContentPane().add(pane);
}

public static void main(String[] args) {
  JFrame f = new CustomEditorExample("Using a Custom Editor");
  f.pack();
  f.setVisible(true);
  f.setDefaultCloseOperation(JFrame.DO_NOTHING_ON_CLOSE);
  f.addWindowListener(new WindowAdapter() {
    public void windowClosing(WindowEvent evt) {
      System.exit(0);
    }
  });
}
}
```

The Example Application

The first part of this application creates a table model by extending
AbstractTableModel, as has been done many times before. This table has two
columns—the left one containing a person's name as a String and the right one
their favorite color as a Color object. Both of these columns will be editable, so the
isCellEditable method is overridden to return true for every cell and
setValueAt is implemented to allow new values to be stored, provided they are of
the correct type for the column that they are being stored into. Because no column-

based editors or renderers are installed, the `getColumnClass` method that is used here is critical, because the value it returns for each column determines which editor and renderer will be used. The first column, which contains strings, will be rendered and edited by the class-based renderer and editor for `Object`—a `JLabel` and a `JTextField`, respectively.

The second column contains `Color` objects. There is no standard renderer or editor for `Color`, so the table would naturally use a `JLabel` to render and a `JTextField` to edit the result of applying the `toString` method to the `Color` object—which would produce a meaningless result. Here, however, our `IconRenderer` and `ColorEditor` will be installed as class-based objects for the `Color` class so that they are used instead. If you run this example with the command:

```
java JFCBook.Chapter11.CustomEditorExample
```

you get a result that looks like Figure 11-16. Although the gray-scale reproduction of this screen shot loses some of the detail, you can see that each person's name is accompanied by a small icon filled with that person's favorite color, or at least its grayscale equivalent!

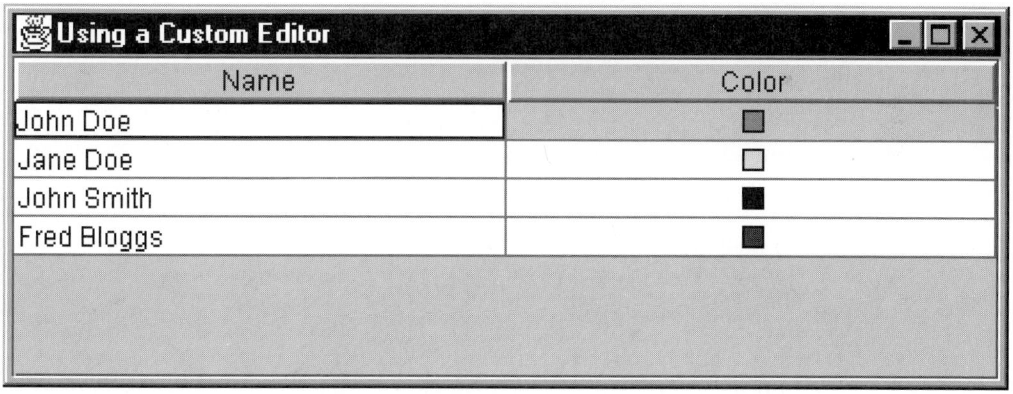

Figure 11-16   A table with a custom renderer for colors.

Implementing a Custom Color Renderer

Next, let's look at the implementation of `IconRenderer`. Like the other renderers that you've seen, this one is derived from `DefaultTableCellRenderer` and uses a `JLabel` as the host component. `JLabel` is a good choice because, as you know, it can display an `Icon` as well as, or instead of, text, so all that needs to be done is to create an icon of the right color for the data in the cell that is being rendered. Chapter 4 built an icon called `ColorFillIcon` that can be used to draw the colored square. This class has a `setFillColor` method that allows us to change the color that it displays. This is essential, because the same renderer instance, and hence the same `ColorFillIcon` instance, will be used to render each row of the second column, so it is necessary to be able to change the icon's fill color for each cell. The code for this simple renderer is shown in Listing 11-14.

Listing11-14   A renderer that displays a colored icon

```
package JFCBook.Chapter11;

import com.sun.java.swing.*;
import com.sun.java.swing.table.*;
import JFCBook.Chapter4.ColorFillIcon;
import java.awt.*;

public class IconRenderer extends DefaultTableCellRenderer {
  public IconRenderer() {
    icon = new ColorFillIcon(Color.white, 10, 10, 1);
    setIcon(icon);
  }

  public Component getTableCellRendererComponent(JTable table,
              Object value,
              boolean isSelected, boolean isFocused,
              int row, int column) {
    Component component =
                super.getTableCellRendererComponent(table,
                value, isSelected, isFocused, row, column);
    if (value != null && value instanceof Color) {
      icon.setFillColor((Color)value);
      ((JLabel)component).setText("");
    } else {
      icon.setFillColor(Color.white);
      ((JLabel)component).setText(value == null ? "" : value.toString());
    }

    return component;
  }

  protected ColorFillIcon icon;
}
```

The constructor is simple—it just creates an icon, initialized arbitrarily to show white, and connects it to the `JLabel` from which the renderer is derived. The size of the icon is also fairly arbitrary—in this case, a 10-pixels square icon was chosen because it fits comfortably with the default row height of 16 pixels. The only other method that needs to provided is `getTableCellRendererComponent`, which configures the label when the cell is being drawn. The value that is supplied to be rendered is simply used to change the fill color of the icon. If the data from the model is, for some reason, not a `Color` object, the icon is made white and the object is displayed in string form as the text part of the label. This will never happen in this particular example, but a `null` value is possible, as you know, when a tool tip is being obtained.

Implementing a Custom Color Editor

All that remains is to implement the custom editor. An editor has to implement the `TableCellEditor` interface, which is much more complex than `TableCellRenderer`. Here is its definition:

```
public interface TableCellEditor extends CellEditor {
   public Component getTableCellEditorComponent(JTable table,
           Object value, boolean isSelected, int row,
           int column);
}
```

You saw the `CellEditor` interface during the discussion of `JTree` in Chapter 10 but, since this example implements it as part of the custom editor, it is repeated here for convenience.

```
public interface CellEditor {
   public Object getCellEditorValue();
   public boolean isCellEditable(EventObject);
   public boolean shouldSelectCell(EventObject);
   public boolean stopCellEditing();
   public void cancelCellEditing();
   public void addCellEditorListener(CellEditorListener);
   public void removeCellEditorListener(CellEditorListener);
}
```

Our custom editor will be derived from `DefaultCellEditor`, which provides implementations for all of these methods, but will only take advantage of its `addCellEditorListener` and `removeCellEditorListener` methods as far as this interface is concerned. As you'll see, two methods that provide for firing events to listeners that register using these methods will also be used.

Before showing the implementation of the editor, let's step through the way in which the edit process is performed. Editing starts when the user clicks in an editable cell. When a click occurs, the editor's `isCellEditable` method is called with the mouse event as its argument, as you saw in Chapter 10. This method usually looks at the click count to determine if it contains the correct number of clicks to start editing, as determined by the `DefaultCellEditor setClickCountToStart` method. By default, one click is enough but text editors usually require two. If editing should begin, `true` is returned. Note that this method is only entered if the table model and the table agree that the cell itself is intrinsically editable, so the editor does not need to concern itself with this issue.

Assuming that true is returned, the table next calls the editor's `getTableCellEditorComponent` method and passes it the current value of the cell, adds the returned component to the table in the place occupied by the cell being edited, and calls its `shouldSelectCell` method. The return value from this method only indicates whether the cell itself should be drawn as if it were selected. The important thing about this method from the editor's viewpoint, however, is that it signals that the editing process has begun—it can assume that it has been mounted on the table. This fact will be used in the editor implementation.

Several things can now happen. Normally, the user will edit the cell's value and the editor will tell the table that editing is completed by firing an event; the table registers to receive this event using the `addCellEditorListener` method. There are other ways for editing to terminate, however. First, the user can stop editing this cell and start editing a different one. This causes the editor's `stopCellEditing` method to be called. In the case of a table, unlike a tree, there is no mechanism for the table to cancel an edit (which abandons any value being typed into the editor), so the `cancelCellEditing` method is never invoked. Since all editors are obliged to provide a `cancelCellEditing` method, our implementation just stops editing whichever method is used.

The editor might also provide a way for the user to abandon the edit (as ours will). In this case, the editor will fire an event to the table that indicates that editing has been canceled. Whether the edit completes normally, is stopped or is canceled, the editor must fire an editing stopped or editing canceled event to the table. If an editing stopped event is fired, the editor's current value is retrieved using `getCellEditorValue` and applied to the table model. Finally, the editor component is removed from the table and the renderer used to redraw the cell with its new value.

Now let's look at the implementation of our color editor, which is shown in Listing 11-15. Our intention, when editing starts, is to pop up a dialog box with a `JColorChooser`, an `OK` button and a `Cancel` button. When the user has selected a color, the `OK` button will signal the table that editing is complete. On the other hand, pressing `Cancel` or dismissing the dialog window will tell the table that the edit has been abandoned.

Even though the editor will show a dialog outside the table, it must return a component to be mounted in the table cell being edited. This example provides a `JTextField` with editing disabled that displays the text "Editing...." You could, if you wanted to, use something else instead, but this is by far the simplest thing to do.

Listing11-15 An editor that creates a dialog box outside the table

```java
package JFCBook.Chapter11;

import com.sun.java.swing.*;
import com.sun.java.swing.preview.*;
import com.sun.java.swing.table.*;
import com.sun.java.swing.event.*;
import java.util.*;
import java.awt.*;
import java.awt.event.*;

public class ColorEditor extends DefaultCellEditor
          implements ActionListener, Runnable {
  public ColorEditor(JTextField textField) {
    super(textField);
    textField.setEditable(false);
    createDialog();
  }

  // These methods implement the TableCellEditor interface
  public Component getTableCellEditorComponent(JTable table, Object value,
              boolean isSelected,
              int row, int column) {
    ((JTextField)editorComponent).setText("Editing...");

    if (value != null && value instanceof Color) {
      currentColor = (Color)value;
    }

    return editorComponent;
  }

  public Object getCellEditorValue() {
    return currentColor;
  }

  public boolean isCellEditable(EventObject evt) {
    if (evt instanceof MouseEvent) {
      if (((MouseEvent)evt).getClickCount() >=
              getClickCountToStart()) {
        return true;
      }
    }
    return false;
  }
```

(Continued)

```java
public boolean shouldSelectCell(EventObject evt) {
  if (isCellEditable(evt)) {
    showDialog();
  }

  return true;
}

public boolean stopCellEditing() {
  canceled = false;
  currentColor = dialog.getValue();
  dismissDialog();
  return true;
}

public void cancelCellEditing() {
  canceled = true;
  dismissDialog();
}

// These are methods that implement the internals
// of the editor itself.
protected void createDialog() {
  if (dialog == null) {
    dialog = new ColorSelectDialog(new Frame("Dummy"), this);
    dialog.addWindowListener(new WindowAdapter() {
      public void windowClosing(WindowEvent evt) {
        JDialog dlg = (JDialog)evt.getSource();
        ColorEditor.this.canceled = true;
        dismissDialog();
      }
    });
  }
}

protected void showDialog() {
  if (showingDialog == false) {
    Thread t = new Thread(this);
    showingDialog = true;
    t.start();
  }
}

protected void dismissDialog() {
  if (showingDialog == true) {
    dialog.hide();
    showingDialog = false;
```

```
    }
  }

  public void run() {
    dialog.setValue(currentColor);
    canceled = false;
    dialog.show();
    if (canceled) {
      fireEditingCanceled();
    } else {
      fireEditingStopped();
    }
  }

  // ActionListener interface
  public void actionPerformed(ActionEvent evt) {
    JButton button = (JButton)evt.getSource();

    if (button.getActionCommand() == "OK") {
      currentColor = dialog.getValue();
      canceled = false;
    } else {
      canceled = true;
    }
    dismissDialog();
  }


  protected Color currentColor;
  protected ColorSelectDialog dialog;
  protected boolean showingDialog;
  public boolean canceled;
}

class ColorSelectDialog extends JDialog {
  public ColorSelectDialog(Frame f, ActionListener l) {
    super(f, "Choose a Color", true);

    // The ColorChooser
    JPanel p =  new JPanel();
    p.setLayout(new BorderLayout());
    p.setBorder(BorderFactory.createEtchedBorder());
    chooser = new JColorChooser();
    p.add(chooser, "Center");

    // The buttons
    okButton = new JButton("OK");
```

(Continued)

```
      cancelButton = new JButton("Cancel");
      okButton.addActionListener(l);
      cancelButton.addActionListener(l);

      JPanel buttonPanel = new JPanel();
      buttonPanel.add(okButton);
      buttonPanel.add(cancelButton);
      p.add(buttonPanel, "South");

      this.getContentPane().add(p);
      this.pack();
   }

   public void setValue(Color color) {
      chooser.setColor(color);
   }

   public Color getValue() {
      return chooser.getColor();
   }


   protected JColorChooser chooser;
   protected JButton okButton;
   protected JButton cancelButton;
}
```

The constructor of this editor is supplied with the text field that it will use as the dummy editing component and just passes it to the `DefaultCellEditor` constructor, making sure that editing of the text field's content is disabled. The other job that the constructor does is to create the dialog that will appear when the cell is edited. Because it is relatively expensive to create a dialog, this is done only once. When the dialog is needed, it is shown and when it is closed, it is just hidden and remains available for re use later.

The `getTableCellEditorComponent` is, as you would expect, trivial—it just puts the "Editing..." text into the text field and returns that to the table. It also stores the current value of the color from the cell being edited in the instance variable `currentColor`. This value will later be used to initialize the `JColorChooser`. This has to be done every time, because successive edits may be in different cells, which could have different colors associated with them. The `getCellEditorValue` method is also simple—it just returns the `currentColor` value that is initially the value that the cell starts with and is later set from the dialog to the newly-chosen color.

Next comes `isCellEditable`, which verifies that the event it has been given is a mouse event and that it has the required number of mouse clicks. If these conditions are satisfied, it returns true to allow editing to begin.

The next three methods are the most important in this editor. As noted earlier, `shouldSelectCell` is the method that is used to start editing. Assuming that it is appropriate to start editing, this method pops up the dialog using our `showDialog` method, which will be described shortly. Similarly, `stopCellEditing` marks the normal end of an edit. It gets the color currently selected in the dialog and stores it in `currentColor`, from where the table will get it using the `getCellEditorValue` method, then uses `dismissDialog` to hide the dialog. Finally, `cancelCellEditing` immediately dismisses the dialog using `dismissDialog`. These two methods set the boolean instance variable `canceled` according to whether the edit was stopped or canceled. You'll see how this variable is used shortly.

The rest of the methods in this class are implementation details that are not part of the `TableCellEditor` interface—their job is to manage the dialog box. The `createDialog` method is called from the constructor to build the dialog. Since dialogs need a `Frame` to act as parent, a dummy one is created for this purpose since there is no natural `Frame` to use. A `WindowListener` is added to the dialog so that the dialog can be dismissed and the `canceled` flag set if the user closes the dialog from the caption bar. This makes it appear to the rest of the code that the dialog's `Cancel` button was pressed. Finally, note that when the dialog is created, the editor object reference is passed to its constructor as an `ActionListener`. The dialog attaches this listener to its buttons; as a result, the editor's `actionPerformed` method will be called when either `OK` or `Cancel` is pressed.

The `showDialog` method is responsible for making the dialog visible. Since the dialog is modal, it will block the calling thread, but we don't want this to happen because this thread is involved in managing the table's editing activity. So, before the dialog is shown, a new thread is created that will execute the editor's `run` method. It is this method that will show the dialog and will be blocked while the original thread returns to executing table code.

To get rid of the dialog, `dismissDialog` is called. This just hides the dialog directly, which causes its `show` method to return. As you can see by looking at the editor's `run` method, immediately after `show` completes, it looks at whether the dialog was canceled by checking the `canceled` instance variable and calls either `fireEditingStopped` or `fireEditingCanceled`, which are methods provided by `DefaultCellEditor` that result in the table being informed that editing is complete.

Finally, the `actionPerformed` method is called when the dialog's buttons are pressed. All this method does is to determine which button was pressed, set `canceled` appropriately, get the newly chosen color value if `OK` was pressed and stores it in `currentColor`, then hides the dialog by calling `dismissDialog`. Whether the dialog is dismissed using one of the buttons or by virtue of its frame being closed by the user clicking on the frame close button on the caption bar, `canceled` is always set appropriately and `dismissDialog` called, resulting in an event to the table to show that editing is complete. This also happens if the user starts editing elsewhere and `stopCellEditing` is invoked—this sets `canceled` (to `false`) and calls `dismissDialog`. You should convince yourself by carefully examining the code that when the editing process ends, `currentColor` is always set to the newly selected color, that `canceled` is `false` if the edit ended normally, and that `currentColor` is left unchanged and `canceled` is `true` if the edit was abandoned from the dialog box.

The last part of the listing shows the implementation of the dialog box. This code is not going to be discussed here because it is relatively simple and you should, by now, be familiar with the creation of dialog boxes. If there is anything in this code that looks unfamiliar, return to Chapters 7 and 8 where dialogs are described in detail.

You can verify that this editor works as expected by running the program and clicking in one of the cells in the right-hand column. This will cause the dialog to appear and the colored icon to be replaced with the text "Editing…," as shown in Figure 11-17. You should also notice that the color chooser is initialized with the original color from the cell. If you choose a new color and press OK, the dialog disappears and the color icon comes back with the new color.

Now start editing the same cell again, or another cell and the dialog will reappear. Pressing `Cancel` or closing the dialog using the close button on the dialog window makes it vanish and leaves the color in the table cell unchanged, even if you started changing the color in the chooser itself before canceling. Finally, bring up the dialog again by editing any color cell and then click once in a different cell. This will stop the edit and the dialog disappears. If, however, you change the color in the chooser before clicking in the other cell, this new color will be applied to the original cell.

Summary

This chapter took an in-depth look at the Swing table component. You will probably have realized that there are many similarities between `JTable` and `JTree` and that, in particular, the techniques used to customize them using standard renderers and editors or by developing ones of your own, are almost identical, which means that once you've understood one of these components, it is much easier to get to grips with the other ones.

During this survey of tables, you saw both simple and complex examples that demonstrate both how quickly you can create some kind of tabular representation of some data and how much you can do to refine that view if you are prepared to spend a little more time and invest a bit more effort. Some of the examples that were shown at the end of the chapter can be used to solve real-world table problems like locking down columns and providing complex editors, the solutions to which might not be obvious at first sight.

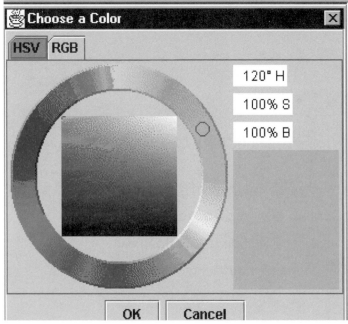

Figure 11-17   A custom table color editor in a separate dialog box.

MULTIPLE-
DOCUMENT
APPLICATIONS

Topics in This Chapter

- Internal Frames and Layered Panes
- The Desktop Manager, Desktop Panes and Icons
- Cascading and Tiling on the Desktop Pane
- Customization of Internal Frames and the Desktop Manager

Chapter 12

U sing the Swing components that you have seen so far, you can create a user interface that consists of a main work area and some controls, such as a menu bar and a toolbar, that allow the user to work with and manipulate whatever is in the work space. While this model works well for some applications, it is very limiting for programs like word processors and spreadsheets where the user may want to work with more than one file a time. In a simple application, the only way to work with multiple documents is to run more than one copy of the program, but this can quickly use up memory resources and makes it more difficult to move information between the documents. In this chapter, we'll examine the facilities that Swing provides to allow you to create multiple-document applications—internal frames, layered panes and the desktop manager.

Internal Frames

Internal frames are miniature versions of an application's top-level window. Like the main window, they have a set of optional decorations, such as maximize, minimize and close buttons and a caption bar that allows the user to move the frame around by clicking on it and dragging it with the mouse. Internal frames are mounted not on the user's desktop, but inside the application main window and are, therefore, always clipped by its boundaries. Figure 12-1 shows four internal frames, each of them an instance of the Swing class JInternalFrame. You can run the example from which Figure 12-1 was generated by using the command:

```
java JFCBook.Chapter.InternalFramesExample1
```

Try running this example and follow through the next few paragraphs to see how internal frames behave.

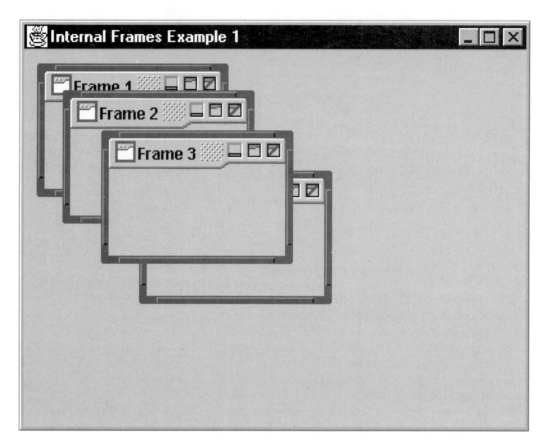

Figure 12-1   Four internal frames in an application window (Metal look-and-feel).

What Internal Frames Look Like

The first thing you'll notice is the neat, cascaded layout of the frames within the application's working area. As you know, usually components are placed and sized by a layout manager but in this case, unfortunately, you would have to do the work of creating this type of arrangement for yourself—there is no standard layout manager that would create such a nice setup for you! Nevertheless, this is such a common way to place internal frames that you'll see later how to write something that will create arrangements like this automatically. You'll also notice that the frames overlap.

This is also relatively unusual—layout managers (apart, of course, from `OverlayLayout`) generally keep components apart and avoid overlaps. The overlap is possible because the container that these internal frames are mounted in doesn't actually have a layout manager at all. As you'll see, this has both advantages and disadvantages.

If you now move your mouse to the caption of the frame entitled "Frame 3" and click once anywhere over the title (and not on any of the title bar decorations), the caption bar will change color, as ordinary frames do when they are selected. Like all components, the appearance of an internal frame depends on the selected look-and-feel. Figure 12-1 shows the Metal look-and-feel; in Figures 12-2 and 12-3, you can see how internal frames are drawn by the Windows and Motif look-and-feel classes, respectively.

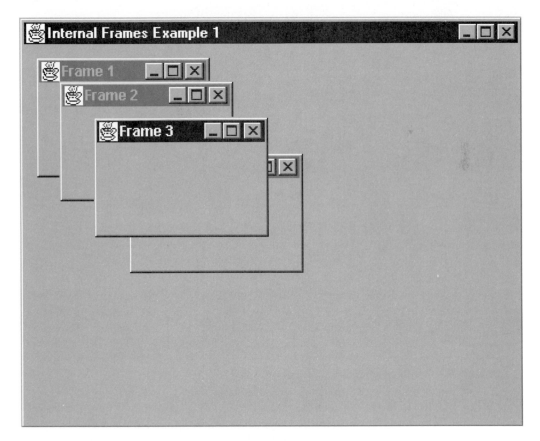

Figure 12-2   Internal frames in the Windows look-and-feel.

In the Metal look-and-feel, the caption bar of a selected window is light blue, for Windows it is dark blue and with Motif it is a kind of purple-red.

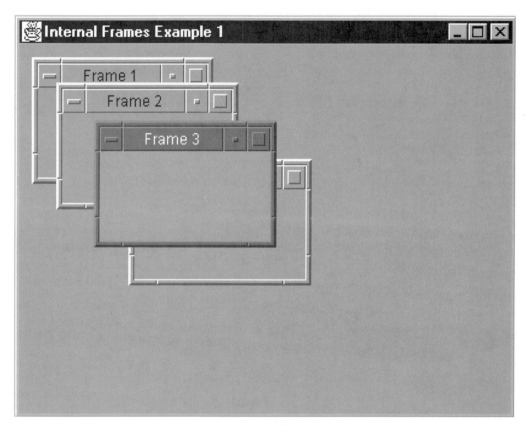

Figure 12-3   Internal frames in the Motif look-and-feel.

To the right of the title there are some buttons. Exactly how many there are depends, again, on the look-and-feel. As you can see, the Motif look-and-feel provides two, while the others have three. In all three cases, the leftmost button is the minimize button, which causes the frame to become an icon when you press it, and the next along is the maximize button, which makes the frame expand to fill its container's window. Unless you're using Motif, you'll have a third button that allows you to close the frame—the Windows version is the usual capital X, while the Metal look-and-feel offers a window icon with a diagonal bar across it. Don't close the frame yet or you won't be able to follow the rest of this example!

Moving to the left of the title bar, what you see again depends on the look-and-feel. In the case of Motif, you see a rectangular area with a bar on it, looking rather like a Motif option menu, while with Windows there is the usual frame icon. Pressing this gives you a drop-down menu of options that we show in Figure 12-4. The items on this menu are equivalent to the buttons on the frame, except, of course, that there is also a `Close` item, which is the only way for the user to close a Motif frame. Three other items are also present, but are currently disabled.

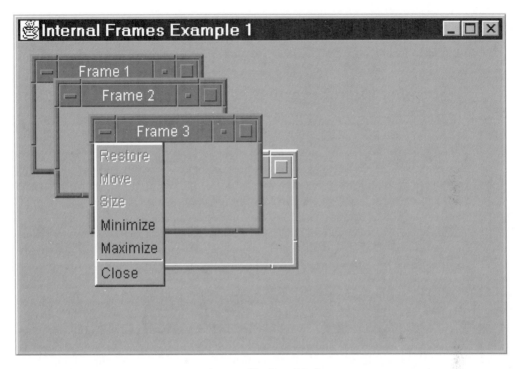

Figure 12-4 The window menu in the Motif look-and-feel.

If you use the Metal look-and-feel, the space to the left of the title is occupied by an icon that looks like a window, but there is no drop-down menu. Move the mouse back to the title on the caption bar of frame 3, press it and hold it down and then drag the mouse sideways. You'll find that this causes the frame to move with the mouse until you release the mouse button, at which point the frame takes up its new position. The frame continues to display its contents as it moves; in some windowing environments, windows that are being moved or resized become transparent or show just an outline until the move or resize operation is complete. Although this behavior is not provided by default, you'll see later how you can implement it and speed up the operation at the same time by saving the overhead of repainting the entire window as it moves or changes size.

Now move the mouse over any edge of frame 3. As you reach the edge of the frame, the cursor changes to indicate that resizing is possible. If you place the mouse over the right or left side of the frame, you'll see a cursor that enables you to resize the frame horizontally, while moving the mouse near one of the corners gives a diagonal cursor that allows a resize in two directions at once. To resize the frame, press the left mouse button and drag while the mouse is over the edge of the frame. When the frame is at the required size, release the mouse button. Again, the frame's contents are on display throughout, which slows the operation down somewhat.

Finally, move the mouse over the title and double-click and you'll find that the window maximizes itself. If you repeat this when the frame is at its maximum size, it returns to its previous size.

Stacking Internal Frames

At this point, you should have three of the original frames together on the left of the application window and the fourth wherever you left it after moving and resizing it. One thing you may have noticed as you dragged frame 3 around was that it always stayed in front of all the other frames. In fact, no matter how much you try, you won't be able to make it do anything other than stay on top, as long as you only move frame 3. If you drag the frame back so that it overlaps frame 4, the frame that was original-ly to the right and below it, and then click anywhere inside frame 4, you'll see that it jumps to the front, covering up the part of frame 3 that it overlaps. At the same time, its caption bar becomes highlighted, while that of frame 3 reverts to its nonhigh-lighted state. You can restore the original situation by clicking on frame 3 to move it to the top.

Perhaps you can do this with all of the frames? Try clicking frame 1 at the top left of the window. This time, its caption bar highlights as you might expect, but it doesn't move to the front—in fact, it stays exactly where it was. Not only that, but the other frame's caption bar remains highlighted as well. You can try the same thing with frame 2 and get the identical effect. In fact, you can end up with three highlighted caption bars, but only frames 3 and 4 will exchange places with each other.

There's more to it than this though: Move the mouse over the caption bar of frame 1 or frame 2 and drag it around the screen. As it moves, you'll see that it always remains under both frame 3 and frame 4. You'll get the same effect if you resize either of these windows—the corner or edge that you're dragging stays under these frames even when you're resizing the frame. Finally, press the maximize button on either of these frames and it will expand to take up the entire window—leaving at least two frames in front of it; if you expand frame 2, it will obscure frame 1, but frame 1 will expand and leave all of the others suspended in front of it.

This behavior is, of course, extremely useful if you want to offer the user the abil-ity to open several documents and work with more than one at the same time; to bring the ones of interest to the front, it is only necessary to click on their caption bars. This functionality is provided not by the internal frames, but by the container that they are placed on—in this example, `JLayeredPane`.

Layered Panes

The Swing `JLayeredPane` control is a container that manages its children in such a way as to create the illusion of multiple overlapping layers. The layers all cover the entire surface of the pane, but they are ordered vertically so that components in one layer appear to be in front of or behind those in another. Every component in the pane is assigned to a single layer, identified by an integer value, with the property that components in layers with higher numbers have precedence in the stacking order over those with lower numbers so that, for example, components in layer 200 always appear to be in front of those in layer 100, but behind those in layer 400. Although the layer numbers are basically arbitrary, JLayeredPane defines a small set of layer numbers as named constants that can be used for certain standard purposes; these constants are listed below, in decreasing order of precedence. Note that these constants are of type Integer, not the primitive type int.

JLayeredPane.DRAG_LAYER	value 400
JLayeredPane.POPUP_LAYER	value 300
JLayeredPane.MODAL_LAYER	value 200
JLayeredPane.PALETTE_LAYER	value 100
JLayeredPane.DEFAULT_LAYER	value 0
JLayeredPane.FRAME_CONTENT_LAYER	value –30000

Later in this chapter, you'll see an example that creates a component in the drag layer, which will appear in front of any other components assigned one of the standard numbers. Although the range of layers is limited only by the number of possible integer values (positive and negative), it is recommended that you try to use only the range of values shown above, so that you don't get unexpected results when using third-party controls that expect certain behavior, such as the fact that the drag layer is above any other component in the pane.

In the example shown in Figure 12-1, four internal frames were placed on a layered pane, assigned to layers as follows:

Frame 1	DEFAULT_LAYER
Frame2	PALETTE_LAYER
Frame 3	POPUP_LAYER
Frame 4	POPUP_LAYER

This layer assignment explains why frame 1 was always behind frame 2 and why both of these stayed behind frames 3 and 4. Frames 3 and 4 occupy the same layer, so which of them should be in front? As you saw earlier, you can arrange for either of them to be on top of the other just by clicking on its caption bar. This is because the layered pane actually has two ways to order its contents—by layer and by *position* within the layer. Every component in a layered pane has both a layer and a position, even if you don't explicitly assign either. Within a layer, a component's position is, like its layer number, an integer. The ordering of position values is the reverse of that for layers however—lower position numbers have greater precedence. Therefore, position number 0 designates the component drawn at the front, position 1 the one next behind it and so on. Also, position numbers are not arbitrary—they always range from 0 to $(n - 1)$, where n is the number of components in the layer. The most recently added component always occupies the highest-numbered position in its layer and therefore always appears behind any others in that same layer. This explains why frame 4 appears behind frame 3 when our example program is started—frame 4 is added after frame 3.

Adding Components and Controlling Layer and Position

In many respects, JLayeredPane is just an ordinary container, so you can just place internal frames and other components on it by using a simple add call. When you do this, your component is placed at the back of the DEFAULT_LAYER:

```
JLayeredPane pane = new JLayeredPane();
JInternalFrame frame = new JInternalFrame("Default settings");
pane.add(frame);  // Frame goes to DEFAULT_LAYER
```

If you only want to use one layer, which is a common requirement, you can just use this simple mechanism and continue to add other components without worrying about layer and position at all. As you'll see shortly, there are methods that allow you to control the position of a component within its layer after it has been added and these are all that you will need for a simple application. Note also that, despite the fact that our examples use internal frames, you can place any AWT or Swing component on a layered pane—the layering is handled by the container, not by the component, so no special support from JComponent is required (although there is an optimization that makes handling of JComponents slighter faster than other components).

 Core Alert

Mixing Swing and AWT components in a JLayeredPane, however, is not a good idea. Because AWT components are heavyweight, they always appear in front of lightweight Swing components, which spoils the layering effect. It is, however, possible to use AWT components in a JLayeredPane that doesn't contain any Swing components.

If your application needs to use more than one layer, you have two ways to control the initial layer of a component. The simplest way is to specify it as a constraint when you add the component to the layered pane. You'll remember from Chapter 2, "Frames, Labels, and Buttons," that there is variant of the add method that looks like this:

```
public void add(Component comp, Object constraints);
```

JLayeredPane supports this variant if you provide your component's initial layer as an Integer. This is usually convenient, because the constants that define the standard layer numbers are, as you have seen, all of type `Integer`. Therefore, you could create and add a couple of frames as follows:

```
JLayeredPane pane = new JLayeredPane();
JInternalFrame frame1 = new JInternalFrame("In default layer");
JInternalFrame frame2 = new JInternalFrame("In palette layer");
pane.add(frame1, JLayeredPane.DEFAULT_LAYER);
pane.add(frame2, JLayeredPane.PALETTE_LAYER);
```

If you insist on using nonstandard layer numbers, you can use the same method, provided that you remember to quote the layer number as an `Integer`:

```
JInternalFrame frame3 = new JInternalFrame("In layer 124");
pane.add(frame3, new Integer(124));
```

If you intend to do this, be aware of the fact that, if you supply your layer number as an `int` instead of as an `Integer`, you will not get a compilation error, because there is a variant of the `add` method that takes a `Component` as its first argument and an `int` as its second. The `int` gives the index in the container's child list at which the component is to be added. This mistake will have strange effects on the way in which your components behave—they will probably appear to be in the wrong layer.

The other way to control a component's layer is to use the `setLayer` method. Both `JLayeredPane` and `JInternalFrame` have a method of this name and they both set the target object's layer. However, they have different signatures. The `JInternalFrame` version is the simpler of the two:

```
public void setLayer(Integer layer);  // JInternalFrame method
```

The `JLayeredPane` method is more general, because it can be used with any component that you want to place on it:

```
public void setLayer(Component comp, int layer);
            // JLayeredPane method
```

Notice that, in this case, confusingly, the layer number is given as an `int`, not an `Integer`! If you want to use either of these two methods, they should be called before you add the component:

```
JInternalFrame frame4 = new JInternalFrame("In popup layer");
frame4.setLayer(JLayeredPane.POPUP_LAYER);
pane.add(frame4);
JInternalFrame frame5 = new JInternalFrame("Also in popup layer");
pane.setLayer(frame5, JLayeredPane.POPUP_LAYER);
pane.add(frame5);
```

As we've already said, you can't determine the initial position of a component within its layer—it always starts at the back. However, once it has been added, you can read or change its layer and/or position using one of the following methods of `JLayeredPane`:

```
public int getLayer(Component c);
```

```
public int getPosition(Component c);

public void setLayer(Component comp, int layer);

public void setLayer(Component comp, int layer, int position);

public void setPosition(Component comp, int position);

public void moveToFront(Component c);

public void moveToBack(Component c);
```

Obviously, the first two of these methods return the component's layer number and position numbers, again as int, not an Integer. The third method you have already seen. The fourth method is a variant on the third that also supplies a position value—use this method to change a component's layer and its position within a layer at the same time. The special value –1, when used as the position argument, moves the component to the back of its layer, while position 0 brings it to the front. If you just want to change a component's position and leave the layer number unchanged, use the setPosition method, which also recognizes the special value –1. Finally, the moveToFront and moveToBack methods make your intentions clearer than, but they are otherwise equivalent to, setPosition(0) and setPosition(-1). Incidentally, you can use the form of setLayer that specifies both a layer and a position before you add a component to the layered pane, but there would be no point in doing so because the position will be ignored.

Let's look at some examples that show how these methods can be used and how the layer and position of a component can be changed. Suppose you created four internal frames f1, f2, f3 and f4 and mounted them all, in the default layer, on a JLayeredPane, as follows:

```
JLayeredPane p = new JLayeredPane();
p.setLayer(f1, JLayeredPane.DEFAULT_LAYER);
   // Must do this before adding
p.add(f1);
p.setLayer(f2, JLayeredPane.DEFAULT_LAYER);
p.add(f2);
p.setLayer(f3, JLayeredPane.DEFAULT_LAYER);
p.add(f3);
p.setLayer(f4, JLayeredPane.DEFAULT_LAYER);
p.add(f4);
```

At this point, since the initial positions are determined by the order in which the components are added, f1 is in position 0, f2 is in position 1, f3 is in position 2 and f4 in position 3. Now suppose you wanted to bring f4 to the top of the stacking order, but not change its layer number. This can be done using any of the following lines of code:

```
p.setLayer(f4, JLayeredPane.DEFAULT_LAYER, 0);
p.setPosition(f4, 0);
p.moveToFront(f4);   // Recommended
```

Doing this pushes all of the other components down in the stacking order and changes their position values accordingly, so that f4 would now be at position 0, f1 in position 1, f2 in position 2 and f3 in position 3. Similarly, a component can be moved to the back of its layer using any of the following:

```
p.setLayer(f1, JLayeredPane.DEFAULT_LAYER, 3)
p.setLayer(f1, JLayeredPane.DEFAULT_LAYER, 24);
p.setLayer(f3, JLayeredPane.DEFAULT_LAYER, -1);
p.setPosition(f1, 3);
p.setPosition(f3, 24);
p.setPosition(f3, -1);
p.moveToBack(f3);    // Recommended
```

In general, it is better not to use setLayer if you only want to change position within a layer, because it makes your intentions less clear. Nevertheless, for completeness, three ways to use it for this purpose are included in the list you have just seen. The first method moves the component directly to position 3 within the layer. This, of course, requires you to know how many components are in the layer. The second variant is even uglier—it moves the component to position 24, which, if there are less than 24 components in the layer, actually moves the component to the back (and sets the position to a legal value—in this case to 3). Only the last alternative, where –1 is quoted as the position, is at all palatable,

The next three cases are exactly the same, but use setPosition instead of setLayer and so omit the layer number. Again, only the last of these should be seriously considered. Undoubtedly the best way to perform this operation is by using the moveToBack method, which is clearer and works no matter how many other components are in the same layer.

JLayeredPane provides a set of methods that allow you to get information about the various layers that are currently active. To discover the highest and lowest active layers, use the methods highestLayer and lowestLayer; to find out how many components are in a given layer, use getComponentCountInLayer; to get a list of all the components in a layer, use getComponentsInLayer. These methods have the following definitions:

```
public int highestLayer();

public int lowestLayer();

public int getComponentCountInLayer(int layer);

public Component[ ] getComponentsInLayer(int layer);
```

How JLayeredPane Works

JLayeredPane creates the layered effect by drawing its child components in the order implied by their layer and position numbers—the one at the back is drawn first and the one at the front is drawn last. This, of course, allows the components to obscure each other naturally, since a component that overlaps another one that should appear behind it will be drawn after that component and will render itself on top of the part of the other component (or components) that it overlaps. Internally, however, JLayeredPane has to use the mechanism provided by Container to manage children.

As you saw in Chapter 2, Container keeps an internal list of child components. You can control the position of a child component within this list by setting its index. In order to make the layering work properly, JLayeredPane has to map the layer and position to an appropriate index, which is the same as ordering the components as they should be drawn. Container draws its child components in order from the *end* of the list—that is, from the component with the highest index, to the *front*—that is, the component with index 0. Therefore, JLayeredPane holds the components that need to appear at the front before those that are at the back.

You know that layers with lower numbers need to appear to be below those with higher numbers, so all of the components in a given layer will be grouped together; the order of these groups will be the reverse of the order in which the layers should be drawn—the members of the lowest numbered layer group will have higher Container indices than those in the highest numbered layer. Within each layer group, components with high position numbers must be drawn before those with lower numbers. Therefore, those with higher position numbers have higher indices than those with lower position numbers. Let's look at example to show how this works in practice.

Let's suppose a JLayeredPane has five JInternalFrames mounted on it, with the layer and position attributes shown here:

Frame 1	POPUP_LAYER	Position 0	Index 0
Frame 2	POPUP_LAYER	Position 1	Index 1
Frame 3	PALETTE_LAYER	Position 0	Index 2
Frame 4	DEFAULT_LAYER	Position 0	Index 3
Frame 5	DEFAULT_LAYER	Position 1	Index 4

If you look at the column that shows the layers, you will see that the list has been sorted so that the layers that appear at the front occur earlier than those that will be at the back: POPUP_LAYER has higher precedence than PALETTE_LAYER, which in turn appears in front of DEFAULT_LAYER. Within the layers, the ordering is such that higher position numbers appear after lower ones. The order shown above is actually how they will be held within the JLayeredPane, with frame 1 at the head of the child list at index 0 and frame 5 at the back with index 4. Container draws from the back of this list, so it will draw frame 5 first, followed by frame 4 and so on. It should be clear that if you read down from the top of the list and draw the components in the order that you meet them, you'll get the correct stacking effects.

If a component's layer or position is changed by called the JLayeredPane setLayer, setPosition, moveToFront or moveToBack methods, this list must be reorganized accordingly and, of course, the component indices will change. Suppose, for example, that frame 2 is moved to the front of its layer by calling moveToFront. This causes the first two components to change places:

Frame 2	POPUP_LAYER	Position 0	Index 0
Frame 1	POPUP_LAYER	Position 1	Index 1
Frame 3	PALETTE_LAYER	Position 0	Index 2
Frame 4	DEFAULT_LAYER	Position 0	Index 3
Frame 5	DEFAULT_LAYER	Position 1	Index 4

On the other hand, if moveToFront were called for frame 5, it moves to the front of its *layer*, but not to the front of the pane. As a result, it is promoted by only one position and is still potentially obscured by frames 1 through 3:

Frame 2	POPUP_LAYER	Position 0	Index 0
Frame 1	POPUP_LAYER	Position 1	Index 1
Frame 3	PALETTE_LAYER	Position 0	Index 2
Frame 5	DEFAULT_LAYER	Position 0	Index 3
Frame 4	DEFAULT_LAYER	Position 1	Index 4

Moving frame 1 from the back of the popup layer to position 1 in the default layer causes slightly more changes:

Frame 2	POPUP_LAYER	Position 0	Index 0
Frame 3	PALETTE_LAYER	Position 0	Index 1
Frame 5	DEFAULT_LAYER	Position 0	Index 2
Frame 1	DEFAULT_LAYER	Position 1	Index 3
Frame 4	DEFAULT_LAYER	Position 2	Index 4

You can obtain the index of any particular component in a layered pane using the JLayeredPane indexOf method:

```
public int indexOf(Component c);
```

In practice, you are unlikely to want to call this method because multiple-document applications don't usually need to be concerned about such low-level details. It is, however, useful if you want to subclass JLayeredPane to produce some customized behavior that involves the order in which components are drawn or managed, or if you just want to write test programs to test your understanding of how the layered pane works. To summarize the use of layers and position with a layer, Figure 12-5 shows how the frames in the final list above would appear on the internal list of the JLayeredPane container, together with the associated layer, position and index numbers.

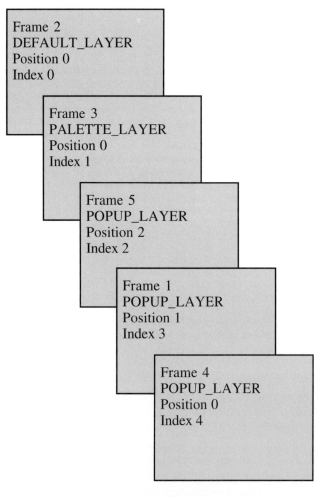

Figure 12-5 How JLayeredPane manages its child components.

Removing a component from the container frees up its position within the layer and its index, since position numbers and indices are always allocated without gaps. For example if, in the example above, frame 1 were removed, then frame 4 would be promoted to position 2 within the default layer and its index would change to 3.

JLayeredPane and Layout Managers

By default, JLayeredPane is created with no layout manager at all. This is almost certainly exactly what you want, because all of the standard layout managers place child components within the container according to strict rules, almost always without overlaps, whereas usually you want to have the children of a layered pane placed in overlapping configurations and you also want to be able to move them around at will.

Using no layout manager does, of course, have some consequences that it is worth reminding you of here. First, without a layout manager, you are responsible for placing and sizing all of the components that you place on the container. Placement is usually a matter of application policy: A common scheme is to cascade successive frames from top left to bottom right, and you'll see how to implement this later in this chapter. Sizing, by contrast, is usually dependent on each component. Generally, you would give each component its preferred size using a construction something like this:

```
// 'comp' is the component that we are adding to the layered
// pane 'pane'
comp.setSize(comp.getPreferredSize());
pane.add(comp, JLayeredPane.DEFAULT_LAYER);
// DEFAULT_LAYER for illustration only
```

Second, with no layout manager, the layered pane won't be able to size itself to a convenient size for its contents. Therefore, doing something like this won't work at all:

```
JLayeredPane pane = new JLayeredPane();
   // Add children - not shown
JFrame f = new JFrame("Layered Pane");
f.getContentPane().add(pane);
f.pack();
f.setVisible(true);
```

The pack method results in the layered pane being asked for its preferred size. This request is normally handled by the layout manager but, when there isn't one, the answer you get won't be particularly useful and it's unlikely to suit the layout of components you add to the container. Usually, multiple-document applications control the size of the layered pane by explicitly sizing the application's JFrame instead of using pack, which will cause the content pane's BorderLayout manager to allocate all of the space in the content pane to the layered pane. An alternative, if you can determine a "best" size for the layered pane, is to use the setMinimumSize, setMaximumSize and setPreferredSize methods of JComponent to set any of these constraints that are applicable. If you use setPreferredSize, you can then use pack as usual to size the frame, as shown above.

If you wish, you *can* associate a layout manager with a layered pane. This will have no affect at all on the way in which it behaves—it will still recognize layers and positions and will continue to order its child components to reflect these attributes. However, if you use a layout manager that tiles its components or ensure that they at least don't overlap (as all the standard ones apart from `OverlayLayout` do), you won't get any benefit from using a layered pane because there won't be any overlap and so the stacking behavior won't be apparent. Once the container has been laid out, you will be able to drag the frames around, but if the container is resized, the layout manager will move them all back to their original locations. In general, unless you are going to write a custom layout manager that works well with the layered pane, it is best to leave it with no layout manager at all.

Working with Internal Frames

Internal frames are the part of a multiple-document application that the user is most aware of. This section examines the pieces that make up and internal frame and the events that internal frames can generate.

The Structure of an Internal Frame

An internal frame is, as near as possible, a miniature replica of a `JFrame`. The similarity extends even to the internal structure: like `JFrame`, `JInternalFrame` has a `JRootPane` and therefore a content pane, a menu bar and a glass pane. In fact, you'll probably recall from Chapter 2 that the main area of a `JRootPane` is actually a `JLayeredPane`: The job of this particular layered pane is to hold the content pane and the menu bar in a layer that resides below the glass pane, so that the latter is always in front when it is visible. Now that you are familiar with `JLayeredPane`, you can, if you need to, use the `JFrame` method `getLayeredPane` to get a reference to it and add your own layers.

Because the internal frame is identical to a frame in structure, you need to use the content pane to create the internal frame's working area. As with `JFrame`, this is a `JPanel` by default but, of course, you can change it. Later in this chapter, you'll see an example application in which the working area is a `JTextArea` wrapped with a `JScrollPane`. You can also add a menu bar to give you a separate menu for each internal frame, in addition to the menu on the frame's caption bar and any menu bar that the application itself might have.

Constructing an Internal Frame

`JInternalFrame` has six constructors:

```
public JInternalFrame();

public JInternalFrame(String title);
```

```
public JInternalFrame(String title, boolean resizable);

public JInternalFrame(String title, boolean resizable,
            boolean closable);

public JInternalFrame(String title, boolean resizable,
            boolean closable, boolean maximizable);

public JInternalFrame(String title, boolean resizable,
            boolean closable, boolean maximizable,
            boolean iconifiable)
```

The various constructors allow you to set explicit values or accept defaults for the five main properties of the frame. All of the boolean values are set to false by default, while using the first constructor gives you a frame with no title. The following boolean properties control both what you can subsequently do with the frame and what appears on its caption bar: Note that some of these properties affect the internal frame's system menu, which is activated from the left side of the caption bar. This menu is, however, not present in the Metal look-and-feel.

- Resizable. If this property is true, you can use the mouse to resize the frame by dragging on its outline. In some look-and-feels, there may be some visual indication that this is the case by the presence of resizing handles on the frame. For example, Figure 12-6 shows the difference between an internal frame with this property set to true (on the left) and one with it set to false in the Motif look-and-feel, which indicates the resizing handles by the presence of notches on the frame outline. All of the look-and-feel implementations change the cursor when the mouse moves over the frame outline if the frame is resizable.

- Closable. This property must be set to true for it to be possible for the user to close an internal frame using the mouse. In the Metal and Windows look-and-feels, it causes a close button to appear on the frame—you can see this button on the right of Figures 12-1 and 12-2. It also creates a Close item on the frame's system menu, which resides on the left side of the caption bar.

- Maximizable. When true, causes a maximize button to appear on the caption bar and a corresponding item on the frame's system menu. Activating either of these makes the frame occupy the full area of its parent's window and may obscure other frames, depending on their layer numbers. When the frame has been maximized, the same button changes its appearance to allow the frame to be restored to its previous size. On the frame's menu, the Maximize item is disabled when the frame is at full size and the Restore item is enabled instead. Note that it is possible to maximize a frame without being able to resize it—these two properties are independent of each other.

- `Iconifiable`. Like the `Maximizable` property, except that it causes a minimize button on the frame and a minimize item on the system menu. Activating either causes the frame to be reduced to an icon (in fact to a `JDesktopIcon` as you'll see later). This icon displays content that is similar to the frame's caption bar, except that the minimize button is replaced by a restore button and the system menu is affected in the same way as it is with the maximize button. This property and the resizable property are independent of each other.

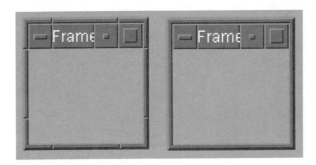

Figure 12-6   Motif internal frames with and without resizing handles.

Changing Internal Frame Properties

All of the properties that can be set using the constructors also have the usual methods that you can use to get their current values, or to change them after the frame has been constructed. It is very unlikely, for example, that you would want to use the default constructor for `JInternalFrame` unless you wanted to conditionally assign attributes using the following methods.

```
public void setClosable(boolean closable);

public boolean isClosable();

public void setResizable(boolean resizable);

public boolean isResizable();

public void setIconifiable(boolean iconifiable);

public boolean isIconifiable();
```

```
public void setMaximizable(boolean maximizable);

public boolean isMaximizable();

public void setTitle(String title);

public String getTitle();
```

Changing any of these attributes (other than the title) once the frame has been made visible for the first time is not advisable. What happens is that the property change becomes effective, but the frame's visual appearance and its menu don't reflect it. For example, if you create a frame that can be closed, the menu (if it exists) will contain a Close item and (unless you are using the Motif look-and-feel) a close button will appear on the frame. If you then invoke setClosable(false), the menu item will and the close button remain, but all attempts to close the frame using either of them will be ineffective.

Setting an Internal Frame's Caption-Bar Icon

Like JFrame, an internal frame can have an icon that is displayed at the left of the title bar. Unlike the JFrame icon which is actually an Image, the icon for an internal frame can be anything that implements the Icon interface, of which ImageIcon is one particular example. If you want to supply an icon, best results are obtained with one that is 16 pixels high and wide. To associate the icon with the frame, use the following method:

```
public void setFrameIcon(Icon icon);
```

Here's an example that puts a small letter J on the top left of the caption bar by using an image loaded as an ImageIcon:

```
JInternalFrame frame = new JInternalFrame("Frame 1", true,
             true, true, true);
frame.setBounds(10, 10, 250, 200);
Icon icon = new
ImageIcon(FrameWithIcon.class.getResource("images/j.gif"));
frame.setFrameIcon(icon);
```

This mechanism of creating an ImageIcon from an image should be familiar by now. In this extract, the image is located by reference to the location of the class FrameWithIcon, of which this code is a part. You can run this example for yourself with the command

```
java JFCBook.Chapter12.FrameWithIcon
```

Figure 12-7 shows what the internal frame looks like with the Metal look-and-feel installed.

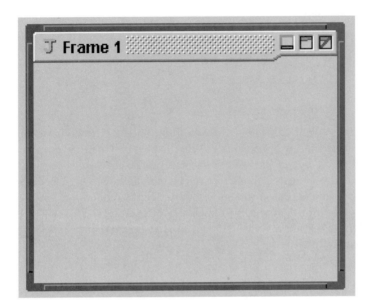

Figure 12-7   An internal frame with a custom frame icon.

Internal Frame State

JInternalFrame has several methods that you can use to get or change its current state:

```
public void setClosed(boolean closed);

public void setIcon(boolean isIcon);

public void setMaximum(boolean maximize);

public void setSelected(boolean selected);

public boolean isClosed();

public boolean isIcon();

public boolean isMaximum();

public boolean isSelected();
```

The setClosed method makes the frame close and removes it from its container. When this method has been called, you should not attempt to use the frame again. setIcon makes the frame minimize to an icon which might look like its caption bar. The exact appearance and location of the icon depends on the look-and-feel in use and on another object called the *desktop manager*, which will be discussed later in this chapter. If you call this method with argument false when the frame is iconified, it will return to its original location and size. Invoking setMaximum with argument true makes the frame expand to fill its container. When you use this method, the frame's original size is saved and used to restore the frame when you setMaximum is later called with argument false.

Finally, setSelected controls whether the frame is the selected frame within its layer. When a frame is selected, it usually highlights its caption bar. Only one frame in each layer can be selected at any given time, so when this method is called for a frame, the frame that was originally selected becomes deselected automatically.

You can call these methods from your application to control your internal frames. They are also invoked by the look-and-feel code associated with the internal frame when the user clicks on buttons on the caption bar to iconify, maximize, restore or close a frame or to bring a frame to the front.

Core Note

Actually, none of these methods directly performs the task it advertises—for example, the setClosed *method does not actually close the frame itself. Instead, they start a chain of events that will usually cause the requested state change to happen. Ultimately, the state of a frame is under the control of the desktop manager, which will be described later. By default, however, all of these methods behave as described above. The default behavior will only be modified if you install your own desktop manager that does different things.*

All of the changes in the frame's state caused by using these methods, whether within the application itself or as a result of user action, can be monitored and, if necessary, in some cases attempts to change the state can be prevented. The frame associates the attributes controlled by these methods with a property and generates a PropertyChangeEvent when a request is made to change any of them; to receive notification of these events, you can register a listener on the internal frame by using the addPropertyChangeListener method. As you've already seen, a PropertyChangeEvent contains the name of the affected property together with the property's old and new values. Table 12-1 lists the properties whose changes can be monitored, the data type of the old and new values and the name of the JInternalFrame method that changes the property.

Table 12-1   Internal Frame Properties

Property	Value Type	Method
CONTENT_PANE_PROPERTY	Container	setContentPane
GLASS_PANE_PROPERTY	Component	setGlassPane
LAYERED_PANE_PROPERTY	JLayeredPane	setLayeredPane
MENU_BAR_PROPERTY	JMenuBar	setMenuBar
ROOT_PANE_PROPERTY	JRootPane	setRootPane
TITLE_PROPERTY	String	setTitle
IS_SELECTED_PROPERTY	Boolean	setSelected
IS_CLOSED_PROPERTY	Boolean	setClosed
IS_MAXIMUM_PROPERTY	Boolean	setMaximum
IS_ICON_PROPERTY	Boolean	setIcon

Changing any of the first six properties generates a PropertyChangeEvent to all registered PropertyChangeListeners. Other than the frame title, it is rare to change any of these items—usually, this will happen only when the frame is created. The consequences of changing the frame's root pane are, of course, vary far-reaching because it changes almost everything in the frame.

Changing any of the last four properties generates two PropertyChangeEvents: the first is sent to any registered VetoableChangeListeners; if any of these listeners throws a PropertyVetoException, the requested change does *not* take place. If no exception is thrown, the change is then notified to all PropertyChangeListeners with an identical PropertyChangeEvent.

These events are, of course, generated both when the methods listed in the Table 12-1 are invoked and when the user attempts to make the same state change using the controls on the frame itself. For example, if the user clicks the title bar to bring a frame that is not in the foreground into the foreground, a PropertyChangeEvent with property name IS_SELECTED_PROPERTY, old value false and new value true is sent to each VetoableChangeListener. If it is acceptable for this frame to move to the foreground, no exception would be thrown and the change would be made. The same event would then be broadcast to all PropertyChangeListeners.

Registering a PropertyChangeListener allows a program to respond to an event that has already happened. For example, in a word processor, when a frame has closed, it might be appropriate to close the file whose content was displayed in it.

By contrast, programs that want to react to an event before it happens and, if necessary, abort it would register a VetoableChangeListener. Using the example of the word processor again, if the user clicked the Close button on a frame that was displaying data that hadn't been written back to the file, it would be useful to be able to display a dialog box asking the user to confirm that the frame should be closed and whether changes to the file should be write back to it. To achieve this, the word processor would register a VetoableChangeListener on each of its internal frames. When it received an event for IS_CLOSED_PROPERTY with the new value true, it would post the dialog box. If the user elected to continue with the close, the file would be saved and the event handler would return normally. On the other hand, if the user decided to cancel the close operation, a PropertyVetoException would be thrown and the close would be abandoned. You'll see this mechanism in action as part of the implementation of an example multiple-document application at the end of this chapter.

Internal Frame Events

Internal frames generate InternalFrameEvents to report certain state changes. These events are delivered to InternalFrameListeners registered with the frame by calling the first of the following two methods:

```
public void addInternalFrameListener(InternalFrameListener l);

public void removeInternalFrameListener(InternalFrameListener l);
```

InternalFrameEvents are the internal frame equivalent of the WindowEvents available to JFrame and the other top-level windows; there is an InternalFrameEvent type corresponding to each WindowEvent type and thus an InternalFrameListener method for each method of WindowListener. Table 12-2 summarizes the listener methods and the event types and describes when the events are generated. Each listener method has a signature similar to this one:

```
public void internalFrameActivated(InternalFrameEvent evt);
```

Table 12-2   Internal Frame Events

Method	*Event*	*When generated*
internalFrameActivated	INTERNAL_FRAME_ACTIVATED	When an internal frame becomes the selected frame in its layer
internalFrameClosed	INTERNAL_FRAME_CLOSED	When an internal frame has completely closed
internalFrameClosing	INTERNAL_FRAME_CLOSING	At the start of an internal frame's close sequence. See the text for further information
internalFrameDeactivated	INTERNAL_FRAME_DEACTIVATED	When an internal frame is no longer the selected frame in its layer

continued

Table 12-2   Internal Frame Events (continued)

Method	*Event*	*When generated*
internalFrameDeiconified	INTERNAL_FRAME_DEICONIFIED	When an internal frame has been restored to the state prior to being iconified
internalFrameIconified	INTERNAL_FRAME_ICONIFIED	When an internal frame has been minimized into an icon
internalFrameOpened	INTERNAL_FRAME_OPENED	When the internal frame is opened for the first time

As you can see, most of these events are generated under the same circumstances as the corresponding WindowEvents and can be treated in the same way. As you know from the previous section, attempts to change the state of an internal frame can be vetoed by application code. These events are only generated when the state change is taking place—in other words, a veto has not occurred. The only tricky cases are the INTERNAL_FRAME_CLOSING and INTERNAL_FRAME_CLOSED events. The way in which these are used is described in "The Role of the Desktop Manager" later in this chapter. Note that it an application closes an internal frame using the setClosed method, an INTERNAL_FRAME_CLOSED event will be generated when the close happens (assuming it is not vetoed), but there will be no INTERNAL_FRAME_CLOSING event. The latter event is generated only when the user attempts to close the frame.

Icons, the Desktop Pane and the Desktop Manager

So far, you've seen JLayeredPane and JInternalFrame, but there are three other classes that you need to know about in order to write multiple-document applications: JDesktopIcon, JDesktopPane and DefaultDesktopManager. Of these, the first is the simplest to deal with—it is the object that you see when you iconify an internal frame. If you go back to the first example in this chapter and minimize all of the frames, you'll get four icons at the bottom of the window, as shown in Figure 12-8. In the standard look-and-feel implementations, the icon for an internal frame is similar to its caption bar and includes buttons that allow you to close, maximize or restore it, provided that the frame is configured to allow these things to happen. If you don't like the default desktop icon, you can, of course, change it by introducing your own look-and-feel implementation.

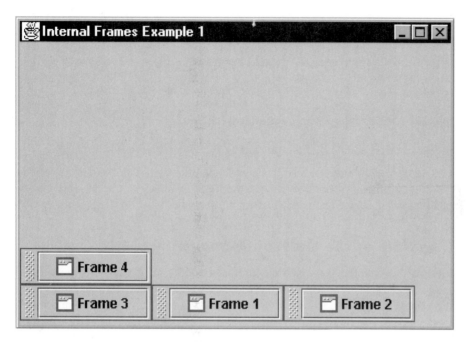

Figure 12-8   Four desktop icons.

Each JDesktopIcon is associated with one internal frame. The icon will be created automatically when the frame is iconified for the first time, but if you wish you can create your own, possibly customized, icon at any time and connect it to the frame using the following JInternalFrame method:

```
public void setDesktopIcon(JDesktopIcon d);
```

When you create the icon, you pass to its constructor a reference to the frame that it will represent:

```
public JDesktopIcon(JInternalFrame f);
```

An internal frame and its icon are never visible at the same time. When the frame is iconified, it is removed from its container and the icon is added instead, then sized and placed appropriately. Similarly, when the frame is deiconified, the icon is removed from the container and the frame replaced at its original location and with its previous size.

The other two classes are very closely related to each other. In our earlier examples, the internal frames have been placed in a JLayeredPane to get the benefit of being able to overlay them and move them around at will. JDesktopPane is a subclass of JLayeredPane that has an associated desktop manager, represented by an instance of the class DefaultDesktopManager. The desktop pane can do everything that the layered pane can do and it also provides the following additional methods:

```
public JInternalFrame[] getAllFrames();

public JInternalFrame[] getAllFramesInLayer(int layer);

public DesktopManager getDesktopManager();

public void setDesktopManager(DesktopManager manager);
```

The first two methods just return arrays of all of the frames on the desktop and all of the frames in a given layer of the desktop. It is the ability of the desktop pane to host a desktop manager that is the important thing about it.

The Role of the Desktop Manager

Earlier in this chapter, you saw that internal frames can be dragged, resized and iconified when they are placed in a layered pane and, of course, this continues to be true when we place them in a desktop pane, which is, in fact, what you would usually do. In fact, as was hinted in the descriptions of the setClosed method and the other methods like it, there is slightly more going on behind the scenes than has been shown so far. The missing piece that you haven't yet seen is the role played by the desktop manager. You'll see how the desktop manager operates by examining what happens when you try to close an internal frame that has been mounted on a JDesktopPane.

An internal frame's close button is part of the caption bar—in fact, it is owned by the caption bar's user interface class. When the close button is pressed, it generates an ActionEvent that is caught by the caption bar's user interface object. If the frame is marked as closable, the UI class will respond to this event by posting an INTERNAL_FRAME_CLOSING event to all registered InternalFrameListeners. What happens next depends on what the internal frame's default close action is.

Core Note

As with JFrame, you can configure an internal frame's default close action using its setDefaultCloseOperation method. Refer to the discussion of this topic in Chapter 2 if you have forgotten the details.

Let's first assume that the selected close operation is DO_NOTHING_ON_CLOSE. If this is the case, then one of the listeners must do something to make the close operation happen. If a listener invokes setVisible with argument false, the frame disappears, but does not actually close—no further events are generated. If a listener invokes dispose, the frame will be closed and an INTERNAL_FRAME_CLOSED event is generated. If neither of these operations is performed by any listener, the close request will be ignored and no further action is taken.

If the default close operation is HIDE_ON_CLOSE, the frame is made invisible and the setClosed method is called. If this is not vetoed, an INTERNAL_FRAME_CLOSED event will be generated. This is the default action.

Finally, if the default close operation is DISPOSE_ON_CLOSE, the setClosed method is invoked and, if this returns without being vetoed, an INTERNAL_FRAME_CLOSED event generated and the frame is disposed.

As you can see from this description, unless the default close action is DO_NOTHING_ON_CLOSE and a close from the user interface is ignored by all registered listeners, all attempts to close an internal frame result in the JInternalFrame setClosed method being called. As noted earlier, the setClosed method creates a PropertyChangeEvent for the property IS_CLOSED_PROPERTY, showing that it is being changed from false to true and sends it to all VetoableChangeListeners and then, if there is no veto, to all PropertyChangeListeners. At this point, of course, nothing has actually happened to the frame itself. When the internal frame was created, a user interface object, distinct from that of its caption bar, was connected to it. One of the things that this object does when it is installed in the frame is to register itself to receive the frame's PropertyChangeEvents, so it will receive the event that notifies the change of IS_CLOSED_PROPERTY.

The UI class does not, however, directly handle this event. Instead, it checks to see whether the internal frame is contained in a JDesktopPane and, if it is, gets a reference to the pane's desktop manager (using the getDesktopManager method) and delegates the close operation to it, by calling its closeFrame method, passing the JInternalFrame reference as its argument. This method can do whatever it wants but in the default desktop manager it removes the frame from its parent container if it is attached to it. It also removes the frame's JDesktopIcon if the frame happened to be iconified when the close request was made. This action actually represents the closing of the frame.

Core Note

An application could also call the setClosed *method and, if it were to do so, the same set of events just described would also occur. The only difference is that an application can call* setClosed *even if the frame is not considered closable, whereas the UI class can not.*

The Desktop Manager Interface

It is the job of the desktop manager to close internal frames. This is only one of its functions because, in fact, it is the desktop manager that does *everything* for a frame that might be requested by user action (or by the programmatic equivalent). The things that a desktop manager must be able to do are specified in the DesktopManager interface, of which DefaultDesktopManager is an implementation. Here are the methods that DesktopManager defines, grouped according to their function:

```
public void openFrame(JInternalFrame f);

public void closeFrame(JInternalFrame f);

public void maximizeFrame(JInternalFrame f);

public void minimizeFrame(JInternalFrame f);

public void iconifyFrame(JInternalFrame f);

public void deiconifyFrame(JInternalFrame f);

public void activateFrame(JInternalFrame f);

public void deactivateFrame(JInternalFrame f);

public void beginDraggingFrame(JComponent f);

public void dragFrame(JComponent f, int newX, int newY);

public void endDraggingFrame(JComponent f);

public void beginResizingFrame(JComponent f, int direction);

public void resizeFrame(JComponent f, int newX, int newY,
            int newWidth, int newHeight);

public void endResizingFrame(JComponent f);

public void setBoundsForFrame(JComponent f, int newX,
            int newY, int newWidth, int newHeight);
```

The first method in this list, openFrame, is not actually called because the application that owns the JDesktopPane is in control of creating and placing frames. It would, however, be useful to have this method invoked when an internal frame is created because it would give the desktop manager an opportunity to enforce a placement policy (such as tiling or cascading) that the application itself did not provide. Instead, if you want to implement some kind of placement policy, you have to implement it in either the application or in the desktop pane. An example of this will be shown later. You have already seen what closeFrame does and the functions of the next four methods should be evident from their names.

The `activateFrame` method is called when a frame becomes selected— that is, when it moves to the front of its layer. In the standard look-and-feel implementations, this happens whenever you click anywhere on the frame. `DefaultDesktopManager`'s implementation of this method makes sure that every other frame in the same layer is not selected and moves the selected frame to the front. By contrast, `deactivateFrame` is called when the selected frame is being deselected. There is nothing for `DefaultDesktopManager` to do in this case, because the caption bar's UI class will repaint itself so that it is not highlighted.

The next six methods are two sets of three that are invoked when the user is moving or resizing a frame. You'll examine these in detail later when implementing a desktop manager that provides customized behavior for these operations. Finally, `setBoundsForFrame` is used to have the desktop manager make the frame occupy a particular location and be a specific size. This is currently only used when the user is dragging a frame's desktop icon.

The important thing to realize about these methods is that it is entirely up to the desktop manager what it does when they are invoked. `DefaultDesktopManager` does the obvious thing in each case and complies with everything asked of it. You could, of course, create a customized desktop manager that refused to allow frames to be resized, by implementing `beginResizingFrame`, `resizeFrame` and `endResizingFrame` as empty methods.

The Shared Desktop Manager

Given that desktop managers do so many critical things and that they are attached to desktop panes, how was it possible to iconify and close frames in our original example (Figure 12-1), in which there was no `JDesktopPane` and hence, apparently, no `DesktopManager`? When the internal frame's UI class is looking for it's container's desktop manager, it find's the internal frame's desktop pane by calling its `getDesktopPane` method. If the internal frame is mounted in a layered pane instead of a desktop pane, this method returns `null`. Since this means that the frame doesn't have an associated desktop manager, it is then assigned to a *shared desktop manager* that is created the first time that it is needed. It is this desktop manager, an instance of `DefaultDesktopManager`, that controls all internal frames that aren't on a desktop. This desktop manager was responsible for closing and iconifying the internal frames in our first example.

A Desktop Pane with Cascade and Tile Support

A common requirement with multiple-document applications is to be able to arrange the document windows in an orderly fashion. Most commercial implementations allow you to create new windows that cascade down from the top left to the bottom right. As well as this, it is usual to be able, at any time, to tidy up the desktop by having all of the document windows rearranged and resized so that they cascade or to arrange for them to be tiled to cover all or almost all of the desktop. These features are not provided by JDesktopPane, but it is easy to add them, as you'll see in this section. Figure 12-9 shows how a desktop would look with five internal frames arranged in a tiled pattern, while Figure 12-10 shows the same frames when they are cascaded.

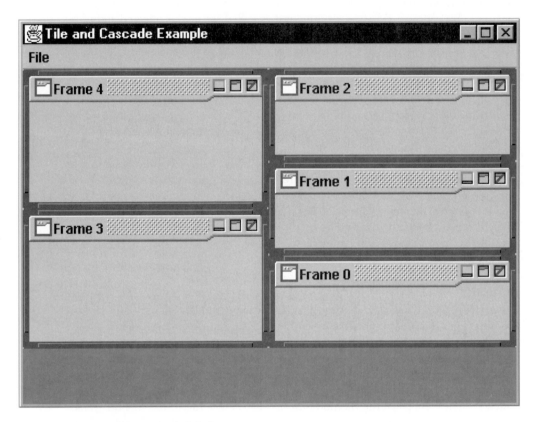

Figure 12-9   A tiled desktop.

The first question to ask is where to put the code that implements the cascading and tiled layout? You might think that this should be in the desktop manager, since it seems to be the place to put desktop policy, but this doesn't work out very well. The fact of the matter is, it might be necessary to be able to provide the user with the ability to create new frames that are automatically cascaded, but the desktop manager doesn't get control when a new frame is created and so can't influence its position or size. It is also advantageous to be able to change the layout of all of the internal frames and put them into a tiled or cascaded configuration at any time. Again, this doesn't fit with the desktop manager interface—there is nothing in this interface that asks for the layout to be changed. The only reasonable place to put this functionality is in the desktop pane itself. In the example in this section, it will be implemented as three new methods in a subclass of JDesktopPane called ExtendedDesktopPane.

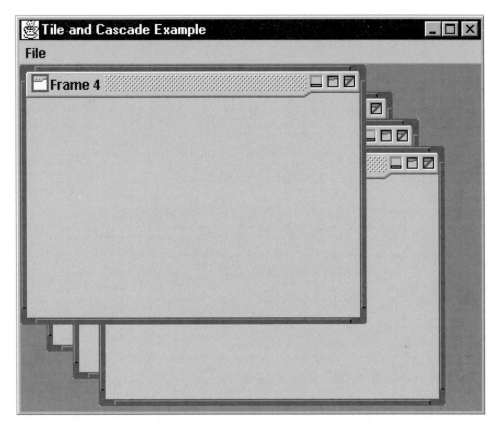

Figure 12-10   A cascaded desktop.

The implementation of this subclass is actually pretty simple, but some of the details make it look more complex than it actually is. The code is presented in Listing 12-1.

Listing 12-1   A tiling and cascading desktop pane

```
package JFCBook.Chapter12;

import com.sun.java.swing.*;
import java.awt.*;

/**
 * A desktop pane that supports tiling and cascading
 */
public class ExtendedDesktopPane extends JDesktopPane {
   // This method allows child frames to
   // be added with automatic cascading
```
continued

```
public void addCascaded(Component comp, Integer layer) {
  // First add the component in the correct layer
  this.add(comp, layer);

  // Now do the cascading
  if (comp instanceof JInternalFrame) {
    this.cascade(comp);
  }

  // Move it to the front
  this.moveToFront(comp);
}

// Layout all of the children of this container
// so that they are cascaded.
public void cascadeAll() {
  Component[] comps = getComponents();
  int count = comps.length;
  nextX = 0;
  nextY = 0;

  for (int i = count - 1; i >= 0; i - ) {
    Component comp = comps[i];
    if (comp instanceof JInternalFrame && comp.isVisible()) {
      cascade(comp);
    }
  }
}

// Layout all of the children of this container
// so that they are tiled.
public void tileAll() {
  DesktopManager manager = getDesktopManager();
  if (manager == null) {
    // No desktop manager - do nothing
    return;
  }

  Component[] comps = getComponents();
  Component comp;
  int count = 0;

  // Count and handle only the internal frames
  for (int i = 0; i < comps.length; i++) {
    comp = comps[i];
    if (comp instanceof JInternalFrame && comp.isVisible()) {
      count++;
```

```
      }
   }

   if (count != 0) {
      double root = Math.sqrt((double)count);
      int rows = (int)root;
      int columns = count/rows;
      int spares = count - (columns * rows);

      Dimension paneSize = getSize();
      int columnWidth = paneSize.width/columns;

      // We leave some space at the bottom that doesn't get covered
      int availableHeight = paneSize.height - UNUSED_HEIGHT;
      int mainHeight = availableHeight/rows;
      int smallerHeight = availableHeight/(rows + 1);
      int rowHeight = mainHeight;
      int x = 0;
      int y = 0;
      int thisRow = rows;
      int normalColumns = columns - spares;

      for (int i = comps.length - 1; i >= 0; i - ) {
         comp = comps[i];
         if (comp instanceof JInternalFrame && comp.isVisible()) {
            manager.setBoundsForFrame((JComponent)comp, x, y, columnWidth, rowHeight);
            y += rowHeight;
            if ( - thisRow == 0) {
               // Filled the row
               y = 0;
               x += columnWidth;

               // Switch to smaller rows if necessary
               if ( - normalColumns <= 0) {
                  thisRow = rows + 1;
                  rowHeight = smallerHeight;
               } else {
                  thisRow = rows;
               }
            }
         }
      }
   }
}

public void setCascadeOffsets(int offsetX, int offsetY) {
   this.offsetX = offsetX;
```

continued

```
      this.offsetY = offsetY;
   }

   public void setCascadeOffsets(Point pt) {
      this.offsetX = pt.x;
      this.offsetY = pt.y;
   }

   public Point getCascadeOffsets() {
      return new Point(offsetX, offsetY);
   }

   // Place a component so that it is cascaded
   // relative to the previous one
   protected void cascade(Component comp) {
      Dimension paneSize = getSize();
      int targetWidth = 3 * paneSize.width/4;
      int targetHeight = 3 * paneSize.height/4;

      DesktopManager manager = getDesktopManager();
      if (manager == null) {
         comp.setBounds(0, 0, targetWidth, targetHeight);
         return;
      }

      if (nextX + targetWidth > paneSize.width ||
         nextY + targetHeight > paneSize.height) {
         nextX = 0;
         nextY = 0;
      }

      manager.setBoundsForFrame((JComponent)comp, nextX, nextY, targetWidth, targetHeight);

      nextX += offsetX;
      nextY += offsetY;
   }

   protected int nextX;      // Next X position
   protected int nextY;      // Next Y position
   protected int offsetX = DEFAULT_OFFSETX;
   protected int offsetY = DEFAULT_OFFSETY;

   protected static final int DEFAULT_OFFSETX = 24;
   protected static final int DEFAULT_OFFSETY = 24;
   protected static final int UNUSED_HEIGHT = 48;
}
```

Cascading on Internal Frame Creation

The first extension provides the ability to add successive frames so that they cascade down the desktop from left to right and top to bottom, as shown in Figure 12-10. This is done by adding a method called addCascaded, defined as follows:

```
public void addCascaded(Component comp, Integer layer);
```

This method will add the component comp to the desktop in the given layer and automatically determine its initial size and location relative to the last component that was added using this method. This is a simple thing to do—the first component is placed at the top left of the pane, while subsequent ones are each placed at a fixed horizontal and vertical offset from the one before. In this example, the offsets that used are instance variables of ExtendedDesktopPane (offsetX and offsetY) which are both set initially to 24 pixels. To allow this to be customized, there is also a method called setCascadeOffsets that changes both offsets to new values given the new offsets either as separate integers or in a Point structure. There is also another method, called getCascadeOffsets, that lets you read the current offsets as a Point.

The next location for a cascaded window is held in the instance variables nextX and nextY which are both initially 0. After each window has been placed, the appropriate offset is added to each of these variables to generate the correct position for the next window. Eventually, however, we will reach a stage where a new window would be clipped by the bottom or right-hand side of the container. When this happens, both nextX and nextY reset to 0 so that subsequent frames are again cascaded from the top left. This behavior is consistent with the cascading scheme used by Windows applications. As far as the size of the component goes, this example always make it three-quarters of the width and height of the entire container. If this isn't appropriate, the component can be explicitly resized after it has been added.

Finally, when the component has be added, it is brought to the front of its layer by calling moveToFront.

Cascading Existing Internal Frames

The second extension that this example provides is a method that will take all of the frames on the desktop and cascade them. This facility is implemented by the cascadeAll method, which implicitly acts on all of the components in the container and so doesn't need any arguments. To implement this, it is necessary to walk through all of the components in the container and move each one to the location it would have had if it were being added with the addCascaded method. It does not, however, need to be added to the container, because it has already been added, and its position in the stacking order must not be changed. The rest of the cascading code can, however, be shared with the addCascaded method. For this reason, the bulk of the cascading logic is in the cascade method, which does everything apart from adding the component to the container and moving it to the front of its layer.

Walking through the list of child components is fairly simple—the list is obtained by using the `getComponents` method of `Container`, which returns an array in ascending order of index—that is, the items that appear at the front of the desktop are at the front of this list. When moving everything, it is important to be careful about the order in which it is done, because everything that is moved will be repainted as it moves. If the array were processed from the front to the back (i.e. from index 0 upwards), the original stacking order would be reversed, because the item that should be at the front first would be drawn first, followed by the second which would then appear on top of the first and so on. For this reason, it is necessary to work from the end of the list toward the front.

There is one other catch to look out for. Most of the layered pane and desktop pane methods allow you to manipulate arbitrary components, but this doesn't work very well for some operations. For example, you can't iconify arbitrary components because there is no way for the desktop pane to know that you want to do this and no way to associate an arbitrary component with its icon—`JInternalFrame` and `JDesktopIcon`, if you recall, keep references to each other so that the desktop manager can easily find the icon for a frame and vice versa. Because of this, it is best to use only internal frames with the desktop pane and refrain from using other components unless you are aware of the restrictions.

Similarly, our cascading code only works for internal frames on the desktop. The reason for this is that the desktop contains other items that you wouldn't want to cascade, the most obvious example being the desktop icons themselves. It isn't really practical to try to avoid this restriction by explicitly checking for and omitting the components that shouldn't be cascaded, because the complete set actually depends on the look-and-feel that's installed—see "The Organic Look-and-Feel Desktop Manager" later in the chapter for a specific (albeit unusual) example of this. Therefore, the loop in `cascadeAll` that processes the desktop pane's child components looks specifically for internal frames and only processes those that are actually visible.

Tiling the Desktop

The third extension is the ability to tile the container. Again, this operation is restricted to visible internal frames only and the basic mechanism used by the `tileAll` method is the same as that used by `cascadeAll`—walking along the list of child components and placing and sizing them appropriately. The interesting problem is deciding where to place all of the windows. The mechanism used in this example makes it behave like Windows applications. First, some unused space is left at the bottom of the container so that you can still access at least some of the icons that might be there (although, as you'll see, this doesn't work very well for the Organic look-and-feel). Our implementation fixes this at 48 pixels, but it is a trivial extension to make this customizable. The rest of the space will be filled by placing the internal frames in columns, working from top to bottom in each column and from left to right across the desktop pane.

The number of rows is determined using a very simple algorithm—just take the integer square root of the number of components that need to be tiled. To get the number of columns, divide the number of components by the number of rows. Because this example works in integer arithmetic, dividing the number of components by its integer square root does not always give you its square root—it gives you something greater than or equal to its square root. If the number of components is a perfect square, this results in a regular layout. For example, with four components, you would have 2 columns with 2 rows in each and with nine components there would 3 columns each with 3 rows. For other values, you get more interesting results.

Suppose you have five components to tile. The integer square root of 5 is 2, so the number of rows would be 2 and the number of columns 5/2, which is 2, working in integer arithmetic. Two columns and two rows gives a total of four tiles, leaving one component that can't be placed. When this happens, the cells in the last column are made shorter and the spare component is placed in that column. Here, there is one spare component, so the last column has 3 rows and the first column has 2.

If there were six components, the solution would be somewhat simpler—the square root is again 2, but 6 divides evenly by 2 to give 3, so there would be 3 columns each with 2 rows. This pattern works well until there are 11 components. The integer square root of 11 is 3, so there would be 3 rows with 11/3 = 3 columns. This provides 9 slots—now there are 2 components unaccounted for. When there was one spare component, it was placed in the last column. This time, one spare component will be placed in each of the last two columns. This is, in fact, the algorithm that is used throughout—calculate the number of spare components and allocate one each to the last columns. Figure 12-11 shows the result obtained with 11 frames.

With this explanation, the code for the `cascadeAll` method should be easy to follow. It starts by counting the number of components to tile by getting the array of components in the container and walking down it, counting only those that are both visible and instances of `JInternalFrame`. It then calculates the number of columns and rows and, from that, works out the number of spares:

```
double root = Math.sqrt((double)count);
int rows = (int)root;
int columns = count/rows;
int spares = count - (columns * rows);
```

Because this code is using integer arithmetic, the integer value of the square root is always smaller than (or the same as) the exact answer, so the number of columns obtained is always larger (or the same as) the number of rows. This code could equally have used the integer part of the square root as the number of columns directly and then there would have been more rows than columns. Next, the width of each column is calculated by dividing the width of the container by the number or columns and the height of each row is obtained by dividing the container height by the row count. However, the last few columns may have more rows than the first ones, so it is necessary to calculate a second row height based on one more row. These two row heights are placed in the variables `mainHeight` and `smallerHeight` respectively.

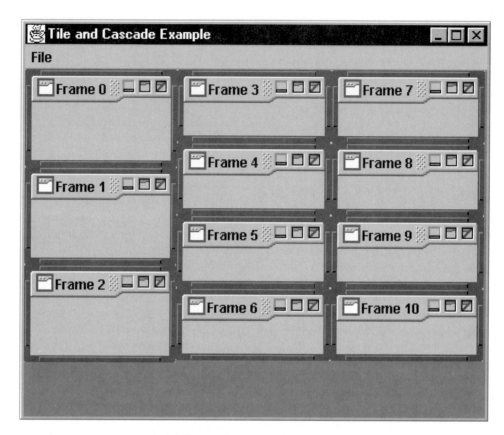

Figure 12-11   A tiled desktop with 11 components.

The `cascadeAll` method then walks down the list of components placing visible internal frames, working from the top left of the container down each column and making each row `mainHeight` pixels high until it fills a column, then moves to the next column. When it reaches the point at which it needs to place one more row in each column, it simply starts using the smaller row height `smallerHeight`. The number of normal columns (i.e. those without extra rows) is given by the expression `columns - spares`, which simply expresses the fact that one spare is placed in each of the last columns. This value is placed in a variable (`normalColumns`) at the start of the loop. Each time a column is filled, `normalColumns` is decremented and when it reaches zero we switch to using the smaller height and packing one more row to each of the remaining columns.

Notice the way in which each frame is placed and sized:

```
manager.setBoundsForFrame((JComponent)comp, x, y,
            columnWidth, rowHeight);
```

The variable `manager` holds a reference to the pane's desktop manager. Rather than explicitly place and size the frame using `setBounds`, this task is delegated to the desktop manager so that it can do whatever it needs to do when a frame is moved or resized. This make it possible to install a desktop manager that disallows any movement of components, for example, without changing the desktop pane implementation. This same method is also used when cascading in the `cascade` method.

You can try out the extended desktop pane using an example program from the CD-ROM that uses it. To run this program, use the command

```
java JFCBook.Chapter12.DesktopPaneExample
```

This brings up an empty desktop with a `File` menu, on which there are options that allow you to create new frames. The `New  Frame` menu item creates a new frame in the middle of the desktop, while `New  Cascaded  Frame` uses the `addCascaded` method to add the frame. The `Tile` and `Cascade` menu items exercise the `tileAll` and `cascadeAll` methods respectively. Try creating various numbers of frames and then tiling them to see how many rows and columns are created and how spares are distributed over the last columns. You'll notice a couple of things about tiling that might, at first, surprise you:

- If you tile the container and resize it, the tiled components don't retile themselves to take up the extra space in the container or shrink if you make the container smaller—they just stay where they are.

- Tiling a container doesn't stop you dragging the components around— but you can put them back later by retiling from the menu.

This behavior is consistent with the way that Windows applications behave. If you want to change this behavior, you can, of course, do so by extending this example desktop pane. You could, for example, make the components tile themselves again when the container resizes by overriding the `setSize` and `setBounds` methods and invoking `tileAll` after allowing the superclass to do the resizing—for example, if you *always* want to tile, you could implement the `setBounds` method like this

```
public void setBounds(Rectangle rect) {
    super.setBounds(rect);
    tileAll();
}
```

Note that there are two variants of `setBounds` and also two forms of `setSize`. To make this scheme work consistently, you have to override all of them. You must, of course, allow the superclass to do its work first, or the `tileAll` method will get the wrong container size to work with.

The Organic Look-and-Feel Desktop Manager

The Organic look-and-feel (formerly known as the Java look-and-feel) is not part of the Swing 1.0 release. It is, however, available as a separate download from JavaSoft. If you want to see how different the Organic desktop is from that of the three standard look-and-feels, download it and follow the example in this section.

If you try the `InternalFramesExample1` program again and iconify the frames with all three look-and-feel styles, you'll find that the icons are identical. This is because the container in this example is a layered pane, which uses the default desktop manager, so the same icons are used in all cases. When you use a `JDesktopPane`, however, the situation changes, because each look-and-feel can install its own desktop manager. The Organic look-and-feel has a customized desktop manager that gives a completely different look-and-feel to icons. You can see this if you run the example from the previous section with the Organic look-and-feel selected and iconify several of the frames. In the top right-hand corner of the desktop pane, you'll see a small multi-colored block, under which there is one thin rectangle for each iconified frame—this is, in fact, the frame icon (Figure 12-12). If you move the mouse over the block or the icons, you get a drop-down menu as shown in Figure 12-13.

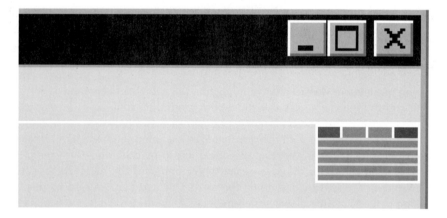

Figure 12-12 Desktop icons in the Organic look-and-feel.

To implement this feature, the Organic look-and-feel class for `JDesktopPane` (`java.awt.swing.plaf.organic.OrganicDesktopPaneUI`) creates a separate component (`OrganicDesktopMenu`) and adds it to the desktop. It also has a custom desktop manager (`OrganicDesktopManager`), which implements the iconifying and deiconifying of frames differently from the basic desktop manager. The presence of the desktop menu is another reason why our extended desktop menu didn't tile and cascade every component it came across on the desktop—if it had done this, it would have tiled or cascaded the desktop menu, with undesirable results!

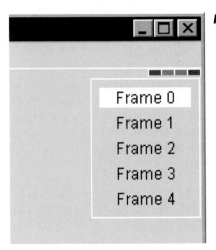

Figure 12-13 The Organic look-and-feel icon menu.

Extending the Desktop Manager

If the standard desktop manager is not suitable for your application you can, of course, develop your own and install it on all of the desktop panes that your application will create. You've already seen the methods that a desktop manager must implement—they are defined by the `DesktopManager` interface. In many cases, though, you only want to redefine a subset of the standard desktop manager's behavior, which you can do by subclassing it and only overriding selected methods.

A Desktop Manager that uses Outline Frames

In this section, you'll see how to develop a subclass of `DefaultDesktopManager` that changes what happens when you drag or resize a frame. As noted in this chapter, these operations are actually performed by the desktop manager, not by the desktop pane or by the frames themselves, and the default implementation redraws the frame as it resizes or moves it so that its content is always visible. This, of course, has a certain performance penalty associated with it, in terms of the speed at which the frame moves or is resized. The effects of this can be reduced by drawing only an outline of the frame as its size or position changes, so that only the cost of drawing the outline is incurred, instead of the whole of the frame and its content.

How Frames are Moved and Resized

Because only the drag and resize behavior of the desktop manager is going to be changed, only the methods that deal with those features need to be overridden. When a frame is dragged, the `beginDraggingFrame` method is called to start the operation, then each time the frame needs to move the `dragFrame` method is

entered and finally, when the frame has reached its final resting point, the
endDraggingFrame method is called. Similarly, a frame resize begins with a call
to beginResizingFrame followed by a series of invocations of resizeFrame
and ends in endResizingFrame. All of these methods receive a reference to the
JComponent being operated on. The resizeFrame method is told what the
frame's new bounds should be and the dragFrame method is given the frame's new
position. As a result, these methods need to get very little state from elsewhere.
However, because there can be only one drag or resize operation in progress on a
desktop pane at any time, it is safe to save state between these methods, provided you
realize that the state becomes invalid after endDraggingFrame or
endResizingFrame has been called.

When a frame is being resized with the default desktop manager, all that happens is that the resizeFrame method calls the setBoundsForFrame
method to change the frame's size based on the current mouse position—the
beginResizingFrame and endResizingFrame methods don't do anything.
Similarly, when a frame is dragged, only the dragFrame method does anything—
it also calls setBoundsForFrame.

Using an Outline Instead of the Real Frame

What we want to do is to move around an outline of the frame, not the frame itself,
so here is the implementation plan:

- In beginDraggingFrame or beginResizingFrame, the actual
  frame will be made invisible and a transparent panel with a thin border will be substituted. This border will act as the outline of the frame.

- In dragFrame or resizeFrame, the transparent panel will be
  moved or resized instead of the frame. This makes the outline appear
  to follow the mouse.

- In endDraggingFrame or endResizingFrame, the outline is
  removed and the original frame will be resized or moved using
  setBoundsForFrame and made visible again,.

With the basic idea in place, let's look at the details, which are shown in Listing 12-2.

**Listing 12-2   A desktop manager that shows outlines when dragging
and resizing frames**

```
package JFCBook.Chapter12;

import com.sun.java.swing.*;
import java.awt.Color;
import java.awt.Cursor;
import java.awt.Rectangle;
```

```
public class ExtendedDesktopManager extends DefaultDesktopManager {
  public ExtendedDesktopManager(JDesktopPane targetPane) {
    ghostPanel = new JPanel();
    ghostPanel.setOpaque(false);
    ghostPanel.setBorder(BorderFactory.createLineBorder(BORDER_COLOR,
              BORDER_THICKNESS));
    this.targetPane = targetPane;
  }

  public void beginDraggingFrame(JComponent f) {
    Rectangle r = f.getBounds();
    ghostPanel.setBounds(r);

    f.setVisible(false);
    targetPane.add(ghostPanel);
    targetPane.setLayer(ghostPanel, JLayeredPane.DRAG_LAYER.intValue());
    targetPane.setVisible(true);
  }

  public void dragFrame(JComponent f, int newX, int newY) {
    setBoundsForFrame(ghostPanel, newX, newY, ghostPanel.getWidth(),
              ghostPanel.getHeight());
  }

  public void endDraggingFrame(JComponent f) {
    Rectangle r = ghostPanel.getBounds();
    f.setBounds(r);
    targetPane.remove(ghostPanel);
    f.setVisible(true);
  }

  public void beginResizingFrame(JComponent f, int direction) {
    oldCursor = f.getCursor();
    super.beginResizingFrame(f, direction);
    Cursor cursor = f.getCursor();
    Rectangle r = f.getBounds();
    ghostPanel.setBounds(r);

    f.setVisible(false);
    targetPane.add(ghostPanel);
    targetPane.setLayer(ghostPanel, JLayeredPane.DRAG_LAYER.intValue());
    ghostPanel.setCursor(cursor);
    targetPane.setVisible(true);
  }

  public void resizeFrame(JComponent f, int newX, int newY, int newWidth,
              int newHeight) {
```

continued

```
    setBoundsForFrame(ghostPanel, newX, newY, newWidth, newHeight);
  }

  public void endResizingFrame(JComponent f) {
    Rectangle r = ghostPanel.getBounds();
    f.setBounds(r);
    ghostPanel.setCursor(oldCursor);
    targetPane.remove(ghostPanel);
    f.validate();
    f.setVisible(true);
  }

  protected JPanel ghostPanel;
  protected JComponent targetComponent;
  protected JDesktopPane targetPane;
  protected Cursor oldCursor;

  protected static final Color BORDER_COLOR = Color.black;
  protected static final int BORDER_THICKNESS = 2;
}
```

The constructor creates the panel that will represent the frame as it is dragged or resized. This panel is just a `JPanel` that it made transparent by calling `setOpaque(false)` and given a line border around its outside. In our case, the border is black and is 2 pixels wide. You could, of course, easily enhance this to make the border color and width configurable or make it sensitive to the selected look-and-feel using techniques that you'll see in Chapter 13. A reference to the panel is held in the instance variable `ghostPanel` for later use. A reference to the desktop pane is also saved, so that the panel can be added to it when necessary.

Core Note

In this example a reference to the desktop pane is passed to the constructor, but it is possible to avoid that and find the desktop pane only when dragging or resizing begins. If we restricted ourselves to handling only `JInternalFrames`, the `getDesktopPane` method could be used to find the desktop pane. However, the desktop manager methods that are being overridden are passed a `JComponent`, so they may, theoretically, be asked to operate on a more general object. If you wanted to support that, you could locate the desktop pane by looking at the ancestors of the object being dragged until you find a `JDesktopPane`. As an exercise, you might want to change this example so that its constructor doesn't take the desktop pane as an argument. One benefit of this would be to make it possible to construct only one instance that could be shared by an arbitrary number of panes.

Implementing the Drag Operation

The implementations for drag and resize are similar, but slightly different so we'll look at them separately. The easier case is dragging the frame. Here, in the beginDraggingFrame method, the ghost panel is substituted for the frame that the user is dragging, setting its initial size from that of the frame and then making the frame invisible. The dragFrame method is very simple—it just calls setBoundsForFrame and passes through the arguments that it was given, except that it passes a reference to the ghost panel instead of the frame itself. Finally, the endDraggingFrame method is the reverse of beginDraggingFrame—the original frame is placed at the current location of the ghost panel, the ghost panel is removed and the original frame made visible again.

Implementing Resize

Frame resizing is, in principle, identical and you'll notice that much of the code is the same. There is, however, one subtle difference. When you move the mouse over the edge of a frame, the cursor changes to reflect the direction in which the frame would be resized by dragging on that edge or corner. This cursor is, of course, associated with the frame itself and it should be preserved when showing the outline ghost panel. To do this, when resizing is started, the frame's cursor is captured and applied to the ghost panel. The previous cursor for the ghost panel is saved and restored later when resizing stops.

Implementation Issues

There are a few points of interest that apply both to dragging and resizing. First, when one of these operations is in progress, the user should be able to see the outline at all times. If the outline were placed in the same layer as the frame it replaces, you could lose sight of it behind other objects, so it is placed instead in the DRAG_LAYER. This is not necessarily the highest layer in the container, but it is the appropriate one to use—anything in a higher layer is probably there for a very good reason.

The second issue relates to the use of various look-and-feels. You can try out the extended desktop manager by running a modified version of the program used to demonstrate the extended desktop pane in the previous section. To run this example, use the following command:

```
java JFCBook.Chapter12.ExtendedDesktopManagerExample
```

If you run this with the Metal look-and-feel, you'll find that you can drag and resize any frames that you create and see the outline panel instead of the complete frame and you should find that the operation is now performed slightly faster. You can see what this example looks like in Figure 12-14.

If you download and use the Organic look-and-feel, you'll also see the Organic look-and-feel desktop menu block at the top right-hand corner but, if you iconify one of the frames, you'll find that it doesn't stack itself under this menu block—instead, it behaves as it would with the Windows look-and-feel. The reason is, of course, that this desktop manager has been created by extending the basic desktop manager, but the Organic look-and-feel desktop manager, which is being replaced here, contains functionality over and above that of the basic one, which has now been lost.

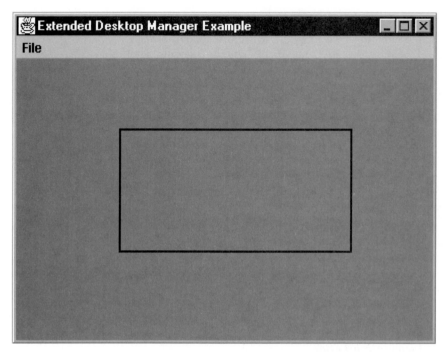

Figure 12-14   Resizing a frame with the extended desktop manager.

There are a couple of ways that you can try to remedy this situation. First, you can use one of the methods that was shown when creating custom tree cell renderers—when your desktop manager is installed, you can hold a reference to the one that you are replacing and delegate to it when all of the methods that you are not going to override are invoked. In the case, you would implement all of the methods of `DesktopManager` and call through to the corresponding method of the desktop manager that had been replaced in all cases apart from the ones implement in the new desktop manager. This would, indeed, work in this case, but it fails if the user should switch the look-and-feel when the application is running, because our desktop manager will be switched out when the new look-and-feel installs its own.

The second way to tackle this problem is to implement a subclass for each look-and-feel that you are going to allow the user to use and install your version instead of the standard one. This will cause every desktop pane to be created with your desktop manager installed and every time the look-and-feel is changed your desktop manager will be used instead of the standard one. You'll see how to deal with this issue in Chapter 13.

An Example Multiple-Document Application

To conclude this chapter, we're going to create a relatively simple, but representative, multidocument application that makes use of most of what you have seen in this chapter. The finished product will be a simple multiple-document editor that will allow you to open files, change their contents and write them back. Because this example uses internal frames, you will be able to open several documents at once and, using the built-in facilities of the Swing text components, you will be able to cut-and-paste between them. You'll also see how to create menu bars for internal frames and how to use dialogs in a multidocument application.

Figure 12-15 shows the completed application with three open files. This example makes use of the extended desktop pane and extended desktop manager, so it is possible, as in this screen shot, to tile the windows, or to cascade them as appropriate. You'll notice that the main application window has a menu bar and so does each internal frame. The main menu bar is used to perform global tasks like cascading, tiling and closing the application, while the individual frame menu bars allow you to save the content of the file in that frame or to close the frame.

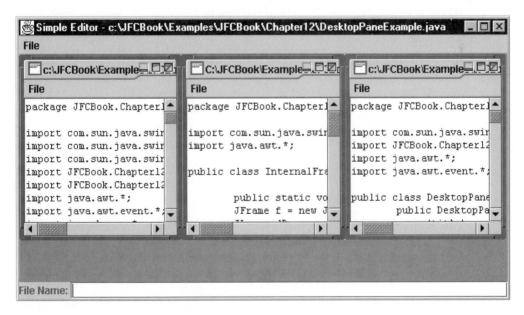

Figure 12-15   An example multiple-document application.

The caption bar of each frame contains the name of the file that it is displaying. If you make changes to the window content, the title bar changes to show that you need to save the file before closing it, by adding an asterisk after the file name. This asterisk is removed when the data has been written back to the file. The name of the currently-active file—that is, the file in the currently-selected frame—also appears in the main window caption bar.

You can try this application yourself using the command

```
java JFCBook.Chapter12.SimpleEditor
```

When the program starts, you get an empty window with a text field at the bottom. As you type file names into here, new frames are opened that allow you to edit the files. If you type the same file name twice, you only get one frame, however. You'll find that the frames are cascaded as they open but, of course, you can use the `File` menu to tile them, or you can drag or resize them as required. Because the extended desktop manager has been installed, you'll notice that the frame turns to an outline as you drag or resize it.

If you try closing the application while there are still open frames, you'll see a dialog box that asks you to close all of your windows before closing the application. This dialog box is created using the `JOptionPane` class that you saw in Chapter 7, "Using Standard Dialogs." If you edit the data in a window and then try to close the window without saving the data, you'll get another dialog box asking if you want to discard the changes, save them, or cancel the close operation. Although it looks very much like the previous dialog box, this one is subtly different because it is housed in an internal frame, not a top-level dialog box. You'll see how to create dialogs that are internal frames later in this section.

The code for this application will be shown piece-by-piece so that you can see more easily what each piece is doing. Because this is quite a long example a complete source listing isn't reproduced here, but you can find it on the CD-ROM that accompanies this book.

Creating the Main Frame

The Simple Editor application is based around a `JFrame`, to which are added a menu bar, a desktop pane, a label and a text field into which the user types file names. This application also uses the extended desktop pane and the extended desktop manager that were built earlier in this chapter to get the benefits of automatic cascading and tiling and the fast frame resize and dragging given by the extended desktop manager. Creating the main window is a simple matter of plugging these components together and using the appropriate layout managers.

The menu bar has its own slot in the frame's `JRootPane`, so there is no need to worry about assigning its position and making sure it resizes properly. As for the rest of the window, the desktop pane should take as much space as it can and the text field and the associated label (see Figure 12-15) should stay at the bottom and grow only horizontally. To make the desktop pane occupy as much space as possible, it should be placed in the Center position of a BorderLayout manager. If the label and text field were then placed in the South position, they would grow horizontally but not vertically. Because they can't both be placed in the South position, they are placed instead on a JPanel that is placed in the South position. JPanel has a FlowLayout manager as the default, which would mean that the label and text field would huddle together in the middle of the strip at the bottom of the frame. What is actually required is for the label to be over to the left, with the text field taking up the rest of the space, so the JPanel is given a BorderLayout manager with the label and text field assigned to the West and Center respectively. This completes the layout of the content pane.

As you know, the desktop pane has no layout manager at all, so it is necessary to either explicitly size it or decide on a size for the main window and let that determine the desktop pane's size. In this case, the width and height of the desktop pane are passed to the SimpleEditor constructor. Just calling setSize on the desktop pane won't work—when the frame is laid out, it will be asked for its preferred size, not its current size. Therefore, the JComponent setPreferredSize method is used to register the values passed to the constructor, which will ensure that the desktop pane is properly sized. You can see the details of this in Listing 12-3.

| Listing 12-3   Creating the Simple Editor main window |

```
package JFCBook.Chapter12;

import com.sun.java.swing.*;
import com.sun.java.swing.text.*;
import com.sun.java.swing.event.*;
import JFCBook.Chapter12.ExtendedDesktopPane;
import JFCBook.Chapter12.ExtendedDesktopManager;
import java.awt.*;
import java.awt.event.*;
import java.beans.*;
import java.io.*;
import java.util.*;

public class SimpleEditor extends JFrame implements ActionListener,
                VetoableChangeListener,
                PropertyChangeListener {
  public SimpleEditor(String caption, int width, int height) {
    super(caption);
    this.caption = caption;
    Container p = this.getContentPane();
    p.setLayout(new BorderLayout());
```

continued

```
// Create the working area
e = new ExtendedDesktopPane();
e.setPreferredSize(new Dimension(width, height));
p.add(e, "Center");
e.setDesktopManager(new ExtendedDesktopManager(e));

// Create the label and file name input fields
JPanel lp = new JPanel();
lp.setBackground(UIManager.getColor("control"));
lp.setLayout(new BorderLayout());
JLabel l = new JLabel("File Name: ", SwingConstants.RIGHT);
l.setFont(new Font("Dialog", Font.BOLD, 12));
lp.add(l, "West");
fileNameField = new JTextField(35);
fileNameField.addActionListener(this);
lp.add(fileNameField, "Center");

p.add(lp, "South");

// Create and add the main window menu
JMenuBar menuBar = new JMenuBar();
this.setJMenuBar(menuBar);
JMenu fileMenu = new JMenu("File");
menuBar.add(fileMenu);

// Action to tile the pane
Action tileAction = new AbstractAction("Tile") {
  public void actionPerformed(ActionEvent evt) {
    e.tileAll();
  }
};
fileMenu.add(tileAction);

// Action to cascade the pane
Action cascadeAction = new AbstractAction("Cascade") {
  public void actionPerformed(ActionEvent evt) {
    e.cascadeAll();
  }
};
fileMenu.add(cascadeAction);

fileMenu.addSeparator();

fileMenu.add(new AbstractAction("Exit") {
  public void actionPerformed(ActionEvent evt) {
```

```
        SimpleEditor.this.doExitCheck();
      }
    });

    // Catch the window close event
    this.addWindowListener(new WindowAdapter() {
      public void windowClosing(WindowEvent evt) {
        SimpleEditor.this.doExitCheck();
      }

      public void windowClosed(WindowEvent evt) {
        System.exit(0);
      }
    });
    this.setDefaultCloseOperation(JFrame.DO_NOTHING_ON_CLOSE);
  }

  // Code omitted here

  public static void main(String[] args) {
    Dimension d = Toolkit.getDefaultToolkit().getScreenSize();
    SimpleEditor f = new SimpleEditor("Simple Editor", 3 *
d.width/ 4, 3 * d.height/4);
    f.pack();
    f.setVisible(true);
  }

  // The working area
  protected ExtendedDesktopPane e;

  // Text field
  protected JTextField fileNameField;

  // This hashtable manages the open windows.
  // It is keyed by file name
  protected Hashtable fileTable = new Hashtable();

  // This hashtable is keyed by frame reference
  protected Hashtable windowTable = new Hashtable();

  // Caption string
  protected String caption;
}
```

The Main Menu Bar

The main frame's menu bar is, of course, an instance of JMenuBar. There's only going to be one menu—the File menu—on this menu bar, to which menu items to close the main window, tile all of the frames on the desktop or cascade them all will be added. As you saw in Chapter 5, the most powerful way to add items to menus is by creating an Action that performs the function of the menu item and place that directly on the menu, so that the same code can be attached to more than one user interface element. In this application, there is no real need to do that, but nevertheless Actions are used here for the sake of consistency and because they make future enhancement (perhaps by adding a tool bar) easier.

The Cascade and Tile actions are very trivial—as you can see in Listing 12-3, they just need to call the appropriate methods exposed by the extended desktop pane. These Actions are implemented as inner classes derived from AbstractAction—all that needs to be added is the label for the menu item (and an icon as well if it were required) and an actionPerformed method that does the actual work.

Closing the main frame is slightly more complex for two reasons. First, the frame can be closed either from the menu or by clicking the frame close button (or, equivalently, the Close item on the caption bar menu) and the same code should be used to handle both cases. Secondly, it isn't a good idea to allow the user to close the frame at any time—there may be windows open that have unsaved data. To prevent possible data loss, this example will require that the user closes all of the open windows before the main window itself will close. As an exercise, you might like to change this so that the main window will close with internal frames open provided that there is no unsaved data in any of them. When you've seen the data structures that are used to manage the internal frames, you should see that this is a fairly simple change to make.

To make it possible to share the frame close code, a method in the SimpleEditor class called doExitCheck contains all the code necessary to initiate the close. An Action labeled Exit is attached to the File menu that will just invoke this method. As far as the frame close button is concerned, to handle this a WindowListener is registered on the main frame. As you know, clicking the frame close button causes the listener's windowClosing method to be entered. In this method, you can either hide or dispose the frame to allow the close to take place, or you can do nothing, in which case the close request is ignored. In fact, windowClosing just calls the doExitCheck method and lets it make the decision. The implementation of this method is shown in Listing 12-4.

Core Note

The description above assumes that the main frame is operating with DO_NOTHING_ON_CLOSE *selected, as described in Chapter 2, "Frames, Labels and Buttons." Since this is not the default, this option is explicitly selected at the end of the constructor.*

Listing 12-4   Handling frame close requests

```
protected void doExitCheck() {
  if (windowTable.isEmpty() == false) {
    JOptionPane.showMessageDialog(SimpleEditor.this,
          "Close all files before closing the main window",
          "Error", JOptionPane.ERROR_MESSAGE);
  } else {
    SimpleEditor.this.dispose();
  }
}
```

As you'll see later, this example has an object that keeps a record of all open internal frames. The doExitCheck method first checks whether this object is empty and, if it is, it disposes of the frame. No matter how this code was entered, this will cause the windowClosed method of the WindowListener to be entered and, as you can see from Listing 12-3, this just exits.

If there is an open internal frame, the main frame should not be closed. Instead, the JOptionPane class that you saw in Chapter 7 is used to create a modal dialog that tells the user why the frame cannot be closed and waits for the OK button to be pressed.

Opening a New Internal Frame

When the user types a file name into the text field and presses return, it generates an ActionEvent, to receive which an ActionListener is registered. The job of the actionPerformed method of this listener is to create a new internal frame and read the content of the named file into it, then place the frame on the main window. However, if the file is already open, a second frame for the same file should not be created—instead, it should just be brought to the front. To make this possible, it is necessary to keep a mapping from file names to internal frames, for which purpose a class that holds information about an internal frame and the file that it is editing is required. A hash table then maps from the file name to the appropriate instance of this class. Listing 12-5 shows the definition of this class. A Hashtable called fileTable is used to map from file name to the FileHolder for a file.

Listing 12-5   Keeping track of open files

```
//
// Helper class.
// This class is used to associate internal frames and
// files. A reference to the class is stored in a Hashtable
// keyed by the name of the file
//
class FileHolder implements DocumentListener {
  FileHolder(String n, JInternalFrame i, JTextArea t) {
    this.fileName = n;
    this.jif = i;
    this.textArea = t;
  }

  void setChanged(boolean changed) {
    if (changed == true && hasChanged == false) {
      jif.setTitle(fileName + "*");
    } else if (changed == false && hasChanged == true) {
      jif.setTitle(fileName);
    }
    this.hasChanged = changed;
  }

  boolean isChanged() {
    return hasChanged;
  }

  String getFileName() {
    return fileName;
  }

  void saveFile() throws IOException, FileNotFoundException {
    File openFile = new File(fileName);
    try {
      FileOutputStream fs = new FileOutputStream(openFile);
      byte[] content = textArea.getText().getBytes();
      fs.write(content);
      fs.close();
      hasChanged = false;
    } catch (FileNotFoundException e) {
      JOptionPane.showInternalMessageDialog(jif,
              "Failed to open \"" + fileName + "\" for writing.",
              "Error", JOptionPane.ERROR_MESSAGE);
      Toolkit.getDefaultToolkit().beep();
      throw e;
    } catch (IOException e) {
```

```
         JOptionPane.showInternalMessageDialog(jif,
               "Failed to write to \"" + fileName + "\".",
               "Error", JOptionPane.ERROR_MESSAGE);
         Toolkit.getDefaultToolkit().beep();
         throw e;
      }
   }

   public void changedUpdate(DocumentEvent evt) {
      setChanged(true);
   }

   public void insertUpdate(DocumentEvent evt) {
      setChanged(true);
   }

   public void removeUpdate(DocumentEvent evt) {
      setChanged(true);
   }

   String fileName;     // The file name
   JInternalFrame jif;   // The Internal Frame
   JTextArea textArea; // The text area
   boolean hasChanged; // true if content changed
}
```

This object is responsible for quite a lot of bookkeeping for the file and internal frame that it represents. To create an instance, you pass the file name, the internal frame that will display the file and the text area that will actually hold the file content. In addition to this, the `FileHolder` class records whether the window content has been changed in its `hasChanged` instance variable, which is initially `false`. It provides a `setChanged` method that allows the state of this variable to be modified and an `isChanged` method to allow it to be read. You'll see later exactly how these methods are used.

It turns out that it is also useful to be able to map from an internal frame to the file which that internal frame contains. To do this, a second hash table that uses an internal frame reference as its key and the `FileHolder` object as the associated value is maintained. A reference to this `Hashtable` is held in the member variable `windowTable`. This is also the hash table that the `doExitCheck` method looks at to determine if there are any open internal frames—if this hash table is empty, there are none open.

Let's now look at the `actionPerformed` method (Listing 12-6) to see how the various pieces that you've seen so far fit together. The first step is to get the new file name from the text field and remove leading and trailing white space, then look for a file of this name in the `fileTable` hash table. If it is found there, the `FileHolder` that corresponds to it is extracted from the hash table. From here, the corresponding internal frame is found and brought to the front of the desktop by using its `setSelected` method. As you'll see in Listing 12-6, this generates several events, one of which will cause the name of this file to become the main window's caption bar title.

Note also that we are obliged to catch a possible `PropertyVetoException` that might occur during the execution of `setSelected`. In this application, this veto will never actually happen, but the compiler forces us to catch the exception anyway. It is simply ignored.

Listing 12-6   Opening a new internal frame

```java
// Act on a new file name in the input area
public void actionPerformed(ActionEvent evt) {
  String fileName = fileNameField.getText().trim();   // File name
  if (fileTable.containsKey(fileName)) {
    // The file is already open in a window
    // Get the file holder object, then
    // make its window the primary view.
    FileHolder h = (FileHolder)fileTable.get(fileName);
    try {
      h.jif.setSelected(true);
    } catch (PropertyVetoException e) {
      // Nothing sensible to do
    }
  } else {
    // Not yet open: create a new one
    SimpleEditor.this.setCursor(Cursor.getPredefinedCursor
                (Cursor.WAIT_CURSOR));
    File f = new File(fileName);
    try {
      fileNameField.setEnabled(false);
      FileInputStream fs = new FileInputStream(f);
      long l = f.length();
      byte[] content = new byte[(int)l];
      fs.read(content);
      fs.close();

      JTextArea ta = new JTextArea(new String(content));
      ta.setEditable(f.canWrite());
      JInternalFrame jif = new JInternalFrame(fileName,
                true, true, true, true);
      jif.setContentPane(new JScrollPane(ta));
      //
      // Enter the window holder and file name
      // in the hash tables to detect duplicate opens
      // and for use at window close time
      //
```

```
    FileHolder h = new FileHolder(fileName, jif, ta);
    fileTable.put(fileName, h);
    windowTable.put(jif, h);

    JMenuBar menuBar = new JMenuBar();
    JMenu fileMenu = new JMenu("File");
    menuBar.add(fileMenu);

    Action saveAction = new SaveAction(jif, h);
    fileMenu.add(saveAction);
    saveAction.setEnabled(f.canWrite());

    Action closeAction = new CloseAction(jif);
    fileMenu.add(closeAction);

    jif.setMenuBar(menuBar);

    e.addCascaded(jif, JLayeredPane.DEFAULT_LAYER);
    jif.addPropertyChangeListener(this);
    jif.addVetoableChangeListener(this);

    // Add a document listener to detect content changes
    ta.getDocument().addDocumentListener(h);

    try {
      jif.setSelected(true);
    } catch (PropertyVetoException e) {
    // Nothing sensible to do here
    }

    fileNameField.setText("");        // Clear file name
  } catch (IOException e) {
    JOptionPane.showMessageDialog((Component)evt.getSource(),
        "Failed to read \"" + fileName + "\".",
        "File Read Error", JOptionPane.ERROR_MESSAGE);
    this.getToolkit().beep();
    return;
  } catch (Exception e) {
    JOptionPane.showMessageDialog((Component)evt.getSource(),
        "Failed to open \"" + fileName + "\".",
        "File Read Error", JOptionPane.ERROR_MESSAGE);
    this.getToolkit().beep();
    return;
  } finally {
    fileNameField.setEnabled(true);
    SimpleEditor.this.setCursor
                (Cursor.getPredefinedCursor(Cursor.DEFAULT_CURSOR));
  }
 }
}
}
```

If this file is not currently open, a new internal frame is created for it, using the file name as its title, and the file content is read into a text area. The details of reading the file are not of any interest here, but note that if an error occurs while trying to open or read the file an internal frame is not created and an error message is posted in a dialog box, which the user must acknowledge. Assuming that the file content is successfully read into memory, a text field (which we make editable if the file itself is writable) and an internal frame are created and the text area, wrapped in a JScrollPane, is placed in the internal frame's content area.

Having constructed the main part of internal frame, the FileHolder instance for it is created, followed by the mappings from file name and from internal frame by making entries in the fileTable and windowTable hash tables. Next, we need to build the internal frame's menu bar. This menu bar, like that on the main frame, has only a File entry, which allows the file data to be saved or the frame to be closed. As with the main menu, these are implemented as Actions and added directly to the File menu. The menu bar is then mounted on the internal frame using its setMenuBar method.

Core Note

There is an inconsistency in the API here that is somewhat annoying: JFrame *has a* setJMenuBar *method to attach a menu, but* JInternalFrame *has* setMenuBar.

With the internal frame complete, it is added to the desktop pane using the addCascaded method. All file frames will be held in the default layer. Next, the SimpleEditor class is registered as both a property listener and a vetoable change listener on the internal frame, for reasons that you'll see later. Then, we register the FileHolder as a document listener to receive notification of changes made to the window content.

Finally, the setSelected method is used to move this new frame to the foreground and make its name appear on the application title bar. The text field is then cleared to invite the user to type a new file name. This completes the processing for a newly-opened file. Everything else that happens is notified as an event and processed by event handlers.

Changes in the document

When the user changes the text displayed in an internal frame, we want to note that this has happened so that we can prompt the user to save the modifications to the file before the frame is closed. As you know from Chapter 9, changes in a text area can be detected by attaching a DocumentListener to its data model. When the internal frame containing the text area was created, the FileHolder object was registered as the listener, so when modifications are made, its changedUpdate, insertUpdate or removeUpdate method will be called. All three of these just call setChanged which sets the changed flag to true and also does one other thing: if this flag was false, in other words the text field is being modified for the first time (or the first time since it was saved to the file, as you'll see), it adds an asterisk to the internal frame's caption bar as a reminder to the user that the content of the frame does not match that in the file.

Moving an Internal Frame to the Foreground

The user can move a frame to the foreground by clicking in it. When this happens, the frame's setSelected method is called with argument true and two property change events are sent for IS_SELECTED_PROPERTY—one to vetoable change listeners and one to property change listeners. This application is not interested in preventing a frame becoming selected, so it ignores the vetoable change event. There is, however, a property change listener registered on the internal frame. Listing 12-7 shows the implementation of the propertyChange method of SimpleEditor. In this section we are interested only in the second part of this method. When the IS_SELECTED_PROPERTY changes to true (and only in this case), the file name of the file in the selected window should be put on the main frame's caption bar, to indicate which file the user is currently working with.

Listing 12-7   Handling property change events

```
public void propertyChange(PropertyChangeEvent evt) {
  JInternalFrame jif = (JInternalFrame)evt.getSource();
  String name = evt.getPropertyName();
  Object value = evt.getNewValue();
  if (name.equals(JInternalFrame.IS_CLOSED_PROPERTY)
      && (Boolean)value == Boolean.TRUE) {
    // Remove it from the hash tables
    FileHolder h = (FileHolder)windowTable.get(jif);
    windowTable.remove(jif);
    fileTable.remove(h.fileName);
  } else if (name.equals(JInternalFrame.IS_SELECTED_PROPERTY)
      && (Boolean)value == Boolean.TRUE) {
    // When a frame moves to the foreground,
    // puts its file name on our title bar
    FileHolder h = (FileHolder)windowTable.get(jif);
    setTitle(caption + " - " + h.getFileName());
  }
}
```

This method receives the internal frame that has been selected as the source of the event, but what it really needs is the name of the file being edited in the frame. One way to get this is directly from the caption bar of the internal frame, since it happens that the file name is displayed there. But coupling between different parts of the application is reduced if this assumption can be avoided. This will also leave us free to change what is in the internal frame caption bar at a later date without having to re-code this event handler. Another problem with using the internal frame's caption bar title is that it may also have an asterisk on it that shows that the file has been modified. The asterisk could be removed with some boring and time-consuming string manipulation, or you could decide to reflect it on the main frame's title bar. If that were done, though, the main title bar would have to be updated whenever the title bar of the internal frame is changed.

Instead of getting involved in these unnecessary complications, it is simpler to use the internal frame reference as the key to the `windowTable` hash table to find the `FileHolder` object and then use its `getFileName` method to retrieve the unadorned file name and write that to the frame's caption bar.

Saving Window Contents to the File

When the user uses the `Save` menu item of the internal frame's file menu, the `actionPerformed` method of the `SaveAction` that was associated with it is invoked. Listing 12-8 shows how this `Action` was defined.

Listing 12-8   The Save Action

```
class SaveAction extends AbstractAction {
  SaveAction(FileHolder h) {
    super("Save");
    this.fileHolder = h;
  }

  public void actionPerformed(ActionEvent evt) {
    try {
      fileHolder.saveFile();
    } catch (Throwable t) {
    }
  }

  FileHolder fileHolder;
}
```

As you can see, this is trivial. When the `Action` is created, its saves a reference to the internal frame's `FileHolder` object so that, when the menu item is activated the `FileHolder`'s `saveFile` method can be invoked directly. If you look back to the creation of this `Action` in Listing 12-6, you'll see that we enabled it only if the file was writable at the time that the internal frame's menu was created, so the menu item itself will be disabled if the file was read-only at that time. Nevertheless, it is possible for a writable file to become read-only later, so it is necessary to cater for this possibility.

Core Note

This example doesn't concern itself with the possibility that a read-only file could become writable after it has been opened. With the current implementation, you won't be able to write to the file (or even change the content of the text area) until you close its window and reopen it.

The code for the `saveFile` method was shown along with the rest of the `FileHolder` class in Listing 12-5, but it hasn't yet been looked at in detail. In principle, it is a simple method—using the file name, just create a `FileOutputStream` and write the content of the text area into it, overwriting whatever was in the file before. The interesting aspect of this method is what happens if the file cannot be opened for writing (because, as noted above, it has now been made read-only to us) or if, for some reason, an error occurs while writing, having successfully opened it. Both of these are notified to us as exceptions. To preserve the simplicity of this example, no attempt is made at complicated error recovery (for example, to be safe you would probably write the new data to a separate file first and then switch the two files around, removing the original data only when you knew you had a safe copy under the new name). The point of interest here is how to notify the user of the problem.

Previously in this application, when there has been a problem, `JOptionPane` has been used to create a dialog and display it over the main window. Those problems were not related to one particular internal frame. In a case like this where the error concerns just one frame, you can use one of a set of `JOptionPane` methods that creates a modal dialog as an internal frame instead of as a separate dialog and places it in the modal layer of the layered pane or desktop. Here are the `JOptionPane` methods that create internal frames:

```
public static void showInternalMessageDialog
            (Component parentComponent, Object message);
public static void showInternalMessageDialog
            (Component parentComponent, Object message,
            String title, int messageType);
public static void showInternalMessageDialog
            (Component parentComponent, Object message,
            String title, int messageType, Icon icon);
```

```
public static int showInternalConfirmDialog(Component parentComponent,
        Object message);
public static int showInternalConfirmDialog(Component parentComponent,
        Object message, String title, int optionType);
public static int showInternalConfirmDialog(Component parentComponent,
        Object message, String title, int optionType,
        int messageType);
public static int showInternalConfirmDialog(Component parentComponent,
        Object message, String title, int optionType,
        int messageType, Icon icon);
public static int showInternalOptionDialog(Component parentComponent,
        Object message, String title, int optionType,
        int messageType, Icon icon, Object options[],
        Object initialValue);
public static String showInternalInputDialog(Component parentComponent,
        Object message);
public static String showInternalInputDialog(Component parentComponent,
        Object message, String title, int messageType);
public static Object showInternalInputDialog(Component parentComponent,
        Object message, String title, int messageType,
        Icon icon, Object selectionValues[],
        Object initialSelectionValue);
```

Apart from the fact that they create internal frames instead of dialogs, these methods are the same as the similarly-named ones that we saw in Chapter 7. In the saveFile method, these methods are used to create and show two internal message dialogs to display error messages.

Closing an Internal Frame

There are two ways to close an internal frame in this application—using the close button (or system menu) on the caption bar, or using the Close item of the File menu on the menu bar. The menu item has an Action associated with it, whose definition is shown in Listing 12-9.

Listing 12-9   The Close action

```
class CloseAction extends AbstractAction {
  CloseAction(JInternalFrame jif) {
    super("Close Window");
    this.jif = jif;
  }

  public void actionPerformed(ActionEvent evt) {
    try {
```

```
            jif.setClosed(true);
        } catch (Throwable t) {
        }
    }

    JInternalFrame jif;
}
```

At the time that the action is created, a reference to the internal frame is saved. When the action is triggered from the menu, this reference is used to call the internal frame's `setClosed` method with argument true. Similarly, as you know, if the user tries to close the frame using the caption bar, the caption bar's UI class will just call `setClosed` itself. What follows applies equally to both cases.

As you saw earlier, calling `setClosed` for an internal frame generates a vetoable change event for `IS_CLOSED_PROPERTY`. If this doesn't cause a `PropertyVetoException`, the close is going to be allowed to proceed and a property change event for the same property will be broadcast and caught by the internal frame's UI class, which arranges for the desktop manager to actually close the frame. However, the frame must not be directly closed if the text field content has been modified and its content has not been written back to the file. The only way to stop this happening is to register a vetoable change listener, which was done during the creation of the internal frame (see Listing 12-6 again). The implementation of the listener method is shown in Listing 12-10.

Core Note

As you have already seen, internal frames also generate
`InternalFrameEvent`*s when they close. Using those events would be another way to handle frame closure.*

Listing 12-10   Handling attempted closure of internal frames

```
public void vetoableChange(PropertyChangeEvent evt)
            throws PropertyVetoException {
    JInternalFrame jif = (JInternalFrame)evt.getSource();
    String name = evt.getPropertyName();
    Object value = evt.getNewValue();
    if (name.equals(JInternalFrame.IS_CLOSED_PROPERTY)
        && (Boolean)value == Boolean.TRUE) {
        FileHolder h = (FileHolder)windowTable.get(jif);
        if (h.isChanged() == true) {
            int result = JOptionPane.showInternalConfirmDialog(jif,
```

continued

```
                "Do you want to save changes to " + h.fileName + "?");
        if (result == JOptionPane.CANCEL_OPTION) {
           throw new PropertyVetoException("Cancelled by user", evt);
        }

        try {
           h.saveFile();
        } catch (Throwable t) {
           result = JOptionPane.showInternalConfirmDialog(jif,
               "Save failed - close anyway?" + h.fileName);
           if (result != JOptionPane.YES_OPTION) {
              throw new PropertyVetoException("Cancelled by user", evt);
           }
        }
      }
   }
}
```

The first step is verify that an internal frame is being closed by checking the property name and the proposed new value. If this is the case, then the internal frame's reference is obtained from the event source and the windowTable hash table is used to locate the FileHolder for the file in that frame. As you saw earlier, this object records whether the data in the text area has been changed—recall that it has a "changed" state that is set when a DocumentEvent occurs. If the text field has been changed, an internal frame dialog is posted that allows the user to decide whether to save the changes, abandon the changes or cancel the close. Figure 12-16 shows what this looks like.

If the user presses the Cancel button, the close should be aborted, so a PropertyVetoException is thrown with the original event and a message indicating why the close has been canceled (this message is not used in this example, but you are obliged to supply one). If the user presses OK, the data should be saved before closing, so the saveFile method of the FileHolder object is invoked to do this. Here, of course, there is the chance that the write might fail, so exceptions from this method are caught and, if one is received, another dialog is posted, offering the user the option of closing anyway. If the user wants to abort the close and sort out the problem, another PropertyVetoException is thrown.

If the save works, or the user opts to abandon a failed save or not to save the data at all, the event handler will return and the close will proceed. The next thing that will happen is a property change event for IS_CLOSED_PROPERTY. You saw the code that handled this in Listing 12-10. At this point, the frame is going to close and the data has been safely written away (or abandoned). The last thing to do is remove the FileHolder entry from the file and window hash tables.

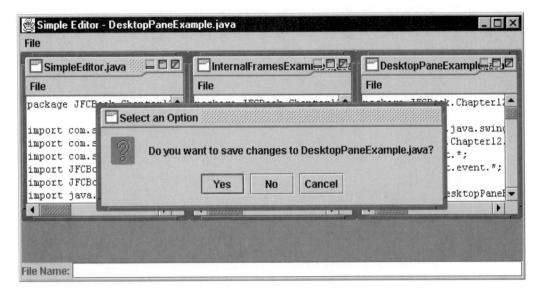

Figure 12-16   Prompting the user to confirm or abandon a close when there is unsaved data.

Summary

This chapter looked at the support that Swing provides for multiple-document applications in the form of internal frames, layered panes, desktop panes, icons and desktop managers.

You first saw the elements of an internal frame and how similar they are to fully-fledged top level frames, then discovered that they can be closed, iconified, resized, maximized and restored to their previous size just like real frames can and that, with the help of the layered pane container, they can be used to create applications that allow windows to overlap and whose relative position can be changed in all three dimensions.

After looking at `JLayeredPane`, we moved on to examine the more powerful `JDesktopPane` which incorporates the idea of a desktop manager that lets you introduce desktop-specific behavior, such as iconifying internal frames, and can be extended to provide customized effects, such as the extended desktop manager that shows frame outlines when they are moved or resized.

Finally, you saw a practical example that demonstrated how multiple-document applications are constructed by building a simple multiple-window editor, in which all of the events and mechanisms that surround internal frames and the desktop manager were shown working together.

THE PLUGGABLE
LOOK-AND-FEEL

Topics in This Chapter

- The LookAndFeel Class
- UIManager and Look-and-Feel Management
- A Customized Button Interface
- Selecting and Changing the Look-and-Feel
- Implementing a New Look-and-Feel

Chapter 13

In the first chapter of this book, you were introduced to the Swing pluggable-look-and-feel mechanism and the Model-View-Controller architecture that enables it, but you only saw enough to allow you to select from the look-and-feels available and to understand how some of the more complex components, such as the text components, trees and tables, separate their data from their visual representation. In this chapter, you'll get a more in-depth look at the classes that manage the look-and-feel of the application.

In reality, you have been making use of the classes that are presented in this chapter all through this book, but most of what you're going to see here is so well-hidden that, unless you are going to create highly-customized components or a whole new look-and-feel, you don't need to know that much about it, because the default behavior is good enough in most cases.

This chapter starts by looking at the three basic pieces of the pluggable look-and-feel mechanism—the `UIManager`, `UIDefaults` and `LookAndFeel` classes and shows how they are used to create the complete look-and-feel implementations that are supplied with Swing. We then move on to show you how to adapt an existing look-and-feel to suit special needs and demonstrate the techniques available by implementing and using a new user interface for buttons. Finally, you'll see what you must provide in order to build a complete new look-and-feel package and how to leverage an existing look-and-feel to minimize your development work.

The Look-and-Feel and the UIManager

This book shows screen shots of applications that use several of the standard Swing look-and-feel packages. In Chapter 1, "Introduction to Java Foundation Classes," you saw how to use the `swing.properties` file to select the default look-and-feel for an application and how changing this setting affected the appearance of the components in the user interface. But what exactly makes up a look-and-feel and how does selecting a particular one cause the application's appearance to change? To answer these questions, we'll look first at what is in a particular look-and-feel, then at how these pieces are used by the `UIManager` class to select the correct appearance for a component.

What Is a Look-and-Feel?

In Swing, a look-and-feel is supplied as a package. Usually, a look-and-feel package will contain a UI class for every Swing component that needs one and a class derived from `LookAndFeel` that provides global information for its particular look-and-feel. Given the number of Swing components, it might seem that this means that a lot of work is required to create a new look-and-feel and, if you really want to fundamentally change the appearance of all of the Swing components, you would be right. However, if you are happy to use a standard look-and-feel but you want to make changes to a particular component or a small number of components, it is possible to make use of the classes in the look-and-feel that you are modifying and so avoid rewriting them all.

Extending an existing look-and-feel is, of course, much simpler than creating a completely new one, so much so that Swing provides a *basic* look-and-feel (`com.sun.java.swing.plaf.basic`) that has fully-functioning implementations of a UI class for every component. This look-and-feel is not used directly in applications (and, in fact, it can't be because its `LookAndFeel` class, `BasicLookAndFeel`, is abstract), but it is used as the basis for all of the other standard Swing look-and-feel packages and use will be made of it to generate our own UI classes in this chapter. The classes that make up the basic look-and-feel package are shown in Table 13-1.

Table 13-1   The Basic Look-and-Feel Package

BasicLookAndFeel	BasicButtonUI	BasicCheckBoxUI
BasicCheckBoxMenuItemUI	BasicColorChooserUI	BasicComboBoxUI
BasicDesktopIconUI	BasicDesktopPaneUI	BasicDirectoryPaneUI
BasicEditorPaneUI	BasicFileChooserUI	BasicInternalFrameUI
BasicLabelUI	BasicListUI	BasicMenuUI

BasicMenuBarUI	BasicMenuItemUI	BasicOptionPaneUI
BasicPasswordFieldUI	BasicPopupMenuUI	BasicProgressBarUI
BasicRadioButtonUI	BasicRadioButtonMenuItemUI	BasicScrollBarUI
BasicScrollPaneUI	BasicSeparatorUI	BasicSliderUI
BasicSpinnerUI	BasicSplitPaneUI	BasicStandardDialogUI
BasicTabbedPaneUI	BasicTableUI	BasicTableHeaderUI
BasicTextAreaUI	BasicTextFieldUI	BasicTextPaneUI
BasicToggleButtonUI	BasicToolBarUI	BasicToolTipUI
BasicTreeUI	AbstractTreeUI	AbstractOptionPaneUI
BasicArrowButton	BasicBorderFactory	BasicButtonBorder
BasicButtonListener	BasicComboBoxEditor	BasicComboBoxRenderer
BasicFieldBorder	BasicGraphicsUtils	BasicInternalFrameTitlePane
BasicLargeTreeModelNode	BasicListCellRenderer	BasicMarginBorder
BasicMenuBarBorder	BasicMenuMouseListener	BasicMenuMouseMotionListener
BasicMenuUtilities	BasicSplitPaneDivider	BasicTextUI
BasicTreeCellEditor	BasicTreeCellEditorContainer	BasicTreeCellRenderer
BasicVisibleTreeNode	LargeTreeModelNode	Spinner
StringSpinner	VisibleTreeNode	

As you can see, every class begins with the name of the look-and-feel itself (in this case `Basic`) and almost all of them end with `UI`. This is actually just a naming convention—the specifics of this are not enforced anywhere, so if you create your own look-and-feel package you are not bound to do the same. But it is recommended that you do, for the sake of clarity.

The classes that end in `UI` are the ones that provide the user interfaces for the Swing components. The methods that must be provided by these classes are, of course, well-defined. You'll see later how to decide what you need to implement to create a UI class for a given component user interface. Some look-and-feel packages also include utility classes that are used within the UI implementations. The basic look-and-feel, for example, has several helper classes that are available for use by all look-and-feels.

Real look-and-feel packages are created by extending the basic look-and-feel. In many cases, a UI class from the basic look-and-feel will be used directly within another look-and-feel. Only where the appearance of the component needs to change in ways that are not related to color and font will a look-and-feel create a UI class of its own. So that you can see the scope of a look-and-feel, Table 13-2 lists the UI classes (excluding helper classes) that make up the Metal look-and-feel package, `com.sun.java.swing.plaf.metal`.

Table 13-2 UI classes in the Metal look-and-feel		
MetalButtonUI	MetalCheckBoxUI	MetalComboBoxUI
MetalDesktopIconUI	MetalInternalFrameUI	MetalLabelUI
MetalProgressBarUI	MetalRadioButtonUI	MetalScrollBarUI
MetalScrollPaneUI	MetalSeparatorUI	MetalSliderUI
MetalTabbedPaneUI	MetalToggleButtonUI	MetalToolBarUI
MetalToolTipUI	MetalTreeUI	

The basic look-and-feel package is much larger than any real look-and-feel and it contains almost as many utility classes as UI classes. You've already seen some of these utility classes in this book—for example, `BasicTreeCellRenderer` was used in Chapter 10, "The Tree Control." This class, along with many of the others in this package, is used directly by the Metal look-and-feel package and by the other look-and-feels.

All of the look-and-feel packages have a class derived from the abstract class `LookAndFeel`. In fact, all of the Swing look-and-feel packages base theirs on `BasicLookAndFeel`, which is itself abstract. This class allows the `UIManager` to use the look-and-feel in such a way that neither it, nor any of the Swing components, need to know specific details of its implementation. Before looking at what the look-and-feel class provides, you need to understand the job of `UIManager`.

The UIManager Class

At any time, an application will have only one look-and-feel selected. Whenever a new component is created, it must attach to itself the corresponding UI class as implemented by the selected look-and-feel and it will need to initialize itself with the color scheme, fonts and so on that are appropriate to that look-and-feel. Because it is undesirable to make the components themselves directly aware of which look-and-feel packages are available, it is not a good idea to hard-code the UI class names or color information into them, even on a per look-and-feel basis. Instead, Swing provides the `com.sun.java.swing.UIManager` class, whose job is to know which look-and-feel is currently selected and to provide the means for components to get look-and-feel-dependent information in a look-and-feel-independent way. The public methods of the `UIManager` class are listed here; you'll find descriptions of most of these methods throughout this chapter.

```
public static LookAndFeel getLookAndFeel();

public static void setLookAndFeel(LookAndFeel lnf);

public static void setLookAndFeel(String className);
```

```
public static ComponentUI getUI(JComponent comp);

public static LookAndFeel[] getAuxiliaryLookAndFeels();

public static UIDefaults getDefaults();

public static Font getFont(Object key);

public static Color getColor(Object key);

public static Icon getIcon(Object key);

public static Border getBorder(Object key);

public static String getString(Object key);

public static Object get(Object key);

public static Object put(Object key, Object value);

public static String getCrossPlatformLookAndFeelClassName();

public static UIManager.LookAndFeelInfo[] getInstalledLookAndFeels();

public static UIDefaults getLookAndFeelDefaults();

public static String getSystemLookAndFeelClassName();

public static void installLookAndFeel(String name, String className);

public static void installLookAndFeel(UIManager.LookAndFeelInfo info);

public static void setInstalledLookAndFeels(UIManager.
          LookAndFeelInfo infos[]) throws SecurityException;

public static synchronized void
          addPropertyChangeListener(PropertyChangeListener l);

public static synchronized void
          removePropertyChangeListener(PropertyChangeListener l);
```

When the first Swing component is created, it will call one of the UIManager "get" methods that access resources from the current look-and-feel; almost certainly, the first UIManager method to be called will be getUI, which locates the UI class for a given component. If this is called when there is no current look-and-feel, it causes UIManager to initialize itself by reading the swing.properties file. In Chapter 1, you saw the format of this file and some of the lines that it can contain. As noted then, this file just holds properties that are loaded into a `Properties` object. Each line, with the exception of comments, has the form:

```
propertyName = propertyValue
```

The set of property names is actually very small and, because of the implementation of `UIManager`, the mechanism is unfortunately not extensible—you can't add properties of your own. The most important property names and their meanings are shown in Table 13-3.

Table 13-3   The swing.properties File

Property Name	Description
`swing.defaultlaf`	Class name of the look-and-feel to be installed when the application starts.
`swing.installedlafs`	A comma-separated list of install look-and-feels
`swing.auxiliarylaf`	A comma-separated list of look-and-feels that can be used with the Multiplexing look-and-feel.
`swing.multiplexinglaf`	The class name of the multiplexing look-and-feel. Defaults to `com.sun.java.swing.plaf.multi.MultiLookAndFeel`.

The `swing.auxiliarylaf` and `swing.multiplexinglaf` properties are used only in conjunction with the multiplexing look-and-feel, which you'll see later in this chapter. The `swing.defaultlaf` property is the one that determines which look-and-feel will be installed when the application starts. The value of this property must be the name of a class that is derived from `LookAndFeel`. To use the Metal look-and-feel, this would be `com.sun.java.swing.plaf.metal.MetalLookAndFeel`, for Windows it would be `com.sun.java.swing.windows.WindowsLookAndFeel` and for Motif it would be `com.sun.java.swing.motif.MotifLookAndFeel`. If you don't have a `swing.properties` file, or the file doesn't contain a valid definition of `swing.defaultlaf`, then `UIManager` makes the Metal look-and-feel the default look-and-feel for the application.

No matter how the initial look-and-feel class is determined, it is made the current look-and-feel by calling the `setLookAndFeel` method. As you can see from the list of `UIManager` methods shown earlier, there are actually two variants of this method—you can supply either a `Class` object or a class name in the form of a `String`. If you choose the latter, the class name is first converted to a `Class` object using the `Class.forName()` method, which may result in an exception if the class can't be found or if it isn't derived from `LookAndFeel`. If, for example, you want your application to use the native platform look-and-feel instead of the Metal look-and-feel, you should use the following code sequence before creating any Swing components or calling any other UIManager methods:

```
try {

UIManager.setLookAndFeel(UIManager.getSystemLookAndFeelClassName());
} catch (UnsupportedLookAndFeelException e) {
    // Not allowed on this platform
} catch (ClassNotFoundException e) {
    // Can't find the class
} catch (InstantiationException e) {
    // Unable to instantiate the class
} catch (IllegalAccessException e) {
    // Class not accessible
}
```

UIManager provides the getCrossPlatformLookAndFeelClassName and getSystemLookAndFeelClassName methods to allow you to find out the name of the default look-and-feel and the native look-and-feel for your platform. The first method, in Swing 1.0, will always return the class name of the Metal look-and-feel. The second, which is used in the code extract above, returns the Windows look-and-feel on a Windows system, the Motif look-and-feel on Solaris and the Metal look-and-feel on any other platform.

The current look-and-feel is actually a bound property of the UIManager class, so when it is changed a PropertyChangeEvent for property name "lookAndFeel" is sent to all registered PropertyChangeListeners. You can register a listener for these events using the addPropertyChangeListener method and later in this chapter you'll see how to make use of this event to make minor changes that affect the look-and-feel and continue to work even if the look-and-feel is switched while the application is running.

Note that, primarily for licensing reasons, there are restrictions that prevent some look-and-feel implementations being used outside of their native platforms. This means that, for example, the Windows look-and-feel cannot be used on the Solaris or Macintosh platforms.

Because of this, UIManager uses a look-and-feel's isSupportedLookAndFeel method (see the description of the LookAndFeel class below) to determine whether it can be used on the current platform. If this method returns false, setLookAndFeel throws an UnsupportedLookAndFeelException.

When a look-and-feel class becomes the currently-selected look-and-feel, its initialize method is called to give it the opportunity to perform any necessary set up. If there is already a look-and-feel installed which is being replaced, its uninitialize method will be called before this happens. Because these methods are called whenever a change of look-and-feel occurs, the initialize method can be called more than once for a particular look-and-feel class. If you are going to create your own look-and-feel implementation and your `initialize` method contains code that should only be executed once, you must provide your own means of ensuring this. Also note that calling `setLookAndFeel` to reinstall the currently selected look-and-feel is not treated specially—the `uninitialize` method will still be called, followed by the `initialize` method. This makes it possible for a look-and-feel class to be reselected with different defaults, provided that it can obtain those defaults from somewhere outside the application, of course. None of the standard look-and-feels supports this.

Apart from organizing the initial selection of the look-and-feel and controlling subsequent changes of it, the major role played by `UIManager` is as a convenient way to access information relating to the current look-and-feel. Components (and other software) can conveniently access font, color, border and other settings from the look-and-feel by using the `UIManager get` methods, most of which extract information from the current `UIDefaults` object. The exceptions to this are `getUI` and `getAuxiliaryLookAndFeels`, both of which you'll see later in this chapter.

Installed Look-and-Feels

As you'll see later in this chapter, it is sometimes useful for an application to know exactly which look-and-feels are installed on the system that it is running on. `UIManager` provides a simple API to make this information available in the form of the static `getInstalledLookAndFeels` method and an inner class called `UIManager.LookAndFeelInfo`. The `LookAndFeelInfo` class has the following definition:

```
public static class LookAndFeelInfo {
  public static LookAndFeelInfo(String name, String className);
  public String getName();
  public String getClassName();
  public String toString();
}
```

When you call `getInstalledLookAndFeels`, you get back an array of `LookAndFeelInfo` objects, one for each installed look-and-feel. A look-and-feel is considered to be installed if, and only if, it has an entry in the `swing.installed-lafs` key in `swing.properties`.

When `UIManager` initializes itself, it reads the `swing.installedlafs` key from `swing.properties` and attempts to build a `LookAndFeelInfo` object for each look-and-feel class in this key. To do this, however, it needs to be able to find two other keys for each look-and-feel that give the official name of the look-and-feel and its `LookAndFeel` class name. The names of these keys begin with the string `swing.installedlaf`, followed by the name of the look-and-feel as given in `swing.installedlafs`, followed by the string `name` or `class`. For example, if your system has Metal, Motif and Windows look-and-feels installed, you should have the following entries in your `swing.properties` file:

```
swing.installedlafs=metal,motif,windows

swing.installedlaf.metal.name=Metal
swing.installedlaf.metal.class=
            com.sun.java.swing.plaf.metal.MetalLookAndFeel

swing.installedlaf.motif.name=CDE/Motif
swing.installedlaf.motif.class=
            com.sun.java.swing.plaf.motif.MotifLookAndFeel

swing.installedlaf.windows.name=Windows
swing.installedlaf.windows.class=
            com.sun.java.swing.plaf.windows.WindowsLookAndFeel
```

You can see the information that is returned by `getInstalledLookAndFeels` by using the command:

```
java JFCBook.Chapter13.InstalledLAFExample
```

The code for this example is extremely simple and is shown in Listing 13-1.

Listing 13-1   Getting information about the installed look-and-feels

```
package JFCBook.Chapter13;

import com.sun.java.swing.*;

public class InstalledLAFExample {
  public static void main(String[] args) {
    UIManager.LookAndFeelInfo[] lfInfo =
            UIManager.getInstalledLookAndFeels();

    System.out.println("Installed look-and-feels are:");
    for (int i = 0; i < lfInfo.length; i++) {
      System.out.println("\tName: " + lfInfo[i].getName() +
                ", Class: " + lfInfo[i].getClassName());
    }
    System.exit(0);
  }
}
```

The output from this on my system is:

```
Installed look-and-feels are:
  Name: Metal, Class: com.sun.java.swing.plaf.metal.MetalLookAndFeel
  Name: CDE/Motif, Class: com.sun.java.swing.plaf.motif.MotifLookAndFeel
  Name: Windows, Class: com.sun.java.swing.plaf.windows.WindowsLookAndFeel
```

If you don't get any output, or if some entries are missing, then your `swing.properties` file has some missing or incorrectly formatted entries. Swing 1.0 does not create a `swing.properties` file when it is installed—it is your responsibility to do this. Try adding the entries shown earlier in this section and rerunning this example. You will need a properly constructed `swing.properties` file to run some of the examples that you'll see towards the end of this chapter.

Core Note

If you don't have a `swing.installedlafs` *key in your* `swing.properties` *file, you will still get the output just shown, because* `UIManager` *has hard-coded defaults that provide exactly the information shown here. However, if you add a* `swing.installedlafs` *key (perhaps because you have a third-party look-and-feel installed), the defaults are discarded and you must provide all of the required keys for each look-and-feel.*

There are a few other methods connected with managing the set of installed look-and-feels that are used by `UIManager` itself during its initialization. You are unlikely to need to use them yourself; they are mentioned here for the sake of completeness. You'll find the definitions of these methods in the description of `UIManager` that you saw earlier.

`UIManager` maintains an array of installed look-and-feels, which is used to provide the information returned by `getInstalledLookAndFeels`. You can make a new entry in this array using one of the the two variants of `installLookAndFeel`. If you provide a name and a class name, a suitable `LookAndFeelInfo` object is created and added to the look-and-feel list. Alternatively, you can create your own `LookAndFeelInfo` object and supply that. You can also replace the entire array of installed look-and-feels with your own by using the `setInstalledLookAndFeels` method.

The UIDefaults Class

There is a great deal of information that components need that cannot be hard-coded into them because of its look-and-feel dependent nature. Obvious examples of this are:

- The UI class to use for each component.
- The font used to display text in various components.
- Components' foreground and background colors.
- Colors used for standard parts of the user interface (caption bars etc).

Some of this information could be coded directly into component UI classes rather than into the components themselves, but even that is not possible for some things—the most obvious of them being the name of the UI class itself. What is needed is a repository in which all of this information can be stored so that it can be retrieved when necessary. This repository is provided by the UIDefaults class.

UIDefaults is actually just a subclass of Hashtable, to which convenience methods have been added to provide type-safe access to certain types of information. Since the content of the UIDefaults table depends on the look-and-feel, there is one copy of it for each look-and-feel. The UIManager requests a particular look-and-feel's specific UIDefaults table by calling its getDefaults method just after its initialize method has been invoked; UIManager saves this reference and uses it whenever its own callers request information that must be obtained from the current look-and-feel. You can get a reference to the current UIDefaults table using the UIManager getDefaults method. Because UIManager provides convenience methods to access information for the current look-and-feel, you don't usually need to directly access the look-and-feel class, so instead of getting the default font for the text displayed by buttons like this:

```
UIManager.getLookAndFeel().getDefaults().getFont("Button.font");
```

you can use the more succinct

```
UIManager.getFont("Button.font");
```

Core Note

You'll see later that there are circumstances under which these two lines of code produce different results.

The following list shows the methods provided by UIDefaults in addition to those of its Hashtable superclass.

```
public synchronized Object get(Object key);

public synchronized put(Object key, Object value);

public synchronized void putDefaults(Object[] keyValues);

public Font getFont(Object key);

public Color getColor(Object key);

public Icon getIcon(Object key);

public Border getBorder(Object key);
```

```
public String getString(Object key);

public ComponentUI getUI(JComponent comp);

public Class getUIClass(String uiClassID);

public synchronized void
            addPropertyChangeListener(PropertyChangeListener l);

public synchronized void
            removePropertyChangeListener(PropertyChangeListener l);
```

Since UIDefaults is a Hashtable, it can store arbitrary objects under arbitrary keys. In practice, all of the keys are strings and they are, of course, all well-known values like "Button.font" that are descriptive of the meaning of the information that they store. Because of this, you can access the table using the usual get and put methods. If you use get, you must cast the returned object to the required type before you use it, for example:

```
UIDefaults defaults = UIManager.getDefaults();
Font buttonFont = (Font)defaults.get("Button.font");
```

The Hashtable put method is overloaded by UIDefaults to generate a PropertyChangeEvent with the key as the property name after the new value has been stored in the table. As usual, you can register to receive these events using the addPropertyChangeListener method; this can be useful if you want to react to a change in the value of some property as soon as that change happens. Components are not automatically informed of changes to properties that they are using so, for example, if a new value were installed for the Button.font property, existing buttons would not change their appearance, but newly-created ones would use the new font. Supplying null as the value of a property removes it from the UIDefaults table and generates a PropertyChangeEvent in which the new value is null.

The putDefaults method allows you to install or change several entries in the table without generating an event for each of them. Instead, a single PropertyChangeEvent with property name "UIDefaults" and old and new values both set to null is broadcast to all PropertyChangeListeners. The argument supplied to putDefaults is an array in which the key and value entries alternate. For example, to change the default button font and the default menu bar font together, you would do this:

```
UIDefaults defaults = UIManager.getDefaults();
Object[] newDefaults = new Object[] {
   "Button.font", new FontUIResource("Dialog", Font.BOLD, 12),
   "MenuBar.font", new FontUIResource("Dialog", Font.BOLD, 12)
};
defaults.putDefaults(newDefaults);
```

Notice that this example doesn't create `Font` objects—instead it uses `FontUIResource`. `FontUIResource` and the other similar classes used by `UIDefaults` will be described, along the reason for their existence, later in this chapter.

The `getFont`, `getColor`, `getIcon`, `getBorder` and `getString` methods are all wrappers around `get` that use the supplied key to access information from the table. If the object returned is of the type requested, it is cast to the appropriate type and returned to the caller. If the information does not exist or it is of the wrong type, then `null` is returned. This enables you to access the `UIDefaults` table in a more type-safe manner and treat an error of type in the same way as lack of information without having to catch a `ClassCastException`. This usually makes your code easier to write, because the error recovery for both cases is usually going to be the same—either write an error message or substitute a hard-coded default. All of these methods have corresponding convenience methods in `UIManager` that make them very simple to use, as you saw earlier.

Finally, the `getUI` method provides the mechanism for a component to find its UI class, as implemented by the active look-and-feel. Although it is probably the most important method in the `UIDefaults` class, further discussion of it and the related `getUIClass` method will be postponed until we look more closely at how to create a new UI class in the section titled "Changing Component Look-and-Feel."

Contents of the UIDefaults Table

Now that you've seen the methods of the `UIDefaults` class, let's look at some of the information that the look-and-feel keeps in it. Since it is only a `Hashtable` (with, as you'll see, a few special properties), you can find all the entries by getting an enumeration of its keys and asking for all of the associated values. If you did this, you would get rather a long list—there are typically over 300 entries! To make it easier to examine this table, there is a simple program on the CD-ROM that allows you to scan for information by giving the first part of the key or by specifying the type of the information that you're looking for. To run this program, use one of the following two commands:

```
java ShowDefaults prefix prefixString
java ShowDefaults type typeName
```

Use the first form to look for keys which begin with `prefixString`; case is ignored when comparing the value to the key. If you want to find all resources connected with buttons, for example, you would use the command:

```
java JFCBook.Chapter13.ShowDefaults prefix button
```

You get the following results from this command if you are using the Metal look-and-feel, where the string `com.sun.java.swing.plaf` has been replaced by ellipsis for brevity:

```
Button.focus : [...].ColorUIResource[r=153,g=153,b=204]
Button.foreground : [...].ColorUIResource[r=0,g=0,b=0]
Button.disabled : [...].ColorUIResource[r=204,g=204,b=204]
Button.border : [...].BorderUIResource@1cd614
Button.background : [...].ColorUIResource[r=204,g=204,b=204]
Button.disabledText : [...].ColorUIResource[r=153,g=153,b=153]
ButtonUI : [...].metal.MetalButtonUI
Button.font : [...].FontUIResource
              [family=Dialog,name=Dialog,style=bold,size=12]
Button.pressed : [...].ColorUIResource[r=153,g=153,b=153]
```

To examine the UIDefaults for a particular look-and-feel, make it the default
in the swing.properties file and run the ShowDefaults command again.

The second form of this command allows you to look for resources of certain types,
identified by the typeName parameter, which must be one of font, color,
insets, dimension, border and icon, where case *is* important. The following
command finds all border resources in the UIDefaults table:

```
java JFCBook.Chapter13.ShowDefaults type border
```

For the Metal look-and-feel, this produces the following result:

```
TextArea.border : [...].BorderUIResource@1cd61f
OptionPane.border : [...].BorderUIResource@1cd905
EditorPane.border : [...].BorderUIResource@1cd61f
Button.border : [...].BorderUIResource@1cd612
MenuBar.border : [...].BorderUIResource@1cd651
Menu.border : [...].BorderUIResource@1cd649
ColorChooser.selectedColorBorder : [...].BorderUIResource@1cd9b7
TitledBorder.border : [...].BorderUIResource@1cd65d
RadioButton.border : [...].BorderUIResource@1cda4c
ToolBar.border : [...].BorderUIResource@1cd645
ToggleButton.border : [...].BorderUIResource@1cd60d
PopupMenu.border : [...].BorderUIResource@1cd64d
ScrollPane.border : [...].BorderUIResource@1cd616
MenuItem.border : [...].BorderUIResource@1cd649
Table.scrollPaneBorder : [...].BorderUIResource@1cd616
Table.focusCellHighlightBorder : [...].BorderUIResource@1cd7aa
List.focusCellHighlightBorder : [...].BorderUIResource@1cd7aa
PasswordField.border : [...].BorderUIResource@1cd61f
TextPane.border : [...].BorderUIResource@1cd61f
InternalFrame.border : [...].BorderUIResource@1cd655
TextField.border : [...].BorderUIResource@1cd61f
DesktopIcon.border : [...].BorderUIResource@1cd65b
```

Core Note

The ability to search for entries of specific types is provided just as a convenience. Nothing in Swing ever searches the UIDefaults *table in this way—components always look for defaults using the key field.*

When showing entries of a particular type, the name of each property is shown first, followed by the value of the object that it is associated with, although this doesn't really show you much more than the name of the class of the object. In the case just shown, you can see that every border has a value that is an instance of the class BorderUIResource, whereas you might have expected it to be of type Border. If you ask for all color resources, you get a similar result, of which the following is an extract:

```
EditorPane.selectionBackground : […].ColorUIResource[r=192,g=192,b=192]
TextField.selectionBackground : […].ColorUIResource[r=204,g=204,b=255]
TableHeader.background : […].ColorUIResource[r=204,g=204,b=204]
PasswordField.selectionForeground : […].ColorUIResource[r=0,g=0,b=0]
TextField.selectionForeground : […].ColorUIResource[r=0,g=0,b=0]
inactiveCaptionText : […].ColorUIResource[r=0,g=0,b=0]
```

Instead of seeing Color objects, you get objects of type ColorUIResource. There are several of these special resource classes:

BorderUIResource

ColorUIResource

DimensionUIResource

FontUIResource

IconUIResource

InsetsUIResource

Each of these classes has two things in common:

- They all implement the UIResource interface.
- Each of them extends the class or implements the interface with which they are associated.

The UIResource interface is actually just a marker—it doesn't contain any methods. The reason for using objects that implement UIResource is to make it easy for the code that installs component resources to decide whether or not the programmer has overridden the default and installed a specific value that should not subsequently be replaced. To see how this works, consider what happens when a button is created. As you'll see later, when the button's UI object is installed, it initializes the button with default foreground and background colors (given by the UIDefaults entries with keys "Button.foreground" and "Button.background," as you can see from the list of button resources shown earlier). These colors will be of type ColorUIResource, which extends Color, so they can be passed directly to the Component setForeground and setBackground methods.

Now suppose that your application allows the user to switch the look-and-feel while the application is running. As part of this switch, the UI object of every user interface component will be removed and replaced by one from the new look-and-feel. The new look-and-feel will have its own default foreground and background colors for buttons, which would get installed automatically by the same means as the initial button colors. But suppose that the program has explicitly set its own colors for the button's foreground and/or background. While it is acceptable to change one default color for another, it probably would not be good to replace colors specifically installed by the application with defaults, because this could destroy the application's carefully chosen color scheme.

To avoid this, all that the new look-and-feel needs to do is check whether the current foreground and background colors are instances of ColorUIResource (or even just of type UIResource) and, if they are, it knows that they were installed by the previous look-and-feel and can be replaced by new defaults. If the user has installed replacement colors, they will be of type Color and so will not be replaced. This same mechanism is used to protect specifically-installed fonts, borders, icons, insets and dimensions. As you'll see later, the task of installing some of these resources is encapsulated in convenience methods of the LookAndFeel class, which implement the mechanism that has just been discussed You'll see an example of this when we implement our own UI class for buttons.

More on UIManager and UIDefaults

Up to this point, the description of UIDefaults and UIManager and how they are related has been simplified to make the basic points clear. Each look-and-feel creates its own UIDefaults table when it becomes the selected look-and-feel and you can gain access to it via the UIManager getDefaults method. So far, it has been implied that the getDefaults method returns you a reference to the actual UIDefaults table of the selected look-and-feel. Actually, this is not the case—in fact, it gives you a reference to a different UIDefaults object of a type called MultiUIDefaults. This class is derived from UIDefaults, so it looks and behaves just like a UIDefaults table, but it can also hold references to two other UIDefaults tables—one for the current look-and-feel and the other containing system defaults that don't change when a look-and-feel switch occurs. This latter table only contains an entry that maps the key FocusManagerClassName to the class name com.sun.java.swing.DefaultFocusManager, which is the default Swing focus manager.

If you use the UIManager getDefaults method or the UIManager get and put methods, you will operate on the MultiUIDefaults object, not on the UIDefaults table of the currently look-and-feel. If, for example, you use the get method to look up the value from its key, MultiUIDefaults first looks to see if it has a local value for that key and returns it if it does. If it doesn't, it looks for the value in the UIDefaults table of the current look-and-feel and then in the system table, returning whatever it finds (or null if it finds nothing).

Now suppose you want to change a default value for the current look-and-feel and call the UIManager put method to do it:

```
UIManager.put("Button.font", new FontUIResource("Dialog", Font.BOLD, 12));
```

What this actually does is to change the value of this key in the MultiUIDefaults table—it does *not* change the current look-and-feel table. When this property is later retrieved using the UIManager get method, MultiUIDefaults will find its own copy and will not go to the look-and-feel for it. This means, of course, that this change is persistent over a change of look-and-feel. Compare this with the following code:

```
UIDefaults defaults =
            UIManager.getLookAndFeel().getDefaults();
defaults.put("Button.font", new FontUIResource("Dialog", Font.BOLD, 12));
```

This causes the current look-and-feel to create a new copy of its UIDefaults table and changes one of its values. This is, of course, a redundant operation because nothing is using this particular copy of the UIDefaults table. Similarly, you *can* read look-and-feel defaults using code like this:

```
UIDefaults defaults = UIManager.getLookAndFeel().getDefaults();
FontUIResource buttonFont = (FontUIResource)defaults.get("Button.font");
```

However, this is expensive, because a new UIDefaults table is created and then discarded. It also will not return the font currently being used for buttons if this has been changed using the UIManager put method.

The LookAndFeel and BasicLookAndFeel Classes

Every look-and-feel package contains a class derived from the Swing class LookAndFeel. As you know, this class is used as the anchor-point for the entire package—you present it to the UIManager when making the look-and-feel active and the UIManager uses it to get the UIDefaults table, which is later used by all of the components to access the rest of the classes and other resources of the current look-and-feel.

The LookAndFeel Class

Despite its importance, LookAndFeel is a very simple class. Its methods are shown below.

```
public abstract String getName();

public abstract String getID()

public abstract String getDescription()

public abstract boolean isNativeLookAndFeel();

public abstract boolean isSupportedLookAndFeel();

public void initialize();

public void uninitialize();

public UIDefaults getDefaults();

public static void installColors
            (JComponent c, String bgName, String fgName);

public static void installColorsAndFont(JComponent c,
            String bgName, String fgName, String fontName);

public static void installBorder(JComponent c,
            String borderName);

public static void uninstallBorder(JComponent c);

public static Object makeIcon(Class baseClass, String fileName);

public String toString();
```

As you can see, many of the methods are abstract, because they can only be implemented in a real look-and-feel package. The strings returned by the getName and getDescription methods are short and long descriptions of the look-and-feel. The string used by getName would typically be used on a menu, as you'll see later in this chapter. In the case of Metal, these return *Metal Look-And-Feel* and *The Metal Look-and-Feel*, respectively. The getID method also returns a short description of the look-and-feel. The intention is that, if a look-and-feel is created from an existing one by changing the appearance of a few components, the getName field should return a unique name to identify the derived look-and-feel, while getID should return the name of the core look-and-feel upon which it was based. The Metal look-and-feel returns the string "Metal" in response to the getID call. You'll see an example of this at the end of the chapter when we look at how to develop a new look-and-feel based on an existing one.

The `isNativeLookAndFeel` method returns true if this is the natural look-and-feel for the platform on which the application is running. The `isSupportedLookAndFeel` method indicates whether the look-and-feel can be used on the current platform and allows licensing restrictions to be implemented. The Windows look-and-feel implements this method by returning the same value as its `isNativeLookAndFeel`, which means that the `UIManager` will only install it as the active look-and-feel on a Windows platform. The Motif look-and-feel, on the other hand, always returns `true`.

The `initialize` and `uninitialize` methods have already been discussed in connection with `UIManager`, and you already know what the `getDefaults` method is used for. Although none of these methods are marked as abstract, they don't have useful implementations in the `LookAndFeel` class itself: The first two do nothing and `getDefaults` returns `null`. In practice, a real look-and-feel package will override `getDefaults` and may implement one or both of the other two, although the Swing look-and-feel packages do not. A more useful implement of the `getDefaults` method is provided in the `BasicLookAndFeel` class, as you'll see shortly.

The `installColors`, `installColorsAndFont` and `installBorder` methods are all static convenience functions that use the `UIDefaults` table to look for the foreground and background colors, font and border for a component and install them using the appropriate `Component` or `JComponent` method (`setForeground`, `setBorder` etc). The programmer supplies the name or names of the properties to look for in the defaults table; for a button, for example, the foreground and background colors would be retrieved using the names "`Button.foreground`" and "`Button.background`" and the font using "`Button.font`," so a typical use of one of these methods would be the following, where it is assumed that `b` is a `JButton`:

```
LookAndFeel.installColorsAndFont(b, "Button.foreground",
        "Button.background", "Button.font");
```

As you can see, there is no explicit mention of the particular look-and-feel to be used to supply the defaults—this method works by using the currently selected look-and-feel, so it can be used in code that needs to be independent of the look-and-feel. It is also typically used in component UI classes—you'll see an example of this later in this chapter. These methods all check before installing any resources that what they are about to replace is either `null` or a `UIResource`, to avoid replacing an explicit color, font or border selection with a default. Because of the need to make this check, the `uninstallBorder` method is not quite as trivial as you might have thought—instead of simply being a shorthand for `setBorder(null)`, it first checks whether the installed border is a `UIResource` before replacing it with `null`.

Lazy Values

The last LookAndFeel method, makeIcon, is an interesting one and to understand its purpose you need to know more about the UIDefaults table. So far, you know that this table is based around a Hashtable and contains mappings from keys to the default values associated with those keys. Because of the nature of a Hashtable, both the key and the associated value have to be stored in the table before they can be retrieved. While this is not an issue for simple objects like colors and fonts, it is not so convenient for things like icons that take up a lot of memory and are time-consuming to load. In the UIDefaults table for the Windows look-and-feel, there are more than a dozen resources that have icons associated with them. If it were necessary to load all of these icons when the Windows look-and-feel is used for the first time, there would be not only a significant waste of memory for those icons that are not going be used by a particular application but also a performance cost due to the time taken to load them.

Instead of loading the resource name and an Icon object into the UIDefaults table, a UIDefaults.LazyValue object is created instead and placed in the table along with the key. UIDefaults.LazyValue is an interface with only one method:

```
public interface LazyValue {
   Object createValue(UIDefaults table);
}
```

The job of the createValue method is to use information from the UIDefaults table that it is associated with and any information stored with the class that it is part of, to construct an object of the type that it represents. This mechanism can be used to store a shorthand form of any kind of object in the defaults table, but it is most commonly used for icons and the LookAndFeel makeIcon method allows you to get an object that implements the LazyValue interface and which can construct an ImageIcon given the means to find the file containing the image to be drawn on it. To see how this works in practice and to demonstrate how to create your own LazyValue shorthand classes for other types of object, let's look at a simple example. Listing 13-2 shows a very basic program that just puts two buttons, each with icons, onto a frame and shows the result. The result of running this program using the command:

```
java JFCBook.Chapter13.LazyValueExample
```

is shown in Figure 13-1.

Listing 13-2   Using LazyValue objects in the UIDefaults table

```
package JFCBook.Chapter13;
import com.sun.java.swing.*;
import java.awt.FlowLayout;
import java.awt.Color;
import JFCBook.Chapter13.LazyColorIcon;

public class LazyValueExample {
   public static void main(String[] args) {
     // Put an image icon in the UIDefaults table
     UIManager.put("Button.okIcon",
         LookAndFeel.makeIcon(LazyValueExample.class,
"images/ok.gif"));

     // Put a LazyColorIcon in the UIDefaults table
     UIManager.put("Button.redIcon",
         new LazyColorIcon(Color.red, 16, 16, 2));

     JFrame f = new JFrame("Lazy Value Example");
     f.getContentPane().setLayout(new FlowLayout());

     JButton button = new JButton("Red icon");
     button.setIcon(UIManager.getIcon("Button.redIcon"));
     f.getContentPane().add(button);

     button = new JButton("OK");
     button.setIcon(UIManager.getIcon("Button.okIcon"));
     f.getContentPane().add(button);
     f.pack();
     f.setVisible(true);
   }
}
```

The first part of the example shows what a look-and-feel class might do to install icon resources.

```
// Put an image icon in the UIDefaults table
UIManager.put("Button.okIcon", LookAndFeel.makeIcon(LazyValueExample.class,
             "images/ok.gif"));
```

Here the makeIcon method is used to get an object that implements the LazyValue interface and which can create an ImageIcon on demand. You don't need to worry about how the class implementing the LazyValue interface is actually implemented—you can just take it on faith that it can create the required Icon when its createValue method is called. For this to be possible, you have to give

Figure 13-1   Icons stored as lazy values.

makeIcon enough information so that the image can be located. Since image files used with components are usually stored near to the class files for the components, makeIcon requires you to specify the image location using a pathname relative to the location of a class. It doesn't actually matter which class this is, as long as the class can be located when the application is running. In this example, we use the class of the example program itself, which is located at JFCBook/Chapter13/LazyValueExample.class, relative to some entry in your CLASSPATH. The parameters given to the makeIcon call in this example require the image to be found at JFCBook/Chapter13/images/ok.gif. When you create a button that needs this icon, all you need to do is invoke the UIManager getIcon method giving the property name under which the LazyValue was installed in the defaults table, in this case "Button.okIcon," and treat the result as a real Icon, which is exactly what it is. As far as the code implementing the user interface is concerned, the UIDefaults table might as well have stored an Icon under the this key and, in fact, there is no way for it to tell that this is not the case.

The key to all of this is the UIDefaults get method, which is used by the getIcon convenience method to access the UIDefaults table. When this method is called to retrieve a value, as it is in the example above to get the button's icon, it presents the key it is given to the Hashtable (remember that UIDefaults is derived from Hashtable) and looks at the object that it gets back. If this object implements the LazyValue interface, it invokes its createValue method and returns the result of this to its caller in place of the object in the Hashtable and also replaces the LazyValue object in the UIDefaults table with the object that it created, for future use.

The other button also has an icon on it, but this time it is a red colored square with a thin black border around it. You can see that this icon was retrieved from the UIDefaults table using the same getIcon method used to get the image on the first button. However, this red square is not an image—it is, in fact, an instance of the ColorFillIcon class that was developed back in Chapter 4. Furthermore, this icon was not stored directly in the UIDefaults table: Instead, it was installed using the following line of code:

```
UIManager.put("Button.redIcon",
              new LazyColorIcon(Color.red, 16, 16, 2));
```

LazyColorIcon is, not surprisingly, a class that implements the LazyValue interface. When it is created, it stores its arguments, which specify the color of the icon, its width, height and the width of the black surrounding border. It also, of course, has a createValue method that manufactures a ColorFillIcon using these stored values. You can see how this class is implemented in Listing 13-3. The advantage of storing the icon in this way, including its color and size, is that the code that uses the icon does not need to know how to get these values and apply them.

Listing 13-3   A LazyValue object to store a ColorFillIcon in the UIDefaults table

```
package JFCBook.Chapter13;

import com.sun.java.swing.*;
import java.awt.Color;
import JFCBook.Chapter4.ColorFillIcon;

public class LazyColorIcon implements UIDefaults.LazyValue {
   public LazyColorIcon(Color color, int width, int height, int borderSize) {
      this.color = color;
      this.width = width;
      this.height = height;
      this.borderSize = borderSize;
   }

   // LazyValue interface implementation
   public Object createValue(UIDefaults defaults) {
      return new ColorFillIcon(color, width, height, borderSize);
   }

   protected Color color;    // Fill color
   protected int width;      // Icon width
   protected int height;     // Icon height
   protected int borderSize;     // Border size
}
```

Active Values

The LazyValue interface, then, allows the programmer of a look-and-feel to store a shorthand in the UIDefaults table that defers creation of an actual object until it is required. There is another type of entry called ActiveValue that is similar to LazyValue, in that it has a createValue method to generate an object on demand. However, whereas the object returned by LazyValue is then stored in the UIDefaults table overwriting the LazyValue object, this doesn't happen with an

ActiveValue—its `createValue` method is invoked *every* time an attempt is made to get its value. This means, of course, that it can potentially return a different object each time it is called. An example of a case in which `ActiveValue` could used would be if you wanted to return a new instance of an object on each occasion. For example, you could create a class that implements this interface that looks like this:

```
class ButtonFactory implements UIDefaults.ActiveValue {
  public Object createValue(UIDefaults defaults) {
    return new JButton("" + count++);
  }
  static int count = 1;
}
```

Now, you can create an entry for this class in the `UIDefaults` table under the key "`Button.factory`:"

```
UIManager.put("Button.factory", new ButtonFactory());
```

This entry will create a new button object each time its value is retrieved from the `UIDefaults` table. For example,

```
JButton button1 = (JButton)UIManager.get("Button.factory");
JButton button2 = (JButton)UIManager.get("Button.factory");
```

creates two `JButton` objects with the labels "1" and "2," respectively.

Active values are used just like this by the Swing look-and-feel packages. Suppose you wanted to get a renderer for a `JComboBox`. You could just create a `BasicComboBoxRenderer` and use that, but if you want to obtain the actual renderer used by the current look-and-feel, you can use code like that shown in the previous example, with the key "`ComboBox.renderer`." This accesses an `ActiveValue` that creates a new instance of whichever class is the default Combo Box renderer for the selected look-and-feel (`MotifComboBoxRenderer` for Motif, `BasicComboBoxRenderer` for Windows):

```
ListCellRenderer renderer =
            (ListCellRenderer)UIManager.get("ComboBox.renderer");
```

BasicLookAndFeel

`LookAndFeel` is the abstract base class from which all look-and-feel classes must be derived. `BasicLookAndFeel` is a slightly more complete, but still abstract, class in the `com.sun.java.swing.plaf.basic` package that contains code common to all of the Swing look-and-feels. When creating a new look-and-feel, you are not obliged to subclass `BasicLookAndFeel`, but you will probably save effort by doing so. `BasicLookAndFeel` implements the abstract `getDefaults` required by `LookAndFeel` and adds the following additional methods:

```
protected void initClassDefaults(UIDefaults defaults);
```

```
protected void initSystemColorDefaults(UIDefaults defaults);

protected void loadSystemColors(UIDefaults defaults,
            String[] systemColors);

protected void initComponentDefaults(UIDefaults defaults);
```

You will notice that these methods are all protected—they are intended to be accessed only by `BasicLookAndFeel` itself and by the real look-and-feel derived from it. In fact, complete implementations of all of these methods, which are biased towards the Windows look-and-feel, are provided in this class. Each method is given a `UIDefaults` table as its argument. The idea is to load information into the `UIDefaults` table and, in fact, three of these methods are invoked by the `BasicLookAndFeel` implementation of `getDefaults`, which creates an empty `UIDefaults` object and then calls them in the following order to populate it:

```
initClassDefaults
```

```
initSystemColorDefaults
```

```
initComponentDefaults
```

The `initClassDefaults` method installs mappings from the UI class identifier to the corresponding UI class name for every component supported by the look-and-feel. For example, buttons always look for their UI class using the key `ButtonUI`; the Metal look-and-feel `initClassDefaults` method would install an entry mapping the key `ButtonUI` to the value `com.sun.java.swing.plaf.metal.MetalButtonUI`, which is the name of the class implementing the UI for buttons in the Metal style. The exact method used by a component to find and install its UI class will be described in "Changing Component Look and Feel" later in this chapter.

The `initSystemColorDefaults` method has the job of installing appropriate values for the system colors that are described by the `java.awt.SystemColor` class. Each color is stored under a key which is the name of the system color from that class, such as "text," "desktop," "activeCaption" and so on. The actual value stored depends on whether the look-and-feel is running on its native platform. If it is, it uses the actual native colors for the platform as currently configured, by using the `java.awt.SystemColor` class to obtain them and installs them in the `UIDefaults` table. If this is not the look-and-feel's natural platform, it installs a hard-coded set of default colors that should represent a particular desktop color scheme from that platform. The choice of which color set to use (i.e. the actual system colors or the default set) is made by the `loadSystemColors` method, which is called by `initSystemColorDefaults` and passed the default color set as its second argument.

Because the process of loading the actual colors is separate from the code that supplies the defaults, you can override `loadSystemColors` to implement a different policy, perhaps choosing to always install the look-and-feel's own colors as supplied by initSystemColorDefaults, instead of using the platform's own colors. At the very minimum, a new look-and-feel would almost certainly override initSystemColorDefaults to supply its own color defaults for the case when it is not the native look-and-feel, and call loadSystemColors to install them when necessary.

Finally, initComponentDefaults is responsible for installing all of the component-specific information, other than the names of the UI classes. This includes font, color and border resources, default renderers, icons and much more. Since there are so many of these resources, there isn't enough room to describe them here. If you are planning to implement your own look-and-feel, you should look at the source code of the BasicLookAndFeel method to get a complete list of these resources.

Changing Component Look-and-Feel

You have now seen all of the classes that are involved in managing the pluggable look-and-feel mechanism. Up to this point, the discussion has been somewhat academic because there has been quite a bit of introductory material to cover. In this section, it is time to start getting practical and look at how you can use what you've seen to change the user interface of a program in various ways, from writing and installing a completely new look-and-feel at one extreme to changing the way that one instance of a particular component looks at the other. To give you something to work with, our first task will be to create a new user interface for the familiar JButton component, in the course of which you'll see in more detail how a UI class interacts with its component and how the UIDefaults mechanism is used to control the component's default appearance.

A New Button User Interface

The first step in implementing a new UI class is, of course, to decide what you want it to do. Buttons are simple objects—about all you can do is press or disable them. Swing manages to make them slightly more interesting than AWT buttons by including icons and a degree of responsiveness to the mouse by allowing you to display a different icon when the mouse is over the button (the "rollover" icon that you saw in Chapter 2) or when the button is disabled. You might think that there is little else you could do to change the way a button looks.

Apart from the text and the icon, a button also has a border and that is where this user interface for the button will be different from the standard one. Usually, the button's border is visible, so that the label appears, in the Metal look-and-feel, with an etched border and level with its surroundings until you press it, when it looks lower than the surrounding area. The user interface that you'll see in this section will make the button look flat and with no etched border, just like a label, under normal circumstances. When the mouse moves over the button or when the button has the focus, the border will appear. The behavior when the button is pressed will be the same as it always is—it will look as if it has been pushed in. When the button is disabled, it won't have a border and it won't respond at all to the mouse or the focus.

Figure 13-2 shows three buttons using the new interface. The button in the center is in the normal state—since it doesn't have the focus and the mouse is not over it, the border is not visible and it looks just like a label. When the button is under the mouse or has the focus, the usual border appears, as is the case with the left button. In this state, it is impossible to tell this user interface apart from the Metal one.

Figure 13-2 Three buttons with a new user interface.

Finally, the right-hand button is disabled and so it also has no border. You can also probably just tell from the gray-scale reproduction that the text and the icon have been grayed-out. In this respect, the new user interface is the same as all of the others in common use. If you want to try this example out for yourself, use the command

```
java JFCBook.Chapter13.CJFCButtonTest
```

When this example starts running, all three buttons are enabled. The right-hand button is periodically disabled for a while and then enabled, to allow you to experiment with the behavior of disabled buttons

Before reading the rest of this section, familiarize yourself with the way in which the new interface works by moving the mouse around and shifting the focus by using the TAB key. Note that it is possible to have two buttons with visible borders by moving the mouse over one of them while another has the focus, but if you click on a button, it grabs the focus causing the other button to lose its border. Also notice that a disabled button doesn't show its border under any circumstances.

The Core JFC Look-and-Feel: The First Step

If you're going to create a new look-and-feel for a component, you might as well use a completely new package for it, so that you can add new user interfaces for other components later if you want to. Of course, as you'll see, you don't need to build an entirely new look-and-feel package or even invent a LookAndFeel subclass to just substitute the user interface for one component and, to show you that this is so, the examples in this section will just change the way that individual buttons look without affecting the rest of the user interface. Later in the chapter, you'll see how to add to this and develop a fully-featured look-and-feel if that is what you want to do. For want of a better title, the new look-and-feel will be called the "Core JFC" look-and-feel and it will reside in the `JFCBook.Cjfc` package.

The Core JFC Button User Interface Classes

As you saw back in Chapter 1, a button is actually made up of several parts, some of which are generic, while others depend on the selected look-and-feel. The most familiar piece of a button is, of course, the `JButton` class, which your application actually deals directly with and which is the same whichever look-and-feel is in use. There are also at least two other pieces—the model and the UI class and, depending on the look-and-feel, there may be others.

The model implements the `com.sun.java.swing.ButtonModel` interface and is usually an instance of `BasicButtonModel`, an implementation of that interface which is supplied by the `com.sun.java.swing.plaf.basic` package. The model is initially installed by `JButton` itself and may be changed by the application program. The look-and-feel does not make any assumptions about which model is installed—all it can assume is that it implements `ButtonModel`.

The UI class that is used is, of course, completely under the control of the installed look-and-feel. It is possible to create a button user interface that is wrapped into a single class, but the standard look-and-feels don't do it that way. Instead, they all use an additional three pieces to implement the user interface:

- The UI class that is responsible for drawing the button and managing the other pieces.
- An implementation of `Border` that draws the button's border.
- A class that reacts to user interaction with the button by monitoring keyboard, mouse and focus activity.

For the Metal look-and-feel, these three pieces are realized by the classes `MetalButtonUI`, `MetalButtonBorder` and `BasicButtonListener`. As discussed in Chapter 1, the interfaces between the UI classes and the corresponding component classes are all defined in the `com.sun.java.swing.plaf` package. To provide a new button interface, you have to create a class that implements all of the methods of the abstract class `com.sun.java.swing.plaf.ButtonUI`, which is defined as follows:

```
public abstract class ButtonUI extends ComponentUI {
   public abstract Insets getDefaultMargin(AbstractButton b);
}
```

The ComponentUI class is, of course, the common piece of every user interface class. Its definition was shown in Chapter 1 and is repeated here for convenience:

```
public abstract class ComponentUI() {
    public static ComponentUI createUI(JComponent c);
    public void installUI(JComponent c);
    public void uninstallUI(JComponent c);
    public void update(Graphics g, JComponent c);
    public void paint(Graphics g, JComponent c);
    public Dimension getPreferredSize(JComponent c);
    public Dimension getMinimumSize(JComponent c);
    public Dimension getMaximumSize(JComponent c);
    public boolean contains(JComponent c, int x, int y);
}
```

At the very least, a button user interface class must implement these ten methods (nine from ComponentUI and one from ButtonUI). The BasicButtonUI class contains implementations of all of them and, by deriving a new interface class from it, you can make use of that code to minimize the amount of work you have to do. The major problem, of course, is to determine which methods can be used unchanged and which need to be overridden. To determine this, you need to refer to the source code for the BasicButtonUI class and to understand what the new class will do that is different. Since the source of the BasicButtonUI class can't be reproduced here, you'll need to refer to the source code that comes with the Swing package to see exactly what each of its methods does. During the implementation of the new user interface, you'll see which methods of BasicButtonUI are being used and which are being overridden.

As well as the UI class itself, there is also the border to consider. Buttons don't use just any border—they install the border specified in the UIDefaults table. The Metal look-and-feel, for example, uses the MetalButtonBorder class as its border. Button borders are all derived from AbstractBorder, but they all have special code that enables them to change their appearance based on the state of the button itself: When the button is pressed, for example, the UI class has to arrange for the border to change its state appropriately. This is, as you'll see, a trivial matter because the border has access to the button's model, which defines its state and hence determines exactly how the border should appear. The new button user interface actually has three border states—normal, lowered and no border at all. There is no border class that can provide all of these states, so it appears that it will be necessary to implement one but, in fact, you can simulate this behavior by installing an empty border when the border should not appear and the usual border when it should. This has the advantage of requiring no new border-drawing code and makes it possible to exploit the ability of the existing button borders to draw themselves according to the button's state. It also means that the button's border is consistent with that of the current look-and-feel, which allows us to mix our button with components from any look-and-feel and still have the correct border.

The last piece to look at is the *controller* in model-view-controller (MVC) terms. This piece listens to mouse, keyboard and focus events and updates the button model state appropriately. To see whether the standard `BasicButtonListener` can be used in conjunction with our new user interface, let's consider exactly what it does and compare this to what our button needs to do. First, let's look at mouse handling. Ordinary buttons react to the mouse as follows:

- When the mouse moves over the button, the "rollover" icon is installed if there is one and rollover is activated (see Chapter 2, "Frames, Labels, and Buttons," for a discussion of button icons).

- When the mouse moves away from the button, the rollover icon is replaced by the standard icon and, if the button appears pressed-in because of a mouse press, it is redrawn in its unpressed state.

- When a mouse button is pressed, the button redraws itself to appear pressed in.

- When the mouse button is released with the mouse still over the button, it is redrawn in its normal state and an `ActionEvent` is generated.

All of this behavior needs to be preserved by our user interface, but a few extra things must be added:

- When the mouse moves over the component, it must be redrawn with a border (unless it is disabled).

- When the mouse moves away from the button, it must be drawn with no border, unless it has the focus, in which case the raised border will be left.

- When the button loses the focus, it must be drawn with no border.

Mouse presses behave in exactly the same way with the new user interface as they do with the standard one. Clearly, this extra behavior requires new code to be written, so it will be necessary to subclass `BasicButtonListener` to fit our purposes and it will be necessary to override some of the mouse-handling code in that class. What about keyboard handling? The `BasicButtonListener` doesn't actually listen to keyboard events at all—instead it registers keyboard actions against the `JButton` that the user interface class is connected to using the keyboard registry. These actions ensure that the button acts as if it had been pressed when it has the focus and the user presses and releases the space key or `RETURN`, or activates the accelerator key on the button's label. They achieve this by modifying the state of the button model just as if mouse buttons had been used to achieve the same effect. This behavior is still appropriate with the new interface and nothing extra is needed, so the methods of `BasicButtonListener` that implement it can be used unchanged.

Last, there is the focus handling. Buttons usually redraw themselves when they gain and lose the focus because they typically provide some visual feedback to the user in the form of a hatched rectangle drawn around the text and/or the icon, depending on the look-and-feel installed. With the new interface, gaining or losing the focus will cause the button to draw or remove its border, so no hatched rectangle should be drawn on the button's surface. It is, therefore, necessary to override the focus-handling methods of `BasicButtonListener`.

Although some extra functionality is required, it seems that there is nothing in `BasicButtonListener` that prevents it from being used as the basis of the controller for the new interface. We conclude, therefore, that the new interface can be created by using the border class unchanged and implementing a view and controller by subclassing `BasicButtonUI` and `BasicButtonListener`. These classes will be part of the Core JFC look-and-feel in the `JFCBook.Cjfc` package, and will be called `CJFCButtonUI` and `CJFCButtonListener`, respectively.

Core Note

Initially, you'll see how to implement the new button interface. This new interface can, as you'll see later, be used with any existing look-and-feel and it will use the button border associated with that look-and-feel by retrieving it from the UIDefaults table. Later, this same button will be part of a new look-and-feel and, without changing any of its code, will use the button border specified for that look-and-feel.

A Quick Look at the Button Model

You can't write a UI class without access to the state of the object that you're trying to represent. In Swing, the state is always held in a model that is separate from both the component itself and from the various views that can represent it. In the case of buttons, the facilities required of a model are specified by the `ButtonModel` interface, of which `DefaultButtonModel` is an implementation. To understand how the CJFC button UI classes work, it is necessary to know what the model contains and what each piece of its state means.

There are five basic attributes that the button model maintains, listed in Table 13-4. These attributes all affect the appearance of the button, so you'll often see the UI class implementation querying the model for their values.

Core Note

`ButtonModel` supports other attributes but, since they don't affect the button's visual representation, they are not listed here. Refer to the API specifications for `ButtonModel` and `DefaultButtonModel` to find out about the other attributes.

Table 13-4	ButtonModel Attributes

Attribute	Meaning
Enabled	This is the most obvious of the five attributes and corresponds exactly to the JComponent "enabled" state. When the button's JComponent is enabled, so will the model be. If the model is disabled, it ignores any further state changes it is asked to make, other than a request to enable itself again.
Pressed	This attribute is true when the button is in the pressed state. The button's controller determines when user action results in a button being "pressed" and when it should be considered released. This attribute can also be changed by the AbstractButton doClick method.
Selected	The selected attribute is only meaningful for buttons like toggle buttons, checkboxes and radio buttons that have a persistent state that is toggled by being clicked with the mouse. For other buttons, a mouse click causes the pressed attribute to go from false to true and then back to false, with no persistent change in the model.
Rollover	The rollover attribute is true when the mouse is positioned over the button itself. The button's controller class is responsible for determining when this is the case and for changing this attribute as necessary.
Armed	When the button is armed, it is able to generate events, typically an ActionEvent caused by the button being pressed.

Each of these attributes is a boolean and has methods that allow its state to be retrieved or to be changed—for example, the setRollover method is used to change the state of the Rollover attribute and isRollover returns its current value. Changes to any of the attributes causes a ChangeEvent to be generated. Typically, the button's UI class or the controller class will register as a ChangeListener and adjust the appearance of the button to reflect the current state of the model.

The CJFCButtonListener Class

Because of its relative simplicity, the first part of the button implementation that you're going to see is the controller part that will directly handle mouse and focus events, which will affect whether the main UI object will display the button's border. The class extends BasicButtonListener to inherit its keyboard handling, so you won't see any key-related code in CJFCButtonListener itself. In fact, there is very little code in BasicButtonListener itself. Because it uses keyboard actions, it doesn't need to catch KeyEvents—it allows the button's JComponent to do that and to invoke the action processing methods registered in the keystroke registry when necessary. If you want to look at the details, refer to the source code for BasicButtonListener. The code for CJFCButtonListener is shown in Listing 13-4.

Listing 13-4   The controller for a button user interface

```
package JFCBook.Cjfc;

import com.sun.java.swing.*;
import com.sun.java.swing.plaf.basic.*;
import com.sun.java.swing.plaf.*;
import java.awt.*;
import java.awt.event.*;

public class CJFCButtonListener extends BasicButtonListener {
  public CJFCButtonListener(AbstractButton b) {
    super(b);
    this.b = b;
  }

  public void mouseEntered(MouseEvent evt) {
    ButtonUI ui = b.getUI();
    if (ui instanceof CJFCButtonUI) {
      ((CJFCButtonUI)ui).setMouseOver(b, true);
    }
    super.mouseEntered(evt);
  }

  public void mouseExited(MouseEvent evt) {
    ButtonUI ui = b.getUI();
    if (ui instanceof CJFCButtonUI) {
      ((CJFCButtonUI)ui).setMouseOver(b, false);
    }
    super.mouseExited(evt);
  }

  public void mouseDragged(MouseEvent evt) {
    ButtonUI ui = b.getUI();
    if (ui instanceof CJFCButtonUI) {
      if (b.contains(evt.getPoint()) == false) {
        ((CJFCButtonUI)ui).setMouseOver(b, true);
      } else {
        ((CJFCButtonUI)ui).setMouseOver(b, false);
      }
    }
    super.mouseDragged(evt);
  }

  public void focusGained(FocusEvent evt) {
    ButtonUI ui = b.getUI();
    if (ui instanceof CJFCButtonUI) {
```

continued

```
      ((CJFCButtonUI)ui).focusChanged(b);
    }
    super.focusGained(evt);
  }

  public void focusLost(FocusEvent evt) {
    ButtonUI ui = b.getUI();
    if (ui instanceof CJFCButtonUI) {
      ((CJFCButtonUI)ui).focusChanged(b);
    }
    super.focusLost(evt);
  }

  protected AbstractButton b;
}
```

When a button is created and the UI component is installed, it will create an instance of CJFCButtonListener. This object will be dedicated to the UI component that creates it and its constructor is passed the button itself in the form of a reference to an AbstractButton, which is the superclass of all Swing button types. Using this reference, it can easily locate the button itself or find its UI object using the JComponent getUI method, as you can see from Listing 13-4.

As explained earlier, the job of this class is to extend the behavior of BasicButtonListener so that mouse and focus events are handled appropriately for our user interface. For this reason, there is very little code—most of the mouse handling is in BasicButtonListener itself. In fact, all this class does is to trap three mouse events and redirect them to the right methods in the button UI class that will be shown later. When the mouse moves over the button, the mouseEntered method will be invoked and this will cause the CJFCButtonUI setMouseOver method to be called. The same method is called when the mouse leaves the button; the difference between these two calls is the second argument, which is true when the mouse enters the button and false when it leaves it.

There is a similar story for focus events—when the button gains or loses the focus, the CJFCButtonUI focusChanged method is called to let it know. In this case, as you'll see, there is no need to pass an argument indicating which focus event occurred, because a JComponent can tell whether or not it has the focus at any given time. Notice that the mouse and focus event handlers all invoke the superclass event handling code as well, to allow it to do anything it needs to do when a focus or mouse event occurs. Table 13-5 shows what BasicButtonListener does with each of these events.

Table 13-5	Handling Mouse and Focus Events for a Button

Event	Response
mouseEntered	If rollover is enabled (see Chapter 2), changes the button model state to show that the button is in rollover mode.
mouseExited	If rollover is enabled, turns off rollover mode in the button model.
focusGained	Calls repaint to have the UI class redraw the component with the appropriate visual cue to show the focus.
focusLost	Calls repaint to remove the visual cue for the focus.

As you can see, all of this is still relevant to our revised user interface because the change of icon on rollover needs to be preserved and it will be necessary to redraw the button when the focus is gained or lost, in order to show the correct border state. Focus and mouse events are also notified to our component UI class by calling setMouseOver or focusChanged to allow the proper state changes within the UI to be made before BasicButtonListener schedules the actions that react to those state changes.

Incidentally, you'll note that mouse enter and exit events just cause the state of the button model to be changed—there is no call to repaint to have the button redrawn with the correct icon, so how is this done? As always in the MVC architecture, changes in the model cause an event which makes the view update itself. In this case, the model generates a ChangeEvent when any if its state is modified. This event is caught by BasicButtonListener, which schedules a repaint. This might seem a little circular in this case, because the original event was originally notified to BasicButtonListener (via CJFCButtonListener), which went to the trouble of updating the model and allowing the model to tell it to redraw the button. This is, of course, a special case and there are other state changes that do not go through the controller—such as those resulting from the application changing the state of the button via the AbstractButton API, like doClick, which programmatically presses and releases the button or setEnabled which will almost certainly require the button to redraw itself.

The last event that CJFCButtonListener receives is the one generated when the user moves the mouse over the button with one of its buttons pressed. This event causes the mouseDragged method to be called periodically as the mouse traverses the button. The only mouse events that should be of any direct interest to this class are the ones for entry and exit because they affect whether the border should be drawn but, if the user is dragging the mouse, these events are not generated. As a result, if only mouse enter and exits events were handled, the border would not always be in the correct state. Suppose, for example, that the mouse enters the button with its buttons released. The mouse entry event will cause the button's border to be drawn. If the user presses a mouse button, the event generated will go to `BasicButtonListener`, because `CJFCButtonListener` doesn't override the `mousePressed` method. If the mouse button remains held down and the mouse leaves the button, there will be no mouse exit event, so the button's border would remain displayed, which is not the desired effect. To avoid this, mouse dragged events, which continue to be generated even when the mouse is no longer over the button, are processed and the mouse's location as reported by these events is used to control the border state. The same mechanism is used by `BasicButtonListener` itself to make the button pop up as the mouse leaves it under these circumstances and to make the button appear pressed again if the mouse enters it with a button still held down.

The CJFCButtonUI Class

The `CJFCButtonUI` class is the real button UI class, whose job it is to implement our specific button look-and-feel. At the very least, it must provide (or inherit) the 10 methods defined by the abstract `com.sun.java.swing.plaf.ButtonUI` class that were listed earlier in this chapter. Some of them can ,of course, be inherited from the `BasicButtonUI` class and some must be overridden to provide customized behavior. The implementation of the `CJFCButtonUI` class is shown in Listing 13-5.

Listing 13-5   The Core JFC look-and-feel button UI class

```
package JFCBook.Cjfc;

import com.sun.java.swing.*;
import com.sun.java.swing.border.*;
import com.sun.java.swing.event.*;
import com.sun.java.swing.plaf.*;
import com.sun.java.swing.plaf.basic.*;
import JFCBook.Cjfc.CJFCButtonListener;
import java.beans.*;
import java.awt.*;

public class CJFCButtonUI extends BasicButtonUI
      implements PropertyChangeListener {
  // ComponentUI implementation
  public static ComponentUI createUI(JComponent c) {
    return new CJFCButtonUI();
  }
```

```
public void installUI(JComponent c) {
  buttonListener = createListener((AbstractButton)c);

  // Connect to listener for mouse and focus events
  c.addMouseListener(buttonListener);
  c.addMouseMotionListener(buttonListener);
  c.addFocusListener(buttonListener);

  // Listen for change events from the model
  ((AbstractButton)c).addChangeListener(buttonListener);

  // Set up keyboard actions
  buttonListener.setupKeyboard((AbstractButton)c);

  // Use convenience methods to install our
  // default colors, fonts and border
  LookAndFeel.installColorsAndFont(c, "Button.background",
              "Button.foreground",
              "Button.font");
  LookAndFeel.installBorder(c, "Button.border");

  // Now replace the border with an empty one
  originalBorder = c.getBorder();
  if (originalBorder != null) {
    createEmptyBorder(originalBorder, c);
  }
  c.setBorder(emptyBorder);

  // Register to receive notification of future border changes
  c.addPropertyChangeListener(this);
}

public void uninstallUI(JComponent c) {
  // Remove listeners
  c.removeMouseListener(buttonListener);
  c.removeMouseMotionListener(buttonListener);
  c.removeFocusListener(buttonListener);
  c.removePropertyChangeListener(this);
  ((AbstractButton)c).removeChangeListener(buttonListener);

  // Remove keyboard actions
  c.resetKeyboardActions();

  // Restore the original border
  c.setBorder(originalBorder);
}
```

continued

```java
public void paint(Graphics g, JComponent c) {
  AbstractButton b = (AbstractButton)c;

  // First install the appropriate border
  changeBorderState(b);

  ButtonModel model = b.getModel();
  Dimension buttonSize = b.getSize();
  FontMetrics fontMetrics = g.getFontMetrics();
  Insets insets = c.getInsets();

  Rectangle drawArea = new Rectangle(buttonSize);
  Rectangle textArea = new Rectangle();
  Rectangle iconArea = new Rectangle();

  drawArea.x += insets.left;
  drawArea.y += insets.top;
  drawArea.width -= insets.right + insets.left;
  drawArea.height -= insets.top + insets.bottom;

  String label = b.getText();
  int textIconGap = TEXT_ICON_GAP;
  if (label == null || label.equals("")) {
    textIconGap = 0;
  }

  label = SwingUtilities.layoutCompoundLabel(fontMetrics,
        b.getText(), b.getIcon(),
        b.getVerticalAlignment(), b.getHorizontalAlignment(),
        b.getVerticalTextPosition(), b.getHorizontalTextPosition(),
        drawArea, iconArea, textArea, textIconGap);

  boolean buttonPressed = model.isArmed() && model.isPressed();
  boolean isEnabled = model.isEnabled();

  // Start by painting the background, but only if the button
  // is opaque
  if (b.isOpaque() == true) {
    g.setColor(b.getBackground());
    g.fillRect(0, 0, buttonSize.width, buttonSize.height);
  }

  // Set up text and icon offsets
  int offsetX = buttonPressed ? PRESSED_SHIFT_X : 0;
  int offsetY = buttonPressed ? PRESSED_SHIFT_Y : 0;

  // Next, select the correct icon and draw that
```

```
   if (b.getIcon() != null) {
      Icon icon = null;
      if (isEnabled == false) {
         icon = b.getDisabledIcon();
      } else if (buttonPressed == true) {
         icon = b.getIcon();
      } else if (b.isRolloverEnabled() == true &&
            model.isRollover() == true) {
         icon = b.getRolloverIcon();
      }

      // If we still don't have an icon, use the default
      if (icon == null) {
         icon = b.getIcon();
      }

      icon.paintIcon(c, g, iconArea.x + offsetX, iconArea.y + offsetY);
   }

   // Finally, render the text
   if (label != null && label.equals("") == false) {
      int accelerator = model.getMnemonic();
      int ascent = fontMetrics.getAscent();
      if (isEnabled == true) {
         g.setColor(b.getForeground());
         BasicGraphicsUtils.drawString(g, label, accelerator,
            textArea.x + offsetX, textArea.y + ascent + offsetY);
      } else {
         g.setColor(b.getBackground().brighter());
         BasicGraphicsUtils.drawString(g, label, accelerator,
            textArea.x, textArea.y + ascent);
         g.setColor(b.getBackground().darker());
         BasicGraphicsUtils.drawString(g, label, accelerator,
            textArea.x - 1, textArea.y + ascent - 1);
      }
   }
}


// PropertyChangeListener interface
public void propertyChange(PropertyChangeEvent evt) {
   if (evt.getPropertyName().equals("border")) {
      JComponent c = (JComponent)evt.getSource();
      Border newBorder = (Border)evt.getNewValue()

      // Don't do anything if this is our border being installed
      if (newBorder != emptyBorder) {
```

continued

```
      if ((emptyBorder == null && newBorder != null) ||
        (emptyBorder != null && newBorder != null &&
          emptyBorder.getBorderInsets(c) != newBorder.getBorderInsets(c))) {
        createEmptyBorder(newBorder, c);
      }
      originalBorder = newBorder;

      // Put back the empty border if we need to
      if (borderShown == false) {
        c.setBorder(emptyBorder);
      }
    }
  } else if (evt.getPropertyName().equals("margin")) {
    AbstractButton b = (AbstractButton)evt.getSource();
    if (emptyBorder != null) {
      emptyBorder = null;
      createEmptyBorder(originalBorder, b);

      // Install the new empty border if we need to
      if (borderShown == false) {
        b.setBorder(emptyBorder);
      }
    }
  }
}

// Create button listener - can be overridden
protected BasicButtonListener createListener(AbstractButton b) {
  return new CJFCButtonListener(b);
}

// Methods called from the button listener
// Change of mouse position relative to the button
public void setMouseOver(AbstractButton b, boolean state) {
  mouseOver = state;
  checkBorderState(b);
}

// Change of focus
public void focusChanged(AbstractButton b) {
  boolean gotFocus = b.hasFocus();
  checkBorderState(b);
}

// Schedule repaint if we need to change border
protected void checkBorderState(AbstractButton b) {
  boolean needBorder = b.isEnabled() && (mouseOver || b.hasFocus());
```

```
    if (needBorder != borderShown) {
      b.repaint();
    }
  }

  // Install the correct border for the current state
  protected void changeBorderState(AbstractButton b) {
    boolean needBorder = b.isEnabled() && (mouseOver || b.hasFocus());

    if (needBorder != borderShown) {
      borderShown = needBorder;
      b.setBorder(needBorder ? originalBorder : emptyBorder);
    }
  }

  // Create the empty border that this component will use
  protected void createEmptyBorder(Border b, Component c) {
    if (emptyBorder == null) {
      Insets insets = b.getBorderInsets(c);
      if (singleEmptyBorder == null) {
        singleEmptyBorder = BorderFactory.createEmptyBorder(insets.top, insets.left,
                  insets.bottom, insets.right);
        emptyBorder = singleEmptyBorder;
      } else if (insets.equals(singleEmptyBorder.getBorderInsets(c))) {
        emptyBorder = singleEmptyBorder;
      } else {
        emptyBorder = BorderFactory.createEmptyBorder(insets.top, insets.left,
                insets.bottom, insets.right);
      }
    }
  }

  // Instance variables
  protected Border originalBorder;       // The programmer's border
  protected boolean borderShown;         // true when the border is visible
  protected boolean mouseOver;           // Mouse over component
  protected Border emptyBorder;          // Our empty border
  protected BasicButtonListener buttonListener;

  // Static members
  protected static Border singleEmptyBorder;
  protected static final int BORDER_SIZE = 4;
  protected static final int TEXT_ICON_GAP = 4;
  protected static final int PRESSED_SHIFT_X = 1;
  protected static final int PRESSED_SHIFT_Y = 1;
}
```

If you scan through the listing, you'll find implementations for only four of the ten required `ButtonUI` methods. The other six (update, `getPreferredSize`, `getMinimumSize`, `getMaximumSize`, contains and `getDefaultMargin`) are inherited directly from `BasicButtonUI` because nothing needs to be added to them for our user interface. The code consists of several distinct pieces, which deal with separate aspects of managing the button's user interface, listed in Table 13-5.

Table 13-5   Aspects of the CJFCButtonUI Class

Function	Description
Management of the UI class	The `createUI`, `installUI` and `uninstallUI` methods allow the `UIManager` to install this UI class for buttons that need it and to remove it if necessary. The `createListener` method is a helper method that creates the `CJFCButtonListener` object for a button.
Drawing the button	The `paint` method is responsible for rendering the button's user interface.
Maintaining the border state	Ensuring that the border is displayed only when it should be is the most important feature of this user interface class, which is why it has six methods associated with it—`propertyChange`, `setMouseOver`, `focusChanged`, `checkBorderState`, `changeBorderState` and `createEmptyBorder`.

Managing the UI Class

Management of the UI class involves creating new instances as necessary, installing them into buttons and removing them when the look-and-feel is changed. The UI class does not, of course, coordinate these activities itself—that job belongs to `UIManager`, using methods defined by `JComponent` and the UI class itself. To understand what the `createUI`, `installUI` and `uninstallUI` methods do, it is necessary to know how a component acquires its UI class. Following is the sequence of events that occurs when a new `JButton` is created; this exact sequence applies to every Swing component except that the component and UI class names will be different.

1. When a new `JButton` is created, a method called from its constructor calls the `updateUI` method that must be implemented by every `JComponent`. The `JButton` implementation of this method is a typical one:

```
public void updateUI() {
    setUI((ButtonUI)UIManager.getUI(this));
}
```

2. The `UIManager getUI` method is passed as its argument the `JComponent` for which the UI class is required. The first thing that this method does is to call that component's `getUIClassID` method, which returns a string that gives the name of the type of UI class that it needs. For every Swing component, the name that must be returned by this method is fixed and in the case of `JButton`, this string will always be `ButtonUI`, which you may recognize from our discussion of `BasicLookAndFeel` earlier in this chapter as a key to the `UIDefaults` table.

3. `UIManager` uses the `UIDefaults` table of the current look-and-feel to look up the value associated with the key `ButtonUI`. While the key is constant, the value returned by this operation will depend on the look-and-feel installed. The value is actually a string which contains the name of the UI class that should be used. If the Core JFC look-and-feel is installed, the string `JFCBook.Cjfc.CJFCButtonUI` would be returned, whereas the Motif look-and-feel would return `com.sun.java.swing.plaf.motif.MotifButtonUI`.

4. Given the name of the class, `UIManager` invokes the `UIDefaults` `getUIClass` method. This uses the class name to get the corresponding `Class` object and then uses the Java reflection mechanism in conjunction with this `Class` object to invoke the UI class's static `createUI` method, passing the `JButton` object as its argument. This `createUI` method is the one shown in Listing 13-5; its job is to return an instance of the button UI class that can be connected to the `JButton` passed as the argument. In some cases, a single UI object can be shared between all objects of the type that it supports, so the `createUI` method would create one UI object the first time it is called, then return the same object on each subsequent call. This is possible if the UI class doesn't need to store any persistent state for each instance of the component. A `JButton`, as managed by the Windows look-and-feel, satisfies this criterion, so the `createUI` method for `JButton` in the Windows look-and-feel creates only one `WindowsButtonUI` object. This is not, however possible for the Core JFC look-and-feel because, as you'll see, there are several pieces of state information that must be held for each button. Therefore, the `CJFCButtonUI createUI` method creates a new `CJFCButtonUI` each time it is called. This completes the `UIManager getUI` call shown in the `updateUI` method above.

5. The button UI class returned by `UIManager` is passed to the `JComponent setUI` method of the `JButton` whose user interface is being installed. This method first looks to see if there is already a UI class installed and, if there is, calls its `uninstallUI` method.

Then, it calls the new UI object's `installUI` method with a reference to the `JButton` as its argument. When this method returns, the UI object has been fully initialized. This completes the process of connecting a UI object to the button.

The installUI and uninstallUI methods

These methods are called when the UI class is being installed into the `JButton` and when it is being removed and replaced by another UI object. Since they are almost mirror images of each other, only the `installUI` method will be described in any detail here—`uninstallUI` just reverses everything that `installUI` does.

When `installUI` is called, its first job is to create the `CJFCButtonListener` object that will be connected to the button. You'll notice if you look at the code in Listing 13-5 that the listener is actually created not in the `installUI` method itself, but in a separate, protected method called `createListener`. This is a common theme that you'll find if you look at the source code for the Swing components—instead of creating helper objects directly, they delegate this job to another method that can be overridden in a derived class. This makes it much easier for a programmer to extend the functionality of a UI class without having to completely rewrite it. Suppose that you want to slightly change what the `CJFCButtonListener` does. To do this, you build a new class, say `MyCJFCButtonListener`, which is derived from `CJFCButtonListener`. To make use of it, you have to arrange for `CJFCButtonUI` to use your class instead of `CJFCButtonListener`. Because the listener is created in `createListener`, all you have to do is override it:

```
public class MyCJFCButtonUI extends CJFCButtonUI {
  public CJFCButtonListener createListener(AbstractButton b) {
    return new MyCJFCButtonListener(b);
  }
}
```

This is much easier than rewriting the entire `installUI` method, which is the only thing you could have done if the `CJFCButtonListener` had been created directly by `installUI`.

Core Tip

As you write new component UI classes, and—indeed—other classes, keep this technique in mind and use it wherever possible.

Having created the `CJFCButtonListener`, `installUI` registers it to receive focus, mouse and mouse motion events from the button itself and to receive `ChangeEvents` from the button's model. If you look back to the implementation of `CJFCButtonListener` in Listing 13-4, you'll see that it doesn't do anything with these `ChangeEvents` and doesn't even claim to implement the `ChangeListener` interface. It is, in fact, its superclass `BasicButtonListener` that needs to receive these events, so we have to register the controller to receive them on its behalf.

Core Note

While reading through this section, it would be a good idea to have the source code for the `BasicButtonUI` *and* `BasicButtonListener` *classes available for reference so that you can see which code has been overridden by our user interface implementation and also see code that is being inherited by it. The source code is part of the Swing package that you can download from the JavaSoft web site.*

The controller also handles keyboard actions, but there is no need for it to receive keyboard events to make this possible. As described earlier, the `JComponent` keyboard handling mechanism is used to connect keys to the actions that the controller will perform when they are pressed. Because all of this keyboard handling is implemented by `BasicButtonListener`, all that is necessary is to call that class's `setupKeyboard` method to have the appropriate keystrokes registered.

Next, `installUI` sets the button's foreground and background colors and its font. Here, you can see a typical use of the `LookAndFeel installColorsAndFont` method that you saw earlier in this chapter. Rather than using hard-coded colors and fonts, this method gets the appropriate values from the `UIDefaults` table. Using this method also avoids overwriting explicit settings that the programmer might have made. Similarly, it is necessary to install the correct border, but this is not so simple.

The border is what this user interface is all about. Unless the mouse is over the button or it has the focus, there should be no visible border. However, it is still necessary to find out which border is appropriate, because it will have to be installed when it should be visible, so `installUI` invokes the `LookAndFeel` method `installBorder` to fetch and install the correct default border. Having done this, it saves a reference to the border in the instance variable `originalBorder`, then creates and installs a suitable empty border instead. The process of creating the empty border is also not quite trivial, as you'll see in the implementation of the `createEmptyBorder` method.

There is one further problem concerning borders that needs to be solved. Suppose that the programmer decides to change the button's border at some time after it has been created and calls `setBorder` to do so. Unless something is done about this unlikely, but possible, event, it will cause a border to be drawn around the button. However, if the button doesn't have the focus and doesn't have the mouse over it, it shouldn't show any border at all. You'll see how this problem is solved in "Maintaining Border State" below. Part of the solution is to have the UI class receive `PropertyChangeEvents` from the button, so the last thing `installUI` does is register the UI class to receive them.

Drawing the Button

The button is drawn by the UI class `paint` method. This method is required to render everything on the button *apart from the border,* which is drawn by the `paintBorder` method of the border itself (recall that `paintBorder` is one of the methods of the `Border` interface, which every border must implement). `paintBorder` is called by the `paint` method of `JComponent` after the UI class paint method has finished. This has two implications for our UI class implementation.

On the positive side, there is no need to worry about drawing over the border when rendering the rest of the button. Therefore, it is possible to fill the whole component with its background color if the button is opaque. This makes the code a little simpler and won't cost anything worth worrying about in performance terms.

On the negative side, it isn't possible to have the border be drawn or not drawn by implementing appropriate code in the paint method. To stop the button drawing the border, it is necessary to convince `JComponent` that there is no border to draw—which requires us to actually install an empty border. If the border had been drawn in the UI class `paint` method, the real border could have remained installed in the `JComponent` and just not drawn when it shouldn't be seen.

Actually, the only real difference between our button user interface and the standard one is the fact that ours doesn't always show the border. But if the `paint` method doesn't have anything to do with the border, why can't the `paint` method of `BasicButtonUI` be used unchanged? Why do we need to override it? One possible reason is that, as noted above, `BasicButtonUI` draws a hatched rectangle on the button when it has the focus, whereas this is not necessary for our user interface, because the presence of the border indicates that the button has the focus. However, you don't actually need to override `paint` to stop this happening, because the rectangle is actually drawn not by `paint` itself, but by the `BasicButtonUI` `paintFocus` method, which is called from `paint`. This is done deliberately so that derived classes can override it and provide different behavior—just as our UI class has a separate `createListener` method. The real reason that `CJFCButtonUI` has its own `paint` method is so that you can see how a typical UI class `paint` method is written. If you wanted to, you could delete this `paint` method and implement an empty `paintFocus` method to achieve exactly the same user interface.

Despite the fact that you've just read that `paint` has nothing to do with drawing the border, the first thing it does is this:

```
// First install the appropriate border
changeBorderState(b);
```

You'll see later exactly why this is necessary. For now, just note that it is safe to install a new border at the start of the `paint` method, because `JComponent` doesn't paint the border until this method has completed and for this reason, `paint` is a very convenient place to switch the border.

When you forget the border and the focus rectangle, all there is left to a button is the text and the icon, either of which may be absent. To draw the button properly, it is necessary to work out which of these is actually present, then decide where they should go, based on the relative icon and text position and the alignment configured in the JButton itself using the methods that you saw back in Chapter 2 (setVerticalTextPosition, setVerticalAlignment, etc.). Before this decision can be made, it is necessary to work out how much space is available for them. This is achieved by getting the size of the button (using getSize from JComponent) and subtracting the button's insets. Since the insets are actually the space occupied by the border, you can see that it is very important that the getInsets method retrieves the size of the actual border that was originally installed in the button, even if it is not currently displayed. The getInsets method works by asking the installed border how much space it occupies, but the original border, as you know, is not always going to be the target of this request. It follows that the empty border that is substituted when necessary must report the same insets as the original border.

Once the available space on the button has been worked out, the job of allocating that space to the text and the icon is actually carried out by the static method layoutCompoundLabel in the SwingUtilities class. SwingUtilities, as its name suggests, is a class that contains methods that are not specific to any one component in the Swing package. Instead, it has facilities, like layoutCompoundLabel, that are of more general use. Think of it as a kind of class-based subroutine library.

The layoutCompoundLabel method is defined as follows:

```
public static String layoutCompoundLabel(FontMetrics fm,
        String text, Icon icon, int verticalAlignment,
        int horizontalAlignment, int verticalTextPosition,
        int horizontalTextPosition, Rectangle viewR,
        Rectangle iconR, Rectangle textR, int textIconGap);
```

The first eight arguments and the last one are all supplied by the caller. The FontMetrics object provides font information used to work out the size of the text given as the second argument, if there is any. The viewR argument describes the rectangular area of the button within which the text and icon must be placed and textIconGap is the distance required between the text and the icon. This is actually a constant of the look-and-feel, which is four pixels in our case. The iconR and textR arguments are supplied by the paint method but are not initialized. Instead, the location and size of the rectangles allocated to the icon and text are returned in these objects. Notice that layoutCompoundLabel returns a String value. What it actually returns is the text to be drawn on the button. This will usually be the same as the text argument, but if there is not enough space to take all of the label as supplied, it is truncated so that three dots appear to the right, along with as many leading characters of the original label as will fit; for example, the label "Press Me" might be replaced by "Pres..." if space is at a premium.

When layoutCompoundLabel returns, the job of actually painting the component starts. First, if the button is opaque, the space that it occupies is filled with its background color as retrieved from the button itself. Next, the appropriate icon to use is chosen. Usually, the standard icon returned by the button's `getIcon` method is used. However, if the button has rollover enabled and there is a rollover icon, this icon will be used if the button is in rollover state. If the button is disabled, the disabled icon is used, if there is one. The UI class determines the button's state by querying the `ButtonModel`—recall from Table 13-4 that all of this information is available as attributes of the `DefaultButtonModel`. Having determined the correct icon, its `paintIcon` method is called to draw it in the rectangular space returned by `layoutCompoundLabel`. Of course, nothing is drawn if the button doesn't have an icon.

You may have noticed what appears to be a flaw in the painting logic while reading the last few paragraphs—first `layoutCompoundLabel` is called to determine where to place the text and the icon, then the `paint` method works out which is the correct icon to use. How can it know that the space returned is large enough for the icon? What if the various icons that the button can use are not all of the same size? Well, the logic here, which is functionally the same as the logic used by `BasicButtonUI`, only works if the icons are all of the same size, which would normally be the case. It would, of course, be simple to rearrange the code so that the correct icon is selected before `layoutCompoundLabel` is called, but this might have the undesirable effect of moving the text and icon around as the icon changes—you may not want your text to jump around as the mouse moves over the button as would happen if the rollover icon were not the same size as the ordinary icon. If you don't agree, feel free to create your own button user interface—that's one of the most useful features of Swing!

The last task is to draw the text. This is a simple job. The only tricky part is simulating grayed-out text when the button is disabled—you saw the details of this back in Chapter 4 and the same technique is used here. A little embellishment that this UI class copies from `BasicButtonUI` is that the text is offset slightly when the button is pressed so that appears to move down and to the right, helping the illusion that the button has been pressed into the screen. Again, the `ButtonModel` state is used to determine whether the button is pressed and to decide whether the text should be offset or not.

Maintaining Border State

A button has only one border, but this one really needs to have two of them. When the button has the focus or the mouse is over it, it needs to have the border that was initially assigned to it, or one explicitly assigned by the programmer, and at other times it needs to appear to have no border at all. The UI class is responsible for making sure that the correct border is displayed.

You may recall from the description of the `installUI` method that a reference to the real border is held in the `originalBorder` variable and a suitable empty border is created to replace it. A button, like all `JComponents`, can have its own border but is not obliged to do so—one way to remove its border to just use `setBorder(null)`. While this would be much simpler than the scheme used in this example, it wouldn't work and the reason why should be clear now that you've seen the `paint` method. In the `paint` method, the insets of the button were obtained from its border and the space available for the text and the icon were determined by subtracting these insets from the overall size of the button. If you take away the border completely, there will be no insets and the text and icon will have more space to occupy. As a result, they will move around as the border is added or removed. To avoid this, the button insets must remain the same at all times, which means that the border size must always be the same size. The most obvious way to achieve this is not to completely remove the border, but to substitute an empty border with exactly the same insets as the real one.

When the button is given its initial border by `installUI`, the `createEmptyBorder` method is called. In principle, this method has a trivial task to perform—get the insets of the border that it is passed and create an empty border with the same insets. It could have been implemented that way and the button would have behaved exactly according to its specification. However, there is a small optimization that is probably worth doing to save memory. Although every button can have its own individual border, in practice all of the buttons in a given application are likely to have exactly the same border (probably the default border of the look-and-feel). Instead of creating a new empty border each time a button is created, the UI class keeps the first empty border that it creates in a static member variable (`singleEmptyBorder`). Each time `createEmptyBorder` is called, it checks whether the insets of the border it is given match those of `singleEmptyBorder` and, if they do, it returns `singleEmptyBorder` as the border to use. In most applications, this will mean that the same empty border is used for all Core JFC buttons. If the new border doesn't match the old one, then a new empty border is created. Because the `BorderFactory createEmptyBorder` method is used to do this, there is still a chance that this empty border will be shared with other buttons or components that need an empty border with the same insets.

Once `installUI` has completed, the button has its original border stored in the `originalBorder` variable and a suitable empty border in the instance variable `emptyBorder` and installed in the component itself. The remaining problem is to arrange for the correct border to be installed in the component at all times. The border may need to be changed at the following times:

- When the mouse moves over the button
- When the button gains the focus
- When the button loses the focus
- When the mouse leaves the button
- When the button is disabled
- When the button is enabled after being disabled

The first four of these events are caught by CJFCButtonListener and result in the CJFCButtonUI setMouseOver or focusChanged methods being called. Both of these methods change instance variables in the UI class to reflect the current state of the mouse, based on the argument passed, or of the focus. Notice that there is no need to pass the current focus state to focusChanged because a JComponent always knows whether it has the focus and you can use the hasFocus method to retrieve this information.

Enabling or disabling a button is done using the setEnabled method of Component. This method is overridden by AbstractButton, which enables or disables the button at the component level and also invokes the ButtonModel setEnabled method to change the button model's Enabled attribute. If this attribute is actually changing, the ButtonModel will generate a ChangeEvent that will be delivered to the button's CJFCButtonListener. The stateChanged method of this class is actually provided by BasicButtonListener, which causes the button to be repainted. Therefore, a change in button state can be detected by the paint method.

Core Note

This is actually the only way to detect this state change. The setEnabled *call is visible in the* JButton *and* AbstractButton *classes, but is not directly seen by the UI class. When you're writing a UI class, the last thing you want to do is require the programmer to subclass the component itself in order to invoke some special functionality in your custom look-and-feel class.*

Because the UI object gets direct notification of the first four events, it is possible to check whether they require the border to be changed. This check is contained in the checkBorderState method, which is called from setMouseOver and focusChanged. This method is shown again here for convenience:

```
protected void checkBorderState(AbstractButton b) {
   boolean needBorder = b.isEnabled() && (mouseOver || b.hasFocus());

   if (needBorder != borderShown) {
     b.repaint();
   }
}
```

The first line determines whether or not the border should be shown—it really just restates the criterion that was given earlier: show the border if the component is enabled *and* either the mouse is over it or it has the focus. As you can see, the enabled state and the state of the focus are obtained directly from the button itself, while the location of the mouse comes from the instance variable mouseOver, which is maintained by setMouseOver. If the event doesn't require a change in border state, there is no need to do anything. This might happen if the mouse moves over the button while it is disabled: the fact that the button is not enabled stops the border being shown. So that a change in state can be detected, the current border state is kept in the `borderShown` member. If a real change is needed, the `repaint` method is called to have the component repainted.

Notice that the border itself wasn't changed by `checkBorderState`—that job is done by the `changeBorderState` method invoked at the beginning of `paint`. The border change is done there to allow it to work when the button is enabled or disabled, because those events just cause the `paint` method to be invoked without any other change in the button state.

```
protected void changeBorderState(AbstractButton b) {
  boolean needBorder = b.isEnabled() && (mouseOver || b.hasFocus());

  if (needBorder != borderShown) {
    borderShown = needBorder;
    b.setBorder(needBorder ? originalBorder : emptyBorder);
  }
}
```

As you can see, much of this method is the same as `checkBorderState`. This is necessary, because `paint` can be invoked for reasons unrelated to border changes and it is a good idea to avoid calling `setBorder` when there is no need to do so. Having changed the border, the new state is stored in `borderShown` for use when the next event that might cause a border change occurs.

That just about covers border management, apart from two minor problems. To make the button user interface function properly, the UI class has to be in full control of when the border is visible. However, the programmer can set a new border with `setBorder` at any time. Since `setBorder` is a `JComponent` method, it can't be overridden by a look-and-feel class. Setting a new border should make the component draw it next time the button should be visible, but shouldn't have any effect if the button is disabled or if doesn't have either the focus or the mouse over it.

Since the UI class can't interfere with `setBorder`, it has to find other ways to detect the change of border. Fortunately, the border is a bound property of `JComponent`—changing the border generates a `PropertyChangeEvent`. This is why the `installUI` method registered the UI object as a `PropertyChangeListener` of the button. When the border is changed, the `propertyChange` method is called.

The other problem is that buttons allow you to define extra space between the border and the text and icon, using the `setMargin` method, which takes an `Insets` argument. The extra space is provided by creating the button's border as a `CompoundBorder`, of which the outer part is the border type used by the look-and-feel (e.g. `MetalButtonBorder`) and the inner part a `BasicMarginBorder`. `BasicMarginBorder` gets its insets by calling the `getMargin` method of the button with which it is associated. As a result, if the programmer changes the margin of a button, the effective size of the border changes accordingly. But, of course, our empty border must always be the same size as the real border or the button itself will not be of the correct size. A possible solution to this would be to implement our own border as a compound, with the empty border on the outside and a `BasicMarginBorder` inside. This would work, until the programmer calls `setBorder` and replaces the standard border with one that is not a compound label (which would, incidentally, stop the margins from appearing). It is, of course, possible to work around even this problem by checking each new border to see whether it is a compound border and trying to mimic what the user is installing. Fortunately, however, there is a simpler solution.

Like the border, the button margin is an attribute of the button itself, not of the UI class. It is also a bound property of the button, so when it is changed a `PropertyChangeEvent` is generated and this can be used to arrange for the margin change to be reflected in the empty border by detecting it in the `propertyChange` method:

```
// PropertyChangeListener interface
public void propertyChange(PropertyChangeEvent evt) {
  if (evt.getPropertyName().equals("border")) {
    JComponent c = (JComponent)evt.getSource();
    Border newBorder = (Border)evt.getNewValue()

    // Don't do anything if this is our border being installed
    if (newBorder != emptyBorder) {
      if ((emptyBorder == null && newBorder != null) ||
         (emptyBorder != null && newBorder != null &&
           emptyBorder.getBorderInsets(c) !=
             newBorder.getBorderInsets(c))) {
        createEmptyBorder(newBorder, c);
      }
      originalBorder = newBorder;

      // Put back the empty border if we need to
      if (borderShown == false) {
        c.setBorder(emptyBorder);
      }
    }
  } else if (evt.getPropertyName().equals("margin")) {
    AbstractButton b = (AbstractButton)evt.getSource();
    if (emptyBorder != null) {
      emptyBorder = null;
      createEmptyBorder(originalBorder, b);

      // Install the new empty border if we need to
      if (borderShown == false) {
        b.setBorder(emptyBorder);
      }
    }
  }
}
```

The first part of this method is concerned with handling border changes made by `setBorder`. The first thing this method does is to get the border just installed and check whether it is our empty border—if it is, there is nothing to do. This will happen regularly, because the UI class uses the same `setBorder` method that the programmer would use to change the border and will get the same `PropertyChangeEvent`. Assuming that this is a new programmer-installed border, it is important to generate an empty border for it if there isn't one already. There are two cases in which this can happen:

- The button might have been initialized with no border. This can be achieved by setting the `Button.border` property in the `UIDefaults` table to `null`.
- The button has a border and the new border has different insets.

As has already been said, it is essential that the empty border matches exactly the button's real border, so a change of border insets must be dealt with by creating a new empty border. When the matter of creating this border has been dealt with, the correct border must be reinstalled in the component. If the border should not be shown because of the button's current state, the empty one is put back using `setBorder`; otherwise, there is no need to do anything, because the current setting is correct.

The second part of `propertyChange` handles a change in the button margin, notified as a change of the `margin` property. When this happens, a new empty border that matches the size of the original border must be created; the size of the original border will include the margin space if it is the default compound border for the button. To create the correct border, you only need to call `createEmptyBorder` again, passing it the border that it has to match. Because this method will only create a new border if is doesn't already have one, `emptyBorder` is set to `null` first to force a new border to be created. Note that this method works whether or not the programmer has installed a nonstandard border that does not take account of the margin, because it creates a border that exactly matches the original border, no matter how its size is calculated.

Changing Component User Interfaces

You've now seen the complete implementation of the Core JFC Button user interface. At this stage, you would undoubtedly want to try it out to see how it works, which brings us to the problem of changing component user interfaces. There are several ways in which you can change the user interface, depending on what changes you want to make and how wide the scope of those changes should be. This section shows all of the techniques available to you.

Changing the User Interface for One Instance of a Component

At this point, what you have is a UI class for a single component and you'd like to try it out. Because you don't have a complete look-and-feel package, you can't just switch in the Core JFC look-and-feel and create a button—that step comes later in this chapter. What you need to be able to do is create a few buttons that have your UI class installed in them. Fortunately, this is very simple.

As you saw earlier, the UI class for a component is installed by calling its `updateUI` method, the default implementation of which locates the UI class from the `UIDefaults` table and passes it to the `JComponent setUI` method. All you need to do to force your own UI class to be used is to override the `updateUI` method as shown in Listing 13-6.

Listing 13-6   Installing a specific UI class in a component

```
JButton b = new JButton("Press...") {
   public void updateUI() {
      setUI(CJFCButtonUI.createUI(this));
   }
};
```

This code creates a subclass of `JButton` with an overridden `updateUI` method. Instead of using the `UIDefaults` table via `UIManager`, a new `CJFCButtonUI` object is created by calling its `createUI` method and installed directly. This technique works for any component as long as you have a replacement UI class available and was used in the `CJFCButtonTest` example that you saw in Figure 13-2.

When you install the UI this way, the `updateUI` method is permanently overridden. This means that if you allow the user to change the look-and-feel of an application that has a button created like this, the button will keep the same UI class even when all of the other components change, because the UI class selected no longer depends on the current look-and-feel. In this case, when the look-and-feel is changed, the `CJFCButtonUI uninstallUI` method will be called to detach the UI object from the button, followed immediately by its `installUI` method.

Changing the User Interface for One Component, Applicationwide

If you create a completely new UI class from scratch or you just modify the UI class of an existing look-and-feel to make it behave slightly differently, you may want to arrange for the new UI class to apply to every component of that type in an application. Using the method shown in the previous section would be very tedious in this case and it might be impractical, because it requires you to find all of the code that creates components of the type that you want to behave differently and change the creation code. If you're using third-party software, or you're modifying something like JButton which is used internally by Swing (for example in JOptionPane), then you won't be able to change this code.

To change the UI class for all instances of a component, you need to go back to the place that the UI class comes from—the UIDefaults table. The simplest way to change the component-to-UI-class mapping is to overwrite the appropriate entry in this table, so that when, say, JButton calls the UIManager getUI method for ButtonUI, it is returned the name JFCBook.Cjfc.CJFCButtonUI. This will result in the right UI class being installed in every JButton.

An example of this technique is shown in Listing 13-7. This program creates a frame onto which places one button. Every 10 seconds, it adds another button and resizes the frame, if necessary, so that all of the buttons can be seen. A GridLayout manager is used to place the buttons in a grid with four columns. As you can see, the buttons are all created in the usual way, with no subclassing or special code attached.

Listing 13-7   Installing a specific UI class in a component

```
package JFCBook.Chapter13;

import com.sun.java.swing.*;
import java.awt.*;

public class AllButtonTest {
   public static void main(String[] args) {
     JFrame f = new JFrame("Change UI of All Buttons");
     f.getContentPane().setLayout(new GridLayout(0, 4));

     // Change the UIDefaults settings
     updateUIDefaults();

     Icon okIcon = new ImageIcon(CJFCButtonTest.class.getResource
                 ("images/ok.gif"));

     JButton b = new JButton("" + count++);
     b.setIcon(okIcon);
     f.getContentPane().add(b);
     f.pack();
     f.setVisible(true);

     try {
       for (;;) {
         Thread.sleep(10000);
         b = new JButton("" + count++);
```

continued

```
            b.setIcon(okIcon);
            f.getContentPane().add(b);
            f.pack();
          }
      } catch (Throwable t) {
      }
   }

   protected static void updateUIDefaults() {
      UIManager.put("ButtonUI", "JFCBook.Cjfc.CJFCButtonUI");
   }

   protected static int count = 1;
}
```

The significant part of this example is the `updateUIDefaults` method, which is called before the first button is created. This simple function just uses the `UIManager` `put` method to associate a new UI class with any component that asks for a UI called `ButtonUI`. This is all you need to do to change the user interface of every `JButton` in the application. You can run this example for yourself using the command:

```
java JFCBook.Chapter13.AllButtonTest
```

Customizing All Instances of One Component

The technique that you saw in the last section can also be used to change any attribute of a component that comes from the `UIDefaults` table. As you know, buttons get several attributes, including their default font and background color, from `UIDefaults`. By changing these defaults, you can arrange for every button to have a non-standard value for these attributes. For example, the code in Listing 13-8 sets the default font for all buttons to a 16-point, bold dialog font and the background color to whatever the selected look-and-feel declares as its "desktop" color. Notice that the value of the "desktop" color is itself obtained from the `UIDefaults` table and that the new font is given not as a `Font`, but as a `FontUIResource`.

Listing 13-8   Customizing button attributes

```
protected static void updateUIDefaults() {
   UIManager.put("ButtonUI", "JFCBook.Cjfc.CJFCButtonUI");
   UIManager.put("Button.font", new FontUIResource("Dialog",
             Font.BOLD, 16));
   UIManager.put("Button.background", UIManager.get("desktop"));
}
```

You can run this example with the command:

```
java JFCBook.Chapter13.CustomizeButtonTest
```

Switching the Look-and-Feel

Switching the look-and-feel of an application is a simple thing to do, but there are a couple of tricky points that you need to be aware of. In this section, you'll see how to create a menu that allows the user to switch the look-and-feel from the application's menu bar and you'll see more clearly the difference between the UIDefaults table of a particular look-and-feel and the one that you can access via UIManager.

To demonstrate the technique for switching look-and-feel, let's build this capability into the graphics program that was first created in Chapter 4, "Graphics, Text Handling, and Printing," and then extended with menus and toolbars in Chapter 6. The aim is to make it use the Core JFC button user interface for all of its buttons and to give it the capability of switching to any of the available look-and-feels via a menu that will be added to its File menu. You've already seen how to make all of the buttons in an application be Core JFC buttons, and this code will be incorporated into the modified graphics program. The only piece that you haven't seen yet is exactly how to switch look-and-feel.

Because the ability to change look-and-feel is likely to be useful in other programs, this example creates a new class that provides a method that will create and return a menu listing the available look-and-feels and the code to handle a switch to any of them. To incorporate this into an existing application, all you have to do is add a call to create the menu and then place the menu somewhere in your application's menu set. The simplest way to explain how this works is to look at the code, which is shown in Listing 13-9.

Listing 13-9 Building a menu that allows a look-and-feel switch

```
package JFCBook.Chapter13;

import com.sun.java.swing.*;
import java.awt.event.*;

public class SwitchLF {
   public static JMenu createSwitchLFMenu(String label,
              JFrame f, boolean verify) {
    // Create a menu entry for each L&F we manage to load
    LookAndFeel lf;
    JMenu menu = new JMenu(label);
    int menuCount = 0;
    UIManager.LookAndFeelInfo[] lfInfo =
              UIManager.getInstalledLookAndFeels();
```

continued

```
  for (int i = 0; i < lfInfo.length; i++) {
    try {
      String className = lfInfo[i].getClassName();
      if (verify) {
        Class cl = Class.forName(className);
        lf = (LookAndFeel)cl.newInstance();
        if (!lf.isSupportedLookAndFeel()) {
          className = null;
        }
      }

      if (className != null) {
        LFSwitchAction switchAction = new LFSwitchAction(lfInfo[i], f);
        JMenuItem mi = menu.add(switchAction);
        mi.setToolTipText(lfInfo[i].getName());
        menuCount++;
      }
    } catch (Throwable t) {
      // Ignore all exceptions - don't add to menu
      System.out.println("Failed loading " + lfInfo[i].getClassName() + ":\n" + t);
    }
  }

  return menuCount == 0 ? null : menu;
}

// Action handler for switching L&F
protected static class LFSwitchAction extends AbstractAction {
  public LFSwitchAction(UIManager.LookAndFeelInfo lfi, JFrame f) {
    super(lfi.getName());
    this.lfi = lfi;
    this.f = f;
  }

  public void actionPerformed(ActionEvent evt) {
    LookAndFeel oldLF = UIManager.getLookAndFeel();
    try {
      UIManager.setLookAndFeel(lfi.getClassName());

      // Switch all component UI's
      SwingUtilities.updateComponentTreeUI(f);
      f.invalidate();
      f.validate();
      f.repaint();
    } catch (Throwable t) {
      // Ignore all exceptions
```

```
         System.out.println("Failed to install " + lfi.getName() + " L&F\n" + t);
         try {
           UIManager.setLookAndFeel(oldLF);
         } catch (Throwable e) {
           System.out.println("Failed to restore old L&F");
           System.exit(0);
         }
       }
     }

     protected UIManager.LookAndFeelInfo lfi;
     protected JFrame f;
   }
 }
```

An application only has to add the following lines of code to make use of this class:

```
JMenu switchMenu = SwitchLF.createSwitchLFMenu("Switch Look-and-Feel…", f, false);
if (switchMenu != null) {
   fileMenu.add(switchMenu);
}
```

The arguments passed to the `createSwitchLFMenu` method are the label to appear on the menu item that the user will see, a reference to the application's top-level frame and a boolean. You'll see why the last two arguments are needed shortly.

The first thing that `createSwitchLFMenu` does is create an empty `JMenu` with the label given as its first argument. It then needs to find out which look-and-feel classes are available and add an entry for each of them to this menu. For this, it uses the `UIManager` `getInstalledLookAndFeels` method that you saw earlier in this chapter. This method returns an array of `LookAndFeelInfo` objects, one for each look-and-feel installed on the system.

Given this array, one possible approach is to just add each entry in it to a menu. If you call this method with its third argument (called `verify`) set to `false`, this is exactly what happens. However, you might want want to check that all of the look-and-feels listed in `swing.properties` are actually available. If you set the `verify` argument to `true`, two checks are performed for each look-and-feel.

First, the `forName` method of `java.lang.Class` is used to get a `Class` object given the look-and-feel class name. If the look-and-feel is not installed, this will throw an exception. Given that the class is present, the next thing to do is to use the `Class` `newInstance` method to instantiate it and, at the same time, cast it to a reference of type `LookAndFeel`. If this does not throw an exception, then the class must represent a valid look-and-feel. Lastly, the `isSupportedLookAndFeel` method of the class is called. If this returns `true`, then this look-and-feel can be used.

At this point, it is time to add a menu entry for the look-and-feel. As you saw earlier, a `LookAndFeelInfo` class has a `getName` method that returns a string that describes the look-and-feel and this strings is used both as the label of the menu item and to create a tooltip that appears if the mouse hovers over the menu for a short time. The `LookAndFeel` class has a more descriptive text string available from its `getDescription` method, but this class will not have been loaded if this method is being called with `verify` set to `false`. The reason for allowing `verify` to be set to `false` is to make it possible to avoid the overhead of loading classes for look-and-feels that are never going to be used, so it would not be a good idea to access the `LookAndFeel` class for each installed look-and-feel to get the full description.

The menu item is created by adding an `Action` to the menu that this method is building. The `Action` is implemented in a static inner class called `LFSwitchAction`, which is derived from the Swing class `AbstractAction` (refer back to Chapter 6 for a full discussion of `AbstractAction`). A single instance of this class will be attached to each menu item that is generated and it will store a reference to the target look-and-feel class in the form of its class name and the reference to the application's top-level frame passed as an argument to `createSwitchLFMenu`. When the menu item is activated, the `actionPerformed` method will be called to make the switch.

Switching look-and-feel is actually a two-step process. The first is obvious—you need to call the `UIManager setLookAndFeel` method and give it the class name that was stored when the menu item was created. This will make the new look-and-feel current and will install its `UIDefaults` table. However, it does *not* change the appearance of the application at all because the UI classes of all of the user interface objects that have been created so far are not changed by this method. To make the interface change, you need to call the `SwingUtilities` method `updateComponentTreeUI`, passing it the top-level frame of the application. This method starts from the component it is given and recursively processes it and all of its children, switching their UI classes by calling their `updateUI` method. When this method has completed, the user interface is redrawn by forcing the frame to resize and repaint itself.

Now let's add this menu item to the graphics program from Chapter 6. At the same time, the `UIDefaults` table will be changed to make the application use the Core JFC user interface for all of its buttons. The code that is going to be modified was presented in Listing 6-8 in Chapter 6.

The new version is shown in Listing 13-10, with the code added highlighted in bold. Note that the class name has also been changed from `GraphicsMenuDemo` to `GraphicsDemo1`, to avoid confusion; this change is not highlighted.

Listing 13-10   Adding look-and-feel switch capability to an application

```
package JFCBook.Chapter13;

import com.sun.java.swing.*;
import com.sun.java.swing.border.*;
import java.awt.*;
import java.awt.event.*;
import JFCBook.Chapter4.GraphicsBorderedCanvas;
import JFCBook.Chapter4.EdgedBorder;
import JFCBook.Chapter6.GraphicsMenuDemoPane;
import JFCBook.Chapter13.SwitchLF;

public class GraphicsDemo1 extends JFrame {
   public GraphicsDemo1(String title) {
      super(title);
      this.getContentPane().setBackground(UIManager.getColor("control"));

      // Create the canvas in which the
      // drawing will be done.
      GraphicsBorderedCanvas c = new GraphicsBorderedCanvas();

      // Create the border and associate it with the canvas
      Border bd = new EdgedBorder(UIManager.getColor("control"));
      c.setBackground(Color.white);
      c.setBorder(bd);

      // Create the pane that holds the user interface
      // including the toolbars
      GraphicsMenuDemoPane gp = new GraphicsMenuDemoPane(c);
      gp.setBackground(UIManager.getColor("control"));

      // Connect panel to canvas so that
      // it can enable/disable buttons
      c.addPropertyChangeListener(gp);

      // Connect the canvas to the panel
      // so that it can action button presses
      gp.setDrawingArea(c);

      // Select the initial color and shape
      // from the button panel.
      gp.selectTools();

      // Create the menu bar
      JMenuBar mb = new JMenuBar();
      this.setJMenuBar(mb);
```

continued

```
    // Build the File menu
    JMenu fileMenu = new JMenu("File");
    mb.add(fileMenu);
    fileMenu.setMnemonic('F');
    gp.buildFileMenu(fileMenu);

    JMenu switchMenu = SwitchLF.createSwitchLFMenu("Switch Look-and-Feel...",
                this, false);
    if (switchMenu != null) {
      fileMenu.addSeparator();
      fileMenu.add(switchMenu);
    }

    fileMenu.addSeparator();
    JMenuItem mi = new JMenuItem("Exit", 'x');
    mi.addActionListener(new ActionListener() {
      public void actionPerformed(ActionEvent evt) {
        System.exit(0);
      }
    });
    fileMenu.add(mi);

    // Add GraphicsDemo1Panel menus to the menu bar
    gp.addToMenuBar(mb);

    this.getContentPane().add(gp);
  }

  public static void updateUIDefaults() {
    UIManager.put("ButtonUI", "JFCBook.Cjfc.CJFCButtonUI");
  }

  public static void main(String[] args) {
    // Change defaults to use our button UI
    updateUIDefaults();

    GraphicsDemo1 f = new GraphicsDemo1("Graphics Demo 1");
    Dimension d = f.getPreferredSize();
    f.setSize(d.width, 500);
    f.addWindowListener(new WindowAdapter() {
      public void windowClosing(WindowEvent evt) {
        System.exit(0);
      }
    });
    f.setVisible(true);
  }
}
```

Notice how simple it is to add the ability to switch look-and-feel when our `SwitchLF` class is used. The `UIDefaults` change is also straightforward and doesn't show anything that you haven't seen before. It is also a temporary measure—in the next section, you'll see how to create a new look-and-feel that incorporates the Core JFC button. You can run this application using the command:

```
java JFCBook.Chapter13.GraphicsDemo1
```

With the Windows look-and-feel, you get an application that looks like Figure 13-3. You can see that only one of the toolbar buttons has a border, indicating that our button user interface is being used here.

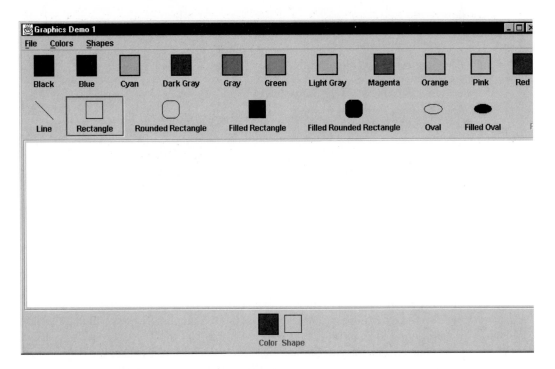

Figure 13-3   An application using the Core JFC button with the Windows look-and-feel.

Now if you pull down the `File` menu, you'll find a menu item labeled `Switch Look-and-Feel...`; if you activate this menu item, you get a drop-down menu that shows the available look-and-feel classes that the `SwitchLF` class found and, if you move the mouse over one of them and let it rest there for a short time, a tool tip will appear as shown in Figure 13-4.

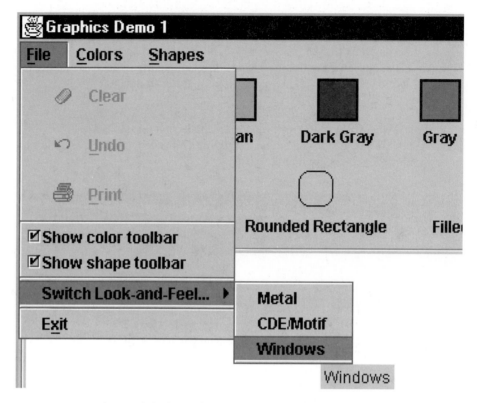

Figure 13-4   The switch look-and-feel menu.

Now select an alternative look-and-feel from the menu. After a short delay, the application will be redrawn with the new look-and-feel in place. Figure 13-5 shows the application after the Windows look-and-feel has been selected. As you'll see, there isn't much difference between them, but the menu bar shows you that they are using different look-and-feel classes.

As you can see, despite the fact that the look-and-feel has changed, the buttons still have the Core JFC user interface installed in them. You might think that, since the use of this UI class was enforced by changing the UIDefaults table while the Windows look-and-feel was selected, the change would be lost and a normal Motif UI class would be used. This is, however, not the case—as you saw earlier in this chapter, changes made via the UIManager put method are persistent because they are held by the MultiUIDefaults object which does not change when the look-and-feel is switched. The same applies to custom colors, fonts and other changes you might have made to the UIDefaults table.

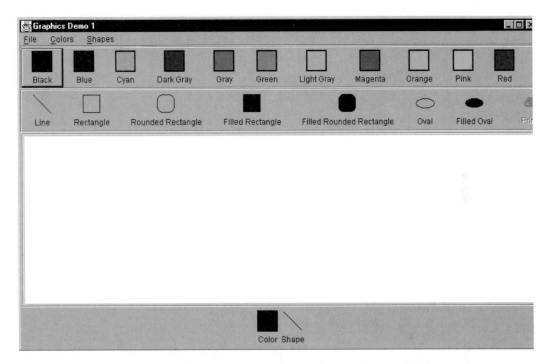

Figure 13-5 The graphics application after switching to the Motif look-and-feel.

The `SwitchLF` class is fine for switching the user interface of an application that has a single top-level frame and all of its components attached to it, but it doesn't work if your application has some hidden components or more than one window, because the `updateComponentTreeUI` method doesn't update the UI of anything not attached to the top-level frame that it is given in the `actionPerformed` method of the menu. For a more complex application, you could extend the `SwitchLF` class to incorporate your extra requirements, but another possibility is to do the extra work in an event handler.

The current look-and-feel is actually a bound property of the `UIManager` class, so you can register a `PropertyChangeListener` to receive notification of changes to it. The event handler will be called after the look-and-feel has been installed, but before the call to `setLookAndFeel` returns. You can use the event handler to perform any extra user interface updates that you need, including calling `updateComponentTreeUI` for frames in addition to the main one or components (such as dialogs) that the application keeps hidden until they are required.

To demonstrate how this is done, Listing 13-11 shows how to add a look-and-feel switch handler to the graphics demo application; only the added lines and a few adjacent lines are shown in this listing.

Listing 13-11   Handling look-and-feel switch using events

```
// Add GraphicsMenuDemoPanel menus to the menu bar
gp.addToMenuBar(mb);

this.getContentPane().add(gp);

// Register for notification of look-and-feel changes
UIManager.addPropertyChangeListener(new PropertyChangeListener() {
  public void propertyChange(PropertyChangeEvent evt) {
    if (evt.getPropertyName().equals("lookAndFeel")) {
      LookAndFeel lf = UIManager.getLookAndFeel();
      System.out.println("Look-and-feel changed to " + lf.getName()
           + " ("   + lf.getDescription() + ")");
    }
  }
});
```

You can run this example using the command:

```
java JFCBook.Chapter13.GraphicsDemo2
```

When you switch look-and-feel, the event handler will print the name and description of the new look-and-feel in the window from which the application was started. In a real application, of course, you would add code to make whatever extra user interface changes you needed in this method.

The Multiplexing Look-and-Feel

The multiplexing look-and-feel allows every component in the application to have more than one look-and-feel associated with it at the same time. This feature is useful in connection with Java Accessibility, because it makes it possible to connect, for example, a text field to the usual visual UI classes and to a separate look-and-feel that can turn the text into sounds. Look-and-feel classes suitable for this type of work are not part of the Swing package and Accessibility is not covered in this book, so this section will just give you a very brief introduction to the multiplexing look-and-feel so that you can see how it fits with the other look-and-feels.

The multiplexing look-and-feel is a complete package—you can find it com.sun.java.swing.plaf.multi. It has a UI class for every Swing component, but they don't contain any component-related code. Instead, they delegate work to *all* of the loaded look-and-feels.

To enable the multiplexing look-and-feel, you have to add a swing. auxiliarylaf line to your swing.properties file and list the extra look-and-feels that should be used, separated by commas. You do not include here any of the standard look-and-feels, which we will refer to as the primary look-and-feels. As an example, suppose you have two extra look-and-feels called `SoundLF` and `BrailleLF` installed on your system and you want to make them available to all applications. To do this, you add the following to `swing.properties`:

```
swing.auxiliarylaf=extraLF.soundLF.SoundLFLookAndFeel,
          extraLF.brailleLF.BrailleLFLookAndFeel
```

where it is assumed that the full package names are `extraLF.soundLF` and `extraLF.brailleLF`, respectively. When `UIManager` finds this line, it loads all of the look-and-feel classes specified and then loads the multiplexing look-and-feel manager which resides in `com.sun.java.swing.plaf.multi.MultiLookAndFeel`. You can, if you wish, customize the multiplexing look-and-feel using another line in `swing.properties`:

```
swing.multiplexinglaf=myMult.MyMultiLookAndFeel
```

You are not obliged to have a `swing.multiplexinglaf` line in `swing.properties` to use this facility, because the default one will be loaded if there is a `swing.auxiliarylaf` line. You can get a list of all of the installed auxiliary look-and-feels using the `getAuxiliaryLookAndFeels` method of `UIManager`.

When the multiplexing look-and-feel is in use, all `UIManager` methods that would normally access the default look-and-feel are directed instead to multiplexing look-and-feel, which invokes them on the current default look-and-feel *and* on all of the auxiliary look-and-feels. Also, the UI classes installed in every component belong not to the current primary UI, but to the multiplexing look-and-feel. As a result, a `paint` request for a button, for example, is directed to the `paint` method of `MultiButtonUI`, which then sends it to the `paint` method of (say) `CJFCButtonUI` if the Core JFC is the default primary UI, followed by the `paint` methods of `SoundLFButtonUI` and `BrailleLFButtonUI`, which will do whatever is appropriate.

If you are writing a look-and-feel package, you don't need to be aware of the multiplexing look-and-feel because it is completely transparent. Switching look-and-feels when it is in use affects only the primary look-and-feel: any auxiliary look-and-feels are left untouched.

Creating a New Look-and-Feel

Creating a completely new look-and-feel is more an artistic exercise than a technical one and this book is not even going to attempt to cover the issues of user interface ergonomics. Instead, in this section you'll see how to start developing a new look-and-feel by putting in place a skeleton that you can use as the basis for your new interface style. If you don't want to build a completely new look-and-feel but just want to modify some irksome feature of an existing one, you'll see how to do that in this chapter as well.

The Core JFC Look-and-Feel

It would be nice to be able to find the time to build a completely new look-and-feel, but I, in common with many software developers, have neither the skill nor the artistic temperament to complete the task in a reasonable space of time. Instead, I settled for implementing a new user interface for buttons (and even that is not an original concept, although the code is) and up to now, it has been necessary to modify the application in some way to use it.

To build a complete look-and-feel, you have to supply a `LookAndFeel` class and a user interface component for all of the Swing components. As you can see from Table 13-1, which shows the content of the Basic look-and-feel package, this is no small undertaking. In practice, even if you do intend to implement all of these classes, you won't be able to develop them all at once and start testing when the implementation is done—I've never yet met a project manager who would be willing to let me take several months to develop something without being able to demonstrate anything at all for a long period. It is much more acceptable (for the developer and the manager) to start with a working skeleton and then add to it. Given that you're going to do it like this, there are two ways that you can go about the task of building a new look-and-feel package.

- You can create a complete `LookAndFeel` class and a dummy UI class for each component.

- You can derive your look-and-feel from another one, create a skeleton `LookAndFeel` class and as many UI classes as you have implemented so far, adding others as you complete them.

If you take the first approach, you'll end up creating around 40 files for the UI classes that you'll eventually implement. Each of these files will contain a skeleton UI class that extends the corresponding one in `com.sun.java.swing.plaf`. You'll also have to provide a dummy implementation for any methods in the superclass that are declared abstract. For example, if the Core JFC look-and-feel were implemented this way, the file I would first create for the UI class for `JOptionPane` would look something like the one shown in Listing 13-12.

Listing 13-12   A dummy UI class for JOptionPane

```
package JFCBook.Cjfc;

import com.sun.java.swing.plaf.*;

public class CJFCOptionPaneUI extends OptionPaneUI {
  public void selectInitialValue() {
      }

      public abstract boolean containsCustomComponents() {
        return false;
      }
}
```

Of course, these files are useful in the long run, because every one of them will get filled in with new code. You'll also have to create a LookAndFeel class that links the UI class name to the UI classes themselves and add all of your classes into it.

While this is a completely workable approach, there is another one that gets you started quicker and allows you to start implementing new UI classes as you need them. It also allows you to create a new UI as a modification of an existing one, which is something that is probably going to be as common as creating a complete new look-and-feel. Let's illustrate the technique by showing how the Core JFC look-and-feel is implemented.

In truth, as I hinted above, the Core JFC look-and-feel has only one new UI class—the button UI that you've seen in this chapter. The rest of its implementation is borrowed from the Metal look-and-feel.

The Core JFC look-and-feel is held in the JFCBook.Cjfc package. The source code for this package has only three files:

CJFCButtonUI.java

CJFCButtonListener.java

CJFCLookAndFeel.java

You've already seen the first two of these. The third file is, of course, the one that pulls the look-and-feel together and it is the one that creates the class file needed by the UIManager. You can see the content of this file in Listing 13-13. In fact, you can create a new look-and-feel class with only the last of these files, since you don't need to add a new component UI class at the beginning: as you'll see, you can just create a skeleton that is identical to the look-and-feel that you are basing the new one on, or just change some colors and so on.

Listing 13-13   The CFJCLookAndFeel class

```
package JFCBook.Cjfc;

import com.sun.java.swing.*;
import com.sun.java.swing.plaf.*;
import com.sun.java.swing.plaf.metal.*;
import java.awt.Font;

public class CJFCLookAndFeel extends MetalLookAndFeel {
  public String getName() {
    return "Core JFC Look and Feel";
  }


  public String getDescription() {
    return "The Core Java Foundation Classes Look-and-Feel";
  }

  public String getID() {
    return "Metal";
  }

  public boolean isNativeLookAndFeel() {
    return false;
  }


  public boolean isSupportedLookAndFeel() {
    return super.isSupportedLookAndFeel();
  }

  protected void initSystemColorDefaults(UIDefaults table) {
    super.initSystemColorDefaults(table);

    // In this array, add any colors that you want to override.
    // As an example, we show how to override the color for "desktop".
    // The value must be in an appropriate form for Color.decode()
    String[] systemColors = {
      "desktop", "#005C5C", /* Color of the desktop background */

      // Add extra overrides here
    };

    // Add override colors
    loadSystemColors(table, systemColors);
  }
```

```
//
// Add to this table the UI classes that override those
// of the look-and-feel being extended.
protected void initClassDefaults(UIDefaults table) {
  super.initClassDefaults(table);

  String cjfcPackageName = "JFCBook.Cjfc.";
  Object[] uiDefaults = {
     "ButtonUI", cjfcPackageName + "CJFCButtonUI",
     // Add extra classes here
  };

  table.putDefaults(uiDefaults);
  }

// Add here any component defaults to override or
// extend the base look-and-feel
//
protected void initComponentDefaults(UIDefaults table) {
  super.initComponentDefaults(table);

  FontUIResource dialogBold14 = new FontUIResource("Dialog",
            Font.BOLD, 14);

  Object[] defaults = {
     "Label.font", dialogBold14,       // Label font.
  };
  table.putDefaults(defaults);
  }

}
```

Most of what is in this file should be familiar from the discussion of `BasicLookAndFeel` earlier in this chapter. Notice first that this class extends `MetalLookAndFeel`, which makes it possible to use the code that installs defaults for Metal and just code the additions that are needed for each class as you go along.

The `getName` and `getDescription` methods just return short and long descriptions for the look-and-feel, while the `getID` method supplies the name of the look-and-feel on which this one is based, When you run the final version of the graphics program that has been used in this chapter, you'll see that these names appear in the menus. The `isNativeLookAndFeel` method obviously should always return `false` (unless you work for a platform vendor and are implementing their look-and-feel...), while the `isSupportedLookAndFeel` always returns `true`, because the Metal look-and-feel from which it is derived is available on all Swing platforms, but actually obtains its returned value by invoking its superclass isSupportedLookAndFeel method in case there is a change of policy at some future time.

The remaining three methods, initSystemColorDefaults, initClassDefaults and initComponentDefaults are really what characterize your look-and-feel. Here, you install specific values for system colors, UI name to UI class name mappings and component defaults that distinguish your look-and-feel; these methods have already been covered in our discussion of the BasicLookAndFeel class. Since this look-and-feel is just extending an existing look-and-feel, each of these methods just invokes the superclass version. Doing this installs almost everything you need—all you have to do is add anything extra or modify what is already there. Because all of these methods are updating a Hashtable, you can replace entries by just adding them again with the same key, as has been done here.

All that is actually needed to build the Core JFC look-and-feel is to change the mapping for the key ButtonUI in the UIDefaults table. Since this key is set up in the initClassDefaults method, you can see that code has been added there to make the change. The code creates a new array of entries, in a form acceptable to putDefaults (which you saw earlier), and uses that method to install it directly into the Hashtable, overwriting the mapping set up by the Metal look-and-feel. Note that the table generated here is the one for the Core JFC look-and-feel only— this is not the same as using the UIManager put method. As you create more UI classes, you should add them in here, progressively replacing the entries installed by Metal.

For illustration, code is also included in initComponentDefaults which changes the font for labels. Again, this method creates an array of replacement entries and calls putDefaults to overwrite the Metal values. If you want to see a good selection of typical component defaults, look at the source file for the BasicLookAndFeel class. Similarly, there is code in the initSystemColorDefaults method that adds to the set of default system colors for this look-and-feel. In this case, the same color mapping is actually installed as would be installed by Metal—this is just a placeholder that shows the format that you should use if you want to actually change any of the system colors.

As you develop your look-and-feel, you will add more and more entries in these three methods until, when you are finished, you won't need to use the superclass methods any more. At this point, you should remove the invocations of the superclass methods and re-parent the class so that it extends BasicLookAndFeel.

Once this class has been compiled, you can use the name JFCBook.Cjfc.CJFCLookAndFeel in swing.properties to use it as your default look-and-feel, or you can use it in conjunction with the example program GraphicsDemo3, which you can run using the command:

```
java JFCBook.Chapter13.GraphicsDemo3
```

Before running this program, however, you need to make another change to your swing.properties file. First, you need to add corejfc to the list of installed

look-and-feels, then you need to add properties for the Core JFC look-and-feel.
Here are some suitable lines:

```
swing.installedlafs=metal,motif,windows,corejfc

swing.installedlaf.corejfc.name=Core JFC
swing.installedlaf.corejfc.class=JFCBook.Cjfc.CJFCLookAndFeel
```

GraphicsDemo3 is a modified version of the one shown in Listing 13-10, in
which the UIDefaults table is no longer changed at the start of the main method
and the updateUIDefaults method has been deleted. As a result, when you start
it, it will take on your default look-and-feel and have the button style appropriate to
that look-and-feel. If you now pull down the file menu and activate the Switch
Look-and-Feel... entry, you should see a menu item with "Core JFC" on it (see
Figure 13-6).

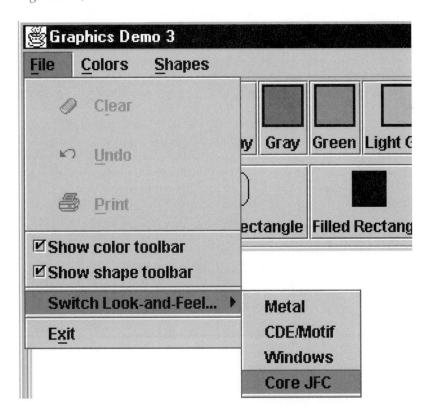

Figure 13-6   The Core JFC look-and-feel on the application look-and-feel menu.

Finally, activate the menu item and the application will change to look like a Metal
program, apart from the buttons which have the Core JFC style, and the text of the
labels at the bottom of the window, which is now in a 14-point, bold font.

Using a New Look-and-Feel to Modify Existing Behavior

In Chapter 10, "The Tree Control," you saw how to develop a file system tree control using the JTree component. The final version of that control had a small flaw, however—it initially showed expansion icons for every directory in the file system, whether or not that directory had any subdirectories. This happens because the UI classes for JTree supplied by the standard look-and-feels do not take into account whether the tree nodes have nodes beneath them when they first draw those nodes—in fact, they always provide an expansion box for a node which is not a leaf until you expand the node, whether or not it actually has any child nodes. Now that you know how to create your own look-and-feel, you can change the behavior of the tree so that it only provides expansion boxes when you would expect them.

The key to obtaining the proper behavior is to extend the tree's UI implementation so that it draws expansion boxes only for those nodes that actually have child nodes. Here, you'll see how to extend the Core JFC look-and-feel so that its JTree controls exhibit this behavior. To find out where the UI class determines whether to draw expansion boxes, you need to look through the source code for the tree UI class. The Core JFC look-and-feel is derived from Metal, so the first place to look is in the Metal implementation of TreeUI. The Swing package supplied by JavaSoft includes a ZIP file with the Swing source code. If you unzip this file, you'll find the source code for the Metal TreeUI class in src\com\sun\java\swing\plaf\metal\MetalTreeUI.java. If you're using JDK 1.2 and you installed the source code, you'll find the corresponding source in src\java\awt\swing\plaf\metal\MetalTreeUI.java. If you look through this file, you won't see anything that influences whether expansion boxes are drawn. You will notice, however, that MetalTreeUI is derived from BasicTreeUI, so the next file to look at (for JFC 1.1—you can easily work out the correct file name for JDK 1.2) is src\com\sun\java\swing\plaf\basic\BasicTreeUI.java. This file contains the following method, which is the one you are looking for:

```
protected boolean shouldPaintExpandControl(VisibleTreeNode
            parentNode, VisibleTreeNode childNode);
```

Core Note

Working out what to change to modify the behavior of a look-and-feel always involves looking through the source code because Sun didn't provide javadoc *documentation for the look-and-feel packages. This case is particularly simple because the method name helps you to find the code whose behavior needs to change. In general, though, you would probably need to spend some time working out how the UI class works to find the right place to make a modification.*

To arrange for expansion controls to be used only when appropriate for the file system tree, you need to override the shouldPaintExandControl method in the Core JFC look-and-feel by implementing a Core JFC UI class for the tree control.

Creating the Core JFC Tree UI

Once you know what to change, it is a relatively simple matter to make the change itself. Here, you need to create a modified TreeUI class that has different behavior for the shouldPaintExandControl method. The Core JFC look-and-feel is derived from Metal, so the new TreeUI class should be derived from MetalTreeUI. To do this, create a new file called CJFCTreeUI.java in the Cjfc directory of the example code installed from the CD-ROM. This file should contain the code shown in Listing 13-14.

Listing 13-14   The Core JFC TreeUI class

```
package JFCBook.Cjfc;

import com.sun.java.swing.*;
import com.sun.java.swing.plaf.*;
import com.sun.java.swing.plaf.basic.*;
import com.sun.java.swing.plaf.metal.*;

public class CJFCTreeUI extends MetalTreeUI {
  // ComponentUI implementation
  public static ComponentUI createUI(JComponent c) {
    return new CJFCTreeUI();
  }

  // Paint an expand control only if the node has children.
  protected boolean shouldPaintExpandControl(VisibleTreeNode
              parentNode, VisibleTreeNode childNode) {
    boolean result = super.shouldPaintExpandControl(parentNode,
                childNode);
    if (result == true) {
      result = childNode.getModelChildCount() != 0;
    }
    return result;
  }
}
```

This code is very much simpler than the implementation of CJFCButtonUI that you saw in Listing 13-5, because it is only making a minor change to an existing UI class. The static createUI method must be implemented so that the correct TreeUI class is installed. If you didn't implement this method, a `MetalTreeUI` object would be used instead. The rest of this class is the modified `shouldPaintExpandControl` method. This method is called with two objects of type `VisibleTreeNode`. `VisibleTreeNode` is an abstract class used internally by `BasicTreeUI` to represent nodes of the tree that have been created to mirror the nodes in the tree's data model. These nodes are used to control the way in which the tree is drawn and they are created only when needed—nodes in the data model do not have corresponding `VisibleTreeNodes` in the `BasicTreeUI` until they become visible. If you look at the implementation of this class (in `src\com\sun\java\swing\plaf\basic\ VisibleTreeNode.java`), you'll find that it has a method called `getModelChildCount` that returns the number of children that the corresponding node in the tree's data model has. This is exactly what you need to know in order to decide whether a node should have an expansion box.

The implementation of `shouldPaintExpandControl` in Listing 13-14 uses this method to determine its return value. You'll notice that it first calls the `MetalTreeUI` implementation of `shouldPaintExpandControl`—this is necessary because there is special behavior for the root node of the tree which is implemented by the `MetalTreeUI` version of this method. If this method returns `false`, there is no need to change the result, since the only case that should be trapped is the one in which child nodes are being shown when they shouldn't be. Hence, the child count in the model is only checked when the result to be returned would be `true`.

Adding the Tree UI to the Core JFC Look-and-Feel

Creating a new UI class is the first half of the process. To use the new look-and-feel class, you need to arrange for it to be returned from the `UIDefaults` table of the look-and-feel when a new `JTree` object is being created. In the case of the Core JFC look-and-feel, you need to edit the `initClassDefaults` method in the `CJFCLookAndFeel.java` file, as shown in Listing 13-15.

Listing 13-15   Enabling the Core JFC TreeUI class

```
protected void initClassDefaults(UIDefaults table) {
  super.initClassDefaults(table);

  String cjfcPackageName = "JFCBook.Cjfc.";
  Object[] uiDefaults = {
    "ButtonUI", cjfcPackageName + "CJFCButtonUI",
    "TreeUI",   cjfcPackageName + "CJFCTreeUI",
    // Add extra classes here
  };

  table.putDefaults(uiDefaults);
}
```

Testing the Core JFC Tree UI

If you now compile both the CJFCTreeUI.java and CJFCLookAndFeel.java files, you'll have a Core JFC look-and-feel that incorporates the new behavior for the tree. To see that it works, you need to change your default look-and-feel to Core JFC and then try the FileTreeTest program that was developed in Chapter 10. Changing the default look-and-feel is a matter of modifying the swing.properties file— just change the swing.defaultlaf property as shown here:

```
swing.defaultlaf=JFCBook.Cjfc.CJFCLookAndFeel
```

Now run the FileTreeTest program:

```
java JFCBook.Chapter10.FileTreeTest C:
```

When you do this, you'll find that directories that do not have subdirectories don't have expansion controls. You may need to navigate around the file system a little to find such a subdirectory. Finally, you have a tree that provides the appropriate behavior for a file system tree control.

Summary

This chapter took an in-depth look at the Swing pluggable look-and-feel mechanism. First, you saw the UIManager class and saw how it interacts with the application to install a default look-and-feel. Next, the UIDefaults table was introduced. This table holds the defaults for individual look-and-feel classes. Using these defaults, the look-and-feel independent parts of the Swing components are able to install the correct UI classes for the current look-and-feel and those classes can correctly set colors, fonts and other attributes. The description of UIDefaults was followed by a discussion of the two classes that underpin all of the Swing look-and-feel packages— LookAndFeel and BasicLookAndFeel.

In the second part of the chapter, you had a detailed look at a UI class that implements a different user interface for a button and saw how to install and test this in a existing application. Finally, the last part of the chapter showed you how to go about creating a skeleton look-and-feel package of your own, beginning with a single source file and described how to incrementally expand it to produce a complete look-and-feel of your own.

Using the techniques you've seen in this chapter, you can do anything from change the font of an individual component to replacing the complete look-and-feel of an application, without changing a single line of the application's code, proving just how powerful and open-ended the Swing component set is.

CLASS DIAGRAMS

Appendix A

This appendix contains diagrams that show how the classes in the Swing packages relate to each other and to their subclasses from other packages. The symbols used in these diagrams are shown in the key in Figure A-1.

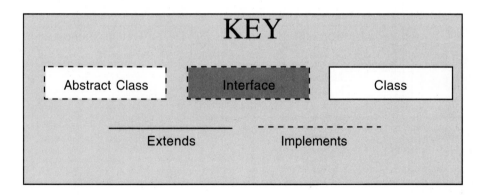

KEY

Abstract Class | Interface | Class

Extends | Implements

Figure A-1   Key to class diagrams.

The Swing Package

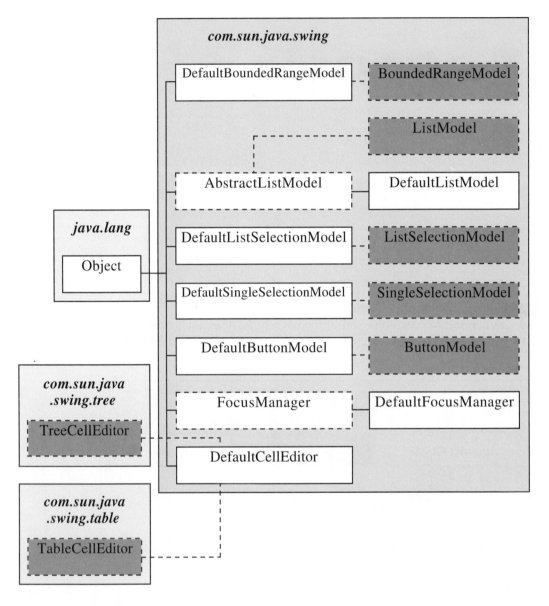

Figure A-2   Swing Classes (part 1).

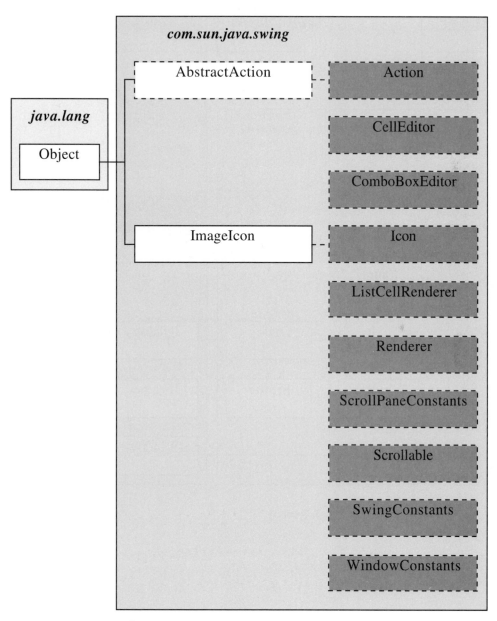

Figure A-3   Swing Classes (part 2).

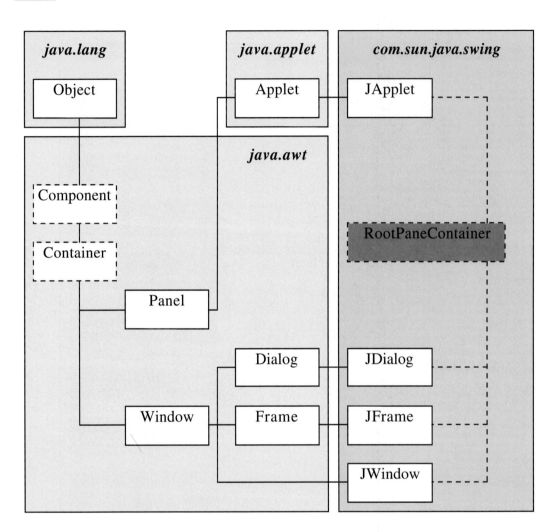

Figure A-4   Swing Classes (part 3).

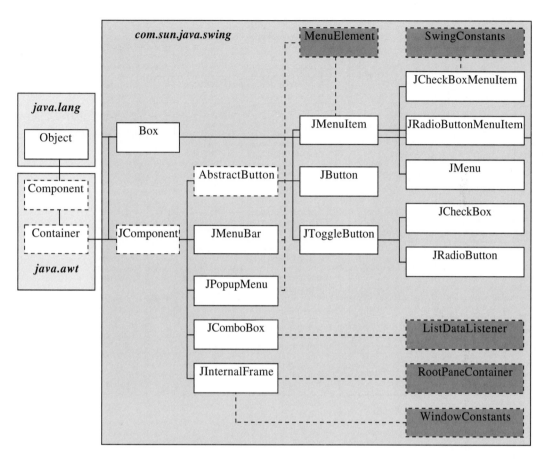

Figure A-5   Swing Classes (part 4).

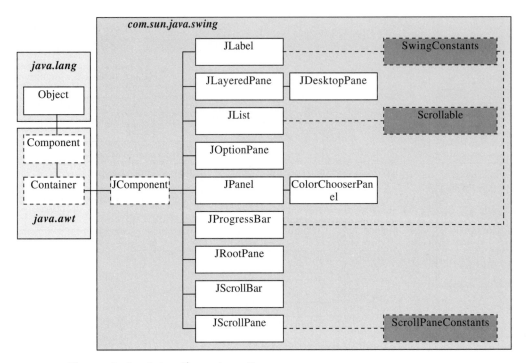

Figure A-6   Swing Classes (part 5).

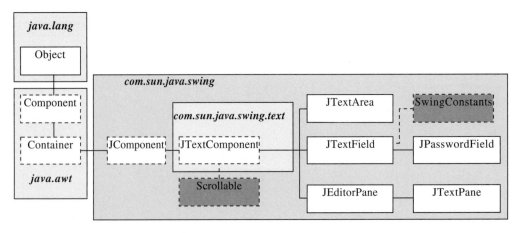

Figure A-7   Swing Classes (part 6).

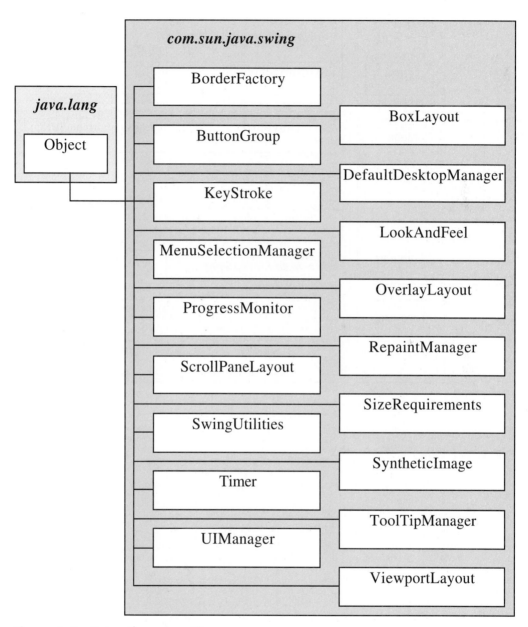

Figure A-8   Swing Classes (part 7).

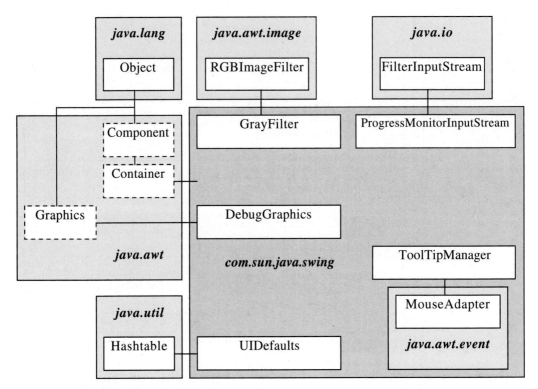

Figure A-9   Swing Classes (part 8).

The Swing Border Package

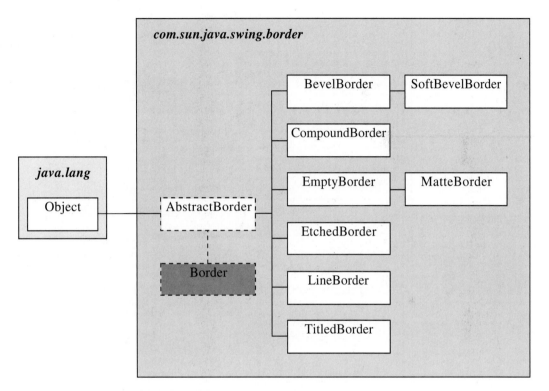

Figure A-10   Swing Border Classes.

The Swing Events Package

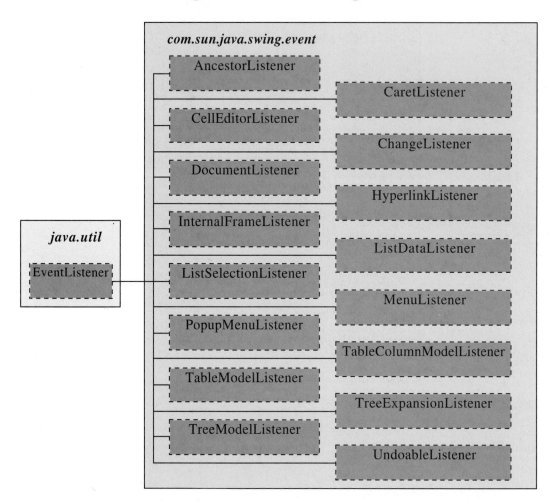

Figure A-11   Swing Events Package (part 1).

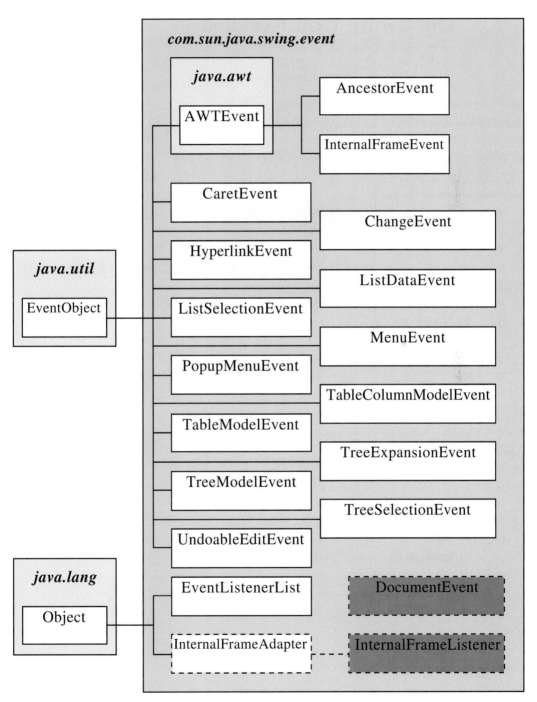

Figure A-12   Swing Events Package (part 2).

The Swing Tree Package

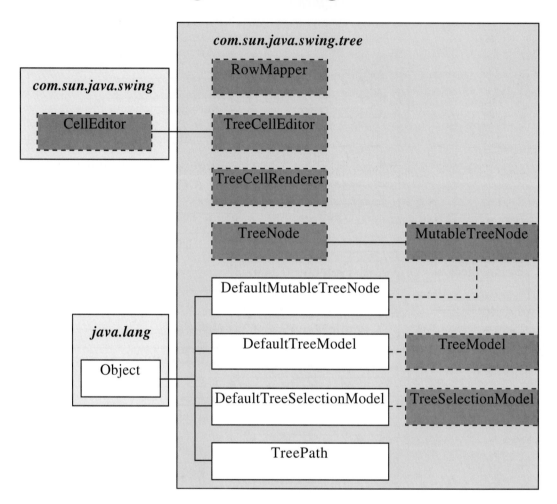

Figure A-13   Swing Tree Package.

The Swing Table Package

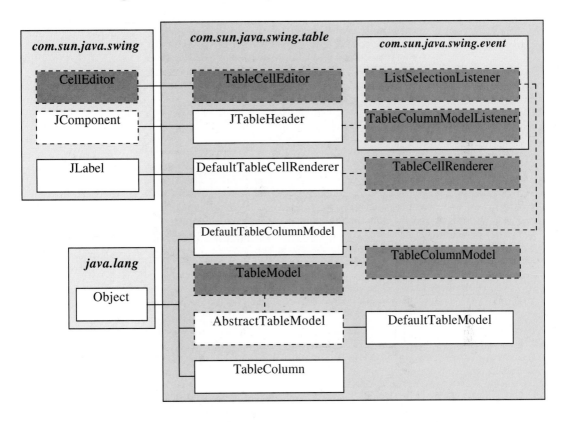

Figure A-14   Swing Table Package.

The Swing Text Package

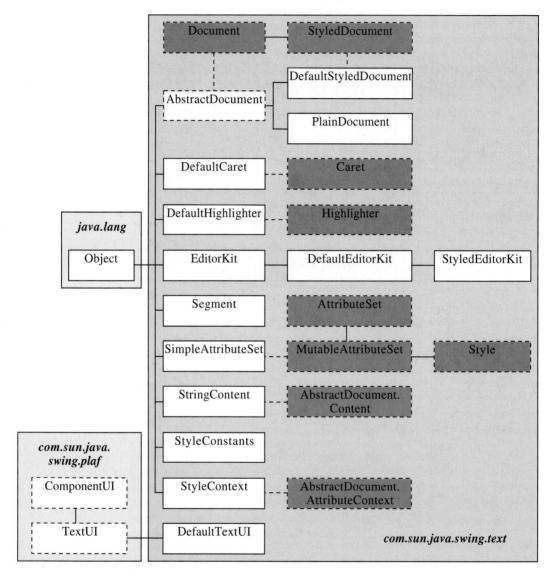

Figure A-15 Swing Text Package (part 1).

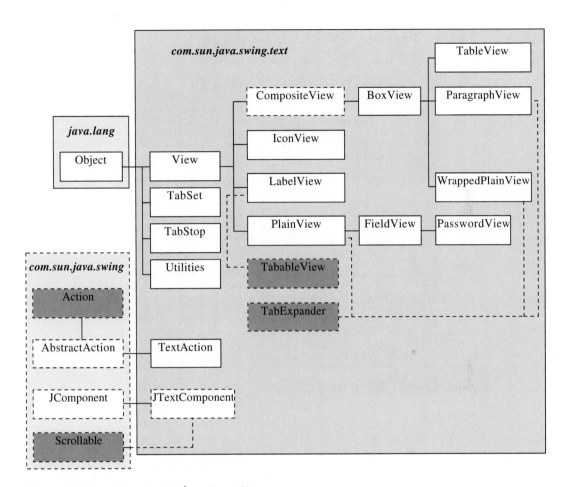

Figure A-16   Swing Text Package (part 2).

The Swing Undo Package

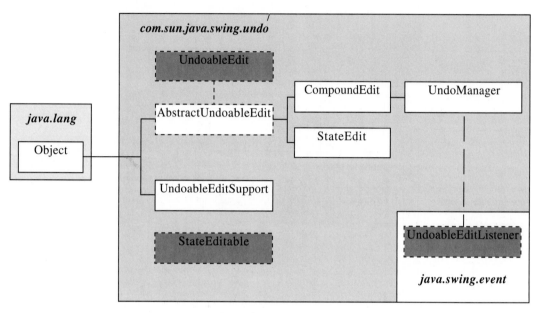

Figure A-17   Swing Undo Package.

SWING COMPONENTS AND MULTI-THREADING

Appendix B

In Chapter 8, you saw how to use the Swing `ProgressMonitorInputStream` and `ProgressMonitor` classes to keep track of operations that might take a long time to complete. Two examples were presented, in Listings 8-18 and 8-19, that showed how these classes are typically used. Although the code in those two listings seems correct and almost certainly worked as you might have expected, both of the examples as presented potentially contain a subtle bug that could be disastrous in a more complex application.

If you look back at either of those examples, you'll see that the main work of the application is done in a thread that is started when the user supplies a file name. A separate thread is created in order not to block the AWT event processing while the file's content is being read. As was explained in Chapter 8, blocking the AWT event thread by reading the file would stop the program's GUI being painted and would also prevent the progress monitor's dialog box from doing its job, which would defeat the purpose of the example. Using background threads in this way is a sound implementation principle, but it can also lead to problems.

Swing Components and Multithreading

The potential problem inherent in the design used for the `WordCounter` and `WordCounterTime` examples from Chapter 8 is that the background thread needs access to the `ProgressMonitor` after it has been created. In Listing 8-19, for example, the `setNote` and `setProgress` methods of `ProgressMonitor` are called from the background thread at essentially arbitrary times as the program makes its way through the content of the file being processed. This is not usually a problem, unless the ProgressMonitor receives an AWT event while the background thread is calling one of the these two methods.

The ProgressMonitor uses a JProgressBar to show the progress made reading the file. When the program calls the ProgressMonitor setProgress method, the JProgressBar setValue method is used to update the state of the progress bar. As you know, AWT events, such as requests to paint a component, are always handled in a dedicated event thread. If such an event coincides with a setValue call in the background thread, there will be two threads attempting to access the JProgressBar control at the same time. The problem is that Swing controls do not protect themselves from the potentially disastrous effects of this—in other words, they are not *thread-safe*. As a result, the background thread of the test program could be updating the state of the control while the paint method is trying to draw it, as shown in figure 14-1. Depending on the implementation of the JProgressBar and its UI classes, this could be benign, it could cause the on-screen appearance of the control to be incorrect, or it could leave the component in an inconsistent state, resulting in incorrect behavior and perhaps even an exception.

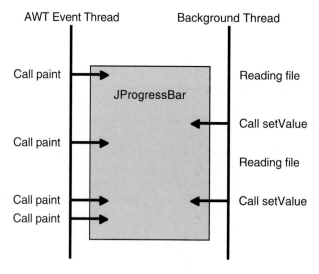

Figure B-1   Two threads accessing a JProgressBar control.

Core Note

Figure 14-1 is, of course, a simplification of the truth. In fact, the job of painting the control belongs to the JProgressBar's *UI class, which will read the* BoundedRangeModel *that maintains the progress bar's value. When the* JProgressBar setValue *method is called, it will update the same* BoundedRangeModel. *Whether or not this causes a problem will depend on the implementation details of the* BoundedRangeModel *and of the methods in* JProgressBar *and its UI classes that use it.*

In Figure 14-1, the AWT event thread is shown on the left and the background thread used to read the file is on the right. Time increases as you move from the top of the figure to the bottom. Looking at the events as they occur, the first paint call happens when the progress bar is first displayed. Shortly afterward, a file read completes and the setValue method is called from the background thread. This call causes the BoundedRangeModel to be updated, which in turn causes an event to the JProgressBar UI class, which needs to redraw the control. Instead of painting the control directly, however, the UI class calls repaint, which defers this work to the AWT event thread. The actual drawing takes place in the second paint call on the left of Figure 14.1, while the background thread is reading more data from the file.

The problem occurs when a paint call in the event thread coincides with a setValue call from the background thread, as is the case with the third paint call in Figure 14.1. This call could be caused by the user uncovering an obscured part of the window that the progress bar resides in. The timing of this call is, of course, not under the control of the application, so there always exists the possibility of a collision of this kind.

The Rule Governing Access to Swing Components

Since Swing components are not thread-safe, all access to them should be made from a single thread. Furthermore, because painting operations always take place in the AWT event thread, this must be the event thread. The Swing development team produced an article that appeared at the same time as the release of Swing 1.0 that stated this restriction as follows:

> *Once a Swing component has been realized, all code that might affect or depend on the state of that component should be executed in the event-dispatching thread.*

You'll see later what is meant by the term 'realized' in the statement of this rule and you'll also see some special circumstances in which you don't need to use the event thread to access Swing components. First, however, let's look at how to change the example in Listing 8-19 so that it conforms to this rule.

Core Note

When the Swing team first posted the article that contained this rule, much concern was expressed that this restriction makes Swing unusable, or at least unpleasant to use. In fact, as you'll see, most applications are not affected because they are naturally written in such a way as to satisfy the single-threaded requirement. Other people found it hard to believe that this restriction actually existed, based on the fact that they had written applets or applications that didn't adhere to it and had not experienced any problems.

The truth of the matter is, of course, that if you do this, most of the time you'll get away with it, just as you would if you wrote a multithreaded application that updated data shared between the threads without proper synchronization. You only see a problem when two threads happen to operate on the same Swing component at the same time and, even then, depending on the component involved and the operation being performed, you may still not suffer any adverse effects. However, as has already been said, the results of ignoring this rule depend on the implementation details of the individual components and their UI classes. It would be unwise to use the fact that you haven't seen a problem with your use of a component to justify ignoring the rule, because the component's implementation may change. This is more of an issue with Swing than it is in other areas of Java, because you may not be able to test your application with every possible look-and-feel that your customers might use. A third-party look-and-feel might expose a problem not shown by the ones you regularly test with.

Using the AWT Event Thread

If you examine the code for the second version of the word counting program shown in Listing 8-19, you'll see that most of it is contained in the `actionPerformed` method that is executed when the user presses return after supplying the name of the file to be read. To avoid blocking the AWT event thread, this method immediately spawns a new thread in which the word counting is performed, allowing the `actionPerformed` method itself to return, freeing the event thread to handle updates to the user interface as required. The work performed in the background thread in this version of the program is as follows:

1. Disable the file name text input field so that the user can't select a new file.

2. Clear the text of the label showing the count of words found so far.

3. Open the named file. If this fails, display an error message.

4. Create the `ProgressMonitor` that will eventually display progress through the file

5. Read the file content. For each line, count the words in that line. Update the number of bytes read, the number of words found and the projected time to completion.

6. Change the text of the label showing the number of words read.

7. Update the `ProgressMonitor` with the number of bytes read and the new projected time to completion.

8. If an error occurs while reading the file, display an error message.

9. When the file has been read to its end, or if an error occurs, close the input stream.

10. Close the `ProgressMonitor`

11. Allow the user to type a new file name by enabling the text input field.

Many of these steps involve access to Swing components and therefore violate the single-thread access rule. Step 1, for example, changes the state of the Swing `JTextField` while it is displayed. Strictly speaking, this is not a thread-safe operation and neither is changing the text of the label showing the number of words counted so far, which is done in steps 2 and 6. To make the program thread-safe, the Swing component accesses that might clash with painting operations in the AWT event thread must be moved out of the background thread and performed in the event thread itself. This poses two problems—how to identify which operations might cause a problem and how to arrange for them to be carried out in the event thread.

Identifying Potential Problems

Finding potential problems is not a simple task. The rule provided by the Swing team states that *all* operations on a Swing component *must* take place in the event thread once the component has been realized to guarantee that there will never be a conflict between these operations and the unpredictable `paint` calls that are serviced by the component's UI class. To apply this rule, you need to know what is meant be 'realizing' a component.

Realizing AWT Components

As you know, AWT components are actually made up of two separate pieces—a pure Java piece that you create and interact with and a 'peer' component that is created when necessary. The peer component interfaces with native code in the platform-specific AWT toolkit to create the necessary platform object that you manipulate through the Java AWT object. For example, an AWT `Button` consists of an instance of the class `java.awt.Button` class which is written in Java, which creates and manipulates a `java.awt.peer.ButtonPeer` object that contains native code. An AWT component is *realized* when it creates its peer object. Usually, you don't care about exactly when a component is realized. However, the Swing access rule requires to be concerned about this, at least to some degree. So exactly when does a component create its peer? Here are the rules:

1. Components which are not `Containers` create their peer object when instructed to by their parent `Container`.

2. A `Component` or `Container` is told to create its peer when added to a `Container` which already has a peer (that is, to a `Container` that has already been realized).

3. When a `Container` creates its own peer, it arranges for all of its child `Components` to create their own peers. If the `Container` contains other `Containers`, this will recursively create the peers for the children of those `Containers` so that everything within a `Container` is realized when the `Container` itself is realized.

4. Top-level windows (`Frame`, `Dialog` and `Window`), which are, of course, all `Containers`, create their peers (and therefore realize themselves and all of their child `Components` and `Containers`) when one of the `pack`, `show` or `setVisible(true)` methods is called for the first time. An `Applet` is realized and has a peer object by the time its `init` method is called.

In summary, if you create a `Frame`, `Dialog` or `Window` and add components to it, none of them are realized until you call `pack` on it or make it visible with `show` or `setVisible(true)`. Once a `Frame`, `Dialog` or `Window` is packed or made visible, everything it contains is realized and any new components or containers you add to it are realized as soon as they are added.

Realizing Swing Components

The discussion to this point has all revolved around AWT components and peers—you may be wondering what the connection is with Swing components which are supposed to be lightweight and not have peers—how can a peerless object be realized? There are actually two distinct cases to consider, depending on whether the Swing components is derived from `JComponent` or not.

Swing components that are not derived from `JComponent` are the top-level objects `JFrame`, `JWindow`, `JDialog` and `JApplet`. All of these are derived directly from the corresponding AWT components (`Frame`, `Window`, `Dialog` and `Applet`). Therefore, they are all heavyweight objects and create their peers as described above for the AWT objects.

The other Swing components are derived from `JComponent`. Although these are lightweight in the sense that they don't have a physical window of their own in the native windowing system, they *do* have peers—each of them has an associated instance of `java.awt.peer.LightweightPeer`. This peer does not, however, have any native code associated with it. A Swing component derived from JComponent is realized when its LightweightPeer object is created, which follows the rules already listed for heavyweight AWT components. In other words, lightweight components are realized when their parent container is realized, which ultimately means that they are realized when the top-level JFrame, JDialog, JWindow or JApplet is packed or made visible. This is exactly the same as for heavyweight components.

Safe and Unsafe Use of Swing Components

According to the single-threading rule, you can manipulate Swing components outside of the event thread until they have been realized. Combining this rule with the information in the previous section, this means that you don't need to worry about the event thread interfering with your use of a newly-created Swing component until you add it to a realized container or you realized the container that it is contained in. Once either of these has happened, however, you must only access the component from the event thread.

Now let's apply this to the WordCounterTime example. Let's take the items in the numbered list under 'Using the AWT Event Thread' one at a time and consider whether each of them constitutes a safe use of Swing components. As you read this description, refer to the original code in Listing 8-19.

1. Disable the file name text input field so that the user can't select a new file: Like everything else in this list, this operation takes place in a background thread. The component it operates on is in a visible (hence realized) container, so it is *not* thread-safe.

2. Clear the text of the label showing the count of words found so far: Again, this operates on a visible component, so it is *not* thread-safe.

3. Open the named file. If this fails, display an error message: If you refer to the code, you'll see that the error message is displayed by creating a dialog using a JOptionPane convenience method. Since the Swing component is being *created* in a background thread, some of this operation may be thread-safe and some of it may not. This issue will be discussed below.

4. Create the ProgressMonitor that will eventually display progress through the file: again, this involves the creation of a Swing component in a background thread, an issue that will be discussed below.

5. Read the file content. For each line, count the words in that line. Update the number of bytes read, the number of words found and the projected time to completion: These steps do not involve any Swing components, so they are thread-safe.

6. Change the text of the label showing the number of words read: As with operations in steps 1 and 2, this one is *not* thread-safe.

7. Update the `ProgressMonitor` with the number of bytes read and the new projected time to completion: This is *not* thread-safe.

8. If an error occurs while reading the file, display an error message: This is the same as step 3 and will be discussed below.

9. When the file has been read to its end, or if an error occurs, close the input stream: Does not involve Swing components and hence is thread-safe.

10. Close the `ProgressMonitor`: This requires access to the `ProgressMonitor` in a background thread and hence is likely not to be thread-safe.

11. Allow the user to type a new file name by enabling the text input field: Because it changes the state of the component, this operation is probably not thread-safe.

Core Note

You'll notice the use of the word 'probably' in some of the descriptions in this section. The word is there because, unless you want to read the source code, you can't be sure whether there will be a problem or not if you perform this operation outside the event thread. If you follow the Swing rule to the letter, you have to assume that all of the operations noted above are safe only *in the event thread. In practice, however, some of them may not cause threading problems because of their implementation. To be on the safe side, you should always assume the worst.*

The result of the initial investigation is that steps 1, 2, 6, 7, 10 and 11 are not thread-safe. The code that implements these operations must be moved out of the background thread. By contrast, steps 5 and 9 are safe and can remain in the background thread. That leaves steps 3, 4 and 8.

These three steps involve the creation of a Swing component. The issue is whether this can safely be done outside the event thread. Since the new component will probably be created by placing Swing components on an invisible top-level container and the realizing the container, it is very likely that some of the creation work will actually be thread-safe. The problem is, however, the code that creates these compound components is not yours—even if you can inspect the code as it is today and determine that it is entirely safe to build a `ProgressMonitor` outside the event thread, the code could be changed in such a way as to invalidate this assumption. In the worst case, different Swing vendors could provide different implementations that have different characteristics. This being the case, the safest approach is to assume that all three of steps 3, 4 and 8 are not thread-safe and to ensure that they are carried out in the AWT event thread.

Moving Work to the Event Thread

As you can see, there is quite a bit of work that needs to be moved out of our example program's background thread and into the event thread in order to make it completely thread-safe. In fact, though, things are not quite as bad as they seem: if you look at the list of items that need to be moved and at the code in Listing 8-19 that implements them, you'll see that they fall into three categories:

1. Initialization work—this covers steps 1 through 4
2. Work in the main loop—steps 6, 7 and 8
3. Completion work—steps 10 and 11.

The most obvious way to handle the initialization work is to take it out of the background thread altogether. If you recall, the background thread is started from the AWT event thread, so performing the initialization before the new thread is started places it in the AWT thread without any special measures. The main loop and the completion work will, however, need to be in the background thread.

Handling Initialization

Moving the initialization steps out of the main loop is a simple matter of relocating code—all of the initialization steps will simply be executed before the new thread is created. To make this possible, some variables that were created locally to the thread must now become instance variables of the `WordCounterTime` class so that they can be initialized in the AWT thread and then used in the background thread. This applies to the following variables:

`name`	the name of the file being read
`p`	a reference to the `ProgressMonitor` being used to provide the progress display to the user
`guessTime`	the current estimate of how long it will take to complete the operation
`bytesRead`	the number of bytes read from the file
`words`	the number of words counted in the file
`size`	the size of the file in bytes
`is`	the input stream being used to read the file.

Having moved the variables to the class, it is a simple matter to reorder the code so that the `ProgressMonitor` is created and the input stream to the file opened before the background thread is started. Opening the input stream at this stage allows a `JOptionPane` containing an error message to be displayed safely should there be any problem opening the file. At this stage, the file name field will also be disabled and label on the main window displaying the number of words so far counted will be cleared. This addresses steps 1 through 4. You can see how this part is implemented in Listing B-1, which shows a revised version of this example, called WordCounterTime2.

Listing B-1   A thread-safe word counting program

```java
package JFCBook.AppendixB;

import com.sun.java.swing.*;
import java.awt.*;
import java.awt.event.*;
import java.io.*;
import java.util.*;

public class WordCounterTime2 extends JPanel implements ActionListener {
    public WordCounterTime2() {
        this.setLayout(new GridBagLayout());
        GridBagConstraints c = new GridBagConstraints();
        Insets i = new Insets(3, 3, 3, 3);

        c.gridx = 0;
        c.gridy = 0;
        c.gridwidth = 1;
        c.gridheight = 1;
        c.insets = i;
        c.anchor = GridBagConstraints.EAST;
        c.fill = GridBagConstraints.NONE;
        c.weightx = 0.0;
        c.weighty = 0.0;
        JLabel l = new JLabel("File Name: ", JLabel.RIGHT);
        this.add(l, c);

        c.gridy = 1;
        l = new JLabel("Words Found: ", JLabel.RIGHT);
        this.add(l, c);

        c.gridx = 1;
        c.gridy = 0;
        c.fill = GridBagConstraints.HORIZONTAL;
        c.weightx = 1.0;
        fileName = new JTextField(40);
        this.add(fileName, c);

        c.gridy = 1;
```

```
      wordsFound = new JLabel("          ", JLabel.LEFT);
      this.add(wordsFound, c);

      fileName.addActionListener(this);
}

public void actionPerformed(ActionEvent evt) {
   // These operations are performed in the event thread...
   fileName.setEnabled(false);
   wordsFound.setText("");
   name = fileName.getText().trim();
   bytesRead = 0;
   words = 0;
   guessTime = -1;

   try {
      is = new DataInputStream(
             new BufferedInputStream(
               new FileInputStream(name)));

      size = (float)new File(name).length();    // Total size of file
      p = new ProgressMonitor(WordCounterTime2.this,
                   "Counting words in " + name,
                   TIME_STRING,
                   0, (int)size);
   } catch (FileNotFoundException e) {
      JOptionPane.showMessageDialog(WordCounterTime2.this,
                   "Cannot find " + name, "File Error",
                   JOptionPane.ERROR_MESSAGE);
      fileName.setEnabled(true);
      return;
   }

   Thread t = new Thread() {
      public void run() {
         String str;
         long startTime;
         long currentTime;
         long lastCheckTime;

         try {
            startTime = System.currentTimeMillis();
            lastCheckTime = startTime;
            while ((str = is.readLine()) != null) {
               bytesRead += str.length();
               words += new StringTokenizer(str).countTokens();
```

continued

```
      currentTime = System.currentTimeMillis();
      if (currentTime - lastCheckTime > CHECK_INTERVAL) {
        lastCheckTime = currentTime;
        float bytes = (float)bytesRead;
        float sizeLeft = size - bytes;

        // Save new guess time for event thread
        guessTime = (int)((((currentTime - startTime)/bytes) *
                sizeLeft)/1000);
      }

      if (updateScheduled == false) {
        updateScheduled = true;
        SwingUtilities.invokeLater(new Runnable() {
          public void run() {
            wordsFound.setText("" + words);
            p.setProgress(bytesRead);
            if (guessTime != -1) {
              p.setNote(TIME_STRING + guessTime +
                  seconds");
            }
            updateScheduled = false;
          }
        });
      }
    }
  } catch (IOException e) {
    SwingUtilities.invokeLater(new Runnable() {
      public void run() {
        JOptionPane.showMessageDialog(WordCounterTime2.this,
            "I/O Exception while reading " +
            WordCounterTime2.this.name,
            "File Read Error",
            JOptionPane.ERROR_MESSAGE);
        wordsFound.setText("");
      }
    });
  } finally {
    SwingUtilities.invokeLater(new Runnable() {
      public void run() {
        fileName.setEnabled(true);
        try {
          if (is != null) {
            is.close();          // Always close!
            is = null;
```

```
                   }
               } catch (IOException ioe) {
                   // Nothing to do
               }

               if (p != null) {
                   p.close();       // Close the ProgressMonitor
                   p = null;
               }
             }
         });
       }
     }
   };
   t.start();
}

public static void main(String[] args) {
   JFrame f = new JFrame("Timed Word Counter");
   f.getContentPane().add(new WordCounterTime2());
   f.addWindowListener(new WindowAdapter() {
     public void windowClosing(WindowEvent evt) {
        System.exit(0);
     }
   });
   f.pack();
   f.setVisible(true);
}

protected JTextField fileName;
protected JLabel wordsFound;
protected static final String TIME_STRING = "Time remaining: ";
protected static final long CHECK_INTERVAL = 500;

// These fields are accessed from the AWT event thread
protected ProgressMonitor p;
protected int guessTime = -1;
protected int bytesRead;
protected int words;
protected DataInputStream is;
protected float size;
protected String name;
protected boolean updateScheduled;
}
```

Scheduling Work to the AWT Event Thread

The main loop of the revised program reads file data and counts bytes and words, as before. While doing this, it also periodically updates its estimate of how long it will take to process the rest of the file. As it reads through the file, it needs to update the number of words read (step 6) and change the value of the progress bar and the estimated time to completion in the `ProgressMonitor`'s note field (step 7). Neither of these operations can be safely performed inline in the background thread—they have to be delegated to code running in the AWT event thread. This raises two questions:

- How can you arrange to have these updates made in the AWT event thread?

- How can you communicate the values to be used to update these fields to the code that runs in the AWT event thread?

One way to schedule work into the AWT event thread is to use a timer, as described in Chapter 8—code executed on the expiration of a timer always runs in the event thread. However, there is a more elegant method—Swing provides two static methods in the `SwingUtilities` class that you can use to schedule work in the event thread, without undue delay:

```
public static void invokeLater(Runnable obj);
public static void invokeAndWait(Runnable obj) throws
         InterruptedException;
```

Both of these methods are given a `Runnable` as their only argument. When called, they arrange for the `run` method of this object to be called some time later from the AWT event thread. It is guaranteed that any events currently in the AWT event queue will be processed to completion before the `run` method is called.

The `invokeLater` method returns control as soon as it has arranged for the `run` method to be executed, which it does by scheduling an event into the AWT event queue, whereas `invokeAndWait` suspends the calling thread until the target object's run method has been executed to completion. The `invokeAndWait` method cannot be called from the AWT event thread itself and throws `java.lang.Error` if you attempt to do so. If you need to use `invokeAndWait` in circumstances in which you might sometimes already be in the AWT event thread, you can either catch the exception and execute the target code directly in the exception handler or you can detect that you are running in the event thread using the following `SwingUtilities` method:

```
public static boolean isEventDispatchThread();
```

Updating the ProgressMonitor in the Event Thread

To update the `ProgressMonitor` in the event thread, you need to use `invokeLater`. The code that will be run by this method needs to be packaged in the run method of some `Runnable` and must have access to the total number of words found, the number of bytes read and the estimated time to completion of the counting operation. All of these values are held in the `WordCounterTime2` object, so a simple way to implement this is to use an inner class of `WordCounterTime2` that implements the `Runnable` interface. Such an object can be passed to `invokeLater` and will also have access to the various counters held by `WordCounterTime2`. Here is how the code is actually implemented:

```
if (updateScheduled == false) {
  updateScheduled = true;
  SwingUtilities.invokeLater(new Runnable() {
    public void run() {
      wordsFound.setText("" + words);
      p.setProgress(bytesRead);
      if (guessTime != -1) {
        p.setNote(TIME_STRING + guessTime + seconds");
      }
      updateScheduled = false;
    }
  });
}
```

As you can see, the object passed to `invokeLater` is actually an anonymous inner class that just performs the steps that used to be carried out in the background thread itself. Because it may be some time before the code is executed in the event thread, there is a possibility that one or more further reads may complete before that time, causing invokeLater to be called several times. To avoid this, a simple interlock mechanism is used: before invokeLater is called, the instance variable `updateScheduled` is set to true. While it remains true, no further calls to `invokeLater` will be made. When the update code is executed in the event thread, it will use the latest values from the `WordCounterTime2` object and then set `updateScheduled` to `false`. Of course, there is a possible race condition here because no attempt is made to synchronize access to `updateScheduled` between the background thread and the AWT event thread. This is, however, a benign race condition—if the event thread sets `updateScheduled` to `false` just after the background thread determines that it shouldn't call `invokeLater`, one update will be lost. Of course, this won't matter because the correct values will be used on the next update. Synchronizing the two threads would be expensive and wasteful because the likelihood of contention between these two threads is small and the result is completely harmless.

The code you have just seen implements steps 6 and 7 of our original list. The implementation of the remaining steps is very similar. Reporting an error while reading the file (step 8) is performed by creating a `JOptionPane` in the run method of another anonymous class implementing `Runnable` and passed to `invokeLater`. Steps 10 and 11 are handled in the same way. You should be able to identify the code that performs these steps packaged into inner classes in Listing B-1.

Core Note

This example does not use invokeAndWait, *although it could easily do so. In general, you should use* invokeLater *instead of* invokeAndWait *whenever possible because it avoids suspending the thread that is doing the useful work of the application.*

Constructing the User Interfaces of Applications and Applets

Earlier in this Appendix, we said that it was safe to manipulate Swing components outside the AWT event thread so long as they haven't been realized. In fact, many Swing applications and applets will create their user interfaces in the thread in which they start executing, which is not the event thread. The obvious question is whether this is safe.

Application User Interfaces

Consider the simple example shown in Listing B-2.

Listing B-2   Creating the initial user interface of an application

```java
public class SimpleApp {
   public static void main(String[] args) {
      JFrame f = new JFrame("Simple App");
      f.getContentPane().add(new JLabel("Constructed in the main thread"));
      f.pack();                             // Realizes the frame
      f.setVisible(true);                   // Is this safe?
   }
}
```

All of the code in this listing executes outside the AWT event thread. Up to and including the `pack` call, there is no possible problem because none of the components have yet been realized. The only possible issue here is whether it is safe to call `setVisible` as shown. You might think that it is obviously safe to do so—after all, the frame is not yet visible, so how can it get a `paint` request in the AWT event thread? The Swing team describes this situation as follows:

> *...as long as the program doesn't have a visible GUI, it's exceedingly unlikely that the* JFrame *or its contents will receive a paint call before* f.setVisible(true) *returns. Because there's no GUI code after the* f.setVisible(true) *call, all GUI work moves to the event-dispatching thread and this code is, in practice, thread-safe.*

If you're not comforted by this description, you can always take the following approach:

```
f.pack();                            // Realizes the frame
SwingUtilities.invokeLater(new Runnable() {
  public void run() {
    f.setVisible(true);
  }
});
```

To make this work, you'll have to change the declaration of the JFrame as follows:

```
final JFrame f = new JFrame("Simple App");
```

Applet User Interfaces

The situation is slightly different for an applet than it is for an application because, as you saw earlier, the user interface of an applet is realized by the browser (or the appletviewer) before the init method is called. Therefore, there is no safe time to manipulate the applet's user interface unless you can do so in its constructor. If this is not possible, you will have to build the applet's GUI in the AWT event thread by calling the invokeLater or invokeAndWait method from init. Listing B-3 shows a trivial Swing applet that constructs its interface in a thread-safe manner. It's not elegant, but it is guaranteed to work.

Listing B-3   Creating the initial user interface of an applet

```
public class SimpleApplet extends JApplet {
  public void init() {
    SwingUtilities.invokeLater(new Runnable() {
      public void run() {
        getContentPane().add(new JLabel("Simple Applet"));
        validate();
      }
    });
  }
}
```

Notice that after constructing the user interface (in this case just adding a label), it is necessary to call validate to have the layout manager size and place the components. Usually, this would be done automatically, but you must do it yourself when interface construction is deferred to the event thread.

Summary

In this appendix, you've seen how to identify potential timing problems when handling Swing components and how to work around them. Bear in mind that, unlike AWT components, Swing controls are not thread-safe and ensuring consistent operation is your responsibility. Fortunately, many applications and applets will not need to take special steps to ensure this, because all of their work after initialization will take place in the AWT event thread. Even if your application does use other threads, the `invokeLater` and `invokeAndWait` methods make it relatively painless to ensure that they interact properly with Swing controls.

Index

Java(tm) Development Kit Version 1.1.6 Binary Code License

This binary code license ("License") contains rights and restrictions associated with use of the accompanying software and documentation ("Software"). Read the License carefully before installing the Software. By installing the Software you agree to the terms and conditions of this License.

1. Limited License Grant. Sun grants to you ("Licensee") a non-exclusive, non-transferable limited license to use the Software without fee for evaluation of the Software and for development of Java(tm) compatible applets and applications. Licensee may make one archival copy of the Software and may re-distribute complete, unmodified copies of the Software to software developers within Licensee's organization to avoid unnecessary download time, provided that this License conspicuously appear with all copies of the Software. Except for the foregoing, Licensee may not re-distribute the Software in whole or in part, either separately or included with a product. Refer to the Java Runtime Environment Version 1.1.6 binary code license (http://java.sun.com/products/JDK/1.1/index.html) for the availability of runtime code which may be distributed with Java compatible applets and applications.

2. Java Platform Interface. Licensee may not modify the Java Platform Interface ("JPI", identified as classes contained within the "java" package or any subpackages of the "java" package), by creating additional classes within the JPI or otherwise causing the addition to or modification of the classes in the JPI. In the event that Licensee creates any Java-related API and distributes such API to others for applet or application development, Licensee must promptly publish an accurate specification for such API for free use by all developers of Java-based software.

3. Restrictions. Software is confidential copyrighted information of Sun and title to all copies is retained by Sun and/or its licensors. Licensee shall not modify, decompile, disassemble, decrypt, extract, or otherwise reverse engineer Software. Software may not be leased, assigned, or sublicensed, in whole or in part. Software is not designed or intended for use in on-line control of aircraft, air traffic, aircraft navigation or aircraft communications; or in the design, construction, operation or maintenance of any nuclear facility. Licensee warrants that it will not use or redistribute the Software for such purposes.

4. Trademarks and Logos. This License does not authorize Licensee to use any Sun name, trademark or logo. Licensee acknowledges that Sun owns the Java trademark and all Java-related trademarks, logos and icons including the Coffee Cup and Duke ("Java Marks") and agrees to: (i) to comply with the Java Trademark Guidelines at http://java.sun.com/trademarks.html; (ii) not do anything harmful to or inconsistent with Sun's rights in the Java Marks; and (iii) assist Sun in protecting those rights, including assigning to Sun any rights acquired by Licensee in any Java Mark.

5. Disclaimer of Warranty. Software is provided "AS IS," without a warranty of any kind. ALL EXPRESS OR IMPLIED REPRESENTATIONS AND WARRANTIES, INCLUDING ANY IMPLIED WARRANTY OF MERCHANTABILITY, FITNESS FOR A PARTICULAR PURPOSE OR NON-INFRINGEMENT, ARE HEREBY EXCLUDED.

6. Limitation of Liability. SUN AND ITS LICENSORS SHALL NOT BE LIABLE FOR ANY DAMAGES SUFFERED BY LICENSEE OR ANY THIRD PARTY AS A RESULT OF USING OR DISTRIBUTING SOFTWARE. IN NO EVENT WILL SUN OR ITS LICENSORS BE LIABLE FOR ANY LOST REVENUE, PROFIT OR DATA, OR FOR DIRECT, INDIRECT, SPECIAL, CONSEQUENTIAL, INCIDENTAL OR PUNITIVE DAMAGES, HOWEVER CAUSED AND REGARDLESS OF THE THEORY OF LIABILITY, ARISING OUT OF THE USE OF OR INABILITY TO USE SOFTWARE, EVEN IF SUN HAS BEEN ADVISED OF THE POSSIBILITY OF SUCH DAMAGES.

7. Termination. Licensee may terminate this License at any time by destroying all copies of Software. This License will terminate immediately without notice from Sun if Licensee fails to comply with any provision of this License. Upon such termination, Licensee must destroy all copies of Software.

8. Export Regulations. Software, including technical data, is subject to U.S. export control laws, including the U.S. Export Administration Act and its associated regulations, and may be subject to export or import regulations in other countries. Licensee agrees to comply strictly with all such regulations and acknowledges that it has the responsibility to obtain licenses to export, re-export, or import Software. Software may not be downloaded, or otherwise exported or re-exported (i) into, or to a national or resident of, Cuba, Iraq, Iran, North Korea, Libya, Sudan, Syria or any country to which the U.S. has embargoed goods; or (ii) to anyone on the U.S. Treasury Department's list of Specially Designated Nations or the U.S. Commerce Department's Table of Denial Orders.

9. Restricted Rights. Use, duplication or disclosure by the United States government is subject to the restrictions as set forth in the Rights in Technical Data and Computer Software Clauses in DFARS 252.227-7013(c) (1) (ii) and FAR 52.227-19(c) (2) as applicable.

10. Governing Law. Any action related to this License will be governed by California law and controlling U.S. federal law. No choice of law rules of any jurisdiction will apply.

11. Severability. If any of the above provisions are held to be in violation of applicable law, void, or unenforceable in any jurisdiction, then such provisions are herewith waived to the extent necessary for the License to be otherwise enforceable in such jurisdiction. However, if in Sun's opinion deletion of any provisions of the License by operation of this paragraph unreasonably compromises the rights or increase the liabilities of Sun or its licensors, Sun reserves the right to terminate the License and refund the fee paid by Licensee, if any, as Licensee's sole and exclusive remedy.

JDK Version 1.2 Beta 3 Binary Code Evaluation License

SUN MICROSYSTEMS, INC., THROUGH ITS JAVASOFT BUSINESS ("SUN") IS WILLING TO LICENSE THE JAVA DEVELOPMENT KIT VERSION 1.2 BETA 3 SOFTWARE AND THE ACCOMPANYING DOCUMENTATION INCLUDING AUTHORIZED COPIES OF EACH (THE "SOFTWARE") TO LICENSEE ONLY ON THE CONDITION THAT LICENSEE ACCEPTS ALL OF THE TERMS IN THIS AGREEMENT.

PLEASE READ THE TERMS CAREFULLY BEFORE INSTALLING THE SOFTWARE. BY INSTALLING THE SOFTWARE, LICENSEE ACKNOWLEDGES THAT LICENSEE HAS READ AND UNDERSTANDS THIS AGREEMENT AND AGREES TO BE BOUND BY ITS TERMS AND CONDITIONS.

IF LICENSEE DOES NOT ACCEPT THESE LICENSE TERMS, SUN DOES NOT GRANT ANY LICENSE TO THE SOFTWARE, AND LICENSEE SHOULD NOT INSTALL THE SOFTWARE.

1. EVALUATION LICENSE PERIOD
Licensee may use the binary Software for a period of ninety (90) days from the date Licensee installs the Software (the "Term"). At the end of the Term, Licensee must immediately cease use of and destroy the Software or, upon request from Sun, return the Software to Sun. The Software may contain a mechanism which (i) disables the Software at the end of the Term or (ii) advises the end user that the license has expired.

2. LICENSE GRANT
(A) License Rights
Licensee is granted a non-exclusive and non-transferable license to download, install and internally use the binary Software for beta testing and evaluation purposes only. Licensee may make one copy of the Software only for archival purposes in support of Licensee's use of the Software, provided that Licensee reproduce all copyright and other proprietary notices that are on the original copy of the Software.

(B) License Restrictions
The Software is licensed to Licensee only under the terms of this Agreement, and Sun reserves all rights not expressly granted to Licensee. Licensee may not use, copy, modify, or transfer the Software, or any copy thereof, except as expressly provided for in this Agreement. Except as otherwise provided by law for purposes of decompilation of the Software solely for inter-operability, Licensee may not reverse engineer, disassemble, decompile, or translate the Software, or otherwise attempt to derive the source code of the

Software. Licensee may not rent, lease, loan, sell, or distribute the Software, or any part of the Software. No right, title, or interest in or to any trademarks, service marks, or trade names of Sun or Sun's licensors is granted hereunder.

(C) Acknowledgment that Software is Experimental

Licensee acknowledges that Software furnished hereunder is experimental and may have defects or deficiencies which cannot or will not be corrected by Sun and that Sun is under no obligation to release the Software as a product. Licensee will release and discharge Sun from any liability from any claims that any product released by Sun is incompatible with the Software. Further, Licensee will defend and indemnify Sun from any claims made by Licensee's customers that are based on incompatibility between the Software and any products released by Licensee. Licensee will have sole responsibility for the adequate protection and backup of Licensee's data and/or equipment used with the Software.

(D) Aircraft Product and Nuclear Applications Restriction

SOFTWARE IS NOT DESIGNED OR INTENDED FOR USE IN ON-LINE CONTROL OF AIRCRAFT, AIR TRAFFIC, AIRCRAFT NAVIGATION OR AIRCRAFT COMMUNICATIONS; OR IN THE DESIGN, CONSTRUCTION, OPERATION OR MAINTENANCE OF ANY NUCLEAR FACILITY. SUN DISCLAIMS ANY EXPRESS OR IMPLIED WARRANTY OF FITNESS FOR SUCH USES. LICENSEE REPRESENTS AND WARRANTS THAT IT WILL NOT USE THE SOFTWARE FOR SUCH PURPOSES.

3. CONFIDENTIALITY

The Software is the confidential and proprietary information of Sun and/or its licensors. The Software is protected by United States copyright law and international treaty. Unauthorized reproduction or distribution is subject to civil and criminal penalties. Licensee agrees to take adequate steps to protect the Software from unauthorized disclosure or use.

4. TERM, TERMINATION AND SURVIVAL

(A) The Agreement is effective until expiration of the Term, unless sooner terminated as provided for herein.

(B) Licensee may terminate this Agreement at any time by destroying all copies of the Software.

(C) This Agreement will immediately terminate without notice if Licensee fails to comply with any obligation of this Agreement.

(D) Upon termination, Licensee must immediately cease use of and destroy the Software or, upon request from Sun, return the Software to Sun.

(E) The provisions set forth in paragraphs 2(B), 3, 7, 8, 9, and 10 will survive termination or expiration of this Agreement.

5. NO WARRANTY

THE SOFTWARE IS PROVIDED TO LICENSEE "AS IS". ALL EXPRESS OR IMPLIED CONDITIONS, REPRESENTATIONS, AND WARRANTIES, INCLUDING ANY IMPLIED WARRANTY OF MERCHANTABILITY, SATISFACTORY QUALITY, FITNESS FOR A PARTICULAR PURPOSE, OR NON-INFRINGEMENT, ARE DISCLAIMED, EXCEPT TO THE EXTENT THAT SUCH DISCLAIMERS ARE HELD TO BE LEGALLY INVALID.

6. MAINTENANCE AND SUPPORT

Sun has no obligation to provide maintenance, support, updates or error corrections for the Software under this Agreement. In the event Sun, in its sole discretion, provides updates to Licensee, Licensee agrees to install and update the Software with such updates within fifteen (15) days from notification by Sun of the updates availability. Updates will be deemed Software hereunder and unless subject to terms of a specific update license, will be furnished to Licensee under the terms of this Agreement.

7. LIMITATION OF DAMAGES

TO THE EXTENT NOT PROHIBITED BY APPLICABLE LAW, SUN'S AGGREGATE LIABILITY TO LICENSEE OR TO ANY THIRD PARTY FOR CLAIMS RELATING TO THIS AGREEMENT, WHETHER FOR BREACH OR IN TORT, WILL BE LIMITED TO THE FEES PAID BY LICENSEE FOR SOFTWARE WHICH IS THE SUBJECT MATTER OF THE CLAIMS. IN NO EVENT WILL SUN BE LIABLE FOR ANY INDIRECT, PUNITIVE, SPECIAL, INCIDENTAL OR CONSEQUENTIAL DAMAGE IN CONNECTION WITH OR ARISING OUT OF THIS AGREEMENT (INCLUDING LOSS OF BUSINESS, REVENUE, PROFITS, USE, DATA OR OTHER ECONOMIC ADVANTAGE), HOWEVER IT ARISES, WHETHER FOR BREACH OR IN TORT, EVEN IF SUN HAS BEEN PREVIOUSLY ADVISED OF THE POSSIBILITY OF SUCH DAMAGE. LIABILITY FOR DAMAGES WILL BE LIMITED AND EXCLUDED, EVEN IF ANY EXCLUSIVE REMEDY PROVIDED FOR IN THIS AGREEMENT FAILS OF ITS ESSENTIAL PURPOSE.

8. GOVERNMENT USER

Rights in Data: If procured by, or provided to, the U.S. Government, use, duplication, or disclosure of technical data is subject to restrictions as set forth in FAR 52.227-14(g)(2),

Rights in Data-General (June 1987); and for computer software and computer software documentation, FAR 52-227-19, Commercial Computer Software-Restricted Rights (June 1987). However, if under DOD, use, duplication, or disclosure of technical data is subject to DFARS 252.227-7015(b), Technical Data-Commercial Items (June 1995); and for computer software and computer software documentation, as specified in the license under which the computer software was procured pursuant to DFARS 227.7202-3(a). Licensee shall not provide Software nor technical data to any third party, including the U.S. Government, unless such third party accepts the same restrictions. Licensee is responsible for ensuring that proper notice is given to all such third parties and that the Software and technical data are properly marked.

9. EXPORT LAW

Licensee acknowledges and agrees that this Software and/or technology is subject to the U.S. Export Administration Laws and Regulations. Diversion of such Software and/or technology contrary to U.S. law is prohibited. Licensee agrees that none of this Software and/or technology, nor any direct product therefrom, is being or will be acquired for, shipped, transferred, or reexported, directly or indirectly, to proscribed or embargoed countries or their nationals, nor be used for nuclear activities, chemical biological weapons, or missile projects unless authorized by the U.S. Government. Proscribed countries are set forth in the U.S. Export Administration Regulations. Countries subject to U.S. embargo are: Cuba, Iran, Iraq, Libya, North Korea, Syria, and the Sudan. This list is subject to change without further notice from Sun, and Licensee must comply with the list as it exists in fact. Licensee certifies that it is not on the U.S. Department of Commerce's Denied Persons List or affiliated lists or on the U.S. Department of Treasury's Specially Designated Nationals List. Licensee agrees to comply strictly with all U.S. export laws and assumes sole responsibility for obtaining licenses to export or reexport as may be required.

Licensee is responsible for complying with any applicable local laws and regulations, including but not limited to, the export and import laws and regulations of other countries.

10. GOVERNING LAW, JURISDICTION AND VENUE

Any action related to this Agreement shall be governed by California law and controlling U.S. federal law, and choice of law rules of any jurisdiction shall not apply. The parties agree that any action shall be brought in the United States District Court for the Northern District of California or the California superior Court for the County of Santa Clara, as applicable, and the parties hereby submit exclusively to the personal jurisdiction and venue of the United States District Court for the Northern District of California and the California Superior Court of the county of Santa Clara.

11. NO ASSIGNMENT

Neither party may assign or otherwise transfer any of its rights or obligations under this Agreement, without the prior written consent of the other party, except that Sun may assign its right to payment and may assign this Agreement to an affiliated company.

12. OFFICIAL LANGUAGE

The official text of this Agreement is in the English language and any interpretation or construction of this Agreement will be based thereon. In the event that this Agreement or any documents or notices related to it are translated into any other language, the English language version will control.

13. ENTIRE AGREEMENT

This Agreement is the parties' entire agreement relating to the Software. It supersedes all prior or contemporaneous oral or written communications, proposals, warranties, and representations with respect to its subject matter, and following Licensee's acceptance of this license by clicking on the "Accept" Button, will prevail over any conflicting or additional terms of any quote, order, acknowledgment, or any other communications by or between the parties. No modification to this Agreement will be binding, unless in writing and signed by an authorized representative of each party.

LICENSE AGREEMENT AND LIMITED WARRANTY

READ THE FOLLOWING TERMS AND CONDITIONS CAREFULLY BEFORE OPEN-
ING THIS DISK PACKAGE. THIS LEGAL DOCUMENT IS AN AGREEMENT BETWEEN YOU AND
PRENTICE-HALL, INC. (THE "COMPANY"). BY OPENING THIS SEALED DISK PACKAGE, YOU
ARE AGREEING TO BE BOUND BY THESE TERMS AND CONDITIONS. IF YOU DO NOT AGREE
WITH THESE TERMS AND CONDITIONS, DO NOT OPEN THE DISK PACKAGE. PROMPTLY
RETURN THE UNOPENED DISK PACKAGE AND ALL ACCOMPANYING ITEMS TO THE PLACE
YOU OBTAINED THEM FOR A FULL REFUND OF ANY SUMS YOU HAVE PAID.

1.   **GRANT OF LICENSE:** In consideration of your payment of the license fee, which is part of the
price you paid for this product, and your agreement to abide by the terms and conditions of this Agreement,
the Company grants to you a nonexclusive right to use and display the copy of the enclosed software program
(hereinafter the "SOFTWARE") on a single computer (i.e., with a single CPU) at a single location so long as
you comply with the terms of this Agreement. The Company reserves all rights not expressly granted to you
under this Agreement.

2.   **OWNERSHIP OF SOFTWARE:** You own only the magnetic or physical media (the enclosed disks)
on which the SOFTWARE is recorded or fixed, but the Company retains all the rights, title, and ownership to the
SOFTWARE recorded on the original disk copy(ies) and all subsequent copies of the SOFTWARE, regardless of
the form or media on which the original or other copies may exist. This license is not a sale of the original SOFT-
WARE or any copy to you.

3.   **COPY RESTRICTIONS:** This SOFTWARE and the accompanying printed materials and user
manual (the "Documentation") are the subject of copyright. You may not copy the Documentation or the
SOFTWARE, except that you may make a single copy of the SOFTWARE for backup or archival purposes only.
You may be held legally responsible for any copying or copyright infringement which is caused or encouraged
by your failure to abide by the terms of this restriction.

4.   **USE RESTRICTIONS:** You may not network the SOFTWARE or otherwise use it on more than
one computer or computer terminal at the same time. You may physically transfer the SOFTWARE from one
computer to another provided that the SOFTWARE is used on only one computer at a time. You may not distribute copies of the SOFTWARE or Documentation to others. You may not reverse engineer, disassemble,
decompile, modify, adapt, translate, or create derivative works based on the SOFTWARE or the
Documentation without the prior written consent of the Company.

5.   **TRANSFER RESTRICTIONS:** The enclosed SOFTWARE is licensed only to you and may not
be transferred to any one else without the prior written consent of the Company. Any unauthorized transfer of
the SOFTWARE shall result in the immediate termination of this Agreement.

6.   **TERMINATION:** This license is effective until terminated. This license will terminate automatically without notice from the Company and become null and void if you fail to comply with any provisions or
limitations of this license. Upon termination, you shall destroy the Documentation and all copies of the SOFT-
WARE. All provisions of this Agreement as to warranties, limitation of liability, remedies or damages, and our
ownership rights shall survive termination.

7.   **MISCELLANEOUS:** This Agreement shall be construed in accordance with the laws of the
United States of America and the State of New York and shall benefit the Company, its affiliates, and assignees.

8.   **LIMITED WARRANTY AND DISCLAIMER OF WARRANTY:** The Company warrants that
the SOFTWARE, when properly used in accordance with the Documentation, will operate in substantial con-
formity with the description of the SOFTWARE set forth in the Documentation. The Company does not war-
rant that the SOFTWARE will meet your requirements or that the operation of the SOFTWARE will be unin-
terrupted or error-free. The Company warrants that the media on which the SOFTWARE is delivered shall be

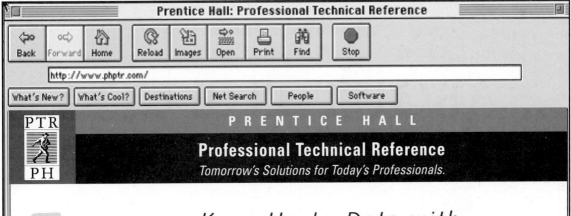

ABOUT THE CD

The CD-ROM that accompanies this book has the following directory structure:

```
COREJFC
    JDK1.1
            CJFC11.ZIP
    JDK1.2
            CJFC12.ZIP

WINDOWS
    JDK1.1
    JDK1.2

SOLARIS
    JDK1.1
    JDK1.2
```

There is also an empty SWING directoy on the CD-ROM (not shown above) that should be ignored. The COREJFC directory contains the source code and compiled class files for the examples in this book. The WINDOWS directory contains a version of JDK1.1 for Windows 95 and Windows NT (version 4 or later) and a beta version of JDK 1.2 for Windows platforms. The SOLARIS directory has the same software for use with the Solaris operating system.

Since Swing can be used either with JDK 1.1 or JDK 1.2, you have a choice as to how to use the CD-ROM. If you want to use Swing with JDK 1.1, you need to do the following:

- Install the appropriate version of JDK 1.1 for your platform.
- Download and install the appropriate version of Swing for your platform.
- Install the JDK 1.1 examples.
- Optionally compile the example source files.

On the other hand, if you are going to use Swing with JDK 1.2, then you should

- Install the version of JDK 1.2 appropriate for your platform.
- Install the examples for JDK 1.2.
- Optionally compile the example source files.

Because Swing is an integral part of JDK 1.2, you don't need to download the Swing package if you intend to work with JDK 1.2.

Please refer to the complete installation instructions contained in the preface.